T0237015

Lecture Notes in Computer Science   9917

Commenced Publication in 1973
Founding and Former Series Editors:
Gerhard Goos, Juris Hartmanis, and Jan van Leeuwen

More information about this series at http://www.springer.com/series/7409

Enqing Chen · Yihong Gong
Yun Tie (Eds.)

Advances in Multimedia Information Processing – PCM 2016

17th Pacific-Rim Conference on Multimedia
Xi'an, China, September 15–16, 2016
Proceedings, Part II

 Springer

Editors
Enqing Chen
Zhengzhou University
Zhengzhou
China

Yun Tie
Zhengzhou University
Zhengzhou
China

Yihong Gong
Jiaotong University
Xi'an
China

ISSN 0302-9743   ISSN 1611-3349 (electronic)
Lecture Notes in Computer Science
ISBN 978-3-319-48895-0   ISBN 978-3-319-48896-7 (eBook)
DOI 10.1007/978-3-319-48896-7

Library of Congress Control Number: 2016959170

LNCS Sublibrary: SL3 – Information Systems and Applications, incl. Internet/Web, and HCI

Printed on acid-free paper

This Springer imprint is published by Springer Nature
The registered company is Springer International Publishing AG
The registered company address is: Gewerbestrasse 11, 6330 Cham, Switzerland

Preface

The 17th Pacific-Rim Conference on Multimedia (PCM 2016) was held in Xi'an, China, during September 15–16, 2016, and hosted by the Xi'an Jiaotong University (XJTU). PCM is a leading international conference for researchers and industry practitioners to share their new ideas, original research results, and practical development experiences from all multimedia-related areas.

It was a great honor for XJTU to host PCM 2016, one of the most longstanding multimedia conferences, in Xi'an, China. Xi'an Jiaotong University, located in the capital of Shaanxi province, is one of the key universities run by the Ministry of Education, China. Recently its multimedia-related research has been attracting increasing attention from the local and international multimedia community. For over 2000 years, Xi'an has been the center for political and economic developments and the capital city of many Chinese dynasties, with the richest cultural and historical heritage, including the world-famous Terracotta Warriors, Big Wild Goose Pagoda, etc. We hope that our venue made PCM 2016 a memorable experience for all participants.

PCM 2016 featured a comprehensive program. The 202 submissions from authors of more than ten countries included a large number of high-quality papers in multimedia content analysis, multimedia signal processing and communications, and multimedia applications and services. We thank our 28 Technical Program Committee members who spent many hours reviewing papers and providing valuable feedback to the authors. From the total of 202 submissions to the main conference and based on at least three reviews per submission, the program chairs decided to accept 111 regular papers (54 %) among which 67 were posters (33 %). This volume of the conference proceedings contains the abstracts of two invited talks and all the regular, poster, and special session papers.

The technical program is an important aspect but only achieves its full impact if complemented by challenging keynotes. We are extremely pleased and grateful to have had two exceptional keynote speakers, Wen Gao and Alex Hauptmann, accept our invitation and present interesting ideas and insights at PCM 2016.

We are also heavily indebted to many individuals for their significant contributions. We thank the PCM Steering Committee for their invaluable input and guidance on crucial decisions. We wish to acknowledge and express our deepest appreciation to the honorary chairs, Nanning Zheng, Shin'chi Satoh, general chairs, Yihong Gong, Thomas Plagemann, Ke Lu, Jianping Fan, program chairs, Meng Wang, Qi Tian, Abdulmotaleb El Saddik, Yun Tie, organizing chairs, Jinye Peng, Xinbo Gao, Ziyu Guan, Yizhou Wang, publicity chairs, Xueming Qian, Xiaojiang Chen, Cheng Jin, Xiangyang Xue, publication chairs, Jun Wu, Enqing Chen, local Arrangements Chairs, Kuizi Mei, Xuguang Lan, special session chairs, Jianbing Shen, Jialie Shen, Jianru Xue, demo chairs, Yugang Jiang, Jitao Sang, finance and registration chair, Shuchan Gao. Without their efforts and enthusiasm, PCM 2016 would not have become a reality. Moreover, we want to thank our sponsors: Springer, Peking University, Zhengzhou University,

Ryerson University. Finally, we wish to thank all committee members, reviewers, session chairs, student volunteers, and supporters. Their contributions are much appreciated.

September 2016

Meng Wang
Yun Tie
Qi Tian
Abdulmotaleb El Saddik
Yihong Gong
Thomas Plagemann
Ke Lu
Jianping Fan

Organization

Honorary Chairs

Nanning Zheng   Xi'an Jiaotong University, China
Shin'chi Satoh   National Institute of Informatics, Japan

General Chairs

Yihong Gong   Xi'an Jiaotong University, China
Thomas Plagemann   University of Oslo, Norway
Ke Lu   University of Chinese Academy of Sciences, China
Jianping Fan   University of North Carolina at Charlotte, USA

Program Chairs

Meng Wang   Hefei University of Technology, China
Qi Tian   University of Texas at San Antonio, USA
Abdulmotaleb El Saddik   University of Ottawa, Canada
Yun Tie   Zhengzhou University, China

Organizing Chairs

Jinye Peng   Northwest University, China
Xinbo Gao   Xidian University, China
Ziyu Guan   Northwest University, China
Yizhou Wang   Peking University, China

Publicity Chairs

Xueming Qian   Xi'an Jiaotong University, China
Xiaojiang Chen   Northwest University, China
Cheng Jin   Fudan University, China
Xiangyang Xue   Fudan University, China

Publication Chairs

Jun Wu   Northwestern Polytechnical University, China
Enqing Chen   Zhengzhou University, China

Local Arrangements Chairs

Kuizi Mei   Xi'an Jiaotong University, China
Xuguang Lan   Xi'an Jiaotong University, China

Special Session Chairs

Jianbing Shen   Beijing Institute of Technology, China
Jialie Shen   Singapore Management University, Singapore
Jianru Xue   Xi'an Jiaotong University, China

Demo Chairs

Yugang Jiang   Fudan University, China
Jitao Sang   Institute of Automation, Chinese Academy of Sciences,
                            China

Finance and Registration Chair

Shuchan Gao   Xi'an Jiaotong University, China

Contents – Part II

Contents – Part I

A Global-Local Approach to Extracting Deformable Fashion Items from Web Images

Lixuan Yang[1,2(✉)], Helena Rodriguez[2], Michel Crucianu[1], and Marin Ferecatu[1]

[1] Conservatoire National des Arts et Metiers,
292 Rue Saint-Martin, 75003 Paris, France
{lixuan.yang,michel.crucianu,marin.ferecatu}@cnam.fr
[2] Shopedia SAS, 55 Rue La Boétie, 75008 Paris, France
{lixuan.yang,helena.rodriguez}@shopedia.fr

Abstract. In this work we propose a new framework for extracting deformable clothing items from images by using a three stage global-local fitting procedure. First, a set of initial segmentation templates are generated from a handcrafted database. Then, each template initiates an object extraction process by a global alignment of the model, followed by a local search minimizing a measure of the misfit with respect to the potential boundaries in the neighborhood. Finally, the results provided by each template are aggregated, with a global fitting criterion, to obtain the final segmentation. The method is validated on the Fashionista database and on a new database of manually segmented images. Our method compares favorably with the Paper Doll clothing parsing and with the recent GrabCut on One Cut foreground extraction method. We quantitatively analyze each component, and show examples of both successful segmentation and difficult cases.

Keywords: Clothing extraction · Segmentation · Active contour · GrabCut

1 Introduction and Related Work

With the recent proliferation of fashion web-stores, an important goal for online advertising systems is to propose items that truly correspond to the expectations of the users in terms of design, manufacturing and suitability. We put forward here a method to extract, without user supervision, clothes and other fashion items from web images. Indeed, localizing, extracting and tracking fashion items during web browsing is an important step in addressing the needs of professionals of online advertising and fashion media: present the users with relevant items from a clothing database, based on the content of the web application they are consulting and its context of use. Users usually look for characteristics expressed by very subjective concepts, to describe a style, a brand or a specific design. For this reason, recent research focused in the development of detection, recognition and search of fashion items based on visual characteristics [11].

© Springer International Publishing AG 2016
E. Chen et al. (Eds.): PCM 2016, Part II, LNCS 9917, pp. 1–12, 2016.
DOI: 10.1007/978-3-319-48896-7_1

A popular approach is to model the target items based on attribute selection and high-level classification, for example [5] trains attribute classifiers on fine-grained clothing styles formulating the retrieval as a classification problem, [2] extracts low-level features in a pose-adaptive manner and learns attribute classifiers by using conditional random fields (CRF), while [3] introduced a novel double-path deep domain adaptation network for attribute prediction by modeling the data jointly from unconstrained photos and the images issued from large-scale online shopping stores. A complementary approach is to use part-based models to compensate for the lack of pose estimation. The idea is to automatically align patches of human body parts by using different methods, for example sparse coding as in [16] or graph parsing technique as in [12].

Segmentation and aggregation to select cloth categories was employed either by using bottom-up cloth parsing from labels attached to pixels [19] or by over-segmentation and classification [8]. Deep learning was also used with success for clothing retrieval (deep similarity learning [13], Siamese networks [18]) or to predict fashionability [15].

(a) Original image   (b) Desired output

Fig. 1. Our goal is to produce a precise segmentation (extraction) of the fashion items as in (b).

Unlike the above-mentioned methods, our proposal aims to *precisely* segment the object of interest from the background (foreground separation, see Fig. 1(b)), without user interaction and without using an extensive training database. Extracting such complex objects by simply optimizing a local pixel objective function is likely to fail without an awareness of the object's global properties. To take this into account, we propose a Global-Local approach based on the idea that a local search is likely to converge to a better fit if the initial state is coherent with the expected global appearance of the object.

Our method is validated on the Fashionista database [19][1]and on a new database of manually segmented images that we specifically built to test fashion objects extraction and that we make available to the community. Our method compares favorably with the well-known Paper Doll [19] clothing parsing and with the recent GrabCut on One Cut [17] generic foreground extraction method. We provide examples of successful segmentation, analyze difficult cases and also quantitatively evaluate each component.

---

[1] http://vision.is.tohoku.ac.jp/~kyamagu/research/paperdoll/.

In Sect. 2 we describe our proposal, followed by a detailed presentation of each component. After the experimental validation in Sect. 3, we conclude the paper with Sect. 4 by a discussion of the main points and extension perspectives.

2   Our Proposal

Detecting clothes in images is a difficult problem because the objects are deformable, have large intra-class diversity and may appear against complex backgrounds. To extract objects under these difficult conditions and without user intervention, methods solely relying on optimizing a local criterion (or pixel classification based on local features) are unlikely to perform well. Some knowledge about the global shape of the class of objects to be extracted is necessary to help a local analysis converge to a correct object boundary. In this paper we use this intuition to develop a framework that takes into account the local/global duality to select the most likely object segmentation.

We investigate here fashion items that are worn by a person. This covers practically most of the situations encountered by users of fashion and/or news web sites, while making possible the use of a person detector to restrict the search regions in the image and to serve as reference for alignment operations.

First, we prepare a set of images containing the object of interest and we manually segment them. These initial object masks (called templates in the following) provide the prior knowledge used by the algorithm. Of course, a given manual segmentation will not match exactly the object in an unknown image. We use each segmentation (after a suitable alignment) as a template to initiate an active contour (AC) procedure that will converge closer to the true boundaries of the real object in the current image. We then extract the object with a suitable GrabCut procedure to provide the final segmentation. Thus, at the end we have as many candidate segmentations as hand-made templates. In the final step we choose the best of them according to a criterion that optimizes the coherence of the proposed segmentation with the edges extracted from the image. In the following subsections we detail each of these stages (see also Fig. 2 for an illustration).

(a)   (b)   (c)   (d)   (e)   (f)   (g)

Fig. 2. Different stages of our approach: (a) original image, (b) a template segmentation, (c) output of the person detector, (d) result after the alignment step, (e) result after the active contour step, (f) the GrabCut band, (g) result after the GrabCut step.

To summarize, the main contributions of this paper are: we introduce a new framework for the extraction of fashion items in web images that combines local and global object characteristics, framework supported by a new active contour that optimizes the gap with respect to the global segmentation model, and by a new measure of fit of the proposed segmentation to the real distribution of the contours. Also, we prepare a new benchmark database and make it available to the community.

2.1 Person Detector

For clothing extraction, it is reasonable to first apply a person detector. As in many other studies (*e.g.* [8,12,20]), we use the person detector with articulated pose estimation algorithm from [21] that was extensively tested and proved to be very robust in several other fashion-related works (see Sect. 1). It is based on a deformable model that sees the object as a combination of parts [21]. The detection score is defined as the fit to parts minus the parts deformation cost. The mixture model not only encodes object structure but also captures spatial relations between part locations and co-occurrence relations between parts. The output of the detector is a set of parts (rectangular boxes) centered on the body joints and oriented correctly. The boxes are used as reference points for alignment by translation and re-scaling in several stages of our proposal (see below).

To train the person detector, we manually annotate a set of 800 images. Each person is annotated with 14 joint points by marking the articulations and main body parts. When the legs are covered by long dresses, the lower parts are placed on the edges of the dress rather than on the legs. This not only improves detection accuracy, but also hints to the location of the contours. Figure 2(c) shows the output of the person detector on an unannotated image. Boxes usually slightly cover the limbs and body joints.

2.2 Template Selection

As we have seen, each initial template can provide a candidate segmentation for a new, unknown image. However, this is redundant and may slow down unnecessarily the procedure. Since we focus on the fashion items that are worn by a person, the number of different poses in which an object may be found is relatively small, and many initial templates are thus quite similar. Intuitively, templates that are alike in shape should also produce similar segmentation masks. To reduce their number, the initial templates are clustered into similar-shape clusters by using the K-Medoid procedure [9]. We employ 8 clusters for each object class, which is a reasonable choice in our case because the number of person poses is not very large. Each resulting cluster is a configuration of deformable objects that share a similarity in pose, viewpoint and clothing shape. The dissimilarity of two object masks is defined by the complement of the Jaccard index:

$$d(S_1, S_2) = 1 - \frac{\text{Surface}(S_1 \cap S_2)}{\text{Surface}(S_1 \cup S_2)}$$

where S_1 and S_2 are the binary masks of two objects.

Fig. 3. Medoids of the 8 clusters of template segmentations for three classes: jeans (top), long dress (middle) and coat (bottom).

Each cluster represents a segmentation configuration and its prototype is used in the next stages of the procedure. However, we do not simply choose the medoid as the prototype of the cluster, but rather the element in the cluster that is visually closest to the corresponding box parts produced by the person detector on the unknown image. To do so, we apply the object detector on both the unknown image and the template image and we compare the boxes that contain the object in the template with the corresponding ones in the unknown image by using the Euclidean distance. To represent the content of the boxes we first considered HOG features [4] (to favor similar shape content) but finally settled for Caffe features [7] that provide better results. This suggests that mid-level features give better clues to identifying the correct pose of an object compared to local pure shape features. Shape is relevant for comparing the boundaries of two objects but less so when comparing what is inside those boundaries.

Specifically, we use the AlexNet model in [10] within the Caffe framework [7]. The network was pre-trained on 1.2 million high-resolution images from ImageNet, classified into 1000 classes. To fine-tune the network to our image domain, we replace the last layer by a layer of ten outputs (the number of classes considered here) and then retrain the network on our training database with back-propagation to fine-tune the weights of all the layers. After the fine-tuning, the feature we employ is the vector of responses for layer fc7 (second to last layer) obtained by forward propagation.

To illustrate this step we show in Fig. 3 the medoids (centers) of the 8 clusters obtained for three classes of our benchmark database. We notice the diversity in poses, scale and topology. For example, some coats are segmented into several disjoint parts, some have openings and some jeans are covered by a vest.

2.3   Template Alignment

The output of the previous stage is a set of segmentation templates (8 in our case) for each object class. They will be used one by one to initiate an active contour process. But they first need to be aligned into the unknown image at the right site and with the correct angle and scale. We propose an SVM alignment technique based on the observation that the person detector places the boxes centered on the body joints. Thus, the line joining adjacent boxes represents the body limbs. Since the clothing's spatial distribution highly depends on the pose of human body, and thus on limb placement, we use the vector of distances from a pixel to the limbs as a feature vector to learn a pixel-level SVM classifier that predicts if a pixel belongs to the object. Learning is performed on the template image and prediction on the unknown image. Pixels predicted as positives form the mask whose envelope serves as initialization for the active contour step. The SVM uses a Gaussian kernel with a scale parameter $\sigma = 1$ found through experiments.

2.4   Active Contour

Once the template is embedded in the image, we use it to initialize an active contour (AC) that should converge to the boundaries of the object. The result is highly dependent on the initial contour, but usually one of the 8 segmentation templates leads to a final contour that is quite close to the true boundary. The AC is initialized with the aligned segmentation contour produced by the previous step and has as input the gray-level image. We use the AC introduced in [1] because it can segment objects whose boundaries are not necessarily well-supported by gradient information. The AC minimizes an energy defined by contour length, area inside the contour and a fitting term:

$$F(c_1, c_2, C) = \mu \cdot \text{Length}(C) + \nu \cdot \text{Area}(\text{in}(C)) + \lambda_1 \int_{in(C)} |u(x,y) - c_1|^2$$
$$+ \lambda_2 \int_{out(C)} |u(x,y) - c_2|^2 \quad (1)$$

where C is the current contour, c_1 and c_2 are the average pixel gray-level values $u(x,y)$ inside and respectively outside the contour C. The curvature term is controlled by μ and the fitting terms by λ_1 and λ_2. The averages c_1 and c_2 are usually computed on the entire image. Because of the large variability of the background in real images, these values can be meaningless locally. Consequently, in our case we replace them by averages computed in a local window of size 40×40 pixels around each contour pixel.

To reinforce the influence of the global shape of the template on the position of the AC, we include a new term in the energy function (Eq. 1) that moderates the tendency to converge too far away from the template:

$$F_t(C) = \eta \int_{on(C)} D_m(x,y) \quad (2)$$

where $D_m(x,y)$ is the distance between pixel (x,y) and the template. By including this term, the contour will converge to those image regions that separate best the inside from the outside and, at the same time, are not too far away from the template contour.

2.5   Segmentation

The contours obtained in the previous step suffer from two implicit problems: (1) only the grey-level information is used by the AC process, and (2) possible alignment errors may affect the result. To compensate for these problems, an "exclusion band" of constant thickness is defined around the contour produced by the previous step, then the inside region is labeled as "certain foreground" and the outside area as "certain background". A GrabCut algorithm [14] is then initialized by these labels to obtain the final result. GrabCut takes into account the global information of color in the image and will correct the alignment errors within the limits of the defined band.

2.6   Object Selection

After obtaining the segmentation proposals initiated from each template, we need to select a single segmentation as the final result. For this, we propose a score based on a global measure of fit to the image:

$$F(C) = \frac{\int_{on(C)} D_e(x,y)ds}{\int_{on(C)} ds} \tag{3}$$

where $D_e(x,y)$ is the distance from the current pixel to the closest edge detected by [6] and C is the boundary of the segmentation proposal. This score measures the average distance from the segmentation boundary to the closest edges in the image. A small value indicates a good fit to the image. See Table 1 for an illustration of this step.

Table 1. Segmentation selection from the results based on the 8 templates of the class, using the corresponding fit values. The test image is given top left, with the extracted edges shown bottom left. The best score is the smallest (outlined in boldface).

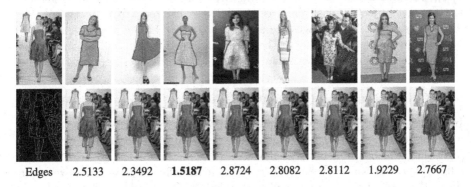

| Edges | 2.5133 | 2.3492 | **1.5187** | 2.8724 | 2.8082 | 2.8112 | 1.9229 | 2.7667 |

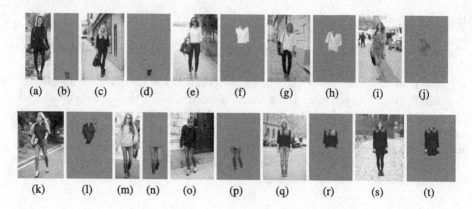

(a)   (b)   (c)   (d)   (e)   (f)   (g)   (h)   (i)   (j)

(k)   (l)   (m)   (n)   (o)   (p)   (q)   (r)   (s)   (t)

Fig. 4. Qualitative evaluation: are original images and associated segmentation results.

3   Experimental Results

To assess the performance of the proposed method, we perform two sets of experiments. In the first set, our method is compared to a recent improvement of GrabCut [14] that is the standard approach in generic object extraction, on a novel fashion item benchmark we built. The second set of experiments compares our proposal to the recent PaperDoll [19] fashion item annotation method on the Fashionista database [20].

3.1   RichPicture Database

Since, to our knowledge, at this time there is no public benckmark specifically designed for clothing extraction from fashion images, we introduce a novel dataset called RichPicture, consisting of 1000 images from Google.com and Bing.com. It has 100 images for each of the following fashion items: Boots, Coat, Jeans, Shirt, T-Shirt, Short Dress, Mid Dress, Long Dress, Vest and Sweater. Each target object in each class is manually segmented. To train the person detector (see Sect. 2.1), images are also annotated by 14 key points. This database will be made available with the paper and open to external contributions. We shall further extend it with new classes and more images per class.

3.2   Comparison with GrabCut in One Cut

In this set of experiments, we compare our proposal to GrabCut in one cut [17], a recent improvement on the well-known GrabCut [14] foreground extraction algorithm, which is frequently used as a baseline method in the literature. Grab-Cut in One Cut was shown in [17] to have higher effectiveness, is less resource demanding and has an open implementation. These reasons makes it a good candidate as a benchmark baseline. For the purpose of this evaluation, we split each class of our database in 80 images for training (template selection) and 20 images for test.

Table 2. Comparison with the One Cut algorithm. The comparison measure is the Jaccard index.

Class	Boots	Coat	Mid dress	Jeans	Shirt	T-shirt	Short dress	Long dress	Vest	Pull
Our method	**0,54**	**0,74**	**0,84**	**0,78**	**0,77**	**0,67**	**0,80**	**0,74**	**0,65**	**0,74**
One Cut	0,26	0,31	0,54	0,71	**0,77**	0,45	0,47	0,57	0,35	0,36

The segmentation produced by the algorithms is tested against the ground truth obtained by manual segmentation. As performance measure we employ the Jaccard index, traditionally used for segmentation evaluation, and averaged over all the testing images of a class. To outline the object for One Cut we use the external envelope of the relevant parts (the ones that contain parts of the object) identified by the person detector. Table 2 shows a class by class synthesis of the results (best results are in boldface).

It can be seen that the proposed method performs significantly better on all the classes except "Shirt" where the scores are equal. While both segmentation methods are automatic (do not require interaction), these results speak in favor of including specific knowledge into the algorithm (by the use of segmentation templates in our case).

3.3 Comparison with Paper Doll

To our knowledge, there is no published method concerning fashion retrieval that aims to precisely extract entire fashion items from arbitrary images. The closest we could find is the Paper Doll framework, cited above, that in fact attributes label scores to a set of blobs in the image. By taking the union of all the blobs that correspond to a same clothing class, one can extract objects of that class. The authors of Paper Doll also introduced the Fashionista database, used to test annotation algorithms, which we use for this evaluation. Table 3 presents the synthesis of the results of Paper Doll vs. One Cut vs. our method. The object classes we selected for tests are those that correspond to fashion items that are worn by persons (compatible with our method).

For our method, training and template selection are performed on the same part of the database that Paper Doll employed for training. As seen from Table 3, on most object classes we compare favorably to Paper Doll. For objects like "Boots", our method needs a more dedicated alignment process, since the object is very small compared to the frame given by the person detector that serves as alignment reference. For objects of the "Jeans" class, the problem also comes from the alignment stage, because the boxes proposed by the person detector are not very well positioned when the legs are crossed. It is necessary to increase the number of training examples with this specific pose.

3.4 Qualitative Evaluation

We illustrate here the results of the proposed method with some examples taken from the our test database. First, Table 1 shows the final segmentation selection

Table 3. Comparison (using Jaccard index) with Paper Doll and One Cut on Fashionista.

Class	Vest	Jeans	Shirt	Boots	Coat	Dress	Skirt	Sweater
Our method	**0,32**	0,72	**0,35**	0,35	**0,56**	**0,52**	**0,62**	**0,52**
Paper Doll	0,19	**0,74**	0,24	**0,44**	0,28	**0,52**	0,52	0,07
One Cut	0,23	0,62	0,29	0,01	0,23	0,33	0,32	0,25

Fig. 5. Comparison with One Cut: original image (left), our method (middle) and One Cut (right)

stage, based on the values of fit associated to the results obtained from each of the 8 templates of the class. Visually, the object segmentation in the test image is close to the template.

A first example of successful segmentation was shown in Fig. 2(g). In Fig. 4 we present other difficult but successful segmentations: (a, c) for small object extraction, (e, g, i) for clothes against confusing or cluttered background, and (k, m, o) for deformed clothes. Figure 4 also shows examples where the segmentation is not perfect: in (r) the extracted object includes some hair and in (t) also part of the leggings. These inclusions probably occur here because the energy term we introduced in the active contour encourages the contour to stay close to the global shape of the segmentation template.

A visual comparison with One Cut is shown in Fig. 5. As hinted by the quantitative results, One Cut includes larger parts of external objects, mainly due to the lack of prior shape information. This occurs on most of the images in the database, explaining the significantly lower performance of One Cut in Tables 2 and 3.

4 Conclusion

We proposed a novel framework for extracting deformable clothing objects from web images. Our proposal combines a three stage global-local approach that injects specific knowledge about the object by using segmentation templates to guide an active contour process. Comparisons with GrabCut in One Cut and with Paper Doll show that the proposed approach is promising and performs favorably compared to generic or more dedicated object extractors. The method can easily be extended to new object classes at relatively low cost, *i.e.* by manually segmenting objects from these classes. We intend to continue adding new object classes to the RichPicture database. Also, a better alignment solution should benefit the proposed method, as well as the annotation of more images for training the person detector with other class-specific poses.

References

1. Chan, T.F., Vese, L.A.: Active contours without edges. IEEE Trans. Image Process. **10**(2), 266–277 (2001)
2. Chen, H., Gallagher, A., Girod, B.: Describing clothing by semantic attributes. In: Fitzgibbon, A., Lazebnik, S., Perona, P., Sato, Y., Schmid, C. (eds.) ECCV 2012. LNCS, vol. 7574, pp. 609–623. Springer, Heidelberg (2012). doi:10.1007/978-3-642-33712-3_44
3. Chen, Q., Huang, J., Feris, R., Brown, L.M., Dong, J., Yan, S.: Deep domain adaptation for describing people based on fine-grained clothing attributes. In: CVPR, June 2015
4. Dalal, N., Triggs, B.: Histograms of oriented gradients for human detection. In: CVPR, pp. 886–893 (2005)
5. Di, W., Wah, C., Bhardwaj, A., Piramuthu, R., Sundaresan, N.: Style finder: fine-grained clothing style detection and retrieval. In: IEEE International Workshop on Mobile Vision, CVPR, pp. 8–13, June 2013
6. Dollár, P., Zitnick, C.L.: Fast edge detection using structured forests. arXiv (2014)
7. Jia, Y., Shelhamer, E., Donahue, J., Karayev, S., Long, J., Girshick, R., Guadarrama, S., Darrell, T.: Caffe: convolutional architecture for fast feature embedding. arXiv preprint arXiv:1408.5093 (2014)
8. Kalantidis, Y., Kennedy, L., Li, L.J.: Getting the look: clothing recognition and segmentation for automatic product suggestions in everyday photos. In: ACM International Conference on Multimedia Retrieval, pp. 105–112 (2013)
9. Kaufman, L., Rousseeuw, P.: Clustering by means of meds. In: Dodge, Y. (ed.) Statistical Data Analysis Based on the L1-Norm and Related Methods, pp. 405–416. North-Holland, Amsterdam (1987)
10. Krizhevsky, A., Sutskever, I., Hinton, G.E.: Imagenet classification with deep convolutional neural networks. In: Bartlett, P., Pereira, F., Burges, C., Bottou, L., Weinberger, K. (eds.) NIPS, vol. 25, pp. 1106–1114 (2012)
11. Liu, S., Feng, J., Song, Z., Zhang, T., Lu, H., Xu, C., Yan, S.: Hi, magic closet, tell me what to wear! In: ACM Multimedia, pp. 619–628. ACM (2012)
12. Liu, S., Song, Z., Liu, G., Xu, C., Lu, H., Yan, S.: Street-to-shop: cross-scenario clothing retrieval via parts alignment and auxiliary set. In: CVPR, pp. 3330–3337 (2012)
13. M. Hadi, K., Xufeng, H., Svetlana, L., Alexander, C.B., Tamara, L.B.: Where to buy it: matching street clothing photos in online shops. In: ICCV (2015)
14. Rother, C., Kolmogorov, V., Blake, A.: GrabCut - interactive foreground extraction using iterated graph cuts. ACM Trans. Graph. **23**, 309–314 (2004)
15. Simo-Serra, E., Fidler, S., Moreno-Noguer, F., Urtasun, R.: Neuroaesthetics in fashion: modeling the perception of fashionability. In: CVPR (2015)
16. Song, Z., Wang, M., sheng Hua, X., Yan, S.: Predicting occupation via human clothing and contexts. In: ICCV, pp. 1084–1091. IEEE Computer Society, Washington, DC (2011)

17. Tang, M., Gorelick, L., Veksler, O., Boykov, Y.: Grabcut in one cut. In: ICCV, pp. 1769–1776. IEEE Computer Society, Washington, DC (2013)

18. Veit, A., Kovacs, B., Bell, S., McAuley, J., Bala, K., Belongie, S.: Learning visual clothing style with heterogeneous dyadic co-occurrences. In: ICCV, Santiago, Chile (2015)

19. Yamaguchi, K., Hadi, K., Luis, E., Tamara, L.B.: Retrieving similar styles to parse clothing. IEEE TPAMI **37**, 1028–1040 (2015)

20. Yamaguchi, K., Kiapour, M.H., Berg, T.L.: Paper doll parsing: retrieving similar styles to parse clothing items. In: ICCV, Washington, DC, pp. 3519–3526 (2013)

21. Yang, Y., Ramanan, D.: Articulated human detection with flexible mixtures of parts. IEEE TPAMI **35**, 2878–2890 (2013)

Say Cheese: Personal Photography Layout Recommendation Using 3D Aesthetics Estimation

Ben Zhang, Ran Ju, Tongwei Ren, and Gangshan Wu[✉]

State Key Laboratory for Novel Software Technology,
Collaborative Innovation Center of Novel Software Technology and Industrialization,
Nanjing University, Nanjing 210023, China
{zhangben,juran}@smail.nju.edu.cn, {rentw,gswu}@nju.edu.cn

Abstract. Many people fail to take exquisite pictures in a beautiful scenery for the lack of professional photography knowledge. In this paper, we focus on how to aid people to master daily life photography using a computational layout recommendation method. Given a selected scene, we first generate several synthetic photos with different layouts using 3D estimation. Then we employ a 3D layout aesthetic estimation model to rank the proposed photos. The results with high scores are selected as layout recommendations, which is then translated to a hint for where people shall locate. The key to our success lies on the combination of 3D structures with aesthetic models. The subjective evaluation shows superior preference of our method to previous work. We also give a few application examples to show the power of our method in creating better daily life photographs.

Keywords: Personal photography · Layout recommendation · Aesthetic estimation

1 Introduction

Photographing is one of the favorite things to do for human nowadays. In stark contrast to the matchless enthusiasm, most people don't master professional photography knowledge well. When seeing an amazing view, people always appear struggling in creating satisfactory photographs. In this paper, we propose to solve the problem from the specific perspective of layout recommendation. As shown in Fig. 1, given a scene as background, our method supplies professional advice for people's layout. The final photographs following our guidance get better aesthetic feelings. For example, the left image shows a best visual balance of the scene elements. The middle image shows a good feeling of symmetry. The right image has an obvious direction feeling corresponding to the depth intensity. In fact, photography aesthetics cannot be concluded in several rules. Many other aesthetic rules which have not been established can be learned by our method.

© Springer International Publishing AG 2016
E. Chen et al. (Eds.): PCM 2016, Part II, LNCS 9917, pp. 13–23, 2016.
DOI: 10.1007/978-3-319-48896-7_2

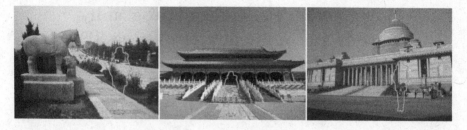

Fig. 1. Illustration of our method. The left image shows a best visual balance of the scene elements. The middle image shows a good feeling of symmetry. The right image has an obvious direction feeling corresponding to the depth intensity.

The challenges for making such professional layout suggestions come from two aspects. First, since a photo is a two-dimensional media, it is difficult to synthesize reasonable photo proposals with different layouts. Second, previous aesthetic models appear to be less discriminative for these synthetic photos for the lack of consideration of layout, especially 3D structures. To solve the two problems, we propose a novel method works as follow. First, we build human models and detect the ground in order to get reasonable synthetic images. Next, we estimate the 3D layout of the photo using a supervised learning approach based on Markov Random Field (MRF) model. Novel synthetic photos of different layouts are then generated using a grid traversal method. At last, we employ a learning based aesthetic estimation model to rank the synthesized photos with the consideration of photography guideline, color palette, scene layout, 3D structure and elements' saliency. The novel synthetics with top ranking scores are selected and translated to where people shall stand and be visualized on the screen.

To evaluate the effectiveness of the proposed method, we build a novel dataset including 630 photos with rating scores from 12 volunteers. The subjective evaluation results show that the proposed method performs best in the layout recommendation task.

The contributions of this paper are as follows.

– We proposed a novel photo synthesis method based on 3D layout estimation, which is used to generate photography recommendation candidates.
– A novel aesthetic estimation model for photography recommendation is presented, which combines several cues like photography rules, color and scene layout, 3D structure and image elements' saliency.
– We built a dataset designed for the task of making professional photography layout suggestions.

2   Related Work

We briefly review the relevant researches on photo layout recommendation, 3D layout estimation and photo aesthetic estimation as follows.

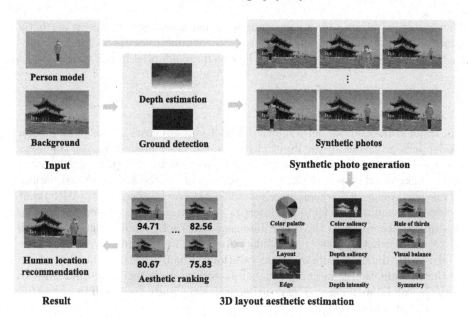

Fig. 2. The framework of our method. Take background and human model as input, ground detection and depth estimation will be executed to generate a set of synthetic photos as shown in the upper right block. Then we combine four features, two saliency intensities and photography guidelines to assess the synthetic photos as shown in the bottom right block. The photo with highest score will be the recommended as shown in the final result.

Photo layout recommendation. Photo layout recommendation is a novel topic proposed in recent years. Many related methods have been proposed but few of them study the problem of photography layout with human and scene [1–3]. Xu *et al.* propose a learning-based method to solve the problem of human position recommendation using 3D point cloud model [4]. However, this work only considers the similarities in social media which limits its application in daily life photography.

3D layout estimation. 3D layout estimation is a challenging problem in computer vision especially for monocular images. Lots of attention has been paid to 3D information extraction and 3D object detection [5–7]. Large and specific data are always necessary to support 3D layout estimation from monocular images [8]. In this work we adopt the supervised learning method proposed by Saxena *et al.* to predict the depthmap [9].

Photo aesthetic estimation. Photo aesthetic estimation aims to assess the quality of photos from the aesthetic point of view. Ke *et al.* propose a principled method for designing high level features for photo quality assessment which can be one of the earliest representatives [10]. Later Luo *et al.* propose a content-based photo quality assessment method using regional and global features [11].

Marchesotti *et al.* propose to use generic image descriptors to assess aesthetic quality [12]. Besides, computational rules in photography are utilized for aesthetic assessment in much work [13,14], which are adopted in our work.

3 Approach

The framework of our model is shown in Fig. 2. Our application provides a human model package as one of the input elements. For more precise results, the users can set their own model by taking several human photos. When a human model and a background photo are set, the algorithm will call the 3D layout estimation. In this part, we use a discriminatively-trained Markov Random Field (MRF) that incorporates multi-scale for depth inferring [9]. Next, a coarse ground region map is acquired according to the depth intensity and background image [15], which makes the synthetic photos reasonable. After that, we generate several synthetic images with different human figure positions. Finally, we implement a photo aesthetic evaluation combining saliency factors and photography guidelines to rank the candidate images. The position with the highest score will be suggested as a mark region to users.

3.1 3D Layout Estimation

We employ a supervised learning approach by training a set of images with unstructured outdoor environments, which is proposed by Saxena *et al.* to infer the depth for the input image [9]. This model chooses Markov Random Field (MRF) to incorporate local and global features. The algorithm will generate several typical features including haze, texture gradients and variations. The method is trained on images collected from Internet and part of SUN2012 dataset [16], and shows satisfying results to support our work. The depth images are visualized in grayscale where higher intensity indicates nearer and vice versa.

3.2 Human Model and Ground Detection

In our work we assume that only color and posture would slightly influence the final recommendation score. Therefore, we only consider the standing posture and users can choose main color of their own clothes. Meanwhile, users can set their own simple model by taking several human photos for more precise results.

The ground map restricts where people shall stand in synthetic images. We use a Hidden Markov Model (HMM) model with depth intensity to detect coarse ground region [15]. We generate a superpixels map based on the SLIC method [17]. The algorithm will train a HMM model and enact a threshold on depth intensity image. It may not be a necessary part because the wrong layout synthetic images would receive a low ranking in layout aesthetic evaluation. However, this map is a limit condition for synthetic layout generation so that we can improve the efficiency and avoid the obvious ridiculous image like a man standing in the air or on a tree.

3.3   Synthetic Photo Generation

The key of our application is to generate the best synthetic layout images. In our application, we also give an alternative selection on whether salient regions shall be remained. In our method, we consider the human figure to be the candidate component and the ground as a support plane. The image is separated into $n*n$ grids. We put the geometry center of human figure image at each grid center. The algorithm will traverse the grid image to generate the candidate synthetic images.

In each grid, we compute the depth intensity at the human figure bottom point. Human model will be proportionally resized according to the grid depth:

$$Z = \frac{k}{D} \qquad (1)$$

where Z is the coefficient of human model size and D is the depth intensity of current human figure bottom point. k is a parameter to control the basic size of human figure according to the camera parameters. Besides, the human figure will slightly be modified in contrast and luminance corresponding to the background. Along with the $n*n$ grid image, if the depth process has been done and the candidate synthetic images have been generated, we plan to increase the accurate aesthetic of the human figure position. To accomplish that, we shrink the basic grid into $m*m$, and repeat the traversal steps. However, this process is alternative, one condition is that the human figure position is not at the saliency region if the saliency region requested well preserved. The other one is that running time of this model should be limited in a threshold which is set to 0.5 s in our application.

3.4   Assessment for Synthesis Images

Computational Photography Model. We adopt many photography guidelines (PG) in our work such as symmetry and patterns, rule of thirds and visual balance [13,18,19]. Rule of thirds (RT) may be the most popular photography guidelines which is based on the golden ratio. The image is split into 9 parts equally with two average horizontal and vertical lines. The main object should be put in the intersection, which is formalized as follows

$$Score(RT) = \max_{j=1,2,3,4} \frac{1}{\sum_{i \in S} d(S_i, I_j)} \sum_{i \in S} d(S_i, I_j) \exp(-\frac{d^2(S_c, I_j)}{2\sigma}) \qquad (2)$$

where S is the salient region set, I is the interaction set and c is the center point in salient region. σ is a parameter to control the range of score and set to 0.18.

Visual balance (VB) suggests the visual mass to be put in the center of a scene. We compute the saliency and depth intensity to get the visual center score as follows

$$Score(VB) = \frac{S_i}{\phi D_i} \exp(-\frac{\sum_{i \in S} d^2(S_i, C)}{2v}) \qquad (3)$$

where D is the depth intensity and C is the center point of the image. ϕ is a parameter to control the fusion rate of saliency intensity and depth intensity and set to 0.5. v is a parameter to control the range of score and set to 0.2.

Symmetry and patterns (SP) is a special rule in our model. If the image get a high score of symmetry, we will intend to put the human figure in the center which is corresponding to the visual balance. We compute the correspondence split by middle vertical line.

$$Score(SP) = \lambda \exp(-\frac{\sum_{\substack{i+p=H \\ j+q=W}} |(x_i, y_j) - (x_p, y_q)|^2}{2\omega}) \qquad (4)$$

where H is the height of the image, W is the width of the image and (x, y) is each point divided by the middle vertical line. λ and ω is parameters to control the range of score and set to 0.7 and 0.18. Finally, we combine those three computational photography guidelines to be a complete model and compute the final score.

Photo Aesthetic Evaluation. We use an instance-based approach for photo aesthetic evaluation algorithm [14]. Four features are selected as the main components including layout composition, edge composition, color palette and global texture features. Besides, several features such as blur feature, dark channel, contrasts and HSV counts are taken into consideration.

Furthermore, we employ the 3D structure for our aesthetic evaluation. We arrange the high-quality images in dataset and generate a few high-quality templates in depth intensity form, as well as low quality ones. The difference between high-quality (hq) and low-quality (lq) templates is considered as a unique feature. Totally it is 24 features and a binary classifier by using support vector machine (SVM) is utilized to train our dataset, which is formalized as follows

$$Score(AE) = \frac{w^T x - b}{|w^T x_{hq} - b|} \exp(-\frac{|w^T x - b|^2}{2\mu}) \qquad (5)$$

where w^T and b is the coefficient vector trained by SVM, and x is the features defined above. μ is a parameter to control the range of score and set to 0.2.

Saliency Evaluation. Except for the aesthetic evaluation mentioned above, we consider a further step to enhance the difference between 'good' and 'bad' synthetic images. As a common sense, people expect figures or objects to be salient in the scene. Accordingly, we consider both color (c) saliency and depth (d) saliency in our aesthetic evaluation model.

We use a saliency method that based on anisotropic center-surround difference [20]. We can get a initial saliency map according to the measure map which is resulted to [0, 255]. Besides, we use a soft image abstraction representation method to generate a saliency map based on color intensity [21]. Based on the formal steps, the saliency map is generated with a global uniqueness indicator

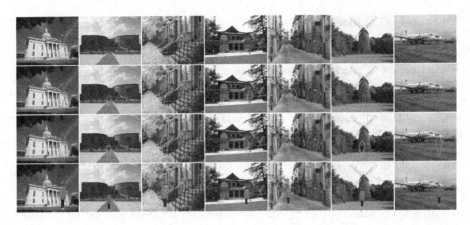

Fig. 3. Several results of our application. The first row is the photography scene. The second row is the professional photographer recommendation. The third row is best results of our method. The fourth row is the abridged view of synthetic images to show an intuitive feeling.

and a color spatial distribution indicator. We combine this map and the depth based map as complex saliency (CS) component in assessment module as follows

$$Score(CS) = \frac{a_{dm} + a_{cm}}{\xi A} exp(-\frac{\sum_{a \in s}(a_d + a_c)}{2\nu A}) \qquad (6)$$

where a is the pixel area of salient objects summed by depth based area a_d and color based area a_c. m is the pixel area of human figure region. A is the total pixel area of the photo. ξ and ν is parameters to control the range of score and set to 0.7 and 0.18 (Fig. 3).

Finally, we combine three components as one image quality assessment model. We find the dominate images which gets the highest score as follows

$$Dom\{i\} = \underset{i \in synthesis}{argmax} \; \alpha CS(i) + \beta AE(i) + \gamma PG(i) \qquad (7)$$

where i is each synthetic image. α controls the influence of complex saliency, β controls the influence of aesthetic evaluation model, γ controls the influence of photography guidelines. We linearly set complex saliency, aesthetic evaluation and computational photography guidelines factors with the equal weight 0.33.

4   Experiments and Analysis

4.1   Experimental Settings

To the best knowledge of ours, professional personal photography layout suggestion is a relatively minor area. Thus, we establish a small-scale dataset for our application experiment. We choose 21 scenes as our initial data structure.

All of them is outdoor environments with or without salient objects. For each scene, we take a background and three people in the photo with different positions and photography layouts. Moreover, one person is dressed in clothes with different colors to check the color palette effect. One person stands in different positions especially form an obvious unsightly layout. Therefore, we totally collect 630 images as our dataset. And we simply labeled non-person images as 'background', deliberately ugly setting images as 'unsight',and the remains as 'normal'. Moreover, we attach a rating score to each photos which is not used in this paper's work. This dataset can be used as a basal one for the task of making professional photography layout recommendation.

We invited 4 professional photographers to give their advice on where is the best position to stand. Because of the workload limit, we select 100 photos from our dataset, the Internet and SUN2012 dataset [16] for them and use the professional suggestion as a contrast. Besides, we downsample the photo to 640 × 480 resolution for unity. Moreover, we arrange a user study to check the accuracy of our method, we design a computational guidelines only assessment, an aesthetic only assessment, a saliency only assessment to show the enhancement and shortcoming in our method. We invited 12 volunteers with various backgrounds including 4 females and 8 males to test those synthetic photos based on saliency only method, aesthetic only method, computational guidelines only method and our combined method. Each photo is requested to mark 'Perfect', 'Satisfied', 'Mediocrity' and 'Bad'. 'Perfect' is the exactly best position in the users' mind. 'Satisfied' is that the current position is not the best but remain good aesthetic. 'Mediocrity' is the photo looks common and user can not say it is beautiful or ugly. 'Bad' is the photo looks ugly and not willing to show them to others. The professional photography contrast will show the disparity between our method and professional photography aesthetic. The user study will show the public view on our method.

4.2   Experimental Results and Discussion

Our experiments are based on the user study and professional photography contrast. From Fig. 4, we can see the great superiority of our method. The accurate data of our 'Perfect' is 62.42% and 'Satisfied' is 26.33%. Therefore, in 88.75% situation, users think our method is pleasing and applicable. While only 4.92% is bad and when it comes to separate method, it increase a lot. 27.58% saliency only method and 23.08% guideline only method is bad. Nearly half of the aesthetic method is 'Mediocrity' and 'Bad'. Therefore, our method is not just based on one main method. It can not be applicable if only one of those method considered. Moreover, the most satisfied situation is the guideline only method. It shows that guideline is the most common method to make people feel aesthetic about a photo, which is corresponding to the traditional photography rules. The saliency only method shows the worst 'Perfect' rate. But when it is combined by some aesthetic methods, it shows an obvious improvement.

The distance between our method result and professional photographer result shows that most of the distance is less than 60 pixels. Totally it is 400 photos and

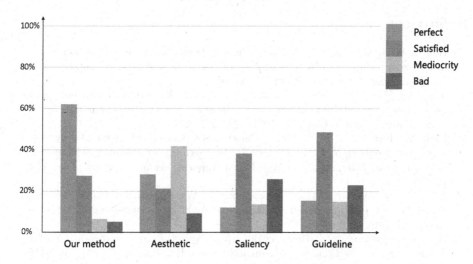

Fig. 4. The comparison of four assessment on user markings: Photography guidelines only method, saliency only method, aesthetic only method and our proposed method

each block is 20 pixel distance plus from darkness to the brightness. 20 pixels less distance occupies 23.75% and $[20, 40]$ pixel distance is 32.5%. Therefore, along with 18.5% of the $[40, 00]$ pixel distance, totally 74.75% situation is less than 60 pixel distance. Considering the photo is 640×480 resolution, we can tell that three quarters of our results are similar with professional view. However, about 20% situation is far away from the professional recommendation. Professional photography aesthetic is a complex problem in various scenes, but our method can be applied with most situations and satisfied with amateur photographers.

5 Conclusions

In this paper, we propose a method to the specific perspective of layout recommendation. Combining 3D structures into aesthetic estimation models along with saliency intensity shows a better discrimination. We also built a dataset designed for the task of making professional photography layout suggestion. According to the scene, our method supplies professional advice for human locations.

Acknowledgments. This work is supported by National Science Foundation of China (61321491, 61202320), Research Project of Excellent State Key Laboratory (61223003), Research Fund of the State Key Laboratory for Novel Software Technology at Nanjing University (ZZKT2016B09), and Collaborative Innovation Center of Novel Software Technology and Industrialization.

References

1. Bourke, S., McCarthy, K., Smyth, B.: The social camera: a case-study in contextual image recommendation. In: Proceedings of the 16th International Conference on Intelligent User Interfaces, pp. 13–22. ACM (2011)
2. Tian, Y., Wang, W., Gong, X., Que, X., Ma, J.: An enhanced personal photo recommendation system by fusing contextual and textual features on mobile device. IEEE Trans. Consum. Electron. **59**(1), 220–228 (2013)
3. Elahi, N., Karlsen, R., Holsbø, E.J.: Personalized photo recommendation by leveraging user modeling on social network. In: Proceedings of International Conference on Information Integration and Web-Based Applications and Services, p. 68. ACM (2013)
4. Xu, P., Yao, H., Ji, R., Liu, X.M., Sun, X.: Where should I stand? Learning based human position recommendation for mobile photographing. Multimedia Tools Appl. **69**(1), 3–29 (2014)
5. Xiang, Y., Savarese, S.: Estimating the aspect layout of object categories. In: 2012 IEEE Conference on Computer Vision and Pattern Recognition (CVPR), pp. 3410–3417. IEEE (2012)
6. Geiger, A., Wojek, C., Urtasun, R.: Joint 3D estimation of objects and scene layout. In: Advances in Neural Information Processing Systems, pp. 1467–1475 (2011)
7. Andriluka, M., Roth, S., Schiele, B.: Monocular 3D pose estimation and tracking by detection. In: 2010 IEEE Conference on Computer Vision and Pattern Recognition (CVPR), pp. 623–630. IEEE (2010)
8. Kumar, S., Hebert, M.: Discriminative fields for modeling spatial dependencies in natural images. In: NIPS (2003)
9. Saxena, A., Chung, S.H., Ng, A.Y.: Learning depth from single monocular images. In: Advances in Neural Information Processing Systems, pp. 1161–1168 (2005)
10. Ke, Y., Tang, X., Jing, F.: The design of high-level features for photo quality assessment. In: 2006 IEEE Computer Society Conference on Computer Vision and Pattern Recognition, vol. 1, pp. 419–426. IEEE (2006)
11. Luo, W., Wang, X., Tang, X.: Content-based photo quality assessment. In: 2011 IEEE International Conference on Computer Vision (ICCV), pp. 2206–2213. IEEE (2011)
12. Marchesotti, L., Perronnin, F., Larlus, D., Csurka, G.: Assessing the aesthetic quality of photographs using generic image descriptors. In: 2011 IEEE International Conference on Computer Vision (ICCV), pp. 1784–1791. IEEE (2011)
13. Liu, L., Chen, R., Wolf, L., Cohen-Or, D.: Optimizing photo composition. In: Computer Graphics Forum, vol. 29, pp. 469–478. Wiley Online Library (2010)
14. Lo, K.Y., Liu, K.H., Chen, C.S.: Assessment of photo aesthetics with efficiency. In: 2012 21st International Conference on Pattern Recognition (ICPR), pp. 2186–2189. IEEE (2012)
15. Gupta, S., Girshick, R., Arbeláez, P., Malik, J.: Learning rich features from RGB-D images for object detection and segmentation. In: Fleet, D., Pajdla, T., Schiele, B., Tuytelaars, T. (eds.) ECCV 2014. LNCS, vol. 8695, pp. 345–360. Springer, Heidelberg (2014). doi:10.1007/978-3-319-10584-0_23
16. Xiao, J., Hays, J., Ehinger, K.A., Oliva, A., Torralba, A.: Sun database: large-scale scene recognition from abbey to zoo. In: 2010 IEEE Conference on Computer Vision and Pattern Recognition (CVPR), pp. 3485–3492. IEEE (2010)
17. Achanta, R., Shaji, A., Smith, K., Lucchi, A., Fua, P., Susstrunk, S.: SLIC super-pixels compared to state-of-the-art superpixel methods. IEEE Trans. Pattern Anal. Mach. Intell. **34**(11), 2274–2282 (2012)

18. Grill, T., Scanlon, M.: Photographic Composition. Amphoto Books, New York (1990)
19. Krages, B.: Photography: The Art of Composition. Skyhorse Publishing, Inc., New York (2012)
20. Ju, R., Ge, L., Geng, W., Ren, T., Wu, G.: Depth saliency based on anisotropic center-surround difference. In: 2014 IEEE International Conference on Image Processing (ICIP), pp. 1115–1119. IEEE (2014)
21. Cheng, M.M., Warrell, J., Lin, W.Y., Zheng, S., Vineet, V., Crook, N.: Efficient salient region detection with soft image abstraction. In: Proceedings of the IEEE International Conference on Computer Vision, pp. 1529–1536 (2013)

Speech Enhancement Using Non-negative Low-Rank Modeling with Temporal Continuity and Sparseness Constraints

Yinan Li$^{(\boxtimes)}$, Xiongwei Zhang, Meng Sun, Xushan Chen, and Lin Qiao

Lab of Intelligent Information Processing,
PLA University of Science and Technology, Nanjing, China
{649447934,735865867}@qq.com, xwzhang@gmail.com,
sunmengccjs@gmail.com, chenxushan87@163.com

Abstract. Conventional sparse and low-rank decomposition based speech enhancement algorithms seldom simultaneously consider the non-negativity and continuity of the enhanced speech spectrum. In this paper, an unsupervised algorithm for enhancing the noisy speech in a single channel recording is presented. The algorithm can be viewed as an extension of non-negative matrix factorization (NMF) which approximates the magnitude spectrum of noisy speech using the superposition of a low-rank non-negative matrix and a sparse non-negative matrix. The temporal continuity of speech is also considered by incorporating the sum of squared differences between the adjacent frames to the cost function. We prove that by iteratively updating parameters using the derived multiplicative update rules, the cost function finally converges to a local minimum. Simulation experiments on NOIZEUS database with various noise types demonstrate that the proposed algorithm outperforms recently proposed state-of-the-art methods under low signal-to-noise ratio (SNR) conditions.

Keywords: Sparse and low-rank decomposition · Speech enhancement · Non-negative matrix factorization · Temporal continuity

1 Introduction

The goal of single-channel speech enhancement is typically to improve the quality and intelligibility in a single-channel recording of a noisy speech signal. According to [1], we know that traditional algorithms which have long been proposed and commercialized include spectral subtraction, Wiener filtering, minimum mean square error estimation and subspace methods. These algorithms are popular and widely used as they do not require the identity of the specific speaker, i.e. they are speaker independent. An estimation of the noise model is normally enough to make these algorithms work. However, most of these algorithms relay heavily on the estimation of noise power spectral density (PSD), and their enhancement performance decrease drastically in the presence of non-stationary noises [2].

© Springer International Publishing AG 2016
E. Chen et al. (Eds.): PCM 2016, Part II, LNCS 9917, pp. 24–32, 2016.
DOI: 10.1007/978-3-319-48896-7_3

Inspired by source separation techniques, non-negative matrix factorization (NMF), which is a powerful model for extracting perceptually meaningful components from mixtures due to its additive nature [3], has recently been extensively investigated for speech enhancement [4,5]. Most of these methods require a prior learning procedure of the involved source model/models (i.e., noise model or/and speaker dependent/independent speech model). Though these methods often yield better performance than traditional enhancement methods when dealing with non-stationary noises [6], the problem that training data of the encountered speech or/and noise is not always available beforehand and the possible mismatch with training samples greatly limit their applications in practice.

As an emerging technique, sparse and low-rank decomposition (or low-rank modeling), such as Robust Principle Component Analysis (RPCA) [7] and REPET-SIM [8] together with their extensions [9–11] have gained much attention. The basic principle is that repeating background is dense and low-rank (typically the background noise), while the non-repeating foreground (typically the speech) is sparse and varied. Based on these assumptions, the enhancement is conducted through a well-behaved convex optimization framework [12] or using a similarity matrix [13]. These techniques are intrinsically suitable for designing systems for unsupervised source separation since they require neither prior training nor hand-crafted features. However, these algorithms consider each frame as an individual observation and often neglect the temporal structure of speech. In the context of speech enhancement, incorporating the temporal continuity criterion may increase the robustness of enhancement, especially when dealing with non-repeating impulse noise or the input signal to noise ratio (SNR) is low. Therefore, we propose a robust version of NMF (RNMF) with temporal continuity which we will refer as TC-RNMF for the task of unsupervised speech enhancement.

The rest of this paper is organized as follows. Descriptions of the proposed robust non-negative matrix factorization (RNMF) with temporal continuity is illustrated Sect. 2. The enhancement algorithm is explained and summarized in Sect. 3. The experimental results of the proposed method are shown in the simulation experiments in Sect. 4. Finally, we conclude the paper in Sect. 5.

2   RNMF with Temporal Continuity

This section investigates the problem of robust non-negative matrix factorization with temporal continuity, and derives the corresponding multiplicative updating rules. Finally, the proof of the convergence of the proposed algorithm is given.

2.1   Formulation of the Optimization Problem

Given the magnitude spectrum of mixtures $\mathbf{V}$, we assume that $\mathbf{V}$ is the superposition of a low-rank repeating background magnitude $\mathbf{WH}$ and a sparse varied foreground $\mathbf{S}$.

The goal of RNMF is to minimize the divergence between the non-negative matrix $\mathbf{V}$ (magnitude of the mixtures) and its approximation $\mathbf{WH} + \mathbf{S}$, with all the matrices constrained to be non-negative. Our previous study [14] has shown that by imposing a threshold, which can be seen as an element-wise Boole operation, a sparse estimation of $\mathbf{S}$ will be obtained. Here, an alternative method is considered through a regularization term of sparsity. Moreover, the temporal continuity of speech is also considered through adding a regularization term measuring the changes between adjacent frame s_t and s_{t-1} (i.e. the adjacent columns of $\mathbf{S}$) to the divergence to be minimized. The problem of RNMF with temporal continuity can thus be formulated as follows:

$$\underset{\mathbf{W,H,S}}{\arg\min} D\left(\mathbf{V} \| \mathbf{WH} + \mathbf{S}\right) + \alpha c_t\left(\mathbf{S}\right) + \beta \|\mathbf{S}\|_1$$
$$s.t. \quad \mathbf{V} \in \mathbb{R}_{\geq 0}^{m \times n}, \mathbf{W} \in \mathbb{R}_{\geq 0}^{m \times r}, \mathbf{H} \in \mathbb{R}_{\geq 0}^{r \times n}, \mathbf{S} \in \mathbb{R}_{\geq 0}^{m \times n} \tag{1}$$

By choosing a small integer r, the matrix production of $\mathbf{W}$ and $\mathbf{H}$ acts as a low-rank approximation of $\mathbf{V}$ with the protection of $\mathbf{S}$ against outlier corruption. The matrix $\mathbf{S}$ is constrained to be non-negative and sparse with the parameter α to control the weight of temporal continuity (the regularization term $c_t\left(\mathbf{S}\right)$ is defined as $\frac{1}{2}\sum_{t=2}^{n} \|s_t - s_{t-1}\|_2^2$) and the parameter β is used to control the sparsity. Among all the possible choices of divergence [15], we use the generalized K-L divergence as cost function since it is a better approximation of human auditory perception compared with Euclidean distance. Its definition is presented in Eq. (2).

$$D\left(x \| y\right) = x\left(\log x - \log y\right) + \left(y - x\right) \tag{2}$$

Note that the learned basis vectors of $\mathbf{W}$ reflect the repeating patterns of background noises coupled with $\mathbf{H}$ as its activation matrix.

2.2 Updating Rules of RNMF

The optimization problem of RNMF can be solved using the multiplicative updating strategy similarly to that in normal NMF. By carefully choosing the step size of the gradient descent method, we can derive the update algorithms and represent them into multiplicative forms as follows:

$$W_{i,k} \leftarrow W_{i,k} \cdot \left\{ \sum_{j=1}^{n} \frac{V_{i,j}}{\sum_{k=1}^{r} W_{i,k}H_{k,j} + S_{i,j}} H_{k,j} \right\} \Bigg/ \sum_{j=1}^{n} H_{k,j} \tag{3}$$

$$H_{k,t} \leftarrow H_{k,t} \cdot \left\{ \sum_{i=1}^{m} \frac{V_{i,t}}{\sum_{k=1}^{r} W_{i,k}H_{k,t} + S_{i,t}} W_{i,k} \right\} \Bigg/ \sum_{i=1}^{m} W_{i,k} \tag{4}$$

$$S_{i,t} \leftarrow S_{i,t} \cdot \frac{\dfrac{V_{i,t}}{S_{i,t} + \sum\limits_{k=1}^{r} W_{i,k}H_{k,j}} + \alpha\left(S_{i,t-1} + S_{i,t+1}\right)}{\beta + 1 + 2\alpha S_{i,t}} \tag{5}$$

where we use the same symbols to notate the elements from their corresponding matrices with the subscript to identify their positions.

To solve the optimization problem of RNMF, we simply initialize the three matrices with non-negative random values and iteratively update them using Eqs. (3)–(5) alternatively until the cost function converges to a local minimum (the proof will be given later). Note that once the parameters are initialized with non-negative values, their sign always hold during iterations.

2.3   Proof of Convergence

We analyze the convergence of TC-RNMF and prove that the cost function keeps decreasing until it converges to a local minimum.

Definition. $G(\theta||\hat{\theta}, \mathbf{S})$ is an auxiliary function for cost function $C(\theta||\mathbf{S})$ if it satisfies the condition,

$$\begin{aligned} G(\theta||\hat{\theta}, \mathbf{S}) &\geq C(\theta||\mathbf{S}) \\ G(\hat{\theta}||\hat{\theta}, \mathbf{S}) &= C(\hat{\theta}||\mathbf{S}) \end{aligned} \tag{6}$$

here, we use the notation θ to denote $\mathbf{W}$ or $\mathbf{H}$ as the their symmetry when given a particular value of $\mathbf{S}$. The auxiliary function with the generalize K-L divergence exists and its detail form can be found in [16].

Theorem. The cost function of RNMF keeps decreasing until it converges to a local minimum by updating the three randomly initialized non-negative matrices using Eqs. (3)–(5).

Proof. Let t denotes the index of iterations, the cost function $C^{(t)}$ obtained by conducting Eqs. (3)–(5) are denoted as $C_1^{(t)}$, $C_1^{(t)}$ and $C_3^{(t)}$ respectively.

On one hand, as there exists an auxiliary function of $C(\theta^{(t)}||\mathbf{S}^{(t)})$, and the optimization of $G(\theta^{(t+1)}||\theta^{(t)}, \mathbf{S}^{(t)})$ over $\theta^{(t+1)}$ is straightforward, we can use an intuitive optimization presented in Eq. (7) to replace the optimization of $C(\theta^{(t)}||\mathbf{S}^{(t)})$.

$$\theta^{(t+1)} = \underset{\theta^{(t+1)}}{\arg\min}\, G\left(\theta^{(t+1)}||\theta^{(t)}, \mathbf{S}^{(t)}\right) \tag{7}$$

Then, the minimization can be conducted iteratively as follows:

$$\begin{aligned} C(\theta^{(t)}||\mathbf{S}^{(t)}) &= G(\theta^{(t)}||\theta^{(t)}, \mathbf{S}^{(t)}) \\ &\geq G(\theta^{(t+1)}||\theta^{(t)}, \mathbf{S}^{(t)}) \geq C(\theta^{(t+1)}||\mathbf{S}^{(t)}) \end{aligned} \tag{8}$$

Thus, we get $C_3^{(t)} \geq C_1^{(t+1)} \geq C_2^{(t+1)}$.

On the other hand, by applying the Jensen inequality, we obtain the following inequality:

$$
\begin{aligned}
& D\left(\mathbf{V}\|\mathbf{WH}+\mathbf{S}\right) \\
& = \sum_{i,j} D\left(V_{i,j}\| [\mathbf{WH}]_{i,j}^{(t)} + S_{i,j}^{(t+1)}\right) \\
& = \sum_{i,j} D\left(V_{i,j}\| \frac{S_{i,j}^{(t)}}{[\mathbf{WH}]_{i,j}^{(t)} + S_{i,j}^{(t)}} \cdot \left([\mathbf{WH}]_{i,j}^{(t)} + S_{i,j}^{(t)}\right) \frac{S_{i,j}^{(t+1)}}{S_{i,j}^{(t)}}\right. \\
& \left. \quad + \frac{[\mathbf{WH}]_{i,j}^{(t)}}{[\mathbf{WH}]_{i,j}^{(t)} + S_{i,j}^{(t)}} \cdot \left([\mathbf{WH}]_{i,j}^{(t)} + S_{i,j}^{(t)}\right)\right) \\
& \leq \sum_{i,j} \frac{S_{i,j}^{(t)}}{[\mathbf{WH}]_{i,j}^{(t)} + S_{i,j}^{(t)}} D\left(V_{i,j}\| \left([\mathbf{WH}]_{i,j}^{(t)} + S_{i,j}^{(t)}\right) \frac{S_{i,j}^{(t+1)}}{S_{i,j}^{(t)}}\right) \\
& \quad + \sum_{i,j} \frac{[\mathbf{WH}]_{i,j}^{(t)}}{[\mathbf{WH}]_{i,j}^{(t)} + S_{i,j}^{(t)}} D\left(V_{i,j}\| [\mathbf{WH}]_{i,j}^{(t)} + S_{i,j}^{(t)}\right) = F\left(\mathbf{S}^{(t+1)}\|\mathbf{S}^{(t)}\right)
\end{aligned}
\tag{9}
$$

We can build an auxiliary function for $\mathbf{S}$ by utilizing F as well as introducing the remaining terms regarding $\mathbf{S}$ in Eq. (1):

$$
G\left(\mathbf{S}^{(t+1)}\|\mathbf{S}^{(t)}\right) = F\left(\mathbf{S}^{(t+1)}\|\mathbf{S}^{(t)}\right) + \alpha c_t\left(\mathbf{S}\right) + \beta\|\mathbf{S}\|_1
\tag{10}
$$

Calculating the derivation of the auxiliary function G with respect to $\mathbf{S}$, we can obtain the update rule of $\mathbf{S}$ in Eq. (5). Given the property of the auxiliary function, we thus have proved that $C_2^{(t+1)} \geq C_3^{(t+1)}$.

Therefore, the cost function keeps decreasing by alternatively updating $\mathbf{W}$, $\mathbf{H}$ and $\mathbf{S}$, i.e.

$$
C_1^{(1)} \geq C_2^{(1)} \geq C_3^{(1)} \geq C_1^{(2)} \geq \cdots \geq C_1^{(t)} \geq C_2^{(t)} \geq \cdots
\tag{11}
$$

Since the cost function is monotonically decreasing, we have shown that the value of cost function converges to a local minimum.

3   Unsupervised Speech Enhancement

The overall framework using RNMF with temporal continuity for unsupervised speech separation is illustrated in the diagram of Fig. 1. The involved procedures can generally be divided into two steps: sparse and low-rank decomposition and post processing.

We first store the noisy speech into a buffer and calculate the noisy magnitude spectrogram using short time Fourier transformation (STFT). The phase of noisy speech denoted by $\angle\cdot$ is stored for clean speech synthesis later.

Then, RNMF with temporal continuity is adopted to decompose the spectrogram into three components, namely the low-rank non-negative matrix which

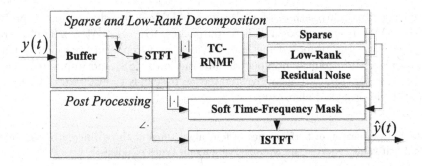

Fig. 1. The diagram of the proposed unsupervised framework for speech enhancement based on the proposed TC-RNMF.

is the product of two low-rank non-negative matrices, the sparse non-negative matrix representing the estimated clean speech and the residual noise matrix.

Finally, we use the soft time-frequency mask **M**, whose value is in the range of 0–1, to further improve the performance of enhancement,

$$\hat{\mathbf{S}} = \mathbf{M} \odot \mathbf{V} = \frac{\mathbf{S}}{\mathbf{WH} + \mathbf{S}} \odot \mathbf{V} \tag{12}$$

The waveform of estimated clean speech can be calculated using the noisy phase $\angle\cdot$ and the inverse STFT of $\hat{\mathbf{S}}$.

4   Experimental Evaluation

In the experiments, the clean speech samples are chosen from the NOIZEUS dataset which contains 30 short English sentences spoken by three male and three female speakers. Stationary noises from NOISEX-92 database [17] and highly non-stationary noises in [6] are respectively added to clean speech to synthesize the noisy speech with SNR ranges from −10 dB to 10 dB. Five types of stationary noises (white, pink, f16, factory1 and volvo) and five non-stationary noises (frogs, computer keyboard, casino, eating chips and machinegun) are tested in our experiments. Each file is resampled to 8 kHz and the spectrograms are calculated using a Hamming window of 64 ms (512 points) with a frame shift of 16 ms (128 points).

All the involved methods are evaluated by using the widely used signal-to-distortion ratio (SDR) in BSS-EVAL toolbox [18]. For SDR, higher value means better performance. To evaluate the impact of random initialization, the results of the proposed methods are averaged across 5 different random initializations. Without loss of generality, we report the mean values for different noise types.

We compare the proposed method, which is referred to as TC-RNMF (i.e. RNMF with Temporal Continuity), with our previous work [19] which uses the alternating direction method of multipliers (ADMM) to solve a similar problem of RNMF. Two recent established approaches, REPET-SIM and RPCA, are compared with the proposed method. Besides, as a representative of the traditional algorithm, multiband spectral subtraction (MSS) and minimum mean square error (MMSE) are also investigated as baselines to evaluate the performance of the proposed algorithm.

Table 1. Comparison of performance of four algorithms at three different input SNR levels. Each value reported are averaged among all types of noises

Input SNR	−10 dB	−5 dB	0 dB	5 dB	10 dB
ADMM	−5.76	−0.11	4.32	6.87	**7.79**
REPET-SIM	−6.64	−2.31	3.62	5.63	6.65
RPCA	−6.43	−1.97	3.79	6.48	6.78
MSS	−7.16	−2.43	3.11	5.39	6.43
MMSE	−9.47	−4.46	3.20	5.53	6.62
TC-RNMF	**−2.53**	**−1.43**	**5.28**	**6.91**	7.74

The performance of all the involved methods at different input SNR levels are presented in Table 1. It is obvious that the sparse and low-rank decomposition based methods such as ADMM, REPET-SIM, RPCA and TC-RNMF are superior to the baseline methods such as MSS and MMSE. This is expected as the stationary assumption of the baseline methods deviates severely from the reality when dealing with non-stationary noises.

We observe that the proposed TC-RNMF almost always performs better than the rest methods. Particularly, our method shows significant improvement under low SNR conditions. This boils down to the usage of temporal continuity constraint since the acoustic characteristics of speech vary not that drastically as a function of time. When the background noise is overwhelming and the time-frequency structures of speech spectrum are severely damaged or buried by the noise spectrum, imposing the temporal continuity constraint helps to better reveal the underlying pitch structure of original speech. Thus, the TC-RNMF yields a significant improvement of the enhancement quality under low SNR conditions.

5   Conclusion

This paper proposed an unsupervised algorithm for single channel speech enhancement which combines RNMF with temporal continuity. The existing algorithms based on sparse and low-rank decomposition are limited in a sense that they consider each frame as an individual observation. The proposed method incorporating the sum of the squared differences between the estimated adjacent frames of spectrum to the cost function is a straightforward and efficient way of including the temporal continuity to the unsupervised enhancement framework. Experimental results confirm the effectiveness of the proposed method especially when the input SNR is low.

Acknowledgments. This work is supported by NSF of China (Grant No. 61471394, 61402519) and NSF of Jiangsu Province (Grant No. BK20140071, BK20140074).

References

1. Loizou, P.C.: Speech Enhancement: Theory and Practice. CRC Press, Boca Raton (2007)
2. Mohammadiha, N., Smaragdis, P., Leijon, A.: Supervised and unsupervised speech enhancement using non-negative matrix factorization. IEEE Trans. Audio Speech Lang. Process. **21**(10), 2140–2151 (2013)
3. Smaragdis, P., Fevotte, C., Mysore, G.J., Mohammadiha, N.: Static and dynamic source separation using nonnegative matrix factorizations: a unified view. IEEE Sig. Process. Mag. **31**(3), 66–75 (2014)
4. Virtanen, T.: Monaural sound source separation by non-negative matrix factorization with temporal continuity and sparseness criteria. IEEE Trans. Audio Speech Lang. Process. **15**(3), 1066–1074 (2007)
5. Wilson, K.W., Raj, B., Smaragdis, P.: Regularized non-negative matrix factorization with temporal dependencies for speech denoising. In: INTERSPEECH, pp. 411–414 (2008)
6. Duan, Z., Mysore, G.J., Smaragdis, P.: Online PLCA for real-time semi-supervised source separation. In: Theis, F., Cichocki, A., Yeredor, A., Zibulevsky, M. (eds.) LVA/ICA 2012. LNCS, vol. 7191, pp. 34–41. Springer, Heidelberg (2012). doi:10. 1007/978-3-642-28551-6_5
7. Huang, P., Chen, S.D., Smaragdis, P., Hasegawa-Johnson, M.: Sing-voice separation from monaural recording using robust principal component analysis. In: IEEE International Conference on Acoustics, Speech and Signal Processing (ICASSP), pp. 57–60. IEEE Press, Kyoto (2012)
8. Rafii, Z., Pardo, B.: Online repet-sim for real-time speech enhancement. In: IEEE International Conference on Acoustics, Speech and Signal Processing, pp. 848–852. IEEE Press, Vancouver (2013)
9. Sun, C., Zhu, Q., Wan, M.: A novel speech enhancement method based on constrained low-rank and sparse matrix decomposition. Speech Commun. **60**, 44–55 (2014)
10. Chen, Z., Eills, D.P.W.: Speech enhancement by sparse, low-rank, and dictionary spectrogram decomposition. In: IEEE Workshop on Applications of Signal Processing to Audio and Acoustics, pp. 1–4. IEEE Press, New Paltz (2013)
11. Li, Y., Zhang, X., Sun, M., Min, G., Yang, J.: Adaptive extraction of repeating non-negative temporal patterns for single channel speech enhancement. In: IEEE International Conference on Acoustics. Speech and Signal Processing (ICASSP), pp. 494–498. IEEE Press, Shanghai (2016)
12. Candes, E.J., Li, X., Ma, Y., Wright, J.: Robust principle component analysis? J. ACM. **58**(3), 1–37 (2011)
13. Rafii, Z., Pardo, B.: Music/voice separation using the similarity matrix. In: 13th International Society for Music Information Retrieval, Porto, Portugal, pp. 583–588 (2013)

14. Sun, M., Li, Y., Gemmeke, J.F., Zhang, X.: Speech enhancement under low SNR conditions via noise estimation using sparse and low-rank NMF with Kullback-Leibler divergence. IEEE Trans. Audio Speech Lang. Process. **23**(7), 1233–1242 (2015)

15. Fevotte, C., Bertin, N., Durrieu, J.-L.: Nonnegative matrix factorization with the Itakura-Saito divergence: with application to music analysis. Neural Comput. **21**(3), 793–830 (2009)

16. Fevotte, C., Idier, J.: Algorithms for nonnegative matrix factorization with the beta-divergence. Neural Comput. **23**(9), 2421–2456 (2011)

17. Varga, A., Steeneken, H.: Assessment for automatic speech recognition: II. NOISEX-92: a database and an experiment to study the effect of additive noise on speech recognition systems. Speech Commun. **12**(3), 247–251 (1993)

18. Vincent, E., Gribonval, R., Fvotte, C.: Performance measurement in blind audio source separation. IEEE Trans. Audio Speech Lang. Process. **14**(4), 1462–1469 (2006)

19. Li, Y., Zhang, X., Meng, M., Min, G.: Speech enhancement based on robust NMF solved by alternating direction method of multipliers. In: IEEE International Workshop on Multimedia Signal Processing, pp. 1–5. IEEE Press, Xiamen (2015)

Facial Animation Based on 2D Shape Regression

Ruibin Bai, Qiqi Hou, Jinjun Wang$^{(\boxtimes)}$, and Yihong Gong

Institute of Artificial Intelligence and Robotics, Xi'an Jiaotong University,
28 West Xianning Road, Xi'an 710049, Shaanxi, China
{bairuibin,houqiqi}@stu.xjtu.edu.cn,
{jinjun,ygong}@mail.xjtu.edu.cn

Abstract. We present a facial animation system for ordinary single-camera videos based on 2D shape regression. Unlike some prior facial animation techniques, our system doesn't need complex equipment. The system consists of firstly a Cascade Multi-Channel Convolutional Neural Network (CMC-CNN) model to accurately detect facial landmarks from 2D video frames. Based on these detected 2D points, the facial motion parameters, including the head pose and facial expressions, are recovered. Then the system animates a bone-driven 3D avatar with the facial motion parameters. Experiments show that our system can accurately detect facial landmarks and the animation results are visually plausible and similar to the user's facial motion.

Keywords: Facial animation · Video tracking · 3D avatars

1 Introduction

Facial animation aims to generate and animate images or models of a character face. This approach has become well known and popular through animated feature films and computer games to control a digital avatar's head pose and facial expressions. This technique also plays an important role in many more areas such as education and scientific simulation.

Some facial animation systems have been proposed and achieved great success in film and game production by utilizing special motion-capture equipments, such as camera arrays [1], structured light projectors [20], and facial markers [9]. These methods can provide highly reliable facial animation, but the complex equipment makes them less practical for general users. With depth maps and video from Microsofts Kinect camera, Weise et al. [19] demonstrated impressive facial animation results, but this method can only work in indoor environments.

In this paper, we present a facial animation system for ordinary single-camera videos, which is more broadly practical. We firstly use Cascade Multi-Channel Convolutional Neural Network (CMC-CNN) like in [8] to get accurate face landmark detection. Then we generate facial animation data (e.g., head pose and facial expression parameters) based on the detected 2D landmark positions, and apply them to a digital avatar to generate the corresponding animation.

© Springer International Publishing AG 2016
E. Chen et al. (Eds.): PCM 2016, Part II, LNCS 9917, pp. 33–42, 2016.
DOI: 10.1007/978-3-319-48896-7_4

A key component of facial animation system is getting accurate facial landmarks. This problem has attracted a lot of research efforts and many detection algorithms have been proposed in recent years. These algorithms can be divided into two categories: optimization-based and regression based. Active Shape Model (ASM) [6] and Active Appearance Model (AAM) [5] reconstruct the face shape appearance by optimization approaches. These methods can only work effectively on certain datasets. Regression-based methods, especially cascade regression, have made great progress by learning a regression function that maps the input face image to the target output. For example, Cascade Pose Regression (CPR) [7] and Explicit Shape Regression (ESR) [3] progressively regress the shape stage by stage. Weise et al. [19] used the motion priors derived from pre-recorded animations in conjunction with a 3D face model and their method demonstrated striking real-time facial animation results. Cao et al. [2] showed comparable results using a single web camera by developing a user-specific 3D shape regressor.

Two 3D face models often used for facial animation are respectively blendshape model and bone-driven model [14]. The blendshape model allows a single 3D mesh to deform to achieve numerous pre-defined basis shapes and linear combinations of the basis shapes, such as Lewis et al. [11] and Seo et al. [17]. This model is specific to each character. The bone-driven model can generate subtle facial expressions based on the highly articulated facial skeleton structure and the articulation joints [12,13]. Compared with blendshapes, this animation model can get smoother results in spite of more preparation need to be done. In our system we utilize the bone-driven model to get the facial animation.

The remaining of this paper is organized as follows: Section 2 presents the overview of our system. Sections 3 and 4 respectively introduce the two main parts of our system, including the face landmark detection and the facial animation. In Sect. 5, we show the experiment results and user study. Section 6 concludes our paper.

2   System Overview

As shown in Fig. 1, our system consists of two major steps: face landmark detection and facial animation. An ordinary single-camera video will be input into the system, used to animate a bone-driven 3D model. The first face landmark detection step is proposed to obtain accurate facial landmarks by utilizing a CMC-CNN regression-based model. Then based on the detected 2D shape points, the facial motion parameters are recovered. During the facial animation step, we construct an articulated bone-driven model including 5 curve-controllers and 30 joint-controllers. Then the facial motion parameters are transferred to a bone-driven model to generate the corresponding animation.

3   Face Landmark Detection

In this paper, our face landmark detection algorithm resembles the regression in [8]. Specifically, it takes a single video frame $\mathbf{I}$ with initial face shape $\mathbf{S}^0$ and

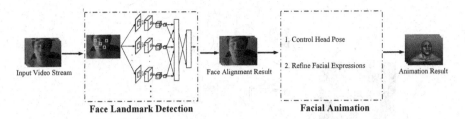

Face Landmark Detection   Facial Animation

Fig. 1. Overview of our system

ground truth shape $\hat{\mathbf{S}}$ as input, where $\mathbf{S} \in \mathbb{R}^{2*p}$ denotes the 2D positions of facial landmarks, and p is the number of facial landmarks. The whole model works in a cascade way. The next subsection briefly introduces the CMC-CNN model.

3.1 The Cascade Process

For the input facial image $\mathbf{I}_i$ and the corresponding initial shape $\mathbf{S}_i^0$, we predict the face shape $\mathbf{S}_i$ in a cascade manner. At stage t, the facial shape $\mathbf{S}_i^t$ is updated by refining $\mathbf{S}_i^{t-1}$ with the shape increment $\Delta\mathbf{S}_i^t$. The process can be presented as follows:

$$\mathbf{S}_i^t = \mathbf{S}_i^{t-1} + \mathbf{R}^t(\mathbf{I}_i, \mathbf{S}_i^{t-1}), \tag{1}$$

where $\mathbf{R}^t$ denotes the regressor at stage t, which computes the shape increment $\Delta\mathbf{S}_i^t$ based on the image $\mathbf{I}_i$ and previous facial shape $\mathbf{S}_i^{t-1}$.

In the training process, we learn the $t-th$ stage regressor $\mathbf{R}^t$ by minimizing the alignment error on the training set $\{\mathbf{I}_i, (\hat{\mathbf{S}})_i, \mathbf{S}_i^0\}_{i=1}^N$. This process can be expressed as follows:

$$\mathbf{R}^t = \underset{\mathbf{R}^t}{arg min} \sum_{i=1}^{N} \left\| \hat{\mathbf{S}}_i - \mathbf{S}_i^{t-1} - \mathbf{R}^t(\mathbf{I}_i, \mathbf{S}_i^{t-1})) \right\|_2, \tag{2}$$

where $\hat{\mathbf{S}}_i$ denotes the ground truth shape of image $\mathbf{I}_i$.

The predicted facial shape $\mathbf{S}_i$ will be more and more close to the ground truth shape $\hat{\mathbf{S}}_i$ through the cascade regression process. The process iterates until the predicted shape $\mathbf{S}_i$ converges.

3.2 The Structure of CMC-CNN

Figure 2 illustrates the form of one of the stages in CMC-CNN. For the input facial image $\mathbf{I}_i$ and the corresponding initial shape $\mathbf{S}_i^0$, we first get local patches around the region of each landmark. Then we transfer these patches to the convolutional layers. In practice, two convolutional layers are set after each input layer. Next the outputs of all local convolutional layer are connected by a fully-connected layer. Finally, the network outputs the predicted shape increment $\Delta\mathbf{S}_i$ for the initial shape $\mathbf{S}_i^0$. The following paper of this subsection will elaborate the details.

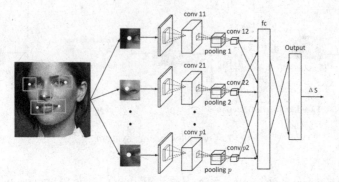

Fig. 2. One of the stages in CMC-CNN

Neuron. Rectified Linear Units (ReLU) is adopted as our neurons for the convolutional layer, which can be represented as follow:

$$\mathbf{O}_{i,j,k} = max(\sum_{x=0}^{h-1}\sum_{y=0}^{w-1}\sum_{z=0}^{c-1}\mathbf{I}_{i-x,j-y,z} \cdot \mathbf{W}_{x,y,z,k} + \mathbf{B}_k, 0), \tag{3}$$

where $\mathbf{O}$ denotes the output and $\mathbf{I}$ denotes the input to the convolutional layer. h, w, c and k are the width, height and channel of the $k-th$ filter. $\mathbf{W}$ denotes the weight and $\mathbf{B}$ denotes the bias.

Pooling Layer. In the network, pooling layers can summarize the output of neighboring groups of neurons in the same kernel map. In our work, we use the max pooling, which can be represented as follows:

$$\mathbf{O}_{i,j,k} = \max_{0 \leq x \leq p, 0 \leq y \leq p}(\mathbf{I}_{i \cdot d+x, j \cdot d+y, k}). \tag{4}$$

Loss Layer. Euclidean-loss is used as the loss layer in our work, which can be represented as follows:

$$loss = \frac{1}{2N}\sum_{i=1}^{N}\left\|\mathbf{O}_i - \Delta\mathbf{S}_i\right\|_2, \tag{5}$$

where $\mathbf{O}$ is the network output, $\Delta\mathbf{S}$ denotes the difference between ground truth shape and current shape, and N denotes the batch-size.

Dropout technique is a very effective way to reduce test errors. Instead of combining many different models, this technique can reduce complex co-adaptations of neurons. In our work, we set the output of each hidden neuron to zero with probability 0.5 in the train time. And in our test time, we multiply all neurons output by 0.5 as a reasonable approximation.

4   Facial Animation

The facial motion parameters, including the head pose and facial expression parameters, are calculated from the 2D facial landmarks detected in Subsect. 3.2, and they are then applied to animate a pre-constructed bone-driven avatar. As shown in Fig. 3, we create an articulated bone-driven 3D avatar, which presents facial animation by means of 5 curve-controllers and 30 joint-controllers. The 5 curve-controllers are located around the neck, aiming to control the avatar's head pose. The 30 joint-controllers, located around the typical facial landmark positions such as cheek, mouth lips, nose, eyelids, eyebrows and so on, are used to refine the facial expressions. Next we will elaborate the two animation processes: control head pose and refine facial expression.

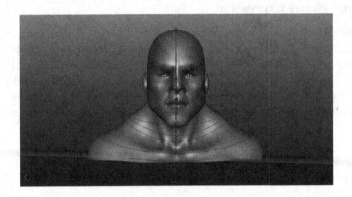

Fig. 3. Bone-driven 3D avatar

4.1   Control Head Pose

Two different ordinate systems are used in our work: 3D mesh ordinate and 2D image ordinate.

The constructed bone-driven model is a kind of 3D mesh composed of a set of vertices. The position of each vertex in 3D mesh coordinate is denoted as $\mathbf{u}_i$ in our work, and the position of a 3D vertex $\mathbf{u}$ can be projected into the 2D image ordinate with homogenous ordinates $\mathbf{s}_h = (x_h, y_h, m)$ by $\mathbf{s}_h = \mathbf{P}\mathbf{u}$, where $\mathbf{P}$ is a 3×3 camera matrix. The corresponding 2D point can be computed as $\mathbf{s} = (x, y)$, where $x = x_h/m$, $y = y_h/m$. In this paper, we represent this process as follows:

$$\mathbf{s} = \mathbf{P} \circ \mathbf{u}. \tag{6}$$

The avatar's head pose can be controlled by rotation $\mathbf{R} \in \mathbb{R}^{3*3}$, translation $\mathbf{t} \in \mathbb{R}^{3*1}$ and scale $w \in \mathbb{R}$ transformation. $\mathbf{R}$, $\mathbf{t}$, and w can be solved as follows:

$$\mathbf{R}, \mathbf{t}, w = \underset{\mathbf{R}, \mathbf{t}, w}{argmin} \sum_{k=1}^{p} \left\| \mathbf{s}^k - \mathbf{P} \circ [w(\mathbf{R}\mathbf{u}^{v_k} + \mathbf{t})] \right\|_2, \tag{7}$$

where p is the number of facial landmarks, $\mathbf{s}^k$ is the position of the $k - th$ landmark in 2D face shape, v^k is the corresponding vertex index on the 3D face mesh, and $\mathbf{P}$ is the camera matrix, which can be presented as follows:

$$\mathbf{P} = \begin{vmatrix} f_x & 0 & c_x \\ 0 & f_y & c_y \\ 0 & 0 & 1 \end{vmatrix}, \tag{8}$$

where f_x and f_y denote the focal length in terms of pixel units, and (c_x, c_y) represents the principle point which is usually at the image center.

Finally, we can control our avatar's head pose by transferring the facial motion parameters $\mathbf{R}$ and $\mathbf{t}$ to the avatar's curve-controller.

4.2   Refine Facial Expression

These landmark vertices, which correspond to facial features such as cheek, mouth lips, eyelids, nose, eyelids and eyebrows, play an important role in refining facial expression. Though the joint controllers located around these landmark vertices, we can animate the facial expressions of the bone-driven avatar.

Firstly, we project the 2D face shape $\mathbf{S}$ to 3D face shape $\mathbf{U}$ by means of the transformation parameters gained in Subsect. 4.1, which can be expressed as:

$$\mathbf{S} = \mathbf{P} \circ [w(\mathbf{RU} + \mathbf{t})]. \tag{9}$$

Then we calculate the shape increment $\Delta \mathbf{u}^{v_k}$ at the position of each 3D landmark $\mathbf{u}^{v_k}$ which attaches to the joint-controller, and this process can be presented as:

$$\Delta \mathbf{u}^{v_k} = \mathbf{u}^{v_k} - \mathbf{u}_0^{v_k}, \tag{10}$$

where v^k is the vertex index on the 3D face mesh $\mathbf{U}$, and $\mathbf{u}_0$ denotes the initial 3D facial landmark.

Finally, we apply the shape increment $\Delta \mathbf{U}$ to the initial neutral 3D face shape by means of 30 joint-controllers to generate various facial expressions.

5   Experiments

We implemented our experiments on a PC with an Intel Core i7-3770(3.40GHz) CPU and a NVDIA GeForce GTX TITAN X graphics card. We trained our CMC-CNN model on the *300-W* [16] dataset. The dataset contains several sub-datasets, including *AFW, LFPW, Helen, XM2VTS*, and *IBUG*. Following the protocol in *LBF* [15], we constructed the training dataset with the training set of *LFPW*, the training set of *Helen*, and the whole *AFW*, containing 3148 images in total.

To test the avatar animation of our system, we used several facial videos from the *300-VW* [4,18] dataset, which contains 114 facial videos in the wild, and all videos were captured at 30 fps. We also tested the system using the single face images from the dataset *300-W*. For quantitative evaluation of facial animation results, a user study is given.

Table 1. Parameters of our network.

Network	Stage 1	Stage 2	Stage 3	Stage 4
Patch ratio	0.3	0.2	0.1	0.1
Input	$15^2 \times 1$	$15^2 \times 1$	$15^2 \times 1$	$15^2 \times 1$
conv.1	$5^2 \times 16$	$5^2 \times 16$	$5^2 \times 16$	$5^2 \times 16$
conv.2	$3^2 \times 8$	$3^2 \times 8$	$3^2 \times 8$	$3^2 \times 8$
fc	1024	1024	1024	1024
Output	136	136	136	136

5.1 Experiments Setting

We used the well-known Caffe [10] to train the CMC-CNN model in the experiments. The neural network was trained by stochastic gradient descent method, and the momentum was set as 0.9. In our work, the learning rate was equally set as 0.01 in all layers, and the layer's weight at first stage was initialized by a zero-mean Gaussian distribution with σ set as 0.01. Table 1 shows other parameters of our network, where *patchratio* is the ratio between the local patch size and face rectangle, fc is the fully connected layer structure, and *Input*, *conv*.1 and *conv*.2 denote the structure of each local patch.

5.2 Results

Figure 4 shows several examples of the results generated by our system. Each row shows, from left to right, the input face image, the face landmark detection result and the avatar animation result. In spite of differences in facial expression, head pose and lighting, our system can get realistic results. During the animation test, the face alignment process takes 35 ms for one 500×500 image on average, and the animation process is performed at 12 ms per frame. The whole system runs at about 20 fps, which is fast enough for consumer-level applications.

5.3 User Study

To obtain quantitative evaluation of facial animation results, we conducted a user study. For this evaluation, we tested 30 persons, consisting of 4 PhD students, 9 post-graduate students, 12 undergraduates and 5 professors. There were 15 males and 15 females among the participants, and all of them were not related to this work. We showed each participant 5 videos of facial animation results, and each animation video consisted of 10 video clips, respectively containing different head pose and facial expressions. Each video clip lasted for 5 seconds and was presented at 640×320 pixels.

We asked the participants to rate the animation results, containing 50 video clips in total, on a scale of one to zero. Two criterions are applied in the user study: similarity of head pose and similarity of facial expressions. For the similarity of head pose, a score of 0 represents that user can find obvious mistake

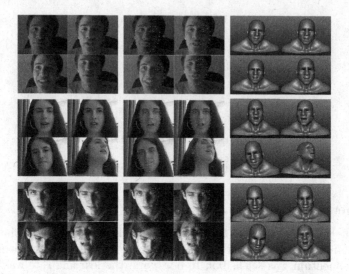

Fig. 4. Several examples of the facial animation results.

in the head pose of the avatar animation results. For example, the head pose of avatar is completely wrong at least in one angle, such as pitch, compared with the input video clip. A full score of 10 represents that user find the animation avatar's head pose is exactly same as the input video clip. For the similarity of facial expressions, a score of 0 means that user find the result of facial expression animation is completely wrong and artificial. For example, the avatar's facial expressions are seriously distorted and user can't make out them. A score of 10

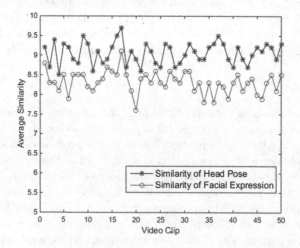

Fig. 5. Average similarity of head pose and facial expression

represents the facial expression animation is exactly same as the input video clip. In our work, a score of 7 is set as the consumer-level criteria.

As shown in Fig. 5, we counted the average similarity of head pose and facial expressions of each video clip. For the 50 video clips, the average scores of head pose and facial expressions were respectively 9.1 and 8.3. None of the animation results had a score below 7. These results indicate that our results are of high quality and the facial animation are realistic.

6   Conclusion

In this paper, we present a facial animation system based on 2D shape regression. Our system only needs ordinary web camera videos as the inputs to driven a digital avatar, which is broadly practical. The experiments show that the whole system can generate realistic and plausible facial animation results.

Acknowledgement. This work is partially supported by the National Science Foundation of China under Grant No. 61473219, and the National High Technology Research and Development Program of China (863 Program) under Grant No. 2014AA015205.

References

1. Bradley, D., Heidrich, W., Popa, T., Sheffer, A.: High resolution passive facial performance capture. ACM Trans Graph (TOG) **29** (2010). ACM. Article No. 41
2. Cao, C., Weng, Y., Lin, S., Zhou, K.: 3d shape regression for real-time facial animation. ACM Trans. Graph. (TOG) **32**(4), 41 (2013)
3. Cao, X., Wei, Y., Wen, F., Sun, J.: Face alignment by explicit shape regression. Int. J. Comput. Vis. **107**(2), 177–190 (2014)
4. Chrysos, G., Antonakos, E., Zafeiriou, S., Snape, P.: Offline deformable face tracking in arbitrary videos. In: Proceedings of the IEEE International Conference on Computer Vision Workshops, pp. 1–9 (2015)
5. Cootes, T.F., Edwards, G.J., Taylor, C.J.: Active appearance models. IEEE Trans. Pattern Anal. Mach. Intell. **6**, 681–685 (2001)
6. Cootes, T.F., Taylor, C.J., Cooper, D.H., Graham, J.: Active shape models-their training and application. Comput. Vision Image Underst. **61**(1), 38–59 (1995)
7. Dollár, P., Welinder, P., Perona, P.: Cascaded pose regression. In: 2010 IEEE Conference on Computer Vision and Pattern Recognition (CVPR), pp. 1078–1085. IEEE (2010)
8. Hou, Q., Wang, J., Cheng, L., Gong, Y.: Facial landmark detection via cascade multi-channel convolutional neural network. In: 2015 IEEE International Conference on Image Processing (ICIP), pp. 1800–1804. IEEE (2015)
9. Huang, H., Chai, J., Tong, X., Wu, H.T.: Leveraging motion capture and 3D scanning for high-fidelity facial performance acquisition. ACM Trans. Graphics (TOG) **30** (2011). ACM. Article No. 74
10. Jia, Y., Shelhamer, E., Donahue, J., Karayev, S., Long, J., Girshick, R., Guadarrama, S., Darrell, T.: Caffe: convolutional architecture for fast feature embedding. In: Proceedings of the ACM International Conference on Multimedia, pp. 675–678. ACM (2014)

11. Lewis, J., Anjyo, K.: Direct manipulation blendshapes. IEEE Comput. Graph. Appl. **4**, 42–50 (2010)
12. McLaughlin, T., Cutler, L., Coleman, D.: Character rigging, deformations, and simulations in film and game production. In: ACM SIGGRApPH 2011 Courses, p. 5. ACM (2011)
13. McLaughlin, T., Sumida, S.S.: The morphology of digital creatures. In: SIGGRAPH Courses, p. 1 (2007)
14. Orvalho, V., Bastos, P., Parke, F., Oliveira, B., Alvarez, X.: A facial rigging survey. In: Proceedings of the 33rd Annual Conference of the European Association for Computer Graphics-Eurographics, pp. 10–32 (2012)
15. Ren, S., Cao, X., Wei, Y., Sun, J.: Face alignment at 3000 fps via regressing local binary features. In: Proceedings of the IEEE Conference on Computer Vision and Pattern Recognition, pp. 1685–1692 (2014)
16. Sagonas, C., Tzimiropoulos, G., Zafeiriou, S., Pantic, M.: 300 faces in-the-wild challenge: the first facial landmark localization challenge. In: Proceedings of the IEEE International Conference on Computer Vision Workshops, pp. 397–403 (2013)
17. Seo, J., Irving, G., Lewis, J., Noh, J.: Compression and direct manipulation of complex blendshape models. ACM Trans. Graph. (TOG) **30** (2011). ACM. Article No. 164
18. Shen, J., Zafeiriou, S., Chrysos, G.G., Kossaifi, J., Tzimiropoulos, G., Pantic, M.: The first facial landmark tracking in-the-wild challenge: benchmark and results. In: Proceedings of the IEEE International Conference on Computer Vision Workshops, pp. 50–58 (2015)
19. Weise, T., Bouaziz, S., Li, H., Pauly, M.: Realtime performance-based facial animation. ACM Trans. Graph. (TOG) **30** (2011). ACM. Article No. 77
20. Weise, T., Li, H., Van Gool, L., Pauly, M.: Face/off: live facial puppetry. In: Proceedings of the 2009 ACM SIGGRAPH/Eurographics Symposium on Computer animation, pp. 7–16. ACM (2009)

A Deep CNN with Focused Attention Objective for Integrated Object Recognition and Localization

Xiaoyu Tao, Chenyang Xu, Yihong Gong$^{(\boxtimes)}$, and Jinjun Wang

Institute of Artificial Intelligence and Robotics,
Xi'an Jiaotong University, Xi'an 710049, Shaanxi, China
{txy666793,xu6666}@stu.xjtu.edu.cn,
{ygong,jinjun}@mail.xjtu.edu.cn

Abstract. We propose a novel deep convolutional neural network (CNN) architecture able to perform the integrated object recognition and localization tasks. We propose the Focused Attention (FA) objective that aims to optimize the network to learn features only from objects of interest while suppress those features from the background. As a result, the features extracted by the learned models can be used to accurately predict both the object category and the bounding box of the recognized object in the input image. Experimental results show that the proposed CNN architecture trained with the FA objective achieves better performances than original AlexNet in both the object localization and recognition tasks.

Keywords: CNN · AlexNet-FCN · FA objective

1 Introduction

Deep convolutional neural networks (CNNs) have achieved great successes in many computer vision and pattern recognition tasks, such as image classification [9,11,14], object localization [3–5], semantic segmentation [4,10], etc. For example, Krizhevsky et al. [9] developed an eight-layer CNN model (AlexNet in short) and trained the model using 1.2 million images from the ImageNet 2012 dataset [2] for image classification. The model won the ILSVRC 2012 competition by a significant margin. VGG-Net from [12] consists of a very deep network structure with up to 19 convolution layers, and is trained for image classification in a greedy way by initializing weight parameters from shallower models. Its object localization counterpart is realized by replacing the top convolution layer with a regressor which outputs the (x, y) location and (width, height) of the bounding box of the recognized object. The two models won the first and second places for the object localization and image classification tasks at the ILSVRC 2014 competition. GoogLeNet from [13] increases the depth to 22 layers with the "inception" building blocks and multiple Softmax loss functions, and won the first place for the image classification task of the ILSVRC 2014 competition.

© Springer International Publishing AG 2016
E. Chen et al. (Eds.): PCM 2016, Part II, LNCS 9917, pp. 43–53, 2016.
DOI: 10.1007/978-3-319-48896-7_5

The latest CNN model from MSRA [6] consists of a whopping 152 convolution layers, and won the image classification task at the ILSVRC 2015 competition.

There have been some problems in recent research and developments for deep learning neural networks. First, as evidenced above, many research works attempt to improve CNN performances by dramatically increasing the network complexity of CNN models. However, this approach is unsustainable, because very deep models, such as GoogLeNet [13], Google BN-Inception [7], MSRA-Net [6], not only become very difficult to train and use, but also require large CPU/GPU clusters, complex distributed computing platforms and ultra-large training data, which are out of reach for many research groups with a limited research budget, as well as many real applications. Second, unlike the human vision system that can quickly and accurately recognize and localize objects of interest at the same time, usually separate CNN models with different loss functions and training examples are required to accomplish the two closely related tasks, which is a waste of time, human efforts, and computing resources. Third and not the last, existing CNN models trained with the Softmax loss function learn and extract features from not only the target objects, but also the surrounding backgrounds. This will cause overfitting to the training data, and will especially harm CNN performances for localization.

In this paper, we propose a novel CNN architecture that is able to accurately recognize and localize objects of interest at the same time. We use the original AlexNet as the base model, and replace its top three fully connected layers with three convolutional ones, and its output layer with an average-pooling layer. To improve both the object recognition and localization accuracies, we introduce a novel objective function to optimize the model to learn features only from objects of interest while suppress those features from the background. We name it the *Focused Attention* objective, or FA objective in short. Comprehensive experimental evaluations show that the proposed FA objective remarkably improves not only object localization accuracy, but also object recognition accuracy on the ILSVRC dataset.

In summary, the contributions of our work are as follows:

- We propose a novel CNN architecture that is able to accurately recognize and localize objects of interest at the same time.
- We propose the FA objective that aims to optimize the model to learn features only from objects of interest while suppress those features from the background.
- We conduct comprehensive experimental evaluations to show that the proposed CNN architecture trained with the FA objective achieves superior performances in both the object localization and classification tasks.

The remaining of this paper is organized as follows: Section 2 describes the details of our proposed FA objective and fully convolutional network methods. Section 3 presents the experimental evaluations of our methods and our top-down visualization techniques. Section 4 draws a conclusion of our work.

2 The Proposed Method

2.1 Integrated Recognition and Localization

In this paper, we propose a fully convolutional architecture that accomplishes the tasks of object recognition and localization simultaneously. We start from the original AlexNet, retain its 1–5 convolution layers, and replace its three fully-connected layers to three convolutional ones. The 1000 feature maps of size 6×6 in the top convolution layer are average-pooled to produce an 1000-dimensional output vector for object category prediction. Thanks to the alternative to the fully-connected layers, the number of weight parameters are reduced from about 60M to less than 6M. We name the proposed fully convolutional network as AlexNet-FCN, as shown in Table 1.

Table 1. Architecture of our AlexNet-FCN model. "max" denotes the 3×3, $stride = 2$ max-pooling operation after convolution. The feature map of the top convolutional layer is average pooled to a C-dimensional vector.

Layer	Stage	Filters	Filter size	Conv stride	Pad	Output size
1	conv + max	64	11×11	4	4	55×55
2	conv + max	192	5×5	1	2	27×27
3	conv	384	3×3	1	1	13×13
4	conv	256	3×3	1	1	13×13
5	conv + max	256	3×3	1	1	6×6
6	conv	1024	3×3	1	1	6×6
7	conv	1024	1×1	1	0	6×6
8	conv + avg	1000	1×1	1	6	6×6

At the inference phase, AlexNet-FCN takes a cropped 224×224 patch from the input image, and outputs an 1000-dimensional vector that indicates a confidence score for each of the 1000 object categories. The category with the highest confidence score (denoted as c_i) is regarded as the top-1 prediction for the input image. Meanwhile, the c_i-th 6×6 feature map from the top convolution layer is used to compute the bounding boxes of the recognized objects directly. For convenience, we name the c_i-th feature map as the *heatmap*.

We use a graph method to compute the left, top, right and bottom margins of the bounding box(es) for the single or multiple recognized object instances from the heatmap. Let $\mathbf{G} = <\mathbf{V}, \mathbf{E}>$ denote an undirected graph where $\mathbf{V}$ is the vertex set to represent the heatmap pixels being activated and $\mathbf{E}$ the edge set. All pixels in the heatmap are normalized to $[0, 1]$ and a threshold t is introduced to determine whether a heatmap pixel is being activated or not. Each pixel p in the heatmap is represented by $v_p = \{z_p, (x_p, y_p)\}$, where z_p is the response value and (x_p, y_p) is its coordinates in the heatmap. v_p is added to $\mathbf{V}$ if it is activated.

An edge denoted by e_{pq} is added to $\mathbf{E}$ if vertices v_p and v_q are spatially adjacent in the horizontal or vertical direction. In summary, $\mathbf{V}$ and $\mathbf{E}$ are defined as:

$$\mathbf{V} = \{v_p | z_p > t\}, \quad \mathbf{E} = \{e_{pq} | \exists v_p, v_q \in \mathbf{V}, p \neq q, \; s.t. \; |x_p - x_q| + |y_p - y_q| = 1\} \quad (1)$$

Note that in localization task, object instances are mostly appeared once or twice and better separated in an image, which is much easier to localize than the detection task. We use the Breadth First Search algorithm (BFS) to find the connected components (maximal connected subgraphs) of $\mathbf{G}$. Denote by $\mathcal{G} = \{\mathbf{G}_k \in \mathbf{G} | k = 1, ..., K\}$ the set of K connected components in $\mathbf{G}$. Each connected component $\mathbf{G}_k \in \mathcal{G}$ corresponds to the k-th object instance. The coordinates of vertices in $\mathbf{G}_k$ are resized to the input scale and a bounding box is generated to contain all the vertices in $\mathbf{G}_k$. Examples of the generated bounding boxes are shown in Fig. 1.

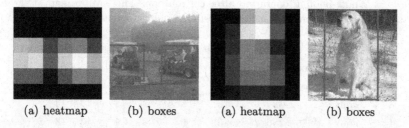

(a) heatmap   (b) boxes   (a) heatmap   (b) boxes

Fig. 1. Bounding boxes generated from the heatmap. (a) Heatmaps produced by AlexNet-FCN. (b) Bounding boxes computed using the graph method.

The final prediction is made by cropping 224×224 patches from four corners and the center as well as their horizontal reflections of the input image, performing recognition and localization for each patch and averaging the results. Bounding boxes predicted from all patches are merged using the Non-Maximum Suppression method (NMS). More details are presented in Sect. 3.

2.2   FA Objective

Our proposed FA objective enforces CNNs to learn features mainly from objects of interest while suppress those from the background. The FA objective is applied to high-level convolutional layers where features with high abstractions are represented. The method is elaborated as follows.

Let $D = \{(\mathbf{X}_i, c_i, B_i), i = 1, ..., N\}$ be the set of training samples, where $\mathbf{X}_i$ denotes the i-th image of size $H_i \times W_i \times 3$, $c_i \in \{1, ..., C\}$ the ground-truth category label, and $B_i = \{b_{im} | m = 1, ..., M_i\}$ the ground-truth bounding boxes of the objects in $\mathbf{X}_i$. M_i is the number of object instances in $\mathbf{X}_i$, and $b_{im} = \{a_l, a_t, a_r, a_b\}_{im}$ consists of 4 coordinates representing the left, top, right and bottom margins of the m-th bounding box in B_i. If a pixel of $\mathbf{X}_i$ locates in any bounding boxes of B_i, it is considered as an object pixel. Otherwise, it is a non-object pixel. Although the region enclosed by a ground-truth bounding box may contain non-object pixels in reality, we still deem all the pixels inside a bounding box as object pixels in order to simplify the computation. For each bounding box (object region) $b_{im} \in B_i$, its size changes in the feature maps of different layers. We simply resize the bounding box to fit the scale of the ith layer feature map so that neural responses in *object regions* and *non-object regions* could be separated reasonably.

The recursive function for each convolutional layer $k = 1, \ldots, K$ is defined as:

$$\mathbf{Z}_i^{(k)} = f(\mathbf{U}_i^{(k)}), \quad \mathbf{Z}_i^{(0)} \equiv \mathbf{X}_i,$$
$$\mathbf{U}_i^{(k)} = \mathcal{W}^{(k)} * \mathbf{Z}_i^{(k-1)}, \tag{2}$$

where K denotes the number of layers, the superscript (k) denotes the layer index, $\mathbf{Z}_i^{(k)}$ is the feature maps produced by input image $\mathbf{X}_i$ at layer k, $\mathbf{U}_i^{(k)}$ is the convolved responses before neural activation, $\mathcal{W}^{(k)}$ denotes the convolution weights absorbing the bias term, $*$ denotes the convolution operation, and $f(\cdot)$ is the neuron activation function on convolved responses $\mathbf{U}_i^{(k)}$. In this paper, we adopt ReLU [1] nonlinearity $f(x) = max(0, x)$ as the activation function to produce non-negative neural responses. Weights from all the layers are combined as $\mathcal{W} = \{\mathcal{W}^{(1)}, ..., \mathcal{W}^{(K)}\}$. Neural responses of $\mathbf{Z}_i^{(k)}$ are separated into two groups: responses of object regions and others of non-object regions:

$$\mathcal{O}_i^{(k)} = \{z \in \mathbf{Z}_i^{(k)} | z \text{ in object regions}\},$$
$$\mathcal{C}_i^{(k)} = \{z \in \mathbf{Z}_i^{(k)} | z \text{ in non-object regions}\},$$
$$s.t. \quad \mathcal{O}_i^{(k)} \cup \mathcal{C}_i^{(k)} = \mathbf{Z}_i^{(k)}, \ \mathcal{O}_i^{(k)} \cap \mathcal{C}_i^{(k)} = \emptyset. \tag{3}$$

For embedding the FA objective into layer k, we define the overall cost function as:

$$\min_{\mathcal{W}} L = \sum_{i=1}^{N} \{\mathcal{L}(\mathbf{W}, \mathbf{X}_i, c_i) + \lambda \ell(\mathbf{Z}_i^{(k)}, \mathcal{O}_i^{(k)}, \mathcal{C}_i^{(k)})\}, \tag{4}$$

where $\mathcal{L}(\mathbf{W}, \mathbf{X}_i, c_i)$ is the classification loss function, such as Softmax loss, and $\ell(\mathbf{Z}_i^{(k)}, \mathcal{O}_i^{(k)}, \mathcal{C}_i^{(k)})$ is the proposed FA objective embedded to layer k. λ is a coefficient to balance the strength of the FA objective relative to the classification loss. The grouped responses $\mathcal{O}_i^{(k)}$ and $\mathcal{C}_i^{(k)}$ defined by Eq. (3) are the inputs of the FA objective.

Let S_o, S_c denote the sum of responses in $\mathcal{O}_i^{(k)}$ and in $\mathcal{C}_i^{(k)}$, respectively, our FA objective is defined by the following subtraction form:

$$\ell = -(S_o - S_c). \tag{5}$$

Our goal is to enforce an overall increase of numeric values in $\mathcal{O}_i^{(k)}$ and decrease of numeric values in $\mathcal{C}_i^{(k)}$ by increasing the numeric difference between S_o and S_c.

This can be implemented by minimizing the above FA objective, which can be expanded as follows:

$$\ell(\mathbf{Z}_i^{(k)}, \mathcal{O}_i^{(k)}, \mathcal{C}_i^{(k)}) = -(\sum\nolimits_{z_o \in \mathcal{O}_i^{(k)}} z_o - \sum\nolimits_{z_c \in \mathcal{C}_i^{(k)}} z_c). \tag{6}$$

The gradients of ℓ with respect to z_o and z_c are

$$\frac{\partial \ell(\mathbf{Z}_i^{(k)}, \mathcal{O}_i^{(k)}, \mathcal{C}_i^{(k)})}{\partial z_o} = -1, \frac{\partial \ell(\mathbf{Z}_i^{(k)}, \mathcal{O}_i^{(k)}, \mathcal{C}_i^{(k)})}{\partial z_c} = 1. \tag{7}$$

Notice that the gradients are constant values during back-propagation. We need to tune the prefixed coefficient λ carefully to make sure that sensitivities are in a proper range. Otherwise, the SGD process tends to be unstable, which may lead to explosion.

The gradients of the overall cost function L with respect to $\mathbf{Z}_i^{(k)}$ is computed by adding the gradients of $\mathcal{L}$ and ℓ multiplied by λ. In practice, we adjust the strength of the FA objective by tuning λ in a proper range to balance with the classification loss. More implementation details for the AlexNet-FCN model are discussed in Sect. 3.

2.3   Improving AlexNet-FCN with FA Objective

We improve the performance of AlexNet-FCN by embedding the FA objective (see Sect. 2.2) to the top convolutional layer of the network. We only apply the objective to the c_i-th feature map in the top layer, where c_i is the ground-truth category label of the i-th training sample. In this way, only the feature map that corresponds to the object's category is enforced to represent the object regions. Here, we make some modifications to the original form of the FA objective:

$$\ell(\mathbf{Z}_i^{(k)}, \mathcal{O}_i^{(k)}, \mathcal{C}_i^{(k)}) = -(\sum\nolimits_{z_o \in \mathcal{O}_i^{(k)}} \gamma z_o - \sum\nolimits_{z_c \in \mathcal{C}_i^{(k)}} z_c), \quad \mathbf{F}_i^{(k)} = (\mathbf{Z}_i^{(k)})_{c_i}, \tag{8}$$

$$\mathcal{O}_i^{(k)} = \{z \in \mathbf{F}_i^{(k)} | z \text{ in object-regions}\},$$

$$\mathcal{C}_i^{(k)} = \{z \in \mathbf{F}_i^{(k)} | z \text{ in context-regions}\},$$

where $\mathbf{F}_i^{(k)}$ denotes the c_i-th feature map of $\mathbf{Z}_i^{(k)}$, which means the FA objective only affects the feature map specified by the ground-truth category label. An additional coefficient γ is introduced to balance between the object and non-object regions. The gradient is computed as:

$$\frac{\partial \ell}{\partial z_o} = -\gamma, \quad \frac{\partial \ell}{\partial z_c} = 1. \tag{9}$$

The overall gradient for the c_i-th feature map is

$$\frac{\partial L}{\partial z_o} = p_{c_i} - 1 - \lambda\gamma, \quad \frac{\partial L}{\partial z_c} = p_{c_i} - 1 + \lambda, \tag{10}$$

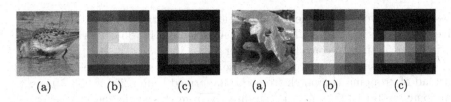

(a)   (b)   (c)   (a)   (b)   (c)

Fig. 2. Heatmap visualization. (a) Input images. (b), (c) The heatmaps produced by AlexNet-FCN before and after using the FA objective, respectively.

where $(p_{c_i} - 1)$ is the gradient back-propagated from the c_i-th output neuron in the average-pooling layer (p_{c_i} denotes the probability of the ground-truth label c_i). λ is set to a "big" value (but no bigger than 1) so that the non-object region responses are suppressed to a great extent, and γ is used to prevent an over-enhancement of the object region responses which may result in the gradient exploding problem.

As shown in Fig. 2, after introducing the FA objective, the heatmap becomes much "cleaner". Only the neurons related to the object regions are significantly activated while other neural responses are suppressed close to zero. Consequently, the heatmap is able to compute bounding boxes more accurately.

3   Experiments

The object recognition and localization experiments are conducted using the ImageNet ILSVRC 2012 dataset. Data for the object recognition task consists of about 1.28 million training, 50,000 validation and 150,000 test images. Each training and validation image is labeled with one of the 1000 object categories. Data for the single-class object localization task consists of the same images as those for the recognition task, except that every object instance belonging to the labeled category in an image is annotated with an axis-aligned bounding box.

Experiments are performed with cuda-convnet2 [8]. We train the models using SGD with a mini-batch size of 128, momentum of 0.9, and weight decay of 0.0005. The learning rate is initialized to 0.01 and decreases three times to 0.0001. Each model is trained for 90 epochs through the training set of 1.28 million images. To measure the improvement brought by our method in a fair setting, the comparison between different CNN models is under the same complexity. Models are trained and tested in single-scale, and test results are based on single model predictions.

3.1   Recognition Evaluation

For the object recognition task, we conduct experimental evaluations for the following models: (1) the original AlexNet, (2) AlexNet trained with the FA objective (denoted as AlexNet+FA), (3) the proposed AlexNet-FCN trained without the FA objective, and (4) the proposed AlexNet-FCN trained with the FA objective (denoted as AlexNet-FCN+FA). For AlexNet, our FA objective is introduced to its layer 5 (the top convolutional layer).

We first resize the training images so that the shortest side equals to 256. Instead of cropping the patch from the uniformed center 256×256 image, we randomly crop the 224×224 patch directly from the whole $256 \times N$ image, so that background pixels could be included in the input patch to a certain extent. All models take the cropped 224×224 patch as the input, and output an 1000-dimensional vector to specify the confidence scores for each of the 1000 object categories. Note that the effect brought by the FA objective can not be too strong (which may result in gradient exploding or overwhelm the Softmax loss) or too weak. Therefore, the coefficient λ of the objective function must be set to a proper range. We evaluate the average gradient of layer 5 from a pre-trained AlexNet model and set $\lambda = 10^{-6}$ for the FA objective function (Eq. (6)) when training the AlexNet+FA model. To make the model converge more stably, we manually decrease λ once from 10^{-6} to 5×10^{-7} at 50% of the training progress. For the proposed AlexNet-FCN+FA model, we initialize its weight parameters of the first 5 convolution layers from a pre-trained AlexNet model to speed up the training process. We evaluate the average gradient of the top convolution layer of the AlexNet-FCN model (Eq. (9)), and set $\lambda = 10^{-2}$, $\gamma = 10^{-3}$ for the modified FA objective function (Eq. (8)). At the test stage, we perform multiview test on the validation set. Our reproduced accuracy of the AlexNet model is 60.8%, about 1.5% higher than 59.3% of the original version in [9]. This is mainly because the multiview test is performed on the whole $256 \times N$ validation image instead of the center 256×256 patch. In this way, the whole image is preserved for testing and all pixels of the object would be evaluated.

Table 2. Object recognition results on ILSVRC 2012 validation set.

Model	Top-1 acc. (%)	Top-5 acc. (%)
AlexNet	60.8	82.4
AlexNet+FA	61.7	83.3
AlexNet-FCN	60.7	82.4
AlexNet-FCN+FA	61.6	83.2

Table 2 shows the evaluation results of the four models using the ILSVRC 2012 validation set. The results can be summarized as follows.

- AlexNet trained with the proposed FA objective improves the top-1 and top-5 recognition accuracies by 0.9%–1.0%.
- The proposed AlexNet-FCNs trained with and without the FA objective achieve the object recognition accuracies on par with the results from the corresponding AlexNets. This is not a surprise because AlexNet-FCN has the same complexity as AlexNet, with much less network parameters. The main

difference between the two networks is that the three fully connected layers of AlexNet are replaced by the three convolution ones.

3.2 Localization Evaluation

For the object localization task, we compare the proposed AlexNet-FCN with the localization version of AlexNet using the ILSVRC 2012 dataset. We adopt the evaluation metric used by the ILSVRC competition, that is, the predicted bounding box is deemed correct if it overlaps the ground-truth bounding box over 50%, and the predicted top-5 categories contain the ground-truth one. The training of both the AlexNet-FCN and AlexNet-FCN+FA models has been described in Sect. 3.1. At test stage, we compute the bounding box predictions on the validation set using the method described in Sect. 2.1. Since Krizhevsky et al. [9] did not publish the localization version of AlexNet, we reproduced the model by replacing the classifier with a regressor in a way similar to that of the OverFeat and the VGG-Net models. The regressor is added onto the pooled feature map from layer 5 (the top convolutional layer) and outputs a 4-D vector representing the 4 coordinates of a bounding box. We performed SCR (single-class regression) with Euclidean loss to train the regressor on the ILSVRC dataset. At test stage, the final bounding box prediction is made by merging predictions from multi-view patches (four corners and the center as well as their horizontal reflections, the same as AlexNet-FCN merging approach in Sect. 2.3). The reproduced AlexNet for localization has achieved the accuracy of 57.3% on single scale, as shown in Table 3.

Table 3. Localization accuracy on ILSVRC 2012 validation set.

Model	Localization acc. (%)
AlexNet	57.3
AlexNet-FCN	51.5
AlexNet-FCN+FA	60.1

Table 3 shows the localization accuracy of the three models on ILSVRC 2012 validation set. As we can see, AlexNet-FCN without the FA objective yields poor performance on localization. After applying the FA objective to train AlexNet-FCN, only the object-pixels of the heat-map are activated (see Fig. 2), and the model becomes more effective to localize the recognized object. We may notice that the AlexNet-FCN model without FA objective performs worse than the AlexNet model when localizing an object, because the produced heatmap does not provide an accurate saliency response for localization. By introducing the proposed FA objective, the heatmap becomes sufficient for bounding box computation, and significantly improves AlexNet-FCN's localization accuracy by 8.6%. Finally, the proposed AlexNet-FCN+FA model achieves the localization accuracy 2.8% better than that of the reproduced AlexNet model. Examples on localization results are shown in Fig. 3.

Fig. 3. Localization examples of AlexNet-FCN with FA objective

4   Conclusion

In this paper, we focus recent deep learning problems and propose a novel CNN architecture to accurately recognize and localize objects of interest at the same time. We implement an FCN model based on AlexNet for integrated recognition and localization and introduce our FA objective to optimize the network to learn features mainly from objects of interest while suppress those from the context. Experimental results show that our proposed CNN architecture with FA objective remarkably improves both object localization accuracy and object recognition accuracy on the ILSVRC dataset.

Acknowledgments. This work is supported by National Basic Research Program of China (973 Program) under Grant No. 2015CB351705, and the National Natural Science Foundation of China (NSFC) under Grant No. 61332018.

References

1. Dahl, G.E., Sainath, T.N., Hinton, G.E.: Improving deep neural networks for LVCSR using rectified linear units and dropout. In: 2013 IEEE International Conference on Acoustics, Speech and Signal Processing (ICASSP), pp. 8609–8613. IEEE (2013)
2. Deng, J., Dong, W., Socher, R., Li, L.J., Li, K., Fei-Fei, L.: Imagenet: a large-scale hierarchical image database. In: 2009 IEEE Conference on Computer Vision and Pattern Recognition, CVPR 2009, pp. 248–255. IEEE (2009)
3. Erhan, D., Szegedy, C., Toshev, A., Anguelov, D.: Scalable object detection using deep neural networks. In: 2014 IEEE Conference on Computer Vision and Pattern Recognition (CVPR), pp. 2155–2162. IEEE (2014)
4. Girshick, R., Donahue, J., Darrell, T., Malik, J.: Rich feature hierarchies for accurate object detection and semantic segmentation. In: 2014 IEEE Conference on Computer Vision and Pattern Recognition (CVPR), pp. 580–587. IEEE (2014)
5. He, K., Zhang, X., Ren, S., Sun, J.: Spatial pyramid pooling in deep convolutional networks for visual recognition. In: Fleet, D., Pajdla, T., Schiele, B., Tuytelaars, T. (eds.) ECCV 2014. LNCS, vol. 8691, pp. 346–361. Springer, Heidelberg (2014). doi:10.1007/978-3-319-10578-9_23

6. He, K., Zhang, X., Ren, S., Sun, J.: Deep residual learning for image recognition. arXiv preprint arXiv:1512.03385 (2015)
7. Ioffe, S., Szegedy, C.: Batch normalization: accelerating deep network training by reducing internal covariate shift. arXiv preprint arXiv:1502.03167 (2015)
8. Krizhevsky, A.: One weird trick for parallelizing convolutional neural networks. arXiv preprint arXiv:1404.5997 (2014)
9. Krizhevsky, A., Sutskever, I., Hinton, G.E.: Imagenet classification with deep convolutional neural networks. In: Advances in Neural Information Processing Systems, pp. 1097–1105 (2012)
10. Long, J., Shelhamer, E., Darrell, T.: Fully convolutional networks for semantic segmentation. arXiv preprint arXiv:1411.4038 (2014)
11. Sermanet, P., Eigen, D., Zhang, X., Mathieu, M., Fergus, R., LeCun, Y.: Overfeat: integrated recognition, localization and detection using convolutional networks. arXiv preprint arXiv:1312.6229 (2013)
12. Simonyan, K., Zisserman, A.: Very deep convolutional networks for large-scale image recognition. arXiv preprint arXiv:1409.1556 (2014)
13. Szegedy, C., Liu, W., Jia, Y., Sermanet, P., Reed, S., Anguelov, D., Erhan, D., Vanhoucke, V., Rabinovich, A.: Going deeper with convolutions. arXiv preprint arXiv:1409.4842 (2014)
14. Zeiler, M.D., Fergus, R.: Visualizing and understanding convolutional networks. In: Fleet, D., Pajdla, T., Schiele, B., Tuytelaars, T. (eds.) ECCV 2014. LNCS, vol. 8689, pp. 818–833. Springer, Heidelberg (2014). doi:10.1007/978-3-319-10590-1_53

An Accurate Measurement System for Non-cooperative Spherical Target Based on Calibrated Lasers

Hang Dong[✉], Fei Wang, Haiwei Yang, Zhongheng Li, and Yanan Chen

Xi'an Jiaotong University, Xi'an, Shaanxi, China
dhunter1230@gmail.com, wfx@mail.xjtu.edu.cn,
{yanghw.2005,chenyanan}@stu.xjtu.edu.cn, lizhongheng2010@gmail.com

Abstract. Strong demands for accurate measurement of non-cooperative targets have been arising for the tasks of assembling and capturing recently. Spherical object is one of the most common targets in these applications. The existing measurement system has limitations in detecting textureless target in spite of their high price. In this paper, we propose a novel measurement system for textureless non-cooperative spherical target based on four calibrated lasers and a vision camera. By using the pre-calibrated lasers, our system can definitely reconstruct the 3-D positions of the laser spots on target without any depth sensor. The experiment results show that the pose and the radius of spherical target can be estimated with high accuracy in real time.

Keywords: Non-cooperative · Measurement system · Spherical target · Calibrated laser

1 Introduction

Measurement for non-cooperative targets is the precondition of assembling and capturing tasks, which has received attention in various areas such as autonomous robotics [2,3], marine transportation [6–8] and aerospace [11,12]. Non-cooperative targets refer to those objects which cannot provide effective cooperation information, their structure, size and motion information are completely or partly unknown.

In measuring and capturing of a non-cooperative target, computer vision is exclusively used as the primary feedback sensor to acquire the pose information of the target. According to the amounts of the camera, vision measurement methods for non-cooperative targets can be classified as monocular vision based, multi-vision based, and multi-sensor fusion based. For the methods using monocular vision, Zhang Shijie et al. [14] proposed a robust algorithm based on R-RANSAC in 2009, using monocular vision to acquire the relative pose of a spacecraft. Fang et al. [15] presents a novel two-level scheme for adaptive active visual servoing to determine relative pose between a camera and a target. For the methods using multi-vision, Xu Wenfu et al. [13] reconstructs the 3-D model of

© Springer International Publishing AG 2016
E. Chen et al. (Eds.): PCM 2016, Part II, LNCS 9917, pp. 54–63, 2016.
DOI: 10.1007/978-3-319-48896-7_6

non-cooperative spacecraft and calculate the pose of spacecraft based on stereo vision. In [10] Segal et al. employs a stereoscopic vision system for determining the relative pose of the target non-cooperative spacecraft by tracking feature points on it.

In recent years, with the rapid development of multisensor fusion technology, camera-only based methods are gradually replaced by multi-sensor fusion based methods in the study of non-cooperative object measurement. To enhance accuracy of pose estimation, a camera is combined with 2-D or 3-D laser scanners in [1,4], which can resolve the inaccuracy of depth in stereo-vision system by directly measuring the depth of correspondence points. Myung et al. in [5,9] proposed a structured light system illuminates patterns of light to calculate the plane-to-plane relative position. This system is composed of two screen planes at both ends, each having one or two laser pointers and a camera installed onto the screen. Recently, a non-contact 6-DOF pose sensor system with three laser one-dimensional sensors and a camera was developed to track the dynamic motions of a cargo ship [6–8]. This system can accurately measure a 6-DOF pose from a distance by tracking feature points of the object.

In this paper, we are focusing on proposing a novel and fully-portable system to measure the geometric parameters of non-cooperative sphere in near distance($<2\,$m), which can be widely used in industrial quality detection and objects capturing tasks. Also, the aim of this study is to mitigate the limitations of the existing systems and to provide an inexpensive embedded solution for engineering application.

Inspired by multi-sensor fusion methods, the proposed system is composed of four calibrated lasers and a vision camera, which can directly measure the positions and radius of textureless sphere without any extra sensor units on the target. By using the calibrated lasers and camera projection model, our method can achieve a high accuracy without using any depth sensor, such as 1-D laser sensor and 3-D scanner. The performance of the proposed system is validated in an embedded system with field experiment.

2   Measurement Algorithm Description

2.1   System Description

As Fig. 1 shows, the designed measurement system is composed of two parts: four calibrated lasers and a vision camera. Four lasers are placed on the front panel of camera in a square configuration with a width of 50 mm. The lens of vision camera is installed at the center of the four lasers. Noticing that both the projection matrix of camera and the linear parameter of each laser beam with respect to (w.r.t.) world coordinate frame are pre-calibrated. An illustration of proposed measurement method is shown in Fig. 2(a).

2.2   Description of Coordinate Frame

The measurement system has three different coordinate frames: {W} is the world (ground) coordinate frame with its origin at the installation location of

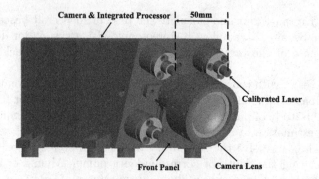

Fig. 1. 3-D model of the measurement system

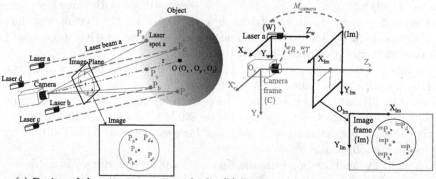

(a) Design of the measurement method   (b) Diagram of reference coordinate frames

Fig. 2. Illustration of measurement method and its reference coordinate frames

Laser a; {C} is the camera coordinate frame with its origin at the center of camera aperture. {Im} is the image coordinate frame with its origin at the top left corner of the image plane. The relationship between camera coordinate frame and image coordinate frame can be described by pinhole model. All of these coordinate frames are orthogonal. The principle of measuring a unknown spherical target is solving for the geometric parameters: $^{w}O = [^{w}O_x, ^{w}O_y, ^{w}O_z]^T$, the 3-D positions of sphere center with respect to frame {W}, and r, the radius of sphere. A diagram of coordinate frames is shown in Fig. 2(b).

2.3   Equation of ^{w}P

In order to calculate the parameter of a unknown sphere, at least three non-coplanar points on the surface of sphere are needed to fit the sphere. As shown in Fig. 2(a), the front panel of camera consists of four lasers which project their laser beams onto the surface of target. Assuming $^{w}P_i = [^{w}P_{ix}, ^{w}P_{iy}, ^{w}P_{iz}]^T$,

Table 1. List of Symbols

$\{W\}$	World coordinate frame
$^{w}P_i$	Positions of laser spot i w.r.t. $\{W\}$
$\{C\}$	Camera coordinate frame
$^{w}L_i$	Installation positions of laser i w.r.t. $\{W\}$
$\{Im\}$	Image coordinate frame
$^{w}D_i$	Direction vector of laser beam i w.r.t. $\{W\}$
^{w}O	Positions of center of sphere w.r.t. $\{W\}$
$^{c}P_i$	Positions of one laser spot i w.r.t. $\{C\}$
r	Radius of sphere
$^{im}P_i$	Image coordinates of laser spot i
M_{camera}	Camera projection matrix
$^{im}P_o$	Image coordinates of the center of projected circle

$i = \{a, b, c, d\}$ are the 3-D positions of laser spot i on the target surface, its coordinate should satisfy the following formula of sphere:

$$(^{w}P_{ix} - {}^{w}O_x)^2 + (^{w}P_{iy} - {}^{w}O_y)^2 + (^{w}P_{iz} - {}^{w}O_z)^2 = r^2. \qquad (1)$$

Meanwhile, the laser spot i is also restricted by the linear equation of laser beam i. The linear constraint can be given as follows: Table 1

$$\begin{bmatrix} ^{w}P_{ix} \\ ^{w}P_{iy} \\ ^{w}P_{iz} \end{bmatrix} = {}^{w}D_i t_i + {}^{w}L_i \qquad (2)$$

where t_i is an arbitrary scale factor, $^{w}L_i = [^{w}x_{io}, {}^{w}y_{io}, {}^{w}z_{io}]^T$ are the installation positions of laser sensor i and $^{w}D_i = [m_i, n_i, p_i]^T$ is the direction vector of laser beam i with respect to frame $\{W\}$.

Combining (2) and (1), a quadratic equation of t_i can be given as follows:

$$Q_{sphere} \begin{bmatrix} t_i^2 \\ 2t_i \\ 1 \end{bmatrix} = 0, \qquad (3)$$

where

$$Q_{sphere} = \begin{bmatrix} q_{11}, q_{12}, q_{13} \end{bmatrix}$$

$$= \begin{bmatrix} m_i^2 + n_i^2 + p_i^2 \\ m_i(^{w}x_{io} - {}^{w}O_x) - n_i(^{w}y_{io} - {}^{w}O_y) + p_i(^{w}z_{io} - {}^{w}O_x) \\ (^{w}x_{io} - {}^{w}O_x)^2 + (^{w}y_{io} - {}^{w}O_y)^2 + (^{w}z_{io} - {}^{w}O_x)^2 - r^2 \end{bmatrix}^{T}.$$

Considering that the laser spot can not be located on the far side of sphere, the only reasonable solution of t_i can be easily solved from (3):

$$t_i = \frac{-q_{12} - \sqrt{q_{12}^2 - q_{11}q_{13}}}{q_{12}}. \qquad (4)$$

Finally, by substituting (4) into (2), the 3-D positions of laser spot i with respect to frame {W} can be represented as follows:

$$
\begin{bmatrix} {}^w P_{ix} \\ {}^w P_{iy} \\ {}^w P_{iz} \end{bmatrix} = \begin{bmatrix} {}^w x_{io} - \dfrac{m_i(q_{12} + \sqrt{q_{12}^2 - q_{11}q_{13}})}{q_{12}} \\[3mm] {}^w y_{io} + \dfrac{n_i(q_{12} + \sqrt{q_{12}^2 - q_{11}q_{13}})}{q_{12}} \\[3mm] {}^w z_{io} - \dfrac{p_i(q_{12} + \sqrt{q_{12}^2 - q_{11}q_{13}})}{q_{12}} \end{bmatrix}. \tag{5}
$$

Since the installation positions ${}^w L_i$ and direction vector ${}^w D_i$ of laser sensor are pre-calibrated, the 3-D positions of each laser spot only depend on the geometric parameters of sphere $[{}^w O_x, {}^w O_y, {}^w O_z, r]^T$.

2.4 Projection Model

In order to solve the geometric parameters of sphere, the perspective projection relationship are used to describe the relationship between 3-D positions of laser spot i and its pixel coordinate.

With camera projection matrix M_{camera}, the 3-D positions of laser spot i with respect to frame {W} can be mapped into the pixel coordinate of frame {Im}, ${}^{im} P_i = [{}^{im} P_{ix}, {}^{im} P_{iy}]^T$, which can be detected in image. The projection model can be expressed as follows:

$$
\begin{bmatrix} {}^{im} P_{ix} \\ {}^{im} P_{iy} \\ 1 \end{bmatrix} = M_{camera} \begin{bmatrix} {}^w P_{ix} / {}^c P_{iz} \\ {}^w P_{iy} / {}^c P_{iz} \\ {}^w P_{iz} / {}^c P_{iz} \\ 1 / {}^c P_{iz} \end{bmatrix} \tag{6}
$$

where

$$
M_{camera} = \begin{bmatrix} f_x & 0 & c_x & 0 \\ 0 & f_y & c_y & 0 \\ 0 & 0 & 1 & 0 \end{bmatrix} \begin{bmatrix} {}^w_c R & {}^w_c T \\ 0 & 1 \end{bmatrix}, \tag{7}
$$

and ${}^c P_{iz}$ is the depth of laser spot i in the frame {C}, ${}^w_c R$ and $({}^w_c T)$ are the relative rotation and translation matrices of the world frame {W} with respect to the camera frame {C}.

As mentioned before, all the parameters in (7) are determined by pre-calibration. Therefore, ${}^c P_i$, the 3-D positions of laser spot i with respect to frame {C}, can be represented by ${}^w P_i$:

$$
{}^c P_i = \begin{bmatrix} {}^c P_{ix} \\ {}^c P_{iy} \\ {}^c P_{iz} \\ 1 \end{bmatrix} = \begin{bmatrix} {}^w_c R & {}^w_c T \\ 0 & 1 \end{bmatrix} \begin{bmatrix} {}^w P_{ix} \\ {}^w P_{iy} \\ {}^w P_{iz} \\ 1 \end{bmatrix} \tag{8}
$$

By substituting ${}^c P_{iz}$ in (8) into (6), the relationship between ${}^{im} P_i$ and ${}^w P_i$ is built. According to the derived ${}^w P_i$ in (5), the 3-D positions of laser spot only depend on the geometric parameters of sphere, which means two equations contain geometric parameters of sphere can be acquired from (6) with one spot detected in image. Therefore, three detected laser spots can make sure the equation set are fully solvable.

Furthermore, avoiding the situation that all the detected spots are coplanar, the detected center of projected sphere in image is also applied. In the pinhole model, the projection point of center of sphere should coincide with the center of its projected circle in image, which can be described as:

$$
{}^{im}P_o = \begin{bmatrix} {}^{im}P_{ox} \\ {}^{im}P_{oy} \\ 1 \end{bmatrix} = M_{camera} \begin{bmatrix} {}^{w}O_x/{}^{c}O_z \\ {}^{w}O_y/{}^{c}O_z \\ {}^{w}O_z/{}^{c}O_z \\ 1/{}^{c}O_z \end{bmatrix}
\tag{9}
$$

where ${}^{im}P_o = [{}^{im}P_{ox}, {}^{im}P_{oy}]^T$ are the image coordinates of center of circle and ${}^{c}O_z$ is the depth of the center of sphere with respect to $\{C\}$.

Combining the (9) with the projection equations of laser spots, a more precise and robust solution of the geometric parameters of target sphere can be calculated.

3   Experimental Results

In this section, we design a series of computer simulation and field experiment to validate the performance of our measure system. In order to represent a realistic measuring environment, the measurement scenario is designed as follow:

$$
\begin{cases}
r \in [30\,mm, 100\,mm] \\
{}^{w}O_z \in [200\,mm, 1200\,mm] \\
{}^{w}O_x, {}^{w}O_y \in [-20\,mm, -20\,mm]
\end{cases}
\tag{10}
$$

The image resolution is of 1024×1024 pixels, and the camera parameters are given by calibration.

3.1   Simulation

In reality, the detection of laser spots can be influenced by the inappropriate exposure parameter and image noise, which will introduce random noise in calculation. To ascertain the effects of noise on the proposed system, two different levels of random noise are added in ${}^{im}P_i$ respectively: random variation of $[-0.5, 0.5]$ pixel error and $[-1, 1]$ pixel error. After taking error into account, the geometric parameters were calculated for the simulated sphere with radius around 60 mm at 2000 different positions over a 500 mm distance. The results for all the noise levels are shown with the box plot in Fig. 3. The maximum positions and radius errors in noise simulation were less than 3.4 mm and 3 mm, for an added noise of 0.5 pixel. The errors increased to 6.3 mm and 4.3 mm at higher pixel noises.

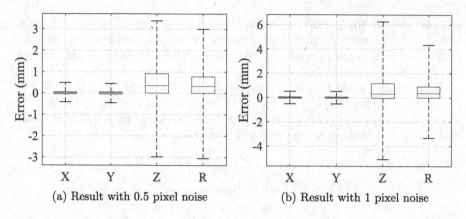

(a) Result with 0.5 pixel noise   (b) Result with 1 pixel noise

Fig. 3. Simulation of pose errors over a 500 mm distance with random noise levels of 0.5 pixel (above) and 1 pixel (below)

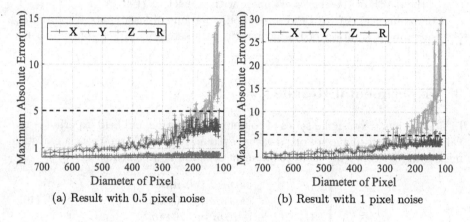

(a) Result with 0.5 pixel noise   (b) Result with 1 pixel noise

Fig. 4. Simulation of pose errors with different pixel of diameter

It's known that the accuracy of pose estimation for cooperative target has strong relationship with the distance. However, our target is non-cooperative, which means the accuracy is influenced by the distance and the size of target simultaneously. Thus, the pixel of diameter of target is used to represent the effective measuring range of our system. We repeat twenty thousands times simulations which randomize the radius and positions of the simulated sphere within the designed scenario and calculate its geometric parameters with noise added. The statistic of maximum absolute error under different pixel of diameter is shown as Fig. 4.

The results of simulation in Fig. 4 show that: (1) the performance of our system slightly decreases as the pixel of diameter decreases at first and becomes dramatically when the diameter is lower than 300 pixels. (2) The absolute calculation error of our system is less than 5 mm if the pixels of diameter are higher than 200 pixels for an added noise of 0.5 pixel. The lower bound increased to

300 pixels for a higher noise of 1 pixel. (3) A better performance may be achieved by implementing more robust laser spots detection methods and a high quality camera with higher resolution.

3.2   Field Experiment

The proposed system in this paper has been implemented with an industry camera and four low-powered lasers. The image processing and other numeric calculations can be real-time with a XC4VSX55 FPGA and a TMS320C6701 DSP integrated in the camera. The performance was evaluated by conducting field experiment in which the targets with various radius were placed in designed scenario. Target in our application is textureless as shown in Fig. 5. The acquired images are used to detect the laser spots and center of circle for the geometric parameters calculation in (6) and (9). The value of ground truth is acquired via a set of theodolites.

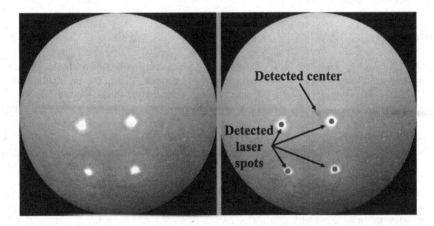

Fig. 5. The image of target sphere (left) and detected laser spots and center point (right)

Finally, the overall accuracies for the positions and radius are 4 mm and 3.8 mm, respectively. Slight difference of the accuracy between the experiment and simulation could have been caused by image processing error and calibration error of lasers. Furthermore, our measurement system also shows good performance in estimating the positions of the center of spherical-like target, such as polyhedron: the overall accuracy for the polyhedron with 26 facets in the field experiment is 8 mm within a distance of 1200 mm, which shows the generality and flexible of our system.

4   Conclusion

In this paper, a new vision measurement system with four calibrated lasers is proposed to accurately calculate the geometric parameters of a unknown spherical-like target. Compared to other systems, the proposed system requires neither the geometry information nor the texture information of the target in advance, and is suitable for a variety of engineering occasions because of its simplicity, fully-portable and low-power consumption.

Field experiment conducted within the designed scenario demonstrates that the overall performance of the system corresponds to the accuracies of 4 mm and 3.8 mm for the positions and radius, and still ensures 8 mm accuracy when the target switches to polyhedron with 26 facets.

In the future work, a new algorithm should be developed to measure the geometric parameters of a target with unknown curved surface and shape. Also a simple and precise method to calibrate the lasers should be proposed.

Acknowledgement. This work is supported by National Natural Science Foundation of China (No. 61231018, No. 61273366), National Science and technology support program (2015BAH31F01) and Program of introducing talents of discipline to university under grant B13043.

References

1. Bok, Y., Jeong, Y., Choi, D.-G., Kweon, I.S.: Capturing village-level heritages with a hand-held camera-laser fusion sensor. Int. J. Comput. Vision **94**(1), 36–53 (2011)
2. Chung, T.H., Hollinger, G.A., Isler, V.: Search and pursuit-evasion in mobile robotics. Auton. Robots **31**(4), 299–316 (2011)
3. Fang, Y., Liu, X., Zhang, X.: Adaptive active visual servoing of nonholonomic mobile robots. IEEE Trans. Industr. Electron. **59**(1), 486–497 (2012)
4. Frueh, C., Jain, S., Zakhor, A.: Data processing algorithms for generating textured 3D building facade meshes from laser scans and camera images. Int. J. Comput. Vision **61**(2), 159–184 (2005)
5. Jeon, H., Bang, Y., Myung, H.: A paired visual servoing system for 6-DOF displacement measurement of structures. Smart Mater. Struct. **20**(4), 045019 (2011)
6. Kim, Y.K., Kim, K.S., Kim, S.: A portable and remote 6-DOF pose sensor system with a long measurement range based on 1-D laser sensors. IEEE Trans. Industr. Electron. **62**(9), 5722–5729 (2015)
7. Kim, Y.K., Kim, Y., Jung, Y.S., Jang, I.G., Kim, K.S., Kim, S., Kwak, B.M.: Developing accurate long-distance 6-DOF motion detection with one-dimensional laser sensors: three-beam detection system. IEEE Trans. Industr. Electron. **60**(8), 3386–3395 (2013)
8. Kim, Y.K., Kim, Y., Kim, K.S., Kim, S., Kwak, B.M., Jang, I.G., Jung, Y.S., Kim, E.H.: Developing a robust sensing system for remote relative 6-DOF motion using 1-d laser sensors. In: Proceedings of IEEE International Systems Conference (SysCon), pp. 1–4 (2012)
9. Myung, H., Lee, S., Lee, B.: Paired structured light for structural health monitoring robot system. Structural Health Monitoring (2010)
10. Segal, S., Carmi, A., Gurfil, P.: Stereovision-based estimation of relative dynamics between noncooperative satellites: theory and experiments. IEEE Trans. Control Syst. Technol. **22**(2), 568–584 (2014)
11. Li, W.Y., Xu, G.L., Zhou, L., Wang, B., Tian, Y.P., Li, K.Y.: Research on measurement of relative poses between two non-cooperative spacecrafts. Aero Weaponry **3**, 14–17 (2012)

12. Xu, W., Liang, B., Li, C., Liu, Y.: Measurement, planning approach of space robot for capturing non-cooperative target. Jiqiren Robot **32**(1), 61–69 (2010)
13. Xu, W.F., Liang, B., Li, C., Liu, Y., Qiang, W.Y.: The approach, simulation study of the relative pose measurement between spacecrafts based on stereo vision. J. Astronaut. **30**(4), 1421–1428 (2009)
14. Zhang, S., Cao, X., Zhang, F., He, L.: Monocular vision-based iterative pose estimation algorithm from corresponding feature points. Sci. China Inf. Sci. **53**(8), 1682–1696 (2010)
15. Zhang, X., Fang, Y., Liu, X.: Motion-estimation-based visual servoing of nonholonomic mobile robots. IEEE Trans. Robot. **27**(6), 1167–1175 (2011)

Integrating Supervised Laplacian Objective with CNN for Object Recognition

Weiwei Shi[✉], Yihong Gong, Jinjun Wang, and Nanning Zheng

Institute of Artificial Intelligence and Robotics,
Xi'an Jiaotong University, Xi'an 710049, Shaanxi, China
shiweiwei.math@stu.xjtu.edu.cn, {ygong,jinjun,nnzheng}@mail.xjtu.edu.cn

Abstract. Methods to improve object recognition accuracies of convolutional neural networks (CNNs) mainly focus on increasing model complexity and training samples, introducing training strategies, etc. Alternatively, in this paper, inspired by "manifolds untangling" mechanism from human visual cortex, we propose a novel and general method to improve object recognition accuracies of CNNs by embedding the proposed *supervised Laplacian objective* (SLO) into a high layer of the models during the training process. The SLO explicitly enforces the learned feature maps with a better within-manifold compactness and between-manifold margin, and it can be universally applied to different CNN models. Experiments with shallow and deep models on four benchmark datasets including CIFAR-10, CIFAR-100, SVHN and MNIST demonstrate that CNN models trained with the SLO achieve remarkable performance improvements compared to the corresponding baseline models.

Keywords: CNN · Object recognitiuon · Supervised Laplacian objective

1 Introduction

Recent years have witnessed the bloom of convolutional neural networks (CNNs) in many computer vision and pattern recognition applications [4,11,22]. The main reasons that lead to these great successes of CNN models include: (1) the rapid progress of modern computing technologies represented by GPGPUs and CPU clusters has allowed researchers to dramatically increase the scale and complexity of neural networks, and to train and run them within a reasonable time frame, (2) the availability of large-scale datasets with millions of labeled training samples has made it possible to train CNNs without a severe overfitting, and (3) the introduction of many training strategies can help to generate better deep network models from the BP-based training process.

Apparently, the strategies to improve object recognition accuracies by increasing model complexity and training data scale are unsustainable, and are approaching their limits, as evidenced by latest research studies in [8,19].

The crux of object recognition is the invariant features. Research studies in the areas of neuroscience, psychology, physiology, etc. [3] have revealed that,

© Springer International Publishing AG 2016
E. Chen et al. (Eds.): PCM 2016, Part II, LNCS 9917, pp. 64–73, 2016.
DOI: 10.1007/978-3-319-48896-7_7

object recognition in human visual cortex is modulated via the ventral stream which is composed of the V1, V2, V4 and IT layers. When an object undergoes identity-preserving transformations (such as shift in position, change in illumination, shape, viewing angle, etc.), it will produce different feature vectors of neuron population activities. The feature vectors corresponding to all possible identity-preserving transformations define a low-dimensional manifold in the high-dimensional feature space (with the same dimension as that of the feature vectors). At lower level of human visual channel such as the retinal ganglion cells, different manifolds belonging to different object categories will be highly curved, and "tangled" together. At higher stages, neurons gradually gain their selectivity for object classes, which implies that the manifolds are more untangled. At the end stage, the invariance is accomplished when each manifold belonging to a specific object category becomes compact, and the between-manifold margins become large.

Inspired by the above "manifolds untangling" mechanism of human visual cortex, we propose a novel objective, called *supervised Laplacian objective* (SLO), to improve object recognition accuracies of CNN models. The SLO enforces the following properties for the features learned by a CNN model: (1) each manifold belonging to a specific object category is as compact as possible, and (2) the between-manifold margins are as large as possible. In theory, the proposed SLO is independent of any CNN structures, and can be applied to any layers of a CNN model. Our experimental evaluations show that applying the SLO to the top layer is most effective for improving object recognition accuracies of the models.

The main contributions of this paper can be summarized as follows:

- Inspired by the "manifolds untangling" mechanism, we propose a novel and general method to improve object recognition accuracies of CNNs by embedding the proposed *supervised Laplacian objective* (SLO) into a high layer of the models during the training process, to enhance within-manifold compactness and between-manifold margins of the learned features.
- Rather than directly regulating model weights and connecting structures as in typical deep learning algorithms, in our framework, the SLO directly modulates the learned feature maps of the embedded layer.
- Experiments with shallow and deep models on four benchmark datasets demonstrate that CNN models trained with the SLO achieve remarkable performance improvements compared to the corresponding baseline models.

The remainder of this paper is organized as follows: Section 2 reviews related works. Section 3 describes the proposed method, including the general framework, the formulation of the *supervised Laplacian objective* (SLO) and its detailed implementation. Section 4 provides the experiments and analysis. Section 5 presents discussions about the proposed method, and Sect. 6 concludes our work.

2   Related Work

There are many methods that aim to improve training of CNN models to enhance performances. These works can be broadly divided into the following three categories: (1) improvement in activation function, (2) improvement in regularization, and (3) improvement in network structure. This section reviews representative works for each category.

Different types of activation functions, such as ReLU [11], PReLU [7], maxout [5], etc., have been used to handle the gradient exploding and vanishing effect in BP algorithm.

The dropout strategy [18] is proven to be effective at preventing neural networks from overfitting, by randomly dropping units from the neural network during training, i.e. setting to zero the output of each hidden neuron in chosen layers with some probability (in general 0.5). The DropConnect [21] method is another effective technique in reducing overfitting by setting to zero the weights in chosen layers with certain probability (in general 0.5). Batch normalization [8] can be used to accelerate deep network training by reducing internal covariate shift.

SPP-net [6] is used to eliminate the requirement that input images must be a fixed-size for CNN with fully connected layers. Lin *et al.* [14] proposed the Network-In-Network (NIN) structure in which the convolution operation was substituted by a micro multi-layer perceptron (MLP) that slides over the input feature maps in a similar manner to the conventional convolution operation. The Deeply-Supervised Nets (DSN) proposed by Lee *et al.* [13] used a classifier, such as SVM or *softmax*, at each layer during training to minimize both the final output classification error and the prediction error at each hidden layer.

3   The Proposed Method

3.1   General Framework

Let $\mathcal{X} = \{\mathbf{X}_i\}_{i=1}^n$ be the set of input training data, where sample $\mathbf{X}_i$ denotes the ith raw input data (i.e. raw image), and n is the number of training samples. Let $\mathbf{c} = \{c_i\}_{i=1}^n$, $\forall c_i \in \{1, \cdots, C\}$ be the set of corresponding labels where C is the number of image classes. The goal of training CNN is to learn filter weights and biases to minimize the classification error at the last output layer. For simplicity, defining the CNN's depth to be M, we can denote a recursive function for each layer as follows:

$$\mathbf{X}_i^{(0)} = \mathbf{X}_i, \; i = 1, 2, \cdots, n, \tag{1}$$

$$\mathbf{X}_i^{(m)} = f(\mathbf{W}^{(m)} * \mathbf{X}_i^{(m-1)} + \mathbf{b}^{(m)}), \; m = 1, 2, \cdots, M, \tag{2}$$

where $\mathbf{W}^{(m)}$ and $\mathbf{b}^{(m)}$ denote the filter weights and biases of the mth layer respectively, $*$ denotes the convolution operation, $f(\cdot)$ is an element-wise nonlinear activation function such as ReLU, and $\mathbf{X}_i^{(m)}$ represents the feature maps generated at layer m for sample $\mathbf{X}_i$. The total parameters of the CNN model is a combination of the filter weights and biases from each layer, denoted as $\mathcal{W} = \{\mathbf{W}^{(1)}, \cdots, \mathbf{W}^{(M)}; \mathbf{b}^{(1)}, \cdots, \mathbf{b}^{(M)}\}$.

As described in Sect. 1, We expect to improve object recognition accuracies of a CNN model by embedding the SLO into certain layer of the model during the training process. In general, for embedding the SLO into the kth layer, the overall objective function could be expressed as:

$$\min_{\mathcal{W}} L = \sum_{i=1}^{n} \ell(\mathcal{W}, \mathbf{X}_i, c_i) + \lambda \mathcal{L}(\mathcal{X}^{(k)}, \mathbf{c}), \tag{3}$$

where $\ell(\mathcal{W}, \mathbf{X}_i, c_i)$ is the classification error cost function for sample $\mathbf{X}_i$ (such as cross entropy loss for *softmax*, hinge loss for SVM, etc.), $\mathcal{X}^{(k)} = \{\mathbf{X}_i^{(k)}, \cdots, \mathbf{X}_n^{(k)}\}$ denotes the set of produced feature maps at layer k for all training data, and accordingly $\mathcal{L}(\mathcal{X}^{(k)}, \mathbf{c})$ denotes the SLO with respect to the corresponding feature maps. λ controls the trade-off between the classification error and the SLO.

Note that $\mathcal{X}^{(k)}$ depends on $\mathbf{W}^{(1)}, \cdots, \mathbf{W}^{(k)}$. Hence directly constraining $\mathcal{X}^{(k)}$ will modulate the filter weights from 1th to k^{th} layer (i.e. $\mathbf{W}^{(1)}, \cdots, \mathbf{W}^{(k)}$) by feedback propagation during training process.

3.2   Supervised Laplacian Objective (SLO)

For $\mathcal{X}^{(k)} = \{\mathbf{X}_1^{(k)}, \cdots, \mathbf{X}_n^{(k)}\}$, the column expansion of $\mathbf{X}_i^{(k)}$ is denoted by $\mathbf{x}_i$. The goal of the proposed SLO is to enhance within-manifold compactness and between-manifold margins of the learned features. Inspired by the spectral clustering research from [20], we construct a similarity graph $\mathcal{G}$ to characterize the within-manifold compactness and between-manifold separability simultaneously. The similarity graph $\mathcal{G} = (\mathcal{V}, \mathcal{E})$ is a fully connected and undirected graph, where $\mathcal{V} = \{\mathbf{x}_1, \mathbf{x}_2, \cdots, \mathbf{x}_n\}$ is the vertex set, $\mathcal{E} = \{(i,j) | i, j = 1, 2, \cdots, n, i \neq j\}$ is the edge set, and edge (i, j) denotes the edge between vertex $\mathbf{x}_i$ and $\mathbf{x}_j$. We assume that the graph $\mathcal{G}$ is weighted, the weight of edge (i, j) represents the similarity of vertex $\mathbf{x}_i$ and $\mathbf{x}_j$, and it can be defined as:

$$s_{ij} = \begin{cases} 1, & \text{if } \mathbf{x}_i \text{ and } \mathbf{x}_j \text{ have the same label,} \\ -1, & \text{otherwise,} \end{cases} \tag{4}$$

The similarity matrix can be defined by $\mathbf{S} = (s_{ij})_{n \times n}$. Because $s_{ij} = s_{ji}$, so $\mathbf{S}$ is a symmetric matrix.

Based on the above description, We propose the SLO which can be expressed as:

$$\mathcal{L} = \sum_{i,j=1}^{n} s_{ij} \|\mathbf{x}_i - \mathbf{x}_j\|^2, \tag{5}$$

Obviously, minimizing the SLO is equivalent to enforce within-manifold compactness and between-manifold margins simultaneously. Taking it back into Eq. (3), the SLO results in the following cost function:

$$\min_{\mathcal{W}} L = \sum_{i=1}^{n} \ell(\mathcal{W}, \mathbf{X}_i, c_i) + \lambda \sum_{i,j=1}^{n} s_{ij} \|\mathbf{x}_i - \mathbf{x}_j\|^2, \tag{6}$$

In next subsection, we will elaborate the optimization process for Eq. (6).

3.3 Implementation

Back-propagation (BP) algorithm is adopted to train the CNN model, which is carried out based on mini-batch. In fact, we only need calculate the error flows, i.e. the gradients of objective function with respect to the features of the corresponding layer.

The SLO can be written as:

$$\mathcal{L} = \sum_{i,j=1}^{n} s_{ij}\|\mathbf{x}_i - \mathbf{x}_j\|^2 = 2tr(\mathbf{M}\mathbf{\Omega}\mathbf{M}^{\top}), \tag{7}$$

where $\mathbf{M} = [\mathbf{x}_1, \cdots, \mathbf{x}_n]$, $\mathbf{\Omega} = \mathbf{D} - \mathbf{S}$, $\mathbf{D} = diag(d_{11}, \cdots, d_{nn})$, $d_{ii} = \sum_{j=1, j\neq i}^{n} s_{ij}$, $i = 1, 2, \cdots, n$, i.e. $\mathbf{\Omega}$ is the Laplacian matrix of similarity matrix $\mathbf{S}$.

The gradients of the $\mathcal{L}$ with respect to $\mathbf{x}_i$ is

$$\frac{\partial \mathcal{L}}{\partial \mathbf{x}_i} = 2\mathbf{M}(\mathbf{\Omega} + \mathbf{\Omega}^{\top})_{(:,i)} = 4\mathbf{M}\mathbf{\Omega}_{(:,i)}. \tag{8}$$

where, $\mathbf{\Omega}_{(:,i)}$ denotes the ith column of matrix $\mathbf{\Omega}$.

To further improve the effectiveness of the proposed SLO, we also consider using the **kernel trick** [1], i.e. Gaussian similarity function to define the similarity matrix, that is, s_{ij} can be defined as:

$$s_{ij} = \begin{cases} \exp\{-\frac{\|\mathbf{x}_i - \mathbf{x}_j\|^2}{\sigma^2}\}, & \text{if } \mathbf{x}_i \text{ and } \mathbf{x}_j \text{ have the same label,} \\ -\exp\{-\frac{\|\mathbf{x}_i - \mathbf{x}_j\|^2}{\sigma^2}\}, & \text{otherwise,} \end{cases} \tag{9}$$

where the parameter σ controls the width of the neighborhoods. Then, the gradients $\frac{\partial \mathcal{L}}{\partial \mathbf{x}_i}$ for the kernel version of the SLO can be derived as follows.

$$\frac{\partial \mathcal{L}}{\partial \mathbf{x}_i} = 4\mathbf{M}(\mathbf{\Omega} + \mathbf{\Psi})_{(:,i)}. \tag{10}$$

where, $\mathbf{\Psi}$ denotes the Laplacian matrix of $\mathbf{H} = (h_{ij})_{n \times n}$, $h_{ij} = -\frac{s_{ij}}{\sigma^2}\|\mathbf{x}_i - \mathbf{x}_j\|^2$.

The total gradient with respect to $\mathbf{x}_i$ is simply the combination of the gradient from the conventional CNN model and the above gradient from the SLO.

4 Experiments and Analysis

4.1 Overall Settings

To evaluate the effectiveness of the proposed SLO and its kernel version, We conduct experimental evaluations using shallow and deep models, respectively. Since our experiments show that embedding the proposed objective into the top layer of a CNN model is most effective for improving its object recognition performance, in all experiments, we only embed the proposed objective into the top layer of the models and keep the other parts of networks unchanged. For the settings of those hyper parameters (such as the learning rate, weight decay, drop ratio, etc.), we follow the published configurations of the original networks. All the models are implemented using the Caffe platform [9] from scratch without pre-training. During the training phase, the parameter λ is empirically selected from the interval $[10^{-5}, 10^{-8}]$, σ^2 is empirically selected from $\{0.1, 0.5\}$, and it is possible that better results can be obtained by tuning σ^2.

4.2 Datasets

Four benchmark datasets including CIFAR-10, CIFAR-100, MNIST and SVHN are selected for the performance evaluations. The reason for choosing these datasets is because they contain a large amount of small images (about 32×32 pixels), so that models can be trained using computers with moderate configurations within reasonable time frames. Because of this, the four datasets have become very popular choices for deep network performance evaluations in the computer vision and pattern recognition research communities.

CIFAR-10 Dataset. The CIFAR-10 dataset [10] consists of 10 classes of 32×32 RGB natural images, $50,000$ for training and $10,000$ for testing.

CIFAR-100 Dataset. The CIFAR-100 dataset [10] is the same in size and format as the CIFAR-10 dataset, except that it has 100 classes. The number of images per class is only one tenth of the CIFAR-10 dataset.

MNIST Dataset. The MNIST dataset [12] consists of hand-written digits $0-9$ which are 28×28 gray images, $60,000$ for training and $10,000$ for testing.

SVHN Dataset. The Street View House Numbers (SVHN) dataset [16] consists of $630,420$ color images of 32×32 pixels in size, which are divided into the training set, testing set and an extra set with $73,257$, $26,032$ and $531,131$ images, respectively. Multiple digits may exist in the same image, and the task of this dataset is to classify the digit located at the center of an image.

4.3 Experiments with Shallow Model

In this experiment, the "quick" CNN model from the Caffe package[1] (named Quick-CNN) is selected as the baseline model. This model consists of 3 convolution layers and 1 fully connected layers. The test set error rates of CIFAR-10, CIFAR-100 and SVHN, respectively, are shown in Table 1[2]. In this Table, SLO and kSLO correspond to the models trained with the SLO and its kernel version respectively. As can be seen from Table 1, when no data augmentation is used, compared with the corresponding baseline model, the proposed SLO and its kernel version can remarkably reduce the test error rates by 4.90%, 5.42% respectively on CIFAR-10, by 4.01%, 4.52% respectively on CIFAR-100, and by 3.29%, 3.70% respectively on SVHN. The improvements on SVHN in terms of absolute percentage are not as large as those on the other two datasets, because the baseline Quick-CNN model already achieves a single-digit error rate of 8.92%. However, in terms of relative reductions of test error rates, the numbers have reached 36.9% and 41.5%, respectively, which are quite significant. These remarkable performance improvements demonstrate the effectiveness of the proposed objectives.

---

[1] The model is available from Caffe package [9].
[2] The MNIST dataset can't be used to test the model because images in the dataset are 28×28 in size, and the model only takes 32×32 images as its input.

Table 1. Comparison results of test error rates for the CIFAR-10, CIFAR-100 and SVHN.

Method	CIFAR-10	CIFAR-100	SVHN
Quick-CNN	23.47	55.87	8.92
Quick-CNN+SLO	**18.57**	**51.86**	**5.63**
Quick-CNN+kSLO	**18.05**	**51.35**	**5.22**

4.4 Experiments with Deep Model

Next, we apply the proposed SLO and its kernel version to the well-known NIN models [14]. NIN consists of 9 convolution layers and no fully connected layer. Indeed, it is a very deep model, with 6 more convolution layers than that of the Quick-CNN model. Four benchmark datasets are used in the evaluation, including CIFAR-10, CIFAR-100, MNIST and SVHN.

We adopted the same pre-processing for these datasets as in [13,14], and followed the training and testing protocols in [13,14]. To be consistent with the previous works, for CIFAR-10, we also augmented the training data by zero-padding 4 pixels on each side, then corner-cropping and random horizontal flipping. In the test phase, no model averaging was applied, and we only cropped the center of a test sample for evaluation.

Table 2 shows the evaluation results on the four benchmark datasets in terms of test error rates. For fairness, for the baseline NIN model, we list the test results from both the original paper [14] and our own experiments. In this table, we also include the evaluation results of some representative methods, including Stochastic Pooling [23], Maxout Networks [5], Prob. Maxout [17], and DSN [13], which is the state-of-the-art model on these four datasets. It is worth mentioning that DSN [13] is also based on the NIN [14] structure with layer-wise supervisions.

From Table 2, we can see that our proposed objectives achieves the best performance against all the compared methods. The evaluation results shown in the table can be summarized as follows.

Table 2. Comparison results of test error rates for the CIFAR-10, CIFAR-100, MNIST and SVHN.

Method	CIFAR-10	CIFAR-10 (Augment.)	CIFAR-100	MNIST	SVHN
Stochastic pooling [23]	15.13	— —	42.51	0.47	2.80
Maxout [5]	11.68	9.38	38.57	0.45	2.47
Prob. Mxout [17]	11.35	9.39	38.14	— —	2.39
NIN [14]	10.41	8.81	35.68	0.47	2.35
DSN [13]	9.78	8.22	34.57	0.39	1.92
NIN (Our baseline)	10.20	8.72	35.50	0.47	2.55
NIN+SLO	**9.35**	**7.64**	**34.04**	**0.32**	1.92
NIN+kSLO	**9.16**	**7.26**	**33.55**	**0.30**	**1.86**

- Compared with the corresponding baseline models, the proposed SLO and its kernel version can remarkably reduce the test error rates on the four benchmark datasets.
- On CIFAR-100, the improvement is most significant: NIN+kSLO achieved 33.55% test error rate which is 1.95% better than the baseline NIN model, and 1.02% better than the state-of-the-art DSN model.
- Although the test error rates are almost saturated on the MNIST and SVHN datasets, the models trained by the proposed objectives still achieved noticeable improvements on the two datasets compared to the baseline NIN model and the state-of-the-art DSN model. In terms of relative reductions of test error rates, compared with the corresponding baseline models, the numbers have reached 36% and 27% respectively on these two datasets, which are significant.

These results once again substantiate the effectiveness of the proposed SLO.

4.5 Visualization

To get more insights of the proposed SLO, we visualize the embedded layer features obtained from Quick-CNN and NIN models on the CIFAR-10 test set. Figure 1 shows the feature visualizations. It can be seen that, in both models, the proposed SLO can help to make the learned features with better within-manifold compactness and between-manifold margins as compared to the corresponding baseline models[3].

Moreover, it is clear from Fig. 1(a) and (c) that through many layers of nonlinear transformations, a deeper network is able to learn good invariant features that can sufficiently separate objects of different classes in a high dimensional feature space. In contrast, features learned by a shallower network are not powerful enough to appropriately "untangle" those different object classes. This explains why the proposed SLO is more effective for improving object recognition accuracies when applied to shallower networks.

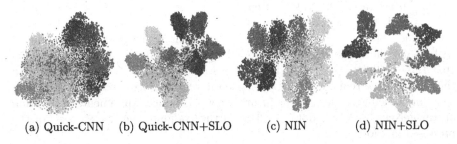

(a) Quick-CNN   (b) Quick-CNN+SLO   (c) NIN   (d) NIN+SLO

Fig. 1. Feature visualization of the CIFAR-10 test set by t-SNE [15]. A point denotes a test sample, and different colors represent different classes.

---

[3] The kSLO produces quite similar visualization results to SLO.

5   Discussions

To investigate the effect of the embedded position of the SLO on the performance, we conducted experiments with Quick-CNN on the CIFAR-10 dataset by embedding the SLO into different layers of the model, and the results of test error rates are shown in Table 3. We can clearly see that the higher the embedded layer, the better the performance[4]. In the experiments, we also found that, for a given embedded layer, as long as the order of magnitude of λ is appropriate, the performance of our method does not change much, and the higher the embedded layer, the higher the order of magnitude of the optimal λ.

In our method, during training phase, the additional computational cost is to calculate the gradients of the SLO (or kSLO) with respect to the features of the embedded layer. According to Sect. 3.3, the gradients have the closed-form computational formula, which make the additional computation cost very low based on a mini-batch. In practise, the additional computational cost is negligible compared to that of the corresponding baseline CNN model.

Table 3. The effect of embedded position of the SLO on the performance on CIFAR-10 dataset with Quick-CNN model (i.e. Quick-CNN+SLO). *conv#* denotes a convolutional layer, *fc* denotes the fully connected layer.

Embedded layer	*conv*1	*conv*2	*conv*3	*fc*
Test error (%)	20.47	19.40	18.97	18.57

6   Conclusion

In this paper, motivated by "manifolds untangling" mechanism of human visual cortex, we propose a novel and general framework to improve the performance of CNN by embedding the proposed *supervised Laplacian objective* (SLO) into the training procedure. The SLO can explicitly enforce the learned object feature maps with better within-manifold compactness and between-manifold separability, and can be universally applied to different CNN models. Experiments with shallow and deep models on four benchmark datasets including CIFAR-10, CIFAR-100, SVHN and MNIST demonstrate that CNN models trained with the SLO achieve remarkable performance improvements compared to the corresponding baseline models. In the future, we will conduct experimental evaluation on ImageNet (ILSVRC) dataset [2] to further validate the effectiveness of the proposed method.

Acknowledgments. This work is supported by National Basic Research Program of China (973 Program) under Grant No. 2015CB351705, and the National Natural Science Foundation of China (NSFC) under Grant No. 61332018.

---

[4] For NIN model, the conclusion is the same as that of Quick-CNN.

References

1. Chen, B., Zhao, S., Zhu, P., Principe, J.C.: Quantized kernel recursive least squares algorithm. IEEE Trans. Neural Netw. Learn. Syst. **24**(9), 1484–1491 (2013)
2. Deng, J., Dong, W., Socher, R., Li, L., Li, K., Fei-Fei, L.: Imagenet: A large-scale hierarchical image database. In: CVPR (2009)
3. DiCarlo, J., Zoccolan, D., Rust, N.: How does the brain solve visual object recognition? Neuron (2012)
4. Girshick, R., Donahue, J., Darrell, T., Malik, J.: Rich feature hierarchies for accurate object detection and semantic segmentation. In: CVPR (2014)
5. Goodfellow, I., Warde-Farley, D., Mirza, M., Courville, A., Bengio, Y.: Maxout networks. In: ICML (2013)
6. He, K., Zhang, X., Ren, S., Sun, J.: Spatial pyramid pooling in deep convolutional networks for visual recognition. In: Fleet, D., Pajdla, T., Schiele, B., Tuytelaars, T. (eds.) ECCV 2014. LNCS, vol. 8691, pp. 346–361. Springer, Heidelberg (2014). doi:10.1007/978-3-319-10578-9_23
7. He, K., Zhang, X., Ren, S., Sun, J.: Delving deep into rectifiers: surpassing human-level performance on imagenet classification. CoRR (2015)
8. Ioffe, S., Szegedy, C.: Batch normalization: accelerating deep network training by reducing internal covariate shift. In: ICML (2015)
9. Jia, Y., Shelhamer, E., Donahue, J., Karayev, S., Long, J., Girshick, R., Guadarrama, S., Darrell, T.: Caffe: convolutional architecture for fast feature embedding. In: ACM MM (2014)
10. Krizhevsky, A., Hinton, G.: Learning multiple layers of features from tiny images. Master's thesis (2009)
11. Krizhevsky, A., Sutskever, I., Hinton, G.E.: Imagenet classification with deep convolutional neural networks. In: NIPS (2012)
12. LeCun, Y., Bottou, L., Bengio, Y., Haffner, P.: Gradient-based learning applied to document recognition. Proc. IEEE **86**(11), 2278–2324 (1998)
13. Lee, C., Xie, S., Gallagher, P., Zhang, Z., Tu, Z.: Deeply-supervised nets. In: NIPS (2014)
14. Lin, M., Chen, Q., Yan, S.: Network in network. In: ICLR (2014)
15. van der Maaten, L., Hinton, G.: Visualizing data using t-SNE. J. Mach. Learn. Res. JMLR **9**, 2579–2605 (2008)
16. Netzer, Y., Wang, T., Coates, A., Bissacco, A., Wu, B., Ng, A.: Reading digits in natural images with unsupervised feature learning. In: NIPS (2011)
17. Springenberg, J., Riedmiller, M.: Improving deep neural networks with probabilistic maxout units. In: ICLR (2014)
18. Srivastava, N., Hinton, G., Krizhevsky, A., Sutskever, I., Salakhutdinov, R.: Dropout: a simple way to prevent neural networks from overfitting. J. Mach. Learn. Res. JMLR **15**(1), 1929–1958 (2014)
19. Szegedy, C., Liu, W., Jia, Y., Sermanet, P., Reed, S., Anguelov, D., Erhan, D., Vanhoucke, V., Rabinovich, A.: Going deeper with convolutions. In: CVPR (2015)
20. Von Luxburg, U.: A tutorial on spectral clustering. Stat. Comput. **17**(4), 395–416 (2007)
21. Wan, L., Zeiler, M., Zhang, S., LeCun, Y., Fergus, R.: Regularization of neural networks using dropconnect. In: ICML (2013)
22. Wang, N., Yeung, D.Y.: Learning a deep compact image representation for visual tracking. In: NIPS (2013)
23. Zeiler, M., Fergus, R.: Stochastic pooling for regularization of deep convolutional neural networks. In: ICLR (2013)

Automatic Color Image Enhancement Using Double Channels

Na Li[1(✉)], Zhao Liu[2], Jie Lei[2], Mingli Song[2], and Jiajun Bu[2]

[1] Zhejiang International Studies University,
Hangzhou 310012, People's Republic of China
nli@zisu.edu.cn
[2] Zhejiang University, Hangzhou 310027, People's Republic of China
{liuzhao,ljaylei,brooksong,bjj}@zju.edu.cn

Abstract. Digital cameras have been widely used in taking photos. However, some photos lack details and need enhancement. Many existing image enhancement algorithms are patch-based and the patch size is always fixed. Users have to tune the parameter to obtain the appropriate enhancement. In this paper, we propose an automatic consumer image enhancement method based on double channels and adaptive patch size. The method enhances an image pixel by pixel using both dark and bright channels. The local patch size is selected automatically by contrast feature. Our proposed method is able to automatically enhance both foggy and under-exposed consumer images without any user interaction. Experiment results show that our method can provide a significant improvement to existing patch-based image enhancement algorithms.

Keywords: Image enhancement · Contrast enhancement · Dark channel · Bright channel · Adaptive patch-based processing

1 Introduction

Digital cameras and smart phones have been widely used in taking photos. However, due to limitations of photosensitive instruments and influences of environment, digital cameras are always insensitive to the variation of input lighting, which leads to low contrast in dim lighting environment or loss of details. Therefore, taking good photos remains a challenge for normal users. Many devices have provided built-in applications to help end users interactively improve photo quality. However, these applications require end users to be experienced in image processing and are also time-consuming. To address the problem, some automatic enhancement algorithms have been proposed to solve consumer image problems. Dark channel prior [1] is proposed for image haze removal and bright channel prior [2] for correcting under-exposed images. Both problems are common among consumer images. Although these patch-based image processing methods improved image quality significantly, we cannot execute batch process on any images unconditionally. The reasons are: (1) the algorithms are specific problem

© Springer International Publishing AG 2016
E. Chen et al. (Eds.): PCM 2016, Part II, LNCS 9917, pp. 74–83, 2016.
DOI: 10.1007/978-3-319-48896-7_8

orientated; and (2) the patch size is fixed and tuned for each image, otherwise the processed images may suffer from halo effects.

In this paper, we propose a novel image enhancement framework based on both dark and bright channels with adaptive patch size. The inspiration is that existing patch-based methods are essentially local histogram stretching. In another words, when we enhance a pixel according to its neighborhood, we actually stretch the histogram of the local patch and pick up the enhanced value for the target pixel. If the histogram is sharp, the stretching will fail. To solve this issue, we propose a contrast feature for automatic patch size selection. In addition, we combine dark and bright channels to deal with general problems in consumer images. Experimental results on various image enhancement tasks demonstrate that our strategy can produce more compelling results.

2 Related Work

Image enhancement techniques are considered thoroughly throughout the image-processing literature and depend significantly on the underlying application. We discuss related works dealing with consumer images rather than those from specific areas such as medical images, remote sensing images and so on.

The majority of image enhancement techniques are global-based. The simplest global exposure correction employs histogram equalization (HE) [3]. HE is improved as Differential gray-levels Histogram Equalization (DHE) [4] by differentiating the gray-levels histogram which contains edge information of an image. Another improvement is Exposure based Sub-Image Histogram Equalization (ESIHE) [5] where an image is divided into sub-images of different intensity levels according to exposure thresholds and the individual histogram of sub images is equalized independently. Channel selection [6] is proposed to reconstruct over-exposed image since the RGB components are unusually over-exposed at the same position. S-curve is a common global-based technique. By estimating the best image specific non-linear tone curve for a given image [7], the dynamic range of the image can be reasonably adjusted.

Model-based methods are another typical branch for global image enhancement, which is usually proposed for airlight correction. A physical model is proposed and optimized with multiple images [8]. The physical model was refined via shading and transmission functions and worked on a single image [9]. Oakley and Bu [10] assumed that the airlight was constant throughout the image and minimized a global cost function to estimate the airlight. Kopf et al. [11] utilized a sufficiently accurate match between a photograph and a geometric model to enhance an image. Generally, global methods cannot concentrate on local regions and hardly deal with backlight photos.

On the contrary, some algorithms only consider local patch information and enhance an image pixel by pixel. An early method is adaptive histogram equalization (AHE) [12] that transforms each pixel based on the histogram of a square surrounding the pixel. Discrete Cosine Transform (DCT) is employed to enhance image block on DC and AC coefficients [13]. Similarly, spatial entropy of pixels using spatial distribution is employed to perform non-linear data mapping [14].

Using channel priors to enhance images is a special kind of patch-based algorithms. He et al. [1] proposed dark channel prior to dehaze foggy images lacking of shadow part. Wang et al. [2] proposed bright channel prior to enhance underexposed images lacking highlight part. Algorithms based on channel priors are patch-based since the prior of a pixel is calculated by the patch surrounding it as in AHE. All mentioned local-based enhancement algorithms considered only fixed patch size, which results in artifacts such as halo effects.

3   Automatic Image Enhancement Pipeline

Our automatic image enhancement is a local patch-based method and the pipeline is depicted in Fig. 1 There are four main steps: color space conversion, automatic patch size selection, dark and bright channel extraction, and adaptive patch-based image enhancement.

The input image is converted to YUV color space at first. As we know, the main purpose of the RGB color model is for representing images in electronic systems, but nonintuitive for us humans. On the other hand, the YUV color model is a linear combination of RGB channels, and represents a color with one luminance channel and two color channels. Researchers have shown that YUV is in a way similar to human vision [15]. For image enhancement, the YUV color model can help significantly enhance the luminance and simultaneously avoid over-enhanced color. The YUV color space is derived as follows:

$$
\begin{bmatrix} Y \\ U \\ V \end{bmatrix} = \begin{bmatrix} 0.299 & 0.587 & 0.114 \\ -0.147 & -0.289 & 0.436 \\ 0.615 & -0.515 & -0.100 \end{bmatrix} \begin{bmatrix} R \\ G \\ B \end{bmatrix} \tag{1}
$$

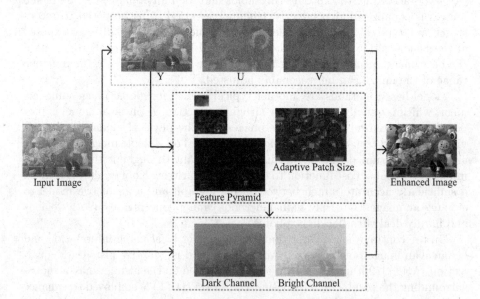

Fig. 1. The proposed automatic image enhancement pipeline.

The heart of our pipeline is the automatic selection of the local patch size (see Sect. 4.1). For each pixel, we select a best-fit local patch for consequent enhancement. The patch surrounding the to-be-enhanced pixel should contain some sufficient contrast; otherwise the patch may be flat and cannot provide any information for further enhancement. Additionally, in order to speed up the process, we build a pyramid of the contrast feature for automatic patch size selection (see Sect. 4.2).

After patch size selection, we extract the dark and bright channels from the original RGB image (see Sect. 5.1). Different from conventional patch-based image enhancement algorithms whose patch size is always fixed, we calculate the dark and bright channels with adaptive patch size for each pixel.

The final step is adaptive patch-based image enhancement using both dark and bright channels (see Sect. 5.2). Each image pixel is enhanced locally and linearly from its local patch with both dark and bright channel. As the image is represented by the YUV color model, our algorithm enhances Y channel and UV channels separately.

4 Automatic Patch Size Selection

The aim of automatic patch size selection is to infer a best-fit local patch for the consequent pixel enhancement using double channels. To achieve this goal, we first need to define the best-fit local patch and estimate its adaptive size.

4.1 Best-Fit Local Patch

To enhance a pixel based on its local patch, we need the information within the patch and enhance the pixel accordingly. As introduced in Sect. 1, our algorithm is using both dark and bright channels, which is essentially a local-histogram stretching process. Figure 2(b) shows two different types of possible local patches and their corresponding histograms. Figure 2(c) shows the enhanced result of the histogram stretching strategy. Obviously, the sky pixels are stretched differently. The reason is that if there is only one narrow and steep peak in the histogram, the local patch will be too flat to be stretched. When stretched inappropriately, it will introduce improper enhancement such as halo effects.

For patch-based image enhancement, the best-fit local patch for a pixel should contain some contrast at least, that is the patch cannot be totally flat. Thus, we define a feature $f(\omega)$ for a patch ω, where $f(\omega)$ represents the contrast level of the patch. The larger the $f(\omega)$, the more contrast within the patch. If the $f(\omega)$ is very low, the patch is too flat to be a proper local patch. Thus, given a threshold σ, the best-fit patch is define as $f(\omega) > \sigma$.

To figure out what a suitable feature $f(\omega)$ is, we observed a lot of image patches and find out that the standard deviant of luminance over a patch is a

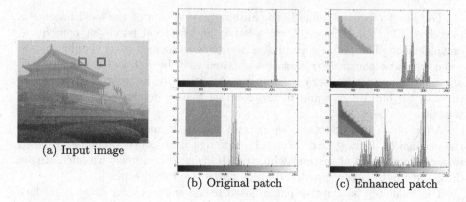

(a) Input image   (b) Original patch   (c) Enhanced patch

Fig. 2. The histograms for different types of local patch.

good choice. A flat patch is always of low standard deviant values. For a given patch, its contrast feature is defined as follows:

$$f(\omega) = \sqrt{\frac{\sum_{\mathbf{p} \in \omega}(Y(\mathbf{p}) - \overline{Y(\mathbf{p})})^2}{M}} \qquad (2)$$

where ω is the patch region with M pixels, $Y(\mathbf{p})$ is the luminance value of pixel $\mathbf{p}$ and $\overline{Y(\mathbf{p})}$ is the luminance average over the patch. In our algorithm, $Y(\mathbf{p})$ is simply the Y channel in (1). The threshold σ is set with 2 for all cases. Using standard deviation as the contrast feature representation, we can effectively select the best fit patches.

4.2   Fast Pyramid Based Patch Size Selection

Technically speaking, given an image we could directly use the above contrast feature definition (2) and its corresponding threshold to obtain the best patch size for each pixel, while the brute-force search is definitely time-consuming. In our proposed algorithm, the adaptive patch size selection is implemented with a pyramid which includes two main steps: build a contrast feature pyramid and search within the pyramid. The result may be not as precise as the brute-force search, but its accuracy is sufficient for our purpose, since the search is to find a proper local patch with some contrast not with a specific contrast.

Build Contrast Feature Pyramid. We first build a bottom-up pyramid over the luminance channel of an input image as follows: The first level of the pyramid includes the $f(\omega)$ values of all 1×1 patches, the second includes all 2×2 patches, the third includes all 4×4 patches, and so on. In general, the nth level of the pyramid is used to store the $f(\omega)$ values of all $2^{n-1} \times 2^{n-1}$ patches. For each level, the pyramid is built as:

$$L_n(\mathbf{p}) = f(\omega_n(\mathbf{p})) \qquad (3)$$

where $\mathbf{p} = (p_x, p_y)$, f is defined in (2) to extract patch contrast feature, and $\omega_n(\mathbf{p})$ is a square patch in the original image whose center is $(p_x \times 2^{n-1} + 2^{n-2}, p_y \times 2^{n-1} + 2^{n-2})$ and radius is 2^{n-1} pixels. Suppose N is the number of the pyramid levels, n ranges from 1 to N. The upper the level of the pyramid, the larger patches involved in the contrast feature extraction.

Search the pyramid. After the pyramid has been built, we compute a patch size map $I_{winsize}$ for each pixel of the input image. In the proposed method, we search the pyramid from the bottom, i.e. the first level and finish till the following criteria is reached: $L_t(\mathbf{p}) > \sigma$, where σ is the feature threshold introduced in Sect. 4.1. Suppose that the search stops at the level t for a given pixel $\mathbf{p}$, the patch size map is computed as $I_{winsize}(\mathbf{p}) = 2^t$. Note that 2^t is the patch size of one level higher than t. We choose a larger one to ensure that the local patch has sufficient contrast in any case, e.g. the pixel is on the edge of the corresponding square patch at the level t. The patch size map stores the best-fit patch size for each pixel. One patch size map example is shown is Fig. 1. The darker the pixel, the smaller the patch size.

5 Patch-Based Image Enhancement Using Double Channels

The main stage of our proposed method is automatically enhancement the input image. Using the combination of dark and bright channels, the algorithm can deal with both foggy and under-exposed images at the same time. The adaptive patch size map helps ensure correct enhancement. The algorithm is performed on the luminance channel Y and the two color channels UV separately based on human vision perception.

5.1 Double Channels

In most existing patch-based algorithms, one channel prior is used to adjust a particular type of problematic images. The dark channel is for image dehazing [1] while the bright channel is for under-exposure correction [2]. The reason is that the shortage of shadow details is represented by dark channel while the shortage of highlight is represented by bright channel. In our proposed algorithm, both the dark and bright channels are adopted for the sake of general image enhancement.

Given the patch size map $I_{winsize}$, the dark channel of the input image I_{rgb} is computed as follows:

$$I_{dark}(\mathbf{p}) = \min_{\mathbf{x} \in \omega(\mathbf{p}), c \in \{r,g,b\}} I_{rgb}^c(\mathbf{x}) \tag{4}$$

where $\omega(\mathbf{p})$ is the adaptive local patch centered at the pixel $\mathbf{p}$, and its radius is $I_{winsize}(\mathbf{p})$. The dark channel is computed as the minimum value of all the RGB values over the local patch. Similarly, the bright channel is computed as follows:

$$I_{bright}(\mathbf{p}) = \max_{\mathbf{x} \in \omega(\mathbf{p}), c \in \{r,g,b\}} I_{rgb}^c(\mathbf{x}) \tag{5}$$

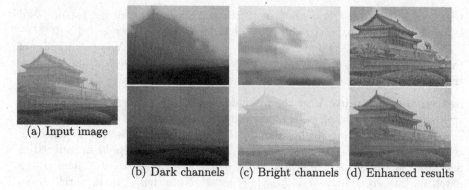

(a) Input image
(b) Dark channels   (c) Bright channels (d) Enhanced results

Fig. 3. Comparison between fixed and adaptive patch size. Top: fixed size; bottom: adaptive size.

To avoid block effects, both the dark and bright channels are filtered by guided filter [16], where the guided image is the luminance channel of the input image.

Thanks to the adaptive patch size map, the dark and bright channels are free of halos. We compared the proposed adaptive patch size selection algorithm with the one using fixed patch size (15×15 pixels for a 600×450 image). The cause of the halo has been explained in Fig. 2. The result shown in Fig. 3 demonstrates the effectiveness of our proposed algorithm.

5.2 Image Enhancement

After both the dark and bright channels are extracted, we reach the final step of the whole pipeline: image enhancement. In our proposed algorithm, the enhancement is performed pixel by pixel on the one luminance channel Y and the two color channels UV separately. The Y channel is enhanced as follows:

$$Y_{en}(\mathbf{p}) = \frac{Y(\mathbf{p}) - I_{dark}(\mathbf{p})}{Y(\mathbf{p}) - I_{bright}(\mathbf{p})} \tag{6}$$

and the UV channel is enhanced as follows:

$$\begin{cases} U(\mathbf{p}) = \frac{U(\mathbf{p})}{I_{bright}(\mathbf{p}) - I_{dark}(\mathbf{p})} \\ V(\mathbf{p}) = \frac{V(\mathbf{p})}{I_{bright}(\mathbf{p}) - I_{dark}(\mathbf{p})} \end{cases} \tag{7}$$

To avoid over-flow or under-flow of the enhanced UV channels which cause over-enhancement, the result of the formula (7) will be normalized to $[-128, 127]$.

We compared the adopted YUV color model with the original RGB color model. The result shown in Fig. 4 presents that the color of the toys hair is over enhanced under the RGB color model in Fig. 4(b), while the detail is preserved under the YUV color model in Fig. 4(c).

(a) Input image   (b) RGB color model   (c) YUV color model

Fig. 4. The comparison between YUV and RGB color model.

6 Experimental Results

In our experiment, all the input images are enhanced with one fixed parameter: the threshold for the contrast feature is set as $\omega = 2$. In the previous section, Figs. 3 and 4 have shown our image enhancement results and demonstrated the advantages of the automatic patch size selection and the YUV color model. In this section, we mainly compare our results with existing image enhancement algorithms using channel priors to demonstrate the advantage of our proposed double channels.

6.1 Image Dehaze

In Fig. 5, we compare our approach with [1]. In the implementation of the algorithm [1], the patch size is set to 15×15 for a 600×400 image as in the article.

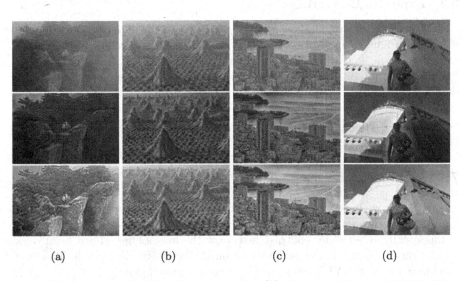

(a)   (b)   (c)   (d)

Fig. 5. Comparison with He's dehaze algorithm [1]. Top: input images. Middle: He's results. Bottom: our results.

(a)   (b)   (c)   (d)

Fig. 6. Comparison with Wang's exposure correction algorithm [2]. Top: input images. Middle: Wang's results. Bottom: our results.

Both algorithms can remove the haze significantly. Overall, our results are more vivid. The color of [1] is somewhat dull due to the single dark channel prior. Moreover, the patch size is fixed in Hes algorithm, which usually introduces halo effects as shown in Fig. 5(c). In addition, the input image in Fig. 5(d) is under-exposed which cannot be corrected by [1].

6.2   Exposure Correction

Next, we compare our method with [2] which corrects under-exposed images using the bright channel prior. Similarly, the patch size is set to 15×15 for a 600×400 image. The comparison results are illustrated in Fig. 6. Both algorithms lighten the input images. Comparatively, our results recover much more color details. The reason is that our algorithm is based on adaptive patch size and involves more information from a pixels neighborhood. Moreover, due to the single bright channel prior, [2] is unable to remove a foggy image as shown in Fig. 6(d).

7   Conclusion

In this paper, we have proposed an automatic image enhancement method using double channels and adaptive patch size. The patch size of a given pixel is automatically selected by contrast feature with thresholding. Then both dark and bright channels are extracted based on the adaptive local patch. The final enhancement on the YUV color model is simple and effective.

The only one parameter in our algorithm is the threshold of contrast feature, which is an empirical value. In the future work, we can figure out this threshold systematically. Additionally, some inhomogeneous regions will be occasionally produced by only employing local patches in the algorithm. With some global information being introduced, the enhancement result could be more natural on the whole.

Acknowledgments. This research was supported by Zhejiang Provincial Natural Science Foundation of China under Grant No. LQ14F020003 and in part by the National Natural Science Foundation of China (61572428, U1509206).

References

1. He, K., Sun, J., Tang, X.: Single image haze removal using dark channel prior. IEEE Trans. PAMI **33**(12), 2341–2353 (2011)
2. Wang, Y., Zhuo, S., Tao, D., Bu, J., Li, N.: Automatic local exposure correction using bright channel prior for under-exposed images. Sig. Process. **93**(11), 3227–3238 (2013)
3. Gonzalez, R.C., Woods, R.E.: Digital Image Processing. Addison-Wesley Longman Publishing Co. Inc., Boston (2001)
4. Nakai, K., Hoshi, Y., Taguchi, A.: Color image contrast enhancement method based on differential intensity/saturation gray-levels histograms. In: Proceedings of International ISPACS Symposium, pp. 445–449 (2013)
5. Singh, K., Kapoor, R.: Image enhancement using exposure based sub image histogram equalization. Pattern Recogn. Lett. **36**, 10–14 (2014)
6. Assefa, M., Poulie, T., Kervec, J., Larabi, M.C.: Correction of over-exposure using color channel correlations. In: Proceedings of IEEE GlobalSIP, pp. 1078–1082 (2014)
7. Yuan, L., Sun, J.: Automatic exposure correction of consumer photographs. In: Proceedings of ECCV, pp. 771–785 (2012)
8. Narasimhan, S.G., Nayar, S.K.: Contrast restoration of weather degraded images. IEEE Trans. PAMI **25**(6), 713–724 (2003)
9. Fattal, R.: Single image dehazing. ACM Trans. Graph. **27**(3), 1–9 (2008)
10. Oakley, J.P., Bu, H.: Correction of simple contrast loss in color images. IEEE Trans. Image Process. **16**(2), 511–522 (2007)
11. Kopf, J., Neubert, B., Chen, B., Cohen, M., Cohen-Or, D., Deussen, O., Uyttendaele, M., Lischinski, D.: Deep photo: model-based photograph enhancement and viewing. ACM Trans. Graph. **27**(5), 1–10 (2008)
12. Pizer, S.M., Amburn, E.P., Austin, J.D., Cromartie, R., Geselowitz, A., Greer, T., Romeny, B.T.H., Zimmerman, J.B., Zuiderveld, K.: Adaptive histogram equalization and its variations. Comput. Vis. Graph. Image Process. **39**(3), 355–368 (1987)
13. Sugimura, D., Mikami, T., Yamashita, H., Hamamoto, T.: Enhancing color images of extremely low light scenes based on RGB/NIR images acquisition with different exposure times. IEEE Trans. Image Process. **24**(11), 3586–3597 (2015)
14. Celik, T.: Spatial entropy-based global and local image contrast enhancement. IEEE Trans. Image Process. **23**(12), 5298–5308 (2014)
15. Podpora, M., Korbas, G.P., Kawala-Janik, A.: YUV vs RGB-choosing a color space for human-machine interaction. In: Proceedings of FedCSIS, pp. 29–34 (2014)
16. He, K., Sun, J., Tang, X.: Guided image filtering. IEEE Trans. PAMI **35**(6), 1397–1409 (2013)

Deep Ranking Model for Person Re-identification with Pairwise Similarity Comparison

Sanping Zhou, Jinjun Wang[✉], Qiqi Hou, and Yihong Gong

Institute of Artificial Intelligence and Robotics,
Xi'an Jiaotong University, Xi'an 710049, China
jinjun@mail.xjtu.edu.cn

Abstract. This paper presents a deep ranking model with feature learning and fusion supervised by a novel contrastive loss function for person re-identification. Given the probe image set, we organize the training images into a batch of pairwise samples, each probe image with a matched or a mismatched reference from the gallery image set. Treating these pairwise samples as inputs, we build a part-based deep convolutional neural network (CNN) to generate the layered feature representations supervised by the proposed contrastive loss function, in which the intra-class distances are minimized and the inter-class distances are maximized. In the deep model, the feature of different body parts are first discriminately learned in the convolutional layers and then fused in the fully connected layers, which makes it able to extract discriminative features of different individuals. Extensive experiments on the public benchmark datasets are reported to evaluate our method, shown significant improvements on accuracy, as compared with the state-of-the-art approaches.

Keywords: Person re-identification · Deep model · Pairwise comparison

1 Introduction

Given one single shot or multiple shots of a target pedestrian, the aim of person re-identification is to match the same individuals among a set of gallery candidates captured from a disjoint camera network. It is a critical computer vision task that can provide useful cues for many surveillance applications, such as person association [12], multi-target tracking [17] and behavior analysis [7]. Despite years of efforts from researchers, the problem is still extremely challenging due to large variations of body poses, lighting conditions, view angles, scenarios across time and cameras in surveillance videos, as shown in Fig. 1. Besides, pedestrian images captured by surveillance cameras are usually in small sizes, which makes many visual details such as facial components are indistinguishable, and different pedestrians may look similar in appearance.

To address these challenges, extensive works have been reported in the past few years, which could be roughly divided into two classes: (1) developing robust descriptors to handle the variations in pedestrian appearance, and

© Springer International Publishing AG 2016
E. Chen et al. (Eds.): PCM 2016, Part II, LNCS 9917, pp. 84–94, 2016.
DOI: 10.1007/978-3-319-48896-7_9

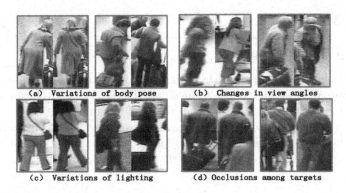

(a) Variations of body pose   (b) Changes in view angles

(c) Variations of lighting   (d) Occlusions among targets

Fig. 1. The challenges to person re-identification problem in public space. (a–d) The two images in each bounding box refer to the same person observed in different cameras, and the data is available at http://www.lrs.icg.tugraz.at/downloads.php.

(2) designing discriminative distance metrics to measure the similarity of pedestrian images. For the first category, different cues (color, shape, texture) from pedestrian images are employed for distinctive feature representation. Representative descriptors in person re-identification include local binary pattern (LBP) [15], ensemble of local feature (ELF) [6], mid-level filter [18] and local maximal occurrence (LOMO) [10]. For the second category, a distance metric is learned from the labeled training samples, under which the inter-class and intra-class variations of pedestrian images get increased and decreased, respectively. Typical metric learning methods include locally adaptive decision function (LADF) [9], large margin nearest neighbor (LMNN) [14], information theoretic metric learning (ITML) [3], and pairwise constrained component analysis (PCCA) [11].

The deep learning methods are becoming popular in person re-identification, because they can incorporate the two above-mentioned aspects into an integrated framework [1,4,8,16]. Despite the great success of these deep models in person re-identification, the lack of labeled training data may limit the generalization ability of them on the test data. To address this problem, we build a part-based deep CNN to extract features, in which different body parts are discriminately learned in the convolutional layers and then fused in the fully connected layers to generate discriminative image representations for different individuals. By organizing the training images into pairwise samples, we feed the fused feature representations into the siamese neural networks for similarity comparison, in which the intra-class distances are minimized and the inter-class distances are maximized. Compared with the popular approaches, our method has achieved the state-of-the-art the performance on the benchmark datasets.

The rest of the paper is organized as follows. In Sect. 2, we introduce our deep feature learning and fusion framework with pairwise similarity comparison. Experimental results and analysis are presented in Sect. 3. Conclusion comes in Sect. 4.

2   Our Method

2.1   Deep Ranking Model

In order to incorporate the feature representation learning into an end-to-end learning framework, we introduce a novel part-based deep convolutional neural network to extract discriminative features of different individuals. The deep architecture of the proposed model is shown in Fig. 2, which is consisted of convolutional layers, max pooling layers and fully connected layers. In the following paragraphs, we will focus on explaining the detail of the architecture.

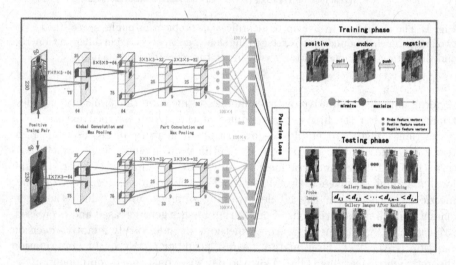

Fig. 2. The siamese-based deep feature learning and fusion framework. The left half shows the siamese deep architecture, the top right panel shows the training stage, and the bottom right panel shows the testing stage.

Global Convolution and Max Pooling. The first layer of our network is a global convolutional layer, which is used to compute low-level features on each input image separately. In order for the features to be comparable across the pairwise samples in later layers, our global convolutional layer shares parameters across the two views to ensure that they use same filters to compute features. In the global convolutional layer, we first pass the input pairwise samples of RGB images of size $230 \times 80 \times 3$ through 64 learned filters of size $7 \times 7 \times 3$. Then, the resulting feature maps are passed through a max pooling kernel of size $3 \times 3 \times 3$ with stride 3. Finally, these feature maps are passed through a rectified linear unit (ReLU).

Local Convolution and Max Pooling. In the local convolutional layer, we first averagely divided the global max pooling layer into four horizontal patches across the height channel, which introduces 4×64 local feature maps of different body parts. Compared with the existing part strategy [16] in the deep model, our method can reserve much more useful information to be discriminately learned in the following layers. Specially, we first pass the part-based feature maps into four local small convolutional layers through 32 learned filters of size 3×3. Then, the resulting local feature maps are passed through four small local max pooling kernels of size 3×3 with stride 1, respectively. Finally, we add a rectified linear unit (ReLU) after each local max pooling layer. In order to learn the feature representation of different body parts discriminately, we do not share the parameters of the four local small convolutional layers in the same view, while do share the parameters of the corresponding local small convolutional layers across the two different views.

Feature Learning and Fusion. In order to capture higher-order feature representations of the pairwise training samples, we implement the feature learning and fusion step by using the fully connected layers. Firstly, the local feature maps of different body parts are discriminately learned by following a local small fully connected layer after each local small max pooling layer. Secondly, the obtained local feature maps are summarized by adding a global large fully connected layer, which feeds the four local small fully connected layers as input. For robust feature representation, we also add the second local small fully connected layer after each of the first local small fully connected layer. The dimension of the local small fully connected layer is 100, while the dimension of the global large fully connected layer is 400. A rectified linear unit (ReLU) is added between two fully connected layers. Finally, the resulting 800 dimensional feature vector of each image in pairwise samples is fed into the contrastive loss layer, in which we minimize the intra-class distances and maximize the inter-class distances.

2.2 Contrastive Loss Function

Let $\{X_i\}_{i=1}^{N}$ be the set of input training data, where X_i denotes the ith raw input data, and N is the number of training samples. The goal of training CNN is to learn filter weights and biases that minimize the ranking error from the output layer. A recursive function for an M-layer CNN can be defined as follows:

$$\mathbf{X}_i^{(m)} = \Psi(\mathbf{W}^{(m)} * \mathbf{X}_i^{(m-1)} + \mathbf{b}^{(m)}),$$
$$i = 1, 2, \cdots, N; m = 1, 2, \cdots, M; \mathbf{X}_i^{(0)} = \mathbf{X}_i. \tag{1}$$

where $\mathbf{W}^{(m)}$ denotes the filter weights of the mth layer to be learned, $\mathbf{b}_i^{(m)}$ refers to the corresponding biases, $*$ denotes the convolution operation, $\Psi(\cdot)$ is an element-wise non-linear activation function such as ReLU, and $\mathbf{X}_i^{(m)}$ represents the feature maps generated at layer m for sample $\mathbf{X}_i$. For simplicity, we consider the parameters in the network as a whole and define $\mathbf{W} = \{\mathbf{W}^{(1)}, \cdots, \mathbf{W}^{(M)}\}$ and $\mathbf{b} = \{\mathbf{b}^{(1)}, \cdots, \mathbf{b}^{(M)}\}$.

For each pair of person samples $\mathbf{X}_i$ and $\mathbf{X}_j$, they can be represented as $f(\mathbf{X}_i) = \mathbf{X}_i^{(M)}$ and $f(\mathbf{X}_j) = \mathbf{X}_j^{(M)}$ at the output layer. The pairwise distance metric can be measured by computing the squared Euclidean distance between the most top level representations, which is defined as follows:

$$d(\mathbf{X}_i, \mathbf{X}_j) = \|f(\mathbf{X}_i) - f(\mathbf{X}_j)\|_2^2 \qquad (2)$$

The smaller the distance $d(\mathbf{X}_i, \mathbf{X}_j)$ is, the more similar the two person images $\mathbf{X}_i$ and $\mathbf{X}_j$ are. The definition formulates the similar person image ranking problem as nearest neighbor search problem in Euclidean space, which can be efficiently solved via relative comparison algorithms.

As described in Sect. 1, we aim to improve person image ranking accuracies of a CNN model by embedding the pairwise comparison metric into the output layer of the model during the training process. Embedding this metric into the Mth layer is equivalent to using the following loss function to train the model:

$$\arg\min_{\mathbf{W},\mathbf{b}} L = \sum_{i=1}^{N} P(f(\mathbf{X}_i), f(\mathbf{X}_j)) + \lambda R(\mathbf{W}, \mathbf{b}) \qquad (3)$$

where $R(\mathbf{W}, \mathbf{b})$ is a regularization term which makes the parameters of the deep model smooth, $P(f(\mathbf{X}_i), f(\mathbf{X}_i))$ denotes the contrastive loss function which minimize the intra-class distances and inter-class distances. Parameter λ controls the balance between the regularization term and the contrastive loss term. Note that the output $f(\mathbf{X}_i)$ depends on $\mathbf{W}^{(1)}, \cdots, \mathbf{W}^{(M)}$ and $\mathbf{b}^{(1)}, \cdots, \mathbf{b}^{(M)}$, therefore directly constraining $f(\mathbf{X}_i)$ will modulate the filter weights from 1th to M^{th} layers by feedback propagation during the training phase.

To explore discriminative information from the output of the deep ranking model, we expect that there is a large margin between positive pairs and negative pairs. Specially, $d(\mathbf{X}_i, \mathbf{X}_j)$ is smaller than M_1 if $\mathbf{X}_i$ and $\mathbf{X}_j$ are from the same subject, $d(\mathbf{X}_i, \mathbf{X}_j)$ is larger than M_2 if $\mathbf{X}_i$ and $\mathbf{X}_j$ are from the different subjects. The formulation can be represented as the following hinge-like loss function:

$$P(\mathbf{X}_i, \mathbf{X}_j) = \mu(1 - y_{ij})\max\{M_2 - d(\mathbf{X}_i, \mathbf{X}_j), 0\} + y_{ij}\max\{d(\mathbf{X}_i, \mathbf{X}_j) - M_1, 0\} \quad (4)$$

where $0 \leq M_1 \leq M_2$ are the margin parameters, μ is the weight parameter, and $y_{ij} = 1$ denotes $\mathbf{X}_i$ and $\mathbf{X}_j$ are from the same subject, while $y_{ij} = 0$ denotes $\mathbf{X}_i$ and $\mathbf{X}_j$ are from the different subjects. Different from the contrastive loss function[1], we improve it from two aspects: (1) A margin parameter M_1 is introduced to avoid the overfitting problem, in which the positive pairs in the training set can get pushed too close together in the embedding space during training. (2) A weight parameter is introduced to strengthen the learning of hard negative pairs, in which we set $\mu > 0$ if the negative pairs looks more similar than the positive pairs.

Notice that the margin parameters M_1 and M_2 are hard to choose in the training process, because given M_1, smaller M_2 will lead to the poor ranking accuracy, and larger M_2 will increase the expensive computation. Therefore, we propose a soft margin strategy to adaptively solve the problem, in which

---

[1] The contrastive loss function: $P(\mathbf{X}_i, \mathbf{X}_j) = (1 - y_{ij})\max\{M_c - d(\mathbf{X}_i, \mathbf{X}_j), 0\} + y_{ij}d(\mathbf{X}_i, \mathbf{X}_j)$, where M_c is the margin parameter.

we use the average positive distance to indicate the punishment standard to the corresponding negative pairs. Incorporate this formulation into Eq. (4), the hinge-like loss function can be rewritten as follows:

$$P(\mathbf{X}_i, \mathbf{X}_j) = \mu(1 - y_{ij})\max\{M_2 + \frac{1}{M}\sum_{k=1}^{M} y_{ik}d(\mathbf{X}_i, \mathbf{X}_k) - d(\mathbf{X}_i, \mathbf{X}_j), 0\}$$
$$+ y_{ij}\max\{d(\mathbf{X}_i, \mathbf{X}_j) - M_1, 0\} \tag{5}$$

where N is the number of positive pairs.

In order to smooth the parameters of the whole neural network, we define the following regularization term, which can be formulated as follows:

$$R = \sum_{m=1}^{M} \|\mathbf{W}^{(m)}\|_F^2 + \|\mathbf{b}^{(m)}\|_2^2 \tag{6}$$

By applying the hinge-like loss function in Eq. (5) and the regularization term in Eq. (6) into the general loss framework in Eq. (3), we formulate our optimization problem as follows:

$$\arg\min_{\mathbf{W}, \mathbf{b}} L = \sum_{i=1}^{N} \mu(1 - y_{ij})\max\{M_2 + \frac{1}{M}\sum_{k=1}^{M} y_{ik}d(\mathbf{X}_i, \mathbf{X}_k) - d(\mathbf{X}_i, \mathbf{X}_j), 0\}$$
$$+ y_{ij}\max\{d(\mathbf{X}_i, \mathbf{X}_j) - M_1, 0\} + \lambda\sum_{m=1}^{M} \|\mathbf{W}^{(m)}\|_F^2 + \|\mathbf{b}^{(m)}\|_2^2 \tag{7}$$

where the first term maximizes the inter-class distances and minimizes the intra-class distances, the second term regularizes the parameters of the whole neural network, and λ balances the contribution of different term to alleviate the over-fitting problem.

2.3 Learning Algorithm

To solve the optimization problem in Eq. (7), we employ the batch gradient descent scheme to obtain the parameters $\mathbf{W} = \{\mathbf{W}^{(1)}, \cdots, \mathbf{W}^{(M)}\}$ and $\mathbf{b} = \{\mathbf{b}^{(1)}, \cdots, \mathbf{b}^{(M)}\}$. For simplicity, we consider the parameters in the network as a whole and define $\mathbf{\Omega}^{(m)} = [\mathbf{W}^{(m)}, \mathbf{b}^{(m)}]$ and $\mathbf{\Omega} = \{\mathbf{\Omega}^{(1)}, \cdots, \mathbf{\Omega}^{(M)}\}$. The gradient of the objection function L with respect to can be computed as follows:

$$\frac{\partial L}{\partial \mathbf{\Omega}} = \sum_{i=1}^{N} p(\mathbf{X}_i, \mathbf{X}_j) + 2\lambda\sum_{m=1}^{M} \mathbf{\Omega}^{(m)} \tag{8}$$

By the definition of $P(\mathbf{X}_i, \mathbf{X}_j)$ in Eq. (5), we obtained the gradient as follows:

$$p(\mathbf{X}_i, \mathbf{X}_j) = \begin{cases} \frac{\partial P}{\partial \mathbf{\Omega}}, \ if \ y_{ij} = 1, \ and \ d(\mathbf{X}_i, \mathbf{X}_j) > \alpha; \\ 0, \ if \ y_{ij} = 1, \ and \ d(\mathbf{X}_i, \mathbf{X}_j) \le \alpha; \\ -\frac{\partial P}{\partial \mathbf{\Omega}}, \ if \ y_{ij} = 0, \ and \ d(\mathbf{X}_i, \mathbf{X}_j) < \beta; \\ 0, \ if \ y_{ij} = 0, \ and \ d(\mathbf{X}_i, \mathbf{X}_j) \ge \beta. \end{cases} \tag{9}$$

Algorithm 1. Siamese-based gradient descent training algorithm

---

Input:

   Training siamese units S, learning rate τ, maximum iterative number C, weight parameter λ, weight parameter margin μ, margin parameter M_1 and M_2.

Output:

   The network parameters Ω.

repeat

   1. Calculate outputs $f(\mathbf{X}_i)$ of image $\{\mathbf{X}_i\}$ by forward propagation.

   repeat

   a) Calculate $\frac{\partial d}{\partial f(\mathbf{X}_i)}$, $\frac{\partial d}{\partial f(\mathbf{X}_j)}$ for image $\mathbf{X}_i$ and $\mathbf{X}_j$ according to Eq. (2);

   b) Calculate $\frac{\partial P}{\partial \Omega}$ according to Eq. (10);

   c) Increment the gradient $\frac{\partial L}{\partial \Omega}$ according to Eq. (8) and Eq. (9);

   until Traverse all the pairwise samples in the training set $\{\mathbf{X}_i^a, \mathbf{X}_i^p, \mathbf{X}_i^n\}_{i=1}^N$;

   2. Update $\Omega_{c+1} = \Omega_c - \tau_c \frac{\partial L}{\partial \Omega_c}$ and $c \leftarrow c - 1$.

until $c > C$

---

where $\alpha = M_1$ and, and $\beta = M_2 + \sum_{k=1}^{M} y_{ik} d(\mathbf{X}_i, \mathbf{X}_k)/M$ is formulated as follows:

$$\frac{\partial P}{\partial \Omega} = 2(f(\mathbf{X}_i) - f(\mathbf{X}_j))' \cdot \frac{\partial f(\mathbf{X}_i) - \partial f(\mathbf{X}_j)}{\partial \Omega} \tag{10}$$

It is clear that the gradient of each pairwise sample can be easily calculated given the values of $f(\mathbf{X}_i)$, $f(\mathbf{X}_j)$ and $\frac{\partial f(\mathbf{X}_i)}{\partial \Omega}$, $\frac{\partial f(\mathbf{X}_j)}{\partial \Omega}$, which can be obtained by separately running the forward and backward propagation for each image in the pairwise units. As the algorithm needs to go through all the pairwise units to accumulate the gradients in each iteration, we call it the siamese-based gradient descent algorithm. Algorithm 1 shows the overall process.

3   Experimental Results

3.1   Dataset Description and Data Augmentation

Dataset Description. In order to evaluate the performance, we test our method on two challenging and widely used benchmark datasets: the VIPeR dataset [6], the i-LIDS dataset [2].

   VIPeR dataset[2]: It contains 632 pedestrians captured from two cameras in an outdoor environment. Each pedestrian has one image per camera view. This dataset is very challenging due to large variations in viewpoint, illumination and pose.

   i-LIDS dataset[3]: It is constructed from video images of a busy airport arrival hall. It contains 479 images from 119 persons and each person has four images in average. These images are captured by two cameras, and are subject to large illumination changes and occlusions.

---

[2] The data set is available at http://vision.soe.ucsc.edu/?q=node/178.

[3] The data set is available at http://www.homeoffice.gov.uk/science-research/hosdb/i-lids/.

Data augmentation. As an important mechanism for alleviating the over-fitting problem, in our implementation, we first resize the image into 250×100 pixel in size, then in the training iteration, we crop a region of size 230×80 with a small random perturbation for each image to augment the training data.

3.2   Parameter Setting and Evaluation Protocol

Parameter Setting. The weights were initialized from two zero-mean Gaussian distribution with standard deviation from 0.01 to 0.001, respectively. The bias terms were initialized with constant value 0. The network learning rate $\tau = 0.001$, the weight parameters $\lambda = 0.01$ and $\mu = 0.8$, and the margin parameters $M_1 = 0.1$ and $M_2 = 1.0$.

Evaluation Protocol. We adopt the widely used cumulative match curve (CMC) approach for quantitative evaluation, in which half of the persons are chosen for training and the remainders are used for testing. For each image in the probe set, we return the k nearest images in the gallery set using the Euclidean distance with the features produced by the trained network. If the returned list contain an image featuring the same person as that in probe image, this probe is considered as success of rank k. We repeated the procedure 10 times, and use the average rate as the metric.

3.3   Experimental Results

Our person re-identification method mainly contains two novel ingredients: (1) the part-based deep CNN, and (2) the improved pairwise loss. To reveal how each ingredient contributes to the performance improvement, we implement the following four variants of the proposed method, and compare them with a dozen of representative methods in the literature:

Variant 1 (denoted as GCNN-C): We replace the four body part channels from the proposed deep architecture with a global convolution layer and use the original contrastive loss function to train the network.

Variant 2 (denoted as GCNN-IC): We replace the four body part channels from the proposed deep architecture with a global convolution layer and use the improved contrastive loss function to train the network.

Variant 3 (denoted as PCNN-C): We use the same loss as GCNN-C, but use the proposed part-based deep architecture to extract the features.

Variant 4 (denoted as PCNN-IC): We use the same network as PCNN-C, but train it with the improved contrastive loss function.

Comparison Results. The evaluation results on the VIPeR dataset and i-LIDS dataset, using Top 1, 5, 10 and 20 ranking accuracies, are shown in Table 1. We compare our method with 5 representative methods that have reported evaluation results on the two datasets. Ding's method [4] uses the deep learning method to deal with person re-identification problem and Sakrapee's [13] method combines several different approaches to boost the performance. Compared with the

Table 1. Matching rates (%) of Different state-of-the-art methods on the VIPeR dataset and i-LIDS dataset

VIPeR					i-LIDS				
Method	Top 1	Top 5	Top 10	Top 20	Method	Top 1	Top 5	Top 10	Top 20
LMNN [14]	6.2	19.7	32.6	52.3	LMNN [14]	28.0	53.8	66.1	82.3
PCCA [11]	19.3	48.9	64.9	80.3	MCC [5]	31.3	59.3	75.6	88.3
ITML [3]	11.6	31.4	45.8	63.9	ITML [3]	29.0	54.0	70.5	86.7
ELF [6]	12.0	31.0	41.0	58.0	Adaboost [6]	29.6	55.2	68.1	82.4
Sakrapee's [13]	45.9	--	--	--	Sakrapee's [13]	50.3	--	--	--
Ding's [4]	40.5	60.8	70.4	84.4	Ding's [4]	52.1	68.2	78.0	88.8
GCNN-C	29.8	56.0	64.2	74.4	**GCNN-C**	42.4	57.6	71.2	84.8
GCNN-IC	38.0	58.2	67.1	75.3	**GCNN-IC**	49.2	69.5	85.1	89.9
PCNN-C	42.7	61.1	66.8	77.2	**PCNN-C**	57.6	81.4	84.7	89.9
PCNN-IC	46.2	67.1	76.3	85.1	**PCNN-IC**	61.0	81.4	85.1	91.5

Table 2. The influence of M_1 and M_2 to Top 1 performance (%) on the VIPeR dataset.

M_1	0			0.1			0.2		
M_2	0.8	1.0	1.2	0.8	1.0	1.2	0.8	1.0	1.2
Top 1	39.24	45.25	42.41	43.04	46.20	43.35	39.87	44.62	41.46

above representative works, the PCNN-IC model has achieved the top performances on the two datasets, with all the four ranking measurements. Specially, compare with Sakrapee's method, which is the state-of-the-art method on the VIPeR dataset so far, our PCNN-IC model is better 0.3 % on Top 1; and compare with Ding's method, which is the state-of-the-art method on the i-LIDS dataset so far, our PCNN-IC model is better 8.9 % on Top 1. what's more, compare with the Top 1 accuracies of GCNN-C and PCNN-C, GCNN-IC and PCNN-IC, our part-based deep neural network beats the global based deep neural network with 12.9 %, 8.2 % and 15.2 %, 11.8 % on the two datasets, respectively; compared with the Top 1 accuracies of GCNN-C and GCNN-IC, PCNN-C and PCNN-IC, our improved contrastive loss beats the original one with 8.2 %, 6.0 % and 3.5 %, 3.4 % on the two datasets, respectively.

Parameters Analysis. The margin parameters M_1 and M_2, and the weight parameter μ play an important role in our method. We analyze the results with varying M_1, M_2 and μ on the two datasets to show the influences. In particular, given a weight parameter $\mu = 0.8$, we change the initial values of M_1 and M_2 to evaluate the performance on the VIPeR dataset. The results are shown in Table 2, in which the best performance of our method is achieved by setting $M_1 = 0.1$ and $M_2 = 1.0$. In order to explore the influence of μ to our method, we set $M_1 = 0.1$ and $M_2 = 1.0$ to evaluate the performances of our method on the two dataset. The results are shown in Fig. 3, which shows that the best performances of our method on the two datatset are achieved by setting $\mu = 0.8$. Therefore, we set $M_1 = 0.1$, $M_2 = 1.0$ and $\mu = 0.8$ in all the experiments for best performance.

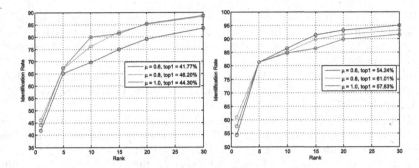

Fig. 3. The varying matching rate of our method according to μ at specified M_1 and M_2 on the two datasets.

4 Conclusion

In this paper, we present a novel part-based convolutional neural network with feature learning and fusion for person re-identification problem, which is formulated under a siamese framework via a improved contrastive loss function. In this framework, we construct a part-based CNN architecture with feature learning in the convolutional layers and feature fusion in the fully connected layers. The architecture is trained by a set of pairwise samples to produce features that the distance of the same person is smaller than that of different persons, with a large margin in the learned feature space. Our method have obtained the state-of-the-art performance on the benchmark datasets for person re-identification. In the future work, we will extend our framework to specific tasks, such as face recognition, fine-grained classification and image retrieval.

Acknowledgments. This work is partially supported by National Basic Research Program of China (973 Program) under Grant No. 2015CB351705, and the National Science Foundation of China under Grant No. 61473219.

References

1. Ahmed, E., Jones, M., Marks, T.K.: An improved deep learning architecture for person re-identification. Differences **5**, 25 (2015)
2. Branch, H.: Imagery library for intelligent detection systems (i-lids). In: The Institution of Engineering and Technology Conference on Crime and Security, 2006, pp. 445–448. IET (2006)
3. Davis, J.V., Kulis, B., Jain, P., Sra, S., Dhillon, I.S.: Information-theoretic metric learning. In: Proceedings of the 24th International Conference on Machine learning, pp. 209–216. ACM (2007)
4. Ding, S., Lin, L., Wang, G., Chao, H.: Deep feature learning with relative distance comparison for person re-identification. Pattern Recogn. **48**(10), 2993–3003 (2015)
5. Globerson, A., Roweis, S.T.: Metric learning by collapsing classes. In: Advances in Neural Information Processing Systems, pp. 451–458 (2005)

6. Gray, D., Tao, H.: Viewpoint invariant pedestrian recognition with an ensemble of localized features. In: Forsyth, D., Torr, P., Zisserman, A. (eds.) ECCV 2008. LNCS, vol. 5302, pp. 262–275. Springer, Heidelberg (2008). doi:10.1007/978-3-540-88682-2_21

7. Hu, W., Tan, T., Wang, L., Maybank, S.: A survey on visual surveillance of object motion and behaviors. IEEE Trans. Syst. Man Cybern. C Appl. Rev. **34**(3), 334–352 (2004)

8. Li, W., Zhao, R., Xiao, T., Wang, X.: DeepReID: deep filter pairing neural network for person re-identification. In: 2014 IEEE Conference on Computer Vision and Pattern Recognition (CVPR), pp. 152–159. IEEE (2014)

9. Li, Z., Chang, S., Liang, F., Huang, T.S., Cao, L., Smith, J.R.: Learning locally-adaptive decision functions for person verification. In: 2013 IEEE Conference on Computer Vision and Pattern Recognition (CVPR), pp. 3610–3617. IEEE (2013)

10. Liao, S., Hu, Y., Zhu, X., Li, S.Z.: Person re-identification by local maximal occurrence representation and metric learning. In: Proceedings of the IEEE Conference on Computer Vision and Pattern Recognition, pp. 2197–2206 (2015)

11. Mignon, A., Jurie, F.: PCCA: a new approach for distance learning from sparse pairwise constraints. In: 2012 IEEE Conference on Computer Vision and Pattern Recognition (CVPR), pp. 2666–2672. IEEE (2012)

12. Morris, B.T., Trivedi, M.M.: A survey of vision-based trajectory learning and analysis for surveillance. IEEE Trans. Circ. Syst. Video Technol. **18**(8), 1114–1127 (2008)

13. Paisitkriangkrai, S., Shen, C., van den Hengel, A.: Learning to rank in person re-identification with metric ensembles. In: Proceedings of the IEEE Conference on Computer Vision and Pattern Recognition, pp. 1846–1855 (2015)

14. Weinberger, K.Q., Blitzer, J., Saul, L.K.: Distance metric learning for large margin nearest neighbor classification. In: Advances in Neural Information Processing Systems, pp. 1473–1480 (2005)

15. Xiong, F., Gou, M., Camps, O., Sznaier, M.: Person re-identification using kernel-based metric learning methods. In: Fleet, D., Pajdla, T., Schiele, B., Tuytelaars, T. (eds.) ECCV 2014. LNCS, vol. 8695, pp. 1–16. Springer, Heidelberg (2014). doi:10.1007/978-3-319-10584-0_1

16. Yi, D., Lei, Z., Liao, S., Li, S.Z.: Deep metric learning for person re-identification. In: 2014 22nd International Conference on Pattern Recognition (ICPR), pp. 34–39. IEEE (2014)

17. Zhang, S., Wang, J., Wang, Z., Gong, Y., Liu, Y.: Multi-target tracking by learning local-to-global trajectory models. Pattern Recogn. **48**(2), 580–590 (2015)

18. Zhao, R., Ouyang, W., Wang, X.: Learning mid-level filters for person re-identification. In: 2014 IEEE Conference on Computer Vision and Pattern Recognition (CVPR), pp. 144–151. IEEE (2014)

Cluster Enhanced Multi-task Learning for Face Attributes Feature Selection

Yuchun Fang[✉] and Xiaoda Jiang

School of Computer Engineering and Science, Shanghai University,
Shanghai, China
ycfang@shu.edu.cn

Abstract. The research on face attribute analysis has received tremendous attention recently for wide range of applications. Considering face attributes are related, we can improve the generalization performance by exploiting the shared features. In such scenario, multi-task feature learning approaches are very promising for face attributes classification. In this paper, inspired by several classic multi-task learning methods, we propose clustering enhanced multi-task learning (CEMTL) which can be applied in feature selection for effectively representing human face attributes through considering both the intra and inter class correlation of multi-tasks. By using CEMTL, we can select useful features to train an efficient model for face attributes classification. Experiments on LFW database prove the advantage of the proposed method in binary and multiple classification.

Keywords: Multi-task learning · Face attributes · Face recognition

1 Introduction

The human face conveys important perceptible information related to individual traits. The face attributes, such as gender, age, expression, are valuable demographic characteristics. Face attributes have received tremendous attention recently and their effectiveness have been applied successfully in a wide range of applications including face verification [1, 2], attribute search [25] and etc. We can solve these verification and search problems by using different methods. For example, Scheirer et al. [3] proposed a Bayesian network approach to utilize the human attributes for face identification. Kumar et al. [4] created one the first image search engine based entirely on face attributes. With the retrieval system, users can find the needed face through over 3.1 million faces which have been automatically labeled on the basis of several facial attributes. Chen et al. [5] aimed to utilize automatically detected human attributes by constructing semantic codewords for efficient large-scale face retrieval. Lei et al. [6] proposed a novel way to search for face photos by simultaneously considering attributes positions, and sizes of the target faces. An implicit assumption of these methods is that the attributes are split. There are very few approaches to estimate all attributes together.

Conventional machine learning methods often only consider data represented by Single-Task Learning (STL), even though these tasks often have relationship. Different

© Springer International Publishing AG 2016
E. Chen et al. (Eds.): PCM 2016, Part II, LNCS 9917, pp. 95–104, 2016.
DOI: 10.1007/978-3-319-48896-7_10

from STL, Multi-Task Learning (MTL) approaches have received increasing studies and they often outperform STL approaches. Thus, we choose MTL to take into account the connection of attributes to capture the shared features when they are in the learning process.

In recent years, MTL [7] has attracted significant interest in the Machine Learning community [8]. MTL has been applied successfully in many applications including object recognition [7], speech recognitions [9] and handwritten digit recognition [10]. MTL aims to improve the generalization performance by exploiting the shared features among multiple related tasks. A critical ingredient in these applications is how to model the shared structures. In traditional MTL methods [11, 12], all tasks are interrelated, they can be put together to train a model; for example, Yu et al. [13] presented an approach based on a hierarchical Bayesian framework, which exploits the equivalence between parametric linear models and nonparametric Gaussian processes. Srijith et al. [14] proposed a novel Gaussian Process (GP) approach in multi-task learning based on joint feature selection. The key assumption of these multi task learning algorithms is that all tasks are related to each other through sharing features.

Simply assuming all tasks share a structure may degrade the performance. Therefore, Cluster Multi-Task Learning (CMTL) algorithms [15, 16] cluster the given task into different groups and impose the tasks in the same groups to share a certain common structure [17]. For example, Thrun et al. [18] explored the hidden task relations by establishing the relationship among tasks. Kang et al. [19] introduced new clustering variables, and the optimal parameters were obtained using the alternate optimization method.

Moreover, considering outlier tasks often exist in face attributes, another solution in real-world applications, Robust Multi-Task Learning (RMTL) [20], has been proposed to capture the common feature and identifies the outlier tasks. RMTL takes into considerations more factors than the other MTL methods. When there are a small number of tasks that are not related to most of the tasks, MTL is performed on all tasks. Because of the existing of outlier tasks, using common methods cannot achieve the optimal solution. For example, in [20], the gradient descent method is used to solve the optimization problem. The optimization is used to capture the characteristic relation of the related tasks and to determine the outliers. Inspired by RMTL, Cheng et al. [21] projected image into a low dimensional hash feature subspace by using the hash method. This method can not only reveal the attribute correlation, but also can capture the task related degree. An illustration of these three MTL methods is shown in Fig. 1.

Considering that all face attributes are related to each other by the presumed structures, we can use MTL algorithms to solve attribute classification problem. As the face attribute is an integral structure, we seek a new approach for face attributes classification by using MTL. We present a new framework which is effective on classification of human face attributes called Cluster Enhanced Multi Task Learning (CEMTL).

In this paper, CEMTL is presented to enhance the recognition in face attributes classification and this method can approximate the underlying true weights of face attributes. We present an algorithm to capture the shared features among tasks and the intra class relationship. By using this method, we can achieve a higher recognition rate in the case of dimension reduction. Our experiments demonstrate the efficiency of the proposed method.

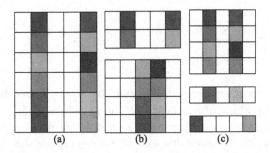

Fig. 1. Illustration of weight matrix decomposition for three MTL method, where squares with white background denote zero entries and squares with color denote non-zero entries. (a) Parameter sharing model. (Traditional MTL) (b) Task clustering model. (CMTL) (c) Outlier task model. (RMTL) (Color figure online)

The remainder of the paper is organized as follows. Section 2 presents different MTL methods, Sect. 3 introduces our proposed CEMTL. Experiments and analysis are depicted in Sect. 4. At last, we conclude the paper in Sect. 5.

2   Multi-task Learning Method

2.1   Preliminaries

Given t learning tasks associated with the training data $\{(X_1, y_1), (X_2, y_2), \ldots, (X_t, y_t)\}$ and a linear model:

$$y_i = f_i(X_i) = X_i w_i + \delta_i, i \in \{1, \ldots, t\}, \tag{1}$$

where $X_i \in \mathbb{R}^{d \times s_i}$ is the data matrix of the i-th task as a sample; $y_i \in \mathbb{R}^{s_i}$ is the response of the i-th task, d is the data dimensionality; s_i is the number of samples for the i-th task. For each task, $w_i \in \mathbb{R}^d$ is the underlying weight of the i-th task and δ_i is the noise vector. The multi-task learning model is formulated as the following problem:

$$\min_W \sum_{i=1}^{t} ||X_i w_i - y_i||^2 + \lambda P(W), \tag{2}$$

where $|| \cdot ||$ is the Euclidean norm, $W = [w_1, w_2, \ldots, w_t] \in R^{d \times t}$ is the weight matrix. λ is a nonnegative regularized parameter, $P(W)$ is the regularization term for W.

2.2   RMTL

In robust MTL, different regularization terms on $P = [p_1, \ldots, p_d]$ and $Q = [q_1, \ldots, q_t]$ represent the inner relationship and the relevance of the classes. RMTL can be solved with the following regularization imposed on P, Q:

$$\min_{W,P,Q} \sum_{i=1}^{t} ||X_i w_i^T - y_i||^2 + \lambda_1 ||P||_{2,1} + \lambda_2 ||Q||_{2,1}, \tag{3}$$

$$s.t. \ W = P + Q,$$

where $|| \cdot ||_{2,1}$ denotes squared matrix $\ell_{2,1}$-norm; the weight vector W of the labeling function is the composition of two factors: P and Q. Where P can capture the shared features and Q discovers the outlier tasks; λ_1 and λ_2 are nonnegative parameters to control these two terms. By using this method, we can capture shared features among tasks and identify outlier tasks.

2.3 CMTL

In CMTL, in order to discover a better clustering relationship between multiple tasks, we can solve the Eq. (2) by optimizing the following function:

$$\min_{W} \sum_{i=1}^{t} ||X_i w_i - y_i||^2 + \lambda_3 \sum_{g} ||WR_g||, \tag{4}$$

where R_g denotes task group assignment matrix of g-th group. By grouping the attributes according to their correlation, we can cluster the t tasks into k classes; $\{(X_1, y_1), (X_2, y_2), \ldots, (X_t, y_t)\} \in \{R_1, \ldots, R_k\}$; $\lambda_3 > 0$ are regularized parameters. CMTL is useful in analysis of the correlation tasks in the group.

3 CEMTL

Group constraints are performed by using CMTL. But CMTL cannot capture the relationship among classes. So CMTL is weak in the weight constraint. Though RMTL takes advantage of two regularization terms to capture the relationship among tasks, it is not efficient to capture the relationship within the classes. Inspired by CMTL and RMTL, we propose CEMTL model as follows:

$$\min_{W} \sum_{i=1}^{t} ||X_i w_i - y_i||^2 + \alpha ||W||_{2,1} + \beta \sum_{g=1}^{k} ||WR_g||. \tag{5}$$

CEMTL has two regularization items that serve to take into consideration both inter- and intra- task group constraints. The CEMTL can be solved by alternatively computing the following two problems:

$$\min_{M \in \mathbb{R}^{d \times t}} \left\{ \sum_{i=1}^{t} ||X_i m_i - y_i||^2 + \lambda_4 ||M||_{2,1} \right\}, \tag{6}$$

$$\min_{N} \left\{ \sum_{i=1}^{k} ||X_i n_i - y_i||^2 + \lambda_5 \sum_{g=1}^{k} ||NR_g|| \right\}, \tag{7}$$

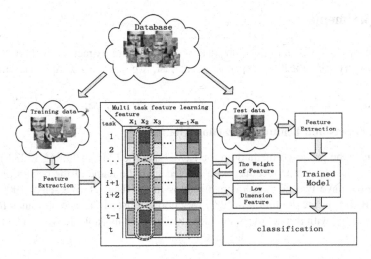

Fig. 2. The framework of our proposed multi task feature learning algorithm

where $M = [m_1, m_2, \ldots, m_t]$ and $N = [n_1, n_2, \ldots, n_k]$ are weight matrix, $W = M + N$; λ_4, $\lambda_5 > 0$ are regularized parameters. We use brute-force method to obtain the optimum solution of $\lambda_4, \lambda_5 \in [0, 1]$. We introduce two kinds of regularization terms. M captures the shared features among tasks and N captures the intra class relationship, as shown in Fig. 2.

Algorithm 1. Heuristic solution to CEMTL

Input: face attributes $\{x_l, y_l\}_{l=1}^t \in \{R_g\}_{g=1}^k$; regularization λ_4 and λ_5

1 Initialization: M_0, N_0;

2 for $i = 1, 2, \ldots, t$

 3   Update M using Equation (6);

 4   Update N using Equation (7);

5 end

 6 $W = M + N$;

 7 Output: optimization solution of M, N, W

By assuming $\{m_1, m_2\} \in \{n_1\}, \ldots, \{m_{t-2}, m_{t-1}, m_t\} \in \{n_t\}$, we propose an alternating algorithm as an approximation solution to the optimization problem in Eq. (5) as summarized in Algorithm 1. Simply adding two weight matric obtained with Eqs. (6) and (7), we obtain very promising experimental results.

The CEMTL feature is selected according to W. The value of W determines the importance of the feature. We select the feature with high weight and remove the negative correlation feature. With the proposed CEMTL for feature selection, we can achieve a high recognition rate in the case of dimension reduction.

4 Experiments

In this section, we first introduce our data sets and feature extraction method; then we present binary classification experiment; at last, we present multiple classification experiment.

4.1 Data Sets and Feature Extraction Method

We evaluate the proposed method on the LFW database [24], including 13233 images from 5749 subjects. Each face has been labeled with the name of the person pictured. 1680 people have two or more distinct photos in the data set. We select 10000 face images. Based on the definition in [28], we choose a list of 26 face attributes that are relatively stable with respect to person identity as shown in Table 1. We conduct 5 fold

Table 1. The average classification accuracy (%) of 26 face attributes with five methods

Attribute		STL	MTL	RMTL	CMTL	CEMTL
Gender	Male	93.53	97.73	96.90	97.34	**97.92**
Race	White	78.44	93.34	92.70	93.00	**93.45**
	Black	80.81	**85.77**	83.39	85.34	85.74
	Indian	77.64	89.29	88.27	88.33	**89.35**
Age	Youth	76.44	**95.66**	94.71	95.30	95.64
	Middle aged	74.47	88.08	86.96	87.59	**88.39**
	Senior	73.14	97.53	**97.54**	97.31	97.45
Face shape	Oval Face	78.67	**93.61**	91.78	91.99	93.52
	Square Face	77.28	94.73	92.90	94.19	**94.75**
	Round Face	73.10	89.86	87.34	89.70	**90.31**
	Chubby	71.88	**88.95**	87.08	87.97	88.56
Fringe	Receding Hairline	85.56	97.16	**97.83**	95.69	97.75
	Bangs	86.88	95.9	91.78	93.85	**95.95**
Nose	Big Nose	82.61	95.24	93.13	91.35	**95.24**
	Pointy Nose	78.78	95.07	93.06	94.12	**95.19**
Eyebrows	Bushy Eyebrows	78.17	96.36	92.76	95.18	**96.47**
	Arched Eyebrows	78.89	92.00	88.23	85.77	**92.13**
Beard	Mustache	86.68	96.11	95.74	**97.48**	96.32
	No Beard	88.58	96.14	94.3	**96.43**	96.13
Jaw	Double Chin	85.96	**96.63**	95.32	93.35	95.56
	Round Jaw	84.70	96.59	94.91	92.41	**96.60**
Appeal	unAttractive Man	79.44	93.47	91.74	**94.44**	93.42
	Attractive Woman	79.51	92.52	91.02	91.97	**92.70**
Forehead	Fully Visible	67.14	92.78	**92.89**	90.56	92.96
	Partially Visible	81.51	**89.56**	86.30	88.29	89.02
	Obstructed	84.00	96.57	95.57	96.19	**96.64**
Average		80.15	93.72	92.08	92.51	**93.74**

cross-validation of binary classification and multiple classification experiments to verify CEMTL we proposed.

In research on face recognition, local feature matching approaches show inspiring results. The most representative one is the local binary pattern (LBP) method [22, 23]. The core idea of this method is that the gray value of the center pixel is a threshold value, and the corresponding binary code is used to represent the local texture characteristics. ULBP feature [27] is an improved algorithm of LBP feature. In our experiments, the face images are divided into 8 * 7 blocks. Every block is denoted with a 59 dimensional histogram vector. Thus, we can obtain 3304 dimensional ULBP feature for each image.

Our method and other MTL models introduced in Sect. 2 are trained in the extracted ULBP feature space. The libsvm [26] is used as classifier. We employ the classification accuracy as the performance metric.

4.2 Binary Classification Experiment Design and Results

In this section, we evaluate the effectiveness of CEMTL by comparing with STL, MTL, CMTL and RMTL. For each attribute, 1000 images are sampled to construct the training set, including 500 positive samples and 500 negative samples; 800 images are used as the test set, including 400 positive samples and 400 negative samples. To observe the variation of accuracy with respect to number of dimensions, the recognition rate is calculated from 10, 20, ... to 100, and from 100, 200, ..., to 3304.

Because the recognition rates tend to be stable from over 100 dimensions, we calculate the average recognition rate from 100 to 1200 dimensions as shown in Table 1. From the results, we have the following observations: (1) The MTL method can enhance the performance in face attributes classification. This is because all the attributes are related to each other, so we can use MTL to find the feature correlations. (2) CEMTL is also efficient for most attributes, especially for labels that have semantic correlations, such as "Big Nose", "Pointy Nose", "square face", "round face". This is because CEMTL adjust weights partly based on the group constraints.

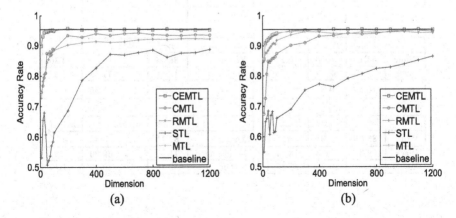

Fig. 3. Example of attribute classification with five methods: (a) Big Nose (b) Pointy Nose

As shown in Fig. 3, we use the 'Nose' attribute as an example: 'Big Nose' and 'Pointy Nose' to further illustrate the performance of CEMTL. The horizontal coordinate represents the dimension, and the vertical coordinate represents the recognition rate. Recognition rate is obtained by using 3304 ULBP features as the baseline shown as the horizontal line in the diagrams. From these results, we have the following observations: (1) CEMTL can achieve good recognition rate with very lower dimensional feature and is robust with the increase of dimensions. (2) The accuracy of CEMTL can exceed the baseline. This is because a larger number of useful features are selected and the negative correlation features are eliminated.

4.3 Multiple Classification Experiment Design and Results

We conduct multiple classification experiment with two natural attribute groups, i.e. 'Age' and 'Race'. We use 500 positive samples for each task as training samples and 400 positive samples for each task as test samples. The average recognition rate is calculated from 100 to 1200 dimension. As shown in Table 2, CEMTL prominently outperforms MTL and CMTL due to introducing the prior knowledge of the attribute group in the multi-task learning and thus effectively improve the recognition rate. We can also notice that taking into account the differences among attribute groups, CEMTL experts at the attribute clustering. Hence, we can conclude that CEMTL utilizes the neighbor structure and archives better results than MTL and CMTL in multiple classification problems. In Table 2(a), the CEMTL outperforms MTL and CMTL for the label of 'White' and 'Asia' but has no superiority for the label 'Indian' due to the less discrimination of this label with the other labels.

Table 2. Confusion matrice of recognition rate (%): (a) MTL + Race (b) MTL + Age (c) CMTL + Race (d) CMTL + Age (e) CEMTL + Race(f) CEMTL + Age

(a)

	White	Black	Indian
White	**83.10**	7.30	9.60
Black	8.73	**68.31**	22.96
Indian	16.84	14.20	**68.96**

(b)

	Youth	Middle aged	Senior
Youth	**85.65**	9.29	5.06
Middle aged	11.40	**76.58**	12.02
Senior	3.75	6.28	**89.97**

(c)

	White	Black	Indian
White	**83.16**	6.60	10.24
Black	8.13	**68.79**	23.08
Indian	18.55	14.86	**66.59**

(d)

	Youth	Middle aged	Senior
Youth	**86.44**	9.26	4.30
Middle aged	12.48	**77.35**	10.17
Senior	3.17	6.36	**90.47**

(e)

	White	Black	Indian
White	**85.38**	6.01	8.61
Black	9.81	**71.58**	18.61
Indian	18.13	14.70	**67.17**

(f)

	Youth	Middle aged	Senior
Youth	**87.15**	8.32	4.62
Middle aged	11.33	**80.00**	8.67
Senior	2.36	6.35	**91.29**

Compared with the binary classification, the advantage of CEMTL is more prominent. CEMTL is not only more suitable for multi-class feature learning, but also show that the group constraints are effective in multi-class feature learning.

5 Conclusions

In this paper, we present a cluster enhanced multi-task feature learning method for face attributes classification. Specially, this feature learning framework can simultaneously utilize the intra class relationship information and the relationship between class groups. We compare with other multi-task feature learning methods to evaluate the effectiveness of the proposed CEMTL. Experimental results show that the CEMTL can obtain high recognition rate with very low dimensional of feature. The experiments also prove the superiority of CEMTL in multiple classification problem. In the future, we will deduce better solution, consider the negative correlation and analyze outlier tasks.

Acknowledgement. The work is funded by the National Natural Science Foundation of China (No. 61170155).

References

1. Nowak, E., Jurie, F.: Learning visual similarity measures for comparing never seen objects. In: CVPR (2007)
2. Kumar, N., Berg, A.C., Belhumeur, P.N., Nayar, S.K.: Attribute and simile classifiers for face verification. In: Proceedings of IEEE International Conference on Computer Vision, pp. 365–372, September/October 2009
3. Scheirer, W., Kumar, N., Ricanek, K., Boult, T.E., Belhumeur, P.N.: Fusing with context: a Bayesian approach to combining descriptive attributes. In: International Joint Conference on Biometrics (2011)
4. Kumar, N., Belhumeur, P., Nayar, S.: FaceTracer: a search engine for large collections of images with faces. In: Forsyth, D., Torr, P., Zisserman, A. (eds.) ECCV 2008. LNCS, vol. 5305, pp. 340–353. Springer, Heidelberg (2008). doi:10.1007/978-3-540-88693-8_25
5. Chen, B.C., Chen, Y.Y., Kuo, Y.H., et al.: Scalable face image retrieval using attribute-enhanced sparse codewords. Multimedia IEEE Trans. **15**(5), 1163–1173 (2013)
6. Lei, Y.H., Chen, Y.Y., Chen, B.C., et al.: Where is who: large-scale photo retrieval by facial attributes and canvas layout. In: International ACM SIGIR Conference on Research and Development in Information Retrieval, pp. 701–710. ACM (2012)
7. Caruana, R.: Multitask learning. Mach. Learn. **28**(1), 41–75 (1997)
8. Blei, D.M., Griffiths, T.L., Jordan, M.I., Tenenbaum, J.B.: Hierarchical topic models and the nested Chinese restaurant process. In: Advances in Neural Information Processing Systems, vol. 16, pp. 17–24. MIT Press, Cambridge (2004)
9. Parameswaran, S., Weinberger, K.: Large margin multi-task metric learning. In: NIPS, vol. 23, pp. 1867–1875 (2010)
10. Quadrianto, N., Smola, A., Caetano, T., Vishwanathan, S., Petterson, J.: Multitask learning without label correspondences. In: NIPS (2010)

11. Quattoni, A., Collins, M., Darrell, T.: Transfer learning for image classification with sparse proto type representations. In: Proceedings of the IEEE Conference on Computer Vision and Pattern Recognition, vol. **68**, no. 1, pp. 49–67 (2006)
12. Hwang, S.J., Sha, F., Grauman, K.: Sharing features between objects and their attributes. In: Proceeding Soft the IEEE Conference on Computer Vision and Pattern Recognition, pp. 1761–1768 (2011)
13. Yu, K., Tresp, V., Schwaighofer, A.: Learning Gaussian processes from multiple tasks. In: International Conference on Machine Learning (2005)
14. Srijith, P.,K., Shevade, S.: Gaussian process multi-task learning using joint feature selection. In: Calders, T., Esposito, F., Hüllermeier, E., Meo, R. (eds.) ECML PKDD 2014. LNCS (LNAI), vol. 8726, pp. 98–113. Springer, Heidelberg (2014). doi:10.1007/978-3-662-44845-8_7
15. Jacob, L., Bach, F., Vert, J.: Clustered multi-task learning: a convex formulation. In: NIPS (2008)
16. Zhou, J., Chen, J., Ye, J.: Clustered multi-task learning via alternating structure optimization. In: NIPS (2011)
17. Xue, Y., Liao, X., Carin, L., Krishnapuram, B.: Multi-task learning for classification with dirichlet process priors. JMLR **8**, 35–63 (2007)
18. Thrun, S.: Discovering structure in multiple learning tasks: the TC algorithm. In: International Conference on Machine Learning, pp. 489–497 (1996)
19. Kang, Z., Grauman, K., Sha, F.: Learning with whom to share in multi-task feature learning. In: International Conference on Machine Learning (2011)
20. Gong, P., Ye, J., Zhang, C.: Robust multi-task feature learning. In: Proceedings of the 18th ACM SIGKDD International Conference on Knowledge Discovery and Data Mining, pp. 895–903. ACM (2012)
21. Deng, C., Liu, X., Mu, Y., et al.: Large-scale multi-task image labeling with adaptive relevance discovery and feature hashing. Signal Process. **112**, 137–145 (2015)
22. Ojala, T., Pietikinen, M., et al.: A comparative study of texture measures with classification based on feature distribution. Pattern Recogn. **29**, 51–59 (1996)
23. Ahonen, T., Hadid, A., Pietikainen, M.: Face description with local binary patterns: application to face recognition. IEEE Trans. Pattern Anal. Mach. Intell. **28**(12), 2037–2041 (2006)
24. Huang, G.B., Mattar, M., Berg, T., Learned-Miller, E.: Labeled faces in the wild: a database for studying face recognition in unconstrained environments. In: Workshop on Faces in 'Real-Life' Images: Detection, Alignment, and Recognition (2008)
25. Scheirer, W.J., Kumar, N., Belhumeur, P.N., Boult, T.E.: Multi-attribute spaces: calibration for attribute fusion and similarity search. In: 2012 IEEE Conference on Computer Vision and Pattern Recognition, pp. 2933–2940. IEEE Press (2012)
26. Chang, C.C., Lin, C.J.: LIBSVM: A library for support vector machines. ACM Trans. Intell. Syst. Technol. **2**(3), 1–27 (2011)
27. Ahonen, T., Hadid, A., Pietikainen, M.: Face description with local binary patterns: application to face recognition. IEEE Trans. Pattern Anal. Mach. Intell. **28**(12), 2037–2041 (2006)
28. Kumar, N., Berg, A.C., Belhumeur, P.N., et al.: Attribute and simile classifiers for face verification. In: IEEE International Conference on Computer Vision, pp. 365–372 (2009)

Triple-Bit Quantization with Asymmetric Distance for Nearest Neighbor Search

Han Deng[1], Hongtao Xie[1(✉)], Wei Ma[1], Qiong Dai[1], Jianjun Chen[1,2], and Ming Lu[3]

[1] National Engineering Laboratory for Information Security Technologies,
Institute of Information Engineering, Chinese Academy of Sciences, Beijing, China
xiehongtao@iie.ac.cn
[2] School of Computer and Communication Engineering,
Changsha University of Science and Technology, Changsha, China
[3] School of Information Engineering, HeNan Radio and Television University,
Zhengzhou, China

Abstract. Binary embedding is an effective way for nearest neighbor (NN) search as binary code is storage efficient and fast to compute. It tries to convert real-value signatures into binary codes while preserving similarity of the original data, and most binary embedding methods quantize each projected dimension to one bit (presented as 0/1). As a consequence, it greatly decreases the discriminability of original signatures. In this paper, we first propose a novel quantization strategy triple-bit quantization (TBQ) to solve the problem by assigning 3-bit to each dimension. Then, asymmetric distance (AD) algorithm is applied to re-rank candidates obtained from hamming space for the final nearest neighbors. For simplicity, we call the framework triple-bit quantization with asymmetric distance (TBAD). The inherence of TBAD is combining the best of binary codes and real-value signatures to get nearest neighbors quickly and concisely. Moreover, TBAD is applicable to a wide variety of embedding techniques. Experimental comparisons on BIGANN set show that the proposed method can achieve remarkable improvement in query accuracy compared to original binary embedding methods.

Keywords: Triple-bit quantization · Asymmetric distance · Binary embedding · Nearest neighbor search

1 Introduction

Nearest neighbor (NN) search has been one of the key problems of visual applications including image retrieval [1, 10], object recognition [2, 11] and copy detection [3, 12]. NN search consists in finding the closest matches of a given query signature in large amounts of reference signatures. When searching similar signatures in a large-scale database composed of float-point values, it usually computes the Euclidean distance between the query and all the reference signatures, which is quite costly. As a consequence, handling these large quantities of data has become a challenge on its own.

© Springer International Publishing AG 2016
E. Chen et al. (Eds.): PCM 2016, Part II, LNCS 9917, pp. 105–115, 2016.
DOI: 10.1007/978-3-319-48896-7_11

When coping with massive amounts of data, there exist two most influential factors: one is the computational cost, and the other is memory usage. Binary codes can exactly handle the two problems. On one hand, the calculation of hamming distance between two binary codes is extremely efficient, which requires just a small number of machine instructions. On the other hand, the memory cost of binary codes is much less than real-value signatures. These considerations directly lead to the growing interests in embedding real-value signatures in compact binary codes. There are various existing binary embedding methods. Principal component analysis (PCA) [7] is a statistical procedure that uses an orthogonal transformation to convert a set of observations of possibly correlated variables into a set of values of linearly uncorrelated variables to reduce the dimension of correlated coefficients. The locality sensitive hashing (LSH) [5] measures the similarity between two vectors using the inner product operation. The hashing function of LSH projects the raw features into hyper-planes, the coefficients of which are drawn from the multivariate normal distribution. The spectral hashing (SH) [3] finds the best codes for given feature vectors by solving the optimization problem, which is expressed by the sum of weighted differences between raw feature vectors. The key idea of iterative quantization (ITQ) [8] simply rotates the data to minimize the error that is defined by the difference between the binary hashing code and the low-dimensional vector acquired in dimensionality reduction. Note that existing methods such as LSH, PCA, SH and ITQ assume that input features are zero-centered and the element of the projected feature vector is mapped into 1, if it is positive, otherwise, mapped into 0.

Despite of its remarkable advantages, the drawback is also obvious: it greatly reduces the distinctiveness between different signatures. For example, the possibilities of Euclidean distance between 32-dimensional real-value signatures are endless, namely all the real-value ranging from 0 to 32. However, the hamming distance between two 32-bit binary codes only has limited 33 kinds of possibilities from 0 to 32. So presenting real-value signatures in binary codes undoubtedly results in lower accuracy.

To take advantages and avoid the weaknesses of both binary codes and real-value signatures, the framework of triple-bit quantization with asymmetric distance (TBAD) is proposed in this paper, as demonstrated in Fig. 1. We firstly map all the signatures in database to binary codes. Then one binary index is built to organize those binary codes. For a given query, we map it to binary code in the same way, and preserve its intermediated real-value data as well. Next, we select the top-k similar binary codes in hamming space and apply asymmetric distance [4] to the candidates for re-ranking. Finally, the nearest neighbors are achieved through above processes. Summarily, we mainly concentrate on two points of the above framework including both dataset and query aspects:

- In the aspect of dataset, we propose a novel quantization method which assigns triple-bit to each dimension. In this way, can we not only take advantages of binary to store and compare signatures efficiently, but also preserve more discriminability of the original signatures.
- In the aspect of query, asymmetric algorithm is employed to compute the distance between compressed reference signatures and uncompressed query signatures for re-ranking, as uncompressed query signatures have more discriminability than binary codes.

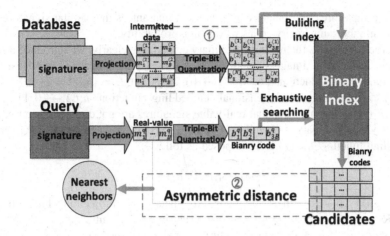

Fig. 1. Framework of the proposed method. Each signature is projected into B-dimensional real-value intermediate data. Then triple-bit quantization converts intermediate data into 3B-bit binary codes. We select the top-K neighbors in hamming space as candidates. Asymmetric distance is used to re-rank candidates to get final results.

We evaluate our approach on BIGANN dataset and apply our framework to a variety kinds of binary embedding methods, such as locality sensitive hashing (LSH) [5], principal component analysis embedding (PCAE) [6], spectral hashing (SH) [7]. In experiments, our method shows significant progress on accuracy over original methods followed by asymmetric distance with the same dimensionality. In some cases, TBAD can provide precision on the order of 10%–15% against original methods.

The rest of the paper is organized as follows. In Sect. 2, we precisely describe the novel triple-bit quantization and improved asymmetric distance algorithm. Section 3 presents the experimental results on BIGANN for NN search. Finally, conclusions are given in Sect. 4.

2 Proposed Method

In this section, we propose TBAD to improve query accuracy for NN search. Firstly, we will briefly introduce binary embedding. Next, the novel triple-bit quantization method is given. Then, we present the improved asymmetric distance scheme and the integration of TBAD which is applicable to a wide variety of binary embedding techniques.

2.1 Signature Quantization

2.1.1 Binary Embedding
The prominent advantages of binary codes lead to the explosion in binary embedding techniques. Several successful binary embedding methods have been proposed, such as LSH [5], SH [7], PCAE [6] and PCAE-ITQ [8]. Binary embedding aims to transform

real-value signatures into binary codes, while it guarantees that similar signatures are mapped into the same binary codes with a high probability.

In order to express the meaning of binary embedding clearly, we introduce a set of notations. Let s be an image signature with K dimensions in space Ω and let h_k be a binary embedding function, i.e., $h_k: \Omega \to \{0, 1\}$. A set $H = \{h_k, k = 1 \dots K\}$ of K functions define a multidimensional embedding function $h: \Omega \to \{0, 1\}^K$ with $h(s) = [h_1(s) \dots h_K(s)]'$. Note that real-value signatures are not directly converted into binary codes via binary embedding. For LSH, SH, PCAE and PCAE-ITQ, binary embedding function h_k can be decomposed as follows:

$$h_k(s) = q_k[g_k(s)], \tag{1}$$

where $g_k(s): \Omega \to \mathcal{R}$ (the intermediated space) is projection function and $q_k(s): \mathcal{R} \to \{0, 1\}$ is quantization function. That is, binary embedding firstly projects image signature s to real-value multidimensional vector $g(s) = [g_k(s), k = 1 \dots K]'$, which is an extremely good approximation to the original signature. Next, the real-value will be quantized into binary codes by thresholding (0 is often set as the threshold). That is, if $g_i(s) > 0$, s_i is mapped to 1. Otherwise, s_i will be mapped to 0. Thus, traditional quantization function just roughly divides each dimension into two parts decoded as 0 or 1, which greatly reduces the discriminability [4]. To alleviate this problem, we propose to retain more information of the original by assigning triple-bit to each dimension of the intermediated data.

2.1.2 Triple-Bit Quantization

In the previous section, we elaborate that binary embedding methods greatly reduce the discriminability of original signatures. To achieve higher accuracy, a lot of related works mainly concentrate on improving the performance of projection functions g_k. Instead, we propose a triple-bit quantization function to assign triple-bit to each dimension of the intermediated data.

The steps of triple-bit quantization are summarized below:

(1) Signature projection and normalization. For a given signature x with K dimensions, we firstly use a multidimensional projection function $g(s) = [g_k(s), k = 1 \dots K]'$ to map original signature x to real-value vector $g(x)$ (the intermediated data). Next, to enhance the efficiency of comparisons, the vector is normalized by its l_1 norm $\mathcal{N}$ for each dimension and the normalized intermediated data $l(x) = [l_k(s), k = 1 \dots K]'$ are obtained with

$$l_i(s) = \mathcal{N}[g_i(s)]. \quad i = 1 \dots K \tag{2}$$

(2) Data partition. We divide the intermediate data for each dimension into two categories according to the sign of the corresponding element, after which we get the medians of both two categories for all the dimensions. The medians of the negative and positive parts in dimension i are represented symbolically by nm_i and pm_i respectively. Based on the sign and two medians, each element of the intermediated

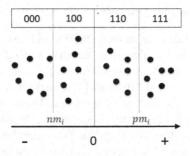

Fig. 2. Encoding signature. Each dimension is divided into four parts by the sign and two medians

vectors can be divided into four categories, shown as Fig. 2. Despite its crude nature, we will see that the partition scheme leads to competitive results on a variety of binary embedding methods.

(3) Binary quantization. After the partition, a novel quantization function needs to be raised, as positional relations of elements in each dimension via original quantization function have only two cases: either on the same side or the opposite side. In order to handle the new partition scheme, we quantize each dimension into triple-bit. By this way, the quantization method may adapt well to the four relations of the elements in each dimension, as showed in Fig. 2. For i_{th} dimension, triple-bit quantization function TBQ is defined as:

$$TBQ_i(s) = \begin{cases} 111, & if \ l_i(s) \geq pm_i \\ 110, & if \ l_i(s) \geq 0 \ and \ l_i(s) < pm_i \\ 100, & if \ l_i(s) < 0 \ and \ l_i(s) \geq nm_i \\ 000, & if \ l_i(s) < nm_i \end{cases} \tag{3}$$

Since intermediate data preserves good approximation to the similarity of original signatures, it has a high probability to map $g_i(x)$ and $g_i(y)$ to the same category if x is the nearest neighbor of y. Conversely, if signature x and y are far from each other, $g_i(x)$ and $g_i(y)$ are more likely to be mapped far apart. Thus, the quantization scheme can naturally preserve the similarity between two signatures. For example, assume x and y are near neighbors, and $g_i(x)$ is decoded as 000. Then $g_i(y)$ is most likely to be decoded as 00 in which case the hamming distance between them is 0. But beyond that, $g_i(y)$ is likely to be decoded as 100 as well, due to the error estimation of projection function, and the hamming distance between them is 1. Similarly, the least likely result is 111, of which the hamming distance is 3. Therefore, the inherence of this coding scheme gives more weight to the data close to query signature. Despite the length of binary codes increases three times, TBAD outperforms other successful binary embedding methods with equal number of bits, as illustrated in our experiments.

2.2   Re-rank with Asymmetric Distance

As stated before, binary codes are storage efficient and fast to compute. Millions of binary codes can be compared to a query in less than a second. For a given query, we will firstly find the top-k closest signatures in hamming space as candidates. To further increase query accuracy, asymmetric distance [4] is carried out. Most binary embedding methods binarize both database and query signatures. However, it is not mandatory to transform the query signature into binary code, because the additional memory cost of a single non-binarized signature is negligible. The algorithm computes the distance between uncompressed data and compressed data is referred to as asymmetric distance, as the distance is computed in two different spaces. A major benefit of asymmetric distance is that it can achieve higher accuracy for binary codes because they take advantage of the more precise position information of the query.

Albert et al. propose an algorithm for asymmetric distance based on expected value [4], which is defined as:

$$d_E(x, y) = \sum_k d(g_k(x), \mathrm{E}[g_k(u)|h_k(u) = h_k(y)]), \tag{4}$$

where $d(.)$ presents the Euclidean distance, and E means the expectation value. d_E is simply computed as the Euclidean distance between the query and the corresponding expected value of the intermediated data $g_k(u)$ such that $h_k(u) = h_k(y)$. In our method, we utilize the concept of the d_E and revise it to satisfy our triple-bit quantization, as we get four subsets rather than two for each dimension. Note that we replace h_k with our proposed TBQ_k in (4). Firstly, we draw a set of signatures $S\{s_i, i = 1 \dots N\}$ randomly from Ω. For each dimension k, we partition S into four clusters S_k^{cu}, $cu = 000, 100, 110, 111$. Each cluster contains signatures s such that $TBQ_k(s) = cu$. Then we compute the expected value c_k for each subsets offline:

$$c_k^{cu} = \frac{1}{|S_k^{cu}|} \sum_{v \in S_k^{cu}} g_k(v). \tag{5}$$

For a given query x, we calculate the distance (see Fig. 3) between uncompressed query and quantized database signature online, which is defined as:

$$d_E(x, y) = \sqrt{\sum_k (g_k(x) - c_k^{TBQ_k(x)})^2}. \tag{6}$$

It shows that the asymmetric distance algorithm takes full advantage of the non-binarized signature, which retains the information of the original. For example, for i-th dimension of a given query q and reference signature x, $g_i(q)$ locates in area1 and $TBQ_i(x)$ is mapped to area2. The asymmetric distance between them is the Euclidean distance between $g_i(q)$ and the expected value of all the intermediated data mapped to area2 in dimension i. Along with the benefit of TBQ, the discriminability is further improved, due to different signatures possessing four possible position relations instead of two for original methods via the revised asymmetric distance.

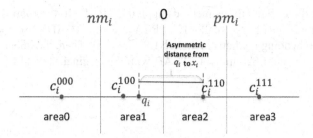

Fig. 3. Asymmetric distance

In our implementation, to compare the performance objectively, we select k = 1000 in which the recall of the nearest neighbor is in close proximity to 100% in most cases. Even though extra floating-point multiplication is involved in the process, it shows negligible time consumption, because we calculate the asymmetric distance only for limited number of signatures which are considered as the candidates.

3   Experiments

In this section, we show the benefits of the TBAD. We first introduce the dataset and evaluation metrics used in the experiments. Then intensive comparisons between methods applying TBAD and traditional binary embedding methods are given.

3.1   Dataset and Evaluation Metrics

We use 1M SIFT [9] signatures from the well-known BIGANN dataset to evaluate our method, which consists of three vector subsets: a 100K training set, a 1M database set and a 10K query set. Each SIFT signature is a 128D real value vector.

There is no difference in time cost between traditional binary embedding methods and those adopting TBAD, as all the methods execute exhaustive search in binary codes of the same dimensionality and involve re-ranking. In our experiments, the precision and recall with respect to the number of bits are used to evaluate our method. For experimental evaluation, we use precision and recall to measure the performance of our method. The precision and recall is defined as follows:

$$precision = \frac{count(relevant \cap retrieved)}{retrieved},$$

$$recall = \frac{count(relevant \cap retrieved)}{relevant},$$

where *retrieved* is the NN search results of our method, and *relevant* is the linear search results. Note that the number of bits of the binary codes we use is multiple of three, as 3-bit in hamming space represents 1 real-value in intermediate space in our method. Therefore, we let the binary codes converted from original binary embedding methods have the same dimensionality as methods applying TBAD. In the following, we first compare the precision@1 and recall@10 of PCA applying TBAD with other representative binary embedding methods including LSH and SH. Then, the intensive comparisons between SH and LSH applying TBAD with the original SH and LSH are made respectively.

3.2 Results

Figure 4(a) shows the precision@1 of TBAD-PCA, original SH and LSH methods and those methods with AD, with respect to the length of the binary codes. We observe a remarkable result on precision. For example, when comparing TBAD-PCA to AD-SH, the precision improvement of 4.75% and precision relative 19.19% is observed on average. Figure 4(b) shows the recall@10 of TBAD-PCA and others. Just like precision, the recall of TBAD-PCA is improved consistently over other traditional methods.

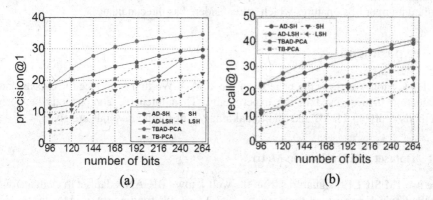

Fig. 4. Influence of PCA applying TBAD with Euclidean-NN. PCA with TBAD is denoted as TBAD-PCA. TB-PCA stands for PCA with triple-bit quantization. SH and LSH followed by asymmetric distance are denoted as AD-SH and AD-LSH, respectively.

However, abnormal results appear in two conditions. First, the precision of TB-PCA is lower than original SH with 96 and 120 bits. The second is that the result of TBAD-PCA and TBAD-SH is not a noticeable contrast when the number of bits is 96. The reason is that our method converts each dimension of the intermediated data into 3-bit, while other methods into only 1-bit. So, when the number of bits is not big enough, our method preserves insufficient information. However, with the increase of the number of bits, the effect of our method is obvious. In our method, we make use of characteristic of PCA, in which each dimension contains different discriminability after projection, to assign triple-bit to the dimensions which are gained more discriminability. Due to the limits on the dimensionality of signatures processed by PCA, we can't compare the retrieval accuracy of TBAD-PCA to original PCAE. So, contrast experiments have been conducted to compare TBAD-PCA with other binary embedding methods, including SH and LSH, and those methods with AD.

To verify the effectiveness of TBAD, the comparisons between TBAD-SH, AD-SH and original SH are given. Figure 5(a) shows the divergence of precision@1 between three methods which has the same number of binary codes, with respect to the dimensionality. We can see that TBAD-SH consistently improves the results over the original SH and AD-SH. On average, we observe a relative precision improvement of 12.93%. Furthermore, the recall between those methods, as Fig. 5(b) shows, has a relative recall enhancement of 11.30%, on average.

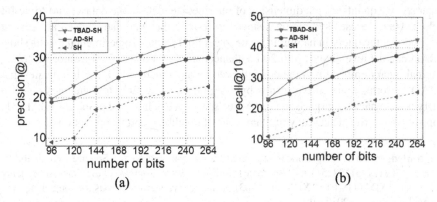

Fig. 5. Influence of SH applying TBAD with Euclidean-NN. Original SH, SH with AD and SH applying TBAD are denoted as SH, AD-SH and TBAD-SH respectively.

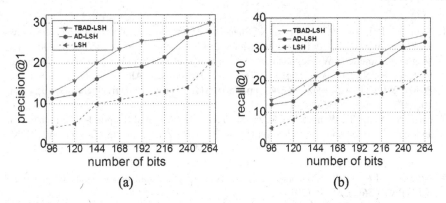

Fig. 6. Influence of LSH applying TBAD with Euclidean-NN. Original LSH, LSH with AD and LSH applying TBAD are denoted as SH, AD-SH and TBAD-SH respectively.

Figure 6 demonstrates the effect of TBAD by comparing TBAD-LSH with AD-LSH and the original LSH with respect to the number of bits. The red line indicates that TBAD-LSH consistently improves the results over other methods. At first, we can see the remarkable improvements made by asymmetric distance through LSH comparing with original LSH. Then, we apply TBAD to LSH to further improve the retrieval accuracy. We can see that TBAD-LSH improves the results over original LSH and AD-LSH significantly in most of the cases. On average, we observe a relative precision and recall improvement of 19.53% and 12.43% respectively over AD-LSH.

4 Conclusion

In this paper, we propose a novel method for fast nearest neighbor search which takes advantages of both compressed data and real-value signatures. To improve retrieval accuracy, we quantize each dimension of intermediate data in the dataset into triple-bit offline. Then we use asymmetric distance to re-rank the candidates which are nearest neighbors of the query in hamming space to get final results. Experimental results show TBAD can achieve about up to 20% enhancements on precision@1 compared to the original binary embedding methods followed by asymmetric distance. It indicates that TBAD performs competitive results by assigning more weight to signatures close to query both in hamming space and real-value space. We believe the proposed TBAD can improve the retrieval accuracy of many nearest neighbor search applications.

Acknowledgements. This work is supported by the National Nature Science Foundation of China (61303171, 61303251), the "Strategic Priority Research Program" of the Chinese Academy of Sciences (XDA06031000, XDA06010703), Xinjiang Uygur Autonomous Region Science and Technology Project (201230123).

References

1. Yahiaoui, I., Hervé, N., Boujemaa, N.: Shape-based image retrieval in botanical collections. In: Proceedings of the 7th PCM 2006, China, 2–4 November 2006, pp. 357–364 (2006)
2. Megrhi, S., Souidène, W., Beghdadi, A.: Spatio-temporal SURF for human action recognition. In: Huet, B., Ngo, C.-W., Tang, J., Zhou, Z.-H., Hauptmann, Alexander, G., Yan, S. (eds.) PCM 2013. LNCS, vol. 8294, pp. 505–516. Springer, Heidelberg (2013). doi: 10.1007/978-3-319-03731-8_47
3. Chen, S., Wang, T., Wang, J., Li, J., Zhang, Y., Lu, H.: A spatial-temporal-scale registration approach for video copy detection. In: Huang, Y.-M.R., Xu, C., Cheng, K.-S., Yang, J.-F.K., Swamy, M.,N.,S., Li, S., Ding, J.-W. (eds.) PCM 2008. LNCS, vol. 5353, pp. 407–415. Springer, Heidelberg (2008). doi:10.1007/978-3-540-89796-5_42
4. Albert, G., Florent, P., Yunchao, G., et al.: Asymmetric distances for binary embeddings. IEEE PAMI **36**(1), 33–47 (2014)
5. Raginsky, M., Lazebnik, S.: Locality-sensitive binary codes from shift-invariant kernels. In: Proceedings of NIPS, pp. 1509–1517 (2009)
6. Jégou, H., Tavenard, R., Douze, M., Amsaleg, L.: Searching in one billion vectors: re-rank with source coding. In: IEEE ICASSP, pp. 861–864. IEEE (2011)
7. Weiss, Y., Torralba, A., Fergus, R.: Spectral hashing. In: Proceedings of NIPS (2008)
8. Gong, Y., Lazebnik, S.: Iterative quantization: a procrustean approach to learning binary codes. In: Proceedings of IEEE Conference on CVPR, pp. 817–824 (2011)
9. Lowe, D.G.: Distinctive image features from scale-invariant keypoints. IJCV **60**, 91–110 (2004)
10. Xie, H., Gao, K., Zhang, Y., et al.: Pairwise weak geometric consistency for large scale image search. In: Proceedings of the 1st ACM ICMR, pp. 1–8. ACM (2011)

11. Lei, Z., Yongdong, Z., Richang, H., et al.: Full-space local topology extraction for cross-modal retrieval. IEEE TIP **24**(7), 2212–2224 (2015)
12. Yahiaoui, I., Hervé, N., Boujemaa, N.: Shape-based image retrieval in botanical collections. In: Advances in Multimedia Information Processing – 7th PCM 2006, Hangzhou, China, 2–4 November 2006, pp. 357–364 (2006)

Creating Spectral Words for Large-Scale Hyperspectral Remote Sensing Image Retrieval

Wenhao Geng[1], Jing Zhang[1(✉)], Li Zhuo[1,2], Jihong Liu[1],
and Lu Chen[1]

[1] Signal and Information Processing Laboratory,
Beijing University of Technology, Beijing 100124, China
{gengwh, kev, chenlu}@emails.bjut.edu.cn,
{zhj, zhuoli}@bjut.edu.cn
[2] Collaborative Innovation Center of Electric Vehicles in Beijing,
Beijing 100124, China

Abstract. Content-Based Image Retrieval (CBIR) for common images has been thoroughly explored in recent years, but little attention has been paid to hyperspectral remote sensing images. How to extract appropriate hyperspectral remote sensing image feature is a fundamental task for retrieving large-scale similar images. At present, endmember as hyperspectral image feature has presented more spectral descriptive ability. Visual words feature is a feasible method to describe image content, which can achieve scalability for large-scale image retrieval. In this article, spectral words are created for hyperspectral remote sensing image retrieval by combining both spatial and spectral information. Firstly, spatial and spectral features are extracted respectively using spectral saliency model and endmember extraction. Then a spectral vocabulary tree is constructed by feature clustering, in which the cluster centers are considered as the spectral words. Finally, the spectral words are compared for finding the similar hyperspectral remote sensing images. Experimental results on NASA datasets show that the spectral words can improve the accuracy of hyperspectral image retrieval, which further prove our method has more descriptive ability.

Keywords: Hyperspectral remote sensing images · Content-Based Image Retrieval (CBIR) · Spectral words · Spectral saliency model · Endmember extraction

1 Introduction

In recent years, hyperspectral imaging has been an area of active remote sensing research and development. Hyperspectral remote sensors collect image data simultaneously in dozens or hundreds of narrow, adjacent spectral bands [1]. These measurements make it possible to derive a continuous spectrum for each image cell. Nowadays, hyperspectral remote sensing images have been widely applied into many fields such as ocean, agriculture, resources, environment, city and so on. With the rapid development of remote sensing technique, the amount of hyperspectral images has explosively increased, which allows users to search the hyperspectral images from the

© Springer International Publishing AG 2016
E. Chen et al. (Eds.): PCM 2016, Part II, LNCS 9917, pp. 116–125, 2016.
DOI: 10.1007/978-3-319-48896-7_12

database. Hence, how to accurately describe a hyperspectral image content has become a very fundamental task for large-scale hyperspectral image retrieval.

For large-scale hyperspectral image retrieval, the methods of image description based on endmember and spectral curve shape are frequently utilized [2–4]. However, due to the phenomenon of same object with different spectra, different objects with same spectrum, endmember and spectral curve shape cannot fully describe a hyperspectral remote sensing image content.

Image description methods have been widely developed [5–7]. Recently, the method of image description based on visual words has attracted more and more attention. Inspired by the text content analysis, an image can be viewed as a series of words combination. Visual words are created by clustering the feature descriptors from the images. Considering high dimensionality and spectral characteristics of hyperspectral image, visual words method cannot be directly introduced into hyperspectral image. Reference [8] proposed to use the visual words of base image to represent a remote sensing image. But the base images selection method is not strict and easy to ignore the spectral characteristics.

In this article, the notion of spectral words is proposed by combining spatial and spectral information from hyperspectral remote sensing images in order to improve the feature descriptive ability. In this work, spatial and spectral features are firstly extracted respectively using spectral saliency model and endmember extraction. Then, a spectral vocabulary tree is constructed by feature clustering, in which a leaf node is considered as a spectral word. At last, the spectral words similarity between the query image and images are measured by Euclidean distance and the images are ranked with descending and the first M retrieved images are returned.

The remainder of this article is organized as follows: Sect. 2 states how to create the spectral words in detail; spectral words are applied into large-scale hyperspectral remote sensing image retrieval in Sect. 3; experimental results are analyzed in Sect. 4 and the conclusions are drawn in Sect. 5.

2   Spectral Words Creation

Traditional visual words creation consists of two steps: (1) extracting Scale-Invariant Feature Transform (SIFT) descriptors; (2) clustering to create visual words. Considering the high dimensionality and abundant spectral information of hyperspectral image, SIFT descriptors have insufficient descriptive ability and are difficult to be directly extracted for hyperspectral images. In this Section, we will create the spectral words for hyperspectral images, which's the overall architecture is shown in Fig. 1. Firstly, the spatial feature and spectral feature are extracted from hyperspectral image. Then, spectral words are constructed by combining spectral and spatial features.

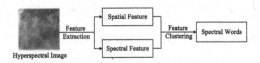

Fig. 1. The process of spectral words creation

2.1 Spatial Feature Extraction

The key problem of spatial feature extraction for hyperspectral image is how to convert hyperspectral data into 2D data as well as remain spatial information. In this article, spectral saliency map is utilized to obtain 2D data [9].

The spectral saliency map is obtained by spectral saliency model, which is inspired by the well-known Itti & Koch's model [10]. For hyperspectral image, we extract four conspicuity features: the first three principal components $C_{PC(1-3)}$, orientations Co, spectral angle C_θ, and visible spectral band opponent C_{OPP}. This detailed work can be seen in our previous work [9].

(1) $C_{PC(1-3)}$. The conspicuity map $C_{PC(1-3)}$ of the first three principal components is defined as the Euclidean distance between $\mathbf{f}_1$ and $\mathbf{f}_2$, in which $\mathbf{f}_1$ represents the center scale and $\mathbf{f}_2$ represents the surround scale.

$$C_{PC(1-3)} = \sqrt{\sum_{n=1}^{3} (\mathbf{f}_1(PC_n) - \mathbf{f}_2(PC_n))^2} \tag{1}$$

(2) C_o. The conspicuity map C_o of orientations is obtained by applying four Gabor filters (at $0°$, $45°$, $90°$ and $135°$) to the first principal component of the spectral dataset, then computing the Euclidean distance between $\mathbf{f}_1$ and $\mathbf{f}_2$. GF is Gabor filters function.

$$Co = \sqrt{\sum_{n=1}^{3} (\mathbf{f}_1(GF(PC_n)) - \mathbf{f}_2(GF(PC_n)))^2} \tag{2}$$

(3) C_θ. The spectral angle between $\mathbf{f}_1$ and $\mathbf{f}_2$ is defined as θ:

$$\theta = (\mathbf{f}_1; \mathbf{f}_2) = \cos^{-1}(\frac{\mathbf{f}_1.\mathbf{f}_2}{\|\mathbf{f}_1\|\|\mathbf{f}_2\|}) \tag{3}$$

The conspicuity map of spectral angle is defined as C_θ.

$$C_\theta = \sum \cos^{-1}(\frac{\mathbf{f}_1.\mathbf{f}_2}{\|\mathbf{f}_1\|\|\mathbf{f}_2\|}) \tag{4}$$

(4) C_{OPP}. The conspicuity feature of visible spectral band opponent is obtained by replacing the color opponents with groups of spectral bands that are approximately correspondence to these color channels. The double opponency of band group can be computed as follows:

$$Opp_1(c, s) = |(G1(c) - G3(c))\Theta(G3(s) - G1(s))|_1 \tag{5}$$

$$Opp_2(c, s) = |(G2(c) - G4(c))\Theta(G4(s) - G2(s))|_1 \tag{6}$$

Where $G1$ to $G4$ are vectors extracted from the corresponding group of spectral bands, Θ is the cross-scale center-surround difference operator, $||_1$ is the 1-norm of a vector. The conspicuity map of visible spectral band opponent is defined as C_{OPP}.

$$C_{opp} = \sum RG(c, s) + BY(c, s) \tag{7}$$

At last, the four conspicuity maps ($C_{PC(1-3)}$, C_O, C_θ and C_{OPP}) are normalized and summed into the final saliency map S.

$$S = \frac{1}{4}(C_{PC(1-3)} + C_O + C_\theta + C_{OPP}) \tag{8}$$

Scale-invariant feature transform (SIFT) [11] is an algorithm in computer vision to detect and describe local features in images. Hyperspectral image contains spatial and spectral domain, in which SIFT features are extracted in spatial domain. Thus SIFT features can represent spatial features of hyperspectral image. As we know SIFT features performance better with the problem of mismatching caused by geometric transformation, affine distortions, etc. Hence, SIFT features extracted from spectral saliency map would be more efficient and reasonable.

2.2 Spectral Feature Extraction

Hyperspectral images are acquired simultaneously in many narrow, adjacent wavelength bands. And a continuous spectrum can be extracted from endmembers, which can be used to identify surface materials [1]. An endmember can be defined as an idealized pure signature for a class, which is a spectral signature that is completely specified by the spectrum of a single material substance [4, 12]. As we known, endmembers have a good descriptive ability of spectral feature for hyperspectral image. Because of the limitation of spatial resolution, the pixels in hyperspectral image acquired by the hyperspectral imaging instruments usually contain more than one feature spectrum [1]. Therefore, pure endmembers need to be extracted firstly.

In our previous work [13], we proposed an automatic endmember extraction using pixel purity index (PPI) for hyperspectral image by improving the projection principle of PPI. The comparisons of projection principles before and after improvement are shown in Fig. 2.

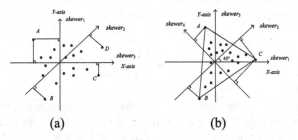

(a)   (b)

Fig. 2. The improved projection principle: (a) The projection principle of traditional PPI (b) The improved projection principle

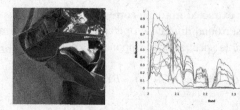

Fig. 3. The sample image and the corresponding spectral curves of extracted endmembers

As can be seen, in traditional PPI, the skewers may be generated in a few directions so that some pixels which located at the extreme positions may be ignored. After improvement, the skewers are generated in different angles of the projection vector in certain directions.

We use improved PPI to extract pure endmembers for constructing spectral words. Figure 3 shows the sample image and the result of endmembers extraction.

2.3 Spectral Words Creation

In Sects. 2.2 and 2.3, we have extracted the spatial and spectral features. We assume that the feature vectors of a hyperspectral image are $A(\alpha_1, \alpha_2,..., \alpha_n)$ and $B(\beta_1, \beta_2,..., \beta_m)$ (A is spatial feature vectors set and B is spectral feature vectors set). Then set A and B are clustered by k-means, for each clustering center being a spectral word. Figure 4 shows the flowchart of the spectral words creation.

The detailed procedure of k-means is as follows:

Step 1. Initialization: Set the number of clustering centers $(m, m_2,.., m_{1k})$ randomly, such as k;

Step 2. Assignment: Compute the distance between each element x_i and clustering centers, assign elements to the nearest centers;

Step 3. Update: Calculate the new means to be the centers of the elements in the new clusters;

$$m_i = \frac{1}{N_i} \sum_{i=1}^{N_i} x_{ij}, i = 1, 2, \cdots, k \tag{9}$$

Step 4. Convergence judgment: Compute difference J, algorithm terminates when J is convergence, otherwise, return to Step 2

$$J = \sum_{i=1}^{k} \sum_{j=1}^{N_i} \|x_{ij} - m_i\| \tag{10}$$

We set $k = 500$, and the normalized spectral words histogram of hyperspectral images are shown in Fig. 5, in which the first line images are original images and the second line are the corresponding histogram of spectral words.

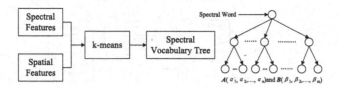

Fig. 4. Flowchart of spectral words creation

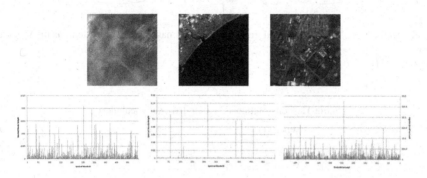

Fig. 5. The sample images and the histogram of spectral words of hyperspectral images

3 Applying Spectral Words to Hyperspectral Remote Sensing Image Retrieval

After creating spectral words, the hyperspectral image retrieval process is performed. Figure 6 shows the overall architecture of hyperspectral remote sensing image retrieval system using spectral words. As shown in Fig. 6, spatial and spectral features are extracted firstly. Spectral words can be obtained by feature clustering. After spectral words construction, the image in database is represented by vectors of the occurrence of spectral words.

As shown in Table 1, these vectors are normalized to be stored in a kind of queue structure which called spectral words vocabulary.

We created a table for each spectral word to store the image ID and word frequency. If a new image is added to database, the image ID and word frequency should be recorded in the corresponding list of the spectral word.

Finally, the similarity between two hyperspectral images is determined by comparing the spectral words. The spectral words representations of the query image and an image in the database are denoted by $Q(Q_1, Q_2,..., Q_k)$ and $D(D_1, D_2,..., D_k)$. The similarity of two images is then measured by

$$S = \sum_{i=1}^{k} |Q_i - D_i|^2 \tag{11}$$

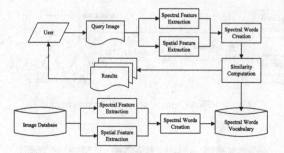

Fig. 6. Architecture of hyperspectral remote sensing image retrieval system using spectral words

Table 1. Construction of spectral words vocabulary

Word ID	i			
Image ID	I_1	I_2	...	I_N
Word frequency	ω_1	ω_2	...	ω_3

Where k is the total number of spectral words, and Q_i and D_i represent the occurrence frequency of word i in the query and database images, respectively.

Then, we use the computed similarity S to retrieve a list of images which are ranked according to their distances from the query image.

4   Experimental Results and Analysis

We conducted experiments with a collection of the high-resolution hyperspectral data sets obtained from German Aerospace Center's (DLR) in Oberpfaffenhofen in Germany and NASA over the World Trade Center (WTC) area in New York. The AVIRIS images contain 125 spectral bands between 0.4 and 2.5 μm. The spatial resolution is 20 m, and the spectral resolution is 10 nm. The experimental platform is a PC with 3.30 GHz CPU, 4.00 G memory, Windows 7 operating system. Our dataset contains 1500 hyperspectral remote sensing images and the size of images is not the same.

Figure 7 shows the Top-10 hyperspectral image retrieval results for a key image based on spectral words.

Three methods of hyperspectral remote sensing image retrieval are compared with our proposed method in this experiment. One method is based on endmember extraction using APPI (defined as M.APPI). The method in Ref. [14] used both spectral and spatial features to represent images (defined as M.SS). The image features in

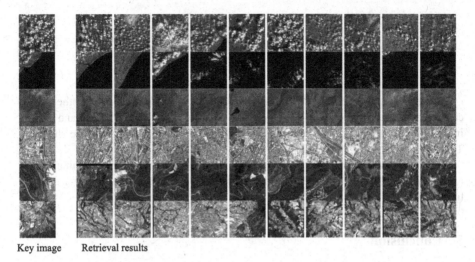

Key image   Retrieval results

Fig. 7. The retrieval results of hyperspectral remote sensing images.

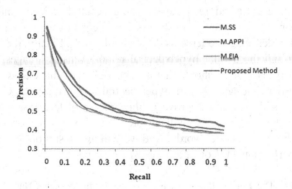

Fig. 8. The precision-recall curves of different methods

Ref. [2] are the endmember signatures obtained from the image data by endmember induction algorithms (defined as M.EIA).

To make quantitative analysis for the hyperspectral images retrieval methods, we calculate the precision and recall curve with different methods. The definition of precision and recall can be denoted as:

$$Precision = \frac{SIR}{SIR + NSIR} \tag{12}$$

$$Recall = \frac{SIR}{SIR + SINR} \tag{13}$$

The precision and recall curves of four methods are show in Fig. 8, in which the vertical axis is precision ratio and the horizontal axis is recall ratio.

Table 2. The precision ratios of different methods

Methods	M.SS	M.EIA	M.APPI	Our method
Precision ratios	0.7322	0.7318	0.7849	0.7984

As can be seen from Fig. 8, our method has a better performance than others. This can be explained by the fact the spectral words contain both spectral and spatial information of hyperspectral images. The corresponding precision ratios are shown in Table 2.

It can be observed in Table 2, the proposed method has higher accuracy than M.SS, M.EIA and M.APPI. Therefore, the proposed spectral words have a stronger descriptive ability.

5 Conclusion

In this article, spectral words are created for large-scale hyperspectral remote sensing image retrieval by combining both spatial and spectral information. Firstly, spatial and spectral features are extracted respectively using spectral saliency model and endmember extraction. Then a spectral vocabulary tree is constructed by feature clustering, in which the leaf nodes are considered as the spectral words. Finally, the spectral words are compared to find the similar hyperspectral remote sensing images. Experimental results on NASA datasets have shown that the spectral words have a strong descriptive ability, thus improves the accuracy of hyperspectral image retrieval. Current spectral words framework still needs to improve in the process of feature extraction, feature clustering, etc. In the next work, we will consider combining other features to improve the description ability of spectral words. And we will also test more hyperspectral data to evaluate the performance of our proposed spectral words.

Acknowledgments. The work in this paper is supported by the National Natural Science Foundation of China (No. 61370189, No. 61531006, No. 61372149, and No. 61471013), the Beijing Natural Science Foundation (No. 4163071, No. 4142009), the Importation and Development of High-Caliber Talents Project of Beijing Municipal Institutions (No. CIT&TCD20150311, CIT&TCD201404043), the Science and Technology Development Program of Beijing Education Committee (No. KM201410005002, No. KM201510005004), Funding Project for Academic Human Resources Development in Institutions of Higher Learning Under the Jurisdiction of Beijing Municipality.

References

1. Smith, R.B.: Introduction to hyperspectral imaging. Microimages (2012). http://www.microimages.com/documentation/Tutorials/hyprspec.pdf
2. Grana, M., Veganzones, M.A.: An endmember-based distance for content based hyperspectral image retrieval. Pattern Recogn. 45(9), 3472–3489 (2012)

3. Li, F., Zhou, C.H., Chen, R.G.: Spectral curve shape feature-based hyperspectral remote sensing image retrieval. Spectro. Spectral Anal. **28**(11), 2482–2486 (2008)
4. Xu, M.M., Du, B., Zhang, L.P.: Spatial-spectral information based abundance-constrained endmember extraction methods. IEEE J. Sel. Top. Appl. Earth Obs. Remote Sens. **7**(6), 2004–2015 (2014)
5. Wang, M., Li, W.S., Liu, D., Ni, B.B., Shen, J.L., Yan, S.C.: Facilitating image search with a scalable and compact semantic mapping. IEEE Trans. Cybern. **45**, 1561–1574 (2015)
6. Wang, M., Gao, Y., Lu, K., Rui, Y.: View-based discriminative probabilistic modeling for 3D object retrieval and recognition. IEEE Trans. Image Process. **22**, 1395–1407 (2013)
7. Wang, M., Li, H., Tao, D.C., Lu, K., Wu, X.D.: Multimodal graph-based reranking for web image search. IEEE Trans. Image Process. **21**(11), 4649–4661 (2012)
8. Yang, J., Liu, J.B., Dai, Q.: An improved bag-of-words framework for remote sensing image retrieval in large-scale image databases. Int. J. Digit. Earth **8**(4), 273–292 (2015)
9. Cao, Y., Zhang, J., Tian, Q., Zhuo, L., Zhou, Q.L.: Salient target detection in hyperspectral images using spectral saliency. In: 2015 IEEE China Summit and International Conference on Signal and Information Processing, China SIP, pp. 1086–1090 (2015)
10. Itti, L., Koch, C., Niebur, E.: A model of saliency-based visual attention for rapid scene analysis. IEEE Trans. Pattern Anal. Mach. Intell. **11**, 1254–1259 (1998)
11. Lowe, D.G.: Object recognition from local scale-invariant features. In: The Proceedings of the Seventh IEEE International Conference on Computer Vision, vol. 2, pp. 1150–1157 (1999)
12. Kowkabi, F., Ghassemian, H., Keshavarz, A.: Using spatial and spectral information for improving endmember extraction algorithms in hyperspectral remotely sensed images. In: 2014 4th International Conference on Computer and Knowledge Engineering, ICCKE, pp. 548–553 (2014)
13. Zhou, Q., Zhang, J., Tian, Q., Zhuo, L., Geng, W.: Automatic endmember extraction using pixel purity index for hyperspectral imagery. In: Tian, Q., Sebe, N., Qi, G.-J., Huet, B., Hong, R., Liu, X. (eds.) MMM 2016. LNCS, vol. 9517, pp. 207–217. Springer, Heidelberg (2016). doi:10.1007/978-3-319-27674-8_19
14. Veganzones, M.A., Graña, M.: A spectral/spatial CBIR system for hyperspectral images. IEEE J. Sel. Top. Appl. Earth Obser. Remote Sens. **5**(2), 488–500 (2012)

Rapid Vehicle Retrieval Using a Cascade of Interest Regions

Yuanqi Su, Bonan Cuan$^{(\boxtimes)}$, Xingjun Zhang, and Yuehu Liu

Xi'an Jiaotong University, Xi'an, China
{yuanqisu,xjzhang,liuyh}@mail.xjtu.edu.cn, cuanbonan@gmail.com

Abstract. We propose a method to retrieve the vehicle instance in a massive dataset, that utilizes a cascaded structure to rapidly discard most irrelevant instances. The structure gradually locates the discriminative parts of a vehicle. Rather than focusing on complex and complicated features, we employ a set of prime locating and matching methods successively. During the process, texture features are utilized for localizing the windshield and license plate. Afterwards, vehicle color and type matching are conducted in the located regions of interest. To evaluate the proposed algorithm, we build a dataset comprising approximately 1000 pictures, and experiments show that our algorithm works on the dataset.

Keywords: Image retrieval · Color matching · Cascaded structure · License plate locating · Visual focus of attention

1   Introduction

Vehicle retrieval [2,12] is a necessary step towards automatic analysis of the surveillance videos of traffic environment. To find the exact vehicle, the intuitive way is to localize the similar instances and then check them one by one. For each instance, we can check the license plate number, the vehicle color, vehicle model and symbols on the windshield. However, this way is indeed time-consuming when confronted with immense data. For the sake of time saving, we propose a cascaded structure that uses simple features to rapidly reject irrelevant instances and simultaneously localizes and checks the potential instances.

In the paper, we focus on the vehicle retrieval based on the front view. We fulfill the retrieval task by examining the discriminative components, such as the windshield and license plate. From the point of view of human vision, these regions correspond to the focus of attention when a human is required to do the task. These regions provide the key information that helps human make the decision. Take the engine hood for example, it lies right between the windshield and the license plate, color in the region can effectively discriminate the specific vehicle from other ones. So in this paper, we firstly search vehicles out of the entire image, and then locate sequentially windshield and license plate for each detected vehicle. Subsequently, vehicle type and color are checked in corresponding interest regions.

© Springer International Publishing AG 2016
E. Chen et al. (Eds.): PCM 2016, Part II, LNCS 9917, pp. 126–135, 2016.
DOI: 10.1007/978-3-319-48896-7_13

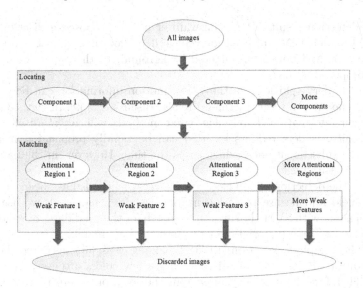

Fig. 1. The proposed framework for vehicle instance retrieval using a cascade of interest regions

At the other end, the massive volume data require the proposed method to run in real-time. Motivated by the cascaded structure for object detection [10], this paper proposes a framework that gradually localizes these interest regions. Weak features extracted from these interest regions are then cascaded to quickly prune out irrelevant instances. At the same time, we noticed that for a specific region, simple feature, such as the color histogram, can work efficiently to discriminate the vehicle from others. The way saves the computational time.

Proposed framework is summarized in Fig. 1. A sequence of calculation units is cascaded to simultaneously localize and check the significant components of a vehicle. Each unit corresponds to an interest region; weak features extracted from these regions are used for validating the similarity. The progressive way significantly discard many irrelevant cases. The rest of this paper is organized as follows. In Sect. 2, we briefly review the related work. In the subsequent Sects. 3 and 4, we describe our algorithm in detail. Experimental evaluations are then presented in Sect. 5. Based on those results, we draw the conclusion in Sect. 6.

2   Related Work

To query a given vehicle, the strategy we used is first to localize a vehicle, and then calculate the similarity measure between the localized one and the given instance. To localize the vehicle, there are many methods proposed [7,9]. Z. Sun et al. [9] supplied an early survey. In the survey, they discussed a list of knowledge-based vehicle detection methods. It is reported that simple features like symmetry, color, shadow or vehicle light, when solely used, never produce accurate detection results. P. Felzenswalb et al. [6] proposed a discriminative part-based model. When utilized for vehicle detection, it is robust to variation of vehicle type and potential cluttered background. In the paper, we adopted method proposed in [6].

When to query vehicle from the video, motion information can be used for efficiency. The motion-based methods are also discussed in [9]. In fact, combined with motion information, knowledge-based methods will act more effectively. Once a vehicle is detected, its location can be rapidly propagated from one frame to the subsequent ones, which saves the time. However, in the paper, we focus on the still image.

Besides the detection of vehicles, some success methods have been proposed for windshield and license plate localization. As for windshield, we use HOG feature [5] along with SVM classifier [4] to search for the candidates of windshield corners, then utilize a pictorial model to find the best match.

As for license plate detection (LPD), S. Chang et al. [3] considered the color information of LP. They observed that only a few colors are used for making a plate. Therefore, a plate may appear in the location where there are color edges of specific patterns, e.g. red-white and green-white ones. They built the detection algorithm based on the assumption. Besides, D. Zheng et al. [11] have noticed that lots of short vertical edges cluster together in the license plate area, in compared with the background. For the reason, vertical edge extraction is first applied to remove most horizontal edges in the background and then long vertical curves and random noises are discarded.

V. Petrovic and T. Cootes [7] extract the texture information around the license plate for recognizing the type pattern of the vehicle. As for extraction approaches, they compared many responses such as Sobel edge, edge orientation, direct normalized gradients, locally normalized gradients, and so on. Matching/classification results are good when license plates are well located (which means the interest region are precise).

3 Localization and Verification of Instances

3.1 Vehicle Detection

In the paper, we focus on the still images. Thence, we use exactly the algorithm of [6] to localize the vehicle. Some localization results are shown in Fig. 2(a). All the vehicles detected are separated into two datasets, one for training and the other one for testing. Details of the two datasets are summarized in Sect. 5.1. With the help of the localization results, we search for the locations of windshield and LP. The accurate localization results make the calculation of similarity measure more accurate. Next, we explain the procedure in detail.

3.2 Windshield Localization

To detect the windshield, we first search for its corners, and then use the geometric constraints for the best match.

(a)   (b)   (c)   (d)

Fig. 2. Sequence of locating and pertinent results. (a) shows the results of vehicle locating and (b) shows windshield locating result of a single detected vehicle; the highlighted area surrounded by red dashes in (c) is the license plate detection (LPD) interest region determined by the windshield; (d) blue bounding box in the brightened area shows the LPD result. (Color figure online)

Windshield Corner Detection. As for corner detection, we use HOG features [5] along with the SVM classifiers. Before detection, the vehicles found in Sect. 3.1 are all normalized such that each has a diagonal length of 500 pixels. In the training phase, we calculate the HOG features for the four corners respectively. Each HOG feature is extracted from a 64×64 pixel patch centered on the corresponding corner. Four linear SVM classifiers are trained separately for each corner.

For each test image, a 64×64 pixel window is slided across the image for feature extraction with horizontal and vertical step 8 pixels. Four voting maps are generated according to the SVM responses. Voting values in all the four maps are normalized to $[0, 1]$. Local maximums of each map are recorded, along with their voting values, as candidates for the corresponding corner.

Windshield Detection with Geometric Constraint. In Fig. 3(a), the quadrilateral represents the windshield. Each of its vertex $V_i, i = 1, 2, 3, 4$ has N_i feasible states. A feasible state for vertex V_i is recorded by $Cand_i^m = (x_i^m, y_i^m)$, $m = 1, \cdots, N_i$. With the description, the localization task is then

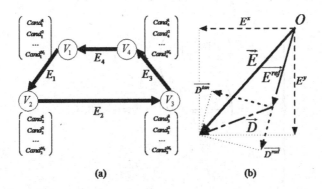

(a)   (b)

Fig. 3. The quadrilateral representing the windshield; (b) the vectors utilized in edge energy calculation.

reduced to select proper states for each vertex to maximize the total energy $\mathcal{E}$ of this quadrilateral,

$$\mathcal{E} = \sum_{i=1}^{4} \alpha_i \phi_i(Cand_i) + \sum_{i=1}^{4} \beta_i \psi_{i,j}(Cand_i, Cand_j) \tag{1}$$

where α_i and β_i are coefficients, and energy of a vertex or a pairwise term is denoted by ϕ_i and ψ_{ij} respectively. We number the vertexes of the quadrilateral in a counter-clockwise way. When $i \in \{1, 2, 3\}$, the pariwise term $\psi_{i,j}$ is $\psi_{i,i+1}$; when for $i = 4$, the term becomes to $\psi_{4,1}$. For clarity, we unify the representation of pairwise term as $\psi_{i,i+1}$. Next, we define ϕ_i as follows.

$$\phi_i(Cand_i^m) = p_i^m \tag{2}$$

where $Cand_i^m$ is the mth feasible state of vertex V_i, with p_i^m the voting value which has been normalized in Sect. 3.2.1.

The pairwise term is defined in Eq. 3, whose domain is $[-\infty, 1]$.

$$\psi_{i,i+1} = 1 - \gamma_i^{rad} d_i^{rad} - \gamma_i^{tan} d_i^{tan} - \gamma_i^{scale} d_i^{scale} \tag{3}$$

This term measures the geometric distortion between the vertexes. As shown in Fig. 3(b), we record the geometric priori for the adjacent pair of vertexes as $\overrightarrow{E_i^{ref}}$. Given the candidate $Cand_i^m$ and $Cand_{i+1}^n$, the relative position between them is recorded by $\overrightarrow{E_i}$. The difference between the candidate pair and the prior is then calculated by,

$$\overrightarrow{D_i} = \overrightarrow{E_i} - \overrightarrow{E_i^{ref}} \tag{4}$$

However, using $\overrightarrow{D_i}$ as the difference is not robust to the deformation. Experiments show that the deformation along the direction of $\overrightarrow{E_i^{ref}}$ is different from that tangent to $\overrightarrow{E_i^{ref}}$. Thus, the difference is decomposed with respect to $\overrightarrow{E_i^{ref}}$, resulting in the radial component $\overrightarrow{D_i^{rad}}$ and tangential one $\overrightarrow{D_i^{tan}}$. With the decomposition, all the 3 terms in Eq. 3 are defined as follows.

$$\begin{cases} d_i^{rad} = \left(\dfrac{\left\| \overrightarrow{D_i^{rad}} \right\|}{\sigma_{rad} \left\| \overrightarrow{E_i^{ref}} \right\|} \right)^2 , i = 1, 2, 3, 4 \\[3ex] d_i^{tan} = \left(\dfrac{\left\| \overrightarrow{D_i^{tan}} \right\|}{\sigma_{tan} \left\| \overrightarrow{E_i^{ref}} \right\|} \right)^2 , i = 1, 2, 3, 4 \\[3ex] d_i^{scale} = \left(\dfrac{\left\| \overrightarrow{D_i} \right\|}{\left\| \overrightarrow{E_i^{ref}} \right\|} - \dfrac{\left\| \overrightarrow{D_{i-1}} \right\|}{\left\| \overrightarrow{E_{i-1}^{ref}} \right\|} \right)^2 , i = 2, 3, 4 \end{cases} \tag{5}$$

where σ_{tan} is often much less than σ_{tan}, which restricts the deformation in radial direction more strictly than that along the tangential direction. The term d_i^{scale}

is introduced for scale consistency. Theoretically speaking, a greater γ_i^{scale} in Eq. 3 results in a windshield resembling the referenced one.

Furthermore, some geometrical constraints are tested for $\overrightarrow{E_i} = (\overrightarrow{E_{i,x}}, \overrightarrow{E_{i,y}})$. If the metric fails the test, ∞ is assigned to the corresponding pairwise term. For example, $\overrightarrow{E_{1,y}}$ should be positive, since V_2 represents the lower-left corner and it should be geometrically below V_1, which represents the upper-left corner.

With all the definitions introduced, we propose a method based on Viterbi Algorithm to optimize the windshield of greatest energy. The procedure is sketched in the pseudo-code in Fig. 4.

Input: states of all V_i, $i = 1, 2, 3, 4$
Output: optimal state for $\{V_i\}$
for each state $Cand_1^m$ of V_1 **do**
    for each state $Cand_4^n$ of V_4 **do**
        $O^{(k)}(S_i, T_j) \leftarrow O^{(k)}(S_i, T_j) + D_k(S_i(T_j))$
        Search for a pair of optimal $(Cand_2^p, Cand_3^q)$ to maximize Eq.1
        Calculate the optimal value $\mathcal{E}|_{m,n}$ with $Cand_1^m$ and $Cand_4^n$ fixed
    end for
end for
$\epsilon = \max\{\mathcal{E}|_{m,n}\}$, and decode the optimal state for $\{V_i\}$

Fig. 4. Algorithm for windshield detection with geometric constraint

The output is the most probable combination of corner positions for the windshield. Figure 2(b) shows an example of windshield localization result.

3.3   License plate

As for license plate, the precise vehicle scale and knowledge of the plain background are two critical requirements of the LPD method [1,11]. Since the windshield is located, the requirements can be easily satisfied. Width of the windshield provides a precise estimation of license plate size, while the area below the windshield becomes the interest area for license plate locating (see Fig. 2(c)). For this reason, this simple rapid method yields much better and more robust results.

4   Similarity Checking

The foregoing work has figured out the positions of some important components of a vehicle. Based on these regions, a similarity measure between each testing vehicle and the queried one is calculated. It is comprised of two components, one for the type checking and the other for the color. With the metric, we further prune the majority of the testing vehicles.

Fig. 5. The geometric configuration for type checking and color matching.

4.1 Type Checking

We employ exactly the same algorithm in [11] to match the vehicle type. As shown in Fig. 5, the attentional region of vehicle type matching is set around the license plate, in terms of plate width w_p. Among the extraction approaches examined, we choose the Local Normalized Gradients,

$$\left(g_x^{DN}, g_y^{DN}\right) = \left(\frac{s_x}{\sqrt{s_x^2 + s_y^2}}, \frac{s_y}{\sqrt{s_x^2 + s_y^2}}\right) \qquad (6)$$

where s_x, s_y are response of Sobel edge detection along x and y direction respectively.

Difference between a testing instance and the queried instance is accumulated pixel by pixel, and then it is as the distance. A smaller difference value indicates that the test instance is more likely to be the queried instance.

4.2 Color Matching

As mentioned before, engine hood is the main part of the interest region. Let h_e denotes the height between the lower base of windshield and the bottom of vehicle (here we use the bottom of type matching interest region). Given w_w the width of the windshield, the interest region for color matching is then set to $\frac{3}{2}w_e \times w_w$, as shown in Fig. 5. At the same time, this region is partitioned for incorporating the spatial information. The sub-part in the region that contains richer color information is intuitively more important and thus assigned higher weight.

For each sub-part, color histogram is extracted for vehicle retrieval. In the RGB color space, we discretize each color channel into N_c bins and let $B_{r,g,b}$ denote the bin whose center are r, g and b respectively.

In this way, chromatic and spatial information of all pixels is collected into a histogram. The histogram is then normalized. In the experiments, we evenly divide the region of interest as shown in Fig. 5 into 3×3 blocks, as we can see in

Fig. 4(c). We set $N_c = 8$, which means one block is represented by a vector of 8^3 elements. There are many metrics for comparing two histograms, e.g. Euclidean distance, Mahalanobis distance, etc. Among these, we finally select Earth Movers Distance (EMD)[11]. Its mathematical form is defined as below:

$$d_{color} = \frac{\sum_1^9 w_i \text{EMD}(\text{Blk}_i^{testing}, \text{Blk}_i^{retrieval})}{\sum_{i=1}^9 w_i} \tag{7}$$

Apparently, the engine hood area contains richer chromatic information than the part of windshield, wherefore we put more weight on the blocks in the second and the third row. Weights for the final matching is given by Eq. 8.

$$W = [1\,1\,1;\ 4\,4\,4;\ 2\,2\,2] \tag{8}$$

When for the EMD distance, a similarity metric is introduced as recommended in [7]. The matrix D, which determines the ground distance between two chromatic bins, is defined in Eq. 9.

$$D(B_{r_1,g_1,b_1}, B_{r_2,g_2,b_2}) = |r_1 - r_2| + |g_1 - g_2| + |b_1 - b_2| \tag{9}$$

Similar to the type distance defined in the previous section, a testing image with more similar color distribution gets a smaller color distance to the querying instance.

5   Experimental Evaluation

5.1   Datasets

We separate the dataset into training and testing ones. Images in the dataset are all taken in the natural on-road traffic scenes. The training set is prepared for the windshield locating (Sect. 3.2) while all experiments are conducted in the testing one. Summary information is listed in Table 1.

5.2   Experimental Results

Results of Separate Matching Methods. We present separately here results of the 2 matching methods. We choose 4 vehicles with different colors and types as demonstration (see Fig. 6(a)) and a ranking measure is applied, as shown in Tables 2 and 3.

Table 1. Summary info of the datasets

	Training set	Testing set
Number of images	740	913
Number of instances	923	990

Table 2. Ranking of color matching results

Positive matching	First 30	First 50	First 100	Last 100
Vehicle 1	30	50	100	0
Vehicle 2	30	50	86	0
Vehicle 3	30	50	97	0
Vehicle 4	28	35	44	0

Table 3. Ranking of type matching results

Positive matching	First 30	First 50	First 100	Last 100
Vehicle 1	30	50	97	3
Vehicle 2	28	45	89	5
Vehicle 3	26	43	89	3
Vehicle 4	27	43	89	3

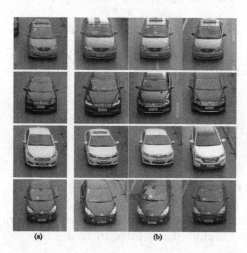

(a)   (b)

Fig. 6. Examples of cascade matching results. (a) Shows the 4 instances we have chosen, and (b) Shows respectively the first 3 matched vehicles.

The Influence of Cascade Structure. The two matching methods are then combined together. After filtered by color matching, the preserved vehicles pass through type matching process. In the experiments, we preserve the first 100 vehicles matched in color matching, and then put them into the type filter. The final results are similar to the instances both in color and type. Some of the results are shown in Fig. 6(b).

6   Conclusion

The proposed cascade structure completes well the vehicle retrieval task. Images were correctly trimmed in every phase and the final results show great relevance to the given instance. When integrated, different locating and matching methods can share results, which not only improves the precision but also saves computational time. In our future work, videos will be used, which means motion information can contribute to the task.

References

1. Abolghasemi, V., Ahmadyfard, A.: An edge-based color-aided method for license plate detection. Image Vis. Comput. **27**(8), 1134–1142 (2009)
2. Brown, L.M.: Example-based color vehicle retrieval for surveillance. In: Advanced Video and Signal Based Surveillance (AVSS), pp. 91–96, August 2010
3. Chang, S.-L., Chen, L.-S., Chung, Y.-C., Chen, S.-W.: Automatic license plate recognition. IEEE Trans. Intell. Transp. Syst. **5**(1), 42–53 (2004)
4. Chang, C.C., Lin, C.J.: LIBSVM: a library for support vector machines. ACM Trans. Intell. Syst. Technol. **2**(3), 27 (2011)
5. Dalal, N., Triggs, B.: Histograms of oriented gradients for human detection. In: CVPR 2005, vol. 1, pp. 886–893, June 2005
6. Felzenszwalb, P.F., Girshick, R.B., McAllester, D., Ramanan, D.: Object detection with discriminatively trained part-based models. IEEE Trans. Pattern Anal. Mach. Intell. **32**(9), 1627–1645 (2010)
7. Petrovic, V.S., Cootes, T. F.: Analysis of features for rigid structure vehicle type recognition. In: British Machine Vision Conference, pp. 587–596 (2004)
8. Rubner, Y., Tomasi, C., Guibas, L.J.: The earth mover distance as a metric for image retrieval. Int. J. Comput. Vision **40**, 2000 (2000)
9. Sun, Z., Bebis, G., Miller, R.: On-road vehicle detection: a review. IEEE Trans. Pattern Anal. Mach. Intell. **28**(5), 694–711 (2006)
10. Viola, P., Jones, M.: Rapid object detection using a boosted cascade of simple features. In: CVPR, vol. 1, pp. 511–518 (2001)
11. Zheng, D., Zhao, Y., Wang, J.: An efficient method of license plate location. Pattern Recogn. Lett. **26**(15), 2431–2438 (2005)
12. Zheng, Q., Liang, C., Fang, W., Xiang, D., Zhao, X., Ren, C., Chen, J.: Car re-identification from large scale images using semantic attributes. In: MMSP, pp. 1–5 (2015)

Towards Drug Counterfeit Detection Using Package Paperboard Classification

Christof Kauba$^{(\boxtimes)}$, Luca Debiasi, Rudolf Schraml, and Andreas Uhl

Department of Computer Sciences, University of Salzburg,
Jakob Haringer Str. 2, 5020 Salzburg, Austria
{ckauba,ldebiasi,rschraml,uhl}@cosy.sbg.ac.at

Abstract. Most approaches for product counterfeit detection are based on identification using some unique marks or properties implemented into each single product or its package. In this paper we investigate a classification approach involving existing packaging only in order to avoid higher production costs involved with marking each individual product. To detect counterfeit packages, images of the package's interior showing the plain structure of the paperboard are captured. Using various texture features and SVM classification we are able to distinguish drug packages coming from different manufacturers and also forged packages with high accuracy while a distinction between single packages of the same manufacturer is not possible.

Keywords: Drug counterfeit detection · Paper structure classification · Texture classification

1 Introduction

Counterfeit products are a serious world wide issue affecting all industries. A recent OECD study [13] reports that in 2013 about 2.5 % of the world wide traded products were faked ones. For the European Union (EU) a remarkably higher value of 5 % for faked and imported products is reported.

In case of medical products counterfeit medicines and drugs lead to an economic loss and are all the worse a threat for the health of the consumers and patients. The International Medical Products Taskforce (IMPACT) of the World Health Organization (WHO) estimated a share of 1 % of faked products in the developed countries and 10 to 30 % in many developing countries [16]. Consequently, medical product authentication is becoming increasingly important. On European level the Falsified Medicines Directive (FMD) 2011/62/EU should be implemented until 2018. The overall aim is to improve patient safety stipulating an efficient anti-counterfighting system. Unique identifiers (2D barcodes) will be used to track and authenticate each medical package along the supply chain. A central repository system is required to enable authentication of each package. Such a system will not be available in developing countries. Furthermore, it suffers costs and is exposed to getting compromised by the forgers.

© Springer International Publishing AG 2016
E. Chen et al. (Eds.): PCM 2016, Part II, LNCS 9917, pp. 136–146, 2016.
DOI: 10.1007/978-3-319-48896-7_14

Another approach to verify the originality of a product is to use intrinsic features visible on the packaging or the product itself. For this work we focus on authentication of a medical product using intrinsic features from the packaging surface. Literature in this field relates to package fingerprinting based on the theory of physically uncloneable functions (PUFs). Paper PUFs use the fiber structure of paper as physical/intrinsic characteristic. The approaches presented in [1,3,10] show that the micro-structure in a certain region of a paper or package material is discriminative enough to identify it. Detailed investigations on paper identification, using a public available microstructure dataset [18], are presented in [4,5]. In [5] the authors explore the applicability of two approaches to overcome geometric distortions. The same approaches and a hybrid one are used to investigate package identification using mobile phones in [4]. Furthermore, in [6] a new feature descriptor for micro-structure identification using mobile phones is introduced. By comparing the performances for different PUFs the results in [20] indicate that the approach by [3] outperforms the approaches by [4,5,18] but it requires a commodity scanner. Thus, in [19] the authors showed that mobile devices and the camera built-in flash lights can also be used to capture images as required for [3].

As shown, research exclusively deals with identification of paper or packages. To the best of our knowledge no works which consider paper or package classification have been presented so far. Like in the work of [17] we assume that the fibre structure pattern of the packaging material is suited for classification, i.e, for a certain medical product the packaging fibre structure shows constant features. If so, one step for checking the authenticity of a medical product could be to assess if the packaging material is the same as used for the original product. To answer this question, we perform a preliminary study for nine different medical products from three different manufacturers and some forged packages for one medical product. The results of this work enable to draw conclusions which are a first step towards medical product authentication using the packaging material.

Section 2 introduces the basic concept of paper classification. The experimental setup and the data set acquisition are described in Sect. 3. Our experimental results together with a discussion of these results can be found in Sect. 4. Section 5 concludes this paper.

2   Paper Texture Classification

This section describes our proposed approach using paper texture classification for package counterfeit detection. The general procedure is the following: At first an image of the interior of the package is taken and several patches are extracted from random positions in the image. These patches are then preprocessed. Afterwards different features are extracted from the preprocessed patches. Based on these features a classifier returns a decision predicting the class a questioned image is belonging to (by utilizing a pre-trained SVM). The steps are explained in the following.

2.1 Image Acquisition

Several images of the package's interior are captured at different positions. For the image acquisition a Canon 70D (100 mm lens and flash light), mounted on a tripod, was utilized. The flashlight was placed besides the package. The camera is set to the smallest possible distance from the package (about 30 cm) trying to capture as most as possible of the paper's fibre-structure. An image of the acquisition setup can be seen in Fig. 1 together with an acquired image from the interior of a sample package.

Fig. 1. Set-up for image acquisition of the fiber structure on the inside of a drug package (left) and acquired image sample (right).

2.2 Preprocessing

During preprocessing of the images a contrast limited adaptive histogram equalization (CLAHE) [21] is applied in order to improve contrast and enhance the paper structure. After this contrast enhancement all images are converted to grayscale and several patches are extracted from random positions in the images to reduce the computational effort and increase the amount of data that can be extracted from each package. Figure 2 shows the paper structure of different packages extracted from the random patches after preprocessing.

Fig. 2. Example preprocessed image patches

2.3 Feature Extraction Techniques

All techniques tested in this work are usually used for texture classification, image tampering detection and printer/paper identification and are applied on the preprocessed images taken from the inside of the package. The techniques utilized in this work are briefly described in the following list, further information on the single techniques can be found in the corresponding papers.

- Histogram
  Gray-level histogram of all pixels as the extracted feature.
- LBP: Local Binary Patterns
  The local binary patterns (LBP) by Ojala *et al.* [14] observe the variations of pixels in a local neighbourhood and are represented in a histogram.
- DMD: Dense Micro-block Difference
  Texture classification approach by Metha *et al.* [9] which captures the local structure from the image patches at high scales, but instead of the pixels small blocks which capture the micro-structure of the image are processed.
- RI-LPQ: Rotation-Invariant Local Phase Quantization
  The rotation-invariant local phase quantization (RI-LPQ) by Ojansivu *et al.* [15] consists of two stages: Estimation of the local characteristic orientation for a given image patch and directed descriptor extraction.
- Dense SIFT: Dense Scale Invariant Feature Transform
  Lowe [8] proposed a technique used in object recognition which is commonly known as scale invariant feature transform (SIFT). This technique is invariant to image scale and rotation and robust against various affine distortions, addition of noise, illumination changes and changes of the viewpoint.
  GLCM: Gray-level Co-occurence Matrix
  Mikkilineni *et al.* proposed to use gray-level co-occurence features for printer identification in [11]. The features model the spatial relationships among the pixels of an image to represent its texture information.
- WP: Weber Pattern
  In [12] Muhammad proposed a multi-scale local texture descriptor which was applied as part of an image forgery framework.
- BSIF: Binarized Statistical Image Features
  The Binarized Statistical Image Features (BSIF) proposed by Kannala *et al.* in [7] rely on pre-computed local image descriptors which efficiently encode texture information.
- LSB+JD: Least Significant Bitplane + Jaccard Distance
  Extraction of the images least significant bitplane (LSB-plane) and calculate the Jaccard distance between the LSB-planes of two images.

2.4 Classification Approach

The features extracted with the techniques described in the previous section are used to classify the images of the various kinds of drug packages.

The classifier is designed according to the improved Fisher vector (IFV) SVM classifier in [2]. The features are soft-quantized using a Gaussian mixture model (GMM), decorrelated and dimensionality reduced by PCA to obtain a Fisher vector (FV) encoding. A pre-trained linear SVM is then used to classify the IFV encoded features. The SVM is trained using a subset of the package's images which is subsequently not used for the testing (evaluation) step.

3   Experimental Settings

The following section describes the dataset used in this work, which contains images showing the paper structure of different forged and original drug packages. Furthermore a description of the two different dataset splits and our evaluation methodology to avoid overlapping between training and testing data is given.

3.1   Dataset

Unfortunately, only a limited number of drug packages was available for our work. In particular we have packages of 9 different kinds of drugs from 3 different manufacturers denoted by A, B and C.

For all 9 kinds of drugs we have genuine packages and for 2 of them we also have forged packages. The forged packages for the *Levitra* drug (ID 1) are real counterfeits confiscated by customs, while the forged packages for the *Neradin* drug (ID 8) have been purpose-made by the manufacturer of the drug.

Table 1 lists the number of genuine and forged packages for each kind of drug (ID 1...9). We acquired 10 to 20 slightly shifted and overlapping images from each of the packages' interiors from which 5 patches of 512×512 pixels are extracted at random position within each image. The extracted patches correspond to a section of approximately 4.1×4.1 mm, or 16.81 mm^2, of the package. From this data we generated two distinct data sets to analyze two different issues using the paper structure of the packages:

1. Is it possible to distinguish different packages of the same manufacturer?
2. Is it possible to distinguish packages of different manufacturers?

The first data set, *SMDP* (Same Manufacturer Different Packages), contains images from packages of the same manufacturer, which correspond to the

Table 1. Number of genuine (G) and forged (F) packages in the data set with drug name, corresponding ID and manufacturer (MF).

ID	Name	# G	# F	MF
1	Levitra	3	4	A
2	Kijimea Reizdarm	2	0	B
3	Kijimea Immun	1	0	B
4	Kijimea Derma	2	0	B
5	Narumed	3	0	B
6	Deseo	4	0	B
7	Signasol	2	0	B
8	Neradin	4	2	B
9	Unistop	2	0	C

manufacturer B in Table 1. We only considered packages of this manufacturer since it is the only one from which we had more than one different type of drug package.

The second data set, *FGDM* (Forged and Genuine Different Manufacturers), contains images from all the packages, genuine and forged, from all manufacturers in Table 1.

3.2 Evaluation Methodology

To investigate the two questions of Sect. 3.1, we split the evaluation according to the two data sets SMDP and FGDM.

For the SMDP data set, where we want to find out if it is possible to distinguish between different types of drug packages from the same manufacturer, images having the same drug ID are defined as corresponding to the same class. A class thus can contain images from different packages of the same drug. Forged and genuine packages are furthermore split into different classes. This yields 8 different classes, because we have 7 different types of drug packages for manufacturer B and for one drug we also have 2 packages, which have been forged by the manufacturer.

To find out if it is possible to distinguish packages of different manufacturers (FGDM data set), images having the same manufacturer ID are defined as corresponding to the same class. Forged and genuine packages are again split into different classes for the *Levitra* drug produced by manufacturer A, but not for the *Neradin* drug of manufactuer B because these forgeries have been produced by the manufacturer and use the same material as the genuine packages. The different classes for the SMDP and FGDM data set are summarized in Table 2.

Table 2. Evaluation classes and corresponding IDs with number of packages

Name	# Packages	SMDP Class ID	FGDM Class ID
Levitra forged	4	-	1
Levitra genuine	3	-	2
Kijimea Reizdarm genuine	2	1	3
Kijimea Immun genuine	1	2	3
Kijimea Derma genuine	2	3	3
Narumed genuine	3	4	3
Deseo genuine	4	5	3
Signàsol genuine	2	6	3
Neradin forged	2	7	3
Neradin genuine	4	8	3
Unistop genuine	2	-	4

The acquired images of the drug packages are slightly overlapping, this might lead to patches of the same image belonging to both, the training and the testing subset. Hence we used leave one package out (LOPO) for the selection of the training and testing images/patches: Training is done with randomly selected patches from all images except the images from one specific package. The patches for the testing subset are then randomly selected only out of images from this package. If there is only a single package in a class, like for the class with ID 2 in the case of the SMDP data set, the patches for this class are only used to train the classifier. Thus, no intra-class comparisons for this class exist and the average precision is not calculated and shown as 0 in the plots. By using the LOPO approach for the evaluation, the slight overlap of images from the same package does not introduce any bias to the results.

4   Experimental Results

This section presents the results of the conducted experiments and the conclusions made from those. We analysed the two cases, at first the separation according to manufacturer (FGDM) and second the separation of packages all from the same manufacturer (SMDP).

Table 3 lists the mean accuracies (mAcc) and mean average precisions (mAP) for both cases. The mean accuracy corresponds to the mean of the values of the confusion matrix diagonal. It can be seen that for FGDM the results for DenseSIFT and DMD are close to 100 % meaning that almost a perfect classification of the paper and thus the manufacturer is possible. Consequently, the true forgeries (corresponding to class 1) can be seperated from the other classes well.

Some example confusion matrices using a heat map for selected feature types (DMD, DenseSIFT and GLCM) can be seen in Figs. 3 and 5 for the FGDM and SMDP case, respectively. The numbers on the axes denote the classes according

Table 3. Mean accuracies (mAcc) and mean average precisions (mAP)

Data set	FGDM		SMDP	
Method	mAcc	mAP	mAcc	mAP
BSIF	0.428	0.403	0.138	0.171
DMD	0.97	1	0.328	0.423
DenseSIFT	0.91	1	0.37	0.476
GLCM	0.953	0.964	0.14	0.18
Histogram	0.603	0.662	0.145	0.176
LBP	0.758	0.863	0.265	0.272
LSB	0.71	0.818	0.113	0.182
RI-LPQ	0.842	0.888	0.158	0.226
WP	0.861	0.896	0.158	0.197

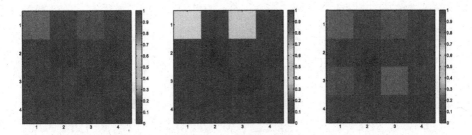

Fig. 3. Confusion matrix for DMD, DenseSIFT and GLCM in the FGDM case

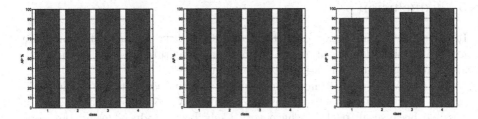

Fig. 4. Average precision for DMD, DenseSIFT and GLCM in the FGDM case

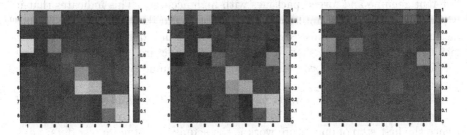

Fig. 5. Confusion matrix for DMD, DenseSIFT and GLCM in the SMDP case

to Table 2, which shows the correspondence of the class labels to the drug packages. Figures 4 and 6 show the corresponding average precision plots for FGDM and SMDP, respectively. These confirm that the recognition works well if the split is done according to different manufacturers and does not work if the split is done according to different drugs all from the same manufacturer.

We do not have any information about which kind of paper is used for the different drug packages. But the experimental results suggest (distinction between different types of drugs from the same manufacturer was not possible) that one manufacturer uses the same kind of paper and the same printing facility/printing process for his drug packages. As long as the forgers do not have access to the same kind of printing facility the genuine manufacturers utilizes, drug counterfeit detection is feasible using our proposed approach.

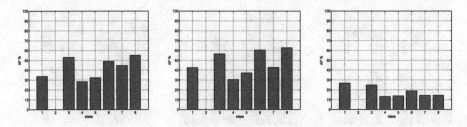

Fig. 6. Average precision for DMD, DenseSIFT and GLCM in the SMDP case

5 Conclusion

In this paper we investigated whether counterfeit drug package detection using texture classification based on the intrinsic paper texture is possible. The available data was split to investigate two different issues.

In the SMDP case (same manufacturer) a distinction between single packages of the same manufacturer was not possible. We concluded that this is not possible because all packages have very likely been produced using the same manufacturing process and therefore share a very similar paper structure.

In the FGDM case (different manufacturers) it was indeed possible to classify different genuine and forged packages with high accuracy. This indicates that it is possible to identify counterfeit packages not produced by the original manufacturer, since they are most likely being produced in a different manufacturing facility and hence do not share a similar paper structure. The class containing the forged packages and the classes containing genuine packages could all be clearly separated in this case.

This promising results however have to be taken with a grain of salt because of the small data set size and the availability of only a few real counterfeit packages. Hence the first step of our future work is the acquisition of more test data, i.e. a higher number of distinct types of drug packages and even more important more counterfeit and genuine packages of the same type of drug. In addition we want to acquire further information about the printing and manufacturing process of the packages.

Acknowledgments. This work is supported by the Munich based software venture eMundo which receives funding from the Central Innovation Program for SMEs by Germany's Federal Ministry of Economics and Technology (project "FakeFinder" no. ZIM-EP150145).

References

1. Buchanon, J., Cowburn, R., Jausovec, A.-V., Petit, S.: Forgery: fingerprinting documents and packaging. Nature **436**(7050), 475 (2005)
2. Cimpoi, M., Maji, S., Kokkinos, I., Mohamed, S., Vedaldi, A.: Describing textures in the wild. In: Proceedings of the IEEE Conference on Computer Vision and Pattern Recognition (CVPR) (2014)

3. Clarkson, W., Weyrich, T., Finkelstein, A., Heninger, N., Halderman, J.A., Felten, E.W.: Fingerprinting blank paper using commodity scanners. In: Proceedings of the 30th IEEE Symposium on Security and Privacy, pp. 301–314 (2009)

4. Diephuis, M., Voloshynovskiy, S., Holotyak, T., Stendardo, N., Keel, B.: A framework for fast and secure packaging identification on mobile phones. In: Proceedings of SPIE Photonics West, Electronic Imaging, Media Forensics and Security V, San Francisco, USA, 23 January, 2014

5. Diephuis, M., Voloshynovskiy, S., Beekhof, F.: Physical object identification based on famos microstructure fingerprinting: comparison of templates versus invariant features. In: 8th International Symposium on Image and Signal Processing and Analysis, Trieste, Italy, 4–6 September, 2013

6. Diephuis, M., Voloshynovskiy, S., Holotyak, T.: Sketchprint: physical object microstructure identification using mobile phones. In: European Signal Processing Conference (EUSIPCO), Nice, France, 31 August - 4, September 2015

7. Kannala, J., Rahtu, E.: BSIF: binarized statistical image features. In: Proceedings of the 21st International Conference on Pattern Recognition, ICPR, Tsukuba, Japan, November 11–15, pp. 1363–1366 (2012)

8. Lowe, D.G.: Distinctive image features from scale-invariant keypoints. Int. J. Comput. Vis. **60**(2), 91–110 (2004)

9. Mehta, R., Egiazarian, K.: Texture classification using dense micro-block difference (DMD). In: Cremers, D., Reid, I., Saito, H., Yang, M.-H. (eds.) ACCV 2014. LNCS, vol. 9004, pp. 643–658. Springer, Heidelberg (2015). doi:10.1007/978-3-319-16808-1_43

10. Metois, E., Yarin, P., Salzman, N., Smith, J.: Fiberfingerprint identification. In: Proceedings of the 3rd Workshop on Automatic Identification, New York City, USA (2002)

11. Mikkilineni, A.K., Chiang, P.-J., Ali, G.N., Chiu, G.T.C., Allebach, J.P., Delp, E.J.: Printer identification based on graylevel co-occurrence features for security and forensic applications, vol. 5681, pp. 430–440 (2005)

12. Muhammad, G.: Multi-scale local texture descriptor for image forgery detection. In: IEEE International Conference on Industrial Technology (ICIT), pp. 1146–1151 (2013)

13. OECD and EUIPO: Trade in counterfeit and pirated goods, p. 138. OECD Publishing (2016)

14. Ojala, T., Pietikainen, M., Harwood, D.: Performance evaluation of texture measures with classification based on kullback discrimination of distributions. In: Proceedings of the 12th IAPR International Conference on Pattern Recognition, vol. 1, pp. 582–585, October 1994

15. Ojansivu, V., Rahtu, E., Heikkila, J.: Rotation invariant local phase quantization for blur insensitive texture analysis. In: 2008 19th International Conference on Pattern Recognition, ICpPR 2008, pp. 1–4, December 2008

16. W.H. Organization. International medical products taskforce - brochure. http://apps.who.int/impact/FinalBrochureWHA2008a.pdf?ua=1. Accessed 29 Apr 2016

17. Varma, M., Zisserman, A.: A statistical approach to material classification using image patch exemplars. IEEE Trans. Pattern Anal. Mach. Intell. **31**(11), 2032–2047 (2009)

18. Voloshynovskiy, S., Diephuis, M., Beekhof, F., Koval, O., Keel, B.: Towards reproducible results in authentication based on physical non-cloneable functions: the forensic authentication microstructure optical set (famos). In: Proceedings of IEEE International Workshop on Information Forensics and Security, Tenerife, Spain, 2–5 December 2012

19. Wong, C.W., Wu, M.: Counterfeit detection using paper PUF and mobile cameras. In: 2015 IEEE International Workshop on Information Forensics and Security (WIFS), pp. 1–6, November 2015
20. Wong, C.W., Wu, M.: A study on PUF characteristics for counterfeit detection. In: IEEE International Conference on Image Processing (ICIP), pp. 1643–1647, September 2015
21. Zuiderveld, K.: Graphics gems iv. chapter contrast limited adaptive histogram equalization, pp. 474–485. Academic Press Professional Inc, San Diego, CA, USA (1994)

Dynamic Strategies for Flow Scheduling in Multihoming Video CDNs

Ming Ma[1]([⊠]), Zhi Wang[2], Yankai Zhang[1,3], and Lifeng Sun[1]

[1] Tsinghua National Laboratory for Information Science and Technology,
Department of Computer Science and Technology,
Tsinghua University, Beijing, China
{mm13,zyk12}@mails.tsinghua.edu.cn, sunlf@tsinghua.edu.cn
[2] Graduate School at Shenzhen, Tsinghua University, Shenzhen, China
wangzhi@sz.tsinghua.edu.cn
[3] Electrical and Computer Engineering, Carnegie Mellon University, CA, USA
yankaiz@cmu.edu

Abstract. Multihoming for a video Content Delivery Network (CDN) allows edge peering servers to deliver video chunks through different Internet Service Providers (ISPs), to achieve an improved quality of service (QoS) for video streaming users. However, since traditional strategies for a multihoming video CDN are simply designed according to static rules, e.g., simply sending traffic via a ISP which is the same as the ISP of client, they fail to dynamically allocate resources among different ISPs over time. In this paper, we perform measurement studies to demonstrate that such static allocation mechanism is inefficient to make full utilization of multiple ISPs' resources. To address this problem, we propose a *dynamic flow scheduling strategy for multihoming video CDN*. The challenge is to find the control parameters that can guide the ISP selection when performing flow scheduling. Using a data-driven approach, we find factors that have a major impact on the performance improvement in the dynamic flow scheduling. We further utilize an information gain approach to generate parameter combinations that can be used to guide the flow scheduling, i.e., to determine the ISP each request should be responded by. Our evaluation results demonstrate that our design effectively performs the flow scheduling. In particular, our design yields near optimal performance in a simulation of real-world multihoming setup.

1 Introduction

Content Delivery Networks (CDNs) have been massively used by video service providers to deliver video chunks using the geo-distributed servers. In such video CDNs, multihoming, that allows one edge peering server to deliver video chunks through networks of different Internet Service Providers (ISPs) to different users (referred to as *flow scheduling* in this paper), has become a promising way to improve the quality of services (QoS) for data-intensive video delivery, e.g., improving the service availability [12].

© Springer International Publishing AG 2016
E. Chen et al. (Eds.): PCM 2016, Part II, LNCS 9917, pp. 147–158, 2016.
DOI: 10.1007/978-3-319-48896-7_15

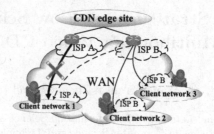

Fig. 1. A simple case to illustrate the inefficiency of rule-based strategy.

In multihoming CDNs, traditional approaches schedule flows using static rule-based strategies, e.g., a user is scheduled to receive data from the CDN server's outgoing ISP which is the same ISP as the user's ISP (referred to as same ISP-based strategy) [1,6]. Such static rule-based strategies fail to make full use of network resources that are dynamically changing over time and across locations [3,8]. Figure 1 is a simple case that illustrates this inefficiency. In this case, a CDN edge site, multihomed to 2 ISPs, delivers videos with the same ISP-based strategy. Thus even when the path "CDN network (ISP A) → Client network (ISP A)" has congestions, the peering server still delivers the contents along this congested path ignoring a better choice "CDN network (ISP B) → Client network (ISP A)".

Thus it is intriguing to study dynamic strategies for flow scheduling in multihoming video CDNs. In this paper, we carry out measurement and strategy designs to answer the following questions: (a) How much gain can we achieve from the dynamical flow scheduling strategy compared to a static one in multihoming video CDN? (b) Which factors will influence the performance gain? And (c) how can we design strategies that can be used by today's CDNs to achieve such performance gain?

To answer questions (a) and (b), we use both real-world and simulation experiments to verify the advantages of using dynamical strategies to allocate network resources, and investigate the network factors which affect the performance of dynamical flow scheduling, e.g., the hops between the server and clients. For question (c), based on the measurement insights, we select a set of parameters, and these parameters can be used by video CDN providers to actively and dynamically control *which flow will go through which ISP's network from a peering server at a given time*.

Our contributions are summarized as follows:

▷ We conduct extensive real-world and simulation experiments to confirm the fact that dynamical flow scheduling significantly outperforms conventional static strategies in multihoming CDNs, i.e., in the controlled simulation experiments, we observe that the throughput of dynamical strategy can even be 2x higher than the static strategy.

▷ We further identify the parameters that affect the performance gain by observing and comparing network information under all possible flow schedule strategies, and find the most influential parameters are link coverage, overlap and the total bandwidth of bottlenecks.

▷ We design a local selection scheme using a combination of parameters, to determine which flow goes through which ISP's network. Our evaluation verify the effectiveness of our design, yielding near optimal performance (up to 90 % of the optimal gain) in most of scenarios under the real-world multihoming simulation.

The rest of this paper is organized as follows. Sect. 2 discusses the related works. Sect. 3 gives some key definitions in this paper. In Sect. 4, we carry out real-world measurements to confirm that dynamic flow scheduling is a must in today's multihoming CDN. In Sect. 5 we investigate the factors that affect the performance gain of dynamic flow scheduling. In Sect. 6, we design a local selection scheme to schedule flows and evaluate our design in Sect. 7. We conclude the paper in Sect. 8.

2   Related Works

Video content constitutes a dominant fraction of online entertainment traffic today. There are abundant techniques [11,15] used in the content-distribution systems. To this end, multihoming has becoming the mainstream solution for CDN providers to improve the service reliability and performance. In this multihoming CDN context, rule-based strategies have been used to schedule flows in a static way due to the charge between ISPs or other commercial polices [1,6]. However, according to Akella et al.'s study [2,3], strategical scheduling traffic across the ISPs can improve performance by 25 %. And Valancius et al. [14] claim that an online service provider can provide tangible improvement (4.3 %) over the state of the art by controlling both the selection of CDN sites and the multiple ISPs between the clients and their associated CDN sites.

As multihoming is a promising approach to enhance the performance of content delivery, some existing works explore the problem of dynamic flow scheduling. Akella et al. [2] choose the outgoing ISP with the least round-trip time (RTT), and propose a method to reduce the ping probes in the link-performance monitoring process of the route optimization. Goldenberg et al. [7,9] develop algorithms for optimizing both cost and RTT for multihomed networks.

These existing studies are not suitable for the CDN of data-intensive video streaming, which pays more attention to high throughput. How to design a more practical strategy to schedule flows for a video peering server is still a challenging problem. In this paper, we study parameters that can be used in real-world flow scheduling for multihoming video CDNs.

3   Key Definitions

Before we present the experiments to motivate the dynamic flow scheduling in multihoming CDN, we define three important terms used in this paper.

▷ **Multihoming ISP and client network.** $\mathcal{F}$ denotes the set of ISPs to which the peering server multihomed. $f \in \mathcal{F}$. $\mathcal{C}$ denotes the set of client networks. $c \in \mathcal{C}$.

▷ **Flow schedule strategy.** We define the flow schedule strategy as an *outgoing ISP vector.* Let k denote a flow scheduling strategy. $k = (f_1, f_2, ..., f_{|\mathcal{C}|})$, where $f_i \in \mathcal{F}$ indicates the outgoing ISP selected for the ith client network. To explore the optimal performance gain of flow scheduling, we assume the CDN peering server can enumerate all possible flow strategies. The number of flow scheduling strategies is $|\mathcal{F}|^{|\mathcal{C}|}$.

▷ **Performance gain.** On account of the characteristic of video streaming, we focus on the evaluation of the throughput improvement achieved by dynamic flow scheduling. And the performance gain is defined as the maximal throughput achieved within all of the flow scheduling strategies divide the throughput achieved by a static flow schedule strategy.

4   Motivation: Real-World Experiments

In this section, we carry out real-world experiments to assess the performance gain of dynamic scheduling in multihoming CDN. We deploy 2 peering severs in a Internet Data Center (IDC) site of Cycomm, a commercial IDC provider in China, to simulate a 2-multihomed CDN server. These 2 peering servers are connected to the ISP China-Unicom (labeled as ISP A) and the ISP China-Telecom (labeled as ISP B) respectively. We have 2 client networks, i.e., Tsinghua campus network (labeled as Client Network 1) and an ADSL network (labeled as Client Network 2). All of the server and client networks are deployed in Beijing. As illustrated in Fig. 2(a), The flow schedule then has the following strategies, (A, A), (A, B), (B, A) and (B, B). For example, (A, B) represents that the server delivers chunks to Client network 1 using ISP A and delivers chunks to Client network 2 using ISP B. We carry out experiments for 14 days. Every 15 min, all clients concurrently download video chunks whose size varies from several megabytes to tens of megabytes from the peering server using 4 strategies in turns, and we record the download speed of each strategy.

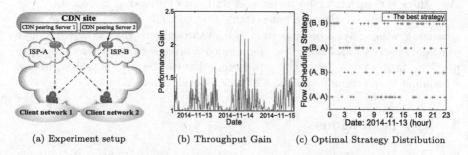

(a) Experiment setup   (b) Throughput Gain   (c) Optimal Strategy Distribution

Fig. 2. Real-world experiment with controlled clients.

Based on the traces recorded for the two controlled client networks, we plot the performance gain over three days in Fig. 2(b). The performance gain is that the maximal throughput achieved among all of the four strategies divides the throughput achieved by a static flow schedule strategy (always using (A, B) in our calculation). Our observations are as follows: (1) The best flow schedule strategy in multihoming CDN can significantly improve the throughput to both client networks (up to 2x); (2) The performance gain is varying over time following a daily pattern, and large gain is achieved during busy hours (daytime).

Furthermore, we investigate which strategies achieve the largest throughput over time. As illustrated in Fig. 2(c), we plot the *best strategies* for each time slot (15 min). We observe that the best strategy varies significantly over time and may be different in consecutive time slots, which indicates that in a real-world network condition, multihoming CDN needs to schedule flows in a dynamic manner by adjusting outgoing ISPs.

5   Performance Gain in Multihoming Video CDN

In this section, we analysis the performance gain of flow scheduling in different scenarios. We perform the controlled simulations to study the factors that intrinsically affect the the performance gain in multihoming CDN.

5.1   Simulation Settings

▷ **Network Topology.** Our simulation experiments are based on two types of network topologies: (1) Generated topologies. We use BRITE [13], a topology generation tools, to create different network topologies with the algorithms *Waxman* (a flat topology model) and *Transit-Stub* (referred to as TS, a hierarchical topology model); (2) Real-world topologies. We use four public datasets of network topologies (referred to as Real 1, Real 2, Real 3 and Real 4), from Route Views Project and Caida Website[1] in our experiments.

▷ **Network Link Capacity.** Due to the distribution of the link capacity is hard to know [16], we set the link capacities in the network following the heavy-tailed distribution ranging from 1 Gbps to 50 Gbps.

▷ **In-network Routing.** Conventional OSPF strategy is used to routing the packets between other nodes in our experiments, and the each link costs is setted as $10^8/Bandwidth$, following the default configuration of Cisco[2].

▷ **Multihoming CDN Settings.** 500 different topologies are generated for the same configuration (i.e., topology structure, client request, etc.) in our experiments. For each topology, we randomly choose one node which has three edges as the 3-multihoming CDN peering server, i.e., $|\mathcal{F}| = 3$ and $\mathcal{F} = \{A, B, C\}$, and 5 other nodes as client nodes (a client node represents a client networks in the

---

[1] http://www.routeviews.org/; http://www.caida.org/.

[2] http://www.cisco.com/c/en/us/support/docs/ip/open-shortest-path-first-ospf/
7039-1.html.

simulation), i.e., $|\mathcal{C}| = 5$ and we set the static flow strategy k as (A, A, B, B, C) for each topology simulation.

▷ **Throughput Calculation under a Flow Scheduling Strategy.** Given a topology with CDN servers and multiple client networks, we can calculate the server throughput of any flow scheduling strategy by formulating this question as a traffic engineering problem in [4], constrained by the capacities of links in the network and the bandwidth requirement of each client.

Note that we carry out other experiment with different setting and the results exhibit similar patterns, thus we only present the results of the simulation settings above in this paper due to page limitation.

5.2   What Influences the Performance Gain

We present the impact of different network topologies on the performance gain in Table 1. The client demands are set unconstrained (from 0 to ∞) to learn the maximum throughput we can get from the network. In this table, we denote the number of nodes as N, the number of links as M, and the minimal hop distance between the server and clients as H. This table shows the significant improvements ranging from 17 % to 56 %.

Next, we control three factors which characterize the network topology and reflects the dynamics of the network, to examine their influence on the performance gain of dynamic flow scheduling. Our observation and analysis are as follows.

More hops between server and clients lead to lower performance gain. BRITE allows us to generate topologies with different scales, i.e., different number of nodes and links between them. When the topology scales varying from 600 nodes to 100,000 nodes, the number of hops between a server and client networks is varying from 3 to 12. In Fig. 3(a), we observe a general trend that a larger number of hops between clients and a server leads to a smaller performance gain, i.e., the performance gain drops by around 10 % when the number of hops increases from 3 to 10.

Larger average node degree leads to lower performance gain. In Fig. 3(b), we plot the performance gain against the average node degrees, using

Table 1. Factors of network topology that affect performance gain in flow schedule.

Dataset	N	M	H	Performance gain (%)
Waxman	1000	2000	8	136.6
TS[1]	3000	6020	17	117.30
Real 1	22963	48436	8	131.96
Real 2	190920	607616	15	128.12
Real 3	54	58	6	156.55
Real 4	135	338	4	118.47

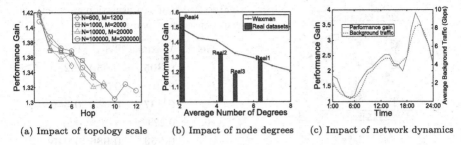

(a) Impact of topology scale   (b) Impact of node degrees   (c) Impact of network dynamics

Fig. 3. Factors of network topology structure and network dynamics that affect performance gain in multihoming flow scheduling.

topologies both generated and from real-world. We observe that the performance gain is usually smaller in topologies with a larger number of degrees. For example, the performance gain decreases by 20 % when the number of average degrees increases from 2 to 7.

Higher background load in the network leads to higher performance gain. We set the average background traffic in each hour based on the realword network workload as showed in Fig. 3(c). When the average background traffic increases, the performance gain improves, which indicates that the dynamic flow schedule can potentially make full use of the available capacity in a network topology.

6 Dynamical Flow Scheduling in Multihoming Video CDN

In this section, we design a local selection scheme to schedule flows from a multihoming CDN server to client networks. Firstly, we using an information gain approach to discover a set of parameters that have the most important impact on server throughput. Secondly, we present our local heuristic strategy, i.e., form a parameter combination to choose the outgoing ISP, which maximizes the information gain, so as to eventually improve the server throughput.

Next, we present the details of our design.

6.1 Parameter Selection Based on Measurement Insights

Based on our previous experiments and analysis in Sect. 5, we study the path characteristics between the server and clients, and design the following parameters for the flow scheduling. We define $TOPO_k$ as the set of links and nodes (e.g., routers) in the network topology that are involved in a flow scheduling strategy k. The parameters below are calculated from $TOPO_k$.

▷ **Parameters of Network Topology.** The parameters of a network topology are as follows, which can be collected by the server using network measurement tools like Traceroute: (1) P_k: the sum of links in all routing paths from the

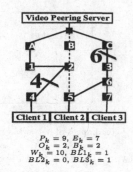

$P_k = 9,\ E_k = 7$
$O_k = 2,\ B_k = 2$
$W_k = 10,\ BL1_k = 1$
$BL2_k = 0,\ BL3_k = 1$

Fig. 4. Strategy $k = (A, C, C)$.

Table 2. Mutual information gain between throughput and parameters.

Metric	Waxman	TS	Real 1
E_k	**0.305**	**0.653**	**0.289**
P_k	0.195	0.541	0.254
O_k	**0.337**	**0.612**	**0.340**
B_k	0.228	0.412	0.296
W_k	**0.753**	**0.986**	**0.945**
$BL1$	0.160	0.234	0.264
$BL2$	0.110	0.298	0.129
$BL3$	0.098	0.184	0.165

server to clients; (2) E_k: the number of unique links in all routing paths from the server to clients; (3) $O_k = (P_k - E_k)$, which represents an "overlap" level of links among the paths to all the clients.

▷ **Parameters of Network Dynamics.** The parameters of network dynamics are designed as follows, which can be collected using tools like Pathneck [10]: (1) B_k: the number of "bottlenecks" in the delivery paths. A bottleneck is a link whose capacity constraints the video traffic delivery; (2) W_k: the sum of bandwidths of all bottleneck links. Furthermore, We split the paths between peering server and clients into three parts, and define parameter: (3) $BL1_k$: the number of bottlenecks that are located nearby the peering server; (4) $BL2_k$: the number of bottlenecks that are located in network; (5) $BL3_k$: the number of bottlenecks that are located nearby the clients.

To illustrate these parameters, Fig. 4 represents the strategy of $k = (A, C, C)$. In this topology, the solid segments represent the links that are actually used for delivering the flows (e.g., the flow goes through a path $A \to 1 \to 2 \to 4$ to client 1), and the slashes are bottlenecks. Then we calculate the value of these parameters as follows: $P_k = 9$, $E_k = 7$, $O_k = 2$, $B_k = 2$, $W_k = 6 + 4 = 10$, $BL1_k = 1$, $BL2_k = 0$, and $BL3_k = 1$.

We use an information gain approach [5] to identify the correlation between the parameters designed above and the throughput. The information gain of the parameter and the throughput is calculated as $I(\beta) = \frac{H(Y) - H(Y|\beta)}{H(Y)}$, where X denotes a parameter which we design, Y is fixed to be the throughput, and $H(X)$ denotes the entropy of the variable X. Table 2 shows the *information gain* of the parameters and the throughputs with the dataset of Waxman, TS and Real 1. We observe that parameters E_k, O_k and W_k tend to have the most significant impact on the throughput. To this end, we use them in our flow scheduling.

6.2 Local Heuristic Strategy for Flow Scheduling

Based on the selected parameters, E_k, O_k and W_k, we perform local selection scheme to schedule flows with a combination of parameters. A parameter combination $\mathcal{X} \in \mathbf{P}(\{E_k, O_k, W_k\})$, where $\mathbf{P}(\cdot)$ is a power set function. For a given parameter combination $\mathcal{X}$, a strategy k satisfies the combination if k optimize all the parameters. Since parameters E_k, W_k have positive correlations with the throughput, O_k has negative correlation with the throughput, the optimization goals for these parameters are different. For example, if the parameter combination is $\{E_k, O_k\}$, a strategy k, which maximizes the number of links in the delivery paths and minimizes the number of overlapped links, is a valid strategy.

Next section, we run experiments to demonstrate the effectiveness of the different combinations of parameters.

7 Evaluation

In this section, we verify the effectiveness of our design, and run experiments to demonstrate the performance of different combinations of parameters. We let param performance gain denote the performance gain achieved by strategies that satisfy the parameter combinations.

▷Effectiveness of Parameter Combination: We present the param performance gain achieved by strategies that satisfy the parameter combinations in Table 3, The "baseline" is the maximum performance gain. We observe that such simple parameters can significantly help a multihoming CDN to schedule flows efficiently. In particular, the param performance gain with a set of parameters is usually better than a single parameter. For example, in the Real 1 topology dataset, using a single parameter E_k to guide the flow scheduling achieves up to 40 % of the optimal performance gain, while a combination of $\{E_k, O_k, W_k\}$ can achieve 90 % of the optimal improvement.

▷ Performance under Dynamic Networks: We study the param performance gain in a dynamic network condition (i.e., changing background traffic over links). In Fig. 5, we plot the param performance gain with a varying background traffic over time. We observe that the performance gain is up to 32 %–98 % of the optimal performance gain (baseline) at 8 pm. We also observe that parameter

Table 3. Effectiveness of the selected parameters: param performance gain.

Metric	Waxman (%)	TS (%)	Real 1 (%)
Baseline	136.6	117.30	131.96
$\{E_k\}$	112.80	107.29	112.49
$\{O_k\}$	127.60	111.51	118.59
$\{W_k\}$	115.95	112.63	125.87
$\{E_k, O_k\}$	128.96	113.23	123.00
$\{E_k, W_k\}$	124.15	113.82	127.90
$\{O_k, W_k\}$	130.33	113.43	124.79
$\{E_k, O_k, W_k\}$	130.63	115.06	128.97

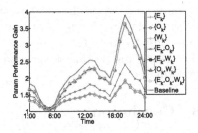

Fig. 5. Effectiveness of the selected parameters: param performance gain.

W_k plays an important role when the background traffic level is high. When the background traffic level is low (e.g., around 6 am), all these parameters achieve relatively similar performance gain.

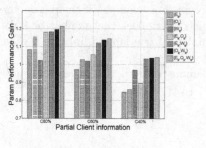

(a) Information loss of client networks.

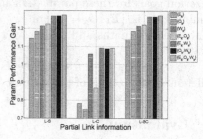

(b) Information loss of links.

Fig. 6. Impact of incomplete information.

7.1   Impact of Incomplete Information

In a real-world deployment, it may not be easy to collect complete information on all the parameters. We verify the effectiveness of the local selection scheme when information is incomplete.

▷ **Partial client information.** We first evaluate the performance when some client information is missing. Figure 6(a) shows the param performance gain when we calculate the parameters based on 80 %, 60 % and 40 % of the client' information. We observe that performance gain decreases as the information loss increases. In Particular, there is almost no performance gain anymore when the client information loss is 60 %.

▷ **Partial link information.** We may also lose information on links. We split the paths between the server and clients into three parts. L-S indicates we only have information about 2/3 links that are close to the server, L-C indicates we only have information about 2/3 links that are close to the clients, and L-SC indicates that we have information about 1/3 links close to the server and 1/3 links close to the clients. From Fig. 6(b), we observe that the information of links close to the server is more important, e.g., L-C misses the link information nearby the peering server, and its performance is obviously lower than the performance of the other two.

8   Conclusion

Multihoming has become a norm for video CDNs to improve the performance of content delivery. Our real-world experiments reveal that conventional rule-based flow scheduling strategies fail to provide good throughput in dynamic network conditions. In this paper, we study the impact of different network factors, including the network topology and the network dynamics, on the performance in dynamic flow scheduling, in a multihoming CDN. Based on our experiments studies, a set of parameters are selected to guide flow schedule in multihoming CDNs. We use an information gain approach to identify the importance of different parameters, and form a parameter combination to generate the flow scheduling strategy. Our evaluation results show the effectiveness of parameter combination, which achieves a throughput improvement up to 90 % of the optimal solution.

Acknowledgement. This work is supported in part by the National Natural Science Foundation of China (NSFC) under Grant No. 61272231, 61133008 and 61531006, Beijing Key Laboratory of Networked Multimedia, and the SZSTI under Grant No. JCYJ20140417115840259.

References

1. http://drpeering.net/white-papers/ecosystems/evolution-of-the-u.s.-peering-eco-system.html
2. Akella, A., Maggs, B., Seshan, S., Shaikh, A.: On the performance benefits of multihoming route control. IEEE/ACM Trans. Network. **16**, 91–104 (2008)
3. Akella, A., Maggs, B., Seshan, S., Shaikh, A., Sitaraman, R.: A measurement-based analysis of multihoming. In: SIGCOMM, pp. 353–364. ACM (2003)
4. Altin, A., Fortz, B., Thorup, M., Umit, H.: Intra-domain traffic engineering with shortest path routing protocols. Ann. Oper. Res. **204**(1), 65–95 (2013)
5. Balachandran, A., Sekar, V., Akella, A., Seshan, S., Stoica, I., Zhang, H.: Developing a predictive model of quality of experience for internet video. In: SIGCOMM 2013. ACM (2013)
6. Bindal, R., Cao, P., Chan, W., Medved, J., Suwala, G., Bates, T., Zhang, A.: Improving traffic locality in BitTorrent via biased neighbor selection. In: ICDCS 2006, p. 66. IEEE (2006)
7. Dhamdhere, A., Dovrolis, C.: ISP and Egress path selection for multihomed networks. In: INFOCOM (2006)
8. Genin, D., Splett, J.: Where in the internet is congestion? arXiv preprint arXiv:1307.3696 (2013)
9. Goldenberg, D.K., Qiuy, L., Xie, H., Yang, Y.R., Zhang, Y.: Optimizing cost and performance for multihoming. In: SIGCOMM CCR. ACM (2004)
10. Hu, N., Li, L.E., Mao, Z.M., Steenkiste, P., Wang, J.: Locating internet bottlenecks: algorithms, measurements, and implications. In: SIGCOMM 2004, pp. 41–54. ACM (2004)
11. Li, B., Wang, Z., Liu, J., Zhu, W.: Two decades of internet video streaming: a retrospective view. ACM Trans. Multimedia Comput. Commun. Appl. **9**(1s), 33 (2013)
12. Liu, X., Xiao, L.: A survey of multihoming technology in stub networks: current research and open issues. IEEE Netw. **21**(3), 32–40 (2007)
13. Medina, A., Lakhina, A., Matta, I., Byers, J.: BRITE: an approach to universal topology generation. In: MASCOTS. IEEE (2001)
14. Valancius, V., Ravi, B., Feamster, N., Snoeren, A.C.: Quantifying the benefits of joint content and network routing. In: SIGMETRICS. ACM (2013)

15. Wang, Z., Zhu, W., Chen, M., Sun, L., Yang, S.: CPCDN: Content delivery powered by context and user intelligence. IEEE Trans. Multimedia **17**(1), 92–103 (2015)
16. Yu, M., Jiang, W., Li, H., Stoica, I.: Tradeoffs in CDN designs for throughput oriented traffic. In: CoNEXT 2012. ACM (2012)

Homogenous Color Transfer Using Texture Retrieval and Matching

Chang Xing, Hai Ye, Tao Yu, and Zhong Zhou[(✉)]

State Key Laboratory of Virtual Reality Technology and Systems,
Beihang University, Beijing 100191, China
{xingchang,zz}@buaa.edu.cn

Abstract. Color transfer is a simple but effective technique of realistic rendering. Most methods of color transfer select the source image manually, which makes an inconsistent transformation in semantic areas. We propose a novel approach of homogenous color transfer by using texture retrieval and matching. Several images are found out from a database using the texture features of a target image, then the image with the highest texture similarity is set as the source image. With a simple interaction of brush stroke in the target image, the texture features of the covered pixels are used to extract a homogenous region in the source image and match between such regions. Afterwards, an adaptive color transfer scheme is applied in the matched regions. Owing to the texture retrieval and matching, this method produces a consistent visual effect results. We demonstrate experiments in image colorization, style conversion and exposure adjustment to verify the characteristics.

Keywords: Color transfer · Texture retrieval · Regions matching

1 Introduction

Color transfer is a research hotspot of image processing, which aims at changing the color style of a target image from a source image. It is widely used in many applications, such as movie making and artistic-designing. Most existing methods tried to avoid manual interaction so that they could be much more efficient and convenient than specialized tools such as Photoshop etc. Figure 1 demonstrates an example of color transfer which shows that the transferred result keeps both the content of the target image and the color style of the source image.

In the last decades, color transfer techniques have attracted increasing attention. Reinhard et al. [1] proposed a color transfer method by estimating the mean value and deviation of each channel, which is the basis of most color transfer methods based on statistical features. Pitie and Kokaram [2] proposed the best linear color transfer method, which used Monge-Kantorovicth theory of mass

Electronic supplementary material The online version of this chapter (doi:10.1007/978-3-319-48896-7_16) contains supplementary material, which is available to authorized users.

E. Chen et al. (Eds.): PCM 2016, Part II, LNCS 9917, pp. 159–168, 2016.
DOI: 10.1007/978-3-319-48896-7_16

(a)	(b)	(c)

Fig. 1. Example of color transfer. (a) Target image. (b) Source image. (c) Transfer result.

transportation to minimize the amount of color changes. Considering the spatial variation of color distribution, some methods using local features of images are presented. Tai et al. [3] optimized local color matching via probabilistic segmentation and apply an Expectation-Maximization scheme to infer the natural connectivity among pixels. Pouli et al. [4] proposed a novel histogram reshaping method that manipulated histograms at different scales and allows coarse and fine features to be considered separately. HaCohen et al. [5] presented a method that uses Generalized PatchMatch and a coarse-to-fine scheme to enhance the correspondence regions between two images with shared contents. Kagarlitsky et al. [6] proposed a method that performs color mapping between pairs of images under various acquisition conditions.

The source image is chosen manually in most color transfer methods. In many cases, the corresponding regions don't have any consistency in their physical attributes, such as semantic category. Undesirable results may be produced if the source image is inappropriate. e.g. the skin of a person in the target image would turn blue if the source image is a sunshine landscape. Besides, the manual selection increases the workload and the instability of the transferred results.

In this paper, a novel approach of homogenous color transfer based on texture retrieval and matching is proposed. Texture features of a target image are used to search a source image with similar content. Then, the color style is transferred between the corresponding texture regions from the source to the target. The main contributions of this paper are as follows:

- We propose a novel approach of color transfer using texture retrieval and matching. The source image is selected according to its texture similarity to the target image to ensure the rationality of the source selection.
- The corresponding regions of the source image and the target image are extracted and matched according to the features of a manual selected texture kernel. Then, the luminance and chrominance are processed respectively in the corresponding texture regions for the color transfer.
- The proposed approach is used in image colorization, style conversion and exposure adjustment to extend its applicability.

2 Our Approach

This section presents the processing procedures of the homogenous texture matched color transfer approach. First of all, a source image is selected from an image dataset according to the texture features of the target image. Then, the corresponding texture regions are extracted from the two images using the texture kernel which is estimated by drawing a simple brush stroke in the target image. Finally, the color style of the target image is transferred to the source image.

2.1 Image Retrieval Based on Texture Features

Generally speaking, geometry shape, color and texture provide most contributions to our awareness and understanding of an image. As a basic property of an image, texture reflects the content of an image, which decides its semantic category. The color transfer will be much more credible when the image contents of the source and the target belong to a same category than the others. Hence, it's better to choose the source image having a similar texture with the target.

Image retrieval is realized using texture features of the target image to determine the required source image. A variety of texture descriptors have been presented in the existing work over the past decades, such as gray level co-occurrence matrix (GLCM) [7], markov model algorithm (MRF) [8], discrete wavelet transform (DWT) [9] and local binary pattern (LBP) [10]. These typical descriptors each have their respective properties, and fit for describing a variety of different scenes.

The texture extract by GLCM gives out a good description for roughness of the texture. The LBP feature reflects the details of the image and it has the rotational and brightness invariance which is often used to classify the texture. The DWT feature reflects both the frequency domain information and the spatial information of the image, which can be used to do the multi-scale analysis. We introduce a texture descriptor with multi-features by combining GLCM, LBP and DWT. It is operated by merging the three feature vectors to be a comprehensive feature. At the beginning, the three feature vectors of a given image are extracted respectively. Setting the texture feature vector extracted by GLCM is $V_{GLCM} = [x_1, x_2, x_3, ..., x_i]$, the feature vector of the rotation invariant unified LBP model is $V_{LBP} = [y_1, y_2, x_3, ..., y_j]$ and the feature vector of DWT is $V_{DWT} = [z_1, z_2, z_3, ..., z_k]$. The merged vector is represented as $V = [x_1, x_2, ..., x_i, y_1, y_2, ..., y_j, z_1, z_2, ..., z_k] = [f_1, f_2, ..., f_N]$, thus the dimension of the vector $N = (i + j + k)$. Since the element value of the three vectors vary in the range, a Gaussian normalization is taken to limit the value range into $[0, 1]$, the Gaussian normalization is given by:

$$F_{p,q} = \frac{v_{p,q} - \mu_q}{\delta_q} \qquad (1)$$

where $I_1, I_2...I_M$ represent the images in the dataset, $v_{p,q}$ represent the vector f_q of I_p, μ_q represent the average value of f_q in all the images. $F_{p,q}$ represent the

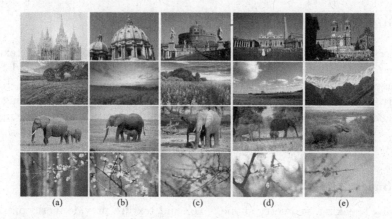

(a)   (b)   (c)   (d)   (e)

Fig. 2. Retrieved results. (a) Target image. (b), (c), (d), (e) are the retrieved results sorted by their texture similarity.

normalized result of $v_{p,q}$. In the source image retrieval, Mahalanobis distance [11] is used to estimate the texture similarity between the retrieved image and the target image. The distance of two images is defined as:

$$D = (F_s - F_t)^T S^{-1}(F_s - F_t) \tag{2}$$

where S represents the covariance matrix, F_s and F_t represent the normalized vector of the source and target image. GLCM descriptor is suitable for global texture, LBP descriptor is fit for detailed texture and DWT descriptor contains scale invariance. In order to be applied to images with different textures, the Mahalanobis distance of the three feature vectors are estimated respectively, and calculate a weighted sum. The weights of the three vectors are set to be adjustable. It is written as:

$$D(I_1, I_2) = \omega_1 D_{GLCM}(I_1, I_2) + \omega_2 D_{LBP}(I_1, I_2) + \omega_3 D_{DWT}(I_1, I_2) \tag{3}$$

where $\omega_1 + \omega_2 + \omega_3 = 1$ are weight coefficient of three descriptor.

Several images are picked out from the retrieved results according to the Mahalanobis distance as candidate source images for user preferences. Figure 2 demonstrates some examples of the retrieved results. The images in the figure are from Corel dataset and our own image library. It is shown that all of the retrieved results have a similar texture with the corresponding target image.

2.2 Texture Feature Based Region Matching

The texture features used in the image retrieval is estimated from the statistical information of the texture features within the global image. Actually, the similar textures between the target image and the retrieved image only occupy parts of the images. Extracting and matching the corresponding regions, and making

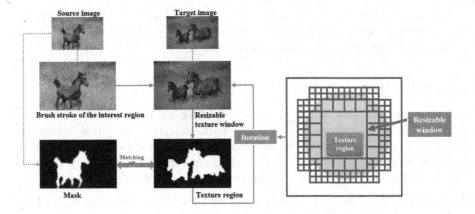

Fig. 3. Texture extraction and matched result.

the color transfer in the regions would improve the visual effect and credibility of the transferred result owing to their similar textures.

The procedure of the matching method is illustrated in Fig. 3. The first step of the method is to acquire a region of interest in the target image, which is operated by drawing a brush stroke in the image. The texture features of the covered pixels are extracted by GLCM and LBP are merged as a standard texture. Then, the retrieved source image is segmented into windows for finding the similar texture regions. The texture feature vector of each window is calculated, and compared with the extracted standard texture using Mahalanobis distance. The one having the smallest distance is selected as the core region of the textures and the features of this region is set as the texture kernel. Subsequently, the core region are expanded to enlarge the texture area. In order to make the expanded boundary as accurate as possible, a resizable texture window is used to update the boundary iteratively.

As shown in Fig. 3, large windows are used near the core area to ensure the consistency of the texture features, while the windows near the boundary are diminished to find an exact edge. The resizable windows are set as the same size with the core window starting from which the adjacent windows are set to be new members of the region if the relative texture distance is smaller than a preset threshold σ. Consequently, a rough edge is generated by the windows expansion. The size of the windows at the edge is zoomed out and the texture features of the zoomed windows are recalculated to get a more elaborate texture detail. Let μ be the texture feature of a window u within the boundary of the texture region, let l be the texture feature of a window v near u. Then the window v is merged in the texture region if $|\mu - l| < \sigma$ to refine the boundary. The process is executed iteratively to further update the region. Texture is a regional concept, which cannot be constituted by a single pixel. Thus, when the window size is too small to carry on enough texture information, the texture region is determined. In addition, to prevent the divergence of the texture area, the gradient descent is also used to restrict the boundary. Finally, the extracted texture region in the retrieved source image is matched to the mask of the target image which is extracted by user-specified segmentation mask [15].

2.3   Color Transfer Scheme

Color transfer consists of two parts: the transfer for the luminance and the transfer for the chrominance. For the first part, standard cumulative histogram method [12] is used to realize the luminance transfer, while for the chrominance transfer, Monge-Kantorovitch [2] linear color mapping method is used to transfer the color from the source image to the target in the color space LAB.

Luminance Transfer. We use the standard cumulative histogram method to transfer the luminance features. With this method, the detailed information of the image can be saved in the case of transforming the brightness histogram. The brightness distribution of the target and source images can become consistent by stretching the cumulative histogram of two images. The standard histogram of transfer function is defined as: $L_t = H^{-1}(T_l)$. H represents the normalized cumulative distribution function of irradiance, and T_l denotes the cumulative probability under the specified value in channel L within the target image. L_t means the irradiance value after migration. The result of the luminance of this target image after migration is shown in Fig. 4.

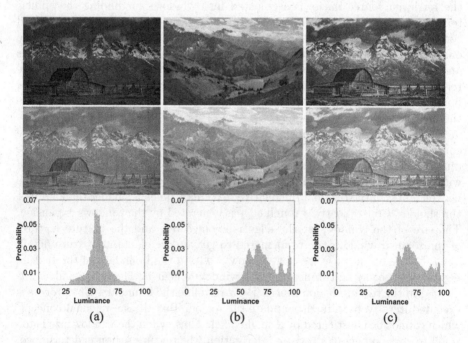

Fig. 4. Luminance cumulative histogram. (a) Target (b) Source (c) Transfer result

Fig. 5. Chrominance transfer. (a) Target image (b) Source image (c) Transfer result

Chrominance Transfer. Chrominance transfer means transferring the color information from the source image to target image. The method proposed in this paper is based on mass transfer in the field of theoretical Monte Carlo. This algorithm for color change depends on the orthogonal color space, so we need to convert the images into a three-channel decoupled Lab color space. Firstly, we use self-adaptive clustering algorithm based on K-medoids clustering method [13] to divide the image into three brightness band with the luminance information of each pixel. The Monge-Kantorovitch Linear Color Mapping is such a method that abstracts both the source image and the target image to a function, whose density distribution is continuous. With equations, a continuous T_{st} can thus be acquired so that the density distribution of the source image and the target image after transformation are similar.

The general formula description of image transform can be defined as:

$$t(u(a,b)) = T_{st}u(a,b) + t_0 \tag{4}$$

When the density function f for target image u and g for the source image v are in concordance with the Gaussian distribution, the Monte Carlo transform has the unique solution.

$$T_{st} = \sum\nolimits_t^{-1/2} (\sum\nolimits_t^{-1/2} \sum\nolimits_s \sum\nolimits_t^{-1/2})^{1/2} \sum\nolimits_t^{-1/2} \tag{5}$$

$\sum_t$ and $\sum_s$ represent the covariance matrix of the target image and the source image respectively. Figure 5 is the result of the chrominance transfer.

Weight Adjustment. In order to make the picture endowed with the characteristics of two images, variable parameters are set to adjust the weight relationship between the source and the target. As for luminance, we use ratio parameter to reset the brightness band: $L_{combine} = L_{target} * Rate \oplus L_{source}(1 - Rate)$. L_{target} represents the brightness band of the target, and L_{source} represent the brightness band of the source image. According to this formula, the luminance information of the $L_{combine}$ is re-divide and clustered. After that, the new clustering result can be used to adjust the luminance of the target image. As for chrominance, the chrominance a_t and b_t of a target image pixel are transferred to the corresponding a_t' and b_t':

$$\begin{bmatrix} a_t' \\ b_t' \end{bmatrix} = T_{st} \begin{bmatrix} a_t - \mu_{at} \\ b_t - \mu_{bt} \end{bmatrix} + \begin{bmatrix} \mu_{as} \\ \mu_{bs} \end{bmatrix} * Rate_{source} + \begin{bmatrix} \mu_{at} \\ \mu_{bt} \end{bmatrix} * Rate_{target} \tag{6}$$

Fig. 6. Weight adjustment. (a) Target image (b) Source image (c) Transfer result (d) Weight adjustment

Where μ_{as}, μ_{at}, μ_{bs}, μ_{bt} denote the mean values of a and b channel in the source and target image respectively. We set weight coefficient $Rate_{source}$ and $Rate_{target}$ for the source and target image respectively to adjust the weight relationship between the images. Through this method, the luminance and chrominance of the result image have both the characteristic of the source image and the target image. As shown in Fig. 6, through the adjustment of the weight ratio, the result image has both the characteristic of the source image and the target image.

3   Experiments

Colorization is a hot issue in the field of image processing to adding color to a monochrome image. However, it's an expensive task to established chrominance mapping to convert an 8-bit monochrome image into a 24-bit color image automatically. Most existing methods need time-consuming and careful adjustment to obtain a good result [14]. By our method, since the foregrounds of the target image is extracted and matched to a source image using its texture features. The color transfer of the monochrome image foregrounds is constrained by the matching area in the source image. Hence, the reliability of the corresponding color transfer is improved owing to their homogenous textures. Figure 7 demonstrates a colorization example to illustrate the effectiveness of our approach. Figure 7(a) presents the target image and the user-specified segmentation to be adjusted. Then, a brush stroke is drawn in the region of interest. With its texture feature, the segment result with homogenous texture in the source image is obtained in Fig. 7(c). The transfer result is illustrated in Fig. 7(d). The color transfer makes a natural and reality effect. More examples are given in supplementary materials, different types of the target images are experimented using our approach, the results show a consistent effect with human visual experience.

Since the retrieved image is highly similar with the target image, the proposed approach achieves a favorable color style conversion. Some results are demonstrated in Fig. 8 (and supplementary materials).

The colorization on monochrome gets ideal results, similarly, our method can process the image that is lack of brightness as well. For instance, we could use our method on exposure adjustment. Although the underexposed image is poor in visual perception, the local luminance variation keeps enough details of the texture information. Hence, the proposed approach based on texture is fit for

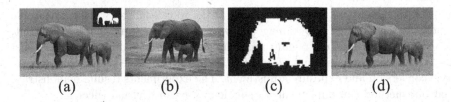

Fig. 7. Region mapping color transfer based on texture feature. (a) Target image with the mask and the interest area (b) Source image (c) Segment result (d) Transfer result

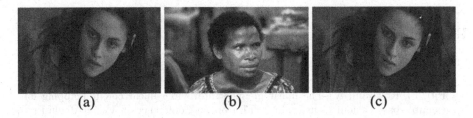

Fig. 8. Style conversion result. (a) Target image (b) Source image (c) Transfer result

Fig. 9. Exposure adjustment. (a) Underexposed (b) Normal (c) Adjustment result

such situation. In contrast, luminance stretching used in many existing methods to adjust the brightness often produces a loss of details and an excessive contrast. With our method, the details of the image is preserving by the correspondence of the texture region in the case of transforming the brightness feature from the source image. As shown in Fig. 9 (and supplementary materials), the results are nature and have an excellent visual experience.

4   Conclusion

In this paper, a novel approach of homogenous color transfer based on texture retrieval and matching is proposed. A source image is selected according to the texture similarity to the target image. With a simple interaction of brush stroke on the target image, we get the regions of interest through artificial selection.

In order to search for the similar texture in the source image, we use a resizable window to segment the source image and withdraw the texture region. After that, the corresponding texture regions are extracted and mapped for the color transfer. In the experiments, we used our method to process the image colorization, style conversion and exposure adjustment. The experiments results demonstrate that our method can implement a realistic and natural visual effect.

Acknowledgments. This work is supported by the National 863 Program of China under Grant No. 2015AA016403 and the Natural Science Foundation of China under Grant No. 61472020.

References

1. Reinhard, E., Ashikhmin, M., Gooch, B., Shirley, P.: Color transfer between images. IEEE Comput. Graph. Appl. **5**, 34–41 (2001)
2. Piti, F., Kokaram, A.: The linear monge-kantorovitch linear colour mapping for example-based colour transfer. In: 4th European Conference on Visual Media Production, vol. 1, pp. 1–9. IET, November 2007
3. Tai, Y.W., Jia, J., Tang, C.K.: Local color transfer via probabilistic segmentation by expectation-maximization. In: IEEE Computer Society Conference on Computer Vision and Pattern Recognition, vol. 1, pp. 747–754. IEEE, June 2005
4. Pouli, T., Reinhard, E.: Progressive color transfer for images of arbitrary dynamic range. Comput. Graph. **35**(1), 67–80 (2011)
5. HaCohen, Y., Shechtman, E., Goldman, D.B., Lischinski, D.: Non-rigid dense correspondence with applications for image enhancement. ACM Trans. Graph. (TOG) **30**(4), 70 (2011)
6. Kagarlitsky, S., Moses, Y., Hel-Or, Y.: Piecewise-consistent color mappings of images acquired under various conditions. In: 12th International Conference on Computer Vision, pp. 2311–2318. IEEE, September 2009
7. Haralick, R.M., Shanmugam, K., Dinstein, I.H.: Textural features for image classification. IEEE Trans. Syst. Man Cybern. **6**, 610–621 (1973)
8. Chellappa, R., Chatterjee, S.: Classification of textures using Gaussian Markov random fields. IEEE Trans. Acoust. Speech Signal Process. **33**(4), 959–963 (1985)
9. Mallat, S.G.: A theory for multiresolution signal decomposition: the wavelet representation. IEEE Trans. Pattern Anal. Mach. Intell. **11**(7), 674–693 (1989)
10. Ojala, T., Pietikainen, M., Maenpaa, T.: Multiresolution gray-scale and rotation invariant texture classification with local binary patterns. IEEE Trans. Pattern Anal. Mach. Intell. **24**(7), 971–987 (2002)
11. Mahalanobis, P.C.: On the generalized distance in statistics. Proc. Nat. Inst. Sci. (Calcutta) **2**, 49–55 (1936)
12. Tanaka, G., Suetake, N., Uchino, E.: Color transfer based on normalized cumulative hue histograms. JACIII **14**(2), 185–192 (2010)
13. Park, H.S., Jun, C.H.: A simple and fast algorithm for K-medoids clustering. Expert Syst. Appl. **36**(2), 3336–3341 (2009)
14. Levin, A., Lischinski, D., Weiss, Y.: Colorization using optimization. ACM Trans. Graph. (TOG) **23**(3), 689–694 (2004). ACM
15. Bai, X., Wang, J., Simons, D.: Video snapcut: robust video object cutout using localized classifiers. ACM Trans. Graph. (TOG) **28**(3), 70 (2009)

Viewpoint Estimation for Objects with Convolutional Neural Network Trained on Synthetic Images

Yumeng Wang, Shuyang Li, Mengyao Jia, and Wei Liang[✉]

School of Computer Science, Beijing Institute of Technology, Beijing, China
liangwei@bit.edu.cn

Abstract. In this paper, we propose a method to estimate object viewpoint from a single RGB image and address two problems in estimation: generating training data with viewpoint annotations and extracting powerful features for the estimation. We first collect 1780 high quality 3D CAD object models of 3 categories. Then we generate a synthetic RGB image dataset with viewpoint annotations, in which each image is generated by placing one model in a realistic panorama scene and rendering the model with a random camera parameters. We train a CNN model on our synthetic dataset to predict the object viewpoint. The proposed method is evaluated on PASCAL 3D+ dataset and our synthetic dataset. The experiment results show good performance.

Keywords: Viewpoint estimation · Convolutional neural network · Synthetic image · Panorama scene rendering

1 Introduction

When a person observes objects in a scene, he or she tends to perceive the coarse information, e.g. viewpoints, layout etc., before getting more details [1]. Estimating the viewpoint from a single image is important for the applications of traffic surveillance, robotic perception, object recognition and so on. Take the task of manipulating a cup by a robot as an example, even if a robot localizes the position of the cup in a RGB image, it can't grasp or move the cup without knowing the viewpoint of it.

To estimate the object viewpoint, the Convolutional Neural Network (CNN) model is an optional method which benefits from its ability of handling powerful features. In recent years, CNN method has achieved great success on a variety of computer vision tasks, such as image classification, detection, pose estimation and segmentation. Handling large labeled datasets for training and extracting stronger features helps to outperform state-of-art methods in these topics. In this paper, we apply a CNN model to estimate object viewpoint from a single image.

The obstacle of CNN method application is to get large-scale training data. For the problem of the viewpoint estimation, it is more difficult because annotating viewpoints mannually is time-consuming and inaccuracy. Take the dataset

© Springer International Publishing AG 2016
E. Chen et al. (Eds.): PCM 2016, Part II, LNCS 9917, pp. 169–179, 2016.
DOI: 10.1007/978-3-319-48896-7_17

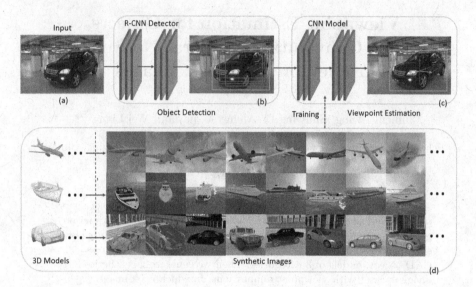

Fig. 1. The framework of our method. (a) Input a single RGB image. (b) A R-CNN detector. (c) The viewpoint estimation by a trained CNN. (d) Some examples of synthetic data for CNN training.

of PASCAL 3D+ [2] as an example, it provides about 22K annotated images for viewpoint estimation, which are far from meeting the requirement of CNN training. In this paper, we design a rendering pipeline which generates realistic RGB images with viewpoint annotations for CNN training.

Figure 1 demonstrates the framework of our method. Given a RGB image in Fig. 1(a), our method runs R-CNN firstly to detect objects in this scene (Fig. 1(b)). Then the viewpoint is estimated by a trained CNN model in Fig. 1(c). We collected three categories of 3D models, comprising aeroplane, boat and car. These models are rendered in 3DS MAX for the CNN model training (Fig. 1(d)).

There are three contributions in this paper:

(i) We design a pipeline to generate realistic synthetic images with annotation in panorama scenes automatically. This method is able to be generalized to other computer vision tasks easily.

(ii) We generated a high resolution synthetic image dataset for viewpoint estimation. The dataset includes 2.76M annotated images of 3 categories totally.

(iii) We train a CNN model to estimate object viewpoints. The results of experiment show a good performance on the benchmark dataset.

2   Related Work

Viewpoint estimation. Recently, computer vision community has been growing interest of the problem of viewpoint estimation for objects [3,4]. Herdtweck and Curio [5] used Random forest to estimate viewpoint. Fidler et al. [6] proposed a deformable 3D cuboid model for 3D object detection and viewpoint estimation. Some work [7,8] linked parts across views to represent continuous viewpoints. It is notable that CNN models have shown their remarkable performance in the estimation task [9,10].

Syntheitc data methods. In recent years, there is also a growing amount of work which used synthetic images to solve computer vision problems [11–16]. Peng et al. [13] used 3D models to render images for training object detectors. Stark et al. [17] used CAD models for recognizing 3D object. Gupta et al. [14] solved the problem of inferring 3D object pose with synthetic images. Lim et al. [15] used 250 chair models to render tens of thousands training images, which are then used to train deformable part models. In the meantime, Ubry et al. [16] expanded the number of models by one order of magnitude. They collected about 1.3K chair models for building key point correspondences between 2D images and rendered 3D views.

Dataset. ImageNet is a huge image dataset including 14.2M real images in 22K categories for object recognition [18]. Xiang et al. [2] provided a novel and challenging dataset which includes 22K images of 12 categories with 3D annotations. Besides, they also released an annotation tool to get continuous 3D viewpoint annotations. More recently, Su et al. [10] utilized the ShapeNet [19] to generate about 2.4M synthetic images for viewpoint estimation. They consider of adding background image after rendering models and then crop it, which improved the performance of the methods in [15,16]. Because images rendered with a fully transparent background cause the problem of overfitting. In this work, we design a synthetic image generating pipeline to get more realistic images, which renders models in a panoramic scene rather than overlapping the rendered images on a RGB image.

3 Approach

Given a single RGB image, our approach aims to estimate the viewpoint of an object in 3D space. The viewpoint of an object in 3D space is defined as a tuple $\Theta = (\theta_a, \theta_e, \theta_c)$, where $\theta_a, \theta_e, \theta_c$ are the azimuth, elevation and cyclorotation angle respectively. We model the estimation of viewpoint Θ as a regression problem. Compared with classification-based formulations [10,20], regression-based formulation output an exact value which is essential in most situations, e.g. robot grabbing. In this section, we design a CNN model to estimate Θ, which is trained on synthetic images.

3.1 Synthetic Dataset

Annotating training data with accurate viewpoint is impractical, because the process is expensive and involves ambiguous decisions. We propose to generate

Fig. 2. Rendering synthetic dataset. (a) An illustration of our rendering setting in a panoramic scene. (b) Some rendered images in this scene.

synthetic images by rendering techniques for two reasons: (i) getting accurate ground truth for each viewpoint; (ii) getting much denser data than real data.

Model Collection. We collected 3D models from online repositories such as TurboSquid (about 300K models) and cgtrader (about 250K models). While many of the downloaded models are not in good visual quality, we handpick the data carefully and normalize the center of all 3D models to the origin. As a result, we retain in total of 1780 high-quality 3D models of 3 categories.

Image Rendering. We select an appropriate panoramic scene, and place our model in the center of the scene. Utilizing 3DS MAX Script and VRay renderer, we render the 3D models by adjusting the parameters of the camera automatically. Instead of assuming the distance between camera and model center be fixed, we adjust the camera distance automatically according to the model size. By self-adjusting the camera distance, we obtain a suitable camera view in which the model occupies most of the rendered image.

We also sample the number of light sources, their positions and energies to get close to the real scene. Moreover, we set the azimuth, elevation and cyclorotation angles correspond with the distribution of the statistics of PASCAL 3D+ dataset, rather than randomly sampling the model from all possible views. More details will be discussed in Sect. 4.1.

It is worth noting that, the images rendered in our method is better than the ones rendered in transparent background which is highly contrasted. Our rendering method prevents the CNN model from overfitting by rendering in a panoramic scene rather than overlapping the rendered image on a random RGB image. The result dataset contains a total of 2, 670, 000 synthesized images, each annotated with the ID indicating the different style, as well as the viewpoint parameters Θ.

3.2   Building CNN Model

Inspired by the work in [21], we build a CNN model to estimate the viewpoint in this section.

Architecture of the CNN. The architecture of our CNN is demonstrated in Fig. 3. The structure of the network can be described by the size of feature maps

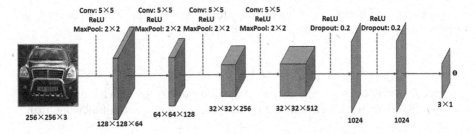

Fig. 3. Architecture of our proposed CNN. The input is a $256 \times 256 \times 3$ image cropped and rescaled from the detection process. The output is the viewpoint Θ.

at each layer as *input* $(256 \times 256 \times 3)$ - *conv*1 $(128 \times 128 \times 64)$ - *relu*1 - *pool*1 - *conv*2 $(64 \times 64 \times 128)$ - *relu*2 - *pool*2 - *conv*3 $(32 \times 32 \times 256)$ - *relu*3 - *pool*3 - *conv*4 $(32 \times 32 \times 512)$ - *relu*4 - *pool*4 - *fc*5 (1024) - *relu*5 - *dropout*5 - *fc*6 (1024) - *relu*6 - *dropout*6 - *output* (3×1).

In details, the input of the network is a cropped single RGB image and rescaled from detection process with a fixed size of 256×256 pixels. The output is the estimated values of viewpoint Θ. Our CNN consists of four convolutional layers to extract features and two fully connected layers to estimate viewpoint. For each convolutional layer, the size of the kernel is 5×5 pixels and its stride is 2 pixel. We then apply max-pooling operations after convolutional layers to increase the performance despite the reduction of resolution. The stride for pooling is 2 and we set the pooling operator size as 3×3. For feature extraction stage, the numbers of features in these four convolutional layers are 64, 128, 256 and 512 respectively. Following the four convolutional layers, there are two fully connected layers with 1024 hidden units. Instead of traditional sigmoid neurons, we use Rectified Linear Units (ReLUs) [22] in the two fully-connected layers to accelerate the stage of training without making a significant difference to generalisation accuracy. To reduce overfitting in training the neural network, we bring in a regularization method called dropout, which has been proven to be very efficient in [23]. At last, in the output layer, there is a linear activation function to predict the parameters of viewpoint Θ.

Loss Function and Training. Assume that $D = \{(I_n, \Theta_n) | n \in [1, N]\}$ means the training set, where I_n is the synthesis image, Θ_n is the viewpoint parameters and N is the amount of train images. Then the learning task is to minimize our defined loss function $L(w)$:

$$L(w) = \frac{1}{N} \sum_{n=1}^{N} f(I_n; w) + \lambda r(w)$$
$$w^* = \arg\min_w L(w) \tag{1}$$

where $r(w)$ is a regularization term which penalizes large weights to improve generalization. The parameter λ represents the weight decay that determines how you trade off between Euclidean loss and large weights. $f(I_n; w)$ is the loss term computed as the output of layers by the given w:

$$f(I_n; w) = \frac{1}{2}\|\psi(I_n; w) - \Theta_n\|_2^2 \qquad (2)$$

Similar with the work in [23], we train our model by stochastic gradient descent (SGD) with momentum and update weight decay in the following form:

$$
\begin{aligned}
w_t &= w_{t-1} + V_t \\
V_t &= r_t V_{t-1} - \alpha \nabla L(w_t) \\
r_t &= \begin{cases} \dfrac{t}{T}r_e + (1 - \dfrac{t}{T})r_s, & t < T \\ r_t, & t \geqslant T \end{cases}
\end{aligned}
\qquad (3)
$$

where w_t and V_t are weight and momentum variable respectively at epoch t, α is learning rate, r_t is momentum coefficient, r_s is starting momentums and r_e is ending momentums, T is a threshold to control how the momentum changes with the number of epochs.

4   Experiments

In this section, we demonstrate the results of our method for viewpoint estimation. We evaluate our viewpoint estimation system on both the PASCAL 3D+ dataset [2] and our synthetic dataset.

4.1   Dataset

Our dataset includes 2,670,000 synthetic images rendered from 1,780 high quality CAD models in 3 types: aeroplane, boat and car. In details, we collected 580 aeroplanes, 324 boats and 876 cars from web. Each model was rendered in total of 1500 times in specified camera parameters in different panoramic scenes.

The rendering parameters of viewpoints follow the statistical distribution of PASCAL 3D+ dataset. We use polar histogram to illustrate the distribution of azimuth angles of azimuth angles for both PASCAL 3D+ dataset and our rendered dataset in Fig. 4, where $0°$ corresponds to the front view of a model. The distribution of PASCAL 3D+ dataset is depicted by blue lines, whereas ours is depicted by red lines. Figure 4(b) denotes the distribution of elevation angles where $0°$ corresponds to the horizontal view of the model. Solid bars and shadowed bars represent PASCAL 3D+ dataset and our dataset respectively. Besides, bars in different colors mean different object category. As expected, the distribution of viewpoints is biased. For example, there is a high bias towards the front view (azimuth $\in [0°, 60°] \cup [300°, 360°]$) of car, and the elevation angles are most aggregated in $[-5°, 15°]$. These statisticses show that our dataset has a fairly good distribution in viewpoint variation to characterize the real scene.

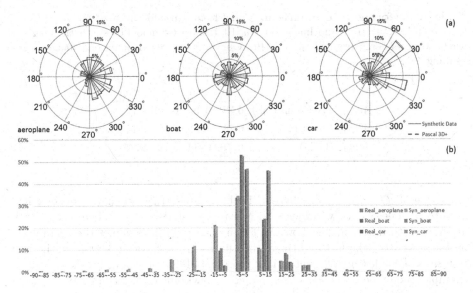

Fig. 4. Distribution of the data. The distribution of azimuths is displayed by three polar histograms in (a), blue lines represent PASCAL 3D+ dataset and red lines represent our dataset. (b) shows the elevation distribution histogram. Solid bars represent PASCAL 3D+ dataset and shadowed bars represent our dataset. Different color means different object category. (Color figure online)

4.2   Viewpoint Estimation

The detection results influence the viewpoint estimation. We consider the accuracy of viewpoint estimation in different detection settings in Fig. 5. In particular, the X-axis is the overlap ratio and the Y-axis is the accuracy. The overlap ratio O is the proportion of how much the detected bounding box overlapping the ground truth. We define an angel range δ. If the predicted value is within

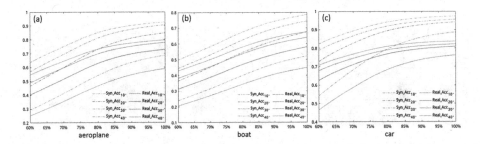

Fig. 5. Viewpoint estimation performance. The accuracy Acc_δ is a function of overlap ratio O and angel tolerance δ. The lines in different colors depict different angel tolerances. The solid lines and the dashed lines represent the accuracy on PASCAL 3D+ dataset and on synthetic dataset respectively. (Color figure online)

Table 1. Performance comparison. Model from Tulsiani [4] based on TNet was trained on VOC 12 train and ImageNet. Su [10] trained his model by synthetic images which were rendered from ShapeNet [19]. Ours used rendered panorama images for training.

Method	aero	boat	car	mean
$Acc_{30°}$ (Tulsiani et al.)	0.78	0.49	**0.90**	0.72
$Acc_{30°}$ (Su et al.)	0.74	0.52	0.88	0.71
$Acc_{30°}$ (Ours)	**0.79**	**0.64**	0.82	**0.75**

the range of $[G - \delta, G + \delta]$, where G is the ground truth, then we consider it as correct. The accuracy subjects to δ is represented by Acc_δ. The change of accuracy with different δ is shown in Fig. 5. The solid lines depict the accuracy on PASCAL 3D+ dataset and the dashed lines depict the accuracy on synthetic test set. The lines in different colors represent different error thresholds. For example, the green one means the predicted viewpoint error within 10°.

Fig. 6. The results of viewpoint estimation. The detected object is bounded by green boxes. We transform the object coordinate into the camera coordinate by the estimated parameters θ_a, θ_e, θ_c. The three colors of red, green, and blue represent three axes of objects in the camera coordinate. (Color figure online)

When the angel tolerance is fixed, the higher 2D detection performance (i.e. overlap ratio) of R-CNN is, the better accuracy we get. The performance on the synthetic test set is better than PASCAL 3D+, because the synthetic test images are more similar with the training data. Comparing with the results of synthetic test set in Fig. 5, when the overlap is 100% and angle range is 40°, the accuracy of car category on synthetic data is around 0.96 while the boat is just 0.79. We believe that the good performance of car category is because cars have similar shapes and more appearance features, such as headlights, automotive glass and so on. Meantime, we can see that the change of green lines in Fig. 5(c) is not as gentle as others, because global appearance features are necessary for cars. It's insufficient to estimate viewpoint if we just own local parts of cars.

Although we train the CNN model on pure synthetic data, our method achieves good performance on real data since the synthetic data provides enough features to estimate the viewpoint. The performance of our method and the comparative methods are shown in Table 1. We compare our method with two recent state-of-the-art work as Tulsiani [4] and Su [10]. They used similar network architectures (TNet/AlexNet) while their loss layer is different. From the comparison results, it is clear that our method outperforms the existing methods.

5   Conclusions

In this paper, we propose a pipeline to generate synthetic panorama images with annotations and design a CNN model trained on synthetic images to estimate object viewpoint. Our pipeline overcomes the limitation of lacking large-scale real images with annotations in CNN training. Our dataset includes in total of 2,760,000 images rendered from 1,780 models. It's worth mentioning that our synthetic images are rendered in panoramic scene using Vray renderer, they are more realistic and have high resolution. We evaluated our method on both synthetic and real data. Our method shows good performance on three object classes form both synthetic and real dataset and outperforms existing methods with the mean accuracy of 0.75.

References

1. Navon, D.: Forest before trees: the precedence of global features in visual perception. Cogn. Psychol. **9**(3), 353–383 (1977)
2. Xiang, Y., Mottaghi, R., Savarese, S.: Beyond PASCAL: a benchmark for 3d object detection in the wild. In: 2014 IEEE Winter Conference on Applications of Computer Vision (WACV), pp. 75–82. IEEE (2014)
3. Gu, C., Ren, X.: Discriminative mixture-of-templates for viewpoint classification. In: Daniilidis, K., Maragos, P., Paragios, N. (eds.) ECCV 2010. LNCS, vol. 6315, pp. 408–421. Springer, Heidelberg (2010). doi:10.1007/978-3-642-15555-0_30
4. Tulsiani, S., Malik, J.: Viewpoints and keypoints. In: 2015 IEEE Conference on Computer Vision and Pattern Recognition (CVPR), pp. 1510–1519. IEEE (2015)

5. Herdtweck, C., Curio, C.: Monocular car viewpoint estimation with circular regression forests. In: 2013 IEEE Intelligent Vehicles Symposium (IV), pp. 403–410. IEEE (2013)
6. Fidler, S., Dickinson, S., Urtasun, R.: 3d object detection and viewpoint estimation with a deformable 3d cuboid model. In: Advances in Neural Information Processing Systems, pp. 611–619 (2012)
7. Payet, N., Todorovic, S.: From contours to 3d object detection and pose estimation. In: 2011 IEEE International Conference on Computer Vision (ICCV), pp. 983–990. IEEE (2011)
8. Su, H., Sun, M., Fei-Fei, L., Savarese, S.: Learning a dense multi-view representation for detection, viewpoint classification and synthesis of object categories. In: 2009 IEEE 12th International Conference on Computer Vision, pp. 213–220. IEEE (2009)
9. Mottaghi, R., Xiang, Y., Savarese, S.: A coarse-to-fine model for 3d pose estimation and sub-category recognition. In: 2015 IEEE Conference on Computer Vision and Pattern Recognition (CVPR), pp. 418–426. IEEE (2015)
10. Su, H., Qi, C.R., Li, Y., Guibas, L.J.: Render for CNN: viewpoint estimation in images using cnns trained with rendered 3d model views. In: Proceedings of the IEEE International Conference on Computer Vision, pp. 2686–2694 (2015)
11. Oliver, N.M., Rosario, B., Pentland, A.P.: A Bayesian computer vision system for modeling human interactions. IEEE Trans. Pattern Anal. Mach. Intell. **22**(8), 831–843 (2000)
12. Nevatia, R., Binford, T.O.: Description and recognition of curved objects. Artif. Intell. **8**(1), 77–98 (1977)
13. Peng, X., Sun, B., Ali, K., Saenko, K.: Exploring invariances in deep convolutional neural networks using synthetic images. CoRR, abs/1412.7122, vol. 2 (2014)
14. Gupta, S., Arbeláez, P., Girshick, R., Malik, J.: Inferring 3d object pose in RGB-D images. arXiv preprint arXiv:1502.04652 (2015)
15. Lim, J.J., Khosla, A., Torralba, A.: FPM: fine pose parts-based model with 3D CAD models. In: Fleet, D., Pajdla, T., Schiele, B., Tuytelaars, T. (eds.) ECCV 2014. LNCS, vol. 8694, pp. 478–493. Springer, Heidelberg (2014). doi:10.1007/978-3-319-10599-4_31
16. Aubry, M., Maturana, D., Efros, A., Russell, B., Sivic, J.: Seeing 3d chairs: exemplar part-based 2d–3d alignment using a large dataset of cad models. In: Proceedings of the IEEE Conference on Computer Vision and Pattern Recognition, pp. 3762–3769 (2014)
17. Stark, M., Goesele, M., Schiele, B.: Back to the future: learning shape models from 3d cad data. In: BMVC, vol. 2, p. 5 (2010)
18. Deng, J., Dong, W., Socher, R., Li, L.J., Li, K., Fei-Fei, L.: Imagenet: a large-scale hierarchical image database. In: IEEE Conference on Computer Vision and Pattern Recognition, CVPR 2009, pp. 248–255. IEEE (2009)
19. Chang, A.X., Funkhouser, T., Guibas, L., Hanrahan, P., Huang, Q., Li, Z., Savarese, S., Savva, M., Song, S., Su, H., et al.: Shapenet: an information-rich 3d model repository. arXiv preprint arXiv:1512.03012 (2015)
20. Juranek, R., Herout, A., Dubska, M., Zemcik, P.: Real-time pose estimation piggybacked on object detection. In: Proceedings of the IEEE International Conference on Computer Vision, pp. 2381–2389 (2015)
21. Krizhevsky, A., Sutskever, I., Hinton, G.E.: Imagenet classification with deep convolutional neural networks. In: Advances in neural information processing systems, pp. 1097–1105 (2012)

22. Nair, V., Hinton, G.E.: Rectified linear units improve restricted Boltzmann machines. In: Proceedings of the 27th International Conference on Machine Learning (ICML-10), pp. 807–814 (2010)
23. Zhang, X., Sugano, Y., Fritz, M., Bulling, A.: Appearance-based gaze estimation in the wild. In: Proceedings of the IEEE Conference on Computer Vision and Pattern Recognition, pp. 4511–4520 (2015)

Depth Extraction from a Light Field Camera Using Weighted Median Filtering

Changtian Sun and Gangshan Wu[✉]

State Key Laboratory for Novel Software Technology,
Nanjing University, Nanjing 210023, China
chantesun@gmail.com, gswu@nju.edu.cn

Abstract. The invention of light field camera provides an approach of extracting depth from a collection of refocused photos. However, current depth from focus methods are suffering from the problem of inaccuracy, especially in the regions of object boundaries. In this paper, we propose a novel method to extract an accurate depth map from several refocused images. We first render a collection of images by uniformly changing the focal length. Then we deduce a rough depth map according to the amount of blur, which is measured by a multi-scale gradient operator. Finally, we apply a weighted median filter for refinement, which suppresses depth noise and supplies a well recovery of object boundaries and fine structures. The experimental results show that our method outperforms the built-in method from Lytro light field camera.

Keywords: Depth extraction · Light field · Weighted median filtering

1 Introduction

Depth from focus aims to recover the depth information from a set of refocused images [1]. Given a few images with different focusing parameters, we can calculate the implicit depth information. And this cast a light on the recovery of explicit depth information from the implicit information. It has been widely utilized in numerous multimedia applications, such as image-based rendering [2] and photo editing [3].

Many previous works capture different focused images sequentially, which are limited to static scenes. To illustrate, two images are acquired by varying the intrinsic parameters of the camera in [4] and two observations are obtained by two sets of lens parameters in [5]. Nowadays, the current light field camera [6] can capture 4D light field images in one shot, which enables rendering of arbitrary focused images of the same scene. Light field camera benefits various multimedia research [7,8], including depth extraction [9,10]. However, the efficiency or accuracy are still far from desired. Most previous studies involving depth recovery pay little attention to the refinement of depth maps, leaving out defects of inaccurate boundaries between different depths, wavy edges or noises in the depth maps.

© Springer International Publishing AG 2016
E. Chen et al. (Eds.): PCM 2016, Part II, LNCS 9917, pp. 180–189, 2016.
DOI: 10.1007/978-3-319-48896-7_18

In this paper, we propose a novel approach for depth from focus, which is featured for its effectiveness. We observed that depth images are full of smooth areas. Consequently, patch based depth inferring is far more robust than pixel-wise calculation. Though the patch based calculation will lead to flattening effects, it can be corrected by current joint edge-preserving filtering. Specially, we first obtain a rough depth map from a set of images refocused to different degrees, which are acquired by a light field camera in a single shot. In the camera, when the distance from the center of the lens and the image plane is viewed as a constant, the variance in focal length brings about different degree of blurring. When the blurring reaches its smallest, say, all the light rays radiated by an object point and refracted by the lens converges at a single point on the image plane, the object distance can be deduced from the focal length and the distance from the image plane to the lens center. Next, a multi-scale gradient operator and small windows are employed to work out the gradient of each pixel in images with distinct camera parameters in order to achieve higher accuracy and to get rid of the impacts of noise. However, these methods may give rise to vague boundaries or wavy edges which do not cater to the original input light field image. Therefore, at last, we need a filtering step under the guidance of the original image. Our work adapts constant time weighted median filtering [11] as a way of refining the rough depth map.

With the combination of gradient analysis of the input image and a refinement step guided by the original image, we can assure an accurate and reliable refined depth map.

Our approach outperforms the built-in depth map of the software, Lytro Desktop [12] in the way that it can recover more of the original outlines of objects. Moreover, the measure we take, constant time weighted median filtering [11], works better than the simple guided filtering [13] on the implicit depth map as it pays more attention to the actual depth of field than the outlines of objects.

2   Related Work

A number of current works devote to the recovery of depth in the images. However, nearly each of them has several defects.

In [14], a spatial constant σ needs to be evaluated. It needs two images that are identical except for the aperture size and therefore depth of field. Two σs can be derived from them and we can thereby work out the depth map. By contrast, our method works in a light field camera and images with different focal lengths can be gained. As a consequence, the parameter σ needn't be evaluated and large amount of time can be saved. Apart from this, our method does not possess the "overconstraint" problem that Alex's work has: if three or more views are obtained in the process, ambiguity of depth will be caused.

In a real-time focus range sensor [15], a passive way of evaluating the depth was adopted: an illumination pattern is projected onto the scene via the same optical path used to image the scene. This leads to a dominant frequency in the images gained and a depth map can be acquired by two images of the same view with different optical settings. Meanwhile, in [16], active measures are taken to get the depth map from the two images with distinct camera settings. However, the depth map derived from either of them is not precise and filters to refine the map need to be applied.

For passive depth from defocus, rational filters [17] can be adopted. In [17], median filtering was used in one example and *adaptive coefficient smoothing* in another. However, as we will point out, there are some defects in the simple median filtering. In addition, *adaptive coefficient smoothing* is only suitable for an image with background which lacks texture. Our method has overcome this disadvantage.

In our work, each of the series of images will be put to good use and a fine approach to filter the depth map will be utilized.

3   Approach

In this section, the input light field image is broken up into numbers of images and n images with different focal lengths are drawn from them uniformly, where n is a parameter given by hand according to our demand on the precision of the depth map. The gradient images are derived from the n differently refocused images using a multi-scale gradient operator. A rough depth map is acquired analyzing the gradient images. And a refined depth map is gained by filtering the rough one, as shown in Fig. 1.

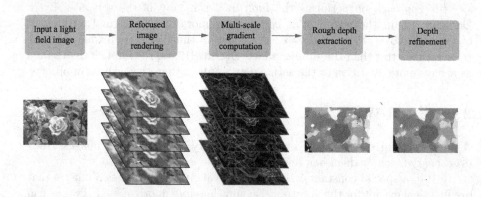

Fig. 1. A framework of our method.

3.1   Images with Different Focal Length

When the light rays radiated by an object point and refracted by the lens converge at a single point on the image plane, the following equation is satisfied:

$$\frac{1}{f} = \frac{1}{u} + \frac{1}{v}, \tag{1}$$

gradient (far focus)   gradient (medium focus)   gradient (near focus)

Fig. 2. The gradient maps with different focal lengths.

where f refers to the focal length, u refers to the object distance, and v represents the image distance.

Suppose an image plane is placed at a distance of v from the lens. Any object point placed behind the focus on the other side of the lens, which does not possess a distance of u from the lens, will cast a circle of confusion on the image plane. Whether the object is placed behind or in front of the intended distance u, a blurring of image can not be avoided.

In light field cameras, images with different camera parameters can be acquired from a single shot. What we need is a change in the focus to utilize the Eq. (1) to help us recover the field depth.

In practice, we need a uniform change in focal length, either from far to near or from near to far, so as to gain convenience in the processing procedure. In this paper, n refocused images can be gained from the input light field image with uniform change in focal length from far to near, with the help of the matching photo processing software of the light field camera.

In addition, an all-clear image with the largest f-number (the ratio of the focal length to the diameter of the aperture) is also available by the camera.

3.2 Acquisition of Rough Depth

A gradient map for each of the n images need to be worked out in the first place. A multi-scale gradient operator as shown in Eqs. (2) and (3) will work. It is superior to a simple Sobel or Scharr operator as the former ones may ignore the effects of smooth edges and are prone to noise.

$$P_{l,k}(x,y) = A_k(2^l x, 2^l y),\qquad(2)$$

$$G_k(x,y) = \sum_{l=0}^{m} Q_{l,k}\left(\frac{x}{2^l}, \frac{y}{2^l}\right),\qquad(3)$$

where l refers to the lth layer of the Gaussian Pyramid, whose maximum m can be adapted according to the characteristics of the input image; k refers to the index of the image picked and A_k refers to the pixel values of the kth image; $P_{l,k}$ is an image resizing A_k to its $\frac{1}{2^l}$. Being the lth layer of the Gaussian Pyramid; $Q_{l,k}$ is $P_{l,k}$ processed with the Sobel operator, and all $Q_{l,k}$s add up to the final gradient image G_k of A_k.

As shown in Fig. 2, the gradient varies as the focal length changes.

In order to raise precision and eliminate the effects of noise, a window at a certain width can be used to analyze the gradient of the very pixel at its center, as shown in Eq. (4). In this equation, $w(x)$ indicates the window at whose center is x. This also helps us reduce the impact of small trembles when shooting the series of images, which leads to dislocation in some of the n images.

$$\widetilde{G}_k(x) = \sum_{y \in w(x)} G_k(y). \tag{4}$$

In practice, integral image [18], which is also known as summed area table, is used in order to speed up the processing procedure. What's more, the edges of the images need to be paid attention to, and a mirror reflection of pixels on the edge tends to be a good solution.

A 25×25 or 15×15 window is usually used according to the objects' structures which make up the image. Small windows are appropriate for images with fine structures.

In this way, an optimized gradient value $\widetilde{G}_k(x)$ is gained for each pixel according to the values of its neighbors. For the pixels with the same coordinate in the n images, the maximum optimized gradient indicates that the pixel is at its sharpest, leading to a rough estimation of the optimal focus length of the very pixel.

Suppose that a pixel reaches its sharpest at the image indexed k, where

$$k = \underset{k}{\operatorname{argmax}} \, \widetilde{G}_k(x), k \in \mathbb{N}^+, k \leqslant n. \tag{5}$$

The largest focal length being $\max(f)$ and the smallest being $\min(f)$ in all n images, the optimal focal length of the pixel can be roughly represented as the following:

$$f_o = \frac{n - k + 1}{n}(\max(f) - \min(f)) + \min(f). \tag{6}$$

Therefore, according to Eq. (1), the rough depth of the very pixel can be estimated as:

$$\widetilde{u} = \frac{f_o v}{v - f_o}. \tag{7}$$

where v is a known camera parameter.

3.3   Attainment of Accurate Depth

Median filtering needs to be used so as to remove outlier noise. However, a simple median filter may result in the loss of sharp features of an image. Consequently, in order for suppressing the influence of nearby pixels in different colors along with preserving sharp edges and fine structures, the method of weighted median filtering is used:

$$f(\boldsymbol{x}, i) \triangleq \delta(V(\boldsymbol{x}) - i), \tag{8}$$

$$h(\boldsymbol{x}, i) = \sum_{\boldsymbol{x}' \in \mathcal{N}(\boldsymbol{x})} b(\boldsymbol{x}, \boldsymbol{x}') f(\boldsymbol{x}', i), \tag{9}$$

where $\boldsymbol{x}$ represents the pixel's coordinate; $V(\boldsymbol{x})$ represent its value in the rough depth map; V equals to $\widetilde{u}$ in Eq. (7); δ is the delta function which equals to 0 when $V(\boldsymbol{x}) = i$ and 1 otherwise.

Meanwhile, $h(\boldsymbol{x}, i)$ can be illustrated as a local histogram and $b(\boldsymbol{x}, \boldsymbol{x}')$ is the weight function. In order for the feature of the input image to be preserved, we can use guided filter weights for $b(\boldsymbol{x}, \boldsymbol{x}')$.

In a guided filter [13], the local linear model is represented as:

$$\mathbf{a}_k = (\Sigma_k + \epsilon U)^{-1}(\frac{1}{|w|} \sum_{i \in w_k} \mathbf{I}_i p_i - \mu_k \bar{p}_k), \tag{10}$$

$$b_k = \bar{p}_k - \mathbf{a}_k^T \mu_k, \tag{11}$$

$$q_i = \bar{\mathbf{a}}_i^T \mathbf{I}_i + \bar{b}_i, \tag{12}$$

where $\mathbf{a}_k$ is a 3×1 coefficient vector, q is a linear transformation of $\mathbf{I}$ in the window w_k centered at the pixel k, Σ_k is a 3×3 covariance matrix of $\mathbf{I}$ and U is a 3×3 identity matrix.

input light field image   rough depth map   refined depth map

Fig. 3. Rough depth map refinement. The refined depth map in the third column is gained from the second column by constant time weighted median filtering [11] under the guidance of the image with largest f-number.

In Fig. 3, a refined depth map is gained from a rough one under the guidance of the image with the largest f-number. Compared with the rough depth map, noises have been removed and the outlines of objects tend to be more accurate. Additionally, the depth map of the background has a tendency to be softer, which conforms to our real life perception.

4   Experiments

4.1   Experimental Settings

In our experiments, $n = 64$ is used for drawing images at different focal lengths from the input light field image. A 25×25 window and $m = 2$ is used for calculating the optimized gradient of images with few fine structures. In the mean time, 15×15 windows and $m = 0$ is used for images with fine structures. Windows too small may lead to extra black edges or white holes for objects while windows too large may result in blocks of colors.

As we want to make full use of the 8 digits of the grayscale images for a depth map, we apply $[0, 1, 2,..., 255]$ for the vector of disparities. However, if the calculating process were too time-consuming on a certain machine, especially for images with big sizes, the number of disparities could be reduced. A little sacrifice on the diversity of gray scale of the depth map can save a great amount of time. In addition, the local window radius for guided filter weights is usually set to $\frac{1}{40}$ of the maximum of the input image's width and height. The regularization parameter is $\epsilon = 10^{-4}$.

4.2   Results and Discussions

Our depth map has proven to correspond more with the original image. It can be seen from Fig. 4, the built-in depth maps of Lytro Desktop tend to have wavy edges while constant time weighted median filtering [11] helps us smooth the structures. On the other hand, the outlines of objects in the built-in depth map is not so accurate as ours. Our method can show fine structures which appear in the original image.

The use of constant time weighted median filtering [11] also helps us erase some white or black blocks in the rough depth maps caused by the ambiguity of gradient change of small areas in the input light field image, just as shown in Fig. 5. The lack of texture results in this ambiguity, and a smooth surface or highlights on objects may accounts for the lack of texture.

In order for a better result, images with high variance in focal length is preferred. This contributes to the n images having greater discrimination in gradient with each other. In practice, objects which are close enough to the camera lens and objects which are far away enough in the input images are preferred so as to achieve high variance in focal length.

Compared to the results of the simple guided image filtering [13], this weighted median filtering [11] using guided filter weights pays more attention to the actual depths of the original image. As is shown in Fig. 6, the former method may produce halo effects and pays too much to the structure of the objects as well as the lighting condition on the surface of the objects. However, the latter method only reflects the depth information we need, which leads to accuracy.

There are still some limitations in our method. For objects with large textureless areas like the sky, our method will fail to predict the accurate depth for

input light field image   Lytro Desktop's built-in   our method

Fig. 4. A comparison between the Lytro Desktop's built-in depth map and our depth map. The first two light field images are available at http://lightfield-forum.com/.

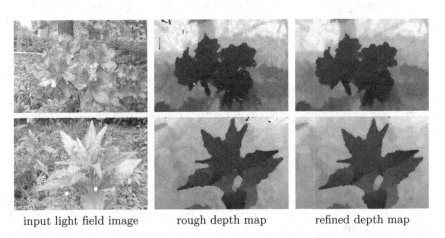

input light field image   rough depth map   refined depth map

Fig. 5. Constant time weighted median filtering [11] removes black and white blocks caused by the ambiguity in the gradient change.

| input light field image | guided image filtering | weighted median filtering |

Fig. 6. A comparison between guided image filtering [13] and constant time weighted median filtering [11]. The light field images are available at http://lightfield-forum.com/.

the lack of gradients. Fortunately, textureless regions can be easily detected to prevent errors in applications.

5   Conclusion

In this paper, we have presented a novel depth from focus method from a series of images using a light field camera. By employing the multi-scale gradient operator, we achieved a robust measurement for the amount of blur. Besides, by using the constant time weighted median filtering, accurate depth maps with clear boundaries are obtained. The experiments have proven that our measure surpasses the built-in measure in the Lytro light field camera.

Acknowledgments. This work is supported by National Science Foundation of China (61321491) and Collaborative Innovation Center of Novel Software Technology and Industrialization.

References

1. Grossmann, P.: Depth from focus. Pattern Recogn. Lett. **5**(1), 63–69 (1987)
2. Shum, H.-Y., Chan, S.-C., Kang, S.B.: Image-Based Rendering. Springer, Heidelberg (2008)
3. Oh, B.M., Chen, M., Dorsey, J., Durand, F.: Image-based modeling and photo editing. In: Annual Conference on Computer Graphics and Interactive Techniques, pp. 433–442. ACM (2001)

4. Ziou, D., Deschenes, F.: Depth from defocus estimation in spatial domain. Comput. Vis. Image Underst. **81**(2), 143–165 (2001)
5. Namboodiri, V.P., Chaudhuri, S.: On defocus, diffusion and depth estimation. Pattern Recogn. Lett. **28**(3), 311–319 (2007)
6. Ng, R., Levoy, M., Brdif, M., Duval, G., Horowitz, M., Hanrahan, P.: Light field photography with a hand-held plenoptic camera. Comput. Sci. Tech. Rep. CSTR **2**(11), 1–11 (2005)
7. Zhang, X., Wang, Y., Zhang, J., Liangmei, H., Wang, M.: Light field saliency vs. 2D saliency: a comparative study. Neurocomputing **166**, 389–396 (2015)
8. Zhang, J., Wang, M., Gao, J., Wang, Y., Zhang, X., Wu, X.: Saliency detection with a deeper investigation of light field. In: International Joint Conference on Artificial Intelligence, pp. 2212–2218 (2015)
9. Zhou, C., Lin, S., Nayar, S.K.: Coded aperture pairs for depth from defocus and defocus deblurring. Int. J. Comput. Vis. **93**(1), 53–72 (2011)
10. Tao, M., Hadap, S., Malik, J., Ramamoorthi, R.: Depth from combining defocus and correspondence using light-field cameras. In: IEEE International Conference on Computer Vision, pp. 673–680 (2013)
11. Ma, Z., He, K., Wei, Y., Sun, J., Wu, E.: Constant time weighted median filtering for stereo matching and beyond. In: IEEE International Conference on Computer Vision, pp. 49–56 (2013)
12. Lytro Desktop. https://illum.lytro.com
13. He, K., Sun, J., Tang, X.: Guided image filtering. In: European Conference on Computer Vision, pp. 1–14 (2010)
14. Pentland, A.P.: A new sense for depth of field. IEEE Trans. Pattern Anal. Mach. Intell. **4**, 523–531 (1987)
15. Nayar, S.K., Watanabe, M., Noguchi, M.: Real-time focus range sensor. IEEE Trans. Pattern Anal. Mach. Intell. **18**(12), 1186–1198 (1996)
16. Chaudhuri, S., Rajagopalan, A.N.: Depth from Defocus: A Real Aperture Imaging Approach. Springer, New York (2012)
17. Watanabe, M., Nayar, S.K.: Rational filters for passive depth from defocus. Int. J. Comput. Vis. **27**(3), 203–225 (1998)
18. Lewis, J.P.: Fast template matching. Vis. Interface **95**(120123), 15–19 (1995)

Scale and Topology Preserving SIFT Feature Hashing

Chen Kang[1], Li Zhu[1], and Xueming Qian[1,2,3](✉)

[1] School of Software Engineering, Xi'an Jiaotong University,
Xi'an 710049, China
kangchen@stu.xjtu.edu.cn,
{zhuli, qianxm}@mail.xjtu.edu.cn
[2] The Ministry of Education Key Laboratory for Intelligent Networks
and Network Security, Xi'an Jiaotong University, Xi'an 710049, China
[3] School of Electronic and Information Engineering, Xi'an Jiaotong University,
Xi'an 710049, China

Abstract. In recent years, content based image retrieval has been concerned because of practical needs on Internet services, especially methods that can improve retrieving speed and precision. Thus, we propose a hashing scheme called Geometry and Topology Preserving Hashing for content based image retrieval. A training process of hashing function involves both of geometric information and topology information is introduced. Compared with state-of-the-art methods, our method gives better precision in experiment on the Oxford Building dataset.

Keywords: CBIR · Hashing · Geometric information · SIFT · GTPH

1 Introduction

Due to the explosive increasing of multimedia data on the Internet, searching for the wanted information has become a problem for all users. An attractive domain in this issue is retrieving similar visual data. Efforts have been made to improve the precision and speed in Content Based Image Retrieval (CBIR) [1, 2, 16, 23–27]. While keeping the matching precision, one solution to increase the searching speed in CBIR is by using hashing method to embed high-dimensional visual features of an image to lower dimension like Hamming space, as it is more efficient in similarity search [1].

The aim of hashing is to learn binary representations of an existing dataset to make sure that the neighbourhood structure in original space is the same with that in Hamming space. However, because of the embedding and the limit of binary code length, a loss of original data is usually caused, which will lead to a decrease of precision in image retrieval. Thus, making less loss is very important.

The aim of this paper is to gain a hash function that can not only preserve the topology information of the data, but also the geometric information of SIFT descriptors [1, 18, 23–27], so that retrieving precision can be improved.

In our work, scale factor of SIFT descriptor is involved into hashing embedding as geometric information. It is involved into training process to make the hashed features

© Springer International Publishing AG 2016
E. Chen et al. (Eds.): PCM 2016, Part II, LNCS 9917, pp. 190–199, 2016.
DOI: 10.1007/978-3-319-48896-7_19

not only preserve distance relation in Euclidean space, but also preserve the scale relation to refine the embedded features.

This paper has following contributions: (1) the proposed method has considered geometric information with topology preserving hashing, which improves the differentiation in hash function training; (2) it gives a significant improvement in precision comparing to the state-of-art methods.

In the following sections, the related work is described in Sect. 2; the description of our method is in Sect. 3; experiments and results are shown in Sect. 4; Sect. 5 is the conclusion.

2 Related Work

Many methods have been proposed to involve different factors in LSH hashing methods. Hashing involved methods are very popular in efficient ANN search [1]. Locality Sensitive Hashing (LSH) [3] method is one of the most well-known data-independent methods, as hash functions use simple random projections [4–6]. In theory, the longer the code length is, the more of the similarity between data preserves.

Data-dependent LSH methods like K-means Locality Sensitive Hashing (KLSH) [7] and PCA-hashing (PCAH) [8] are proposed to make hash functions more specified. As Yu et al. proposed in [8], it uses Principal Component Analysis (PCA) to reduce dimensions and preserve the principal component of a given dataset. Later, Gong et al. improved PCAH in [9] (ITQ) by adding an orthogonal rotation matrix to refine the projection matrix to improve the precision of quantization.

Many efforts have been made to involve geometric information into different methods to work out different situations as well. For example, Vyshali et al. [10] proposed showing a normalized scale contour coding to preserve shape description, but it is very limited in complex pictures. Zhang et al. [11] proposed making a geometry preserving visual phrases (GVP) to combine bag-of-visual-words method and spatial information. Yang et al., propose to utilize the salient visual phrase mined from multiple queries by mobile end [24, 25]. It shows that the contextual saliency information can improve the retrieval performance and reduce the required bandwidth dramatically. Scalable Graph Hashing (SGH) [12] can approximate the whole graph without explicitly computing the similarity graph matrix and preserve the entire similarity information in the dataset. Many supervised and semi-supervised methods such as [13–17] involve tagged data in training process to capture more data variance and sematic neighborhood as well.

One of the most advanced methods is Topology Preserving Hashing (TPH) [18, 19], which is proposed after ITQ by Zhang et al. In their work, a neighborhood distance difference matrix used for exploits the neighborhood rankings and a topo-weighting matrix are presented to preserve the topology of given data in training process based on ITQ.

However, these methods have limited outcome, since the descriptor has lacked of some original information already. Therefore, adding more elements into hash function training becomes feasible.

Talking about descriptors, local features like SIFT [20], PCA-SIFT [8] and SURF [21] are better in detail preserving. In SIFT feature extraction, Difference of Gaussian (DoG) detector is used to find interest points < x, y, scale, orientation >, and theses interest points are described by the 128-dimension SIFT descriptor. While SURF gets least time cost and best robust to changes of illumination in experiment on the same dataset, it has no interest point in extraction. SIFT finds more matches than SURF and PCA-SIFT, and it is invariant to scale, rotation and blur [22]. Especially, the geometric information explored from the location, scale and orientation makes the retrieval more robust against various variations [23–27].

3   Scale and Topology Preserving Hashing Method

In this paper, we propose a Geometry and Topology Preserving Hashing (GTPH) for SIFT feature matching. We first give the system overview of our approach. Then we give the corresponding models in training the GTPH, and at last we describe the similarity measurement.

3.1   System Overview

The flow chart is as Fig. 1. SIFT features of dataset should be extracted off-line. In extraction, we can get a 128-dimensional descriptor and a scale value for each feature point. Then, picking out training set to train a hash function following our steps in Sect. 3.2. We use the hash function to hash descriptors of each image, after which we can have binary descriptors of all images. When a query is given, use similarity evaluating method represented in Sect. 3.3 to get similarity scores. The smaller the score is, the more similar two images are.

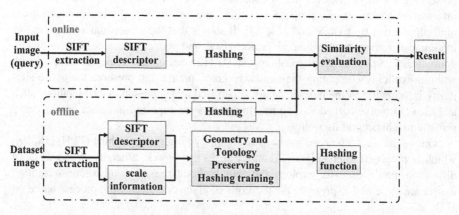

Fig. 1. Flow chart of the proposed scale and topological preserved hashing

3.2 Geometry and Topology Preserving Hashing for SIFT

Hashing-based similarity search methods are popular in image retrieval with big data. In order to acquire effective hash function, topology has been taken into consideration. Topology Preserving Hashing (TPH) [18, 19] shows that using topology preserving is acceptable in some cases. Adding more elements into hash function training can cover the shortage that the 128-dimension SIFT descriptor has lacks of scale factor, which is very useful in similarity evaluation.

In this paper, geometric information is considered in training process. Here we describe Geometry and Topology Preserving Hashing (GTPH) as following.

- Dataset Generation

To make the trained GTPH robust to the different applications, we need to prepare a large scale SIFT point dataset, in which SIFT points can be down-sampling from 5 K images.

A zero-centered matrix $X_{128 \times n}$ is consisted of all SIFT descriptors from a dataset; each column is a descriptor, and the related feature points are defined as a dataset X'. n training samples should be chosen randomly from X'. For each sample (i.e. the selected SIFT point), we get its nearest k neighbor points which are measured by the Euclidean distance of 128 dimensional SIFT feature descriptors, and l points are selected randomly from the points that far away from its nearest neighbors as well. These nearest points and non-neighbor points build up a neighbor set N_i.

The training set and all neighbor sets build up a set defined as $T' = \{x_i\}_{i=1}^{n} \cup \{N_i\}_{i=1}^{n}, x_i \in X', N_i \in X'$, which makes up a training matrix $T_{128 \times t}(t = n(1 + k + l))$. Its rows and columns are ranked in the same order, which will be emphasized in our later description. l points are used for getting more robustness, and usually l is less than k. In our experimentation, we use $k = 4$ and $l = 1$.

- Geometry and Topology Extraction and Regulation

To involve geometry and topology information into hash training in the next part, we need to propose a matrix Γ_t which takes the geometric and topology relationships among training samples. Thus we build up four matrices: Γ_r, Γ_s, S_r and S_s. These four matrices build up Γ_t. When computing them, the order of columns and rows should be the same with T's correspondingly.

Rank-Weighting matrix Γ_r and Simi-Weighting matrix Γ_s are defined with the method proposed in [18]. Γ_r represents Euclidean distance deviation and Γ_s means the relative ranking of each sample point's neighbors' distances.

To involve geometric information, we address $t \times t$ matrices S_r and S_s that can preserve the scale ranking and similarity into hash training.

First, we shall have S_r to keep the scale ranking. The normalised scale distance of feature points x_i and x_j is written as $ds(s_i, s_j) = |s_i - s_j|/\max(s_i, s_j)$. x_i is a sample from training set, and is no more than the number of training samples. x_j is a neighbor point of x_i in N_i. For every sample x_i expressed as a 128×1 SIFT descriptor matrix in the training set, the average scale difference is calculated as function (1) and scale deviation $S_r(i, j)$ is as function (2).

$$\bar{s}_i = \sum_{x \in N_i} \mathrm{ds}(s_i, s_j)/|N_i| \tag{1}$$

$$\mathbf{S}_r(i,j) = \begin{cases} \bar{s}_i - \mathrm{ds}(s_i, s_j) \\ 0 \end{cases} \tag{2}$$

where N_i represents the neighbor set, and $|N_i|$ is the member number of it. The bigger of s_j means it is less similar to s_i, as the larger value $\mathbf{S}_r(i,j)$ will be, which leads to s_j is more specific in the training set.

$\mathbf{S}_s$ involves the scales' relation in the following function (3).

$$\mathbf{S}_s(i,j) = 2 \times \exp\{-\mathrm{ds}^2(x_i, x_j)/\sigma_s^2\} - 1 \tag{3}$$

where σ_s is the average Euclidean distance of points' scales, and is calculated with 2% of X'. A larger absolute value of $\mathbf{S}_s(i,j)$ means x_j is more different with x_i.

These two matrices can enhance the geometry relationship between training points in training process.

Here, we have got four matrices to emphasis the geometry and topology relationship between training points. The last process is to integrate the four matrices, as function (4).

$$\boldsymbol{\Gamma}_t = \beta[(1-\gamma)\boldsymbol{\Gamma}_r + \gamma\boldsymbol{\Gamma}_s] + (1-\beta)[(1-\gamma)\mathbf{S}_r + \gamma\mathbf{S}_s] \tag{4}$$
$$\gamma, \beta \in (0,1)$$

where γ is the weight to balance the matrix $\boldsymbol{\Gamma}_r$ and $\mathbf{S}_r$ with neighborhood relationship preserving matrix $\boldsymbol{\Gamma}_s$ and $\mathbf{S}_s$, while weights the importance of the 128-dimension feature to the scale.

- Hash Function Training

In this part, we use the basic method in [9, 19] to train our hash function. A hash function is to map descriptors into a lower dimension while making the most similar ones in original space still has a large possibility being similar in the lower dimension. Thus, the training consists of two steps: First, use PCA [9] to get the principal component of geometry and topology emphasized dataset. Second, use SVD to minimize the loss of quantization. They are described as following.

1. Principal Component Extraction

Follow PCA [9] method to solve an eigen-decomposition of matrix $\mathbf{A}$ given by

$$\mathbf{G} = \mathbf{T} \times (\boldsymbol{\Gamma}_t + \boldsymbol{\Gamma}_t^{\mathrm{T}}) \times \mathbf{T}^{\mathrm{T}} + \mathbf{X} \times \mathbf{X}^{\mathrm{T}} \tag{5}$$

$$\mathbf{A} = \mathbf{G} + \mathbf{G}^{\mathrm{T}} \tag{6}$$

where $\times$ represents matrix multiplication. $\mathbf{X}$ is the matrix built up with all 128-dimensional descriptors of all images in the dataset.

G is a matrix that can carry both of neighborhood ranking and relationship information. From the first term $\mathbf{T} \times (\mathbf{\Gamma}_t + \mathbf{\Gamma}_t^T) \times \mathbf{T}^T$ we can extract the principal components of descriptors that preserve geometric and topology relationship of the training set. The second term $\mathbf{X} \times \mathbf{X}^T$ is for preventing overfitting.

G is not a symmetric matrix, thus we should process it as function (6).

The m largest eigenvalues of the decomposition construct a projection matrix $\mathbf{W}_{128 \times m}$, where decides the bit number of hashing result.

2. Minimize the Loss of Quantization

Find an orthogonal matrix $\mathbf{R}_{m \times m}$ that can minimize the quantization loss $Q(\mathbf{Y}, \mathbf{R})$. If $\mathbf{X}$ is a matrix of n, then $\mathbf{Y}_{m \times m} = \text{sgn}(\mathbf{R} \times \mathbf{Z})$ represents the hashed $\mathbf{X}$. A hashing function is denoted as $F(\mathbf{X}) = \text{sgn}(\mathbf{P}^T \times \mathbf{X})$, and $\mathbf{P} = \mathbf{W} \times \mathbf{R}^T$. So the loss should be calculated as function (7).

$$Q(\mathbf{Y}, \mathbf{R}) = \|\mathbf{Y} - \mathbf{R} \times \mathbf{Z}\|_F^2 \qquad (7)$$

where $\mathbf{Z} = \mathbf{W}^T \times \mathbf{X}$ and $\|\cdot\|_F^2$ is the Frobenius norm. $\mathbf{X}$ is the same dataset descriptor matrix with (5). $\mathbf{R}$ is a random square matrix with an $m \times m$ size in the beginning. The detail procedure of getting $\mathbf{R}$ can be seen from [18].

The final hash function is $F(\mathbf{X}) = \text{sgn}(\mathbf{P}^T \times \mathbf{X})$, in which $\mathbf{P} = \mathbf{W} \times \mathbf{R}^T$, $\mathbf{X}$ is the input matrix built up with descriptors and $\text{sgn}(\cdot)$ is the symbolic function. $F(\mathbf{Y})$ means the corresponding output binary descriptors in columns as a matrix.

3.3   Similarity Evaluation

In this part, the steps of our similarity evaluation is given.

SIFT features of dataset should be extracted off-line. In extraction, we can get a 128-dimensional descriptor and a scale value for each feature point. Then, picking out training set to train a hash function following our steps in 3.2. We use the hash function as $F(\mathbf{X}) = \text{sgn}(\mathbf{P}^T \times \mathbf{X})$ where the $\mathbf{X}$ is the 128-dimensional SIFT descriptors in columns of each image, after which we can have binary descriptors of all images.

After a query is given, with SIFT feature extraction and hashing, we can get binary descriptors of query's feature points.

Defining the feature points in the query as a set $Q = \{q_1, q_2, \ldots, q_n\}$, and those of the i-th image in a dataset as $P_i = \{p_1, p_2, \ldots, p_m\}$. $H(q, p)$ means the hamming distance between feature point q and p.

If we call q_k and p_j are a match, it means that they are the feature points that in an image $\mathbf{P}_i$, p_j and p_{j+1} are the closest and the second-closest feature points to q_k in query Q among all of feature points in Hamming space, which leads to $H(q_k, p_j) < H(q_k, p_{j+1})$. Ratio $\dfrac{H(q_k, p_{j+1})}{H(q_k, p_j)}$ decides the reliable match, as described in [20].

When $\dfrac{H(q_k, p_{j+1})}{H(q_k, p_j)} \geq r$, q_k and p_j are a reliable match. We choose $r = 1.25$ in this paper.

We use the average Hamming distance of reliable pairs in each image as its score. The smaller the score is, the more similar to the query.

4   Experimentation and Results

To express the precision of our method, we implement experiments on Oxford Building benchmark dataset [2]. Average precision comparison are made among SGH, ITQ, TPH and our method. We use the precision of top 2, 5, 10, 15, 20, 25 and 30 as the criteria to compare methods. The ground truth is taken by hand.

Oxford Building benchmark dataset consists of 5062 photos of Oxford landmarks images provided by "Flickr", grouped by 11 landmarks. In our experiments, we randomly selected 29 queries in 3 manually selected groups based on the 11 landmarks and manually choose 11 ground truth sets.

4.1   Dataset Processing

During the experiment, we shrink every image to 0.3×0.3 of its original size to extract SIFT descriptors. σ and σ_s are calculated by 2% of all feature points collected in random. In training process, 2000 feature points are randomly selected from all feature points as the training set. γ is 0.2. Each training point's 4 nearest neighbor feature points are chosen in Euclidean space, and 1 non-neighbor random feature point is added to increase adaptability, leading to and.

4.2   Compared Methods and Their Parameter Settings

ITQ [9], SGH [12], and TPH [18, 19] methods are used as comparisons. ITQ improves the way to get hash function with PCA methods; SGH involves a whole graph matrix; TPH involves topology consideration. They are in the same parameter values with our methods, while training feature points are chosen in the same way if necessary.

4.3   Experimentation Description and Results

We set $m = 32$ that leads to 32-bit descriptors to see the precision rate. Top 30's average precision comparison of ITQ, SGH, TPH and our method in $\beta = 0.8$ is shown in Table 1.

Also, we give Table 2 to discuss the top 30 average precision in three parameter β values: 0.16, 0.4 and 0.8. The best result of each row is in bold.

It is easy to find that our method has a better precision, even though it is fluctuating with the parameters. Oxford Building dataset consists of spot pictures with complex background and architectures in similar style, including patterned decorations and parts. These pictures are especially easy to become similar images to all kinds of queries due to the limit of descriptor length. Thus, methods that keep more relations between similar points in Euclidean space perform better. ITQ focuses on the principle

Table 1. $m = 32$ top 30's average precision comparison between ITQ, SGH, TPH and GTPH

Top	ITQ	SGH	TPH	GTPH $\beta = 0.8$
2	0.138	0.569	0.534	**0.586**
5	0.055	0.262	0.283	**0.317**
10	0.031	0.152	0.183	**0.224**
15	0.028	0.117	0.133	**0.166**
20	0.021	0.102	0.114	**0.133**
25	0.018	0.088	0.098	**0.110**
30	0.020	0.080	0.089	**0.099**

Table 2. GTPH $m = 32$ Top 30's average precision comparison in different parameter β

Top	$\beta = 0.8$	$\beta = 0.4$	$\beta = 0.16$
2	0.586	**0.603**	0.552
5	0.317	**0.324**	0.317
10	**0.224**	0.193	0.210
15	**0.166**	0.147	0.156
20	**0.133**	0.131	0.129
25	0.110	**0.113**	0.109
30	0.099	**0.102**	0.099

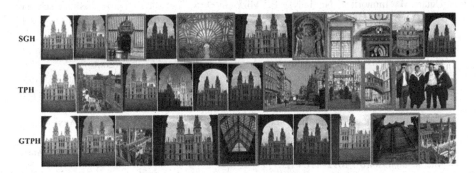

Fig. 2. A top 10 comparison of SGH, TPH and GTPH

components to make less loss in quantization, and SGH focuses more on the whole graph. TPH considers topology relationship, but GTPH has involved geometric information.

A group of top 10 typical results are shown in Fig. 2 as well. Irrelevant images are in red rectangular. The first image of each figure is both the query and the first result. In SGH, the 3rd, 5th, 7th–9th are wrong answers; in TPH, the 2nd, 7th–10th are incorrect; in GTPH, only the 5th and 9th are wrong. It can be seen that our GTPH method has improvement than SGH and TPH methods.

5 Conclusions

This paper proposes Geometry and Topology Preserving Hashing method to acquire a hash function considered both of geometric relation and topological distance between SIFT feature points, and deal with the problem of inaccuracy in image retrieval to an extent. This method improves the shorting of only considering distance relationship of feature points in training by adding scale factor. An obvious improvement in precision with a comparison between ITQ, SGH, TPH and our GTPH, along with the comparison of different factor values in Oxford Building benchmark dataset are shown in experiment part. In future work, we will improve the precision by adjusting the geometric information and discuss the parameters in detail.

Acknowledgement. This work was supported in part by the Program 973 under Grant 2012CB316400, in part by the NSFC under Grant 61373113, Grant 61173109, and Grant 61332018, and in part by Microsoft Research Asia.

References

1. Zhang, Y., Zhang, L., Tian, Q.: A prior-free weighting scheme for binary code ranking. IEEE Trans. Multimedia **16**(4), 1127–1139 (2014)
2. Philbin, J., Chum, O., Isard, M., Sivic, J., Zisserman, A.: Object retrieval with large vocabularies and fast spatial matching, pp. 1–8 (2007)
3. Datar, M., Immorlica, N., Indyk, P., Mirrokni, V.S.: Locality-sensitive hashing scheme based on p-stable distributions. In: Twentieth Symposium on Computational Geometry, vol. 34, pp. 253–262. ACM (2004)
4. Andoni, A., Indyk, P.: Near-optimal hashing algorithms for approximate nearest neighbor in high dimensions. Found. Comput. Sci. Annu. Symp. **51**(1), 117–122 (2006)
5. Lv, Q., Josephson, W., Wang, Z., Charikar, M., Li, K.: Multi-probe LSH: efficient indexing for high-dimensional similarity search. In: International Conference on Very Large Data Bases, University of Vienna, Austria, September, pp. 950–961 (2007)
6. Ji, J., Li, J., Yan, S., Zhang, B., Tian, Q.: Super-bit locality-sensitive hashing. Adv. Neural Inf. Process. Syst. **1**, 108–116 (2012)
7. Kulis, B., Grauman, K.: Kernelized locality-sensitive hashing. IEEE Trans. Pattern Anal. Mach. Intell. **34**(6), 1092–1104 (2011)
8. Yu, X., Zhang, S., Liu, B., Zhong, L., Metaxas, D.N.: Large scale medical image search via unsupervised pca hashing, vol. 13, no. 4, pp. 393–398 (2013)
9. Gong, Y., Lazebnik, S., Gordo, A., Perronnin, F.: Iterative quantization: a Procrustean approach to learning binary codes for large-scale image retrieval. In: Proceedings of the 2011 IEEE Conference on Computer Vision and Pattern Recognition, vol. 35, pp. 2916–2929. IEEE Computer Society (2011)
10. Vyshali, S., Subramanyam, M. V., Raajan, K.S.: Geometry preserving image retrieval using normalized scale coding. In: International Conference on Electrical, Electronics, Signals, Communication and Optimization. IEEE (2015)
11. Zhang, Y., Jia, Z., Chen, T.: Image retrieval with geometry-preserving visual phrases. In: IEEE Conference on Computer Vision & Pattern Recognition, vol. 42, pp. 809–816 (2011)

12. Jiang, Q.Y., Li, W.J.: Scalable graph hashing with feature transformation. In: International Conference on Artificial Intelligence, vol. 9, pp. 331–337. AAAI Press (2015)
13. Shen, F., Shen, C., Liu, W., Shen, H.T.: Supervised discrete hashing. In: Computer Science, pp. 37–45 (2015)
14. Salakhutdinov, R., Hinton, G.: Semantic hashing. Int. J. Approximate Reasoning **50**(7), 969–978 (2009)
15. Kulis, B., Darrell, T.: Learning to hash with binary reconstructive embeddings. In: Advances in Neural Information Processing Systems, Conference on Neural Information Processing Systems 2009. Proceedings of a Meeting held 7–10 December 2009, Vancouver, British Columbia, Canada, pp. 1042–1050 (2009)
16. Wang, J., Kumar, S., Chang, S.F.: Semi-supervised hashing for large-scale search. IEEE Trans. Pattern Anal. Mach. Intell. **34**(12), 2393–2406 (2012)
17. Wang, J., Kumar, S., Chang, S.F.: Semi-supervised hashing for scalable image retrieval. IEEE Conf. Comput. Vis. Pattern Recogn. **23**, 3424–3431 (2010)
18. Zhang, L., Zhang, Y., Gu, X., Tang, J., Tian, Q.: Scalable similarity search with topology preserving hashing. IEEE Trans. Image Process. Publication IEEE Signal Process. Soc. **23**(7), 3025–3039 (2014)
19. Zhang, L., Zhang, Y., Tang, J., Gu, X., Li, J., Tian, Q.: Topology preserving hashing for similarity search. ACM International Conference on Multimedia, pp. 123–132. ACM (2013)
20. Lowe, D.G.: Distinctive image features from scale-invariant keypoints. Int. J. Comput. Vis. **60**(60), 91–110 (2004)
21. Bay, H., Tuytelaars, T., Gool, L.V.: Surf: speeded up robust features. Comput. Vis. Image Underst. **110**(3), 404–417 (2006)
22. Luo, J., Gwun, O.: A comparison of SIFT, PCA-SIFT and SURF. Int. J. Image Process. **3**(4), 143–152 (2009)
23. Qian, X., Xue, Y., Yang, X., Tang, Y.Y.: Landmark summarization with diverse viewpoints. IEEE Trans. Circ. Syst. Video Technol. **25**(11), 1 (2014)
24. Yang, X., Qian, X., Xue, Y.: Scalable mobile image retrieval by exploring contextual saliency. IEEE Trans. Image Process Publication IEEE Sig. Process. Soc. **24**(6), 1709–1721 (2015)
25. Yang, X., Qian, X., Mei, T.: Learning salient visual word for scalable mobile image retrieval. Pattern Recogn. **48**(10), 3093–3101 (2015)
26. Qian, X., Zhao, Y., Han, J.: Image location estimation by salient region matching. IEEE Trans. Image Process. Publication IEEE Sig. Process. Soc. **24**(11), 4348–4358 (2015)
27. Qian, X., Tan, X., Zhang, Y., Hong, R.: Enhancing sketch-based image retrieval by re-ranking and relevance feedback. IEEE Trans. Image Process. **25**(1), 1 (2015)

Hierarchical Traffic Sign Recognition

Yanyun Qu$^{(\boxtimes)}$, Siying Yang, Weiwei Wu, and Li Lin

Computer Science Department, Xiamen University, Xiamen, China
quyanyun@gmail.com

Abstract. Traffic Sign Recognition (TSR) is very important for driverless systems and driver assistance systems. Because of the large number of the traffic sign classes and the unbalanced training data, we propose a hierarchical recognition method for traffic sign recognition. A classification tree is constructed, where the non-leaf node is constructed based on shape classification with aggregated channel features and a leaf node is constructed based on random forest classifiers with histogram of gradient for multi-class traffic sign recognition in the non-leaf node. The proposed method can overcome the inefficiency of flat classification scheme and imbalance of training data. Extensive experiments are done on three famous traffic sign datasets: the German Traffic Sign Recognition Benchmark (GTSRB), Swedish Traffic Signs Dataset (STSD), and the 2015 Traffic Sign Recognition Competition Dataset. The experimental results demonstrate the efficiency and effectiveness of our methods.

1 Introduction

Traffic Sign Recognition (TSR) is an active topic in the intelligence traffic systems. It is important for automatic driverless vehicle and driver assistant systems [1]. For example, driver assistance systems could warn drivers to take strategies ahead of time to avoid accidents [2]. The task of traffic sign recognition usually contains two main stages: traffic sign detection (TSD) and traffic sign classification (TSC). Traffic sign detection aims at locating the position of the traffic signs accurately in an image or each frame of video. Traffic sign classification focuses on labeling a traffic sign. Although the two stages may overlap such as feature representation of traffic sign, they are usually studied independently. In this paper, we focus on the second task which is usually named traffic sign recognition.

Traffic sign recognition is challenging due to the complicated dynamic nature scene, which faces four difficulties: (1) Appearances of traffic signs change with variations of viewpoint and illumination, weather condition like rain or fog, motion-blur during driving, occlusions, physical damage, colors fading, graffiti, stickers and so on. (2) Traffic sign recognition should be of real time speed and high recognition accuracy for the purpose of the practical application. (3) The training data are unbalanced. The frequencies of occurrences of traffic signs are different greatly. For example, the speed limit signs appear more frequently than the no-entry signs in the German Traffic Sign Recognition Benchmark (GTSRB) [3] and the Swedish Traffic Signs Dataset (STSD) [4]. (4) The number of traffic sign classes is large. For example, there are 112 important warning sign templates in Chinese traffic signs.

© Springer International Publishing AG 2016
E. Chen et al. (Eds.): PCM 2016, Part II, LNCS 9917, pp. 200–209, 2016.
DOI: 10.1007/978-3-319-48896-7_20

There are many literatures to deal with the first two difficulties. Some popular machine learning methods are implemented on traffic sign recognition, such as Bayesian classifiers [5], boosting [6], support vector machines (SVM) [7], and random forest classifier [8]. These methods used hand-crafted features such as Histogram of Oriented Gradient (HOG) [9] and Scale-invariant feature transform (SIFT) [6–8]. In [10], Zaklouta used a tree classifier of K depth combined with HOG as well as the distance transforms. Maldonado [11] designed a recognition system based on SVMs, whose results showed high recognition accuracy and a very low false positive rate. Convolutional Neural Network (CNN) is used for traffic sign recognition [3, 12, 13] and achieved high recognition accuracy. Recently, CNN is hot in the field of computer vision. It has achieved several state-of-the-art performances in ILSVRC2012 [14–16] and the 2011 International Joint Conference on Neural Networks (IJCNN) competition [3, 4, 17].

However, few work discussed how to deal with the imbalance of training data and how to improve the efficiency of multi-class prediction for traffic sign recognition. Most of the current multi-class prediction schemes are flat, that is, a one-vs.-all or a one-vs.-one classification scheme is used for label prediction. The flat classification scheme is time-consuming. Moreover, the imbalance of training data has negative influence on the classification performance. As we know, the traffic signs are man-made signs of special shapes, which can be divided three shape classes: circle, triangle, and square. We construct a tree structure of two layers for traffic sign. The first layer contains the coarse shape classes and the second layer contains the fine classes which is the traffic sign identification. Thus, we propose a hierarchical traffic sign recognition method. The advantage of our method is to improve the efficiency of traffic sign recognition.

The paper is organized as follows. Section 2 introduces the hierarchical recognition method for traffic sign recognition. Section 3 introduces the experimental results. Conclusion are given in Sect. 4.

2 Hierarchical Class Prediction Algorithm

In this section, we detail the implementation of the hierarchical traffic recognition. Figure 1 shows the framework of our method. In the training stage, a classification tree $G = (V, E)$ is constructed which has two layers. In the first layer, the traffic signs are divided into three groups based on the Adaboost classifier combined with Aggregate Channel Features (ACF) [18]. The non-leaf nodes are the shape nodes in the first layer, and in the second layer, each node contains traffic sign identification. A leaf node is identified by a random forest classifier which is learned on the data of classes contained in its parent node. In the testing stage, a query traffic sign image will traverse the classification tree. In each layer, the query image is given to the node with the maximum confidence value. Finally, the leaf node label with the maximum confidence value is regarded as the label of traffic sign.

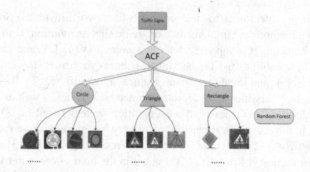

Fig. 1. The framework of the hierarchical recognition for traffic signs

2.1 Building the Non-leaf Node for Shape Classification

In this subsection, we introduce the construction of the non-leaf nodes based the shape classification. Aggregated channel features (ACF) [18] are proved to be useful for pedestrian detection with high speed and detection accuracy [19]. Motivated by the success in pedestrian detection, we use ACF for feature representation of traffic signs. The basic structure of the aggregated channel features is channel. We use ten channels: three color channels of the image with RGB color space, the gradient magnitudes, the six oriented gradient maps. Figure 2 shows the ACF used in our method. In our implementation, six oriented gradient filters are used: horizontal, vertical, 30°, 60°, 120°, and 150°. A traffic sign image is firstly normalized into a 10×10 image. And then its ACF are computed. We use all the obtained map for training an Adaboost classifier.

For the shape classification in the first layer, we adopt the Adaboost framework of Viola and Jones (VJ) framework [20]. As we know, the Adaboost classifier contains many weak classifiers called weak learners which can be combined into a strong classifier. It has been proven to converge to the optimal solution with a sufficient number of weak classifiers. AdaBoost assigns weights to weak classifiers based on their quality, and the resulting strong classifier is a linear combination of weak classifiers with the appropriate weights.

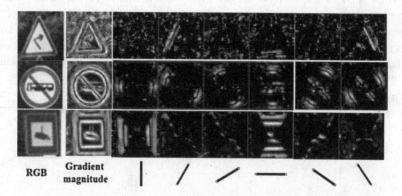

Fig. 2. Aggregated channel features for shape classification

We use depth-2 decision trees for boosting [21], where each node is a simple decision stump, defined by rectangular region, a channel, and a threshold [23]. We carry out the VJ framework and the final classifier is a weighted linear combination of boosted depth-2 decision trees of weak classifier. Because each weak classifier is a depth-2 decision tree, it implements only two comparing operations to apply a weak classifier, so the shape classification is quite fast.

2.2 Building the Leaf Node for Traffic Sign Identification

In this subsection, we detail how to build the leaf node based on random forest classifier. Because each shape node contains several traffic sign classes, we build a random forest classifier for the traffic sign classes contained in a shape node. In order to train a random forest classifier, each training sample is normalized to a 40×40 image. If a shape node contains N classes of traffic signs, the samples from the N classes of traffic signs are used to train the random forest classifier, and each leaf node contains a traffic sign class. In order to train a random forest classifier, we use multiple features which include the following features: Histogram of Oriented Gradients (HOG), Local Binary Pattern (LBP), and HSV.

HOG: An image is converted from the RGB color space to gray scale space. And then it is divided into 7×7 blocks and each block contains 4 cells. In each cell, a gradient oriented histogram with 9 bins is computed. Thus, HOG is 1764-dimensional.

LBP: Just like HOG, an image firstly is transformed to gray scale space. LBP has low computing complexity with rotation invariant and gray scale invariance performances. In this paper, a 256-dimensional LBP descriptor is used.

HSV: Because RGB color space is very sensitive to illumination, HSV color space is used in this paper. An image is firstly converted to HSV color space. For each pixel, values of hue and saturation are scaled to the range [0, 255]. For the H channel and S channel, the two components of two similar colors are numerically much closer, thus, HSV is less sensitive to illumination. A histogram is computed for each channel, and the two histograms are concatenated into a vector of 512 dimensions, which is treated as the color feature.

The tree types of features are concatenated and form a 2532-dimensional vector. In our experiments, 500 trees are used to form a random forest classifier. The prediction label is predicted by the ensemble learning of all the trees.

2.3 Class Prediction Scheme

If a query image is input, it traverses the classification tree. In the first layer, it can be scored by the classifiers in shape nodes and the shape node is retained whose score is the maximum among the three shape nodes. And then, the query image is scored by the random forest classifier in the retained shape node. The label of traffic sign whose score is the maximum is given to the query image.

3   Experimental Results

We estimate the proposed hierarchical recognition method on three traffic sign data-bases: GTSRB, STSD, and the 2015 Traffic Sign Recognition Competition Dataset (Mutil-72TSD).

GTSRB: This database is famous, because it is used in the 2011 IJCNN competition of traffic sign recognition [4]. It contains 43 classes. There are 39209 training images in the training set and the testing set contains 12630 testing images. The sizes of traffic sign images vary from 15×15 to 250×250 pixels. They have reliable ground-truth data due to semi-automatic annotation. GTSRB has two test sets: final_test and online_test. We will give the result on both datasets.

STSD: It was built in 2011 by Department of Electronic Engineering in Linkoping University. It is mainly used for traffic sign detection. Some scene images contain one or many traffic signs. In order to test our method, we crop the traffic signs in the scene image. In order to test further the algorithm performance, we create a sub-dataset of STSD: Swedish30. And training set contains all of the samples with four statuses. The first 18 classes are those which occurred most frequently in STSD, other 12 are those appearing STSD at least 5 times. Swedish30 includes 3129 traffic signs.

Mutil-72TSD: It is a multi-class traffic sign dataset used in the 2015 China Traffic Sign Recognition Competition. Figure 3 shows some examples in Mutil-72TSD. In the training set, there are 66 video sequences containing 72 traffic classes. They are split into 7 main categories: (1) warning signs, (2) prohibitory or restrictive signs, (3) mandatory signs, (4) tourism districts signs, (5) road construction safety sign (6) direction, position, or indication signs and (7) assist sign. According to the image quality, they are divided into visible, blurred, occluded, shaded and sloping. The training dataset contains 10611 training images and test dataset contains 8520 test images.

Additionally, in Mutil-72TSD, the number of the traffic signs with low occurrence frequency is very few, which result in the imbalance of training data. Thus, we augment the training data for robust learning to potential deformations in the test set. We build a synthesizing dataset by adding 5 transformed versions of the original training set;

Fig. 3. Some examples in Mutil-72TSD.

enhance the number of training samples. Samples are randomly perturbed in position ([−0.2, 0.2] pixels), in scale ([0.1, 5] ratio) and rotation ([−10, +10] degrees).

3.1 The Imbalance of Traffic Sign Classes

We analyze the distribution of training data for the three traffic sign datasets. The histograms of the class frequencies are given in Fig. 4. It demonstrates that the imbalance of traffic sign classes exist in all the three dataset. The plots of histogram of the class frequencies are of long tails. In GTSRB, the biggest class set contains more than 2000 samples while the smallest class set contains only dozens of samples. In Swedish30, the biggest set contains about 600 samples, while the smallest set contains only several samples. In Mutil-72TSD, the biggest set contains about 1000 samples while the smallest set contains only dozens of samples. The imbalance of training data has negative influence on the classification performance. It implies that our method is required for multi-class classification.

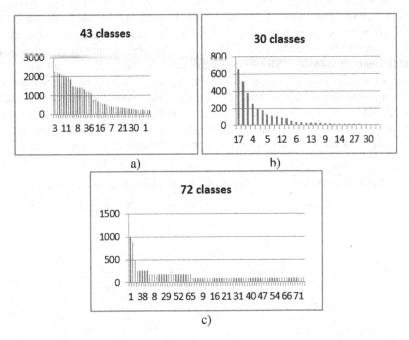

Fig. 4. The histogram of the class frequencies in traffic sign dataset. The x-axis is the label of each class; the y-axis is the number of samples in train dataset. (a) the histogram for GTRSB. (b) the histogram for Swedish30. (c) The histogram for Mutil-72TSD.

3.2   The Analysis of Computational Complexity

The main computational complexity of our method comes from the complexity of building the decision tree. Building the random forest model is an ensemble method, so it's going to be close to the sum of the complexities of building the individual decision trees in the model. If each model has the same complexity, then it would be the complexity of the individual model times the number of models you build. If having n instances and m attributes, the computational cost of building a tree is O(mn log n). If growing M trees, then the complexity is O(M(mn log n). This is not an exact complexity, because the trees in the model are grown using a subset of the features, and additional time may be added in to handle the randomization processes. However, this would get close to the complexity. The parameters here are n, m, and M - the of instances in the training data, the number of attributes, and the number of trees you build. The number of trees is a parameter you set yourself when you run the model [24].

We compare the flat classification scheme with the proposed hierarchical scheme in terms of the computational complexities. We give the number of classes contained in shape nodes in Table 1. Take the GTSRB for example. This database contains 43 classes, in which 26 classes are circle, 16 classes are triangle and 1 class is rectangle. For the flat classification scheme, 43 classifiers are used and the label with the largest score is given to the query image. Instead, for our method, 3 shape classifiers and 16 classifiers identifying traffic signs are used, thus, the total number of classifier is 19, which is more time-saving. Moreover, in the training stage, all data are loaded for training, while our method does not load all data for all classifiers, that is, the classifiers in the leaf nodes do not load all data. We also show the distribution of training data of Mutil-72TSD in the non-leaf nodes in Fig. 5. The horizontal axis denotes the shape nodes, and the vertical axis denotes the number of samples in each shape node. It demonstrates that our method can overcome the imbalance of classes.

Table 1. The class number in the classification tree for the three datasets

Classifiers		GTSRB	Swedish30	Mutil72
Flat		43	30	72
Hierarchical	Shape nodes	3		
	Circle	26	22	29
	Triangle	16	5	19
	Rectangle	1	3	25

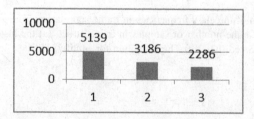

Fig. 5. The distribution of classes in the shape nodes for Mutil-72.

3.3   The Performance of the Proposed Method

In this subsection, we estimate the performance of the proposed method in term of the recognition accuracy. We first implement our method on GTSRB, which is famous because of the 2011 IJCNN traffic sign competition. In Table 2, we compare the methods of traffic sign recognition in terms of recognition accuracy. For the purpose of fair comparison, we only compare the method based on tree classifiers and SVM classifiers with HOG. The result demonstrates that our method is superior to other tree based methods. We also compare our method with the CNN [22] method trained on GTSRB. The result proves that our method performs CNN method with the same amount of train samples.

In Swedish30, we compare our method with the random forest classifier used in [25] which discusses the performances of HOG and LBP in different color channels. Table 3 shows the comparison results in which our result is the average of five testing results. HH means three HOG is computed in the three channels of HSV color space and the feature vector is the concatenation of the three channels of HOG. HL means that LBP is computed in the three channels of HSV color space, and H+L means that the histogram of color in HSV color space and LBP histogram are concatenated to form a feature vector. Table 3 demonstrates that our method can achieve the comparable results while the dimension of features used in our method is lower than the comparison method [25].

We also implement the proposed method on Multi-72STD. The results are shown in Table 4. Furthermore, we compare the flat classification scheme with the hierarchical classification method. In Table 4, we give the comparison results on the three datasets. We also compare the flat classification scheme with the hierarchical classification scheme.

Table 2. Comparison of traffic sign recognition in GTSRB

Method	Accuracy (%)
Ours	95.97
CNN	92.82
HOG_02-L2RL2SVM[a]	95.89
logistic23[a]	95.82
Linear SVM[a]	95.81
RandomForest_Hog_Hue_100tree[a]	94.74
KdTree+HOG 9720 KNN 5[a]	93.40
KdTree+HOG 2520[a]	92.90
Random trees HOG3[a]	92.13

[a]All the compared methods come from the 2011 IJCNN. http://benchmark.ini.rub.de

Table 3. Comparison of traffic sign recognition in Swedish30.

Method	HH	HH+HL	H+L	Ours
Accuracy (%)	97.69	97.49	97.91	97.94

Table 4. Comparison between the flat classification and the hierarchical classification

Method	GTRSB Final_test (%)	GTRSB Online_test (%)	Swedish30 (%)	Mutil-72TSD (%)
Random forest	95.20	–	97.49	86.68
Ours	95.97	99.87	97.94	88.87

4 Conclusion

In this paper, we focus on traffic sign recognition in a hierarchical classification scheme. A classification tree is firstly constructed, in which the non-leaf nodes are constructed based on shape classification and the leaf nodes are constructed based on traffic sign identification. For the shape classification, aggregated channel features are used for feature representation of a traffic sign image and the Adaboost classifier based on weak decision tree are used for shape classification. In each shape node, a random forest classifier is trained based on HOG. The proposed method can overcome the inefficiency of flat classification scheme and the imbalance of the training data. The proposed method is implemented on three famous traffic sign recognition datasets and the experimental results demonstrate the efficiency and effectiveness of our method.

References

1. Mogelmose, A., Trivedi, M.M., Moeslund, T.B.: Vision-based traffic sign detection and analysis for intelligent driver assistance systems: perspectives and survey. IEEE Trans. Intell. Transp. Syst. **13**(4), 1484–1497 (2012)
2. Cai, Z., Gu, M.: Traffic sign recognition algorithm based on shape signature and dual-tree complex wavelet transform. J. Central South Univ. **20**, 433–439 (2013)
3. Cireşan, D., Meier, U., Masci, J., et al.: A committee of neural networks for traffic sign classification. In: The 2011 International Joint Conference on Neural Networks (IJCNN), pp. 1918–1921. IEEE (2011)
4. Stallkamp, J., Schlipsing, M., Salmen, J., et al.: The German traffic sign recognition benchmark: a multi-class classification competition. In: The 2011 International Joint Conference on Neural Networks (IJCNN), pp. 1453–1460. IEEE (2011)
5. Meuter, M., Nunn, C., Görmer, S.M., et al.: A decision fusion and reasoning module for a traffic sign recognition system. IEEE Trans. Intell. Transp. Syst. **12**(4), 1126–1134 (2011)
6. Ruta, A., Li, Y., Liu, X.: Robust class similarity measure for traffic sign recognition. IEEE Trans. Intell. Transp. Syst. **11**(4), 846–855 (2010)
7. Greenhalgh, J., Mirmehdi, M.: Real-time detection and recognition of road traffic signs. IEEE Trans. Intell. Transp. Syst. **13**(4), 1498–1506 (2012)
8. Zaklouta, F., Stanciulescu, B.: Real-time traffic-sign recognition using tree classifiers. IEEE Trans. Intell. Transp. Syst. **13**(4), 1507–1514 (2012)
9. Dalal, N., Triggs, B.: Histograms of oriented gradients for human detection. In: IEEE Computer Society Conference on Computer Vision and Pattern Recognition, CVPR 2005, vol. 1, pp. 886–893. IEEE (2005)
10. Zaklouta, F., Stanciulescu, B., Hamdoun, O.: Traffic sign classification using KD trees and random forests. In: The 2011 International Joint Conference on Neural Networks (IJCNN), pp. 2151–2155. IEEE (2011)

11. Maldonado-Bascon, S., Lafuente-Arroyo, S., Gil-Jimenez, P., et al.: Road-sign detection and recognition based on support vector machines. IEEE Trans. Intell. Transp. Syst. **8**(2), 264–278 (2007)

12. LeCun, Y., Bottou, L., Bengio, Y., et al.: Gradient-based learning applied to document recognition. Proc. IEEE **86**(11), 2278–2324 (1998)

13. Sermanet, P., LeCun, Y.: Traffic sign recognition with multi-scale convolutional networks. In: The 2011 International Joint Conference on Neural Networks (IJCNN), pp. 2809–2813. IEEE (2011)

14. He, K., Zhang, X., Ren, S., et al.: Deep residual learning for image recognition. arXiv preprint arXiv:1512.03385 (2015)

15. Russakovsky, O., Deng, J., Su, H., et al.: Imagenet large scale visual recognition challenge. Int. J. Comput. Vis. **115**(3), 211–252 (2015)

16. Szegedy, C., Vanhoucke, V., Ioffe, S., et al.: Rethinking the inception architecture for computer vision. arXiv preprint arXiv:1512.00567 (2015)

17. Jin, J., Fu, K., Zhang, C.: Traffic sign recognition with hinge loss trained convolutional neural networks. IEEE Trans. Intell. Transp. Syst. **15**(5), 1991–2000 (2014)

18. Dollár, P., Appel, R., Belongie, S., et al.: Fast feature pyramids for object detection. IEEE Trans. Pattern Anal. Mach. Intell. **36**(8), 1532–1545 (2014)

19. Benenson, R., Omran, M., Hosang, J., Schiele, B.: Ten years of pedestrian detection, what have we learned? In: Agapito, L., Bronstein, Michael M., Rother, C. (eds.) ECCV 2014. LNCS, vol. 8926, pp. 613–627. Springer, Heidelberg (2015). doi:10.1007/978-3-319-16181-5_47

20. Viola, P., Jones, M.: Robust real-time object detection. Int. J. Comput. Vis. **57**(2), 137–154 (2007)

21. Dollár, P., Tu, Z., Perona, P., et al.: Integral channel features. In: Proceedings of British Machine Vision Conference, BMVC 2009, London, UK, 7–10 September 2009 (2009)

22. Wang, T., Wu, D.J., Coates, A., et al. End-to-end text recognition with convolutional neural networks. In: 2012 21st International Conference on Pattern Recognition (ICPR), pp. 3304–3308. IEEE (2012)

23. Mathias, M., Timofte, R., Benenson, R., et al.: Traffic sign recognition—how far are we from the solution? In: The 2013 International Joint Conference on Neural Networks (IJCNN), pp. 1–8. IEEE (2013)

24. Biau, G.Ã.Š.: Analysis of a random forests model. J. Mach. Learn. Res. **13**, 1063–1095 (2012)

25. Yang, X., Qu, Y., Fang, S.: Color fused multiple features for traffic sign recognition. In: Proceedings of the 4th International Conference on Internet Multimedia Computing and Service, pp. 84–87. ACM (2012)

Category Aggregation Among Region Proposals for Object Detection

Linghui Li[1], Sheng Tang[1(✉)], Jianshe Zhou[2], Bin Wang[1], and Qi Tian[3]

[1] Key Lab of Intelligent Information Processing, Institute of Computing Technology,
CAS, Beijing 100190, China
{lilinghui,ts,wangbin1}@ict.ac.cn
[2] Beijing Advanced Innovation Center for Imaging Technology,
Capital Normal University, Beijing 100048, People's Republic of China
zhoujianshe@cnu.edu.cn
[3] Department of Computer Science, University of Texas at San Antonio,
San Antonio, TX 78249-1604, USA
qitian@cs.utsa.edu

Abstract. Recently, an overwhelming majority of object detection methods have focused on how to reduce the number of region proposals while keeping high object recall without consideration of category information. It may lead to a lot of false positives due to the interferences between categories especially when the number of categories is very large. To eliminate such interferences, we propose a novel category aggregation approach based upon our observation that more frequently detected categories around an object have the higher probabilities to be present in an image. After further exploiting the co-occurrence relationship between categories, we can determine the most possible categories for an image in advance. Thus, many false positives can be greatly filtered out before subsequent classification process. Our extensive experiments on the well-known ILSVRC 2015 detection dataset show that our approach can achieve 49.0% of mAP in the validation dataset and 45.36% of mAP in the test dataset ranked *5th* in the ILSVRC 2015 detection task.

Keywords: Object detection · Convolutional network · Region proposal

1 Introduction

Recently, with the great progress by deep learning technology, visual object detection has become a very hot and important research topic in the field of computer vision. In order to overcome the tension between computational tractability and high detection quality, an overwhelming majority of researchers are shifting from the traditional sliding window paradigm such as [1,2] to region proposal methods [3,4,6]. Most of such frameworks [6,7,19] usually consist of three

This work was supported by 863 Project (2014AA015202), National Nature Science Foundation of China (61572472), Beijing Natural Science Foundation (4152050) and Beijing Advanced Innovation Center for Imaging Technology (BAICIT-2016009).

© Springer International Publishing AG 2016
E. Chen et al. (Eds.): PCM 2016, Part II, LNCS 9917, pp. 210–220, 2016.
DOI: 10.1007/978-3-319-48896-7_21

main processes: (1) Extract region proposals which are likely to contain objects; (2) Extract Convolution Neural Network (CNN) features of these proposals; and (3) Classify the proposals with classifiers trained with CNN features.

Compared with the widely used CNN features and relatively mature classification methods, how to obtain small number of region proposals with good localization capability while keeping high object recall is very crucial for training detectors with excellent performances, and still remains a challenging problem which is attracting more and more attentions from researchers throughout the world. Recent representative works on region proposals are Objectness [8], Selective Search [9], BING [10], Edge Boxes [11], Region Proposal Network (RPN) [12], MultiBox [13], and MCG [14]. However, almost all of them are category-independent which do not consider category information. But when the number of categories is very large, the interferences between categories may lead to a lot of false positives.

Actually, object categories in real world do not exist in isolation. They naturally interact with each other at the semantic level [15]. For instances, chairs and tables are very likely to appear simultaneously in an image, while "seal" and "bench" commonly do not co-occur. Early research work on image and video annotation, classification and retrieval [15–18,24] indicates that contextual information can help improve performance to a certain degree. Through our observation, we find that more frequently detected categories around an object have the higher probabilities to be present in an image. So we propose a novel category aggregation approach among region proposals, and through further exploitation of the co-occurrence relationship between categories, we can determine the most possible categories for an image in advance. Thus, many false positives of proposals can be greatly filtered out.

The main contribution of this paper is that we propose a novel category aggregation approach together with co-occurrence refinement to reduce large number of region proposals to keep only those with good localization

(a)   (b)   (c)   (d)

Fig. 1. Illustration of comparison between different detection results (the coordinate of the detected objects, its category with the high confidence score) on the ILSVRC 2014 detection dataset. (a) is ground truth. Compared with the result of Fast R-CNN result (b), our proposed category aggregation (c) can remove the false positive "watercraft" due to its relatively smaller frequency detected in this image. After further co-occurrence refinement, our proposed method (d) can filter out the false positive "bench" since seal and bench often do not co-occur in this dataset.

capability while keeping high object recall for visual object detection. Our extensive experiments on the well-known ILSVRC 2015 detection dataset show that our proposed category aggregation can remove the false positive as shown in Fig. 1. Totally, our approach can achieve 49.0% of mAP in the validation dataset and 45.36% of mAP in the test dataset.

The rest of our paper is organized as follows. We first review the related work in Sect. 2 and elaborate on the details of the proposed category aggregation and co-occurrence refinement in Sect. 3. Experiments are described in Sect. 4. Finally, we draw our conclusive remarks along with discussion for future work in Sect. 5.

2   Related Work

The performance of object detection mainly benefits from region proposal generation and region proposal classification. One of the most successful method of object detection is R-CNN [6] which takes advantage of high quality region proposals (Selective Search method [9]) and CNN features which recently have achieved impressive performance due to its discriminative nature and made a big breakthrough in the field of object detection.

Based on the R-CNN framework, large numbers of outstanding models using region proposals for object have been proposed [7,12,18,19]. Thus, generating high quality region proposals has become a typical trend. Most of methods focus on generating more accurate region proposals and reducing the total number of region proposals. For instance, Erhan [13] proposes a saliency-inspired neural network model named MultiBox to directly learn the bounding boxes. Girshick [7] integrates region classification and bounding box regression in a deep neural network using a multi-task loss to improve detection accuracy.

Category-related context information has been applied to image and video annotation and classification [15,18,20]. Qi [15] shows that contextual relationship can help improve performance stably for video annotation. DeepId-Net [18] uses the classification score of the whole image as contextual information to refine the classification score of the candidate box. Choi [21] uses a tree graphical model to learn dependencies among object categories. Galleguillos [22] uses a conditional random field to model object co-occurrence and location to detect object. Different from those methods which obtain the category relationship by learning from data, we propose a novel category aggregation approach along with further exploitation of the co-occurrence relationship between categories.

3   Our Proposed Method

3.1   Framework of Our Approach

An overview of our approach is shown as Fig. 2. Our proposed approach consists of the following four processes: (a) **Region proposal extraction:** Generating category-independent candidate bounding boxes using region proposal method. (b) **Category aggregation and co-occurrence refinement:** Filtering out false positives using category aggregation along with co-occurrence refinement among region proposals. (c) **Region classification:** Classifying region proposals. (d) **Region fusion:** Fusing different region proposals for object detection.

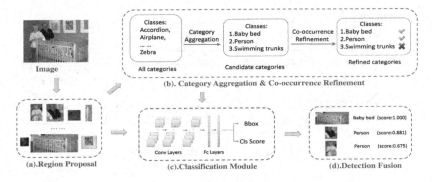

Fig. 2. Illustration of our proposed object detection framework based on category aggregation and co-occurrence refinement among region proposals

3.2 Category Aggregation

As discussed above, existing object detection methods may generate many false positives due to the errors of both classification and localization. In order to filter out the false positives, we propose a category aggregation method for predicting the possible classes contained in an image as a candidate category set. The process of our proposed category aggregation method is shown in Fig. 3.

The goal of category aggregation is to obtain all the possible object category in a given image which essentially is a multi-label detection problem. Liking multi-label method [23], we first sample patches from the given image which may contain one or more objects, background, or a part of the object. Different from randomly or sliding sampling patches in previous method, our method uses the region proposal methods to extract patches which can get high quality patches and can help to infer the possible categories. For a given image, we use region proposal method to generate region proposals $R = \{R_1, R_2, ..., R_m\}$. m is the number of proposals generated from a given image I and varies with images. Then we score those generated region proposals. Because of the high performance of CNN (Convolutional Neural Network) in image recognition task, we use the well-known VGG16 model to score those proposals. The VGG16 [5] model is pre-trained on ImageNet classification dataset and then fine-tuned on ImageNet detection dataset.

After we score the generated region proposals, we rank each proposal according the scores and select the category c_i of the highest score, c_i denotes the selected category of the i-th proposal. Then we aggregate categories of the image I by combining the category of each proposal except background category which is denoted by 0, $i.e$:

$$o_I = \bigcup_{i=1,..,m} (c_i \quad if \quad c_i! = 0) \tag{1}$$

Where o_I denotes the result of category aggregation, i.e., the predicted possible category set of image I.

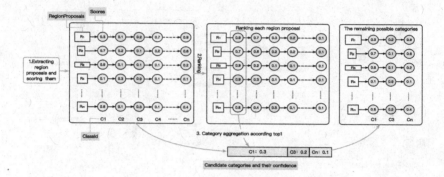

Fig. 3. Illustration of our proposed category aggregation method.

Finally, we sort the category set o_I in descending order according to each confidence, and select the category with highest confidence as reference category which will be used in the next process of co-occurrence refinement. We define the confidence of category i according to the following equation:

$$c_I^i = 1/m \sum_{n=1}^{m} I(c_n), I(c_n) = \begin{cases} 1 & \text{if } c_n = i. \\ 0 & \text{else.} \end{cases} \quad (2)$$

3.3   Co-occurrence Refinement

In order to get more accurate category information of an image I, we further utilize the co-occurrence relationship between categories to refine the possible category set o_I. The left of Fig. 4 illustrates the heat map of the co-occurrence matrix and the right of Fig. 4 illustrates the procedure how to apply it to refine candidate categories.

The co-occurrence matrix M shows the co-occurrence relationship between categories. Generally, the co-occurrence relationship among categories can be determined by experts or based on large lexical database, for instance, WordNet and Wikipedia, *etc.* In this paper, we get the co-occurrence relationship on large database using data-driven approach. Because the ImageNet object detection training set is large enough to cover most of category co-occurrence information, we count the category co-occurrence information from the ground truth labels of the training set. Let $M = (m_{i,j})_N^N$ denotes the co-occurrence matrix generated from training set. The matrix M can be generated by the following equation:

$$m_{i,j} = \begin{cases} 0 & \text{if } \nexists I \text{ s.t. } i\text{-}th \text{ category} \in I \text{ and } j\text{-}th \text{ category} \in I. \\ 1 & \text{if } \exists I \text{ s.t. } i\text{-}th \text{ category} \in I \text{ and } j\text{-}th \text{ category} \in I. \end{cases} \quad (3)$$

where $m_{ij} = \{0, 1\}$ represents whether the i-th category co-occurs with the j-th category. If there is one image in which the i-th category object and the j-th category object simultaneously appear, then $m_{i,j}$ is assigned to 1, otherwise, $m_{i,j}$ is assigned to 0.

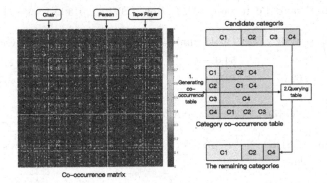

Fig. 4. The illustration of the degree of co-occurrence among 200 categories in the ImageNet. Each pixel represents degree of co-occurrence between two categories. The brighter of the pixel is, the higher the degree of co-occurence is.

After we get the co-occurrence matrix, we apply this co-occurrence matrix to the aforementioned candidate category set o_I of each image I to refine the category aggregation results. The right of Fig. 4 shows, for each input candidate category set, we have a reference category Rc_1 with the highest confidence whose definition is in Sect. 3.2. Then we filter the candidate category according to the reference category by using the following equation:

$$\widehat{o}_I^1 = \{Rc_1\}$$

$$\widehat{o}_I^{t+1} = \begin{cases} \widehat{o}_I^t & \text{if} \nexists Rc_j \in \widehat{o}_I^t \text{ s.t. } m_{Rc_j, Rc_t} ! = 0. \\ \widehat{o}_I^t \bigcup \{Rc_t\} & \text{if} \exists Rc_j \in \widehat{o}_I^t \text{ s.t. } m_{Rc_1, Rc_t} ! = 0. \end{cases} \quad (4)$$

where $\widehat{o}_I$ represents the remained candidate category set after filtering by employing co-occurrence relationship. Rc_t is the number of category; $t \in \{1, 2, ..., K\}$ and K is the size of candidate category set o_I.

3.4 Region Classification

Our final goal is to detect objects using the candidate category set o_I or $\widehat{o}_I$. As the right of Fig. 3 shows, we only detect object on the candidate categories.

The main difference between our detection pipeline from the existing detection method is the candidate category set which is changed from the whole dataset category set to a subset o_I. In our experiments, the size of whole category set Y is 200 and the average size of o_I is 4. By utilizing this new candidate category set, the interference with other categories can be largely suppressed so as to improve the performance of detection.

4   Experiments Results

We participated in the ImageNet Large Scale Visual Recognition Challenge 2015 and achieved 5th in detection task using our proposed method. This detection

Table 1. Top5 ranked detection mAP (%) on ILSVRC 2015 test set and val_2 set.

Method	MSRA [25]	QualcommResearch	CUImage	Adelaide	Ours
val_2	-	54.6	57.3	-	49.0
test	62.07	53.57	52.57	51.44	45.36

Table 2. Detection mAP (%) on ImageNet val_2.

Method	FastRCNN	DeepID-Net (sgl)	DeepId-Net (avg)	Ours (sgl)
val_2	46.7	48.2	50.7	49.0

dataset contains 200 object categories including 450,000 training images, 20,121 validation images and 51, 294 test images, respectively. We divide the validation data into two parts just same as R-CNN [6] does: val_1 set and val_2 set. val_1 set and training set is merged as "trainval" set to train the models, val_2 set is used to evaluate the performance.

Table 1 summarizes the results from ILSVRC 2015 object detection challenge. It contains the *top5* ranked approaches on the test data submitted to ILSVRC 2015. As Table 1 shows, the MSRA [25] achieved the best performance of 62.07% mAP by utilizing a 152 layers deep model. The Qualcomm Research proposed NeoNet ensemble with bounding box regression which achieved 53.57% mAP. The CUImage achieved 52.57% mAP based on combining DeepID-Net [18] with Faster RCNN [12] model. The University of Adelaide fused multiple VGG16 and VGG19 networks which is in total of 9 models to achieve 51.44% of mAP. Our proposed category aggregation method achieved 45.36% of mAP in the test dataset.

Table 2 shows detection performance of Fast R-CNN [7] and DeepID-Net [18]. We can see that on the val_2 set we achieve 49.0% mAP in single model (shorten to "sgl" in Table 2). The results of Fast R-CNN is fine-tuned as our baseline. Compared with the baseline, our model can improve 2.3% of mAP. This shows the effectiveness of our proposed method.

We train our model with the fusion of region proposals extracted by Selective Search method [9] and Edge Boxes method [11]. During testing, we take different region proposals as candidate bounding boxes, such as Selective Search (SS), Edge Boxes (EB), RPN, etc. In the following part, we will detail our category aggregation experiments, co-occurrence refinement experiments, and region proposal fusion experiments respectively.

4.1   Category Aggregation Experiments

Table 3 compares the detection performance of the Fast R-CNN and our model with/without category aggregation. From Table 3, we can see that experimental results with category aggregation is better than that of Fast R-CNN (without category aggregation) no matter what kind of region proposal is used. By using

Table 3. Experimental results (with/without category aggregation)

Proposal method	SS	EB	RPN	SS+EB	SS+RPN	Average
Fast R-CNN (without cg-agg)	46.7	46.9	46.5	46.5	47.0	46.72
Ours (with cg-agg)	47.5	46.9	46.8	48.1	48.4	47.54

Table 4. Part of results on 200 categories of ILSVRC2015 detection dataset.

ClassName	mAP	accordian	airplane	ant	antelope	apple	armadillo	artichoke
Fast R-CNN	46.7	62.3	59.7	45	62.5	34.4	90.9	49.6
Ours	47.5	63.9	61.2	47.2	69.2	34.8	90.5	55.6
Improved	+0.8	+1.6	+1.5	+2.2	+6.7	+0.4	−0.4	+6.0
ClassName	pack	banana	bandAid	bear	basketBall	bagel	baseball	bathingCap
Fast R-CNN	14.4	33.4	46.8	88.7	78.5	37.4	51.7	48.0
Ours	15.0	38.6	63.5	87.5	80.4	44.0	59.4	49.1
Improved	+0.6	+5.2	+16.7	−1.2	+1.9	+6.6	+7.7	+1.1

category aggregation, we achieve mAP of 48.4% using region fusion, 0.78% higher mAP on average than without using region fusion. Taking advantage of classification information in advance, our method can filter a number of false positives, eventually improving the detection performance.

Table 4 shows part of results on 200 categories only using category aggregation. From Table 4, we can see that for some categories, using category aggregation can improve the performance 16.7%. Because on those categories, common detection pipeline often classifies some bounding boxes to incorrect categories with relative higher confidence score. In our experiments, the average number of elements in candidate categories is only about 3 which is rather smaller than the original 200 categories. This will reduce the probability of misclassification. Although there are also some categories whose mAP is reduced to some extent because some true categories are filtered out during category aggregation process, the overall mAP over all the 200 categories increases finally.

Besides, our experiments shows the mAPs by using different region proposal method. In Table 3, using single region proposal methods, the Selective Search has the best performance. Fusing different region proposals can improve the detection performance in that they are complementary.

4.2 Co-occurrence Refinement Experiments

Table 5 compares detection precision for with/without co-occurrence relationship using different region proposals. From Table 5, we can see that experimental results with co-occurrence relationship are constantly better than those without co-occurrence refinement. By using co-occurrence information, we further improve the detection mAP 49.0% with mAP increasing 0.36% on average compared to without using co-occurrence refinement.

Table 5. Experimental results (with/without co-occurrence refinement)

Proposal method	SS	EB	RPN	SS+EB	SS+RPN	Average
Without co-occur	47.5	46.9	46.8	48.1	48.4	47.54
With co-occur	47.9	47.2	47.2	48.4	49.0	47.9

(b) With co-occur ref   (a) Without co-occur ref

Fig. 5. Illustration of removal of false positives ("without co-occur ref" denotes "without co-occurrence refinement", "with co-occur ref" denotes "with co-occurrence refinement"): (a) Before applying co-occurrence relationship, there are three category which are wrongly detected—ray, chair, drum; (b) After applying co-occurrence relationship, the wrong categories are removed with only correct category "train" left.

As shown in Fig. 5, utilizing the co-occurrence relationship of categories can further reduce the false positives of region proposals.

From Tables 3 and 5 we can also discover that region proposal fusion is a simple and effective method. By using region fusion, we can improve mAP from 48.4% to 49.0%. Because region proposals extracted by using different methods complement each other, we can get higher quality candidate bounding boxes resulting in better detection precision after fusion.

5   Conclusion

In this paper, we propose a novel category aggregation approach together with co-occurrence refinement to filter out false positives of region proposals before subsequent classification. Several issues are worth further investigation: First, we plan to investigate the adoption of more complex relationship than co-occurrence between categories through using graph model. The second is how to fine tune the deep neural network on the ILSVRC 2015 detection dataset to get better performance for object detection.

References

1. Sermanet, P., Eigen, D., Zhang, X., et al.: Overfeat integrated recognition, localization and detection using convolutional networks. arXiv preprint arXiv:1312.6229 (2013)
2. Felzenszwalb, P.F., Girshick, R.B., McAllester, D.: Cascade object detection with deformable part models. In: 2010 IEEE Conference on Computer Vision and Pattern Recognition (CVPR), pp. 2241–2248. IEEE (2010)
3. Krizhevsky, A., Sutskever, I., Hinton, G.E.: ImageNet classification with deep convolutional neural networks. In: Advances in Neural Information Processing Systems, pp. 1097–1105 (2012)
4. Szegedy, C., Liu, W., Jia, Y., et al.: Going deeper with convolutions. In: Proceedings of the IEEE Conference on Computer Vision and Pattern Recognition, pp. 1–9 (2015)
5. Simonyan, K., Zisserman, A.: Very deep convolutional networks for large-scale image recognition. arXiv preprint arXiv:1409.1556 (2014)
6. Girshick, R., Donahue, J., Darrell, T., et al.: Rich feature hierarchies for accurate object detection and semantic segmentation. In: Proceedings of the IEEE Conference on Computer Vision and Pattern Recognition, pp. 580–587 (2014)
7. Girshick, R.: Fast R-CNN. In: Proceedings of the IEEE International Conference on Computer Vision, pp. 1440–1448 (2015)
8. Alexe, B., Deselaers, T., Ferrari, V.: What is an object? In: 2010 IEEE Conference on IEEE Computer Vision and Pattern Recognition (CVPR), pp. 73–80 (2010)
9. Uijlings, J.R.R., van de Sande, K.E.A., Gevers, T., et al.: Selective search for object recognition. Int. J. Comput. Vision **104**(2), 154–171 (2013)
10. Cheng, M.M., Zhang, Z., Lin, W.Y., et al.: BING: binarized normed gradients for objectness estimation at 300fps. In: Proceedings of the IEEE Conference on Computer Vision and Pattern Recognition, pp. 3286–3293 (2014)
11. Zitnick, C.L., Dollár, P.: Edge boxes: locating object proposals from edges. In: Fleet, D., Pajdla, T., Schiele, B., Tuytelaars, T. (eds.) ECCV 2014. LNCS, vol. 8693, pp. 391–405. Springer, Heidelberg (2014). doi:10.1007/978-3-319-10602-1_26
12. Ren, S., He, K., Girshick, R., et al.: Faster R-CNN: towards real-time object detection with region proposal networks. In: Advances in Neural Information Processing Systems, pp. 91–99 (2015)
13. Erhan, D., Szegedy, C., Toshev, A., et al.: Scalable object detection using deep neural networks. In: Proceedings of the IEEE Conference on Computer Vision and Pattern Recognition, pp. 2147–2154 (2014)
14. Arbelez, P., Pont-Tuset, J., Barron, J., et al.: Multiscale combinatorial grouping. In: Proceedings of the IEEE Conference on Computer Vision and Pattern Recognition, pp. 328–335 (2014)
15. Qi, G.J., Hua, X.S., Rui, Y., et al.: Correlative multi-label video annotation. In: Proceedings of the 15th International Conference on Multimedia, pp. 17–26. ACM (2007)
16. Jiang, W., Chang, S.F., Loui, A.C.: Active context-based concept fusion with partial user labels. In: 2006 IEEE International Conference on Image Processing, pp. 2917–2920. IEEE (2006)
17. Gidaris, S., Komodakis, N.: Object detection via a multi-region and semantic segmentation-aware CNN model. In: Proceedings of the IEEE International Conference on Computer Vision, pp. 1134–1142 (2015)

18. Ouyang, W., Wang, X., Zeng, X., et al.: DeepID-net: deformable deep convolutional neural networks for object detection. In: Proceedings of the IEEE Conference on Computer Vision and Pattern Recognition, pp. 2403–2412 (2015)

19. He, K., Zhang, X., Ren, S., et al.: Spatial pyramid pooling in deep convolutional networks for visual recognition. IEEE Trans. Pattern Anal. Mach. Intell. **37**(9), 1904–1916 (2015)

20. Weng, M.F., Chuang, Y.Y.: Multi-cue fusion for semantic video indexing. In: Proceedings of the 16th ACM International Conference on Multimedia, pp. 71–80. ACM (2008)

21. Choi, M.J., Lim, J.J., Torralba, A., et al.: Exploiting hierarchical context on a large database of object categories. In: 2010 IEEE Conference on Computer Vision and Pattern Recognition (CVPR), pp. 129–136. IEEE (2010)

22. Galleguillos, C., Rabinovich, A., Belongie, S.: Object categorization using co-occurrence, location and appearance. In: IEEE Conference on Computer Vision and Pattern Recognition, CVPR 2008, pp. 1–8. IEEE (2008)

23. Oquab, M., Bottou, L., Laptev, I., et al.: Learning and transferring mid-level image representations using convolutional neural networks. In: Proceedings of the IEEE Conference on Computer Vision and Pattern Recognition, pp. 1717–1724 (2014)

24. Zheng, L., Wang, S., Liu, Z., et al.: Packing, padding: coupled multi-index for accurate image retrieval. In: Proceedings of the IEEE Conference on Computer Vision and Pattern Recognition, pp. 1939–1946 (2014)

25. He, K., Zhang, X., Ren, S., et al.: Deep residual learning for image recognition. arXiv preprint arXiv:1512.03385 (2015)

Exploiting Local Feature Fusion
for Action Recognition

Jie Miao, Xiangmin Xu[✉], Xiaoyi Jia, Haoyu Huang, Bolun Cai,
Chunmei Qing, and Xiaofen Xing

School of Electronic and Information Engineering,
South China University of Technology, Wushan RD., Tianhe District,
Guangzhou, People's Republic of China
xmxu@scut.edu.cn

Abstract. Densely sampled local features with bag-of-words models
have been widely applied to action recognition. Conventional approaches
assume that different kinds of local features are totally uncorrelated, and
they are separately processed, encoded, and then fused at video-level representation. However, these local features are not totally uncorrelated
in practice. To address this problem, multi-view local feature fusion is
exploited for local descriptor fusion in action recognition. Specifically,
tensor canonical correlation analysis (TCCA) is employed to obtain a
fused local feature that carries the high-order correlation hidden among
different types of local features. The high-order correlation local feature
improves the conventional concatenation based fusion approach. Experimental results on three challenging action recognition datasets validate
the effectiveness of the proposed approach.

Keywords: Action recognition · Multi-view · Local feature

1 Introduction

Vision-based action recognition has been an active research area in the recent
decades, and it is the central part in many computer vision applications, such as
intelligent video surveillance, human-computer interaction, video content analysis, and video retrieval. It is a changeling problem to recognize actions from
unconstrained videos due to complex backgrounds, large intra-class variances,
etc. To obtain a better feature for classification, videos are usually represented
in different ways using multiple types of features. This kind of representation is
termed as the multi-view features. In this paper, we exploit the multi-view local
feature fusion for action recognition.

This work is supported in part by the National Natural Science Founding of China
(61171142, 61401163), Science and Technology Planning Project of Guangdong
Province, China (2011A010801005, 2014B010111003, 2014B010111006), Guangzhou
Key Lab of Body Data Science (201605030011) and the Fundamental Research Funds
for the Central Universities (2015ZZ032).

E. Chen et al. (Eds.): PCM 2016, Part II, LNCS 9917, pp. 221–230, 2016.
DOI: 10.1007/978-3-319-48896-7_22

Approaches based on densely sampled local features with bag-of-words models have been successfully applied to complex action recognition tasks. In these approaches, different types of local features are encoded independently by bag-of-words models, and then concatenated together as final representation for classification. This fusion strategy is regarded as the representation fusion. It is proposed by assuming that different types of local features are totally uncorrelated. In this way, they are processed separately without losing valuable information.

However, different types of local features are not totally uncorrelated in practice. There might be some correlation exist among these features that are useful for feature representation. A straightforward solution is the local feature fusion, which simply concatenate local features before feature encoding. This concatenation cannot capture the hidden connections among local features effectively. Furthermore, due to the increased input dimensionality, the conventional bag-of-words model in local feature fusion fails to encode features as good as that in representation fusion.

In this paper, we propose the high-order correlation local feature (HCF) to utilize the correlation among different types of local features. In our work, different types of local features are regarded as different views, tensor canonical correlation analysis [12] is employed to capture the high-order correlation among different views. Experimental results on three challenging action recognition datasets show that a significant improvement can be achieved by proposed approach.

2   Related Work

Recently, approaches based on densely sampled local features and bag-of-words models have been shown to be particularly successful. [25] first evaluated various local features and sampling strategies, and showed the effectiveness of densely sampled local features for action recognition. After that, more sampling strategies and local features were proposed. Dense trajectories [23] samples local patches in a dense grid from each frame and tracks them as trajectories using dense optical flow, it then extracts local features along trajectories and encodes them for video representation. Then the improved dense trajectories (IDT) was introduced by removing camera motion in videos [24]. A two-stream CNN was proposed by training two independent networks for appearance and motion representation, respectively [21]. All of these approaches use the representation-level fusion, which neglects the correlation be-tween different types of local features, and simply concatenating different features as final video representation. In our work, we propose a better fusion approach for different types of local features.

Correlation is a powerful way to investigate and describe the relationship between two sets of data. There are many approaches proposed by utilizing correlation. [20] proposed a gradient-based subspace phase correlation for efficient image alignment estimations. Statistical methods was introduced to estimate vehicle count based on correlation estimation [18]. Canonical correlation analysis (CCA) is a straightforward method utilizing correlation for data fusion, it has been widely used for multi-view applications, such as classification [6], regression [7] and clustering [1]. However, these approaches based on conventional CCA are limited by two views. Although the multi-view fusion can be achieved by enumerating each pair of views, the high-order correlation among multiple views will be ignored. Tensor canonical correlation analysis (TCCA) [12] was proposed as a multi-view dimension reduction method to handle the data of an arbitrary number of views by analyzing the covariance tensor of different views. Besides of correlation, lots of approaches for multi-view fusion based on different principles have been proposed. A non-linear multi-view dimension reduction method was proposed by utilizing the common structure among different views [27].

There are only few studies on the fusion of local features have been proposed. A local feature fusion approach using coupled multi-index frame was proposed for accurate image retrieval [29], but its performance is limited by nearest neighbor based bag-of-words models. Three types of simple concatenation based fusion strategy were investigated [17], and fused them as hybrid representation. Experimental results suggested that the representation-level fusion is the best fusion among three strategies, and more useful information can be obtained from different types of fusions. But this approach is inefficient due to the simple concatenating based fusion, and the improvement was mainly introduced by the large number of clusters used in bag-of-words models. A mixture model of probabilistic CCA was proposed to learn shared latent variables for utilizing the common part of different features in action recognition [2]. Similar to other approaches based on CCA, it is also limited by two views. Therefore, it fails to utilize rich correlation among all views.

3 Local Feature Fusion

In this section, we detail the proposed high order correlation local feature (HCF) for action recognition. An illustration of our approach is shown in Fig. 1. First of all, we extract different types of local features using IDT [24]. Briefly, points are densely sampled in a grid from each frame and tracked as trajectories by dense optical flow, and then the features are extracted aligned with tracked trajectories.

There are four kinds of local features extracted by IDT. Histograms of oriented gradients (HOG) [4] encodes static edges and textures, which represent appearance information for action recognition. HOG is extracted directly from video frames. Histograms of oriented optical flow (HOF) [10] is obtained from horizontal and vertical optical flows. It captures both magnitudes and directions of motion. Horizontal and vertical motion boundary histograms (MBHx and MBHy) [5] are extracted from horizontal and vertical optical flow respectively. MBHx and MBHy utilize the gradient of optical flows, and they carry horizontal and vertical motion information respectively. These four kinds of local features represent different information of local video cubes. In conventional approach, they are assumed to be totally uncorrelated to each other. Therefore, they are processed and encoded independently, and then concatenated as the final feature for the classification.

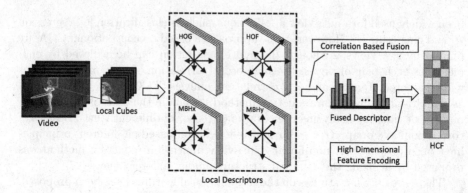

Fig. 1. The framework of the proposed approach.

We suggest that there are some important correlations hidden among them, which are neglected in conventional approaches. Regarding each type of features as a unique view, we perform a fusion by tensor canonical correlation analysis (TCCA) [12] to extract high-order correlation among different features. TCCA projects multiple views of features into a new subspace that maximizes correlation of multiple views. Different from other multi-view approaches that keep similar information among different views, TCCA is able to obtain new representation that carries high-order correlations among different views. These correlations encode the relationship of different types of features in each local video cubes. TCCA can be summarized as follows.

Assuming that m views of features $\{X_l\}_{l=1}^m$ of N instances are given, where each view $X_l = [\mathbf{x}_{l1}, \mathbf{x}_{l2}, \cdots, \mathbf{x}_{lN}] \in \mathbb{R}^{d_l \times N}$ has been whitened, the covariance tensor among all views is represented as

$$\mathcal{C} = \frac{1}{N} \sum_{n=1}^{N} \mathbf{x}_{1n} \circ \mathbf{x}_{2n} \circ \cdots \circ \mathbf{x}_{mn}, \tag{1}$$

where the operate $\circ$ is the tensor outer product, and $\mathcal{C}$ is of dimension $d_1 \times d_2 \times \cdots \times d_m$.

According to [12], the major problem of TCCA is to maximize the correlation ρ among multiple types of features. It can be described as

$$\underset{\{\mathbf{h}_l\}}{\text{argmax}} \ \rho = corr(\mathbf{z}_1, \mathbf{z}_2, ..., \mathbf{z}_m),$$
$$s.t. \ \mathbf{z}_l^T \mathbf{z}_l = 1, l = 1, ..., m, \tag{2}$$

where $corr(\mathbf{z}_1, \mathbf{z}_2, ..., \mathbf{z}_m) = (\mathbf{z}_1 \odot \mathbf{z}_2 \odot ... \odot \mathbf{z}_m)^T \mathbf{e}$ is the canonical correlation, the operator $\odot$ is the element-wise product, and $\mathbf{e} \in \mathbb{R}^N$ is an all ones vector. Specifically, $\mathbf{z}_l = X_l^T \mathbf{h}_l, l = 1, ..., m$ are canonical variables, and $\mathbf{h}_l$ are called canonical vectors. Problem (2) is equivalent to solving the following formulation:

$$\underset{\{\mathbf{h}_l\}}{\text{argmax}} \ \rho = \mathcal{C} \times_1 \mathbf{h}_1^T \times_2 \mathbf{h}_2^T \cdots \times_m \mathbf{h}_m^T,$$
$$s.t. \ \mathbf{h}_l^T (C_l + \epsilon I) \mathbf{h}_l = 1, l = 1, ..., m, \tag{3}$$

where I is an identity matrix, ϵ is a nonnegative trade-off parameter. The operator $\times_p$ is the p-mode production.

Specifically, C_l are self-covariance matrices represented as

$$C_l = \frac{1}{N} \sum_{n=1}^{N} \mathbf{x}_{ln} \mathbf{x}_{ln}^T, \ l = 1, ..., m.$$

The reformulated optimization problem is

$$\underset{\{\mathbf{u}_l\}}{\mathrm{argmax}} \ \rho = \mathcal{M} \times_1 \mathbf{u}_1^T \times_2 \mathbf{u}_2^T \cdots \times_m \mathbf{u}_m^T,$$

$$s.t. \ \mathbf{u}_l^T \mathbf{u}_l = 1, l = 1, ..., m, \tag{4}$$

where $\mathbf{u}_l = \tilde{C}_l^{1/2} \mathbf{h}_l$ are latent transform variables. And the definition of $\mathcal{M}$ is

$$\mathcal{M} = \mathcal{C} \times_1 \tilde{C}_1^{-1/2} \times_2 \tilde{C}_2^{-1/2} \cdots \times_m \tilde{C}_m^{-1/2}, \tag{5}$$

where $\tilde{C}_l = C_l + \epsilon I$.

The problem (4) is equivalent to

$$\underset{\{\mathbf{u}_l\}}{\mathrm{argmax}} \left\| \mathcal{M} - \hat{\mathcal{M}} \right\|_F^2, \tag{6}$$

where $\hat{\mathcal{M}} = \rho \mathbf{u}_1 \circ \mathbf{u}_2 \circ \cdots \circ \mathbf{u}_m$. The problem (6) can be solved by Alternating Least Square (ALS) algorithm [8].

Obtaining the solution $\mathbf{u}_l$, the canonical variable is $\mathbf{z}_l = X_l^T \tilde{C}_l^{-1/2} \mathbf{u}_l$. Define r as the dimensionality after the reduction ($r \leqslant min\{d_1, \cdots, d_m\}$), and let $U_l = [\mathbf{u}_l^{(1)}, \cdots, \mathbf{u}_l^{(r)}]$ and $\mathbf{z}_l^{(1)}, \cdots, \mathbf{z}_l^{(r)}$ be the column vectors of Z_l, the projected feature of the l-th view is

$$Z_l = X_l^T \tilde{C}_l^{-1/2} U_l. \tag{7}$$

Finally $\{Z_l\}_{l=1}^m$ are concatenated as $Z \in \mathbb{R}^{mr \times N}$ for subsequent processing. Regarding HOG, HOF, MBHx and MBHy as four different views, TCCA is performed to project them into a new subspace to obtain a fused feature-level representation that carries the high-order correlation among them.

4 Experiments

In this section, we report the experimental results of the proposed HCF. Firstly, we introduce the datasets used to evaluate the performance of HCF and detail the implementation parameters. Then we report the evaluation of different parameters used in our work. And we compare the performance of HCF with other feature fusion approaches for action recognition. Lastly, we compare our method with state-of-the-art approaches. We evaluate the proposed approach on three challenging action recognition datasets: HMDB51, UCF50 and Hollywood2. Some example frames of these datasets are shown in Fig. 2.

Climb	Run	Laugh	Kiss	Drink
Skiing	BaseballPitch	PommelHorse	PushUps	GolfSwing
HandShake	GetOutCar	AnswerPhone	HugPerson	Run

Fig. 2. Example frames from the action recognition datasets used in this paper. Rows from top to bottom are HMDB51, UCF50 and Hollywood2 respectively.

The HMDB51 dataset [9] consists of 51 action categories with 6,766 video sequences from different movies. We report the mean accuracy (mAcc.) over 3 train/test splits proposed in [9]. The UCF50 dataset [19] consists of 50 action categories divided into 25 groups. Following the standard evaluation protocol proposed in [19], we report the mean accuracy over 25 cross validation sets. The Hollywood2 dataset [13] consists of 3,669 movie clips collected from 69 different Hollywood movies. We follow the standard evaluation protocol proposed by [13], and report the mean average precision (mAP) over all classes.

4.1 Implementation Details

Here, we describe the implementation details of our experiments. All experiments were performed as described here, unless stated otherwise.

To extract local features, we follow the default parameters proposed in IDT [24]. Four kinds of local features were extracted, i.e. HOG, HOF, MBHx and MBHy. For preprocessing, principle component analysis (PCA) and whitening were performed to reduce the dimensionality by a factor of two. As the baseline approach, the representation-level fusion was performed. Here, for each type of local features, 256,000 features were randomly sampled from a dataset to train a GMM with 256 clusters, and Fisher vector was performed to get the encoded feature. After encoding, four kinds of feature were concatenated together as the final representation.

Instead of encoding fused features by conventional Fisher vector, we use sparse coding based Fisher vector [11] for encoding the fused features. The dimensionality r of each type of features after processed by TCCA was set to 45.

Thus the dimensionality of fused feature was 180. The dictionary size for sparse coding based Fisher vector was 256. And the number of nonzero coefficients for sparse coding was set to 15. Similar to conventional Fisher vector, normalization is required for better feature representation. In our work, we apply intra-normalization and L_2-normalization to the encoded feature. We concatenate HCF with conventional features for final classification. To better utilize both conventional single view features and the proposed HCF, an extra L_2-normalization is performed after the concatenation of all encode features. A one-against-all linear support vector machine was used for classification. The evaluation protocols for each dataset were then applied to produce the final results.

4.2 Experimental Results

First, we evaluate the impact of parameters in HCF on the HMDB51 dataset. Following the feature extraction process, we study the dimensionality of each view r kept by TCCA. As shown in Fig. 3, a proper r can capture more valuable connections among all views, but some interferences will be introduced while using a large r. In our experiments, the best performance is achieved at the point $r = 45$.

Second, we conduct experiments to evaluate the performance of HCF compared with other local feature fusion approaches. The results are shown in Table 1. Here the baseline approach use only representation-level fusion was proposed in [24]. The extra concatenation-based local feature fusion is able to slightly improve the recognition accuracy. As shown in Table 1, the proposed method outperforms MVSV and all kinds of fusion methods. Using both the correlation and the independence of multiple types of features, the proposed approach performs better than MVSV, which unable to make full use of the correlation information among four types of features. This indicates that HCF is more effective to capture the high-order correlation among different views simultaneously.

As shown in Table 2, we compare the propose approach with state-of-the-art action recognition approaches. Results show that the proposed method can achieve competitive results on the three challenging action recognition datasets compared with other approaches. Here, IDT can be considered as the baseline

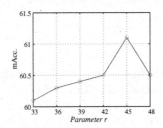

Fig. 3. Evaluation of the parameters on the HMDB51 dataset.

Table 1. The comparison of different fusion approaches.

	HMDB51 (mAcc.)	UCF50 (mAcc.)	Hollywood2 (mAP)
Baseline [24]	57.2%	91.2%	64.3%
Concatenation	58.6%	92.0%	66.7%
MVSV [2]	59.5%	92.0%	66.2%
Proposed	**61.1%**	**93.8%**	**67.3%**

Table 2. Comparison of different action recognition approaches on HMDB51, UCF50 and Hollywood2 datasets.

HMDB51	mAcc	UCF50	mAcc	Hollywood2	mAP
Causality [14]	58.7%	Movement [3]	90.0%	FV [15]	63.3%
SHVLAD [16]	59.8%	FV [15]	90.0%	IDT [24]	64.3%
Hybrid [17]	61.1%	IDT [24]	91.2%	GNMF [22]	56.8%
CNN [21]	59.4%	Causality [14]	92.5%	ICA [28]	54.1%
Pooling [26]	59.7%	Hybrid [17]	92.3%	Pooling [26]	67.5%
Proposed	**61.1%**	Proposed	**93.8%**	Proposed	**67.3%**

approach. Lots of efforts have been made for better feature encoding. Fisher vector was introduced to action recognition in [15], which compact feature set can be used. Granger causality is used to encode relationship of trajectory pairs [14]. SHVLAD employs high-order statistics and supervised learning to improve feature encoding [16]. A hybrid approach was proposed by combining many kinds of feature encoding approaches, and it gains lots of improvements on recognition accuracy. Using high-order correlation features, our approaches outperforms these approaches. Movement patterns histogram was proposed for action representation using motion information [3]. And the two-stream CNN was proposed by using CNN on both RGB video frames and stacked optical flows. Withe the motion information obtained from stacked optical flows, good results can be achieved by these approaches. The proposed approaches outperforms these action recognition approaches on HMDB51 and UCF50 datasets. And competitive results on Hollywood2 dataset can be achieved.

5   Conclusion

In this paper, we highlight the high-order correlation information among different types of local features in action recognition, which is neglected in conventional approaches. In particular, we proposed the high-order correlation local feature as an axillary feature to utilize these information. Experimental results show that the proposed approach able to improve conventional approach as an axillary feature. The proposed approach is by all means not limited to an action recognition representation and could be applied in other applications that rely on densely sampled local features and bag-of-words models.

References

1. Blaschko, M.B., Lampert, C.H.: Correlational spectral clustering. In: IEEE Conference on Computer Vision and Pattern Recognition, CVPR 2008, pp. 1–8. IEEE (2008)
2. Cai, Z., Wang, L., Peng, X., Qiao, Y.: Multi-view super vector for action recognition. In: 2014 IEEE Conference on Computer Vision and Pattern Recognition (CVPR), pp. 596–603. IEEE (2014)
3. Ciptadi, A., Goodwin, M.S., Rehg, J.M.: Movement pattern histogram for action recognition and retrieval. In: Fleet, D., Pajdla, T., Schiele, B., Tuytelaars, T. (eds.) ECCV 2014. LNCS, vol. 8690, pp. 695–710. Springer, Heidelberg (2014). doi:10.1007/978-3-319-10605-2_45
4. Dalal, N., Triggs, B.: Histograms of oriented gradients for human detection. In: Computer Vision and Pattern Recognition, vol. 1, pp. 886–893 (2005)
5. Dalal, N., Triggs, B., Schmid, C.: Human detection using oriented histograms of flow and appearance. In: European Conference on Computer Vision, pp. 428–441 (2006)
6. Farquhar, J., Hardoon, D., Meng, H., Shawe-taylor, J.S., Szedmak, S.: Two view learning: SVM-2K, theory and practice. In: Advances in Neural Information Processing Systems, pp. 355–362 (2005)
7. Kakade, S.M., Foster, D.P.: Multi-view regression via canonical correlation analysis. In: Bshouty, N.H., Gentile, C. (eds.) COLT 2007. LNCS, vol. 4539, pp. 82–96. Springer, Heidelberg (2007). doi:10.1007/978-3-540-72927-3_8
8. Kroonenberg, P.M., De Leeuw, J.: Principal component analysis of three-mode data by means of alternating least squares algorithms. Psychometrika $45(1)$, 69–97 (1980)
9. Kuehne, H., Jhuang, H., Garrote, E., Poggio, T., Serre, T.: HMDB: a large video database for human motion recognition. In: 2011 IEEE International Conference on Computer Vision (ICCV), pp. 2556–2563. IEEE (2011)
10. Laptev, I., Marszalek, M., Schmid, C., Rozenfeld, B.: Learning realistic human actions from movies. In: Computer Vision and Pattern Recognition, pp. 1–8 (2008)
11. Liu, L., Shen, C., Wang, L., van den Hengel, A., Wang, C.: Encoding high dimensional local features by sparse coding based fisher vectors. In: Advances in Neural Information Processing Systems, pp. 1143–1151 (2014)
12. Luo, Y., Tao, D., Wen, Y., Ramamohanarao, K., Xu, C.: Tensor canonical correlation analysis for multi-view dimension reduction. arXiv preprint arXiv:1502.02330 (2015)
13. Marszalek, M., Laptev, I., Schmid, C.: Actions in context. In: IEEE Conference on Computer Vision and Pattern Recognition, CVPR 2009, pp. 2929–2936. IEEE (2009)
14. Narayan, S., Ramakrishnan, K.R.: A cause and effect analysis of motion trajectories for modeling actions. In: 2014 IEEE Conference on Computer Vision and Pattern Recognition (CVPR), pp. 2633–2640. IEEE (2014)
15. Oneata, D., Verbeek, J., Schmid, C.: Action and event recognition with fisher vectors on a compact feature set. In: 2013 IEEE International Conference on Computer Vision (ICCV), pp. 1817–1824. IEEE (2013)

16. Peng, X., Wang, L., Qiao, Y., Peng, Q.: Boosting VLAD with supervised dictionary learning and high-order statistics. In: Fleet, D., Pajdla, T., Schiele, B., Tuytelaars, T. (eds.) ECCV 2014. LNCS, vol. 8691, pp. 660–674. Springer, Heidelberg (2014). doi:10.1007/978-3-319-10578-9_43

17. Peng, X., Wang, L., Wang, X., Qiao, Y.: Bag of visual words and fusion methods for action recognition: comprehensive study and good practice. Eprint Arxiv (2014)

18. Peng, Z., Yi, S., Bei, H.: Statistical methods to estimate vehicle count using traffic cameras. Multidimension. Syst. Signal Process. **20**(2), 121–133 (2009)

19. Reddy, K.K., Shah, M.: Recognizing 50 human action categories of web videos. Mach. Vis. Appl. **24**(5), 971–981 (2013)

20. Ren, J., Vlachos, T., Zhang, Y., Zheng, J., Jiang, J.: Gradient-based subspace phase correlation for fast and effective image alignment. J. Vis. Commun. Image Represent. **25**(7), 1558–1565 (2014)

21. Simonyan, K., Zisserman, A.: Two-stream convolutional networks for action recognition in videos. In: Advances in Neural Information Processing Systems, pp. 568–576 (2014)

22. Wang, H., Yuan, C., Hu, W., Ling, H., Yang, W., Sun, C.: Action recognition using nonnegative action component representation and sparse basis selection. IEEE Trans. Image Process. **23**(2), 570–581 (2014)

23. Wang, H., Kläser, A., Schmid, C., Liu, C.L.: Dense trajectories and motion boundary descriptors for action recognition. Int. J. Comput. Vision **103**(1), 60–79 (2013)

24. Wang, H., Schmid, C.: Action recognition with improved trajectories. In: IEEE International Conference on Computer Vision, ICCV 2013, pp. 3551–3558, December 2013

25. Wang, H., Ullah, M.M., Klser, A., Laptev, I., Schmid, C.: Evaluation of local spatio-temporal features for action recognition. In: British Machine Vision Conference (2009)

26. Wang, P., Cao, Y., Shen, C., Liu, L., Shen, H.T.: Temporal pyramid pooling based convolutional neural networks for action recognition. arXiv preprint arXiv:1503.01224 (2015)

27. Xia, T., Tao, D., Mei, T., Zhang, Y.: Multiview spectral embedding. IEEE Trans. Syst. Man Cybern. B Cybern. **40**(6), 1438–1446 (2010)

28. Zhang, S., Yao, H., Sun, X., Wang, K., Zhang, J., Lu, X., Zhang, Y.: Action recognition based on overcomplete independent components analysis. Inf. Sci. **281**, 635–647 (2014)

29. Zheng, L., Wang, S., Liu, Z., Tian, Q.: Packing and padding: coupled multi-index for accurate image retrieval. In: IEEE Conference on Computer Vision and Pattern Recognition, pp. 1947–1954 (2014)

Improving Image Captioning by Concept-Based Sentence Reranking

Xirong Li[1,2] and Qin Jin[1,2(✉)]

[1] Key Lab of DEKE, Renmin University of China, Beijing, China
qjin@ruc.edu.cn
[2] Multimedia Computing Lab, Renmin University of China, Beijing, China

Abstract. This paper describes our winning entry in the ImageCLEF 2015 image sentence generation task. We improve Google's CNN-LSTM model by introducing *concept-based sentence reranking*, a data-driven approach which exploits the large amounts of concept-level annotations on Flickr. Different from previous usage of concept detection that is tailored to specific image captioning models, the propose approach reranks predicted sentences in terms of their matches with detected concepts, essentially treating the underlying model as a black box. This property makes the approach applicable to a number of existing solutions. We also experiment with fine tuning on the deep language model, which improves the performance further. Scoring METEOR of 0.1875 on the Image-CLEF 2015 test set, our system outperforms the runner-up (METEOR of 0.1687) with a clear margin.

Keywords: Image captioning · Sentence reranking · Neural language modeling · ImageCLEF 2015 benchmark evaluation

1 Introduction

In this paper we tackle the challenging task of image captioning. Given an unlabeled image, the task is to automatically generate a natural language sentence that describes main entities and events present in the image. See Fig. 1 for some example sentences.

There has been a considerable progress on the topic in the last few years, thanks to powerful image representation derived from deep convolutional neural networks (CNN) [1] and trainable recurrent neural networks (RNN) capable of modeling long term dependency in natural language [2]. Joint models of CNN and RNN have demonstrated quite promising results for image captioning [3–5].

Since the number of model parameters to be optimized is at a million scale, what also matters are the growing amounts of training images associated with manually written descriptions, e.g., Flickr8k [7], Flickr30k [8], MSCOCO [9] with more than 100k images, and Flickr8k-CN [10] as a bilingual extension of Flickr8k. Even though the number of captioned images has increased from a few thousands to over 100k, sentence-level annotations remain in shortage when compared to

© Springer International Publishing AG 2016
E. Chen et al. (Eds.): PCM 2016, Part II, LNCS 9917, pp. 231–240, 2016.
DOI: 10.1007/978-3-319-48896-7_23

(1) a plane taking off from a runway
(2) a plane taking off from the runway
(3) a plane flying in the sky
(4) an airplane flying in the sky
(5) a plane flying in the air
(6) an airplane is flying in the sky
(7) a plane taking off into the sky

(3) a plane flying in the sky
[flying | plane | sky]

(a)

(1) a plant with green leaves
(2) a cluster of yellow flowers
(3) a plant is growing in a garden
(4) a plant with green leaves and green leaves
(5) a plant with green leaves and purple flowers
(6) a cluster of yellow flowers in a garden
(7) a cluster of yellow flowers in a field

(5) a plant with green leaves and purple flowers
[purple | plant | green]

(b)

Fig. 1. Examples illustrating concept-based sentence re-ranking for improving image captioning. Candidate sentences generated by a CNN-LSTM image captioning model are shown in descending order on the left side, while the chosen sentences are shown on the right side. In square brackets are concepts predicted by the neighbor voting algorithm [6]. The candidate sentence best matching the predicted concepts are chosen as the final description. (Color figure online)

concept-level annotations. For instance, one can easily obtain one million learning examples of 'dog' from Flickr[1]. How to exploit such large amounts of (noisy) concept-level annotations to improve image captioning is important.

Works on utilizing concept detection for image captioning exist, but are tailored to specific models. For instance, in the work by Fang *et al.* [11], concept

---

[1] Over 6 million images tagged with 'dog' on Flickr, https://www.flickr.com/search/? tags=dog, retrieved on April-29-2016.

detection results are used as part of input features for a maximum entropy language model. Gong *et al.* [12] leverage Flickr data to improve image and text embedding within a kernel Canonical Correlation Analysis framework. These works are inapplicable to other models, e.g., the popular CNN+LSTM architecture.

Contributions of this work. For improving image captioning by exploiting concept-level annotations, we propose concept-based sentence reranking. The proposed technique treats the underlying sentence generation model as a black box, making it applicable to a number of existing solutions. Moreover, by deriving concept detectors from Flickr images, better image descriptions are predicted with no extra cost of manual annotation. In addition, we show that a fine tuning on a trained deep language model further improves the performance. Putting all this together, our system is the winning entry in the ImageCLEF 2015 image sentence generation task [13,14].

2   Related Work

Depending on whether candidate sentences are given in advance, we see two lines of research, namely retrieval approaches and generative approaches.

The retrieval approaches sort a predefined set of candidate sentences in terms of their relevance with respect to a given image, and then selects the top ranked sentence to annotate the image [7,12,15]. To compute cross-media relevance between images and sentences, representing them in a common space is a prerequisite. In [7], this space is derived by Kernel Canonical Correlation Analysis, while normalized linear Canonical Correlation Analysis is used in [12] for scaling to larger training sets. In the DeViSE model [15], the common space is formed by a pretrained *Word2Vec* [16], where the embedding vector of a sentence is obtained by averaging over the vectors of its words. Compared to bag-of-words used in [7,12], the use of *Word2Vec* enables DeViSE to handle a much lager vocabulary. In [17], the common space is implemented as a visual CNN feature space in order to better capture visual and semantic similarity. One strength of the retrieval approaches is that a predicted sentence is syntactically and grammatically correct. However, they lack the ability to generate novel sentences.

The generative approaches typically consist of two main components, i.e., image encoding and sentence decoding [3–5]. For image encoding, a pretrained deep convolutional neural network (CNN) is employed to project a specific image into a visual feature space. For cross-media comparison, images and words are embedded into a latent common space before they are fed to a recurrent neural network (RNN), which eventually outputs a sequence of words as the caption. Variants of RNN have been investigated, including multi-modal RNN [4], bidirectional RNN [5], and Long Short-Term Memory (LSTM) [3]. Recent benchmark evaluations, e.g., the MSCOCO Captioning Challenge [9] and the ImageCLEF 2015 image sentence generation task [14], have demonstrated outstanding performance of LSTM based solutions [3,13].

3 Our Approach

We aim to improve the performance of an existing image captioning model by re-ranking its generated sentences in terms of concept detection results. More concretely, given an image, the model first generates k best sentences. Each sentence, indicated by *hypoSent*, is associated with a confidence score, denoted as *sentenceScore(hypoSent)*. Meanwhile, suppose we have access to a concept detection system that predicts m concepts deemed to be relevant with respect to the given image. If a detected concept appears in a *hypoSent*, we call it a matched concept. Our assumption is that a sentence covering more matched concepts is more likely to be a good description of the image. Hence, the final caption shall be the sentence that maximizes the prediction confidence score and the concept matches. The new sentence confidence score is therefore computed as a linear combination of these two factors, i.e.,

$$newScore(hypoSent) = \theta \cdot concScore(hypoSent) + (1-\theta) \cdot sentScore(hypoSent), \tag{1}$$

where *concScore(hypoSent)* is the averaged confidence score of all the matched concepts in the hypothesis sentence, and $\theta \in [0,1]$ is a trade-off parameter. Figure 1 show cases some examples of how this simple strategy helps produce better image descriptions.

The proposed approach treats the image captioning component as a black box, meaning any captioning model can be applied in theory. In this work we adopt Google's CNN-LSTM framework [3] for its state-of-the-art performance. The framework is described in Sect. 3.1. We then discuss in Sect. 3.2 how to adapt the model to new target data, followed by our choices of concept detection in Sect. 3.3.

3.1 The CNN-LSTM Model for Sentence Generation

To generate the hypothesis sentences for a specific image, we employ the CNN-LSTM model proposed by Vinyals *et al.* [3]. At the heart of the model is an LSTM based recurrent neural network, which computes the posterior probability of a (novel) sentence conditioned on the image.

The network is trained by maximum likelihood estimation using many pairs of image and sentence. As an image and a sentence are of different modalities and thus not directly comparable, an image projection matrix and a word projection matrix are deployed to embed the image and the sentence from their initial representations into a common space before feeding them into the network. We use a CNN feature, i.e., the last fully connected layer of a pretrained 16-layer VGGNet [18], as the initial representation of an image. Each word in a sentence is represented by a one-hot vector.

In the sentence generation stage, a hypothesis sentence of the input image is generated as a sequence of words in a greedy manner. In particular, the CNN vector of the input image, after projection, is fed into the LSTM network to initialize its memory units. The posterior probability over all words is re-estimated based on the memory status and the words already been chosen in previous iterations. Consequently, the word with the highest probability is selected, while its embedding vector will be fed into the LSTM network in the next iteration. The generation process stops once a predefined STOP token is chosen. Similar to [3], we use beam search to obtain a list of hypothesis sentences.

3.2   Model Adaptation by Fine Tuning

We use stochastic gradient descent to train the LSTM based sentence generation model. Such an incremental learning strategy makes it relatively ease to adjust an existing model with respect to novel data. In particular, we leverage a transfer learning strategy similar to the ones used in the context of object recognition for fine tuning a CNN model [19]. That is, re-train the LSTM model using a novel training dataset but with a relatively lower learning rate.

3.3   Concept Detection

Notice that the output of the CNN model corresponds to the 1,000 labels defined in the Large Scale Visual Recognition Challenge [20]. We do not directly use this as concept detection results, because the labels are often over specific to be overlapped with words used in image captions. Instead, we consider two methods for concept detection, i.e., neighbor voting [6] and hierarchical semantic embedding [21], both of which are capable of learning from large amounts of weakly labeled Flickr images, and thus predict words used in daily life.

Neighbor voting (NeiVote) [6]. Given an image, this method first retrieves a set of neighbor images visually close to the given image, and then count the occurrence of a specific concept in textual annotations associated with the neighbors. The concepts are sorted in descending order by their occurrence and the top m ranked ones are preserved. Despite its simplicity, a recent comparison [22] shows that the method remains competitive when compared to more complicated alternatives. The visual distance between images are computed in terms of the Euclidean distance between their CNN features.

Hierarchical Semantic Embedding (HierSE) [21]. Developed in the context of zero-shot image tagging, HierSE casts concept detection into cross-media relevance computation. In particular, HierSE embeds both concept and image into a *Word2Vec* space. The embedding vector of the concept is obtained by convex combination of the embedding vectors of the concept and its ancestors tracing back to the root in WordNet. The embedding vector of an image is obtained by convex combination of the embedding vectors of the top ten labels predicted by the CNN model. Consequently, the image-concept relevance score is computed as the cosine similarity between the corresponding embedding vectors. The top m concepts with the largest scores are preserved.

A conceptual diagram of the proposed approach is given in Fig. 2.

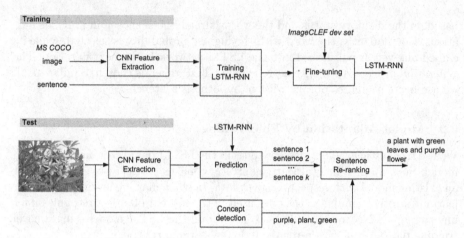

Fig. 2. An illustration of the proposed solution. We improve the popular CNN+LSTM architecture through (1) model adaption by fine tuning and (2) sentence reranking using auto-detected visual concepts. (Color figure online)

4   Evaluation

To verify the effectiveness of our approach, we participated in the ImageCLEF 2015 image sentence generation task [14]. In this task, participants were asked to generate sentence-level textual descriptions for 500k images crawled from the web, from which the task organizers selected a subset of 3,070 images for performance assessment. Notice that we have no access to ground-truth annotations, as the test set is used for blind testing by the organizers only.

In ImageCLEF 2015, a dev set of 2k images with manually written captions are provided for system development. The number of captions per image ranges from 5 to 51 per image, with a mean of 9.5 and a median of 8 descriptions. In order to tune the weighting parameter θ in Eq. 1, we randomly split the dev set into three disjoint subsets, i.e., 1,600 images for training, 200 images for validation and the remaining 200 images for internal test.

Table 1. Performance of our solution under varied settings on the ImageCLEF 2015 image sentence generation task.

Training data	Data for fine tuning	Concept detection	METEOR score
ImageCLEF dev	–	–	0.1659
MSCOCO	ImageCLEF dev	–	0.1759
ImageCLEF dev	–	HierSE	0.1781
ImageCLEF dev	–	NeiVote	0.1806
MSCOCO	ImageCLEF dev	HierSE	0.1684
MSCOCO	ImageCLEF dev	NeiVote	**0.1875**

4.1   Experiment 1. The Influence of Fine Tuning

We compare two runs. One run is to train the sentence generation model on the ImageCLEF dev set. The other run is to first train the model on the MSCOCO dataset [9], and then fine tune it on the ImageCLEF dev set using a lower learning rate. Following the protocol [14], we use the METEOR score to assess the performance of image captioning. As shown in the first two rows of Table 1, the fine-tuned model, with METEOR of 0.1759, performs better.

4.2   Experiment 2. The Effect of Concept-Based Sentence Reranking

Given detection results either from NeiVote or from HierSE, we apply concept-based sentence reranking on sentences generated by the CNN-LSTM models with and without fine tuning, respectively. For NeiVote, we retrieve neighbor images from a collection of 2 million Flickr images. For HierSE, we adopt an existing *Word2Vec* model pre-trained on Flickr tags [21].

As we see from Table 1, the performance of the model (without fine tuning) consistently improves after sentence reranking, with the METEOR score increases from 0.1659 to 0.1781 (HierSE) and 0.1806 (NeiVote), respectively. For the fine-tuned model, using HierSE for concept detection causes some performance drop, while NeiVote remains effective, reaching the best METEOR score

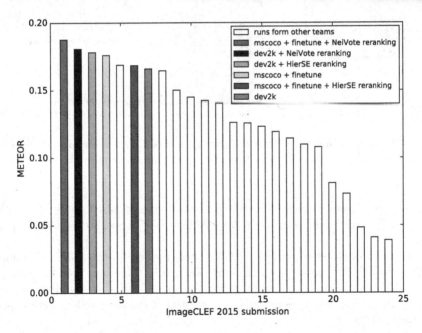

Fig. 3. Comparing with submissions from other teams in the ImageCLEF 2015 image sentence generation task. Our results given varied settings are highlighted in color bars. The submissions have been sorted in descending order according to their METEOR scores. (Color figure online)

Fig. 4. Some test images with sentences generated by the proposed system. The images are hand picked that showing our system performs well. (Color figure online)

of 0.1875. The results justify the effectiveness of concept-based sentence reranking, and NeiVote appears to be a better choice for concept detection in this context.

Figure 3 plots the performance of our system in the context of all submissions in ImageCLEf 2015, showing our leading position in the evaluation. Image captioning results of some selected examples are given in Fig. 4. The quantitative and qualitative results demonstrate the potential of the proposed concept-based sentence reranking.

Note that due to the unavailability of the ground truth of the test dataset as aforementioned, we have compared mainly with submissions from other ImageCLEF participants. In our future work we will compare other state-of-the-art methods on other benchmarks, e.g., MSCOCO.

5   Conclusions

We present in this paper *concept-based sentence reranking*, a data-driven approach to improve image captioning. As demonstrated by our participation in the ImageCLEF 2015 benchmark evaluation, the proposed approach is found to be effective for improving the popular CNN-LSTM image captioning model. In essence the improvement is gained by exploiting the large amount of noisy concept-level annotations associated with Flickr images. In addition, fine tuning on the deep language model helps its generalization to novel data.

Acknowledgements. The authors are grateful to the ImageCLEF coordinators for the benchmark organization efforts [14,23]. This research was supported by the Fundamental Research Funds for the Central Universities and the Research Funds of Renmin University of China (No. 16XNQ013).

References

1. Krizhevsky, A., Sutskever, I., Hinton, G.: ImageNet classification using deep convolutional neural networks. In: Proceedings of NIPS (2012)
2. Sutskever, I., Vinyals, O., Le, Q.V.: Sequence to sequence learning with neural networks. In: Proceedings of NIPS (2014)
3. Vinyals, O., Toshev, A., Bengio, S., Erhan, D.: Show and tell: a neural image caption generator. In: Proceedings of CVPR (2015)
4. Mao, J., Xu, W., Yang, Y., Wang, J., Huang, Z., Yuille, A.: Deep captioning with multimodal recurrent neural networks (m-RNN). In: Proceedings of ICLR (2015)
5. Karpathy, A., Fei-Fei, L.: Deep visual-semantic alignments for generating image descriptions. In: Proceedings of CVPR (2015)
6. Li, X., Snoek, C., Worring, M.: Learning social tag relevance by neighbor voting. IEEE Trans. Multimedia **11**(7), 1310–1322 (2009)
7. Hodosh, M., Young, P., Hockenmaier, J.: Framing image description as a ranking task: data, models and evaluation metrics. J. Artif. Int. Res. **47**(1), 853–899 (2013)
8. Young, P., Lai, A., Hodosh, M., Hockenmaier, J.: From image descriptions to visual denotations: new similarity metrics for semantic inference over event descriptions. TACL **2**, 67–78 (2014)
9. Lin, T., Maire, M., Belongie, S., Hays, J., Perona, P., Ramanan, D., Dollár, P., Zitnick, C.L.: Microsoft COCO: common objects in context. CoRR abs/1405.0312 (2014)
10. Li, X., Lan, W., Dong, J., Liu, H.: Adding Chinese captions to images. In: Proceedings of ICMR (2016)
11. Fang, H., Gupta, S., Iandola, F., Srivastava, R., Deng, L., Dollar, P., Gao, J., He, X., Mitchell, M., Platt, J., Zitnick, L., Zweig, G.: From captions to visual concepts and back. In: Proceedings of CVPR (2015)
12. Gong, Y., Wang, L., Hodosh, M., Hockenmaier, J., Lazebnik, S.: Improving image-sentence embeddings using large weakly annotated photo collections. In: Fleet, D., Pajdla, T., Schiele, B., Tuytelaars, T. (eds.) ECCV 2014. LNCS, vol. 8692, pp. 529–545. Springer, Heidelberg (2014). doi:10.1007/978-3-319-10593-2_35
13. Li, X., Jin, Q., Liao, S., Liang, J., He, X., Huo, Y., Lan, W., Xiao, B., Lu, Y., Xu, J.: RUC-tencent at ImageCLEF 2015: concept detection, localization and sentence generation. In: CLEF Working Notes (2015)

14. Gilbert, A., Piras, L., Wang, J., Yan, F., Dellandrea, E., Gaizauskas, R., Villegas, M., Mikolajczyk, K.: Overview of the ImageCLEF 2015 scalable image annotation. In: CLEF Working Notes, Localization and Sentence Generation Task (2015)
15. Frome, A., Corrado, G., Shlens, J., Bengio, S., Dean, J., Ranzato, M., Mikolov, T.: DeViSE: a deep visual-semantic embedding model. In: Proceedings of NIPS (2013)
16. Mikolov, T., Sutskever, I., Chen, K., Corrado, G., Dean, J.: Distributed representations of words and phrases and their compositionality. In: Proceedings of NIPS (2013)
17. Dong, J., Li, X., Snoek, C.G.M.: Word2VisualVec: cross-media retrieval by visual feature prediction. CoRR abs/1604.06838 (2016)
18. Simonyan, K., Zisserman, A.: Very deep convolutional networks for large-scale image recognition. In: Proceedings of ICLR (2015)
19. Agrawal, P., Girshick, R., Malik, J.: Analyzing the performance of multilayer neural networks for object recognition. In: Fleet, D., Pajdla, T., Schiele, B., Tuytelaars, T. (eds.) ECCV 2014. LNCS, vol. 8695, pp. 329–344. Springer, Heidelberg (2014). doi:10.1007/978-3-319-10584-0_22
20. Russakovsky, O., Deng, J., Su, H., Krause, J., Satheesh, S., Ma, S., Huang, Z., Karpathy, A., Khosla, A., Bernstein, M., Berg, A.C., Fei-Fei, L.: Imagenet large scale visual recognition challenge. Int. J. Comput. Vision **115**(3), 211–252 (2015)
21. Li, X., Liao, S., Lan, W., Du, X., Yang, G.: Zero-shot image tagging by hierarchical semantic embedding. In: Proceedings of SIGIR (2015)
22. Li, X., Uricchio, T., Ballan, L., Bertini, M., Snoek, C.G.M., Del Bimbo, A.: Socializing the semantic gap: a comparative survey on image tag assignment, refinement and retrieval. ACM Comput. Surv. **49**(1), 14:1–14:39 (2016)
23. Villegas, M., et al.: General overview of ImageCLEF at the CLEF 2015 Labs. In: Mothe, J., Savoy, J., Kamps, J., Pinel-Sauvagnat, K., Jones, G.J.F., SanJuan, E., Cappellato, L., Ferro, N. (eds.) CLEF 2015. LNCS, vol. 9283, pp. 444–461. Springer, Heidelberg (2015). doi:10.1007/978-3-319-24027-5_45

Blind Image Quality Assessment Based on Local Quantized Pattern

Yazhong Zhang, Jinjian Wu, Xuemei Xie[✉], and Guangming Shi

School of Electronic Engineering, Xidian University, Xi'an, China
yzzhang@stu.xidian.edu.cn, {jinjian.wu,xmxie}@mail.xidian.edu.cn,
gmshi@xidian.edu.cn

Abstract. No-reference (NR) image quality assessment (IQA) metrics
have attracted great attention in the area of image processing. Since
there is no access to the reference images, the generic NR IQA metrics
have made less progress than the full-reference and reduced-reference
IQA metrics. In this paper, we aim to propose an effective quality-aware
feature based on the local quantized pattern (LQP) for quality evaluation. Firstly, a codebook is learned by K-means clustering the LQP
descriptors of a corpus of pristine images. Based on the codebook, the
LQP descriptors of images are then encoded to derive the quality-aware
features. Finally, the image features are mapped to the subjective quality scores using the support vector regression. Experimental results on
several public databases indicate the propose method performs highly
consistent with the human visual perception.

Keywords: Image quality assessment (IQA) · No-reference · Local
quantized pattern (LQP) · Visual codebook · Human visual system
(HVS)

1 Introduction

The advent of the information era has brought great changes to the lifestyle of
human beings. We prefer to capture information around the scene visually via
digital images and videos. The good quality of images or videos are crucial for
image understanding and perception. However, too many factors may introduce
distortions to the images before arriving to human eyes, such as thermal noise
and dithering of imaging devices, or lossy compression format. To distinguish
the spotty quality of images on the Internet, it is necessary for the computers to
automatically measure the image degradation in accordance with human visual
system (HVS) [1].

Up to now, researchers have made great progress to propose a large number of image quality assessment (IQA) metrics. Generally speaking, the quality
evaluation algorithms can be divided into three types depending on the information required from the reference images, which are full-reference (FR), reduced-
reference (RR) and blind/no-reference (NR) [2]. FR metrics need the original

© Springer International Publishing AG 2016
E. Chen et al. (Eds.): PCM 2016, Part II, LNCS 9917, pp. 241–251, 2016.
DOI: 10.1007/978-3-319-48896-7_24

reference image to evaluate the image quality, such as the classic metric: peak signal noise ratio (PSNR). The FR metrics usually have low computational complexity and can provide universally good performance for different types of distorted images. RR metrics are proposed based on a small number of features extracted from the reference image. Both FR and RR metrics require the whole or partial access to the reference image, which may be impossible for the practical application. In this case, NR metrics is introduced since it can evaluate image quality without any knowledge of the reference image [3].

The early work about NR IQA is mainly distortion-specific, which means that the metric is proposed to evaluate one specific type of distortion and can't be generalized for other distorted images. Fang et al. introduce a quality assessment of contrast-distorted images based on the entropy and moment features [4]. Li et al. utilize the discrete orthogonal moments to evaluate the blur effect [5]. The blocking artifacts of JPEG compressed images are detected using gradient profiles [6]. Algorithms presented in [7] can estimate the quality of JP2K compressed images. This type of metrics can only measure the quality of images suffering from single distortion. Usually, the images are contaminated by multiple distortions and the distortion is not known in advance. Thus, non-distortion-specific or general NR metrics are required to evaluate the quality of distortion-unknown images.

Recently, the general NR metrics usually follow two main trends: natural scene statistics (NSS)-based and learning-based. The NSS-based metrics extract the image features using the statistical property of natural images, while the learning-based metrics involve in learning and testing based on the neural network or support vector regression (SVR). The two categories of NR metrics are not absolute distinct. Specifically, NSS model assumes that there exists certain statistical regularity in spatial and transform domain for the natural scene [8]. Distortions will vary the statistical properties held by natural images. Moorthy et al. proposed the DIIVINE index by employing generalized Gaussian distribution (GGD) to model the wavelet coefficients [9]. Saad et al. extracted the NSS features in DCT domain and introduced the BLIINDS-II index [10]. In [11], Mittal et al. derived the BRISQUE index using GGD and asymmetric GGD to model the spatial pixels. The NSS-based algorithms hold a hypothesis that distorted images also follow the statistical regularity as the natural images do. However, Zhou Wang et al. pointed out that distortions may disturb the statistical regularity [12]. There exists fitting errors between the real distribution and the fitted NSS model which influence the prediction accuracy [13].

The learning-based metrics usually extract features based on the entropy, structural information or phase congruency instead of NSS model. The image quality is predicted through a regression model which maps the image features to subjective perceptive scores. Li et al. used the phase congruency, entropy and gradient as image features to evaluate image quality based on the general regression neural network [14]. Liu et al. extracted the image entropy features in both spatial and DCT domain and introduced the SSEQ index using SVR model [15]. Entropy has been considered as an efficient feature, while it can not represent the local information of images. Xue et al. utilized the joint statistics of gradient magnitude and Laplacian features to measure image quality [16]. However, gradient only reflects the intensity property but it can not well deliver the orientation information and spatial correlation. It is known that the performance of an IQA metric mainly depends on the image features. Thus, the quality-aware features which can effective summary the images and be sensitive to distortions are crucial for IQA algorithms.

Researches have demonstrated that human eyes are more likely to extract the image structural information for visual perception. The perceptive changes of image structure can be considered as effective indicators to reflect the image quality. As an efficient local structural descriptor, local binary pattern (LBP) has achieved great progress for quality evaluation [17]. However, the existing algorithms usually employ the fix layout of neighborhood pixels of LBP which limits the multiscale analysis. Recently, a generalized form of local pattern called local quantized pattern (LQP) is proposed in [18] that can overcome the disadvantage of LBP. It has the ability to encode larger radius of neighborhood pixels and deeper pattern quantization than LBP. We introduce the LQP descriptor to represent the image content and propose a novel NR IQA metric. The image features are extracted through a codebook constructed based on the LQP descriptor of a set of natural images. Concretely, the proposed method consists of three steps: (1) codebook construction. The codebook is constructed by K-means clustering the LQP descriptors extracted from a corpus of natural images across various contents. (2) image representation. Based on the codebook, any givens image can be encoded as the occurrence histogram of each codeword. (3) quality prediction. The image quality is predicted using the SVR model learned based on the training dataset.

It is noted that the idea of codebook-based NR metric has been proposed in [19], while our proposed algorithm differs from it on two points of codebook construction. Firstly, reference [19] constructed the codebook based on distorted images with specific distortions. So, the codebook should be re-constructed when evaluating images with other distortion types. In our metric, the codebook is constructed based on a set of natural images and the codebook is only needed to be constructed once. The obtained codebook can be reused for different types of distorted images quality assessment. In addition, the algorithm in [19] required large size of codebook to achieve good performance. In our algorithm, only several hundreds or thousands of codeword are enough to give reliable performance. The small codebook size can reduce the computational complexity to train the regression model.

The reminder of this paper is organized as follows. In Sect. 2, the detailed representation of the proposed method is given to evaluate the image quality. Section 3 presents the experimental results to demonstrate the effectiveness of the proposed algorithm. The conclusion is drawn in Sect. 4.

2   The Proposed Metric

In this section, we will present the detailed procedure of evaluating the image quality. Firstly, the LQP descriptor of images are extracted. Then, a codebook is constructed based on a set of natural images. Next, the image is represented by the statistical histogram by mapping into the codebook. Finally, the SVR model is trained to predict the image quality.

2.1   LQP Descriptor Extraction

Researches have demonstrated that larger neighborhood radius and deeper pattern quantization are more sensitive to distortions and can better represent the image structural information [20]. Therefore, we select the circular local ternary pattern (LTP) with 24 neighborhood pixels and neighborhood radius of 2 in our algorithm. To reduce the number of possible pattern codes, the splitting strategy is adopted by splitting the ternary pattern into two binary patterns: "positive" and "negative" patterns. Figure 1 shows the diagram of the 24-bit LTP and its split "positive" and "negative" LBP of an image block.

As shown Fig. 1, notation s_r^i represents the i-th sample point on the circle with radius of r, and s_0 denotes the central pixel. Many samples on the circle such as s_1^2, s_1^4 and s_2^2, s_2^4, s_2^{16} do not exactly fall on any image coordinates, so the sample intensity should be interpolated. For simplicity, we employ the bilinear interpolation for pixel interpolation. Given the threshold t, the LTP of the central pixel s_0 can be calculated by comparing s_0 and its corresponding neighborhood sample points. The comparison result c_r^i of sample point s_r^i can be defined as

$$c_r^i = \begin{cases} 1 & s_r^i - s_0 > t \\ 0 & |s_r^i - s_0| \leqslant t \\ -1 & s_r^i - s_0 < -t \end{cases} \tag{1}$$

As the ternary pattern will be split into "positive" and "negative" binary pattern. Then, the comparison results c_r^i in Eq. 3 are further decomposed as

$$c_r^{i+} = \begin{cases} 1 & c_r^i > 0 \\ 0 & c_r^i \leqslant 0 \end{cases} \tag{2}$$

and

$$c_r^{i-} = \begin{cases} 1 & c_r^i < 0 \\ 0 & c_r^i \geqslant 0 \end{cases} \tag{3}$$

where c_r^{i+} and c_r^{i-} respectively denote the positive and negative comparison result between the sample point s_r^i and the central pixel s_0.

Based on the pixel-comparison, the "positive" pattern p^+ and "negative" pattern p^- are defined as

$$\begin{aligned} p^+ &= [c_1^{1+}, c_1^{2+}, \ldots, c_1^{8+}, c_2^{1+}, c_2^{2+}, \ldots, c_2^{16+}] \\ p^- &= [c_1^{1-}, c_1^{2-}, \ldots, c_1^{8-}, c_2^{1-}, c_2^{2-}, \ldots, c_2^{16-}] \end{aligned} \tag{4}$$

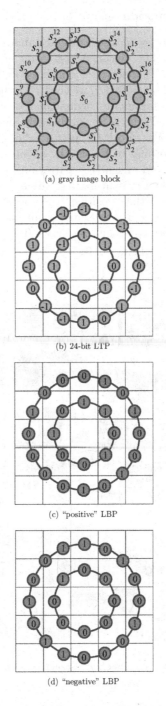

(a) gray image block

(b) 24-bit LTP

(c) "positive" LBP

(d) "negative" LBP

Fig. 1. An example to show the LTP and its split "positive" and "negative" LBP.

2.2   Codebook Construction

The 24-bit splitting ternary pattern will produce about 17 million pattern codes from all-zeros to all-ones. The obtained histogram is too spare and meaningless for feature extraction. Therefore, we utilize a codebook to encode the huge number of pattern codes. In this paper, we construct the codebook based on the natural images instead of specific-distortion images. 60 natural images across various contents are selected from SUN database [21] for codebook construction, which are shown in Fig. 2. The "positive" patterns and "negative" patterns of all images are calculated according to Eq. 4. The occurrence of each pattern code are counted in "positive" and "negative" pattern sets separately. To avoid the effect of outliers, a threshold τ is utilized to discard the pattern codes which occur less than τ. Based on the "positive" (or "negative") pattern codes and their corresponding occurrence, the weighted K-means using Euclidean distance is used to cluster the pattern codes into k centers. Then, two codebooks denoted by Cb^+ and Cb^- are obtained by grouping the clustering centers of "positive" and "negative" patterns respectively.

Fig. 2. 60 natural images for codebook construction. The images are presented in proportion to the original size.

2.3   Image Representation

For any given image, the "positive" and "negative" pattern codes of each pixel are computed based on Eq. 4. Each "positive" (or "negative") pattern code can be mapped to the nearest codeword of Cb^+ (or Cb^-) by minimizing the Euclidean distances between the pattern code and the codewords. The occurrences of each codeword in Cb^+ and Cb^- are separately counted and normalized to calculate the histograms h^+ and h^-. Then, the two histograms of "positive" and "negative" patterns are concatenated to make a large histogram as

$$h = [h^+, h^-] \tag{5}$$

Then, h is the proposed quality-aware structural feature of images.

Obviously, there are strong correlation between the histograms of "positive" and "negative" patterns. In addition, the codewords intra the "positive" and "negative" codebook also correlate to each other. To reduce the redundancy of the histogram h, we employ the principle component analysis (PCA) to project h to a low-dimensional space. Then, the dimension of histogram features can be reduced further.

2.4   Quality Prediction

Based on the training dataset, a regression model is learned to map the image features to the corresponding subjective perception scores, such as mean opinion score (MOS) or different mean opinion score (DMOS). Then, the quality of an quality-unknown image can be predicted using the trained regression model. In this paper, we employ the SVR technique [22] to learn the regression function. The radial basis function (RBF) kernel is selected to implement the ε-SVR model. In addition, the libSVM package [23] is adopted to run the training and testing process of SVR.

3   Experimental Results

3.1   Protocol

To verify the performance of the proposed NR metric, three public benchmark IQA databases are deployed. LIVE database [24] contains 29 reference images and 779 corresponding distorted images over five distortion types: JPEG2000 compression (JP2K), JPEG compression (JPEG), white noise (WN), Gaussian blurring (Gblur) and fast fading Rayleigh channel (FF). CSIQ [25] is composed of 866 distorted images built from 30 reference images with 6 distortion types. We select four common distortions: WN, JPEG, JP2K and Gblur, which consist of 600 distorted images. TID2013 [26] covers 24 distortion types, each of which consists of 5 distorted levels generated from 25 reference images. Four common distortion types (WN, JPEG, JP2K and Gblur) containing 480 distorted images are used.

The threshold value t to calculate the LTP of images in Eq. 3 is set as 0. And the threshold value τ to discard the outliers pattern codes is set as 10. The codebook sizes of "positive" and "negative" patterns are both 1800. The number of components of PCA is set as 50. As the proposed metric involves in training process based on SVR model, the dataset is randomly split into two non-overlap subsets: a training set and a testing set. The training set contains the distorted image corresponding to 80% reference images, and the rest belongs to the testing set. To avoid the partitioning bias, the experiments are repeated 1000 times and the median results are marked.

3.2 Performance Comparisons on Individual Database

Five state-of-the-art NR IQA metrics: DIIVINE [9], BRISQUE [11], CBIQ [19], NIQE [27], IL-NIQE [28], and two classical FR metrics: PSNR and SSIM [29] are selected for performance comparisons. Three common criteria are computed to evaluate the prediction accuracy and monotonicity between the subjective perceptual scores and the predicted quality scores. The criteria contain Pearson Linear Correlation Coefficient (PLCC), Spearman Rank-Order Correlation Coefficient (SROCC) and Root Mean Squared Error (RMSE). The higher PLCC and SROCC values and lower RMSE represent a better performance of the IQA algorithm.

The performance comparisons on four distortion types of TID2013 database across 1000 iterations are shown in Table 1. The two best results measured by PLCC, SROCC and RMSE are emphasized in bold. It can be found that the proposed metric performs quite well on JP2K and JPEG compression distortions.

Table 1. Performance comparison across 1000 train-test iterations on four distortion types of TID2013 database. The two best results are emphasized in bold.

Dist.	Crit.	NR						FR	
		Proposed	DIIVINE	BRISQUE	CBIQ	NIQE	IL-NIQE	PSNR	SSIM
JP2K	PLCC	**0.9489**	0.9136	0.9156	0.9003	0.9250	0.9152	**0.9305**	0.9140
	SROCC	**0.9192**	0.9073	0.9015	0.8942	0.9054	**0.9106**	0.8907	0.9063
	RMSE	**0.5303**	0.6855	0.6838	0.7399	0.6393	0.6803	**0.6227**	0.6900
JPEG	PLCC	**0.9608**	0.9438	0.9313	0.8637	0.9389	0.9105	0.9177	**0.9551**
	SROCC	0.9038	0.9034	0.8757	0.8477	0.8826	0.8835	**0.9188**	**0.9317**
	RMSE	**0.4140**	0.4954	0.5429	0.7445	0.5173	0.6282	0.5919	**0.4415**
WN	PLCC	0.8571	0.9241	**0.9359**	0.7475	0.8619	0.9008	**0.9625**	0.8731
	SROCC	0.8342	0.9208	**0.9323**	0.8037	0.8493	0.8923	**0.9436**	0.8661
	RMSE	0.3612	0.2705	**0.2529**	0.4696	0.3567	0.3150	**0.1920**	0.3450
Gblur	PLCC	0.9272	0.9253	0.8893	0.9015	0.8682	0.8611	**0.9664**	**0.9640**
	SROCC	0.9192	0.9292	0.8939	0.9023	0.8450	0.8616	**0.9666**	**0.9667**
	RMSE	0.4568	0.4703	0.5648	0.5293	0.6112	0.6309	**0.3201**	**0.3310**
Overall	PLCC	**0.9337**	**0.9225**	0.9089	0.8209	0.8346	0.8749	0.9140	0.8329
	SROCC	**0.9134**	0.9079	0.8930	0.7938	0.8450	0.8830	**0.9244**	0.8522
	RMSE	**0.5014**	**0.5376**	0.5812	0.8014	0.7684	0.6731	0.5671	0.7737

Table 2. Overall performance comparison across 1000 train-test iterations on LIVE and CSIQ databases. The two best results are emphasized in bold.

DB	Crit.	NR						FR	
		Proposed	DIIVINE	BRISQUE	CBIQ	NIQE	IL-NIQE	PSNR	SSIM
LIVE	PLCC	**0.9238**	0.9182	**0.9476**	0.9200	0.9122	0.9092	0.8723	0.9042
	SROCC	**0.9221**	0.9203	**0.9501**	0.9190	0.9113	0.9035	0.8756	0.9104
	RMSE	**6.1599**	9.1499	**7.3668**	12.3611	11.1746	11.4353	13.3597	11.6694
CSIQ	PLCC	**0.9238**	0.8958	**0.9266**	0.8300	0.9097	0.8837	0.9073	0.8513
	SROCC	**0.9090**	0.8757	0.9018	0.8173	0.9012	0.8867	**0.9219**	0.8767
	RMSE	**0.1071**	0.1237	**0.1036**	0.1582	0.1152	0.1305	0.1188	0.1483

It performs a little worse than the best NR metrics and PSNR on WN. On Gblur distortion, the proposed metric performs better than other NR metrics while worse than the FR metrics. The overall performance of the proposed metric is much better than other NR and FR metrics. In addition, the overall performance comparisons on LIVE and CSIQ databases are presented in Table 2. The proposed metric performs as well as the state-of-the-art NR metric BRISQUE and better than other NR and FR metrics, although the FR metrics require the whole reference images. In summery, the proposed metric performs quite well on the three databases and is highly consistent with human perception.

4   Conclusion

This paper proposed a novel NR IQA metric using the codebook-based LQP features. The codebook is constructed through clustering the LQP descriptors of a group of natural images across various contents, which can be employed for general image representation and has strong generalization ability. The codebook-based features are extracted by counting the occurrence of images LQP descriptors on each codeword. The experimental results indicated that the proposed metric can predict the image quality in accordance with the human perception.

Acknowledgement. This work was supported by the Major State Basic Research Development Program of China (973 Program, No. 2013CB329402), the National Natural Science Foundation of China (Nos. 61401325, 61472301, 61301288, 61227004), the Research Fund for the Doctoral Program of Higher Education (No. 20130203130001), International cooperation project of Shaanxi science and technology R&D program (No. 2014KW01-02).

References

1. Bovik, A.C.: Automatic prediction of perceptual image and video quality. Proc. IEEE **101**(9), 2008–2024 (2013)
2. Manap, R.A., Shao, L.: Non-distortion-specific no-reference image quality assessment: a survey. Inf. Sci. **301**, 141–160 (2015)
3. Wang, Z., Bovik, A.C.: Reduced-and no-reference image quality assessment. IEEE Signal Process. Mag. **28**(6), 29–40 (2011)

4. Fang, Y., Ma, K., Wang, Z., Lin, W., Fang, Z., Zhai, G.: No-reference quality assessment of contrast-distorted images based on natural scene statistics. IEEE Signal Process. Lett. **22**(7), 838–842 (2015)
5. Li, L., Lin, W., Wang, X., Yang, G., Bahrami, K., Kot, A.C.: No-reference image blur assessment based on discrete orthogonal moments. IEEE Trans. Cybern. **46**(1), 39–50 (2016)
6. Brandão, T., Queluz, M.P.: No-reference image quality assessment based on DCT domain statistics. Signal Process. **88**(4), 822–833 (2008)
7. Sheikh, H.R., Bovik, A.C., Cormack, L.: No-reference quality assessment using natural scene statistics: JPEG 2000. IEEE Trans. Image Process. **14**(11), 1918–1927 (2005)
8. Ruderman, D.L., Bialek, W.: Statistics of natural images: scaling in the woods. Phys. Rev. Lett. **73**(6), 814 (1994)
9. Moorthy, A.K., Bovik, A.C.: Blind image quality assessment: from natural scene statistics to perceptual quality. IEEE Trans. Image Process. **20**(12), 3350–3364 (2011)
10. Saad, M.A., Bovik, A.C., Charrier, C.: Blind image quality assessment: a natural scene statistics approach in the DCT domain. IEEE Trans. Image Process. **21**(8), 3339–3352 (2012)
11. Mittal, A., Moorthy, A.K., Bovik, A.C.: No-reference image quality assessment in the spatial domain. IEEE Trans. Image Process. **21**(12), 4695–4708 (2012)
12. Wang, Z., Wu, G., Sheikh, H.R., Simoncelli, E.P., Yang, E.H., Bovik, A.C.: Quality-aware images. IEEE Trans. Image Process. **15**(6), 1680–1689 (2006)
13. Zhang, Y., Wu, J., Xie, X., Shi, G.: Blind image quality assessment with improved natural scene statistics model. Digital Signal Process. (2016, accepted)
14. Li, C., Bovik, A.C., Wu, X.: Blind image quality assessment using a general regression neural network. IEEE Trans. Neural Networks **22**(5), 793–799 (2011)
15. Liu, L., Liu, B., Huang, H., Bovik, A.C.: No-reference image quality assessment based on spatial and spectral entropies. Signal Process. Image Commun. **29**(8), 856–863 (2014)
16. Xue, W., Mou, X., Zhang, L., Bovik, A.C., Feng, X.: Blind image quality assessment using joint statistics of gradient magnitude and Laplacian features. IEEE Trans. Image Process. **23**(11), 4850–4862 (2014)
17. Li, Q., Lin, W., Xu, J., Fang, Y., Thalmann, D.: No-reference image quality assessment based on structural and luminance information. In: Tian, Q., Sebe, N., Qi, G.-J., Huet, B., Hong, R., Liu, X. (eds.) MMM 2016. LNCS, vol. 9516, pp. 301–312. Springer, Heidelberg (2016). doi:10.1007/978-3-319-27671-7_25
18. ul Hussain, S., Triggs, B.: Visual recognition using local quantized patterns. In: Fitzgibbon, A., Lazebnik, S., Perona, P., Sato, Y., Schmid, C. (eds.) ECCV 2012. LNCS, vol. 7573, pp. 716–729. Springer, Heidelberg (2012). doi:10.1007/978-3-642-33709-3_51
19. Ye, P., Doermann, D.: No-reference image quality assessment using visual codebooks. IEEE Trans. Image Process. **21**(7), 3129–3138 (2012)
20. Tan, X., Triggs, B.: Enhanced local texture feature sets for face recognition under difficult lighting conditions. IEEE Trans. Image Process. **19**(6), 1635–1650 (2010)
21. Xiao, J., Hays, J., Ehinger, K., Oliva, A., Torralba, A., et al.: Sun database: large-scale scene recognition from abbey to zoo. In: IEEE Conference on Computer Vision and Pattern Recognition (CVPR), pp. 3485–3492 (2010)
22. Gu, B., Sheng, V., Tay, K., Romano, W., Li, S.: Incremental support learning for ordinal regression. IEEE Trans. Neural Netw. Learn. Syst. **26**(7), 1403–1416 (2015)

23. Chang, C.C., Lin, C.J.: LIBSVM: a library for support vector machines. ACM Trans. Intell. Syst. Technol. (TIST) **2**(3), 27 (2011)
24. Sheikh, H.R., Sabir, M.F., Bovik, A.C.: A statistical evaluation of recent full reference image quality assessment algorithms. IEEE Trans. Image Process. **15**(11), 3440–3451 (2006)
25. Larson, E.C., Chandler, D.: Categorical image quality (CSIQ) database (2010). http://vision.okstate.edu/csiq
26. Ponomarenko, N., Ieremeiev, O., Lukin, V., Egiazarian, K., Jin, L., Astola, J., Vozel, B., Chehdi, K., Carli, M., Battisti, F., et al.: Color image database TID2013: peculiarities and preliminary results. In: 4th European Workshop on Visual Information Processing (EUVIP), pp. 106–111 (2013)
27. Mittal, A., Soundararajan, R., Bovik, A.C.: Making a blind image quality analyzer. IEEE Signal Process. Lett. **20**(3), 209–212 (2013)
28. Zhang, L., Zhang, L., Bovik, A.: A feature-enriched completely blind image quality evaluator. IEEE Trans. Image Process. **24**(8), 2579–2591 (2015)
29. Wang, Z., Bovik, A.C., Sheikh, H.R., Simoncelli, E.P.: Image quality assessment: from error visibility to structural similarity. IEEE Trans. Image Process. **13**(4), 600–612 (2004)

Sign Language Recognition with Multi-modal Features

Junfu Pu, Wengang Zhou[✉], and Houqiang Li

CAS Key Laboratory of Technology in Geo-spatial
Information Processing and Application System,
Department of Electronic Engineering and Information Science,
University of Science and Technology of China, Hefei 230027, China
pjh@mail.ustc.edu.cn, {zhwg,lihq}@ustc.edu.cn

Abstract. We study the problem of recognizing sign language automatically using the RGB videos and skeleton coordinates captured by Kinect, which is of great significance in communication between the deaf and the hearing societies. In this paper, we propose a sign language recognition (SLR) system with data of two channels, including the gesture videos of the sign words and joint trajectories. In our framework, we extract two modals of features to represent the hand shape videos and hand trajectories for recognition. The variation of gesture is obtained by 3D CNN and the activations of fully connected layers are used as the representations of these sign videos. For trajectories, we use the shape context to describe each joint, and combine them all within a feature matrix. After that, a convolutional neural network is applied to generate a robust representation of these trajectories. Furthermore, we fuse these features and train a SVM classifier for recognition. We conduct some experiments on large vocabulary sign language dataset with up to 500 words and the results demonstrate the effectiveness of our proposed method.

Keywords: Sign language recognition · Joint trajectory · Gesture recognition

1 Introduction

Sign language is wildly used in communication between the deaf and hearing societies. It has attracted considerable attention thanks to the broad social impact. Sign language recognition (SLR) targets on automatically translating sign language into text or interpreting it into spoken language. Besides, SLR has great potential applications in other fields such as human-computer interaction systems [19,23] and image retrieval [17].

Sign language conveys semantic information through gestures and the movements of hands and elbows. There are many previous studies focusing on the joint trajectories or gestures. The trajectory based sign language recognition method achieved promising results [16]. Lin et al. [16] presented a curve matching method

© Springer International Publishing AG 2016
E. Chen et al. (Eds.): PCM 2016, Part II, LNCS 9917, pp. 252–261, 2016.
DOI: 10.1007/978-3-319-48896-7_25

from the view of manifold for sign language recognition. They divided the trajectory of the sign word into several linear segments, and calculated the distances between these two sets of segments. Their method achieved good performance both on two datasets which contain 370 and 1000 sign words, respectively. There are also other trajectory based methods for sign language or action recognition such as [1,4,5,20].

The above works are commonly based on trajectory recognition. However, these methods are not able to handle the recognition for signs with gestures. Murakami et al. [18] designed a gesture recognition system for Japanese sign language. They used a recurrent neural network that employed a three-layered back propagation algorithm to recognize the finger alphabet, with the gesture and character pairs as the input of the system. Furthermore, there were also some other works which combined different kinds of features, including gestures and hand trajectories [15,27,31]. Wang et al. [27] proposed a SLR framework using trajectories, RGB videos and depth videos. They used the method introduced in their paper to select key frames. After that, HMMs were used to model each sign word with the features extracted in each key frame. This method cost less time while maintaining a high recognition rate.

Some early SLR systems achieved great successes with data gloves [18,25]. The main advantage of data gloves is that they can capture the finger joints information and hand trajectory accurately. One typical SLR framework with data gloves was proposed by Gao et al. [8]. They employed the temporal clustering algorithm to cluster a large amount of transition movements for automatic segmentation. However, the data gloves were expensive and inconvenient in real application for the signers. Hence, more and more researchers turned to sign language recognition based on Kinect [9,27,30]. Microsoft Kinect [32] can provide the RGB and depth data as well as skeleton joint coordinates in real time, which makes a great contribution to SLR. The method based on Kinect proposed in [26] achieved an average accuracy of 74.4% on a large dataset with 1000 sign words.

Our approach is based on multi-modal features extracted from RBG data and joint coordinates. We use 3D CNN to obtain the representation of RGB video captured by Kinect. At the same time, LeNet [14] is used for joint trajectory based feature extraction. After that, we use SVM to recognize each sign word with these two kinds of features.

The rest of the paper is organized as follows. In Sect. 2, we describe the framework of our sign language recognition system and present the main procedures to represent the sign words with skeleton joint coordinates and RGB data. The ·SVM classifier is also briefly introduced in this section. The experimental results are reported in Sect. 3. Finally, the paper ends with some conclusions in Sect. 4.

2   Our Approach

In this section, we first give an overview of our SLR system. By using Kinect, we obtain 3D coordinates of 25 skeleton joints including hands, elbows, head,

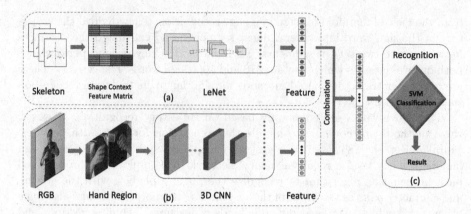

Fig. 1. The framework of our SLR system. (a) Feature extraction on skeleton trajectory from LeNet with shape context feature matrix as input. (b) Using 3D CNN to represent the hand videos formed by patches with hands from original RGB videos. (c) Classification with SVM.

and so on. Besides, the RGB videos is also captured. With the original data, we extract robust features for signs representation and the details will be introduced next. At the end of this section, we use SVM to recognize each sign word.

2.1   System Overview

Figure 1 gives the illustration for the main flowchart of the proposed method in this paper. In this method, we extract both skeleton based features and video based features for recognition. Figure 1(a) shows the procedure of feature extraction from skeletons. We first extract shape context for each point in motion trajectory, and integrate them to form a feature matrix. After that, we use these feature matrixes as the input of a convolutional neural network, and extract deep convnet features which are the intermediate response of fully connected layer from LeNet [14]. The RGB data based feature extraction process is illustrated in Fig. 1(b). Kinect [32] can help us track the skeletons of signer's hands. Hence, we can easily identify the corresponding regions of both hands and extract features from them for recognition. Thus, we get a video with lower resolution which only contains hand shape. With these videos, we can get a good representation by learning with 3D convolutional neural network [22]. These two kinds of features are concatenated for fusion. Finally, we use SVM [3] for classification of sign words.

2.2   Trajectory Representation

When we focus on a specific skeleton, we can get a trajectory formed with a set of 3D coordinates captured in each frame. Then the motion of a skeleton can be modeled by this trajectory. In this section, we will introduce how to build robust features with an effective representation of the 3D trajectory curve.

Preprocessing. In SLR, the trajectories are quite different when performed by different signers. Even for the trajectories performed by the same signer, they may be quite different in velocities. To address these problems, there are two aspects for data preprocessing, including normalization and re-sampling. The location of head and height of spine are used for normalization. In this way, the effect of various scales can be avoid. Another aspect in preprocessing is re-sampling, which will remove the noise and make the trajectory much more smooth. We use the $1 algorithm [29] for re-sampling. We use this method to sample the trajectory with a fixed number of points, making the distribution of the sampling points more uniform. In our experiments, the number of points for sampling is set to be 250.

Shape Context. Shape context [2] is a kind of feature which has been wildly used in shape recognition. It describes the distribution of other points in the neighborhood of a reference point. Denote C as a trajectory curve consisting of a set of 3D points. For a point p_i on curve C, each element of shape context feature is defined as a histogram of voting with the remaining $N - 1$ points in the corresponding bins. The $log - polar^2$ coordinate system is used to make it more sensitive to nearby points. Besides, we project 3D trajectory along three orthogonal plans and obtain three 2D curves. We extract shape context feature in each coordination and concatenate them all together. There are 3 bins for log r and 12 bins for θ. Hence, we get a 108-D ($3 \times 12 \times 3$) shape context feature for each point p_i on C.

Feature Extraction from LeNet. In sign language recognition, we focus on 4 joints which are most informative to recognize a sign word, including both two hands and elbows. Hence, we get four trajectories while a signer performing a sign word. Using the method introduced in above section, the trajectory curve are sampled into a fixed points which we set as 250 in our experiments. For each point p_i on curve C, we extract a 108-D feature. Thus, we can combine all the features extracted in 4 trajectories with the method shown in Fig. 2(c). For each trajectory, we get a 250×108 feature matrix, and the 4 feature matrixes are concatenated row by row. In this way, we get a 250×432 matrix to represent a sign word.

As we know, convolutional neural network (CNN) performs very well in feature learning for a variety of tasks, such as image classification, object detection, and video tracking. Motivated by that fact, we use these feature matrix to train a CNN model. In our system, LeNet [11] is adopted for feature extraction process. For the last fully connected layer, we change it into 1000 neurons. We use the intermediate response of the last fully connected layer as a descriptor for a sign word.

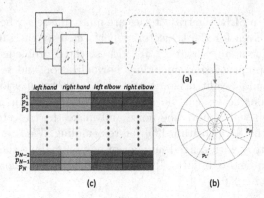

Fig. 2. Main steps for feature matrix. (a) Sampling with $1 algorithm to decrease the effect of different velocities. (b) Shape context extraction for each point. (c) The formation of feature matrix with different trajectories which include both hands and elbows.

2.3   RGB-Data Based Feature Extraction

Hand Shape Segmentation. The Kinect provides us the body skeletons, including both hands. And we use the Kinect mapping function to get the corresponding location in RGB video. Hence, we can easily get an approximate region of hand. For each frame of a video, we take out a 70 by 70 image patch centered on the hand joint. We combine the two patches from both hands and get a low resolution video which only contains hands from the original video. The motion of other parts of body will be removed and we are able to focus on hand shape only. Figure 3(a) gives an illustration for fetching the patches with hand shapes, and several selected frames are shown in Fig. 3(b).

Representation with 3D CNN. To effectively extract the motion information in video analysis, [10] proposed to perform 3D convolutional layers of CNNs so that discriminative features along both spatial and temporal directions are captured. We use 3D CNN to analyze the motion of signer's hand. We follow the network architecture which is similar to Alex Net [13, 22]. The main difference is that the 3D convolution kernels take the place of 2D kernels in Alex Net, and the number of kernels in each layer is also a little different. This network has 5 convolutional layers, 5 pooling layers, followed by 2 fully connected layers, and a softmax output layer. Figure 4 gives a simple illustration of network architecture.

For each video with hand shape, we split it into clips of 16 frames. SGD is adopted to train the networks with mini-batch size of 30 examples. Initial learning rate is 0.001, and divided by 5 every 20k iterations. The training stage lasts for about 310k iterations. The clips from each video are passed to the 3D convolutional neural network to extract fc6 or fc7 activations. These activations are averaged to form a 2048-dim descriptor. This representation for each video is used for sign words recognition.

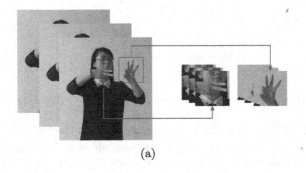

(a)

left hand

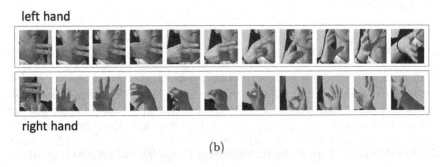

right hand

(b)

Fig. 3. (a) A simple illustration for fetching the hand shapes. (b) Selected frames with left hand (first row) and corresponding right hands (second row).

Fig. 4. 3D CNN architecture. The network has 5 convolutional, 5 max-pooling, and 2 fully connected layers, followed by a softmax output layer. The number of filter in each layer is denoted at the bottom of each box. Each fully connected layer has 2048 output units.

2.4   Recognition with SVM

Support vector machine (SVM) [24] is one of the most successful statistical pattern classifiers which has recently gained popularity within visual pattern recognition [21]. In this section we provide a brief review of SVM. Consider a training data set $T = \{(\mathbf{x_i}, y_i)|i = 1, 2, 3, ..., N\}$ with N samples, where $\mathbf{x_i} \in \mathbb{R}^D$ is the feature vector and $y_i \in \{-1, +1\}$ is class label. The basic task of SVM is to separate the samples in T into two classes. Assume that the training data set is linearly separable in feature space, so that we can find at least a hyperplane $\omega \cdot \mathbf{x} + b = 0$ separating samples into two classes. The support vector method aims at constructing a classifier of the form:

$$y(\mathbf{x}) = \text{sign}(\sum_{i=1}^{N} \alpha_i y_i \Psi(\mathbf{x}, \mathbf{x_i}) + b), \tag{1}$$

where α_k are positive real constants and b is a real constant, and Ψ is a kernel function.

We use LIBSVM [6] to classify the sign words with the features extracted in Sects. 2.2 and 2.3. It implements the one-against-one approach [12] for multiclass classification. Denote k is the number of classes, then $k(k-1)/2$ classifiers are constructed and each one trains data from two classes and a voting strategy is used in classification.

3   Experiments

In this section, we provide some experimental illustrations and relative evaluations of our method on real dataset. We use the Chinese sign language dataset built by ourselves with Kinect. Firstly, the experiments with different features are conducted to evaluate the efficiency of these features. Then we compare the performance of our method with other SLR methods, including the SLR system proposed by Lin et al. [16] and the improved Dense Trajectories (iDTs) [28].

3.1   Dataset

The dataset in our experiments is collected by different sign language signers with Kinect. It contains 500 isolate Chinese sign language words in our daily life. There are 50 signers with different ages taking part in the data collection, which will make this dataset more various and challenging. For each sign word, it is performed by these 50 signers for 5 times. Hence, the dataset consists of 125k ($500 \times 50 \times 5$) samples. To evaluate the effectiveness of our method for signer independent, we choose 200 samples of each word performed by 40 signers for training, and the rest samples performed by the other 10 signers for testing.

3.2   Evaluation of Different Features

Different kinds of features have different discriminative abilities. We represent a sign word by hand trajectory and gestures. They both play important roles in SLR, since the hand trajectory describe the dynamic motion and gesture describe the static appearance. We conduct some experiments with gesture based features and trajectory based features, respectively. As introduced in Sect. 2.3, we split a video into several clips with every 16 frames, then calculate the average activations of fc6 (or fc7) from 3D CNN with all these clips as the representation of a sign word video within hands. Both fc6 and fc7 features are 2048D vectors. With the same idea for trajectory, the activations of the last fully connected layer of LeNet is used for recognition.

Table 1. Recognition rates with different features

Feature		Dimension	Accuracy
Video (Gesture)	clip-softmax	-	0.361
	fc6.ave-knn	2048	0.529
	fc7.ave-knn	2048	0.550
Skeleton (Trajectory)	fc-softmax	1000	0.773

Table 2. Performance comparison

Method		Top1	Top5	Top10
iDTs [28] (RGB)		0.685	0.888	0.927
CM_VoM [16] (Trajectory)		0.546	0.820	0.897
Ours	fc6-3DCNN+fc-LeNet	0.847	0.970	0.987
	fc7-3DCNN+fc-LeNet	0.858	0.973	0.988

The experimental results with different features are shown in Table 1. For sign words with videos, the accuracy in clip level is about 36.1%. The we classify the videos with the average fc6 (or fc7) activations from the network using KNN [7] classifier. The recognition rates increase to 52.9% for fc6 and 55.0% for fc7, which is higher than accuracy in clip level. The accuracy with trajectory features is 77.3%. For better performance, we combine the trajectory features and hand shape features for recognition.

3.3 Comparison with Other Methods

In this part, the baseline improved Dense Trajectories (iDTs) [28] and curve matching from the view of manifold for SLR (CM_VoM) [16] are evaluated on our dataset for comparisons. The recognition rates for different methods are shown in Table 2. The iDTs method is proposed for action recognition, and it also works for SLR task with a top1 accuracy of 68.5%. Another method CM_VoM is based on 3D trajectories, and it reaches the accuracy of 54.6%. In our method, we fuse the trajectory features and hand shape features, and use SVM for classification. The recognition rate is improved significantly with our method. The best recognition rates can reach up to 85.8%, 97.3% and 98.8% in top 1, top 5 and top 10, respectively. Among these results, our method achieves much higher accuracy and outperforms the baselines by a large margin on our SLR dataset.

4 Conclusions

This paper presents a framework for analyzing Chinese sign language using gestures and trajectories of skeletons. We implement the shape context for trajectory representation and extract features from LeNet with the feature matrix.

Meanwhile, we fetch out the hand region with a bounding box of 70×70 pixels in the original RGB videos, and then use 3D CNN to extract features for representing the sign words. Furthermore, these two kinds of features are fused for classification and demonstrate state-of-the-art results. We conduct some experiments with a large isolate Chinese sign language dataset. From the experimental results, it can be seen that the features extracted with neural networks demonstrate strong discriminative capability. Comparing to the baselines, the framework proposed in this paper achieves superior performance. In our future work, we will explore more robust feature fusion strategies among RGB data, depth data, and the skeleton coordinate to improve the performance of our sign language recognition system.

Acknowledgement. This work is supported in part to Prof. Houqiang Li by the 973 Program under Contract 2015CB351803 and the National Natural Science Foundation of China (NSFC) under Contract 61390514 and Contract 61325009, and in part to Dr. Wengang Zhou by NSFC under Contract 61472378, the Natural Science Foundation of Anhui Province under Contract 1508085MF109, and the Fundamental Research Funds for the Central Universities.

References

1. Amor, B.B., Su, J., Srivastava, A.: Action recognition using rate-invariant analysis of skeletal shape trajectories. TPAMI **38**(1), 1–13 (2016)
2. Belongie, S., Malik, J., Puzicha, J.: Shape matching and object recognition using shape contexts. TPAMI **24**(4), 509–522 (2002)
3. Burges, C.J.: A tutorial on support vector machines for pattern recognition. Data Min. Knowl. Disc. **2**(2), 121–167 (1998)
4. Cai, X., Zhou, W., Li, H.: An effective representation for action recognition with human skeleton joints. In: SPIE/COS Photonics Asia, 92731R. International Society for Optics and Photonics (2014)
5. Cai, X., Zhou, W., Wu, L., Luo, J., Li, H.: Effective active skeleton representation for low latency human action recognition. TMM **18**(2), 141–154 (2016)
6. Chang, C.C., Lin, C.J.: LIBSVM: a library for support vector machines. ACM Trans. Intell. Syst. Technol. (TIST) **2**(3), 27 (2011)
7. Cover, T.M., Hart, P.E.: Nearest neighbor pattern classification. IEEE Trans. Inf. Theory **13**(1), 21–27 (1967)
8. Gao, W., Fang, G., Zhao, D., Chen, Y.: Transition movement models for large vocabulary continuous sign language recognition. In: FG, pp. 553–558 (2004)
9. Huang, J., Zhou, W., Li, H., Li, W.: Sign language recognition using 3D convolutional neural networks. In: ICME (2015)
10. Ji, S., Xu, W., Yang, M., Yu, K.: 3D convolutional neural networks for human action recognition. TPAMI **35**(1), 221–231 (2013)
11. Jia, Y., Shelhamer, E., Donahue, J., Karayev, S., Long, J., Girshick, R., Guadarrama, S., Darrell, T.: Caffe: convolutional architecture for fast feature embedding. In: ACM MM, pp. 675–678 (2014)
12. Knerr, S., Personnaz, L., Dreyfus, G.: Single-layer learning revisited: a stepwise procedure for building and training a neural network. In: Neurocomputing, pp. 41–50 (1990)

13. Krizhevsky, A., Sutskever, I., Hinton, G.E.: ImageNet classification with deep convolutional neural networks. In: Advances in Neural Information Processing Systems, pp. 1097–1105 (2012)
14. LeCun, Y., Bottou, L., Bengio, Y., Haffner, P.: Gradient-based learning applied to document recognition. Proc. IEEE **86**(11), 2278–2324 (1998)
15. Lee, G.C., Yeh, F.H., Hsiao, Y.H.: Kinect-based taiwanese sign-language recognition system. Multimedia Tools Appl. **75**(1), 261–279 (2016)
16. Lin, Y., Chai, X., Zhou, Y., Chen, X.: Curve matching from the view of manifold for sign language recognition. In: Jawahar, C.V., Shan, S. (eds.) ACCV 2014. LNCS, vol. 9010, pp. 233–246. Springer, Heidelberg (2015). doi:10.1007/978-3-319-16634-6_18
17. Liu, Z., Li, H., Zhou, W., Hong, R., Tian, Q.: Uniting keypoints: local visual information fusion for large-scale image search. TMM **17**(4), 538–548 (2015)
18. Murakami, K., Taguchi, H.: Gesture recognition using recurrent neural networks. In: SIGCHI Conference on Human Factors in Computing Systems (1991)
19. Pavlovic, V.I., Sharma, R., Huang, T.S.: Visual interpretation of hand gestures for human-computer interaction: a review. TPAMI **19**(7), 677–695 (1997)
20. Pu, J., Zhou, W., Zhang, J., Li, H.: Sign language recognition based on trajectory modeling with HMMs. In: Tian, Q., Sebe, N., Qi, G.-J., Huet, B., Hong, R., Liu, X. (eds.) MMM 2016. LNCS, vol. 9516, pp. 686–697. Springer, Heidelberg (2016). doi:10.1007/978-3-319-27671-7_58
21. Schüldt, C., Laptev, I., Caputo, B.: Recognizing human actions: a local SVM approach. In: ICPR, vol. 3, pp. 32–36 (2004)
22. Tran, D., Bourdev, L., Fergus, R., Torresani, L., Paluri, M.: Learning spatiotemporal features with 3D convolutional networks. In: ICCV, pp. 4489–4497 (2015)
23. Ueoka, R., Hirose, M., Kuma, K., Sone, M., Kohiyama, K., Kawamura, T., Hiroto, K.: Wearable computer application for open air exhibition in expo 2005. In: PCM, pp. 8–15 (2001)
24. Vapnik, V.N., Vapnik, V.: Statistical Learning Theory, vol. 1. Wiley, New York (1998)
25. Wang, C., Gao, W., Xuan, Z.: A real-time large vocabulary continuous recognition system for Chinese sign language. In: Shum, H.-Y., Liao, M., Chang, S.-F. (eds.) PCM 2001. LNCS, vol. 2195, pp. 150–157. Springer, Heidelberg (2001). doi:10.1007/3-540-45453-5_20
26. Wang, H., Chai, X., Chen, X.: Sparse observation (so) alignment for sign language recognition. Neurocomputing **175**, 674–685 (2016)
27. Wang, H., Chai, X., Zhou, Y., Chen, X.: Fast sign language recognition benefited from low rank approximation. In: FG, vol. 1, pp. 1–6 (2015)
28. Wang, H., Kläser, A., Schmid, C., Liu, C.L.: Action recognition by dense trajectories. In: CVPR, pp. 3169–3176 (2011)
29. Wobbrock, J.O., Wilson, A.D., Li, Y.: Gestures without libraries, toolkits or training: a $1 recognizer for user interface prototypes. In: Annual ACM Symposium on User Interface Software and Technology, pp. 159–168 (2007)
30. Zhang, J., Zhou, W., Li, H.: A threshold-based HMM-DTW approach for continuous sign language recognition. In: ICIMCS, p. 237 (2014)
31. Zhang, J., Zhou, W., Li, H.: Chinese sign language recognition with adaptive HMM. In: ICME (2016)
32. Zhang, Z.: Microsoft kinect sensor and its effect. IEEE MultiMedia **19**(2), 4–10 (2012)

Heterogeneous Convolutional Neural Networks for Visual Recognition

Xiangyang Li, Luis Herranz, and Shuqiang Jiang[✉]

Key Laboratory of Intelligent Information Processing,
Institute of Computing Technology, Chinese Academy of Sciences,
Beijing 100190, China
{xiangyang.li,luis.herranz}@vipl.ict.ac.cn, sqjiang@ict.ac.cn

Abstract. Deep convolutional neural networks (CNNs) have shown impressive performance for image recognition when trained over large scale datasets such as ImageNet. CNNs can extract hierarchical features layer by layer starting from raw pixel values, and representations from the highest layers can be efficiently adapted to other visual recognition tasks. In this paper, we propose heterogeneous deep convolutional neural networks (HCNNs) to learn features from different CNN models. Features obtained from heterogeneous CNNs have different characteristics since each network has a different architecture with different depth and the design of receptive fields. HCNNs use a combination network (i.e. another multi-layer neural network) to learn higher level features combining those obtained from heterogeneous base neural networks. The combination network is also trained and thus can better integrate features obtained from heterogeneous base networks. To better understand the combination mechanism, we backpropagate the optimal output and evaluate how the network selects features from each model. The results show that the combination network can automatically leverage the different descriptive abilities of the original models, achieving comparable performance on many challenging benchmarks.

Keywords: Deep learning · Object classification · Scene recognition · Convolutional neural networks · Heterogeneous convolutional neural networks

1 Introduction

Convolutional neural networks (CNNs) [10] trained using supervised backpropagation were successful in certain controlled tasks such as digit recognition. In recent years, CNNs have shown their real potential in large-scale visual recognition [7,9,11,14,17,18,20,26]. The first breakthrough was made by Krizhevsky *et al.* [9], showing that CNNs can improve the state-of-the-art accuracy in large scale object recognition with a large margin. The availability of large datasets such as ImageNet [13] or Places [26] and high-performance computing systems such as GPUs are the main factors responsible for this dramatic improvement.

© Springer International Publishing AG 2016
E. Chen et al. (Eds.): PCM 2016, Part II, LNCS 9917, pp. 262–274, 2016.
DOI: 10.1007/978-3-319-48896-7_26

CNNs extract features from the raw pixels in a feed-forward basis, where the output of a layer is the input of the next layer. The convolution operation of the input image with the specific filters introduces local invariance. The filters in CNNs are learned from data and contribute greatly to obtain very discriminative image features. Another key of the success of CNNs is their ability to learn complex high level features by building increasingly abstract representations hierarchically.

A number of works have been focused on how to improve the performance of CNNs. The first strategy is to train and test CNNs with multiple scales rather than using only a fixed size [7,14]. Sermanet et al. [14] proposed OverFeat, which shows how a multi-scale sliding window can be efficiently implemented within CNNs. It uses the same fixed size approach proposed by Krizhevsky et al. [9] when training CNNs, but turns to multi-scale during test. He et al. [7] proposed spatial pyramid pooling convolutional networks (SPP-net), which adds a spatial pyramid pooling layer between the last convolutional layer and the first fully-connected layer. Another strategy to improve recognition accuracy is to increase the depth and width of the architecture [11,17,18]. Lin et al. [11] propose Network in Network (NIN), which aims to enhance model discriminability for local patches within the receptive field by building micro neural networks. In NIN, convolutional filters are replaced by micro networks which increase the depth of the global network. Simonyan et al. [17] propose models with very deep layers. Their work demonstrated that the representation depth is beneficial for the classification accuracy. Similarly, Szegedy et al. [18] propose GoogLeNet which contains 22 layers. In their work, the inception module is the key component, which not only increases the width but also computes multi-scale features.

Preivous methods use more complex architectures to learn discriminative features. Another way to increase the performance is averaging the results (i.e. probabilities for each class) obtained from multiple instances of the same network, each of them trained under different settings [3,6,9,16,17,21]. In this way the variance of the joint model decreases, with an improvement in the recognition accuracy. However, in this case, since the architecture is fixed, the features extracted from each instance have similar properties.

In contrast to combining decisions or probabilities, we can also combine the mid-level features extracted from CNNs. Agrawal et al. [1] suggest that units in CNNs may be classified into grandmother cells (GMC), which have strong response to specific object classes, or part of distributed codes in which a single response is not discriminative, but a group of responses jointly can be very discriminative. Features extracted from different architectures have different characteristics due to different number of layers and filter designs (related with different receptive fields). Thus, these different features can have complementary characteristics. For example, Fig. 5 shows the response of units from two CNNs with very different architectures (corresponding to those in Fig. 2) to different images. Responses from each of these heterogeneous networks focus on different parts of the original images. To recognize a lizard, one unit in one CNN focuses on the middle part of its body, while one of the other CNN is sensitive to its tail. Features from different models are learned jointly with the rest of its units, so each model has its specific characteristics. The combination of features from heterogeneous networks can make the resulting features more discriminative.

In this paper, we propose heterogeneous convolutional neural networks (HCNNs) as an efficient approach to combine features obtained from heterogeneous architectures using a multi-layer combination network that replaces the top layers of the individual networks and combines them (see Fig. 1). The combination mechanism is also trained from data, learning additional network parameters which can better integrate features obtained from base networks with different architectures. The advantages of HCNNs are:

- First, higher level features resulting from the combination of features from heterogeneous CNNs lead to richer and more discriminative feature representations. HCNN can automatically leverage different descriptive abilities of the original models, achieving better performance on many challenging benchmarks than single network.
- Second, the combination network strategy is flexible and it can benefit from large datasets and fine tuning to specific tasks.

The rest of the paper is organized as follows. Section 2 describes the proposed method. Section 3 describes the experiments and Sect. 4 concludes the paper.

2   Heterogeneous Convolutional Neural Networks

Our motivation is to combine the different capabilities of two (or more) base networks. The architecture and the training process of a HCNNs is illustrated in Fig. 1 for two base networks.

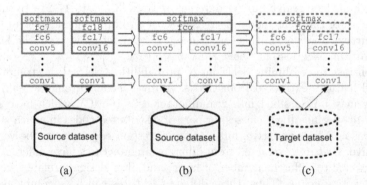

Fig. 1. Heterogeneous convolutional neural networks (HCNNs): (a) pre-training base networks (or reuse available networks), (b) pre-training the combination network, and (c) fine tuning. The example shows two base networks with different architectures, and a two layer combination network.

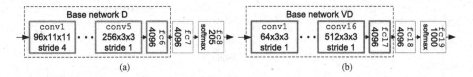

(a)   (b)

Fig. 2. Architectures used in the experiments: (a) deep network D (8 layers), and (b) very deep network VD (19 layers).

2.1 Base Networks

The base networks are the components we want to combine. Although any number of networks can be combined, we focus on the case of two networks. We prefer that both networks have different architectures, since different architectures may provide different expressive capabilities due to different depth and receptive field sizes.

Figure 2 shows two examples of heterogeneous CNN architectures that we will use as base networks. For simplicity, in the rest of the paper we will refer to this particular two architectures as deep (D) and very deep (VD) networks. D has 8 layers and the filters in D have certain sizes, such as 11×11, 5×5 and 3×3, while VD has 19 layers and its convolutional filters have the same size 3×3. The convolution of the input images or feature maps with the learned kernels can capture local invariance, and pooling can increase the invariance to small deformations as well as small shifts. Following the same process layer by layer, the units in high layers have progressively larger receptive field sizes, so they can extract more complex features.

2.2 Combination Network

In order to learn complementary features from base networks, we combine they (two or more) by concatenating the features from the base networks and stack another network (see Fig. 1b). It is a way to learn new features from base networks and can also retain their strength. This combination network may have multiple layers, typically fully connected. The parameters of the combination network are learned from data, so the joint network can freely combine features from any of the networks. Note that this contrasts with simply averaging the probabilities after the softmax classifier. Our method is more flexible, but also has a large number of parameters that must be learned properly. The architecture of the combination network should be designed carefully to maximize the benefit from the available models.

A first question that arises is where should the features be concatenated. In order to keep as much as possible of the abstract knowledge learned by the pretrained base networks, we would like to connect them at a high layer. However, high layer units are too specialized to the original task, so reusing them may decrease the generalization to a new task or a new setting [25]. Thus, we drop several top layers (see Fig. 1a), so the base networks can "forget" too specific

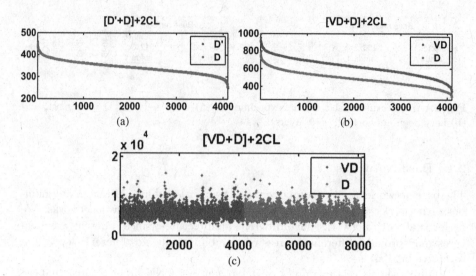

Fig. 3. Average distribution of activations in the concatenation layer, obtained by maximizing the posterior probability (in descending order) when combining (a) homogeneous architectures and (b) heterogeneous architectures, and (c) activations in the concatenated layer for heterogeneous architectures. Best viewed in color.

knowledge, which can be learned again in the combination network from a combination of features from all the base networks. To decide how many layers to remove, a reasonable rule seems to remove as many top layers from each base network as the number of layers in the combination network. In this way, the number of layers from each of the input layers to the output (i.e. the depth) is not changed. In our standard architecture we remove two layers (softmax and top fully connected) and stack two fully connected layers (softmax and fully connected). The number and size of the layers in the combination network is also related with the number of parameters to be learned, and thus has impact over the generalization capability of the network and training cost.

2.3 Training the Network

A HCNN is trained in three steps (see Fig. 1). First the base networks are pretrained with a suitable large scale dataset such as ImageNet. This step requires far more computational resources and training time than the rest. The training cost can be significantly reduced by reusing models already available, and combining their architectures. In this paper, we reuse publicly available models for fast implementation.

The second step is training the combination network, which typically uses backpropagation over a large scale dataset. The third step is fine tuning the network. This step is optional and only necessary when the target dataset is not the same dataset used from training. In principle we only fine tune the last layer or the layers of the combination network, although it could be extended to layers in the base networks or even the whole joint network, but that would increase the training cost significantly.

There is another implicit trade-off with the training cost: the more layers to be trained, the higher the computational cost and the training time. Training a combination network is much faster than training a deep network from scratch, because the number of layers and parameters to be learned is significantly small (which is also less prone to overfitting).

2.4   Understanding the Combination Mechanism

In order to understand how the combination network selects features from the base networks we follow the visualization methods proposed in [5,15], but stopping at the concatenation layer. Instead of computing the input image that maximizes the posterior probability (i.e. softmax) for a given class, we back-propagate the optimal output for each class and check the corresponding input value. Then we average the values across all the classes and sort them in descending order. The results are shown in Fig. 3, where we separately plot the values corresponding to units from each base network.

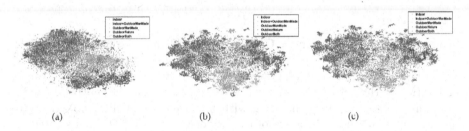

(a)   (b)   (c)

Fig. 4. t-SNE visualization of deep features for SUN397: (a) `fc7` of D, (b) `fc18` of VD, and (c) `fcα` of the joint network [D,VD]+2CL (see Sect. 4 for details). Best viewed in color.

Focusing on SUN397, Fig. 3a shows the case where two homogeneous architectures are combined. As both base networks have the same architecture and learned similar units, the distributions for both networks are similar, showing no particular preference for either of them. In contrast, if we combine two different heterogeneous networks (denoted as D and VD in Fig. 3b) there is a clear dominance of the best performing network. In order to check that this is not caused by different scales in the activations from each base network, we checked the average activations at the same fully connected layer (obtained by forward processing each image and averaging the activations), which shows that both networks are in the same scale (see Fig. 3c). This suggests that the combination network tends to rely more on VD than on D, as expected, because VD is deeper, has better performance and its features are likely to be more discriminative. In contrast, in the case of base networks with the same architecture, the filters learned by each base network capture similar patterns, so Fig. 3a shows almost the same distribution for each base network.

In contrast to averaging, the combination network can generate deep features by taking the output of a fully connected layer. In order to get some insight about how different groups of classes are represented by these deep features, we visualize the 4096-dimensional features obtained from the last fully connected layer (before the softmax) using a two-dimensional t-SNE embedding [19]. Figure 4 shows the heterogeneous case, comparing features from both individual networks and the combined one for SUN397. The difference between the visualizations of D and VD is relatively clear, with VD visualization showing the groups of classes somewhat more separated. The difference between VD and the HCNNs is more subtle. This agrees with the previous conclusion, suggesting that units from VD are selected with higher weights by the combination network, and thus the deep features are more similar to those obtained from VD. However, some discriminative units from D are also integrated in the joint network, which leads to a more discriminative space with a gain of 7.53% over VD in this particular case (see Table 3).

3   Experiments

3.1   Settings

In our experiments we rely on the Caffe framework [8], and the available models[1]. We downloaded the reference BVLC caffenet [8] and the VGG [17] models (see Fig. 2) trained over ILSVRC2012, which are publicly available in Caffe format. In addition to the network D, we trained from scratch another network D′ with the same architecture for comparing with homogeneous architectures. Due to the time limit, we did not train another very deep network VD' from scratch as it will cost a lot of time. So here we only use D and D' to show the performance of homogeneous architectures. In most of the experiments we fine tuned only the combination network for target datasets other than ILSVRC2012.

We compare two combination methods: averaging and the proposed combination network. For convenience we introduce the following notation to compactly describe a particular variation: [A,B]+kCL denotes a HCNN which concatenates the features from two base networks A and B with a combination network with k layers. Similarly, [A,B]+avg denotes the model resulting from averaging the predictions of A and B. In our experiments we only used the central crop of size 227×227 of the image previously resized to 256×256, and compare with other architectures in the same setting.

3.2   Combination Network Architecture

We evaluated combination networks consisting of stacked fully connected layers on top of the concatenated features of the two base networks. We refer to them

---

[1] http://caffe.berkeleyvision.org.

as combination layers (CLs). The most important parameters are the number of CLs and the size. In our standard architecture (see Fig. 5a), there are two CLs, where the top one is the softmax. The only free parameter is the size of the other layer $fc\alpha$. We compared three sizes for the number, and the performance is very similar (see Table. 1), so we keep the two layer network with a size of 4096 for the rest of the experiments.

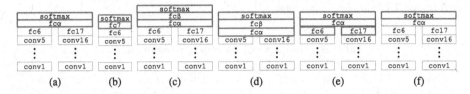

Fig. 5. Variations of architectures and fine tuning strategies in the experiments: (a) standard architecture [V,VD]+2CL with 2 CL fine tuned, (b) single network D with the two top-layers fine tuned, (c) three-layer CL, (d) three-layer CL with one additional top-layer removed from the base networks, (e) fine tuning down to the first top layer of the base networks, and (f) only fine tune the top layer (i.e. retrain the softmax).

We also compared with a deeper combination network with three layers. In this case we considered two variations. The first one adds one additional layer between $fc\alpha$ and the softmax (see Fig. 5c). This increases the total depth of the network, and increases the parameters to be learned and the training cost. However, the accuracy decreases slightly. We also compared with a second variation with three layers, but with another fully connected layer from the base networks removed, so the two base networks are concatenated after the last convolutional layer (the total depth is the same as in the standard architecture).

Table 1. Comparison of different architectures for the combination network.

Architecture	Layer size		Accuracy (%)	
	$fc\alpha$	$fc\beta$	Top 1	Top 5
2CL (Fig. 5a)	4096	-	69.87	89.67
	5192	-	70.10	89.50
	6144	-	70.08	89.44
3 CL (Fig. 5c)	4096	6144	69.43	89.02
3 CL (Fig. 5d)	4096	6144	66.73	87.24

3.3   Object Recognition Performance

We first evaluate the performance for object recognition, and compare the proposed method with averaging the outputs of the two networks. The results are shown in Table 2. In general we can observe that averaging performs well for homogeneous base networks, but the gain is more limited for heterogeneous networks (except for Caltech 101). In contrast, HCNNs seem to achieve higher gains when the architectures are heterogeneous, while achieving marginal or even negative gains for homogeneous ones.

Table 2. Accuracy (%) for object recognition.

Method	ILSVRC 2012 (top 1)		ILSVRC 2012 (top 5)		Caltech101		Caltech256	
	Acc	Gain	Acc	Gain	Acc	Gain	Acc	Gain
D	57.47	-	80.41	-	88.38	-	66.33	-
D'	57.45	-	80.34	-	88.31	-	66.06	-
VD[a]	68.56	-	88.53	-	90.32	-	76.87	-
[D,D']+avg	59.25	1.78	81.68	1.27	89.18	0.80	68.39	2.06
[D,VD]+avg	69.10	0.54	88.15	-0.38	92.55	2.23	77.32	0.45
[D,D']+2CL	58.25	0.78	80.75	0.34	88.55	0.17	65.81	-0.52
[D,VD]+2CL	**70.10**	1.54	**89.50**	0.97	**92.82**	2.50	**79.07**	2.20
VGG[b]	**75.6**		92.5		-		-	
GoogLeNet[c]	-		89.93 (92.11)		-		-	
GoogLeNet[d]	-		91.91 (**93.33**)		-		-	
GoogLeNet[e]	67.44 (68.44)		88.24 (89.01)		-		-	
[2]	-		86.9		91.4		77.61	

[a]Caffe implementation of VGG using only the central crop and one scale [17].
[b]Using multiple scales, dense evaluation and 7 networks. ILSVRC submission [17].
[c]ILSVRC submission. 1 crop (144 crops)[18].
[d]ILSVRC submission. 7 networks, 1 crop (144 crops)[18].
[e]Caffe implementation of GoogLeNet, 1 crop (10 crops)[23].

3.4   Scene Recognition Performance

We also evaluated the performance for scene recognition using the MIT67 [12] and SUN397 [24] datasets (see Table 3). Similarly to the results for object recognition, we observe that averaging is a better solution for combining homogeneous architectures, while a combination network is more suitable for heterogeneous ones. The gain is particularly significant for SUN397, with a very competitive performance of 57.30%, 7.53% better than the best performing base network. As networks trained on scene-oriented datasets are more suitable for scene classification [26], we also report the performance of the networks trained on Places, donated as Dp and VDp. The results verify the effectiveness of the proposed HCNNs.

Table 3. Accuracy (%) for scene recognition.

Method	MIT67		SUN397	
	Acc	Gain	Acc	Gain
D	59.34	-	46.41	-
D'	59.52	-	45.85	-
VD	69.70	-	49.41	-
[D,D']+avg	62.68	3.16	47.77	1.36
[D,VD]+avg	70.75	2.05	52.28	2.87
[D,D']+2CL	58.27	−1.25	45.54	−0.87
[D,VD]+2CL	72.31	2.61	57.30	7.53
SFV_ImageNet [4]	72.86	-	54.4	-
Meta_Objects [22]	78.90	-	58.11	-
SFV [4]	79.01	-	61.72	-
[Dp,VDp]+2CL	**80.52**	-	**64.91**	-

Table 4. Accuracy (%) for different fine tuning strategies for [D,VD]+2CL.

Architecture	Accuracy (%)			
	Cal101	Cal256	MIT67	SUN397
Only softmax	91.89	78.07	79.93	64.08
Softmax, FCα	92.82	79.07	80.52	64.91
Softmax, FCα FC6, FC17	**93.18**	**79.50**	**81.06**	**65.32**

3.5 Impact of Fine Tuning

Fine tuning can improve the recognition accuracy by refining the parameters of the network. We analyze its impact on the recognition accuracy for our standard architecture [D,VD]+2CL, with one, two and three layers refined (see Table 4). First we consider retraining only the softmax layer (see Fig. 5f). We see that the performance improves compared to individual networks. However retraining the two layers of the combination network (see Fig. 5a) improves the performance significantly around 1–3%. Further propagating fine tuning to the next layer, which actually corresponds to layers in the base networks (see Fig. 5e), can still improve the performance. The lower the layer, the less related to the task (less specific), so the gain is marginal. However, the training cost increases significantly.

4 Conclusion

In this paper we studied the unusual case of combining deep networks with heterogeneous architectures, and proposed HCNNs which combine them by concatenating high-layer features and stacking another (combination) network. The proposed method achieves significant performance on many challenging benchmarks. To understand the combination mechanism, we backpropagate the optimal output and evaluate how HCNNs select features from each model. The results show that it can automatically leverage the different descriptive abilities of the original models. Compared with the conventional model averaging method (i.e. ensemble), HCNNs can generate new features from different base networks not just combining probabilities. This allows them to work better when the features are heterogeneous, while averaging often works better for homogeneous (similar model, so the ensemble reduces the variance). The combination network strategy is flexible and it can benefit from large datasets and fine tuning to specific tasks. In this work, we only implement two existing models to show the effectiveness of HCNNs. In the future, more heterogeneous models can be included in the proposed method, where the models can either be publicly available models or trained from scratch.

Acknowledgements. This work was supported in part by the National Basic Research 973 Program of China under Grant No. 2012CB316400, the National Natural Science Foundation of China under Grant Nos. 61532018, 61322212 and 61550110505, the National High Technology Research and Development 863 Program of China under Grant No. 2014AA015202, Beijing Science And Technology Project under Grant No. D161100001816001. This work is also funded by Lenovo Outstanding Young Scientists Program (LOYS).

References

1. Agrawal, P., Girshick, R., Malik, J.: Analyzing the performance of multilayer neural networks for object recognition. In: Fleet, D., Pajdla, T., Schiele, B., Tuytelaars, T. (eds.) ECCV 2014. LNCS, vol. 8695, pp. 329–344. Springer, Heidelberg (2014). doi:10.1007/978-3-319-10584-0_22
2. Chatfield, K., Simonyan, K., Vedaldi, A., Zisserman, A.: Return of the devil in the details: delving deep into convolutional nets. In: Proceedings of the British Machine Vision Conference, BMVC 2014 (2014)
3. Ciregan, D., Meier, U., Schmidhuber, J.: Multi-column deep neural networks for image classification. In: Proceedings of the IEEE Conference on Computer Vision and Pattern Recognition, CVPR 2012, pp. 3642–3649 (2012)
4. Dixit, M., Chen, S., Gao, D., Rasiwasia, N., Vasconcelos, N.: Scene classification with semantic fisher vectors. In: Proceedings of the IEEE Conference on Computer Vision and Pattern Recognition, CVPR 2015, pp. 2974–2983 (2015)
5. Erhan, D., Bengio, Y., Courville, A., Vincent, P.: Visualizing higher-layer features of a deep network. Technical report, Department of IRO, Université de Montréal (2009)
6. Hansen, L.K., Salamon, P.: Neural network ensembles. IEEE Trans. Pattern Anal. Mach. Intell. **12**(10), 993–1001 (1990)
7. He, K., Zhang, X., Ren, S., Sun, J.: Spatial pyramid pooling in deep convolutional networks for visual recognition. IEEE Trans. Pattern Anal. Mach. Intell. **37**(9), 1904–1916 (2015)

8. Jia, Y., Shelhamer, E., Donahue, J., Karayev, S., Long, J., Girshick, R., Guadarrama, S., Darrell, T.: Caffe: convolutional architecture for fast feature embedding. In: Proceedings of the 2014 ACM Conference on Multimedia, MM 2014. pp. 675–678 (2014)
9. Krizhevsky, A., Sutskever, I., Hinton, G.E.: Imagenet classification with deep convolutional neural networks. In: Proceedings of the 26th Annual Conference on Neural Information Processing Systems, NIPS 2012, vol. 2, pp. 1097–1105 (2012)
10. LeCun, Y., Boser, B., Denker, J.S., Henderson, D., Howard, R.E., Hubbard, W., Jackel, L.D.: Backpropagation applied to handwritten zip code recognition. Neural Comput. 1(4), 541–551 (1989)
11. Lin, M., Chen, Q., Yan, S.: Network in network. In: Proceedings of the International Conference on Learning Representations, ICLR 2014 (2014)
12. Quattoni, A., Torralba, A.: Recognizing indoor scenes. In: Proceedings of the IEEE Conference on Computer Vision and Pattern Recognition Workshops, CVPR Workshops 2009, pp. 413–420 (2009)
13. Russakvovsky, O., Deng, J., Su, H., Krause, J., Satheesh, S., Ma, S., Huang, Z., Karpathy, A., Kholsa, A., Bernstein, M., Berg, A., Fei-Fei, L.: Imagenet large scale visual recognition challenge. Int. J. Comput. Vis. 115(3), 211–252 (2015)
14. Sermante, P., Eigen, D., Zhang, X., Mathieu, M., Fergus, R., LeCun, Y.: Overfeat: integrated recognition, localization and detection using convolutional networks. In: Proceedings of the International Conference on Learning Representations, ICLR 2014 (2014)
15. Simonyan, K., Vedaldi, A., Zisserman, A.: Deep inside convolutional networks: visualising image classification models and saliency maps. In: Proceedings of the International Conference on Learning Representations Workshops, ICLR Workshops 2014 (2014)
16. Simonyan, K., Zisserman, A.: Two-stream convolutional networks for action recognition in videos. In: Proceedings of the 28th Annual Conference on Neural Information Processing Systems, NIPS 2014, vol. 1, pp. 568–576 (2014)
17. Simonyan, K., Zisserman, A.: Very deep convolutional networks for large-scale image recognition. In: Proceedings of the International Conference on Learning Representations, ICLR 2015 (2015)
18. Szegedy, C., Liu, W., Jia, Y., Sermanet, P., Reed, S., Anguelov, D., Erhan, D., Vanhoucke, V., Rabinovich, A.: Going deeper with convolutions. In: Proceedings of the IEEE Conference on Computer Vision and Pattern Recognition, CVPR 2015, pp. 1–9 (2015)
19. Van Der Maaten, L., Hinton, G.: Visualizing data using t-SNE. J. Mach. Learn. Res. 9, 2579–2605 (2008)
20. Wang, S., Jiang, S.: INSTRE: a new benchmark for instance-level object retrieval and recognition. ACM Trans. Multimedia Comput. Commun. Appl. (TOMM) 11(3), 1–21 (2015)
21. Wu, C., Fan, W., He, Y., Sun, J., Naoi, S.: Cascaded heterogeneous convolutional neural networks for handwritten digit recognition. In: Proceedings of the 21st International Conference on Pattern Recognition, ICPR 2012, pp. 657–660 (2012)
22. Wu, R., Wang, B., Wang, W., Yu, Y.: Harvesting discrimnative meta object with deep CNN features for scene classification. In: IEEE International Conference on Computer Vision, ICCV 2015 (2015)
23. Wu, Z., Zhang, Y., Yu, F., Xiao, J.: A GPU implementation of GoogLeNet. Technical report, Priceton University (2014)

24. Xiao, J.*, Hays, J., Ehinger, K.A., Oliva, A., Torralba, A.: Sun database: large-scale scene recognition from abbey to zoo. In: Proceedings of the IEEE Conference on Computer Vision and Pattern Recognitions, CVPR 2010, pp. 3485–3492 (2010)
25. Yosinski, J., Clune, J., Bengio, Y., Lipson, H.: How transferable are features in deep neural networks? In: Proceedings of the 28th Annual Conference on Neural Information Processing Systems 2014, NIPS 2014, vol. 4, pp. 3320–3328 (2014)
26. Zhou, B., Lapedriza, A., Xiao, J., Torralba, A., Oliva, A.: Learning deep features for scene recognition using places database. In: Proceedings of the 28th Annual Conference on Neural Information Processing Systems 2014, NIPS 2014, vol. 1, pp. 487–495 (2014)

Recognition Oriented Feature Hallucination
for Low Resolution Face Images

Guangheng Jia, Xiaoguang Li$^{(\boxtimes)}$, Li Zhuo, and Li Liu

Signal and Information Processing Lab,
Beijing University of Technology, Beijing, China
{jiagh, liu_li}@emails.bjut.edu.cn,
{lxg, Zhuoli}@bjut.edu.cn

Abstract. In face recognition, Low Resolution (LR) images will lead to the decline of the recognition rate. In this paper, we propose a novel recognition oriented feature hallucination method to map the features of a LR facial image to its High Resolution (HR) version. We extract the principal component analysis (PCA) features of LR and HR face images. Then, canonical correlation analysis is applied to establish the coherent subspaces between the PCA features of the LR and HR face images. Furthermore, a recognition rate guided prediction model is proposed to map the LR features to the HR version, which is employed an adaptive Piecewise Kernel Partial Least Squares (P-KPLS) predictor. Finally, a weighted combination of the hallucinated PCA features and the Local Binary Pattern Histogram (LBPH) features are adopted for face recognition. Experimental results show that the proposed method has a superior recognition rate.

Keywords: Feature hallucination · PCA · Canonical correlation analysis · KPLS · Face recognition

1 Introduction

Face recognition technology [1] has a wide range of applications, such as video surveillance, evidence collection and other aspects. However, due to the limit of acquisition devices, capturing distance and the light environment, the acquired facial images are tend to be low-resolution and low-quality. While the low-resolution (LR) face images are used to identify, the performance of face recognition algorithms will decline [2, 3]. In order to solve this problem, super-resolution (SR) [4] is necessary, which reconstruct a high-resolution (HR) face image for recognition.

Many effective SR algorithms have been proposed in the past decades. However most of them are to improve the visual quality, which may not be able to improve the face recognition rate [5].

In order to improve the recognition rate of LR facial images, we proposed a novel recognition oriented feature hallucination method in this paper. The contributions of our paper include: (1) A recognition rate guided feature selection scheme. We select the features under the guidance of the face recognition rate. By extracting effective PCA features, we can improve the recognition rate. (2) A recognition rate guided feature hallucination model is proposed. An adaptive piecewise KPLS predictor is employed to

© Springer International Publishing AG 2016
E. Chen et al. (Eds.): PCM 2016, Part II, LNCS 9917, pp. 275–284, 2016.
DOI: 10.1007/978-3-319-48896-7_27

predict the HR features. We determine the number of piecewise according to the recognition rate of the training set. (3) A new feature that combined the hallucinated global feature and the local LBPH feature are applied to further improve the recognition rate of the LR image. Experimental results have shown that the proposed method can achieve better results.

2   The Proposed Method

In this section, we will describe our recognition oriented feature hallucination method in details. The framework of the proposed method is shown in Fig. 1. It includes two stages: the offline training stage and the online hallucination stage. Note that to evaluate the performance of the proposed method, a testing stage is also embedded into the framework.

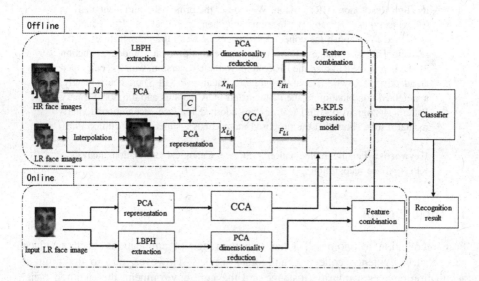

Fig. 1. The Framework of the proposed method.

First of all, a training set is collected. In the training set, each sample includes an HR face image and it corresponding LR version. In the offline stage, the principal component analysis (PCA) feature is extracted [6] for each LR and HR face image. Then, the Canonical Correlation Analysis (CCA) [7, 8] is applied to maximize the correlation between the LR and HR PCA features [9, 10]. A Piecewise KPLS (P-KPLS) regression model is trained with the LR and HR features in the CCA space. During the training procedure, the recognition rate of the training set is used to determine the best number of piecewise for the P-KPLS regression model.

In the online stage, for a testing LR face image, we extract PCA features and LBPH features. Then, the LR testing PCA feature vectors is projected to the CCA space and the coherent LR feature is obtained. After that, the pre-trained P-KPLS predictor is employed to predict the coherent HR features. Finally, a weighted combination of the coherent LR feature and the LBPH [11] feature is used for face recognition.

In the testing stage, we suppose that the input face image is a LR image and the record face database is made up HR face images. The combined features of the record face images is extracted and used to match with the input testing LR image.

2.1   Offline Training Stage

Feature Selection Feature hallucination is to estimate HR features from LR features with the help of a training set [12, 13]. According to [14, 15], PCA and LBPH features may be more robust in the LR face recognition. Therefore, we take these two kinds of features into account.

For a training set $\{I_{Li}, I_{Hi}\}_{i=1}^{N}$ with N samples, all LR images are interpolated to the size of HR image with bicubic, the HR PCA feature were extracted from the HR face images, as shown in (1):

$$X_{Hi} = C^T(I_{Hi} - M), \tag{1}$$

where M and C denote the mean face and the eigenface matrix of HR training images. We calculate the PCA coefficients of the LR image as follows.

$$X_{Li} = C^T(I_{Li} - M), \tag{2}$$

where X_{Hi} and X_{Li} denote the PCA features of the HR and LR training images, they are N dimensional vectors. Note that the M and C are the mean face and the eigenface matrix of HR faces as (1).

Then, we obtained the PCA feature vectors of HR and LR training sets as $X_H = \{X_{H1}, X_{H2}, ..., X_{HN}\}$ and $X_L = \{X_{L1}, X_{L2}, ..., X_{LN}\}$.

However, not all dimensions of the PCA features should be used. Here, we select the number of Eigen faces according to the LR face recognition rate of the training set. We evaluate the recognition rate of the LR training images for different number of Eigen faces is selected. Then, The most discriminative M ($M < N$) dimension of the PCA features is selected. $X_{Hi} = \{x_{H1}, x_{H2}, ..., x_{HM}\}$ and $X_{Li} = \{x_{L1}, x_{L2}, ..., x_{LM}\}$ denote the M-dimensional PCA features of a pair of HR and LR face image. In order to learn the relationship between LR and HR feature vectors more efficiently, both of the X_{Hi} and X_{Li} sets are converted to the coherence feature space via CCA [10]. Let $\{F_{Li}, F_{Hi}\}_{i=1}^{N}$, $F_{Hi} = \{f_{H1}, f_{H2}, ..., f_{HM}\}$ and $F_{Li} = \{f_{L1}, f_{L2}, ..., f_{LM}\}$ represent the coherent features of a pair of HR and LR face images.

In addition to the global PCA features, we have also extracted local LBPH features. For the input LR image and the HR images in the testing set, we tile the image into $m \times n$ non-overlapped blocks, viz. the number of blocks is $m \times n$. The LBPH are extracted with $LBP_{8,2}^{u2}$ model. The subscript represents using the operator in a $(8, 2)$ neighborhood, namely with 8 pixels. Superscript u_2 stands for uniform patterns. Then, the LBPH feature is dimension reduced via PCA and normalized by Z-score. Here, the number of feature dimension T and m, n are determined according to the recognition rate of the training set.

The LBPH features are extracted from both the input LR face image for testing and the HR face images in the HR testing set. Let $\{Y_{Hi}\}_{i=1}^{N}$, $Y_{Hi} = \{y_{H1}, y_{H2}, \cdots, y_{HT}\}$ and $\{Y_{Li}\}_{i=1}^{N}$, $Y_{Li} = \{y_{L1}, y_{L2}, \cdots, y_{LT}\}$ denotes the LBPH features of an HR and a LR face image respectively.

The Piecewise Kernel Partial Least Squares (P-KPLS) Predictor After obtained the coherent features, a Piecewise Kernel Partial Least Squares (P-KPLS) predictor is designed and trained to map the LR coherent features to the HR ones. The KPLS is one of a multivariate statistical analysis. More details about KPLS model can be found in [16]. The radial basis kernel is selected in our implementation.

In the Feature Selection stage, we have obtained the coherent features $\{F_{Li}, F_{Hi}\}_{i=1}^{N}$, where $F_{Hi} = \{f_{H1}, f_{H2}, \ldots, f_{HM}\}$ and $F_{Li} = \{f_{L1}, f_{L2}, \ldots, f_{LM}\}$. Then, the coherent features vector is divided into S equal dimensional sub-vectors. Thus, the dimension of each sub-vector is $P = M/S$. The piecewise feature of the HR and the LR coherent features can be denoted as $F_{Hi} = \{p_{Hj}\}_{j=1}^{s} = \{p_{H1}, p_{H2}, \cdots, p_{Hs}\}$, $F_{Li} = \{p_{Lj}\}_{j=1}^{s} = \{p_{L1}, p_{L2}, \cdots, p_{Ls}\}$ and sub-vector $p_{Hj} = \{(f_{H((j-1)*P+1)}, f_{H((j-1)*P+2)}, \ldots, f_{H(j*P)})\}$, $p_{Lj} = \{(f_{L((j-1)*P+1)}, f_{L((j-1)*P+2)}, \ldots, f_{L(j*P)})\}$. Then, for each sub vectors set, a sub-KPLS regression model is trained. There are S sub-KPLS predictors. The P-KPLS predictor is the collection of all the piecewise sub-KPLS predictor. S is determined according to the recognition rate of LR face training samples. The coherent feature vector is divided into different number of sub-vectors, the recognition rate will be different. Therefore, we can find out the best parameter to improve the recognition rate.

In this section, a well-trained P-KPLS predictor can be obtained.

2.2   Online Feature Hallucination Stage

For an input LR face image, its PCA feature X_L' is calculated first. Then, the X_L' is projected to the CCA coherent LR feature F_L'. The coherent HR features F_H' can be predicted from F_L' via the well-trained P-KPLS predictor. Further, the LBPH feature of the testing image is computed, then dimension reduced and normalized via PCA and Z-score, which is denoted as Y_L'. The significant of the Y_L' and F_H' features are not same. Therefore, we further combine these two features as (3):

$$Z = \left(\omega \cdot F_H', (1 - \omega) \cdot Y_L' \right), \tag{3}$$

where $0 \le \omega \le 1$. The value of ω is determined according to the recognition rate of the training set.

The combined feature Z will be used to face recognition in the testing stage.

2.3   Testing Stage

In the testing stage, the combined feature Z should be extracted for the HR testing database. As described in the above sections, the coherent features of the testing HR and LR face images $\{F_{Li}, F_{Hi}\}_{i=1}^{N}$ can be obtained. The LBPH features of HR face images $Y_H = \{Y_{H1}, Y_{H2}, \ldots, Y_{HN}\}$ also should be extracted for testing procedure. The Y_H and $F_H = \{F_{Hi}\}_{i=1}^{N}$ are used to establish an HR recorded face image feature database.

$$\left\{ Z'_{Hi} \right\} = (\omega \cdot F_{Hi}, (1 - \omega) \cdot Y_{Hi}), \tag{4}$$

Finally, we use Z in (3) as a probe feature to match in $\{Z'\}$ for face recognition. In our experiments, the Nearest Neighbor classification with l_2 norm is employed.

3   Experiments and Discussion

3.1   Evaluation on the ORL Database

In this section, we will evaluate the performance of our proposed method on the ORL database. The ORL database includes 40 individuals, and each has 10 different face images. The face images were taken at different time, lighting, facial expressions and facial details. The size of each image is 92×112 pixels, with 256 grey levels per pixel.

In our experiments, all images are aligned and normalized based on the positions of eyes. Two sets of face images are used in the experiments. Set A has its HR and LR face images of sizes 48×48 pixels and 16×16 pixels, respectively, while Set B has its HR and LR face images of sizes 72×72 pixels and 24×24 pixels, respectively. For each subject in the dataset A and B, we choose five images for training and the other five for testing. Therefore, there are only 200 facial images for training. Figure 2 shows some images from the datasets A and B, respectively.

In order to evaluate the effectiveness of our algorithm, we compare the face recognition rate of our method with 7 algorithms, they are LR-PCA, HR-PCA, LBPH, PCA-LBPH, PCA-KPLS, CCA-KPLS and Lin Reg+GCCA [17]. The method recognizes the PCA feature extracted from the interpolation image that is obtained by enlarging the input LR image to the size of the HR image by bicubic interpolation (LR-PCA); and the method using original HR face images (HR-PCA). The method extracted the LBPH feature from the interpolation image (LBPH). The method extracted the LBPH feature and PCA feature from the interpolation image (PCA-LBPH). The PCA-KPLS method applies KPLS model to obtain HR face features for recognition. While the CCA-KPLS employs KPLS to obtain the coherent HR features for recognition.

In the experiment, to determine the value of ω, we have searched the range $\{0, 0.1, 0.2, 0.3, \cdots, 1\}$. As shown in Fig. 3, the recognition rates for the feature Z, based on the datasets A and B. The results show that the best performance can be achieved at $\omega = 0.3$. These two values are used in the rest of our experiments. Both the

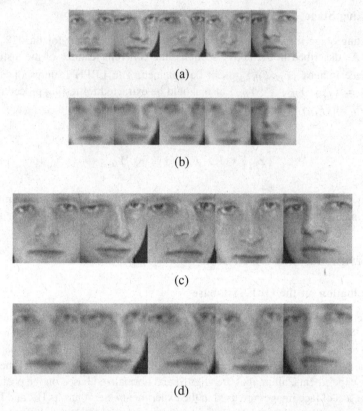

(a)

(b)

(c)

(d)

Fig. 2. Face images of one individual in dataset *A* and *B*. (a) HR training face images with size 48 × 48. (b) LR training face images with size 16 × 16. (c) HR training face images with size 72 × 72. (d) LR training face images with size 24 × 24. (a) and (b) are from the dataset *A*. (c) and (d) are from the dataset *B*.

m and *n* are set to 7 for dataset *A* and 4 for dataset *B*. *M* is set to 96 and 28. *T* is set to 51 and 53, respectively.

The recognition rates with different methods are listed in Table 1. Our method achieves the highest recognition rate of 0.900 in dataset *B*. The recognition rates achieved by LR-PCA, HR-PCA, PCA-KPLS, CCA-KPLS, PCA-LBPH and LBPH are 0.750, 0.780, 0.765, 0.785, 0.755 and 0.835, respectively. On the other hand, the recognition rates achieved by LR-PCA, HR-PCA, PCA-KPLS, CCA-KPLS, PCA-LBPH and LBPH are 0.745, 0.770, 0.745, 0.755, 0.765 and 0.775 in dataset *A*. For Lin Reg+GCCA's method, the recognition rates are 0.831 and 0.866 in dataset *A* and *B*, respectively. *S* is set to 2. Thus, our proposed method is more effectively.

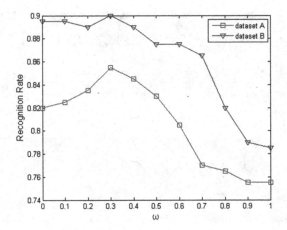

Fig. 3. The recognition rates of the proposed method with different values of ω on the ORL datasets.

Table 1. Recognition results with different methods for the dataset A and B

Algorithm	Recognition rate (dataset A)	Recognition rate (dataset B)
LR-PCA	0.745	0.750
HR-PCA	0.770	0.780
LBPH	0.775	0.835
PCA-LBPH	0.765	0.755
PCA-KPLS	0.745	0.765
CCA-KPLS	0.755	0.785
Lin Reg+GCCA [17]	0.831	0.866
Our method	0.855	0.900

3.2 Evaluation on the AR Database

In this section, we evaluate the performance of our proposed method on the AR face database. The AR database includes 100 individuals, and each has 26 different face images. AR database each face image includes 14 different facial expressions, lighting, and 12 images contain obstructions (sunglasses, scarves). The size of each image is 120×165 pixels.

In our experiments, we choose 7 images for training and the other 7 images for testing from different facial expressions, lighting images. So, there are 700 face images for training. Figure 4 shows some images from the AR database. Set AR database has its HR and LR face images of sizes 120×160 pixels and 15×20 pixels, respectively.

In this experiment, the results show that the best performance can be achieved when ω is set to 0.4. As shown in Fig. 5, the recognition rates for the feature Z, based on the AR database. M is set to 201. T is set to 121. m and n are set to 12 and 16.

As shown in Table 2, our method achieves the highest recognition rate of 0.842 compared to other methods in the AR database. The recognition rates achieved by

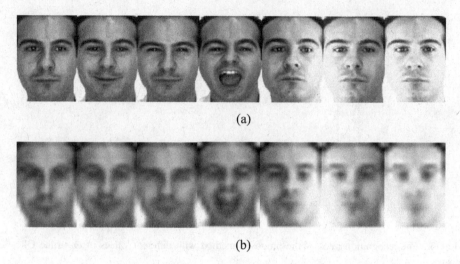

(a)

(b)

Fig. 4. Face images of one individual in AR database. (a) HR training face images with size 160×120. (b) LR training face images with size 15×20.

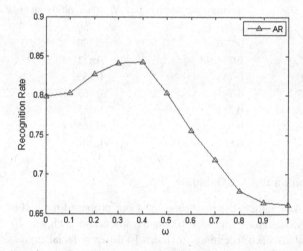

Fig. 5. The recognition rates of the proposed method with different values of ω on the AR database.

LR-PCA, HR-PCA, PCA-KPLS, CCA-KPLS, PCA-LBPH and LBPH are 0.551, 0.718, 0.580, 0.661, 0.575 and 0.637, respectively. S is set to 77. Therefore, our proposed method is more effectively.

All experiment was conducted using MATLAB on Windows 7 with 3.30 GHz Intel® Core(TM) i5-4590 CPU and 20 GB RAM.

Table 2. Recognition rates with different methods for the AR database

Algorithm	Recognition rate
LR-PCA	0.551
HR-PCA	0.718
LBPH	0.637
PCA-LBPH	0.575
PCA-KPLS	0.580
CCA-KPLS	0.661
Our method	0.842

4 Conclusions

For the problem of LR face images declining recognition rate, a novel recognition oriented feature hallucination method for low resolution face images is proposed in this paper. In our algorithm, CCA was applied to obtain the coherent features between the LR and HR PCA features, and a P-KPLS model was proposed to model the relationship between the coherent features. Moreover, a weighted combination of the LBPH and the hallucinated coherent HR features is employed, which can enhance the representational efficiency of the combined features. Compared to the traditional approaches, the experimental results show that our proposed method can improve the recognition rates of the low resolution face images.

The drawback of our work is that only PCA and LBPH features are investigated. Furthermore, the segmented of piecewise KPLS model is equal length. In our future work, more features and more flexible adaptive P-KPLS model will be explored.

Acknowledgments. The work in this paper is supported by the National Natural Science Foundation of China (No. 61471013, No. 61531006, No. 61372149 and No. 61370189), the Importation and Development of High-Caliber Talents Project of Beijing Municipal Institutions (No. CIT&TCD201404043, CIT&TCD20150311), the Beijing Natural Science Foundation (No. 4142009, No. 4163071), the Science and Technology Development Program of Beijing Education Committee (No. KM201510005004, No. KM201410005002), Funding Project for Academic Human Resources Development in Institutions of Higher Learning under the Jurisdiction of Beijing Municipality.

References

1. Zhao, W., Chellappa, R., Phillips, P.J., Rosenfeld, A.: Face recognition: a literature survey. ACM Comput. Surv. **35**(4), 399–458 (2000)
2. Wang, M., Gao, Y., Lu, K., Rui, Y.: View-based discriminative probabilistic modeling for 3D object retrieval and recognition. IEEE Trans. Image Process. **22**(4), 1395–1407 (2013). A Publication of the IEEE Signal Processing Society
3. Wang, M., Liu, X., Wu, X.: Visual classification by ℓ_1-hypergraph modeling. IEEE Trans. Knowl. Data Eng. **27**(9), 2564–2574 (2015)

4. Ouwerkerk, J.D.V.: Image super-resolution survey. Image Vis. Comput. **24**(10), 1039–1052 (2006)
5. Fookes, C., Lin, F., Chandran, V., Sridharan, S.: Evaluation of image resolution and super-resolution on face recognition performance. J. Vis. Commun. Image Represent. **23**(1), 75–93 (2012)
6. Shen, H., Li, S.: Hallucinating faces by interpolation and principal component analysis. In: International Symposium on Computational Intelligence and Design, pp. 295–298. IEEE Computer Society (2009)
7. Hotelling, H.: Relations between two sets of variates. Biometrika **28**(28), 321–377 (1935)
8. Liu, Y.Y., Cao, H.R., Wang, J.G., Zhao, Y.B.: Improved two-dimensional canonical correlation analysis and its application in face recognition. Comput. Eng. **38**(10), 151–153 (2012)
9. Huang, H., He, H., Fan, X., Zhang, J.: Super-resolution of human face image using canonical correlation analysis. Pattern Recogn. **43**(7), 2532–2543 (2010)
10. Huang, H., He, H.: Super-resolution method for face recognition using nonlinear mappings on coherent features. IEEE Trans. Neural Netw. **22**(1), 121–130 (2011)
11. Ahonen, T., Hadid, A., Pietikäinen, M.: Face description with local binary patterns: application to face recognition. IEEE Trans. Pattern Anal. Mach. Intell. **28**(12), 2037–2041 (2006)
12. Li, B., Chang, H., Shan, S., Chen, X.: Hallucinating facial images and features. In: 19th International Conference on IEEE Pattern Recognition, ICPR 2008, pp. 1–4 (2008)
13. Baker, S., Kanade, T.: Hallucinating faces. In: IEEE International Conference on Automatic Face and Gesture Recognition, pp. 83–83. IEEE Computer Society (2000)
14. Luo, Y., Wu, C.M., Zhang, Y.: Facial expression recognition based on fusion feature of PCA and LBP with SVM. Optik Int. J. Light Electron Opt. **124**(17), 2767–2770 (2013)
15. Wang, J., Wang, M., Hu, X., Yan, S.: Visual data denoising with a unified Schatten-p norm and ℓ_q norm regularized principal component pursuit. Pattern Recogn. **48**(10), 3135–3144 (2015)
16. Li, X., Xia, Q., Zhuo, L., Lam, K.M.: A face hallucination algorithm via KPLS-eigentransformation model. In: IEEE International Conference on Signal Processing, Communication and Computing, pp. 462–467 (2012)
17. Pong, K.H., Lam, K.M.: Gabor-feature hallucination based on generalized canonical correlation analysis for face recognition. In: International Symposium on Intelligent Signal Processing and Communications Systems, pp. 1–6 (2011)

Learning Robust Multi-Label Hashing
for Efficient Image Retrieval

Haibao Chen[1], Yuyan Zhao[1], Lei Zhu[2]([✉]), Guilin Chen[1], and Kaichuan Sun[1]

[1] School of Computer and Information Engineering,
Chuzhou University, Chuzhou, China
[2] Singapore Management University, Singapore, Singapore
leizhu0608@gmail.com

Abstract. Supervised hashing generally achieves superior performance over unsupervised or semi-supervised approaches by leveraging semantic labels. However, most existing supervised hashing techniques only deal with image samples with single label. Few of them properly address the practical problem concerning images with multiple labels, which is very common in real applications. In this paper, we seek to address the limitations of the existing schemes by proposing a novel approach, dubbed as Robust Multi-Label Hashing (RMLH). A label hypergraph is constructed to effectively capture high-order semantic correlations of images. And they are preserved into hashing codes with hypergraph consistency and direct label-hashing correlation. Besides, we impose a nuclear norm regularization on correlation matrix to maintain label correlations and robustly accommodate missing labels. Furthermore, an efficient algorithm based on Alternate Direction Method of Multipliers (ADMM) is developed to calculate the optimal hashing codes. Experiments demonstrate that RMLH can outperform state-of-the-art schemes and enjoy much better robustness against missing labels.

Keywords: Robust Multi-Label Hashing · Label hypergraph · Correlation matrix

1 Introduction

Driven by the rapid growth of social media, facilitating similarity search over large scale image collection becomes more and more important. Hashing has recently been developed as a promising technique to address the problem. Its core idea is to map high-dimensional vector into compact binary codes, and search process can be completed with simple but efficient bit operations. Accordingly, storage cost of image collection can be greatly reduced and search process can be significantly accelerated. Due to these desirable advantages, hashing has received great attention from multimedia research community.

In view of the superior performance compared with data-independent techniques, learning based approaches have been emerging as popular paradigm [6, 10, 12, 13]. Among them, supervised hashing generally performs better than

© Springer International Publishing AG 2016
E. Chen et al. (Eds.): PCM 2016, Part II, LNCS 9917, pp. 285–295, 2016.
DOI: 10.1007/978-3-319-48896-7_28

unsupervised and semi-supervised hashing by leveraging semantic labels. Representative supervised hashing approaches include: Binary Reconstructive Embedding (BRE) [9], Kernel Supervised Hashing (KSH) [10], Supervised Discrete Hashing (SDH) [12], and etc. These methods mainly exploit image instances with only single label to compute hashing codes. However, in real world, each image instance is usually associated with multiple labels. Ignoring this important characteristic could lead to the limited performance in terms of robustness and effectiveness. CCA-ITQ [6] and Multi-label Least Squares Hashing (MLSH) [13] are developed to deal with multi-label images. But they simply assume that image instances are assigned with complete labels and thus cannot robustly accommodate the missing labels.

In this paper, we propose Robust Multi-Label Hashing (RMLH). The main objective is to effectively exploit available semantic labels for hashing and simultaneously accommodate missing labels. First, label correlations are captured with a label hypergraph, where images are considered as vertices and their assigned labels are determined as hyperedges. Then, hypergraph consistency and direct label-hashing correlation are proposed to integrate label correlations into binary hashing codes. Besides, a nuclear norm regularization is introduced on correlation matrix to maintain label correlations and cope with missing labels. Furthermore, we propose an efficient algorithm based on Alternate Direction Method of Multipliers (ADMM) [4] to iteratively solve RMLH.

The contributions of the paper are highlighted as follows:

1. RMLH addresses the practical problem concerning on learning robust hashing for multi-label images. To the best of our knowledge, no similar work has been reported in the literature.
2. Label correlations are captured by label hypergraph and direct label-hashing correlation. A nuclear norm regularization is introduced on correlation matrix to robustly address missing labels. An efficient algorithm based on ADMM is proposed to compute the optimal hashing codes.
3. Extensive experiments demonstrate that RMLH can achieve state-of-the-art performance and enjoy superior robustness against missing labels.

2   Related Work

Hashing has recently received considerable attention. Existing research work can be coarsely divided into two major categories: data-independent and data-dependent hashing. Locality Sensitive Hashing (LSH) [5] is one of the typical methods in the first category. Its hashing functions are randomly generated from certain distributions.

To overcome the limitation, recent efforts have been made by applying advanced machine learning mechanisms, ranging from unsupervised to supervised settings. Supervised hashing learns binary codes with the supervision of semantic labels, and thus demonstrates better performance than unsupervised hashing. Binary Reconstructive Embedding (BRE) [9] is one of the pioneering research works. It learns hashing functions by minimizing reconstruction error between original metric space and Hamming space corresponding to binary hashing codes. Liu *et al.* present Kernel Supervised Hashing (KSH) [10] where Hamming distances of similar pairs are minimized and that of dissimilar pairs are maximized simultaneously. In recent literature, Supervised Discrete Hashing (SDH) [12] is developed to directly learn discrete binary codes within a supervised linear classification framework.

In particular, to better employ multiple labels, several multi-label hashing methods are developed. As the first technical development in this direction, CCA-ITQ [6] applies supervised Canonical Correlation Analysis (CCA) [7] to project visual feature into low-dimensional space, and then learns an orthogonal rotation matrix to minimize the quantization error. Boosted Shared Hashing (BSH) [11] can also address multi-label images. However, it requires queries consisting of both visual image and text, which cannot be satisfied in content-based image retrieval where no texts are provided. Multi-label Least-Squares Hashing (MLSH) [13] integrates CCA and least square method together to project the original multi-label images into lower-dimensional Hamming space.

Although existing supervised hashing methods can achieve promising results, they mainly focus on the hashing with only one label or complete multi-labels. While in real applications, it is common that each image instance is associated with a set of labels with incompleteness. Ignoring this important fact may limit the hashing performance.

3   The Proposed Method

Denote multi-label image set as $\{\mathbf{x}_i, \mathbf{y}_i\}_{i=1}^N$ with N instances, where $\mathbf{x}_i \in \mathbb{R}^d$ and $\mathbf{y}_i \in \{0,1\}^L$ represent d dimensional visual feature and L dimensional label vector, respectively. The label vectors construct label matrix $\mathbf{Y} = [\mathbf{y}_1, ..., \mathbf{y}_N] \in \{0,1\}^{L \times N}$, while feature vectors comprise feature matrix $\mathbf{X} = [\mathbf{x}_1, ..., \mathbf{x}_N] \in \mathbb{R}^{d \times N}$. Each entry in label vector denotes whether image instance is associated with the corresponding label or not. Since image instances are multi-labeled, $\sum_{l=1}^L y_{li} \geq 1$. The aim of RMLH is to learn hashing functions $\mathbf{F} = \{\mathbf{f}_1, ..., \mathbf{f}_K\}$ which map $\mathbf{X}$ to binary codes $\mathbf{B} = [\mathbf{b}_1, ..., \mathbf{b}_N] \in \{0,1\}^{K \times N}$, where $\mathbf{b}_i$ corresponds to the hashing codes of i_{th} image instance, $\mathbf{f}_k$ is a mapping $\mathbb{R}^d \mapsto \{0,1\}$, K is hashing code length.

3.1   Overall Learning Framework

The proposed RMLH can be formally stated as the following framework

$$\min_{\mathbf{B}} \mathcal{L}(\mathbf{B}, \mathbf{C}, \mathbf{Y}) + \eta \Phi(\mathbf{B}, \mathbf{Y}) + \gamma \Psi(\mathbf{C}) \ s.t. \ \mathbf{B} \in \{0,1\}^{K \times N} \tag{1}$$

where $\mathcal{L}(\mathbf{B}, \mathbf{C}, \mathbf{Y})$ is the label-hashing correlation term, it measures the correlation loss between label matrix $\mathbf{Y}$ and hashing codes $\mathbf{B}$, $\mathbf{C}$ is correlation matrix, $\Phi(\mathbf{B}, \mathbf{Y})$ is the label correlation preserving term which controls the label smoothness by enforcing the instances to be close in Hamming space when they are close in label space, $\Psi(\mathbf{C})$ is missing label accommodation term which deals with missing labels. Moreover, $\eta, \gamma > 0$ are hyper-parameters which adjust the trade-off between regularization terms. In the following, we will present the details of these formulation terms.

Label-Hashing Correlation. Image labels are high-level and explicit concept description, while hashing codes to be learned can be understood as the discrete representation of latent concepts. In this case, a hashing bit may be shared with multiple labels and a label may be described by multiple hashing bits. There principally exist correlations between hashing codes and labels. To capture them, we introduce a correlation matrix $\mathbf{C} \in \mathbb{R}^{L \times K}$ whose elements directly measure the relations between semantic labels and hashing bits. In particular, we minimize the loss between hashing codes transformed by $\mathbf{C}$ and the label matrix $\mathbf{Y}$. Formally

$$\mathcal{L}(\mathbf{B}, \mathbf{C}, \mathbf{Y}) = ||\mathbf{CB} - \mathbf{Y}||_F^2 \tag{2}$$

Label Correlation Modeling and Preserving. In multi-label setting, a label may be described by several image samples and an image may be associated with more than one label. Also, different labels may be correlated with more than one image sample. Hence, label correlations of image samples are actually high-order. It is intuitive that the learned hashing codes should preserve high-level label correlations. In other words, if two points are associated with similar labels, they should be mapped in Hamming space with short distance.

This paper proposes a Label Hypergraph (LHG) to model label correlations. In LHG, image samples and labels are considered as vertices and hyperedges, respectively. Image samples associated with same label comprise a hyperedge. With this design, high-order label correlations are effectively modeled. Formally, we define $LHG = (\mathbf{V}, \mathbf{E}, \mathbf{W})$, $\mathbf{V} = \{v_i\}_{i=1}^N$ is the vertex set, where $\mathbf{E} = \{e_l\}_{l=1}^L$ is the hyperedge set, $\mathbf{W} = \{w(e_l)\}_{l=1}^L$ is the weight set for hyperedges. $w(e_l)$ is weight of hyperedge e_l. LHG can be mathematically represented with an $L \times N$ incidence matrix $\mathbf{H}$. And it is actually equal to label matrix $\mathbf{Y}$ in our case. With $\mathbf{H}$, we calculate the degree of hyperedge as the number of image samples included. Hence, for hyperedge e_l, its degree $\delta(e_l)$ is $\sum_{i=1}^N \mathbf{H}(e_l, v_i)$. For simplicity, the weights of hyperedge are all set to 1, $w(e_l) = 1$. The degree of each vertex $\varepsilon(v_i)$ is defined as the number of hyperedges that the vertex belongs to, $\varepsilon(v_i) = \sum_{l=1}^N w(e_l)\mathbf{H}(e_l, v_i) = \sum_{l=1}^N \mathbf{H}(e_l, v_i)$.

With LHG modeling, image samples included in more hyperedges will be more semantically similar. They should be mapped into Hamming space with closer distance. Therefore, we can derive that

$$\Phi(\mathbf{B}, \mathbf{Y}) = \frac{1}{2} \sum_{k=1}^K \sum_{i,j=1}^N \mathbf{H}'(e_l, v_i) \sum_{k'=1}^K \left(\frac{b_{k'i}}{\sqrt{\varepsilon(v_i)}} - \frac{b_{k'j}}{\sqrt{\varepsilon(v_j)}} \right)^2, \ \mathbf{H}'(e_l, v_i) = \frac{\mathbf{H}(v_i, e_l)\mathbf{H}(v_j, e_l)}{\delta(e_l)}$$

$$\tag{3}$$

Since $\sum_{j=1}^{N} \frac{H(v_j, e_l)}{\delta(e_l)} = 1$ and $\sum_{l=1}^{L} \frac{H(v_i, e_l)}{\varepsilon(v_i)} = 1$, we get

$$
\begin{aligned}
\Phi(\mathbf{B}, \mathbf{Y}) &= \sum_{i=1}^{N} \sum_{k'=1}^{K} b_{k'i}^2 - \sum_{k'=1}^{K} \sum_{l=1}^{L} \sum_{i,j=1}^{N} \frac{H(v_j, e_l) H(v_i, e_l) (\sum_{k'=1}^{K} b_{k'i} b_{k'j})}{\delta(e_l) \sqrt{\varepsilon(v_i)\varepsilon(v_j)}} \\
&= \sum_{k'=1}^{K} \left(\sum_{i=1}^{N} b_{k'i}^2 - \frac{1}{2} \sum_{l=1}^{L} \sum_{i,j=1}^{N} \frac{H(v_j, e_l) H(v_i, e_l) b_{k'i} b_{k'j}}{\delta(e_l) \sqrt{\varepsilon(v_i)\varepsilon(v_j)}} \right) \\
&\Rightarrow \Phi(\mathbf{B}, \mathbf{Y}) = \mathrm{Tr}(\mathbf{B} \boldsymbol{\Delta} \mathbf{B}^{\mathrm{T}})
\end{aligned} \tag{4}
$$

where $\boldsymbol{\Delta} \in \mathbb{R}^{N \times N}$ is Laplacian matrix of LHG, it is calculated as $\boldsymbol{\Delta} = \mathbf{I} - \mathbf{D}_v^{-1/2} \mathbf{H} \mathbf{D}_w \mathbf{D}_e^{-1} \mathbf{H}^T \mathbf{D}_v^{-1/2}$, where $\mathbf{D}_v$, $\mathbf{D}_e$, and $\mathbf{D}_w$ are the diagonal matrices of the vertex degrees, edge degrees, and hyperedge weights, respectively.

Missing Label Accommodation. It is common in practical application that many image instances are partially labeled. In image annotation, there are large-scale candidate concepts to be annotated. Thus, human annotators may only annotate each training image with a part of labels. Therefore, it is important for hashing to robustly address the missing labels. This paper proposes to address this problem by introducing a low-rank based nuclear norm on correlation matrix.

With Singular Value Decomposition (SVD), correlation matrix $\mathbf{C}$ can be represented as $\mathbf{C} = \sum_{i=1}^{r} p_i(\mathbf{C}) \sigma_i(\mathbf{C}) q_i(\mathbf{C})^{\mathrm{T}}$, where $r = min\{L, K\}$ is the rank of $\mathbf{C}$, $p_i(\mathbf{C}) \in \mathbb{R}^L$ is the i_{th} left singular vector, $q_j(\mathbf{C}) \in \mathbb{R}^K$ is the j_{th} right singular vector, $\sigma_i(\mathbf{C})$ is the i_{th} singular value. The transformed hashing codes of i_{th} instance $\mathbf{b}_i$ with $\mathbf{C}$ can be given by $\mathbf{C} \mathbf{b}_i = \sum_{i=1}^{r} p_i(\mathbf{C}) [\sigma_i(\mathbf{C}) q_i(\mathbf{C})^{\mathrm{T}} \mathbf{b}_i]$. The resulting vector is label vector. Since $\sigma_i(\mathbf{C}) q_i(\mathbf{C})^{\mathrm{T}} \mathbf{b}_i$ is scalar, $\mathbf{C} \mathbf{b}_i$ can be considered as linear combination of label component vectors $\{p_i(\mathbf{C})\}_{i=1}^{r}$, each of which represents latent label correlations. Via minimizing the rank of $\mathbf{C}$, we can capture intrinsic and meaningful label correlations. Therefore, correct labels can still be recognized with weighted label component vectors and learned hashing codes, even when there exist missing labels.

Since $\{\sigma_i(\mathbf{C})\}_{i=1}^{r}$ are all real and non-negative, r can be measured by the sum of singular values. Accordingly, the minimization of rank can be achieved by minimizing the nuclear norm of $\mathbf{C}$. Therefore

$$
\Psi(\mathbf{C}) = ||\mathbf{C}||_* = \sum_{i=1}^{r} \sigma_i(\mathbf{C}) \tag{5}
$$

By integrating label-hashing correlation term in Eq. (2), label correlation preserving term in Eq. (4), and missing label accommodation term in Eq. (5), we derive the overall objective function of RMLH

$$
\min_{\mathbf{C}, \mathbf{B}} ||\mathbf{C}\mathbf{B} - \mathbf{Y}||_F^2 + \eta \mathrm{Tr}(\mathbf{B} \boldsymbol{\Delta} \mathbf{B}^{\mathrm{T}}) + \gamma ||\mathbf{C}||_* \ s.t. \ \mathbf{B} \in \{0,1\}^{K \times N} \tag{6}
$$

3.2 Solution with ADMM

Solving the problem in Eq. (6) is NP-hard due to the discrete constraint. To make the problem solvable, we relax the discrete constraint $\mathbf{B} \in \{0,1\}^{K \times N}$. We first obtain real values of $\mathbf{Y}$, and then binarize it to hashing codes via mean thresholding. We derive the following relaxed problem

$$\min_{\mathbf{C},\mathbf{B}} \|\mathbf{CB} - \mathbf{Y}\|_F^2 + \eta \mathrm{Tr}(\mathbf{B}\mathbf{\Delta}\mathbf{B}^{\mathrm{T}}) + \gamma \|\mathbf{C}\|_* \tag{7}$$

We propose an effective optimization algorithm based on ADMM to iteratively solve the problem in Eq. (7). By introducing an auxiliary matrix $\mathbf{A} \in \mathbb{R}^{L \times K}$, we can formulate the augmented Lagrange function of Eq. (7) as

$$\min_{\mathbf{C},\mathbf{B}} \frac{1}{2}\|\mathbf{CB} - \mathbf{Y}\|_F^2 + \frac{\eta}{2}\mathrm{Tr}(\mathbf{B}\mathbf{\Delta}\mathbf{B}^{\mathrm{T}}) + \gamma \|\mathbf{A}\|_* + \frac{\beta}{2}\|\mathbf{C} - \mathbf{A}\|_F^2 + \mathrm{Tr}(\mathbf{\Lambda}^{\mathrm{T}}(\mathbf{C} - \mathbf{A})) \tag{8}$$

where $\mathbf{\Lambda} \in \mathbb{R}^{L \times K}$ is Lagrange multiplies, $\beta > 0$ is hyper-parameter. The above proxy problem can be tackled by optimizing one variable while fixing others alternatively.

Step 1: Optimizing C with Others Fixed. By fixing $\mathbf{A} = \mathbf{A}^m$, $\mathbf{\Lambda} = \mathbf{\Lambda}^m$ and $\mathbf{B} = \mathbf{B}^m$ (m is iteration index), the optimal $\mathbf{C}$ can be solved by

$$\min_{\mathbf{C}} \frac{1}{2}\|\mathbf{CB}^m - \mathbf{Y}\|_F^2 + \frac{\eta}{2}\mathrm{Tr}(\mathbf{B}^m\mathbf{\Delta}(\mathbf{B}^m)^{\mathrm{T}}) + \frac{\beta}{2}\|\mathbf{C} - \mathbf{A}^m\|_F^2 + \mathrm{Tr}((\mathbf{\Lambda}^m)^{\mathrm{T}}(\mathbf{C} - \mathbf{A}^m)) \tag{9}$$

By calculating its derivation to $\mathbf{C}$ and setting it to $\mathbf{0}$, we can derive

$$\mathbf{CB}^m(\mathbf{B}^m)^{\mathrm{T}} - \mathbf{Y}(\mathbf{B}^m)^{\mathrm{T}} + \beta\mathbf{C} - \beta\mathbf{A}^m + \mathbf{\Lambda}^m = 0 \tag{10}$$

We get the updating of $\mathbf{C}$ at $(m+1)_{th}$ iteration as

$$\mathbf{C}^{m+1} = (\mathbf{Y}(\mathbf{B}^m)^{\mathrm{T}} + \beta\mathbf{A}^m - \mathbf{\Lambda}^m)(\mathbf{B}^m(\mathbf{B}^m)^{\mathrm{T}} + \beta\mathbf{I}_K)^{-1} \tag{11}$$

Step 2: Optimizing B with Others Fixed. By fixing $\mathbf{A} = \mathbf{A}^m$, $\mathbf{\Lambda} = \mathbf{\Lambda}^m$ and $\mathbf{C} = \mathbf{C}^{m+1}$, the optimal $\mathbf{B}$ can be solved by

$$\min_{\mathbf{B}} \frac{1}{2}\|\mathbf{C}^{m+1}\mathbf{B} - \mathbf{Y}\|_F^2 + \frac{\eta}{2}\mathrm{Tr}(\mathbf{B}\mathbf{\Delta}\mathbf{B}^{\mathrm{T}}) \tag{12}$$

By calculating the derivation to $\mathbf{B}$ and setting it to $\mathbf{0}$, we obtain that

$$(\mathbf{C}^{m+1})^{\mathrm{T}}\mathbf{C}^{m+1}\mathbf{B} + \eta\mathbf{B}\mathbf{\Delta} = (\mathbf{C}^{m+1})^{\mathrm{T}}\mathbf{Y} \tag{13}$$

Equation (13) is a Sylvester equation [1], which can be solved with the Lyapunov function in Matlab.

Step 3: Optimizing A with Others Fixed. Similarly, by fixing $\mathbf{C} = \mathbf{C}^{m+1}$, $\mathbf{\Lambda} = \mathbf{\Lambda}^m$, the optimal $\mathbf{A}$ can be solved by

$$\min_{\mathbf{A}} \frac{\beta}{2}\|\mathbf{C}^{m+1} - \mathbf{A}\|_F^2 + \mathrm{Tr}((\mathbf{\Lambda}^m)^{\mathrm{T}}(\mathbf{C}^{m+1} - \mathbf{A})) + \gamma \|\mathbf{A}\|_* \tag{14}$$

It can be transformed as a compact form

$$\min_{\mathbf{A}} \frac{1}{2}||(\mathbf{C}^{m+1} + \frac{\mathbf{\Lambda}^m}{\beta}) - \mathbf{A}||_F^2 + \frac{\gamma}{\beta}||\mathbf{A}||_* \tag{15}$$

It is convex and has unique minimum solution. The optimal $\mathbf{A}^{m+1}$ can be calculated with a closed form solution via Singular Value Thresholding (SVT) operator [2] $\mathtt{SVT}_{\frac{\gamma}{\beta}}(\cdot)$ as

$$\mathbf{A}^{m+1} = \mathtt{SVT}_{\frac{\gamma}{\beta}}(\mathbf{C}^{m+1} + \frac{\mathbf{\Lambda}^m}{\beta}) = \mathbf{U}\mathtt{SVT}_{\frac{\gamma}{\beta}}(\mathbf{\Sigma})\,\mathbf{V}^{\mathrm{T}} \tag{16}$$

where $\mathbf{U}\mathbf{\Sigma}\mathbf{V}^{\mathrm{T}}$ is SVD of $\mathbf{C}^{m+1} + \frac{\mathbf{\Lambda}^m}{\beta}$. The columns of $\mathbf{U}$ and $\mathbf{V}$ are left-singular vectors and right-singular vectors of $\mathbf{C}^{m+1} + \frac{\mathbf{\Lambda}^m}{\beta}$ respectively. $\mathbf{\Sigma} = \mathtt{diag}(\{\sigma_i\}_{i=1}^r)$, σ_r is r_{th} singular value of $\mathbf{\Sigma}$, $\mathtt{SVT}_{\frac{\gamma}{\beta}}(\mathbf{\Sigma}) = \mathtt{diag}(\{\mathtt{sgn}(\sigma_i)\mathtt{max}(|\mathbf{C}^{m+1} + \frac{\mathbf{\Lambda}^m}{\beta}| - \frac{\gamma}{\beta}, 0)\}_{i=1}^r)$.

Step 4: Optimizing $\mathbf{\Lambda}$ with Others Fixed. Once we get $\mathbf{C} = \mathbf{C}^{m+1}$ and $\mathbf{A} = \mathbf{A}^{m+1}$, $\mathbf{\Lambda}$ can be updated with the difference of $\mathbf{C}$ and $\mathbf{A}$. The updating formula is

$$\mathbf{\Lambda}^{m+1} = \mathbf{\Lambda}^m + \beta(\mathbf{C}^{m+1} - \mathbf{A}^{m+1}) \tag{17}$$

We perform the above steps iteratively to obtain the optimal relaxed hashing codes. Based on the proof in [4], our proposed ADMM based optimization can be converged to a optimal solution.

3.3 Out of Sample Extension

In this paper, we leverage linear projection to learn hashing functions. Formally $\mathbf{B} = \mathbf{P}^{\mathrm{T}}\mathbf{X}$, where $\mathbf{P} \in \mathbb{R}^{d \times K}$ denotes the projection matrix. The main objective is to reduce the loss between the new generated hashing codes and the projected ones. It can be solved by $\min_{\mathbf{P}} ||\mathbf{B} - \mathbf{P}^{\mathrm{T}}\mathbf{X}||^2 + \xi||\mathbf{P}||_F$, where $\xi > 0$ is the hyper-parameter. The $\mathbf{P}$ is the projection matrix, which is given as $\mathbf{P} = (\mathbf{X}\mathbf{X}^{\mathrm{T}} + \xi\mathbf{I}_D)^{-1}\mathbf{X}\mathbf{B}^{\mathrm{T}}$. With $\mathbf{P}$, the hashing functions can be constructed as $\mathbf{F}(\mathbf{x}) = \mathtt{binary}(\mathbf{P}^{\mathrm{T}}\mathbf{x})$, where $\mathtt{binary}(\cdot)$ is the operator which is defined as $\mathtt{binary}(x) = 1, x > 0, \mathtt{binary}(x) = 0, x \le 0$.

3.4 Complexity Analysis

The subsection provides time complexity analysis for the training cost of RMLH. The updating for $\mathbf{C}$ in Eq. (11) requires the calculation of two matrices $\beta\mathbf{A}^m - \mathbf{\Lambda}^m$ and $\mathbf{B}^m(\mathbf{B}^m)^{\mathrm{T}} + \beta\mathbf{I}_K$, which will cost $O(LK)$ and $O(K^2N)$ respectively. The inverse of $\mathbf{B}^m(\mathbf{B}^m)^{\mathrm{T}} + \beta\mathbf{I}_K$ consumes $O(K^3)$. Consequently, the updating of $\mathbf{C}$ will cost $O(LK + K^2N + K^3)$. The updating of $\mathbf{B}$ solves Sylvester equation which consumes $O(KN)$. The main cost of updating $\mathbf{A}$ in Eq. (16) is brought from SVT operator, whose computation complexity is $\min\{O(KL^2), O(K^2L)\}$. The updating for $\mathbf{\Lambda}$ in Eq. (17) is completed via matrix plus or minus operations, which will cost $O(LK)$. Thus, the overall time complexity of our proposed solution is linear to the training size N which is quite efficient.

4   Experiments

4.1   Experimental Setting

In this paper, experiments are conducted on two publicly available multi-label image datasets: **Corel5K** [3] and **MIR Flickr** [8]. **Corel5K** is comprised of 4999 images labeled with 260 concepts. **MIR Flickr** contains 25,000 images from 38 semantic categories, which are collected from the Flickr. On both datasets, visual contents of images in **MIR Flickr** are represented by 1000-D dense SIFT histogram. For retrieval setting, 1% images are used as queries, 3% images comprise learning image set, and the remaining images are database images to be retrieved. For performance evaluation, images are considered to be relevant only if they share at least one concept.

Mean Average Precision (MAP) [12,13] is adopted as the evaluation metric. In experiments, we set the number of returned images as 100 to collect results. Furthermore, *Precision-Scope* curve is also reported to reflect the retrieval performance variations with respect to the number of retrieved images.

4.2   Compared Approaches

We compare RMLH with several state-of-the-art single label and multi-label hashing approaches. Single label hashing approaches used for comparison include: Binary Reconstructive Embedding (BRE) [9], Kernel Supervised Hashing (KSH) [10], Supervised Discrete Hashing (SDH) [12]. These single label hashing approaches can be applied to multi-label images by modifying corresponding label matrix. Multi-label hashing approaches include: Multi-label Least Squares Hashing (MLSH) [13]. For these baselines, we carefully adjust the involved parameters according to relevant literature and report the best performance. For RMLH, the best performance is achieved when $\beta = 1$, $\gamma = 1$, $\eta = 10^{-3}$. Λ and **A** are all initialized to **0**, **B** is initialized with random numbers.

4.3   Experimental Results

Performance Comparison. We first report the MAP results of RMLH and all compared approaches on different code lengths and datasets in Table 1. Their

Table 1. MAP of all approaches on **Corel5K** and **MIR Flickr**.

Methods	Corel5K			MIR Flickr		
	16 bits	24 bits	32 bits	16 bits	24 bits	32 bits
BRE	0.2583	0.2755	0.2835	0.6261	0.6159	0.6147
SKH	0.3164	0.3002	0.3047	0.6181	0.6047	0.6174
MLSH	0.3059	0.3444	0.3495	0.6308	0.6305	0.6361
SDH	0.3154	0.3108	0.3346	0.6035	0.6168	0.6106
RMLH	**0.3294**	**0.3631**	**0.3634**	**0.6352**	**0.6500**	**0.6567**

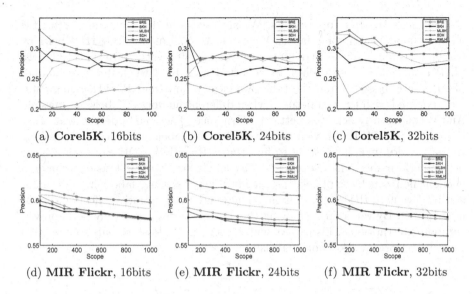

(a) **Corel5K**, 16bits (b) **Corel5K**, 24bits (c) **Corel5K**, 32bits

(d) **MIR Flickr**, 16bits (e) **MIR Flickr**, 24bits (f) **MIR Flickr**, 32bits

Fig. 1. *Precision-Scope* curves of compared approaches.

Table 2. MAP of all approaches on **MIR Flickr** when labels are missing.

Methods	24 bits				32 bits			
	1	2	3	4	1	2	3	4
BRE	0.6231	0.6289	0.6226	0.6294	0.6301	0.6301	0.6279	0.6284
SKH	0.6250	0.6387	0.6099	0.6204	0.6380	0.6351	0.6281	0.6259
MLSH	0.5890	0.6358	0.6279	0.6205	0.5855	0.6381	0.6298	0.6237
SDH	0.6039	0.6061	0.6129	0.6124	0.6273	0.6294	0.6105	0.6003
H2ML	**0.6408**	**0.6453**	**0.6410**	**0.6402**	**0.6576**	**0.6494**	**0.6463**	**0.6405**

corresponding *Precision-Scope* curves on two datasets are shown in Fig. 1. From the results, we can clearly observe that RMLH outperforms the compared approaches in most cases. The retrieval performance of RMLH increases steadily with hashing code length. Besides, we easily find that BRE does not perform well among the competitors. This is because BRE simply preserves pairwise label relations into hashing codes. Please note that SKH also depends on pairwise label relations. However, it employ kernel extension to capture non-linear inner data structure. Therefore, it usually performs better than BRE. In addition, it is not hard to find that MLSH always achieve better performance among the compared approaches. This is mainly attributed to the label correlation capturing via CCA. SDH is reported to be effective in single label based supervised hashing. But, in multi-label setting, we fail to observe its superior performance. The reason is that SDH ignores the label correlation preservation, which is important in multi-label hashing.

Robustness to Missing Labels. We also evaluate the robustness of RMLH on accommodating missing labels. We conduct experiments on **MIR Flickr** by training hashing model on training images associated with more than 10 labels. MAP results of all approaches are reported in Table 2 when different number of labels are missed. From the table, we clearly find that, RMLH is more stable compared with the competitors when different number of labels are missing. And it consistently achieves better performance. The results demonstrate that the proposed RMLH can well cope with missing labels when learning hashing codes. Besides, it is interesting to find that RRE, SKH, SDH can even achieve better performance when several missing labels are existed. This experimental phenomenon can be explained as: In multi-label setting, labels may be noisy and irrelevant to the visual contents. They may bring negative effects on hashing learning. By randomly removing them, their performance may be improved without interruption. This experimental phenomenon also reveals that RMLH can still perform well on noisy labels.

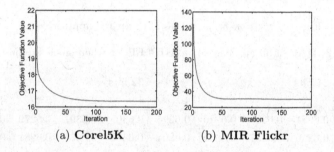

(a) **Corel5K**   (b) **MIR Flickr**

Fig. 2. Convergency of the proposed approach.

Convergency Analysis. Figure 2 presents the variations of objective function value in Eq. (7) with the number of iterations on two datasets. We can observe from the figure that, objective function value first decreases with the number of iterations and becomes steady after certain iterations (about 50). This experimental result demonstrates that the convergency of RMLH can be obtained.

5   Conclusions

This paper proposes an effective approach RMLH to robustly accommodate the missing labels in multi-label hashing settings. RMLH preserves label correlation with direct label-hashing correlation and high-order label correlation preserving. It imposes low-rank based regularization on correlation matrix to cope with missing labels. The optimization based on ADMM can effectively solve optimal hashing codes. Experimental results on standard datasets demonstrate the promising effectiveness of the proposed approach.

References

1. Bartels, R.H., Stewart, G.W.: Solution of the matrix equation ax + xb = c [f4]. Commun. ACM **15**(9), 820–826 (1972)
2. Cai, J.F., Candès, E.J., Shen, Z.: A singular value thresholding algorithm for matrix completion. SIAM J. Optim. **20**(4), 1956–1982 (2010)
3. Duygulu, P., Barnard, K., Freitas, J.F.G., Forsyth, D.A.: Object recognition as machine translation: learning a lexicon for a fixed image vocabulary. In: Heyden, A., Sparr, G., Nielsen, M., Johansen, P. (eds.) ECCV 2002. LNCS, vol. 2353, pp. 97–112. Springer, Heidelberg (2002). doi:10.1007/3-540-47979-1_7
4. Ghadimi, E., Teixeira, A., Shames, I., Johansson, M.: Optimal parameter selection for the alternating direction method of multipliers (ADMM): quadratic problems. IEEE Trans. Autom. Control **60**(3), 644–658 (2015)
5. Gionis, A., Indyk, P., Motwani, R.: Similarity search in high dimensions via hashing. In: VLDB, pp. 518–529 (1999)
6. Gong, Y., Lazebnik, S., Gordo, A., Perronnin, F.: Iterative quantization: a procrustean approach to learning binary codes for large-scale image retrieval. IEEE Trans. Pattern Anal. Mach. Intell. **35**(12), 2916–2929 (2013)
7. Hotelling, H.: Relations between two sets of variates. Biometrika **28**, 321–377 (1936)
8. Huiskes, M.J., Lew, M.S.: The MIR flickr retrieval evaluation. In: MIR, pp. 39–43 (2008)
9. Kulis, D., Darrell, T.: Learning to hash with binary reconstructive embeddings. In: NIPS, pp. 1042–1050 (2009)
10. Liu, W., Wang, J., Ji, R., Jiang, Y.G., Chang, S.F.: Supervised hashing with kernels. In: CVPR, pp. 2074–2081 (2012)
11. Liu, X., Mu, Y., Lang, B., Chang, S.: Mixed image-keyword query adaptive hashing over multilabel images. ACM Trans. Multim. Comput. **10**(2) (2014)
12. Shen, F., Shen, C., Liu, W., Shen, H.T.: Supervised discrete hashing. In: CVPR, pp. 37–45 (2015)
13. Wang, S., Huang, Z., Xu, X.: A multi-label least-squares hashing for scalable image search. In: SDM, pp. 954–962 (2015)

A Second-Order Approach for Blind Motion Deblurring by Normalized l_1 Regularization

Zedong Chen, Faming Fang, Yingying Xu, and Chaomin Shen[✉]

Shanghai Key Laboratory of Multidimensional Information Processing,
East China Normal University, Shanghai 200241, China
cmshen@cs.ecnu.edu.cn

Abstract. We propose a second-order approach for blind motion deblurring. Our idea is to define an energy functional, and the convolution kernel corresponds to the minimum of the functional. After the kernel is obtained, the problem is solved by existing non-blind deconvolution algorithms. To avoid that the minimizer of energy functional does not correspond to the unblurred image, which is often encountered in many algorithms, in the literature the normalized l_1 norm regularization term for the original or first-order gradient image was adopted. We further extend the idea using the second-order gradient image, which is the main novelty of the paper. This method favours a piecewise linear transition in the unblurred image, and thus efficiently attenuates the staircase and ring effects in the original or first-order case. Comparing with other state-of-the-art algorithms, the proposed method is effective in estimating the blur-kernel and restoring the unblurred image.

Keywords: Blind motion deblurring · Normalized l_1 norm · Second-order gradient · Staircase effects

1 Introduction

Motion blur is one of the most common phenomena encountered in image processing. Therefore, recovering an unblurred image from a motion blurred one has long been a fundamental topic. This problem can be reduced to image deconvolution, if the blur-kernel, i.e. the point spread function (PSF), is shift-invariant. Image deconvolution can be further separated into the blind and non-blind cases. In real situations, the blind deconvolution is more common and more difficult to handle. Its difficulty lies on that the blind deconvolution is highly ill-posed, since both the blur-kernel and the latent sharp image are unknown. To solve this problem, appropriate prior assumptions should be imposed [1,2].

In this paper we focus on the shift-invariant blur, which is commonly modeled as a convolution process:

$$g = u \otimes k + n, \tag{1}$$

where g represents the observed blurred image, u the sharp image, n the Gaussian noise, k the shift-invariant PSF, and $\otimes$ the 2D convolution operator. Our aim

© Springer International Publishing AG 2016
E. Chen et al. (Eds.): PCM 2016, Part II, LNCS 9917, pp. 296–305, 2016.
DOI: 10.1007/978-3-319-48896-7_29

is to recover u, given g. Unavoidably, we also need to estimate k in order to obtain u.

Most existing deblurring methods are formed as follows:

$$\min_{u,k} \|u \otimes k - g\|_2^2 + \alpha_u R_u(u) + \alpha_k R_k(k), \qquad (2)$$

where α_u and α_k are positive tuning parameters, and $R_u(u)$, $R_k(k)$ are the regularization terms corresponding to the priors on the latent sharp image u and the blue-kernel k respectively.

Most image priors are imposed on the image itself or the image gradients. Table 1 lists some choices of $R_u(u)$ and $R_k(k)$ in several state-of-the-art methods. All these $R_u(u)$'s are based on the first-order gradient of image. This approach favors piecewise constant pixel transitions, which tends to produce staircase effects in the recovered image. For the purpose of comparison, we also put our $R_u(u)$ and $R_k(k)$ at the last row, which will be discussed in detail later.

Note that many image deblurring algorithms have a fetal problem: the minimum of the objective functional does not correspond to the true sharp image [3]. The reason is that blur attenuates high frequency components and the response of any derivative-type filter will also be reduced [4]. To solve this problem, a number of complicated methods have been proposed, such as marginalization over all possible images [1,5], re-weighting of the image edges [6], dynamic adaptation of the cost function [7], and selective edge suppression [8].

To solve the problem, we employ the so called normalized l_1 norm to ensure the correspondence of the functional minimizer and the unblurred image. The core contribution is that we initially apply the second-order gradient to remove motion blur. Our approach has greater potential for producing a sharp image while restraining staircase artifacts. It is also quick by taking advantage of existing fast l_1 methods to estimate the kernel and the sharp image.

Table 1. $R_u(u)$ and $R_k(k)$ proposed in recent methods

Method	$R_u(u)$	$R_k(k)$
[2]	$\|\nabla u\|_0 + \frac{\beta_u}{\alpha_u}\|\nabla u\|_2^2$	$\|\nabla k\|_0 + \frac{\beta_k}{\alpha_k}\|\nabla k\|_2^2$
[4]	$\frac{\|\nabla u\|_1}{\|\nabla u\|_2}$	$\|k\|_1$
[9]	$\Sigma_m \min(1, \frac{|(\nabla u)_m|^2}{\epsilon^2})$	$\|k\|_2^2$
[10]	$\|\nabla u\|_p^p, p : 0.8 \to 0.6 \to 0.4$	$\|\nabla k\|_2$
[11]	$\|\nabla u\|_{0.3}^{0.3}$	$\|k\|_1$
[12]	$\Sigma_m \log |(\nabla u)_m|$	$\log \|k\|_2$
[13]	$(\nabla u)^T W(|\nabla u|)\nabla u$	$\|k\|_2^2 + \varsigma\|k\|_{0.5}^{0.5}$
Ours	$\frac{\|\nabla^2 u\|_1}{\|\nabla^2 u\|_2}$	$\|k\|_1$

2   Motivation

The regularization function we propose is the normalized l_1 norm in the second-order gradient domain of the image. To the best of our knowledge, the second-order gradient has not been applied to blind deconvolution yet.

2.1   Second-Order Gradient

As referred in [2,4,10,11], the first-order regularization with sparsity constraint is commonly used as an image prior for blind deconvolution. This approach favors piecewise constant pixel transitions, removes noise and/or blur and preserves edges reasonably well. However, the so-called staircase effects are likely to appear: smoothly changing transitions are approximated by a step-by-step change [14], especially when gradual changes are present in the scene.

To recover a sharp image while restraining staircase artifacts, instead of using the first-order gradient, we use the second-order gradient regularization. Second-order gradient of an image contains more spatial details, and favors piecewise linear pixel transitions to circumvent the possibility that the staircase effects may arise [15]. The second-order gradient (also called Hessian matrix) is defined as:

$$\nabla^2 u = \begin{bmatrix} u_{xx} & u_{xy} \\ u_{yx} & u_{yy} \end{bmatrix}. \tag{3}$$

2.2   The Normalized l_1 Regularization

Here, we express the normalized l_1 norm as the l_1/l_2 norm which is one of the scale-invariant sparsity-inducing regularizer [16]. An image of sharp edges tends to minimize the l_1/l_2 norm [3]. If applied to the high frequency parts of an image, the l_1/l_2 norm is equivalent to the l_1 norm of the edges rescaled by their total energy. Adding blur and noise to the image, the value of l_1 norm is increased: although blur decreases both the l_1 and l_2 norms, crucially the latter is reduced more [4]. Most of the energy in images is contained in the low and mid frequency parts, which are barely affected by blur.

Therefore, using the normalized l_1 in the second-order gradient domain of the image as image prior can ensure the minimum of the objective function correspond to the true sharp image, and recover an unblurred image while restraining staircase artifacts.

3   The Proposed Approach

In this paper, the overall scheme for blind motion deblurring include three steps: (i) generate a high frequency image $\nabla^2 g$ by applying second-order derivative filters to g; (ii) estimate the blur-kernel k and the sharp high frequency image $\nabla^2 u$ from $\nabla^2 g$ by alternating iteration; and (iii) recover sharp image u using the non-blind algorithm of [17] with the estimated blur-kernel k.

3.1   Blur-Kernel Estimation

Similar to (2), our cost function for blind motion blur-kernel estimation is given as:

$$\min_{\nabla^2 u,k} \lambda\|\nabla^2 u \otimes k - \nabla^2 g\|_2^2 + \frac{\|\nabla^2 u\|_1}{\|\nabla^2 u\|_2} + \alpha_k\|k\|_1, \quad \text{s.t. } k_{i,j} \geqslant 0, \ \sum_{i,j} k_{i,j} = 1, \quad (4)$$

where ∇^2 is the second-order derivative operator, $R_{\nabla^2 u}(\nabla^2 u)$ are the normalized l_1 norm. To reduce noise in the kernel, we add l_1 regularizer on blur-kernel k as $R_k(k)$. The output blur-kernel should be non-negative as well as normalized.

Because (4) is highly non-convex, our numerical scheme is deployed for alternatingly computing $\nabla^2 u$ and k starting, by the methods of inner-outer iteration [4] and the unconstrained iterative re-weighted least squares (IRLS) [18].

3.1.1   Update k

The kernel update sub-problem is given by:

$$\min_k \lambda\|\nabla^2 u \otimes k - \nabla^2 g\|_2^2 + \alpha_k\|k\|_1, \quad \text{s.t. } k_{i,j} \geqslant 0, \ \sum_{i,j} k_{i,j} = 1. \quad (5)$$

It can be efficiently solved by the unconstrained IRLS. Then we project the resulting k onto the constraints (setting negative elements to zero, and renormalizing). During the iterations we run IRLS for just one iteration, with the weights being computed from the kernel of the previous k update. We solve the inner IRLS system to a low level of accuracy, using a few conjugate gradient iterations.

To increase robustness to noise, we threshold small elements of the kernel to zero after recovering the kernel at the finest level. This is similar to other blind deconvolution methods [1,4].

3.1.2   Update ∇^{2u}

Substitute $\nabla^2 u$ with x, this sub-problem becomes:

$$\min_x \lambda\|x \otimes k - \nabla^2 g\|_2^2 + \frac{\|x\|_1}{\|x\|_2}. \quad (6)$$

The function (6) is non-convex and hard to optimize directly. However, it becomes a convex l_1-regularized problem if the denominator of the regularizer is fixed by the previous iterate. The iterative shrinkage-thresholding algorithm (ISTA) [19] is simple and fast to solve such general linear inverse problems like the form:

$$\min_x \lambda\|Kx - \nabla^2 g\|_2^2 + \|x\|_1, \quad (7)$$

where $K \in \mathbb{R}^{W \times W}$ is the convolution matrix corresponding to k, and W is the number of image pixels.

We use the ISTA step as the inner iteration in x-update. The outer loop then simply re-estimates the weights in (6) by updating the denominator $\|x\|_2$. In practice this inner-outer iteration is effective in reducing the cost function in (6). The overall x-update algorithm is presented in Algorithm 1.

Algorithm 1. Update x

Require: blurred image g, initial x^0 and k^0, regularization parameter λ, threshold t, maximum outer iterators M, and inner iterators N
1: **for** $i = 0$ to $M - 1$ **do**
2:      $\lambda' = \lambda\|x^i\|_2$
3:      **for** $j = 0$ to $N - 1$ **do**
4:          $v = x^j - \lambda' t K^T (K x^j - \nabla^2 g)$
5:          $x^{j+1} = \max(|v| - t, 0) sign(v)$
6:      **end for**
7:      $x^i = x^N$
8: **end for**
9: **return** Update image x

3.2   Image Recovery

After the blur-kernel k has been estimated, we use the non-blind deconvolution method from [17], rather than our second-order regularization, to recover the unblurred u from g. This is because the non-blind deconvolution problem is much less ill-posed than the blind one, and the method of [17], which is based on the hyper-Laplacian image prior, works well and fast. This algorithm uses a continuation method to solve the following cost function:

$$\min_u \beta\|u \otimes k - g\|_2^2 + \|\nabla u\|_\alpha^\alpha, \tag{8}$$

where $\nabla u = [u_x, u_y]^T$ is the gradient operator.

3.3   Implementation Details

In order to account for the large-scale motion blur-kernel estimation as well as to further reduce the risk of getting stuck in a poor local minimum, we perform multi-scale (L scales) estimation of the kernel using a coarse-to-fine pyramid of image resolutions, similar to some top-performing methods [1,2,4]. We use levels with a size ratio of $\sqrt{2}$ between them (in each dimension). The number of levels L is computed by:

$$q \times \sqrt{2}^L \leq h, \tag{9}$$

where h is the maximum kernel size, and q is the value of kernel size at the coarsest level setting as $q = 3$.

Algorithm 2. Multi-scale blind deconvolution with second-order model

---

Require: Blurred image g, h, x^0, λ, M, N, t, β, α

1. Blind estimation of blur-kernel k from g (Section 3.1).
    For
        For
            - Update blurring kernel k (Section 3.1.1).
            - Update sharp high-freqencies image $\nabla^2 u$ (Section 3.1.2).
        Until the maximum number of iteration is reached.
        Interpolate solution to finer level as initialization.
    Until the maximum scale level is reached.
    Output blur-kernel k
2. Image recovery using the non-blind algorithm of [17] (Section 3.2).
return Sharp image u.

We downsample the input blurry image, and at each level generate the second-order gradient image $\nabla^2 g$. Once a kernel estimate k and sharp high-frequency image ∇u are computed, they are upsampled to act as the initialization of the kernel and sharp image at the next finer level. All of the resizing operations are done using bilinear interpolation.

The pseudo-code of the overall scheme is presented in Algorithm 2.

4 Experiments and Comparisons

In this paper, we perform 200 alternatingly updates of $\nabla^2 u$ and k at each scale level. The α_k parameter depends on the user-specified maximum kernel size h, according to the formula $\alpha_k = \frac{3}{13} h$, similar as [4]. We set other parameters as follows: $\lambda = 32$, $M = 2$, $N = 2$, $t = 0.001$, $\beta = 3000$, and $\alpha = 0.8$. We use the same settings for all results throughout the paper. This robustness is a major advantage of our algorithm over existing schemes requiring parameter adjustment for different input images.

Furthermore, our methods have comparable speed with other methods. For example, our algorithm takes 2 min to estimate a 27×27 kernel for a 255×255 image, compared to 6 min for the method of [1]. Most worthy of mention is that we only use a single-threaded Matlab on a 2.50 GHZ CPU and our method is amenable to speedups GPU acceleration.

4.1 Synthetic Data

We test our approach on a benchmark image dataset proposed by Levin et al. [5][1] This dataset consists of 32 blurred images generated by 4 images of size 255×255 and 8 different kernels ranging from 13×3 to 27×27.

Our kernels are compared with the blind deconvolution algorithms of Fergus et al. [1] and Krishnan et al. [4]. After obtaining these three kernels, we perform non-blind deconvolution using the algorithm in [17] with the same parameter settings.

---

[1] www.wisdom.weizmann.ac.il/~levina/papers/LevinEtalCVPR2011Code.zip.

The error metric used the SSD (sum of squared differences) error ratio between the images deconvolved respectively with the estimated blur-kernel (its size set as same as the true one) and the ground truth blur-kernel, as defined in [5].

In Fig. 1, we plot the histograms of the SSD deconvolution error ratios across 32 test images for 3 algorithms. Following convention of earlier work, the r'th bin in the figure counts the percentage of the motion blurred images in the dataset achieving error ratio below r [5]. For each bin, the higher the bar, the better the deblurring performance. As pointed out by Levin et al. [5], deblurred images are visually plausible in general and the blind deblurring is considered to be successful, if their SSD error ratios are below 3. The cumulative histogram in Fig. 1 shows the high success percentage of our method is 93.75%. As for Algorithms [1,4], their percentages of success are 68.73% and 81.25%.

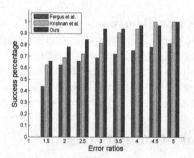

Fig. 1. The cumulative histogram of the SSD error ratios across the dataset of [5] archived by [1,4] and ours.

For visual perception and considering the limited space, we only show the deblurring results and the corresponding PSNR in Fig. 2 produced by each approach for the blurred image Image04-kernel04.

4.2   Real Data

We test the proposed approach on some real-world color blurred images, and comparing them with some previously mentioned methods $[2,4,7,8]+[9]^2$ We first use different algorithms to generate the blur-kernel utilizing the codes and parameter settings provided and suggested by the authors, and then use the same non-blind deblurring algorithm (that of [17]) with identical parameter settings to produce the final deconvolution image.

In Fig. 3, from left to right, top to bottom are the blurred image, the result of $[4,7,9]+[2,8]$ and our method, respectively. Note that staircase effects in the deblurred image by [2,4] are clearly seen, for example, in the foreheads of

---

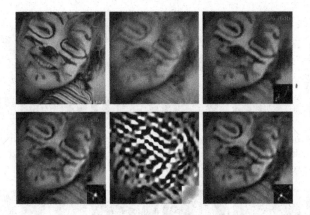

Fig. 2. Blind deblurring for Image04-kernel04 in the dataset [5]. Top-left: original image; top-middle: blurred image; top-right: deblurred image with ground truth kernel; bottom-left: deblurred image with kernel of [1]; bottom-middle: deblurred image with kernel of [4]; bottom-right: deblurred image with our estimated kernel. Recovered kernels (of size 27 × 27) are shown as insets.

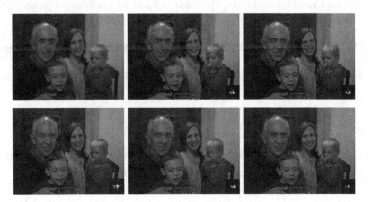

Fig. 3. Results for the blurred image. From left to right, top to bottom are the blurred image, deblurred image with kernel of [4,7,9] + [2,8] and ours. Recovered kernels (of size 27 × 27) are shown in the lower-right corners of each image.

the man. The details of the blue rectangle boxes show that the letters on kids are much better deblurred and less artifacts are observed by our method than [4,9] + [8].

The blurred image in Fig. 4 comes from the online code of Krishnan et al. [4]. From Fig. 4, we can see that other results produce staircase effects at the junction of woman's forehead and hair, except ours. Specifically, [2,7] introduced very visible artifacts on her hand. On the other hand, compared with [8] + [9], our method is effective in restoring image details, for example, the clothes crease. Figure 5 shows another picture with more details. The staircase effects can be observed in some regions in the results of [2,4]. For example, in the cheeks of

Fig. 4. Results for the blurred image. From left to right are the blurred image, deblurred image with kernel of $[4,7,9]+[2,8]$ and ours. Recovered kernels (of size 27×27) are shown in the lower-right corners of each image.

Fig. 5. Results for the blurred image. From left to right are the blurred image, deblurred image with kernel of $[4,7,9]+[2,8]$ and ours. Recovered kernels (of size 25×25) are shown in the lower-right corners of each image.

the statue. By contrast, our deblurred result is much clearer than others with almost no staircase effects.

5   Conclusion

In this paper, we have proposed an effective blind motion deblurring method for single blurred image. The estimation of convolution kernel is crucial to deblurring, since spatially invariant deblurring can be regard as deconvolution. To overcome the staircase effects caused by gradient based methods, we calculate the kernel on second-order gradient domain. Moreover, we propose to minimize the normalized l_1-norm (termed as l_1/l_2-norm) of second-order gradient image incorporate with the kernel's sparse regularization, which contributes to a more accurate blur kernel estimation. Whereafter, a desirable deblurring result is achieved by using the non-blind deblurring algorithm based on the estimated blur-kernel.

Our model is validated via a series of experiments on both benchmark image datasets and real-world blurred images. The results demonstrate that the proposed method effectively restrains staircase artifacts while obtaining an unblurred image. It is fast as well as robust to the choices of parameters. In the future work, we will study how our algorithm be extended to the case of shift-variant blur.

Acknowledgments. This work is supported by the National Science Foundation of China (No. 61273298), and the Science and Technology Commission of Shanghai Municipality under research grant No. 14DZ2260800.

References

1. Fergus, R., Singh, B., Hertzmann, A., Roweis, S.T., Freeman, W.T.: Removing camera shake from a single photograph. ACM Trans. Graph. **25**(3), 787–794 (2006)
2. Shao, W.Z., Li, H.B., Elad, M.: Bi-l_0-l_2-norm regularization for blind motion deblurring. J. Vis. Commun. Image Represent. **33**, 42–59 (2015)
3. Ji, H., Li, J., Shen, Z., Wang, K.: Image deconvolution using a characterization of sharp images in wavelet domain. Appl. Comput. Harmon. Anal. **32**(2), 295–304 (2012)
4. Krishnan, D., Tay, T., Fergus, R.: Blind deconvolution using a normalized sparsity measure. In: IEEE Conference on CVPR, pp. 233–240 (2011)
5. Levin, A., Weiss, Y., Durand, F., Freeman, W.T.: Understanding blind deconvolution algorithms. IEEE Trans. Pattern Anal. Mach. Intell. **33**(12), 2354–2367 (2011)
6. Cho, S., Lee, S.: Fast motion deblurring. ACM Trans. Graph. **28**(5), 145–152 (2009)
7. Shan, Q., Jia, J., Agarwala, A.: High-quality motion deblurring from a single image. ACM Trans. Graph. **27**(3), 73–82 (2008)
8. Xu, L., Jia, J.: Two-phase kernel estimation for robust motion deblurring. In: Daniilidis, K., Maragos, P., Paragios, N. (eds.) ECCV 2010. LNCS, vol. 6311, pp. 157–170. Springer, Heidelberg (2010). doi:10.1007/978-3-642-15549-9_12
9. Xu, L., Zheng, S., Jia, J.: Unnatural L_0 sparse representation for natural image deblurring. In: IEEE Conference on CVPR, pp. 1107–1114 (2013)
10. Almeida, M.S., Almeida, L.D.: Blind and semi-blind deblurring of natural images. IEEE Trans. Image Process. **19**(1), 36–52 (2010)
11. Kotera, J., Šroubek, F., Milanfar, P.: Blind deconvolution using alternating maximum a posteriori estimation with heavy-tailed priors. In: Wilson, R., Hancock, E., Bors, A., Smith, W. (eds.) CAIP 2013. LNCS, vol. 8048, pp. 59–66. Springer, Heidelberg (2013). doi:10.1007/978-3-642-40246-3_8
12. Babacan, S.D., Molina, R., Do, M.N., Katsaggelos, A.K.: Bayesian blind deconvolution with general sparse image priors. In: Fitzgibbon, A., Lazebnik, S., Perona, P., Sato, Y., Schmid, C. (eds.) ECCV 2012. LNCS, vol. 7577, pp. 341–355. Springer, Heidelberg (2012). doi:10.1007/978-3-642-33783-3_25
13. Krishnan, D., Bruna, J., Fergus, R.: Blind deconvolution with re-weighted sparsity promotion. arXiv:1311.4029 (2013)
14. Bauer, S., Stefan, J., Michelsburg, M., Laengle, T., Leon, F.P.: Robustness improvement of hyperspectral image unmixing by spatial second-order regularization. IEEE Trans. Image Process. **23**(12), 5209–5221 (2014)
15. Liu, P., Xiao, L., Zhang, J., Naz, B.: Spatial-Hessian-feature-guided variational model for pan-sharpening. IEEE Trans. Geosci. Remote Sens. **54**(4), 2235–2253 (2016)
16. Hurley, N., Rickard, S.: Comparing measures of sparsity. IEEE Trans. Inf. Theor. **55**(10), 4723–4741 (2009)
17. Krishnan, D., Fergus, R.: Fast image deconvolution using hyper-Laplacian priors. In: NIPS, pp. 1033–1041 (2009)
18. Levin, A., Fergus, R., Durand, F., Freeman, W.T.: Image and depth from a conventional camera with a coded aperture. ACM Trans. Graph. **26**(3), 70–79 (2007)
19. Beck, A., Teboulle, M.: A fast iterative shrinkage-thresholding algorithm for linear inverse problems. SIAM J. Imaging Sci. **2**(1), 183–202 (2009)

Abnormal Event Detection and Localization by Using Sparse Coding and Reconstruction

Jing Xue, Yao Lu[✉], and Haohao Jiang

Beijing Laboratory of Intelligent Information Technology,
School of Computer Science, Beijing Institute of Technology,
Beijing 100081, China
vis_yl@bit.edu.cn

Abstract. In this paper, we present a novel approach using a local feature called Histograms of Sparse Codes (HSC) and sparse reconstruction for an accurate localization of abnormal events in surveillance videos, and we design a way of dual threshold to do further modification on reconstruction error. In addition, we formulate abnormal event detection as an optimal path discovery problem solved by Max-Path algorithm in a spatio-temporal space, and our method can detect multiple occurrences of abnormal events simultaneously. The proposed method can obtain the global optimal solution and improve the overall accuracy of detection and localization. Experimental results on UCSD dataset and comparison with the state-of-the-art methods show the effectiveness and advantages of our approach.

Keywords: Abnormal event detection · Histograms of Sparse Codes · Sparse reconstruction error

1 Introduction

Abnormal event detection is a key application in automatic video surveillance and hence much research. It refers to the problem of finding patterns in the videos that do not conform to expected behaviors. By finding suspicious events automatically, it significantly reduces the cost of heavy burden of manual annotation. However, abnormal event detection is a challenging problem because of the camera viewpoint distortion, intra- and inter-classes variations of normal events and the versatility and uncertainty of anomalies.

Research in abnormal event detection has made great progresses in recent years. Kratz et al. [10] proposed to combine the spatio-temporal gradient feature and Hidden Markov Model (HMM) for anomaly detection. Adam et al. [1] used histograms to represent the probability of optical flow in a local patch. Mahadevan et al. [12] modeled the normal crowd behavior by the mixtures of dynamic textures. Tang et al. [14] proposed to sparsely code the motion features directly to describe the crowd. To evaluate anomaly in pixel level, Cong et al. [4] measured the normalness by using sparse reconstruction cost, though

© Springer International Publishing AG 2016
E. Chen et al. (Eds.): PCM 2016, Part II, LNCS 9917, pp. 306–314, 2016.
DOI: 10.1007/978-3-319-48896-7_30

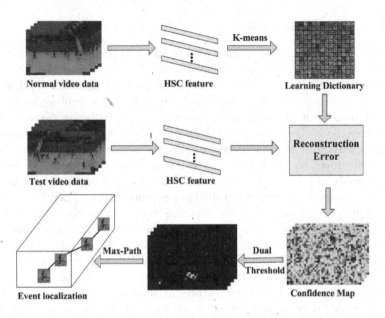

Fig. 1. The overview of our approach for abnormal event detection and localization

finding sparse bases at each test sample is a time-consuming process, it is a worth learning for the idea of detecting abnormal via reconstruction from normal data.

In our paper, we propose an improved approach for accurate abnormal event localization by using an effective anomaly evaluation method. First, we adopt Histograms of Sparse Codes (HSC) [13] as our feature descriptor, which has never been used for abnormal event detection, and we demonstrate its advantages from our following experiment results. Second, we use reconstruction error from normal videos to describe the anomaly possibility at each location of video frames, and design a way of dual threshold to do further modification. Finally, in order to improve the accuracy of localization and reduce computational complexity, we regard abnormal detection as an optimal spatio-temporal path discovery problem solved by Max-Path algorithm [6]. Our approach can also detect multiple occurrences of abnormal events simultaneously. The overview of our proposed approach is depicted in Fig. 1.

2 Anomaly Evaluation

Abnormal video detection is a challenging problem in that it is difficult to define anomaly in an explicit manner [7], and we can never know an abnormal event may occurs in what content and which form, so anomaly localization in pixel level becomes much harder. We determine the likelihood of being abnormal is to find the difference between the normal videos and the test videos. Two factors are very important in this process, one is the feature to describe video frames, and the other is the way to judge the difference.

2.1   Feature Representation

An effective feature to represent the video frames is very important for anormly detection. A mixtures of dynamic textures in [12] can represent the dynamic background effectively, but it need much time cost for training. Optical flow has been widely used in anomaly detection, like [16], which is robust to multiple object motions, but it can not represent spatial-temporal flow properties. Therefore, more methods used local spatio-temporal features to represent the underlying intrinsic structure. Motion histograms, like Histogram of Optical Flow (HOF) [5] has been proved to be effective in [1], but it is not every suitable for crowd motion analysis in that motion orientation computation on histogram is time-consuming and error-prone due to the aligning problem [11]. Therefore, we urge to find a kind of more advanced and effective feature for anomaly detection.

Histograms of Sparse Codes (HSC) is proposed in [13] by aggregating per-pixel sparse codes to form local histograms, which performs much better than Histogram of Oriented Gradient (HOG) in object detection but has never been used for abnormal event detection and localization so far. We underline two advantages of HSC over the above features in anomaly detection. The first one is that it can learn richer structures on patches. As dictionary size and patch size grow, more and more useful structures can be found (such as thin lines, line endings, corners, and high-frequency gratings). The second one is there are very few ad-hoc design choices in feature extraction, that means only change several settings, such as dictionary size, patch size or sparsity level, allowing to adapt to the needs of different problems. Moreover, it can avoid the high time cost.

In the HSC feature extraction, we firstly divide each frame into a set of image patches, the size of which we choose is 5×5. For dictionary learning, we use K-SVD algorithm [2], the sparsity level is 1 and dictionary size is 100. Then we can get the sparse code at each pixel, whose dimension equals the dictionary size. We adopt the sliding window framework to divide the image into regular cells (composed by 8×8 pixels) and aggregate those sparse codes into histograms. Finally, we normalize HSC feature with its L2 norm, and to increase the discriminative power, the power transform we set is 0.25.

2.2   Anomaly Discrimination

Motivated by [4], we use reconstruction error to represent the likelihood of being abnormal at each location. Given $y \in R^m$, we can reconstruct it by a sparse combination $y = \beta x$ from an over-complete normal bases set $\beta \in R^{m \times D}$, where $m < D$. A normal event is likely to be reconstructed with a low reconstruct error, while an abnormal event can be reconstructed with greater cost or even cannot be constructed. Considering the balance between time cost and accuracy, instead of updating sparse bases at each test sample of [4], we get the reconstruct error through a more simple and effective way.

For training, only normal videos are used for a dictionary of normalness. We extract HSC features at location and use K-means algorithm to cluster the result features, and group those clustering centers to a normal bases set $\beta = [b_1, ..., b_m]$, by which any feature vector can be represented as a sparse combination. Then the problem to reconstruct a feature vector y is formulated by l_1 regularized least squares:

$$\min_x \frac{1}{2} \|\beta x - y\|_2^2 + \lambda \|x\|_1 \tag{1}$$

where $\|x\|_1 = \sum_i^n x_i$ denotes the l_1 norm of x and $\lambda > 0$ is the regularization parameter. Equation 1 will yield a sparse vector x^*, that is that has relatively few non-zero coefficients [9]. And when reconstruction coefficient x^* is resolved, we use Eq. 2 to compute the error between feature vector y and its reconstructed vector.

$$C = \frac{1}{2} \|\beta x^* - y\|_2^2 + \lambda \|x^*\|_1 \tag{2}$$

therefore, given a video sequence F, we can build a set of confidence maps constituted by the construction errors. At each location of video frames, the larger the reconstruction error, the higher the likelihood of being abnormal.

2.3 Method of Dual Threshold

Threshold setting on the reconstruct errors can directly lead to the discriminative capability of result. A large threshold can remove most of the noise but may loss some effect information, while a small threshold can get more information but still retain much noise.

To combine the advantages of both, we design a way of dual threshold to deal with the reconstruct errors for the formation of discriminative confidence maps. For a confidence map, we first get its binary image I_a through a small threshold F_a, I_b through a large threshold F_b. We regard each connected region as a unit, then compute the intersection of I_a and I_b denoted by I_c for an accuracy location, and for reserving more effective information, we get the connected regions from I_a combining with I_c as the mask. Then we adopt the small threshold F_a on the mask's region, and adopt the small threshold F_b on the rest of region. Then we can form a 3D array of positive and negative scores as the confidence maps with the priori knowledge of the video sequence, the examples showed in Fig. 2.

3 Anomaly Localization

In surveillance videos, an abnormal event occurs not from an individual frame but from a series of continuous frames. We formulate abnormal event detection and localization as an optimal path discovery problem in a spatio-temporal space showed in Fig. 3. Supposed the size of space is $w \times h \times n$, because the start and end location of a path is unknown for us, as well as the detail abnormal status, if we use an exhaustively searching way, the computational complexity becomes $O(w^3 h^3 n^3)$. Therefore, we adopt Max-Path algorithm [6], an improved way of dynamic programming, whose complexity is only $O(whn)$ with a globally

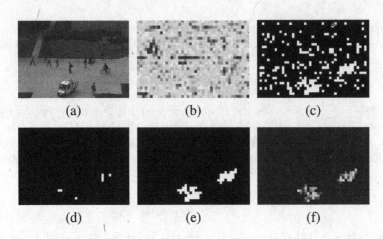

Fig. 2. Dual threshold processing: (a) original frame (b) confidence map (c) binary image by a small threshold (d) binary image by a large threshold (e) binary image after the combination of b and c (f) the final result

optimal solution. It has been proved to be robust to the cluttered and dynamic backgrounds, and intra-class variations of the video events.

Given a set of confidence maps consisted of the construction errors at location, we denote by $w_t^{x,y}$ the local window centered at (x, y, t). By treating each local window as a node, we form a 3 dimension trellis model G with the size of $w \times h \times n$. Denote a path by a set of local windows from continuous frames $p = \{w_{t1}, ..., w_{tm}\}$, if it satisfies two fundamental conditions: (1) connectivity constraints: $x_i - 1 \leq x_{i+1} \leq x_i + 1, y_i - 1 \leq y_{i+1} \leq y_i + 1, t_{i+1} = t_i + 1$ and (2) boundary constraints: $1 \leq x_i \leq w, 1 \leq y_i \leq h, 1 \leq t_{i_1} \leq t_{i_k} \leq n$. Condition (1) specifies the spatial and temporal proximities for a path. Condition (2) bounds the location of a path. We define the i-th optimal path p_i^* by Eq. 3:

$$p_i^* = \arg\max_{p_i \in G_i} \sum_{t=t_1}^{t_n} M(w_t) \tag{3}$$

where G_i is the grid model of i-th path discovery, $M(w_t)$ is the abnormal score of the patch w_t. We denote a set of l optimal paths by $P_l = \{p_1^*, ..., p_l^*\}$.

The path discovery problem is solved by the Max-Path algorithm. Considering more than one abnormal event may occur in some cases, we do iterations over the trellis model G. That is, after finding the optimal path p_i^*, we update G_{i+1} for a new iteration $i + 1$ by removing the previous i paths from G. We denote by $s(p_i^*)$ the maximum accumulated score of optimal path p_i^* and the result is positive. However, the score of optimal path decreases monotonically, namely $s(p_{i+1}^*) \leq s(p_i^*)$, and finally will become none-positive. Denote $S(P_l)$ the total scores of l previous optimal paths, which is a convex function with respect to l.

$$S(P_{l^*-1}) \leq S(P_{l^*}) \geq S(P_{l^*+1}) \tag{4}$$

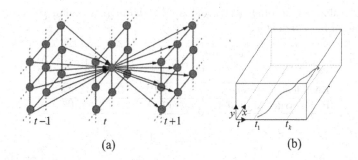

(a)   (b)

Fig. 3. Optimal path discovery problem in a spatio-temporal space (a) 9 incoming and 9 outgoing neighbors for node. (b) The visualization of one spatio-temporal path, including the start and end in the video and the detail location in each frame.

We set Eq. 4 as the stopping criterion of Max-Path algorithm. To avoid erroneous splitting of paths, we select the smallest one among all consecutive values that satisfy the above condition [3]. Therefore, our way is globally optimal with the complexity of $O(whn(k+1))$. Algorithm 1 describes the overall algorithm of the proposed approach.

Algorithm 1. Overall algorithm of the proposed approach.

Require: normal video frames V_s, a test video frames sequence V_p;
Ensure: a set of optimal paths representing abnormal events, $P_k = \{p_1^*, ..., p_k^*\}$;
Training:
  1. Extract HSC features F_s from V_s;
  2. Build the normal bases set β by clustering F_s;
Testing:
  1. Extract HSC features F_p from V_p;
  2. Construct F_p based on β from Eq. 1 and compute the construction error C from Eq. 2;
  3. Do dual threshold on C to build a 3D grid model G;
  4. Find i-th optimal path p_i by Max-Path algorithm[6], and compute previous i path total abnormal score $S(P_{i^*})$;
  5. if $S(P_{i^*-1}) \leq S(P_{i^*}) \geq S(P_{i^*+1})$
        return P_i
      else
          $i = i + 1$, update G and go to Step 4

---

4   Experiments

We evaluate the proposed method on well-established UCSD abnormal event detection dataset [12] which contains pixel-level groundtruth. This dataset consists of two sections (UCSDped1 and UCSDPed2) under two different pedestrian-walkway scenarios with image size 238×158 and 360×240 separately. UCSDPed1

Table 1. Localization accuracy (RD) compared with different combinations of features and evaluation measurements.

RD Feature Method	HOF-HOG	HSC
Euclidean Distance	37.1%	43.6%
Reconstruct & dual-T	42.5%	**51.4%**

has 34 video sequences for training and 16 for testing, and UCSDPed2 has 16 video sequences for training and 12 for testing. The anomalies in the dataset contains bikers, skaters, wheelchairs and small cars. We extract HSC feature with a dictionary size $D = 100$ and sparsity level $K = 1$ using 5×5 patches. Then the scene is tiled with a 37×24 grid model for UCSDped1, 43×28 grid model for UCSDped2. We suppose 30% of the data contributed to the abnormal model and use a small threshold T_a and a large one T_b working on the grid model, where $T_a = 0.8T_b$. Assuming that abnormal events may occur across different scales, we use integral image [15] to compute the scores of different scales local windows at each frame.

To highlight the advantages of our anomaly evaluation method, we compare the localization accuracy on pixel-level (RD [12]) using different features and anomaly measurements showed in Table 1 (where we use HOF and HOG feature with 8×8 patches, Max-Path algorithm for abnormal event detection). From the results, we can see that HSC feature performs significantly better than the traditional feature for anomaly detection, and anomaly measurement based on construction with modification by dual-threshold achieves a better performance than the measurement based on distance.

We also compare with the state-of-art approaches on frame-level (detection accuracy [12], AUC, area under ROC over different thresholds) and pixel-level (localization accuracy, RD). The results in Table 2 indicate that the proposed approach outperform other approaches. And Fig. 4 shows the resulting images compared with MDT method. Our approach has ability to detect wheelchair case and people walking across grassland case but MDT can not, and the anomaly localization of our result is more accurate. Finally, experimental results show that our approach can detect multiple occurrences of abnormal events effectively, and automatically discover the starting and ending points.

Table 2. Compared with the state-of-art methods on frame level and pixel level.

Algorithm	MPPCA [8]	MDT [12]	Context [4]	Our method
Frame AUC	64.2%	82.4%	86.0%	**88.1%**
RD	18%	45%	46%	**51.4%**

Fig. 4. Comparison with MDT method. Each row shows the results of different algorithms (first row: proposed method, second row: temporal MDT. Anomalous objects are labeled with a red color. (Color figure online)

5 Conclusion

The purpose in our paper is to detect and locate abnormal events accurately in surveillance videos. And to realize it, we design a novel way of anomaly evaluation at each location of video frames. First, we adopt a local sparse coding representation called Histograms of Sparse Codes (HSC). The likelihood of being abnormal is represented by reconstruction error over normal video data, and then we use a way of dual threshold to do further modification for our anomaly evaluation. Moreover, our method can detect multiple occurrences of abnormal event simultaneously. From the experiment results on the published UCSD compared to other approaches, our approach can locate anomalies more accurately.

References

1. Adam, A., Rivlin, E., Shimshoni, I., Reinitz, D.: Robust real-time unusual event detection using multiple fixed-location monitors. PAMI **30**(3), 555–560 (2008)
2. Aharon, M., Elad, M., Bruckstein, A.: K-SVD: an algorithm for designing overcomplete dictionaries for sparse representation. IEEE Trans. Sig. Process. **54**(11), 4311–4322 (2006)
3. Berclaz, J., Fleuret, F., Turetken, E., Fua, P.: Multiple object tracking using k-shortest paths optimization. IEEE Trans. Softw. Eng. **33**(9), 1806–1819 (2011)
4. Cong, Y., Yuan, J., Liu, J.: Abnormal event detection in crowded scenes using sparse representation. Pattern Recogn. **46**(7), 1851–1864 (2013)
5. Dalal, N., Triggs, B., Schmid, C.: Human detection using oriented histograms of flow and appearance. In: Leonardis, A., Bischof, H., Pinz, A. (eds.) ECCV 2006. LNCS, vol. 3952, pp. 428–441. Springer, Heidelberg (2006). doi:10.1007/11744047_33
6. Du, T., Junsong, Y., David, F.: Video event detection: from subvolume localization to spatio-temporal path search. IEEE Trans. PAMI **36**(2), 404–416 (2013)
7. Jiang, F., Yuan, J., Tsaftaris, S.A., Katsaggelos, A.K.: Anomalous video event detection using spatiotemporal context. Comput. Vis. Image Underst. **115**(3), 323–333 (2011)
8. Kim, J., Grauman, K.: Observe locally, infer globally: a space-time MRF for detecting abnormal activities with incremental updates. In: CVPR, pp. 2921–2928 (2009)

9. Kim, S.J., Koh, K., Lustig, M., Boyd, S.: An interior-point method for large-scale l1-regularized least squares. IEEE J. Sel. Top. Sig. Process. **1**(4), 606–617 (2007)
10. Kratz, L., Nishino, K.: Anomaly detection in extremely crowded scenes using spatio-temporal motion pattern models. In: CVPR, pp. 1446–1453 (2009)
11. Li, T., Chang, H., Wang, M., Ni, B., Hong, R., Yan, S.: Crowded scene analysis: a survey. IEEE Trans. Circ. Syst. Video Technol. **25**(3), 367–386 (2015)
12. Mahadevan, V., Li, W., Bhalodia, V., Vasconcelos, N.: Anomaly detection in crowded scenes. In: CVPR, pp. 1975–1981 (2010)
13. Ramanan, D.: Histograms of sparse codes for object detection. In: CVPR, pp. 3246–3253 (2013)
14. Tang, X., Zhang, S., Yao, H.: Sparse coding based motion attention for abnormal event detection. In: ICIP, pp. 3602–3606 (2013)
15. Viola, P., Jones, M.: Rapid object detection using a boosted cascade of simple features. In: CVPR, p. 511 (2001)
16. Zhang, Y., Qin, L., Yao, H., Huang, Q.: Abnormal crowd behavior detection based on social attribute-aware force model. In: ICIP. pp. 2689–2692 (2012)

Real-Time Video Dehazing Based on Spatio-Temporal MRF

Bolun Cai[1], Xiangmin Xu[1(✉)], and Dacheng Tao[2]

[1] South China University of Technology, Guangzhou, China
caibolun@gmail.com, xmxu@scut.edu.cn
[2] University of Technology Sydney, Ultimo, Australia
dacheng.tao@uts.edu.au

Abstract. Video dehazing has a wide range of real-time applications, but the challenges mainly come from spatio-temporal coherence and computational efficiency. In this paper, a spatio-temporal optimization framework for real-time video dehazing is proposed, which reduces blocking and flickering artifacts and achieves high-quality enhanced results. We build a Markov Random Field (MRF) with an Intensity Value Prior (IVP) to handle spatial consistency and temporal coherence. By maximizing the MRF likelihood function, the proposed framework estimates the haze concentration and preserves the information optimally. Moreover, to facilitate real-time applications, integral image technique is approximated to reduce the main computational burden. Experimental results demonstrate that the proposed framework is effectively to remove haze and flickering artifacts, and sufficiently fast for real-time applications.

Keywords: Video dehazing · Spatio-temporal MRF · Intensity value prior

1 Introduction

Haze is a traditional phenomenon where dust, smoke and other dry particles obscure the clear atmosphere, which makes the image/video contrast lost and/or vividness lost. The light scattering through the haze particles results in a loss of contrast in the photography process. Video dehazing has broader and broader prospects for real-time processing (e.g. automatic driving, video surveillance, automobile recorder). Since the haze concentration is spatio-temporal relevant, recovering the haze-free scene from hazy videos becomes a challenging problem.

X. Xu—This work is supported in part by the National Natural Science Founding of China (61171142, 61401163), Science and Technology Planning Project of Guangdong Province of China (2011A010801005, 2014B010111003, 2014B010111006), Guangzhou Key Lab of Body Data Science (201605030011) and Australian Research Council Projects (FT-130101457 and DP-140102164).

© Springer International Publishing AG 2016
E. Chen et al. (Eds.): PCM 2016, Part II, LNCS 9917, pp. 315–325, 2016.
DOI: 10.1007/978-3-319-48896-7_31

Various image enhancement techniques [7,12] are proposed to deal with static image dehazing, which transform the color distribution without considering the haze concentration. Moreover, methods based on multi-image [11] or depth-information [8] are employed, but the additional information is hard to be acquired in real application scenes. Due to the use of strong priors, single image dehazing methods have made significant progresses recently. Dark channel prior [5] shows at least one color channel has some pixels with very low intensities in most of non-haze patches; Meng et al. [10] propose an effective regularization method to recover the haze-free image by exploring the inherent boundary constraint. Since the above algorithms only focus on static image dehazing, they may yield flickering artifacts due to the lack of temporal coherence when applied to video dehazing.

Little work has been done on video dehazing compared to extensive works on static image dehazing. Tarel et al. [13] segment a car vision video into motorial objects and a planar road, then update the depth for haze removal based on a image dehazing scheme [12]. Therefore, this method is unable to apply in unrestraint conditions. To improve the spatio-temporal coherence, an optical flow method [16] is introduced to optimize the haze concentration map, which requires high computational complexity and is hard for real-time applications. Kim et al. [6] optimize contrast enhancement by minimizing a temporal coherence cost to reduce flickering artifacts. If the contrast is overstretched, some saturation values are truncated resulting in computationally intensive. In [8], authors combine depth and haze information to recover the clear scene. However, depth reconstruction depending on Structure-from-Motion (SfM) requires high complexity, and cannot get satisfying performance in the distance.

Extending image dehazing algorithm to video is not a trivial work. The challenges mainly come from the following aspects:

- Spatial consistency. There are two constraints of spatial consistency. The haze concentration is locally constant to overcome the estimation noise. In addition, the recovered video should be as natural as the original one to handle inner-frame discontinuity.
- Temporal coherence. Human visualization system is sensitive to temporal inconsistency. However, applying static image dehazing algorithm naively on frame-by-frame may break the temporal coherence, and yield a recovered video with severe flicking artifacts.
- Computational efficiency. The algorithm must be able to efficiently process the large number of pixels in video sequences. In particular, a practical real-time dehazing method should reach a speed of at least 15 frames per second.

In this paper, we build a spatio-temporal MRF with IVP to optimize haze concentration estimation. This method effectively assures the spatial consistency and temporal coherence of video dehazing. In addition, integral image technique [14] is used for efficiently computing in $O(N)$ time to reduce the main computational burden. Typically, the only single CPU implementation achieves approximately 120 frames per second for real-time video with the size of 352×288.

2   Real-Time Video Dehazing

Currently, all of the static images dehazing algorithms can obtain truly good results on general outdoor images. However, when applied to each frame of a hazy video sequence independently, it may break spatio-temporal coherence and produce a recovered video with blocking and flickering artifacts. Moreover, its high computational complexity prohibits real-time applications. In this section, we propose a spatio-temporal optimization framework for real-time video dehazing, which is shown in Fig. 1.

2.1   Single Image Haze Removal

Single image haze removal is a classical image enhancement problem. According to empirical observations, existing methods propose various assumptions or prior (e.g. dark channel [5], maximum contrast [6] and hue disparity [1]) to estimate the haze concentration. Based on the atmospheric scattering model and the haze concentration, the haze-free image is recovered easily.

Atmospheric Scattering Model. To describe the formation of a hazy image, the atmospheric scattering model is proposed by McCartney [9]. The atmospheric scattering model can be formally written as

$$I(x) = J(x) T(x) + A(1 - T(x)),\qquad(1)$$

where $I(x)$ is the observed hazy image, $J(x)$ is the real scene to be recovered, $T(x)$ is the medium transmission, A is the global atmospheric light, and x indexes pixels in the image. The real scene $J(x)$ can be recovered after A and $T(x)$ are estimated. The atmosphere light A is constant in the whole image, so it is easy to estimate. The medium transmission map $T(x)$ describes the light portion that is not scattered and reaches the camera. Therefore, it is the key to estimate an accurate haze concentration map.

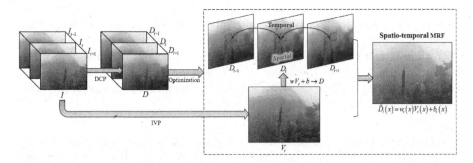

Fig. 1. Spatio-temporal MRF for video dehazing. DCP is used to estimate the haze concentration and an MRF is built based on IVP between inner-frame and inter-frame.

(a)Synthetic image   (b)Intensity value   (c)Concentration   (d)Residual error

Fig. 2. Intensity Value Prior. The residual error is close to zero, and shows that the haze concentration is highly correlated with the intensity value.

Medium Transmission Estimation. Dark Channel Prior [5] (DCP) is discovered based on empirical statistics of experiments on outdoor haze-free images. In most of haze-free images, at least one color channel has some pixels whose intensity values are very low and even close to zero. The dark channel is defined as the minimum channel in RGB color space:

$$D(x) = \min_{c \in \{r,g,b\}} I^c(x), \tag{2}$$

where $I^c(x)$ is a RGB color channel of $I(x)$. The dark channel prior has a high correlation to the amount of haze in the image, and is used to estimate the medium transmission directly as $\tilde{T}(x) = 1 - \omega D(x)/A$, where a constant parameter ω is introduced to map dark channel value to the medium transmission. We fix it to 0.7 for all results reported in this paper.

2.2 Spatio-Temporal MRF

To handle blocking and flickering artifacts, the haze concentration map should be refined by spatio-temporal coherence. Based on an intensity value prior, a spatio-temporal MRF is built to fine-tune the haze concentration map, as which the dark channel map $D(x)$ is regarded in this paper.

Intensity Value Prior. With the wide observation on hazy images, the intensity values of pixels in a hazy image vary sharply along with the change of the haze concentration. To show how the intensity value of pixels vary within a hazy image, Fig. 2 gives an example with an image synthetized by known haze concentration. It can be deduced from $A(1 - T(x))$ in the atmosphere scattering model, that the effect of the white or gray airlight on the observed values is related to the amount of haze. Thus, caused by the airlight, the intensity value is increased while haze concentration is enhanced.

Spatial Consistency. The pixel-level concentration estimation may fail to work in some particular situations. For instance, outlier pixel values in an image result in inaccurate estimation of the haze concentration. Based on the assumption that the haze concentration is locally constant, local filters (e.g. minimum filter [17], maximum filter [2] and medium filter [4]) are commonly to overcome this problem. However, blocking artifacts appear in the haze concentration map because of these local filters. To handle the locally constant and inner-frame continuity, a spatial MRF is built based on IVP. In spatial neighborhood, the intensity value $V(x)$ is linear transformed to the haze concentration $D(x)$, and the transformation fields $W = \{w(x)\}_{x \in \forall}$ and $B = \{b(x)\}_{x \in \forall}$ are only correlated with the contextual information. The spatial likelihood function is

$$P_s(w, b) \propto \prod_{y \in \Omega(x)} \exp\left(-\frac{\|w(x)V(y) + b(x) - D(y)\|_2^2}{\sigma_s^2}\right), \qquad (3)$$

where $\Omega(x)$ is a local patch centered at x with the size of $r \times r$, and σ_s is the spatial parameter.

Temporal Coherence. Flicking artifacts can be avoided by the relevant information between consecutive frames. The haze concentration changes due to camera and object motions. As an object approaches in the camera, the observed radiance gets closer to the original scene radiance. On the contrary, when an object moves away from the camera, the observed radiance becomes more similar to the atmospheric light. Thus, we can modify the haze concentration of a scene point adaptively according to its intensity value change. As shown in Fig. 3, the haze concentration of the neighbor frame can be transformed to the current frame's by IVP, which is similar to block-matching of optical flow estimation. As with the spatial consistency, a temporal MRF is used for temporal coherence, and at time t its likelihood function is defined by

$$P_\tau(w_t, b_t) \propto \prod_{\tau \in [-f, +f]} \exp\left(-\frac{\|w_t(x)V_t(x) + b_t(x) - D_{t+\tau}(x)\|_2^2}{\sigma_\tau^2}\right), \qquad (4)$$

where f is the number of neighbor frames, and σ_τ is the temporal parameter.

Along the spatio-temporal dimension, we improve the spatial consistency and temporal coherence with an uniform likelihood function, which is rewritten as

$$P(w_t, b_t) = \prod_{\tau \in [-f, +f]} \prod_{y \in \Omega(x)} \exp\left(-\frac{\|w_t(x)V_t(y) + b_t(x) - D_{t+\tau}(y)\|_2^2}{\sigma_\tau^2}\right), \qquad (5)$$

where σ_s is omitted because it is assumed as a constant in this paper.

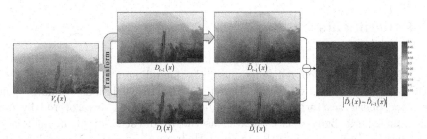

Fig. 3. Inter-frame correlation of the haze concentration. The intensity map $V_t(x)$ in current frame is transformed to the haze concentration map $D_{t,t-1}(x)$ in neighbor frames. The absolute error map between $\tilde{D}_t(x)$ and $\tilde{D}_{t-1}(x)$ is close to zero.

2.3 Maximum Likelihood Estimation

The log-likelihood function is more convenient to work with maximum likelihood estimation. Taking the derivative of a log-likelihood function and solving for the parameter, is often easier than the original likelihood function. Let temporal weights $\lambda_\tau = 1/\sigma_\tau^2$ ($s.t. \sum_\tau \lambda_\tau = 1$) to express conveniently, and the log-likelihood function of Eq. 5 is given by:

$$L(w_t, b_t) = \sum_{\tau \in [-f, +f]} \sum_{y \in \Omega(x)} -\lambda_\tau \|w_t(x) V_t(y) + b_t(x) - D_{t+\tau}(y)\|_2^2 \quad (6)$$

To find the optimal random fields W and B, the maximum log-likelihood estimation is written as $(w_t, b_t) = \arg\max L(w_t, b_t)$. We maximize the probability by solving the linear system from $\partial L(w_t, b_t)/\partial w_t = 0$ and $\partial L(w_t, b_t)/\partial b = 0$, and generate the final haze concentration map by $\tilde{D}_t(x) = w_t(x) V_t(x) + b_t(x)$.

$$\begin{cases} w_t(x) = \dfrac{\sum_\tau \lambda_\tau \left(\mathcal{U}_\Omega [V_t(x) D_{t+\tau}(x)] - \mathcal{U}_\Omega [V_t(x)] \mathcal{U}_\Omega [D_{t+\tau}(x)] \right)}{\mathcal{U}_\Omega [V_t^2(x)] - \mathcal{U}_\Omega^2 [V_t(x)]} \\ b_t(x) = \sum_\tau \lambda_\tau \mathcal{U}_\Omega [D_{t+\tau}(x)] - w_t(x) \mathcal{U}_\Omega [V_t(x)] \end{cases} \quad (7)$$

Here, $\mathcal{U}[\cdot]$ is a mean filter defined as $\mathcal{U}[F(x)] = (1/|\Omega|) \sum_{y \in \Omega(x)} F(y)$, and $|\Omega|$ is the cardinality of the local neighborhood.

2.4 Complexity Reduction

A main advantage of the spatio-temporal MRF built in this paper is that it naturally has an $O(N)$ time non-approximate acceleration. The main computational burden is the mean filter $\mathcal{U}[\cdot]$ with the local neighborhood. Fortunately, the mean filter can be efficiently computed in $O(N)$ time using the integral image technique [14], which allows for fast computation of box type convolution filters. The entry of an integral image represents the sum of all pixels in the input image within a rectangular region formed by the origin and current position. Once the integral image has been computed, it takes three additions to calculate the sum of the intensities over any rectangular area. Hence, the calculation time of the mean function is independent of its size, and the maximum likelihood estimation in Sect. 2.3 is naturally $O(N)$ time.

3 Experiments

We analyze the validity of the proposed framework and compare it with the state-of-art image/video dehazing methods, including DCP [5], BCCR [10], MDCP [4], IVR [13], OCE [6]. Based on the transmission estimated and the atmospheric scattering model, a haze-free video can be recovered by (1). The atmospheric light A is estimated as the brightest color [3] in an image: $A = \max_{x \in \forall} (\min_{y \in \Omega(x)} V(y))$. At the t-th frame, the airlight is updated by $A_t = \rho A + (1 - \rho) A_{t-1}$, where $\rho = 0.1$ is a learning parameter. The other parameters mentioned in Sect. 2.2 are specified as follows: the number of neighbor frames f is set to 1, and the temporal weights λ_τ is set to a Hanning window.

3.1   Temporal Coherence Analysis

Temporal coherence is the main challenge compared to static image dehazing. However, the evaluation of temporal coherence is difficult on real videos since no reference is available. To show the proposed framework can suppresses flickering artifacts well, we compare the mean intensity value (MIV) between consecutive frames on five hazy videos, which are synthesized from non-haze videos[1] with flat haze $T(x) = 0.6$.

Figure 4 plots MIV between consecutive frames in *Suzie* and *Foreman*. When the static dehazing algorithms (including DCP [5], BCCR [10], MDCP [4]) are independently applied to each frame, the MIV curves experience relatively large fluctuations as compared with the original sequences, especially between 50–75 frames in Fig. 4(a) and 175–225 frames in Fig. 4(b). We also quantify the flickering artifacts based on the correlation analysis of MIV between the dehazing result and the original video, shown in Table 1. In contrast, our video dehazing method alleviates the fluctuations and reduces the flickering artifacts efficiently.

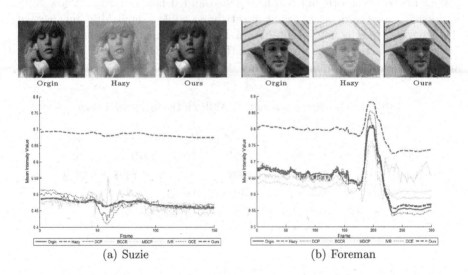

(a) Suzie   (b) Foreman

Fig. 4. Comparsion of the mean intensity value in consecutive frames.

3.2   Quantitative Results on Synthetic Videos

To verify the dehazing effectiveness, the proposed framework is tested on hazy videos synthesized from stereo videos [15] with a known depth map[2], and it is compared with 5 representative methods. Among the competitors, MDCP [4], IVR [13] and OCE [6] are the most recent state-of-the-art video dehazing

---

[1] http://trace.eas.asu.edu/yuv/.

[2] http://www.cad.zju.edu.cn/home/gfzhang/projects/videodepth/data/.

Table 1. The correlation coefficients of MIV between dehazing and original videos

	DCP [5]	BCCR [10]	MDCP [4]	IVR [13]	OCE [6]	Ours
Suzie	0.783	0.612	0.641	0.584	0.649	0.976
Foreman	0.980	0.920	0.015	0.949	0.994	0.995
Container	0.929	0.703	0.927	0.998	1.000	0.955
Hall	0.784	0.429	0.444	0.824	0.845	0.991
Silent	0.853	0.898	0.936	0.892	0.770	0.990
Avg.	0.866	0.712	0.592	0.849	0.851	0.982

methods; DCP [5] and BCCR [10] are classical static image dehazing methods which are used as comparison baselines. The hazy video is generated based on (1), where we assume pure white atmospheric airlight $A = 1$.

To quantitatively assess these methods, we calculate Mean Square Error (MSE) between the original non-haze video and dehazing result. A low MSE represents that the dehazed result is satisfying while a high MSE means that the dehazing effect is not acceptable. In Table 2, our method is compared with 5 state-of-the-art methods on three synthetic video. Our method achieves the lowest MSEs outperforming the others.

Table 2. The dehazing results of MSE on the synthetic videos

	DCP [5]	BCCR [10]	MDCP [4]	IVR [13]	OCE [6]	Ours
Flower	0.0228	0.0240	0.0257	0.0479	0.0174	0.0034
Lawn	0.0198	0.0176	0.4902	0.0141	0.0408	0.0166
Road	0.0141	0.0191	0.0108	0.0364	0.0274	0.0092
Avg.	0.0189	0.0202	0.1756	0.0328	0.0285	0.0097

3.3   Qualitative Results on Real-World Videos

In addition, we also evaluate the performance of the proposed framework on the real-world videos collected in related works. Figure 5 shows the results on four representative sequences with different methods[3]. The contrast maximizing methods (BCCR [10], IVR [13], OCE [6]) are able to achieve impressive results, but they tend to produce over-saturated and spatial inconsistency (for example, the mountain in *Bali* and the halo of the sky in *Playground*). In Fig. 5(c) and (d), it is observed that the static image dehazing methods (DCP [5] and BCCR [10]) yield severe flickering artifacts (such as, the road region in *Cross* and the sky region in *Hazeroad*). Although, the OCE [6] method uses overlapped block

---

[3] More comparisons can be found at http://caibolun.github.io/st-mrf/.

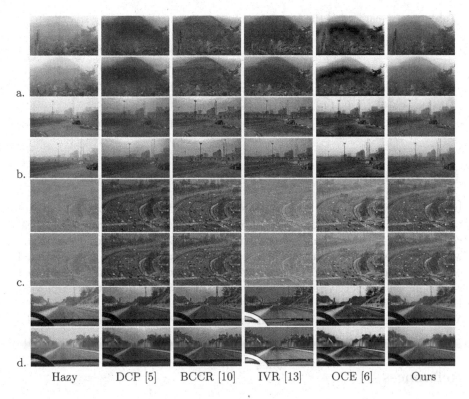

| | Hazy | DCP [5] | BCCR [10] | IVR [13] | OCE [6] | Ours |

Fig. 5. Qualitative comparison of different methods on real-world hazy videos, including (a) Bali, (b) Playground, (c) Cross, (d) Hazeroad.

filter to reduce blocking artifacts, there are still a small number of blocking artifacts in the results. Compared with the other methods, our results avoid image over-saturation and keep spatio-temporal coherence.

3.4 Real-Time Analysis

We evaluate the computational complexity of the proposed framework on hazy videos with different sizes of general video standards. The experiments are run on a PC with Intel i7 3770 CPU (3.4 GHz), and we report the average speed (in fps) comparison with DCP [5], BCCR [10], MDCP [4], IVR [13], and OCE [6]. According to Table 3, our method is significantly faster than others and achieves efficient processing even when the given hazy video is large. Typically, our framework achieves the processing speed of about 120 fps on Common Intermediate Format (CIF, 352 × 288), which is close to quadruple that of the real-time criterion. Thus, the proposed framework leaves a substantial amount of time for other processing, and is transplanted into embedded system easily.

Table 3. Comparision of the processing speeds in terms of frames per second (fps)

	DCP [5]	BCCR [10]	MDCP [4]	IVR [13]	OCE [6]	Ours
CIF (352 × 288)	1.485	1.322	7.343	1.205	97.076	116.371
VGA (640 × 480)	0.566	0.467	2.430	0.171	30.539	36.609
D1 (704 × 576)	0.414	0.358	1.830	0.102	22.930	27.493
XGA (1024 × 768)	0.216	0.197	0.842	0.028	12.106	14.515

4   Conclusion

In this work, we propose a real-time video dehazing framework based on spatio-temporal MRF. We introduce the notion of spatial consistency and temporal coherence to yield a dehazed video without blocking and flickering artifacts. Moreover, the integral image technique is applied to reduce the computational complexity significantly. Experimental results demonstrate that the proposed algorithm can efficiently recover a hazy video at low computational complexity. However, DCP is unable to estimate the haze concentration in high accuracy. Moreover, this spatio-temporal framework can be extended for other real-time video processing. We leave these problems for future research.

References

1. Ancuti, C.O., Ancuti, C., Hermans, C., Bekaert, P.: A fast semi-inverse approach to detect and remove the haze from a single image. In: Kimmel, R., Klette, R., Sugimoto, A. (eds.) ACCV 2010. LNCS, vol. 6493, pp. 501–514. Springer, Heidelberg (2011). doi:10.1007/978-3-642-19309-5_39
2. Cai, B., Xu, X., Jia, K., Qing, C., Tao, D.: Dehazenet: an end-to-end system for single image haze removal. arXiv preprint arXiv:1601.07661 (2016)
3. Chiang, J.Y., Chen, Y.C.: Underwater image enhancement by wavelength compensation and dehazing. IEEE Trans. Image Process. 21(4), 1756–1769 (2012)
4. Gibson, K., Vo, D., Nguyen, T.: An investigation in dehazing compressed images and video. In: OCEANS 2010, pp. 1–8 (2010)
5. He, K., Sun, J., Tang, X.: Single image haze removal using dark channel prior. IEEE Trans. Pattern Anal. Mach. Intell. 33(12), 2341–2353 (2011)
6. Kim, J.H., Jang, W.D., Sim, J.Y., Kim, C.S.: Optimized contrast enhancement for real-time image and video dehazing. J. Vis. Commun. Image Represent. 24(3), 410–425 (2013)
7. Kim, T.K., Paik, J.K., Kang, B.S.: Contrast enhancement system using spatially adaptive histogram equalization with temporal filtering. IEEE Trans. Consum. Electron. 44(1), 82–87 (1998)
8. Li, Z., Tan, P., Tan, R.T., Zou, D., Zhou, S.Z., Cheong, L.F.: Simultaneous video defogging and stereo reconstruction. In: IEEE Conference on Computer Vision and Pattern Recognition (CVPR), pp. 4988–4997 (2015)
9. McCartney, E.J.: Optics of the Atmosphere: Scattering by Molecules and Particles. Wiley, New York (1976)

10. Meng, G., Wang, Y., Duan, J., Xiang, S., Pan, C.: Efficient image dehazing with boundary constraint and contextual regularization. In: IEEE International Conference on Computer Vision (ICCV), pp. 617–624 (2013)
11. Narasimhan, S.G., Nayar, S.K.: Contrast restoration of weather degraded images. IEEE Trans. Pattern Anal. Mach. Intell. **25**(6), 713–724 (2003)
12. Tarel, J.P., Hautiere, N.: Fast visibility restoration from a single color or gray level image. In: IEEE International Conference on Computer Vision, pp. 2201–2208 (2009)
13. Tarel, J.P., Hautiere, N., Cord, A., Gruyer, D., Halmaoui, H.: Improved visibility of road scene images under heterogeneous fog. In: 2010 IEEE conference on Intelligent Vehicles Symposium (IV), pp. 478–485. IEEE (2010)
14. Viola, P., Jones, M.: Rapid object detection using a boosted cascade of simple features. In: IEEE Conference on Computer Vision and Pattern Recognition (CVPR), vol. 1, pp. I–511 (2001)
15. Zhang, G., Jia, J., Wong, T.T., Bao, H.: Consistent depth maps recovery from a video sequence. IEEE Trans. Pattern Anal. Mach. Intell. **31**(6), 974–988 (2009)
16. Zhang, J., Li, L., Zhang, Y., Yang, G., Cao, X., Sun, J.: Video dehazing with spatial and temporal coherence. Vis. Comput. **27**(6–8), 749–757 (2011)
17. Zhu, Q., Mai, J., Shao, L.: A fast single image haze removal algorithm using color attenuation prior. IEEE Trans. Image Process. **24**(11), 3522–3533 (2015)

Dynamic Contour Matching for Lossy Screen Content Picture Intra Coding

Hu Yuan[✉], Tao Pin, and Yuanchun Shi

Tsinghua National Laboratory for Information Science and Technology (TNList),
Department of Computer Science and Technology, Tsinghua University, Beijing
100084, China
hu-yl5@mails.tsinghua.edu.cn,
{taopin,shiyc}@tsinghua.edu.cn

Abstract. Video coding was proposed and developed by JCT-VC. Screen content video generally contains some complex texture, such as text, graphics, images and other natural mix and so on. The most popular coding scheme is H2.264. But for the screen content video H2.264 can not achieve significant performance as it works on natural video. In this paper, we proposed-pixel prediction method based on dynamic contour matching. First, apply rearrangement procedure for avoiding error spreading by pixel prediction. Then, build a dynamic contour including sets of pixels for each pixel to be predicted as a template to search for the most similar template. Meanwhile, using hash table for accelerating searching procedure. This method takes advantage of more repetitive pattern for designing a novel framework. Experimental results show that Our proposed method improves about 2.612 dB and saves 12.5% bitrate in comparison with the HEVC range extension software HM12.0+RExt4.1.

Keywords: Template matching · Dynamic contour · Screen content picture · Intra coding

1 Introduction

Many important applications based screen content video coding, such as: online game broadcast, desktop sharing and so on. The JCT-VC (Joint Collaborative Team on Video Coding) project group of HEVC (High Efficiency Video Coding) presented the screen content video coding and it has been rapid developed. Compared with natural images of the camera, the screen image has many different characteristics, such as screen image doesn't include noise, and the edges is not continuous, complex textures and so on. Currently popular encoding methods, such as AVC/H2.264, HEVC/H2.265, etc., mainly work for camera-capture images, but these coding methods are not suitable for the screen content video. JCT-VC project group of HEVC proposed a new way of extend codes for the screen image in 2010. The extension version of the HECV standard is mainly used to solve the screen content videos/images.

The differences between the screen content videos/images and the camera-capture images include:

© Springer International Publishing AG 2016
E. Chen et al. (Eds.): PCM 2016, Part II, LNCS 9917, pp. 326–334, 2016.
DOI: 10.1007/978-3-319-48896-7_32

1. Screen image has many repeat structures, unlike the camera-capture, mostly because the screen content videos/images generated by computer program. So there are many repeat textures. As for the camera-capture videos/images, it does not have such properties.
2. As the generation process of screen image is controlled by the program, there is no noise; and the camera image is acquired with noise, mainly for the process of image acquisition.
3. The value of screen content image usually contains non-continuous value, which is different from the camera-capture videos/images whose pixel values on edge is continuous. Screen content videos/images is mainly used for displaying text, specific computer screen and icons and etc. whose edge usually has a lot change on pixel values.
4. The screen image has smaller color space compared to the camera image. The screen image generated by the computer program usually contain complex textures, such as text, graphics, etc., but has relatively few color distribution.

These characteristics of the screen content videos/images makes the-state-of-the-art coding scheme including AVC/H.264 perform not satisfying on screen content videos/images coding. Then, for the characteristics of the screen content videos/images, a number of methods have been proposed for increasing the encoding efficiency of screen image, such as palettes method, intra block copy, template matching and so on. Template matching method for inter frame prediction [1] was proposed in 2004 by Kazuo Sugimoto et al. In 2006 intra picture coding [2] was presented by Thiow Keng Tan et al. Based on previous works, some further work of [3–8] showed that the template matching can improve the screen content videos/images coding efficiency. The size of the matching block in template matching scheme is usually 2×2, 4×4, 8×8 or greater. For pixel-level template matching whose matching block is 1×1, there are shortcomings including error propagation and time consuming process on prediction, so that it is not applicable compared to other matching block with bigger size. But the Pixel Granularity Template Matching & Rearrangement (PGR) proposed in the [9] solved the above two challenges, so that the pixel-level template matching can also be used. One of the key issues of template matching is how to choose the best prediction value from the candidate templates, the average value is selected in [5], the best prediction value is selected in [6], and in [4] a linear model is used to be predicted. The size of template for matching is typically fixed, however, those template always make some region not to be matched which could be successfully matched in some other template.

In this paper, we proposed a template matching scheme based on dynamic contour search for lossy screen content picture intra coding. In Sect. 2 of this paper, we will describe the template matching method based on a fixed template PGR in detail. In Sect. 3, we present a template matching scheme based on dynamic contour and a detailed description of the algorithm; Sect. 4 shows the experimental results; Sect. 5, we summarize this paper.

2 Fixed Template Matching Method Based on PGR Method

Overall, the size of template in the template matching scheme conventionally used is generally 2×2, 4×4, 8×8 or larger. The larger size of template block, the faster matching. But target block will be more likely to be mismatch. In the PGR template matching, it use pixel-level template matching method after resampling, to minimize the mismatch in the block area and avoid the error propagation. What's more, one VLCU [9] can do template matching prediction for all of the points in parallel, which in turn overcomes the slowly—match problem of template matching on the 1×1 block.

Main steps of PGR algorithm are as follows. First, all Intra picture pixels of a screen content videos/images are resampled into VLCU. Figure 1 shows a resampling schematic of 4×4. VLCU units. Then pixels in VLCU units are predicted by the template matching on pixel-level (1×1). The search area of traditional template matching is generally the upper left portion of the decoded region, but in PGR, the search region is expanded to the all VLCU block which had been decoded. In VLCU, more than 80% pixels will be correctly predicted, which means 80% prediction residual is 0. In the end, only the remaining non-zero residuals are encoded into the final code stream by the entropy coding method.

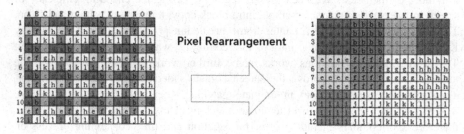

Fig. 1. An example of resampling schematic

The challenge after using the template matching on pixel-level in PGR is that it will spend much more time to find best candidate template and the scope of the search becoming larger. Pick out the best template from many candidate templates is a very time-consuming thing. To address this challenge, template matching algorithm in PGR adopts fixed template of 21 points [9], and use pixel value of the 21 points to get one hash value. And it takes advantage of the hash table—fast searching to accelerate the process of prediction. However, the fixed template will lead to some mismatches that some template could correctly predicted, but actually it is failed. In Fig. 2, according to fixed template of 21 points, T(x) is the template of the pixel X and T(y) is the template of the pixel y. The contour of T(x) and T(y) is not the same, but part of the template T(x) and T(y) can be matched successfully. Thus, for adopting fixed template, the template of pixel y will not be correctly matched with x in the template gallery. To address this challenge, we propose a method based on dynamic contour template matching.

TX, HABCX

16	17	18	19	20	21
15	8	9	10	11	12
14	7	2	3	4	5
13	6	1	X		

pixel and its template in the
original picture

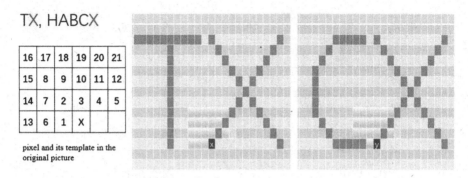

Fig. 2. Fixed template matching in PGR

3 Dynamic Contour Template Matching Frame

For that in fixed template matching some template can be locally matched as shown in Fig. 2, we proposed a dynamic contour template method to solve the mismatching in the fixed template. Not only fixed templates still can be found and correct match, but more pixels can also be correctly match by using locally similarity of fixed template, so that it improves the coding efficiency.

3.1 Dynamic Contour Template

Dynamic contour template method presented in this paper is intended to extract the dynamic contour of the shape of texture region. We will use that extract the dynamic contour of pixel y as an example to introduce the details of our algorithm.

Some items defined as follow:

- minimum degree of similarity, the point that is below this similarity will refused to join the dynamic template.
  MIN_SIMIALRITY ← 0.2;
- maximum distance between the pixel in the dynamic template to the pixel to be predicted. If the distance is excess the maximum distance, it will refused to join the dynamic template.
  MAX _EXTAG ← 16;
- maximum number of pixels contained in the dynamic template.
  MAX _TEPLATE ← 24

Select the lowest similarity of pixels in 8—neighboring window of y pixels and add it in the dynamic template

As Fig. 3 shows, y is the pixel to be predicted, and a selected window (W) involved the vi (i = 1, 2… 8) pixels that must be decoded. If the W including no decoded pixels, just return a empty template. If the W including some decoded pixels, it will do as flowing. Use the following formula to calculate every pixel's similarity in the W window, and select the pixel with the lowest similarity to be added into dynamic

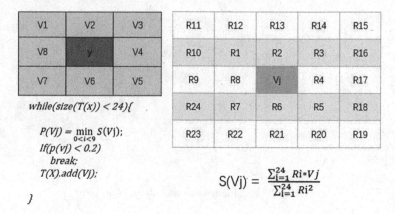

$$S(Vj) = \frac{\sum_{i=1}^{24} Ri * Vj}{\sum_{i=1}^{24} Ri^2}$$

Fig. 3. Calculate the lowest similarity of pixels in 8—neighboring window

template T(y). In the same time, the distance should calculated before one pixel was added into the dynamic. if the distance id over the MAX_EXTAG, the pixel will be refused to be added into the dynamic template. The next pixel add in the dynamic template should meet two conditions: (1) it's distance should less than or equal to MAX_EXTAG; (2) It's similarity is the first bigger than the refused one.

1. After successfully adding one pixel into the dynamic template, repeating step 1
   In the process of repeating step 1, if the similarity of the pixel to be added is below the certain threshold: MIN_SIMIALRITY, or the number of the dynamic template is greater than or equal to the MAX _TEPLATE, or no pixels can be find it the window W, it should stop all acts, and returns the current dynamic template. Finally, the returned template of pixel y is the dynamic template T(y) as shows in Fig. 4.

TX,HABCX

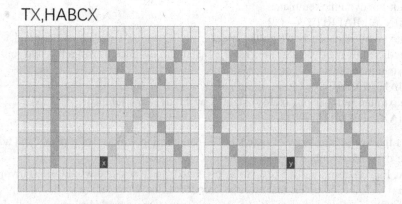

Fig. 4. Dynamic contour template matching method

2. Calculates two hash Value: the hash value based on contour information and the hash value based on color values after getting the dynamic template of pixel y (Fig. 5).

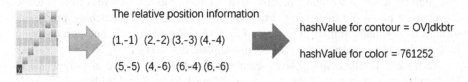

The relative position information

(1,-1) (2,-2) (3,-3) (4,-4)

(5,-5) (4,-6) (6,-4) (6,-6)

hashValue for contour = OVJdkbtr

hashValue for color = 761252

Fig. 5. Calculates two hash Value

The steps of how to calculate the two hash value are described in pseudocode:

i. The hash value based on contour information
String hashValue = ""
For each pixel of the Template T(y)
CurrentPixel;
dx = CurrentPixel's relative position of the horizontal
dy = CurrentPixel's relative position of the vertical
hashValue += MAX_EXTAG * (dx + MAX_EXTAG) + (dy + MAX_EXTAG);
Each hash value can be corresponded to the contour information of template T(x).
Therefore, it is able to uniquely identify each contour information by the hash value.

ii. the hash value based on color values
In order to construct the hash value of the corresponding template based color value, first of all, based on the current sequence of pixel in the template, templates can be divided into the following eight groups.

- G1:{1}
- G2:{2}
- G3:{3}
- G4:{4, 5}
- G5:{6, 7, 13, 14}
- G6:{8, 15, 16, 17}
- G7:{9, 10, 18, 19}
- G8:{11, 12, 20, 21, 22, 23,………}

Each group will add to template sequentially. Group G1, G2 and G3 contain one pixel. Group G4 contains two pixels. Group G5, G6 and G7 contain four pixels. And group G8 includes all the remaining pixels. In the process of dividing the group, it will immediately stop when the last one pixel is divided into the group. Regardless of whether classified into Group 8. Finally, each group get the average of all pixel values (the average of the group that does not exist is 0). Then take the first three bit of each average value to combine a 24 bits value as the last hash value based on the color value.

3.2 Two-Level Hash Table Searching

Hash table is a data structure according to keywords to quickly find the target data's location. The advantage of hash table is that searching is very fast, the disadvantage is that a hash function construction must be reasonable and needs extra storage space. Although the template matching prediction method has good predictive accuracy, led to the time of prediction increasing exponentially. The template matching prediction method is essentially similar to process of finding the best template, and introducing a hash method can accelerate the process of template discovery.

Hash table has the constant level searching speed at the expense of storage space. Hash table can directly find the object which need to be found without exhaustive comparison, and that one of the key step is that map the object through hash function into memory storage location. Hash function is the critical issue of design for hash table, construction of the hash function typically requires shorter computing time and guarantee the storage locations distributed as evenly as possible, to minimize the conflict that the different objects are mapped into the same position. Most hash functions can not guarantee no conflict strategy, and for dealing with conflict, it generally adopts the list link to record the search target with confliction strategy. Figure 6 shows an example of hash table described.

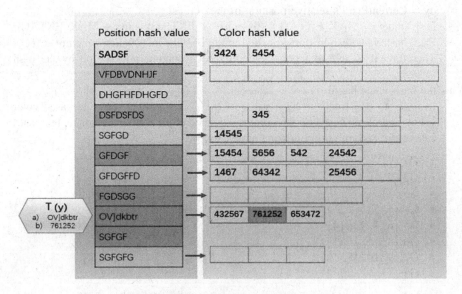

Fig. 6. The process of hash table searching

The process of hash searching in our proposed method as follow:

Using the hash value of template T(y) based on the contour information as the first key and search the target in the first hash table to check if the target exists. If not, which means it is failed to search this target, and this key and the template T(y) will be insert the first hash table as one key-value pair; if exist, then get the object as the head pointer.

Meanwhile, using the hash value of template T(y) based on the color information as the second key and search the target in the second hash table to check if the target exists. If not, it shows that it is failed to search the target and this second key and the template T (y) will be inserted in the second hash table that start with the head pointer. If exist, it shows it is successful to search the target, and the second key and the template T(y) will be returned as the template matching.

4 Experimental Results

The proposed methods are implemented based on the HEVC reference software HM12.0+RExt4.1. Four typical sequences, including Console, Map, Programing and WebBrowsing, are tested using the proposed method and experimental results are compare with the fixed template matching methods proposed by [9]. The test condition of our test software is all-intra configuration and with flag TransquantBypassEnableFlag and CUTransquantBypassFlagForce are both set to 1 which means Discrete Cosine Transform (DCT) transform was used. Respectively, the QPs used in our test is 17, 22, 27, 32.

For all of those four test sequences, we test both lossy and lossless compress in comparing with the paper [9]. Not only, in lossless compression, we contain the highly correct prediction ratio as the paper [9] do, but, in lossy compression, the compression ratio is improved. The main reason of improvement is that Map and WebBrowsing involve much more irregular graphic patch, which makes our proposed method work well on them. Experimental results are shown in Table 1 and it shows the method we proposed improves about 2.612 dB and saves 12.5% bitrate in comparison with the fixed template matching method proposed by [9] in lossy compression condition.

Table 1. Experimental result

Sequences	QP	PGR		Proposed		Ave. Bit increse (excel)	Ave. dB gain (excel)
		PSNR-YUV (old)	Bitrate (old)	PSNR-YUV (new)	Bitrate (new)		
Average						−12.05%	2.612
Console	17	49.3113	1,783,444.8000	49.0535	1,600,259.0400	−5.52%	1.108
	22	44.6375	1,468,556.1600	44.4324	1,305,689.2800		
	27	40.1484	1,156,933.4400	39.8622	1,013,095.6800		
	32	34.9013	857,028.0000	34.3719	747,238.0800		
Map	17	45.5457	908,575.6800	45.5914	791,700.4800	−16.27%	3.501
	22	41.1053	769,810.0800	41.1820	657,324.4800		
	27	36.3010	631,315.6800	36.2179	521,654.4000		
	32	31.5933	495,592.3200	31.2695	386,366.8800		
Programming	17	46.5875	890,538.7200	46.3615	802,751.5200	−11.83%	2.806
	22	42.1130	758,292.0000	42.2255	675,345.1200		
	27	37.3734	625,233.6000	37.3109	546,845.2800		
	32	32.5454	496,187.5200	32.4679	423,197.7600		
WebBrowsing	17	47.8004	396,745.4400	47.8078	346,625.0400	−14.57%	3.032
	22	43.5334	328,068.4800	43.5372	285,596.1600		
	27	38.6388	265,382.1600	38.4865	224,713.6800		
	32	33.7179	205,726.0800	33.6554	163,605.8400		

5 Conclusion

In this paper, we proposed an adaptive chosen dynamic template matching method for Screen Content video. Based on the discovery of shortcomings of fixed template matching method. Experimental results showed new method improve the compression efficiency significantly for screen coding video.

In feature work, better entropy encoder and residuals transform method should be discussed.

References

1. Sullivan, G.J., Ohm, J.R., Han, W.J., et al.: Overview of the high efficiency video coding (HEVC) standard. IEEE Trans. Circuits Syst. Video Technol. **22**(12), 1649–1668 (2012)
2. Tan, T.K., Boon, C.S., Suzuki, Y.: Intra prediction by template matching. In: 2006 IEEE International Conference on Image Processing, pp. 1693–1696. IEEE (2006)
3. Lan, C., Xu, J., Wu, F., et al.: Intra frame coding with template matching prediction and adaptive transform. In: 2010 17th IEEE International Conference on Image Processing (ICIP), pp. 1221–1224. IEEE (2010)
4. Moinard, M., Amonou, I., Duhamel, P., et al.: A set of template matching predictors for intra video coding. In: 2010 IEEE International Conference on Acoustics Speech and Signal Processing (ICASSP), pp. 1422–1425. IEEE (2010)
5. Tan, T.K., Boon, C.S., Suzuki, Y.: Intra prediction by averaged template matching predictors. In: 4th IEEE Consumer Communications and Networking Conference, CCNC 2007, pp. 405–409. IEEE (2007)
6. Zheng, Y., Yin, P., Divorra Escoda, Ò., et al.: Intra prediction using template matching with adaptive illumination compensation. In: 15th IEEE International Conference on Image Processing, ICIP 2008, pp. 125–128. IEEE (2008)
7. Su, H., Han, J., Xu, Y.: An optimized template matching approach to intra coding in video/image compression. In: IS&T/SPIE Electronic Imaging. International Society for Optics and Photonics, p. 902904-6 (2014)
8. Wige, E., Yammine, G., Amon, P., et al.: Sample-based weighted prediction with directional template matching for HEVC lossless coding. In: IEEE Picture Coding Symposium (PCS 2013), pp. 305–308 (2013)
9. Feng, L., Tao, P., Guang, D., Wen, J., Yang, S.: Pixel granularity template matching method for screen content lossless intra picture. In: Ooi, W.T., Snoek, C.G.M., Tan, H.K., Ho, C.-K., Huet, B., Ngo, C.-W. (eds.) PCM 2014. LNCS, vol. 8879, pp. 143–152. Springer, Heidelberg (2014). doi:10.1007/978-3-319-13168-9_15

A Novel Hard-Decision Quantization Algorithm Based on Adaptive Deadzone Offset Model

Hongkui Wang, Haibing Yin[✉], and Ye Shen

China Jiliang University, No. 258, Xueyuan Street, Hangzhou 310018, People's Republic of China
1550661343@qq.com, haibingyin@163.com, 04A0303080@cjlu.edu.cn

Abstract. In video encoder, the soft-decision quantization (SDQ) achieves superior coding performance however suffering from deadly sequential processing dependency. Comparatively, deadzone hard-decision quantization (HDQ) is dependency-free and suitable for hardwired parallel processing, however suffering from non-negligible coding performance degradation. In this paper, a content-adaptive HDQ algorithm is proposed by employing an adaptive deadzone offset. The contributions of this paper are characterized as follows. On one hand, this work applies offline statistic analysis, Bayes method, to explore the distribution characteristics of the desired deadzone offsets obtained from huge amounts of samples by fully simulating the behaviour of SDQ, and then derives adaptive deadzone offset model by maximizing the probability of right judgment of offset-induced rounding in HDQ. On the other hand, the deadzone offset model is constructed heuristically as functions of quantization step size, the distribution parameter of DCT coefficients and the number of possible significant coefficients prior to the current coefficient in the block. Simulation results verify that the proposed adaptive HDQ algorithm, in comparison with fixed-offset HDQ, achieves 0.08836 dB PSNR increment and 3.097 % bit rate saving with almost negligible complexity increase. In addition, this work, in comparison with the SDQ, achieves less than 0.03921 dB PSNR loss and 1.51 % bit rate increment. The proposed HDQ is well-suited for hardware encoder design.

Keywords: Video coding · Soft Decision Quantization · Hard Decision Quantization

1 Introduction

In MPEG-like hybrid video encoders, quantization plays an overwhelmingly important role in coding rate-distortion (RD) performance. It not only determines the quantization distortion, but also has prominent impacts on the consumed coding rate. Since video coding standards only define the inverse quantization, many research works have explored how to efficiently quantize discrete cosine transform (DCT) coefficients while remaining compliant with respective video coding standards [1].

In early video codecs, DCT coefficients were quantized generally using a uniform scalar quantizer (USQ). Later on, a USQ with deadzone (USQ + DZ) was adopted in MPEG-4 and early H.264/AVC reference codes [1]. In USQ + DZ, fixed rounding offsets

© Springer International Publishing AG 2016
E. Chen et al. (Eds.): PCM 2016, Part II, LNCS 9917, pp. 335–345, 2016.
DOI: 10.1007/978-3-319-48896-7_33

are usually employed and determined in a heuristic and empirical way. Coefficient-independent rounding based quantization in USQ and USQ + DZ is the so-called hard-decision quantization (HDQ), in which correlation among adjacent coefficients and their effects on quantization are not considered. The coefficient-wise processing in HDQ makes it friendly to hardwired video coder with parallel implementation. However, HDQ even deadzone HDQ both suffer from non-negligible rate distortion performance loss.

Soft decision quantization (SDQ) is a better alternative achieving superior RD performance contributed by full utilization of inter-coefficient correlation. A popular SDQ implementation is Viterbi trellis search [3], which was implemented for H.263+ [2] and for H.264/AVC [3]. However, running dynamic programming over the full trellis graph is computationally expensive. To get around this, in H.264/AVC and HEVC reference softwares JM and HM, a simplified suboptimal SDQ, called rate distortion optimized quantization (RDOQ) [4], was adopted. RDOQ is a simplified version of SDQ, implemented by employing dynamic programming in a similar way. SDQ achieves superior coding RD performance, approximately 6 ~ 8% bit rate saving as opposed to HDQ. In SDQ and RDOQ, multiple candidate results of quantization are competed and chosen using rate distortion optimization. As a result, heavy computation burden is one major challenge for SDQ and RDOQ. Moreover, dynamic programming based path search in SDQ results in severe sequential dependency, and serial processing in CABAC aggravates the data dependency in CABAC based SDQ [5].

Accounting for this issue, some literatures had made meaningful explorations to alleviate the computation burden of the SDQ [5–7]. These works decrease the computation of SDQ by decreasing the candidates of quantized results [5], employing fast computation for rate distortion of candidate coefficient levels [6, 7], and using fast bit rate evaluation [7]. These methods alleviate the computation burden in SDQ to certain extent, however they still suffer from some sequential dependency, or mainly designed for soft-targeted video coder optimization. In comparison, data dependency does not appear in the HDQ, such as the prevalent deadzone based HDQ. Coefficient level parallel processing can be achieved in coefficient-wise HDQ with obviously increased throughput by employing hardwired pipelining. As a result, HDQ is well-suited for hardwired video coder in terms of satisfactory throughput efficiency. Unfortunately, there is a nontrivial rate distortion performance gap between HDQ and SDQ.

In summary, it is meaningful to further improve the RD performance of HDQ for hardwired video coder, taking the inter-coefficient correlation into account by simulating the behavior pattern of SDQ. On one hand, the distribution characteristics of DCT coefficients have great influence on quantization results, and thus DCT distribution parameter and quantization parameter are taken as consideration factor from the viewpoint of macro level. On the other hand, context modelling is used in CABAC and the number of possible significant coefficients plays important role in determining the quantization results. From the viewpoint of micro level manipulation, the deadzone offset is supposed to be tuned taking inter-coefficient influence into consideration according to the number of the possible significant coefficients in the block.

According to the above analysis, this paper aims to optimize rounding offset model for deadzone HDQ to improve the coding RD performance. Bayes classification method is used to derive the coefficient-wise deadzone offset model which is described as functions of these three parameters, i.e. the quantization parameter, the parameter of component-wise DCT coefficients, and the number of possible significant coefficients prior to the current coefficient. In addition, the behaviour pattern of SDQ is analyzed and used as guidance for offset modelling to improve the RD performance of the proposed offset model based HDQ. This algorithm that proposed in this paper is well-suited for hardware coder design and achieves superior RD performance compared with deadzone HDQ thanks to considering the inter-coefficient correlation by offline methods to analyze the number of significant coefficients in the block.

The rest of this paper is organized as follows. Problem formulation is given in Sect. 2. The proposed HDQ algorithm is given in Sect. 3. Section 4 gives the experimental results. Finally, Sect. 5 concludes the paper.

2 Background and Problem Formulation

2.1 Difference Between Deadzone HDQ and SDQ

In CABAC-based SDQ, the output level of one coefficient not only depends on the levels of the anterior coefficients, i.e. backward dependency, but has influence on the following coefficients, i.e. forward influence. Intrinsically, dynamic programming such as Viterbi search is desired to track the inter-coefficient dependency in SDQ [5]. There are multiple sequentially scanned coefficients in one block, and each coefficient is described as a trellis stage in the graph [5]. There are multiple candidate quantized levels to be checked at each stage in SDQ, and they are described as candidate context states. The sequential coefficients and their candidate quantized levels form a trellis graph, and so the SDQ is actually a problem of searching for a path in the graph with minimum coding cost. The optimal path is composed by multiple adjacent branches, one survivor branch at one stage. The SDQ algorithm achieves superior coding performance, approximately 6~8 % bit rate saving, at the cost of high dependency caused by Viterbi algorithm and CABAC.

The HDQ algorithm is coefficient-wise based on memoryless source assumption, i.e. there is no dependency among adjacent coefficients. As a result, HDQ is well-suited for parallelism implementation. Compared with USQ, the USQ + DZ achieves considerable RD performance improvement by employing the statistical characteristics of entropy coding [1]. However, fixed offsets, 1/3 and 1/6 for intra and inter modes, are used in deadzone HDQ in H.264 JM and HEVC HM codecs [8]. Memoryless source assumption does not hold for the context based entropy coding, such as CABAC. It means that the fixed-offset HDQ is not fully optimized compared with optimal SDQ in terms of rate distortion optimization.

It is meaningful to excavate the inner characteristics of SDQ as guidance to propose adaptive offset model for new deadzone HDQ. The goal is to approach the RD performance of the SDQ and maintain the advantage of coefficient-wise processing in HDQ. The source distribution parameter and inter-coefficient influence will be taken into consideration.

2.2   Challenge in Adaptive Coefficient-wise HDQ

A deadzone offset δ is employed to adjust the quantization result φ in deadzone HDQ, and that can be described as follows.

$$\phi = floor(\frac{|u|}{q} + \delta) \tag{1}$$

Here, q is the quantization step size determined by the quantization parameter Qp. In H. 264/AVC and HEVC, q is equal to pow(2,(Qp-4)/6). floor is the rounding operator. u is the DCT coefficients to be quantized. | | is the absolute value of the operation. There are several factors that should be considered in designing optimal coefficient-wise deadzone HDQ.

Firstly, the deadzone offset δ in HDQ is supposed to be determined in a coefficient-wise way. In general, Laplacian distribution is used to model the DCT coefficient, and the probability density function is described as follows.

$$f_i = \frac{1}{2\Lambda_i}e^{-\frac{|u_i|}{\Lambda_i}} \ and \ \Lambda_i = \frac{\sigma_i}{\sqrt{2}} = \frac{1}{n}\sum_{j=1}^{n}|u_{ij}| \tag{2}$$

Λ_i and σ_i are the model parameter and the standard deviation of the ith frequency component. u_{ij} is the DCT coefficient and u_{ij} is the jth DCT coefficient of the ith frequency component. Based on Laplacian DCT distribution model, the deadzone offset δ of HDQ is typically determined as follows using rate distortion optimization [1].

$$\delta = \frac{q}{2} - \frac{\lambda}{2\ln 2 \times \Lambda} \tag{3}$$

Here, λ is Lagrange multiplier and equals to ln2(power(q-δ,2)-power(δ,2))/q in [1]. However, there is an egg-and-chicken problem because the parameters λ and δ are dependent with each other. The coefficient-wise model in (3) is built in a macroscopic way based on statistical analysis. However, the SDQ algorithm manipulates the quantization result in a microscopic way, specifically according to the probabilities of the contexts in CABAC. Moreover, based on λ equals to ln2(power(q-δ,2)-power(δ,2))/q, coefficient level solutions are theoretically desired for Eq. (3), which is not easy to be solved.

Thirdly, the adaptive deadzone offset in Eq. (3), derived from coefficient-level models without considering inter-coefficient influence, will unavoidably suffer from RD performance degradation. In CABAC, coding bit of a quantization coefficient is determined by the probability state of the context, which is modelled according to the numbers of coefficients with intensity equal to 1 and larger than 1, i.e. Numeq1 and NumLg1, prior to the current coefficient. Under the criterion of rate distortion optimization, SDQ considers the inter-coefficient correlation and adjusts the quantization coefficient level. The code rate of the quantization coefficient is related to the number of nonzero (significant) quantization coefficients which are in current block and in the adjacent block.

Therefore, this paper take this factor into consideration in a micro way, i.e. employing the number of significant coefficients in one block in determining the deadzone offset and quantization results. However, the number of significant coefficient of a certain coefficient is not available before the SDQ algorithm finish the trellis search. Thus, it is not possible to measure the accurate number of significant coefficient in deadzone HDQ. By striking a compromise, we define the number of possible significant coefficients for the i-th coefficient η_i according to the HDQ quantization results as follows.

$$\eta_i = \sum_{j=i+1}^{N} \varpi(|u_i| - \frac{q}{2}) \text{ and } \varpi(x) = \{^{1;\ x>0}_{0;\ x\leq 0} \tag{4}$$

When the amplitude of the DCT coefficient is larger than q/2, the coefficient is considered as a possible significant coefficient. η_i is the number of possible significant coefficients prior the current i-th coefficient. For all coefficients on one block, their η_i can be estimated in parallel due to the coefficient-wise processing in HDQ as shown in (4). Suppose N is the number of the last DCT coefficient in the adjacent block, so η_i is an integer ranging from 0 to N-i.

Here we first quantitatively evaluate the degree of which η_i affect the quantization result of the current i-th coefficient. We use $\varphi_{HDQ(u)}$ and $\varphi_{SDQ(u)}$ to distinguish the quantization amplitude of u in HDQ and SDQ respectively. There are two possible situations according to the condition whether $\varphi_{HDQ(u)}$ is equal with $\varphi_{SDQ(u)}$ or not, i.e. $\varphi_{HDQ} = \varphi_{SDQ}$ and $\varphi_{HDQ} \neq \varphi_{SDQ}$. Taking 4×4 transform block as an example, the statistical distribution of η_i of sequences in the Table 1 is counted respectively. Figure 1 shows these sequences' average results of the statistical distribution of η_i in the case of two cases. We can make comparison between the η_i results of two cases, i.e. $\varphi_{HDQ} = \varphi_{SDQ}$ and $\varphi_{HDQ} \neq \varphi_{SDQ}$, as shown and in Fig. 1. The result shows that the distribution of η_i is more dispersed when

Table 1. The BD-PSNR loss of the deadzone HDQ algorithms using fixed-offset and the proposed adaptive offset compared with optimal SDQ

Sequences	BD-PSNR (dB)		BD-RATE (%)		Sequences	BD-PSNR (dB)		BD-RATE (%)	
	fixed-offset	Proposed	fixed-offset	Proposed		fixed-offset	Proposed	fixed-offset	Proposed
City	-0.1123	-0.0809	2.7651	2.0926	SlideShow	-0.2011	-0.0951	3.1697	1.5151
Harbour	-0.1505	-0.1145	3.2987	2.4996	720p Average	-0.1146	-0.0429	2.9833	1.1345
Crew	-0.1396	-0.0442	1.3462	0.7649	Proposed vs fixed-offset	0.0717		-1.8488	
ICE	-0.0711	-0.0350	1.9779	0.9418	Kimono1	-0.1675	-0.0186	6.1667	0.8812
Soccer	-0.1675	-0.0807	3.7417	1.7785	ParkScene	-0.0647	-0.0468	2.0155	1.4357
D1 Average	-0.1282	-0.0710	2.6259	1.6155	riverbed	-0.1542	-0.0093	3.1231	0.2450
Proposed vs fixed-offset	0.0572		-1.2968		Basketball	-0.0881	-0.0542	4.1461	2.6046
Cyclists	-0.0627	-0.0353	2.3778	1.3271	Cactus	-0.0892	-0.0189	4.4226	0.3890
Harbour	-0.1013	-0.0308	2.4938	0.9619	sunflower	-0.2016	-0.0874	7.76895	3.5057
Optis	-0.0759	-0.0079	2.6692	0.3354	1080p Average	-0.1275	-0.0392	4.6072	1.5102
Raven	-0.132	-0.0455	4.2062	1.5328	Proposed vs fixed-offset	0.08836		-3.0969	

$\varphi_{HDQ} = \varphi_{SDQ}$, while η_i are mainly concentrated in the vicinity of zero comparatively in the case of $\varphi_{HDQ} \neq \varphi_{SDQ}$. This statistical differences of η_i in two opposite cases give us the insight that η_i can be employed to aid in deriving deadzone offset model in terms of simulating SDQ. This work will adjust the deadzone offset δ according to the actual distribution of η_i to simulate the SDQ decision mechanism as far as possible.

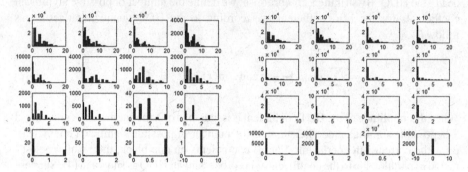

Fig. 1. The histogram results of η_i in the case of $\varphi_{HDQ} = \varphi_{SDQ}$ and $\varphi_{HDQ} \neq \varphi_{SDQ}$

3   Improved HDQ with the Proposed Adaptive Deadzone Offset

3.1   Heuristic Deadzone Offset Modelling

As analyzed above, deadzone offset modelling is supposed to be built adaptively for deadzone HDQ. Instead of RD model based derivation method shown in Eq. (3), this work attempts to estimate optimal deadzone offset model by simulating the behavior of SDQ and construct an adaptive deadzone offset model based on statistical analysis method.

As shown in Fig. 2, statistical analysis and heuristic method for model derivation is employed. We use the classification method in II-C to distinguish two kinds of situations. The "inlier" and "outlier" which represent DCT coefficients samples of two categories respectively, are collected for offline deadzone offset modeling. The "inlier" samples are the DCT coefficients in the case of $\varphi_{HDQ} = \varphi_{SDQ}$; the "outlier" samples are the DCT coefficients in the case of $\varphi_{HDQ} \neq \varphi_{SDQ}$. Taking the inter-coefficient correlation into consideration as analyzed in (3), the deadzone offset δ is related with the quantization parameter Qp, the Laplacian distribution parameter Λ and the number of possible significant coefficients prior to the current coefficient, i.e. η_i. As a result, the parameter (Qp, Λ, η) combination samples of the "inlier" and "outlier" coefficients are collected for statistical analysis. In addition, the "inlier" offset range $(\delta_{min1}, \delta_{max1})$ and the "outlier" offset range $(\delta_{min2}, \delta_{max2})$, in which the resulting results of HDQ are equal to those of SDQ of two kinds of samples, are also recorded simultaneously. These statistic samples will be used for off-line offset modeling.

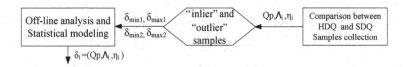

Fig. 2. Heuristic deadzone offset model derivation.

3.2 Analysis on Optimal Offset Distribution

When the HDQ fails to track the optimality of SDQ, the quantizaton results of HDQ will be different from those of SDQ, i.e. $\varphi_{HDQ} \neq \varphi_{SDQ}$. In these samples, we find that the probability of $\varphi_{HDQ(u)} = \varphi_{SDQ(u)} + 1$ is very close to 1, and this phenomenon can be explained that smaller quantization level in SDQ, with changed level intensity equal to 1, will result in predominate rate saving, which is larger than the increased distortion. The algorithm design of adaptive deadzone HDQ is just to find adaptive deadzone offset (δ_{best}) which is suitable for both of two kinds of samples.

The method of deriving the ranges of the possibly reasonable offsets is analyzed as follows. A well-designed offset δ for deadzone HDQ may achieve right classification with result identical with SDQ, or wrong classification with result differing from SDQ. δ_{best} will be determined from a great amount of samples using statistical analysis method, i.e. Bayes method. Intuitively, we estimate appropriate deadzone offset range that can make HDQ achieving the identical result as SDQ. The suitable deadzone offset ranges of two cases are estimated respectively, and their upper and lower bounds of offset ranges of two kinds of simples, i.e. (δ_{min1}, δ_{max1}) and (δ_{min2}, δ_{max2}), are estimated as follows.

$$(\delta_{min1}, \delta_{max1}) = \underset{\delta_{best}}{\arg}(floor(\frac{|u|}{q} + \delta_{best}) = \phi_{HDQ(u)})$$

$$(\delta_{min2}, \delta_{max2}) = \underset{\delta_{best}}{\arg}(floor(\frac{|u|}{q} + \delta_{best}) = \phi_{HDQ(u)} - 1) \qquad (5)$$

Here, $\varphi_{HDQ(u)} = floor(|u|/q + 0.5)$ is HDQ quantization intensity. As for the "inlier" samples, we get the possible range of the optimal δ under the constraint that $floor(|u|/q + \delta_{best})$ is equal to $\varphi_{HDQ(u)}$. As for the "outlier" samples, we get the possible range of the optimal δ under the constraint that $floor(|u|/q + \delta best)$ is equal to $\varphi_{HDQ(u)}-1$. In a word, we estimate the possible ranges of the optimal δ under the constraint of $\varphi_{HDQ(u)} = \varphi_{SDQ(u)}$ for both kinds of samples.

Offline statistic analysis is carried out using a great amount of two kinds of samples and their offset ranges. Histogram based non-parametric analysis is employed to estimate these two probability density function curves. The maximal possible solution range for (δ_{min}, δ_{max}), i.e. (0,1), is partitioned into N segments, and the actual range (δ_{min}, δ_{max}) of all samples are compared for grouping and classification respectively. Then, ranges (δ_{min}, δ_{max}) of all samples are compared for classification respectively. If one segment is within range (δ_{min}, δ_{max}), its histogram count $\theta_y(k)$ is increased by $\zeta(k)$. $\theta_y(k)$ is expressed as follows.

$$\theta_y(k) = \theta_y(k) + \zeta(k); \quad if(\frac{k-1}{N}, \frac{k}{N}) \in (\delta_{min_y}, \delta_{max_y})$$
$$\theta_y(k) = \theta_y(k); \qquad otherwise \qquad y = 1 \ or \ 2 \tag{6}$$

In this work, different weight is used for histogram estimation accounting for statistical characteristics. That is, different weight $\zeta(k)$ is sued for different each subsection for δ_{best} histogram statistical analysis. Gaussian function is used for modeling the weight of each sub section ($\zeta(k)$). Gaussian function based $\zeta(k)$ is employed and expressed as follows.

$$\zeta(k) = \frac{1}{\sigma_1 \times \sqrt{2 \times \pi}} \times e^{(-\frac{(k-\mu_1)^2}{2 \times \sigma_1^2})} \ and \ \mu_1 = \frac{\delta_{max} + \delta_{min}}{2}, \sigma_1 = \frac{\delta_{max} - \delta_{min}}{\alpha} \tag{7}$$

Here, α is equal to 6. The segment-wise histogram results of δ_{best}, $cnt_y(Qp, \Lambda)$ are obtained independently in the case of different Qp and Λ. $y = 1$ and $y = 2$ correspond to the "inlier" and "outlier" samples. It is well-known that Λ is related with the coefficient position index (i). One example of $cnt_y(Qp, \Lambda(i))$ of different coefficients with two kinds of samples is shown in Fig. 3.

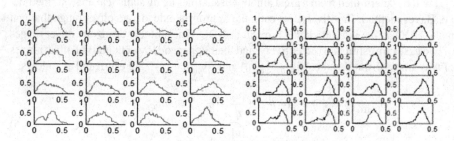

Fig. 3. The histogram results of possible δ_{best} $cnt_1(Qp, \Lambda)$ and $cnt_2(Qp, \Lambda)$

3.3 The Adaptive Deadzone Offset Model

According to the statistical samples, we build an adaptive model $\delta_i = (Qp, \Lambda_i)$ using heuristic method for deadzone offset. The model is constructed by maximizing the positive judgment probability and minimizing the probability of wrong judgment. In fact, $\theta_1(k)$ and $\theta_2(k)$ actually reflect the right classification probabilities of the "inlier" and "outlier" coefficients. We perform normalization for the histogram results, $\theta_y(k)$, to derive the condition probability p_y, i.e. $p_1(\delta)$ and $p_2(\delta)$ respectively. Therefore, δ_{best} can be determined by taking the peak value of the weighted histogram as shown in Eq. (8). The schematic diagram and the actual statistics results are shown respectively in Fig. 4.

$$\delta_i = \underset{\delta_i(\Lambda_i, Qp)}{\arg\max} \{p_1(\delta_i) + p_2(\delta_i)\} \tag{8}$$

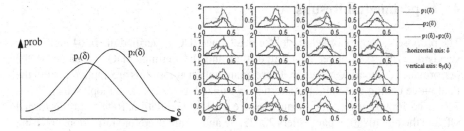

Fig. 4. The sketch map of δ_{best} and the statistical results of δ_{best}

On the basis of the above model, we built a factor $\phi(\eta_i)$ which can adjust the deadzone offset according to the number of possible significant coefficients in the adjacent block. Here, i is the coefficient position index and the factor $\phi(\eta_i)$ is expressed as follows.

$$\varphi(\eta_i) = \beta \times \arctan(\eta_i - \frac{\eta_{i max}}{\gamma}) \quad and \quad \eta_{i max} = N - i \qquad (9)$$

Here, N is the number of the last DCT coefficient in the adjacent block. $\eta_{i max}$ is equal to N-i. We had evaluated the RD performance in the cases of different combinations between (β, γ). The simulation results indicate that superior RD performance appear when β is equal to 0.03 and γ is equal to 3, as shown in Fig. 5. Therefore, the adaptive deadzone offset model with η_i is expressed as flowers.

$$\delta_i^* = \arg_{\delta_i(\Lambda_i, Qp)} \max\{p_1(\delta_i) + p_2(\delta_i)\} + \varphi(\eta_i) \qquad (10)$$

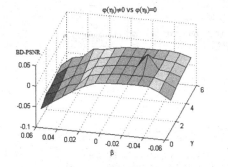

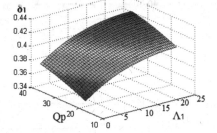

Fig. 5. The RD performance of different combinations between β and γ

Fig. 6. The surf results of δ_{best}

According to the method of modeling above, in the case of $\eta_1 = 10$, one example of the surf results of δ_1, in the case of different combinations between Qp and Λ_1, is shown in Fig. 6.

4   Experimental Results

The proposed adaptive offset model for deadzone HDQ is verified in H.264 and H.265 standards. The fixed-offset HDQ algorithm and the optimal SDQ are taken as the performance comparision anchor. These quantization algorithms are applied in both the final mode coding and the rate distortion optimized mode decision loop. Standard D1, 720p, and 1080p format video sequences are used for simulation. Rate control is turned off, and the quantization parameters 22, 27, 32 and 37 are used for simulation, covering low, medium and high bit rate applications. IPBBPBB GOP structure is used, and 100 frames are tested for all resolution video sequences. The PSNR degradation (BD-PSNR) and rate increment percentage (BD-RATE) are used for performance comparison [8].

The rate distortion curves of the 1080p BasketballDrive sequence are taken as example shown in Fig. 7. The anchor optimal SDQ, the fixed-offset deadzone HDQ, and the proposed algorithm are compared. In addition, Table 1 gives the detailed BD-PSNR and BD-RATE results [8]. Relatively, larger RD performance improvement is observed in higher resolution video sequences. Intensive results show that the proposed algorithm only has 0.03921 dB BD-PSNR loss on average, with 1.51 % average BD-RATE increment, in comparison with the SDQ algorithm in the case of 1080p sequences. In addition, the proposed algorithm achieves 0.08836 dB BD-PSNR improvement on average, with 3.097 % average rate saving (BD-RATE), in comparison with the fixed-offset deadzone HDQ algorithm. The proposed adaptive offset HDQ algorithm is considerably superior than the fixed-offset HDQ, and has close performance with the optimal SDQ algorithm. Compared to the SDQ algorithm, the proposed algorithm has much smaller complexity and is well-suited for hardwired video coder in terms of satisfactory throughput efficiency.

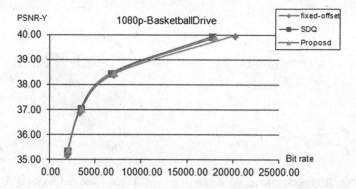

Fig. 7. The RD performance of three kinds of quantization algorithms.

As for complexity, the additional computation of the proposed algorithm, in comparison with the fixed-offset HDQ algorithm, is just simple function call as shown in Eq. (10) or tabulation shown in Fig. 6, so it is almost ignorable.

5 Conclusions

Sequential processing hinders soft-decision quantization (SDQ) from effective hardware implementations, while hard-decision quantization (HDQ) suffers from obvious coding performance loss compared with SDQ. Based on statistics analysis and heuristic modelling, this paper proposes a content-adaptive deadzone quantizer to minimize the rate distortion performance difference between the deadzone HDQ and SDQ. An adaptive deadzone offset model is built according to the quantization parameter, the coefficient-wise DCT distribution parameter, and the number of possible significant coefficients in the block. Simulation results verify that the proposed adaptive HDQ algorithm, in comparison with fixed-offset HDQ, achieves 0.08836 dB PSNR increment and 3.097 % bit rate saving in 1080p sequences with almost negligible complexity increase. In addition, this work, in comparison with the SDQ, achieves less than 0.03921 dB PSNR loss and 1.51 % bit rate increment.

Acknowledgment. This work was supported in part by the National Natural Science Foundation of China under Grants 61572449, in part by the Zhejiang Natural Science Foundation under Grants LY15F020022 LY12F01011, and LY13H180011.

References

1. Sullivan, G.J.: Efficient scaler quantization of exponential and laplacian random variables. IEEE Trans. Inf. Theor. **42**, 1365–1374 (1996)
2. Wen, J., Luttrell, M., Villasenor, J.: Trellis-based R-D optimal quantization in H.263+. IEEE Trans. Image Process. **9**, 1431–1434 (2000)
3. Yang, E.-H., Yu, X.: Rate distortion optimization of H.264 with main profile compatibility. In: Proceedings of IEEE International Symposium on Information Theory, Seattle, WA, pp. 282–286, 9–14 July 2006
4. Karczewicz, M., Ye, Y., Chong, I.: Rate Distortion Optimized Quantization. ITU-T SG16/Q. 6 Doc. VCEG-AH21, Antalya, Turkey, 12–13 January 2008
5. Yin, H., Yang, E., Xiang, Y.: Fast soft decision quantization with adaptive preselection and dynamic trellis graph. IEEE Trans. Circ. Syst. Video Technol. **25**(8), 1362–1375 (2015)
6. Huang, T.-Y., Chen, H.H.: Efficient quantization based on rate-distortion optimization for video coding. IEEE Trans. Circ. Syst. Video Technol. **26**, 1099–1106 (2015). doi:10.1109/TCSVT. 2015.2444732
7. Lee, H., Yang, S., Park, Y., Jeon, B.: Fast quantization method with simplified rate-distortion optimized quantization for HEVC encoder. IEEE Trans. Circ. Syst. Video Technol. (2015). doi:10.1109/TCSVT.2015.2450151
8. Sun, J., Duan, Y., Li, J., Liu, J., Guo, Z.: Rate-distortion analysis of dead-zone plus uniform threshold scalar quantization and its application–part I: fundamental theory. IEEE Trans. Image Process. **22**(1), 202–214 (2013)

Comparison of Information Loss
Architectures in CNNs

Song Wu[✉] and Michael S. Lew

The Leiden Institute of Advanced Computer Science,
Leiden University, Leiden, Netherlands
{s.wu,m.s.lew}@liacs.leidenuniv.nl

Abstract. Recent advances in image classification have been achieved
with deep convolutional neural networks (CNNs). The pooling and subsampling operations in the CNNs introduce invariance to local transformations, but result in accuracy loss in the image applications. In this
paper, we propose a novel deep network called "Weighted Integration
Architecture Network" (WIAN) which can effectively recover the information loss due to the pooling operation in the CNNs. The proposed
WIAN reuses the information from the previous layers in the network
and assigns a weight to each according to the responses or entropy in
the layer and then element-wise summing them to further enhance the
image classification performance. Exhaustive experiments on four standard benchmark datasets (CIFAR-10, CIFAR-100, MNIST and SVHN)
demonstrate the effectiveness as well as an improved performance of
WIAN.

Keywords: Image classification · Convolutional neural network ·
Weighted integration architecture network

1 Introduction

Significant performance gain on the task of image classification has been made
with deep convolutional neural networks (CNNs) [1,2]. This is mainly due to
the advances in CNN architectures as well as the availability of very larger and
more comprehensive datasets.

Traditional convolutional neural networks consist of several stacked convolutional layers (optionally followed by normalization layer and pooling layer), fully
connected layers and a softmax layer on the top. Convolutional layers take the
inner product of the linear filter and the underlying receptive field followed by a
nonlinear activation function at every local region of the input. The outputs from
each convolutional layer are named as feature maps. The fully connected layer
has full connections to all activations in the feature maps from previous layer and
the resulting vector can be fed into the softmax layer for classification (as shown
in Fig. 1). Variants of this basic design are proposed to improve the performance
of the network. Most recent methods increase the depth of network layer as well

© Springer International Publishing AG 2016
E. Chen et al. (Eds.): PCM 2016, Part II, LNCS 9917, pp. 346–354, 2016.
DOI: 10.1007/978-3-319-48896-7_34

as the width of each layer to enhance the performance of CNNs [3,4], and adopt dropout to address the issue of over-fitting [5]. The approach of GoogleNet [6] is designed by increasing the depth and width of the network while keeping the computational budget constant. The Network in Network (NIN) [3] replaces the linear convolution by a nonlinear convolution function to enhance the abstraction ability of the neural network. Deeply supervised network [7] focuses on the importance of minimizing the output classification error while reducing the prediction error of each individual layer. A Siamese network [8] is trained with a pairwise loss that minimises the distance between the same class and maximises the distance between different classes, and a similar triplet network [9] employs the triplet ranking loss to preserve relative similarity relations.

The convolutional layer is usually followed by a pooling layer. The pooling operation reduces the spatial resolution by computing a summary statistic over a local spatial region (typically a max or average operation). The main motivation behind the use of pooling is to promote invariance to local input transformations (such as translation, occlusion and truncation of the local stimulus). This is due to the resulting outputs by pooling being invariant to spatial location within the pooling region. This is particularly important for the performance of image classification where local image transformations obfuscate object identity. Therefore the pooling layer plays a vital role in preventing over-training while reducing computational complexity for the task of image classification. However, the invariance achieved by pooling comes at the price of information loss. Several researches attempt to make up the loss caused by pooling operation. Sun et al. [10] proposed to use cascaded networks to improve the accuracy of facial landmarks detection. Tompson et al. [11] designed a heat-map regression model to refine the position of human body joints localization. Yang et al. [12] extracted multi-scale features across multiple layers and further integrated them for image recognition. In this paper, we introduce a novel architecture called weighted integration architecture network (WIAN) to boost the performance. WIAN starts by adjusting the convolutional layers to the same shape by a convolution operation, and automatically learns a weight value according to the responses or entropy on each reshaped convolution layer. Then these convolutional layers are multiplied by the assigned weight respectively, and finally combined into a single layer by element-wise summing, as illustrated in Fig. 3.

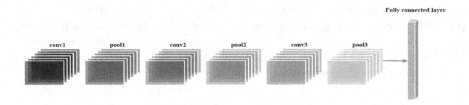

Fig. 1. The illustration of the standard deep convolutional neural networks (CNNs).

The remainder of this paper is organized as follows. Section 2 gives an overview of the convolutional neural network based image classification. Section 3 provides a detailed description of the proposed weighted integration architecture network. Section 4 presents the experimental results and conclusions are given in Sect. 6.

2   Convolutional Neural Networks Classification

Considering a standard CNN architecture, as shown in Fig. 1, there are N convolutional layers, denoted as $C^1, ..., C^N$. Each convolutional layer is followed by a pooling layer, and the pooling layers are denoted as $P^1, ..., P^N$. The training of traditional CNNs is to maximize the probability of the correct class, which is achieved by minimizing the softmax loss function. For a specific training set which includes m images: $\{(I^{(i)}, L^{(i)}); i = 1, ..., m\}$, where $I^{(i)}$ is the ith image and the $L^{(i)} \in 1, ..., K$ is the class label. Let $\{x_j^{(i)}; j = 1, ..., K\}$ be the output of the activation j in the last fully connected layer, then the probability that the label of $I^{(i)}$ is j is given by

$$p_j^{(i)} = \frac{exp(x_j^{(i)})}{\sum_{j=1}^{K} exp(x_j^{(i)})} \tag{1}$$

The output of the fully connected layer is then fed into the softmax layer which aims to minimize the following loss function:

$$J_\theta = -\frac{1}{n}[\sum_{i=1}^{n} \sum_{j=1}^{K} 1\{L^{(i)} = j\} \log(p_j^{(i)})] \tag{2}$$

where $1\{.\}$ is the indicator function. The standard back-propagation is utilized to optimize the parameters of the network through computing the derivatives of the defined loss function.

3   Integration Architecture Network

As the architecture of the standard CNNs did not take into account the information loss caused by the pooling operation, in this section, we explore several useful practices to integrate the information from the previous convolutional layers to recover the accuracy loss in the CNNs, and the evaluation results demonstrate that the reuse of the previous convolutional layers could effectively increase the performance of image classification.

3.1   Concatenate Architecture Network

Inspired by the architecture of GoogleNet [6], a simple and effective way to train a high quality model is to concatenate the previous convolutional layer into a

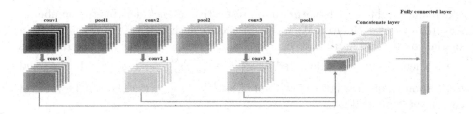

Fig. 2. The illustration of the concatenate architecture network (CONCAT).

new layer. The illustration of the concatenate architecture network (CONCAT) is in Fig. 2. In this architecture, we first reshape these existing convolutional layers into the same shape by a convolution operation, and then concatenate them together. The fully connected layer takes all neurons in the concatenate layer and connects it to every single neuron it has and finally fed the output from the fully connected layer into the softmax loss function to optimal the network.

3.2   Weighted Integration Architecture Network

The concatenate operation significantly increases the width of the integration layer, which means a larger number of parameters are stored in this layer. However, large amount of parameters make the network more easy to over-fitting, especially if the amount of labeled data in the training set is small. Additionally, because of the existing redundant information between two adjacent layers, we propose to assign each previous convolutional layer (reshape to the same dimensions by a convolution operation) a weight value, respectively, and then combine them by the element-wise summing. Two weight schemes are explored in this paper, one is based on the responses on the convolutional layer and the other one is based on the entropy on the convolutional layer.

Responses based weight scheme: as shown in Fig. 3, for the given N convolutional layers in the network, we denote the feature maps from layer C^n as $F^n, n = 1, ..., N$. These features maps on each convolutional layer can be represented as a vector with the dimensions of $w^k \times h^k \times c^k$, where w^k and h^k are the

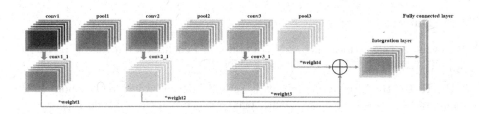

Fig. 3. The illustration of the proposed weighted integration architecture network (WIAN).

width and height of each feature map, respective, and c^k denotes the number of feature maps at each layer. We further associate each unit in feature maps with a spatial coordinates (x, y) and the activation of this unit is $a(x, y)$. The responses of each feature map is calculated as $r^c = \sum_{x=1}^{w^k} \sum_{y=1}^{h^k} a(x, y), c = 1, ..., c^k$ and the responses of each layer is computed as $R^n = \sum_{c=1}^{c^k} r^c$. The weight value of each layer is defined as:

$$weight_R^n = \frac{R^n}{\sum_{n=1}^{N} R^n} \tag{3}$$

We need to note the specific case that the weight from each layer is equal to $1/N$, which is named as average integration architecture network (AIAN).

Entropy based weight scheme: we further employ the entropy information [13] on each convolutional layer to define the weight value. The activation of each unit $a(x, y)$ in the feature maps can be treated as a state p_i, and the entropy on each feature map is measured according to $e^c = \sum_{x=1}^{w^k} \sum_{y=1}^{h^k} (p_i \times \lg p_i), c = 1, ..., c^k$ and the responses of each layer is computed as $E^n = \sum_{c=1}^{c^k} e^c$. The weight value of each layer is then defined as:

$$weight_E^n = \frac{E^n}{\sum_{n=1}^{N} E^n} \tag{4}$$

Finally, the activation value of each unit $a^{n+1}(x, y)$ in the integration layer is calculated as:

$$a^{n+1}(x, y) = \sum_{n=1}^{N} weight^n \times a^n(x, y) \tag{5}$$

4 Experiments

The proposed WIAN is implemented using the Caffe [14], and the experimental environment is 32 GB RAM, NVIDIA TITANX. The training of WIAN starts from the initial weights and learning rates, and the learning rates are lowered by a factor of 10 according to an epoch schedule determined on the validation set. The source code of WIAN is available at: http://press.liacs.nl/researchdownloads/.

4.1 Datasets

We evaluate the performance of WIAN on four benchmark datasets: CIFAR-10 [1], CIFAR-100 [1], MNIST [15] and SVHN [16].

CIFAR-10: the CIFAR-10 dataset is established for object recognition. It is composed of 10 object classes, with 6000 images per class. 50000 images are selected for training, and remaining 10000 images are used for testing. Each image is an RGB format with size 32×32.

CIFAR-100: the CIFAR-100 dataset is similar to CIFAR-10 dataset (both are with the same image size and format), except that the CIFAR-100 contains 100 classes with 600 images per class. CIFAR-100 also uses 50000 images for training and the remaining 10000 image for testing.

MNIST: the MNIST dataset consists of hand written digits number images which are 28×28 in size. There are 60000 training images and 10000 testing images in total. For this dataset, all images have been resized to a fixed resolution of 32×32 in the experiments.

SVHN: the Street View House Numbers(SVHN) dataset is a collection from house numbers in the Google Street View images. It is composed of over 600000 color images with a fixed resolution of 32×32 pixels.

5 Results and Discussion

The architecture of the network in the evaluation contains three convolutional layers, followed by RELU normalization and pooling operation. Moreover, for the integration layer, we convolute them to the same shape and combine them together. According to the parameter configuration of each layer, the architecture of the WIAN in the performance evaluation can be described concisely by layer notations with layer sizes:

$INPUT(32 \times 32 \times 3)$
$CONV1(32 \times 32 \times 32) \rightarrow RELU1 \rightarrow POOL1(16 \times 16 \times 32)$
$CONV2(16 \times 16 \times 32) \rightarrow RELU2 \rightarrow POOL2(8 \times 8 \times 32)$
$CONV3(8 \times 8 \times 64) \rightarrow RELU3 \rightarrow POOL3(4 \times 4 \times 64)$
$CONV1 \rightarrow CONV1\_1(4 \times 4 \times 64)$
$CONV2 \rightarrow CONV2\_1(4 \times 4 \times 64)$
$CONV3 \rightarrow CONV3\_1(4 \times 4 \times 64)$
$CONV1\_1 + CONV2\_1 + CONV3\_1 + POOL3 \rightarrow FC$

5.1 Results of Weighted Integration Architecture

We present the performance of our proposed WIAN (with two weight schemes based on responses and entropy) and make a comprehensive comparison with general CNNs, average integration architecture network (AIAN) as well as the directly concatenate (CONCAT) of the previous convolutional layers in the CNN architecture. The concatenation operation is similar as the inception module in GoogleNet [6]. Softmax is employed to predict the classification accuracy. The evaluation results of classification accuracy are demonstrated in Table 1, and the test classification error at each epoch during the training is also displayed in Fig. 2.

It turns out that the integration (WIAN, AIAN and CONCAT) of the previous layers in the network gets improved performance when compared with general CNNs. The scheme of WIAN shows much better results than other approaches, and the WIAN based on the weight calculated according to responses

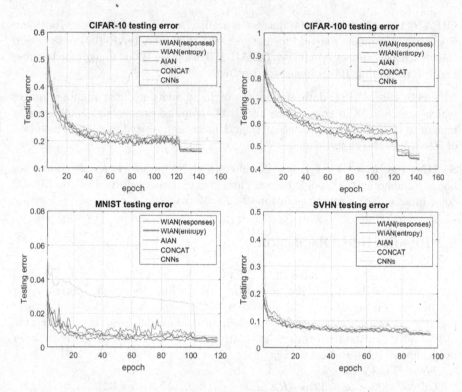

Fig. 4. The comparison results among several possible architectures to recover the information loss on four benchmark datasets.

Table 1. The performance comparison of different convolutional neural network architectures on four benchmark datasets.

Methods	CIFAR-10	CIFAR-100	MNIST	SVHN
WIAN (responses)	**83.92**	**55.84**	**99.65**	**95.21**
WIAN (entropy)	83.86	55.25	99.58	94.95
AIAN	82.9	54.1	99.46	94.68
CONCAT [6]	83.3	55.06	99.51	94.94
CNNs [1]	81.5	53.5	99.3	94.15

on each layer gets the best performance on all the benchmarks. Based on the curves displayed in Fig. 4, it shows that the WIAN reaches the smallest testing error faster than others. This further demonstrates that the weighted integration of previous convolutional layers can boost the performance of the network.

6   Conclusions

In this paper, we propose to reuse the information in the previous layers in the network to recover the precision loss due to the pooling operation in the CNN. We present a novel weighted integration architecture network (WIAN) to enhance the performance of CNN based image classification, where each layer is multiplied by a weight generated according to the responses or entropy and then element-wise summed together. The evaluation results demonstrated that the WIAN can yield high accuracy on image classification, and also show better performance than the schemes of the directly concatenation and the average element-wise summing of the previous convolutional layers in the CNN architecture.

Acknowledgments. This work was supported by the LIACS Media Lab at Leiden University. We are also grateful to the support of NVIDIA for this work.

References

1. Krizhevsky, A., Hinton, G.: Learning multiple layers of features from tiny images (2009)
2. He, K., et al.: Delving deep into rectifiers: surpassing human-level performance on imagenet classification. In: Proceedings of the IEEE International Conference on Computer Vision (2015)
3. Lin, M., Chen, Q., Yan, S.: Network in network. arXiv preprint arXiv:1312.4400 (2013)
4. Zeiler, M.D., Fergus, R.: Visualizing and understanding convolutional networks. In: Fleet, D., Pajdla, T., Schiele, B., Tuytelaars, T. (eds.) ECCV 2014. LNCS, vol. 8689, pp. 818–833. Springer, Heidelberg (2014). doi:10.1007/978-3-319-10590-1_53
5. Srivastava, N., et al.: Dropout: a simple way to prevent neural networks from overfitting. J. Mach. Learn. Res. **15**(1), 1929–1958 (2014)
6. Szegedy, C., et al.: Going deeper with convolutions. In: Proceedings of the IEEE Conference on Computer Vision and Pattern Recognition (2015)
7. Lee, C.-Y., et al.: Deeply-supervised nets. arXiv preprint arXiv:1409.5185 (2014)
8. Bromley, J., et al.: Signature verification using a Siamese time delay neural network. Int. J. Pattern Recogn. Artif. Intell. **7**(04), 669–688 (1993)
9. Hoffer, E., Ailon, N.: Deep metric learning using triplet network. In: Feragen, A., Pelillo, M., Loog, M. (eds.) SIMBAD 2015. LNCS, vol. 9370, pp. 84–92. Springer, Heidelberg (2015). doi:10.1007/978-3-319-24261-3_7
10. Sun, Y., Wang, X., Tang, X.: Deep convolutional network cascade for facial point detection. In: Proceedings of the IEEE Conference on Computer Vision and Pattern Recognition (2013)
11. Tompson, J., et al.: Efficient object localization using convolutional networks. In: Proceedings of the IEEE Conference on Computer Vision and Pattern Recognition (2015)
12. Yang, S., Ramanan, D.: Multi-scale recognition with DAG-CNNs. In: Proceedings of the IEEE International Conference on Computer Vision (2015)
13. Lin, M., et al.: Multiple feature fusion via weighted entropy for visual tracking. In: Proceedings of the IEEE International Conference on Computer Vision (2015)

14. Jia, Y., et al.: Caffe: convolutional architecture for fast feature embedding. In: Proceedings of the ACM International Conference on Multimedia. ACM (2014)
15. LeCun, Y., et al.: Gradient-based learning applied to document recognition. Proc. IEEE **86**(11), 2278–2324 (1998)
16. Netzer, Y., et al.: Reading digits in natural images with unsupervised feature learning. In: NIPS Workshop on Deep Learning and Unsupervised Feature Learning, Granada, Spain, vol. 2011 (2011)

Fast-Gaussian SIFT for Fast and Accurate Feature Extraction

Liu Ke[1,2(✉)], Jun Wang[1,3], and Zhixian Ye[4]

[1] SYSU-CMU Shunde International Joint Research Institute, Guangzhou, China
keliu@mail2.sysu.edu.cn
[2] Department of Electrical and Systems Engineering,
Washington University in St. Louis, St. Louis, USA
[3] School of Electronics and Information Technology,
Sun Yat-Sen University (SYSU), Guangzhou, China
wangj387@mail.sysu.edu.cn
[4] School of Data and Computer Science, Sun Yat-Sen University (SYSU), Guangzhou, China
yezhx3@mail2.sysu.edu.cn

Abstract. Scale invariant feature transform (SIFT) is an algorithm to extract distinctive and invariant features from images to achieve reliable object matching between different images in variant scales and rotations, which is an essential method for object recognition in computer vision field. However, SIFT's huge computation for the Gaussian Scale Space (GSS) impedes its real-time implementation. In this paper, a Fast-Gaussian SIFT (FG-SIFT) is proposed. FG-SIFT separates SIFT's 2-D difference of Gaussian (DoG) into two 1-D DoG in x and y dimensions, and reduces the level of scales in DoG pyramid in GSS. The experiment shows that FG-SIFT reduces the computational complexity about 95% in GSS, also increases the accuracy of keypoint localization. Subsequently, the accuracy of the generated feature (UF) is increased about 130%, and the accuracy of matched feature (AMF) is increased about 20%.

1 Introduction

Feature-Based object recognition is a common image object recognition method in computer vision. Feature extraction and matching are essential tasks to recognize objects in an image, collecting the correspondence between two images containing the same scene or object. Feature-Based object recognition consists 3 main steps. (1) *Detector* selects distinctive points as keypoints in images, such as corners or blobs. The requirement for keypoint *detector* is repeatability, which means it can reliably find the same keypoints under different condition of viewing. (2) A feature vector for each keypoint is generated based on the keypoints neighbors as the keypoints *descriptor*. The *descriptor* should be distinctive and robust to noise. (3) *Descriptor matcher* compares the feature vectors between different images to find the best matched feature pairs. The matching is based on the distance between vectors, like Euclidean distance.

Many *detectors* and *descriptors* have been proposed. First widely used keypoint detector is Harris corner detector [3]. However, Harris corner detector is not scale-invariant. The widely used feature extraction algorithm is the scale-invariant feature

E. Chen et al. (Eds.): PCM 2016, Part II, LNCS 9917, pp. 355–365, 2016.
DOI: 10.1007/978-3-319-48896-7_35

transform (SIFT) [7]. SIFT features are invariant to image scale, rotation and illumination. Because its distinctive and invariant characteristic, SIFT feature can be correctly matched against a large database of features from other images to achieve stable and reliable object recognition.

Several works have been proposed to optimize SIFT in algorithm level. Ke and Sukthankar proposed PCA-SIFT [13] applying principal components analysis to the normalized gradient patch instead of smoothed weighted histograms. Bay et al. proposed Speed Up Robust Features (SURF) [4] which uses integral images for image convolution and Fast-Hessian *detector*. SURF reduces the computation time from 1036 ms for SIFT to 354 ms on a Linux PC (Pentium IV, 3 GHz). S. Govindarajulu et al. [9] did a comparison between the three algorithms: SIFT, PCA-SIFT and SURF. Both PCA-SIFT and SURF reduce the computation time by sacrificing the accuracy of extracted features. SURF has the best performance in time. SIFT has more reliable features to achieve the best stability in feature extraction and matching, although it is slow.

Some researchers focus on accelerating SIFT in hardware level. [10] uses GPU parallel optimization and [8] implements SIFT on multicore processors. FPGA hardware architectures also have been proposed to accelerate SIFT. [1,5,11,12] work on small image resolution or limited number of SIFT features to achieve real-time requirement. [2] works on VGA and can detect up to 890 SIFT features per frame in 33 ms. [6] works on both VGA and HD sizes, and can detect up to 11000 SIFT features in HD size of image per frame in 33 ms.

In this paper, we focus on optimizing SIFT in algorithm level, and a novel Fast-Gaussian SIFT (FG-SIFT) is proposed. It is aimed to reduce the computational complexity in constructing Gaussian scale space (GSS). First, DoG in x dimension is calculated from the convolution of the difference of two 1-D Gaussian kernels in x dimension with the input image. Then, the final DoG is computed from the convolution of x dimension DoG with the difference of two 1-D Gaussian kernels in y dimension. Then, extrema points are detected. Finally, accurate keypoints are located after rejecting low contrast and edge extrema points. The execution time is reduced. Unlike PCA-SIFT and SURF sacrificing the accuracy of extracted features, the accuracy of keypoint localization is increased which can raise the accuracy of feature generation and matching.

This paper is organized as follows. Section 2 generally explains SIFT. Section 3 presents the FG-SIFT's detail. Section 4 compares the complexity and accuracy between SIFT and FG-SIFT. Section 5 concludes the paper.

2   Overview of SIFT

In SIFT, the major computation stages to generate the set of image features consist of: (1) scale-space extrema detection, (2) accurate keypoint localization, (3) orientation assignment, (4) keypoint descriptor generation.

In first stage, scale space extrema detection, the extrema *detector* builds up a GSS (Fig. 1) to detect locations that are invariant to scale change of images. GSS consists of Gaussian-filtered image (GFI) pyramid, difference of Gaussian (DoG) Pyramid and extrema pyramid.

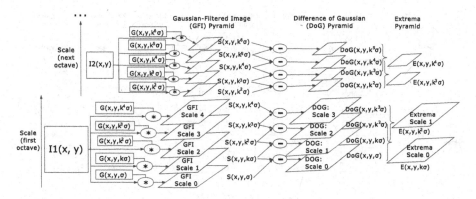

Fig. 1. SIFT GSS

Each level of the GFI pyramid, denoted by $S(x,y,\sigma)$, is produced from the convolution of a 2-D Gaussian kernel $G(x,y,\sigma)$ with an input image $I(x,y)$:

$$S(x,y,\sigma) = G(x,y,\sigma) * I(x,y), \tag{1}$$

where $*$ is the 2-D convolution operation in x and y dimensions,

$$G(x,y,\sigma) = \frac{1}{2\pi\sigma^2}e^{-(x^2+y^2)/2\sigma^2} \tag{2}$$

$DoG(x,y,\sigma)$ is the difference of two scale-nearby GFI. DoG pyramid is constructed by subtracting two adjacent GFIs in GFI pyramid:

$$DoG(x,y,\sigma) = S(x,y,k\sigma) - S(x,y,\sigma) \tag{3}$$

To detect the local maximum and minimum extrema of $DoG(x,y,\sigma)$ as keypoint candidates (Fig. 2), each sample point is compared to its 8 neighbors in the same DoG scale and nine neighbors in the above and below DoG scales.

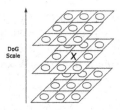

Fig. 2. Maxima and minima of DoG are located by comparing a pixel(X) to its 26 neighbors (circles) in the same and two nearby scales

In the accurate keypoint localization, Taylor expansion of the scale-space function, $DoG(x,y,\sigma)$, is used to reject the low contrast extrema points. A 2×2 Hessian matrix can compute the principal curvatures. The points located on edges are also rejected.

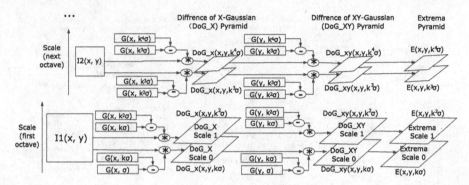

Fig. 3. FG-SIFT GSS

In the orientation assignment step, a 36 bins gradient histogram of orientation is computed from the neighbors of each keypoint in the corresponding GFI. Then, the peak of the histogram is the principal orientation of the keypoint.

In the descriptor generation, taking a keypoint as the center, based on the keypoint's principal orientation, its neighbor region is divided into 4×4 square subregions. The gradient histogram of orientation is computed for each subregion, and each histogram has 8 orientation bins. So, feature vector of each *descriptor* has $16 \times 8 = 128$ elements.

3   Proposed FG-SIFT Algorithm

Based on SIFT, FG-SIFT optimizes extrema *detector*'s GSS construction to achieve low computational complexity and high accuracy. Figure 3 shows the GSS of FG-SIFT, consisting of DoG_X pyramid, DoG_XY pyramid and extrema pyramid.

3.1   DoG Calculation

First, DoG in x dimension $DoG\_x(x,y,k\sigma)$ is computed. In Eq. (4), $G\_X(x,y,\sigma)$ is the convolution result of 1-D Gaussian kernel in x dimension $G(x,\sigma)$ ($1 \times n$ matrix) with input image $I(x,y)$. $DoG\_x(x,y,k\sigma)$ is the difference of two nearby scales of G_X. From Eq. (4), $DoG\_x(x,y,k\sigma)$ can be directly produced from the convolution of the difference of two Gaussian kernels with the input image. It can reduce one image convolution computation and the number of subtraction from $W \times H$ to n (W and H are the width and height of the image).

$$
\begin{aligned}
DoG\_x(x,y,k\sigma) &= G\_X(x,y,k\sigma) - G\_X(x,y,\sigma) \\
&= G(x,k\sigma)*I(x,y) - G(x,\sigma)*I(x,y) \\
&= (G(x,k\sigma) - G(x,\sigma))*I(x,y)
\end{aligned} \tag{4}
$$

Next, $DoG\_xy(x,y,k\sigma)$ is computed from the convolution of $DoG\_x(x,y,k\sigma)$ with the difference of two 1-D Gaussian kernel in y direction ($n \times 1$ matrix):

$$
DoG\_xy(x,y,k\sigma) = (G(y,k\sigma) - G(y,\sigma))*DoG\_x(x,y,k\sigma) \tag{5}
$$

Fig. 4. Stop sign example

In terms of computation: in one octave, five 2-D convolution computations in SIFT are decreased to four 1-D convolution in FG-SIFT. The substraction are reduced from four images' substraction to four Gaussian kernels' subtraction in one octave.

In terms of accuracy: taking the stop sign (Fig. 4(a)) as an example, in scale 0 of first octave (Fig. 3), $DoG\_x(x,y,k\sigma)$ (Fig. 4(b)) is firstly computed from the convolution of the original image with difference of two x dimension gaussian kernels. In Fig. 4(b), edges in x dimension are eliminated and edges in y dimension are enhanced. Next, $DoG\_xy(x,y,k\sigma)$ (Fig. 4(c)) is computed from the convolution of $DoG\_x(x,y,k\sigma)$ (Fig. 4(b)) with the difference of two gaussian kernels in y dimension. In Fig. 4(c), edges in y dimension are eliminated, and corners and curves are enhanced. Comparing the DoG in SIFT (Fig. 4(f)) with DoG_XY in FG-SIFT, SIFT's DoG has higher edge response than FG-SIFT's DoG_XY. The lower edge response in FG-SIFT's DoG_XY can increase the accuracy in the following extrema detection step, because the local maximum and minimum points are more concentrated on corners and curves.

3.2 Extrema Detection

Local peak of $DoG\_xy(x,y,k\sigma)$ is needed to be selected as potential keypoints. Instead of using $3 \times 3 \times 3$ point window (Fig. 2) to detect extrema point in original SIFT, a 3×3 point window (Fig. 5) is utilized to detect extrema points in FG-SIFT. The computation is reduced compared with SIFT, since each points is compared to its 8 neighbors in the current scale in FG-SIFT, instead of compared to 26 neighbors in SIFT. Meanwhile the accuracy is still improved. In the stop sign example, after the extrema points detection (Fig. 4(d)), the extrema points are mainly concentrated on the color changing region, because of the low edge response in FG-SIFTs DoG_XY. Extrema points in SIFT (Fig. 4(g)) are decentralized and distributed all region of the image.

Next, like SIFT, the low contrast and edge extrema points are rejected in FG-SIFT. Most of noise candidates are eliminated. In the stop sign example, the final

Fig. 5. Maxima and minima of FG-DoG_XY are located by comparing a pixel(X) to its 8 neighbors (circles) in the same scale

Fig. 6. Test image: (a) flower, (b) butterfly, (c) cafe, (d) dorm desk, (e) mountain, (f) building

keypoints (Fig. 4(e)) are located at the corners and curves. Comparing FG-SIFT's keypoints (Fig. 4(e)) with SIFT's keypoints (Fig. 4(h)), FG-SIFT's keypoints are more accurate than SIFT. Many SIFT keypoints are located on edges and background.

In the orientation assignment and descriptor generation steps, in original SIFT, orientation, magnitude and descriptor of a keypoint are computed from neighbors of the keypoint in the corresponding GFIs. However, in FG-SIFT, different scales of GFIs are not computed. The neighbors of keypoints are selected from the image I(x, y) in the corresponding octave (the original image I1(x, y) (Fig. 3) or down sampled image I2(x, y)).

4   Experiment

Figure 6 shows the test VGA (640 × 480) images for the complexity and accuracy analysis, which contain one simple object in one image ((a), (b)), multiple objects in one image ((c), (d)) and complex outdoor scenes ((e), (f)). In the following, we will show the low computational complexity and high accurate feature extraction in FG-SIFT.

4.1   Computational Complexity Analysis

The computational complexity of scale-space extrema detection in FG-SIFT is much less than original SIFT. Table 1 shows the complexity analysis of SIFT and FG-SIFT for [octave, extrema-scale] = [2, 2], A is the number of pixels in the original image and the sampled down image. B denotes the number of keypoints detected by SIFT *detector*. C is the number of keypoints detected by FG-SIFT *detetor*.

Table 1. Computation complexity of SIFT and FG-SIFT

Algorithm stage	Multiplication		Division		Addition		Subtraction	
	SIFT	FG-SIFT	SIFT	FG-SIFT	SIFT	FG-SIFT	SIFT	FG-SIFT
Scale-space extrema	1037 A	64 A	0	0	1032 A	56 A	4 A	48
Keypoint localization	59 A	59 A	50 A	50 A	132 B	132 C	6 B	6 C
Orientation assignment	2 A	2 A	1 A	1 A	2A + 98 B	2A + 98 C	2 A	2 A
Descriptor generation	148229 B	148229 C	0	0	150677 B	150677 C	0	0

From Table 1, multiplications is reduced about 95.19%. Additions is reduced about 95.76%. Subtraction is reduced about 99.996%. Table 2 shows the execution time in scale-space extrema detection of two algorithms. Two size of images, VGA (640×480) and HD (1920×1080), are tested in the Matlab on Intel i5 2.8 GHz, 8 GB DDR desktop. The execution time is reduced more than 71.13%.

Table 2. SIFT and FG-SIFT's Exe-Time in scale-space extrema detection

Algorithm	VGA size	HD size
SIFT	0.755 s	3.251 s
FG-SIFT	0.218 s	0.729 s
Save	71.13%	77.58%

FG-SIFT's execution time in descriptor generation is also less than SIFT. Because the difference of the two keypoint *detectors* in SIFT and FG-SIFT, the number of keypoint features for the same image are also different. In Table 4, the number of features of the 6 original test images in FG-SIFT is less than features in SIFT. FG-SIFT's average execution time in descriptor generation is about 70% of the descriptor generation's execution time in SIFT.

We did another experiment to compare the execution time of FG-SIFT with SURF. FG-SIFT has the similar timing performance with the fastest feature extraction algorithm SURF. The total execution time for SURF to extract features from a VGA image is about 3.4447 s. The number of features is about 1000. The total execution time of FG-SIFT to extract 1000 features from the same VGA image is about 4.1507 s, which is only 0.7 s less than SURF.

4.2 Accuracy Analysis

The accuracy analysis contains two parts: (1) accuracy in keypoint localization, (2) accuracy of features generation and matching. The location of keypoints can effect the accuracy of extracted feature, because the generation of features are based on the neighbors of keypoints. The more distinctive region the keypoint's location is, the higher probability the keypoint's features can be matched in the feature database. The following content first analyzes the accuracy of keypoint localization, and then analyzes the accuracy of extracted feature based on the location of keypoints.

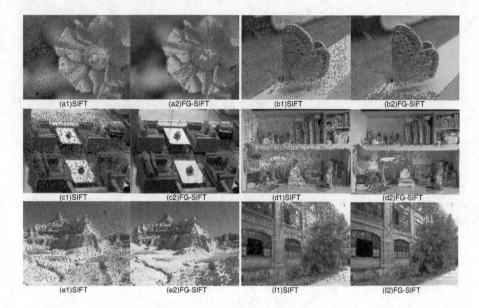

Fig. 7. SIFT and FG-SIFT keypoints in test images

Accuracy of Keypoint Localization. The goal of feature extraction is to find the features for objects in the picture, so it is better to detect keypoints on objects other than the background. As shown in Fig. 7, in the object images (a, b, c, d), the FG-SIFT keypoints are mainly concentrated on objects other than the background in images, like flower, sofa. The SIFT keypoints are decentralized and distributed all region of the images. In the scene images (e, f), the plenty of SIFT keypoints are detected at the defocus region, like sky and road, while the FG-SIFT keypoints are located at the distinctive region, like mountains, trees and windows.

Accuracy of Keypoint Features. The accurate keypoint localization can reduce the complexity in the following feature generation and matching, since the number of keypoints are much less. The execution time of descriptor generation can be reduced a lot. However, even though the number of feature are decreased, the number of matched feature is still needed to be ensured to achieve stable object or scene recognition.

Table 3 shows the conditions for testing the accuracy of SIFT and FG-SIFT. Figure 8 shows the FG-SIFT's matching result of *building* image for different cases.

The matching performance is measured by 2 parameters: (1) utilization of features(UF), (2) accuracy of matched features(AMF):

$$UF = \frac{Number\ of\ Matched\ Features}{Number\ of\ Features} \tag{6}$$

$$AMF = \frac{Number\ of\ Correct\ Matched\ Features}{Number\ of\ Matched\ Features} \tag{7}$$

Table 3. Test condition

Case	Rotation (angle)	Resize (ratio)
Best case	3	0.95
Normal case	10	0.8
Worst case	30	0.6

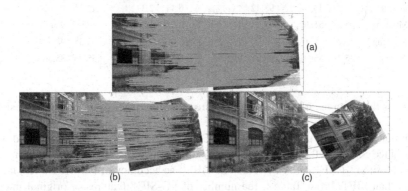

Fig. 8. *Building* FG-SIFT matching: (a) best match, (b) normal match, (c) worst match

The number of features in the original image is selected as the denominator of Eq. (6). Matched feature means that keypoint features in two different images have the similar feature vectors. A feature is utilized for matching when a matched feature is found in the transformed image. Because the keypoints localization are more accurate, features generated based on keypoints in FG-SIFT are more representative for the image, and therefore the accuracy of features is improved. UF indicates the accuracy of generated features, and a higher UF is expected in the simulation.

Table 4. SIFT and FG-SIFT 's features generation and matching in Normal Case

	Feature in original image		Features in scale-angle changed image		Matched features		Correct matched features		UF (%)		AMF (%)	
	SIFT	FG	SIFT	FG	SIFT	FG	SIFT	FG	SIFT	FG	SIFT	FG
Flower	11048	4622	2961	2389	426	725	422	720	3.9	15.7	99.0	99.3
Butterfly	6390	3812	3884	3318	215	467	204	466	3.4	12.3	94.8	99.8
Cafe	3691	3754	3278	2542	72	438	65	420	1.9	11.7	88.9	95.8
DormDesk	5850	3752	2191	2938	366	428	264	425	6.3	11.4	72.1	99.3
Mountain	7472	6916	4163	4627	287	475	277	474	3.8	6.9	96.5	99.8
Building	6783	5883	5661	4386	253	387	251	387	3.7	6.6	99.2	100
Average	6869	4790	3689	3366	269	487	247	482	3.9	10.2	91.8	99.0

Correct match feature means that two matched features with the identical information have the same coordinates after the transformation of angle and size. AMF

Table 5. SIFT and FG-SIFT's UF and AMF in best and worst case

	Best case UF (%)		Best case AMF (%)		Worst case UF (%)		Worst case AMF (%)	
	SIFT	FG-SIFT	SIFT	FG-SIFT	SIFT	FG-SIFT	SIFT	FG-SIFT
Flower	17.77	30.31	98.37	99.79	0.69	1.10	30.26	58.82
Butterfly	20.44	24.42	99.77	1	1.24	1.63	58.23	82.26
Cafe	14.22	21.31	97.71	99.5	0.19	1.36	71.43	92.16
DormDesk	29.21	44.64	98.42	1	0.44	2.37	92.31	96.67
Mountain	36.83	51.30	99.13	1	0.08	0.59	50	92.68
Building	32.73	47.97	1	1	0.04	0.46	33.33	92.59
Average	25.2	36.66	98.9	99.88	0.45	1.25	55.93	85.86

expresses the accuracy of the matched feature. A higher AMF is expected in the simulation.

In our experiment, the accuracy of FG-SIFT's extracted features is compared with SIFT, since SIFT has the best accuracy in feature generation and matching among the three algorithms (SIFT, PCA-SIFT and SURF). The accuracy of FG-SIFT's features is higher than SIFT. From Table 4, the number of FG-SIFT features in original images and scale-angle changed images is less than SIFT. However, the number of matched FG-SIFT features is about 45% more than matched SIFT features. FG-SIFT's UF is about two times of SIFT. In addition, correctness rate of matched FG-SIFT features is also higher than matched SIFT features. In Table 5, FG-SIFT's UF and AMF in best case matching and worst case matching are also higher than SIFT's UF and AMF. Especially in worst case, FG-SIFT's UF is about 3 times of SIFT's UF. And FG-SIFT has a great increase in the accuracy of matched features. So, the accurate keypoints localization not only can reduce the complexity in generating keypoints' *descriptors*, but also can increase the accuracy in feature generation and matching.

In addition, FG-SIFT has better performance in object recognition. Lots of SIFT features are located at the background or defocus region, and many correct matched features are not useful for object recognition. For example (Fig. 9(a)), 237 correct matched features are located on the background. Only 44% of correct matched features can be used to recognize the flower in the image. However, all FG-SIFT correct matched features are located on the flower (Fig. 9(b)) in the image.

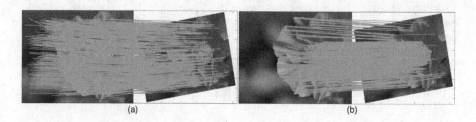

(a)   (b)

Fig. 9. Flower Matching: (a) SIFT matching, (b) FG-SIFT matching

5 Conclusion

This paper proposed a novel FG-SIFT algorithm. In scale-space extrema detection stage, FG-SIFT first computes the DoG in x dimension, and then computes the DoG in y dimension. The extrema points are detected based on one DoG scale. Then, accurate keypoints are located after rejecting low contrast and edge extrema points. Descriptors are generated based on neighbors of keypoints in the input image in the corresponding octave. FG-SIFT not only reduces the complexity of GSS, but also increases the accuracy of feature extraction and matching and has better performance in object recognition.

References

1. Borhanifar, H., Naeim, V.: High speed object recognition based on SIFT algorithm. In: International Conference on Image, Vision and Computing (2012)
2. Ker, J.-W., Huang, F.-C., Huang, S.-Y., Chen, Y.-C.: High-performance SIFT hardware accelerator for real-time image feature extraction. IEEE Trans. Circuits Syst. Video Technol. **22**, 340–351 (2012)
3. Harris, C., Stephens, M.J.: A combined corner and edge detector. In: Alvey Vision Conference, pp. 147–152 (1988)
4. Bay, H., Tuytelaars, T., Gool, L.: SURF: speeded up robust features. In: Leonardis, A., Bischof, H., Pinz, A. (eds.) ECCV 2006. LNCS, vol. 3951, pp. 404–417. Springer, Heidelberg (2006). doi:10.1007/11744023_32
5. Kim, E.S., Lee, H.-J.: A novel hardware design for SIFT generation with reduced memory requirement. J. Semicond. Technol. Sci. **13**, 157–169 (2013)
6. Chen, J.-Y., Chiu, L.-C., Chang, T.-S., Chang, N.Y.-C.: Fast SIFT design for real-time visual feature extraction. IEEE Trans. IP **22**(8), 3158–3167 (2013)
7. Lowe, D.G.: Distinctive image features from scale-invariant keypoints. IJCV **60**(2), 91–110 (2004)
8. Zhang, Y., Zhang, Q., Chen, Y., Xu, Y.: SIFT implementation and optimization for multi-core systems. In: IEEE International Symposium Workload Characterization (2008)
9. Reddy, K.N.K., Govindarajulu, S.: A comparison of SIFT, PCA-SIFT and SURF. IJIRES (2012)
10. Smolic, A., Heymann, S., Müller, K., Froehlich, B.: SIFT implementation and optimization for general-purpose GPU. In: 15th International Conference in Central Europe on Computer Graphics, Visualization and Computer Vision (2007)
11. Wang, J., Zhong, S., Yan, L.: A real-time embedded architecture for SIFT. J. Syst. Archit. **59**, 16–29 (2013)
12. Marques, E., Bonato, V., Constantinides, G.: A parallel hardware architecture for scale and rotation invariant feature detection. IEEE Trans. Circuits Syst. Video Technol. **18**, 1703–1712 (2008)
13. Sukthankar, R., Ke, Y.: PCA-SIFT: a more distinctive representation for local image descriptors. In: CVPR (2006)

An Overview+Detail Surveillance Video Player: Information-Based Adaptive Fast-Forward

Lele Dong[1], Qing Xu[1(✉)], Shang Wu[1], Xueyan Song[1],
Klaus Schoeffmann[2], and Mateu Sbert[1,3]

[1] School of Computer Science and Technology, Tianjin University,
Yaguan Road #135, Tianjin 300350, China
dongletju@gmail.com, qingxu@tju.edu.cn, qingxu.itcn@gmail.com,
tjuwushang@gmail.com
[2] Klagenfurt University, Institute of Information Technology,
Universitaetsstr. 65-67, 9020 Klagenfurt, Austria
ks@itec.aau.at
[3] Graphics and Imaging Lab, Universitat de Girona,
Campus Montilivi, 17071 Girona, Spain
mateu@ima.udg.edu

Abstract. In this paper, we propose an adaptive fast playback framework where multi-features are used to support arbitrary frame-rate video playback. We introduce a Jenson noise-based difference (JSND) as a distance measure between adjacent frames for video key frame extraction, and then present an interest learning model to control the playback rate according to the user preference. The proposed "smart-skip" frame schema not only helps users navigate the video content non-uniformly for any variable playback rate, but also preserves video semantic information to avoid the omission of important events. An overview+detail video player offering users an immersive experience is implemented to browse and comprehend the video content. Experimental results show that users can quickly skim the video, understand the content, and navigate into the content of interest.

Keywords: Video playback · Adaptive fast-forward · Interest learning model · Overview+detail · Frame skipping transcoding

1 Introduction

Remote mobile video surveillance (RMVS) has a broad application prospect in civil security, transportation and other fields. This type of mobile application is not bound by time and place. However, due to the limitation of the network environment such as bandwidth, heterogeneity and instability, RMVS brings little effect in the process of real-time transmission. Furthermore, having limited patience or time to watch the entire length of a video, users are obliged to manually skim and fast-forward to locate content of interest so as to watch more detailed information. This often involves tedious work on users' part.

© Springer International Publishing AG 2016
E. Chen et al. (Eds.): PCM 2016, Part II, LNCS 9917, pp. 366–375, 2016.
DOI: 10.1007/978-3-319-48896-7_36

Frame skipping transcoding technology is one of the key technologies to solve the problems mentioned above, such as the methods in [2,15,16]. Via transforming a precoded video bitstream into different formats to reduce the time resolution of video stream, it becomes an effective method to meet the requirement of heterogeneous network environment. The architecture of RMVS transcoding diagram is shown in Fig. 1.

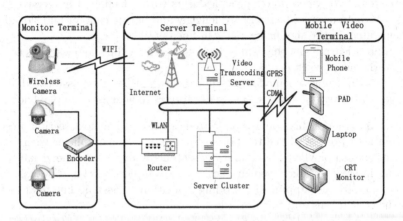

Fig. 1. The architecture of RMVS transcoding diagram

Traditional fixed interval frame skipping strategy is simple and low-cost. But due to neglect of video frame features, this strategy may well result in "bad" frame sequences, where static segments [17] with huge information redundancy take up a larger proportion than dynamic segments with significant activities. Worse still, the significant segments are too short to be captured by the human eye in the process of video acceleration. These "bad segments" can cause discontinuous motions which affect the visual perception and degrade the overall video quality.

Recently, Many content-based video players have been realized, such as the work in [7,9,10]. Höferlin presents a method to adapt the playback velocity of the video to the temporal information density in [7]. The author also proposes a blending approach to cope with arbitrary playback speeds. However, the blending of multiple similar frames with subtle distinction or small motions will result in blurry frames which are so difficult to identify that users misunderstand video content. In [9,10], X. Zhang et al. put forward a non-uniform sampling function based on mutual information.

Video interaction tools can greatly improve the efficiency of browsing videos such as [13]. Schoeffman et al. in [14] have carried out a survey of recent work on interaction tools. In [4], Christmann et al. introduce a dynamic 3D picture collections system to visual search.

In this paper, we present an adaptive fast playback framework and design an overview+detail interface to skim the lengthy video content fastly in overview mode and browse interested parts in detail mode. In general, the advantages of our proposed method are as follows:

- We improve our proposed relative entropy measure [6,17] by changing the difference between video frames to the difference between the temporal noise and the frame difference distribution. Such an improvement avoids the static changes and enhances robustness to noise.
- The interface of video player provides users with a feeling of immersive experience to help users to fast-forward lengthy and boring content and slow down when watching the significant parts in fine detail.
- An interest learning mechanism is adopted to adjust the playback rates according to the user preference.
- A smart-skip frame schema for sub-shots helps to delete the possible redundant frames and select the most salient set of frames to achieve ideal playback rate.

The remainder of this paper is organized as follows. The next section presents the quantified process of the temporal video data. A smart player with smart-skip fast forward playback mode is stated detailedly in Sect. 3. The visualization browsing interface is displayed in Sect. 4. We compare regular frame skipping and dynamic frame skipping transcoding algorithm in Sect. 5. The final section gives the conclusions and future work.

2   Quantization of Temporal Video Data

2.1   Video Data Modeling Using JSND

In this paper, a distance measure (JSND) between the temporal noise and the frame difference distribution based on JSD is introduced. Concretely, we compute the distance between each two adjacent frames, f_i and f_{i+1}, by Eq. 1 on behalf of the activity intensity for the f_i frame, which is defined as:

$$JSND(i) = JSND(D_i \| N_i) = \sum_i p(d_j) \log_2 \left(\frac{p(d_j)}{p(n_j)} \right) \tag{1}$$

Here, $p(d_j)$ and $p(n_j)$ are respectively the discrete difference image distribution and the estimated noise probability distribution of f_i, and the D_i is the absolute frame difference between f_i and $f_{(i+1)}$, and then N_i is the temporal noise of f_i. The index i and j denote a particular bin of the distribution histogram and order of the temporal frame sequence, respectively.

Combined with the powerful extreme studentized deviate (ESD) test [6], the proposed measure can detect shot boundaries with distance ratios of inter-frame JSND automatically. Then a shot is partitioned into a succession of concatenated sub-shots, by using the borders of all the sub-shots with significant content changes. These sub-shots are dynamic parts with abrupt content changes. Namely, the remaining parts are all static sub-shots. Finally, key frames are selected from these two type sub-shots with different extraction algorithms.

2.2   User Behavior Learning Model

We present a method to adapt the playback rate of the video according to temporal JSND so that users can browse videos under controlled cognitive load. Different users have respective preferences and tolerances with respect to playback rate. Except the basic control buttons (play, pause, previous and next), we further employ an interest learning model that adapts playback speed according to the user preference. Users can stop the playing video and then circle the interested parts in red rectangle as shown in Fig. 2. Then the player calculates the similarity between the subsequent frames and picked parts [12] in the background. The left and right side ① of the player are lined with the "past" and "future" scenery as well as interested events, respectively. The "past" shows viewed events and the "future" indicates coming events. Besides, we design an interest learning interface ② which influences the value of the interest level (IL) in Eq. 2.

$$IL(i) = \frac{i * (max(JSND(i)) - min(JSND(i)))}{5} \qquad (2)$$

where the index of IL i is between 1 and 5. The color of circle represents event types and the radius expresses interest levels which will change synchronously with the number of same color clicks of user in the other sub-shots. If, for instance, users add the green one (current IL values 1) in the third sub-shot, then the same color in the fourth sub-shot changes synchronously in Fig. 2.

In this paper, JSND and IL are joint considered as the complexity measure to define the importance degree (ID) of the i-th frame in Eq. 3.

$$ID(i) = \omega_1 JSND(i) + \omega_2 IL(i) \qquad (3)$$

where ω_1 and ω_2 (both initial values are 0.5) are corresponding weights. The bigger the value is, the greater the impact on ID is. Meanwhile, the player can also learn users' underlying behavior pattern by some factors ⑤ such as sliding speed, direction and frequency on the time bar [1,5,8]. These factors have an effect on the value of ω_2.

After the above video sequence processing, we can obtain the temporal quantized video sequence with the corresponding ID and key frames in each sub-shot. Accordingly, we allocate the playback time in proportion to the ID. However, in general users prefer to gradually increase the playback speed, allowing their eyes to accommodate to a higher playback speed. So we apply the average of the ID within a sub-shot to maintain a constant playback speed in Eq. 4.

$$v_{out} = \frac{(\frac{1}{U}) \sum_i ID_i}{r_{target}} v_{original} \qquad (4)$$

where U is the number of the sub-shot, $v_{original}$ is the original playback speed, v_{out} is the output speed with a sub-shot and r_{target} is the desired activity intensity [11]. Accordingly, the system plays the video content automatically similar to the car inertial navigation and fast-forwardly similar to the car high-speed operation.

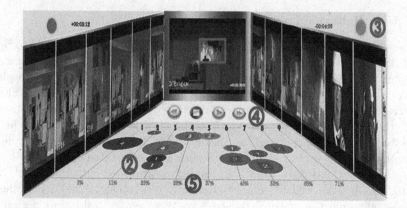

Fig. 2. The interest learning model: ① is the viewed and upcoming interest events; ② is an interest learning interface; red and green button ③ is used to switch back and forth between Figs. 2 and 5; ④ is the sub-shot sequence marked at regular intervals in ascending order; ⑤ is the time progress for every sub-shot.

3 A Smart Player with Smart-Skip Fast Forward Playback Mode

Having a video with long duration, users hope to do content-based fast-forward playback that preserves important semantic information. A smart-skip algorithms is adopted to sampling each sub-shot. Considering users' limited browsing time and constraints of processor frame rate, selecting a larger sampling interval arises as a natural solution. Along with visual dithering phenomenon, it is not an ideal solution. Hence, we come up with a novel frame skipping algorithm, the core of which has two steps. The first is to obtain a proper number of video frames depending on the loss function. The next step is similar to the integration of the human eyes when playing the video at a high rate.

In this paper, whether a frame should be skipped or not is determined by two factors (activity continuity and the loss of importance). Due to video encoding, motion vectors are available, which explains how fast the content changes. Suppose that the temporal quantified data in sub-shots can be represented by a set of f in Eq. 5.

$$\{\underbrace{f_1\cdots f_{i-1}}_{Q_1}|\underbrace{f_i\cdots f_j}_{Q_2}|f_{j+1}\cdots|\underbrace{f_a\cdots f_k\cdots f_b}_{Q_i}|\cdots f_{m-1}|\underbrace{f_m\cdots f_N}_{Q_L}\} \qquad (5)$$

where f_i denotes the $i-th$ frame and the subset from f_a to f_b is Q_i.

Motion vector considers only the motion of current frame corresponding to previous frame without analyzing the motion change. If there are continuous frames having high motion vector values without obvious difference, that means no abrupt change will happen. Here, we use motion change instead of motion vector [15] to express the activity continuity. If motion vector between f_{i-1} and

f_i is $\mathbf{mv}_{f_i}$, the motion change from f_{i-1} to f_{i+1} is $\nabla \mathbf{mv}_{f_i} = \mathbf{mv}_{f_{i+1}} - \mathbf{mv}_{f_i}$. If we skip the frame f_i, then the motion change is $\nabla \overline{\mathbf{mv}_{f_i}} = \mathbf{mv}_{f_{i+1}} + \mathbf{mv}_{f_i}$. Thus, we get the motion change of the $i - th$ frame $\| \nabla \mathbf{mv}_{\overline{f_i}} - \nabla \mathbf{mv}_{f_i} \|$ to represent the loss of continuity and the impacts on jerky effect. The other impact factor is the ID. Then, we define the loss degree due the lack of f_i and get the minimum value of $min\{\nabla f_i\}$ in Eq. 6. Hence, the loss function of a sub-shot is defined in Eq. 7.

$$\nabla f_i = \| \nabla \mathbf{mv}_{\overline{f_i}} - \nabla \mathbf{mv}_{f_i} \| * ID(f_i) \tag{6}$$

$$F_{loss} = \sum_{i=1}^{L} min(\nabla f_i). \tag{7}$$

The whole blending procedure is shown as follows:

Suppose that we label the original sub-shot as $\{f_1 \sim f_N\}$, the output blending frame sequence as $\{r_1 \sim r_M\}$, and the middle transition sequence as $\{m_1 \sim m_L\}$ $(m_i \in Q(i))$. L is given by the accelerated magnification adjusted by users. Sequencely, one frame is extracted from a certain subset Q_i with the interval of b-a+1 frames. If the frame index at time i $(1 \leq i \leq N)$ is denoted by $I(i)$. According to the above definitions of parameters, we get the relations in Eq. 8.

$$\begin{cases} I(f_a) = (I(m_i) + I(m_{i-1}))/2 & (1 \leq i \leq L) \\ I(m_i) = \sum_{i=a}^{b} [I(f_i) * ID(f_i)] \Big/ \sum_{i=a}^{b} ID(f_i) \end{cases} \tag{8}$$

The updated method of $\{Q_i\}$ is as same as that proposed in [9], so we can get intermediary layer$\{m_1 \sim m_L\}$ with the lowest distortion.

While considering a condition of the human eye called persistence of vision, Human Visual System (HVS) is insensitive to the filtered frame sequence during the fast-forward playing. Via throwing suitable L frames to cope with the restraint of playback frame rate, the video quality will be reduced but not affect browsing experience. Then we adopt the blending theory proposed in [7] to fuse the middle sequence into M output frames. The final output $\{r_1 \sim r_M\}$ is got as shown in Fig. 3(3).

The superiority compared with [7] is mainly embodied in introducing the concept of shot, which reduces the cognitive psychological burden caused by many similar frames and has better performance than that simply employing the JSND of a frame. What's more, we utilize the video encoding which creates many motion vector for each recoding blending frame.

When users implement the deceleration operation, the current output frame is probably blended. Note that all the speed adjustments are based on (1) in Fig. 3, so we should configure the start point for replaying. In other words, we need to select a mapping between the output (2) and the input (3). Suppose that the frame rate remains unchanged and the current frame r_i is blended with t_i and t_{i+1} at time $t_{current}$. We apply the mapping rule with the start point at the first frame t_i at t2 instead of the proportional way at t3 so that the output start point at m_i not m_{i+3} ensures the continuity of "layer-to-layer" skipping between frames and avoids loses the information of frame t_i.

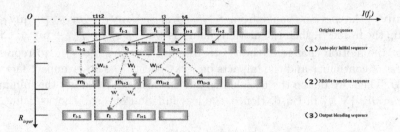

Fig. 3. The method of selecting the replay point during deceleration

4   User Interface

An overview+detail navigation with the metaphor of "scenic car driving" [3] assists users to understand the video content quickly in Fig. 4. Similar to drivers who adjust their speeds according to road conditions, we propose the following features.

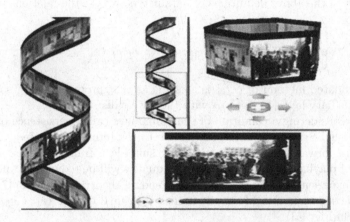

Fig. 4. Browsing video frames in details

- The browsing interface in detail mode [17]: when the scenery is complex and interesting, drivers tend to slow down to get a better look. In Fig. 4, users can see the details from a different perspective and get a deep understanding of video content.
- The fast forward interface in overview mode: when the scenery is boring, drivers tend to speed up and skip it. A user-centric "car steering wheel" in the middle of control panel dashboard, see Fig. 5, is put into effect by user's manual speed adjustment for preferred speeds. It consists of two speed controllers, where the left counts the integer part and the right counts the fractional part. Here, we label S_{normal} as initial speed, S_{min} and R_{min} as the minimum speed

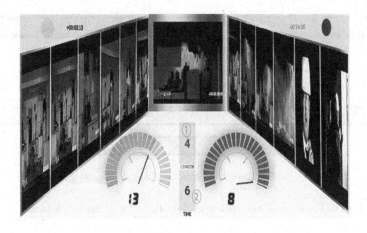

Fig. 5. Detail manual speeds adjustment

and times, and S_{max} and R_{max} as the maximum speed and times. All of
them are within physical limitation of the device. What's more, the part in
the middle of two controllers is used to express that how long user's desirable
time ② is when the player goes somewhere at normal speed, as shown in Fig. 5
①. The adjusted speed S_{output} is given in Eq. 9.

$$S_{output} = (R_{input} - 1)\frac{S_{max} - S_{normal}}{R_{max} - 1} + S_{normal} \qquad (9)$$

5   Experimental Results

To evaluate the performance of our method on a long time RMVS, we collect
over 30 videos involving surveillance videos of traffic intersection, home fire and
test them by arranging a group of users to watch the final sampling results. We
compare our method with the standard video player without the content-based
fast-forward video playing.

A video of the fire scene(07:28 min duration) is encoded in MPEG-4 with
25 frame rate and 640 × 480 frame size. The whole video has 10107 frames, a
large value of R_{input} (84.2 with the video segments from frame #252 to #1010)
is tested. The result shown in Fig. 6 shows that when the large R_{input} is set,
the standard player (a) loses events such as the 4th and 14th frame in red.
The user study has, thus, demonstrated that our method can grasp the salient
information, and avoid the omission of the important events ignored by the
traditional method without the constraint of playback rate.

Besides, eighteen undergraduate students (six female) participated in the
experiment. Then we asked them for their subjective impressions and preferences regarding the two player. Sixteen of them prefer our system than standard
interface; one people doesn't have clear preference and he thinks the standard

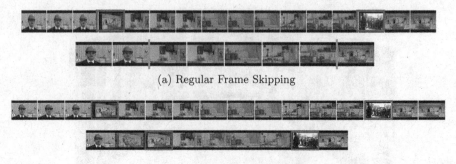

(a) Regular Frame Skipping

(b) Dynamic Non-uniform Frame Skipping

Fig. 6. Example of two different algorithms for video fast forward.

one has already satisfied his requirement; one people prefers the traditional one due to familiarity and less effort demand; eight users express that the automatic playback mode has provides them a wonderful experience.

6   Conclusion

In this paper, we propose a smart player which allows users browsing surveillance videos in a "smart-skip" fast-forward mode based on the semantic video content. This player automatically adjusts playback speed utilizing the JSND measure. In addition, it is capable of studying behaviour pattern of user by an interest learning model and playback habit on the time slider. Moreover, we propose an adaptive frame skipping algorithm for any variable playback rate. An overview+detail interface with the metaphor of "driving scene", is implemented on mobile platform, to help users to browse video content quickly. Experimental results show that our algorithm avoids users blundering away their interested parts effectively and provides them a rich and wonderful experience.

As for the future work, we intend to carry out a more user study to compare our video browser with the other video players to evaluate the browsing performance.

Acknowledgment. This work has been funded by Natural Science Foundation of China (61471261, 61179067, U1333110), and by grants TIN2013-47276-C6-1-R from Spanish Government and 2014-SGR-1232 from Catalan Government (Spain).

References

1. Al-Hajri, A., Miller, G., Fong, M., Fels, S.S.: Visualization of personal history for video navigation. In: Proceedings of the SIGCHI Conference on Human Factors in Computing Systems, pp. 1187–1196. ACM (2014)
2. Chen, C.Y., Hsu, C.T., Yeh, C.H., Chen, M.J.: Arbitrary frame skipping transcoding through spatial-temporal complexity analysis. In: TENCON 2007–2007 IEEE Region 10 Conference, pp. 1–4. IEEE (2007)

3. Cheng, K.Y., Luo, S.J., Chen, B.Y., Chu, H.H.: Smartplayer: user-centric video fast-forwarding. In: Proceedings of the SIGCHI Conference on Human Factors in Computing Systems, pp. 789–798. ACM (2009)

4. Christmann, O., Carbonell, N., Richir, S.: Visual search in dynamic 3d visualisations of unstructured picture collections. Interact. Comput. **22**(5), 399–416 (2010)

5. Glance, N.S.: Recommender system and method for generating implicit ratings based on user interactions with handheld devices, US Patent 6,947,922, 20 September 2005

6. Guo, Y., Xu, Q., Sun, S., Luo, X., Sbert, M.: Selecting video key frames based on relative entropy and the extreme studentized deviate test. Entropy **18**(3), 73 (2016)

7. Höferlin, B., Höferlin, M., Weiskopf, D., Heidemann, G.: Information-based adaptive fast-forward for visual surveillance. Multimedia Tools Appl. **55**(1), 127–150 (2011)

8. Hu, Y., Koren, Y., Volinsky, C.: Collaborative filtering for implicit feedback datasets. In: Eighth IEEE International Conference on Data Mining, ICDM 2008, pp. 263–272. IEEE (2008)

9. Jiang, J., Zhang, X.P.: A new player-enabled rapid video navigation method using temporal quantization and repeated weighted boosting search. In: 2010 IEEE Computer Society Conference on Computer Vision and Pattern Recognition Workshops (CVPRW), pp. 64–71. IEEE (2010)

10. Jiang, J., Zhang, X.P.: A smart video player with content-based fast-forward playback. In: Proceedings of the 19th ACM International Conference on Multimedia, pp. 1061–1064. ACM (2011)

11. Peker, K.A.: Method and system for playing back videos at speeds adapted to content, US Patent 7,796,860, 14 September 2010

12. Petrovic, N., Jojic, N., Huang, T.S.: Adaptive video fast forward. Multimedia Tools Appl. **26**(3), 327–344 (2005)

13. Ramos, G., Balakrishnan, R.: Fluid interaction techniques for the control and annotation of digital video. In: Proceedings of the 16th Annual ACM Symposium on User Interface Software and Technology, pp. 105–114. ACM (2003)

14. Schoeffmann, K., Hudelist, M.A., Huber, J.: Video interaction tools: a survey of recent work. ACM Comput. Surv. (CSUR) **48**(1), 14 (2015)

15. Shu, H., Chau, L.P.: Variable frame rate transcoding considering motion information [video transcoding]. In: IEEE International Symposium on Circuits and Systems, ISCAS 2005, pp. 2144–2147. IEEE (2005)

16. Vetro, A., Christopoulos, C., Sun, H.: Video transcoding architectures and techniques: an overview. IEEE Sig. Process. Mag. **20**(2), 18–29 (2003)

17. Xu, Q., Liu, Y., Li, X., Yang, Z., Wang, J., Sbert, M., Scopigno, R.: Browsing and exploration of video sequences: a new scheme for key frame extraction and 3d visualization using entropy based jensen divergence. Inf. Sci. **278**, 736–756 (2014)

Recurrent Double Features: Recurrent Multi-scale Deep Features and Saliency Features for Salient Object Detection

Ziqin Wang[⊠], Peilin Jiang, Fei Wang, and Xuetao Zhang

Xi'an Jiaotong University, Xi'an, Shaanxi, China
wangziqin@stu.xjtu.edu.cn, {pljiang,wfx,xuetaozh}@mail.xjtu.edu.cn

Abstract. Fully convolutional networks can be used to perform end-to-end saliency detection, but pooling operations generate low resolution results. We propose a novel recurrent architecture to generate and to refine the saliency maps. We firstly train a deep FCN (fully convolutional networks) to extract multi deep features and saliency features(denote as *double features*), then we feed the *double features* into the recurrent FCN. After each loop, the recurrent architecture generates new saliency features and saliency maps with higher resolutions and quality. We evaluate our method on many datasets, and our *RDF* outperforms state-of-the-art saliency detection methods.

Keywords: Salient object detection · Recurrent · Double feature · Fully convolutional networks · Refinement · Multi scale · RDF

1 Introduction

Salient object detection is a challenging computer vision task. It aims to find the most visually distinctive objects in an image. Different from predicting eye-fixations in images, a salient object detection algorithm need to find the object position and segment the object boundaries. Salient object detection is more useful in many computer vision tasks and it can serve as a pre-processing step.

Salient object detection can be saw as a dense estimation task, which uses saliency maps to show estimation results. Thus, a pixel-wise estimation is needed. Recently, convolutional neural networks (CNNs) are employed and achieve better results than previous state-of-the-art methods [14,16,18]. ConvNet exact more robust features than handcrafted, and it has been widely used in many computer vision tasks. More importantly, convolutional layers generate features with local information, and this characteristic has been used in many dense estimation tasks, such as scene labeling [21], semantic segmentation [18], depth estimation [5], etc. Most these works use fully convolutional networks in their approaches, as FCNs maintain more local information than traditional CNNs. But, unfortunately, pooling operations in FCNs generate low resolution feature maps and loss local information.

© Springer International Publishing AG 2016
E. Chen et al. (Eds.): PCM 2016, Part II, LNCS 9917, pp. 376–386, 2016.
DOI: 10.1007/978-3-319-48896-7_37

Thus, Refinement is an important part for dense estimation using fully convolutional networks. Recently, many approaches proposed methods for refinement, such as deconvolution and unpooling [19], using fine feed forward networks [5]. Besides, some approaches [9,16,27] use pre-segmentations to generate high resolution results. However, we notice that each pooling layer loses local information, while deconvolution, unpooling and some other methods only recover a part of local information. We aim to refine the results using all the local information, and we propose a novel approach to refine the dense maps step by step using a recurrent fully convolutional network. In this way, all the features before pooling layers are used for refinement.

In conclusion, this paper has the following contributions:

- We propose an architecture to extract deep features and saliency features for refining the dense estimation results.
- In each step, we proposed a method to merge the new saliency features and deep features as new *double features*, and we use these features to generate high-resolution and high quality saliency map.
- Most importantly, we introduce recurrent fully convolutional networks to refine the dense estimation recurrently. We treat the multi-scale deep features and the generated saliency features in each step as time sequences, which can be used in recurrent architecture.

2   Related Works

2.1   Saliency Object Detection

For most saliency detection methods [6,7,13,23,24], low-level features, including colors, intensities, contrasts are important information for detecting salient objects. However, learning technique was also used in saliency detection models [9,12,16,17,22,27], but most of them were based on the hand-crafted features. Recently, with the development of segmentation algorithm [2], region based methods become popular. Above all, region or superpixel based methods [4,8,9,16,20,25,27] maintain the shape of objects, while a pixel-based method always generate a fuzzy estimation [1,11,17]. Since the advantage of region based features and learning technic, some powerful methods such as MC and MDF based on both superpixel segmentation and deep learning achieved better results. Nevertheless, we propose a novel coarse-to-fine approach.

2.2   Convolutional Neural Networks for Dense Estimation

Many computer vision tasks, including salient object detection, can be saw as a dense estimation task. [18] employ a FCN for semantic segmentation with no refinement, thus the objects have unclear boundaries. [5] use two deep networks to estimate depth in a single image, the results of the first network are directly fed into the other fine network. [21] introduce recurrent convolutional network for scene labeling, the results are refined by recurrently inputting the previous outputs and the source images, but the final results only have a few improvements over the first results.

Unlike the previous approaches, we extract multi-scale deep features as local information and saliency features as salient information instead of directly using previous outputs as [5, 21].

3   Our Approach

We introduced a deep architecture based on fully convolutional networks for salient object detection. We employ a pre-trained deep network (VGG16Net) to extract deep features and to generate a small saliency map with low resolution by fine turning. Specially, We use features from two layers for fine turning. And we introduce a recurrent architecture to generate fine and high resolution saliency maps. For each loop, deep features from two different layers are concatenated in depth. A layer in the pre-trained deep networks provides the local information, and a layer before the output layer provides the features for saliency detection. And we call the those features **double feature**. Then those features are fed into a small fully convolutional neural networks which have the same parameters in all the loops. The architecture of our networks is described in Sect. 3.1, and we discuss how the deep features are looped for saliency detection in Sect. 3.2 (Fig. 1).

3.1   Deep Networks for Generating Double Features

Our architecture can be divided into two parts, a feed forward fully convolutional network and a recurrent FCN.

In the first part, a 16 layers' VGGNet is employed. We remove all the fully connected layers and add four extra convolutional layers, then fine turn the new network. Notice that only the extra layers are updated during training. Specially, for fine turning the network and generating saliency maps with higher resolution, we upsample the features from the last convolutional layer in the original VGGNet, and concatenate them with the features from the convolutional layer before the nearest pooling layer. For training, we pad the source images with zero to square instances and then resize them to the size of 256×256. Finally, this feed forward FCN generates a saliency map at the size with 32×32. And giving the ground truth G, the lost function is a binary cross-entropy between the predicted saliency map and G.

3.2   Recurrent Refinement Approach

For refinement, we introduce a recurrent architecture to combine deep features and saliency features. As described in Sect. 1, FCN is effective and efficient in dense estimation task, but pooling layers subsample of the feature maps. In order to recover the lost information, we combine the saliency features, which

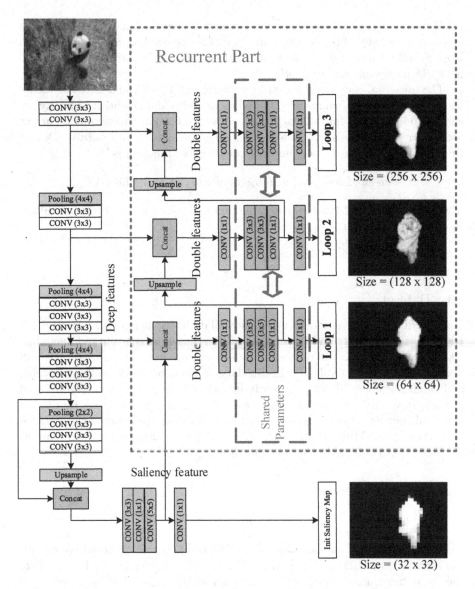

Fig. 1. The architecture of our model. The recurrent part is shown using time-unfolded computation graph. The convolutional layers in white have fixed weights, while yellow instances have shared weights, and blue instances have unshared weights. (Color figure online)

are useful for saliency detection, and the deep features with higher resolutions, which maintain more local information.

In each step, we concatenate the upsampled saliency features and the deep features which have twice width and height than the saliency features. Then the concatenated *double features* are fed into a convolutional layer which has different parameters but has the same channels of convolutional kernels in each loop. So that the feature maps that inputted into the recurrent convolutional networks have same size in depth.

The initial saliency maps have the resolution of 32×32, and after each loop, we get refined saliency maps with twice size of width and height. And finally, we can get full size and fine saliency maps. Giving an input image, our recurrent architecture generates three saliency maps (*Loop*1, *Loop*2 and *Loop*3). Denote their ground truths as G_1, G_2 and G_3, and the lost function is

$$L = a_1 L_E(Loop1, G_1) + a_2 L_E(Loop2, G_2) + a_3 L_E(Loop3, G_3) \qquad (1)$$

where L_E is a binary cross-entropy function and a_1, a_2, a_3 are constant values. In our work, we use $a_1 = a_2 = a_3 = 1$.

4   Experiment

4.1   Dataset

For experiment and evaluation, we use several datasets, including MSRA10K [4], HKU-IS [16], ASD [1] and iCoseg [3]. MSRA10K is a large dataset including 10000 images, and most of our training instances are from this dataset. HKU-IS was introduced by Li et al. [16]. In this dataset, there are more multi-object, big and small instances. iCoseg was firstly introduced for image segmentation, and recently it was used for evaluating saliency detection. ASD is popularly used in many saliency detection approaches, but there are overlaps between the instance of ASD and MSRA10K, so we remove the overlapped images in the ASD dataset, thus more than 900 images are used for testing.

4.2   Implement Details

As described in Sect. 3.1, we cut the three fully connected layers of the original VGGNet, and multi-scale features from two convolutional layers are combined by a upsample layer and a concatenate layer. We add four convolutional layers with the kernel sizes of $1024 \times 3 \times 3, 512 \times 1 \times 1, 256 \times 5 \times 5$ and $1 \times 1 \times 1$, where the three dimensions respective represent kernel channels, width and height.

In the recurrent model, we extract upsampled saliency features and deep features with batch normalization [10] and concatenate them. Then, in order to unify the channels of the feature maps in each loop, the *double features* are passed thought a convolutional layer which has the kernel size of $256 \times 1 \times 1$. The recurrent fully convolutional networks consist of four convolutional layers, which have the kernel sizes of $256 \times 3 \times 3, 128 \times 3 \times 3, 96 \times 1 \times 1$, and $1 \times 1 \times 1$, and the last one is a output layer with a sigmoid activation function.

We randomly divided MSRA10K dataset into three parts, 8000 for training, 1000 for validation and 1000 for testing. For training, we use the training set of HKU-IS and MSRA10K. And we use the validation set of those two datasets

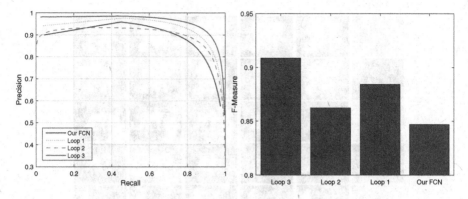

Fig. 2. Evaluate our results by PR-curve and F-Measure on MSRA10K testing dataset. Including our deep FCN and the three output of the recurrent refinement network.

for validation. We pad the source images to square images and then subsample them to the size of 256×256 as input. Firstly, we train the feed forward part using a fixed learning rate. Secondly, we fix the parameters in the feed forward networks and train our recurrent networks using a fixed learning rate.

While testing, we use the same strategy of padding and resizing, and then generate fixed size (256×256) saliency maps. And after cropping and resizing, we can achieve the final saliency maps.

4.3 Evaluate Our Results

In this section, we evaluate and compare our results generated by the proposed model, including the initial results of the deep FCN (denoted as $OurFCN$), the results after each looping (denoted as $Loop1, Loop2$, and $Loop3$). Additionally, $Loop3$ is our final result, it is also denoted as RDF.

On MSRA10K dataset, we calculate the PR-curve and max F-Measure as shown in Fig. 2. The max F-Measure calculated from the PR-curve of $OurFCN$ is 0.8469, while the final refined result achieve the score of 0.9085, which improve the performance about 7.28%. It can be inferred that the recurrent architecture improve the performance a lot.

4.4 Comparison with the State of the Art

We also compare our method with several state of the art method. Including MDF [16], MC [27], DRFI [9], RRWR [15], RC [4], HS [26] and FT [1]. We use four datasets to evaluate the performances, including HKU-IS, MSRA10K, iCoseg and ASD, Due to that some methods used training sets which overlap with the MSRA10K and ASD dataset, we didn't compare with these methods on the overlapped datasets.

We show the saliency maps of these methods in Fig. 3. The proposed method RDF can better detect salient objects. As shown in the first five images, our

Fig. 3. Compare with the state of the art methods. Each two rows make up a group of instances. From left to right in the first row of each group: source image, our FCN, our loop 1 result, our loop 2 result, our RDF (loop 3), Ground Truth. From left to right in the second row of each group: FT, MDF, RC, MC, HS, RRWR

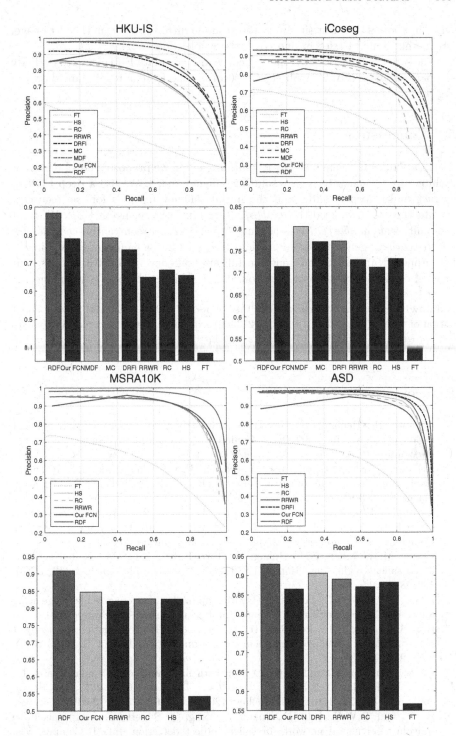

Fig. 4. PR-curves and F-Measures. We compare our method with other seven methods on four datasets. Our *RDF* has huge improvement over other state-of-the-art methods

RDF method is the most similar to the ground truth. However, in the last image, our method failed to detect and cover the whole object area.

The same as [16], we draw the PR-curve and calculate F-Measure to evaluate the performances of salient object detection methods. The results are shown in Fig. 4.

5   Conclusion

As traditional FCN generate low resolution results, we propose a novel recurrent architecture to generate high resolution saliency maps. We use a deep FCN to extract multi deep features and the initial saliency features for the recurrent architecture, then we feed the *double features* into the recurrent FCN. We treat the multi scale *double features* as time sequences, and recurrently feed the new *double features* generated from previous time step into a recurrent FCN. Finally, the proposed approach can generate full size saliency maps. We evaluate our method on 4 popular datasets, and our *RDF* achieves the best performance.

Acknowledgments. We acknowledge the support of National Natural Science Foundation of China (No. 61231018, No. 61273366), National Science and technology support program (2015BAH31F01), Program of introducing talents of discipline to university under grant B13043.

References

1. Achanta, R., Hemami, S., Estrada, F., Susstrunk, S.: Frequency-tuned salient region detection. In: 2009 IEEE Conference on Computer Vision and Pattern Recognition (2009)
2. Achanta, R., Shaji, A., Smith, K., Lucchi, A., Fua, P., Susstrunk, S.: SLIC superpixels compared to state-of-the-art superpixel methods. IEEE Trans. Pattern Anal. Mach. Intell. **34**(11), 2274–2282 (2012)
3. Batra, D., Kowdle, A., Parikh, D., Luo, J., Chen, T.: iCoseg: interactive cosegmentation with intelligent scribble guidance. In: 2010 IEEE Computer Society Conference on Computer Vision and Pattern Recognition (2010)
4. Cheng, M.M., Mitra, N.J., Huang, X., Torr, P.H.S., Hu, S.M.: Global contrast based salient region detection. IEEE Trans. Pattern Analy. Mach. Intell. **37**(3), 569–582 (2015)
5. Eigen, D., Puhrsch, C., Fergus, R.: Depth map prediction from a single image using a multi-scale deep network. In: Neural Information Processing Systems (2014)
6. Han, S.H., Jung, G.D., Lee, S.Y., Hong, Y.P., Lee, S.H.: Automatic salient object segmentation using saliency map and color segmentation. J. Cent. S. Univ. **20**(9), 2407–2413 (2013)
7. He, S., Lau, R.W.H.: Saliency detection with flash and no-flash image pairs. In: Fleet, D., Pajdla, T., Schiele, B., Tuytelaars, T. (eds.) ECCV 2014. LNCS, vol. 8691, pp. 110–124. Springer, Heidelberg (2014). doi:10.1007/978-3-319-10578-9_8
8. He, S., Lau, R.W.H., Liu, W., Huang, Z., Yang, Q.: SuperCNN: a superpixelwise convolutional neural network for salient object detection. Int. J. Comput. Vis. **115**(3), 330–344 (2015)

9. Huaizu, J., Jingdong, W., Zejian, Y., Yang, W., Nanning, Z., Shipeng, L.: Salient object detection: a discriminative regional feature integration approach. In: 2013 IEEE Conference on Computer Vision and Pattern Recognition (2013)
10. Ioffe, S., Szegedy, C.: Batch normalization: accelerating deep network training by reducing internal covariate shift (2015). arXiv:1502.03167
11. Itti, L., Koch, C., Niebur, E.: A model of saliency-based visual attention for rapid scene analysis. IEEE Trans. Pattern Anal. Mach. Intell. **20**(11), 1254–1259 (1998)
12. Khuwuthyakorn, P., Robles-Kelly, A., Zhou, J.: Object of interest detection by saliency learning. In: Daniilidis, K., Maragos, P., Paragios, N. (eds.) ECCV 2010. LNCS, vol. 6312, pp. 636–649. Springer, Heidelberg (2010). doi:10.1007/978-3-642-15552-9_46
13. Klein, D.A., Frintrop, S.: Center-surround divergence of feature statistics for salient object detection. In: 2011 International Conference on Computer Vision (2011)
14. Krizhevsky, A., Sutskever, I., Hinton, G.E.: Imagenet classification with deep convolutional neural networks. In: Pereira, F., Burges, C.J.C., Bottou, L., Weinberger, K.Q. (eds.) Advances in Neural Information Processing Systems 25, pp. 1097–1105. Curran Associates, Inc. (2012). http://papers.nips.cc/paper/4824-imagenet-classification-with-deep-convolutional-neural-networks.pdf
15. Li, C., Yuan, Y., Cai, W., Xia, Y., Feng, D.D.: Robust saliency detection via regularized random walks ranking. In: 2015 IEEE Conference on Computer Vision and Pattern Recognition (CVPR) (2015)
16. Li, G., Yu, Y.: Visual saliency based on multiscale deep features. In: 2015 IEEE Conference on Computer Vision and Pattern Recognition (CVPR) (2015)
17. Liu, T., Yuan, Z., Sun, J., Wang, J., Zheng, N., Tang, X., Shum, H.Y.: Learning to detect a salient object. IEEE Trans. Pattern Anal. Mach. Intell. **33**(2), 353–367 (2011)
18. Long, J., Shelhamer, E., Darrell, T.: Fully convolutional networks for semantic segmentation. In: 2015 IEEE Conference on Computer Vision and Pattern Recognition (CVPR) (2015)
19. Noh, H., Hong, S., Han, B.: Learning deconvolution network for semantic segmentation. In: 2015 IEEE International Conference on Computer Vision (ICCV), pp. 1520–1528 (2015)
20. Peng, H., Li, B., Xiong, W., Hu, W., Ji, R.: RGBD salient object detection: a benchmark and algorithms. In: Fleet, D., Pajdla, T., Schiele, B., Tuytelaars, T. (eds.) ECCV 2014. LNCS, vol. 8691, pp. 92–109. Springer, Heidelberg (2014). doi:10.1007/978-3-319-10578-9_7
21. Pinheiro, P., Collobert, R.: Recurrent convolutional neural networks for scene labeling. In: International Conference on Machine Learning, pp. 82–90 (2014)
22. Rahtu, E., Kannala, J., Salo, M., Heikkilä, J.: Segmenting salient objects from images and videos. In: Daniilidis, K., Maragos, P., Paragios, N. (eds.) ECCV 2010. LNCS, vol. 6315, pp. 366–379. Springer, Heidelberg (2010). doi:10.1007/978-3-642-15555-0_27
23. Sun, J., Lu, H., Li, S.: Saliency detection based on integration of boundary and soft-segmentation. In: 2012 19th IEEE International Conference on Image Processing (2012)
24. Tong, N., Lu, H., Zhang, Y., Ruan, X.: Salient object detection via global and local cues. Pattern Recogn. **48**(10), 3258–3267 (2015)
25. Wei, Y., Wen, F., Zhu, W., Sun, J.: Geodesic saliency using background priors. In: Fitzgibbon, A., Lazebnik, S., Perona, P., Sato, Y., Schmid, C. (eds.) ECCV 2012. LNCS, vol. 7574, pp. 29–42. Springer, Heidelberg (2012). doi:10.1007/978-3-642-33712-3_3

26. Yan, Q., Xu, L., Shi, J., Jia, J.: Hierarchical saliency detection. In: 2013 IEEE Conference on Computer Vision and Pattern Recognition (2013)
27. Zhao, R., Ouyang, W., Li, H., Wang, X.: Saliency detection by multi-context deep learning. In: 2015 IEEE Conference on Computer Vision and Pattern Recognition (CVPR) (2015)

Key Frame Extraction Based on Motion Vector

Ziqian Qiang[1], Qing Xu[1(✉)], Shihua Sun[1], and Mateu Sbert[1,2]

[1] School of Computer Science and Technology, Tianjin University,
Yaguan Road #135, Tianjin 300350, China
`qzq199334@gmail.com`, `qingxu@tju.edu.cn`, `qingxu.itcn@gmail.com`,
`sunshihua.stu@gmail.com`
[2] Graphics and Imaging Lab, Universitat de Girona,
Campus Montilivi, 17071 Girona, Spain
`mateu@ima.udg.edu`

Abstract. Video key frame extraction is a video summarization technique which is used to recapitulate and describe the most important segments of video sequence. Video clips containing motion information are more likely to draw users' attention. Accordingly, we propose a novel key frame extraction scheme based on motion vector. A video sequence is partitioned into shots by distance between consecutive video frames calculated by Relative Entropy (RE). Difference of magnitude of motion vector between neighboring video images within a shot is computed to localize video clips containing significant content changes. And such segments are defined as active sub-shots in this paper. The key frames are extracted from each active sub-shots and other inactive sub-shots by exploiting different algorithms. Experimental results show that our proposed method obtains exact and complete results in video key frame extraction.

Keywords: Key frame extraction · Motion vector

1 Introduction

With the sustained development of Internet video technology, video browsing becomes a principal way of obtaining information for people. Due to the explosive growth of video data volume, it is hard to understand the meaning of a huge amount of video information efficiently. Video key frame satisfies this requirement and provides an effective, comprehensive and accurate way for users to understand main content of video [11,15]. In order to obtain optimized results of key frame extraction, the design of extraction algorithm should conform to users' thought as much as possible. Apparently, more attention should be paid to the clips containing obvious changes than others [9]. It is crucial to localize significant video clips for improving accuracy of extraction. Therefore, a video sequence is firstly partitioned into a succession of concatenated shots based on the previously proposed methods in [5]. Then we exploit motion information as a an objective criteria directly, and propose a delicate sub-shots detection

© Springer International Publishing AG 2016
E. Chen et al. (Eds.): PCM 2016, Part II, LNCS 9917, pp. 387–395, 2016.
DOI: 10.1007/978-3-319-48896-7_38

approach based on motion vector. Magnitude of motion vector of each frame within a shot is calculated as a measure. If difference of magnitude of motion vector between current frame and next frame is larger than the mean value of this shot, current frame is considered as an active frame. Then weakly continuous active frames (it may have a few inactive frames) construct a video clip including significant content changes, namely, active sub-shot. Key frames are selected from each active sub-shot to obtain a result satisfying users' concerns and inactive sub-shots whose time duration is long enough to draw users' attention. It ensures the proposed technique could provide more exact and complete results of video key frame extraction. Consequently, our new approach has better performance than that of video key frame extraction simply employing RE.

The remainder of the paper is structured as follows. In Sect. 2, related work of segmenting video shot boundary is reviewed. Our proposed method of extracting key frames based on motion vector is summarized in Sect. 3. Experimental results are reported in Sect. 4, and finally Sect. 5 concludes the paper.

2   Related Work

Previous researchers have conducted copious studies on key frames extraction algorithms. Survey works [11,15] are the summarization of them for readers to consult. Since its compact mechanism and high efficiency, shot-based key frame extraction technique is considered as a best choice for practical application [7,14]. It has been demonstrated that information theoretic measures are suitable to be a measure of distance between video frames in key frame extraction algorithms [2,3], some characteristic examples based on information theory are shown in [10,13,16,17]. Mentzelopoulos *et al.* [10] propose a simple technique that difference between Shannon entropies of consecutive frames is calculated as a metric to determine video key frames. Key frames will be picked when the sum of Entropy Difference reaches threshold. Although the method is efficient, the result is not very satisfactory. Černeková *et al.* [16] present a work that compute the joint probability distribution between two images to obtain Mutual Information, which reflects the variation of video content. It really works, but fails to guarantee correctness in the case of conspicuous motion occurs. Omidyeganeh *et al.* [13] exploit the Kullback-Leibler divergence to measure distance between frames and detect shot and sub-shot boundaries. And then, key frames are picked from sub-shots. Due to the mechanism of selecting key frames requires a large number of compare to obtain a unique frame which is most-similar to the frames in the sub-shot and the most dissimilar to the others, its execution efficiency is very low. A scheme based on Jensen-Renyi Divergence has a great performance on key frame selection is shown in [17]. However, the accurate result relies on presetting an optimum value and each video has its own optimum value. Therefore, it is hard to get a standard value to adapt any type of video. An efficient and general method based on RE and Extreme Studentized Deviate Test is shown in [5], which provide an adaptive optimum value to segment shots for any kind of video. Moreover, it also has a good performance on significant content change detection, but it is insensitive to the motion without significant color change. Chong-Wah Ngo *et al.* [12] proposed a thinking which exploits motion attention modeling to highlight significant video clips. In this paper, we proposed a novel sub-shot detection method based on motion vector. It is on the basis of exact shot partition by previous work [5] and improves the results of motion detection than before.

3 Proposed Approach for Key Frame Extraction

For a shot-based video key frame extraction method, firstly video sequence is divided into shots by a robust shot boundary detection method proposed in our previous work [5], and then we reform process of detecting sub-shots by replacing information theoretic measures based on color histogram with motion vector. Within a shot, video clips with obvious change of motion vector is marked as active sub-shots, the other segments are inactive sub-shots. We extract one key frame in each active sub-shot and long enough inactive sub-shot. We are going to give a detailed description of motion vector and sub-shot detection method in Subsects. 3.1.1 and 3.1.2, respectively.

3.1 A New Sub-shot Boundary Detection Method

Sub-shot boundary detection implement on the basis of shots partition. Firstly, motion vector is computed to represent how video contents change. Then, active sub-shots is detected by matching weakly continuous pattern which are detailed in Subsects. 3.1.2.

3.1.1 Motion Vector

Motion vector is a measure of the degree of contents change. The higher magnitude of motion vector is, the faster video contents change. The core computational mechanism of motion vector is that each frame is divided into blocks, and each block has a most similar matching block in next frame. Displacement between current block and best matching block is computed to become the motion vector of current block. We exploit a well-known search algorithm "Three Step Search" [6] which has low search times and preferable result with Mean Absolute Difference (MAD) to search the best matching block. If there exists displacement (i_0, j_0) let MAD get the minimal value, then this displacement is the motion vector of current block (MV_{block}),

$$MAD_{block}(i,j) = \frac{1}{MN} \sum_{m=1}^{M} \sum_{n=1}^{N} |f_c(m,n) - f_{c+1}(m+i, n+j)|, \qquad (1)$$

here (i,j) is displacement, M and N is the height and width of a block. f_c is current frame, f_{c+1} is next frame. $f_c(m,n)$ is the pixel value of point (m,n). Sum

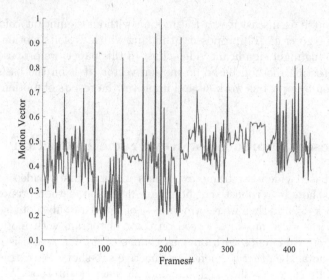

Fig. 1. A motion vector curve of test video.

of blocks motion vector represents how fast content of current frame changes,

$$MV_{frame} = \sum_{t=1}^{T} MV_{block}(t), \qquad (2)$$

$$MV_i = \frac{MV_{frame}(i)}{max(MV_{frame})}, \qquad (3)$$

here T is the total block number of a frame. MV_{frame} is the sum of all MV_{block} within current frame, MV_i is a normalized metric of current frame and final result obtained from the original video. With frames changing, the curve of motion vector is shown in Fig. 1.

3.1.2 Sub-shot Boundary Detection

Several undulant segments can be observed in motion vector curve shown in Fig. 1. These curve segments practically match active sub-shots. The core mechanism of sub-shot detection scheme is locating undulant parts of motion vector curve and thus active sub-shots is detected. We are going to ensure the boundary of active sub-shots and extract key frames by the result of sub-shot detection.

In order to detect the boundary of undulant fragment, within a shot, absolute value of motion vector difference between two consecutive frames (DMV) is calculated to evaluate the degree of fluctuation,

$$DMA_a = |MV_a - MV_{a+1}|, \qquad (4)$$

here DMV_a is a measure of degree of fluctuation at frame a. A higher DMV_a value of current frame represents the frame has obvious changes of state of motion

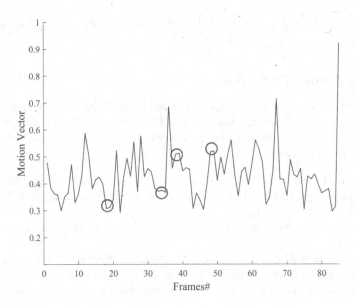

Fig. 2. An example of weakly continuous pattern. Frames corresponding low DMV value are marked by red circles. (Color figure online)

between frame a and $a+1$, and *vice versa*. We exploit DMV as a measure rather MV, because MV just represents how fast video contents change and is similar to "velocity". If there are continuous high MV value without obvious difference, no abrupt change will happen. Contents change can be found in such clips, but it is regular and internal frames are parallel. For instance, there is a man running fast in a video clip, which will cause continuous high MV occurs, but its value is subequal. Such clips with regular motion cannot be classified as active sub-shots. Relatively, DMV is more like "acceleration" which could reflect how MV changes. We consider that clips corresponding continuous high DMV value match the undulant segments, and namely ensure active sub-shots. In reality, due to the uncertainly of motion, the situation that continuous high DMV value mixed a handful of low DMV value may happen. If we detect sub-shots boundary in according with the principle that high DMV value must be continuous, an entire movement process is likely to being divided into several relevant active sub-shots, which will result in the generation of redundancy. In order to guarantee the integrity of motion and reduce redundancy, we locate the boundary of active sub-shots by matching the pattern of weakly continuous high DMV value. Weakly continuous pattern allow the appearance of continual frames corresponding low DMV value whose length is less than L. Weakly continuous pattern can also be considered as a combination of strict sub-shots detection and clustering. This procedure ensures the integrity of each movement and reduces noise interference. An example of weakly continuous pattern is shown in Fig. 2. According to our repetitive test, here L is taken as 12 (FPS of test video is 24 and we consider half second is a appropriate length).

3.2   Key Frames Extraction

The strategy of key frame extraction is based on the result of sub-shots boundaries detection. We obtain the boundaries of active sub-shots and namely ensure the inactive sub-shots. In terms of the partition of sub-shots, the criteria of key frames extraction is as follows.

1. If there is at least one active sub-shot in a shot, we extract key frames from all active sub-shots and inactive sub-shots whose length is more than 24 frames (FPS of test video is 24).
2. If there is no active sub-shots in a shot, we consider such shots as inactive sub-shots.
3. For the active sub-shots, we choose the frames which have minimum sum of RE difference between other frames and itself as key frames.
4. For the inactive sub-shots, we select the middle frame as key frames.

4   Experimental Result

In order to verify the effect of the proposed scheme and guarantee the accuracy of results, we exploit same shot boundary detection algorithm (RE). The main distinction is that basis of dividing sub-shots is change of color or motion vector. Therefore, in our experiment, we compare previous method based on RE with our proposed motion vector driven technique.

Test videos consist of common videos containing obvious motion and some sports videos. Sports videos, such as football videos and basketball videos, usually have a lot of object and camera motions and less changes of scene.

For instance, test video "NBA04" is divided into 6 shots by RE driven shot detection method. Due to the few scene changes and color changes caused by motion of players within a basketball video shot, there is no sub-shots found

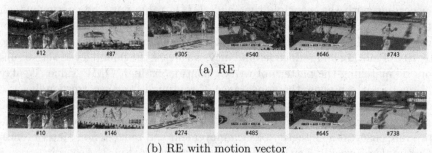

(a) RE

(b) RE with motion vector

Fig. 3. Contrast of two methods on video "NBA04".

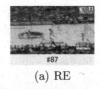

(a) RE

(b) RE with motion vector

Fig. 4. Contrast of two methods in a shot of video "NBA04". More detailed and significant key frames are extracted by our new method. Five key frames extracted within this shot respectively represent "interception", "dribble", "positioning", "shoot" and "defence".

by previous method. Comparatively, on one hand, our new method can provide robust results in the case of no motion occurs. One the other hand, our new scheme provides more meaningful results for users than RE. As is shown in Fig. 3, previous method simply extracts middle frames as key frames while our new scheme extracts key frames from detected active sub-shots. Besides, our new method can provide more detailed results. As is shown in Fig. 4, for a same shot,

Table 1. VSE and FID of test video.

RE						RE with MV					
No	FID	VSE	No	FID	VSE	No	FID	VSE	No	FID	VSE
1	0.81	76.32	15	0.25	790.4	1	0.81	60.91	15	0.32	587.59
2	0.60	73.07	16	0.38	667.17	2	0.60	60.14	16	0.44	490.47
3	0.36	493.39	17	0.22	812.36	3	0.37	454.17	17	0.33	533.84
4	0.371	665.45	18	0.37	656.89	4	0.40	507.64	18	0.47	433.46
5	0.36	673.56	19	0.28	778.08	5	0.37	586.93	19	0.36	485.82
6	0.40	625.45	20	0.30	730.34	6	0.42	407.46	20	0.41	520.75
7	0.28	762.84	21	0.29	736.25	7	0.40	467.78	21	0.35	574.46
8	0.33	690.30	22	0.33	689.92	8	0.37	414.70	22	0.31	615.23
9	0.34	672.12	23	0.34	744.33	9	0.37	452.96	23	0.44	526.58
10	0.31	728.44	24	0.37	651.34	10	0.40	438.6	24	0.42	434.97
11	0.40	642.93	25	0.33	682.41	11	0.50	385.73	25	0.47	440.45
12	0.40	654.13	26	0.21	813.94	12	0.47	482.83	26	0.32	551.22
13	0.35	671.02	27	0.27	753.53	13	0.45	429.24	27	0.32	551.50
14	0.43	580.01	28	0.30	717.94	14	0.48	374.18	28	0.33	589.61

the middle frame (#87) is simply picked as key frame by RE driven method, but five frames (#50, #120, #146, #171, #194) which respectively represent "interception", "dribble", "positioning", "shoot" and "defence" are selected by our new method. For sports enthusiasts, our new method apparently offer a better user experience.

Video Sampling Error (VSE) [8] and Fidelity (FID) [1,4] are used to measure the difference between initial video and extracted key frames and thus an objective evaluation of proposed method is obtained. A larger FID and a lower VSE demonstrates that the approach has a great performance on key frame extraction. Although results of our new method usually have more key frames than RE and there is a positive correlation between the number of key frames and VSE value, the VSE value of our new method is still less than RE. The VSE and FID of test video is shown in Table 1, which indicates that RE with motion vector performs better than RE [5].

5   Conclusion and Future Work

We propose a novel key frame extraction scheme based on motion vector. Based on the shot boundaries detected by our previous work, motion vector is utilized as a measure to locate active sub-shots in order to extract more significant key frames within these sub-shots. Experimental results demonstrate that utilizing motion vector to detect sub-shots can obtain better video summarization on motion than the previous work, especially for sports videos. In addition, our method has been proved to be integral on improving accuracy of video key frame extraction.

For the future work, several improvements will be carried out. We are going to utilize motion vector extracted from video bitstream to reduce the calculation cost of motion vector, and enhance the performance of shot detection for video sequence with gradual content change.

Acknowledgments. This work has been funded by Natural Science Foundation of China (61471261, 61179067, U1333110), and by grants TIN2013-47276-C6-1-R from Spanish Government and 2014-SGR-1232 from Catalan Government (Spain).

References

1. Chang, H.S., Sull, S., Lee, S.U.: Efficient video indexing scheme for content-based retrieval. IEEE Trans. Circ. Syst. Video Technol. **9**, 1269–1279 (1999)
2. Escolano, F., Suau, P., Bonev, B.: Information Theory in Computer Vision and Pattern Recognition. Springer, London (2009)
3. Feixas, M., Bardera, A., Rigau, J., Xu, Q., Sbert, M.: Information Theory Tools for Image Processing. Morgan & Claypool, San Rafael (2014)
4. Gianluigi, C., Raimondo, S.: An innovative algorithm for key frame extraction in video summarization. J. Real-Time Image Proc. **1**, 69–88 (2006)
5. Guo, Y., Xu, Q., Sun, S., Luo, X., Sbert, M.: Selecting video key frames based on relative entropy and the extreme studentized deviate test. Entropy **18**(3), 73 (2016)

6. Li, R., Zeng, B., Liou, M.L.: A new three-step search algorithm for block motion estimation. IEEE Trans. Circ. Syst. Video Technol. 4(4), 438–442 (1994)
7. Lienhart, R., Pfeiffer, S., Effelsberg, W.: Video abstracting. Commun. ACM **40**, 54–62 (1997)
8. Liu, T., Kender, J.R.: Computational approaches to temporal sampling of video sequences. ACM Trans. Multimedia Comput. Commun. Appl. **3**, 217–218 (2007)
9. Ma, Y.F., Lu, L., Zhang, H.J., Li, M.: A user attention model for video summarization. In: Proceedings of the Tenth ACM International Conference on Multimedia, pp. 533–542. ACM (2002)
10. Mentzelopoulos, M., Psarrou, A.: Key-frame extraction algorithm using entropy difference. In: Proceedings of the 6th ACM SIGMM International Workshop on Multimedia Information Retrieval, pp. 39–45. ACM. New York, October 2004
11. Money, A.G., Agius, H.: Video summarisation: a conceptual framework and survey of the state of the art. J. Vis. Commun. Image Represent. **19**, 121–143 (2008)
12. Ngo, C.W., Ma, Y.F., Zhang, H.J.: Video summarization and scene detection by graph modeling. IEEE Trans. Circ. Syst. Video Technol. **15**(2), 296–305 (2005)
13. Omidyeganeh, M., Ghaemmaghami, S., Shirmohammadi, S.: Video keyframe analysis using a segment-based statistical metric in a visually sensitive parametric space. IEEE Trans. Image Process. Publ. IEEE Signal Process. Soc. **20**, 2730–2737 (2011)
14. Souza, C.L., Pádua, F.L.C., Nunes, C.F.G., Assis, G.T., Silva, G.D.: A unified approach to content-based indexing and retrieval of digital videos from television archives. Artif. Intell. Res. **3**(3), 49–61 (2014)
15. Truong, B.T., Venkatesh, S.: Video abstraction: a systematic review and classification. ACM Trans. Multimedia Comput. Commun. Appl. **3**, 3 (2007)
16. Černeková, Z., Pitas, I., Nikou, C.: Information theory-based shot cut/fade detection and video summarization. IEEE Trans. Circ. Syst. Video Technol. **16**, 82–91 (2006)
17. Xu, Q., Liu, Y., Li, X., Yang, Z., Wang, J., Sbert, M., Scopigno, R.: Browsing and exploration of video sequences: a new scheme for key frame extraction and 3D visualization using entropy based Jensen divergence. Inf. Sci. **278**, 736–756 (2014)

Haze Removal Technology Based on Physical Model

Yunqian Cui and Xinguang Xiang[✉]

School of Computer Science and Engineering,
Nanjing University of Science and Technology,
Nanjing 210094, People's Republic of China
yunqiancui@gmail.com, xgxiang@njust.edu.cn

Abstract. In this paper, we present a novel image dehazing method based on physical model. In this new approach, we get the scene transmission by calculating the scattering coefficient and the scene depth. In the process of solving the scattering coefficient, haze particle diameter is considered. In different weather conditions, we pick appropriate haze particle diameter to achieve the best dehazing effect. The scene depth is estimated by factorizing from a single hazy image. Moreover, we can estimate better scene depth using stereo matching method. The results demonstrate that our algorithm achieves more accurate dehazing effect compared with several state-of-the-art methods.

Keywords: Dehazing · Physical model · Scattering coefficient · Depth

1 Introduction

In most cases, the outdoor computer vision system is built on the clear and accurate image features. However, outdoor computer vision system is sensitive to the weather, light and many other conditions. Among the numerous meteorological conditions, haze and fog are the most common natural phenomena. The captured images in hazy weather will be seriously degraded. So, it is important to improve the visual effect of the degraded images.

Dehazing or defogging is the process to remove haze effects in captured images and reconstruct the original colors of natural scenes. Dehazing from image is a promising and significant issue, research results can be widely used in aerial photography, topographic survey, intelligent driving and video surveillance. There are many methods to deal with degraded images, generally divided into two broad classes: contrast enhancement techniques and image restoration methods based on physical degraded model. Contrast enhancement techniques mainly include histogram equalization and contrast stretching. Stark [1] proposes generalized local histogram equalization method, will expand the scope of the histogram equalization. However, bad weather effects depend strongly on the depth of scene point, simple contrast enhancement techniques can not achieve the expectation [2]. Image restoration methods mainly include single image and multiple images dehazing. Nayar [3] removes the haze effects through two or more

© Springer International Publishing AG 2016
E. Chen et al. (Eds.): PCM 2016, Part II, LNCS 9917, pp. 396–405, 2016.
DOI: 10.1007/978-3-319-48896-7_39

images taken with different conditions of weather. Although this method can provide acceptable result, the requirement cannot always be satisfied. Recently, single image dehazing methods have made significant progresses. The success of these methods is largely dependent on strong priors and assumptions. Fattal [4] estimates the albedo of the scene and the medium transmission under the assumption that the transmission and the surface shading are locally uncorrelated. Tarel [5] uses improved median filter to estimate atmospheric dissipation function assuming that atmospheric dissipation function in the feasible region approaching the maximum. He [6] proposes a novel dark channel prior based on the statistics of outdoor haze-free images that most local patches contain some pixels whose intensity are very low in at least one color channel.

In this paper, we propose a novel dehazing method based on physical model. This method is based on the assumption that the haze particles are round and have same size. According to atmospheric light model we derive that transmission has relationship with scattering coefficient and scene depth. So, we get a relatively accurate transmission map by calculating scattering coefficient and scene depth. In the process of solving the scattering coefficient, we consider the diameter of haze particles as an important parameter. Next, we estimate the scene depth by probabilistic method. Then we get the global atmospheric light by dark channel of the hazy image. Finally, according to hazy image degradation model, we can get a clear haze-free image.

This paper is organized as follows. We begin by introducing the background in Sect. 2. Sections 3 and 4 present the physical-based dehazing method we proposed. Section 5 presents the experiment results. Finally, in Sect. 6 we conclude this paper.

2   Background

In computer vision, the model widely used to describe the formation of a hazy image is [2–6]:

$$I(x) = J(x)t(x) + A(1 - t(x)) \tag{1}$$

where $I(x)$ denotes the observed hazy image, $J(x)$ denotes the scene radiance (the clear haze-free image), A denotes the global atmospheric light treated as a constant, $t(x)$ denotes the medium transmission reflecting the ability of light to penetrate the haze. The higher value of $t(x)$ indicates that more reflected light penetrates the haze and reaches the viewer's field of scene. Figure 1 shows the pictorial description of this model.

This physical model of hazy image is the theoretical basis of our research. From Eq. (1) we can see that the goal of haze removal is to recover $J(x)$, A and $t(x)$ from $I(x)$. This is an ill-posed problem owing to A and $t(x)$ are unknown. Therefore, we need to estimate transmission $t(x)$ and atmospheric light A.

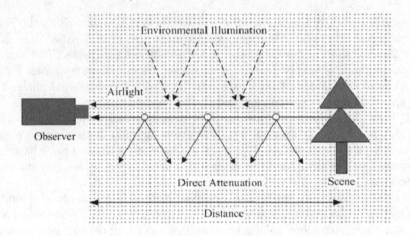

Fig. 1. The pictorial description of the atmosphere model.

3   Estimating the Transmission

According to the physical model of hazy image, when the atmosphere is homogeneous, transmission can be defined as:

$$t(x) = e^{-\beta d(x)} \tag{2}$$

where β is the scattering coefficient of the atmosphere and $d(x)$ is the scene depth. Obviously, if we want to estimate the transmission, we can estimate β and $d(x)$.

3.1   Estimating the Scattering Coefficient

We assume that the particles of haze are homogeneous and have same size. Under this assumption, we can get the expression of scattering coefficient [7]:

$$\beta = 1.5 * Q_s * \frac{f_v}{D} \tag{3}$$

where Q_s is scattering efficiency, f_v is the volume percentage which is set 10^{-6} in this paper, D is spherical particle diameter, i.e. haze particle diameter here. The scattering efficiency follows from the integration of the scattered power over all directions [8], determined by the following formula:

$$Q_s = \frac{2}{x^2} \sum_{n=1}^{\infty} (2n+1)(\mid a_n \mid^2 + \mid b_n \mid^2) \tag{4}$$

where a_n, b_n are Mie coefficients, $x = k * a$ is size parameter, a is radius of the haze particle and $k = 2\pi/\lambda$ is the wave number, λ is wavelength in the ambient medium. The Mie coefficients are given in BH [9]:

$$a_n = \frac{m^2 j_n(mx)\,[x j_n(x)]' - \mu_1 j_n(x)\,[m x j_n(mx)]'}{m^2 j_n(mx)\left[x h_n^{(1)}(x)\right]' - \mu_1 h_n^{(1)}(x)\,[m x j_n(mx)]'} \tag{5}$$

$$b_n = \frac{\mu_1 j_n(mx)\,[x j_n(x)]' - j_n(x)\,[m x j_n(mx)]'}{\mu_1 j_n(mx)\left[x h_n^{(1)}(x)\right]' - h_n^{(1)}(x)\,[m x j_n(mx)]'} \tag{6}$$

where m is the refractive index of the sphere relative to the ambient medium, μ_1 is the ratio of the magnetic permeability of the sphere to the magnetic permeability of the ambient medium. The functions $j_n(z)$ and $h_n^{(1)}(z) = j_n(z) + i y_n(z)$ are spherical Bessel functions of order $n(n = 1, 2, ...)$ and of the given arguments, $z = x$ or mx, respectively, and primes mean derivatives with respect to the argument. We acquire the values of a_n and b_n according to Eqs. (5) and (6). Putting a_n and b_n into Eq. (4), we can get scattering efficiency Q_s. Putting Q_s into Eq. (3), we can get the scattering coefficient.

It is worth mentioning that past haze removal approaches do not consider the diameter of haze particles. In this paper, we consider haze particle diameter as an important parameter. We find that, choosing appropriate haze particle diameter in different weather conditions will get better dehazing result. Based on the statistics of outdoor hazy and foggy images, we find that, degraded images can be separated into three classes: hazy, thin foggy and dense foggy images. Hazy images have the smallest particle diameter and the average is $2\,\mu$m. The average diameter of thin foggy images is $10\,\mu$m and dense foggy is $30\,\mu$m. The process of classifying the degraded images is shown in Fig. 2.

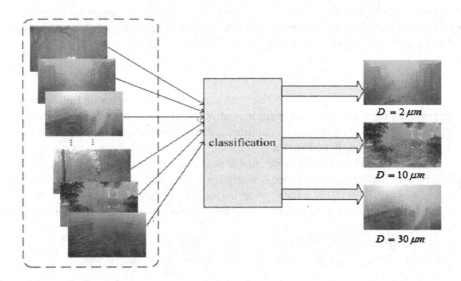

Fig. 2. The classification of the degraded images.

3.2 Estimating the Scene Depth

Scene depth indicates the structural information of the scene, can be seen the distance from the target point to the camera plane. We factorize the scene depth from a single hazy image via maximizing the Bayesian posterior probability [10]. Firstly, we normalize the hazy image model Eq. (1) by A and simple algebraic rearrangements:

$$ln(\frac{I(x)}{A} - 1) = ln(\rho(x) - 1) - \beta d(x) \tag{7}$$

where $\rho(x) = J(x)/A$ is the scene albedo. To simplify the expression, the Eq. (7) can be expressed:

$$\widetilde{I}(x) = C(x) + D(x) \tag{8}$$

where $\widetilde{I}(x)$ denotes the log of airlight-normalized input image offset by 1, $C(x)$ denotes the $ln(\rho(x) - 1)$, $D(x)$ denotes the $-\beta d(x)$. Afterwards, modeling the image with a Factorial Markov Random Field [11] (FMRF) in which the scene albedo($C(x)$) and depth($D(x)$) are two statistically independent latent layers. According to natural statistics of both the albedo and depth of the scene, we model the gradient distribution of the hazy image's chromaticity by fitting an exponential power distribution to the histogram and use it as a prior on the albedo. For scene depth, we impose a Laplace distribution prior. Simultaneously, we assume the noise inherent in the observations with Gaussian distributions, which is independent both componentwise and pixelwise, with zeros mean and variance σ^2:

$$p(\widetilde{I} \mid C, D) = \prod_x N(\widetilde{I} \mid C(x) + D(x), \sigma^2) \tag{9}$$

Finally, we factorize the albedo and depth from the hazy image by maximizing the Eq. (10) posterior probability via a canonical Expectation Maximization algorithm. The recovered depth results are shown in Fig. 3b.

$$p(C, D \mid \widetilde{I}) \propto p(\widetilde{I} \mid C, D)p(C)p(D) \tag{10}$$

From the results, we can see that the top and middle rows of Fig. 3b have accurate depth map due to the simple spatial information of the original image. When the spatial information is complicated, the depth result has many errors shown in red rectangle of Fig. 3b.

In order to get more accurate depth map, stereo matching method [12] is used in this paper. We use a stereo matching algorithm named a non-local cost aggregation (NLCA) [13] which performs non-local cost aggregation over the image with a minimum spanning tree (MST). The process of this algorithm is as follows:

1. Constructing the MST based on weight formula

Letting s and r be a pair of neighboring pixels, the weight between s and r is

$$w(s, r) = w(r, s) = |I(s) - I(r)| \tag{11}$$

2. Defining the similarity between two image pixels using a MST

(a)   (b)

Fig. 3. (a) Input hazy images. (b) The depth maps. (Color figure online)

The distance between the two nodes is the evaluation indicator of measuring the degree of similarity of two pixels.

$$S(p,q) = S(q,p) = exp(-\frac{D(p,q)}{\sigma})$$ (12)

3. Matching cost aggregation

The formula of cost aggregation is as follows:

$$C_d^A(p) = \sum_q S(p,q)C_d(q) = \sum_q exp(-\frac{D(p,q)}{\sigma})C_d(q)$$ (13)

4. Disparity choose

According to the Winner-Take-All principle to choose the optimal disparity. The finally disparity, i.e. depth map, is shown in Fig. 4c. With scattering coefficient and scene depth, we can get transmission map.

(a)   (b)   (c)

Fig. 4. (a) and (b) are the input image set. (c) is the depth map.

4   Estimating the Atmospheric Light

In the previous single image haze removal methods, the color of the most haze-opaque region is usually regarded as the atmospheric light. Tan [14] selects the highest intensity pixel in hazy image as the value of atmospheric light A. However, the highest intensity pixel may be on a white object such as a white car or a white building.

In this paper, we estimate the global atmosphere light via dark channel. The dark channel can be described as: non-sky patches in outdoor images often have some low intensity pixels in at least one color channel. For an image J, the dark channel value of a pixel x is defined as:

$$J^{dark}(x) = min_{y \in \Omega(x)}(min_{c \in \{r,g,b\}} J^c(y)) \tag{14}$$

where J_c is a color channel of J, J is an outdoor hazy image, $\Omega(x)$ is a local patch around pixel x. Due to the additive airlight, a hazy image is brighter than its haze-free version. So, the dark channel of a hazy image will have higher intensity in regions with denser haze. We can find the most haze-opaque region from dark channel. Therefore, We first select the top 0.1 % brightest pixels from the dark channel of hazy image. Then we choose the pixel with brightest intensity as the atmospheric light A from the corresponding pixels in hazy image. The process is shown in Fig. 5.

Fig. 5. The process of estimating the atmosphere light.

5   Experimental Results

In this section, the results of the proposed method will be shown and compared
with several state-of-the-art haze removal methods. Figure 6 shows the results of
our method compared with He's method based on dark channel. We used haze
particle diameter of 10 µm. Note that He's method has residual haze at the edge
of image, but our method achieves perfect and nature results.

In Fig. 7, we compare our approach with Fattal's work. We used haze particle diameter of 10 µm. From Fig. 7, we can see that our approach outperforms
Fattal's method. Though his result has higher brightness than our result, the
result loses the original color of image. Our approach can better restore the
original image color.

Next, we compared our approach with Kratz's work. We used haze particle
diameter of 30 µm. Kratz factorizes the scene albedo from a single hazy image
to approximate the clear haze-free image. The results of this method have over-
saturated colors shown in Fig. 8. Our approach gives more natural color and
accurate results.

In Sect. 3.2, we know that making use of the stereo matching method in image
set can get more accurate depth map, thereby, get more accurate transmission
map. So, we compare our single image dehazing method with image set dehazing
in Fig. 9. Note that the results of image set dehazing have more clear vision effect
than single dehazing. Moreover, single dehazing method result has residual haze
not removed in the red rectangle of Fig. 9 compared with image set dehazing.

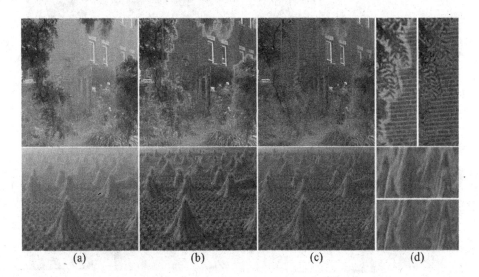

Fig. 6. Comparison with He's work [6]. (a) Input hazy images. (b) He's haze removal
results. (c) Our haze removal results. (d) Close-up of the red rectangles in (b) and (c).
(Color figure online)

(a)   (b)   (c)   (d)

Fig. 7. Comparison with Fattal's work [4]. (a) Input image. (b) Estimated transmission map. (c) Fattal's result. (d) Our haze removal result. (Color figure online)

(a)   (b)   (c)

Fig. 8. Compare with Kratz's work [10]. (a) Input hazy images. (b) Kratz's haze removal results (c) Our results (Color figure online)

(a)   (b)   (c)   (d)   (e)

Fig. 9. Comparison with image set dehazing. (a) Input images. (b) Depth maps using probabilistic method. (c) Depth maps using stereo matching method. (d) Single image dehazing results. (e) Image set dehazing results. (Color figure online)

6   Conclusion

In this paper, we have proposed a novel image dehazing method based on physical model. We get a relatively accurate transmission map by calculating scattering coefficient and scene depth. During computing the scattering coefficient, we pick the appropriate haze particle diameter to achieve the best dehazing effect in different weather conditions. We next factorize the depth from hazy image by maximizing posterior probability. Then we estimate the atmospheric light via the dark channel of hazy image. Finally, we obtain a clear image from the physical model formulation. Moreover, we find that if using stereo matching method, the dehazing effect will be better.

Acknowledgments. This work was supported in part by the 863 Program (2014AA015101), and the Natural Science Foundation of China under Grant 61301106 and 61327013.

References

1. Stark, J.A.: Adaptive image contrast enhancement using generalizations of histogram equalization. IEEE Trans. Image Process. **9**(5), 889–896 (2000)
2. Narasimhan, S.G., Nayar, S.K.: Vision and the atmosphere. Int. J. Comput. Vis. **48**(3), 233–254 (2002)
3. Schechner, Y.Y., Narasimhan, S.G., Nayar, S.K.: Instant dehazing of images using polarization. In: Proceedings of the 2001 IEEE Computer Society Conference on Computer Vision, Pattern Recognition, CVPR 2001, p. 325 (2011)
4. Fattal, R.: Single image dehazing. ACM Trans. Graph. **27**(3), 1–9 (2008)
5. Tarel, J.P., Hautiere, N.: Fast visibility restoration from a single color or gray level image. In: IEEE International Conference on Computer Vision, pp. 2201–2208 (2009)
6. He, K., Sun, J., Tang, X.: Single image haze removal using dark channel prior. In: Conference on Computer Vision, Pattern Recognition, pp. 2341–2353. IEEE Computer Society (2011)
7. Hespel, L., Mainguy, S., Greffet, J.J.: Radiative properties of scattering and absorbing dense media: theory and experimental study. J. Quant. Spectrosc. Radiat. Transfer **77**(2), 193–210 (2003)
8. Tien, C.L., Drolen, B.L.: Thermal radiation in particulate media with dependent and independent scattering. Ann. Rev. Heat Transfer **1**(1) (1987)
9. Bohren, C.F., Huffman, D.R., Kam, Z.: Book-review - absorption and scattering of light by small particles. Nature **306**(306), 675 (1983)
10. Kratz, L., Nishino, K.: Factorizing scene Albedo and depth from a single foggy image, pp. 1701–1708 (2009)
11. Kim, J., Zabih, R.: Factorial markov random fields. In: Heyden, A., Sparr, G., Nielsen, M., Johansen, P. (eds.) ECCV 2002. LNCS, vol. 2352, pp. 321–334. Springer, Heidelberg (2002). doi:10.1007/3-540-47977-5_21
12. Scharstein, D., Szeliski, R.: A taxonomy and evaluation of dense two-frame stereo correspondence algorithms. In: Stereo and Multi-Baseline Vision, pp. 131–140. IEEE (2002)
13. Yang, Q.: A non-local cost aggregation method for stereo matching. In: IEEE Conference on Computer Vision Pattern Recognition, pp. 1402–1409 (2012)
14. Tan, R.T.: Visibility in bad weather from a single image, pp. 1–8 (2008)

Robust Uyghur Text Localization in Complex Background Images

Jianjun Chen[1,2], Yun Song[1], Hongtao Xie[2(✉)], Xi Chen[1], Han Deng[2], and Yizhi Liu[3]

[1] School of Computer and Communication Engineering,
Changsha University of Science and Technology, Changsha, China
[2] Institute of Information Engineering, Chinese Academy of Sciences,
Beijing, China
xiehongtao@iie.ac.cn
[3] School of Computer Science and Engineering,
Hunan University of Science and Technology, Xiangtan, China

Abstract. Text localization in complex background images remains a challenging task, especially for Uyghur text. Since the existing methods mostly focus on English and Chinese. Uyghur as a minority language is paid less attention. This paper proposes a robust and precise method for locating Uyghur texts in complex background images. Firstly, a multi-color-channel enhanced Maximally Stable Extremal Regions (MSERs) extraction scheme is used to capture text components robustly. Then, the strong classification and retrieve strategy (SCRS) accurately identifies text components. Finally, our method precisely connects text components into lines according to component connectivity. The proposed method is evaluated on the UICBI400 dataset, and the *F-measure* is over 82.8%, which is much better than the state-of-the-art performance of 61.6%.

Keywords: Text detection · Text localization · MSERs · Uyghur extraction

1 Introduction

Text in images commonly contains valuable information. Text localization in images has been the key of image/video text recognition and analysis applications [1, 10]. Although, text localization has been studied for recent years, it still is a challenging task, especially for Uyghur text localization. The current related works concentrate on English and Chinese [2–8, 13], and cannot achieve good Uyghur text localization results, as because of the Uyghur character is very different from English or Chinese on aspect ratio, stroke and join-up writing. In this paper, we focus on Uyghur language localization in the complex background images. Since 8 ~ 11 millions of people using Uyghur language in all over the world[1], the Uyghur text localization has a wide application prospect.

---

[1] The statistical data comes from http://en.wikipedia.org/wiki/Uyghur_language.

© Springer International Publishing AG 2016
E. Chen et al. (Eds.): PCM 2016, Part II, LNCS 9917, pp. 406–416, 2016.
DOI: 10.1007/978-3-319-48896-7_40

Recently, the Maximally Stable Extremal Regions (MSERs) based text localization methods are widely used [5–7]. These methods extract MSERs as text components, and have achieved state-of-the-art performance on the widely used ICDAR 2011 dataset [9]. However, several problems of the MSERs remain to be addressed. First, the MSER region detector is sensitive to blur, which may misses text components during component extraction, and the missed text components cannot be recovered in following stages. Second, the MSER extracts a lot of repeating components. These repeating components are redundant for latter processes, and the current methods for MSERs pruning [4, 6] are complex. Third, existing approaches [3–8] for component classification can be categorized as manual-feature based and learning-feature based methods, both work well but are still insufficient. The component classification with manual-feature [4–7] usually extracts text features depend on experience of human, which is time-consuming. While the component classification with learning-feature [8] learns text features by a convolution neural network (CNN) automatically, which shows good performance but the training and calculation are complex. Finally, the extracted Uyghur text components are multi-level, and may be a character or a joined-up writing of several characters. But current component classification methods is mainly effective for character-level component differentiation [5–7].

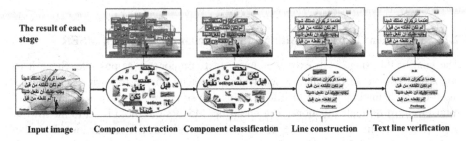

Fig. 1. Flowchart of the proposed method and the corresponding result of each stage. The components/lines are labeled by red bounding rectangles.

In order to tackle the problems mentioned above, this paper proposes a robust Uyghur text localization method with multi-color-channel enhanced MSERs and the strong classification and retrieve strategy (SCRS). The flowchart of our method is illustrated in Fig. 1. The main contributions of this paper are:

(1) We propose a multi-color-channel enhanced MSERs extraction, which is highly robust to blur, low-resolution and low-contraction. The MSER extraction contains two steps, the multi-color-channel MSER extracting and the rapid duplication removing, to enhance the raw MSER. The former makes our system reach a high recall. The latter reduce the redundancy for the following processes.

(2) We use the SCRS to precisely distinguish texts from a large number of non-text components. The SCRS includes two phases, the strong classification and the retrieve. In the strong classification phase, two strong classifiers cause low recall, but which also accurately identify texts form non-texts. So in the retrieve phase, to

restore the recall, the misclassification text is found back according to the similarity between it and the identified texts.

(3) Our method automatically learns the spacing between words by the effective line construction scheme, which precisely groups text components into text lines.

The remainder of the paper is organized as follows. Section 2 describes the proposed method of Uyghur localization in complex background images in detail. Section 3 presents the classifier training method and the experimental result. Finally, the conclusion is drew in Sect. 4.

2 Proposed Method

The main processes of our Uyghur text localization method are shown in Fig. 1. The proposed method consist of four stages: (1) component extraction, (2) component classification, (3) line construction, and (4) text line verification. In the first stage, components are extracted using the multi-color-channel enhanced MSERs. In the second stage, text components are identified by the SCRS. In the third stage, lines are constructed via component connection. Finally, lines corresponding to true text lines are verified by the text line classifier.

2.1 Component Extraction with Multi-color-channel Enhanced MSER

The goal of this stage is to extract as many text components as possible. Since it is almost impossible to find the missed text components in the following stages. The multi-color-channel enhanced MSER contains two strategies, which make our method robust to most difficult situations. The one is the MSERs threshold is set to the lowest value 1, and the other is the multi-color-channel MSER extraction. For the multi-color-channel MSER extraction, the input image is split into three channel images, and then MSERs are extracted separately in each channel image. The final component extraction result is the merged MSERs of all channels. Although these two strategies increase a lot of non-text components and repeating components, they also reduce the loss of text components in challenging cases. The two strategies make the proposed method achieve a high recall. The illustration of the multi-color-channel MSERs extraction is presented in Fig. 2.

As mentioned above, the merged result contains a lot of repeating MSERs, which will cause slow computation. So the repetitions have to be removed before subsequent stages. Here, if the area coincidence ratio of two MSERs is over 85%, then discard one. The area coincidence ratio $r_{a,b}$ of MSER a and b is defined as follows:

$$r_{a,b} = area(a \cap b)/area(a \cup b), \qquad (1)$$

where $area(x)$ is a function to measure area of MSER x.

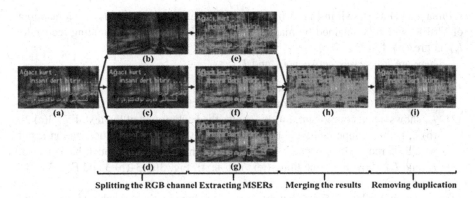

Splitting the RGB channel   Extracting MSERs   Merging the results   Removing duplication

Fig. 2. The multi-color-channel MSERs extraction. The MSERs are labeled by green bounding rectangles. (a) A text edge blur image. (b) The R-channel image. (c) The G-channel image. (d) The B-channel image. (e), (f) and (g) are the result of the extracted MSERs in corresponding channel. (h) The merged result. (i) The result after removing duplication.

2.2 Component Classification with SCRS

In this subsection, we propose a SCRS component classification to differentiate text/non-text components. The SCRS includes two steps, the strong classification step and the retrieve step. In the strong classification step, two strong classifiers divide the extracted component set C into three subsets, the text component subset (C_T), the ambiguity component subset (C_A) and the non-text component subset (C_N). These three subsets correspond to three cases of the two strong classifiers judgment results, the consistent positive case, the inconsistent case and the consistent negative case. In the retrieve step, the identified text components in C_T retrieve text components in C_A according to the similarity between them. After that, the subset C_N and C_A are discarded directly, and C_T is the final result of text component. The SCRS component classification is illustrated in Algorithm 1.

Why use two strong classifiers to identify components? Actually, the extracted MSER is a point set P. Usually a MSER is presented by its bounding rectangle. When we capture the bounding rectangle from the original color image, we can get the local

Fig. 3. (a) The original image; (b) The subimage I_{os}; (c) The mapped binary image I_{mb}.

subimage (I_{os}) as shown in Fig. 3(b). The component binary image (I_{mb}) is a mapping of MSER, which is obtained by mapping MSER points to MSER bounding rectangle. I_{mb} is presented in Fig. 3(c).

There are four cases between I_{os} and I_{mb}:

(1) The text in I_{os} is more intact than the text in I_{mb}. Since the trunk is disconnected to the widgets (such as points) in some Uyghur characters. Figure 3(c) 1–(b) 1.
(2) I_{os} shows a text component, but I_{mb} shows the background of the text, Fig. 3(c) 2–(b) 2. If this component were text component, the precision of localization result would be reduced, as because of the component contains too much background.
(3) I_{os} and I_{mb} show the same thing (text/non-text), Fig. 3(c) 3–(b) 3 and Fig. 3(c) 4–(b) 4.
(4) I_{os} contains a lot of noises that may generate classification mistake. However, the text in I_{mb} is clearer than in I_{os}, Fig. 3(c) 5–(b) 5.

We train two support vector machines (SVMs) with radial basis function (RBF) kernel to deal with the above cases. Since the histogram of oriented gradient (HoG) + SVM system has been applied to a number of object detection tasks in computer vision, and has achieved excellent performance [11]. The one SVM distinguish text/non-text components with the HoG feature of I_{os}, similarly the other is an expert of I_{mb}. The SVM training method and parameter selection will be described in Subsect. 3.2 in detail.

Algorithm 1. SCRS component classification

Input: Component set C; The trained SVM_{os}(by HoG feature of I_{os}); The trained SVM_{mb}(by HoG feature of I_{mb}).
Output: Text component set C_T
Procedure:

1: For i=1→|C| Do
2:     extract HoG feature of I_{os_i}, H_{os_i}
3:     extract HoG feature of I_{mb_i}, H_{mb_i}
4:     If $SVM_{os}.predict(H_{os_i}) > 0$ and $SVM_{mb}.predict(H_{mb_i}) > 0$ then
5:         move C_i to text component set C_T
6:     Else If $SVM_{os}.predict(H_{os_i}) > 0$ or $SVM_{mb}.predict(H_{mb_i}) > 0$ then
7:         move C_i to ambiguity component set C_A
8:     Else
9:         discard C_i
10:     End If
11: End For
12: For j=1→|C_A| Do
13:     For k=1→|C_T| Do
14:         If C_{A_j} is similar to C_{T_k} then
15:             move C_{A_j} to C_T
16:             Break
17:         End If
18:     End For
19: End For

Definition 1 (component similarity): Given component a and b, a and b is similar to each other if $dist_B(hist_c(a), hist_c(b)) \leq \varepsilon$. Where $hist_c(a)$ is the color histogram of a, $dist_B(h_a, h_b)$ is the Bhattacharyya distance between histogram h_a and h_b, and ε is the threshold.

SCRS is powerful, but it has expensive computation. So a pre-filter is designed to reduce non-text components in C, which can improve the whole computation performance of our method. Generally, the Uyghur text stroke is solid. The corresponding I_{mb} of Uyghur text component contains virtually no pin-hole. If a component has a lot of pin-holes, it most likely is a non-text component. The pin-hole detector is a 3×3 matrix with the value be set to 1 except the center.

2.3 Line Construction

Our system mainly processes horizontal lines. The difficult comes from two aspects. In one hand, sometimes there are more than one line in the same horizon. The line localization result is inaccurate as illustrate in Fig. 4(b), if line is directly constructed via component vertical connection. So it is necessary to know the spacing between words during line construction. In the other hand, the spacing changes with the font size. To solve these problems, the line construction includes two phases, the vertical connection phase and the horizontal connection phase. In the first phase, the upper and lower connected components are organized into a group. The minimum of component width in a group is considered to be a character width (w_c), and the spacing is $2w_c$. In the second phase, the group is divided into lines according to horizontal connectivity. The final result of line construction is shown in Fig. 4(c).

(a)   (b)   (c)

Fig. 4. (a) The result of text components classification. (b) The result of components horizontal connection. This result contains too much background and is not precise. (c) The final result of lines construction.

Definition 2 (vertical connectivity): A component a is vertically connected with a component b, if $(a.tl.y + a.br.y)/2 \in [b.tl.y, b.br.y]$. Where $x.tl.y$ is the y coordinate value of the top left point in the component x, and $x.br.y$ is the y coordinate value of the bottom right point.

Definition 3 (horizontal connectivity): A component a is horizontally connected with a component b, if $i_{ab} \leq 2w_c$. Where i_{ab} is the horizontal interval between component a and b, and w_c is character width.

After line construction, the lines corresponding to true text lines are verified by the text line classifier. Similarly, the text line classifier is a SVM that trained by line samples. Both line classifier training and parameters selection are declared in Subsect. 3.2.

3   Experiments

In this section, our method is evaluated on the UICBI400 dataset. Since the widely used databases mainly contain English and Chinese. Subsection 3.1 recommends our UICBI400 dataset and introduces widely used evaluation protocol. Subsection 3.2 describes the SVM training method, and the window size and block size selection of HoG. Subsection 3.3 gives the experiment on UICBI400.

3.1   Dataset and Evaluation Protocol

Dataset: Uyghur In Complex Background Image (UICBI) dataset consists of 400 color images with various size (from $52 \times 52 \sim 1024 \times 768$), and the dataset includes 200 training images and 200 testing images. All the images are download from Internet. They are public service slogans, scene images or posters. The challenging cases of UICBI include changeable font, low-resolution, illumination, blur and complex background. UICBI400 images contain a plenty of Uyghur texts and little English and Chinese texts. The text regions in UICBI400 are labeled as lines. Some sample images of UICBI400 are presented in Figs. 7 and 8.

Evaluation Protocol: Previously, most algorithms are assessed base on the area criterion. The area precision and the area recall are defined as follows:

$$\begin{cases} precision = \frac{area(G_i \cap D_i)}{area(D_i)} \\ recall = \frac{area(G_i \cap D_i)}{area(G_i)} \end{cases}, \tag{2}$$

where G is a list of ground truth object rectangles $G_i, i = 1, 2, \cdots, |G|$, and D is a list of detected object rectangles $D_i, i = 1, 2, \cdots, |D|$. Later, in ICDAR 2011 Wolf *et al.* [12] propose a new protocol, which considers three matching cases between G and D: one-to-one, one-to-many and many-to-one. The definition of precision and recall are follows:

$$\begin{cases} precision(G, D, t_r, t_p) = \frac{\sum_j Match_D(D_j, G, t_r, t_p)}{|D|} \\ recall(G, D, t_r, t_p) = \frac{\sum_i Match_G(G_i, D, t_r, t_p)}{|G|} \end{cases}, \tag{3}$$

where $t_r \in [0, 1]$ is the constraint on area recall, and $t_p \in [0, 1]$ is the constraint on area precision. Generally, $t_r = 0.8$ and $t_p = 0.4$.

3.2   Classifier Training and Parameter Selection

Classifier Training. The three SVM classifiers are trained separately. Some training samples are shown in Fig. 5. The component level samples are generated by MSER extraction algorithm, and the line level samples are obtained by the proposed method without text line verification. The composition of three classifiers training set and testing set is listed in Table 1.

Fig. 5. Training samples. (a) The negatives of I_{mb}. (b) The positives of I_{mb}. (c) The negatives of I_{os}. (d) The positives of I_{os}. (e) The negatives of lines. (f) The positives of lines.

Table 1. The constitution of training set and testing set

Classifier name	Training set		Testing set	
	Positives	Negatives	Positives	Negatives
Component classifier of I_{mb}	3000	5400	1640	2000
Component classifier of I_{os}	4000	4500	2000	2000
Text line classifier	3118	2508	759	2200

Parameter Selection. According to Dalal [11], HoG + SVM system parameters are selected as follows: gradient scale $\sigma = 0$, the number of orientation bins is 9, using L2 − Hys normalization methods and Gaussian kernel SVM kernel width $\gamma = 3e − 2$. In order to extract the same length HoG feature of the components which have different size, the cell size is unfixed and is used to be the base unit of window and block. The block stride is fixed as one cell. To obtain the window and block size decision graph, the SVM is trained by training samples at first. Then, the trained SVM is verified by testing sample. The miss rate of the SVM verification is used to measure the performance of HoG + SVM system. Here the miss rate denotes as 1 − recall. Finally, window and block size decision graph are acquired as Fig. 6.

3.3   Experimental Results

The results on UICBI400 dataset are summarized in Table 2. The localization results on several challenging images are displayed in Fig. 7. The proposed method achieve excellent performance on UICBI400 dataset. Our method improves the compared

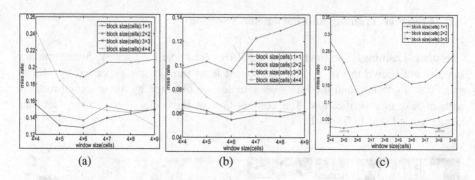

Fig. 6. The miss rate as the block and window sizes change. Here (a) and (b) are parameters decision diagram of two component classifiers, 3 × 3 block of cells and 4 × 6 window of cells perform best. (c) The parameters decision diagram of line classifier, both 2 × 2 block of cells and 2 × 5 window of cells and 3 × 3 block of cells and 3 × 8 windows of cells perform well, but the feature dimension of the former is lower.

Table 2. The left table is the results on the UICBI400 dataset measured with protocol (2). The right table is measured with protocol (3).

Algorithm	Precision	Recall	F-measure
Proposed	**0.948**	**0.814**	**0.876**
Yin *et al.*	0.822	0.534	0.647

Algorithm	Precision	Recall	F-measure
Proposed	**0.888**	**0.776**	**0.828**
Yin *et al.*	0.749	0.522	0.616

performance with 13.9 ∼ 25.4% in all three terms and reach the *F-measure* over 82.8%. The improvements by our method mainly come from two facts. On the one hand, the multi-color-channel enhanced MSER extraction scheme is able to capture the most text components in challenging cases, which is the main reason of high *recall*. On the other hand, the component classification with SCRS robustly classifies text from non-text components, which result in high *precision*.

Figure 7 presents several successful localization results on some difficult cases. These results mean that the proposed approach is robust to text variations including blurring, shadow and font size. The results also show that the presented method is robust to highly noise and complex background effects. There are three failure cases in our experiments as shown in Fig. 8. The left one misses some texts in component classification since their font style is infrequent in training set. For the mid one, the missed texts are discarded by component pre-filter. Due to its stroke pin-holes are more than 5. The right one has a false positive. Due to the curly ribbons are similar to Uyghur text.

Fig. 7. Successful text localization results

Fig. 8. Failure cases

4 Conclusion

This paper presents an effective method for Uyghur text localization in complex background images. First, we propose a robust multi-color-channel enhanced MSERs component extraction scheme, which robustly extracts most text components in challenging images. Second, we propose a SCRS component classification with high accuracy to discriminate texts from a large amount of non-text components. Our method can effectively construct lines using the two-stages component connection algorithm. Our approach has achieved superior performance over the state-of-the-art method on UICBI400 dataset.

Acknowledgement. This work is supported by the National Nature Science Foundation of China (61303171), Natural Science Foundation of Hunan Province (2016JJ2005), the "Strategic Priority Research Program" of the Chinese Academy of Sciences (XDA06031000), Xinjiang Uygur Autonomous Region Science and Technology Project (201230123), Hunan Provincial University Innovation Platform Open Fund Project of China (14K037).

References

1. Yin, X-C., et al.: Robust vanishing point detection for mobilecam-based documents. In: International Conference on Document Analysis & Recognition, Beijing, China, pp. 136–140 (2011)

2. Ye, Q., Doermann, D.: Text detection and recognition in imagery: a survey. IEEE Trans. Pattern Anal. Mach. Intell. **37**(7), 1480–1500 (2015)
3. Lee, J-J., et al.: AdaBoost for text detection in natural scene. In: Proceedings of the 2011 International Conference on Document Analysis and Recognition, IEEE Computer Society, pp. 429–434 (2011)
4. Epshtein, B., Ofek, E., Wexler, Y.:. Detecting text in natural scenes with stroke width transform. In: 2013 IEEE Conference on Computer Vision and Pattern Recognition, pp. 2963–2970. IEEE (2010)
5. Neumann, L., Matas, J.: Text localization in real-world images using efficiently pruned exhaustive search. In: 2011 International Conference on Document Analysis and Recognition (ICDAR), pp. 687–691. IEEE (2011)
6. Matas, J.: Real-time scene text localization and recognition. In: IEEE Conference on Computer Vision & Pattern Recognition, pp. 3538–3545 (2012)
7. Yin, X.-C., et al.: Robust text detection in natural scene images. IEEE Trans. Pattern Anal. Mach. Intell. **36**(5), 970–983 (2013)
8. Huang, W., Qiao, Y., Tang, X.: Robust scene text detection with convolution neural network induced MSER trees. In: Fleet, D., Pajdla, T., Schiele, B., Tuytelaars, T. (eds.) ECCV 2014. LNCS, vol. 8692, pp. 497–511. Springer, Heidelberg (2014). doi:10.1007/978-3-319-10593-2_33
9. Shahab, A., Shafait, F., Dengel, A.: ICDAR 2011 robust reading competition challenge 2: reading text in scene images. In: International Conference on Document Analysis & Recognition, pp. 1491–1496. IEEE (2011)
10. Halima, M.B., Karray, H., Alimi, A.M.: A comprehensive method for arabic video text detection, localization, extraction and recognition. In: Qiu, G., Lam, K.M., Kiya, H., Xue, X.-Y., Kuo, C.-C.J., Lew, M.S. (eds.) PCM 2010. LNCS, vol. 6298, pp. 648–659. Springer, Heidelberg (2010). doi:10.1007/978-3-642-15696-0_60
11. Dalal, N., Triggs, B.: Histograms of oriented gradients for human detection. In: IEEE Conference on Computer Vision & Pattern Recognition, pp. 886–893 (2005)
12. Wolf, C., Jolion, J.M.: Object count/area graphs for the evaluation of object detection and segmentation algorithms. Int. J. Doc. Anal. Recogn. **8**(4), 280–296 (2006)
13. Liu, S., Zhou, Y., Zhang, Y., Wang, Y., Lin, W.: Text detection in natural scene images with stroke width clustering and superpixel. In: Ooi, W.T., Snoek, C.G.M., Tan, H.K., Ho, C.-K., Huet, B., Ngo, C.-W. (eds.) PCM 2014. LNCS, vol. 8879, pp. 123–132. Springer, Heidelberg (2014). doi:10.1007/978-3-319-13168-9_13

Learning Qualitative and Quantitative Image Quality Assessment

Yudong Liang, Jinjun Wang$^{(\boxtimes)}$, Ze Yang, Yihong Gong, and Nanning Zheng

Institute of Artificial Intelligence and Robotics, Xi'an Jiaotong University,
28 West Xianning Road, Xi'an 710049, Shaanxi, China
{liangyudong,yangze}@stu.xjtu.edu.cn,
{jinjun,ygong,nnzheng}@mail.xjtu.edu.cn

Abstract. Quantitative human evaluations give a much finer description while qualitative human evaluations are more stable, consistent and can be much easier to be obtained. Quantitative assessments have been widely explored, while the interaction between qualitative and quantitative evaluations has barely been exploited. A deep convolutional neural network with multi-task learning framework was utilized to perform quantitative evaluations and qualitative evaluations at the same time. The supervision of qualitative evaluations could help the model overcome the inconsistency existed in quantitative evaluations. Further, multi-task learning gives more information to facilitate the learning of discriminative features to describe image quality. As shown in the experiments, referring to qualitative evaluations has boosted the performance of quantitative assessments and the state of art performance has been achieved.

Keywords: Quantitative · Qualitative · Multi task learning · Deep convolutional neural network

1 Introduction

Image quality assessment (IQA) attempts quantifying the image quality to be consistent with human evaluations. Assessing the image quality is essential for designing and evaluating imaging and image processing systems. For instance, image and video compression algorithms aim to reduce the amount of data required while restore the resulting images with sufficiently high quality. Quality assessment algorithms are essential to analysis performance of algorithms and systems such as denoising, enhancement and restoration. Besides, bandwidth efficiency of applications such as online video can be improved using quality assessment systems to evaluate the effects of channel errors. The image quality assessment is a fundamental problem and draws a lot of attentions. Quantitative human evaluations refers to continuous descriptions that quantify the image quality to certain scores. Qualitative human evaluations means discrete assessments, such as dividing image quality into several grades [5] or ranking image quality with preference image pairs [3].

© Springer International Publishing AG 2016
E. Chen et al. (Eds.): PCM 2016, Part II, LNCS 9917, pp. 417–427, 2016.
DOI: 10.1007/978-3-319-48896-7_41

For IQA algorithms which learn from human evaluations, the accuracy and reliability of human evaluations contained in IQA dataset are very important. The subjective evaluation experiments must be performed in critical viewing conditions and procedures [3,13,17]. Sufficient images with each distortion type should be collected at diverse levels [1]. Experiments should be executed continuously and the experimental time must be strictly controlled to avoid observer fatigues [1,13]. Thus IQA dataset is hard to extended and requires heavy workload.

However, it is elaborated that the subjective scores are imprecise, biased, and inconsistent [3,15]. For instance, subjective scores may be biased by image content or aesthetic perception of the image [3]. The quality evaluation may not be perceptually similar across different distortion type [3] as Fig. 1(a). The sculpture picture with white noises is assessed as smaller DMOS than building picture with jpeg distortion, which indicates a better image quality. However, it looks much more annoyed.

Some efforts [3,5] towards utilizing qualitative description have been proposed, based on the psychological evidence that human prefer to get a qualitative evaluation rather than numerical one [6]. Hou *et al.* [5] developed blind IQA model to learn rules from qualitative linguistic description. Gao *et al.* explored preference image pairs (PIPs) to train a blind image quality assessment model. The preference image pairs (PIPs) associate with the preference labels, such as quality of image I_1 is better than quality of image I_2. It proved that evaluations of PIPs were generally precise and consistent, and not sensitive to image content, distortion type, viewing conditions, or subject identity [2,3,15]. Besides, it can be generated at a very low cost [2,3] and easily extended to new distortion types.

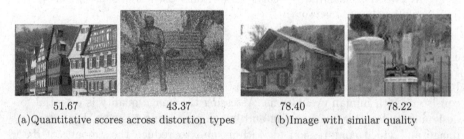

51.67   43.37   78.40   78.22
(a)Quantitative scores across distortion types   (b)Image with similar quality

Fig. 1. Examples of LIVE dataset with subjective scores (DMOS)

On the other hand, MOS/DMOS values give a much finer image quality description than PIPs, the performance of method only based on PIPs [3] was still much inferior to the state of art IQA methods which learned from human perceptual scores to directly predict image quality scores [8,20]. Thus, this paper attempts to combine information from quantitative human perceptual scores and qualitative descriptions especially preference image pairs (PIPs) with a multi-task deep convolutional neural network (CNN) learning framework, to figure out finer description and to make the assessment stable and consistent at the same time. Unlike [3] which discarded PIPs with similar quality, the image pairs with similar quality as Fig. 1(b) are classified into another group. In this case, the quality comparison of this two images can be more accurately described as 'similar' in a qualitative evaluation way.

The deep CNN is designed as the architecture of Fig. 2, with one part to do IQA regression for quantitative IQA scores and another part to accomplish qualitative preference image quality label prediction as a classification problem. As shown in the experiments, our network has achieved state of art performance even compared with full reference IQA methods. In addition, we believe our methods can further improve the existed quantitative evaluation of CNN network with qualitative description.

2   Related Work

Existing IQA methods could be broadly classified into the following three categories: full reference (FR) IQA methods [16,18,21], reduced referenced (RR) IQA methods [14], and no reference (NR) IQA methods [8,20], also called blind image quality assessment methods. The storage inefficiency and non-existence problem of reference images make no reference (NR) IQA methods hot issues and evolving rapidly recent years.

The focus of most NR-IQA methods is to obtain discriminative features. Machine learning techniques have helped IQA methods especially no reference (NR) IQA methods [8,20] develop greatly. Nowadays many NR IQA algorithms prefer to learn features from data rather than propose handcrafted ones. For

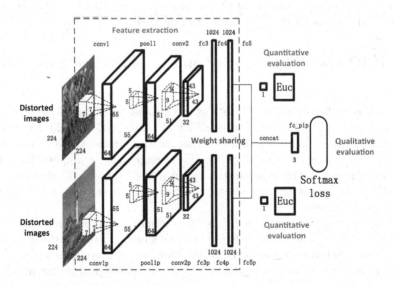

Fig. 2. The architecture of multi-task learning deep CNN with qualitative and quantitative evaluations

example, the CORNIA [20] method performed unsupervised learning from local image patches to encode features, then regressor was trained to evaluate the quality of a distorted image. Recent years, deep convolutional neural network (CNN) has achieved great success [9,10] due to its great feature description ability. Kang *et al.* designed a CNN architecture inspired by the coding process of CORNIA [20], to learn features for NR IQA [8] and it achieved impressive result that approaches state of the art FR-IQA performance.

From another perspective, the consistency and preciseness of human evaluation contained in image quality databases are crucial for IQA task. Many observers are recruited and plenty of distorted images are degraded at diverse level for each type to give a meaningful evaluations [1,13,17]. Sheikh *et al.* [17] further applied evaluation realignment between different subjects and distortion types to improve the human evaluations. Qualitative human evaluations such as PIPs or linguistic descriptions have draw more and more attentions. Gao *et al.* [3] explored preference image pairs (PIPs) to train a blind image quality assessment model. They divided the IQA problem into two step: first, a multiple kernel learning algorithm was utilized to solve the preference label learning problem. Then test images were combined with many training images to form multiple preference image pairs (PIPs). Preference labels were obtained and further converted into perceptual IQA quality scores through a simple linear mapping.

The preference image pairs (PIPs) evaluated by observers largely relax the rigid requirements of experimental conditions. The evaluation of PIPs can be easily extended to new distortion types. Moreover, existed quantitative scores can be easily converted to PIPs. Besides, even with fewer observers, consistent and meaningful PIPs can be achieved. All these efforts have motivated us to take advantage of both the much finer descriptive IQA quantitative scores and qualitative description such as intuitive, consistent and stable preference image pairs (PIPs). The next section depicts our approach.

3   NR IQA with Qualitative and Quantitative Evaluations

In this section, a deep convolutional neural network under a multi-task learning framework is utilized to do IQA as Fig. 2. One task performs IQA regression for quantitative IQA scores while the other task accomplishes qualitative preference image quality label prediction as a classification problem. Both tasks share feature extraction layers, then different linear mappings are applied for different tasks. For qualitative comparison, two distorted images are evaluated via two paths, and weight sharing strategy between paths ensures the preference comparison reasonable.

For our deep CNN, image quality is first evaluated in local sub images, then assessment of the whole image is figured out by simply averaging the local evaluations based on the assumption that distortions are homogeneous. One obvious advantage with deep learning technology is discriminative feature learning from raw data, which maximally preserves information from images. Only simple local contrast normalization is applied to the grayscale image I to ensure numeric stability. The intensity value of pixel $I(i,j)$ is normalized as [8], which can also be understood as a data whiten process.

$$I(x,y)_N = \frac{I(x,y) - u(x,y)}{\sigma(x,y) + \epsilon}$$

$$u(x,y) = \sum_{a=\frac{-P}{2}}^{a=\frac{P}{2}} \sum_{b=\frac{-Q}{2}}^{b=\frac{Q}{2}} (I(x+a, y+b))$$

$$\sigma(x,y) = \sqrt{\sum_{a=\frac{-P}{2}}^{a=\frac{P}{2}} \sum_{b=\frac{-Q}{2}}^{b=\frac{Q}{2}} (I(x+a, y+b) - u(x,y))^2} \tag{1}$$

$I(x,y)_N$ denotes values at image location (x,y) normalized by neighboring pixels in a $(P \times Q)$ window, and ϵ is a small positive constant. We mainly deal with image distortions from degradation. Intensity shift and contrast variations are ignored, as it is highly subjective to judge the image quality for distortions with these types.

The architecture of deep convolutional neural network applied was represented in Table 1. It consists of the convolutional layer, the nonlinear rectified linear unit, the pooling layer, the concat layer and the full connection layer, denoted as $conv\#$, $relu\#$, $pool\#$ and $fc\#$ respectively.

The $conv$ layers have a set of learnable filters (or kernels), with small receptive field to extract local features. In a recursive fashion, the local information is extracted into deeper layers by Eq. (2), where $*$ denotes the convolution operation, A_i^j denotes the feature map in the jth layer of i_{th} path, W_j and B_j are the shared weight and bias parameters of the j_{th} layer respectively.

$$A_i^{j+1} = W_j * A_i^j + B_j, \tag{2}$$

To increase the nonlinear expression ability and accelerate training, the activation function is selected to be $relu$ as $A_i^{j+1} = max(0, A_i^j)$.

Pooling operation greatly reduces the size of feature representation and computation in the network which largely alleviates overfitting. Both [8] and [20] applied max and min pooling over an entire feature map to reduce the computational cost. Although both work achieved impressive results, these two methods have dropped spatial structure information. Our model integrates information from local to global as the network goes deeper with a larger receptive field. Empirically, max-pooling is applied as Eq. (3), where R is the pooling region of corresponding position.

$$A_i^{j+1} = \max_R A_i^j \tag{3}$$

Discriminative features are further combined and mapped to generate image quality assessment with $fc\#$ layer.

Table 1. The deployment of a multi-task learning deep CNN to do IQA with qualitative and quantitative evaluations

Layer name	Padding	Filter size/stride	Output size
Feature extraction			
*input*1	0		$224 \times 224 \times 3$
*conv*1/*conv*1p	0	$7 \times 7/4$	$64 \times 55 \times 55$
*relu*1/*relu*1p			$64 \times 55 \times 55$
*pool*1/*pool*1p (MAX)		$5 \times 5/1$	$64 \times 51 \times 51$
*conv*2/*conv*2p	0	$9 \times 9/1$	$32 \times 43 \times 43$
*relu*2/*relu*2p			$32 \times 43 \times 43$
*fc*3/*fc*3p			1024
*fc*4/*fc*4p			1024
Quantitative evaluations			
*fc*5/*fc*5p			1
Euc			1
Qualitative evaluations			
concat	Concatenating the features from *fc*4 and *fc*4p		
*fc*_pip			3
softmaxloss			1

3.1   Deep CNN for NR IQA with Quantitative Evaluation Scores

Quantitative human evaluation scores are continuous scores distributed in certain ranges, obtained from carefully designed experiments. They make much finer description for image quality. Generally, to predict quantitative evaluation scores is an regression problem.

The image quality score is predicted to approximate human evaluation by minimizing the following Euclidean loss,

$$L_{quan} = \sum_{s=0}^{S} ||\big(f(I_k); W, B\big) - Eva_k||^2 \tag{4}$$

where S is the number of samples, I_k and Eva_k are the input sub distorted images and corresponding human evaluation respectively, W, B are the parameters of convolutional and fc layers.

3.2   Deep CNN for NR IQA with Qualitative Evaluations

Qualitative evaluation is to predict discrete values which is opposite to quantitative evaluation. In fact, a lot of qualitative evaluations are converted into quantitative assessment scores in carefully designed human assessment experiments [13]. Thus, it is believed that human qualitative evaluation can be utilized to facilitate IQA problem. Approximating human qualitative evaluation would be a classification problem. Here preference image pairs (PIPs) are adopted mainly for the fact that: PIPs which are generated across different sessions or by different subjects keep stable and consistent. Besides, they are easy to be obtained from both human evaluation experiments or existed IQA databases.

The difference of distortion level of the two images may be similar and hard to distinguish (Fig. 2(b)), especially when they contain different contents and types. In these cases, it is hard for observers to give consistent opinions. Thus, these cases are denoted as similar image quality associated with an extra kinds of labels instead of discarding the image pairs as [3]. Three kinds of preference between two images (a, b) are defined, 'better', 'worse', and 'similar'. These relationships could be obtained from subjective evaluations or existed IQA dataset as Eq. (5).

$$L_{PIP} = \begin{cases} 1 & Q_a - Q_b > Thres \\ 0 & |Q_a - Q_b| \leq Thres \\ -1 & Q_a - Q_b < -Thres \end{cases} \quad (5)$$

$Thres$ is a threshold value to both avoid reluctantly assigning preference labels and preserve the preference order to evaluate image quality. The quality difference is measured according to subjective scores as Eq. (6).

$$Q_a - Q_b = -(DMOS_a - DMOS_b) \quad or \quad (MOS_a - MOS_b) \quad (6)$$

To accomplish PIPs classification, a couple of features are extracted from a pair of images respectively through two paths of the deep convolutional neural network with a manner of weight sharing. Then the extracted features are linearly mapped into three classes as $z_k = W_k \cdot A$, where W_k is the weight of the linear mapping. Softmax loss is finally applied to approximate the qualitative evaluation as Eq. (7), where z is the predicted result of the PIPs label L_{PIP}.

$$L_{qua} = -\log(\sigma(z = z_k)) = -\log(\frac{e^{z_k}}{\sum_{k=1}^{3} e^{z_k}}), \quad k \in 1, 2, 3 \quad (7)$$

Finally, the total loss of the multi-task learning deep CNN was obtained by the addition:

$$L_{QQ} = L_{quan1} + L_{quan2} + \alpha \cdot L_{qua}. \quad (8)$$

α makes the L_{quan} and L_{qua} numerical comparable and balances the impacts of qualitative and quantitative evaluations.

3.3 Training

Stochastic gradient descent with the standard back-propagation [9] has been applied during training. In particular, the parameters such as weights of the filters of the *conv* or *fc* layer can be updated as Eq. (9)

$$\triangle_{t+1} = m \cdot \triangle_t - \eta \frac{\partial L}{\partial W_t^j}$$

$$W_{t+1}^j = W_t^j + \triangle_{t+1} - \lambda \eta W_t^j \quad (9)$$

It denotes the momentum factor m, the learning rate η, index of the layer j and the weight decay factor λ. $\triangle_t$ is the gradient increment for training iteration t. Momentum factor and weight decay factor were fixed in 0.9 and 0.0005 respectively in the following experiments.

4   Experiment

In this section, a series of experiments were conducted to validate the benefits of combining qualitative and quantitative evaluations to do IQA. The multi-task deep CNN model for IQA was built upon deep learning toolbox Caffe [7]. Two widely investigated datasets were adopted in the experiments: the LIVE dataset, and the TID2008 dataset. In our experiments, Linear Correlation Coefficient (LCC) and Spearman Rank Order Correlation Coefficient (SROCC) were applied, which are the most commonly evaluated and significant criterions in IQA problem. The correlation of the predicted scores with the ground-truth scores were calculated. Higher correlation indicates better consistency with human assessment, and thus better performance. LCC indicates the linear dependence between two quantities, and SROCC measures the monotonicity between predictions and subjective scores.

Deep CNN combined with qualitative and quantitative methods was denoted as CNN-QQ. The proposed Deep CNN with quantitative evaluation only was reported as baseline methods, denoted as CNN-Q. Our methods were compared with the following methods: FR-IQA methods FSIM [21], PSNR and SSIM [18], and NR-IQA methods CNN-NR [8], BRISQUE [11] and CORNIA [20].

We collected PIPs from existed IQA dataset as qualitative evaluations which were directly generated from subjective assessment evaluations had shown similar behavior in [3]. Sub images were extracted with a stride of 20 to train the deep CNN. For both the LIVE and TID2008 datasets, random selected 80 % of the data was used for training, and the remainders for testing. The results of Tables 2 and 3 appeared in the paper were the median evaluation of five times. As human evaluations applied in **LIVE dataset** and **TID2008 dataset** were different, we modulated the parameters of deep CNN for different dataset.

LIVE dataset consists of 779 distorted images with one of the following distortion types [4]: JP2k compression (JP2K), JPEG compression (JPEG), White Gaussian (WN), Gaussian blur (BLUR) and Fast Fading (FF) derived from 29 reference images. The Differential Mean Opinion Scores (DMOS) are attached for each of the distorted images as subjective evaluation. Larger DMOS demonstrate inferior image quality and roughly range in [0, 112]. The results were listed in Table 2, with loss weight $\alpha = 5$, threshold $Thres = 10$ and learning rate $lr = 10^{-5}$.

TID2008 dataset consists of distorted images derived from 25 reference images. The Mean Opinion Score (MOS) are given as subjective evaluations for each of the distorted images. As in many previous works [8,12,19], in our experiments 4 types of distortions that are common to the LIVE dataset were considered: JPEG2000, JPEG, WN and GB. Loss weight $\alpha = 0.5$, threshold

Table 2. LCC and SROCC scores for the LIVE dataset

	FSIM [21]	PSNR	SSIM [18]	BRISQUE [11]	CNN-NR [8]	CORNIA [20]	CNN-QQ	CNN-Q
LCC	0.960	0.856	0.906	0.942	0.953	0.935	**0.974**	0.968
SROCC	0.964	0.866	0.913	0.940	0.956	0.942	**0.973**	0.967

Table 3. LCC and SROCC scores for the TID2008 dataset

	FSIM [21]	PSNR	SSIM [18]	BRISQUE [11]	CNN-NR [8]	CORNIA [20]	CNN-QQ	CNN-Q
LCC	0.926	0.836	0.893	0.892	0.903	0.880	**0.932**	0.920
SROCC	**0.947**	0.870	0.902	0.882	0.920	0.890	0.925	0.921

$Thres = 0.5$ and learning rate $lr = 10^{-3}$ was applied. As CNN-NR [8] has not released the code, data were cited from the paper which were tested in slight different methods with an logistic regression.

4.1 The Influence of Distortion Type

It is interested to study which type of distortions could be best promoted by qualitative evaluation in our multi-task framework. Hence we further conducted and reported distortion specific experiments in Table 4. Slightly tuned parameters were applied in each type. It is obvious that for most of the stated distortion type, CNN-QQ achieved the best or comparable performance even compared with FR-IQA methods.

4.2 Discussion

Overall, state of art performance has been achieved in most of the above experiments even compared with FR-IQA methods. Although CNN-Q has already gained great performance, CNN-QQ further boosted CNN-Q when it combined human quantitative evaluations with qualitative evaluations. The reasons of the promotion could be analyzed as following: first, the advantages are perfectly complementary. Quantitative evaluations give a much finer description while qualitative evaluations are more stable, consistent and can be easily obtained. With our multi-task learning framework, the supervision of qualitative evaluations could help the model overcome the inconsistency existed in quantitative evaluations and give more information to facilitate learning discriminative features to describe image quality. Second, compared with CNN-Q, a richer output implies higher errors to be propagated from the loss layer which is partly equivalent to increasing the learning rate of deep CNN without gradient exploding. Third, qualitative comparisons make training samples much richer which facilitates the learning of discriminative features for IQA problem. If S training samples existed, CNN-QQ could have $S(S-1)$ combinations of samples which greatly helped the deep CNN to avoid local minima problem.

Table 4. LCC and SROCC score *vs.* Distortion type for the LIVE dataset (the best and second best performance are in bold)

LCC	JPEG2k	JPEG	WN	BLUR	FF	SROCC	JPEG2k	JPEG	WN	BLUR	FF
FSIM [21]	0.910	**0.985**	0.976	0.978	0.912		**0.970**	**0.981**	0.967	0.972	**0.949**
PSNR	0.873	0.876	0.926	0.779	0.870		0.870	0.885	0.942	0.763	0.874
SSIM [18]	0.921	0.955	0.982	0.893	0.939		0.939	0.946	0.964	0.907	0.941
CNN-NR [8]	0.953	**0.981**	**0.984**	0.953	0.933		0.952	0.977	**0.978**	0.962	0.908
CORNIA [20]	0.951	0.965	**0.987**	0.968	0.917		0.943	0.955	0.976	0.969	0.906
BRISQUE [11]	0.922	0.973	0.985	0.951	0.903		0.914	0.965	**0.979**	0.951	0.877
CNN-QQ	**0.972**	**0.981**	0.967	**0.984**	**0.965**		**0.972**	**0.980**	0.923	**0.982**	**0.936**
CNN-Q	**0.972**	0.974	0.969	**0.987**	**0.951**		0.968	0.976	0.921	**0.981**	0.935

5 Conclusion and Future Work

This paper presents a multi-task learning framework with deep convolutional neural network, which combines continuous qualitative and discrete quantitative evaluations for image quality assessment. Assisted with consistent and stable qualitative evaluations, the multi-task learning framework not only boosted NR IQA by deep CNN with quantitative evaluations but also has achieved state of art performance. In the future, obtaining quantitative prediction from qualitative prediction should be carefully investigated. Further, we will explore manners of inference between quantitative and qualitative prediction which could potentially reject inconsistency of the evaluations.

Acknowledgment. This work is partially supported by the National Basic Research Program of China (973 Program) under Grant No. 2015CB351705, and National Science Foundation of China under Grant No. 61473219.

References

1. Assembly, I.R.: Methodology for the subjective assessment of the quality of television pictures. International Telecommunication Union (2003)
2. Bradley, R.A., Terry, M.E.: Rank analysis of incomplete block designs: I. The method of paired comparisons. Biometrika **39**(3/4), 324–345 (1952)
3. Gao, F., Tao, D., Gao, X., Li, X.: Learning to rank for blind image quality assessment. IEEE Trans. Neural Netw. Learn. Syst. **26**(10), 2275–2290 (2015)
4. Sheikh, H.R., Wang, Z., Cormack, L., Bovik, A.C.: LIVE image quality assessment database release 2. http://live.ece.utexas.edu/research/quality
5. Hou, W., Gao, X., Tao, D., Li, X.: Blind image quality assessment via deep learning. IEEE Trans. Neural Netw. Learn. Syst. **26**(6), 1275–1286 (2015)
6. Hutchins, E.: Cognition in the Wild. MIT Press, Cambridge (1995)
7. Jia, Y., Shelhamer, E., Donahue, J., Karayev, S., Long, J., Girshick, R., Guadarrama, S., Darrell, T.: Caffe: convolutional architecture for fast feature embedding. arXiv preprint arXiv:1408.5093 (2014)
8. Kang, L., Ye, P., Li, Y., Doermann, D.: Convolutional neural networks for no-reference image quality assessment. In: 2014 IEEE Conference on Computer Vision and Pattern Recognition (CVPR), pp. 1733–1740. IEEE (2014)

9. Krizhevsky, A., Sutskever, I., Hinton, G.E.: Imagenet classification with deep convolutional neural networks. In: Advances in Neural Information Processing Systems, pp. 1097–1105 (2012)

10. Liang, Y., Wang, J., Zhou, S., Gong, Y., Zheng, N.: Incorporating image priors with deep convolutional neural networks for image super-resolution. Neurocomputing **194**, 340–347 (2016)

11. Mittal, A., Moorthy, A.K., Bovik, A.C.: No-reference image quality assessment in the spatial domain. IEEE Trans. Image Process. **21**(12), 4695–4708 (2012)

12. Moorthy, A.K., Bovik, A.C.: Blind image quality assessment: From natural scene statistics to perceptual quality. IEEE Trans. Image Process. **20**(12), 3350–3364 (2011)

13. Ponomarenko, N., Lukin, V., Zelensky, A., Egiazarian, K., Carli, M., Battisti, F.: TID2008-a database for evaluation of full-reference visual quality assessment metrics. Adv. Mod. Radioelectron. **10**(4), 30–45 (2009)

14. Rehman, A., Wang, Z.: Reduced-reference image quality assessment by structural similarity estimation. IEEE Trans. Image Process. **21**(8), 3378–3389 (2012)

15. Rouse, D.M., Pépion, R., Le Callet, P., Hemami, S.S.: Tradeoffs in subjective testing methods for image and video quality assessment. In: IS&T/SPIE Electronic Imaging, 75270F–75270F. International Society for Optics and Photonics (2010)

16. Sheikh, H.R., Bovik, A.C., De Veciana, G.: An information fidelity criterion for image quality assessment using natural scene statistics. IEEE Trans. Image Process. **14**(12), 2117–2128 (2005)

17. Sheikh, H.R., Sabir, M.F., Bovik, A.C.: A statistical evaluation of recent full reference image quality assessment algorithms. IEEE Trans. Image Process. **15**(11), 3440–3451 (2006)

18. Wang, Z., Bovik, A.C., Sheikh, H.R., Simoncelli, E.P.: Image quality assessment: from error visibility to structural similarity. IEEE Trans. Image Process. **13**(4), 600–612 (2004)

19. Xue, W., Zhang, L., Mou, X.: Learning without human scores for blind image quality assessment. In: Proceedings of the IEEE Conference on Computer Vision and Pattern Recognition, pp. 995–1002 (2013)

20. Ye, P., Kumar, J., Kang, L., Doermann, D.: Unsupervised feature learning framework for no-reference image quality assessment. In: 2012 IEEE Conference on Computer Vision and Pattern Recognition (CVPR), pp. 1098–1105. IEEE (2012)

21. Zhang, L., Zhang, L., Mou, X., Zhang, D.: FSIM: a feature similarity index for image quality assessment. IEEE Trans. Image Process. **20**(8), 2378–2386 (2011)

An Analysis-Oriented ROI Based Coding Approach on Surveillance Video Data

Liang Liao[1,2], Ruimin Hu[1,2,3(✉)], Jing Xiao[2,3,4], Gen Zhan[2],
Yu Chen[2], and Jun Xiao[2]

[1] State Key Laboratory of Software Engineering,
Wuhan University, Wuhan, China
[2] Computer School, National Engineering Research Center
for Multimedia Software, Wuhan University, Wuhan, China
{liaoliangwhu, hrm, jing, zhangen, cynercms,
junxiao}@whu.edu.cn
[3] Hubei Provincial Key Laboratory of Multimedia and Network
Communication Engineering, Wuhan University, Wuhan, China
[4] Research Institute of Wuhan University in Shenzhen, Shenzhen, China

Abstract. Driven by the growing amount of surveillance video data, intelligent video analysis has been applied to manipulate the stored videos automatically. As the most important method of video storage, the conventional coding method with high compression ratio severely degrades the video quality, which restrict the performance of intelligent analysis. In this paper, we propose an analysis-oriented region of interest (ROI) based coding approach to relieve this problem. We qualitatively analyze the effect of video compression on the performance of video analysis, such as feature similarity and object detection. Based on the analysis, we generate the ROI by the prior knowledge of interest objects rather than considering the characteristics of Human Visual System (HVS). Then, a weight-based rate control scheme is proposed to protect the quality of ROI by assigning more bits to encode it. Experimental results show that the proposed approach can reach 5.52% and 4.39% gains average over HEVC on the performance of feature similarity and object detection respectively under the same bitrate.

Keywords: Surveillance video data · Video compression · Video analysis

1 Introduction

With the rapid development of security system, surveillance cameras have been widely deployed. They can not only provide real-time monitoring, but also generate surveillance videos that serve as the key resources for event analysis and incident investigation. Nevertheless, the widely deployed surveillance cameras produce huge amount of video data daily, which leads to large storage and transmission cost. To relieving this problem, the usual method is to shorten the storage period of collected videos or compress with high compression ratio. The former leads to valuable resource lost for a long-term event. Whilst the latter results in the low quality of surveillance videos, which severely degrades the performance in main tasks of videos analysis [1].

© Springer International Publishing AG 2016
E. Chen et al. (Eds.): PCM 2016, Part II, LNCS 9917, pp. 428–438, 2016.
DOI: 10.1007/978-3-319-48896-7_42

Other than conversational video, which is captured for watching purposes, surveillance video is usually captured for intelligent analysis such as key object detection or retrieval [1–3]. Based on this demand, we need to keep the relatively high fidelity of important region, which is the important prerequisites in video analysis.

To protect the quality of important region, namely ROI in videos, there are series of ROI based coding methods have been proposed previous. The common strategy employed by those methods includes two steps: (1) ROI is extracted by either bottom-up or top-down perceptual model according to knowledge of HVS, e.g. bright colors or fast motions; (2) more bits are allocated for ROI to reduce quality distortion by rate control algorithm [4–6]. However, the detected ROI may not be suitable for intelligent analysis due to following reasons: (1) regions with high contrast, such as zebra crossing, are not important for surveillance video analysis; (2) pedestrians or vehicles as the most important objects in surveillance cannot all be preserved by the ROI defined from HVS. Therefore, existing coding methods based on HVS may not achieve desirable performance when directly apply to surveillance videos.

Aiming to keep the analytical performance of surveillance video data after compression, we analyze the effect of video coding distortion on video analysis performance such as feature similarity and object detection accuracy in this paper. Based on the analysis, we propose an analysis-oriented ROI based coding approach on surveillance videos. Rather than considering the characteristics of HVS, the ROI is defined by the prior knowledge of the interest object, adopting the method of object detection. After that, a weight-based R-λ rate control scheme is proposed to reduce the distortion on ROI by assign more bits to encode it.

The main contribution of our paper is that we compress surveillance videos considering the analytic requirement, which is special characters of surveillance video data. Based on this requirement, we establish the relationship between video analysis and video compression by experiments. Then, a modified analysis oriented ROI based surveillance video coding approach is developed guided by the relationship. Experimental results show that the proposed approach can achieve better analytical performance in the ROI of encoded videos under a fixed bitrate compared to HEVC.

2 Analysis

In general, the distortion on the performance of video analysis relies on the distortion of the compressed video. Although the idea is very straightforward, there is no detailed analysis on what is the relationship between video compression and the performance of video analysis. Therefore, this section firstly validates that the video compression ratio has positive correlation on the performance loss of feature similarity and object detection and presents some quantitative results on the correlation by experiments.

2.1 Feature Similarity

The SIFT (Scale Invariant Feature Transform) descriptor is robust to rotation and brightness and widely applied in computer vision tasks [7]. In this experiment, it is utilized in our scheme to measure the feature similarity between the original videos and the decoded videos. It is extracted on video frames with different QPs, and the average similarity is calculated between SIFT features of the original frames and those of the corresponding decoded frames.

Figure 1(a) shows that the sift similarity drops with the increases of QP, which means the compression quality has positive correlation with the performance of sift similarity. It is reasonable since details of textures are lost more when coding under lower quality.

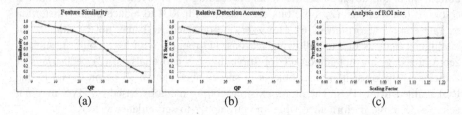

(a)   (b)   (c)

Fig. 1. The effect of video compression quality on (a) feature similarity; (b) object detection accuracy; (c) the effect of ROI size on object detection accuracy. Experiments are conducted on six test videos and the above results are the average. Evaluation algorithms and six test videos are shown later in the experimental section

2.2 Relative Detection Accuracy

Different from the general object detection task, there is no ground truth for surveillance video and all outputs of object detection is used to be key resources for investigation in general. Therefore, we adopt relative detection accuracy to analyze the effect of compression on output of detection results by evaluating the similarity of object detection results between the original videos and the decoded videos frame-wise.

Figure 2(b) shows that the F1 score of object detection is lower in higher QP relative to its original frames, but the declining trend is more moderate than that of sift similarities. It may be explained that the feature of key point is more sensitive to the quality reduction than the feature of region.

Fig. 2. Example frames of the test videos in our experiments

2.3   The Effect of ROI Size

In our scheme, ROI is identified by object detection method and the blocking artifacts in the decoded frames may affect the accuracy of the detection method. To deal with this, we splice a worst quality decoded non-ROI (compressed with QP 47) and higher quality decoded ROI (compressed with QP 2, 12, 22 and 32) together to analyze whether the ROI size has impact on the detection performance. The relative detection accuracy is computed by comparing the detection results of the spliced frame and that of those frames compressed with corresponding QP of ROI.

Figure 2(c) shows that the precision of detection is increasing with the scaling factor when the scaling factor is lower than 1 and the precision starts to steady when the scaling factor beyond 1. Through the analysis, we set scaling factor to 1, namely the size of the output bounding box, to the size of ROI in the experiment section.

3   The Proposed Scheme

3.1   ROI Detection

In the step of ROI detection, we employ deformable part models (DPM) [8] which has a high detection accuracy to segment ROI (pedestrians and vehicles in this paper) and non-ROI. First, we use pre-training DPM to localize the pedestrians and vehicles respectively. Then, the cover region of pedestrians and vehicles is merged as a whole and defined as ROI. It can be formalized as:

$$R = \left(\bigcup_{i=0}^{m} P_i\right) \cup \left(\bigcup_{j=0}^{n} V_j\right) \tag{1}$$

where R is ROI, P_i is the i-th region of the pedestrian and V_j is the j-th region of the vehicle, m and n are the number of the region of pedestrians and vehicles respectively.

3.2   Weight-Based R-λ Rate Control

After the generation of ROI, we develop a weight-based rate control strategy based on the R-λ rate control algorithm [9]. We modify the bit allocation in the unit of the largest coding unit (LCU) while keep the bit allocation in the GOP level and picture level the same as done in HEVC. To make the paper complete, we first make a brief review on the R-λ rate control algorithm of HEVC on the basement of LCU. Then we give a description on the proposed weighted R-λ rate control algorithm.

- **R-λ rate control algorithm of HEVC.**

The algorithm aims to allocate leftover bits to the remaining LCUs according to the weight of each LCU.

$$Target_{LCU} = \frac{Target_{Pic} - Bit_H - Coded_{Pic}}{\sum_{NotCodedLCUs} \omega_i} \cdot \omega_{CurrLCU} \tag{2}$$

$$\omega_i = MAD_i^2 \tag{3}$$

where $Target_{Pic}$ is the total bits of the current picture, Bit_H is the estimated header bits, $Coded_{Pic}$ is the bit cost of the previously coded LCU in current picture. ω_i is the weight for each LCU, which is calculated according to the estimated mean absolute difference (MAD). The MAD is obtained from the prediction error of the collocated LCU in the previously coded picture belonging to the same picture level:

$$MAD_i = \frac{1}{N} \sum_{j=1}^{N} |pred_j - org_j| \tag{4}$$

where N is the number of pixels in the i-th LCU, org_j and $pred_j$ are the pixel value in the original signal and the predicted signal respectively.

After bit allocation for each LCU, a value of λ is determined by the following algorithm:

$$\lambda = \alpha \, bpp^{\beta} \tag{5}$$

$$bpp = Target_{LCU}/N \tag{6}$$

where bpp is the average bits per pixel in current LCU, and α, β is initialized as 3.2003 and −1.367 respectively, which will be further updated by the real cost bpp and real applied λ value.

Then, for a given λ, the QP value is determined by:

$$QP = c_1 \times ln(\lambda) + c_2 \tag{7}$$

where c_1 and c_2 are set to 4.2005 and 13.7122 respectively.

- **Weighted R-λ rate control algorithm**

In the ROI based rate control scheme, we prefer to use low QP in the salient area in order to achieve high quality. Based on the Eqs. (2)–(7), we conclude that QP can be reduced by giving high weight to the MAD value. Therefore, in our weighted R-λ rate control algorithm, we add a weight to the calculation of MAD based on whether the LCU belongs to ROI. The MAD is calculated by:

$$MAD_i = \frac{1}{N} \sum_{j=1}^{N} |pred_j - org_j| \cdot \omega_s \tag{8}$$

where ω_s is obtained by the piecewise function:

$$\omega_s = \begin{cases} \varepsilon_1 & LCU \subset ROI \\ \varepsilon_2 & LCU \subset non\_ROI \end{cases} \tag{9}$$

In our experiment, we use 8, 1 for ε_1, ε_2 respectively.

4 Experimental Results

4.1 Experimental Setup

- **Test video sequences**

We carried out the experiments on six surveillance video clips from both public and private datasets: Gate of resolution 720 p (1280 × 720) from the public PKU-SVD dataset [2], Bank of resolution 720 p and Road of resolution 1080 p (1920 × 1080) from the public PKU-HUMANID dataset [10] and Playground, Villa, Park and Community of resolution 1080 p from private campus surveillance. For each video sequence, we select 300 successive frames and all the video sequences contain pedestrians or vehicles. Examples of the six videos are shown in Fig. 2.

- **Experimental Design**

We design two sets of experiments to test the performance of the proposed ROI based video coding method. In the first set of experiments, comparison on the coding performance with HEVC is conducted by using the main profile of HEVC test model HM 16.2 [11] and the details of the configuration of HEVC are showed in Table 1.

Table 1. Experimental HEVC configuration

Parameter	Value	Parameter	Value
Frame structure	Random access IBBB	GOP size	8
MaxCUwidth	64	MaxCUheight	4
FastSearch	Enable	SearchRanged	64
IntraPeriod	−1	RateControl	1
SAO	1	AMP	1

In the second set of experiments, comparison on the analysis performance with HEVC is carried out in the aspects of feature points matching using the index of feature similarity (FS) and object detection using the index of relative detection accuracy (RDA). The statistical analysis is carried out using similar formula in [12] to compute (1) the average difference on the indexes over the whole range of bitrates; and (2) the average bitrate difference over the whole range of the indexes.

- **Feature similarity**

We generate matched SIFT point pairs based on the original frame and add constraints on the positions of the matched point pairs to eliminating the pairs with points at different locations, ultimately leaving only similar point pairs.

$$s_i = \begin{cases} 1 & if \, ||x_{i1} - x_{i2}|| \leq 1 \, and \, ||y_{i1} - y_{i2}|| \leq 1 \\ 0 & otherwise \end{cases} \quad (i = 1, 2, \ldots, k) \quad (10)$$

where s_i is the flag showing whether the pair is similar or not, (x_{i1}, y_{i1}) and (x_{i2}, y_{i2}) are SIFT points of the i-th matched pair extracted from the original image and the decoded image respectively.

The percentage of SIFT points in the original frame which can find matches in the decoded frame is adopted to represent the FS of one frame:

$$FS = \frac{\sum_{i=0}^{k} s_i}{m} \times 100\% \tag{11}$$

where k is the number of matched point pairs and m is the number of SIFT points in the original frame. The overall FS of a video is calculated by averaging FS of all frames.

- **Relative detection accuracy**

We used DPM trained by PASCAL VOC 2011 dataset [13, 14] on pedestrians and vehicles as detectors to detect pedestrians and vehicles separately on the original frames and the decoded frames, generating a bounding box for each detection. Then, the RDA is computed by evaluating overlaps between the bounding box on the original frames and that on the decoded frames.

$$f(b_i, B_j) = \begin{cases} 1 & if b_i \text{ and } B_j \text{ have more than } T \text{ overlap} \\ 0 & otherwise \end{cases} \tag{12}$$

where f is the flag shows whether the box pair is correct or not, b_i and B_j are the i-th detected object from the decoded frame and the j-th detected object from the original frame. In the experiment, we set the overlap threshold T to 0.9.

$$F_1 = \frac{2 \cdot P_{rda} \cdot R_{rda}}{P_{rda} + R_{rda}} \times 100\% \tag{13}$$

$$P_{rda} = \frac{\sum_{ip}^{m_p} \sum_{jp}^{n_p} f(b_{ip}, B_{jp}) + \sum_{iv=0}^{m_v} \sum_{jv=0}^{n_v} f(b_{iv}, B_{jv})}{n_p + n_v} \tag{14}$$

$$R_{rda} = \frac{\sum_{ip}^{m_p} \sum_{jp}^{n_p} f(b_{ip}, B_{jp}) + \sum_{iv=0}^{m_v} \sum_{jv=0}^{n_v} f(b_{iv}, B_{jv})}{m_p + m_v} \tag{15}$$

where P_{rda} and R_{rda} are the precision and recall of relative detection accuracy respectively, m_p and m_v are the number of detected pedestrians and vehicles on the decoded frame and n_p and n_v are the number of detected pedestrians and vehicles on the original frame. The overall RDA of a video is calculated by averaging F_1 of all frames.

4.2   Comparison on Coding Efficiency

The RD curves of our proposed method and HEVC on each sequence is plotted in Fig. 3, and the statistical comparisons are presented in Table 2. It should be noted that the rate-distortion performance of the proposed methods is slightly lower than HEVC, in average 26.44% higher bitrate and 0.85 dB lower in PSNR. The decrement is under the expectation because the proposed weighted R-λ rate control algorithm will change the optimized coding mode which the conventional rate control algorithm can achieve.

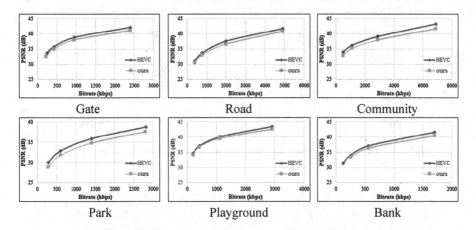

Fig. 3. RD curves comparison for proposed method and HEVC

4.3 Comparison on Video Analysis

- **Feature similarity**

Results on FS of SIFT points are shown in Fig. 4. All curves show that the sift similarities drops with the deceases of bitrate. Another discovery can be found in the figure is that in ROI, we can achieve higher FS in all video clips though the increment of FS does not have clear trend with the increment of bitrate. The statistical analysis in Table 3 shows that under the same bitrate, the FS gains can reach maximum 8.11% with the average of 5.52%. Meanwhile, when we want to obtain the same performance on feature matching, we can save almost 28% bitrate over HEVC.

Table 2. Encoding performance comparison of proposed method versus HEVC

Simulated video	BD-PSNR (dB)	BD-Rate (%)	Simulated video	BD-PSNR (dB)	BD-Rate (%)
Gate	−0.77	23.76	Road	−0.86	23.99
Community	−1.12	39.47	Park	−1.07	33.37
Playground	−0.51	16.91	Bank	−0.74	21.13
			Average	**−0.85**	**26.44**

The increment on the FS reflects that by giving a high weight to the MAD of ROI, more bitrate can be assigned to them. As a result, the FS increases in each video clip, which is of great significance to analysis and recognition of special objects or events.

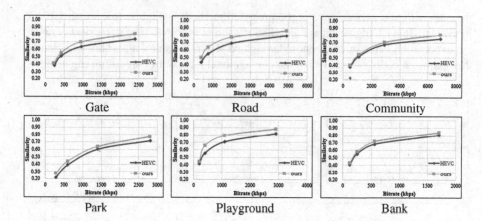

Fig. 4. Comparison of feature similarity between proposed method and HEVC

Table 3. Comparison on feature similarity of proposed method versus HEVC

Simulated video	FS (%)	Bitrate (%)	Simulated video	FS (%)	Bitrate (%)
Gate	5.94	−28.03	Road	7.73	−42.33
Community	3.43	−18.93	Park	4.60	−18.25
Playground	8.11	−41.29	Bank	3.34	−19.17
			Average	**5.52**	**−28.00**

- **Relative detection accuracy**

Results on RDA are shown in Fig. 5. Similar with the results from FS, the object detection has been improved by our proposed method with the improvement of 4.39% on accuracy under the same bitrate. More importantly, the bitrate savings can reach as high as 62.22% when we obtain the same detection accuracy with HEVC (Table 4).

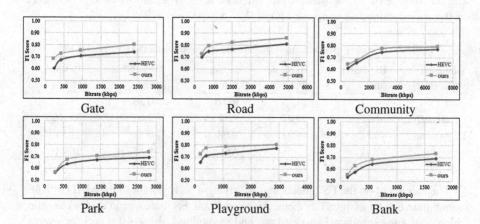

Fig. 5. Comparison of object detection between proposed method and HEVC

Table 4. Comparison on RDA of proposed method versus HEVC

Simulated video	RDA (%)	Bitrate (%)	Simulated video	RDA (%)	Bitrate (%)
Gate	5.48	−70.69	Road	4.93	−74.07
Community	2.75	−37.84	Park	3.49	−52.85
Playground	5.72	−91.73	Bank	3.98	−46.15
			Average	**4.39**	**−62.22**

5 Conclusion

In this work, a novel analysis-oriented ROI based coding scheme for big surveillance videos is proposed. We first analyze the analysis performance of surveillance videos with different coding quality using the index of feature similarity and relative object detection. Based on the analysis, a knowledge-based ROI extraction method is proposed to detect the most important objects in surveillance video analysis. Then a weighted rate control method is proposed to adjust the rate control mechanism in HEVC to give more emphasize on the ROI. The results show that the proposed method is capable of improve the performance of video analysis by 5.52% and 4.39% gains average over HEVC on the performance of feature similarity and object detection respectively under the same bitrate. Further work can be done In the Improvement on the ROI extraction to detect and represent the ROI by powerful and robust features.

Acknowledgements. This work was partly supported by the National Natural Science Foundation of China (61231015, 61502348), the National High Technology Research and Development Program of China (2015AA016306), the EU FP7 QUICK project under Grant Agreement (PIRSES-GA-2013-612652).

References

1. Gao, W., Ma, S.: Advanced Video Coding Systems. Springer International Publishing, Cham (2014)
2. Gao, W., Tian, Y., Huang, T., Ma, S., Zhang, X.: IEEE 1857 standard empowering smart video surveillance systems. Intell. Syst. IEEE **29**(5), 30–39 (2013)
3. Wang, M., Hong, R., Li, G., Zha, Z., Yan, S., Chua, T.: Event driven web video summarization by tag localization and key-shot identification. IEEE Trans. Multimedia **14** (4), 975–985 (2012)
4. Guo, C., Zhang, L.: A novel multiresolution spatiotemporal saliency detection model and its applications in image and video compression. IEEE Trans. Image Process. **19**(1), 185–198 (2010)
5. Hadizadeh, H., Bajic, V.: Saliency-aware video compression. IEEE Trans. Image Process. **23** (1), 19–33 (2014)
6. Xu, M., Deng, X., Li, S., Wang, Z.: Region-of-interest based conversational HEVC coding with hierarchical perception model of face. IEEE Sel. Top. Signal Process. **8**(3), 475–489 (2014)

7. Lowe, D.G.: Distinctive image features from scale-invariant keypoints. Int. J. Comput. Vision **60**(2), 91–110 (2010)
8. Felzenszwalb, P.F., Girshick, R.B., McAllester, D., Ramanan, D.: Object detection with discriminatively trained part-based models. IEEE Trans. Pattern Anal. Mach. Intell. **32**(9), 1627–1645 (2010)
9. Li, B., Li, H., Li, L., Zhang, J.: λ Domain rate control algorithm for high efficiency video coding. IEEE Trans. Image Process. **23**(9), 3841–3854 (2014)
10. Wei, L., Tian, Y., Wang, Y., Huang, T.: Swiss-system based cascade ranking for gait-based person re-identification. In: AAAI Conference on Artificial Intelligence, Austin, pp. 1882–1888 (2015)
11. HM 16.2. http://hevc.hhi.fraunhofer.de/
12. Gisle, B.: Calculation of average PSNR differences between RD-Curves. ITU-T SG16 Q.6 Document, VCEG-M33 (2001)
13. Zhu, L., Chen, Y., Yuille, A., Freeman, W.: Latent hierarchical structural learning for object detection. IEEE Int. Conf. Comput. Vis. Pattern Recogn. **13–18**, 1062–1069 (2010). San Francisco

A Stepwise Frontal Face Synthesis Approach for Large Pose Non-frontal Facial Image

Xueli Wei[1,2], Ruimin Hu[1,2(✉)], Zhen Han[1,2], Liang Chen[1,2], and Xin Ding[1,2]

[1] State Key Laboratory of Software Engineering, Wuhan University, Wuhan, China
hrm1964@gmail.com
[2] School of Computer, National Engineering Research Center
for Multimedia Software, Wuhan University, Wuhan, China
{weixl,2012102110002,ding-xin}@whu.edu.cn,
hanzhen_1980@163.com

Abstract. Frontal face synthesis plays an important role in many fields. The existing methods mainly synthesize frontal face based on the consistency assumption that non-frontal and frontal face manifolds are locally isometric. But the assumption couldn't be held well when non-frontal faces have large variations. To solve this problem, we propose a stepwise frontal face synthesis approach for large pose non-frontal facial image. Considering that the consistency is desirable when the angle variations of different poses are small, we divide frontal face synthesis into multiple stepwise synthesis steps. In each step, the intermediate pose training sets between non-frontal and frontal training sets are used to synthesize intermediate pose faces. Furthermore, in each step, we utilize the geometric structure of target face space with small pose as constraint to represent the input face with larger pose. Experimental results demonstrate that the proposed method outperforms other state-of-the-art methods quantitatively and qualitatively.

Keywords: Frontal face synthesis · Large pose · Intermediate pose training sets

1 Introduction

Frontal face synthesis plays an important role in *image processing, video surveillance, face recognition* etc. [1–4]. Generally, frontal face synthesis is to synthesize one's frontal facial image given his/her non-frontal facial image. In recent decades, many methods have been proposed for synthesizing frontal facial images.

Depending on whether the synthesis is accomplished in the 3D domain or the 2D domain, the existing methods of frontal face synthesis can be classified into two categories: methods based on 2D techniques and methods based on 3D techniques [5]. The 3D techniques, such as 3D morphable model (3DMM) [6] and generic elastic model (GEM) [7], mainly utilize 3D models of human faces to synthesize frontal facial images. These methods can achieve relatively good

© Springer International Publishing AG 2016
E. Chen et al. (Eds.): PCM 2016, Part II, LNCS 9917, pp. 439–448, 2016.
DOI: 10.1007/978-3-319-48896-7_43

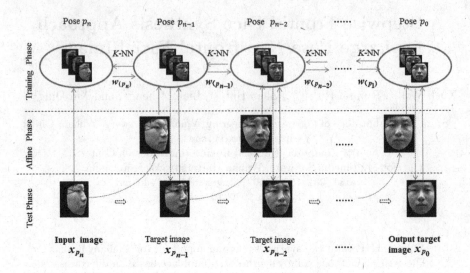

Fig. 1. Illustration of multiple stepwise frontal face synthesis for large pose non-frontal facial image.

performance, but they need good initial values for 3D model fitting; especially the optimization process of 3D model fitting is too slow to be used in real-time tasks.

Methods based on 2D techniques mainly learn the relationship between non-frontal facial images and corresponding frontal facial images, and most of them follow the consistency assumption that non-fontal and frontal face manifolds are locally isometric. Compared with methods based on 3D techniques, the methods based on 2D techniques require relatively less computation. Moreover, these methods can be divided into two categories. One category is synthesizing frontal facial image as a whole. In [8], Vetter et al. use a Linear Object Class (LOC) algorithm to infer frontal facial image. They first separate the input non-frontal face into texture vector and shape vector, and then LOC algorithm is applied to them respectively. Finally, they utilize a basis set of 2D prototypical views to generate a novel frontal face. Huang et al. [9] treat frontal face synthesis as a manifold estimation problem, and the frontal face can be synthesized by subspace reconstruction. The synthesis results of these methods are relatively smooth, but they neglect the local texture feature of faces. Another category is based on the local patch strategy. Chai et al. [10] propose a Locally Linear Regression (LLR) algorithm, in which the facial image are divided into local rectangular patches, and each patch is predicted by linear regression. Zhao et al. [11] divide the facial image into triangle patches and utilize sparse representation to reconstruct the frontal facial image. However, Hao et al. [2] think that the manifold assumption could not be guaranteed well because of the self-occlusion. So they introduce a Unified Regularization Framework (URF), which incorporate the local similarity prior and encircling neighbor patches of the input rectangle patch as constraint.

To some extent, the performance of the above methods is better than other global face synthesis methods in dealing with the facial images with small pose variations. But in practice, the facial images captured by surveillance cameras usually have large variations, which make the self-occlusion much severer. In this situation, the performance of the above methods is relatively poor.

To address the above problem, in this paper, we propose a stepwise frontal face synthesis approach for large pose non-frontal facial image. When the angle variations of different poses are small, we consider that the manifold consistency of two different pose spaces is desirable. Based on the above consideration, we divide frontal face synthesis into multiple stepwise synthesis, as illustrated in Fig. 1. In each step, we utilize the intermediate pose training sets between non-frontal and frontal training sets (such as the pose of 45° is the intermediate pose between the poses of 67.5° and 0°) to synthesize intermediate facial images with different poses. Furthermore, in each step, in order to take full advantage of the geometric structure of target face space which has few self-occlusion, we use it as constraint to represent the input facial image with larger pose.

2   The Proposed Method

2.1   Notations

Assumed that there are non-frontal and corresponding frontal face training sets $I_{p_n} = \{I_{p_n}^1, I_{p_n}^2, ..., I_{p_n}^N\} \in R^{\sigma \times N}$ and $I_{p_0} = \{I_{p_0}^1, I_{p_0}^2, ..., I_{p_0}^N\} \in R^{\sigma \times N}$, where every column in I_{p_n} and I_{p_0} respectively represents the vectorized facial image of the training sets, N represents the number of all the training images in the training set I_{P_0} and I_{p_n}. Given a non-frontal input facial image x_{p_n}, whose pose is p_n, the goal of frontal face synthesis is to reconstruct its frontal facial image by learning the relationship of the non-frontal and frontal face training sets. As for a local patch based method, we divide all the facial images into T triangle patches based on Delauany triangulation [12]. Then the input face can be expressed as $x_{p_0} = \{x_{(1,p_0)}, x_{(2,p_0)}, ..., x_{(T,p_0)}\}$, and the i_{th} patch of the training sets I_{p_0} and I_{p_n} can be respectively described as $I_{(i,p_0)} = \{I_{(i,p_0)}^1, I_{(i,p_0)}^2, ..., I_{(i,p_0)}^N\}$, $I_{(i,p_n)} = \{I_{(i,p_n)}^1, I_{(i,p_n)}^2, ..., I_{(i,p_n)}^N\}$. Later we utilize the reconstruction weights of each input patch and frontal face training patches set to obtain the final frontal facial image.

2.2   Multiple Stepwise Synthesis

In practice, facial images are usually have large pose variations, which make the self-occlusion much severe and the manifold consistency between input non-frontal and frontal face space couldn't be held well. As Fig. 2, with the increase of face pose variations, the neighbor preservation rates of face spaces under different poses will decrease. So we consider that when the angle variations of different poses are small, the manifold consistency of two different pose spaces is desirable. And based on the above consideration, we divide frontal face synthesis into multiple stepwise synthesis.

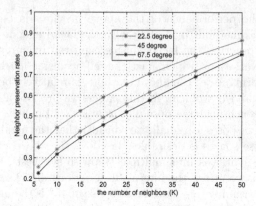

Fig. 2. The neighbor preservation rates of different pose face spaces according to different neighbor number K.

Supposed that the intermediate pose training sets are $I_{p_{n-1}}, I_{p_{n-2}}, ..., I_{p_1}$, where $p_{n-1}, p_{n-2}, ..., p_1$ are the intermediate poses between the poses p_n and p_0. We use similar operations with frontal face training set to represent these different pose training sets. Given an input facial image x_{p_n}, for its i_{th} patch (such as the red triangle patch in Fig. 1), we can get the corresponding frontal face patch $x_{(i,p_0)}$ through multiple stepwise steps. In the first step, we can obtain the intermediate pose target face patch $x_{(i,p_{n-1})}$ under the pose p_{n-1} through two substeps. Firstly, we need to obtain the reconstruction weights of $x_{(i,p_n)}$, and the weights can be described as:

$$J(w_{(i,p_n)}) = \underset{w_{(i,p_n)}}{\operatorname{argmin}} \|x_{(i,p_n)} - \sum_{j=1}^{N} I^j_{(i,p_n)} w^j_{(i,p_n)}\|^2_2 \qquad 1 \le j \le N \qquad (1)$$

where $w_{(i,p_n)} = (w^1_{(i,p_n)}, w^2_{(i,p_n)}, ..., w^N_{(i,p_n)})^T \in R^{N \times 1}$. Secondly, the patch $x_{(i,p_{n-1})}$ can be obtained via:

$$x_{(i,p_{n-1})} = \sum_{j=1}^{N} I^j_{(i,p_{n-1})} w^j_{(i,p_n)} \qquad (2)$$

In the second step, we set $x_{(i,p_{n-1})}$ as a new input patch, following the above two substeps, target facial image patch $x_{(i,p_{n-2})}$ under the pose p_{n-2} can be got easily. Through multiple stepwise iterations, we can finally obtain frontal face patch $x_{(i,p_0)}$. Meanwhile, in order to mitigate the line-like artifacts inherited from the triangulation blocks, we increase overlap for each patch based on the equidistantly similarity. When all triangle patches of the input face have been synthesized, the corresponding frontal face image can be produced by averaging the overlapping regions [13] and merging all the patches according to the position.

2.3   Prior Constraint Neighbors Embedding

In our approach, we utilize Neighbors Embedding (NE) based method [14] to synthesize frontal face. For each step, each target facial image patch is reconstructed by mapping the weights of input face patch to target face training space, without considering the prior information of target face space which has few self-occlusion. As Fig. 2, compared with the pose of $45°$, the correct neighbor number of facial image patch under the pose of $22.5°$ is larger. In order to take use of the information of target face space with smaller pose, we propose to utilize the neighbors of target face space as constraint to represent the neighbors of input facial image.

Algorithm 1. A stepwise frontal face synthesis approach for large pose non-frontal facial image

---

Input: Suppose there are two intermediate pose training sets, so all the training
   sets can be described as I_{p3}, I_{p2}, I_{p1}, I_{p0}, where $I_{(pq)} = \{I^1_{(pq)}, I^2_{(pq)}, ..., I^N_{(pq)} | q \in$
   $0, 1, 2, 3\}$, the input facial image is x_{p3}. The parameters: T, K, $overlap$.
1: Divide all images into T small patches and update each patch through increasing $overlap$, the image can be describes as: $x_{p3} = \{x_{(1,p3)}, x_{(2,p3)}, ..., x_{(T,p3)}\}$,
   and the i_{th} patch of the training set under the pose variations q are $I_{(i,pq)} =$
   $\{I^1_{(i,pq)}, I^2_{(i,pq)}, ..., I^N_{(i,pq)}\}$
2: **for** $i = 1 : T$ **do**
3:    **for** $s = 0 : 2$ **do**
4:       Initialize the virtual target facial image patch $x'_{(i,p3-s-1)} = Affine -$
         $Transform(x_{(i,p3-s)})$.
5:       **for** $j = 1 : N$ **do**
6:          $dist^j_{(i,p3-s-1)} = \|x'_{(i,p3-s-1)} - I^j_{(i,p3-s-1)}\|_2$ $1 \leq j \leq N$
7:       **end for**
8:       Get C_K of $x'_{(i,p3-s-1)}$ according to the Eq. (4).
9:       Establish the objective function: $J(w_{(i,p3-s)}) = \underset{w_{(i,p3-s)}}{argmin} \|x_{(i,p3-s)} -$
         $\sum_{j \in C_K} I^j_{(i,p3-s)} w^j_{(i,p3-s)}\|^2_2$ $1 \leq j \leq N$
10:      Obtain the reconstruction weights of $x_{(i,p3-s)}$ by applying the LcR algorithm.
11:      Get the updated target face patch $x_{(i,p3-s-1)} = \sum_{j \in C_K} I^j_{(i,p3-s-1)} w^j_{(i,p3-s)}$.
12:   **end for**
13: **end for**
14: Combine all frontal face patch $\{x_{(i,p0)}, 1 \leq i \leq T\}$ according to the position of each
   patch. And the frontal facial image can be obtained by averaging the overlapping
   regions.
Output: The frontal facial image x_{p0} .

Given an input facial image under the pose p_n, we first estimate the virtual target facial image $x'_{p_{n-1}}$ under the pose p_{n-1} via *linear affine transformation*. Then, for each patch, we apply the squared Euclidean distance between the intermediate pose facial patch and the patches of intermediate pose training samples to search K nearest neighbors (K-NN). Next we utilize the neighbors to obtain the weights of input face patch. As following, for the i_{th} patch, the reconstruction weights can be optimized by

$$J(w_{(i,p_n)}) = \underset{w_{(i,p_n)}}{\operatorname{argmin}} \|x_{(i,p_n)} - \sum_{j \in C_K} I^j_{(i,p_n)} w^j_{(i,p_n)}\|^2_2 \quad 1 \le j \le N \quad (3)$$

where C_K denotes the index set of K-NN of $x'_{(i,p_{n-1})}$ in the training set $I_{(i,p_{n-1})}$. It can be computed as following,

$$C_K = order(dist_{(i,p_{n-1})}|K) \quad (4)$$

$dist_{(i,p_{n-1})}|K$ refers to the smallest K indexes of $dist_{(i,p_{n-1})} = \{dist^j_{(i,p_{n-1})}\}^N_{j=1}$, which can be represented as

$$dist^j_{(i,p_{n-1})} = \|x'_{(i,p_{n-1})} - I^j_{(i,p_{n-1})}\|_2 \quad 1 \le j \le N \quad (5)$$

Generally speaking, least square representation (LSR) [10] and sparse representation (SR) [11] are usually applied to solve Eq. (3). But LSR may suffer from the over-fitting problem thus does not generalize well, SR overemphasizes the sparsity of the solution without considering the local similarity prior. So in our approach, we utilize Locality-constrained Representation (LcR) [15], which imposes a locality constraint onto the least square inversion problem to obtain the reconstruction weights. Through mapping the weights $w_{(i,p_n)}$ to the training patches set $I_{(i,p_{n-1})}$, we can obtain the updated target face patch $x_{(i,p_{n-1})}$. Then applying the prior constraint neighbor embedding method to each step of multiple stepwise synthesis, we can get the final frontal face patch $x_{(i,p_0)}$. The stepwise frontal face synthesis approach for large pose non-frontal facial image can be summarized as Algorithm 1.

3 Experiments

3.1 Dataset

To evaluate the proposed method effectively, we conduct experiments in the CAS-PEAL-R1 database [16]. There are 30863 images of 1040 subjects with controlled pose, expression, and lighting variations in this database. In our experiments, we make use of the only 79 subjects containing 316 images which cover the poses yawing over $0°$, $22.5°$, $45°$ and $67.5°$. 70 subjects for training and the left for test.

3.2 Parameters Settings

Before the experiments, we manually located 60 landmark points of all the training images. We set the size of each image as 192×228, and the number of

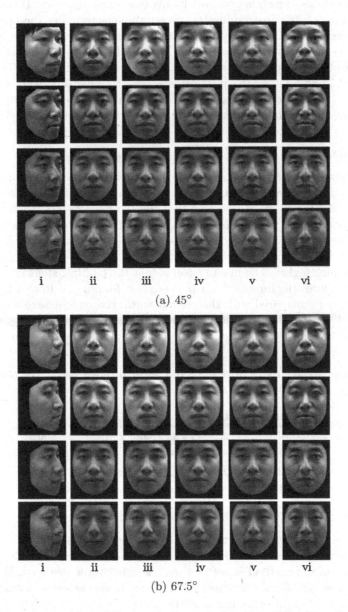

(a) 45°

(b) 67.5°

Fig. 3. Comparisons of frontal face synthesis results based on different methods on the CAS-PEAL-R1 database. (a) represents the synthesis results under 45°; (b) represents the synthesis results under 67.5°. In both subfigures, (i) represents the input non-frontal facial images under different poses; (ii) shows the results of LOC [8]; (iii) shows the results of LLR [10]; (iv) shows the results of URF [2]; (v) shows the results of the proposed method and (vi) shows the ground truth.

triangular patches, which is obtained by dividing each image via Delaunay triangulation as 99. In our experiments, we set the images under the pose of 45° and 67.5° as inputs. Limited by the datasets, when the input face pose is 45°, we set the training set under the pose of 22.5° as the intermediate pose training set. And when the input face pose is 67.5°, we set the training sets under the poses of 22.5° and 45° as the intermediate pose training sets. The number of nearest neighbors K for NE is set to 40. Meanwhile, we increase the overlapping regions for every patch to alleviate the blocking artifacts, and set overlap to 10.

3.3   Experimental Results

Figure 3 shows the comparison of our method with the methods of LOC [8], LLR [10] and URF [2]. Due to space limitation, we don't provide all the face results here. From the Fig. 3, we can observe that the synthesis results under the pose of 45° are better than the pose of 67.5° in the details, which can be easily understood because the smaller the pose, the more the useful information. Meanwhile, under the large pose of 67.5°, compared with other methods, the fidelity of our method is much higher. The main reason is that the multiple stepwise synthesis strategy mitigates the inconsistency between non-frontal and frontal face manifolds. However, compared with the ground truth, the reconstruction results of our method are still slightly smooth, which may be caused by the fact that the overlapping regions are too large and the number of samples is too small.

Table 1. The average PSNR (dB) and SSIM under different poses. The best results are shown in black fronts.

	Methods	LOC [8]	LLR [10]	URF [2]	Ours
45°	PSNR (dB)	23.8841	22.9246	24.1923	**24.3502**
	SSIM	0.8218	0.8160	0.8407	**0.8464**
67.5°	PSNR (dB)	23.4420	22.4994	23.1990	**23.8914**
	SSIM	0.8132	0.8088	0.8308	**0.8458**

Table 1 represents the average PSNR (dB) and SSIM of different methods for frontal face synthesis with different poses. As can be seen from the table, the performance of our method is better than the other three methods. When the input face pose is 67.5°, the average PSNR of our method is higher about 0.45 dB than the best result of other methods. However, the average PSNR of LOC is better than URF under 67.5°. This is mainly because global face synthesis can find smooth geometry for the severe self-occlusion regions of facial image.

4   Conclusion

In this paper, we propose a stepwise frontal face synthesis approach for large pose non-frontal facial image. Based on the intermediate pose training sets with different poses, we divide frontal face synthesis into multiple stepwise synthesis, which can mitigate the manifold inconsistency between non-frontal face space and frontal face space. Meanwhile, in each step, we use the geometric structure of target face space that has few self-occlusion as constraint to represent the input facial image with larger pose. In the future, our work will focus on enhancing facial details and utilizing multiple non-frontal facial images of the same person to jointly synthesize the frontal facial image.

Acknowledgement. The research is supported by the National Nature Science Foundation of China (61231015, 61303114), National High Technology Research and Development Program of China (863 Program, No. 2015AA016306), Internet of Things Development Funding Project of Ministry of industry in 2013 (No. 25), Technology Research Program of Ministry of Public Security (2014JSYJA016), Nature Science Foundation of Hubei Province (2014CFB712).

References

1. Zhu, Z., Luo, P., Wang, X., Tang, X.: Deep learning identity-preserving face space. In: IEEE International Conference on Computer Vision, pp. 113–120 (2013)
2. Hao, Y., Qi, C.: A unified regularization framework for virtual frontal face image synthesis. IEEE Sig. Process. Lett. **22**(22), 559–563 (2015)
3. Ho, H.T., Chellappa, R.: Pose-invariant face recognition using Markov random fields. IEEE Trans. Image Process. **22**(4), 1573–1584 (2013). A Publication of the IEEE Signal Processing Society
4. Ding, C., Xu, C., Tao, D.: Multi-task pose-invariant face recognition. IEEE Trans. Image Process. **24**(3), 980–993 (2015)
5. Ding, C., Tao, D.: A comprehensive survey on pose-invariant face recognition. ACM Trans. Intell. Syst. Technol. **7**(3) (2016)
6. Blanz, V., Grother, P., Phillips, P.J., Vetter, T.: Face recognition based on frontal views generated from non-frontal images. In: IEEE Computer Society Conference on Computer Vision and Pattern Recognition, vol. 2, pp. 454–461 (2005)
7. Prabhu, U., Heo, J., Savvides, M.: Unconstrained pose invariant face recognition using 3D generic elastic models. IEEE Trans. Pattern Anal. Mach. Intell. **33**(10), 1952–1961 (2011)
8. Vetter, T., Poggio, T.: Linear object classes and image synthesis from a single example image. IEEE Trans. Pattern Anal. Mach. Intell. **19**(7), 733–742 (1995)
9. Huang, X., Gao, J., Cheung, S.S., Yang, R.: Manifold estimation in view-based feature space for face synthesis across poses. In: Zha, H., Taniguchi, R., Maybank, S. (eds.) ACCV 2009. LNCS, vol. 5994, pp. 37–47. Springer, Heidelberg (2010). doi:10.1007/978-3-642-12307-8_4
10. Chai, X., Shan, S., Chen, X., Gao, W.: Locally linear regression for pose-invariant face recognition. IEEE Trans. Image Proces. **16**(7), 1716–1725 (2007). A Publication of the IEEE Signal Processing Society
11. Zhao, L., Gao, X., Yuan, Y., Tao, D.: Sparse frontal face image synthesis from an arbitrary profile image. Neurocomputing **128**(5), 466–475 (2014)
12. Cootes, T.F., Taylor, C.J., Cooper, D.H., Graham, J.: Active shape models-their training and application. Comput. Vis. Image Underst. **61**(1), 38–59 (1995)
13. Yang, J., Wright, J., Huang, T.S., Ma, Y.: Image super-resolution via sparse representation. IEEE Trans. Image Process. **19**(11), 2861–2873 (2010)

14. Zhang, C., Wang, J., Zhao, N., Zhang, D.: Reconstruction and analysis of multi-pose face images based on nonlinear dimensionality reduction. Pattern Recogn. **37**(2), 325–336 (2004)
15. Jiang, J., Hu, R., Han, Z., Lu, T., Huang, K.: Position-patch based face hallucination via locality-constrained representation. In: 2012 IEEE International Conference on Multimedia and Expo, pp. 212–217 (2012)
16. Gao, W., Cao, B., Shan, S., Chen, X., Zhou, D., Zhang, X., Zhao, D.: The CAS-PEAL large-scale Chinese face database and baseline evaluations. IEEE Trans. Syst. Man Cybern. Part A Syst. Hum. **38**(1), 149–161 (2008)

Nonlinear PCA Network for Image Classification

Xiao Zhang and Youtian Du[✉]

MOE Key Lab for Intelligent Networks and Network Security,
Xi'an Jiaotong University, Xi'an 710049, China
zhangxiaoz@stu.xjtu.edu.cn, duyt@mail.xjtu.edu.cn

Abstract. In this paper, we propose a simple nonlinear convolutional network, named Nonlinear PCA network (NL-PCANet) for image classification. Compared with previous PCA network, NL-PCANet introduces a nonlinear term in the convolution filters, which ensures that the maps depend on not only the direction of principal components of global distribution but also the location of individual example. Consequently, it is suitable to the nonlinear distribution of data and keeps more information of raw features. The main difference of our method from the traditional nonlinear architecture is that we introduce a nonlinear term in the traditional convolution filter instead of adding the layer of nonlinear transformation. Experiments of face recognition over Extended Yale B, Yale, ORL datasets and object recognition over various sizes of partial CIFAR10 dataset show the effectiveness of our approach.

Keywords: Deep learning · Nonlinear PCA network · Image classification

1 Introduction

Image understanding is a challenging problem mainly due to the gap between low-level representation and high-level human brain's cognition. How to represent images is a kernel issue in this problem. Many traditional methods tend to extract the low-level features to represent an image, including pixel-wise features, color distribution, and scale-invariant feature transform (SIFT) [2]. Usually, low-level features are hand-crafted and can be easily extracted, but they can hardly be extended to new conditions from previous specific data and tasks [3, 4]. Moreover, different kinds of tasks generally need different features. This problem limits flexible frameworks in image representation.

Deep Learning brings an effective architecture for both image recognition and representation tasks [3]. This architecture includes multiple similar layers. Features can be abstracted layer by layer, and the higher-level features represent more abstract semantics than previous. Convolutional network (ConvNet) [5, 6] is a typical model in image classification. The model consists of multiple trainable unsupervised stages, followed by a supervised classifier [7]. In ConvNet [8], each stage comprises three parts, i.e. convolution filters, nonlinear processing, and feature pooling. An important challenge is the parameter learning over a large space of parameters, which needs some expertise tuning and ad hoc tricks. In previous work, almost deep architectures [9–11]

© Springer International Publishing AG 2016
E. Chen et al. (Eds.): PCM 2016, Part II, LNCS 9917, pp. 449–457, 2016.
DOI: 10.1007/978-3-319-48896-7_44

apply nonlinear method in every stage. For example, every stage of Convolutional Neural Network (CNN) [10] includes a convolution layer and a pooling layer. Different with previous work, PCANet [1] proposes a two-stage unsupervised convolutional network, which is comprised of cascaded principal component analysis (PCA), binary hashing, and block-wise histograms. The model is a very simple deep learning network and is generally considered as a baseline for image classification and recognition. In PCANet, the first two stages are regarded as filter banks to learn, and binary hashing and block histogram are to index and pool. Compared with some complex deep learning models, it also gets a relative good performance in classification tasks. However, PCANet is suited to linear distribution of data. For complex and nonlinear distributions, the projection into the linear subspace will lost much information of raw features.

In this work, we propose a new approach, named nonlinear PCA Network (NL-PCANet) based on PCANet. NL-PCANet introduces a nonlinear term in the convolution filters, which ensures that maps depend on not only the direction of principal components of global distribution but also the location of examples. Consequently, it is suitable to nonlinear distribution of data and keeps much information of raw features. The main difference with the traditional nonlinear architectures is that we introduce a nonlinear term in traditional convolution filter instead of adding the layer of nonlinear transformation.

2   Brief Introduction of PCA Network

This section briefly reviews the PCA network [1]. As shown in Fig. 1, PCA network is comprised of two stages of convolution based on principal component analysis (PCA), binary hashing and block-size histogram.

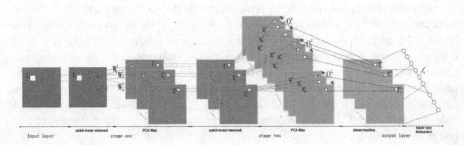

Fig. 1. PCA network

This model works over a set of N images $\{I_i\}_{i=1}^N$, each with size of $m \times n$. PCA network includes only two levels of PCA filters. In the first level of PCA filters, the patch of size $k_1 \times k_2$ centered at k^{th} pixel of the ith image is represented as a vector, denoted by $x_{i,k}$, with the concatenation of all pixels in it, and thus the image can be represented as a matrix of form $\bar{X}_i = \left[\bar{x}_{i,1}, \bar{x}_{i,2}, \ldots, \bar{x}_{i,\bar{m}\bar{n}} \right]$, by keeping the patches together, where $\tilde{m} = m - \lceil k_1/2 \rceil$ and $\tilde{n} = n - \lceil k_2/2 \rceil$. All images in the given set are represented by the matrix $\bar{\mathbf{X}} = [\bar{\mathbf{X}}_i, \bar{\mathbf{X}}_i, \cdots, \bar{\mathbf{X}}_N]$. The kernel idea of PCANet is that the ith filter is constructed by the ith basis derived by PCA over the matrix X. The ith filter is achieved as the following form of matrix:

$$W_l^1 \doteq mat_{k_1,k_2}\left(q_l(XX^T)\right) \in \mathbb{R}^{k_1 \times k_2}, \; l = 1, 2, \ldots, L_1 \tag{1}$$

where $mat_{k_1,k_2}(\mathbf{v})$ maps $\mathbf{v} \in \mathbb{R}^{k_1 k_2}$ to a matrix $W_l^1 \in \mathbb{R}^{k_1 \times k_2}$, and $q_l(XX^T)$ is the ith principal eigenvector of XX^T. The input I_i^l convolves with W_l^1 as follows:

$$O_i^l \doteq \{I_i^l * W_l^1\}_{l=1}^{L_1} \tag{2}$$

The stage two repeats operations of stage one. The output W_l^2 is L_1 times more than stage one and combines L_1 groups, in which each group has L_2 images.

The output layer is comprised of hashing and histogram. The output of stage two is binarized, divided into L_1 groups, and transferred to binary matrix, which is viewed as decimal numbers. After parting matrix into B blocks, the histogram of the decimal values is computed in each block. The output vector is the feature of one input image.

3 Our Approach

3.1 Nonlinear Projection of Data

PCA Network uses a set of orthogonal basis derived from PCA to construct the filters, which is effective for linear distributed data. In other words, it abstracts the information through the linear dimension reduction based on PCA. However, the visual information is located in a high dimensional feature space with extremely complicated distribution rather than only a linear space. Thus, the linear filter is limited to the problem. As is shown in Fig. 2, we find that the projection of data to the principal components derived

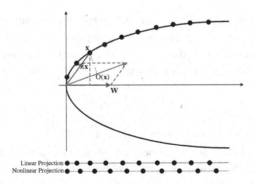

Fig. 2. The projection of samples for a nonlinear distribution the black curve indicates the distribution of data, and the orange line means the direction corresponding to the first principal components achieved by PCA. (Color figure online)

from PCA will lost very much information for nonlinear distribution. Therefore, the linear filter used in PCA network cannot represent the data accurately and completely.

In our work, we consider that the projection result of each example depends on not only the direction of principal components of global distribution but also the location of individual examples. Hence, we formulate the filters in CNNs as follows:

$$O(\mathbf{x}) = (W + \lambda f(\mathbf{x}))^T \mathbf{x} \tag{3}$$

where $f(\mathbf{x})$ is a term associated with the location of example $\mathbf{x}$ and W denotes the vector of principal component. Figure 2 illustrates the filtering process for a nonlinear distribution where $f(\mathbf{x}) := \mathbf{x}$. We can see that our idea considers the manifold structure of data distribution, and combines the principal direction of distribution and the location of each sample together. Consequently, the representation after the filtering process keeps more information, i.e., the relative position among data points, of the raw data in the nonlinear embedded space.

There can be various definitions of $f(\mathbf{x})$, such as polynomial functions and exponential functions. In the practical work, 1-order or 2-order polynomial functions may achieve efficient performance due to their simplicity.

3.2 Nonlinear Network Structure

In our work, we introduce a new method based on the analysis in Sect. 3.1. In this work, we let $f(\mathbf{x}) = \mathbf{x}$ for simplicity, and then obtain the final formulation for each filter:

$$O(\mathbf{x}) = (W + \lambda \mathbf{x})^T \mathbf{x} \tag{4}$$

where λ is a coefficient to control the balance between principal direction of global distribution and location of individual examples. Equation (4) shows that we use a quadratic function to model each filter in the network instead of the linear one used in PCA Network.

Our nonlinear PCA network includes two stages of convolution based on Eq. (4), binary hashing and block-size histogram for representation. Suppose given N input images $\{I_i\}_{i=1}^N$, each with size of $m \times n$. As shown in Fig. 3, we can also get Eq. (1) with same operations in Sect. 2. Based on Eq. (4), we obtain the nonlinear convolution in the stage one of NL-PCANet as follows:

$$O_i^l = I_i^l * \left(W_l^1 + \lambda_l^1 \times I_i^l\right) \tag{5}$$

where I_i^l is the lth patches of the ith input images, $W_l^1 \in R^{k_1 \times k_2}$ is with the same meaning with that in Eq. (1), and λ_l^1 is a coefficient added to individual patches to balance the principal eigenvector of distribution. Our nonlinear PCA network uses a convolution kernel, $W_l^1 + \lambda_l^1 \times I_i^l$, to replace the principal eigenvector W_l^1 in PCA network. The computation process in the stage two of this network is almost the same as the stage one except that its input is the output of the stage one, and L2 filters are used for the

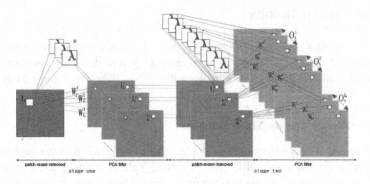

Fig. 3. Nonlinear network structure (partial)

output of one filter of the stage one. In the stage two, W_l^2 means the lth principal component vector that is achieved by PCA over the output of the stage one.

Like the PCANet, a Heaviside step (like) function $H(\bullet)$ is used in the hashing process. The output is one for positive entries and zero for others. It applies in the output $\left\{ I_i^l * \left(W_l^2 + \lambda_l^2 \times I_i^l \right) \right\}_{l=1}^{L_2}$ of the stage two, as $\left\{ H \left(I_i^l * \left(W_l^2 + \lambda_l^2 \times I_i^l \right) \right) \right\}_{l=1}^{L_2}$. We integer the L_2 outputs of each input in the stage two:

$$T_i^l = \sum_{l=1}^{L_2} 2^{l-1} H \left(I_i^l * \left(W_l^2 + \lambda_l^2 \times I_i^l \right) \right) \tag{6}$$

There are L_1 integer images T_i^l, $l = 1, 2, \ldots, L_1$, and each integer is considered as a distinct "word". Next, we divide the integers into B blocks and compute the histogram as $Bhist(T_i^l)$. We define the histogram with the "feature" of input images [1]:

$$f_i \doteq \left[Bhist \left(T_i^1 \right), \ldots, Bhist \left(T_i^{L_1} \right) \right]^T \in \mathbb{R}^{(2^{L_2})L_1 B} \tag{7}$$

According to the above discussion, the quadratic term in Eq. (4) describes the degree of nonlinearity associated to a given principal direction. There are L_1 filters in stage one and L_2 filters in stage two in our nonlinear PCA Network, which correspond to L_1 and L_2 directions respectively. In this work, we have not learned the parameter λ with training algorithms over datasets. We introduce three strategies to set the nonlinear terms in our network.

(1) We fix a uniform value of λ for each filter of the network, which means that the degrees of nonlinearity along all the directions are the same;
(2) A part of filters are chosen to introduce the nonlinear term with the same value of λ, and the rest keeps $\lambda = 0$;
(3) Random value of λ is set for each filter in a pre-defined range.

In the following section of experiments, we show some results about the strategies.

4 Experimental Results

This section evaluates the performance of our NL-PCANet with the tasks of face recognition and object classification over multiple public datasets. They are implemented with Matlab R2014a on a computer with 64-bits Windows 7 and 32 GB RAM.

4.1 Face Recognition on Many Datasets

The experiment of face recognition is implemented over three datasets including the extended Yale B, Yale, and ORL. The Extended Yale B includes 2414 frontal-face images of 38 individuals, around 64 images per individual. These images are made in various laboratory-controlled lighting conditions, having different illumination. In our experiments, we resize them to 32×32 pixels. We randomly select 190 images as learning set, 80 images as validation and the rest as test set. The Yale dataset has 165 gray scale images from 15 individuals, with different facial expression and configurations, like center-light, happy, left-light, w/n glasses, right-light, sad, normal, surprise, wink, and sleepy. We use leave one out procedure to get 60 images as training set, 20 as validation set, and others as test set. ORL dataset has 40 distinct individuals with 10 images of each subjects. The images are taken at different times, lighting, facial expressions and details. We randomly choose 100 images as training set, 100 as validation set, and the rest as test set. Over each dataset, we independently implements 5 times and use the averaged results to evaluate the performance.

For Extended Yale B dataset, we set the patch size to $k_1 = k_2 = 5$, the number of filters to $L_1 = L_2 = 8$, the block size in histogram computation to 8×8 and the overlapping ratio to 0.5. For Yale and ORL, we set the patch size to $k_1 = k_2 = 7$, the number of filters to $L_1 = L_2 = 8$, the block size to 7×7 and the overlapping ratio to 0.5.

To determine the degree of nonlinearity, i.e. the value of λ, we search it over the grid of $\{1, 1 \times 10^{-1}, 1 \times 10^{-2}, ..., 1 \times 10^{-7}, ..., 1 \times 10^{-10}\}$ to choose the best one. The experiment result is shown in Table 1. We test two strategies introduced in Sect. 3.2, one is to fixed λ as a uniform value 1×10^{-7}, and the other is to give λ randomly whose absolute value is in $(1 \times 10^{-6}, 1 \times 10^{-7})$. Compared to the traditional PCANet, both strategies improve the accuracy rate, respectively by 1.54% and 1.45% in Extended Yale B dataset, 1.34% and 2.67% in Yale dataset, 1.32% and 1.63% in ORL dataset. It's noted that although $\lambda = 1 \times 10^{-7}$ seems to be a tiny value, we find that the average $|\lambda \mathbf{x}|| / ||\mathbf{W}||$ is about 1.14%. Therefore, the nonlinear term is necessary.

4.2 Object Recognition on CIFAR10

4.2.1 Fixed λ Value for Different Filters

The experiment is implemented over CIFAR10, a set of 60000 natural RGB images of 32×32 pixels for 10 classes of objects. We choose four different size of training sets including 1000, 2500, 5000 and 10000 training samples, respectively.

We extend the filter to accommodate the RGB images by changing one channel to three. The second difference is that we connect spatial pyramid pooling to the output

Table 1. Experiments in different dataset

Network	PCANet	NL-PCANet	
λ	/	1×10^{-7}	$[-1,1]\times1\times10^{-7}$
Extended Yale B Dataset	79.63%	81.17%	81.08%
Yale Dataset	89.33%	90.67%	92.00%
ORL Dataset	91.87%	93.19%	93.50%

layer. We choose the size of filters $k_1 = k_2 = 5$, the number of filters $L_1 = 40, L_2 = 8$, block size 8×8, and overlapping ratio 0.5. Table 2 shows the classification accuracy. We can find that our NL-PCANet is superior to the PCANet, and the performance is promoted by 0.85% to 1.9%. From the results we also find a phenomenon that the promotion of performance decreases as the size of training set increases. We consider that the most possible reason is that, for the large set the simple nonlinear term used in Eq. (3) is limited to model the nonlinearity of the distribution.

4.2.2 The Analysis of λ Values
In this section, we discuss how the performance changes when the nonlinear term is used in the different combination of filters. The discussion is based on 1000 training and 1000 test images in CIFAR10 dataset.

From Sect. 4.1, we know $\lambda = 1 \times 10^{-7}$ is a good choice for recognition. Hence we use the value in the discussion. First, we choose only one filter to introduce the nonlinear term. We find that no matter which filter is chosen, the error rate is near to 42.5%, which is similar to PCANet. Second, we let $\lambda = 1 \times 10^{-7}$ to two filters and the others equal to zero. Similarly, we choose more filters to introduce the nonlinear term, and obtain the recognition results, as shown in Fig. 4. Different performance is raised when we introduce the nonlinear term into different combination of filters. We think that the most possible reason is different directions over different degrees of nonlinearity. When the combination of filters is consistent to the nonlinearity over different directions, the performance reaches the best one.

Table 2. Experiments in CIFAR-10 with different size of training set

Training set	Accuracy		Promotion
	PCANet	NL-PCANet (Fixed $\lambda=1\times10^{-7}$)	
1000	57.50%	59.40%	1.90%
2500	64.20%	65.40%	1.20%
5000	69.00%	70.00%	1.00%
10000	71.25%	72.10%	0.85%

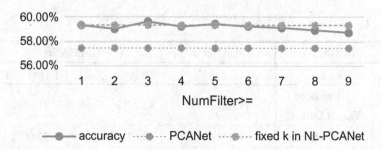

Fig. 4. The results for different combination filters to introduce the nonlinear term

5 Conclusion and Future Work

In this paper, we propose simple nonlinear convolutional network, named Nonlinear PCA network (NL-PCANet) for image classification. We can find that the nonlinear term in our model uses the changeable direction over which raw features are projected. The advantage is that the projected results in the convolution layers keep more information of the raw nonlinear-distributed features in the initial space. In the experiments, we evaluate the performance by object classification over CIFAR10 and face recognition over extended Yale B, Yale, and ORL datasets. The result shows that our approach can increase the accuracy by 0.85%–2.67% compared with the PCA network. As for computational cost, there is nearly similar to the previous PCANet.

In future work, we will explore more effective nonlinear convolution method based on current work, such as a more reasonable nonlinear term $f(\mathbf{x})$ shown in Eq. (3), and test the work over larger dataset for illustrating its effectiveness. Also, another important issue is to study how to automatically learn parameter λ from the datasets.

Acknowledgments. This work is supported in part by the National Natural Science Foundation (61375040, 61572397, 61221063), Natural Science Basic Research Plan in Shaanxi Province (2015JM6299, 2015JM6298), and 111 International Collaboration Program, of China.

References

1. Chan, T.-H., Jia, K., Gao, S., Lu, J., Zeng, Z., Ma, Y.: PCANet: a simple deep learning baseline for image classification? IEEE Trans. Image Process. **24**(12), 5017–5032 (2015)
2. Lowe, D.G.: Distinctive image features from scale-invariant keypoints. Int. J. Comput. Vis. **60**(2), 91–110 (2004)
3. Hinton, G., Osindero, S., Teh, Y.-W.: A fast learning algorithm for deep belief nets. Neural Comput. **18**(7), 1527–1554 (2006)
4. Bengio, Y., Courville, A., Vincent, P.: Representation learning: a review and new perspectives. IEEE TPAMI **35**(8), 1798–1828 (2013)
5. Lee, H., Grosse, R., Ranganath, R., Ng, A.Y.: Convolutional deep belief networks for scalable unsupervised learning of hierarchical representation. In: ICML (2009)

6. Krizhevsky, A., Sutskever, I., Hinton, G.: Imagenet classification with deep convolutional neural network. In: NIPS (2012)
7. Jarrett, K., Kavukcuoglu, K., Ranzato, M., LeCun, Y.: What is the best multi-stage architecture for object recognition. In: ICCV (2009)
8. Kavukcuoglu, K., Sermanet, P., Boureau, Y., Gregor, K., Mathieu, M., LeCun, Y.: Learning convolutional feature hierarchies for visual recognition. In: NIPS (2010)
9. Ciresan, D., Meier, U., Schmidhuber, J.: Multi-column deep neural networks for image classification. In: CVPR (2012)
10. Jia, Y.: Caffe: an open source convolutional architecture for fast feature embedding (2013). http://caffe.berkeleyvision.org/
11. Mikolov, T., Karafiát, M., Burget, L., Cernocký, J., Khudanpur, S.: Recurrent neural network based language model. In: Proceedings of Interspeech (2010)

Salient Object Detection in Video Based on Dynamic Attention Center

Mengling Shao[1,2], Ruimin Hu[1,2,3(✉)], Xu Wang[1,2],
Zhongyuan Wang[1,2,3], Jing Xiao[1,2,3], and Ge Gao[1,3]

[1] State Key Laboratory of Software Engineering,
Wuhan University, Wuhan, China
shaomengling_whu@163.com, hrml964, wzy_hope@163.com,
wangxu9191@gmail.com
[2] National Engineering Research Center for Multimedia Software,
Computer School of Wuhan University, Wuhan, China
[3] Hubei Provincial Key Laboratory of Multimedia and Network
Communication Engineering, Wuhan University, Wuhan, China
{jing,gaoge}@whu.edu.cn

Abstract. Salient object detection in video has attracted enormous research efforts for its wide applicability. But there are still some issues in restraining the disturbance of background, which make it difficult to detect salient object in complex scenarios. Inspired by the hypothesis of center prior in image domain, we novelly introduced the concept of dynamic attention center in video. The distance between specific regions and this center is used as a weighting term to restrain the influence of background disturbance and obtain more accurate spatial and temporal saliency maps. Besides, we develop a dynamic fusion method to combine the temporal and spatial saliency map, leading to higher spatiotemporal consistency. The experiments on Freiburg-Berkeley Motion Segmentation Dataset show that our method outperforms several state-of-art methods on subjective visual perception and objective measurements.

Keywords: Salient object detection in video · Dynamic attention center · Center prior · Spatiotemporal consistency

1 Introduction

The human vision system has a remarkable ability to locate and focus on the object or region of interest among massive visual information, which is called salient object detection in computer vison. Salient object detection for images and videos plays a crucial role in image understanding, content-based image editing, object recognition, which facilitates great reduction in the visual information that needs to be processed. According to early works, Treisman and Gelade [1], Itti et al. [2] suggested that, visual attention is generally classified into two manners: a rapid, bottom-up, saliency-driven, task-independent manner and a slower, top-down, volition-controlled, and task-dependent manner [3]. The bottom-up manner is driven by low-level features, such as color, gradient, edges and boundaries. While the top-down manner is driven by

© Springer International Publishing AG 2016
E. Chen et al. (Eds.): PCM 2016, Part II, LNCS 9917, pp. 458–468, 2016.
DOI: 10.1007/978-3-319-48896-7_45

subjective factors such as age, culture, and experience regulate attention, which is relatively less explored for its high complexity [4]. Here we focus on bottom-up, features driven salient object detection in videos in our wok.

It is widely believed that human vision system always preferentially responds to high contrast stimulus in receptive fields. In static images, contrast-based models have been proved to be effective for salient object detection [2, 5–8]. Considering motion is the primary influential factor in salient object detection in video [4], many researchers have extended existing spatial salient object detection models by taking the additional temporal dimension into account to extract spatiotemporal saliency [9–15]. Zhai and Shah [9] proposed a spatiotemporal model which defined the pixel-level saliency based on a pixel's motion and color contrast to all other pixels. Fu et al. [13] devised three visual attention cues: contrast, spatial, and global correspondence to measure the cluster saliency. Zhou et al. [14] adopted space-time saliency to generate a low-frame-rate video from a high-frame-rate input using region contrast of various low-level features. In these works, spatial features are combined with motion features to measure the saliency frame-by-frame. However, in complex scenarios, the background disturbance becomes a major obstacle to detect accurate salient object. The background could be detected as the target object or the detected salient object in adjacent frames may not be consistent along the time axis, which apparently contradicts with common sense.

In image salient object detection, a hypothesis called center prior proposed by Jiang et al. [16] provides a feasible idea to solve the problem caused by background. This hypothesis is based on the fact that the salient object in an image always locates near the image geometric center. In other words, the background tends to be far away from the image geometric center. Based on this, Cheng et al. [7] introduced a weight of average distance between pixels in specific region and the image geometric center, which effectively restrained the influence of regions located near the boundary of image. In terms of video, which is made up with continuous frames, this hypothesis still make sense. The background in video frames tends to be far away from human attention center. As for video, fixed center is inappropriate for moving salient objects and the salient object may locate at the boundary of the frame. Thus directly adopting the idea of center prior into the salient object detection model in video will cause inaccurate distribution of saliency map. Some modifications should be made to fit the case in video.

To solve this problem, we extended the hypothesis of center prior by introducing the dynamic attention center to make it applicable for video. The distance between specific regions and this center is used as a weighting term, which restrains the influence of background disturbance to obtain more accurate spatial and temporal saliency maps. The attention center is presupposed as the center of extracted salient region in last frame. With the continually updated attention center, the extracted salient region would converge at a more accurate location. Furthermore, we combine the temporal and spatial saliency maps in a dynamic fusion method to obtain the accurate salient object and achieve higher spatiotemporal consistency.

The remainder of this paper is organized as follows: we introduce the detail of ourmodel in Sect. 2; Sect. 3 presents the experiment compared with several state-of-art methods; Finally we conclude our major contributions in Sect. 4.

2 Proposed Method

2.1 Framework of Proposed Model

In this paper, we propose a salient object detection model based on global contrast and combination of spatial and temporal features. Figure 1 shows the framework of proposed model. The process of our model is divided into following three steps.

Firstly, we obtain the segmented image and the optical flow information from video frames. Then we utilize the global region contrast of motion and color to obtain the preliminary temporal and spatial saliency maps. Secondly, we improve the preliminary saliency maps by introducing a distance weight to emphasize the region located near the attention center. Lastly, a dynamic fusion method is proposed to combine the temporal and spatial saliency map together. Moreover, we extract the k-th frame's attention center as the presupposed attention center of the next frame.

2.2 Preliminary Salient Object Detection

Firstly, we utilize the well-known EDSION segmentation [17–19] to divide the frame into separated objects and regions. We obtain the motion vector $\overrightarrow{m_i}(p_i) = (x, y)$ of each pixel p_i by utilizing the optical flow between two adjacent frames. The motion vector $\vec{v}(o_k)$ of the region o_k is computed by (1).

$$\vec{v}(o_k) = w_v(o_k)\overrightarrow{m_a}(o_k) \tag{1}$$

$$w_v(o_k) = exp\left(-\sigma\frac{\sum_{p_i \in o_k}\left|\overrightarrow{m_i}(p_i) - \overrightarrow{m_a}(o_k)\right|^2}{n}\right) \tag{2}$$

where $\overrightarrow{m_a}(o_k) = \frac{1}{n}\sum_{p_i \in o_k} \overrightarrow{m_i}(p_i)$ is the average motion vector of o_k, n is the number of pixels in o_k. $w_v(o_k)$ is the normalized variance of motion vectors in o_k, which measure the consistency of motion vectors in o_k. The value of $\overrightarrow{m_a}(o_k)$ is higher in foreground due to its highly consistent motion vectors, which is quite obvious in Fig. 2(c).

Considering the complicated movements in background, we use a global contrast method to obtain the temporal saliency through motion vectors. For each object or region o_k the temporal saliency is:

$$S_t'(o_k) = \sum_{o_k \neq o_i} exp\left(-\frac{D_t(o_k, o_i)}{\sigma^2}\right)w(o_i)|\vec{v}(o_k) - \vec{v}(o_i)|^2 \tag{3}$$

where $exp\left(\frac{D_t(o_k,o_i)}{-\sigma^2}\right)$ is the normalized distance weight to eliminate the influence of regions located too far. And $D_t(o_k, o_i)$ is the normalized distance between the centers of two regions. Here we use the number of pixels in region o_i as the weight of region o_i to emphasize motion contrast to larger regions.

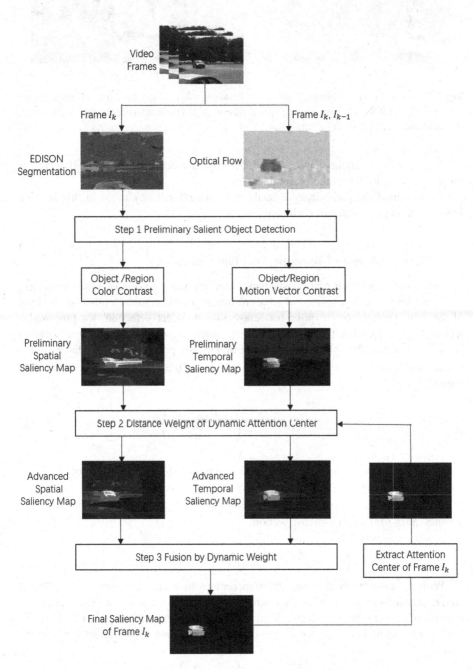

Fig. 1. The framework of proposed model

Fig. 2. Illustration of preliminary process of salient object detection: (a) original frame; (b) result of EDISON segmentation; (c) optical flow map; (d) preliminary temporal saliency map; (e) preliminary spatial saliency map

As for spatial saliency, we adopted the region color contrast method which is proposed in [7] to obtain the preliminary result.

We obtained the preliminary spatial and temporal saliency maps in this section. Figure 2 shows the result in each step.

2.3   Distance Weight of Dynamic Attention Center

The temporal correlation and consistency is an important feature of video sequence, which means the salient regions of adjacent frames are close to each other. In the light of the hypothesis of center prior for image salient object detection, we proposed a weighting term based on the distance between current region and the dynamic attention center to restrain the influence of background. We presuppose the center of the extracted salient object o'_k of the $n-1$ th frame as the attention center of the n th frame.

$$w_t(o_k, n) = exp\left(-\frac{d_k^2(o_k, o'_k)}{\sigma^2}\right) \qquad (4)$$

where $d_k(o_k, o'_k)$ is the distance between the center of o_k and the center of o'_k. Thus, $w_t(o_k, n)$ gives a high value if o_k is close to the attention center and it gives a low value if the o_k is a border region away from the attention center. We improve the temporal saliency $S'_t(o_k)$ introduced in last section.

$$S_t(o_k) = w_t(o_k, n)S'_t(o_k) \qquad (5)$$

With the continually updated attention center, the extracted salient region would converge at a more accurate location, which enhances the accuracy of extracted salient region and weaken the disturbance from background as shown in Fig. 3. For the same reason, we also add the distance weight in the color contrast method in spatial domain.

$$S_s(o_k) = w_s(o_k, n)\sum_{o_k \neq o_i} exp\left(-\frac{D_s(o_k, o_i)}{\sigma^2}\right)w(o_i)D_o(o_k, o_i) \qquad (6)$$

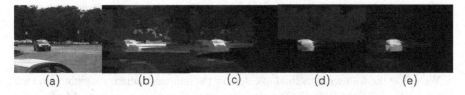

(a)   (b)   (c)   (d)   (e)

Fig. 3. Comparison of preliminary spatial and temporal saliency maps and advanced spatial and temporal maps: (a) original frame; (b) preliminary spatial saliency map; (c) advanced spatial saliency map; (d) preliminary temporal saliency map; (e) advanced temporal saliency map

Via introducing the distance weight of dynamical attention center, we obtain the advanced saliency maps both in spatial and temporal domain.

2.4   Fusion by Dynamic Weight

When we extracting the salient region in temporal domain, the motion of the object and the background is not always identifiable. The proposed method in temporal domain is difficult to obtain satisfying result in this situation. So we fuse the saliency map in spatial and temporal domain together to obtain stable result. According to [9], we proposed an improved fusion method with dynamic weight.

The fusion method is based on the following principle: human vision system is sensitive to the stimuli caused by motion. So if the motion contrast in temporal domain is intense, the temporal saliency map should occupy a larger proportion in the fusion result and vice versa. The optical flow is the direct reflection of motion information. Through the observation of optical flow, we divide the result of the optical flow into the following three types, which are shown in Fig. 4:

1. The optical flow of the whole frame is roughly consistent, which means the motion contrast between the moving object and background is weak;
2. The moving object and background have different but internally consistent optical flow, which means the motion contrast between the moving object and background is strong;

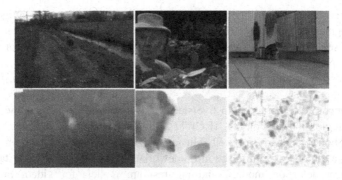

Fig. 4. Three different types of optical flow map

3. The optical-flow of the whole frame is disorder and random, which means it is difficult to distinguish the moving object and background;

Only in the type 2, the moving object is obvious and we need to increase the weight of temporal saliency map in the fusion method.

We utilize the following method to calculate the temporal saliency weight λ and the spatial saliency weight $1-\lambda$. Firstly, we compute the gradient magnitude M of matrix I_m which is made up with the normalized motion vector modulus of each region.

$$M(x, y) = mag(\nabla I_m(x, y)) \tag{7}$$

As for three different types of optical flow map mentioned above, the first type generate a small value of $\sum M(x, y)$, and the third type lead to a large value of $\sum M(x, y)$.

Only the second type achieve stable and reasonable range for value of $\sum M(x, y)$ because only the edge of the motion changed region achieve high gradient magnitude.

Therefore, we make use of M and Gaussian method to calculate the weight of temporal saliency map.

$$\lambda = exp\left(-\frac{\left(\sum M(x, y) - \mu\right)^2}{\sigma^2}\right) \tag{8}$$

where μ means reasonable sum of gradient magnitude, and σ is the convergence rate. Both of them are empirical value and we make $\mu = 300$, $\sigma = 400$ in our experiment. Finally, the temporal saliency map and the spatial saliency map is combined together to obtain the final saliency value.

$$S(I) = \lambda S_t(I) + (1 - \lambda)S_s(I) \tag{9}$$

where $S_t(I)$ and $S_s(I)$ are obtained by (5) and (6) respectively. And $S(I)$ is the final result of our model.

3 Experimental Results

In the experiment, we evaluate our model on the well-known Freiburg-Berkeley Motion Segmentation Dataset (FBMS) [20]. It contains 59 video sequences and a pixel-level segmentation ground-truth for each video is available. Most of videos in FBMS are pretty challenging for salient object detection for the large appearance variation of foreground and background, significant shape deformation, and large camera motion.

We compare our method with five state-of-art methods: frequency-tuned saliency (FT) [5], region based contrast (RC) [7], luminance contrast saliency (LC) [9], quaternion Fourier transform based saliency (QS) [21] and spatial and temporal saliency integration energy minimization framework (SEG) [22]. FT, RC are static image salient object detection models, and the rest are models for video. In order to comprehensively evaluate the performance of our model for salient object detection, we performed two experiments on both subjective and objective measures.

Firstly, we present the subjective visual comparison result in Fig. 5. It shows an intuitional comparison of our model and FT, RC, LC, QS, SEG for some representative frames chosen from the FBMS dataset. Because of lacking inter-frame information, FT, RC cannot identify the salient object accurately, and RC also tend to highlight the back ground for using a distance weight based on fixed center (e.g., cats01). Although LC, QS, SEG are methods for videos, they do not effectively suppress interference from background. As a result, the salient value of the same region may dramatically change in adjacent frames, which means the background may be detected as the salient object (e.g., marple4). The comparison demonstrates that our model performs better especially in video contains complex background (e.g., marple4, various subtle motion in its background). The extracted salient objects have higher spatial-temporal consistency (e.g., cats01, the cat is always highlighted in our saliency maps).

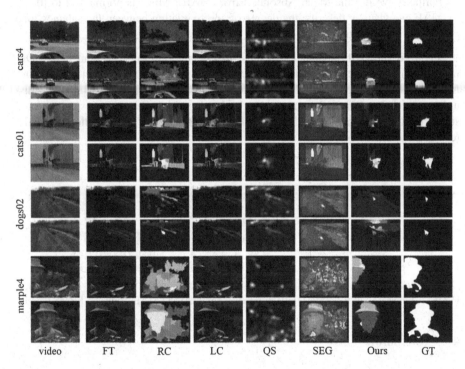

Fig. 5. Video saliency results on the FBMS dataset. From left to right columns: indicative frames of input videos, FT, RC, LC, QS, SEG, our model and the ground truth (GT).

Secondly, we evaluate the objective performance of our model with three quantitative measurements.

1. The first one is the precision versus recall curves (PR curves). For the saliency value of the predicted saliency map is in the range of [0, 255], we convert the saliency

map to a binary mask with a threshold from 0 to 255. For each threshold, we compute the precision and the recall to plot a Precision-Recall (PR) curve to describe the performance of the proposed method. The precision value represents the ratio of the real salient pixels correctly assigned to all the pixels of extracted regions, while the recall value represents the ratio of the detected salient pixels correctly assigned to all the pixels of the ground truth.

2. Then we use the F-Measure combing both precision and recall. The F-Measure is proposed as a weighted harmonic mean of precision and recall with a non-negative weight:

$$F_\beta = \frac{(1+\beta^2) \cdot precision \cdot recall}{\beta^2 precision + recall} \quad (10)$$

β^2 is set to 0.3 as suggested in many salient object detection works.

3. Furtherly we use the Mean Absolute Error (MAE), which is normalized to [0, 1]. MAE can visually describe the degree of approximation between the saliency map and the ground truth.

Figure 6 shows the evaluation results on PR curves, F-measure and MAE. Our model significantly performs better in PR curves and F-measure than other models. Our model achieves a higher value in precision because of effective restraining the disturbance of the background, no matter the background is static or contains complicated subtle motion. Our model achieves the lowest MAE value, which reflects that the results produced by our model are closer to ground truth.

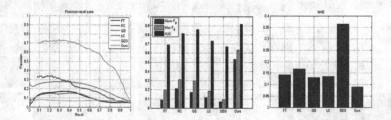

Fig. 6. Comparison of PR curves (left), F-measure (middle) and MAE (right) on FBMS dataset.

4   Conclusion

In this paper, we proposed a novel salient object detection model for video sequence. There are two major contributions of our paper: (1) In order to restrain the disturbance of background, we novelly introduce the concept of dynamic attention center. And the weighting term based on the distance between specific region and the center is used to obtain more accurate spatial and temporal saliency maps; (2) We present a dynamic fusion method combining the temporal and spatial saliency maps to achieve higher spatiotemporal consistency. Experimental results on FBMS dataset show that the proposed model performs better than several state-of-art models especially in the video with a complex background.

As the motion vector is obtained from optical flow which has high complexity in computation, the time complexity of our method mainly depends on the algorithm of optical flow. The acceleration of our method will be further explored in fast extraction of motion information.

Acknowledgements. This work was partly supported by the National High Technology Research and Development Program of China (863 Program) No. 2015AA016306, the National Nature Science Foundation of China (No. 61231015) , the National Natural Science Foundation of China (61502348), the EU FP7 QUICK project under Grant Agreement No. PIRSES-GA-2013-612652.

References

1. Treisman, A.M., Gelade, G.: A feature integration theory of attention. Cogn. Psychol. **12**(1), 97C136 (1980)
2. Itti, L., Koch, C., Niebur, E.: A model of saliency-based visual attention for rapid scene analysis. IEEE trans pami. IEEE Trans. Pattern Anal. Mach. Intell. **20**(11), 1254–1259 (1998)
3. Niebur, E., Koch, C.: Computational architectures for attention. In: The Attentive (1998)
4. Borji, A., et al.: Salient Object Detection: A Survey (2014). eprint arXiv:1411.5878
5. Achanta, R., Hemami, S., Estrada, F., Susstrunk, S.: Frequency-tuned salient region detection. In: IEEE International Conference on Computer Vision and Pattern Recognition (CVPR 2009), pp. 1597–1604 (2009)
6. Zhang, J., Wang, M., Zhang, S., Li, X., Wu, X.: Spatio-chromatic context modeling for color saliency analysis. IEEE Trans. Neural Netw. Learn. Syst. **27**(6), 1177–1189 (2016)
7. Cheng, M., Zhang, G., Mitra, N., Huang, X., Hu, S.: Global contrast based salient region detection. In: IEEE International Conference on Computer Vision and Pattern Recognition (CVPR 2011), pp. 569–582 (2011)
8. Chen, Y., Nguyen, T.V., Katti, H., Yadat, K., Kankanhalli, M., Yuan, J., Yan, S., Wang, M.: Audio matters in visual saliency. IEEE Trans. Circ. Syst. Video Technol. **24**(11), 1992–2003 (2014)
9. Zhai, Y., Shah, M.: Visual attention detection in video sequences using spatiotemporal cues. In: Multimedia Proceedings of Annual ACM International Conference on Multimedia, vol. 2006, pp. 815–824 (2006)
10. Wang, M., Hong, R., Yuan, X.-T., Yan, S., Chua, T.-S.: Movie2comics: towards a lively video content presentation. IEEE Trans. Multimedia **14**(3), 858–870 (2012)
11. Zhang, J., Wang, M., Gao, J., Wang, Y., Zhang, X., Wu, X.: Saliency detection with a deeper investigation of light field. In: International Joint Conference on Artificial Intelligence (IJCAI) (2015)
12. Fang, Y., Lin, W., Chen, Z., Tsai, C.-M., Lin, C.-W.: A video saliency detection model in compressed domain. IEEE Trans. Circ. Syst. Video Technol. **24**(1), 27–38 (2014)
13. Fu, H., Cao, X., Tu, Z.: Cluster-based co-saliency detection. IEEE Trans. Image Process. **22**, 3766–3778 (2013)

14. Zhou, F., Kang, S.B., Cohen, M.F.: Time-mapping using space-time saliency. In: IEEE International Conference on Computer Vision and Pattern Recognition, pp. 3358–3365 (2014)
15. Fang, Y., Wang, Z., Lin, W., Fang, Z.: Video saliency incorporating spatiotemporal cues and uncertainty weighting. IEEE Trans. Image Process. 23(9), 3910–3921 (2014)
16. Jiang, H., Wang, J., Yuan, Z., Liu, T., Zheng, N., Li, S.: Automatic salient object segmentation based on context and shape prior. In: Proceedings of the British Machine Vision Conference (BMVC) (2011)
17. Comaniciu, D., Meer, P.: Mean shift: a robust approach toward feature space analysis. IEEE Trans. Pattern Anal. Mach. Intell. 24(5), 603–619 (2002)
18. Meer, P., Georgescu, B.: Edge detection with embedded confidence. IEEE Trans. Pattern Anal. Mach. Intell. 23(12), 1351–1365 (2001)
19. Christoudias, C., Georgescu, B., Meer, P.: Synergism in low level vision. In: International Conference on Pattern Recognition, pp. 150–155 (2002)
20. Ochs, P., Malik, J., Brox, T.: Segmentation of moving objects by long term video analysis. IEEE Trans. Pattern Anal. Mach. Intell. 36(6), 1187–1200 (2014)
21. Guo, C., Ma, Q., Zhang, L.: Spatiotemporal saliency detection using phase spectrum of quaternion fourier transform. In: Proceedings of the IEEE Computer Society Conference on Computer Vision and Pattern Recognition, CVPR, pp. 1–8 (2008)
22. Rahtu, E., Kannala, J., Salo, M., Heikkilä, J.: Segmenting Salient Objects from Images and Videos. In: European Conference on Computer Vision, pp. 366–379 (2010)

Joint Optimization of a Perceptual Modified Wiener Filtering Mask and Deep Neural Networks for Monaural Speech Separation

Wei Han[1], Xiongwei Zhang[1(✉)], Jibin Yang[1], Meng Sun[1], and Gang Min[1,2]

[1] Lab of Intelligent Information Processing, PLAUST, Nanjing, China
Signal.ICedu@gmail.com
[2] Xi'an Communications Institute, Xi'an, China

Abstract. Due to the powerful feature extraction ability, deep learning has become a new trend towards solving speech separation problems. In this paper, we present a novel Deep Neural Network (DNN) architecture for monaural speech separation. Taking into account the good mask property of the human auditory system, a perceptual modified Wiener filtering masking function is applied in the proposed DNN architecture, which is used to make the residual noise perceptually inaudible. The proposed architecture jointly optimize the perceptual modified Wiener filtering mask and DNN. Evaluation experiments on TIMIT database with 20 noise types at different signal-to-noise ratio (SNR) situations demonstrate the superiority of the proposed method over the reference DNN-based separation methods, no matter whether the noise appeared in the training database or not.

Keywords: Speech enhancement · Deep neural networks · Audible noise suppression · Joint optimization

1 Introduction

The objective of a speech enhancement process is to suppress the noise and improve the perceptual quality of speech in noisy environments. Over the past decades, many approaches have been widely used to extract the target speech from the noisy speech, like spectral subtraction [1], Wiener filter [2], minimum mean squared error (MMSE) estimation [3] and optimally-modified log-spectral amplitude (OM-LSA) speech estimator [4]. Those methods often perform not well when noise is non-stationary and SNR levels are low.

Another set of widely-used techniques is dictionary learning approaches such as non-negative matrix factorization (NMF) [5, 6]. Dictionary learning approaches performance better than statistical speech enhancement approaches in low SNR conditions and non-stationary noise environment, but dictionary learning approaches are not good at capturing the spectra patterns of noises without repeated low rank spectral structures.

Recently, deep learning has achieved state-of-the-art performance in many speech enhancement tasks [7–12]. In general, speech enhancement can be formulated as a

© Springer International Publishing AG 2016
E. Chen et al. (Eds.): PCM 2016, Part II, LNCS 9917, pp. 469–478, 2016.
DOI: 10.1007/978-3-319-48896-7_46

supervised learning problem. A typical supervised speech enhancement system is proposed in [7]. In this system, DNN is developed as a nonlinear approximation function to predict the clean speech spectra from the noisy speech spectra. Extended from the basic DNN, some different training targets, including the ideal binary mask (IBM), the target binary mask (TBM), the ideal ratio mask (IRM), and the Gammatone frequency power spectrum, are evaluated and compared [8]. This study find that masking based targets, in general, are significantly better than spectral envelope based targets. In [9], the authors explored joint optimization of masking functions and deep recurrent neural network (DRNN) for monaural source separation tasks. This method use the soft time-frequency mask as an extra masking layer, which is placed on the top of the original network output as the final output. In [10], the authors investigated a novel method that simultaneously enhances the magnitude and phase spectra by operating in the complex domain. The approach uses a DNN to estimate the real and imaginary components of the IRM in the complex domain.

In general, the masking based targets are widely used in deep learning and achieve good performance for speech enhancement tasks, but the masking properties of the human auditory system was not consider. In this paper, we propose a new DNN architecture for monaural speech enhancement. Firstly, a Wiener-type filtering layer is used to mask the network original output. Then, a perceptually motivated modification is applied to the Wiener filter masking function. Finally, the adjusted Wiener masking function as the network final output to obtain clean speech spectra from noisy speech spectra.

The rest of the paper is organized as follows. Section 2 gives a brief introduction of the perceptual modified Wiener filter mask. The proposed enhancement approach is presented in Sect. 3. The results of the experimental evaluation over the TIMIT database are outlined in Sect. 4. Finally, Sect. 5 concludes our work.

2 A Brief Review on Perceptual Modified Wiener Filter Mask

The noisy signal $y = s + n$ is expressed in terms of speech signal s and noise signal n. Using discrete Fourier transform (DFT) to the observed signal gives

$$Y(m,k) = S(m,k) + N(m,k) \tag{1}$$

where $m = 1, 2, \ldots, M$ is the frame index, $k = 1, 2, \ldots, K$ is the frequency bin index, M is the total number of frames and K is the frame length, $Y(m,k)$, $S(m,k)$ and $N(m,k)$ represent the short-time spectral components of y, s and n, respectively.

Basic speech enhancement approaches usually estimate the frequency component of the clean speech from the noisy speech, as shown

$$\hat{S}(m,k) = H(m,k)Y(m,k) \tag{2}$$

where $H(m,k)$ is a gain estimator chosen according to a suitable criterion. The error signal generated by this gain estimator is

$$\varepsilon(m,k) = \hat{S}(m,k) - S(m,k)$$
$$= (H - I)S(m,k) + HN(m,k) \tag{3}$$

where $(H - I)S(m,k)$ represents the spectrum of speech distortion and $HN(m,k)$ represents the spectrum of residual noise.

The Wiener filtering is one of the widely-used mask methods aimed at reducing residual noise. In this case, the gain estimator is $H(m,k) = W(m,k)$ and $\hat{S}(m,k) = W(m,k)Y(m,k)$ is the Wiener estimate of $S(m,k)$. If clean speech signal and noise signal are zero mean and uncorrelated, the Wiener gain function $W(m,k)$ is obtained as follows:

$$W(m,k) = \frac{E(|S(m,k)|^2)}{E(|S(m,k)|^2) + E(|N(m,k)|^2)} \tag{4}$$

where $E(|S(m,k)|^2)$ and $E(|N(m,k)|^2)$ represents the estimated clean speech power spectrum and noise power spectrum, respectively.

Although the Wiener filtering estimator reduces the level of residual noise, it does not eliminate it [13]. In order to make the residual noise perceptually inaudible, many perceptual gain estimators have been proposed which incorporates the auditory masking properties [14–16]. In these estimators, residual noise is shaped according to an estimate of the clean signal masking threshold. One of the famous perceptual gain estimator $H(m,k) = G(m,k)$ proposed in [15] can be expressed as

$$G(m,k) = \frac{|S(m,k)|^2}{|S(m,k)|^2 + \max(|N(m,k)|^2 - T(m,k), 0)} \tag{5}$$

where $T(m,k)$ is an estimate of the clean speech noise masking threshold (NMT).

In [16], the authors proposed perceptual modified Wiener filtering mask by using a perceptual weighting factor $G(m,k)$ to control the Wiener gain function $W(m,k)$. The proposed perceptual modified Wiener filter mask concatenate perceptual weighting factor $G(m,k)$ and Wiener gain function $W(m,k)$ as follows:

$$H(m,k) = G(m,k)W(m,k)$$
$$= \frac{|\tilde{S}(m,k)|^2}{|\tilde{S}(m,k)|^2 + \max(|\tilde{N}(m,k)|^2 - \tilde{T}(m,k), 0)} W(m,k) \tag{6}$$

where $\tilde{S}(m,k)$ and $\tilde{N}(m,k)$ are clean speech magnitude spectrum and noise speech magnitude spectrum which are separated from noisy spectrum $Y(m,k)$ by Wiener filter $W(m,k)$, respectively. $\tilde{T}(m,k)$ represents the noise masking threshold which is calculated by $\tilde{S}(m,k)$.

3 Proposed Method

3.1 Model Architecture

Joint optimization of masking functions and DNN can improve the separation performance [9]. In this paper, we use this idea and propose a new DNN architecture for speech separation, which jointly optimize DNN together with the perceptual modified Wiener filtering. The proposed DNN architecture is shown in Fig. 1.

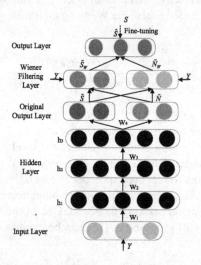

Fig. 1. The architecture of the proposed DNN

The proposed DNN simultaneously predict the clean speech magnitude spectrum $\tilde{S}$ and the noise magnitude spectrum $\tilde{N}$. Then, the Wiener filter mask can be calculated as follows:

$$W_S = \frac{\tilde{S}^2}{\tilde{S}^2 + \tilde{N}^2} \quad W_N = \frac{\tilde{N}^2}{\tilde{S}^2 + \tilde{N}^2} \tag{7}$$

Using the Wiener filter, we obtained the masked separation spectra $\tilde{S}_W$ and $\tilde{N}_W$ from noisy spectra Y, as shown in Eq. (8). Subsequently, the perceptual gain estimator is calculated by both the separation spectra, as shown in Eq. (9).

$$\tilde{S}_W = W_S \cdot Y = \frac{\tilde{S}^2}{\tilde{S}^2 + \tilde{N}^2} \cdot Y \quad \tilde{N}_W = W_N \cdot Y = \frac{\tilde{N}^2}{\tilde{S}^2 + \tilde{N}^2} \cdot Y \tag{8}$$

$$G = \frac{\tilde{S}_W^2}{\tilde{S}_W^2 + \max(\tilde{N}_W^2 - T, 0)} \tag{9}$$

In order to obtain the enhanced clean speech magnitude spectrum, we jointly optimize the DNN and the modified Wiener filtering mask in Eq. (6). The modified Wiener filtering mask together with the noisy speech magnitude spectrum placed on the top of the DNN as the network final output, as follows:

$$\hat{S} = G \cdot W_S \cdot Y$$

$$= \frac{\tilde{S}_W^3}{\tilde{S}_W^2 + \max(\tilde{N}_W^2 - T, 0)} \tag{10}$$

3.2 Training Objective and Optimization

Commonly, modeling both clean speech and noise in a model can improve separation performance due to the complementarity between different sources in the mixture [9]. However, modeling noise source will bring more prior knowledge. In this paper, we only predict the magnitude spectrograms of speech, the optimization training objective as follows

$$J_{MSE}(W) = \frac{1}{2}\|\hat{S}(W) - S\|_2^2 \tag{11}$$

To update the network parameters W corresponding to the clean speech features, the error back-propagation algorithm with stochastic gradient learning is subsequently used.

We derive the derivative of J with respect to the original output-layer weights w_4 which is obtained by using chain rule

$$\frac{\partial J}{\partial w_4^{(1)}} = \frac{\partial J}{\partial \hat{S}} \frac{\partial \hat{S}}{\partial \tilde{S}_W} \frac{\partial \tilde{S}_W}{\partial \tilde{S}} \frac{\partial \tilde{S}}{\partial w_4^{(1)}} + \frac{\partial J}{\partial \hat{S}} \frac{\partial \hat{S}}{\partial \tilde{N}_W} \frac{\partial \tilde{N}_W}{\partial \tilde{S}} \frac{\partial \tilde{S}}{\partial w_4^{(1)}} \tag{12}$$

$$\frac{\partial J}{\partial w_4^{(2)}} = \frac{\partial J}{\partial \hat{S}} \frac{\partial \hat{S}}{\partial \tilde{N}_W} \frac{\partial \tilde{N}_W}{\partial \tilde{N}} \frac{\partial \tilde{N}}{\partial w_4^{(2)}} + \frac{\partial J}{\partial \hat{S}} \frac{\partial \hat{S}}{\partial \tilde{S}_W} \frac{\partial \tilde{S}_W}{\partial \tilde{N}} \frac{\partial \tilde{N}}{\partial w_4^{(2)}} \tag{13}$$

Notably, $w_4^{(1)}$ and $w_4^{(2)}$ are the parameters between the two original output and the last hidden layer. The terms in Eqs. (12) and (13) are yielded as

$$\frac{\partial \hat{S}}{\partial \tilde{S}_W} = \frac{3\tilde{S}_W^2(\tilde{S}_W^2 + \max(\tilde{N}_W^2 - T, 0)) - 2\tilde{S}_W^4}{(\tilde{S}_W^2 + \max(\tilde{N}_W^2 - T, 0))^2} \tag{14}$$

$$\frac{\partial \hat{S}}{\partial \tilde{N}_W} = -\frac{2\tilde{S}_W^3 \cdot M_{1,0} \cdot \tilde{N}_W}{(\tilde{S}_W^2 + \max(\tilde{N}_W^2 - T, 0))^2} \tag{15}$$

$$\frac{\partial \tilde{S}_W}{\partial \tilde{S}} = \frac{2\tilde{S} \cdot \tilde{N}^2}{(\tilde{S}^2 + \tilde{N}^2)^2} \qquad \frac{\partial \tilde{S}_W}{\partial \tilde{N}} = -\frac{2\tilde{S}^2 \cdot \tilde{N}}{(\tilde{S}^2 + \tilde{N}^2)^2} \tag{16}$$

$$\frac{\partial \tilde{N}_W}{\partial \tilde{S}} = -\frac{2\tilde{S} \cdot \tilde{N}^2}{(\tilde{S}^2 + \tilde{N}^2)^2} \quad \frac{\partial \tilde{N}_W}{\partial \tilde{N}} = \frac{2\tilde{S}^2 \cdot \tilde{N}}{(\tilde{S}^2 + \tilde{N}^2)^2}, \tag{17}$$

where $M_{1,0}$ represents the partial derivatives of $u(u = \tilde{N}_W^2 - T)$ with respect to $\max(u, 0)$, the value of $M_{1,0}$ is a matrix consisting of 1 and 0, which depend on u is greater than 0.

For the hidden layers, the partial derivatives can be calculated as the common DNN. Thus, the errors are propagated backwards through all layers to adjust the weights by using optimization methods. In this paper, we use the limited-memory Broyden-Fletcher-Goldfarb-Shanno (L-BFGS) algorithm to update the weights W.

3.3   Proposed Speech Enhancement System

A block diagram of the proposed speech enhancement framework is given in Fig. 2. The proposed method contains two phases: the "training phase" and the "enhancement phase". In the "training phase", the proposed DNN was trained as a mapping function from noisy to clean speech.

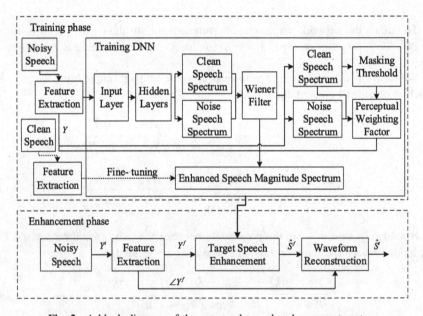

Fig. 2. A block diagram of the proposed speech enhancement system

In the "enhancement phase", the trained DNN was used to obtain the enhanced speech magnitude spectrum from the noisy speech. Then, clean speech signal is reconstructed by using the enhanced spectrum for clean speech and the phase from the noisy input.

4 Evaluation Experiments

4.1 Experiment Setting

In the experiments, we evaluated the performance of the proposed model with the TIMIT corpus. 1200 utterances were randomly selected from 240 different male and female speakers as the training set. All the sentences were resampled to 8 kHz. Twenty types of noise, namely *babble, car, casino, cicadas, f16, factory1, frogs, hfchannel, jungle, restaurant, street, white, airport, pink, birds, exhibition, subway, train, motorcycles* and *ocean* were considered. The training set consists of the first 15 noise types, the last 5 types of noise were used to test the proposed method's generalization ability. The 1200 sentences were added with the above-mentioned 15 types of noise and eleven levels of SNR, at −15 dB, −12 dB, −9 dB, −6 dB, −3 dB, 0 dB, 3 dB, 6 dB, 9 dB, 12 dB, and 15 dB, to build a multi-condition training set.

For testing, we randomly chose 160 clean speech utterances from other 120 different male and female speakers and mixed with above 20 noise types at −5 dB, 0 dB, 5 dB, and 10 dB, respectively.

4.2 Comparison Methods and Evaluation Metrics

To evaluate the proposed method (denoted as 'PW-DNN'), we compared with the basic DNN (denoted as 'DNN') [7], and Wiener filtering masking DNN (denoted as 'W-DNN') [9]. All model architectures were set to 3 hidden layers of 2048 hidden units and Rectified linear unit (ReLU) was chosen as the activation function. The magnitude spectrograms, extracted by applying a 512-point STFT with 50% overlap to the mixture signals, was used as the input features. To capture the context information, a window (11 frames) of features were concatenated together to form a long feature vector. All DNNs were trained from a random initialization, and the network weights were updated using the L-BFGS algorithm.

Three metrics were computed to evaluate the performance of the speech enhancement algorithms, namely the perceptual evaluation of speech quality (PESQ), the log-spectral distortion (LSD), and the frequency-weighted segmental SNR (fwSNRseg). For PESQ and fwSNRseg, a larger score indicates better performance. For LSD, a small value means better enhancement quality.

4.3 Results and Discussions

The Method's General Performance. The PESQ scores, LSD values and fwSNRseg values of the proposed methods as well as the DNN and W-DNN baselines are given in Tables 1, 2 and 3, respectively. From the tables, we see that both PW-DNN and W-DNN show significant improvements over DNN, this mainly due to that the enhancement ability of DNN is dependent on large training date [7]. The PW-DNN performs better perceptual quality than the W-DNN at most SNR situations by obtaining higher scores for PESQ and fwSNRseg. The LSD presented in Table 2 illustrate the capability of PW-DNN to reduce noise without introducing too much distortion. The significant improvements of PW-DNN over the W-DNN mainly owes to that the modified Wiener filtering can mask more audible noise frequency components.

Table 1. The PESQ scores of DNN, W-DNN and PW-DNN at four different input SNR levels. For matched noise case, the numbers are the mean values over all the 15 noise types. For unmatched noise case, the numbers are the mean values over all the 5 noise types.

Methods	Matched noise				Unmatched noise			
	−5 dB	0 dB	5 dB	10 dB	−5 dB	0 dB	5 dB	10 dB
DNN	1.621	1.850	2.067	2.282	1.650	1.913	2.148	2.358
W-DNN	1.766	2.052	2.332	2.618	1.832	2.205	**2.503**	2.786
PW-DNN	**1.806**	**2.107**	**2.385**	**2.671**	**1.853**	**2.209**	2.492	**2.789**

Table 2. The LSD values of DNN, W-DNN and PW-DNN at four different input SNR levels. For matched noise case, the numbers are the mean values over all the 15 noise types. For unmatched noise case, the numbers are the mean values over all the 5 noise types.

Methods	Matched noise				Unmatched noise			
	−5 dB	0 dB	5 dB	10 dB	−5 dB	0 dB	5 dB	10 dB
DNN	2.094	1.885	1.715	1.512	2.104	1.896	1.664	1.450
W-DNN	1.982	1.783	1.572	1.350	**1.942**	**1.725**	1.508	1.302
PW-DNN	**1.920**	**1.727**	**1.534**	**1.336**	1.961	1.751	**1.506**	**1.287**

Table 3. The fwSNRseg values of DNN, W-DNN and PW-DNN at four different input SNR levels. For matched noise case, the numbers are the mean values over all the 15 noise types. For unmatched noise case, the numbers are the mean values over all the 5 noise types.

Methods	Matched noise				Unmatched noise			
	−5 dB	0 dB	5 dB	10 dB	−5 dB	0 dB	5 dB	10 dB
DNN	4.843	5.844	6.914	7.891	4.742	5.914	7.076	8.074
W-DNN	5.415	**6.574**	7.931	8.972	5.182	**7.100**	8.026	9.548
PW-DNN	**5.430**	6.404	**8.104**	**9.296**	**5.584**	6.928	**8.694**	**10.493**

The Method's Performance per Noise Type. To better understand the methods' performance on each noise type, Fig. 3 present the mean PESQ scores over the four SNR levels. From Fig. 3, we can see that, for the 15 matched noise cases, PW-DNN outperforms on most noise types, except the *cicadas*. Furthermore, for the 5 unmatched noise cases, the proposed PW-DNN still performs better.

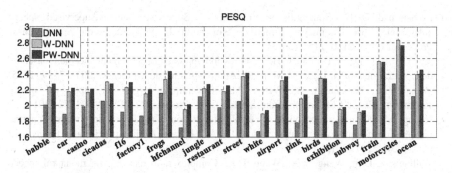

Fig. 3. The PESQ scores of DNN, W-DNN and PW-DNN for the 20 noise types. For each noise type, the numbers are the mean values over four input SNR conditions, i.e. from −5 dB to 10 dB spaced by 5 dB.

5 Conclusion

The main contribution of this paper is incorporating the masking properties of the human auditory system with deep neural networks for monaural speech separation. In order to make the residual noise inaudible, we propose a novel DNN architecture, which jointly train the perceptual modified Wiener filtering masking function and DNN. Experimental evaluation on 15 types of matched noises and 5 types of unmatched noises demonstrated the superiority of the proposed approach over the DNN-based methods. In future work, we believe that combining the masking properties of the human auditory system with DNN need more in-depth study. There will likely be room for future improvement.

Acknowledgments. This work is supported by NSF of China (Grant No. 61471394, 61402519) and NSF of Jiangsu Province (Grant No. BK20140071, BK20140074).

References

1. Paliwal, K., Wjcicki, K., Schwerin, B.: Single-channel speech enhancement using spectral subtraction in the short-time modulation domain. Speech Commun. **52**(5), 450–475 (2010)
2. Lim, J.S., Oppenheim, A.V.: Enhancement and bandwidth compression of noisy speech. Proc. IEEE **67**(12), 1586–1604 (1979)
3. Gerkmann, T., Hendriks, R.C.: Unbiased MMSE-based noise power estimation with low complexity and low tracking delay. IEEE Trans. Audio Speech Lang. Process. **20**(4), 1383–1393 (2012)
4. Cohen, I.: Noise spectrum estimation in adverse environments: improved minima controlled recursive averaging. IEEE Trans. Speech Audio Process. **11**(5), 466–475 (2003)
5. Sun, M., Li, Y.N., Gemmeke, J., Zhang, X.W.: Speech enhancement under low SNR conditions via noise estimation using sparse and low-rank NMF with Kullback-Leibler divergence. IEEE/ACM Trans. Audio Speech Lang. Process. **23**(7), 1233–1242 (2015)

6. Mohammadiha, N., Smaragdis, P., Leijon, A.: Supervised and unsupervised speech enhancement using nonnegative matrix factorization. IEEE Trans. Audio Speech Lang. Process. **21**(10), 2140–2151 (2013)
7. Xu, Y., Du, J., Dai, L.R., Lee, C.H.: A regression approach to speech enhancement based on deep neural networks. IEEE/ACM Trans. Audio Speech Lang. Process. **23**(1), 7–19 (2015)
8. Wang, Y.X., Narayanan, A., Wang, D.L.: On training targets for supervised speech separation. IEEE/ACM Trans. Audio Speech Lang. Process. **22**(12), 1849–1858 (2014)
9. Huang, P.S., Kim, M., Johnson, M.H.: Joint optimization of masks and deep recurrent neural network for monaural source separation. IEEE/ACM Trans. Audio Speech Lang. Process. **23** (12), 2136–2147 (2015)
10. Williamson, D.S., Wang, Y.X., Wang, D.L.: Complex ratio masking for monaural speech separation. IEEE/ACM Trans. Audio Speech Lang. Process. **24**(3), 483–492 (2016)
11. Sun, M., Zhang, X.W., Hamme, H.V., Zheng, T.F.: Unseen noise estimation using separable deep auto encoder for speech enhancement. IEEE/ACM Trans. Audio Speech Lang. Process. **24**(1), 93–104 (2016)
12. Xia, B.Y., Bao, C.C.: Wiener filtering based speech enhancement with weighted denoising auto-encoder and noise classification. Speech Commun. **60**(2), 13–29 (2014)
13. Alam, M.J., O'Shaughnessy, D., Selouani, S.A.: Speech enhancement based on novel two-step a priori SNR estimators. In: INTERSPEECH, pp. 565–568 (2008)
14. Hu, Y., Loizou, P.C.: Incorporating a psychoacoustical model in frequency domain speech enhancement. IEEE Signal Process. Lett. **11**(2), 270–273 (2004)
15. Lin, L., Holmes, W.H., Ambikairajah, E.: Speech denoising using perceptual modification of Wiener filtering. IEE Electron. Lett. **38**(23), 1486–1487 (2002)
16. Amehraye, A., Pastor, D., Tamtaoui, A.: Perceptual improvement of Wiener filtering. In: IEEE International Conference on Acoustics, Speech and Signal Processing (ICASSP), pp. 2081–2084 (2008)

Automatic Extraction and Construction Algorithm of Overpass from Raster Maps

Xincan Zhao, Yaodan Liu, and Yaping Wang[✉]

School of Information Engineering, Zhengzhou University,
Zhengzhou, Henan, China
ieypwang@zzu.edu.cn

Abstract. Aiming at the problems of the complex modeling, large amount and variety of data in the three-dimensional (3D) modeling of overpass in digital city, a novel approach is proposed for the fast extraction and construction of 3D overpass based on the two-dimension grid map. First the centerlines of roads of the three-dimensional overpass are automatically extracted from the two dimensional grid map of local road network. Then the intersections and layers are obtained based on it. The rapid three-dimensional solid modeling of the overpass could be realized through the parametric modeling and texture mapping. The topology of the whole model is consistent with the real surface features, so it is measurable. The experimental results show that the proposed parametric modeling approach of the overpass could greatly reduce the modeling time, and improve the design efficiency with better flexibility and interactivity.

Keywords: Overpass · Raster map · Automatic extraction · Parametric modeling

1 Introduction

In modern society, people have more demands on the urban spatial information. The traditional two-dimensional digital map is hard to meet the demand of people's life, and the construction of three-dimensional digital city has become the goal of the city informatization. As an indispensable part of the traffic network in the virtual 3D digital city, elevated road and interchanges are of great significance for the 3D simulation of the traffic, the optimization of road, vehicle tracking, traffic statistics and emergency treatment. The interchanges consist of the main body, the crossing components and the connection parts in space, which are of complex connection and topology. Thus interchanges are the most complex part of the city traffic network. Researchers have done lots of works on 3D fast modeling of interchanges. Jingjing Wang [1] developed a virtual reality system of the urban interchange based on the graphical platform named PKPM3D. This system could be used to accomplish the design and modeling of many types of bridges with complex structures, while the parameters are required to be adjusted for different components of the interchanges in the modeling process, which makes it more complicated. Bisong Hu [2] put forward the three-dimensional data structure and spatial topology of large interchange, and further proposed the three

© Springer International Publishing AG 2016
E. Chen et al. (Eds.): PCM 2016, Part II, LNCS 9917, pp. 479–489, 2016.
DOI: 10.1007/978-3-319-48896-7_47

dimensional modeling method based on high-resolution aerial images and satellite remote sensing images, but the optimization of its modeling is difficult. Jie Wang [3] proposed an approach for the extraction of the interchange by converting the existing GIS data of road to high-precision three-dimensional road network models. While for the complex interchanges with multiple levels, it is still hard to determine the final relationship of different levels. Min Deng [4] proposed a feature-based data model with three hierarchies, which was used for the mapping and navigation in the traffic network. This method could reflect the simple hierarchy of the interchange, while it is lack of in-depth research on the modeling of the complex interchanges.

Based on the researches on the construction and display of interchanges in recent years, a novel automatic extraction and fast modeling algorithm of interchange based on two-dimensional raster map is proposed, combining with Design Specification for Highway Alignment in China. The proposed method consists of three stages, including the extraction of road centerline, the detection of intersection and layers, and 3D geometric modeling. This approach could automatically detect the intersections of the interchanges, and realize the fast parametric modeling of the key components of the interchanges. In order to enhance the visual effect, the texture mapping technology for 3D rendering is further proposed. Finally the road editor is used to do manual correction about the layered intersection errors.

2 Parametric Description of Interchange

The important parameters of the city interchange include the bridge height, road width, and spacing of the bridge pier. The ratio of interchange bridge height and its span is normally $1:2.5 \sim 1:3$ [5]. The widths of general lanes, car lanes and the median strip are 3.75 m, 3.5 m and 0.5 m respectively. And the width between the left and right edge of the road is 0.5 m. Pier spacing is related to beam structure. The spacing of piers is at above 20 m when box girders are used. In this paper, the interchange extraction algorithm consists of three stages, including preprocessing, centerline processing and intersection stratification, 3D geometric modeling, as shown in Fig. 1.

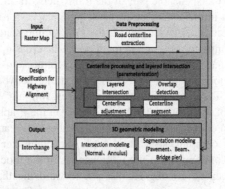

Fig. 1. The interchange extraction algorithm.

The preprocessing stage is mainly the extraction of the road centerline from the raster maps. The stage of centerline processing and intersection stratification includes the detection of overlapping points, stratifying the intersections, the adjustment of centerline, and segmentation, etc. The 3D geometric modeling stage includes the modeling of the interchange and the overlapping area according to the centerline, which uses the texture mapping technology to render the interchange for enhancing the visual effect.

3 Preprocessing of Raster Map Data

3.1 Analysis of World Map Data

World map is an important part of "Digital China", which is the public version of the public information service platform on the national geography, and provides the 2–18 class map resource for public use. The street maps of the World map have different layers. As shown in Fig. 2(left), yellow color represents for main road, white color represents for the path, blue color represents for lakes, and green color represents for parks. In the 14th level of the world map, roads are clear, and there are no greenbelts and buildings. Roads in the 15th level are more refined. Buildings appear in the 16th level. Two-way road appears in the main road in the 17th level with the crossroads more precise. And in the 18th level of the world map, the interchanges are more clear and easily to be distinguished. Figure 2(left) and (right) are the raster map and image map of interchanges in Jinshui Road, Zhengzhou City, which are cut out from the 18th level of the world map.

Fig. 2. The raster map (left) and the image map (right) are cut out from the World map. (Color figure online)

3.2 Extraction of the Road Centerline

The road centerline is extracted according to the following steps, which are given in details. (1) Read the map data. (2) Convert the map data into grayscale data. (3) Divide the data into two areas, which are road region and non-road region. (4) Due to the noise in map data, some unexpected noise should be removed after the region segmentation.

(5) Fill the holes, nick and gap in the roads using image smoothing algorithm to avoid the disconnection phenomenon. (6) Transform the road into the line with one pixel wide. After the extraction process above, the centerline in target road can be extracted. The extracted road centerlines are given in Fig. 3. You can refer to [6, 7] for the extraction of road centerline.

4 Detection and Stratification of Road Intersection

4.1 Intersection Detection

The road centerline is composed of a series of discrete points, as shown in Fig. 4. The three-dimensional coordinates of the discrete points on the road centerlines are stored in the arrays according to the topological relations between points. Thus each centerline of the road corresponds to an array. To realize the stratification of the interchanges, the intersection point should be detected firstly. For each centerline, the intersection sets between it with all the other centerlines should be found out. Then the newly detected intersection could be stored in a new array.

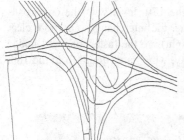   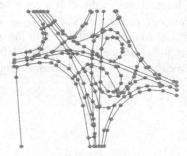

Fig. 3. The extracted road centerlines.   **Fig. 4.** The discrete points on the centerlines of the roads.

4.2 Intersection Stratification

Since each intersection is generated because the centerlines of two roads cross with each other, the level of intersection should be determined first. Through the following two iteration steps, the overpass is divided into three rating levels, which are corresponding to different heights.

The first iteration is executed in the following two steps.

(1) According to the order of the array subscript, the intersections on the centerlines of each road are traversed. If the intersection has been assigned a predefined height level, the next intersection is traversed. If not, the distance between the current intersection and the next intersection should be computed. The neighboring intersections are considered to be continuous when the distance between them is within a certain range (it is set as 50 m in the paper). After traversing the

intersections of all roads, the consecutive intersections with the maximum number of intersections are found. Then the predefined height levels, such as the 1st and 2nd levels, are assigned, and the road centerlines with the intersections on them are recorded.

(2) According to the order of array subscript, the intersections of other road centerlines are traversed in orders. The intersections, which have the same coordinates with the intersections in (1), are assigned the same height level (the 2nd level or the 1st level).

Currently the interchanges just have two levels, and they are assigned different heights according to the level assigned before. As shown in Fig. 5(left), the points $v4$, $v5$, $v6$ are continuous intersections, and they are set as the 1st level. $v2$ and $v4$ are correspondingly set as the 2nd level. $v3$ and $v7$ are the branch points, which could be handled using the method introduced in Sect. 4.3. The point v corresponds to $v1$, thus v is set as the 2nd level, and $v1$ is set as the 1st level.

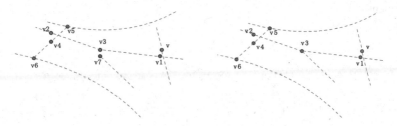

Fig. 5. The two-layered structure (left) and the three-layered structure (right). Here the blue point represents for the 1st level. The red point represents for the 2nd level. And the green point represents for the 3rd level. (Color figure online)

The second iteration is executed as following until the intersections that belong to the 3rd level are assigned the same heights.

(1) The intersections on each road centerline are traversed according to the order of the array subscripts. And the intersection v whose height is non-zero value is found. It is not branch point.

(2) The intersections on other road centerlines are traversed, and the intersection $v1$ that has the same x and y coordinates with point v are found. The level of $v1$ is lower than v, and the road centerline L with intersection $v1$ on it is recorded.

(3) Traverse is executed on the left and right sides of intersection $v1$ on the road centerline L. And the non-branch point $v2$ whose height is non-zero value is found. Then judgement is executed between the intersections $v1$ and $v2$ to make sure if there are branch points between them. If there are branch points existed, all the intersections between $v2$ and $v1$ are assigned the same height as $v2$. v is assigned a bigger value of height, and it is further set the 3rd level. If there is no branch point between $v1$ and $v2$, no processing is done, and it directly goes to step (1).

For the intersections on each road centerline, if there is point with zero height existing between two points with non-zero heights, the height of the zero height point should be enhanced and it should be same with the minimal non-zero height of the two points. As shown in Fig. 5(right), it is a three-layered structure diagram. $v4$, $v5$ and $v6$ are set as the 1st level. $v1$, $v2$ and $v3$ are set as the 2nd level. v is set as the 3rd level.

4.3   The Adjustment of the Road Centerline

After assigning the height values for the intersections, the intersection array should be inserted to the array of the original road centerline. And adjustment should be done for the road centerline. As shown in Fig. 6(left), we can see that the endpoint $v1$ and the intersection $v2$ were wrongly separated in the 1st iteration of Sect. 4.2. First $v1$ and $v2$ could coincide by setting $v2$ the same height with $v1$. If the height value of the $v3$, $v4$ is the same, the overlapped intersection will have the same height value with $v3$, $v4$. If not, the height value is dependent on the neighboring two intersections on the two sides of $v2$. If the neighboring two intersections have the same height with $v2$, then the overlapped point also has the same height value. Figure 6(right) is final result after adjustment.

Fig. 6. Adjustment of the branch ports by separating the endpoints $v1$ and $v2$.

5   3D Geometric Modeling of Interchange

5.1   Three-Dimensional Modeling of Deck

The deck is mainly composed of motor vehicle lane, central separation belt, two-side trip and two-side collision avoidance walls. As shown in Fig. 7, L is the road centerline. By moving L left and right to L1 and L2 respectively according to the width of the central separation belt, the rectangular central separation belt could be drawn, and then be pasted the central strip texture map. With the half width of the central separation belt, the width and the number of lanes, L is shifted to the left and the right at L3 and L4 respectively. Thus two rectangles could be drawn by using L1, L3, L2, L4, and then be pasted the way texture map. Then with the lane and the collision avoidance walls, L is shifted to the left and right at L5 and L6 respectively. Two collision avoidance wall geometry could be drawn by using L3, L5, L4, L6, and finally be pasted the collision avoidance wall texture map.

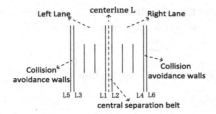

Fig. 7. The schematic diagram for the translation of road centerline.

5.2   3D Modeling of Bridge Pier

Bridge pier mainly consists of three parts. They are fundamental objects, the bridge pier shaft and the bridge pier cap. The foundational bridge is on the bottom of the pier and buried under the ground. The bridge pier shaft refers to the bridge pier, the cross sections of which are generally round, rectangular or round-end shape. Pier cap, which is composed of hat and tray, is located on the upper part of the piers. The bridge pier structure is shown in Fig. 8.

According to the pier spacing, the length of the interchange and the three-dimensional center coordinates of each pier could be calculated. The bottom of single-column pier is a circular contour, so the coordinate points on the circle could be calculated by the following formula:

$$\alpha = 0$$
$$\beta = osg :: PI/18$$
$$\begin{cases} x = R * cos(\alpha + i * \beta) \\ y = R * sin(\alpha + i * \beta) \end{cases} \tag{1}$$

Wherein, α is the starting angle of the arc, R is the radius of the circle. β is an angle. Thus the 2D coordinates could be calculated using these equations. By setting their Z coordinate be 0, the 2D coordinates are converted to 3D coordinates.

As shown in Fig. 9, $v1$, $v2$ is the two three-dimensional coordinates of the circle on the bottom of the bridge pier. By adding them with the height of the pier, the corresponding 3D coordinate point $v1'$, $v2'$ could be obtained. The points on the other side could be computed, and they are put into the same array. The shape of the bridge pier is drawn by drawing primitives QUAD_STRIP in the OSG PrimitiveSet class. Then these

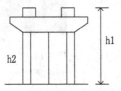

Fig. 8. The composition of bridge structure.

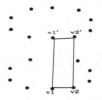

Fig. 9. The cylindrical pier.

points are made the texture map coordinates, and be pasted the texture map. The double column pier is composed of two single column piers.

5.3   3D Modeling of Interchange Intersection

(1) Merging/separation intersection modeling

As shown in Fig. 10(left), L1 and L2 are the centerline of two interchanges and they are intersected at *vCenter*. Taking the *vCenter* as the center of circle and using certain radius to clean the intersection parts, the map cleaned is shown in Fig. 10(right). *v*1 and *v*4 are laying on the line of L1 and L2. By shifting L1 and L2 to L1′ and L2′ correspondingly, and extending them to cross at the point *vOut*, the Bezier curve L3 (from *v*2 to *v*5) could be obtained by the interpolation method from *v*2, *vOut* and *v*5. Similarly, Bezier curve L4 (from *v*3 to *v*6) could be obtained by *v*3, *vIn* and *v*6. The crash barrier geometry could be drawn by discrete points from L3 and L4. In the same way, the crash barrier geometry at the right part of L2 and the centerline of L1 could be drawn out and be made the texture mapping. The merging and separation results are shown in Fig. 11.

(2) Roundabout intersection modeling

As shown in Fig. 12, the intersection of two centerlines of separate interchange is assigned as *v*, which is the center of intersection. The elimination is executed in the intersection areas by setting center on *v* and using radius with *dRadius*. The two intersection road centerlines are divided into four sections. From the distance formulation of 3D coordinate shown below, the distance between two 3D coordinate points *v*1 and *v* can be calculated as *dLength*.

$$d = \sqrt{(x_2 - x_1)^2 + (y_2 - y_1)^2 + (z_2 - z_1)^2} \qquad (2)$$

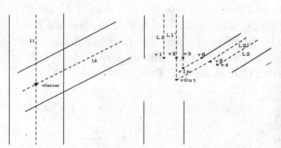

Fig. 10. The interchange intersection processing.   **Fig. 11.** The   merging/separating intersections.

The distance d_{v1v2} between $v1$ and $v2$ is calculated as $dLength - dRadius$. The direction vector from $v1$ to v is set as v_{v1v}. The 3D coordination of $v2$ could be calculated by normalizing v_{v1v}, which is represented as $v1 + d_{v1v2} * v_{v1v}$. The distance between $v1$ and $v3$ is $dLength + dRadius$, so the coordinates of $v3$ is $v1 + d_{v1v3} * v_{v1v}$. Similarly, coordinates of $v6$, $v7$ could be calculated, and the coordinates of the $v2$, $v3$, $v6$, $v7$ are the control points of the intersection of four branch roads.

As shown in Fig. 13(left), after removing the intersection parts, d is set as the length which is calculated by using the half length of the road minus $d1$, with $d1$ be the width of the barrier wall. According to $v2$, v, the vector v_{v2v} could be calculated. Letting v_{v2v} 90° counterclockwise around the Z axis and normalizing it as $vNormal$, these two coordinate points could be obtained with $v21$ be $v2 - vNormal * d$, and points $v22$ be $v2 + vNormal * d$.

Similarly, $v71$, $v72$ could be calculated. $v27$ is the intersection between the line whose endpoints are $v21$ and $v07$ and the line whose endpoints are $v71$ and $v02$. By using three coordinates of points $v21$, $v27$ and $v71$, the Bezier curve interpolation method could be used to compute the line L from $v21$ to $v71$. As shown in Fig. 13 (right), with inner circle radius r1 and cylindrical radius r2, r1 is the half of the minimum width of two separate interchange, and r2 is the minimum distance from point v to Bezier curve L. All the discrete points on the inside and outside of the circle can be calculated according to the formula (1). The annular geometry could be obtained using these coordinates and be made lane texture. $v22$, $v2$, $v21$ and the discrete points on the L form the peripheral 1/4 part. The coordinate points on other parts could be calculated with the same method. So the areas outside the roundabouts can be drawn from these points and the cylindrical coordinates, and finally be made the road texture map. The 3D Roundabout intersection results are shown in Fig. 16(right).

6 Implementation of the Intersection Stratification Correction Algorithm

After stratified the intersection of the road centerline, there may be layered error at some intersections. In this paper, correction work is realized by using road editor to adjust the intersections of centerline. The correction process is divided into four steps:

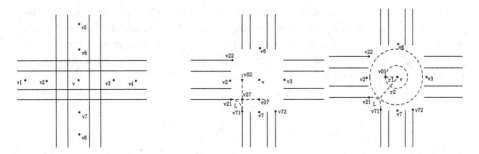

Fig. 12. Interchange intersection.   **Fig. 13.** The diagram for drawing roundabouts.

(1) For the intersections which have layered errors, or which do not conform to the actual situation, the vertical side of the intersection should be calculated. As shown in Fig. 14, by getting the camera's position in the program, the vector i is determined by the position of the camera and the selected intersection v. The vector j is the cross product of vector i and Z axes. The plane where vector j and Z axes exist is the vertical side of the intersection v.

(2) Move the intersection to the appropriate location along the vertical side.

(3) Repeat steps (1) and (2) until the intersection of the centerlines has adjusted to the actual situation.

(4) Reconstruct the model of the interchange using the road centerlines.

Through the above correction steps, the interchanges that conform to the actual situation could be generated, and could stratify the interchange with multiple levels. The correction process is shown in Fig. 15.

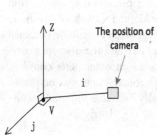

Fig. 14. Sketch map for computing vertical surface.

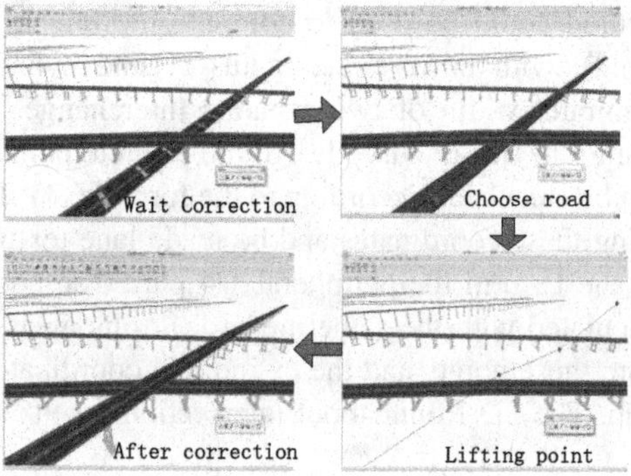

Fig. 15. Stratification correction process.

7 Implementation of Urban Transportation Stereoscopic Three-Dimensional Road Network

In this paper, VS2010 is used as the development platform, and the entire module is dependent on the OpenCascade geometric modeling library. By further combining with the open-source virtual reality engine OSG (OpenSceneGraph) technology, the extraction and construction of urban interchange could be achieved. The overall and partial rendering results of the interchange after stratification are given in Fig. 16(left) and (middle) respectively. Figure 16(right) is the rendering result of the traffic viaduct in three-dimensional road network.

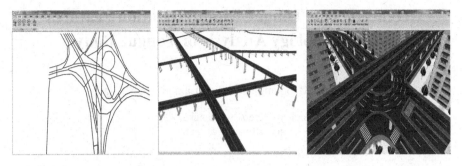

Fig. 16. The overall and partial rendering effect of the interchange after stratification.

8 Conclusion

After comparing the world map image with the street maps of different layers, the method for the rapid extraction of the road centerline based on the two-dimensional raster map, and the rapid construction of three-dimensional interchanges, are proposed. This modeling method is not perfect enough in some details. A large amount of collinear points were removed when obtaining the road centerline, so the constructed interchange is straight. In addition, the stratification is limited to three layers in the program. What we should do next is to improve the smoothing of interchange, and make the multi-level stratification available in the program, which will provide a solid foundation for realizing 3D intelligent traffic simulation.

Acknowledgments. This work was supported by grants U1433106, U1504606, 2016T90679 and 2015M582201.

References

1. Wang, J.-J.: A Virtual Reality System for Urban Overpass Bridges Based on PKPM3D Graphical Platform. Beijing Jiaotong University, Beijing (2007)
2. Hu, B.-S., Gong, J.-H.: A 3-Dimensional modeling method of complex and enormous cloverleaf junction. Sci. Surveying Mapp. **33**(1), 100–102 (2008)
3. Wang, J., Lawson, G., Shen, Y.: Automatic high-fidelity 3D road network modeling based on 2D GIS data. Adv. Eng. Softw. **76**(3), 86–98 (2014)
4. Deng, M., Fei, L.: Research on modeling the overpasses for mapping and navigation. In: Proceedings of the SPIE 7144, Geoinformatics 2008 and Joint Conference on GIS and Built Environment: The Built Environment and Its Dynamics, p. 71442L, 05 November 2008. doi:10.1117/12.812842
5. Chen, J.-H.: Critical factor analysis and development conceiving of structural schemes for urban viaducts. Bridge Constr. **43**(4), 99–104 (2013)
6. Wu, H.-L.: Automatic Road Segmentation and Extraction in the Bitmap. Yunnan Normal University, Yunnan (2007)
7. Kou, M.-M., Wang, Q.-Z., Tan, T.-D.: Recoginition and Extraction of classified Roads from Color Digitial Raster Graphic Image. Comput. Eng. **38**(13), 276–279 (2012)

Geometric and Tongue-Mouth Relation Features for Morphology Analysis of Tongue Body

Qing Cui, Xiaoqiang Li[✉], Jide Li, and Yin Zhang

Shanghai University, Shanghai, China
xqli@shu.edu.cn

Abstract. Traditional Chinese Medicine diagnoses a wide range of health conditions by examining morphology features of the tongue, such as fat, thin and normal. This paper presents an approach of classification for recognizing and analyzing tongue morphology based on geometric features and tongue-mouth relation feature. The geometric features are defined using various measurements of width and length of the tongue body, and ratio between them. In addition, an innovative and important feature is proposed based on the relationship between the width of the tongue body and the width of the oral cavity, named as tongue-mouth relation feature. All these features are used to train a SVM classifier. Experimental results show that the tongue-mouth relation feature is helpful to improve the recognition accuracy for tongue morphology, and the proposed method, tested on a total of 200 tongue samples, achieved an accuracy of more than 92%.

Keywords: Tongue morphology · Tongue-mouth relation feature · SVM

1 Introduction

Diagnosis based on condition of the tongue [1–3] is one of the most important and valuable diagnostic methods in traditional Chinese medicine (TCM) and has been widely used in clinical analysis and applications for thousands of years. According to the principles of TCM, analyzing the appearance of an individual's tongue can provide a greater understanding of his or her overall health. Whenever there is a complex disorder in vivo, examining the tongue may instantly clarify the main pathological processes. However, traditional tongue diagnosis has inevitable limitations that impede its medical applications. First, the clinical competence of tongue diagnosis is determined by the experience and knowledge of the practitioners. Second, tongue diagnosis is usually based on the detailed visual discrimination, so it depends on the subjective analysis of the examiners and the diagnostic results may be unreliable and inconsistent.

In recent years, some research has been done to improve computerized or automated tongue diagnosis by applying the techniques of image analysis and pattern recognition. Chiu et al. [4, 5] proposed a structural texture recognition algorithm which adopted the RGB model for mapping the tongue colors to some known categories and used certain features to verify or identify certain properties of coating on the tongue. [6] presented a

© Springer International Publishing AG 2016
E. Chen et al. (Eds.): PCM 2016, Part II, LNCS 9917, pp. 490–497, 2016.
DOI: 10.1007/978-3-319-48896-7_48

novel computerized tongue inspection method based on two kinds of quantitative features, chromatic and textural measure, and Bayesian networks are employed to model the relationship between these quantitative features and diseases. [7–9] introduced three kinds of tongue image segmentation method. [10] gave a scheme to extract tongue cracks, one of pathological features in tongue diagnosis, which extracts the whole of the line by employing anisotropic nonlinear filter. Base on their work, [11] proposed a new method using statistic feature to identify if a tongue is a cracked tongue. [12] proposed a teeth-marked tongue recognition method performing better than the work [13, 14], which are concentrated on features of convex and the change of brightness of tongue. An in-depth analysis on the statistical distribution characteristics of human tongue color that aims to propose a mathematically described tongue color space for diagnostic feature extraction is presented in [15]. [16] elaborated a research result about a noninvasive method to detect diabetes mellitus and non-proliferative diabetic retinopathy based on three groups of features including color, texture, and geometry extracted from tongue images.

The theory of TCM claims that tongue morphology can objectively reflect some physiological and pathologic changes of human. For example, the fat tongue may indicate spleen-kidney yang-deficiency, gasification disorder and internal stagnation of fluid dampness, while the thin tongue is arising from qi-blood deficiency and yin-blood insufficiency. Recently, some research has been done for tongue morphology recognition. Wei [17] established an automatic tongue body analysis which was based on the curve-fitting parameters. Xu [18] studied and analyzed the tongue shape to establish a kind of tongue diagnosis method, which measured the tongue's length, width and height and established an optimum formula between the body surface area and the sum of the width and height. However, these methods neglect tongue-mouth relation feature, according to tongue diagnosis, which is also key factor to recognize tongue as fat tongue, thin tongue and normal tongue. In addition, machine learning method is not used in these methods. In this paper, we propose a novel medical biometric approach that automatically classifies and recognizes tongue morphology. First, we combined geometric features with tongue-mouth relation feature to represent the tongue morphology. Then, a multi-class SVM is trained based on these statistic features to build a classifier for tongue morphology.

The remainder of this paper is organized as follows. Section 2 introduces how to extract geometric features with tongue-mouth relation feature, and train SVM classifier. Section 3 gives the experimental results and discussion. Finally, this study is concluded in Sect. 4.

2   Feature Extraction and SVM Classifier

This section describes the method to extract the geometry features of tongue and the tongue-mouth relation. First, Automatic contour extraction extracts the geometric contours of the tongue body from its surroundings by using a segmentation method based on histogram projection and matting [9]. Image in Fig. 1 shows that the accurate and precise tongue body in Fig. 1(b) can be segmented from original tongue image showed in Fig. 1(a), which is captured by standard tongue image acquisition.

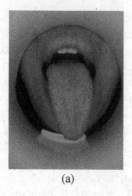 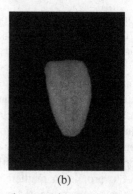

(a)   (b)

Fig. 1. Tongue image segmentation (a) initial tongue image includes the lips, parts of the face, or the teeth; (b) tongue body image

2.1 Geometry Features

After extracting tongue body image, we extract the geometry features based on tongue body region. The width and the length of a tongue were often used in researches related to the analysis of tongue body [19]. Here, the tongue length is the distance between tongue root and tongue tip; the tongue width refers to the distance of the leftmost and rightmost of the different tongue position as showed in Fig. 2.

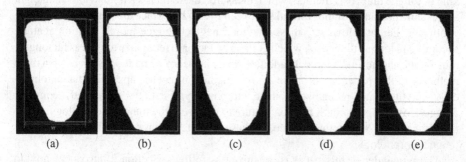

(a)   (b)   (c)   (d)   (e)

Fig. 2. Length of tongue body and width of different part of tongue body. (a) Width and Length of tongue body. (b) Width of tongue root. (c) and (d) With of tongue middle. (e) Width of tongue tip

Given a tongue body image, the pixels which are rendered in the RGB color space are first converted to the grayscale value. Then, the binarization algorithm is conducted for grayscale image, which uses one calculated threshold value to classify pixels into object or background. The new value of each image pixel is modified as:

$$f(x,y) = \begin{cases} 0, & f(x,y) \leq 10 \\ 255, & f(x,y) > 10 \end{cases} \tag{1}$$

in which f(x, y) is the gray value of image pixels. We selected 10 as the threshold. It is very intuitive to get the contour of the tongue in the binary image (see Fig. 2(a)). Drawing a minimum circumscribed rectangle for the tongue body contour, the coordinate of the up-left point of the rectangle is set to (0, 0). The width and the length of the rectangle are denoted as W (width) and L (length) of tongue, respectively, showed in Fig. 2(a). The ratio of the tongue width and length is calculated as follows:

$$F = W/L \tag{2}$$

The relationship between tongue width and length is a very important feature on the judgment of tongue morphology. For fat tongues, the width is basically equal to or more than the length, while the length of thin tongues is much larger than the width.

Then, we extract four width of different position of tongue body based on four different rectangles, showed as green box in Fig. 2(b)–(d), they are located at tongue root, tongue middle and tongue tip respectively. The width of each rectangle is W and the length is 0.1L. The x coordinate sequence of left boundary and right boundary is denoted as

$$x_l = \{x_{li}|i = 1, 2, \cdots, n\} \text{ and } x_r = \{x_{rj}|j = 1, 2, \cdots, m\}$$

respectively. Here, x_{li} represents the x coordinate of the ith pixel on left boundary and x_{rj} represents the x coordinate of the jth pixel on right boundary. The x coordinate of a boundary of different position is presented by the mean value of all pixels' x coordinate on left boundary or right boundary. The widths of four tongue body positions are defined as:

$$W_k - \frac{1}{n}\sum_{i=1}^{n} x_{li} - \frac{1}{m}\sum_{j=1}^{m} x_{rj}, \ k = 1, 2, 3, 4 \tag{3}$$

$$F_i = W_i/W, \ i = 1, 2, 3, 4 \tag{4}$$

Finally, four geometric features are defined as Eq. 4. In our research, we found that the width of the tip and the root part of fat tongue are smaller than the tongue width, in contrast, the width of each part of thin tongue, except the root part, will not be larger than the tongue body width.

2.2 Tongue-Mouth Relation Feature Extraction

The objective of this subsection is to extract the tongue-mouth relation feature on the initial image. The method used to find oral cavity is based on the rectangle drawn in Sect. 2.1. The changes on the rectangle are moving the distance of 0.3 W to the left and move up the distance of 0.4L, moreover the width is set to 1.6 W and the length is unchanged. Thus we get a new rectangle that is named imgROI. The function of creating the new rectangle is defined as follows,

$$imgROI.x = x - 0.3W$$
$$imgROI.y = y - 0.4L \tag{5}$$

$$imgROI.W = 1.6 * W$$
$$imgROI.L = L \tag{6}$$

The oral cavity is surrounded by the rectangle while applying the new rectangle on the initial image. Then split the local image which is contained in the rectangle from the initial image, thus we get the image of oral cavity named mouth.

The detail steps calculating the width of the oral cavity are described as follow:

1. Converting the image mouth to the red channel image.
2. Splitting the red channel image by using threshold operation of parameter inversion. The threshold is selected according to the local area information.
3. There are several contours after image segmentation. These contours are descending sort according to the size of areas which are surrounded by contours. Then, remove areas which are over small or over wide or near the image edge.
4. Retaining two of the largest regions in the residual areas if the number of the rest area is greater than 3. Otherwise, all remaining areas are retained.
5. All pixels for each region are combined together as the oral cavity region.
6. Drawing the minimum enclosing rectangle for oral cavity area.

The area surrounded by the tongue is the gap between the upper lip and the tongue when the tongue is stretched out. Let the width of the rectangle represents the width of the oral cavity area named as mouth.W. The ratio represented the tongue-mouth feature is defined as follow,

$$F_m = (mouth.W - W)/W \tag{7}$$

For fat tongue samples (see Fig. 3(a)), the oral cavity width is less than the width of the tongue. However, for thin tongue samples (see Fig. 3(c)), the oral cavity width is far larger than the width of the tongue.

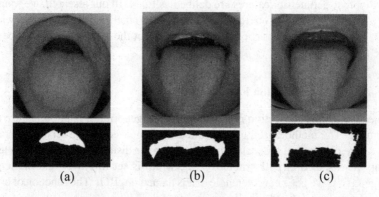

(a)   (b)   (c)

Fig. 3. The space of oral cavity (a) fat tongue; (b) normal tongue; (c) thin tongue

2.3 SVM

Support vector machine is a supervised learning model. Originally it was worked out for linear two-class classification with margin, where margin means the minimal distance from the separating hyperplane to the closest data points. SVM learning machine seeks for an optimal separating hyperplane, where the margin is maximal. The SVM classifier supports binary classification, multiclass classification and regression, the structured SVM allows training of a classifier for general structured output labels. The linear SVM can extended to nonlinear one when the problem is transformed into feature space using a set of nonlinear basis function. In the feature space – which can be very high dimensional – the data points can be separated linearly. An important advantage of the SVM is that it is not necessary to implement this transformation and to determine the separating hyperplane in the possibly very-high dimensional feature space, instead a kernel representation can be used, where the solution is written as a weighted sum of the values of certain kernel function evaluated at the support vectors [20].

In this study, the RBF kernel is chosen to train the SVM model because it has only one parameter for model selection and fewer numberical difficulties. The definition of RBF function is,

$$K(x_i, x) = \exp(-\gamma \|x_i - x\|^2) \tag{7}$$

The parameter gamma(γ) which tunes the training error and the generalization capability needs to be optimized for best performance.

3 Experimental Results and Discussion

Based on the proposed methods of the tongue morphology feature extraction, this section describes the tongues classification using SVM.

3.1 Dataset

According to the diagnosis experience given by the experts, there are three classes of tongue morphology: fat, normal and thin. In our experiment, the image database contains over 200 tongue images and covers various types of tongues. Every image in the database is independently labeled by three or more experts of TCM with opinion agreement.

The typical sample (see Fig. 3) refers to the representative tongue image in the category of tongue. In this study, we select 10 images from the fat tongue type, 10 images from the normal tongue type and 10 images from the thin tongue type to form a set of typical sample. The testing set consists of the rest images in the image database.

3.2 Experimental Results

In this section, we will verify whether the extracted features are valid. As mentioned in Sect. 3.1, some typical samples are selected from the image database to form the SVM training set, and the remaining images are used for testing.

The experiment is conducted on two different feature sets. One set contains all of the six features mentioned in Sect. 2, and another one contains five features which not include the feature representing the relationship between the width of oral cavity and the tongue.

True positive rate (TP) are calculated to evaluate the classification. TP measures the proportion of positives that are correctly identified. In Table 1, we compute TP of two different feature sets on three tongue types respectively according experimental results. The set of five features contains the ratio between tongue width and length and the ratio between different tongue part width and tongue width. These features are much affected by the length of the tongue when it is stretching outside of the mouth, especially the ratio of tongue width and length. Even though the volunteers are required to open their mouth and stretch out their tongue when taking pictures, there are still some images are not perfectly. The experiment shows that the correct rate of classification is greatly improved after added new feature. And it indicates that classification based on all features can recognize the fat tongue and thin tongue correctly, while a few of normal tongue are always recognized as fat tongue or thin tongue, showed as Table 2. Compared with accuracy rate 80% in [17], fat TP rate (93.4%) and thin TP rate (88.57%) [18], the proposed method achieves better performance.

Table 1. True positive base on five features or six features

Feature set	Fat TP	Normal TP	Thin TP
Five features	78.74%	71.67%	76.92%
Six features	98.43%	86.67%	92.31%

Table 2. Classification results of proposed method based on six features

	Fat	Normal	Thin
Fat	125	4	0
Normal	1	52	1
Thin	1	4	12

4   Conclusion

This paper presents a classification approach for automatically recognizing and analyzing tongue morphology based on geometric features and tongue-mouth relation feature. First, we develop five geometric features by using various measurements of width and length of the tongue body, and ratio between them. Then, our main contribution, an innovative tongue-mouth relation feature, the relationship between the width of the tongue body and the width of the oral cavity is computed to add into feature vector representing tongue morphology. Finally, a SVM classifier is trained to classify the tongue into three categories such as fat tongue, normal tongue and thin tongue. Experimental results demonstrated that the tongue-mouth relation feature is helpful to improve the recognition accuracy for tongue morphology, and the proposed method achieves better accuracy.

References

1. Kirschbaum, B.: Atlas of Chinese Tongue Diagnosis. Eastland Press, Seattle (2000)
2. Yiu, H., Shuai, X.Z.: Fundamental of Traditional Chinese Medicine. Foreign Languages Press, Beijing (1992)
3. Li, N., Zhang, D., Wang, K.: Tongue Diagnostics. Shed-Yuan Publishing, Beijing (2006)
4. Chiu, C.C., Lin, H.S., Lin, S.L.: A structural texture recognition approach for medical diagnosis through tongue. Biomed. Eng. Appl. Basis Commun. 7(2), 143–148 (1995)
5. Chiu, C.C.: A novel approach based on computerized image analysis for traditional Chinese medical diagnosis of the tongue. Comput. Methods Programs Biomed. 61(2), 77–89 (2000)
6. Pang, B., Zhang, D., Li, N., et al.: Computerized tongue diagnosis based on Bayesian networks. IEEE Trans. Biomed. Eng. 51(10), 1803–1810 (2004)
7. Pang, B., Zhang, D., Wang, K.: The bi-elliptical deformable contour and its application to automated tongue segmentation in Chinese medicine. IEEE Trans. Med. Imaging 24(8), 946–956 (2005)
8. Ning, J., Zhang, D., Wu, C., et al.: Automatic tongue image segmentation based on gradient vector flow and region merging. Neural Comput. Appl. 21(8), 1819–1826 (2012)
9. Li, X., Li, J., Wang, D.: Automatic tongue image segmentation based on histogram projection and matting. In: 2014 IEEE International Conference on Bioinformatics and Biomedicine (BIBM), pp. 76–81. IEEE (2014)
10. Liu, L.L., Zhang, D.: Extracting tongue cracks using the wide line detector. In: Zhang, D. (ed.) ICMB 2008. LNCS, vol. 4901, pp. 49–56. Springer, Heidelberg (2007). doi:10.1007/978-3-540-77413-6_7
11. Li, X., Shao, Q., Yao, Q.: Cracked tongue recognition using statistic feature. In: 2014 IEEE International Conference on Bioinformatics and Biomedicine (BIBM), pp. 72–73. IEEE (2014)
12. Shao, Q., Li, X., Fu, Z.: Recognition of teeth-marked tongue based on gradient of concave region. In: 2014 International Conference on Audio, Language and Image Processing (ICALIP), pp. 968–972. IEEE (2014)
13. Zhong, S., Wei, Y., Xie, G.: Research on a tooth-marked rapid locating method based on convex hulls. Microcomput. Inf. 25(3), 312–314 (2009)
14. Zhang, Y.T.: Research on analysis method of tongue and teeth-marked tongue. Doctor dissertation, Beijing University of Chinese Medicine (2005)
15. Wang, X., Zhang, B., Yang, Z., et al.: Statistical analysis of tongue images for feature extraction and diagnostics. IEEE Trans. Image Process. 22(12), 5336–5347 (2013)
16. Zhang, B., Kumar, B.V.K., Zhang, D.: Detecting diabetes mellitus and nonproliferative diabetic retinopathy using tongue color, texture, and geometry features. IEEE Trans. Biomed. Eng. 61(2), 491–501 (2014)
17. Wei, B., Shen, L.: Automatic analysis for plumpness and slenderness of tongue. Comput. Eng. 11 (2004)
18. Xu, J., Tu, L., Ren, H., et al.: A diagnostic method based on tongue imaging morphology. In: The 2nd International Conference on Bioinformatics and Biomedical Engineering, ICBBE 2008, pp. 2613–2616. IEEE (2008)
19. Huang, B., Wu, J., Zhang, D., et al.: Tongue shape classification by geometric features. Inf. Sci. 180(2), 312–324 (2010)
20. Joachims T. Introduction to support vector machines (2002)

Perceptual Asymmetric Video Coding for 3D-HEVC

Yongfang Wang[1(✉)], Kanghua Zhu[1], Yawen Shi[1],
and Pamela C. Cosman[2]

[1] School of Communication and Information Engineering,
Shanghai University, Shanghai 200072, China
yfw@shu.edu.cn
[2] Department of Electrical and Computer Engineering,
University of California, San Diego, La Jolla, CA 92093, USA

Abstract. In the scope of stereoscopic 3D video, asymmetric video coding is an effective method in terms of maintaining the perceived quality while reducing the required transmission bandwidth by exploiting the perceptual phenomenon of binocular suppression. On the other hand, just noticeable distortion (JND) has been applied successfully in improving the video coding efficiency by removing human visual redundancies. However perceptual asymmetric coding combined with JND has not been studied. In this paper, the effectiveness of using JND aided asymmetric 3D video coding is explored for 3D-HEVC. We conducted extensive subjective tests, which indicate that if the base view is encoded at perceptual high quality and the dependent view is encoded at a lower perceptual quality, then the degradation in 3D video quality is unnoticeable and asymmetric just-noticeable distortion threshold is gained. Furthermore, we proposed a novel perceptually asymmetric 3D video coding framework by taking full advantage of these observations and subjective test results. Experimental results demonstrate that, compared with HTM, the proposed asymmetric 3D-HEVC video coding demonstrates comparable 3D perceived visual quality with about 13% bitrates savings in the whole view and about 32% bitrates savings for dependent view.

Keywords: Asymmetric 3D video coding · JND · 3D-HEVC

1 Introduction

Recent improvements in 3D video technology led to a growing interest in 3D video. While an efficient compression algorithm for 3D content is vital for the adoption of 3D technology. The state-of-the-art standard for multiview video coding (MVC) was mainly developed for efficient compression of scenes from different viewpoints. Since the bit rate required for MVC increases approximately linearly with the number of coded views, Multiview Video plus Depth (MVD) could be specified as an extension of MVC in order to support different stereoscopic as well as multi-view displays. In 2012, the standardization projects for MVD video were developed by MPEG and by ITU-T/ISO/IEC Joint Collaborative Team on 3D Video Coding Extension Development (JCT-3V) with the goal of developing a new standard for future applications.

E. Chen et al. (Eds.): PCM 2016, Part II, LNCS 9917, pp. 498–507, 2016.
DOI: 10.1007/978-3-319-48896-7_49

JCT-3V drafted two test models for a 3D video coding standard including the AVC-based (3D-AVC) and the HEVC-based (3D-HEVC) [1]. 3D-HEVC provides coding gains better than 3D-AVC, whose reference software implementation is called HTM [2]. Currently, 3D-HEVC is a popular choice for 3D entertainment media distribution. However, the delivery over bandwidth constrained networks exhibits challenges, which enforce the transmission system to perform perception-aware coding to save bitrates.

Binocular suppression show that the binocular perception of stereoscopic image pair is dominated by the high quality component [3], which is better supported with an asymmetric quality. Binocular suppression visual characteristics have been extensively investigated in asymmetric coding [4–10], which is a promising method for stereo compression to reduce bandwidth by the unequal quantization of views or unequal subsampling. In [4], a stereoscopic video coding method is proposed with asymmetric luminance and chrominance qualities based on the suppression theory of binocular vision. For asymmetry by spatial resolution reduction, Fehn et al. [5] have proposed an integration method of mixed-resolution with MVC by modifying the Disparity Compensated Prediction (DCP) loop across the views of different spatial resolutions and achieved significant average bit-rate gains. The study in [6] reports little quality and depth sensation degradations even when the spatial frequency was reduced to half of its original bandwidth. Authors in [7] had subjectively compared the performances of symmetric, asymmetric, and spatially mixed-resolution stereoscopic video coding. It was concluded that the performance of spatially mixed-resolution coding, where the auxiliary view is encoded at half resolution in both dimensions, is similar to that of the symmetric and asymmetric quality coding at full resolution. Low-resolution video coding has been found to be advantageous in terms of processing complexity. For temporal asymmetry, Anil et al. [8] proposed a low-weight frame skipping method for the secondary view to decrease the overall bitrate. Based on the subjective analysis done in [9], the performance of asymmetric quality stereoscopic video coding against that of the symmetric quality coding differs at different operating ranges. Asymmetric coding provides bit-rate gains without perceptually noticeable differences, if the auxiliary view is encoded at a higher quality than a certain threshold, while the other view is encoded at a lower quality but above a certain PSNR threshold.

Erhan et al. [10] proposed a visual attention aided ROI coding method in the context of asymmetric stereoscopic 3D video compression, in terms of achievable bit-rate gains and the dependency to the characteristics of the stereoscopic content. A mixed resolution coding method in [11] have been developed on the presumption of a certain visual fatigue response, which compared two methods of mixed resolution coding, single-eye and alternating-eye blur, in terms of overall quality for short exposures and visual fatigue level for long exposures. It is reported in [9] have concluded that PSNR reduction method is more suitable for asymmetric stereo video coding in the context of adaptive streaming at sufficiently high bitrates.

The aforementioned methods for asymmetric stereoscopic video coding have been proven to be effective as a mean for network adaptation. But only a limited number of works had incorporated just noticeable distortion (JND) model in the scope of asymmetric stereoscopic video coding. In the paper, we investigated the effectiveness of JND coding in the context of asymmetric stereoscopic 3D video compression by jointly considering the perceptual effect of binocular suppression and spatial-temporal JND model. Furthermore, the effect of 3D JND threshold levels based on binocular suppression within the asymmetric coding approach is tested subjectively. A large scale subjective test is conducted and the results are analyzed. The presented scheme can be used in a 3D-HEVC framework and achieve very high compression gains without reducing the overall perceived 3D video quality compared with state-of-the-art algorithm.

2   Perceptual Asymmetric Coding

2.1   Proposed Perceptual Asymmetric Coding Method

A flowchart of the proposed perceptual asymmetric coding method is shown in Fig. 1. Suppose that the left eye is considered as the dominant eye and it is encoded in HTM guided by JND model - J_{st}, which has not perceptual distortion in 2D display, and the right view is compressed with HTM guided by the proposed JND model - J_{3d}, which has perceptual distortion in 2D display but has not perceptual distortion combined with left view in 3D display. We define J_{3d} as following

$$J_{3d}(i,j) = J_{st}(i,j) \times Jb(i,j) \tag{1}$$

where J_{3d} denotes the 3D JND threshold of pixel (i,j),

$J_{st}(i,j)$ is the threshold of spatial and temporal JND model [12]. $Jb(i,j,n)$ is binocular JND threshold based on binocular suppression, which is obtained by the experiment in Sect. 2.2.

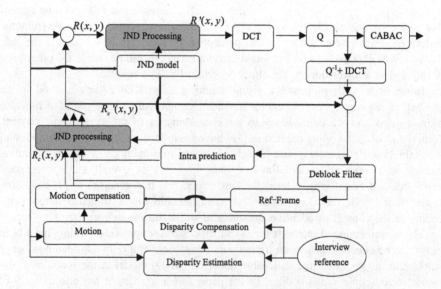

Fig. 1. A flowchart of the proposed perceptual asymmetric coding

The coding method guided by JND model is to pre-process residual coefficients and the distortion coefficient between reconstructed frame and original frame. If the residuals are less than the JND threshold, they can be discarded to save bit rate, or directly subtract the JND threshold from residual value if JND threshold is less than residual value, while maintains subjective quality.

$$R'(i,j) = \begin{cases} R(i,j) - J(i,j), & R(i,j) > J(i,j) \\ 0, & |R(i,j)| \leq J(i,j) \\ R(i,j) + J(i,j), & -R(i,j) > J(i,j) \end{cases} \qquad (2)$$

where $R(i,j)$ and $R'(i,j)$ is the original residual signal and JND-processed residual signal in pixel domain, $J(i,j)$ is the JND threshold, which is $J_{st}(i,j)$ for left view and $J_{3d}(i,j)$ for right view. Besides, In order to further remove the perceptual redundancy, the distortion coefficient $R_c(i,j)$ between reconstructed frame and original frame will be pre-process. The JND processed distortion coefficient $R'_c(i,j)$ is denoted as follow:

$$R'_c(i,j) = \begin{cases} R_c(i,j) - J(i,j), & R_c(i,j) > J(i,j) \\ 0, & |R_c(i,j)| \leq J(i,j) \\ R_c(i,j) + J(i,j), & -R_c(i,j) > J(i,j) \end{cases} \qquad (3)$$

2.2   JND Threshold Based on Binocular Suppression

JND refers to the maximum possible distortion in the signal, which is imperceptible to human eyes. According to the suppression theory of stereo human vision, the HVS can tolerate absence of high frequency information in one of the views; therefore, the two views can be represented at unequal resolutions or bitrates. This means that there exists the unequal maximum possible distortion for two views, which is JND threshold based on binocular suppression. One view is considered as the dominant eye and has not perceptual distortion in 2D display by JND processing. The other view which has perceptual distortion in 2D display but has not perceptual distortion combined with other view in 3D display by 3D JND processing based on binocular suppression.

In order to obtain JND threshold based on binocular suppression $Jb(i,j)$, our experiment is conducted in HTM platform, a typical prediction structure of 3D video coding is a hierarchical B picture (HBP) prediction structure. Left view is independently encoded and right view is encoded with disparity compensated prediction between views. For reference stereoscopic video, we encode in HTM for both left and right views. For asymmetric stereoscopic video, suppose that the left eye is encoded in HTM guided by JND model - J_{st}, and the right view is compressed with HTM guided by the proposed JND model - JND_{3d}. For the left video at each possible quality level (PSNR), Jb has been adjusted from 1 to increased by 1 until the distortion was becoming noticeable in 3D-display compared to reference stereoscopic video.

We have conducted a subjective experiment using 5 stereoscopic video sequences [13]. The test stimuli were shown on a 50-inch Panasonic TH-P50ST30C stereoscopic display with a 2D equivalent resolution of $1920 * 1080$ using polarized glasses. The aspect ratio of this display is 16:9, and the contrast ratio is 2000:1, where the picture height is 74.4 cm, the picture width is 120.4 cm. The distance of the subjects from the 3D display was 3.7 m that is approximately 5 times the picture height. The studio illumination was set to 200 lx to mimic home viewing conditions. This is an interactive subjective test that starts by displaying both views at reference stereoscopic video. A total of 13 subjects were tested, ranging in age from 23 to 29 years, 9 males and 4 female.

During the test, viewers reduce the perceptual quality of right view down to about 30 dB by incrementing JND value processing. The viewers always compare the current quality level against the reference stereoscopic video and continue to decrement the quality until coding artifacts become noticeable. This PSNR value and Jb is recorded. Figure 2 shows the average Jb threshold values for different quality stereoscopic video (over all subjects). Each of the 13 tests was 30 s long, consisting of the 8-second reference video followed by the processed test video shown twice. Preceding each video clip was a 2-second gray screen indicating whether the reference or test video was going to be shown. After each test, the subjects rated the overall quality of the test clip relative to the reference clip, indicating the level of difference or degradation on the following scale: (5) imperceptible, (4) perceptible, but not annoying, (3) slightly annoying, (2) annoying, (1) very annoying. This test design is adapted from the Double-Stimulus Impairment Scale (DSIS) method recommended in [14]. The scores are averaged across subjects and both trials of each video. If the variance between trials was large for any particular subject, that subject's data was discarded for video.

From Fig. 2, we find when $1 < Jb \leq 7$ stereoscopic video has perceptual distortion in 2D display but has not perceptual distortion in 3D-display compared to reference stereoscopic videos. Therefore, $Jb = 7$ is the maximum distortion, which is HVS can tolerate for two views.

3   Experimental Results

To evaluate the performance of the proposed algorithm, it is implemented on HTM12.1 of 3D-HEVC standard [2]. The software first codes center view0 (lift view), then side views1 (right view). The coding order is the following: T0, T1, T2 (in which Ti is the texture frames in the ith view). We mainly followed the common test condition (CTC) [13]. Most of the encoder configuration including QP setting was inherited from the CTC. A group of pictures (GOP) of 8 was considered with an Intra period of 24. The maximum coding unit depth was set to 4, and the maximum coding unit size was set to 64×64. For side view coding, disparity compensated prediction and multiview motion vector prediction were enabled. The following QP combinations for texture and depth respectively were considered: (30;39), (35;42), and (40;45). We have tested our algorithm on five sequences defined in the CTCs (1920×1088 and 1024×768) including Balloons, Kendo, Lovebird1, Poznan-Streets and Shark. The mean opinion score (MOS) scales for the DSIS protocol range from 1 to 5 for the quality from bad to excellent.

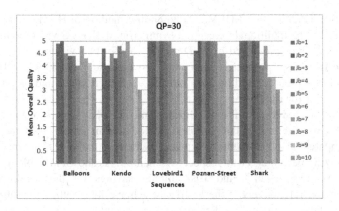

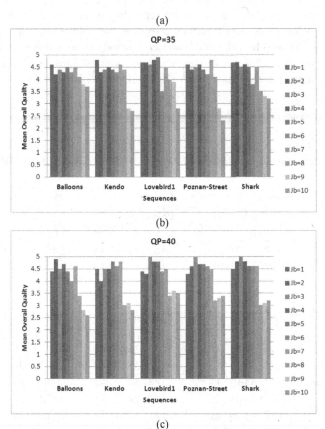

Fig. 2. 3D perceived visual quality evaluation for different *Jb* threshold values

In order to objectively assess how the proposed asymmetric stereoscopic video coding method affects bitrates saving performance, three schemes are designed as follows:

Scheme-I: Traditional 3D-HEVC video coding method in HTM

Scheme-II: The traditional perceptual symmetric 3D-HEVC video coding method in HTM, which is preprocessed by JND model - J_{st} for two views.

Scheme-III: The proposed perceptual asymmetric 3D-HEVC video coding method, which is preprocessed by JND model - J_{st} for left views and preprocessed by JND model - J_{3d} for right views.

Tables 1 and 2 show the PSNR, Bitrates and 3D DSIS scores of three methods. From Table 1 we can see that the proposed method present similar 3D perceived visual quality compared to other method. Suppose Scheme-I to be a benchmark, we can obtain the saving percentage with respect to Scheme-I. As shown in Table 3, Scheme-II contributes to average 11% and 19% bitrates savings for the whole views and dependent view, respectively. Scheme-III can achieve more bitrates savings ranging from 8% to 64% compared to Scheme-II for dependent view. It is because that Scheme-II improves coding efficiency by removing human visual spatial temporal redundancies. While Scheme-III further considers the vision binocular suppression masking effect. We also find that the proposed method can gain more bitrates savings when the left view have better video quality. Besides, we suggest that the modification of the spatial temporal JND model can slightly increase the efficiency of the asymmetric coding.

Table 1. Results comparison of Scheme-III, Scheme-II and Scheme-I in terms of PSNR and 3D DSIS

QP	Test seq.	Scheme-III			Scheme-II			Scheme-I		
		PSNR (dB)		3D MOS	PSNR (dB)		3D MOS	PSNR (dB)		3D MOS
		L	R		L	R		L	R	
30	Balloons	39.60	33.97	4.8	39.59	38.14	4.9	41.14	39.91	5
	Keno	39.57	33.81	5	39.57	38.42	4.7	41.77	40.66	5
	Lovebird1	38.32	32.55	4.7	38.32	35.85	5	38.85	36.84	5
	Poznan-Street	37.29	34.16	4.5	37.29	36.31	4.6	37.88	37.13	5
	Shark	37.05	34.73	4.8	37.05	36.57	5	38.40	37.89	5
35	Balloons	37.35	32.81	4.5	37.35	36.02	4.6	38.53	37.28	5
	Keno	37.55	32.86	4.6	37.55	36.49	4.8	39.25	38.17	4.5
	Lovebird1	35.76	31.46	4.5	35.76	33.50	4.7	36.11	34.27	4.7
	Poznan-Street	35.47	33.16	4.8	35.48	34.73	4.6	35.87	35.25	4.9
	Shark	34.57	33.08	4.5	34.57	34.23	4.7	35.51	35.15	5
40	Balloons	34.88	31.26	4.6	34.87	33.61	4.4	35.70	34.51	4.5
	Keno	35.31	31.59	4.8	35.31	34.27	4.5	36.55	35.54	4.6
	Lovebird1	33.15	30.03	4.5	33.15	31.34	4.4	33.78	31.81	4.8
	Poznan-Street	33.51	31.72	4.5	33.51	32.93	4.3	33.77	33.28	4.7
	Shark	32.22	31.27	4.6	32.22	31.96	4.5	32.86	32.60	4.8

Table 2. Results comparison of Scheme-III, Scheme-II and Scheme-I in terms of Bitrates

QP	Test seq.	Scheme-III		Scheme-II		Scheme-I	
		Bitrates (kbps)		Bitrates (kbps)		Bitrates (kbps)	
		L	R	L	R	L	R
30	Balloons	410.78	95.63	418.78	108.84	476.71	128.95
	Keno	360.70	74.87	360.70	87.08	420.79	110.88
	Lovebird1	567.80	116.63	567.80	152.04	602.07	199.54
	Poznan-Street	881.04	77.32	881.04	131.45	1013.2	202.64
	Shark	2034.7	150.97	2034.7	209.69	2335.9	269.96
35	Balloons	250.17	56.22	250.18	61.21	275.20	68.61
	Keno	217.43	44.76	217.44	49.86	245.70	59.38
	Lovebird1	303.44	57.90	303.44	68.99	313.24	84.85
	Poznan-Street	445.45	38.73	445.45	57.38	484.16	77.60
	Shark	1064.63	78.60	1064.6	102.6	1199.99	124.32
40	Balloons	155.60	34.10	155.60	33.81	165.91	36.97
	Keno	135.69	25.85	135.69	28.2	150.11	32.23
	Lovebird1	163.57	27.73	163.57	31.16	97.35	27.33
	Poznan-Street	238.63	20.15	238.63	27.05	252.19	34.85
	Shark	537.08	42.99	537.08	48.60	595.29	56.95

Table 3. Results comparison of proposed Scheme-III, Scheme-II to HTM encoder

QP	Test seq.	Scheme-II and Scheme-I		Scheme-III and Scheme-I	
		Save bitrates (%) for the whole views	Save bitrates (%) for the dependent views	Save bitrates (%) for the whole views	Save bitrates (%) for the dependent views
30	Balloons	13%	16%	15%	26%
	Keno	16%	22%	18%	32%
	Lovebird1	10%	24%	15%	42%
	Poznan-Street	17%	35%	21%	62%
	Shark	14%	22%	16%	43%
35	Balloons	9%	11%	11%	18%
	Keno	12%	16%	14%	25%
	Lovebird1	6%	19%	9%	32%
	Poznan-Street	10%	26%	14%	50%
	Shark	12%	17%	14%	37%
40	Balloons	7%	9%	7%	8%
	Keno	10%	13%	11%	20%
	Lovebird1	5%	16%	6%	25%
	Poznan-Street	7%	22%	10%	42%
	Shark	10%	15%	11%	25%
Ave.		11%	19%	13%	32%

4 Conclusion

A new perceptually asymmetric 3D video coding method based 3D-JND was presented in this paper. We first analyzed and presented the impact of utilizing JND coding within the framework of asymmetric stereoscopic video coding. Then, extensive subjective tests were evaluated to obtain asymmetric JND threshold considering different operating ranges and content types. Experimental results clearly demonstrated that the proposed algorithm achieves a significant bitrates savings than the conventional perceptually symmetric 3D video coding.

Acknowledgments. This work was supported by National Natural Science Foundation of China (61301113, 6167010863), Natural Science Foundation of Shanghai (13ZR1416500), and Open Project of Key Laboratory of Advanced Display and System Application.

References

1. Domanski, M., Grajek, T., Karwowski, D., Klimaszewski, K., Konieczny, J., Kurc, M., Luczak, A., Ratajczak, R., Siast, J., Stankiewicz, O., Stankowski, J., Wegner, K.: Multi-view HEVC—experimental results. Document JCT-VC (MPEG/VCEG), JCTVCG582, Geneva, Switzerland. Tech Rec, November 2011
2. Joint Collaborative Team on 3D Video (JCT-3V). https://hevc.hhi.fraunhofer.de/svn/svn_3DVCSoftware/tags/HTM-12.1/
3. Seuntiens, P., Meesters, L., Ijsselsteijn, W.: Perceived quality of compressed stereoscopic images: effects of symmetric and asymmetric JPEG coding and camera separation. ACM Trans. Appl. Percept. 3(2), 95–109 (2006)
4. Shao, F., Jiang, G., Wang, X., Yu, M., Chen, K.: Stereoscopic video coding with asymmetric luminance and chrominance qualities. IEEE Trans. Consum. Electron. 56(4), 2460–2468 (2010)
5. Fehn, C., Kauff, P., Cho, S., Kwon, H., Hur, N., Kim, J.: Asymmetric coding of stereoscopic video for transmission over T-DMB. In: Proceedings of 3DTV-CON, Kos, Greece, May 2007
6. Stelmach, L., Tam, W.J., Meegan, D., Vincent, A.: Stereo image quality: effects of mixed spatio-temporal resolution. IEEE Trans. Circuits Syst. Video Technol. 10(2), 188–193 (2000)
7. Aflaki, P., Hannuksela, M.M., Gabbouj, M.: Subjective quality assessment of asymmetric stereoscopic 3D video. Sig. Image Video Process. 9, 331–345 (2013). ISSN 1863–1703
8. Aksay, A., Bilen, C., Kurutepe, E., Ozcelebi, T., Akar, G.B., Civanlar, M.R., Tekalp, A.M.: Temporal and spatial scaling for stereoscopic video compression. In: Proceedings of EUSIPCO, Florence, Italy, pp. 4–8 (2006)
9. Saygili, G., Gurler, C.G., Tekalp, A.M.: Evaluation of asymmetric stereo video coding and rate scaling for adaptive 3D video streaming. IEEE Trans. Broadcast. 57(2), 593–601 (2011)
10. Ekmekcioglu, E., De Silva, V., Pesch, P.T., Kondoz, K.: Visual attention model aided non-uniform asymmetric coding of stereoscopic video. IEEE J. Sel. Top. Sig. Process. 8(3), 402–414 (2014)
11. Jain, A.K., Robinson, A.E., Nguyen, T.Q.: Comparing perceived quality and fatigue for two methods of mixed resolution stereoscopic coding. IEEE Trans. Circ. Syst. Video Technol. 24 (3), 418–429 (2014)

12. Yang, X., Lin, W., Lu, Z., Lin, X., Rahardja, S., Ong, E.P., Yao, S.: Rate control for videophone using local perceptual cues. IEEE Trans. Circ. Syst. Video Technol. **15**(4), 496–507 (2005)
13. Muller, K., Vetro, A.: Common Test Conditions of 3DV Core Experiments. Document JCT3V-G1100, ITU-T SG 16 WP 3 and ISO/IEC JTC1/SC 29/WG 11, January 2014
14. ITU-R: Recommendation ITU-R BT.500-13: Methodology for the subjective assessment of the quality of television pictures. International Telecommunication Union

Recognition of Chinese Sign Language Based on Dynamic Features Extracted by Fast Fourier Transform

Zhengchao Zhang, Xiankang Qin, Xiaocong Wu,
Feng Wang, and Zhiyong Yuan[(✉)]

School of Computer, Wuhan University, Wuhan, China
zhiyongyuan@whu.edu.cn

Abstract. Not only can sign language recognition (SLR) enhance the communications between the hearing-impaired and the healthy, but it facilitates the human-machine interaction. In this paper, a novel approach of dynamic features extraction for recognizing Chinese sign language (CSL) is proposed. At first, after image processing, to acquire dynamic features, the track of positions, the alternation of orientations and the variation of hand shapes are viewed as discrete-time signals to be transformed to the frequency domain through FFT. Afterwards, Principal Components Analysis (PCA) is used to reduce dimensionality. The above procedures yield features capable of fully describing a gesture and transform the problem concerning classification of time-series into one simple.

Random Forest (RF) is committed to recognition. The average accuracy is up to 96.7% in the recognition experiment of 14 gestures with different patterns. Thus this method proves to be effective and robust in SLR, especially those involving complicated movements.

Keywords: Chinese sign language recognition · Vision-based · Fast Fourier Transform (FFT) · Dynamic features · Feature extraction · Time series classification · Random forest

1 Introduction

1.1 Sign Language

Sign language is a stable language system composed of manual and non-manual features. In such a system, manual features contribute a larger number of messages while non-manual ones are playing their complementary roles [1]. According to the morphology of sign language, basic words fall into two categories: fingers letters and gestures. The latter occupy around 89.1% in Chinese sign language [2], hence the focus on gesture, benefiting people to a higher degree, is more significant, which is also why our paper will center around such gestures. An intact gesture could be completely described in terms of its position, orientation, shape and movement [3]. In a dynamic view, we can describe a gesture with manual behaviors consisting of the track of positions, the alternation of orientations and the variation of hand shapes, and different behaviors lead to

© Springer International Publishing AG 2016
E. Chen et al. (Eds.): PCM 2016, Part II, LNCS 9917, pp. 508–517, 2016.
DOI: 10.1007/978-3-319-48896-7_50

four gestures with different patterns, namely, large-scale simple gestures, small-scale reciprocating gestures and gestures only with fingers shaking, as in Fig. 1.

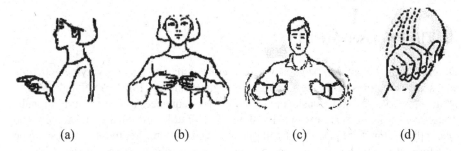

| (a) | (b) | (c) | (d) |

Fig. 1. Four categories of gestures (a) a static gesture for "you"; (b) a large-scale simple gesture for "body"; (c) a small-scale reciprocating gesture for "exercise"; (d) a gesture only with fingers shaking for "can". (Source: [4])

In the following passage, gesture is defined as one word in a sign language and it consists of a series of manual features varying with time.

1.2 Related Work

Although sign language plays a vital role in the communications among the hearing impaired, there exist great barriers in the interactions between them and the healthy, who lack the related competence. Considerable efforts have been made to enable the communications between them, and researches based on different data sources under various models have contributed a lot, such as those based on dataglove or vision [1]. Using datagloves circumvents the difficulty in the extraction of hand shapes from video and enjoys a higher accuracy, an easier access to data and its being highly real-time, and no doubt it abounds, like literature [5]. However, the potential of this approach is highly limited by the glove's inconvenience in use and the ignorance of non-manual features. Vision-based recognition, able to catch manual and non-manual performances, boasts a higher degree of resemblance to the human's way of catching sign language and so has a brighter future [1]. Built upon the above discussions, this paper presents the extraction of manual features through image processing, providing a future possibility of realizing the integration of manual and non-manual information, like [6].

There are many previous works grounded on vision [7]. Yang Quan introduced a recognition method of sign language spatiotemporal appearance model for the vision-based multi-features classifier of Chinese sign language recognition [8]. In his model, he utilized multiple features and adopted the SVMs with linear kernel function to classify 30 groups of the Chinese manual alphabet images. Rybach investigated appearance-based approaches that do not rely on a segmentation of the images or on predefined models of the image content and used the image itself as the feature [9].

To conclude, as giving a gesture is a dynamic and continuous process, if we represent a gesture using manual feature sequences, it would be unworkable to classify them with an ordinary classifier. Meanwhile, such approaches as HMM make it hard to cope with complex gestures and usually demand laborious computations. Therefore, a new method is proposed. It can extract the dynamic features of a gesture, and a general classifier is enough for training and recognition.

2   The Proposed Model

Different from the previous studies, where a series of manual features varying with time was seen as features of the gesture to be recognized using HMM, ANN and SVM to name a few, our research considers manual feature sequences as discrete-time signals. These manual features are extracted with the help of color information from the video where the gestures are performed with gloved hands. Therefore, those samples can be transformed with FFT, producing the spectrum describing those variations in the frequency domain. In the spectrum, the average manual features during a certain period are symbolized by direct components (DC), while dynamic features are indicated by nonzero-frequency components. Later, to increase the value of the higher frequency components, a stepped bandpass filter bank is introduced, whose result fully describes a gesture. Owing to the interdependency among the various dimensions of the vector, PCA is committed to dimensionality reduction. At last, the gestures with the resultant 8-dimensional features are trained and recognized through a Random Forest classifier [10]. The whole model could be illustrated by Fig. 2.

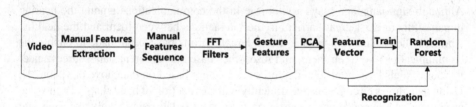

Fig. 2. Overview of the proposed model

2.1 Extraction of Manual Features

At this stage, the task is to acquire the manual features from each frame via image processing. The method mentioned in literature [11] is employed and improved. Each glove is dyed with seven colors to distinguish among the five fingers, the palm and the hand back, as in Fig. 3(a). Then we identify different parts by different colors and revise them with a simple morphological dilation and such information as the continuity of movements, prior knowledge of the size and position. This is a simple and efficient method.

Although this method is a little bit rough, hand shape extraction without many details, hardly affecting the full expression of main messages, is acceptable, as in literature [12].

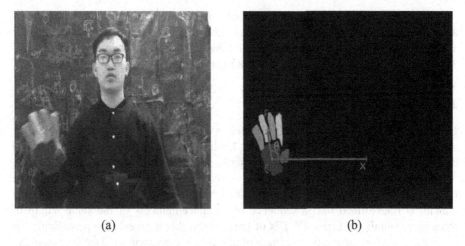

(a)   (b)

Fig. 3. The extraction of hand shape (a) is the collected image of a gesture by a gloved hand; (b) exhibits the hand shape extraction, with θ indicating the orientation of the hand.

In each frame, 12 features are extracted to describe the position, orientation and hand shape of a single hand. Specifically, the position is defined as the mean of the all pixel coordinates of a hand (x for the horizontal axis and y for the vertical); defining F as the center of the five fingers and C as that of the palm and the back, the orientation is expressed by the angle between CF and x, in this way the whole range of $(0, 2\pi)$ can be fully represented, as in Fig. 3(b); the hand shape, or the projection of the hand onto the two-dimensional plane, is represented through the size (the number of pixels), the dispersion degree of fingers (the variance of the center of five fingers) and the respective proportions of seven parts (in terms of their covering area). In light of perspective knowledge, size carries with it the depth information of the position. After the above extraction, a 12-dimensional vector is constructed to represent each hand to the full. Besides, a standardization of the position, size of the hand and the dispersion degree of fingers are conducted to exclude the influence of individual physical distinctions, as Eqs. 1–4.

$$S' = \frac{S}{Ss} \tag{1}$$

$$Y' = \frac{Y - Y_{nose}}{Y_s} \tag{2}$$

$$X' = \frac{X - X_{nose}}{X_s} \tag{3}$$

$$V' = \frac{V}{V_s} \tag{4}$$

X_s is the shoulder breadth; Y_s is the distance between the nose and the center of abdomen; X_{nose} and Y_{nose} are the coordinates of nose on the horizontal and vertical axes; s_s and V_s express the size and the dispersion degree of fingers when the palm is open. The above six values are measured and configured in advance.

2.2 Extraction of Dynamic Features

In the last part, a $12 \times 2 \times 7$ vector is defined in every frame for hand description, then there comes a time series data of gesture. Each of these dimensions can be seen as a discrete- time signal, and the task is to describe how it performs.

The Discrete Fourier transform (DFT) is a mathematical procedure used to determine the frequency content of a discrete signal sequence. The sequence of N samples in time domain is transformed into a sequence of complex numbers of the same length in frequency domain, as Eq. 5. DFT is of great use in that it reveals the periodicities in samples as well as the relative strength of any periodic component. That is always the case when the DFT is implemented via the Fast Fourier transform (FFT) algorithm. FFT manages to reduce the complexity of the DFT from $O(N^2)$ to $O(N \log N)$, where N is the data size [13]. Therefore, it takes little time to extract the gesture features.

$$X_k = \sum_{n=0}^{N-1} x_n e^{-i\frac{2\pi}{N}kn} \quad k = 0, \ldots, N-1 \tag{5}$$

In this way, the frequency spectrum is obtained, as shown in Fig. 4. The DC in this spectrum reflects the global manual features during this period, while nonzero-frequency components express the dynamic features regarding the track of positions, the alternation of orientations and the variation of hand shapes. We retain both amplitude spectrum and phase spectrum because they co-determine the behaviors of a gesture.

DFT used, the sequences varying with time are transformed into those varying with frequency, thus making it not a problem to measure distance in classifying time series [14]. In conclusion, the complicated process of classifying time series is transformed into a general simple classification, which stands as the key of our model. Moreover, the negative relation between range and frequency of a person's movement, coupled with the statistical characteristics [15] of the speed of sign language makes it necessary to design a filter bank for the amplification of higher frequencies and thus for the consideration of such fast manual movements like shaking hand, in this way, it becomes more effective to discriminate among various manual behavior. Simultaneously, this filter bank can serve as a low-pass filter. The highest frequency of a normal gesture is around 3 Hz, as in literature [16]. The components at 0–6 Hz are found to be quite functional to reconstruct the manual feature sequence, as Fig. 4. Therefore, those above 6 Hz, noises mainly incurred by such external factors as light, the moving shadows in the video, are filtered. In this way, the defects resulting from the simple extraction of manual features are repaired to a certain extent, making the model more reliable and robust. The Eq. 6 shows the devised filters bank, w is set according to the statistical

$$F(i) = \begin{cases} X(0) & i = 0 \\ \sum_f w_i X(f) & i < f \leq i+1 \\ 0 & i > 7 \end{cases} \tag{6}$$

characteristics of gestures and human manual movements. In this experiment, $w = (1.0, 1.2, 1.4, 1.6, 1.8, 2.0)$.

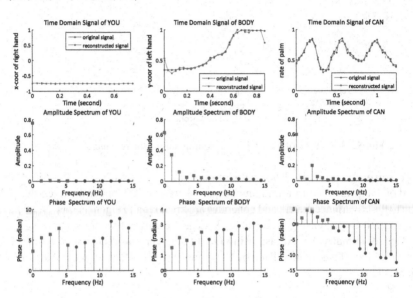

Fig. 4. The feature extraction of three typical gestures using FFT From left to right, they are: the horizontal coordinate of the right hand in gesture "you"; the vertical coordinate of the left hand in gesture "body"; the coordinate of the proportion of palm's area in gesture "can". They respectively stand for static gestures, large-scale simple gestures and gestures only with finger shakings. The small-scale reciprocating gestures are not shown here due to the space limitation. In the three figures of time-domain signals, blue is for the original signal and red is for the reconstructed signal using frequencies under 6 Hz. In the figures of spectrum, red is for the feature and blue is for the noises to be eliminated. (Color figure online)

2.3 Principle Components Analysis (PCA)

The filtering is followed by the production of a $12 \times 2 \times 7 \times 2$ dimensional vector for the depiction of every gesture. The number of dimensions makes it hard to conduct classification. Meanwhile, certain correlation is found among different dimensions of this vector, causing data redundancy, as in Fig. 5. To illustrate, while one is signifying "exercise" (by clenching the hand, bending the elbow and expending the chest twice) the positional tracks of two hands reflected on the horizontal axis are exactly the opposite, giving rise to correlation between the corresponding dimensions.

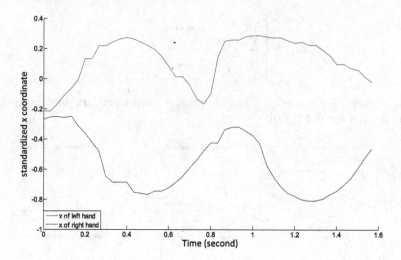

Fig. 5. The tracks of the horizontal coordinates of the two hands in training

To solve this problem, Principal Components Analysis (PCA) comes into effect. Based on the principle of minimizing a squared error, PCA applies an eigen-decomposition to the covariance matrix and generates eigenvalues and eigenvectors. Next, having been ordered in decreasing eigenvalue, K largest eigenvectors are selected to form a transformation matrix A^T. At last, using Eq. 8 to convert the vector of correlated variables, which have been standardized by Eq. 7, into a set of values of linearly uncorrelated variables [17].

$$Z = \frac{F - E(F)}{\sigma(F)} \tag{7}$$

$$X' = A^T Z \tag{8}$$

3 Experiment and Analysis

3.1 Experimental Environment

Videos of fourteen representative gestures [4] are collected using ordinary webcam (Logitech c920), with a resolution of 640×480 and a frame rate of 30fps. Among these gestures, four typical categories are made: static gestures including "you", "I", "good" and "house"; large-scale simple gestures including "welcome", "throw", "gift", "very" and "body"; small-scale reciprocating gestures including "health", "exercise" and "often"; gestures only with fingers shaking including "like" and "can".

In the experiment, we adopt the above mentioned method of hand detection, and use seven distinguishing colors painted on each glove to mark different parts of hands: five fingers, the palm and back, then extract the manual features in each frame. It turns out that, limited by the performance of the camera, moving shadows would appear in some frames, which leads to abnormal data. To settle this problem, the data of these frames are substituted by those of their respective front frames. Better result is produced when *K* is 8 in PCA.

Accordingly, 280 video samples are obtained among which each gesture have 20 samples. Under the proposed approach, manual features of each frame and gesture features of each sample are successfully acquired. Next come the 4-fold cross validations for five times.

3.2 Results and Analysis

At the outset, the recognition is tried through the traditional HMM. We assume Gaussian distribution whose parameters depend on its underlying states for defining the emission probabilities. The number of states Q is configured as 5, the results are shown in Tables 1:

Table 1. Accuracy under the traditional HMM

	Category 1	Category 2	Category 3	Category 4	Average
On training set	0.975	0.972	0.951	0.937	0.959
On test set	0.930	0.954	0.893	0.870	0.912

Category 1: static gestures; category 2: large-scale simple gestures; category 3: small-scale reciprocating gestures; category 4: gestures only with finger shakings.

Then we choose Random Forest (RF) classifier for training and recognizing the gesture features extracted using our model. 50 decision trees are configured, and one-third of the training set is randomly sampled with replacement to train each decision tree. And half of the features are selected for decision split every time. The result is as follows (Table 2):

Table 2. Recognition of features extracted using RF

	Category 1	Category 2	Category 3	Category 4	Average
On training set	0.998	0.996	1.000	0.985	0.995
On test set	0.955	0.964	0.980	0.970	0.967

Comparing the two results, it can be observed that our model outperforms the classical HMM in the aspect of average accuracy, which indicates that the method proposed in this paper is workable and effective. To analyze the reason, our model requires only the configuration of several parameters during the extraction of dynamic manual features and the recognition using RF, whereas HMM entails a large number of parameters of the model to describe a gesture, thus the inadequate training on our small set. This demonstrates the advantage of our model in its convenience in training. What's more, in each category, a higher accuracy of our model is seen in the recognition of complex gestures (category 3 and 4) than HMM, and also what's obvious is a lower accuracy of HMM in recognizing complex gestures than in simple ones. This indicates the disadvantage of HMM when it comes to a more complicated situation, where our model performs quite effectively. In addition, although our model focuses on complex gestures, the experimental results unfold its good adaptability to the recognition of simple ones.

3.3 Discussions

As the experimental results show, for the extraction of gesture features of SL, it is workable and effective to view manual feature sequences as discrete-time signals and to deploy FFT in this process. Moreover, this kind of method has a good adaptability to model for extracting simple gestures and it is indeed robust. In addition, corresponding improvements may be made for putting it into actual use as much as possible.

In the process of standardization, to eliminate the effect of individual physical differences, we configure the position of the nose as a base point after manual measurement. This is applicable in some circumstances such as sign language program and sign language teaching. When it comes to actual communications, however, nose tends to move. If we utilize the techniques in face detection to locate the nose and add to our model the facial expressions [6], which also play a role, though secondary, in the transmission of information, it would be more accurate.

Simultaneously, as the objective of this paper is to test whether our proposed model is feasible, only a small number of isolated gestures are recognized. Under our model, the track of positions, alternation of orientations and the variation of hand shape are combined to form a vector. It works well when the number of samples to be recognized is not large, but it yields the sparsity problem in a system demanding actual realizations. To solve this problem, we could encode all the gestures with treating the track, alternation and variation as three independent characteristics, then recognize them and refer them to lexicon. When recognition of continuous gestures is in question, the researches in speech recognition may shed light: split the feature sequence into frames based on such statistical features like the frequency and the basic behaviors of the gesture of CSL. The above two solutions would significantly decrease the number of categories fallen into, making it easier to train.

4 Conclusion

To conclude, this paper presents a method of extracting gesture features of CSL and conducts a recognition with the Random Forest classifier. A signer is arranged to wear a colored glove and to perform gestures. Then a video of this is shot with an ordinary webcam and the manual feature sequences are extracted based on distinguishing colors which differentiate hand from the background and mark different parts of the hand. These manual feature sequences are considered as discrete-time signals, FFT and filters are used to obtain the gesture features. As the results indicate, features extracted this way work well to represent gestures. It circumvents the problem of the traditional HMM where a large training set is entailed and parameters are hard to be trained. In addition, it offers a thought of how to recognize and analyze the various movements and even how to classify time series. Its applications could also concern with gait and behavior recognitions and its values could be explored in the fields of new human-machine interface and virtual reality (VR) as well.

Acknowledgements. The research work described in this paper was supported by the National Natural Science Foundation of China (Project no. 61373107) and the Project of Scientific Research & Innovative Experiment of National Undergraduate (Project no. 201510486068).

References

1. Cooper, H., Holt, B., Bowden, R.: Sign language recognition. In: Visual Analysis of Humans, pp. 539–562. Springer, London (2011)
2. Dingqian, G.U., Xiaohua, S., Yuanyuan, Y.U.: The analysis of chinese sign language's basic words (basic movements). Chin. J. Spec. Educ., 65–72 (2005)
3. Stokoe, W.C.: Sign language structure: an outline of the visual communication systems of the American Deaf. J. Deaf Stud. Deaf Educ. **10**, 3–37 (2005)
4. China Disabled Persons' Federation, Disabilities, C.A.o.P.w.H.: Chinese Sign Language. Huaxia Publishing House, Beijing, China, 1,9,116,153,158,218,258,268,373,762,805, 1004,1023 (2003)
5. Yuan, Q., Geo, W., Yao, H., Wang, C.: Recognition of strong and weak connection models in continuous sign language. In: Proceedings of 16th International Conference on Pattern Recognition, pp. 75–78. IEEE (2002)
6. Metaxas, D.N., Liu, B., Yang, F., Yang, P., Michael, N., Neidle, C.: Recognition of nonmanual markers in American Sign Language (ASL) using non-parametric adaptive 2D-3D face tracking. In: LREC, pp. 2414–2420. Citeseer (2012)
7. Joudaki, S., bin Mohamad, D., Saba, T., Rehman, A., Al-Rodhaan, M., Al-Dhelaan, A.: Vision-based sign language classification: a directional review. IETE Tech. Rev. **31**, 383–391 (2014)
8. Quan, Y.: IEEE: Chinese sign language recognition based on video sequence appearance modeling. In: 5th IEEE Conference on Industrial Electronics and Applications, pp. 385–390. IEEE, New York (2010)
9. Rybach, D., Ney, I.H., Borchers, J., Deselaers, D.-I.T.: Appearance-based features for automatic continuous sign language recognition. Master's thesis, H.L.T.P.R. Group, RWTH Aachen University, Aachen, Germany (2006)
10. Liaw, A., Wiener, M.: Classification and regression by random forest. R News **2**, 18–22 (2002)
11. Starner, T.E.: Visual recognition of american sign language using hidden Markov models. DTIC Document (1995)
12. Sperling, G., Landy, M., Cohen, Y., Pavel, M.: Intelligible encoding of ASL image sequences at extremely low information rates. Comput. Vis. Graph. Image Process. **31**, 335–391 (1985)
13. Lyons, R.G.: Understanding Digital Signal Processing. Pearson Education, Upper Saddle River (2010)
14. YiMing, Y., Rong, P.A.N., JiaLin, P.A.N., Qiang, Y., Lei, L.I.: A comparative study on time series classification. Chin. J. Comput. **30**, 1259–1266 (2007)
15. Haken, H., Kelso, J.A.S., Bunz, H.: A theoretical-model of phase-transitions in human hand movements. Biol. Cybern. **51**, 347–356 (1985)
16. Hager-Ross, C., Schieber, M.H.: Quantifying the independence of human finger movements: comparisons of digits, hands, and movement frequencies. J. Neurosci. **20**, 8542–8550 (2000)
17. Duda, R.O., Hart, P.E., Stork, D.G.: Pattern Classification, p. 636. Wiley, New York (2012)

Enhanced Joint Trilateral Up-sampling for Super-Resolution

Liang Yuan, Xin Jin[✉], and Chun Yuan

Graduate School at Shenzhen, Tsinghua University, Shenzhen 518055, China
yuanll4@mails.tsinghua.edu.cn,
jin.xin@sz.tsinghua.edu.cn

Abstract. In this work, we propose a new depth image super-resolution method. We use low resolution depth image, refined high resolution color image and generated HR depth image to conduct iterative joint trilateral up-sampling. During the process of up-sampling, we put forward an algorithm to smooth the area in color image with overmuch texture to solve the texture copying problem. Based on the assumption that LR image is a counterpart of HR image with missing pixels, we defined an evaluation criterion to ensure the convergence of iteration and simultaneously make the final generated image close to the true HR depth image as far as possible. Our approach can generate HR depth image with sharp edges, none texture copying and little noises. Experiments are conducted on various datasets including Middlebury to demonstrate the superiority of the proposed method and show the improvement over state-of-the-art methods.

Keywords: Super-resolution · Iterative · HR color image · Convergence criteria

1 Introduction

Depth image is playing a more and more important role in image processing and computer vision. Traditional depth sensing methods cannot provide enough accurate depth information. Laser range canners are only applicable at static scenes and depth images acquired by time-of-flight (TOF) cameras are of relatively low resolution (LR) and always contain a lot of noises. Single depth image super-resolution (SR) is to reconstruct a high resolution (HR) depth image based on one single LR depth image by up-sampling and de-noising at the same time.

According to whether an associated HR color image is used or not, previous single depth image SR methods can be divided into two categories (SR guided by depth image and SR guided by depth and color image). The first category contains two groups, basic interpolation methods [1–4] and learning-based methods [5–12]. Bilinear interpolation [1] and bicubic interpolation [2] are two representatives of the first group. They can quickly generate SR images, but produce blurry edges and low accuracy. Learning-based methods attempt to find the mapping relation between the LR image/block and the HR image/block through training dataset and optimization solution. Freeman *et al.* [5] propose the example-based algorithm using Markov random fields (MRFs). Roweis *et al.* [6] put forward locally linear embedding (LLE) and

© Springer International Publishing AG 2016
E. Chen et al. (Eds.): PCM 2016, Part II, LNCS 9917, pp. 518–526, 2016.
DOI: 10.1007/978-3-319-48896-7_51

Chang *et al.* [7] raise neighborhood embedding algorithm to conduct nonlinear dimensionality reduction. J.C. Yang *et al.* [8] propose a sparse representation model to reconstruct the HR image from an over-complete dictionary generated by training set, and it is further extended by Li *et al.* [9] and R. Zeyde *et al.* [10]. Chao Dong *et al.* [11] use a lightweight structured deep convolutional neural network (CNN) to learn the mapping between low and high resolution images, and jointly optimize all layers of CNN. Samuel Schulter *et al.* [12] directly map the low and high resolution patches through random forests. Learning-based methods can improve high frequency details in the SR image, but suffer from huge computational cost and the requirement in big training sets. The second category takes associated HR color image as a depth cue and assumes the discontinuities in the depth image and color image are consistent [13–17]. The most fundamental method is joint bilateral up-sampling (JBU), proposed by Kopf *et al.* [13]. Yang *et al.* [14] aggregate each layer of the 3D cost volume with joint bilateral filter (JBF) in his cost aggregation-based method. Lo *et al.* [15] use spatial and range information in HR color image and integrate local gradient information of depth image to conduct joint trilateral filtering. He et al. [16] propose guided image filter based on a local linear model. Jiajun Lu *et al.* [17] segment the color image through the guidance of sparse depth samples, But the aforementioned assumption is invalid when color changes in depth consistent area or depth changes in color consistent area. Although the associated color image help get clear and sharp edge, texture copying problem cannot be avoided especially when there is too much change in intensity values.

In this paper, we propose a novel SR approach named enhanced joint trilateral up-sampling (EJTU), which can generate SR depth image with clear and sharp edge, no texture copying problem and high accuracy. Our approach belongs to the second category. It exploits spatial distance from input LR depth image, intensity variance extracted from the refined HR color image and intermediate HR depth image to conduct an iterative joint trilateral up-sampling. The redundant texture information is removed during the process of up-sampling. The LR image is considered as a counterpart of the HR image with pixels missing, and based on that a regularization term is added to make the final result close to the real HR image. The iteration process can converge rapidly with no more than 10 iterations on average.

The remainder of this paper is organized as follows. Section 2 gives a detailed description of the proposed approach. Section 3 shows the experimental results of the proposed approach. Section 4 concludes the paper.

2   Proposed Approach

An overall flowchart of the framework of our proposed approach is provided in Fig. 1. And the detail of each part is introduced in the following subsections.

2.1   Enhanced Joint Trilateral Up-sampling (EJTU)

The proposed enhanced joint trilateral up-sampling method mainly consists of 3 steps:

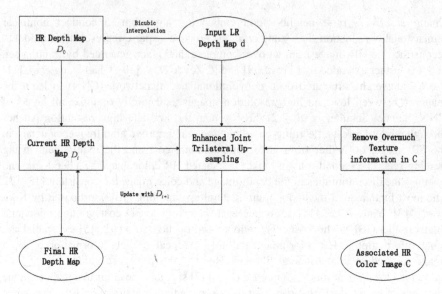

Fig. 1. Flowchart of the framework of our proposed approach.

First, bicubic interpolation is applied to the LR input depth image d to generate the initial depth image D_0. Second, the associated HR color image C is transformed from RGB color space to YCBCR color space and its luminance component L is refined in each window area where the range filter kernel works and then extracted as reference image for depth image up-sampling. Third, based on the geometric distance in d, the intensity of surrounding depth pixels in HR depth image and luminance intensity of reference image L, we conduct joint trilateral up-sampling to generate HR depth image. We consider the LR image as a counterpart of HR image with pixels missing. To take full advantage of the accurate information of LR depth image, we introduce iteration to refine the generated result. In each iteration, the HR depth image D_i is replaced by the new generated D_{i+1}. The equation of EJTU is as follows:

$$\widetilde{S}_p = \frac{1}{k_p} \sum_{q_\downarrow \in \Omega_{p_\downarrow}, q \in \Omega_p} S_{q_\downarrow} f(\|p_\downarrow - q_\downarrow\|) g(\|I_p^1 - I_q^1\|) h(\|I_p^2 - I_q^2\|) \qquad (1)$$

where $\widetilde{S}_p$ is the intensity value at pixel p in the generated HR depth image D_{i+1}; I_p^1 and I_q^1 are the intensity value at pixel p and q in the refined window area where the range filter kernel $g(\bullet)$ works in reference image L, respectively; I_p^2 and I_q^2 are the corresponding intensity value of pixel p and q in D_i; $p_\downarrow$ is the pixel in d corresponding to the pixel p; $q_\downarrow$ stands for a pixel around $p_\downarrow$; $\Omega_{p_\downarrow}$ and Ω_p stands for the window area where filter kernels work around pixel $p_\downarrow$ and p. K_p is the normalization factor, which is given by:

$$k_p = \sum_{q_\downarrow \in \Omega_{p_\downarrow}, q \in \Omega_p} f(\|p_\downarrow - q_\downarrow\|) g(\|I_p^1 - I_q^1\|) h(\|I_p^2 - I_q^2\|) \qquad (2)$$

$f(\bullet)$ is the spatial filter kernel for measuring the spatial similarities between $p_{\downarrow}$ and its neighbors, which is defined as:

$$f(\|p_{\downarrow} - q_{\downarrow}\|) = \exp\left(-\frac{\|p_{\downarrow} - q_{\downarrow}\|^2}{2\sigma_d^2}\right) \tag{3}$$

$g(\bullet)$ is the range filter kernel to measure the luminance similarities between I_p^1 and its neighbors, which is defined as:

$$g(\|I_p^1 - I_q^1\|) = \exp(-\frac{\|I_p^1 - I_q^1\|^2}{2\sigma_r^2}) \tag{4}$$

$h(\bullet)$ is the range filter kernel to measure the depth intensity similarities between I_p^2 and its neighbors, which is defined as:

$$h(\|I_p^2 - I_q^2\|) = \exp(-\frac{\|I_p^2 - I_q^2\|^2}{2\sigma_t^2}) \tag{5}$$

2.2 Removing Overmuch Texture Information in Associated HR Color Image

Traditional color image guided SR methods assume the discontinuities in the depth image and color image are consistent. When there exists lots of color changes in the depth consistent area, texture copying problem cannot be avoided.

To eliminate the texture copying problem, we propose a new algorithm to remove the complex texture in the window area Ω_p where the range filter kernel $g(\bullet)$ works. During the up-sampling process, the associated color image is transformed from RGB color space to YCBCR color space, and the luminance component is extracted and refined in each window area where the range filter kernel works, then served as reference for depth up-sampling. Texture is considered as complex edges here, we use Candy operator [18] to detect the edge, which generates a 0-1 matrix where 1 represents the edge. If the proportion that "1" holds exceeds a pre-defined limit, this window area Ω_p is considered to contain complex texture. Then we project the window area to LR depth image to get $\Omega_{p_{\downarrow}}$, for purpose of judging whether this area contains depth change. If there is no depth change in $\Omega_{p_{\downarrow}}$, the matrix of filtering window Ω_p is filled in with mean value of pixels which have zero value at the corresponding coordinate position in the 0-1 matrix. If there is a depth change in $\Omega_{p_{\downarrow}}$, the area of $\Omega_{p_{\downarrow}}$ is considered to have depth boundaries, pixel value in Ω_p is left unchanged. If the proportion that "1" holds is lower than the pre-defined limit, the window area Ω_p is considered to have no complex texture or the area $\Omega_{p_{\downarrow}}$ of contains depth boundaries, so Ω_p is left unchanged. An example is demonstrated in Fig. 2 to illustrate the algorithm.

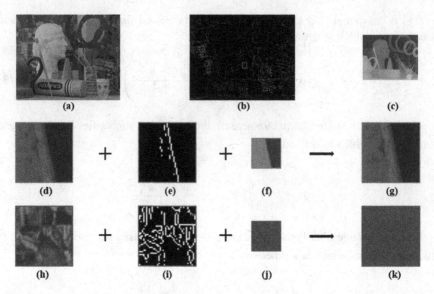

Fig. 2. Illustration of the algorithm of removing overmuch texture. (a) is the luminance map of associated color image. (b) is the edge map of (a). (c) LR input depth image. (d)–(f) and (h)–(j) are the enlargement of corresponding framed area in (a)–(c), respectively. (g) and (k) are optimized results of (d) and (h) after removing overmuch texture information. (Color figure online)

2.3   Proposed Iterative Framework

Iterative framework is introduced to take full advantage of the geometric information from the LR input depth image and luminance information from associated color image to refine the generated HR depth image. Based on the assumption that LR image is a counterpart of HR image with pixels missing, we down-sample D_{i+1} by projecting it to a new image with the same size of LR input depth image d, then calculate the mean squared error (MSE) between d and the projection result. MSE between two consecutive generated HR depth image D_i and D_{i+1} are taken into consideration at the same time. Two different MSEs are endowed with different weights to construct a new evaluation criterion, which is defined as:

$$t = k_1 \cdot MSE(D_i, D_{i+1}) + k_2 \cdot MSE(d, downsample(D_{i+1})) \qquad (6)$$

But for input image with noises, k_2 is always set to 0, as the true value of pixels in image with noises are corrupted.

3   Experiments

Experiments are divided into two groups: SR to depth image without noises and SR to depth image with noises. Datasets without noises from Middlebury [19] and datasets with noises from Ferstl et al. [20] are tested for visual and quantitative comparison.

For datasets from Middlebury [16] without noises, parameters of the proposed algorithm are set as $\sigma_d = 1.5$, $\sigma_r = 0.09$, $\sigma_t = 0.035$, $\Omega_p = 9 \times 9$, $\sigma = 0.01$, $k_1 = 0.02$ and $k_2 = 0.1$ Ground truth image are down-sampled by factor 2 and 4 to generate LR input depth image. Visual comparison based on dataset Art of [19] is shown in Fig. 3.

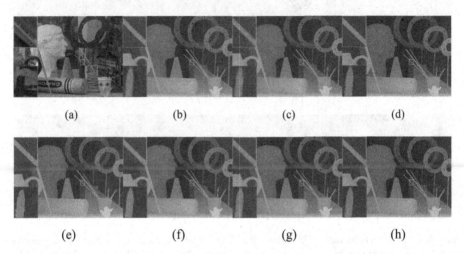

Fig. 3. Experiments on dataset of Art without noises of [19]. Depth map SR methods compared in details (upscaled factor: 2). (a) is the HR color image. (b)–(g) are SR results of He *et al.* [16], Diebel *et al.* [22], Park *et al.* [23], Yang *et al.* [14], Ferstl *et al.* [20] and ours, respectively. (h) Ground truth. (Color figure online)

Mean absolute error (MAE) is used for evaluation criterion for SR effect. The smaller the MAE is, the better the SR result is. Seven well established algorithms are compared in Table 1, and the proposed approach outperforms all the other algorithms.

Table 1. Quantative MAE comparision on the datasets in Middlebury [19].

Algorithms	Art		Books		Moebius		Texture copying
	X2	X4	X2	X4	X2	X4	
Nearest	0.54	1.11	0.20	0.39	0.20	0.41	No
Bilinear	0.56	1.09	0.19	0.35	0.22	0.41	No
Yang *et al.* [14]	0.57	0.70	0.30	0.45	0.39	0.48	Yes
He *et al.* [16]	0.66	1.06	0.22	0.36	0.24	0.38	Yes
Diebel *et al.* [22]	0.62	1.01	0.22	0.33	0.25	0.37	Yes
Park *et al.* [23]	0.57	0.70	0.17	0.31	0.18	0.30	Yes
Ferstl *et al.* [20]	0.49	0.75	0.19	0.28	0.19	0.31	Yes
Ours	**0.21**	**0.41**	**0.11**	**0.16**	**0.12**	**0.18**	No

For datasets from Ferstl *et al.* [20] with noises, parameters of the proposed algorithm are set as $\sigma_d = 5$, $\sigma_r = 0.2$, $\sigma_t = 0.03$, $\Omega_p = 17 \times 17$, $\sigma = 0.01$, $k_1 = 1$, $k_2 = 0$. Down-scaled noisy depth images are served as LR input and the up-scaled factor is 2 and 4. Peak signal-to-noise ratio (PSNR) is adopted to evaluate the SR result. The bigger PSNR is, the better the result is. The subjective comparison is shown in Fig. 4 and objective comparison with eight other algorithms based on PSNR is demonstrated in Table 2. Our algorithm works best among the comparison.

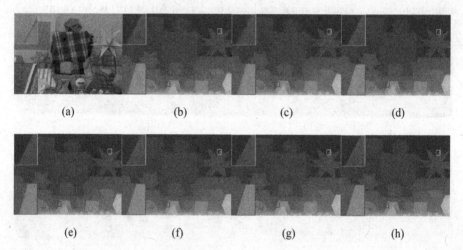

(a)   (b)   (c)   (d)

(e)   (f)   (g)   (h)

Fig. 4. Experiments on dataset Moebius with noises in [20]. Depth map SR methods compared in details (upscaled factor: 2). (a) is the HR color image. (b)–(g) are SR results of He *et al.* [16], Diebel *et al.* [22], Park *et al.* [23], Yang *et al.* [14], Ferstl *et al.* [20] and ours, respectively. (h) Ground truth. (Color figure online)

Table 2. Quantitative PSNR comparision on the datasets with noises used in [20].

Algorithms	Art		Books		Moebius		Texture copying
	X2	X4	X2	X4	X2	X4	
Nearest	31.80	30.65	32.34	32.13	31.75	31.51	No
Bilinear	34.91	33.13	36.20	35.44	35.67	34.95	No
Yang *et al.* [14]	38.57	36.04	42.69	40.60	42.46	40.45	Yes
He *et al.* [16]	37.13	35.24	40.64	39.38	40.24	31.90	Yes
Diebel *et al.* [22]	37.28	35.04	41.85	38.59	41.56	38.28	Yes
Chan *et al.* [21]	37.40	35.14	41.73	39.28	41.77	39.31	Yes
Park *et al.* [23]	36.63	34.94	42.33	39.80	42.29	40.14	Yes
Ferstl *et al.* [20]	38.06	35.95	44.49	41.24	44.78	41.98	Yes
Ours	**47.13**	**43.23**	**48.94**	**45.63**	**48.15**	**44.85**	No

4 Conclusions

An enhanced joint trilateral up-sampling method is put forward in this paper. Based on the assumption that LR depth image is a counterpart of HR depth image with pixels missing, we exploit spatial information from the LR depth image, intensity information from generated HR depth image and refined luminance map of associated color image for up-sampling. During the up-sampling process, redundant texture information in the luminance map is removed to avoid texture copying problem. MSE between two consecutive generated HR depth images and MSE between LR depth image and its counterpart in the newly generated HR depth image are weighted to terminate the iterative up-sampling process. Final SR result generated by the proposed approach has clear sharp edges, little noises and none texture copying problem. Comparison experiments demonstrate the superiority of the proposed approach over state-of-the-art SR methods.

Acknowledgements. This work is supported in part by the NSFC-Guangdong Joint Foundation Key Project (U1201255) and project of NSFC 61371138, China.

References

1. Gribbon, K.T., Bailey, D.G.: A novel approach to real-time bilinear interpolation. In: Second IEEE International Workshop on Electronic Design, Test and Applications, Perth, Australia, pp. 126–131, January 2004
2. Keys, R.G.: Cubic convolution interpolation for digital image processing. IEEE Trans. Acoust. Speech Signal Process. **29**(6), 1153–1160 (1981)
3. Li, X., Orchard, M.T.: New edge-directed interpolation. IEEE Trans. Image Process. **10**, 1521–1527 (2001)
4. Wang, Q., Ward, R.K.: A new orientation-adaptive interpolation method. IEEE Trans. Image Process. **16**(4), 889–900 (2007)
5. Freeman, W.T., Jones, T.R., Pasztor, E.C.: Example-based super-resolution. IEEE Comput. Graph. Appl. **22**(2), 56–65 (2002)
6. Roweis, S., Saul, L.: Nonlinear dimensionality reduction by locally linear embedding. Science **290**(22), 2323–2326 (2000)
7. Chang, H., Yeung, D.Y., Xiong, Y.: Super-resolution through neighbor embedding. In: CVPR, vol. 1, pp. 275–282 (2004)
8. Yang, J.C., Wright, J., Huang, T., Ma, Y.: Image super-resolution via sparse representation. IEEE Trans. Image Process. **19**(11), 2861–2873 (2010)
9. Kiechle, M., Hawe, S., Kleinsteuber, M.: A joint intensity and depth co-sparse analysis model for depth map super-resolution. In: ICCV, pp. 1545–1552 (2013)
10. Zeyde, R., Elad, M., Protter, M.: On single image scale-up using sparse-representations. In: Boissonnat, J.-D., Chenin, P., Cohen, A., Gout, C., Lyche, T., Mazure, M.-L., Schumaker, L. (eds.) Curves and Surfaces 2010. LNCS, vol. 6920, pp. 711–730. Springer, Heidelberg (2012). doi:10.1007/978-3-642-27413-8_47
11. Dong, C., Loy, C.C., He, K., Tang, X.: Learning a deep convolutional network for image super-resolution. In: Fleet, D., Pajdla, T., Schiele, B., Tuytelaars, T. (eds.) ECCV 2014. LNCS, vol. 8692, pp. 184–199. Springer, Heidelberg (2014). doi:10.1007/978-3-319-10593-2_13

12. Schulter, S., Leistner, C., Bischof, H.: Fast and accurate image upscalling with super-resolution forests. In: CVPR 2015, pp. 3791–3799 (2015)
13. Kopf, J., Cohen, M., Lischinski, D., Uyttendaele, M.: Joint bilateral upsampling. ACM TOG 26(3), 96 (2007)
14. Yang, Q., Yang, R., Davis, J.: Spatial-depth super resolution for range images. In: CVPR (2007)
15. He, K., Sun, J., Tang, X.: Guided image filtering. In: ECCV, pp. 1–10 (2010)
16. Lu, J., Forsyth, D.: Sparse depth super resolution. In: CVPR 2015, pp. 2245–2253 (2015)
17. Canny, J.: A computational approach to edge detection. IEEE Trans. Pattern Anal. Mach. Intell. 8(6), 679–698 (1986). PAMI
18. Middlebury stereo database. http://vision.middlebury.edu/stereo/
19. Ferstl, D., Reinbacher, C., Ranftl, R.: Image guided depth upsampling using anisotropic total generalized variation. In: ICCV (2013). http://rvlab.icg.tugraz.at/project_page/project_tofusion/project_tofsuperresolution.html
20. Chan, D., Buisman, H., Theobalt, C.: A noise-aware filter for real-time depth upsampling. In: Workshop on Multi-camera and Multi-modal Sensor Fusion Algorithms and Applications (2008)
21. Diebel, J., Thrun, S.: An application of markov random fields to range sensing. In: Proceedings of Advances in Neural Information Processing System (2005)
22. Park, J., Kim, H., Tai, W.Y.: High quality depth map upsampling for 3D-TOF cameras. In: ICCV (2011)

Learning to Recognize Hand-Held Objects from Scratch

Xue Li[1,2], Shuqiang Jiang[2]([⊠]), Xiong Lv[2], and Chengpeng Chen[2]

[1] College of Information Science and Engineering,
Shandong University of Science and Technology, Qingdao 266590, China
[2] Key Laboratory of Intelligent Information Processing,
Institute of Computing Technology, Chinese Academy of Sciences,
Beijing 100190, China
sqjiang@ict.ac.cn

Abstract. Real-life environments are open-ended and dynamic: unlearned information comes over time. These changes of environments ask for the systems to have the ability of self growth. A reasonable solution is to build an intelligent human-computer interaction system to simulate the mind at birth, and then automatically teach it by human. In this work, we present a hand-held object recognition system which could incrementally enhance its recognition ability from beginning during the interaction with humans. Automatically capturing the images of hand-held objects and the voice of users, our system could refer the interacting person as a strong teacher. This allows the system to learn from scratch and to learn new concepts one after another like humans. Although our system is implemented on hand-held recognition scenario, we also implement experiments on ImageNet dataset to validate the effectiveness of our system. Experimental results illustrate its performance.

Keywords: Learn from scratch · Object recognition · SVM · Human-computer interaction

1 Introduction

Gobet *et al.* [6] propose that the configuration of smaller units of information into large coordinated units might be important in many processes of perception, learning and cognition in humans. A human baby learns everything from scratch. In addition, he can continuously learn new knowledge and build it on what he knows. This leads to a growing interest in the 'developmental' approach, which takes its inspiration from nature (especially the human infant) and attempts to build a human-computer interaction system which could develop its own knowledge and abilities through interaction with the world [7]. The idea of building an artificial baby dates back at least as far as Turing's paper on 'Computing Machinery and Intelligence' [26].

For intelligent human-computer interaction (HCI) systems, it is an important issue to learn new knowledge from scratch based on newly available data, which

© Springer International Publishing AG 2016
E. Chen et al. (Eds.): PCM 2016, Part II, LNCS 9917, pp. 527–539, 2016.
DOI: 10.1007/978-3-319-48896-7_52

makes the system have the ability of self growth like a baby. Then the infant HCI system could be teached much like a human child during interaction, until it reaches an adult level. This kind of self-adjustment during interaction is a kind of on-line improvement which is timely and effectively.

In this paper, we focus on the ability of learning from scratch, by which we mean that such infant HCI systems attempt to build their own knowledge and abilities autonomously (starting with no innate knowledge), and to develop continuously to reach increasingly higher levels of knowledge. Considering an Object Recognition System (ORS), enhance its recognition ability can be regarded as a kind of self-adjustment to increase its knowledge.

Object recognition [8] is a widely studied problem in computer vision. It describes the task of finding and identifying objects in an image or video sequence. Humans recognize a multitude of objects in images with little effort, despite the fact that the image of the objects may vary somewhat in different view points, in many different sizes and scales or even when they are translated or rotated. Objects can even be recognized when they are partially obstructed from view. But it is challenging for machines. Over multiple decades, many approaches have been implemented for this task. In general, an ORS has several parts. These include image sensors, image preprocessing, object detection, object segmentation, feature extraction and object classification [23].

As manipulating objects with hands is a straight way for human-machine interaction [14,15,19], hand-held object recognition is a special and important case in object recognition. The hand-held object can not only help the system obtain a better understanding of user's intention but also a more comprehensive perception about surrounding environment. But during interaction, the system may encounter unknown objects, which asks for the ability of self growth. Fixed models for HCI systems are unable to cope with the changes of the dynamic environments. While new concept instances will be arriving all the time, it is unrealistic and costly to retrain all previously seen images. An on-line learning HCI systems can take the advantage of incoming new concept instances to improve the existing model during interaction.

For humans to accurately understand the world around them, multi-modal integration is essential because it enhances perceptual precision and reduces ambiguity. Multi-modal sensor and feature fusion may contribute to replicate such human ability [17].

Figure 1 illustrates the procedure that our hand-held object recognition systems learn from scratch and improve its recognition ability during interaction. During interaction, our system could learn new concepts from scratch. At first, the system hasn't learn any concepts before, which means no classification model is available. It will initialize a model first, then the system can update the model with newly available objects constantly. In the process of initializing a model, our system would automatically capture the images of hand-held object as positive examples and prepare some negative examples which are not hand-held objects to train a binary classification. In later processes, the system only has to collect images of unidentified objects as positive examples. The existing model

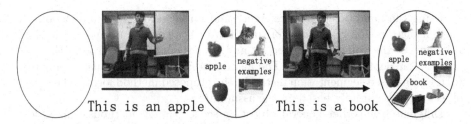

Fig. 1. The procedure that our self-adjustment hand-held object recognition system learn from scratch. At first, the system hasn't learn any concepts. It initializes a model first, and then the system updates the model with newly available objects constantly.

could be updated only based on these new data. RGB feature and depth feature are extracted from RGB and depth images respectively, then we fuse these two kinds of features into one.

The contributions of our recognition system can be summarized as the following:

(1) Our hand-held object recognition system could learn from scratch and update the model constantly; (2) our system could automatically improve its recognition ability incrementally during interaction; (3) we validate the performance of our system on HOD and ImageNet.

The rest of this paper is organized as follows: our proposed framework is illustrated in Sect. 2. And the experimental results are showed in Sect. 3. Section 4 concludes this paper.

2 Our System

We have designed and developed a real-time self-adjustment system to learn from scratch like a human baby. Our self-adjustment framework is under the setting of SVM [12,27]. This framework allows our system to improve the recognition ability during interaction over new obtained data without retrain all previously seen data.

Object Segmentation

With the surge of RGB-D devices, they provide additional depth and skeletal information, which is beneficial to eliminate background noise and make the localization and segmentation of the object easier and more precise. Our system automatically captures color and depth images using an RGB-D camera, whose API also provides additional skeletal data. Before object segmentation, the depth map is preprocessed to filter noise and recover part of the missing depth data. The system interpolates depth information in pixels where more than half of their eight neighbors have valid depth. An estimation of the location of the hand is provided in the skeletal data. We assume that hand-held objects are connected to the hand, so the hand position will typically fall in the object region.

Using the hand position as reference and initial seed, we obtain the object mask using a region-growing algorithm [15]. This algorithm examines the eight neighbors of the points in the seed set and adds them to the seed set if they are at a similar depth as the hand. The algorithm is simple yet robust. Compared with vision-based segmentation methods, the proposed method locates the target object more accurately based on the assumption.

Different from other general object or scene parsing methods, this object segmentation approach is designed specifically for the HOR problem. It utilizes the position of hands but focuses on the object held on the hand, rather than the hand itself. In HOR problem, hands remain mostly static. This approach exploits skeleton information to infer the location of the hand, and focuses on the region of hand to segment the object of interest. By exploiting prior knowledge about the HOR problem, this task-specific detection and segmentation method is more robust for HOR problem than general segmentation methods. It has three inherent advantages: background is eliminated more effectively; recognition is more reliable (as there is only one candidate); computational complexity is significantly reduced.

Feature Extraction and Fusion

Some hand-crafted features have been proposed to represent low-level information, like SIFT [13], spin images [10], Fast Point Features Histogram [16] and Ensembles of Shape Features (ESFs) [9]. They have been proved to be robust to transformations such as rotation and scale. But the major limitation of hand-crafted features is that they are often manually tuned for the specific conditions encountered in datasets. In addition, they can only capture a subset of the cues that are useful for recognition [28]. Except for hand-crafted features, there are also machine-learned features such as deep features. Convolutional neural networks (CNNs) [1] can learn higher order properties leading to features that can describe higher level properties of the images, which are more discriminatory [15]. Therefore, we extract features by CNNs from images. The CNN architecture that we used has eight layers: the first five layers are convolutional layers, while the sixth and the seventh layers are fully connected layers and the final layer is a softmax classifier. We use the output of the seventh layer as a feature (4096-dimensional).

There are two main types of multi-modal systems: one is to integrate signals at the feature level and the other at a semantic level [29]. For the first type, feature fusion may be beneficial to obtain a better representation of the image, and feature fusion has been used in computer vision to improve recognition accuracy. Different features often capture complementary properties of the image: RGB feature and depth feature related with color and shape respectively. Generally, feature fusion is considered more appropriate for closely coupled and synchronized modalities, such as RGB feature and depth feature [25]. There are many ways for feature fusion, we simply concatenate RGB feature and depth feature.

Image Classification

Image classification is an important and challenging task in computer vision. It includes a broad range of decision-theoretic approaches to the identification of images, such as SVM [3,21], deep convolutional neural network [11,22] and decision tree [5,18]. Since image labeling is time consuming and labor intensive, image classification tasks frequently suffer from the problem of lacking sufficiency training data. So we need methods to learn incrementally from scratch.

There are some proposed approaches that could learn new information based on new available data. Ristin *et al.* [20] propose a framework named NCM Forest. They combine Nearest Class Mean classifier and Random Forest to learn new concepts. This algorithm uses hierarchical concepts to make the model can be modified locally when new data comes. Kuzborskij *et al.* [12] propose an algorithm that adds a new classification-plane to source model to learn a new concept. Michael Fink [4] proposes a one-shot learning algorithm which achieves knowledge transfer through the reuse of model parameters.

Support vector machine constructs a set of hyperplanes in feature space, which can be used for classification. The classification-planes describe the separation in feature space and support vectors describe the classification-planes. Because of these properties, it is easier to deal with the new available data for SVM.

Therefore, we extend the method of [12] to our system.

Before presenting the method, we give some preliminaries. We denote lowercase letters as vectors and capital letters as matrices. $A_{k,n}$ is corresponding to the (k, n) entry of matrix A. (x, y) represents a pair of data. x is a feature vector, and y is the corresponding label. α is denoted as Lagrange multiplier. We denote $(x_i, y_i)_{i \in I}$ as new data.

This approach is under the setting of SVM [27]. SVM solves the quadratic programming problem by minimizing an objective function, which consists of two terms: $\min J_p = Risk_{espected} + Complexity$.

It utilize the multi-class LSSVM objective function [24], which turns the quadratic programming into a problem of solving linear equations. LSSVM transfers the inequality constraints to equality constraints, which greatly facilitates the solution of Lagrange multiplier method. The objective function minimizes the regularized risk by making prediction error and the complexity of this model be minimal.

$$\min_{W,b,e} J_p(W, e) = \frac{1}{2} W^T W + \frac{1}{2} C \sum_{k=1}^{N} e_k^2 \tag{1}$$

such that

$$y_k(W^T \varphi(x_k) + b) = 1 - e_k, \ k = 1, \ldots, N$$

e is slack variable.

In [12], it try to find a new classification-plane w_{n+1} for unlearned concept data making N-class source model turn into a $(N + 1)$-class target model. The method could achieve the following targets:

(1) Finding a new group of classification-planes $W^t = [w_1, w_2, \cdots, w_n, w_{n+1}]$ which is close to source classification-planes making N-class source classifier transfer to a $(N+1)$-class target classifier;

(2) Modifying the source classification-planes $W^{t-1} = [w_1, w_2, \cdots, w_n]$ slightly making the performance of source concepts will not decline;

(3) Adjusting all source classification-planes making the prediction error be smaller.

Based on the above mentioned considerations, the objective function as following:

$$\min_{W^t, b, e} J_p(W^t, e) = \frac{1}{2} \left\| W^t - W^{t-1} \right\|^T \left\| W^t - W^{t-1} \right\| \tag{2}$$
$$+ \frac{1}{2} \left\| w_{n+1} - W^{t-1}\beta \right\|^T \left\| w_{n+1} - W^{t-1}\beta \right\| + \frac{C}{2} \sum_{i \in I^k} (e_i)^2$$

such that

$$y_i((W^t)^T \varphi(x_i) + b_i) = 1 - e_i, \ i \in I$$

The first term in Eq. 2 controls the variety of the classification-planes of source model and this term forces the target model to keep close to the source model. The second term makes the new added classification-plane keep close to the linear combination of other existed classification-planes. The linear combination is described by a vector β. This first two terms force the target model to keep close to the source model in both situations of incremental learning, which basically guarantees the performance of other source concepts won't deteriorate. The final term is used to minimize prediction error of new data.

Finally, we can get:

$$A = A' - \left[A'' A'' \beta \right]$$

$$\begin{bmatrix} A' \\ b'^T \end{bmatrix} = M \begin{bmatrix} Y \\ 0 \end{bmatrix}, \quad \begin{bmatrix} A'' \\ b''^T \end{bmatrix} = M \begin{bmatrix} X^T W' \\ 0 \end{bmatrix}$$

$$M = \begin{bmatrix} X^T X + \frac{1}{C} 1 \\ 1^T \quad 0 \end{bmatrix}$$

The solution of this objective function is determined once we set the parameters β, C, L. The optimal β is automatically chosen by a method based on LOO error [12]. And we change C from 10^{-4} to 10^5 using 5-fold cross-validation to find the best value of C.

3   Results

In this section, we show a series of experiments to evaluate our self-adjustment system.

Table 1. N is the number of learned concepts. "New Concept" displays the new concept that the model learned in this step. "New Concept Accuracy" is the accuracy of "New Concept". And "ACC" represents the accuracy of the model. (a): incremental learning method: each column indicates a new class is introduced. (b): retraining method.

N	0	1	2	3	4	5	6	7	8
(a)									
New Concept	-	apple	ball	book	bottle	box	calculator	can	cup
New Concept Accuracy	-	1	0.9	0.9625	0.7525	0.6775	0.7	0.74	0.78
ACC	-	1	0.95	0.9875	0.90812	0.893	0.86833	0.83143	0.84719
(b)									
New Concept	-	apple	ball	book	bottle	box	calculator	can	cup
New Concept Accuracy	-	1	1	0.995	0.9575	0.8775	0.9825	0.8925	1
ACC	-	1	1	0.99833	0.97938	0.9445	0.94208	0.88857	0.9075

Experimental Setup

We validate our system on the subset of HOD [15] and ImageNet [2]. We don't make any pre-selection or pre-processing on images in the dataset. Our dataset is splitted into two parts: train (incremental learning) and test.

Experimental Results

In this section, we show the performance of our on-line learning system. Each experiment is implemented for 5 times and we show the average results.

Learn from Scratch on HOD. HOD consists of 16 concepts and 4 different instances for each concept. There are 200 RGB and depth image pairs for each instance. RGB feature and depth feature are extracted from RGB image and depth image respectively, and we fuse the two kinds of features into one. We randomly selected 160 images for each class considered in train datasets. And 80 images are selected for each class as a test dataset. Depth information are available in HOD, so we cascade the two kinds of features and use RBF kernel which could perform non-linear transformations of the original input features in SVM.

As Table 1(a) shows, our system learns from scratch and every step it learns 160 images of a new concept. Each column indicates a new class is introduced. Previous classes are not used for training in subsequent training steps, but they are used to evaluate the algorithm performance on previously learned classes to make sure that previously acquired knowledge was not lost. The validation on test dataset shows that our framework is able to learn the new classes, success-fully. For the third columns, this step is the process of learning the first concept from scratch. In this step, our system initialize a model. And it updates this

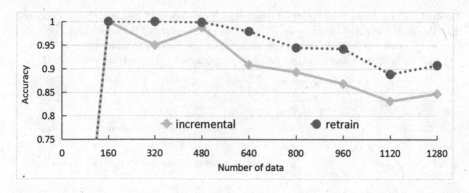

Fig. 2. Accuracies of the model: the solid line and dotted line separately represent the accuracies of incremental learning and retraining methods.

model constantly in the following steps. Because we adjust existing classification-planes while finding the new classification-plane, it can be observed that the accuracy of source concepts does not drop too much, even increases sometimes.

Table 1(b) shows the results of retraining. Every column means one process of retraining. Like the last column, we retrain a 8-class model. "ACC" of this column represents the accuracy this model, "New Concept Accuracy" is the accuracy of concept "cup", which is corresponding to the accuracy of new added concept in incremental learning method.

In Fig. 2, the accuracy of incremental learning method is lower than retraining method. In retraining method, there are always maximum margins between concepts. But in incremental learning method, the margin between new added concept and a similar learned concept may be not maximum. There is a balance between the variety of source classification-planes and prediction error, which are corresponding to the first and last terms in Eq. 2. It is the reason why the accuracy may have a slight decline after incremental learning.

Experiments in this sub section validate the ability of learning from scratch.

Statistical Result on HOD. In this part, we implemented our experiments on a subset of HOD which inludes eleven classes: "apple", "ball", "book", "bottle", "box", "calculator", "can", "cup", "dish", "disk" and "glove".

We split the eleven classes into two parts: one part (the former seven classes (160 imageseach class)) is used for training a source model and another part (the other four classes (160 images each class)) for incremental learning. And 80 images are selected for each class as a test dataset. We concatenate RGB feature and depth feature and use it with RBF kernel.

The source model has learned 7 source concepts ("apple", "ball", "book", "bottle", "box", "calculator", "can") and it will learn 4 new concepts ("cup", "dish", "disk", "glove") continuously in random sequences for 5 times. And each sequence we implemented for 5 times. Figure 3(a) shows the accuracies of incremental learning method (on-line self-adjustment system) and retraining method

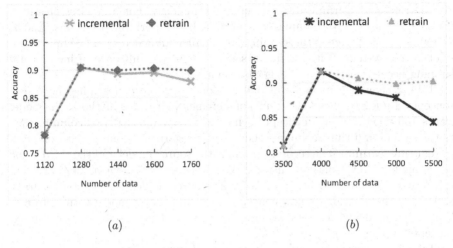

(a)   (b)

Fig. 3. Average total accuracies: the solid line and dotted line separately represent the accuracies of incremental learning and retraining methods. (a): HOD. (b): ImageNet

(off-line adjustment system). The accuracies of our on-line self-adjustment system are slight lower than off-line adjustment system for the reason that incremental learning method learns new information upon previously model without retraining all previously seen images. It adjusts the existing model according to the new examples instead of learning a new model. And this means that the training time of incremental learning method is much shorter than retraining method. The accuracy of the model has a slight drop during the processes of learning new concepts. This is reasonable. As the model getting complex, the accuracy decreases. Figure 3(a) shows that the accuracy in retraining method

Table 2. N is the number of learned concepts. "New Concept" displays the new concept that the model learned in this step. "New Concept Accuracy" is the accuracy of "New Concept". And "ACC" represents the accuracy of the model. (a): incremental learning method: each column indicates a new class is introduced. (b): retraining method.

N	7	8	9	10	11
(a)					
New Concept	-	cup	dish	disk	glove
New Concept Accuracy	-	1	0.94	0.8425	0.905
ACC	0.77875	0.90781	0.905	0.88775	0.87295
(b)					
New Concept	-	cup	dish	disk	glove
New Concept Accuracy	-	1	0.9375	0.9	0.9275
ACC	0.77875	0.90656	0.90722	0.901	0.90227

also decreases as learning new concepts continuously. For a N-class classifier, the smaller the N is, the simpler it is, and the better performance it has. And as we can see that incremental learning has smaller influence to the simpler classifier in our system. With the increasement of N, the influence of incremental learning becomes bigger and bigger to the model.

Table 2 shows an example of one random sequence of learning the 4 new concepts. Table 2(a) shows the results of incremental learning method. The model learns 160 images of new concept each step. Every adjacent two column, such as the second and third columns, they can be regarded as one process of class-incremental learning. The second column is the source model and the third is the target model. "New Concept" displays the new concept that the model learned in this process. The second column is a 7-class source model with a total accuracy of 0.7785. After learning a new concept "cup", the source model turns into a 8-class target model with a total accuracy of 0.90781. The accuracy of new learned concept "cup" is 1.

Table 2(b) shows the results of retraining. Every column means one process of retraining. Like the third column, we retrain a 8-class model. "ACC" of this column represents the accuracy this model, "New Concept Accuracy" is the accuracy of concept "cup", which is corresponding to the accuracy of new added concept in incremental learning method. The results show that "New Concept Accuracy" of incremental learning method are not much lower than retraining method basically.

Validations on ImageNet. We implemented our experiments on a subset of ImageNet which inludes eleven classes: "orange", "strawberry", "coffee mug", "pitcher", "vase", "plate", "trashcan", "envelope", "coffeepot", "park bench" and "lemon".

We randomly selected 500 images each class (the former seven classes) to train a source model. And we randomly select 500 images for each unknown concepts (the last four classes) for incremental learning. And 200 images are selected for each class as a test dataset. There is no depth information available in ImageNet, so we use a single RGB feature with RBF kernel.

The source model has learned 7 source concepts ("orange", "strawberry", "coffee mug", "pitcher", "vase", "plate", "ashcan") and it will learn 4 new concepts ("envelope", "coffeepot", "park bench", "lemon") continuously in random sequences. Each sequence we implemented for 5 times. Figure 3(b) shows the accuracies of incremental learning method (on-line self-adjustment system) and retraining method (off-line adjustment system). The accuracies of our on-line self-adjustment system are slight lower than off-line adjustment system.

Table 3 shows an example of one random sequence of learning the 4 new concepts. Table 3(a) shows the results of incremental learning method. The model learns 500 images of a new concept each step. Table 3(b) shows the results of retraining. Every column means one process of retraining. The results show that "New Concept Accuracy" of incremental learning method are not much lower than retraining method basically.

Table 3. N is the number of learned concepts. "New Concept" displays the new concept that the model learned in this step. "New Concept Accuracy" is the accuracy of "New Concept". And "ACC" represents the accuracy of the model. (a): incremental learning method: each column indicates a new class is introduced. (b): retraining method.

N	7	8	9	10	11
(a)					
New Concept	-	park bench	coffee pot	lemon	envelope
New Concept Accuracy	-	0.99	0.902	0.743	0.993
ACC	0.80963	0.92025	0.88144	0.8627	0.84291
(b)					
New Concept	-	park bench	coffee pot	lemon	envelope
New Concept Accuracy	-	0.99	0.902	0.873	0.98
ACC	0.80963	0.92138	0.89956	0.8861	0.89618

4   Conclusion

In this work, we introduce a new on-line self-adjustment system for hand-held object recognition. The system could learn new information constantly from scratch like a human baby, which reflects the ability improve its interaction experience during interaction. It adds new classification-planes to learn unknown concepts. In the future, our on-line self-adjustment system will be extended to more recognition tasks. Besides, we will include hierarchical concepts and their relations into this framework to make human-computer interaction systems more intelligent.

Acknowledgments. This work was supported in part by the National Basic Research 973 Program of China under Grant No. 2012CB316400, the National Natural Science Foundation of China under Grant Nos. 61532018 and 61322212, the National High Technology Research and Development 863 Program of China under Grant No. 2014AA015202, Beijing Science And Technology Project under Grant No. D161100001816001. This work is also funded by Lenovo Outstanding Young Scientists Program (LOYS).

References

1. Cun, Y.L., Boser, B., Denker, J.S., Henderson, D., Howard, R., Hubbard, W., Jackel, L.: Backpropagation applied to handwritten zip code recognition. Neural Comput. **1**, 541–551 (1989)
2. Deng, J., Dong, W., Socher, R., Li, L.J., Li, K., Fei-Fei, L.: ImageNet: a large-scale hierarchical image database. In: CVPR (2009)
3. Doan, T.N., Poulet, F.: Large scale image classification: fast feature extraction, multi-codebook approach and SVM training. In: Guillet, F., Pinaud, B., Venturini, G., Zighed, D.A. (eds.) Advances in Knowledge Discovery and Management. Studies in Computational Intelligence, vol. 527, pp. 155–172. Springer, Switzerland (2014)

4. Fink, M.: Object classification from a single example utilizing class relevance metrics. In: NIPS, pp. 449–456. MIT Press (2004)
5. Friedl, M.A., Brodley, C.E.: Decision tree classification of land-cover from remotely-sensed data. Remote Sens. Environ. **61**(3), 399–409 (1997)
6. Gobet, F., Lane, P., Croker, S., Cheng, P., Jones, G., Oliver, I., Pine, J.: Chunking mechanisms in human learning. Trends Cogn. Sci. **5**(6), 236–243 (2001)
7. Guerin, F.: Learning like a baby: a survey of artificial intelligence approaches. Knowl. Eng. Rev. **26**(2), 209–236 (2011)
8. Heckerman, D.: An empirical comparison of three inference methods. CoRR (2013)
9. Hinterstoisser, S., Holzer, S., Cagniart, C., Ilic, S., Konolige, K., Navab, N., Lepetit, V.: Multimodal templates for real-time detection of texture-less objects in heavily cluttered scenes. In: Metaxas, D.N., Quan, L., Sanfeliu, A., Gool, L.J.V. (eds.) ICCV, pp. 858–865. IEEE Computer Society (2011)
10. Johnson, A.E., Hebert, M.: Using spin images for efficient object recognition in cluttered 3D scenes. IEEE Trans. Pattern Anal. Mach. Intell. **21**(5), 433–449 (1999)
11. Krizhevsky, A., Sutskever, I., Hinton, G.E.: Imagenet classification with deep convolutional neural networks. In: Bartlett, P.L., Pereira, F.C.N., Burges, C.J.C., Bottou, L., Weinberger, K.Q. (eds.) NIPS, pp. 1106–1114 (2012)
12. Kuzborskij, I., Orabona, F., Caputo, B.: From n to n+1: Multiclass transfer incremental learning. In: 2013 IEEE Conference on CVPR, pp. 3358–3365, June 2013
13. Lowe, D.G.: Distinctive image features from scale-invariant keypoints. Int. J. Comput. Vis. **60**(2), 91–110 (2004)
14. Lv, X., Jiang, S., Herranz, L., Wang, S.: Hand-object sense: a hand-held object recognition system based on RGB-D information. In: Proceedings of the 23rd ACM International Conference on Multimedia, MM 2015, NY, USA, pp. 765–766. ACM, New York (2015)
15. Lv, X., Jiang, S., Herranz, L., Wang, S.: RGB-D hand-held object recognition based on heterogeneous feature fusion. J. Comput. Sci. Technol. **30**(2), 340–352 (2015)
16. Morisset, B., Rusu, R.B., Sundaresan, A., Hauser, K.K., Agrawal, M., Latombe, J.C., Beetz, M.: Leaving flatland: toward real-time 3D navigation. In: ICRA, pp. 3786–3793. IEEE (2009)
17. Noda, K., Arie, H., Suga, Y., Ogata, T.: Multimodal integration learning of robot behavior using deep neural networks. Robot. Auton. Syst. **62**(6), 721–736 (2014)
18. Rajendran, P., Madheswaran, M.: Hybrid medical image classification using association rule mining with decision tree algorithm. CoRR (2010)
19. Ren, X., Gu, C.: Figure-ground segmentation improves handled object recognition in egocentric video. In: CVPR, pp. 3137–3144. IEEE Computer Society (2010)
20. Ristin, M., Guillaumin, M., Gall, J., Van Gool, L.: Incremental learning of random forests for large-scale image classification. IEEE Trans. Pattern Anal. Mach. Intell. **PP**(99), 1 (2015)
21. Sánchez, J., Perronnin, F.: High-dimensional signature compression for large-scale image classification. In: CVPR, pp. 1665–1672. IEEE Computer Society (2011)
22. Simonyan, K., Zisserman, A.: Very deep convolutional networks for large-scale image recognition. CoRR (2014)
23. Smith, B., Gosine, R.: Support vector machines for object recognition (2001)
24. Suykens, J.A.K., Vandewalle, J.: Least squares support vector machine classifiers. Neural Process. Lett. **9**(3), 293–300 (1999)
25. Tang, J., Jin, L., Li, Z., Gao, S.: RGB-D object recognition via incorporating latent data structure and prior knowledge. IEEE Trans. Multimedia **17**(11), 1899–1908 (2015)

26. Turing, A.M.: Computing machinery and intelligence. Mind **59**(236), 433–460 (1950)
27. Vapnik, V.N.: The Nature of Statistical Learning Theory. Springer, New York (1995)
28. Wang, A., Lu, J., Cai, J., Cham, T.J., Wang, G.: Large-margin multi-modal deep learning for RGB-D object recognition. IEEE Trans. Multimedia **17**(11), 1887–1898 (2015)
29. Wu, L., Oviatt, S.L., Cohen, P.R.: Multimodal integration - a statistical view. IEEE Trans. Multimedia **1**(4), 334–341 (1999)

Audio Bandwidth Extension Using Audio Super-Resolution

Jiang Lin[1,3], Hu Ruimin[1,2(✉)], Wang Xiaochen[1,2], and Tu Weiping[1,2]

[1] State Key Lab of Software Engineering, Computer School of Wuhan University, Wuhan, China
jlcdf@163.com, hrm1964@163.com, colwang@163.com,
echo_tuwp@163.com
[2] National Engineering Research Center for Multimedia Software, Wuhan University,
Wuhan, China
[3] Software School, East China University of Technology, Nanchang, China

Abstract. Audio bandwidth extension (BWE) has emerged as an important tool for the satisfactory performance of low bitrate audio and speech codecs. In the existing BWE method, the high frequency (HF) excitation signals are generated by replicating the low frequency (LF) band directly. However, the coding perception quality will degrade if the correlation between LF and HF bands becoming weak. In this paper, we proposed a new algorithm to restore the HF excitation signals using audio super-resolution. The experiments shown the new algorithm have an outstanding performance for rebuilding HF excitation signals compare with the conventional replication method. In addition, we also provided a new BWE scheme based on audio super-resolution. According to our experimental results, in compare with LPC-based BWE, the subjective listening quality increased by 13% under the same bitrates; in compare with eSBR, the bitrates drop by 63.7% and have the approximate subjective listening quality.

Keywords: Audio bandwidth extension · Audio super resolution · Sparse representation

1 Introduction

Audio bandwidth extension (BWE) is a standard technique within contemporary audio codecs to efficiently code audio signals at low bitrates. A BWE method uses the received audio signal and a model for extending the frequency bandwidth. The model can include knowledge of how audio is produced and how audio is perceived by the human hearing system. From the point of view of whether transmitting parameters, the BWE methods have two categories: blind BWE and non-blind BWE. In non-blind BWE, a few parameters of high frequency band are transmitted to decode side for reconstructing the high frequency signals. In this paper, we only discuss about non-blind BWE.

In existing non-BWE techniques, the original audio signals are divided into low frequency (LF) and high frequency (HF) band. On encode side, The LF signals are encoded by selected audio coder, and the HF signals don't be encoded but extract a few HF parameters. On decode side, the HF excitation signals are achieved by replicating

© Springer International Publishing AG 2016
E. Chen et al. (Eds.): PCM 2016, Part II, LNCS 9917, pp. 540–549, 2016.
DOI: 10.1007/978-3-319-48896-7_53

the LF band directly, and then the final HF signals are reconstructed by adjusting the envelope using the transmissive HF parameters. The basic ideal of BWE is shown in Fig. 1.

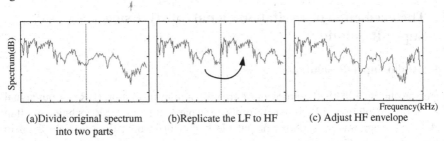

<table>
<tr><td>(a)Divide original spectrum
into two parts</td><td>(b)Replicate the LF to HF</td><td>(c) Adjust HF envelope</td></tr>
</table>

Fig. 1. How BWE works

The approach was again based on the physical properties of the audio signals. There is a correlation between LF and HF bands. Therefore, in the conventional BWE methods, the LF bands are replicated as the HF excitation signals. Previously developed BWE technologies include Linear Predictive Coding (LPC)-based BWE technology in AMR-WB+ audio codec standard [1], Spectral Band Replication (SBR) technology in MPEG Audio coding standard [2], and prediction based technologies that use codebook mapping methods to predict a HF envelope from a LF band [3, 4]. The LPC-based BWE provided a good sound quality for speech-like signal at very bitrates (about 0.8 kbps), but for the music-like signal, the coding quality is decreased. The SBR technology is an outstanding scheme at low bitrates, this scheme provides high sound quality for music-like signals, but not well for speech-like signals. In addition, Yuki Yamamoto et al. provided a new BWE method which was used to MPEG USAC codec [5]. In USAC, predictive vector coding (PVC) is added to SBR formed enhance spectral band replication (eSBR), which improved the subjective quality. The eSBR technology provides an excellent perception quality, but its bitrates reaches about 2.2 kbps, and the calculation complexity is expensive.

In fact, the correlation between LF and HF band is a vital factor for the reconstruction quality of HF bands. In the existing BWE technologies, the HF excitation signals derived from the LF bands by replication method. However, the coding sound quality will degrade obviously if the correlation becoming weak. In addition, even the correlation is high between LF and HF bands, the method of replicating directly also will lead to the coding artifacts, because the difference of excitation signals between LF and HF bands cannot be eliminated completely.

In this paper, our main goal is to restore the HF excitation signals for reducing the coding artifacts. For the correlation between the low and high bands, we have an assumption, if there is a tool with powerful modeling capability, the HF excitation signals could be predict from LF bands. The assumption has been confirmed by our previous work [6]. Different with the provided deep neural network in [6], we used a recent proposed audio super-resolution [7–9] to predict the HF excitation signals. In addition, we also proposed a low bitrate BWE scheme which is similarity with in [6].

In our BWE scheme, we used audio super-resolution to restore HF excitation signals on FFT domain, and extracted the HF subband energies for adjusting the HF envelope.

2 The Prediction of Excitation Signals of HF Using Super-Resolution

2.1 Audio Super-Resolution

Super-resolution (SR) is the problem of creating a high-resolution (HR) output signal from a low-resolution (LR) input. In order to achieve this goal, SR techniques often make use of certain assumptions or outside knowledge about the original signal to achieve their goal. Use of super-resolution for images is one of the most active research areas [10, 11] in image processing. In the field of audio signal processing, the super-resolution problem can be cast as the problem of reconstructing high-frequency portions of audio signals [7]. In the existing audio super-resolution methods, the original signals are transformed into time-frequency domain, the LR spectrogram $Y_l \in \mathbb{R}^{L \times N}$ can be regarded as the remaining part of the HR spectrogram $Y_h \in \mathbb{R}^{H \times N}$ after the removal of the top $H - L$ high-frequency bins of Y_h. The known, HR dictionary matrix is $D_h \in \mathbb{R}^{H \times K}$. By truncating the columns of matrix D_h in frequency, we create a LF dictionary matrix $D_l \in \mathbb{R}^{L \times K}$.

The central problem is to generate a sparse matrix of coefficients $\alpha \in \mathbb{R}^{K \times N}$, such that we minimize the difference between the input Y_l, and $D_l \alpha$, i.e.:

$$\min_{\alpha} \| Y_l - D_l \alpha \|_F, \tag{1}$$

where $\| \cdot \|_F$ denotes the Frobenius norm. In this expression, matrix α contains coefficients that represent the relative weighting of the dictionary atoms in D_l necessary to approximate Y_l.

One key assumption made in audio super resolution is that for audio spectra, there is high correlation between LF and HF band. In a practical sense, this means that the spectrum structure played on any audio signals shares great similarity with other audio signals not only in its lower frequencies, but also in its high frequencies as well. Of cause, the similarity of spectrum structure become worse, the reconstructed quality of excitation signals also will become degraded. From a technical perspective, this assumption means that, given the HR spectrogram Y_h, we assume that finding α such that Eq. (1) is satisfied and will also satisfy the expression

$$\min_{\alpha} \| Y_h - D_h \alpha \|_F. \tag{2}$$

2.2 The Prediction of Excitation Signals of HF

The previously proposed audio super-resolution methods focus on rebuild the HF spectrogram and shown the outstanding performance. As known, the spectrogram is impossible to inverse transform into the original audio signals. In BWE, we need to restore the HF excitation signals, which are represented as frequency spectral coefficients on the time-frequency domain. The prediction process is similarity with in [7].

Our prediction model, shown in Fig. 2, begins with the LF band frequency coefficients S_{LF}. S_{LF} are transformed from the decoded LF signals by time-frequency transformation. D_{LF} and D_{HF} is an analysis dictionary of LF and HF bands, respectively. The dictionary is different with the pre-defined in [7]. Since the analysis dictionary learned from some related data usually has the potential to adapt to a signal better as compared with a pre-defined dictionary. The dictionary is trained by the proposed method in [8]. The technical details of training are omitted due to the limited space. The proposed matching pursuit algorithm in [7], AMP, takes in S_{LF} and D_{LF}, and returns the sparse coefficient matrix α, which is constructed to minimize $\min\|S_{LF} - D_{LF}\alpha\|_F$. On a smaller scale, AMP takes in $S_{LF}(i)$, the ith column of S_{LF}, and generates a sparse column matrix α_i such that $\min\|S_{LF}(i) - D_{LF}\alpha_i\|_2$ is minimized. α_i then becomes the ith column in coefficients matrix α. Lastly, the HF dictionary D_{HF} and the output coefficients matrix α are multiplied to create the HF output excitation signals $S_{HF} = \alpha D_{HF}$. The prediction of the excitation signals of HF is presented in Algorithm 1.

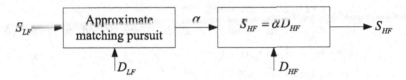

Fig. 2. The prediction block diagram of HF excitation signal

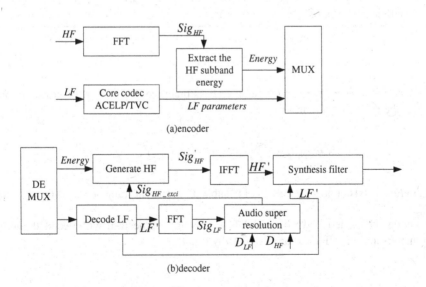

(a)encoder

(b)decoder

Fig. 3. The proposed BWE scheme

3   The Proposed BWE Scheme

In order to improve the perception quality of AVS-M coding standard [12, 13], we proposed a new BWE scheme based on audio super-resolution. The AVS-M is a speech and audio coding standard in China with independent intellectual property. In AVS-M, the BWE system (similarly in [1], called as LPC-based BWE) extracted the LPC coefficients and subband energy ratios of LF and HF bands to reconstruct the HF signals on FFT domain [14]. The new BWE scheme is shown in Fig. 3. The input signal sampled at 25.6 kHz is processed in 20 ms per frame. The pre-processed signal is divided into two 6.4 kHz sampled LF and HF band using an analysis filterbank.

Algorithm 1 Predict the HF excitation signals

Input: S_{LF}, D_{LF}, D_{HF}

Output: S_{HF}, α

Main Iterations:

1. AMP algorithm uses S_{LF} and D_{LF} to generate sparse coefficient matrix α

   ① For each column $S_{LF}(i)$ in D_{LF}, finds column matrix α_i such that $S_{LF}(i) - D_{LF}\alpha_i$ is minimized.

   ② The N generated column matrices α_i are joined to form α, S_{LF} is approximated by $D_{LF}\alpha$.

   ③ Increase the iteration counter: $i=i+1$

   ④ If the stopping criterion is satisfied, quit the iteration. Otherwise, go back to step①.

2. HF excitation signal S_{HF} generated using the HF dictionary D_{HF} and coefficient matrix, $S_{HF} = D_{HF}\alpha$.

On encoder side (Fig. 3(a)), the LF is coded using ACELP/TVC hybrid codec. The HF band first is transform into FFT domain, and then extract HF subband energies as envelope parameters, the energy parameters is quantized by vector quantization. We extract the HF subband energy by Eq. 3:

$$Energy(i) = \sum_{j=1}^{M} (Sig_{HF}(i-1)M+j)^2, \tag{3}$$

where $Energy(i)$ denotes the energy of ith subband in current frame and M is the subband length.

On decoder side (Fig. 3(b)), the HF signals are synthesized with decoded energy parameters and the HF excitation signals by Eq. 4:

$$Sig'_{HF}(i,j) = Energy(i)' * Sig_{HF\_exci}(i,j),$$
$$1 \le i \le N, 1 \le j \le M \tag{4}$$

where $Sig'_{HF}(i,j)$ denotes generated HF signal the jth point of ith suband in current frame, $Sig_{HF\_exci}(i,j)$ is the corresponding excitation signal, $Energy(i)'$ is the decoded energy of ith subband, and N is the number of subband. The Sig'_{HF} is calculated by Algorithm 1. Sig'_{HF} and Sig_{HF_exci} is corresponding S_{LF} and S_{HF} in Algorithm 1, respectively. The analysis dictionary D_{LF} and D_{HF} is stored beforehand in decode side, which are trained by the analysis dictionary learning algorithm in [8]. The technique details are omitted due to the limit space.

4 Experiments and Evaluation

We used 3 baselines in our experiments: LPC-based BWE [14], eSBR [5], DAE-based BWE [6]. LPC-based BWE was developed at low bitrate for speech communication, eSBR faces with all kind type audio signals, DAE-based BWE used deep auto-encoder to predict the fine structure of HF. The selected 3 baselines BWE methods represent the different types the state of the art BWE technology. The selected dictionary training dataset including TIMIT speech, natural sounds and music, which in totals about 1 million frames, 20 ms per frame. For each audio signal, a Hamming window of length 256 with 25% overlap was applied to generate the HF excitation signals using the short-time Fourier transform (STFT). In subjective and objective testing, the MPEG standard test audio file (12 test items, including 3 speech, 9 music and mixed signal) is selected. In order to take evaluation completely, two type experiments are implemented.

4.1 The Performance of Generated the HF Excitation Signals

The first experiment, in order to evaluate the performance of generated the HF excitation signals, we used the audio super-resolution algorithm to instead of the corresponding replication module in LPC-based BWE and eSBR, instead of the deep auto-encoder prediction module in DAE-based BWE.

The spectrum comparison of the rebuilding HF signal is shown in Fig. 4. In LPC-based BWE (Fig. 4(a)), the spectrum shape is rebuild well (red rectangle); in eSBR (Fig. 4(b)), the harmonic structure is retained partly (black rectangle); in DAE-based BWE (Fig. 4(c)), the spectral flatness is more close the original signal (blue rectangle). From the spectrum comparison, the spectral envelope of reconstructed HF is more close to the original signal. As known, the spectral envelope is vital to perception quality. So this experiment illustrates the validity of audio super-resolution algorithm for restoring the HF excitation signals.

In order to evaluate the listening perception quality, the subjective quality test was performed by A/B listening test. 12 listeners participate in the A/B listening test. The subjective test results are listed in Table 1. The subjective listening test results indicate

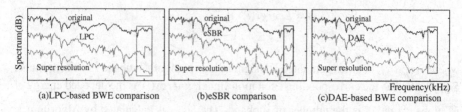

(a)LPC-based BWE comparison   (b)eSBR comparison   (c)DAE-based BWE comparison

Fig. 4. The spectrum comparison of generated HF signal. (Color figure online)

that the audio super-resolution outperforms the 3 baselines system on the restoration of HF excitation signals.

Table 1. A/B listening test comparison between audio super resolution and 3 baselines

BWE method	Prefer audio-super resolution	Prefer baselines	No preference
LPC-based	**50.0%**	41.7%	8.3%
eSBR	**58.3%**	33.3%	16.7%
DAE-based	**41.7%**	33.3%	25.0%

4.2 The Test Results of the Proposed BWE Scheme

In order to improve the listening perception quality of AVS-M codec [12, 13], we proposed a new BWE scheme using audio super-resolution (see Sect. 3, abbreviate as SR-based BWE). In the above first experiment, we have verified the audio super-resolution has an outstanding restoration performance for HF excitation signals. In the second experiments, we will evaluate the overall performance of SR-based BWE. We performed the subjective listening test, objective test, simple runtimes test and bitrates comparison with LPC-based BWE, eSBR and DAE-based BWE.

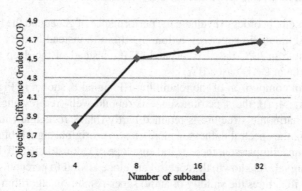

Fig. 5. The ODG under different number of subband

In this experiments, the LPC-based BWE, eSBR, DAE-based BWE, the HF excitation signals are generated by them own way. In our SR-based BWE, the time-frequency transform is STFT, and the sample frequency is 25.6 kHz, means the frequency bandwidth of LF is 0–6.4 kHz, and the HF is 6.4–12.8 kHz, the frame length is 20 ms (256 samples). The suband number N (in Eq. 4) is set 8 according to our test. In our test, we set $N = 4, 8, 16, 32$ respectively, then test the average objective difference grades (ODG, 0–5, from annoying to very imperceptible) by ITU-R BS.1387 PEAQ test method [15]. From the test results (Fig. 5), $N = 8$ is the best trade off selection. In SR-based BWE, therefore, the only spectral parameters (HF subband energies) are send to decoder side with 16 bits (vector quantization) per frame (20 ms per frame), so the bitrates only 0.8 kbps (16 bit * 1000 ms/20 ms). The bitrates comparison is shown in Table 2.

Table 2. The bitrates comparison

BWE method	Bitrates (kbps)
LPC-based BWE	0.8
eSBR[a]	2.2
DAE-based BWE	0.8
SR-based BWE	**0.8**

[a]The bitrate of eSBR is 2.2 kbps, the envelope and control parameters are extracted, and then the parameters are quantized by Huffman coding, its bitrate is flexible, about 2.2 kbps in our experiments.

Table 3. The objective testing results (ODG)

BWE method	Speech	Music/mixed	Average
LPC	3.72	3.64	3.68
eSBR	4.41	4.69	4.55
DAE	4.32	4.46	4.39
SR	**4.38**	**4.56**	**4.47**

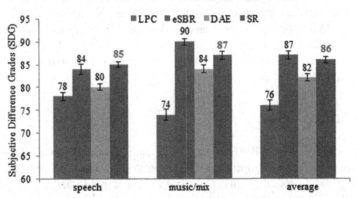

Fig. 6. Subjective listen test results.

We carry out subjective listening test to assess the perception quality of the proposed BWE system using MUSHRA method [16]. 15 expert listeners participate in the test, which is performed for two categories signal, that is, speech and music/mixed contents, and test materials derived from MEPG standard (the same as the first experiment). The subjective listening test results are shown in Fig. 6. In addition, we also use ITU-R BS. 1387 PEAQ [16] test method to evaluate the objective performance, the average objective difference grades (ODG) is listed in Table 3.

In order to assess the calculation complexity, a simple codec runtime is executed. A 368 s wave file is selected as test item, and the run environment of test is also same among different codec. The runtimes of each codec are listed Table 4.

Table 4. The runtimes comparison (unit: second)

BWE method	Encode	Decode	Total
LPC	42.45	14.12	56.57
eSBR	54.67	19.34	74.01
DAE	34.89	18.02	52.91
SR	**32.08**	**28.45**	**60.53**

4.3 Discussion of Results

The performance of codec should be comprehensive evaluation from bitrate, calculation complexity and sound quality. From subjective listening test results (Fig. 6), the proposed method is better than the LPC-based BWE (increased by 13%), is slightly better than DAE-based BWE (increased by 5%), and is comparable with eSBR. The objective testing results (Table 3) also are consistent with the subjective listening testing results. The perception quality further illustrates the super-resolution have an excellent performance for restoring the HF excitation signals. The bitrates comparison (Table 2) show the SR-based BWE drop 63.7% ((2.2–0.8)/2.2 * 100%) compare with eSBR, because only HF subband energy parameters are send to decoder side. The runtimes comparison shows (Table 4) the total runtimes of SR-based BWE have competition than other methods. However, the decoded runtimes are expensive than other methods. This is because an AMP algorithm is used on decoder side. The following study will focus on the fast algorithm to resolve sparse coefficients. From the above test results, the SR-based BWE outperforms LPC-based BWE, is better than DAE-based BWE, and is comparable to eSBR.

5 Conclusions

This paper proposed a new BWE method using audio super resolution. This method provides a new generation algorithm of HF excitation signals on BWE, which is helpful to improving coding sound quality. Our experiments demonstrated the advantage of proposed BWE. However, the decoded calculation complexity is expensive due to solve sparse coefficients by AMP algorithm. The further study will find a fast algorithm for solving sparse coefficients.

Acknowledgments. The research was supported by National Nature Science Foundation of China (No. 61231015, No. 61102127, 61201340, 61201169, 61471271), National High

Technology Research and Development Program of China (863 Program) No. 2015AA016306, the Science and Technology Plan in Jiangxi Province Department of Education (GJJ150585).

References

1. Mäkinen, J., Bessette, B., Bruhn, S., Ojala, P., Salami, R., Taleb, A.: AMR-WB + : a new audio coding standard for 3rd generation mobile audio services. In: IEEE International Conference on Acoustics, Speech, and Signal Processing (ICASSP), Philadelphia, PA, USA, vol. 2, pp. 1109–1112 (2005)
2. Dietz, M., Liljeryd, L., Kjörling, K., Kunz, O.: Spectral band replication, a novel approach in audio coding. In: 112th Convention of the Audio Engineering Society, Munich, Germany (2002)
3. Epps, J., Holmes, W.: A new technique for wideband enhancement of coded narrowband speech. In: Proceedings of IEEE Workshop on Speech Coding, pp. 174–176 (1999)
4. Fuemmeler, J.A., Hardie, R.C., Gardner, W.R.: Techniques for the regeneration of wideband speech from narrowband speech. EURASIP J. Appl. Signal Process. **2001**(4), 266–274 (2001)
5. Neukam, C., Nagel, F., Schuller, G., et al.: A MDCT based harmonic spectral bandwidth extension method. In: Proceedings of IEEE International Conference on Acoustics, Speech and Signal Processing (ICASSP), Vancouver, Canada, 26–31 May 2013. IEEE press, pp. 566–570 (2013)
6. Jiang, L., Hu, R., Wang, X., Zhang, M.: Low bitrates audio bandwidth extension using a deep auto-encoder. In: Ho, Y.-S., Sang, J., Ro, Y.M., Kim, J., Wu, F. (eds.) PCM 2015. LNCS, vol. 9314, pp. 528–537. Springer, Heidelberg (2015). doi:10.1007/978-3-319-24075-6_51
7. Keegan, B.P., Steven, K.T., Liu, K.J.: Super-resolution of musical signals using approximate matching pursuit. In: IEEE Workshop on Applications of Signal Processing to Audio and Acoustics (WASPAA), pp. 81–84 (2011)
8. Dong, J., Wang, W., Chambers, J.: Audio super-resolution using analysis dictionary learning. In: IEEE International Conference on Digital Signal Processing (DSP), pp. 604–608 (2015)
9. Mandel, M.I., Young, S.C.: Audio super-resolution using concatenative resynthesis. In: IEEE Workshop on Applications of Signal Processing to Audio and Acoustics (WASPAA), pp. 1–5 (2015)
10. Park, S.C., Park, M.K., Kang, M.G.: Super-resolution image reconstruction: a technical overview. IEEE Signal Process. Mag. **20**(3), 21–36 (2003)
11. Yang, J., Wright, J., Huang, T.S., Ma, Y.: Image super-resolution via sparse representation. IEEE Trans. Image Process. **19**(11), 2861–2873 (2010)
12. Zhang, T., Liu, C.-T., Quan, H.-J.: AVS-M audio: algorithm and implementation. EURASIP J. Adv. Signal Process. **2011**(1), 1–16 (2011)
13. GB/T 20090.10-2013. Information technology—advanced coding of audio and video—Part 10: Mobile speech and audio. China standard publishing house (2014)
14. Jie, Z., Choo, K., Oh, E.: Bandwidth extension for China AVS-M standard. In: IEEE International Conference on Acoustics, Speech and Signal Processing (ICASSP), pp. 4149–4152 (2009)
15. ITU-R Rec. BS 1387, Methods for objective measurements of perceptual audio quality (1999)
16. ITU-R, Recommendation BS. 1534-1, Method for the subjective assessment of intermediate quality levels of coding systems (MUSHRA). International Telecommunication Union (2003)

Jointly Learning a Multi-class Discriminative Dictionary for Robust Visual Tracking

Zhao Liu[1,2], Mingtao Pei[1(✉)], Chi Zhang[1], and Mingda Zhu[1]

[1] Beijing Laboratory of Intelligent Information Technology,
School of Computer Science, Beijing Institute of Technology,
Beijing 100081, People's Republic of China
{peimt,zhangchi,zhumingda}@bit.edu.cn
[2] People's Public Security University of China,
Beijing 10038, People's Republic of China
zhao.liu@ppsuc.edu.cn

Abstract. Discriminative dictionary learning (DDL) provides an appealing paradigm for appearance modeling in visual tracking due to its superior discrimination power. However, most existing DDL based trackers usually cannot handle the drastic appearance changes, especially for scenarios with background cluster and/or similar object interference. One reason is that they often encounter loss of subtle visual information that is critical to distinguish the object from the distracters. In this paper, we propose a robust tracker via jointly learning a multi-class discriminative dictionary. Our DDL method exploits concurrently the intra-class visual information and inter-class visual correlations to learn the shared dictionary and the class-specific dictionaries. By imposing several discrimination constraints into the objective function, the learnt dictionary is reconstructive, compressive and discriminative, thus can achieve better discriminate the object from the background. Tracking is carried out within a Bayesian inference framework where the joint decision measure is used to construct the observation model. Evaluations on the benchmark dataset demonstrate that the proposed algorithm achieves substantially better overall performance against the state-of-the-art trackers.

1 Introduction

An appearance model is one of the most critical prerequisites for successful visual tracking. Designing an effective appearance model is still a challenging task due to appearance variations caused by background clutter, object deformation, partial occlusions, and illumination changes, *etc.* Efforts dedicated to this issue have leaded to numerous tracking algorithms [8,14,15,19,24,25,27,28,30]. In this paper, we focus on the discriminative tracker using the novel discriminative dictionary learning (DDL) method. The learned dictionary is reconstructive, compressive and discriminative, which can better distinguish the object from the complex background.

Considering visual tracking as a binary classification problem, most DDL based trackers [20,26] have difficulties in discriminating the similar visual patterns, especially for the object sharing similar shape and/or visual appearances

© Springer International Publishing AG 2016
E. Chen et al. (Eds.): PCM 2016, Part II, LNCS 9917, pp. 550–560, 2016.
DOI: 10.1007/978-3-319-48896-7_54

with the background. For example, the differences between the object and background are very minute and subtle, as shown in the left column of Fig. 1. Many DDL based trackers often fail to distinguish the differences successfully, and thus the most likely object location is incorrectly determined. The reason can be explained as follows. Since the object and the background are visually similar, the learnt dictionary is likely to be governed by the common patterns. Since candidates from different classes may be encoded by the same atoms, the representations could share many similar code and the proportion of discriminative codes may be very small. Such a property results in the loss of subtle image information that is critical to differentiate the object from the similar background. Therefore, for a robust tracker, what is desired is a new dictionary learning method which can encode subtle visual differences between the object and the background, especially for the cluttered environments or similar object interference scenarios.

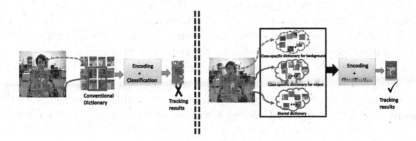

Fig. 1. Left: Most DDL based trackers are likely to encode subtly discriminative objects into the same atoms, resulting in the object drift. Right: Our method can jointly learn the *compact* shared dictionary and the *non-redundant* class-specific dictionaries. Red solid rectangles denote the true object and blue dashed rectangles are candidates. (Color figure online)

The above observations inspire us to design a new tracker via jointly learning the multi-class discriminative dictionary. Our DDL method exploits concurrently the intra-class visual information and inter-class visual correlations. To enhance the discrimination of the dictionaries, the classification error and the different constraints are incorporated into the objective function. The proposed DDL method can learn the *compact* shared dictionary and the *non-redundant* class-specific dictionaries. The class-specific dictionaries are able to capture the most discriminative feature between the object and the background. The shared dictionary can reconstruct the common patterns among all samples. In this way, the learnt dictionary is more compact and more discriminative, thus can achieve better discriminate the object from the background, as shown in the right column of Fig. 1. Tracking is carried out within a Bayesian inference framework where the joint decision measure is used to construct the observation model. The quality of each candidate is measured by the global coding classifier and the learnt linear classifier instead of relying on only one of them. A candidate with the highest measure score is considered as the tracking result. To alleviate the drift problem, both the ground truth information of the first frame and the reliable tracking results obtained online are accumulated to update the dictionaries. The proposed tracker is able to adapt to drastic appearance variations, as validated in our experiments.

2   Related Work

Sparse representation has been shown to give promising results against the object appearance variations for visual tracking. The pioneer work introduced by Mei and Ling [15] models the object appearance as a sparse linear combination of both object templates and trivial templates via ℓ_1 minimization. However, the computational cost of [15] grows linearly with the number of candidates, resulting in quite time consuming. To obtain more efficient solutions, many accelerated algorithms have been employed under the framework of ℓ_1 tracker [3,16]. Although these methods [3,16] are effective in modeling the object, the observation likelihood measured by the reconstruction error under the generative framework is neither efficient nor robust [24]. Therefore, several sparse trackers [9,31] not only propose new sparse models but also introduce construction schemes of the observation likelihood. In comparisons, we propose a joint decision measure to determine the most likely object location. The quality of each candidate is measured by both the global coding classifier and the learnt linear classifier. More details are discussed in Sect. 4.

The aforementioned methods achieve noticeable tracking results. However, since most formulations do not take the background into account, they are less effective for tracking in cluttered environments due to the lack of discrimination. Although [13,23] consider background information during dictionary construction, the fixed dictionary makes them lacks the ability to adapt to appearance changes. [20,21] introduced online tracking algorithms based on dictionary learning. Nevertheless, the dictionary and classifier are learned separately rather than jointly. Different from the method in [21,22], in our tracker, the classification error is incorporated the objective function, thus allowing a linear classifier and the good dictionary being considered simultaneously.

Our tracker also differs from the closely related works [20,26] in terms of both formulation and motivation. Yang et al. [26] presented an online discriminative dictionary learning algorithm for visual tracking, which learns a sparse dictionary and a linear classifier simultaneously. Compared with [26], our dictionary learning method can jointly learn the shared dictionary and the class-specific dictionaries by imposing the inter-incoherence constraint and the intra-incoherence constraint on the objective function. Such dictionary can characterize the discriminative information between the object and the background, especially when the object appearance bears some similarity with the background objects.

3   Joint Multi-class Discriminative Dictionary Learning

In this paper, we use x and $\mathbf{X}$ to denote a vector and a matrix, respectively. Given C classes of individual samples, let $\mathbf{X} = [\mathbf{X}_1, \cdots, \mathbf{X}_c, \cdots, \mathbf{X}_C] \in \mathbb{R}^{d \times N}$ be a training set with N samples. Here $\mathbf{X}_c \in \mathbb{R}^{d \times N_c}$ contains samples of each class and N_c is the number of samples from the c-th class. The class-specific dictionary is denoted by $\mathbf{B}_c \in \mathbb{R}^{d \times K_c}$ with $c = 1, 2, \cdots, C$, and the shared dictionary is denoted by $\mathbf{B}_0 \in \mathbb{R}^{d \times K_0}$, respectively. K_0 and K_c are the number of atoms from the shared dictionary and c-th class-specific dictionary, respectively. $\mathbf{B}_c$ is responsible for describing the class-specific visual properties of each class. $\mathbf{B}_0$ is used to describe the commonly shared visual patterns for all classes. Thus the complete learned dictionary is $\mathbf{B} = [\mathbf{B}_0, \mathbf{B}_1, \cdots, \mathbf{B}_c, \cdots, \mathbf{B}_C] \in \mathbb{R}^{d \times K}$, where K is the number of the atoms with $K = \sum_{c=0}^{C} K_c$. Denote by $\mathbf{A}$ the sparse coefficient matrix of $\mathbf{X}$ over $\mathbf{B}$, i.e., $\mathbf{X} \approx \mathbf{BA}$. Here, $\mathbf{A}$ can be expressed as $\mathbf{A} = [\mathbf{A}_1, \cdots, \mathbf{A}_c, \cdots, \mathbf{A}_C] \in \mathbb{R}^{K \times N}$, where $\mathbf{A}_c \in \mathbb{R}^{K \times N_c}$ is the coefficients matrix of $\mathbf{X}_i$ over $\mathbf{B}$.

In this paper, our consideration is that the learned dictionary $\mathbf{B}$ should well represent $\mathbf{X}_c$, i.e., $\mathbf{X}_c \approx \mathbf{BA}_c$. For each class samples, the representation $\mathbf{A}_c$ can be rewritten as $\mathbf{A}_c = [\mathbf{A}_c^0; \mathbf{A}_c^1; \cdots; \mathbf{A}_c^c; \cdots; \mathbf{A}_c^C] \in \mathbb{R}^{K \times N_c}$, where $\mathbf{A}_c^0 \in \mathbb{R}^{K_0 \times N_c}$ is the coding coefficients of $\mathbf{X}_c$ over the shared dictionary $\mathbf{B}_0$, and $\mathbf{A}_c^c \in \mathbb{R}^{K_c \times N_c}$ is the coding coefficient of $\mathbf{X}_c$ over the sub-dictionary $\mathbf{B}_c$. So there exists $\mathbf{X}_c \approx \mathbf{BA}_c = \sum_{i=0}^{C} \mathbf{B}_i \mathbf{A}_c^i$. In addition, ideally each class sample $\mathbf{X}_c$ should be well represented by $\mathbf{B}_0$ and $\mathbf{B}_c$. That is, only the coefficients associated with $\mathbf{B}_0$ and $\mathbf{B}_c$ can be non-zero, such that $\mathbf{X}_c \approx \mathbf{B}_0 \mathbf{A}_c^0 + \mathbf{B}_c \mathbf{A}_c^c$. Therefore, the discriminative dictionary learning model can be described as

$$\langle \mathbf{B}^*, \mathbf{A}^*, \mathbf{W}^* \rangle = \arg \min_{\mathbf{B}, \mathbf{A}, \mathbf{W}} \left\{ \sum_{c=1}^{C} \left(\left\| \mathbf{X}_c - \mathbf{BA}_c \right\|_F^2 + \left\| \mathbf{X}_c - [\mathbf{B}_0, \mathbf{B}_c][\mathbf{A}_c^0; \mathbf{A}_c^c] \right\|_F^2 \right) \right.$$

$$\left. + \left\| \mathbf{H} - \mathbf{WA} \right\|_F^2 + \beta_1 \left\| \mathbf{W} \right\|_F^2 + \eta \left\| \mathbf{A} \right\|_{\ell_1} \right\} \tag{1}$$

$$s.t. \begin{cases} \sum_{j=1, j \neq c}^{C} \left\| \mathbf{B}_j \mathbf{A}_c^j \right\|_F^2 = 0 \\ \sum_{j=0, j \neq c}^{C} \left\| \mathbf{B}_c^\top \mathbf{B}_j \right\|_F^2 = 0 \\ \left\| \mathbf{B}_c^\top \mathbf{B}_c \right\|_F^2 = \mathbf{I}_{K_c} \end{cases}$$

where $\| \cdot \|_F$ is the Frobenius norm; $\mathbf{I}_{K_c}$ is a $K_c \times K_c$ identity matrix. The first term is able to guarantee the good representation power of the overall dictionary, and the second term ensures that samples of each class can be favorably reconstructed by $\mathbf{B}_0$ and $\mathbf{B}_c$. Obviously, only using the first term is impractical to learn the discriminative class-specific dictionaries. While only adopting the second term is impossible to obtain an optimal shared dictionary $\mathbf{B}_0$, as there exist some commonly shared visual atoms between $\mathbf{B}_0$ and $\mathbf{B}_c$. $\| \mathbf{H} - \mathbf{WA} \|_F^2$ represents the classification error. $\mathbf{W} \in \mathbb{R}^{C \times K}$ denotes the classifier parameters. $\mathbf{H} = \{\mathbf{h}_1, \mathbf{h}_2, \cdots, \mathbf{h}_N\} \in \mathbb{R}^{C \times N}$ is the class labels of $\mathbf{X}$, where class label vector $\mathbf{h}_i = [0, 0, \cdots, 1, \cdots, 0, 0]^\top \in \mathbb{R}^C$. For each sample $\mathbf{x}_i \in \mathbb{R}^d$, if $\mathbf{x}_i$ belongs to the c-th class ($1 \leq c \leq C$), the c-th entry in $\mathbf{h}_i$ is 1 and all the other entries are 0's.

$\|\mathbf{H} - \mathbf{WA}\|_F^2 + \beta_1 \|\mathbf{W}\|_F^2$ not only couples the process of learning classifier, but also generates discriminative sparse coefficients. The discriminative property of $\mathbf{A}$ is very important for the performance of the linear classifier [10].

The constraint $\sum_{j \neq c, j=1}^{C} \|\mathbf{B}_j \mathbf{A}_c^j\|_F^2 = 0$ requires that each class-specific dictionary has poor representation ability for other classes, i.e., $\mathbf{A}_c^j$ should have nearly zero coefficients such that $\|\mathbf{B}_j \mathbf{A}_c^j\|_F^2$ is as small as possible for $j = 1, 2, \cdots, C$ and $j \neq c$. For samples of the c-th class, $\sum_{j \neq c, j=1}^{C} \|\mathbf{B}_j \mathbf{A}_c^j\|_F^2 = 0$ amounts to forcing the coefficients to be zero except the ones corresponding to both the c-th class-specific dictionary and the shared dictionary. Clearly, the sub-dictionaries among the class-specific dictionaries and the shared dictionary are orthogonal, and in this case we regard the learnt dictionary $\mathbf{B}$ as most incoherent. However, it does not mean that the learnt individual dictionaries only contain the visual properties of its corresponding class. The commonly shared visual atoms may appear in the different individual dictionaries, which makes the individual dictionaries redundant and thereby resulting in poor performance [1,4]. Based on the theoretical analysis in [5], the mutual coherence among all class-specific dictionaries and the shared dictionary should be as small as possible. Thus we impose the inter-orthogonality constraint $\|\mathbf{B}_c^\top \mathbf{B}_j\|_F^2$ for $j \neq c$ on the objective function. In addition, the intra-orthogonality constraint $\|\mathbf{B}_c^\top \mathbf{B}_c\|_F^2 = \mathbf{I}_{K_c}$ makes the learnt class-specific dictionary more stable. Without this constraint, many atoms in the class-specific dictionary will be zeros.

For simplicity, we replace $\sum_{j \neq c, j=1}^{C} \|\mathbf{B}_j \mathbf{A}_c^j\|_F^2 = 0$ with $\sum_{c=1}^{C} \mathbf{A}_c^{/0,c} = 0$ which indicates the submatrix by removing $\mathbf{A}_c^0$ and $\mathbf{A}_c^c$ from $\mathbf{A}_c$, i.e., $\mathbf{A}_c^{/0,c} = [\mathbf{A}_c^1; \cdots; \mathbf{A}_c^{c-1}; \mathbf{A}_c^{c+1} \cdots; \mathbf{A}_c^C] \in \mathbb{R}^{(K-K_0-K_c) \times N_c}$. Similarly, $\mathbf{B}_{/c}$ is the submatrix by removing $\mathbf{B}_c$ from $\mathbf{B}$, i.e., $\mathbf{B}_{/c} = [\mathbf{B}_0, \mathbf{B}_1, \cdots, \mathbf{B}_{c-1}, \mathbf{B}_{c+1}, \cdots, \mathbf{B}_C] \in \mathbb{R}^{d \times (K-K_c)}$. Therefore, $\sum_{j=0, j \neq c}^{C} \|\mathbf{B}_c^\top \mathbf{B}_j\|_F^2 = 0$ is converted to $\sum_{c=1}^{C} \|\mathbf{B}_c^\top \mathbf{B}_{/c}\|_F^2 = 0$. The objective function in Eq. (1) is not jointly convex in all variables $\mathbf{A}_c, \mathbf{B}_0, \mathbf{B}_c, \mathbf{W}$, however, it is convex with respect to each variable when others are fixed. Therefore, the optimization procedure of the our model can be divided into four sub-procedures by solving $\mathbf{A}_c, \mathbf{B}_0, \mathbf{B}_c$, and $\mathbf{W}$ alternatively. The alternative procedure is iteratively implemented to find the local optimum of each variable.

4   Our Tracker

In this section, with the joint discriminative dictionary learning method introduced in Sect. 3, we propose a robust tracker based on Bayesian inference where the joint decision measure is used to construct the observation model. In our tracker, a candidate with the highest measure score is considered as the tracking result. The detailed description of the proposed tracking method is summarized in Algorithm 1.

4.1 Bayesian State Inference

Object tracking can be considered as a Bayesian inference task in a Markov model with hidden state variables. Given the observation set of the object $\mathcal{O}_{1:t} = \{o_1, o_2, \cdots, o_t\}$, the optimal state s_t of the tracked object is obtained by the maximum a posteriori estimation $p(s_t^i|\mathcal{O}_{1:t})$, where s_t^i indicates the state of the i-th sample. The posterior probability $p(s_t|\mathcal{O}_{1:t})$ is formulated by Bayes theorem as $p(s_t|\mathcal{O}_{1:t}) \propto p(o_t|s_t) \int p(s_t|s_{t-1})p(s_{t-1}|\mathcal{O}_{1:t-1}) \, ds_{t-1}$. This inference is governed by the dynamic model $p(s_t|s_{t-1})$ and the observation model $p(o_t|s_t)$.

With particle filtering, the posterior $p(s_t|\mathcal{O}_{1:t})$ is approximated by a finite set of N_s samples or particles $\{s_t^i\}_{i=1}^{N_s}$ with importance weights $\{\omega_t^i\}_{i=1}^{N_s}$. We apply an affine image warp to model the object motion between two consecutive frames [17]. The dynamic model $p(s_t|s_{t-1})$ is modeled by Gaussian distribution, $i.e.$, $p(s_t|s_{t-1}) = \mathcal{N}(s_t; s_{t-1}, \sum)$, where $\sum$ is a diagonal covariance matrix whose diagonal elements are the corresponding variances of respective parameters. The observation model $p(o_t|s_t)$ is defined as

$$p(o_t|s_t) \propto SC_t, \tag{2}$$

where $SC_t = \kappa(\tau^{(t)})$ is the classification decision score at time t which will be explained in the next section.

Algorithm 1. The proposed tracking algorithm

Input: Image frames $F_1, F_2, \cdots, F_n$; Object state s_1.
Output: Tracking results $\hat{s}_t$ at time t.

1 **for** $t = 1 \rightarrow n$ **do**
2   **if** $t == 1$ **then**
3   Obtain labeled samples set $\mathbf{X_1} = \mathbf{X}_{N_p} \bigcup \mathbf{X}_{N_n}$;
4   Initialize the sample pool $\mathbf{X}_P = \mathbf{X_1}$;
5   Initialize the sample buffer pool $\mathbf{X}' = []$;
6   Initialize $\mathbf{B}^{(0)}$ and $\mathbf{W}^{(0)}$ with $\mathbf{X}_P$.
7   **end**
8   Sample the object candidates $\widehat{\mathbf{X}}$ according to the motion model $p(s_t|s_{t-1})$;
9   Compute the classification score of each candidate using Eq. (3) and get the best candidate based on Eq. (2);
10   Collect training samples set $\widetilde{\mathbf{X}}$ in the current frame and let $\mathbf{X}' = [\mathbf{X}'; \widetilde{\mathbf{X}}]$;
11   **if** $t\%T == 0$ **then**
12   Update $\mathbf{X}_P$ with $\mathbf{X}'$;
13   **if** $length(\mathbf{X}_P) > \Theta(\mathbf{X}_P)$ **then**
14   randomly remove some samples from $\mathbf{X}_P$.
15   **end**
16   Update dictionaries $\mathbf{B}$;
17       $\mathbf{X}' = []$.
18   **end**
19    $\widehat{\mathbf{X}} = []$.
20 **end**

4.2   Classification Decision

Given a candidate $x \in \mathbb{R}^{d \times 1}$, we encode it over the learnt dictionary $\mathbf{B} = [\mathbf{B}_0, \mathbf{B}_1, \cdots, \mathbf{B}_c, \cdots, \mathbf{B}_C]$, and obtain the spare code $\nu = \arg\min_\nu \|x - \mathbf{B}\nu\|_2^2 + \eta \|\nu\|_1$, where $\nu \in \mathbb{R}^{K \times 1}$. A candidate can be better represented by its corresponding dictionary $\mathbf{B}_c$ and the shared dictionary $\mathbf{B}_0$, then its reconstruction error is $\varepsilon_f = \|x - \mathbf{B}_0\nu_0 - \mathbf{B}_c\nu_c\|_2^2$, where $\nu_0 = [\nu_0^1, \nu_0^2, \cdots, \nu_0^{K_0}]^T \in \mathbb{R}^{K_0 \times 1}$ and $\nu_c = [\nu_c^1, \nu_c^2, \cdots, \nu_c^{K_c}]^T \in \mathbb{R}^{K_c \times 1}$ are the sparse coefficients over $\mathbf{B}_0$ and $\mathbf{B}_c$, respectively. Meanwhile, a candidate should be poor represented by other class-specific dictionaries and the corresponding reconstruction error is $\varepsilon_b = \|x - \sum_{j=1, j \le c} \mathbf{B}_j \nu_j\|_2^2$. For instance, in the case of the single object tracking, a candidate with a smaller foreground error and larger background error is more likely to be the target object, and vice versa. Thus, the golbal coding classifier is formulated as $f_g = \exp\big(-(\varepsilon_f - \varepsilon_b)/\sigma\big)$, where σ is a constant. To enhance the classification accuracy, the linear predictive classifier $f_c = \mathbf{W}_c \nu$ is jointly used to evaluate how a candidate is resembling the target object. Thus, the joint decision measure is defiend as

$$\kappa(x) = \mathbf{W}_c \nu + \exp\big(-(\varepsilon_f - \varepsilon_b)/\sigma\big). \tag{3}$$

For each class candidates, the index corresponding to the largest element of $\kappa(x)$ is considered as the tracking result. Using the measure Eq. (3), we have a more reliable decision score for the candidate x.

4.3   Updating the Dictionary

In the first frame, we draw positive and negative samples around the object location to initialize the dictionaries. Suppose the object is labeled manually, perturbation (e.g., shifting 1 or 2 pixels) around the object is performed for collecting N_p positive samples $\mathbf{X}_{N_p}$. Similarly, N_n negative samples $\mathbf{X}_{N_n}$ are collected far away from the located object (e.g., within an annular region a few pixels away from the object). $\mathbf{X}_1 = \mathbf{X}_{N_p} \bigcup \mathbf{X}_{N_n}$ is the initialized labeled sample set. Using labeled samples, we can obtain the initialized dictionaries via the proposed DDL method.

For each new frame, candidates predicted by the particle filter are denoted by $\widehat{\mathbf{X}}$. According to Eq. (3), we can get the classification score of each candidate. A candidate with higher classification score indicates that it is more likely to be generated from the target class. The most likely candidate is considered as the tracking result for this frame. Then, perturbation (*i.e.*, the same scheme in the first frame) around the tracking result is performed for collecting sample set $\widetilde{\mathbf{X}}$.

To make our tracker more adaptive to appearance changes, we construct a *sample pool* $\mathbf{X}_P$ and a *sample buffer pool* $\mathbf{X}'$ to update the samples and dictionaries. We only keep T collected sample set $\widetilde{\mathbf{X}}$ to constitute the sample buffer pool. Every T frames, $\mathbf{X}'$ is utilized to update $\mathbf{X}_P$. After updating the sample pool, we will empty $\mathbf{X}'$ and then reconfigure it. In our experiment, we set the sample pool capacity $\Theta(\mathbf{X}_P)$[1]. If the total number of samples in the sample pool is larger than $\Theta(\mathbf{X}_P)$, some samples in $\mathbf{X}_P$ will be randomly replaced with samples in $\mathbf{X}'$. To reduce the risk of visual drift, we always retain the samples $\mathbf{X}_1$ obtained from the first frame in the sample pool. That is, $\mathbf{X}_P = [\mathbf{X}_1; \mathbf{X}']$, which is able to better characterize the samples distribution. Then the updated sample pool $\Theta(\mathbf{X}_P)$ is utilized to update the dictionries with our DDL method described in Sect. 3. Similarly, we also retain the dictionary obtained in the first frame for constructing the joint dictionaries to compute the classification decision. Thus the stability and adaptivity in tracking objects of changing appearance are preserved.

5   Experiments

We evaluate the proposed tracker against 14 state-of-the-art tracking algorithms including ONNDL [20], RET [2], CT [29], MLSAM [24], ODDL [26], CN [6], VTD [12], SCM [31], Struck [7], TLD [11], ASLA [9], LSST [18], LSK [13], and LSPT [28] on the benchmark dataset [24]. *Note that we fix the parameters of our tracker for all sequences to demonstrate its robustness and stability.* The number of particles is 600 and the state transition matrix is $[8, 8, 0.015, 0, 0.005, 0]$ in the particle filter. We resize the object image to 10×10 pixels. 64 dimensional gray scale feature using subsampling with a step size of 4 and 288 dimensional HOG feature are extracted from each candidate, and they are concatenated into a single feature vector of 352 dimensions. In the first frame, $N_p = 50$ positive samples and $N_n = 200$ negative samples are used to initialize the dictionaries. Once the tracked object is located, 10 positive samples and 80 negative samples are used for dictionaries updating. The sample pool capacity $\Theta(\mathbf{X}_P)$ is set to 1200, in which the number of positive, negative are 200 and 1000, respectively. The size of each class-specific dictionary and the shared dictionary are 15 and 5, respectively.

Followed by [24], one pass evaluation (OPE) is adopted to measure the overall tracking performance for 14 trackers on 51 sequence. The OPE curve of both the precision plot and success rate are shown in Fig. 2. Only the top 10 trackers are displayed for clarity. For precision plots, we use the results at error threshold of 20 pixels for ranking these 10 trackers. The AUC score for each tracker is shown in the legend. Our tracker is 4.1% above the SCM in success rate, and outperforms the Struck by 10.6% in precision plot. Overall, our tracker outperforms other 14 trackers both in precision plot and success rate.

Apart from summarizing the performance on the whole sequences, we also construct 11 subsets corresponding to different attributes to test the tracking performance under specific challenging conditions. Because the AUC score of success plot is more accurate than the score at one threshold (*e.g.*, 20 pixels) of the precision plot, Fig. 3 only shows the attribute-based performance analysis in success rate. Only the top 10 trackers are displayed for clarity. Our approach

---

[1] The cardinality $\Theta(\mathbf{X}_P)$ denotes the number of samples in the sample pool.

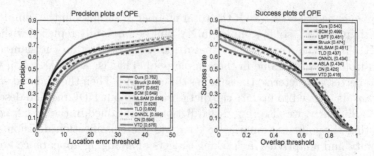

Fig. 2. Overall performance comparisons of precision plot and success rate. The performance score for each tracker is shown in the legend (best viewed on high-resolution display).

performs favorably on 8 out of 11 attributes: background clutter (BC), illumination variation (IV), motion blur (MB), deformation (DEF), out-of-view (OV), in-plane rotation (IPR), out-of-plane rotation (OPR) and occlusions (OCC). In this section, we only illustrate and analyze four attributes which occur more frequently in the benchmark. On the BC subset, our method get better results than others. The results suggest that the learnt dictionaries can characterize the discriminative information between the object and the distracters. On the SV subset, we see that trackers with affine motion models (*e.g.*, our method, SCM, MLSAM, and ASLA) are able to cope with scale variation better than others that only consider translational motion (*e.g.*, Struck and MIL). Similarly, on the OPR and IPR subsets, besides our tracker, the SCM tracker is also able to obtain the satisfactory results. The performance of SCM tracker can be attributed to the efficient spare representations of local image patches.

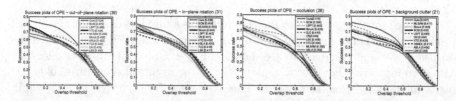

Fig. 3. Attribute-based performance analysis in success rate. The performance score of each tracker is shown in the legend (best viewed on high-resolution display).

It is known that visual trackers can be sensitive to initialization. Followed by [24], temporal robustness evaluation (TRE) and spatial robustness evaluation (SRE) are used to evaluate the initialization robustness. TRE randomly initializes the starting frame and runs a tracker through the rest of the sequences, and SRE randomizes the initial bounding boxes by shifting and scaling the ground truth. 12 different initializations and 20 different segments are evaluated for

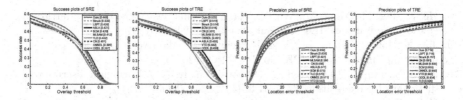

Fig. 4. Success plots and precision plots for TRE and SRE. The performance score of each tracker is shown in the legend (best viewed on high-resolution display).

SRE and STE, respectively. Figure 4 shows the top 10 trackers in the precision plot and success plot for TRE and SRE experiments. In both evaluations, our tracker obtains the best overall performance. For example, in the precision plots, the ranking score of our tracker outperforms the second best score by over 1.0% and 0.9% in TRE and SRE, respectively.

6 Conclusion

In this paper, we have presented a joint discriminative dictionary learning method for visual tracking. Our DDL method can learn the shared dictionary and the class-specific dictionaries, and effectively separate the commonly shared visual patterns from the class-specific ones. The learnt dictionary is more compact and more discriminative, which makes our tracker have better discriminating power to be more adaptive to handle appearance changes. During tracking, the quality of each candidate is measured by the global coding classifier and the learnt linear classifier instead of relying on only one of them. Comparison with 14 state-of-the-art tracking methods on the benchmark dataset have demonstrated that our tracker resists distracters excellently and generally outperforms existing methods.

References

1. Arora, S., Ge, R., Moitra, A.: New algorithms for learning incoherent and over-complete dictionaries. arXiv preprint arXiv:1308.6273 (2013)
2. Bai, Q., Wu, Z., Sclaroff, S., Betke, M., Monnier, C.: Randomized ensemble tracking. In: ICCV, pp. 2040–2047 (2013)
3. Bao, C., Wu, Y., Ling, H., Ji, H.: Real time robust l1 tracker using accelerated proximal gradient approach. In: CVPR, pp. 1830–1837. IEEE (2012)
4. Barchiesi, D., Plumbley, M.D.: Learning incoherent dictionaries for sparse approximation using iterative projections and rotations. TSP **61**(8), 2055–2065 (2013)
5. Candes, E., Romberg, J.: Sparsity and incoherence in compressive sampling. Inverse Probl. **23**(3), 969 (2007)
6. Danelljan, M., Shahbaz Khan, F., Felsberg, M., Van de Weijer, J.: Adaptive color attributes for real-time visual tracking. In: CVPR. IEEE (2014)
7. Hare, S., Saffari, A., Torr, P.H.: Struck: Structured output tracking with kernels. In: ICCV, pp. 263–270 (2011)

8. He, Y., Pei, M., Yang, M., Wu, Y., Jia, Y.: Online visual tracking by integrating spatio-temporal cues. IET Comput. Vis. **9**(1), 124–137 (2015)
9. Jia, X., Lu, H., Yang, M.: Visual tracking via adaptive structural local sparse appearance model. In: CVPR, pp. 1822–1829 (2012)
10. Jiang, Z., Lin, Z., Davis, L.S.: Label consistent K-SVD: learning a discriminative dictionary for recognition. TPAMI **35**(11), 2651–2664 (2013)
11. Kalal, Z., Mikolajczyk, K., Matas, J.: Tracking-learning-detection. TPAMI **34**(7), 1409–1422 (2012)
12. Kwon, J., Lee, K.: Visual tracking decomposition. In: CVPR, pp. 1269–1276 (2010)
13. Liu, B., Huang, J., Yang, L., Kulikowsk, C.: Robust tracking using local sparse appearance model and k-selection. In: CVPR, pp. 1313–1320 (2011)
14. Ma, C., Huang, J.B., Yang, X., Yang, M.H.: Hierarchical convolutional features for visual tracking. In: ICCV, pp. 3074–3082 (2015)
15. Mei, X., Ling, H.: Robust visual tracking using $\ell 1$ minimization. In: ICCV, pp. 1–8 (2009)
16. Mei, X., Ling, H., Wu, Y., Blasch, E., Bai, L.: Minimum error bounded efficient $\ell 1$ tracker with occlusion detection. In: CVPR, pp. 1257–1264. IEEE (2011)
17. Ross, D., Lim, J., Lin, R., Yang, M.: Incremental learning for robust visual tracking. IJCV **77**(1), 125–141 (2008)
18. Wang, D., Lu, H., Yang, M.H.: Least soft-threshold squares tracking. In: CVPR, pp. 2371–2378 (2013)
19. Wang, L., Ouyang, W., Wang, X., Lu, H.: Visual tracking with fully convolutional networks. In: ICCV, pp. 3119–3127 (2015)
20. Wang, N., Wang, J., Yeung, D.Y.: Online robust non-negative dictionary learning for visual tracking. In: ICCV, pp. 657–664. IEEE (2013)
21. Wang, Q., Chen, F., Xu, W., Yang, M.: Online discriminative object tracking with local sparse representation. In: WACV, pp. 425–432 (2012)
22. Wang, Q., Chen, F., Xu, W., Yang, M.H.: Object tracking with joint optimization of representation and classification. IEEE Trans. Circ. Syst. Video Technol. **25**(4), 638–650 (2015)
23. Wu, Y., Lim, J., Yang, M.H.: Online object tracking: a benchmark. In: CVPR, pp. 2411–2418. IEEE (2013)
24. Wu, Y., Ma, B., Yang, M., Jia, Y., Zhang, J.: Metric learning based structural appearance model for robust visual tracking. TCSVT **24**(5), 865–877 (2014)
25. Wu, Y., Pei, M., Yang, M., Yuan, J., Jia, Y.: Robust discriminative tracking via landmark-based label propagation. TIP **24**(5), 1510–1523 (2015)
26. Yang, F., Jiang, Z., Davis, L.S.: Online discriminative dictionary learning for visual tracking. In: WACV (2014)
27. Yang, M., Pei, M., Wu, Y., Jia, Y.: Learning online structural appearance model for robust object tracking. Sci. Chin. Inf. Sci. **58**(3), 1–14 (2015)
28. Yao, R., Shi, Q., Shen, C., Zhang, Y., van den Hengel, A.: Part-based visual tracking with online latent structural learning. In: CVPR, pp. 2363–2370 (2013)
29. Zhang, K., Zhang, L., Yang, M.-H.: Real-time compressive tracking. In: Fitzgibbon, A., Lazebnik, S., Perona, P., Sato, Y., Schmid, C. (eds.) ECCV 2012. LNCS, vol. 7574, pp. 864–877. Springer, Heidelberg (2012). doi:10.1007/978-3-642-33712-3_62
30. Zhang, L., Lu, H., Du, D., Liu, L.: Sparse hashing tracking. TIP **25**(2), 840–849 (2016)
31. Zhong, W., Lu, H., Yang, M.: Robust object tracking via sparsity-based collaborative model. TIP **23**(5), 2356–2368 (2014)

Product Image Search with Deep Attribute Mining and Re-ranking

Xin Zhou[1], Yuqi Zhang[1], Xiuxiu Bai[1], Jihua Zhu[1], Li Zhu[1], and Xueming Qian[1,2(✉)]

[1] School of Software Engineering, Xi'an Jiaotong University, Xi'an 710049, China
{zhouxin0209,zhangyuqi}@stu.xjtu.edu.cn,
{xiuxiubai89,zhujh,zhuli,qianxm}@mail.xjtu.edu.cn
[2] The Ministry of Education Key Laboratory for Intelligent Networks and Network Security,
Xi'an Jiaotong University, Xi'an 710049, China

Abstract. With the high-growing of e-commerce, more and more users have changed to buy from websites rather than in stores. To deal with mass products, the traditional text-based product search has become incompetent to meet use's requirement. In this paper, we explore deep learning with convolutional neural networks (CNN) to resolve query's classification, and propose an efficient approach for product image search. For a query image, we first train a CNN model of a large database containing various product images to discriminate the query's category. Then we search similar products from the established category and utilize these visual results to parse the query with attribute. Finally we use the extracted attribute tags to finish the textual re-ranking and obtain the most relevant retrieved product list. Experimental evaluation shows that our approach significantly outperforms state of art in product image search.

Keywords: Product image search · Visual results · Attribute tags · Textual re-ranking

1   Introduction

With the rapid development of the internet technology, e-commerce websites are becoming increasingly popular as the convenient shopping experience they provide for users. Many shopping search engines are designed to have numerous personalized services to meet user's various demands, like Google, Amazon, and Taobao. For a query, the item retrieval list can be located by category, price, brand and etc.

Nowadays, the shopping search engines are mainly based on textual query. Users can search the item they desired to by inputting several key words, such as "black, tight, dress". However, it is difficult to clearly describe an item by only several brief and rough keywords to query about. Meanwhile, facing a great deal of diverse items, users usually spend a lot of time to select one by one in the tediously item retrieval list. Furthermore, consider such a scene: when reading a magazine or viewing an album, users may find some items they are interested in and take photos intending to have a similar one. In traditional textual search [16], there is no problem if the interested item is a book, electron, or other item with a concrete name. But it turns out to be troublesome when the

© Springer International Publishing AG 2016
E. Chen et al. (Eds.): PCM 2016, Part II, LNCS 9917, pp. 561–570, 2016.
DOI: 10.1007/978-3-319-48896-7_55

items are clothing, bag, or shoes. It is difficult for us to give a clear description from the photo with concrete style details to find out their real needs. Once reaching the wrong text label, the retrieval list may become terrible and useless.

Obviously the traditional textual search is not adequate to deal with the above situation while pictures often provide more important cues for product search. Content-based image retrieval (CBIR) techniques [11–13] have become classical as they provide an effective way to mine semantic information from images. But CBIR was mainly applied to search rigid images (such as building and landscapes). These algorithms are unable to deal with most of product images as they are non-rigid. Especially for clothing, it is apt to folding and geometric deformations. In addition, the style detail of a product often plays an important role in searching, while the traditional algorithms may omit it. SIFT (scare-invariant feature transform) is one of the most robust registration method of correspondence matching [11–15]. And it performs well in our experiment on most categories.

As the query's category is unknown, the search will surely take a long time and make an inaccurate result within multiple categories products. So, we employ CNN to infer query's category. As we all know, recently deep learning has been proposed to solve data learning and analysis problem well for the Big Data.

In this work, we first collect a large dataset of a variety of categories products from the famous e-commerce websites, such as Amazon. Our dataset combines product images and detailed description texts. And we utilize the description information to automatically label each product images with their style attributes. Beyond colors and patterns, users mainly care the styles of the products.

For a query image, we first use the CNN model trained offline to determine the query's category, and consider the visual similarity to retrieve the similar product images in the determined category. Then we use the top examples of initial product list to orderly predict style attributes of the query. Finally we compute the similarity between the predicted tags and each product tags in visual retrieved results to re-rank the initial product list, providing the most similar products to query for users. The main contributions of our work are as follows:

(1) We propose an effective product search with attribute re-ranking approach. This approach uses the visual search results and the textual descriptions for results re-ranking.
(2) We propose an effective approach to estimate the category of the input product image by deep neural networks. This approach makes full use of the excellent discrimination characters of deep learning tools, such as convolution networks, to predict the category of the query.
(3) We propose category constrained search by utilizing visual words of SIFT feature to represent the local feature of the query image, to get the visual similar images. The category refined images is far less than the original product dataset, which can not only guarantee the search performances but also speed up the searching process.

2 Related Works

Product Search Based on Attributes: Nowadays, many e-commerce searching engines mainly depend on textual retrieval and design a fine-grained and all-sided description system for products. The product searching platforms, such as Amazon, Taobao, and 360buy, have defined various attributes (style, color, pattern, etc.) for users to search. With the rapid increase of the product database scale, more refined descriptions for product were created, especially in garment domain. Some work [4, 5] has primarily focused on analyzing the relationships between general clothing attributes, with respect to human activeness and occasion. Bossard et al. [6] presented a classification pipeline for classifying upper-body clothing by visual attributes and related them to occasion, season and lifestyle. In [7], a style-related vocabulary presenting clothing compositions was built for a new garment dataset to improve the search performance. Note that the current work is almost only for clothing, we expand the attributes to wider domains, not only for clothing, but also for shoes, bag, accessory and other product categories.

Product Image Search: Although there are some achievements on general image retrieval, researches on product image search are still limited. Recently some search engines for product image search have been developed. Google Googles and Amazon Flow are well-known commercial mobile product image search engines, but working robustly only for a few near-planar, textual object categories. And the search results are always inaccurate to meet users' real needs. Recently, researchers have devoted some efforts to product image retrieval. Tseng et al. [8] proposed an efficient garment visual search based on shape categories and styles, which did well in solving garment matching on non-rigid geometric deformations. In [9], Mizuochi et al. focused on local similarity of clothing retrieval with multiple images, which allowed user to circle one part of clothing they require while inputting the query image and provide a comprehensive result. Consider that query image always contains body part, Yamaguchi et al. [10] utilized pose estimation to analyze the clothing components in a fashion photograph, and use the analysis results to search similar clothing. As we can see, research on product image search has always been a challenge to cover a wide range of product categories while providing accurate results. In this paper, we consider a simple but efficient approach to make some efforts in this domain.

Deep Learning: Deep learning is a hierarchical model designed to emulate the learning process of the sensorial areas of the neocortex in the human brain. The algorithm can learn low-level features to obtain complex data representations through a hierarchical learning. Moreover, some companies like Google, Microsoft, and IBM have used Deep learning for the project of analyzing the big data of users. To handle the high-dimensional data with Deep learning, CNN are proposed. CNN have achieved impressive accuracy improvements in many areas of computer vision, especially in image parsing. In [1], Huang et al. proposed a Dual Attribute-aware Ranking Network (DARN) for cross-domain clothing image retrieval, which used CNN to recognize the semantic attributes of input clothing. Chen et al. [2] used CNN to resolve clothing style classification and retrieval task. Lin et al. [3] designed a clothing image retrieval framework by combining deep learning with Hash codes. In our work, we use the collected multiple categories product images, not only one clothing category, to train a CNN model for query's category recognition, so that we can finish the subsequent work better.

3   Approach Overview

For a query image, our approach consists of three steps: (1) Recognize query's category through the pre-trained CNN model. (2) Retrieve similar products by visual-based retrieval from the established category. (3) Use the visual results to parse the query's attributes and measure the similarity to re-rank the initial results.

Figure 1 depicts the overall retrieval pipeline. We firstly input the query to the pre-trained CNN model to determine which category the query belongs to. Then we apply the image retrieval approach based on hierarchical vocabulary tree [11] to obtain the initial visual retrieved results from the established category. Note that the visual retrieved results might contain a lot of noise, then we use some textual methods to improve the initial results. The process can be divided into the following steps: (1) K-NN tag prediction to parse query's attributes, (2) Attribute similarity to re-rank the visual results. The detail was discussed in Sects. 3 and 4. For a query image, we recognize its category and compare its visual feature and textual feature to other products in the established category. Therefore, we retrieve an image list ranked by style similarity to the query image.

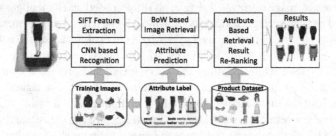

Fig. 1.   The retrieval pipeline of our product searching approach

3.1   CNN Based Recognition

We use the CNN method to solve the problem of query's category recognition. We use the collected product images to train and fine-tune the pre-trained network with latent layers. In the training process, we first select multiple categories product images as training set containing 123700 images, and they are fed into the pre-trained network with the initial training parameters we give. Then we use another test set as input to measure and supervise the accuracy of the classified results. Meanwhile, we fine-tune the training parameters and compare the test results and finally choose the best. After obtaining the best fine-tune network, the query is fed into the network and the outputs of the last layer become the classification results.

Note that the feature vectors generated from the latent layers contains the classification information. Each element value in the vector is the probability of which category the query is determined to. Experiment demonstrates that our trained network works well in classification. The detail of experiment result was discussed in Sect. 4.

3.2 Visual Retrieval

We utilize the image retrieval approach based on BoW [11] to preliminarily obtain a ranking result based on visual similarity, which can be helpful for parsing query item subsequently.

(1) Visual feature descriptor

We consider SIFT feature as visual feature descriptor for style retrieval which is useful for finding styles with similar appearance. SIFT was developed for image feature generation in object recognition applications. The invariant features extracted from images can be used to perform reliable matching between different views of an object or scene. So that we extract the 128-D SIFT feature to describe each image in our database, and carry our hierarchical quantization to obtain the visual word representation [12–16]. In this paper, we experimentally choose depth = 7 and breadth = 10 for hierarchical clustering, and experiment result show that the final number of visual word io 590518.

(2) BoW based retrieval

After the hierarchical clustering and quantization, we utilize the BoW (bag-of-word) model [11] to present an image. The BoW model is built as a visual word histogram by statistics of the number of features of different visual words in an image. By this time, in the established category, we present an image i as a N dimensional BoW histogram named h(k), k = 1, 2,... N. To consider a query image q, we present it as the corresponding dimensional BoW histogram named q(k) in the same way. We use the Euclidean distance to measure the similarity between a pair of tags.

$$D(i, q) = \sum_{k=1}^{N} (h(k) - q(k))^2 \tag{1}$$

where D(i, q) is the similarity score between two images. We rank the results by the score in descending order. Now we obtain a ranked item list with similar appearance.

3.3 Textual Re-ranking

Following the visual retrieval, we start to re-rank the visual results using the textual approach we proposed.

(1) Attribute prediction

Since the visual retrieval returns a result with visual similarity, we then aim to find the most similar items in details in the visual result. It is widely accepted that style may be the most representative attribute for an item. To analyze our dataset, we extract the useful description information as style tags for each item. Then we use K-NN to predict the query's attributes. For a Top K prediction, we record the times each tag appeared in the K re-ranked samples and compute its frequency. In a K samples statistic, the frequency is defined as follow:

$$f = T/K \tag{2}$$

where T is the appearance times of the corresponding tag in K samples. In this paper, we experimentally selected $K = 6$. We also define N_f as the number of the tags whose frequency is f. Then we experimentally make a rule to select the most relevant tags for query:

a. If $f > 0.5$ and $N_f > 5$, the 5 nearest item tags are selected; otherwise $N_f \leq 5$, all the tags that satisfies $f > 0.5$ are selected.

b. If all $f = 0.5$, the nearest sample's tags are selected.

(2) Attribute similarity to re-rank

After finishing parsing the query image in details, we represent a query with several attribute tags. We compute the similarity between tags using *Normalized Google Distance (NGD)*. The Normalized Google Distance is a semantic similarity measure derived from the number of hits returned by the Google search engine for a given set of keywords. Keywords with the same or similar meanings in a natural language sense tend to be "close" in units of *NGD*, while words with dissimilar meanings tend to be farther apart. Experiments demonstrate it works well in our paper. For a pair of tags, the similarity score can be compute as follow:

$$u_{i,j} = \exp \left\{ -\frac{\max\left[\log n(t_i), \log n(t_j)\right] - \log n(t_i, t_j)}{N - \min\left[\log n(t_i), \log n(t_j)\right]} \right\} \tag{3}$$

where $n(t_i)$ is the number of images which contain t_i, $n(t_j)$ is the number of images which contain t_j, $n(t_i, t_j)$ is the number of images which contain both t_i and t_j.

We compute the score of each sample tag with all the query tags using *NGD*, and select the highest score as final score of the sample tag. Then we can compute average *NGD* score of an sample item:

$$Score_{NGD}(n, q) = \sum_{k=1}^{N_{tags}} u_{i,j}/N_{tags} \tag{4}$$

where N_{tags} is the number of tags of the sample item.

Consider that the visual similarity plays an important role in the retrieval, we add the exponentiate visual score $D(n, q)$ to the final relevance score. We also define a weight λ of the textual score, so that the weight of visual score is $1 - \lambda$. The whole score between a query image q and a sample image n is defined as follow:

$$Score(n) = \lambda Score_{NGD}(n, q) + (1 - \lambda) \exp(-D(n, q)) \tag{5}$$

In this paper, the value of λ is experimentally discussed to be 0.5. We re-rank the results above according to the *score(n)* in descending order so as to get the final retrieved item list.

4   Experiment

4.1   Dataset Construction

We collect the product dataset from the famous online shopping website, Amazon.com. In order to enrich the diversity of products, we totally harvested 123700 products with 20 categories. The dataset mainly contains three fields: product images with different visual angles, detailed description information, and the whole users' reviews from the corresponding product.

We note that the product description statements always contain the key words to well present style of the product. So that we consider an automatically tag labeled method to create style tags for each product. For a category (such as skirt), we firstly compute the word frequency from the description statements of all products and sort the words according to the frequency. Then we manually select the most critical descriptive words with high frequency as a benchmark (e.g. pencil, mini, knee-length, etc.) for the category. For a product, we extract the words appearing in the benchmark from the description statements as style tags (e.g. pencil, knee-length). Particularly, different benchmarks were assigned to different labeling tasks so as to reflect the unique characteristics of different category. Table 1 shows some benchmarks of different categories. As thus, we complete the whole dataset labeling (see examples of the labeling interface in Table 2).

Table 1. Benchmark examples of different categories

Category	Attribute benchmarks
Skirt	pencil, maxi, mini&short, A-line, printed, denim, midi, striped,...
Coat	pocket, hood, zip, double-breasted, leather, denim, vest, peacoat,..
Shoes	slippers, sports, boots, canvas, slingback, ballet, martens, leather...

Table 2. Attribute label examples of different categories

category	Skirt			Coat			Shoes		
Attribute label examples	pencil knee-length	flared midi	bohemian printed	woolen zippered	windcoat lapel double-breasted	jacket leather black	asics sports lace-up	sandal	boots leather mid-heel

4.2   CNN Recognition Precision

CNN recognition plays a very important role in our approach as it firstly constraint the category of query to search so as to guarantee our search performance and also speed up the searching process. Figure 2 shows the test results. We can see that the total classification accuracy of the top 1 category achieves 91.3%, and the top 2 categories achieve 96.4%, and the top 3 categories achieve 97.7%. In addition, most categories achieved more than 95%. As for the wrong results, their probabilities of top1 category are less than 0.9, but the right category appears at top2 or top3. So we make a rule for the subsequent search. For a query's classification result:

a. If the top1 category accuracy > 0.9, the subsequent search will be done only in the category.

b. If the top1 category accuracy < 0.9, the subsequent search will be done in the top three categories.

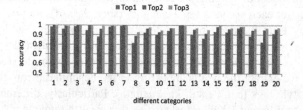

Fig. 2.   Category classification accuracy of different categories

4.3   Product Image Search Precision

In order to evaluate search performance, we selected some product images as queries and manually labeled the ground-truth of them in advance. We measure the performance of our approach by computing the Precision (PR) of Top N retrieved product datum and the total Average Precision (AP) [13–16]. The PR calculation is extended to multiple categories products. We select 600 products from 20 different typical categories as queries to experiment. The whole process of search is based on the whole dataset which contains 123700 products with 20 categories.

To analyze the search performance of our approach, the two methods that SIFT feature and the low-level feature: color and texture (CT), based visual search without textual re-ranking (TR) are selected as traditional baselines. In addition, we compare the low-level feature combined with textual re-ranking (CT+TR) method, and the subsequent textual re-ranking is same to our approach. Figure 3 shows the AP of the above methods. We can observe that our approach is demonstrated obviously superior than others. CT achieves the lowest AP, which may be due to less discriminative to deal with clothing with transformation. The top1–top20 retrieval accuracy of CT+TR improves about 5% AP when compared with CT, demonstrating the contribution of textual re-ranking method we proposed. By comparing SIFT and our approach SIFT +TR, our approach achieves it is clearly that the results turned to be improved a lot after we add to the TR method.

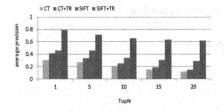
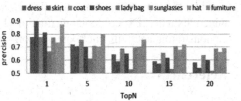

Fig. 3. Average precision on different methods   **Fig. 4.** Precision on different categories

Figure 4 shows the PR of different categories on our approach. We can observe that the PR relatively achieves high score on most categories, and even over 80% on some categories, such as skirt, furniture and shoes. As for other categories, the minimum is higher than 50%, and the Top1 and Top5 perform better than others. The different performance between different categories may be due to the irregularity recognition on categories. For example, the skirt is easier to recognize than lady bag, as bags usually contain more details.

4.4 Examples of Search Results

Figure 5 provides six examples search results. Overall, our approach performs well in the most experimental category. No matter product image is only about the entity or contains human model, there are few influences on the search results. Different from retrieving the same products to query, our approach provide more choices not only based on the same colors. As we can see, our approach is also sensitive to the figure and pattern of products showing the efficient consideration of product details.

Fig. 5. Top 5 retrieved examples.

5   Conclusion

We have proposed an efficient product image search with deep attribute mining and re-ranking. Different from previous approaches, we concentrate on multiple various categories to search. Meanwhile, we constrain category search by CNN classification to guarantee the search performance and speed up the searching process. We innovatively consider the semantic features to refine the search results by using the attribute tags we mined textually. Experimental evaluation shows successful results on most categories, demonstrating a significant boost over previous work.

References

1. Huang, J., et al.: Cross-domain image retrieval with a dual attribute-aware ranking network. In: IEEE International Conference on Computer Vision, pp. 1062–1070. IEEE (2015)
2. Chen, J.C., Liu, C.F.: Visual-based deep learning for clothing from large database. In: ASE Bigdata & Socialinformatics. ACM (2015)
3. Lin, K., et al.: Rapid clothing retrieval via deep learning of binary codes and hierarchical search. In: ACM on International Conference on Multimedia Retrieval, pp. 499–502. ACM (2015)
4. Liu, S., et al.: Hi, magic closet, tell me what to wear! In: Proceedings of the 20th ACM International Conference on Multimedia, pp. 1333–1334. ACM (2012)
5. Nguyen, T.V., et al.: Sense beauty via face, dressing, and/or voice. In: Proceedings of the 20th ACM International Conference on Multimedia, pp. 239–248. ACM (2012)
6. Bossard, L., Dantone, M., Leistner, C., Wengert, C., Quack, T., Gool, L.V.: Apparel classification with style. In: ACCV (2012)
7. Wei, D., Catherine, W., Anurag, B., Robinson, P., Neel, S.: Style finder: fine-grained clothing style recognition and retrieval. In: CVPRW (2013)
8. Tseng, C.H., Hung, S.S., Tsay, J.J.: An efficient garment visual search based on shape context. In: Proceedings of the 9th WSEAS International Conference on Multimedia Systems and Signal Processing. World Scientific and Engineering Academy and Society (WSEAS) (2009)
9. Mizuochi, M., Kanezaki, A., Harada, T.: Clothing retrieval based on local similarity with multiple images. In: Proceedings of the ACM International Conference on Multimedia, pp. 1165–1168. ACM (2014)
10. Yamaguchi, K.: Parsing clothing in fashion photographs. In: IEEE Conference on Computer Vision and Pattern Recognition, pp. 3570–3577 (2012)
11. Qian, X., et al.: Landmark summarization with diverse viewpoints. IEEE Trans. Circuits Syst. Video Technol. 25(11), 1857–1869 (2015)
12. Qian, X., Tan, X., Zhang, Y., Hong, R., Wang, M.: Enhancing sketch-based image retrieval by re-ranking and relevance feedback. IEEE Trans. Image Process. 25(1), 195–208 (2016)
13. Qian, X., Zhao, Y., Han, J.: Image location estimation by salient region matching. IEEE Trans. Image Process. 24(6), 4348–4358 (2015)
14. Yang, X., Qian, X., Xue, Y.: Scalable mobile image retrieval by exploring contextual saliency. IEEE Trans. Image Process. 24(6), 1709–1721 (2015)
15. Yang, X., Qian, X., Mei, T.: Learning salient visual word for scalable mobile image retrieval. Pattern Recogn. 48(10), 3093–3101 (2015)
16. Lu, D., Liu, X., Qian, X.: Tag based image search by social re-ranking. IEEE Trans. Multimedia (2016). doi:10.1109/TMM.2016.2568099

A New Rate Control Algorithm
Based on Region of Interest for HEVC

Liquan Shen[✉], Qianqian Hu, Zhi Liu, and Ping An

Key Laboratory of Advanced Display and System Application, Ministry of Education,
Shanghai University, Shanghai 200072, China
{jsslq,anping}@shu.edu.cn, hqq629@126.com, liuzhisjtu@163.com

Abstract. Although the existing rate control algorithm in HEVC (High Efficiency Video Coding) has achieved relatively high coding efficiency, it is not efficient in ensuring a higher quality for the visually important parts than others in a frame. In this paper, we propose a new rate control algorithm for HEVC based on ROI (Region of Interest), aiming at improving the visual quality while still maintaining the accuracy of rate control. Firstly, a novel method is developed for saliency estimation of the current frame based on spatial and temporal saliency estimation. Then the saliency map is utilized to determine ROI and guide the bits allocation process at the frame level and LCU (Largest Coding Unit) level. Finally the Lagrange multiplier and the quantization parameter will be clipped in a narrow range for smooth visual quality. Experimental results show that the proposed algorithm can make the output bit rate meet the target number and effectively raise the PSNR of ROI. As a result, the overall visual quality of the encoded sequence is highly improved compared to the original HEVC encoder.

Keywords: HEVC · Rate control · ROI · Saliency map · Visual quality

1 Introduction

The High Efficiency Video Coding (HEVC) standard is the most recent joint video project of the ITU-T Video Coding Experts Group (VCEG) and the ISO/IEC Moving Picture Experts Group (MPEG) standardization organizations, working together in a partnership known as the Joint Collaborative Team on Video Coding (JCT-VC) [1]. HEVC represents a number of advances in video coding technology. Its video coding layer design is based on conventional block-based motion compensated hybrid video coding concepts, but with some important differences relative to prior standards, such as the quad-tree structured coding unit (CU), which allows recursive splitting into four equally sized blocks [2]. HEVC significantly improves the coding efficiency over the preceding coding standards.

Rate control is a crucial module in high quality video services which adjusts the encoder's output bit-rate to a specific requirement of target bitrate and avoids over- and under-flow of the buffers in video decoders. In [3], a linear R-λ model based rate control algorithm is proposed for HEVC. Different from traditional models, it controls output

© Springer International Publishing AG 2016
E. Chen et al. (Eds.): PCM 2016, Part II, LNCS 9917, pp. 571–579, 2016.
DOI: 10.1007/978-3-319-48896-7_56

bits by adjusting the value of λ, which is the Lagrange multiplier in the RDO (Rate Distortion Optimization) process. The R-λ model is expressed as

$$\lambda = \alpha \times R^{\beta} \tag{1}$$

where α and β are parameters related to the video source. R is the target bits. QP is determined according to λ value as the following equation

$$QP = 4.2005 \times \ln\lambda + 13.7122 \tag{2}$$

The rate control algorithm based on R-λ model is the recommended rate control algorithm in the present HEVC reference software because of its outstanding coding performance. However, it does not take visual perception of human eyes into consideration, leading to an inefficient bit allocation. Its LCU level bits allocation is based on MAD (Mean Absolute Difference). Nevertheless, such measures could not match the characteristics of the human visual system since an area with high MAD value may not certainly catch much human attention. To fix this problem, the main idea of our proposed algorithm is: how to allocate the limited bit resource on one frame in order to provide a higher quality for the parts that attract the human attention, i.e. the Region-of-Interest (ROI), so that the subjective quality can be improved.

Rate control algorithms for ROI-based video coding have gained much attention from researchers. In [4], an ROI-based bit allocation technique is proposed with consideration of the human faces in conversational video communications. A modified rate control algorithm for H.264/AVC in [5] can accommodate multiple priority levels given a ROI, which allows a better control of the quality of ROIs and gradual variation of the quality in the rest of the frame through a bit redistribution process. In [6], a rate control scheme based on ROI is proposed for H.264/AVC, aiming at allocating more bit resource for ROI and still maintaining the accuracy of the output bit rate. A perceptual rate control algorithm that takes into account visual attention is proposed in our previous work [7], where bits allocated to each frame in a group of pictures (GOP) are related to the local motion attention in it, and more bits are allocated to the frames with strong local motion attention. Similarly, in each frame, more bits are assigned to visually significant macroblocks (MBs), and fewer to visually insignificant MBs.

However, these algorithms are all designed on H.264/AVC platform, which could not be directly applied to HEVC because of different coding structure and technologies. A rate control algorithm for lossless ROI coding in HEVC intra-coding is proposed in [8], which is developed for digital pathology images and allows for random access to the data. Based on an input ROI mask, the algorithm first encodes the ROI losslessly. According to the bit rate spent on the ROI, it then encodes the background by using rate control in order to meet an overall target bit rate.

In this paper, we propose a new ROI-based rate control algorithm for HEVC. First, a novel method considering both spatial and temporal saliency is introduced to generate a saliency map for each frame. Second, ROI and non-ROI (abbreviated as NROI afterwards) in one frame are separately rate-controlled. Third, some constraints are used to adjust λ and QP values for smooth visual quality. In addition to make the actually encoding bit rate meet the target bit rate, the proposed rate control method is better in preserving information contained in ROI, leading to a better subjective quality, compared with the existing rate control algorithms in HEVC.

2   Saliency Map Generation and ROI Determination

2.1   Saliency Map Generation

In our rate control algorithm, saliency map for one frame is generated by the combination of its spatial saliency and temporal saliency. To generate the spatial component of our saliency map S_p, we borrow the well-known Graph-Based saliency model [9]. It consists of two steps: first forming activation maps on certain feature channels, and then normalizing them in a way which highlights conspicuity and admits combination with other maps. The model is simple and biologically plausible insofar as it is naturally parallelized. For more detailed information about generating saliency map by this method, please refer to [9].

Usually, moving objects are of great interest to viewers. Since motion vectors (MVs) can indicate the motion intensity, it is the main feature we adopted here for the saliency estimation in temporal domain. Note that in our algorithm, saliency map for each frame is generated before encoding the video sequence. The MVs are therefore extracted from the previous coded frame. The block size is set to 16×16 and the search range is set to 7. Mean Absolute Difference (MAD) is utilized as the cost function in our algorithm and Adaptive Rood Pattern Search (ARPS) [10] as the searching algorithm because of its relatively low computational complexity. The obtained MV statics cannot be directly used to estimate saliency map because of camera movement, which leads to the competition between apparent motion of the background and fore-ground object motion. To solve this problem, we adopt the iterative least square method [11] to estimate the global motion. Followed by global motion compensation, i.e. subtraction of global motion from the motion field, we obtain one global motion-compensated MV (GMC-MV) per block. By this way, the camera movement is removed. For each block, the magnitude of its GMC-MV is taken as its temporal saliency S_t.

In [12], Mcleod et al. suggest the movement filter hypothesis of visual system and the mixed effect of moving and stationary stimuli. According to their research, we combine the spatial and temporal saliency to obtain the spatiotemporal saliency S_F as follows:

$$S_F = \theta_1 S_t + \theta_2 S_p + \theta_3 S_t S_p \tag{3}$$

where θ_1, θ_2, θ_3 are weighting factors set to 0.5, 0.3, 0.5, respectively in our experiment. The first two terms in (3) allow the spatial and temporal saliency to promote a pixel independently. The third term weighs the spatial saliency value by the temporal saliency value and vice versa. We choose a larger weight for temporal saliency as moving objects are always more attractive to human eyes.

2.2 ROI Determination

ROI can be determined based on the obtained spatiotemporal saliency map. The saliency value of each largest CU (LCU) in a frame is measured as follows:

$$ws(i) = \sum_{m=1}^{M} \sum_{n=1}^{N} S_F(i, m, n) \tag{4}$$

where ws(i) can be regarded as the weight in terms of saliency assigned to the ith LCU, $S_F(i, m, n)$ is the saliency value at the coordinate (m, n) within the ith LCU. M and N are the width and height, respectively, of this block. After calculating all the LCU-level weights in a frame, they are ordered from large to small. The weight value at the quarter of this order is chosen as the threshold T, which means the ROI area occupies a quarter of the frame area. LCU with a weight value larger than T will be classified into ROI and the one with a weight value smaller than T will be classified into NROI. The whole process of generating saliency map and ROI determination is illustrated in Fig. 1.

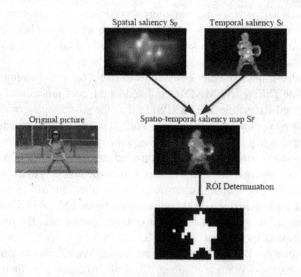

Fig. 1. Generation of saliency map and ROI determination

3 Target Bits Assignment Based on Saliency

Bit allocation for ROI and NROI are separately determined in our algorithm, i.e. ROI and NROI have their own target bits, preventing bits over-occupation by either of them and ensuring sufficient quality improvement for ROI. Note that the bits allocation process of a group of pictures (GOP) is the same as [3]. The frame-level target bits is divided into two portions based on a quality factor K, which is the ratio of the desired bits between ROI and NROI. A larger K leads to a better image quality in ROI. The target bits for ROI and NROI are determined according to the following equations:

$$T = T_{ROI} + T_{NROI} \tag{5}$$

$$T_{ROI} = K \times T_{NROI} \tag{6}$$

where T, T_{ROI}, and T_{NROI} denote the target bits allocated to the current frame, ROI and NROI, respectively. In the LCU-level rate control, the target bits for each LCU should be proportional to its saliency value, which is expressed as

$$R(p) = \hat{T}_{ROI} \times \frac{ws(p)}{\sum_{i=1}^{M_{left}} ws(i)} \tag{7}$$

$$R(q) = \hat{T}_{NROI} \times \frac{ws(q)}{\sum_{i=1}^{N_{left}} ws(i)} \tag{8}$$

where $\hat{T}_{ROI}$ and $\hat{T}_{NROI}$ denote the remaining bits for ROI and NROI, respectively. R(p) and M_{left} are the estimated bits for the p-th LCU in ROI and the number of uncoded LCUs in ROI. R(q) and N_{left} are the estimated bit count for the q-th LCUs in NROI and the number of uncoded LCUs in NROI. After setting target bits, the corresponding λ and QP can be determined by (1) and (2).

4 λ and QP Adjustment

To keep the quality consistency spatially and temporally, the preliminary λ and QP will be clipped in a narrow range according to the coding parameters of previously encoded LCUs. We define R and ΔQP as the adjusting factor that guarantee

$$\lambda_{pLCU} \cdot R^{-1} \leq \lambda_{currLCU} \leq \lambda_{pLCU} \cdot R \tag{9}$$

$$QP_{pLCU} - \Delta QP \leq QP_{currLCU} \leq QP_{pLCU} + \Delta QP \tag{10}$$

$$\lambda_{psamelevel} \cdot R^{-1} \leq \lambda_{currLCU} \leq \lambda_{psamelevel} \cdot R \tag{11}$$

$$QP_{psamelevel} - \Delta QP \leq QP_{currLCU} \leq QP_{psamelevel} + \Delta QP \tag{12}$$

where $\lambda_{currLCU}$, λ_{pLCU}, $\lambda_{psamelevel}$, $QP_{currLCU}$, QP_{pLCU}, $QP_{psamelevel}$ are respectively the λ and QP of the current LCU, the previously encoded LCU and the LCU at the same location on the previously coding frame (with the same temporal level of the hierarchical B prediction structure). R and ΔQP are determined by the rule of thumb and we set them to (2) and (3), respectively.

5   Experimental Results

To evaluate the performance of the proposed algorithm, we implemented the proposed rate control algorithm on HM16.0. The proposed algorithm is evaluated with ten video sequences recommended by JCT-VC. All the sequences are coded in the "Random Access (RA)" case of main profile. The rate control algorithm already included in HM16.0, which is described in [3]. The target bit ratio K in our algorithm is set to 3. The accuracy of bit mismatch is investigated in terms of mismatch error:

$$M = \frac{\left|R_{target} - R_{actual}\right|}{R_{target}} \times 100\% \tag{13}$$

where R_{target} and R_{actual} are the number of target bitrate and the actual output bitrate for a coding sequence.

Table 1 shows the experimental results of different sequences with different target bit rates. It can be seen that the proposed algorithm achieves significant bit-rate accuracy with a negligible mismatch, from 0.02% to 1.65% for different cases. The proposed algorithm gains an improvement of 1.02–2.30 dB on ROI at the cost of 1.30–3.39 dB loss on NROI in PSNR compared to the rate control in HM 16.0.

Table 1. Bit-rate, PSNR and ROI PSNR of HM16.0 with RC and the proposed algorithm

Sequence	R_{target} (kbps)	HM16.0 with RC [3]		Proposed algorithm				ROI PSNR Change (dB)	NROI PSNR Change (dB)
		ROI PSNR (dB)	NROI PSNR (dB)	R_{actual} (kbps)	ROI PSNR (dB)	NROI PSNR (dB)	M		
BQMall	500	31.12	32.74	500.37	32.25	30.38	0.12%	1.13	−2.36
PartyScene	1200	30.03	30.38	1200.64	32.33	28.19	0.08%	2.30	−2.19
RaceHorses	1000	32.40	33.28	1000.28	34.28	31.31	0.06%	1.88	−1.97
BQTerrace	2000	32.95	32.97	2000.21	34.19	30.65	0.02%	1.24	−2.30
Cactus	1000	31.09	31.48	1002.52	32.11	30.32	0.25%	1.02	−1.16
Kimono	600	35.31	35.26	600.35	37.52	32.83	0.12%	2.21	−2.43
ParkScene	1000	34.20	33.34	1000.14	36.31	31.25	0.03%	2.11	−2.09
Tennis	1000	33.80	35.64	1003.21	35.15	34.34	0.64%	1.35	−1.30
PeopleOnStreet	8000	32.55	34.15	7917.80	34.53	31.74	1.65%	1.98	−2.41
Traffic	3500	36.86	38.01	3501.64	38.63	34.62	0.07%	1.77	−3.39
Average							0.30%	1.70	−2.16

ROIs in two algorithms are both detected by the method described in Sect. 2.

In the following, we show results of subjective visual quality tests. The test sequences are presented on a Panasonic TH-P50ST30C plasma display panel TV with a resolution of 1920 1080. The test procedure follows the double stimulus continuous quality scale (DSCQS) method [13]. The score range is from 0 to 100. The proposed algorithm is compared with the rate control algorithm in [3], which is implemented in HM16.0 without consideration of ROI, and the method in [6]. For a fair comparison, both the bit ratio index in [6] and the target bit ratio K in the proposed algorithm are set to 3. Figures 2 and 3 show the comparisons of subjective visual test (for "PartyScene" and "Kimono" video sequence) with different target bitrates. DMOS (Difference Mean Opinion Score) denotes the mean of different opinion score gathered from observers.

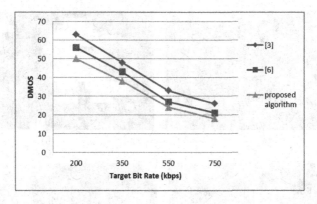

Fig. 2. Subjective visual tests for PartyScene (832 × 480)

Lower number represents the better visual quality. It can be seen from Figs. 2 and 3 that both the proposed algorithm and [6] produce the better visual quality than [3]. This can be inferred by the fact that more bits in more attended regions and less bits in less attended regions lead to the overall visual enhancement. The proposed algorithm performs better than [6] since it has considered the influence of global motion in temporal saliency detection process and allocates bits according to the saliency of each unit. Besides, R-λ model is more efficient than the classical quadratic R-Q model in the HM platform.

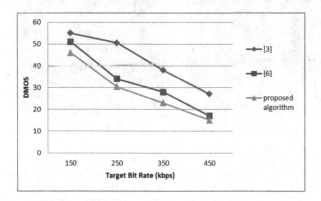

Fig. 3. Subjective visual tests for Kimono (1920 × 1080)

An example of subjective visual quality comparison is shown in Fig. 4. It could be seen that the detected ROI correctly catches the region in the frame that human eyes want to focus on. Although the PSNR value of the reconstructed frame with our algorithm is lower than that resulted by the original rate control algorithm in HM 16.0, the subjective quality is obviously improved. Some distortion may be observed within NROI if we check it very carefully. However, such quality degradation is not sensitive to human eyes and would not annoy the observer.

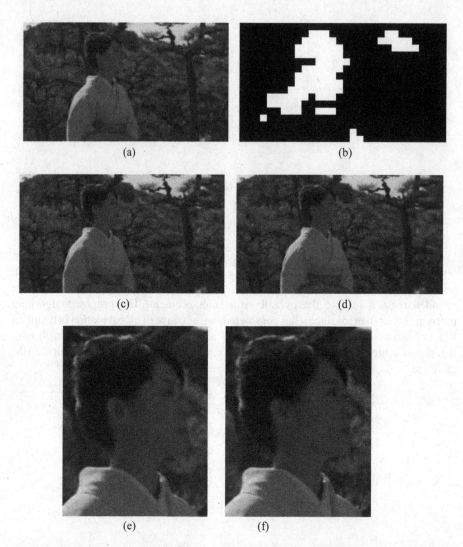

Fig. 4. Analysis of the 137th frame of Kimono (1920 × 1080). (a) Original frame. (b) Detected ROI. (c) Reconstructed frame via rate control in HM16.0 with PSNR = 32.05 dB. (d) Reconstructed frame via the proposed algorithm with PSNR = 30.27 dB. (e) Details of the most sensitive region in (c). (f) Details of the most sensitive region in (d).

6   Conclusion

In this paper, we propose a new HEVC rate control algorithm based on region of interest. We firstly generate a saliency map based on both the spatial and temporal cues for each frame. Then the ROI and NROI are determined so that we can separately allocate bits for ROI and NROI. After λ and QP calculation and adjustment for each LCU, the encoding process can be carried out finally. Experimental results show that the proposed algorithm successfully improved the subjective quality of each sequence while maintaining the accuracy of rate control.

Acknowledgment. This work is sponsored by Shanghai Pujiang Program (15pjd015) and Innovation Program of Shanghai Municipal Education Commission (13ZZ069), and is supported by the National Natural Science Foundation of China under grant No. 61171084, 61172096, 61422111, U1301257, and by the Program for Professor of Special Appointment (Eastern Scholar) at Shanghai Institutions of Higher Learning.

References

1. Sullivan, G., Ohm, J., Han, W.J., et al.: Overview of the high efficiency video coding (HEVC) standard. IEEE Trans. Circuits Syst. Video Technol. **22**(12), 1649–1668 (2012)
2. Kim, I.K., Min, J., Lee, T., Han, W.J., Park, J.: Block partitioning structure in the HEVC standard. IEEE Trans. Circuits Syst. Video Technol. **22**(12), 1697–1706 (2012)
3. Li, B., Li, H., Li, L., Zhang, J.: λ domain rate control algorithm for high efficiency video coding. IEEE Trans. Image Process. **23**(9), 3841–3854 (2014)
4. Liu, Y., Li, Z.G., Soh, Y.C.: Region-of-Interest based resource allocation for conversational video communication of H.264/AVC. IEEE Trans. Circuits Syst. Video Technol. **18**(1), 134–139 (2008)
5. Agrafiotis, D., Bull, D.R., Canagarajah, N., Kamnoonwatana, N.: Multiple priority region of interest coding with H.264. In: IEEE International Conference on Image Processing (ICIP), pp. 53–56 (2006)
6. Chiang, J.-C., Hsieh, C.-S., Chang, G., Jou, F.-D., Lie, W.-N.: Region of interest based rate control scheme with flexible quality on demand. In: IEEE International Conference on Multimedia Expo, pp. 238–242, July 2010
7. Shen, L., Liu, Z., Zhang, Z.: A novel H.264 rate control algorithm with consideration of visual attention. Multimedia Tools Appl. **63**(3), 709–727 (2013)
8. Sanchez, V., Aulí-Llinàs, F., Vanam, R., Bartrina-Rapesta, J.: Rate control for lossless region of interest coding in HEVC intra-coding with applications to digital pathology images. In: IEEE International Conference on Acoustics, Speech and Signal Processing (ICASSP), pp. 1250–1254 (2015)
9. Harel, J., Koch, C.: Graph-based visual saliency. In: 20th Annual Conference on Neural Information Processing Systems, pp. 545–552 (2007)
10. Nie, Y., Ma, K.: Adaptive rood pattern search for fast block-matching motion estimation. IEEE Trans. Image Process. **11**(12), 1442–1448 (2002)
11. Rath, G.B., Makur, A.: Iterative least squares and compression based estimations for a four-parameter linear global motion model and global motion compensation. IEEE Trans. Circuits Syst. Video Technol. **9**(7), 1075–1099 (1999)
12. Mcleod, P., Driver, J., Dienes, Z., et al.: Filtering by movement in visual search. J. Exp. Psychol. Hum. Percept. Perform. **17**(1), 55–64 (1991)
13. Pereira, F., Ebrahimi, T.: The MPEG-4 Book, pp. 669–675. Prentice-Hall, Upper Saddle River (2002)

Deep Learning Features Inspired Saliency Detection of 3D Images

Qiudan Zhang[1,2], Xu Wang[1,2(✉)], Jianmin Jiang[1,2], and Lin Ma[3]

[1] College of Computer Science and Software Engineering, Shenzhen University,
Shenzhen 518060, China
qiudzhang@gmail.com, {wangxu,jiang}@szu.edu.cn
[2] Research Institute for Future Media Computing, Shenzhen University,
Shenzhen 518060, China
[3] Huawei Noah's Ark Lab, Shatin, Hong Kong
forest.linma@gmail.com

Abstract. Saliency detection of 3D images is important for many 3D applications, such as bit allocation in 3D video coding, spatial pooling in stereoscopic image quality assessment and feature extraction in 3D object retrieval. However, traditional saliency detection approaches only target for the 2D images. Meanwhile, the traditional hand-crafted low-level feature extraction process may be not suitable for the 3D images. In this paper, we propose a deep learning feature based 3D visual saliency detection model. The pre-trained CNN model is employed to extract the feature vectors for both color and depth images after multi-level image segmentation. Then, we train a neutral network based classifier to generate the color and depth saliency maps from the feature vectors. Final, the linear fusion method is adopted to obtain the final saliency map for 3D image. Experimental results demonstrate that our proposed model can achieve appealing performance improvement over two public benchmark datasets.

Keywords: Index terms—3D image · Visual saliency · Conventional neural network · Deep learning feature and depth saliency

1 Introduction

With the development of consumer electronic industry, three dimensional (3D) applications become more and more popular in our daily life. Comparing to the traditional 2D viewing experience, 3D applications can offer users with depth perception and immersive viewing experience. However, there are still many open issues that need to be well addressed in 3D processing chain. Saliency detection of stereoscopic images is one of the most fundamental problems in 3D research, which aims to find regions of interest that standout from their neighbors in natural images. It can be applied to optimize the bit allocation in 3D video coding [1], spatial pooling in stereoscopic image quality assessment [2, 3] and compressed domain for image and video [4, 5].

Existing visual saliency detection methods are mostly related to 2D image. These models estimate saliency from color images via hand-crafted low-level features (such

© Springer International Publishing AG 2016
E. Chen et al. (Eds.): PCM 2016, Part II, LNCS 9917, pp. 580–589, 2016.
DOI: 10.1007/978-3-319-48896-7_57

as luminance, color, contrast and texture) [6–8], which did not exploited the depth cues. Thus, traditional 2D saliency detection models are unable to accurately predict where people look in a 3D scene. To improve the prediction accuracy, some researcher modeled the visual saliency of stereoscopic images by considering the depth information. For example, Fang et al. designed a framework that applied the feature contrast of color, luminance, texture, and depth to estimate saliency of a stereoscopic image [9], in which adopted a traditional hand-crafted method to extract low-level features and depth features in computing the stereoscopic saliency. Qi et al. proposed a 3D visual saliency detection model with generated disparity by using low-level features and depth features [10]. For these approaches, the hand-crafted feature extraction stages cannot effectively and accurately extract feature hierarchically from raw pixel [11]. Thus, the performances are limited.

In this paper, we propose a visual saliency detection model for 3D image based on deep learning features. The contributions of our proposed model can be summarized as follows.

- For each stereoscopic image pair, the features map of depth image and color image are extracted by a pre-trained convolution neural network (CNN), respectively.
- The saliency map of a depth image (or color image) is estimated by a fine-tuned deep neural network which is used to infer the saliency value of every image region from the deep learning features maps.
- The final visual saliency map of 3D image is obtained by a linear fusion approach which combines the color saliency map and depth saliency map.

The remaining of this paper is organized as follows. Section 2 surveys the related work in the literature. Section 3 describes the proposed computation model in detail. Section 4 shows the experiment results. Final, Sect. 5 concludes this paper.

2 Background and Motivation

Classical visual saliency model can be classified into two categories, one is bottom-up methods and the other is top-down methods. Bottom-up approaches are low-level features driven which aims to distinguish regions of interest stand out from their background. For example, Itti et al. proposed a model of saliency for rapid scene analysis combined the multi-scale image features into a saliency map [6]. Bruce et al. introduced a saliency measure based on information maximization, in which Shannon's self-information method was applied to the saliency operation [12]. Hou et al. designed a visual saliency detection model based on spectral residual which constructed the saliency map via the log-spectrum of an image [13].

Top-down approaches are specific-task driven to process information of image. For example, Goferman et al. designed an especially context-aware saliency detection model has been proposed to detect the image regions which can present the scene [14]. Yang et al. proposed a visual saliency model based on top–down approach via joint a Conditional Random Field and a discriminative dictionary [15]. Kanan et al. introduced a top-down saliency based on natural image statistics, in which many forms of top-down knowledge was incorporated into saliency detection model [16].

Currently, to further improve the prediction accuracy, combining the bottom-up and top-down approaches together becomes the hot research topic. Itti et al. proposed an overt and covert shifts of visual attention model based on a saliency search mechanism, in which focused on how to combine the information including orientation, intensity, and color information in a specific visual attention task [17]. Cheng et al. put forward a salient object detection algorithm based on a regional contrast. Meanwhile the global contrast and spatial coherence were both applied to detect the salient object [18]. Zhao et al. designed multi-context deep learning framework for salient object detection [19], in which the global context and local context are both considered into saliency detection.

Apart from 2D visual saliency models, a few studies investigated the computation model of 3D visual saliency. Wang et al. added a depth to visual dimension, and utilized the 2D visual features to detect the salient areas in a computation model of 3D visual saliency [20]. The depth saliency map is generated by a Bayesian approach. Fang et al. obtained the feature contrast based saliency map by measuring the spatial distance between image patches [9]. Qi et al. proposed a band-pass filtering based 3D visual saliency detection model [10]. Kim et al. described a saliency prediction model on stereoscopic videos which accounts for diverse low-level features, depth attributes and high-level classifications of scenes [21].

Based on above-mentioned discussions, the performance of computation visual saliency map is significantly influenced by the visual feature representation. Thus, finding the representative visual features is quite important to the 3D visual saliency research. Existing saliency detection model of stereoscopic images are based on hand-crafted features [9, 10, 20]. However, these approaches are difficult to achieve high degree of distinction among saliency region and their neighbors. Besides, due to the lack of knowledge on 3D visual perception, how depth information can contribute to the final visual saliency is still not clear.

Deep convolution neural network (CNN) has already been widely applied in hierarchical feature learning and extraction [22], and achieves significantly success on performance improvement of visual saliency models for 2D images [11]. However, existing works mainly focus on the feature learning for color image but not for depth image. Thus, it is necessary to learn the depth feature representative through the CNN tools.

3   Proposed Visual Saliency Model for 3D Images

The framework of proposed deep learning features based visual saliency model contains three basic stages, including deep features extraction, saliency map generation and saliency map fusion as shown in Fig. 1. First, the deep feature vectors for the color and depth image are extracted by employing the CNN model, respectively. Then, the saliency maps for color and depth image are generated from the feature vector through a three-layer neural network. Final, the saliency map of 3D image is fused by the saliency maps of color and depth image.

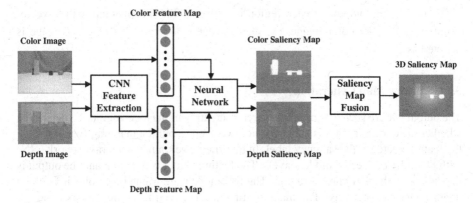

Fig. 1. Framework of proposed visual saliency detection model of 3D image

3.1 Deep Learning Features Extraction

Based the theory of human visual system, the visual attention mechanism contains a hierarchical selection process from the coarsest to finest [23]. Thus, the multi-level image segmentation is employed before feature extraction. Then, the feature extraction is implemented for each region with in the same level. Detailed descriptions are provided as follows.

A. Multi-level Image Segmentation
In this paper, we focus on the depth based 3D image format where each color image is associated with a depth image. For each 3D image, the color image and its associated depth image are decomposed into multi-level non-overlapping regions, respectively. For convenience, we assume the total number of level is L. For each level j, the non-overlapping region sets of color image I_c and depth image I_d are denoted as $A_c^j = \{R_c^{j,i} | i = 1, \ldots, m_j\}$ and $A_d^j = \{R_d^{j,i} | i = 1, \ldots, n_j\}$, respectively. Detailed description of multi-level image segmentation algorithm can be referred in [23].
B. CNN based Feature Extraction
Due to the lack of depth image capturing technology, the amount of ground truth data public available in the 3D saliency detection domain is not very large. Thus, it is hard to training an accuracy CNN model rely on these available datasets. In this stage, the pre-trained AlexNet model is employed to extract the features for both color and depth images. The AlexNet model is trained over the ImageNet dataset [24], which has five convolutional layers and three full-connected layers.

As we know, the saliency of each local region is not only relying on its own characterics, but also influenced by the content of its neighborhood and background (the rest part of the region). Thus, for each level j of depth image, we extract the CNN feature vectors of local region $R_d^{j,k}$, its neighborhood region $H_d^{j,k}$ and background region $B_d^{j,k}$. Detailed description of region segmentation and bounding box determination can be referred in [11, 23]. Each region is resized into a 227×227 square and fed into the

CNN model. The output for each region is with a 12288-dimensional feature vector denoted as $f_d^{j,k}$. For color image, the feature vector of region $R_c^{j,k}$ of color image is denoted as $f_c^{j,s}$.

3.2 Saliency Map Generation

The output feature vector is just a sparse representation of the local region. To determine whether the current region is salient or not, we need to build a mapping function from the feature vector to the saliency label. In this stage, we trained a neural network (NN) with two fully connected hidden layers. The feature vector is the input and the output is the saliency labels of current region. The NN models are trained for color image and depth image, respectively. The mapping function between the saliency label and the feature vector for color and depth image is denoted as $P_c(f_c^{j,i})$ and $P_d(f_d^{j,i})$, respectively. All the pixels belong to the same region share the same saliency labels. Final, the saliency maps of depth image is generated as

$$S_d(x) = \sum_{j=1, x \in R_d^{j,i}}^{L} w_d^j P_d(f_d^{j,i}). \tag{1}$$

The saliency maps of color image is generated as

$$S_c(x) = \sum_{j=1, x \in R_c^{j,i}}^{L} w_c^j P_c(f_c^{j,i}). \tag{2}$$

x is the pixel belongs to the region $f_d^{j,i}$ of depth image and $f_c^{j,i}$ of color image. w_d^j and w_c^j are the weighting factors of depth image and color image, respectively.

3.3 Saliency Map Fusion and Enhancement

Fusing depth saliency map and color saliency map is important for obtaining a accuracy saliency map. After obtaining the saliency maps S_d and S_c, the saliency map of 3D image is generated by a linear fusion approach. The formula is provided as follows.

$$S = w \cdot S_c + (1 - w) \cdot S_d, \tag{3}$$

where w is the parameter to adjust the two components. To further improve the performance, the widely used centre-bias mechanism is also employed to enhance the final saliency map.

4   Experimental Results

4.1   Simulation Setup

To make a fair performance comparison, the computational models including Li's multi-scale features based model [11] (denoted as VSMD), İmamoğlu's wavelet domain based model [25] (denoted as SDLL), Fang's 2D saliency model [9] (denoted as SSDF2D) and 3D saliency model [9] (denoted as SSDF3D) are implemented as benchmark. The VSMD, SDLL and SSDF2D are computation models targeted for 2D images. The SSDF3D model is targeted for 3D images. In our experiment, the number of segmentation level N of our proposed model is set as 15. The parameter w is set as 0.5.

To demonstrate the performance of our proposed 3D visual saliency detection model, we evaluate all the saliency detection models with various datasets. Currently, there are few public available eye-tracking datasets for 3D saliency research. In this paper, we evaluate the saliency detection methods on the two representative datasets, name as NUS3D-Saliency [26] and NCTU-3DFixation [27]. Detailed descriptions of these datasets are provided as follows.

- NUS3D-Saliency dataset (denoted as NUS) has 600 images collected from 80 participants. It involves several 2D and 3D scenes. This dataset provides color stimuli, depth maps, smooth depth maps, 2D and 3D fixation maps.
- NCTU-3DFixation dataset (denoted as NCTU) is consisting of 475 3D images as well as their depth maps. The contents of this dataset are various scenes and mainly came from the existing 3D movies or videos.

4.2   Performance Comparison

To evaluate the performance of the 3D visual saliency detection models, the following three criterions [28] are employed in our experiments for fair comparison.

- Pearson Correlation Coefficient (CC) measures the strength of a linear association between two variables. And it can be used to measure the linear correlation coefficient between the saliency map of an image and the eye-fixation map of the image.
- Earth Mover's Distance (EMD) measures the distance between two probability distributions over a region. Informally, if the distributions are interpreted as two different ways of piling up a certain amount of dirt over the region, the EMD is the minimum cost of turning one pile into the other; where the cost is assumed to be amount of dirt moved times the distance by which it is moved.
- Similarity score (SIM) measures the similarity of the two distributions. A high similarity score indicates the distributions of two maps are quite similar.

These metrics can evaluate the performance of the proposed model. A good saliency model would have a high CC and SIM score, but a low EMD score. Detailed experimental results are provided in Table 1. Our proposed model can achieve better performance than all the 2D saliency models for both the NCTU and NUS datasets as shown in Table 1. For example, the CC, EMD and SIM scores of our proposed 3D model are 0.5225, 2.1547 and 0.4985, respectively. The CC, EMD and SIM scores of VSMD are

586   Q. Zhang et al.

Table 1. Performance of the models for the two datasets in terms of CC, EMD and SIM

Model	NUS			NCTU		
	CC	EMD	SIM	CC	EMD	SIM
VSMD	0.3783	2.8419	0.3812	0.3121	9.106	0.3198
SDLL	0.3397	3.1359	0.3893	0.2678	11.1806	0.321
SSDF2D	0.4430	2.6513	0.4321	0.4531	9.184	0.3951
SSDF3D	0.5033	2.3965	0.4589	**0.5601**	8.3874	0.4356
Proposed	**0.5225**	**2.1547**	**0.4985**	0.4761	**7.2313**	**0.4445**

only 0.3783, 2.8419 and 0.3812. The experimental results show that the performance of saliency prediction model can benefit from fusing color saliency map with depth saliency map.

Fig. 2. From left to right are four images from NUS dataset. From the second row to the last row, the order of the model is SSDF2D model, SDLL model, VSMD model, SSDF3D model, and our proposed model.

The performance comparison between our proposed 3D model and the SSDF3D model on both the NCTU and NUS datasets are also provide in Table 1. It is observed that the CC, EMD, SIM scores of our proposed 3D model is better than those of the SSDF3D model on the NUS dataset. For the NCTU dataset, the CC score of proposed 3D model is less than the SSDF3D model, but the EMD, SIM scores of proposed 3D model are larger than those of SSDF3D model. Experiment results demonstrate that our proposed 3D model have a significantly performance improvement on 3D visual saliency detection. For further illustration, some 3D saliency detection examples among the models are shown in Figs. 2 and 3, where it can be seen that our proposed model can achieve the best performance.

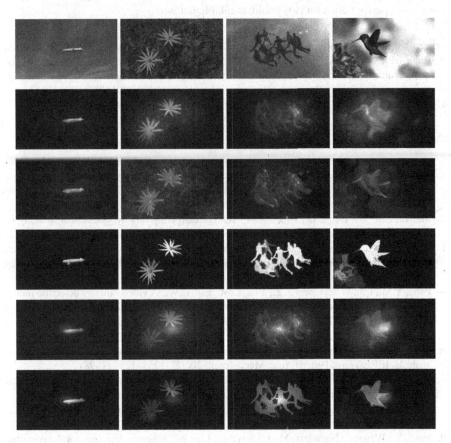

Fig. 3. From left to right are four images from NCTU dataset. From the second row to the last row, the order of the model is SSDF2D model, SDLL model, VSMD model, SSDF3D model, and our proposed model.

5 Conclusion

In this paper, we propose a computation model of 3D image visual saliency based on deep learning features. There are three key factors in our approach. First, we extract deep learning features of color and depth image using multi-scale regions by a CNN model. Second, the saliency map from depth image (or color image) is generated based on deep feature vectors and the saliency labels of regions by a NN model which plays the role as a classifier. Final, we adopt a linear fusion method to combine the color and depth saliency map to generate the final 3D image saliency. The centre bias mechanism is also implemented to enhance the saliency map. The proposed model can achieve the remarkable performance on two public available datasets.

Acknowledgments. This work was supported in part by the National Natural Science Foundation of China under Grants 61501299 and 61373103, in part by the Guangdong Nature Science Foundation under Grant 2016A030310058, in part by the Shenzhen Emerging Industries of the Strategic Basic Research Project under Grants JCYJ20150525092941043 and JCYJ20160226191842793, in part by the Project 2016049 supported by SZU R/D Fund.

References

1. Guo, C., Zhang, L.: A novel multiresolution spatiotemporal saliency detection model and its applications in image and video compression. IEEE Trans. Image Process. **19**(1), 185–198 (2010)
2. Ma, L., Lin, W., Deng, C., Ngan, K.N.: Image retargeting quality assessment: a study of subjective scores and objective metrics. IEEE J. Sel. Top. Sign. Process. **6**(6), 626–639 (2012)
3. Ma, L., Li, S., Zhang, F., Ngan, K.N.: Reduced-reference image quality assessment using reorganized DCT-based image representation. IEEE Trans. Multimedia **13**(4), 824–829 (2011)
4. Fang, Y.M., Lin, W.S., Chen, Z.Z., Tsai, C.M., Lin, C.W.: A video saliency detection model in compressed domain. IEEE Trans. Circuits Syst. Video Technol. **24**(1), 27–38 (2014)
5. Fang, Y.M., Chen, Z.Z., Lin, W.S., Lin, C.W.: Saliency detection in the compressed domain for adaptive image retargeting. IEEE Trans. Image Process. **21**(9), 3888–3901 (2012)
6. Itti, L., Koch, C., Niebur, E.: A model of saliency-based visual attention for rapid scene analysis. IEEE Trans. Pattern Anal. Mach. Intell. **20**(11), 1254–1259 (1998)
7. Song, X., Zhang, J., Han, Y., Jiang, J.: Semi-supervised feature selection via hierarchical regression for web image classification. Multimedia Syst. **22**(1), 41–49 (2016)
8. Zhang, J., Han, Y., Jiang, J.: Tensor rank selection for multimedia analysis. J. Vis. Commun. Image Represent. **30**, 376–392 (2015)
9. Fang, Y., Wang, J., Narwaria, M., Callet, P.L., Lin, W.: Saliency detection for stereoscopic images. IEEE Trans. Image Process. **23**(6), 2625–2636 (2014)
10. Qi, F., Zhao, D., Liu, S., Fan, X.: 3D visual saliency detection model with generated disparity map. Multimedia Tools Appl. (2016). doi:10.1007/s11042-015-3229-6
11. Li, G., Yu, Y.: Visual saliency based on multiscale deep features. In: Proceedings of the IEEE Conference on Computer Vision and Pattern Recognition, pp. 5455–5463 (2015)
12. Bruce, N., Tsotsos, J.: Saliency based on information maximization. In: Advances in Neural Information Processing Systems, pp. 155–162 (2005)

13. Hou, X., Zhang, L.: Saliency detection: a spectral residual approach. In: IEEE Conference on Computer Vision and Pattern Recognition, pp. 1–8 (2007)
14. Goferman, S., Zelnik-Manor, L., Tal, A.: Context-aware saliency detection. IEEE Trans. Pattern Anal. Mach. Intell. **34**(10), 1915–1926 (2012)
15. Yang, J., Yang, M.H.: Top-down visual saliency via joint CRF and dictionary learning. In: IEEE Conference on Computer Vision and Pattern Recognition, pp. 2296–2303 (2012)
16. Kanan, C., Tong, M.H., Zhang, L., Cottrell, G.W.: Sun: Top-down saliency using natural statistics. Visual Cogn. **17**(6–7), 979–1003 (2009)
17. Itti, L., Koch, C.: A saliency-based search mechanism for overt and covert shifts of visual attention. Vision Res. **40**(10), 1489–1506 (2000)
18. Cheng, M., Mitra, N.J., Huang, X., Torr, P.H., Hu, S.: Global contrast based salient region detection. IEEE Trans. Pattern Anal. Mach. Intell. **37**(3), 569–582 (2015)
19. Zhao, R., Ouyang, W., Li, H., Wang, X.: Saliency detection by multi-context deep learning. In: Proceedings of the IEEE Conference on Computer Vision and Pattern Recognition, pp. 1265–1274 (2015)
20. Wang, J., DaSilva, M.P., Callet, P.L., Ricordel, V.: Computational model of stereoscopic 3D visual saliency. IEEE Trans. Image Process. **22**(6), 2151–2165 (2013)
21. Kim, H., Lee, S., Bovik, A.C.: Saliency prediction on stereoscopic videos. IEEE Trans. Image Process. **23**(4), 1476–1490 (2014)
22. Song, H.A., Lee, S.-Y.: Hierarchical representation using NMF. In: Lee, M., Hirose, A., Hou, Z.-G., Kil, R.M. (eds.) ICONIP 2013. LNCS, vol. 8226, pp. 466–473. Springer, Heidelberg (2013). doi:10.1007/978-3-642-42054-2_58
23. Jiang, H., Wang, J., Yuan, Z., Wu, Y., Zheng, N., Li, S.: Salient object detection: a discriminative regional feature integration approach. In: Proceedings of the IEEE Conference on Computer Vision and Pattern Recognition, pp. 2083–2090 (2013)
24. Deng, J., Dong, W., Socher, R., Li, L.J., Li, K., Li, F.: ImageNet: a large-scale hierarchical image database. In: IEEE Conference on Computer Vision and Pattern Recognition, pp. 248–255 (2009)
25. İmamoğlu, N., Lin, W., Fang, Y.: A saliency detection model using low-level features based on wavelet transform. IEEE Trans. Multimedia **15**(1), 96–105 (2013)
26. Lang, C., Nguyen, T.V., Katti, H., Yadati, K., Kankanhalli, M., Yan, S.: Depth matters: influence of depth cues on visual saliency. In: Fitzgibbon, A., Lazebnik, S., Perona, P., Sato, Y., Schmid, C. (eds.) ECCV 2012, Part II. LNCS, vol. 7573, pp. 101–115. Springer, Heidelberg (2012). doi:10.1007/978-3-642-33709-3_8
27. Ma, C.Y., Hang, H.M.: Learning-based saliency model with depth information. J. Vision **15**(6), 19 (2015)
28. Judd, T., Durand, F., Torralba, A.: A benchmark of computational models of saliency to predict human fixations. Massachusetts Inst. Technol., MA, USA, Computer Science and Artificial Intelligence Lab (CSAIL), Technical rep. MIT-CSAIL-TR-2012–001 (2012)

No-Reference Quality Assessment
of Camera-Captured Distortion Images

Lijuan Tang[1,2]([✉]), Leida Li[1], Ke Gu[3], Jiansheng Qian[1],
and Jianying Zhang[1]

[1] School of Information and Electrical Engineering,
China University of Mining and Technology, Xuzhou, China
nttlj@163.com
[2] School of Information and Electrical Engineering,
Jiangsu Vocational College of Business, Nantong, China
[3] Computer Science and Engineering, Nanyang Technological University,
Singapore, Singapore

Abstract. In this paper we address the problem of quality assessment of camera images using three types of features. The first type of features measures the naturalness of an image, inspired by a recent finding that there exists high correlation between structural degradation and free energy entropy on natural scene images and this regulation will be gradually devastated as more distortions are introduced. The second type of features comes from an observation that a broad spectrum of statistics of distorted images can be caught by the generalized Gaussian distribution (GGD) according to natural scene statistics (NSS). These two groups of features are both based on NSS regulations, but they come from the considerations of local auto-regression and global histogram, respectively. The third type of features estimates the local sharpness by computing log-energies in the discrete wavelet transform domain. Finally our quality metric is achieved via an SVR-based machine learning tool and its performance is proved to be statistically better than state-of-the-art competitors on the CID2013 database, which is dedicated to the quality assessment of camera-captured images.

Keywords: Quality assessment · Camera images · No-reference · Natural scene statistics · Local sharpness · Free energy theory · Structural degradation model

1 Introduction

With the soaring development of mobile devices and network, an enormous amount of images are being presented to users every moment. It is challenging to evaluate and control the quality of digital photographs. At the same time, a supreme effort is still made by camera manufacturers to improve the quality of photography. As thus, it is in an urgent pursuit of finding ways to automatically predict the perceptual quality of camera images.

In the past few years, as for the issue of image quality assessment (IQA), many objective metrics of the ability to faithfully evaluate the quality of distorted images have been developed. If the distortion-free reference image that a distorted image can

© Springer International Publishing AG 2016
E. Chen et al. (Eds.): PCM 2016, Part II, LNCS 9917, pp. 590–599, 2016.
DOI: 10.1007/978-3-319-48896-7_58

be compared with is available, the metric is called full-reference (FR) IQA [1]. But in most cases only the distorted image is available, this type of IQA models are called no-reference (NR) IQA. Furthermore, according to the requirement of prior knowledge of the images or their distortions, current NR-IQA algorithms can also be further classified into two categories, namely general-purpose metrics and distortion-specific metrics. Typical distortion-specific blind quality measures are devoted to blockiness [2], noise [3], tone mapping [4], retargeting [5], enhancement [6–8], sharpness/ blurriness [9–15], etc. In recent years, general-purpose NR-IQA metrics have been an active research field [16–24].

Although the aforementioned metrics perform well on the popular databases such as the LIVE [25], they do not perform as well on real photographs which are subjected to many different distortion sources and types, because these image quality metrics have been based on the assumption that an image contains single or simulated distortions which are not representative of what one encounters in practical real scenarios [26]. Unlike most distortions present in the popular databases, camera images contain more practical distortions. The proposed blind quality index for camera images (BQIC) has acquired substantially high performance. It is the only metric with the correlation coefficient beyond 80% in both linear and monotonic performance indices.

The paper is structured as follows. In Sect. 2, we present the details of the BQIC algorithm. Section 3 compares performance measures of our BQIC with state-of-the art blind quality metrics on the CID2013 database [27], which is dedicated to the IQA of camera images. Conclusions and future work are provided in Sect. 4.

2   No-Reference Quality Metric of Camera-Captured Distortion Images

Selecting appropriate features plays an important part in IQA problems. The features of the proposed metric consist of three parts. The flowchart of the proposed NR-IQA metric is shown in Fig. 1.

The first type of features is extracted based on the free-energy principle, which is recently found in brain theory and neuroscience [21], and structural degradation measurement via simple convolutions and nonlinear regression [28]. The free-energy principle operates under the assumption that there always exists a difference between an input genuine visual signal and its processed one by human brain. Human perceptual process is manipulated by an internal generative model, which can infer predictions of the input visual signal and avoid the residual uncertainty information. On this basis, the psychovisual quality of a scene is defined by both the scene itself and the output of the internal generative model. It differs from most traditional signal decomposition based methods.

To facilitate operation, we assume that the internal generative model for visual perception is parametric, which infers perceived scenes by adjusting the parameter vector. In this paper we choose the linear auto-regression (AR) model as the internal generative model, for its ability to approximate a wide range of natural scenes by varying its parameters and describe the local self-similarity of the image [15, 22, 24].

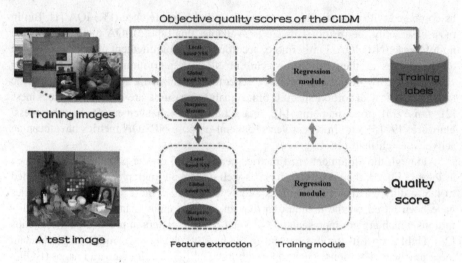

Fig. 1. The framework of the proposed NR-IQA metric.

The AR model is defined as:

$$y_n = \varphi^k(y_n)\theta + \epsilon_n \tag{1}$$

where y_n is a pixel of the distorted image, $\varphi^k(y_n)$ is a row-vector consisting of k nearest neighbors of y_n, $\theta = (\theta_1, \theta_2, ..., \theta_k)^T$ is a vector of AR coefficients, and ϵ_n is the error term. Then, the predicted version of the input distorted visual signal I can be estimated by $\varphi^k(y_n)\,\theta_{opt}$, where θ_{opt} is the optimal estimate of AR parameters for y_n based on the least square method.

It was found that low-pass filtered versions of the distorted images have different degrees of spatial frequency decrease, which inspires the design of the reduced-reference structural degradation model (SDM) [28]. We modify the classical SSIM [30], and define the structural degradation information to be:

$$S(I) = E\left(\frac{\sigma_{(\mu_I \overline{\mu_I})} + C}{\sigma_{(\overline{\mu_I})}\sigma_{(\mu_I)} + C}\right) \tag{2}$$

where μ_I represents the mean intensity, $\sigma_{(\mu_I \overline{\mu_I})}$ denotes the local covariance as the definition in SSIM [30]; E ($\bullet$) is a direct average pooling; C is a small constant to avoid instability when denominator is very close to zero. Since different sizes of Gaussian weighting functions introduce different amounts of information, this paper picks three pairs of (K, L) as (1, 1), (3, 3) and (5, 5). An approximate linear relationship between the structural degradation information and the free energy feature of original image can be seen from the scatter plots in Fig. 2, which are obtained based on thirty images randomly selected from Berkeley database [31]. The linear dependence feature provides possibility to describe distorted image without primitive image.

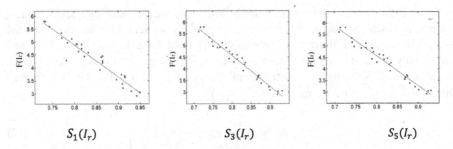

$$S_1(I_r) \qquad\qquad S_3(I_r) \qquad\qquad S_5(I_r)$$

Fig. 2. Scatter plots of the structural degradation information $S_s(I_r)$ ($s = \{1, 3, 5\}$) vs. the free energy feature $F(I_r)$ on thirty images in the Berkeley database [31]. The straight lines are fitted with the least square method.

We define the linear regression model as follows:

$$F(I_r) = \alpha \cdot S(I_r) + \beta \tag{3}$$

where I_r is the original image, α and β are gained by the least square algorithm. We then reduce the dependence of original references by using $FS_I = F(I_d) - \{\alpha \cdot S(I_d) + \beta)\}$ and use it as the feature, where I_d denotes the distorted image.

Note that FS_I values of high-quality images are quite near to zero, and conversely they will be far from zero when distortions are progressively intensive. Finally, we supplement the free energy entropy as the final feature of group one.

The second type of features comes from a classical NSS based model [18, 20]. Runderman observed that the normalized luminance value of natural images without distortions appears Gaussian characteristic [32], and the distribution is broken when the images suffer distortions. However, a wider spectrum of statistics of distorted images can be effectively caught by the generalized Gaussian distribution (GGD). The probability density function of GGD defined as following:

$$f(x; \mu, \alpha, \beta) = \frac{\alpha}{2\beta\gamma\left(\frac{1}{\alpha}\right)} exp\left(-\left(\frac{|x - \mu|}{\beta}\right)^{\alpha}\right) \quad \alpha > 0 \tag{4}$$

where μ is the mean, α is the shape parameter that controls the 'shape' of the distribution:

$$\beta = \sigma\sqrt{\frac{\gamma\left(\frac{1}{\alpha}\right)}{\gamma\left(\frac{3}{\alpha}\right)}} \tag{5}$$

and the gamma function $\gamma(\cdot)$ is given by:

$$\gamma(z) = \int_0^{\infty} t^{z-1}e^{-t}dt \tag{6}$$

where σ is the standard deviation. In this paper, we utilize the mean subtracted contrast normalized (MSCN) coefficients by computing locally normalized luminance via local mean subtraction and divisive normalization [18], for it has a decorrelating effect. And we employ the GGD with zero mean to fit the MSCN, because MSCN is global-based NSS and MSCN coefficients distributions are symmetric [16]. The GGD with zero mean is defined as following:

$$f(x; \alpha, \beta) = \frac{\alpha}{2\beta\gamma\left(\frac{1}{\alpha}\right)} exp\left(-\left(\frac{|x|}{\beta}\right)^\alpha\right)$$ (7)

For each image, two pairs of parameters (α, σ^2) are computed from a GGD fit of the MSCN coefficients. One pair is from the original scale, and another is at the reduced resolution via a low-pass filtering by a down sampling with the factor of 2. These form the second group of four features.

Sharpness plays an important role in image quality assessment. The third type of features is the modified patch-based image sharpness measure [10]. First, using Cohen-Daubechies-Feauveau filters [33] to decompose the input image signal into discrete wavelet transform (DWT) subbands only with one level. Then computing the Log-energy of each subband of discrete wavelet transform (DWT) as follows [10]:

$$E_{xy} = log_{10}(1 + \frac{1}{M}\sum_{i,j} S_{XY}^2(i,j))$$ (8)

where S_{XY} is either S_{HH}, S_{HL} or S_{LH}, and S_{LL} is not used, and M is the number of DWT coefficients in the subband. The addition of one is used to avoid negative values of E_{XY}. In [6], the authors measured the total log-energy at each level via

$$E_n = (1 - \alpha)\frac{E_{LHn} + E_{HLn}}{2} + \alpha E_{HHn}$$ (9)

where the parameter α is 0.8. But according to [34], the authors used predictable sinusoidal, triangular target motions and randomized step-ramp stimuli to compare smooth pursuit in the horizontal and vertical planes, and confirmed that most normal subjects show higher gain values during horizontal than during vertical tracking. Grönqvist [35] also observed that vertical tracking was inferior to horizontal tracking and the proportion of smooth pursuit increased with age. So horizontal tracking and vertical tracking are asymmetry. Thorough experiments are performed to give the result that LH, HL and HH appears auto-adaptive non-linear relationship. Hence we separately use E_{LHn}, E_{HLn} and E_{HHn} as features, instead of directly combining them via Eq. (9). Finally, we use the above algorithm in a block-based way to obtain the sharpness index across the entire image. The block-based procedure is similar to that in [10]. A collection of local sharpness values are computed using the DWT coefficients associated to each 16×16 block of the image, and the index is computed by taking the root mean square of the 1% largest values of the block sharpness indices.

All these extracted features are effective to describe the naturalness and sharpness of real photographs which are subjected to many different distortion sources and types.

After feature extraction, we need to find a proper way that can map the feature space to subjective MOS, and utilize it to produce objective quality scores. In order to make a fair comparison with other NR-IQA methods, we use a support vector regression (SVR) [36] to generate a proper mapping that is learnt from the feature score to human visual system. SVR has been widely used in the IQA field [18]. Here the SVR with a radial basis function (RBF) is adopted by using the LIBSVM package [36].

3 Experimental Results

In this section, the CID2013 database [27] is used as testing bed for performance evaluation and comparison. The CID2013 database consists of 6 image sets with 36 scenarios and the associated 474 distorted images captured by 79 distinct digital cameras. The images in CID2013 do not have reference images because they were captured by real cameras, which make FR- and RR-IQA methods not workable. As for our training-based BQIC algorithm, we use a similar method to what is used in [37]. To be specific, we divide 474 images into 36 subsets based on the scenario of the image. The predicted rating for each image is determined by training an SVR on the other 35 subsets via a leave-one-out cross-validation methodology [37]. We will test the performance of the proposed blind BQIC metric from two aspects. The first is to demonstrate the effectiveness of our BQIC method compared to state-of-the-art general-purpose NR-IQA metrics. The second is to analyze and compare the effectiveness of our BQIC method compared to state-of-the-art distortion-specific NR-IQA metrics. In this paper we follow the video quality experts group (VQEG)'s suggestion and employ a five-parameter nonlinear fitting function to map objective quality scores to subjective human ratings [38]. Then, four performance measures, including SRCC, KRCC, PLCC and RMSE, are exploited.

Recently, extensive general-purpose NR-IQA metrics have been proposed to evaluate the quality of distorted images without knowing the distortion types. Later we will demonstrate and compare the performance of the proposed model with the top general-purpose NR-IQA approaches, including BLIINDS-II [17], BRISQUE [18], SISBLIM [19], NFERM [22], and IL-NIQE [29]. A logistic nonlinear function is used before calculating PLCC, KRCC, PLCC and RMSE. Table 1 summarizes the performance results on the CID2013 database. One can see from Table 1 that the proposed BQIC metric has achieved the highest PLCC, SRCC and KRCC values as well as the smallest RMSE value. The proposed BQIC model correlates highly with human visual perception to image distortions. We also show the scatter plots of the subjective scores versus the predicted scores using different metrics in Fig. 3. A good metric is expected to produce scatter points that are closed to the fitted curve. It can be easily found from Fig. 3 that the proposed metric produces the best fitting results on the CID2013 database.

Sharpness is one of the most important factors in the problem of quality assessment of camera images. In this section, we will demonstrate and compare the performance of the proposed model with 5 popular blind sharpness algorithms BIBLE [11], S_3 [14], FISH [10], $FISH_{bb}$ [10], and ARISM [15]. To estimate the performance of the proposed BQIC metric and aforementioned distortion-specific blind algorithms, experiments are conducted on the CID2013 database. Table 2 lists the performance of the

Table 1. Comparison of our BQIC metric and state-of-the-art general-purpose NR-IQA methods on CID2013. We bold the best performed NR IQA algorithm.

CID2013	PLCC	SRCC	KRCC	RMSE
BLIINDS-II	0.6393	0.6346	0.4539	17.4088
BRISQUE	0.7810	0.7844	0.5902	14.1402
SISBLIM	0.7010	0.6533	0.4762	16.0947
NFERM	0.7933	0.7880	0.5943	13.7833
IL-NIQE	0.4274	0.3065	0.2101	20.4687
BQIC	**0.8285**	**0.8207**	**0.6291**	**12.6759**

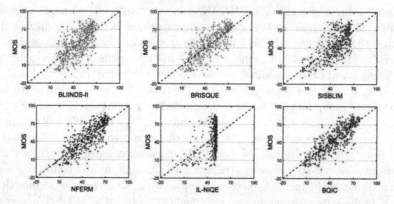

Fig. 3. Scatter plots of objective scores generated by BLIINDS-II, BRISQUE, SISBLIM, NFERM, IL-NIQE and our proposed BQIC metric versus subjective scores reported by CID2013 databases after nonlinear mapping.

comparison methods and Fig. 4 shows the scatter plots between the predicted scores and the corresponding MOSs on the CID2013 database, where a point denotes one image. It can be found that the proposed algorithm not only competes with these specific-distortion metrics, but also outperforms it.

Table 2. Comparison of our BQIC metric and state-of-the-art distortion-specific blind algorithms on CID2013. We bold the best performed NR IQA model.

CID2013	PLCC	SRCC	KRCC	RMSE
BIBLE	0.6335	0.6309	0.4447	17.4616
S$_3$	0.3277	0.2936	0.2019	21.3902
FISH	0.7038	0.6822	0.4956	16.0827
FISH$_{bb}$	0.7553	0.7383	0.5461	14.8375
ARISM	0.4877	0.4408	0.3090	19.7651
BQIC	**0.8285**	**0.8207**	**0.6291**	**12.6795**

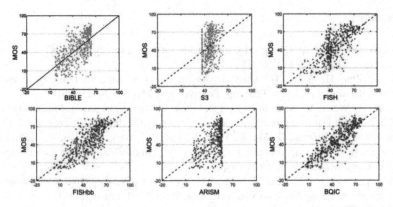

Fig. 4. Scatter plots of objective scores generated by BIBLE, S_3, FISH and FISH$_{bb}$, ARISM and our proposed metric BQIC versus subjective scores reported by CID2013 databases after nonlinear mapping.

4 Conclusion

With the development of networked hand-held devices, a large amount of visual data is presented to users. Many efforts have been made to ensure the end consumers are presented with a satisfactory quality of experience (QoE). Therefore, assessment of camera-captured images is a significant and meaningful topic in scientific research and application development of digital image processing. However, it is struggle to handle the images with many concurrent distortion types for current blind quality metrics. Effective objective quality metrics are expected.

In this paper we have put forward a blind quality index for camera images with natural scene statistics and patch-based sharpness assessment. A comparison of our BQIC with state-of-the-art general-purpose NR-IQA methods and popular blind distortion-specific measures is conducted on CID2013 database. The experiment results have proved the superior performance of the proposed blind quality measure on the CID2013 database. Besides the substantially high prediction accuracy, it is worthy to emphasize two points below. First, experimental results prove the superiority of our proposed method on CID2013 over popular NR-IQA models and blind sharpness measures. Second, the proposed BQIC needs merely 11 features, far less than the majority of general-purpose train-based NR-IQA metrics.

Acknowledgment. This work is supported in part by the National Science Foundation of China (61379143), the Fundamental Research Funds for the Central Universities (2015QNA66, 2015XKMS032) and Science and Technology Planning Project of Nantong (BK2014022).

References

1. Lin, W., Kuo, C.-C.J.: Perceptual visual quality metrics: a survey. J. Vis. Commun. Image Represent. **22**(4), 297–312 (2011)
2. Li, L., Zhu, H., Yang, G., Qian, J.: Referenceless measure of blocking artifacts by Tchebichef kernel analysis. IEEE Sig. Process. Lett. **21**(1), 122–125 (2014)
3. Zoran, D., Weiss, Y.: Scale invariance and noise in natural images. In: Proceedings of the IEEE International Conference on Computer Vision, pp. 2209–2216, September 2009
4. Gu, K., Wang, S., Zhai, G., Ma, S., Yang, X., Lin, W., Zhang, W., Gao, W.: Blind quality assessment of tone-mapped images via analysis of information, naturalness and structure. IEEE Trans. Multimedia (2016, to appear)
5. Fang, Y., Zeng, K., Wang, Z., Lin, W., Fang, Z., Lin, C.-W.: Objective quality assessment for image retargeting based on structural similarity. IEEE J. Emerg. Sel. T. Circ. Syst. **4**(1), 95–105 (2014)
6. Wang, S., Gu, K., Ma, S., Lin, W., Liu, X., Gao, W.: Guided image contrast enhancement based on retrieved images in cloud. IEEE Trans. Multimedia **18**(2), 219–232 (2016)
7. Gu, K., Zhai, G., Yang, X., Zhang, W., Chen, C.W.: Automatic contrast enhancement technology with saliency preservation. IEEE Trans. Circ. Syst. Video Technol. **25**(9), 1480–1494 (2015)
8. Gu, K., Zhai, G., Lin, W., Liu, M.: The analysis of image contrast: from quality assessment to automatic enhancement. IEEE Trans. Cybern. **46**(1), 284–297 (2016)
9. Marziliano, P., Dufaux, F., Winkler, S., Ebrahimi, T.: Perceptual blur and ringing metrics: application to JPEG2000. Sig. Process. Image Commun. **19**(2), 163–172 (2004)
10. Vu, P.V., Chandler, D.M.: A fast wavelet-based algorithm for global and local image sharpness estimation. IEEE Sig. Process. Lett. **19**(7), 423–426 (2012)
11. Li, L., Lin, W., Wang, X., Yang, G., Bahrami, K., Kot, A.C.: No reference image blur assessment based on discrete orthogonal moments. IEEE Trans. Cybern. **46**(1), 39–50 (2016)
12. Ferzli, R., Karam, L.J.: A no-reference objective image sharpness metric based on the notion of just noticeable blur (JNB). IEEE Trans. Image Process. **18**(4), 717–728 (2009)
13. Narvekar, N.D., Karam, L.J.: A no-reference image blur metric based on the cumulative probability of blur detection (CPBD). IEEE Trans. Image Process. **20**(9), 2678–2683 (2011)
14. Vu, C.T., Phan, T.D., Chandler, D.M.: S3: a spectral and spatial measure of local perceived sharpness in natural images. IEEE Trans. Image Process. **21**(3), 934–945 (2012)
15. Gu, K., Zhai, G., Lin, W., Yang, X., Zhang, W.: No-reference image sharpness assessment in autoregressive parameter space. IEEE Trans. Image Process. **24**(10), 3218–3231 (2015)
16. Mittal, A., Soundararajan, R., Bovik, A.C.: Making a completely blind Image quality analyzer. IEEE Sig. Process. Lett. **20**(3), 209–212 (2013)
17. Saad, M.A., Bovik, A.C.: Blind image quality assessment: a natural scene statistics approach in the DCT domain. IEEE Trans. Image Process. **21**(8), 3339–3352 (2012)
18. Mittal, A., Moorthy, A.K., Bovik, A.C.: No-reference image quality assessment in the spatial domain. IEEE Trans. Image Process. **21**(12), 4695–4708 (2012)
19. Gu, K., Zhai, G., Yang, X., Zhang, W.: Hybrid no-reference quality metric for singly and multiply distorted images. IEEE Trans. Broadcast. **60**(3), 555–567 (2014)
20. Moorthy, A.K., Bovik, A.C.: Blind image quality assessment: from natural scene statistics to perceptual quality. IEEE Trans. Image Process. **20**(12), 3350–3364 (2011)
21. Zhai, G., Wu, X., Yang, X., Lin, W., Zhang, W.: A psychovisual quality metric in free-energy principle. IEEE Trans. Image Process. **21**(1), 41–52 (2012)

22. Gu, K., Zhai, G., Yang, X., Zhang, W.: Using free energy principle for blind image quality assessment. IEEE Trans. Multimedia **17**(1), 50–63 (2015)
23. Fang, Y., Ma, K., Wang, Z., Lin, W., Fang, Z., Zhai, G.: No-reference quality assessment of contrast-distorted images based on natural scene statistics. IEEE Sig. Process. Lett. **22**(7), 838–842 (2015)
24. Gu, K., Zhai, G., Lin, W., Yang, X., Zhang, W.: Learning a blind quality evaluation engine of screen content images. Neurocomputing **196**, 140–149 (2016)
25. Sheikh, H.R., Wang, Z., Cormack, L., Bovik, A.C.: LIVE image quality assessment database release 2. http://live.ece.utexas.edu/research/quality
26. Saad, M.A., Corriveau, P., Jaladi, R.: Objective consumer device photo quality evaluation. IEEE Sig. Process. Lett. **22**(10), 1516–1520 (2015)
27. Virtanen, T., Nuutinen, M., Vaahteranoksa, M., Oittinen, P., Hakkinen, J.: CID2013: a database for evaluating no-reference image quality assessment algorithms. IEEE Trans. Image Process. **24**(1), 390–402 (2015)
28. Gu, K., Zhai, G., Yang, X., Zhang, W.: A new reduced-reference image quality assessment using structural degradation model. In: Proceedings of the IEEE International Symposium Circuits and System, pp. 1095–1098, May 2013
29. Zhang, L., Zhang, L., Bovik, A.C.: A feature-enriched completely blind image quality evaluator. IEEE Trans. Image Process. **24**(8), 2579–2591 (2015)
30. Wang, Z., Bovik, A.C., Sheikh, H.R., Simoncelli, E.P.: Image quality assessment: from error visibility to structural similarity. IEEE Trans. Image Process. **13**(4), 600–612 (2004)
31. Martin, D., Fowlkes, C., Tal, D., Malik, J.: A database of human segmented natural images and its application to evaluating segmentation algorithms and measuring ecological statistics. In: Proceedings of the IEEE International Conference on Computer Vision, pp. 416–423 (2001)
32. Ruderman, D.L.: The statistics of natural images. Netw. Comput. Neural Syst. **5**(4), 517–548 (1994)
33. Cohen, A., Daubechies, I., Feauveau, J.-C.: Biorthogonal bases of compactly supported wavelets. Commun. Pure Appl. Math. **45**(5), 485–560 (1992)
34. Rottach, K.G., et al.: Comparison of horizontal, vertical and diagonal smooth pursuit eye movements in normal human subjects. Vis. Res. **36**(14), 2189–2195 (1996)
35. Grönqvist, H., Gredeback, G., Hofsten, C.V.: Developmental asymmetries between horizontal and vertical tracking. Vis. Res. **46**(11), 1754–1761 (2006)
36. Chang, C.-C., Lin, C.-J.: LIBSVM: a library for support vector machines. ACM Trans. Intell. Syst. Technol. **2**(3), 27 (2011)
37. Kee, E., Farid, H.: A perceptual metric for photo retouching. Proc. Nat. Acad. Sci. U.S.A. **108**(50), 19907–19912 (2011)
38. VQEG: Final report from the video quality experts group on the validation of objective models of video quality assessment, March 2000. http://www.vqeg.org/

GIP: Generic Image Prior for No Reference Image Quality Assessment

Qingbo Wu[1]([✉]), Hongliang Li[1], and King N. Ngan[1,2]

[1] University of Electronic Science and Technology of China, Chengdu 611731, China
{qbwu,hlli}@uestc.edu.cn, knngan@ee.cuhk.edu.hk
[2] Chinese University of Hong Kong, ShaTin, Hong Kong

Abstract. No reference image quality assessment (NR-IQA) has attracted great attention due to the increasing demand in developing perceptually friendly applications. The crucial challenge of this task is how to accurately measure the naturalness of an image. In this paper, we propose a novel parametric image representation which is derived from the generic image prior (GIP). More specifically, we utilize the classic fields of experts model to capture the prior distribution of an image with respect to a random field, which is learned from a great deal of natural images. Then, the parameters in modeling this prior distribution are used as the quality-relevant image feature, which is represented by a simple two-dimension vector. Experimental results show that the proposed method achieves competitive quality prediction accuracy in comparison with the state-of-the-art NR-IQA algorithms at the expense of much less memory usage and computational complexity.

Keywords: Generic image prior · No reference image quality assessment · Human perception

1 Introduction

No reference image quality assessment (NR-IQA) aims to estimate the perceptual quality of a test image without accessing to its reference version. Due to the high demand in evaluating and improving the experience of user experience, NR-IQA has attracted a great deal of attentions in the past few years [18]. To adapt to various real-world applications under different platforms, a NR-IQA metric is expected to accurately estimate the image quality at the lowest overhead in terms of memory and computations. Therefore, it is highly desired to develop compact image representation for balancing the quality prediction accuracy against the computational cost.

Recently, the research on NR-IQA has made significant process [4,5,9,11, 12,15,23,24]. By incorporating the quality-aware features into a machine learning framework, many existing algorithms are reported to deliver state-of-the-art performance. An interesting development in this process is the ever-growing dimension of the image feature, where a higher dimensional feature space is usually believed to be beneficial for achieving good classification or regression

© Springer International Publishing AG 2016
E. Chen et al. (Eds.): PCM 2016, Part II, LNCS 9917, pp. 600–608, 2016.
DOI: 10.1007/978-3-319-48896-7_59

performance [1,2,6]. In [9,11,12,15], only tens of statistical indexes are extracted from the transform coefficients on wavelet, DCT and normalized spatial domains. Then, the image feature dimension increases to thousands in [10,21]. By means of unsupervised learning, Ye *et al.* [24] proposed a state-of-the-art NR-IQA method, whose feature dimension is up to twenty thousand. Although a better prediction performance is achieved by extracting richer image information, the extremely increased memorial and computational cost impede their application in many platforms with limited computation resources.

In this paper, we aim to propose a compact image representation which could deliver good prediction performance with limited storage and computation resources. Unlike conventional natural scene statistics [9,11,12,15] which are derived from handcrafted transform basis, we utilize the unsupervised learning method in [14] to train a set of filters whose responses on the natural images present regular student t-distribution [19]. Then, two parameters in modeling the raw distribution of the responses on these learned filters are used as the natural scene statistics. Except for the statistics on the real-value filter response, a statistical index derived from the response on specific local binary pattern [22] is also included in our image representation, which builds a three dimension feature referred to as generic image prior (GIP). Finally, by means of the support vector regression (SVR) [16], we can map the GIP feature to a quantitative image quality score. Experimental results on the popular IQA database – LIVE II [17] demonstrate the effectiveness and high-efficiency of the proposed NR-IQA method.

2   Proposed Method

Accurately measuring the naturalness of an image is crucial for the NR-IQA task. Inspired by the natural scene statistics study in [14], we employ the unsupervised learning method to train a set of filters from a large number of natural images, which contain inherent prior information in measuring the naturalness. Let $\mathbf{x}$ denote the whole input image and $\mathbf{x}_{(k)}$ denote the kth cropped patches from $\mathbf{x}$. Let J_i and α_i denote the ith linear filter and model parameter to be learned. Then, the natural image prior $p(\cdot)$ can be presented as the full product of t-distribution model [20], i.e.,

$$p(x;\Theta) = \frac{1}{Z(\Theta)} \prod_{k=1}^{K} \prod_{i=1}^{N} \phi_i(J_i^T x_{(k)}; \alpha_i) \tag{1}$$

where $\Theta = \{\theta_1, \cdots, \theta_N\}$ and $\theta_i = \{\alpha_i, J_i\}$. The experts ϕ_i can be given by

$$\phi_i(J_i^T x_{(k)}; \alpha_i) = \left(1 + \frac{1}{2}(J_i^T x)^2\right)^{-\alpha_i} \tag{2}$$

where the linear filters J_i and parameters α_i are learned from a set of generic natural images by maximizing its likelihood. It should be noted that there is no any annotation information needed in this training process. Following the configurations in [14], we train the image filers in two sizes, i.e., 3×3 and 5×5. All training images are collected from the Berkeley database [8].

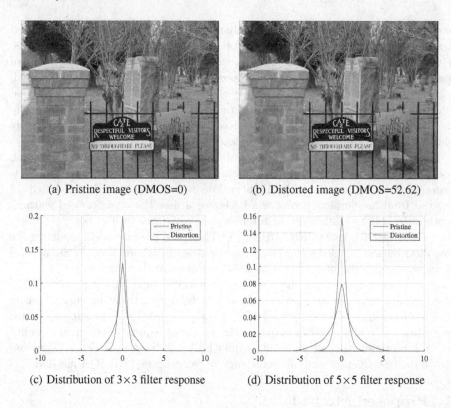

(a) Pristine image (DMOS=0)   (b) Distorted image (DMOS=52.62)

(c) Distribution of 3×3 filter response   (d) Distribution of 5×5 filter response

Fig. 1. The comparison of distributions between the pristine image and its JP2K version.

After training the linear filters and parameters set, we can analyze the statistical property of an image from its response on the learned filters. More specifically, the image response is derived from the gradient of the log-prior, i.e.,

$$\nabla_x \log p(x) = \sum_{i=1}^{N} J_i^- * \psi_i(J_i * x) \tag{3}$$

where $*$ denotes the convolution operation and J_i^- denotes the mirror filter of J_i. The function ψ_i represents the partial differential operator, i.e.,

$$\psi_i(y) = \frac{\partial \log \phi_i(y; \alpha_i)}{\partial y} \tag{4}$$

To highlight the discriminating power of the learned naturalness-aware filters, the filter responses comparison between a pristine image and its distorted version is illustrated in Fig. 1. From the observation in Figs. 1 (c) and (d), it can be seen that the filter response of a natural image exhibits clear non-gaussian and heavy tailed distribution under different filter sizes. When the distortion is present, the distribution of the filter response would become more dispersed and deviate from the image with pristine quality. In order to quantify this variation, we model the filter response of an image with a standard t-distribution, whose probability density function (PDF) is given by,

$$f(t|n) = c(1 + \frac{t^2}{n})^{-(n+1)/2} \tag{5}$$

where c is a constant and $t = \nabla_x \log p(x)$. n is the degree of freedom of a standard t-distribution.

In this paper, the maximum likelihood estimation (MLE) [13] is utilized to solve the parameter n, whose PDF is most likely to approximate the raw density of t. Let $\mathcal{L}(n|t)$ denote the likelihood function, which is defined by reversing the roles of the observed data t and the parameter n in $f(t|n)$, i.e.,

$$\mathcal{L}(n|t) = f(t|n) \tag{6}$$

For computational convenience, the likelihood function is usually converted to its logarithm version, i.e., $\ln \mathcal{L}(n|t)$. Then, the MLE is formulated as

$$\hat{n} = \arg \max_{n \subset \Omega} \ln \mathcal{L}(n|t) \tag{7}$$

where Ω is the parameter set. The Quasi-Newton algorithm [3] is employed to solve the optimization problem in (7).

Since two sizes of filters (i.e., 3×3 and 5×5) are learned in our simulation, we compute two distribution parameters $\hat{n}_{3\times3}$ and $\hat{n}_{5\times5}$ to capture the multi-scale natural scene statistics. Besides the real-value filter responses derived from the original image intensities, we also compute a local pattern statistical index (*LPSI*) [22] which captures the response on specific local binary pattern. By combing these three statistical indexes, we can obtain our GIP feature s, i.e.,

$$s = [\hat{n}_{3\times3}, \hat{n}_{5\times5}, LPSI] \tag{8}$$

In order to map the proposed GIP feature s to a perceptual quality score Q, the SVR is used to train the image quality regression function $R(s)$, i.e.,

$$R(s) = \sum_{k=1}^{K} \alpha_k \mathbb{K}(s, \hat{s}_k) + \beta \tag{9}$$

where α_k and β denote the SVR parameters to be learned from the training samples. $\hat{s}_k$ is the GIP feature of the kth support vector. $\mathbb{K}(\cdot, \cdot)$ is the kernel function, which is used to measure the similarity of two samples. Similar with previous works [9,11,12], the radial basis function kernel is used here, i.e.,

$$\mathbb{K}(s, \hat{s}_k) = \exp(-\gamma \|s - \hat{s}_k\|^2) \tag{10}$$

where γ is the custom parameter which is determined by cross validation.

3 Experimental Results

To verify the performance of the proposed NR-IQA method, we implement the image quality estimation on the LIVE II database [17], which is consist of 29 pristine images and 779 distorted images across 5 distortion types (i.e., JP2K, JPEG, WN, Blur and FF). In our simulation, two metrics are employed to evaluate the performance of the proposed method, which include the Pearson's linear correlation coefficient (LCC) and Spearman's rank ordered correlation coefficient (SROCC). For both metrics, a value which is more close to 1 indicates a better performance in predicting the human perception.

Following the criterion in [9, 11, 15], we randomly divide the LIVE II database into two non-overlap subsets, where the 80% reference images and their associated distorted versions are used to construct the training set, and the left 20% images are used for testing. The splitting procedure is repeated 1000 times and the median LCC and SROCC are reported for evaluating the final performance. Seven state-of-the-art NR-IQA algorithms are included in this comparison, i.e., BIQI [12], DIIVINE [11], BLIINDS-II [15], BRISQUE [9], NIQE [10], CORNIA [25] and TCLT [21].

Figure 2 first shows the scatter plot of predicted image quality via our GIP method against the DMOS on LIVE II database. It is clear that the predicted image quality presents nearly linear relationship with DMOS, which indicates that the proposed objective metric is highly consistent with the subjective perception in terms of the image quality. The median LCC and SROCC results are listed in Tables 1 and 2, respectively. For clarity, the best metric in each column is highlighted by boldface. Although a very compact image representation, which only includes three indexes, is used to capture the perceptual quality, the proposed GIP method delivers highly competitive performance in comparison with the state-of-the-art NR-IQA algorithms.

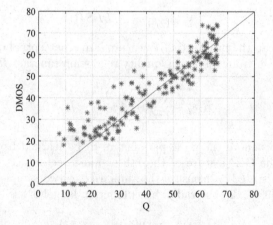

Fig. 2. The scatter plot of the predicted image quality Q versus the ground-truth human opinion scores DMOS on LIVE II database.

Table 1. The median LCC performance on the LIVE II database

Method	JP2K	JPEG	WN	Blur	FF	All
BIQI	0.750	0.630	0.968	0.800	0.722	0.740
DIIVINE	0.922	0.921	0.988	0.923	0.888	0.917
BLIINDS-II	0.963	**0.979**	0.985	0.948	**0.944**	0.923
BRISQUE	0.923	0.974	0.985	0.951	0.903	0.942
CORNIA	0.951	0.965	0.987	**0.968**	0.917	**0.935**
NIQE	0.937	0.956	0.977	0.953	0.913	0.915
TCLT	0.902	0.946	**0.989**	0.954	0.923	0.935
GIP	**0.977**	0.958	0.883	0.931	0.920	0.923

Table 2. The median SROCC performance on the LIVE II database

Method	JP2K	JPEG	WN	Blur	FF	All
BIQI	0.736	0.591	0.958	0.778	0.700	0.726
DIIVINE	0.913	0.910	**0.984**	0.921	0.863	0.916
BLIINDS-II	0.951	0.942	0.978	0.944	0.927	0.920
BRISQUE	0.914	0.965	0.979	0.951	0.877	0.940
CORNIA	0.943	0.955	0.976	**0.969**	0.906	**0.942**
NIQE	0.917	0.938	0.966	0.934	0.859	0.914
TCLT	0.898	0.923	0.979	0.940	0.903	0.934
GIP	**0.978**	0.935	0.897	0.965	**0.929**	0.936

To measure the memory overhead of different NR-IQA algorithms, we summarize their feature dimensions and the corresponding memory usage of storing the feature of an image in Table 3, where the smallest value in each column is highlighted by boldface. It is seen that the proposed GIP method spends smallest memory for sorting the image feature, which is beneficial for saving the storage space and bandwidth in many real-world applications.

To analyze the computational complexity of different NR-IQA algorithms, we compute their running time of training a support vector regressor using all images in the LIVE II database. It is noted that the parameter tuning procedure is included in this evaluation, where two parameters (C, γ) are determined by grid search [7]. The candidate parameter space is 2^S, where S ranges from 0 to 5 with the interval 0.5. The system platform is Intel Core 2 Duo processor of speed 2.0 GHz, 6 GB RAM and Windows 7 64-bit version. All methods are tested using the MATLAB2015a software. Table 4 reports the detailed running time in terms of seconds, where the smallest value is highlighted by boldface. It is seen that the proposed GIP method spends much less running time in comparison with other algorithms, which is highly desired for many low power devices.

Table 3. The memory usage for storing the feature of an image in terms of Kilobyte (KB)

Method	Feature dimension	Memory usage
BIQI	18	0.325
DIIVINE	88	0.880
BLIINDS-II	24	0.368
BRISQUE	36	0.466
CORNIA	20000	149.591
NIQE	1332	8.162
TCLT	4413	9.172
GIP	**3**	**0.198**

Table 4. Running time of different NR-IQA algorithms for training SVR (seconds)

Method	Running time
BIQI	87.821
DIIVINE	214.956
BLIINDS-II	94.121
BRISQUE	117.997
CORNIA	5.243×10^4
NIQE	3.492×10^3
TCLT	1.094×10^4
GIP	**45.716**

4   Conclusion

In this paper, we proposed a GIP based no reference image quality assessment method. Specifically, a set of naturalness-aware filters are learned from large number of pristine images. The distribution of filter responses is used to measure the perceptual quality variation. Meanwhile, the LPSI is used to compensate the image information derived from these real-value filter responses. Finally, a compact image representation, which only computes three statistical indexes, is used as the quality-aware feature. Experimental results demonstrate its effectiveness and high-efficiency in evaluating the image quality.

Acknowledgement. This work was supported in part by National Natural Science Foundation of China (No. 61525102, No. 61271289), and by The program for Science and Technology Innovative Research Team for Young Scholars in Sichuan Province, China (No. 2014TD0006).

References

1. Chen, D., Cao, X., Wen, F., Sun, J.: Blessing of dimensionality: high-dimensional feature and its efficient compression for face verification. In: IEEE Conference on Computer Vision and Pattern Recognition, pp. 3025–3032 (2013)
2. Clarke, B., Fokoue, E., Zhang, H.: Principles and Theory for Data Mining and Machine Learning. Springer Series in Statistics. Springer, New York (2009)
3. Dennis Jr., J.E., Moré, J.J.: Quasi-newton methods, motivation and theory. SIAM Rev. 19(1), 46–89 (1977)
4. Fang, Y., Ma, K., Wang, Z., Lin, W., Fang, Z., Zhai, G.: No-reference quality assessment of contrast-distorted images based on natural scene statistics. IEEE Sig. Process. Lett. 22(7), 838–842 (2015)
5. Fang, Y., Zeng, K., Wang, Z., Lin, W., Fang, Z., Lin, C.W.: Objective quality assessment for image retargeting based on structural similarity. IEEE J. Emerg. Sel. Top. Circ. Syst. 4(1), 95–105 (2014)
6. Han, J., Pei, J., Kamber, M.: Data Mining, Southeast Asia Edition. The Morgan Kaufmann Series in Data Management Systems. Elsevier, Amsterdam (2006)
7. Hsu, C.W., Chang, C.C., Lin, C.J., et al.: A practical guide to support vector classification, Technical report (2003)
8. Martin, D., Fowlkes, C., Tal, D., Malik, J.: A database of human segmented natural images and its application to evaluating segmentation algorithms and measuring ecological statistics. In: IEEE International Conference on Computer Vision, vol. 2, pp. 416–423 (2001)
9. Mittal, A., Moorthy, A.K., Bovik, A.C.: No-reference image quality assessment in the spatial domain. IEEE Trans. Image Process. 21(12), 4695–4708 (2012)
10. Mittal, A., Soundararajan, R., Bovik, A.C.: Making a "completely blind" image quality analyzer. IEEE Signal Process. Lett. 20(3), 209–212 (2013)
11. Moorthy, A.K., Bovik, A.C.: Blind image quality assessment: From natural scene statistics to perceptual quality. IEEE Trans. Image Process. 20(12), 3350–3364 (2011)
12. Moorthy, A., Bovik, A.: A two-step framework for constructing blind image quality indices. IEEE Sig. Process. Lett. 17(5), 513–516 (2010)
13. Redner, R.A., Walker, H.F.: Mixture densities, maximum likelihood and the em algorithm. SIAM Rev. 26(2), 195–239 (1984)
14. Roth, S., Black, M.: Fields of experts: a framework for learning image priors. In: IEEE Computer Society Conference on Computer Vision and Pattern Recognition, vol. 2, pp. 860–867 (2005)
15. Saad, M., Bovik, A.C., Charrier, C.: Blind image quality assessment: a natural scene statistics approach in the dct domain. IEEE Trans. Image Process. 21(8), 3339–3352 (2012)
16. Schölkopf, B., Smola, A.J., Williamson, R.C., Bartlett, P.L.: New support vector algorithms. Neural Comput. 12(5), 1207–1245 (2000)
17. Sheikh, H.R., Wang, Z., Cormack, L., Bovik, A.C.: LIVE Image Quality Assessment Database Release 2. http://live.ece.utexas.edu/research/quality
18. Wang, Z.: Applications of objective image quality assessment methods [applications corner]. IEEE Sig. Process. Mag. 28(6), 137–142 (2011)
19. Welling, M., Osindero, S., Hinton, G.E.: Learning sparse topographic representations with products of student-t distributions. In: Advances in Neural Information Processing Systems, pp. 1359–1366 (2002)

20. Welling, M., Osindero, S., Hinton, G.E.: Learning sparse topographic representations with products of student-t distributions. In: Becker, S., Thrun, S., Obermayer, K. (eds.) Advances in Neural Information Processing Systems, pp. 1383–1390 (2003)
21. Wu, Q., Li, H., Meng, F., Ngan, K.N., Luo, B., Huang, C., Zeng, B.: Blind image quality assessment based on multichannel feature fusion and label transfer. IEEE Trans. Circ. Syst. Video Technol. 26(3), 425–440 (2016)
22. Wu, Q., Wang, Z., Li, H.: A highly efficient method for blind image quality assessment. In: IEEE International Conference on Image Processing, pp. 339–343 (2015)
23. Wu, Q., Li, H., Meng, F., Ngan, K.N., Zhu, S.: No reference image quality assessment metric via multi-domain structural information and piecewise regression. J. Vis. Commun. Image Representation 32, 205–216 (2015)
24. Ye, P., Doermann, D.: No-reference image quality assessment using visual codebooks. IEEE Trans. Image Process. 21(7), 3129–3138 (2012)
25. Ye, P., Kumar, J., Kang, L., Doermann, D.: Unsupervised feature learning framework for no-reference image quality assessment. In: IEEE Conference on Computer Vision and Pattern Recognition, pp. 1098–1105 (2012)

Objective Quality Assessment of Screen Content Images by Structure Information

Yuming Fang[1], Jiebin Yan[1], Jiaying Liu[2], Shiqi Wang[3], Qiaohong Li[3],
and Zongming Guo[2](✉)

[1] Jiangxi University of Finance and Economics, Nanchang, China
[2] Institute of Computer Science and Technology, Peking University, Beijing, China
guozongming@pku.edu.cn
[3] School of Computer Science and Engineering, Nanyang Technological University,
Singapore, Singapore

Abstract. In this paper, we propose a novel full-reference objective quality assessment metric of screen content images by structure information. The input screen content image is first divided into textual and pictorial regions. The visual quality of textual regions is predicted based on perceptual structural similarity, where the gradient information is used as the feature. To estimate the visual quality of pictorial regions, we extract the luminance and structure features as feature representation. The overall quality of the screen content image is measured by fusing those of textual and pictorial parts. Experimental results show that the proposed method can obtain better performance of visual quality prediction of SCIs than other existing ones.

Keywords: Visual quality assessment · Screen content image · Full-reference quality assessment

1 Introduction

Recently, there is one type of images emerging over Internet, which is called screen content images (SCIs). Generally, the SCI includes different forms of visual content, such as texts, pictures, and graphics. It has been emerging and widely used in various multimedia applications, including information sharing system between computer and smart devices [1], cloud computing systems [2,3], remote conference, product advertising, *etc*. With the popularity of smart phones, more and more users would like to share different information with each other by rendering various visual content as the form of SCIs, where various multimedia processing methods might be involved, such as coding [7–9], transmission [3], *etc*. There are a large number of image processing algorithms proposed for SCIs, including SCI compression [4], SCI quality assessment [5], SCI segmentation [6], *etc*.

Z. Guo—This work was supported by the NSFC (No. 61571212), NSF of Beijing (No. 4142021), and NSF of Jiangxi Province (No. 20151BDH80003, 20161ACB21014).

E. Chen et al. (Eds.): PCM 2016, Part II, LNCS 9917, pp. 609–616, 2016.
DOI: 10.1007/978-3-319-48896-7_60

During SCI processing such as acquisition, processing and transmission, there might be various visual distortions generated. When SCIs are created by the camera from smart phones, the noise and blurring distortions might be involved due to the camera motion. For the transmission of SCIs over Internet, the compression distortion might be generated. To evaluate the visual quality of these distorted SCIs, it is highly desired to design effective objective visual quality assessment metrics for various multimedia processing applications.

In the past decades, there have been various quality assessment methods designed for visual content. Traditional signal fidelity methods such as PSNR (Peak Signal-to-Noise Ratio), MSE (Mean Square Error) and MAE (Mean Absolute Error) predict visual quality of images by simply computing pixel differences between the reference and distorted images. These signal fidelity methods are widely used for visual quality assessment (VQA) in both industry and academia due to their simple and efficient implementation. However, they do not consider the properties of the Human Visual System (HVS), and thus, they might not obtain accurate quality prediction results as human beings perceive [14,15]. To overcome the drawbacks of these existing metrics, many advanced perceptual IQA metrics have been proposed during the past decade [14].

Wang et al. proposed the well-known SSIM (structural similarity) by considering the characteristics of human beings' perception on image structure [16]. Following this perceptual VQA metric, there are various types of full-reference VQA metrics proposed in recent ten years [14]: VIF (visual information fidelity) [17], IGM (internal generative mechanism) [18], GSM (gradient similarity metric) [19], etc. Also, many reduced-reference metrics [10] and no-reference metrics [11–13] have been designed in the past decades. These IQA metrics are mainly designed for VQA of general images and they are not effective in VQA of SCIs. Recently, Yang et al. conducted an user study for VQA of SCIs [5]. Based on the detailed analysis of the subjective data on the constructed SCI database, the authors proposed an objective VQA metric to predict visual quality of SCIs [5]. However, the performance of that metric in [5] can be further improved. Thus, it is highly desired to design VQA metrics for SCIs for various potential SCI processing applications.

In this study, we propose a full-reference (FR) VQA metric for SCIs based on structure features. We first divide the SCI into textual and pitorial parts by the text segmentation method. The visual distortion of textual regions is predicted by structural similarity, where gradient information is used to extract the structure feature. For the pictorial regions, we calculate the luminance and structure features to estimate the visual quality. The overall quality of the SCIs can be predicted by fusing those of pictorial and textual regions. Experimental results show that the proposed method can obtain good performance in visual quality prediction of SCIs.

2   The Proposed Method

Our previous study [5] has shown that the statistical features of natural and textual images are totally different. The detailed analysis of subjective data

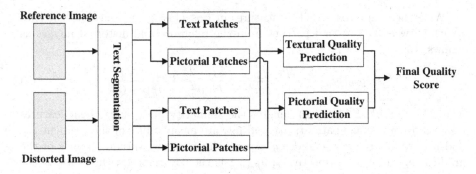

Fig. 1. The proposed framework.

demonstrate that human perception on pictorial and textual regions is different with each other. Specifically, the distortion in textual regions are perceived differently from that of the overall SCI. Observers would be sensitive to the luminance and contrast change in pictorial regions, while for textual regions, they are more sensitive to blurring distortion than other types of distortion. Thus, it is reasonable to design different methods for visual quality assessment of pictorial and textual regions.

The framework of the proposed method is shown in Fig. 1. We first use the texture segmentation method in [20] to segment the SCI into pictorial and textual regions. Then the image is divided into two types of image patches: pictorial and textual patches. For textual patches, we extract the gradient to represent the feature for similarity computation. The luminance and texture features are used for similarity calculation of pictorial patches. The final quality of SCIs is obtained by fusing the visual quality of textual and pictorial patches. We will introduce the proposed method in detail in the following.

The content in the textual region of SCIs mainly includes various characters. Since characters are composed of various edges, we use the gradient to represent the structure feature of textual regions in SCIs. The following filters with two directions are adopted to compute the gradient of textual region: $h_x = [-1/2 \ 0 \ 1/2]$ and $h_y = [-1/2 \ 0 \ 1/2]'$. With these two filters, we can compute the structure feature for reference and distorted SCIs as follows.

$$g_{rx} = h_x \bigotimes T_r, \tag{1}$$

$$g_{ry} = h_y \bigotimes T_r, \tag{2}$$

$$g_{dx} = h_x \bigotimes T_d, \tag{3}$$

$$g_{dy} = h_y \bigotimes T_d, \tag{4}$$

where T_r and T_d represent textual patches in the reference and distorted images, respectively. (g_{rx}, g_{ry}) and (g_{dx}, g_{dy}) denote the gradient features with two directions for the textual patches in the reference and distorted images, respectively.

With the computed structure features in Eqs. (1)–(4), we calculate the similarity between the textual patches from the reference and distorted images as follows [16]:

$$S_i(g_{rk}, g_{dk}) = \frac{2\mu_{g_{rk}}\mu_{g_{dk}} + C_1}{\mu_{g_{rk}}^2 + \mu_{g_{dk}}^2 + C_1} \frac{2\sigma_{g_{rk}g_{dk}} + C_2}{\sigma_{g_{rk}}^2 + \sigma_{g_{dk}}^2 + C_2} \tag{5}$$

where $k \in \{x, y\}$; $S_i(g_{rk}, g_{dk})$ denotes the similarity between gradient features g_{rk} and g_{dk} for image patch i; μ_{rk} and μ_{dk} are mean values of the gradient g_{rk} and g_{dk}, respectively; σ_{rk} and σ_{dk} denote the standard variance values of the gradient g_{rk} and g_{dk}, respectively; $\sigma_{g_{rk}g_{dk}}$ is the covariance of the gradient g_{rk} and g_{dk}; C_1 and C_2 are two constant values.

After we calculate the similarity between gradient features with two directions for textual patches, we estimate the visual score of textual regions S_t in SCI as follows:

$$S_t = \frac{1}{N} \sum_{i=1}^{N} (\alpha S_i(g_{rx}, g_{dx}) + (1 - \alpha)S_i(g_{ry}, g_{dy})) \tag{6}$$

where N is the number of textual patches in the SCI; α is a weighting parameter.

For pictorial patches, we use the structure and luminance features to predict the visual quality. First, the local contrast normalization is applied to the pictorial regions of SCIs to mimic early visual system and remove the redundancy information in the visual scene. The normalization operation can be implemented as [21].

$$P'(i, j) = \frac{P(i, j) - \mu_p}{\sigma_p + C} \tag{7}$$

where $P'(i, j)$ and $P(i, j)$ represent the normalized and original values at location (i, j) in pictorial regions; μ_p and σ_p denote the mean and standard variance values of pictorial regions; C is a constant parameter.

With the local normalized $P'(x, y)$, we can extract the structure feature of pictorial regions by using the rotation invariant uniform LBP descriptor [22]. The general LBP representation can be formulated as follows.

$$LBP_{K,R} = \sum_{i=0}^{K-1} t(p_i - p_c)2^i, \tag{8}$$

$$t(p_i - p_c) = \begin{cases} 1, (p_i - p_c) \geq 0 \\ 0, (p_i - p_c) < 0 \end{cases} \tag{9}$$

where K and R denote the number of neighbors and the radius of the neighborhood; p_c is the normalized luminance value of the center pixel in the local patch; $(p_0, p_1, ..., p_{K-1})$ represent the normalized luminance values of K circularly symmetric neighborhood. Based on the study [22], we can define the local rotation invariant uniform LBP operator as:

$$LBP'_{K,R} = \begin{cases} \sum_{i=0}^{K-1} t(p_i - p_c), U(LBP_{K,R}) \leq 2 \\ K + 1, Otherwise \end{cases} \tag{10}$$

$$U(LBP_{K,R}) = \|t(p_{K-1} - p_c) - t(p_0 - p_c)\|$$
$$+ \sum_{i=0}^{K-1} \|t(p_i - p_c) - t(p_{i-1} - p_c)\| \tag{11}$$

where U is computed as the number of bitwise transitions.

After extracting the LBP features by using the LBP descriptor in Eq. (10), we further calculate the histogram of LBP features in each pictorial patch. Here, we set the bin of the histogram as 10 and thus obtain the structure feature with 10 elements $\{f_1, f_2, ..., f_{10}\}$. Meanwhile, we also calculate the normalized luminance histogram as the luminance feature in the proposed method. Similarly, we set the bin of the histogram as 10, and thus, there are 10 elements $\{f_{11}, f_{12}, ..., f_{20}\}$ in the luminance feature. In total, there is one feature vector with 20 elements for structure and luminance features for each pictorial patch i: $f_i = \{f_1, f_2, ..., f_{20}\}$. We predict the visual quality of pictorial regions in the SCI by the difference between pictorial patches from the reference and distorted SCIs.

$$S_p = \frac{1}{N} \sum_{i}^{N} e^{(-q_i)} \tag{12}$$

$$q_i = \sqrt{\sum_{j=1}^{20} (f_i - f_i')^2} \tag{13}$$

where f_i and f_i' denote the used luminance and structure features from the reference and distorted SCIs.

After computing the visual quality of textual and pictorial regions in SCIs, we predict the final visual quality of each input SCI by combing them as follows.

$$S = \beta S_t + (1 - \beta)S_p \tag{14}$$

where β is a weighting parameter with the range $[0, 1]$.

3 Experimental Results

To demonstrate the advantages of the proposed method, we use the image database in [5] to conduct the comparison experiments. This database includes 20 reference SCIs in total. For each SCI in this database, there are seven distortion types (Gaussian Noise, Gaussian Blur, Motion Blur, Contrast Change, JPEG, JPEG2000, and Layer Segmentation Based Coding) with seven degradation levels and thus there are 980 distorted SCIs. These reference images obtained from webpages, slides, PDF files and digital magazines are diverse with the visual content.

The 11-category Absolute Category Rating (ACR) is used in the subjective experiment. In total, there were 96 subjects involved in the test and each image was rated by at least 30 subjects. The participants' ages range from

Table 1. Experimental results of the proposed method and other existing methods.

Components	PSNR	SSIM	VIF	IFC	MAD	GMSD	SPQA	Proposed
PLCC	0.5869	0.5912	0.8206	0.6395	0.6191	0.7259	0.8584	0.8656
SRCC	0.5608	0.5836	0.8069	0.6011	0.6067	0.7305	0.8416	0.8642

19 to 38 years. After the raw subjective scores were obtained, outliers were removed to obtain the DMOS.

Here, we adopt two commonly used methods to compute the correlation between the subjective and objective scores: SRCC (Spearman Rank-order Correlation Coefficient), and PLCC (Pearson Linear Correlation Coefficient). SRCC can be used to evaluate the prediction monotonicity, while PLCC can be adopted to assess the prediction accuracy. Generally, a better visual quality assessment method has higher SRCC and PLCC values. Given the ith image in the database (with N images in total), its objective and subjective scores are o_i and s_i. We can estimate the PLCC as follows.

$$PLCC = \frac{\sum_{i=1}^{N}(o_i - \overline{o})(s_i - \overline{s})}{\sqrt{\sum_{i=1}^{N}(o_i - \overline{o}) * \sum_{i=1}^{N}(s_i - \overline{s})}} \tag{15}$$

where $\overline{o}$ and $\overline{s}$ denote the mean values of o_i and s_i, respectively.

SRCC can be computed as follows.

$$SRCC = 1 - \frac{6\sum_{i=1}^{N} e_i^2}{N(N^2 - 1)} \tag{16}$$

where e_i is the difference between the ith image's ranks in subjective and objective results.

In this experiment, we perform the comparison experiments by using the proposed method and the following existing visual quality metrics: PSNR, SSIM [16], VIF [17], IFC [23], MAD [25], GMSD [24], SPQA [5]. We compute the correlations in terms of PLCC and SRCC values between the subjective scores and the predicted objective scores from the used compared metrics. The experimental results are shown in Table 1.

From Table 1, we can observe that GMSD can obtain better performance than PSNR, SSIM, IFC and MAD in visual quality prediction of SCIs. Obviously, SPQA an VIF can obtain much better performance than other existing studies. Among all the compared metrics, the proposed method can obtain best performance on visual quality prediction of SCIs, which can be demonstrated by the highest PLCC and SRCC values in Table 1.

4   Conclusion

In this study, we have proposed a new full-reference VQA metric for SCIs based on structural information. For textual regions in SCIs, we extract the structure features by using the gradient information for visual quality prediction of textual regions. For pictorial regions in SCIs, the luminance and structure features are computed by intensity and LBP information, respectively, for visual quality prediction of pictorial regions. The final visual quality of SCIs is estimated by fusing these of textual and pictorial parts. In the future, we will further investigate how to fuse the visual quality scores of textual and pictorial regions to obtain more reasonable quality scores of SCIs.

References

1. Chang, T., Li, Y.: Deep shot: a framework for migrating tasks across devices using mobile phone cameras. In: ACM Proceedings of the SIGCHI Conference on Human Factors in Computing Systems (2011)
2. Lu, Y., Li, S., Shen, H.: Virtualized screen: a third element for cloud-mobile convergence. IEEE Multimedia 18(2), 4–11 (2011)
3. Hu, H., Wen, Y., Chua, T.-S., Li, X.: Toward scalable systems for big data analytics: a technology toturial. IEEE Access 2, 652–687 (2014)
4. Lan, C., Shi, G., Wu, F.: Compress compound images in H.264/MPGE-4 AVC by exploiting spatial correlation. IEEE Trans. Image Process. 19, 946–957 (2010)
5. Yang, H., Fang, Y., Lin, W.: Perceptual quality assessment of screen content images. IEEE Trans. Image Process. 24(11), 4408–4421 (2015)
6. Minaee, S., Wang, Y.: Screen content image segmentation using least absolute deviation fitting. In: IEEE International Conference on Image Processing (2015)
7. Lei, J., Li, S., Zhu, C., Sun, M.-T., Hou, C.: Depth coding based on depth-texture motion and structure similarities. IEEE Trans. Circ. Syst. Video Technol. 25(2), 275–286 (2015)
8. Lei, J., Sun, J., Pan, Z., Kwong, S., Duan, J., Hou, C.: Fast mode decision using inter-view and inter-component correlations for multiview depth video coding. IEEE Trans. Indus. Inf. 11(4), 978–986 (2015)
9. Ma, S., Zhang, X., Zhang, J., Jia, C., Wang, S., Gao, W.: Nonlocal in-loop filter: the way toward next-generation video coding? IEEE MultiMedia 23(2), 16–26 (2016)
10. Wu, J., Lin, W., Shi, G., Liu, A.: Reduced-reference image quality assessment with visual information fidelity. IEEE Trans. Multimedia 12(7), 1700–1705 (2013)
11. Gu, K., Zhai, G., Lin, W., Yang, X., Zhang, W.: No-reference image sharpness assessment in autoregressive parameter space. IEEE Trans. Image Process. 24(10), 3218–3231 (2015)
12. Fang, Y., Ma, K., Wang, Z., Lin, W., Fang, Z., Zhai, G.: No-reference quality assessment for contrast-distorted images based on natural scene statistics. IEEE Signal Process. Lett. 22(7), 838–842 (2015)
13. Li, L., Lin, W., Wang, X., Yang, G., Bahrami, K., Kot, A.C.: No-reference image blur assessment based on discrete orthogonal moments. IEEE Trans. Cybern. 46(1), 39–50 (2016)
14. Lin, W., Kuo, C.C.J.: Perceptual visual quality metric: a survey. J. Vis. Commun. Image Represent. 22(4), 297–312 (2011)
15. Wang, Z., Bovik, A.C.: Mean squared error: love it or leave it? a new look at fidelity measures. IEEE Signal Process. Mag. 26(1), 98–117 (2009)
16. Wang, Z., Bovik, A.C., Sheikh, H.R., Simoncelli, E.P.: Image quality assessment: from error visibility to structural similarity. IEEE Trans. Image Process. 13(4), 600–612 (2004)

17. Sheikh, H.R., Bovik, A.C.: Image information and visual quality. IEEE Trans. Image Process. **15**(2), 430–444 (2006)
18. Wu, J., Lin, W., Shi, G., Liu, A.: Perceptual quality metric with internal generative mechanism. IEEE Trans. Image Process. **22**(1), 43–54 (2013)
19. Liu, A., Lin, W., Narwaria, M.: Image quality assessment based on gradient similarity. IEEE Trans. Image Process. **21**(4), 1500–1512 (2012)
20. Yang, H., Lin, W., Deng, C.: Image acitivity measure (IAM) for screen image segmentation In: IEEE International Conference on Image Processing (2012)
21. Zhang, L., Zhang, L., Bovik, A.: A feature-enriched completely blind image quality evaluator. IEEE Trans. Image Process. **24**(8), 2579–2591 (2015)
22. Ojala, T., Pietikainen, M., Maenpaa, T.: Multiresolution gray-scale and rotation invariant texture classification with local binary patterns. IEEE Trans. Pattern Anal. Mach. Intell. **24**(7), 971–987 (2002)
23. Sheikh, H.R., Bovik, A.C., de Veciana, G.: An information fidelity criterion for image quality assessment using natural scene statistics. IEEE Trans. Image Process. **14**(12), 2117–2128 (2005)
24. Xue, W., Zhang, L., Mou, X., Bovik, A.C.: Gradient magnitude similarity deviation: a highly efficient perceptual image quality index. IEEE Trans. Image Process. **23**(2), 684–695 (2014)
25. Larson, E.C., Chandler, D.M.: Most apparent distortion: full reference image quality assessment and the role of strategy. J. Electron. Imaging **19**(1) (2010). 011006

CrowdTravel: Leveraging Heterogeneous Crowdsourced Data for Scenic Spot Profiling and Recommendation

Tong Guo, Bin Guo$^{(\boxtimes)}$, Jiafan Zhang, Zhiwen Yu, and Xingshe Zhou

School of Computer Science, Northwestern Polytechnical University,
Xi'an 710129, People's Republic of China
guob@nwpu.edu.cn

Abstract. With the prosperity of mobile social networks, more and more people are willing to share their travel experiences and feelings on the Web, which provides abundant knowledge for people who are going to make travel plans. Travel reviews and travelogues are two major ways of social travel sharing. They are complementary in terms of structure, content, and interaction, forming a sort of fragmented travel knowledge. Moreover, the ever-increasing reviews and travelogues may impose the burden on gaining and reorganizing knowledge while making travel plans. Over these issues, this paper proposes CrowdTravel, a multi-source social media data fusion approach for multi-aspect tourism information perception and intelligent recommendation, which can provide travelling assistance for users by crowd intelligence mining. First, we propose a cross-media multi-aspect correlation method to connect fragmented travel information. Second, we mine popular and personalized travel routes from travelogues and make intelligent recommendation based on sequential pattern mining. Finally, we achieve cross-media relevance information based on the similarity between the reviews and image contexts. We conduct experiments over a dataset of eight domestic popular scenic spots, which is collected from two popular social websites about travel, namely Dazhongdianping and Mafengwo. The results indicate that our approach attains fine-grained characterization for the scenic spots and the extracted travel routes can meet different users' needs.

Keywords: Crowd intelligence · Scenic spot profiling · Intelligent recommendation · Social media data fusion · Multi-aspect characterization

1 Introduction

Crowd intelligence [1, 2] refers to implementing multifaceted perception and understanding of the target objects by mining and associating crowd contributed data. Social media shows a diversified development trend in recent years, which forms a variety of online social communities for crowd data and knowledge sharing.

Social tourism is one of the popular social communities, where people often share their opinions and knowledge on scenic spots online after a fantastic journey. This, however, has become an important information source for people to make their travel plans. Travel reviews and travelogues are two major ways of social travel sharing, which

© Springer International Publishing AG 2016
E. Chen et al. (Eds.): PCM 2016, Part II, LNCS 9917, pp. 617–628, 2016.
DOI: 10.1007/978-3-319-48896-7_61

can serve as a reliable knowledge source for tourism information extraction. Although the information in a single review or travelogue may be noisy or biased, the content contributed by numerous travelers as a whole could characterize the essence of scenic spots. Considering sustained increasing massive travel-related information, an automatic tourism information perception and intelligence recommendation method is highly desired to facilitate people to obtain accurate information and prepare for their journeys.

To some extent, the tourism information summarization for travel can be formulated as a multi-document summarization (MDS) problem [3]. During the past decade, a variety of methods have been proposed for MDS. Notable approaches include frequency-based methods [12, 14], semantic-based methods such as probabilistic latent semantic analysis (PLSA) [5] and latent Dirichlet allocation (LDA) [7]. Graph and machine learning-based methods [11] have also been proposed. However, previous MDS methods are mainly designed for well-organized texts, e.g., news articles.

Different from traditional text mining, tourism social information comprises of multiple media types, such as image and text. Besides, tourism information summarization is even more challenging than its usage in other domains. Scenic spots usually contain dozens of distinguished natural, cultural scenes (e.g., the Kunming Lake and the Long Corridor in the Summer Palace). Each tourist is more likely to visit part of them each time, and thus individual reviews cover very different combinations of scenes. Moreover, there is usually only one overall evaluation score on the experience of the scenic spot each time in most cases, making it difficult to gain accurate understanding to each of the scenes. On the other hand, potential tourists need more information than simple statistics on the overall quality of the scenic spot with all sorts of different scenes. They are not only interested in choosing best scenic spots but also keen to know the details of various scenes in a scenic spot, based on previous experiences of other tourists. Therefore, we consider a distinguished natural or cultural scene as one tag of a scenic spot. And people's opinions or descriptions (beautiful, magnificent, interesting, etc.) towards a certain scene of the scenic spot are jointly called the 'scene-feature' characterization, which can help people explicitly understand the scenic spot from different views.

Recently, several attempts [10, 12] have been made to mine tourism knowledge through different perspectives. For example, Rattenbury et al. [10] extracted place semantics from Flickr tags. Hao et al. [12] investigated the mining of location-representative knowledge from travelogues to recommend travel routes. Nonetheless, the performance of these methods are still far from satisfactory because they only depict the scenic spots from a single perspective. The benefits of multi-source social media data fusion are two-folds: (1) Images can supplement the textual content with additional information, especially in the tourism domain, where the text lacks sufficient expressive power; (2) Incorporating concrete multimedia exemplars into summarization can assist users to gain a more visualized understanding of interesting scenes. More recently, Wang et al. [16] proposed a method to generate visualized summarization for scenic spots by mining representative aspects from text reviews and combining it with images from travelogues. However, it did not make full use of the aforementioned travelogues to support further intelligent travel route recommendation.

In this work, we propose a multi-source social media data fusion approach for multi-aspect tourism information perception and intelligent recommendation. First, we propose a cross-media multi-aspect correlation method to connect fragmented travel information. Second, we mine typical travel route from travelogues and make intelligent recommendation based on the sequential pattern mining. Finally, we implement cross-media relevance information based on the similarity between the reviews and the image contexts. We conduct experiments over a dataset of eight domestic popular scenic spots, which is collected from Dazhongdianping[1] and Mafengwo[2]. The results indicate that our approach makes a fine-grained characterization for the scenic spots and the extracted travel routes can meet different users' needs.

2 Related Work

Recently, the application of crowd intelligence has become more and more widely, including event discovery and characterization, business intelligence, activity recommendation, and so on. Especially in the domain of tourism, a large number of users contribute rich information via social media, which has become one of the issues of concern to researchers.

In general, tourism knowledge mining can be divided into two aspects, mining rich tourism knowledge from the massive social network and travel recommendation. Currently, the research about the rich tourism knowledge mining is mostly based on the traditional MDS theory. Lin et al. [17] leveraged position, term frequency and scheme to extract summarization. Wan et al. [18] improved the graph-ranking algorithm by different intra-document and inter-document links between sentences. The clustering approach has been incorporated in the graph model to better evaluate sentences [19]. Li et al. [9] used a structural SVM to learn for sentences selection. However, they just give some general descriptions as a whole while not from different aspects. For travel recommendation, feature mining has recently attracted increasing attention. These approaches [15] normally apply some constraints on high-frequency noun phrases to identify product aspects. As a result, they usually produce too many non-aspects and miss low-frequency aspects [6]. In addition, feature-based approaches require the manual tuning of various parameters which makes them hard to port to other datasets. Besides, probabilistic topic models, e.g., PLSA and LDA, which have been successfully applied to a variety of text mining tasks, owing to their powerful capability of discovering topics from texts and representative documents in a low-dimensional space spanned by the topics. However, to the best of our knowledge, existing models do not consider or address the limitation of short reviews and travelogue data.

In order to better meet the needs of different users, the method we propose supports both rich tourism knowledge mining and intelligent travel recommendation from complementary social networks.

---

[1] http://www.dianping.com/.

[2] http://www.mafengwo.cn/.

3 Problem Formulation

The aim of CrowdTravel is to attain fine-grained characterization for the scenic spots and make intelligent recommendation. The input of it (see Fig. 1) is a collection of reviews, travelogues and scene words $P = \{R, T, N\}$ related to the same scenic spot. R means pieces of reviews. $T = \{C, I\}$ represents the travelogues uploaded by the travelers, where I denotes the images and C means the contexts location adjacent to the images in the travelogues. Besides, N denotes the name of all the main scenes of the scenic spot. The output is informative scene-feature characterizations and representative images regarding the scenes of each scenic spot, which is in the order of the recommended popular travel route.

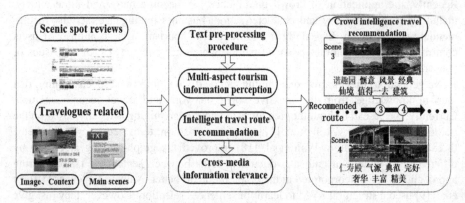

Fig. 1. The CrowdTravel system framework

4 The System Framework

Our system contains the following four components: (1) *Text pre-processing procedure*. We select sentences with at least one scene word and high entropy, which can obtain the important and significant sentences. (2) *Multi-aspect tourism information perception*. We discover multiple textual features for each scene of the scenic spot from the informative review sentences and the collection of scene words. (3) *Intelligent travel route recommendation*. We extract a travel route from each travelogue, and finally get the most popular one. (4) *Cross-media information association*. Through the contexts nearest the images and the similarity between the scene sentences and contexts, we vote to select the representative images associated to the corresponding scene-feature characterization.

4.1   Text Pre-processing Procedure

For the text pre-processing procedure, we firstly build individual vocabulary dictionary V for each scenic spot by segmenting Chinese words using FudanNLP[3] package from all reviews R. We filter stop words, meaningless words, time and numeric words. We give a premise that the information about the scenic spot is uniformly distributed over the review dataset. Besides, it is well-known that the information entropy can reflect that the average amount of information it brings when you know the result of a stochastic event. So we calculate the entropy for each word w as formulated in Eq. (1):

$$H(w) = -p(w)\log p(w) \tag{1}$$

Where $p(w) = \frac{tf(w,R)}{\sum_{w'} tf(w',R)}$ denotes the probability of word w in review sentence set R and tf denotes the term frequency for word w. The entropy of each sentence s with at least one scene word in R can be calculated as summation of entropy for each word w_k in s as Eq. (2):

$$H(s) = \sum_{k} H(w_k) \tag{2}$$

Therefore, we select the significant sentences with high entropy as Eq. (3):

$$S = \{s \mid H(s) > \varepsilon\} \tag{3}$$

where ε is the threshold value for sentences selection and S is the selected informative sentence set from reviews R.

4.2   Multi-aspect Tourism Information Perception

Feature characterization mining suffers from large valiance of noisy sentences and various expressions. To deal with these difficulties, we propose a novel incremental learning method.

Given all sentences S, the set of all the main scenes in a scenic spot P and a couple of sentences $S_n = \{s_i\}_{i=1}^{N} \in S$ of one scene n, we aim to extract feature words for this scene. These feature words including nouns and adjectives should be able to well describe the scene.

We resort to two assumptions [10] and propose a greedy strategy which is simple but effective to solve the problem. In reality, for each scene in a scenic spot, only a small set of words are salient and valuable. Therefore, we perform a pre-filtering step to obtain the words W_F with large values of $F(w_i, S_n)$, where $F(w_i, S_n)$ is the constraint between $p(w_i \mid S_n)$ and $p(w_i \mid S)$, as formulated in Eq. (4).

---

[3] http://nlp.fudan.edu.cn/.

$$F(w_i, S_n) = f(x), \ x = p(w_i \mid S_n) - p(w_i \mid S) > 0 \tag{4}$$

Where we introduce the increasing logistic function $f(x) = \frac{1}{1+\varepsilon^{-x}}$. This can reduce the computational cost to favor the feature words extraction. For feature word extraction, we first select the word $w \in W_F$ with largest value of $F(w, S_n)$ and then choose the next word w_i from $W_F \backslash W^*$ by solving $\arg\max_{wi} \varphi(w_i)$. The feature words set is updated by $W^* = W^* \cup \{w_i\}$ and obtained until $W_F = \varnothing$. The whole procedure for feature words extraction is summarized in Algorithm 1. In the incremental learning procedure, when a feature is augmented by adding a new sentence it is not necessary to process all the words of the scene. Instead, we only need to update the feature words set based on the previous one, which can largely reduce the computational complexity of feature mining.

Algorithm 1. Mining Multiple Features

Input: scene n with S_n , parameter λ
Output: W^*
1. $W_F = \{w \mid F(w, S_n) > \lambda\}$
2. select the word w with largest value of $F(w, S_n)$
3. $W^* = W^* \cup \{w\}$
4. repeat
5. choose the next word from $W_F \backslash W^*$ by solving $\arg\max_{wi} \varphi(w_i)$
6. $W^* = W^* \cup \{w_i\}$
7. until $W_F = \varnothing$
8. return W^*

4.3   Intelligent Travel Route Recommendation

The travel route is the route that tourists followed in the scenic spot. If a large number of tourists choose the same travel route, this route can be regarded as recommending information for users. The contexts and images are organized in travelogues as the user's writing order, which can also be considered as the user's travel route in most cases.

Different from association rule mining, which can mine frequent item sets. The inputs and outputs for this step are orderly, and sequential pattern mining can get frequent sequences or sub sequences from the discrete data sets. Therefore, this paper improves the traditional sequential pattern mining algorithm according to the real needs, and the procedure is shown in Algorithm 2:

Algorithm 2. Travel Route Recommendation

Input: travelogues set T, scene words set N
Output: recommended travel route r
1. *for* each a in T
2. $c \leftarrow FM(N, a)$
3.   IF $Judge(c) == True$
4. $P \leftarrow c$
5. *end*
6. $L_1 = \{n \mid n \in N, support(n) \geq min\_sup\}$
7. *for* $(k = 2; L_{k-1} \neq \varnothing; k++)$ *do*
8. $C_k = GC(L_{k-1})$
9.   *for* each c in P *do*
10.   all candidates of C_k contained in c plus 1
11. $L_k = \{c \mid c \in C_k, support(c) \geq min\_sup\}$
12. *end*
13. $r = L_k$ (the longest sequence)

Where $FM(N, a)$ discovers a travel route from travelogue a by using fuzzy matching algorithm according to the collection of scene words set N. And $Judge(c)$ return $True$ if there is no duplicate scenes and the number of scenes is greater than or equal to the one third of the total number of scenes. This is to ensure that the route extracted from travelogues is completely enough. $support(n)$ denotes the degree of support and min_sup indicates the minimum support threshold. $GC(L_{k-1})$ generates new candidates by using the pruning and connection operation according to the L_{k-1}.

4.4   Cross-Media Information Relevance

According to our observation, people usually give some simple textual description C location adjacent to the uploaded image I in the travelogue. Therefore, we can build the text to image association through the extracted scene-feature characterization sentences and the textual description about the image in travelogue. We use a majority voting scheme to select the correlated images to the scene n. The detail process is as follows:

Image Clustering. We first extract image I which contains some description context c_I in the travelogue to formulate the image set I_P and context C_P about the scenic spot P. Then we apply spectral clustering to group I_P into visually diverse clusters $L_P = \{l_1, l_2, \ldots, l_{|l|}\}$ based on the visual content feature vector. Hence we labeled the corresponding l_i to each context c_I whose adjacent image I is clustered to l_i.

Image Cluster Voting. For each sentence s in S_n, we look for the most similar context sentences C_I from C_P according to the cosines theory. Then we vote to decide the potentially associated image cluster L_a based on the similar context label. The algorithm is shown in Algorithm 3.

Algorithm 3. Cross-Media Information Relevance

    Input: scene n with S_n, C_P, L_P in a scenic spot
    Output: L_a
1. $N(l_{ci}) = 0$ #initial count
2. *for*   each s in S_n *do*
3.   *for*   each c_i in C_P *do*
4. $score(s, c_i) = \cos(s, c_i)$
5.   *end*
6.   choose the top c_i, $N(l_{ci}) = N(l_{ci}) + 1, (l_{ci} \in L_P)$
7. *end*
8. rank $N(l_{ci})$ and choose the top label as L_a
9. return L_a

Until now, we get the associated scene-feature characterization image cluster label L_a for each scene. Then we select the representative images for each scene-feature characterization via the affinity propagation method [8] from image cluster L_a.

5 Experiments

We conduct extensive experiments to evaluate the effectiveness and usefulness of the proposed methods.

5.1 The Dataset and Experimental Settings

We construct the dataset by choosing 8 domestic well-known scenic spots. Our dataset was collected by crawling reviews from Dazhongdianping and travelogues from Mafengwo. We use each scenic spot's name as the search word and all queried reviews and travelogues are collected together with their associated information. The statistics information are shown in Table 1.

The character of reviews from Dazhongdianping is that each piece of review is short and may include only 2 or 3 sentences which depict some scene-feature characterizations about the scenic spot and lacks visual images. Comparatively, the travelogues from Mafengwo are less informative and noisy in opinions but more abundant in high-quality images and corresponding contexts. For each scenic spot, we initially get an average of 2100 reviews and 3100 travelogues. A pre-filtering process is performed on the dataset to remove duplicate reviews, images and travelogues which are not related to the scenic spot, etc. We also restrict to images that they should have completely associated textual contexts. After pre-processing, the dataset for each scenic spot contains around 1800 reviews and 2000 images with the surrounding contexts.

To represent the image content, we extract five types of visual features to form an 809-dimension vector for each image, including 81-dimension color moment, 37-dimension edge histogram, 120-dimension wavelet texture feature, 59-dimension

Table 1. The experimental dataset

Scenic spot	The Summer Palace	The Forbidden City	Lijiang	Zhangjiajie	Jiuzhai Valley	Tang Paradise	Lushan Mountain	Mount Huangshan
Scenes	20	10	15	15	12	15	10	12
Reviews	6415	5256	1543	1116	1102	1023	588	443
Travelogues	2504	1775	4511	3024	4021	412	2018	2860

LBP feature and 512-dimension GIST feature [14]. Based on experiment, the tradeoff parameter λ in Algorithm 2 is empirically set to 0.6. We extract the top 6 feature words to represent each scene.

5.2 Performance Evaluation

Figure 2 shows the official travel routes of The Summer Palace on Mafengwo, which are simply based on the location information and it is hard for users to make the best decision. In reality, the route that most people choose is the most popular and most reasonable, which can be the reference information for users. In this paper, we mine popular travel route from travelogues and make an intelligent recommendation based on the sequential pattern mining.

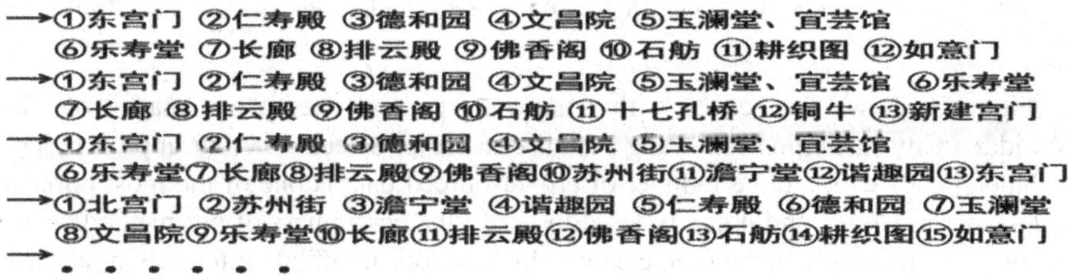

→①东宫门　②仁寿殿　③德和园　④文昌院　⑤玉澜堂、宜芸馆
　⑥乐寿堂　⑦长廊　⑧排云殿　⑨佛香阁　⑩石舫　⑪耕织图　⑫如意门
→①东宫门　②仁寿殿　③德和园　④文昌院　⑤玉澜堂、宜芸馆　⑥乐寿堂
　⑦长廊　⑧排云殿　⑨佛香阁　⑩石舫　⑪十七孔桥　⑫铜牛　⑬新建宫门
→①东宫门　②仁寿殿　③德和园　④文昌院　⑤玉澜堂、宜芸馆
　⑥乐寿堂⑦长廊⑧排云殿⑨佛香阁⑩苏州街⑪澹宁堂⑫谐趣园⑬东宫门
→①北宫门　②苏州街　③澹宁堂　④谐趣园　⑤仁寿殿　⑥德和园　⑦玉澜堂
　⑧文昌院⑨乐寿堂⑩长廊⑪排云殿⑫佛香阁⑬石舫⑭耕织图⑮如意门
→ ● ● ● ● ● ●

Fig. 2. Official travel routes to the Summer Palace

In addition, compared with the traditional research of single data source, the method proposed in this paper depicts the scenes from multiple aspects. Our approach makes good use of multi-source data fusion to visualize the combination of scene-feature characterization. The accuracy rate of scenes and images correlation is shown in Table 2, and the average accuracy rate reached 87.5 %.

Table 2. The accuracy rate of scenes and images correlation

Scenic spot	The Summer Palace	The Forbidden City	Lijiang	Zhangjiajie	Jiuzhai Valley	Tang Paradise	Lushan Mountain	Mount Huangshan
Accuracy	85.0 %	84.4 %	90.0 %	92.5 %	91.7 %	82.5 %	81.3 %	91.7 %

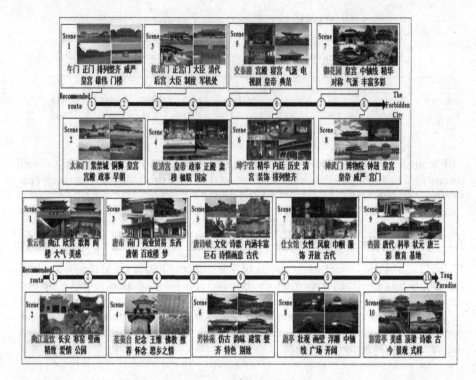

Fig. 3. Scenic spot profiling and recommendation

Figure 3 shows the scenes with feature words and exemplary images of The Forbidden City in Beijing and Tang Paradise in Xi'an detected by our approach. The Forbidden City with a large number of crowdsourced data is one of the most popular scenic spot in China, and it can be used to verify the correctness of our method. Tang Paradise is a relatively niche scenic spot, which is poor in official information, and we can leverage the rich crowdsourced data to demonstrate the practical effect of CrowdTravel.

We conduct a small-scale user study to evaluate the effectiveness of the proposed method and user experience of the novel visualization form. Three criteria are considered:(1) consistency, the level of consistency between the visual content and scene-feature characterization (0: Not consistent, 5: Very consistent); (2) relatedness, the extent that the mined features related to the scene (0: Not related, 5: Very related); and (3) satisfaction, how satisfactory are our framework (0: Not satisfied, 5: Very satisfied) We recruited 25 participants for the user study. The results are averaged over all participants for each scene-feature characterization, as shown in Fig. 4. It is obvious that the participants have given positive feedback to the novel visual scene-feature characterization scheme, which further validates the potential of our framework in advanced travel exploration and related applications.

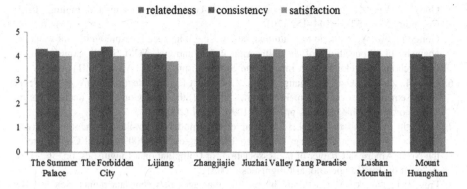

Fig. 4. User study results

6   Conclusion

In this paper, we present a system of multi-aspect information perception and intelligent recommendation for travel by leveraging the multi-source social media data. A cross-media multi-aspect correlation method is introduced to connect fragmented travel information and sequential pattern mining method for popular travel route mining. The mined feature words and corresponding images formulate the scene-feature characterization to generate travel information perception and intelligent recommendation, which help understand the scenic spot better from various perspectives. Based on a large collection of reviews and travelogues, experimental results show the effectiveness of the proposed methods.

As for the future work, we plan to take full advantage of the content of images to improve the performance of image selection and user experience. Besides, it is an interesting direction to take various granularity levels of locations into consideration, so as to better meet application needs.

Acknowledgement. This work is partially supported by the National Basic Research Program of China (No. 2015CB352400), the National Natural Science Foundation of China (No. 6133 2005, 61373119).

References

1. Zhang, D.Q., Guo, B., Yu, Z.W.: The emergence of social and community intelligence. IEEE Comput. **44**(7), 21–28 (2011)
2. Guo, B., Wang, Z., Yu, Z.W., Wang, Y., Yen, N., Huang, R.H., Zhou, X.S.: Mobile crowd sensing and computing: the review of an emerging human-powered sensing paradigm. ACM Comput. Surv. **48**(1), 1–31 (2015)
3. Bian, J., Yang, Y., Chua, T.S.: Multimedia summarization for trending topics in microblogs. In: Proceedings of the 22nd ACM International Conference on Conference on Information and Knowledge Management, pp. 1807–1812. ACM (2013)

4. Guo, B., Yu, Z., Zhang, D., Zhou, X.: Cross-community sensing and mining. IEEE Commun. Mag. **52**(8), 144–152 (2014)
5. Gong, Y., Liu, X.: Generic text summarization using relevance measure and latent semantic analysis. In: Proceedings of the 24th Annual International ACM SIGIR Conference on Research and Development in Information Retrieval, pp. 19–25. ACM (2001)
6. Guo, H., Zhu, H., Guo, Z., Zhang, X., Su, Z.: Product feature categorization with multilevel latent semantic association. In: Proceedings of the 18th ACM Conference on Information and Knowledge Management, pp. 1087–1096. ACM (2009)
7. Haghighi, A., Vanderwende, L.: Exploring content models for multi-document summarization. In: Proceedings of Human Language Technologies: The 2009 Annual Conference of the North American Chapter of the Association for Computational Linguistics, pp. 362–370. Association for Computational Linguistics (2009)
8. Frey, B.J., Dueck, D.: Clustering by passing messages between data points. Science **315** (5814), 972–976 (2007)
9. Li, L., Zhou, K., Xue, G.R., Zha, H., Yu, Y.: Enhancing diversity, coverage and balance for summarization through structure learning. In: Proceedings of the 18th International Conference on World Wide Web, pp. 71–80. ACM (2009)
10. Rattenbury, T., Naaman, M.: Methods for extracting place semantics from flickr tags. ACM Trans. Web (TWEB) **3**(1), 1 (2009)
11. Shen, D., Sun, J.T., Li, H., Yang, Q., Chen, Z.: Document summarization using conditional random fields. IJCAI **7**, 2862–2867 (2007)
12. Hao, Q., Cai, R., Wang, C., Xiao, R., Yang, J.M., Pang, Y., Zhang, L.: Equip tourists with knowledge mined from travelogues. In: Proceedings of the 19th International Conference on World Wide Web, pp. 401–410. ACM (2010)
13. Torralba, A., Murphy, K.P., Freeman, W.T., Rubin, M.A.: Context-based vision system for place and object recognition. In: Proceedings of the Ninth IEEE International Conference on Computer Vision, pp. 273–280. IEEE (2003)
14. Radev, D.R., Jing, H., Sty's, M., Tam, D.: Centroid-based summarization of multiple documents. Inf. Process. Manag. **40**(6), 919–938 (2004)
15. Moghaddam, S., Ester, M.: Opinion digger: an unsupervised opinion miner from unstructured product reviews. In: Proceedings of the 19th ACM International Conference on Information and Knowledge Management, pp. 1825–1828. ACM (2010)
16. Wang, T., Bai, C.: Understand the city better: multimodal aspect-opinion summarization for travel. In: Benatallah, B., Bestavros, A., Manolopoulos, Y., Vakali, A., Zhang, Y. (eds.) WISE 2014, Part II. LNCS, vol. 8787, pp. 381–394. Springer, Heidelberg (2014)
17. Lin, C.Y., Hovy, E.: From single to multi-document summarization: a prototype system and its evaluation. In: Proceedings of the 40th Annual Meeting on Association for Computational Linguistics, pp. 457–464. Association for Computational Linguistics (2002)
18. Wan, X., Yang, J., Xiao, J.: Single document summarization with document expansion. In: Proceedings of the National Conference on Artificial Intelligence, vol. 22, p. 931. AAAI Press, MIT Press, Menlo Park (2007)
19. Wan, X., Yang, J.: Multi-document summarization using cluster-based link analysis. In: Proceedings of the 31st Annual International ACM SIGIR Conference on Research and Development in Information Retrieval, pp. 299–306. ACM (2008)

Context-Oriented Name-Face Association in Web Videos

Zhineng Chen[1], Wei Zhang[2], Hongtao Xie[2], Bailan Feng[1], and Xiaoyan Gu[2(✉)]

[1] Institute of Automation, Chinese Academy of Sciences, Beijing, China
{zhineng.chen,bailan.feng}@ia.ac.cn
[2] Institute of Information Engineering, Chinese Academy of Sciences, Beijing, China
{wzhang,xiehongtao,guxiaoyan}@iie.ac.cn

Abstract. Automatically linking faces in Web videos with their names scattered in the surrounding text (e.g., the user generated title and tags) is an important task for many applications. Traditionally, this task is accomplished either by jointly exploring visual-textual consistency under constraints, or by leveraging external resources, e.g., public facial images. This paper follows the second paradigm and implements the name-face association by matching faces appearing in Web videos with carefully collected Web facial images. Specially, given a Web video, we first identify the relevant and discriminative tags from its surrounding text. The tags are defined as *Contextual Tags* (CTags) as they roughly give the semantic context of the video (e.g., *who* are doing *what* at *when* and *where*). Then, facial images are retrieved by issuing a commercial search engine using the assembled text queries, where each query contains a detected name and one of the top CTags. By doing this, we crawl facial images that are highly relevant to the person in the video context, and thus the task of name-face association can be simply implemented by matching faces. Compared with traditional methods, our novelty lies in the exploration of both visual content of the video and crowdsourced text of the context that aims to find more specific facial images from the Web to facilitate the association. Experimental results on real-world Web videos containing faces and celebrity names show that the proposed method outperforms several existing methods in performance.

Keywords: Web video · Name-face association · Celebrity image · Contextual tag · Image matching

1 Introduction

Face recognition has received considerable attention from both industry and academia over the past several decades. Despite numerous progresses made, automatically recognizing faces under unconstrained capturing conditions nevertheless remains a highly challenging problem, as the faces often appear with large variations in pose, illumination, facial expression, etc. However, with the explosive growth of people-related video services and activities on the Web nowadays, it becomes an urgent demand to develop techniques that could distinguish people in Web videos, at least for those famous ones, i.e., celebrities.

© Springer International Publishing AG 2016
E. Chen et al. (Eds.): PCM 2016, Part II, LNCS 9917, pp. 629–639, 2016.
DOI: 10.1007/978-3-319-48896-7_62

Name-face association is generally regarded as a feasible methodology towards recognizing faces appearing in Web videos. It utilizes surrounding text (e.g., the user generated title and tags) of a video to assist the recognition and can be viewed as the following challenge [1, 2]: given a video with face (track) and name responses, automatically establish the one-to-one alignment between the face and name, where a face can associate with at most one name, or none if no corresponding name is found (i.e., null assignment), and a name can be assigned to at most one face in a frame.

In the literature, the name-face association is mostly investigated using a two-step pipeline. First, every face detected from a video is weakly associated with every name found in its surrounding text. Then, a refinement is conducted to remove false matches. Several refinements are proposed for images or videos from different domains with various available clues [3–8]. For example, in *Graph-based Association* (GA) introduced by Guillaumin *et al.* [5], all faces detected from a News image collection are modeled as a graph and the refinement is determined based upon the jointly visual-textual consistency between faces and names under constraints like the one-to-one assignment. Another idea is utilizing external resources such as online facial images for disambiguation. In [3], celebrity images freely available online are crawled from the Web for automatically face model learning. Then the refinement is carried out in a *kNN* manner. While in [7], the authors proposed the *Image Matching* (IM) method that performs name-face association by matching a face detected from a video to a celebrity whose facial images are most similar to it, and the facial images are obtained by using celebrity names as queries to issue *Google Image Search*. Experimental results show that for faces detected from Web videos which often suffer from low-resolution and even larger visual variations, IM performs better than the well-established GA method in general.

The IM method, despite straightforward, has a disadvantage that it heavily depends on the quality of top searched Web images. In other words, it performs well if there are faces in the top ranked images quite similar to faces detected from the Web video being associated, otherwise it may perform poorly. In [7], the authors use celebrity names purely as queries to retrieve images, which does not sound to be an ideal strategy for two reasons. First, top ranked images retrieved by a celebrity name are representative images of the celebrity covering a wide range of his/her activities. They are relevant to the celebrity rather than his/her appearance in a video. There is no guarantee that the face of a celebrity from a specific video would be well modeled by his/her top ranked facial images. Figure 1 (a) shows an example, where the top ranked images retrieved by "Lady Gaga" are presented. It is seen that their faces are diverse. Second, there are celebrities sharing the same name. For example, Jana Krause is the name of both a Czech TV host[1] and a Germany handball player. Figure 1 (b) gives the top ranked images searched by "Jana Krause", which is ambiguous. However, in case that given a video about "Lady Gaga Poker face", if we could derive that the video is related to *Lady Gaga* (name) and *Poker Face* (context) in advance by visual and textual analysis, we thus could generate a query composed of the two terms to issue Google. The returned images

---

[1] In fact, his true name is Jan Kraus. He is recognized as Jana Krause since he is known as the host of a famous TV show named Jana Krause.

are given in Fig. 1 (c), which are obviously more focused and relevant compared with Fig. 1 (a). Similarly, Fig. 1 (d) shows the images retrieved using "Jana Krause Show", which are clearly pointed to the Czech TV host. Consequently, if context of the video could obtain to some extent, we could generate carefully-assembled text queries instead of celebrity names solely. Thus more relevant facial images are likely to be retrieved from the huge Web resources.

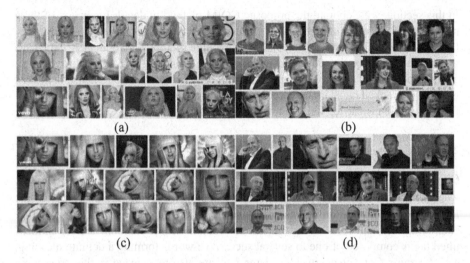

(a)   (b)

(c)   (d)

Fig. 1. Top ranked facial images returned from *Google Image Search* using different queries. (a) Lady Gaga. (b) Jana Krause. (c) Lady Gaga Poker Face. (d) Jana Krause show.

Motivated by this observation, we propose the *Context-Oriented Image Matching* (COIM) method to implement the task of name-face association. Given a Web video containing face and name responses, the COIM method can be viewed as a three-step pipeline. First, *Contextual Tags* (CTags) that roughly depict *who* are doing *what* at *where* and *when* for the video is identified, where tag relevance with respect to the video, tag clarity and tag correlation are jointly evaluated. Then, several relevant and discriminative queries in the form of <CTag, celebrity name> are picked out and are used to retrieve facial images, which are expected to be highly similar to the celebrities' appearance in the video. Thirdly, with the facial images, the task of name-face association is carried out in an image matching manner, i.e., a face from the video is matched with the sets of celebrities' Web facial image one-by-one, and roughly classified as the celebrity whose facial image set are most similar to it. The AT pipeline proposed in [7] is also applied to make sure the name-face assignment is one-to-one, and set the low confident assignments to null assignments. Compared with existing studies such as GA and IM, our novelty is the use of social tag analysis to assist the association, which is an active field with plentiful research output [9–14] but rare connection with the task of name-face association. We carry out experiments on ten people-related topics with hundreds of real-world Web videos containing faces and celebrity names. It is shown that the proposed COIM method outperforms several existing methods, where 4.8%~12.9% and 11.2%~13.9% performance gains in terms of FA and FP are observed when compared with the baselines.

2 Context-Oriented Name-Face Association

In this section, we elaborate the proposed COIM method in detail. It consists of three modules: CTag determination, query construction, and image matching based name-face association. Given a web video, the first module is employed to identify the CTags that roughly describe the video. Then, queries in the form of <CTag, celebrity name> are generated based on tag relevance and their co-occurrence characteristics. In the last module, top ranked facial images are retrieved using these queries and the task of name-face association is carried out in an image matching manner.

2.1 CTag Determination

Given a Web video v_q with faces $\mathcal{F}^q = \{f_0^q, f_1^q, \dots, f_n^q\}$ and tags $\mathcal{T}^q = \{t_0^q, t_1^q, \dots, t_m^q\}$, where the faces are detected from keyframes by commercial software developed by the IS'vision company[2], and the tags are found in surrounding text and are resolved by employing the Wiki-based tag identification method [15]. Using this method, an identified tag is composed of one to several successive words forming a definite meaning, e.g., *Britain's Got Talent*. Besides, name tags are also recognized in this process by checking the tags' Wikipedia pages.

With the tags, the CTag determination aims at picking out the informative and relevant ones with respect to v_q. We thus adopt the multiple tag property exploration (mTagPE) method [16] to implement the task. In mTagPE, the visual duplicate analysis is performed firstly. It utilizes content redundancy in social video platforms to collect a set of videos duplicated with v_q, as well as their associated tags [9, 10]. These videos and tags, defined as $\mathcal{V}_q^\#$ and $\mathcal{T}_q^\#$ respectively, construct a neighborhood for v_q. Then for each tag $t_i \in \mathcal{T}_q^\#$, tag relevance, tag clarity and tag correlation, which describe tag properties from different but complementary aspects, are separately formulated and measured. In the following, a tag relation graph is built with tag relevance and clarity as the node intensity and tag correlation as the edge weight. A random walk process is thus applied to fuse the properties and produce a final relevance score representing how good the tag serves as a contextual tag. Readers are referred to [16] for more details about the mTagPE method. The final relevance score of tag t_i outputted from the method is denoted as $S_{rd}(t_i, v_q)$ in this paper.

---

2 http://www.isvision.com/cn/index.

2.2   Query Construction

Generally, tags with the highest $S_{rd}(t_i, v_q)$ are the most informative tags with respect to a video v_q. They are usually names, locations, and other kinds of name entities. With several of them, context of the video could be largely determined. Assuming there are t name tags found by the mTagPE method. Thus, a straightforward strategy for query construction is building a text query for each name, where the query is formed by the name and other top scored contextual tags (name tags are excluded in advance). This kind of queries describes the video well. However, it is practically not a wise choice for Web facial image crawling, as the query is usually too concrete and strict. Using it in *Google Image Search* or other commercial search engines, the returned images are mostly duplicate images, or some of them are faces of other people related to the context. This is because the query consists of several tags thus the name tag is not a dominating factor. The search engine tends to misunderstand the intention behind query and return faces related to the context mainly.

To address this problem, we propose to construct the query using two tags, i.e., one name tag and one contextual tag that best fits the name. We believe this kind of combination could pick out a reasonable number of different facial images not only belonging to the name searched but also related to the video. Thus, an issue arises naturally: How to select a contextual tag that best fits a given name? Intuitively, the tag should be discriminative and highly relevant to the video, and it together with the name should eliminate the uncertainty of the images to be searched as much as possible. We thus propose to identify the appropriate tag according to two properties, i.e., tag relevance that has been well modeled by the $S_{rd}(t_i, v_q)$ previously, and tag co-occurrence characteristics. More specifically, the tag should be strongly related to the name within the context, but is loosely related to the name beyond the context. This property, denoted as $S_{tc}(t_i, n_j, v_q)$, is thus modeled as

$$S_{tc}(t_i, n_j, v_q) = \frac{\left| \mathcal{NV}^q_{t_i} \cap \mathcal{NV}^q_{n_j} \right|}{\left| \mathcal{NV}^q_{t_i} \right|} + 1 - \frac{\left| \mathcal{V}_{t_i} \cap \mathcal{V}_{n_j} \right|}{\left| \mathcal{V}_{t_i} \right|} \qquad (1)$$

where $\mathcal{NV}^q_{t_i} \subseteq \mathcal{V}^{\#}_q$ is the set of videos in the neighborhood of v_q that simultaneously contain tag t_i. $|\mathcal{V}|$ is the cardinality of set $\mathcal{V}$. $\mathcal{V}_{t_i}$ is the set of videos with tag t_i found in surrounding text in corpus C, which is a large and independent video repository for stable tag occurrence calculation. Here we use the MCG-WEBV [17] as the corpus. A tag with large co-occurrence in the neighborhood and small co-occurrence in corpus C with name n_j will have a large $S_{tc}(t_i, n_j, v_q)$ score. Note that we do not calculate the $S_{tc}(t_i, n_j, v_q)$ scores for all tags in $\mathcal{T}^{\#}_q$. In practice only top T tags with the highest $S_{rd}(t_i, v_q)$ (name tags are excluded) are calculated, where T is empirically set as 3.

Based on the two measurements above, the recommendation score of a tag t_i with respect to name n_j and video v_q, denoted as $S_r(t_i, n_j, v_q)$, is given by

$$S_r(t_i, n_j, v_q) = \alpha \cdot \bar{S}_{rd}(t_i, v_q) + (1 - \alpha) \cdot \bar{S}_{tc}(t_i, n_j, v_q) \tag{2}$$

where $\bar{S}_{rd}, \bar{S}_{tc} \in [0, 1]$ are the normalized S_{rd} and S_{tc}, respectively. $\alpha \in [0, 1]$ is a weight that linearly fuses the two terms. For each name n_j, the tag t_i with the highest $S_r(t_i, n_j, v_q)$ is selected to formulate the query for name n_j, i.e., $<t_i, n_j>$.

2.3 Image Matching Based Name-Face Association

With the determined queries $Q = \{< t_1, n_1 >, \cdots, < t_\tau, n_\tau >\}$, where τ is the number of names found in $\mathcal{T}_q^\#$, τ sets of facial images, each corresponds to a name, can be retrieved by issuing *Google Image Search* using the queries. Faces detected from the sets of Web images, denoted as $\mathcal{JF} = \{\mathcal{JF}^i, \ldots, \mathcal{JF}^\tau\}$, can be viewed as the gallery sets of the names. Therefore, for each face f_i^q detected from v_q, it could be classified as one of the names in $\mathcal{T}_q^\#$, or none of them, according to the similarity between the video face and the image faces belonging to the names, in which the similarity between face f_i^q and name n_j is computed by

$$simi_{ij} = min_{1 \leq t \leq K} e^{-\frac{d^2(f_i^q, f_t^j)}{\sigma}} \tag{3}$$

where f_i^q is the feature vector of the i-th face in video v_q, and f_t^j is the feature vector for of the t-th face in $\mathcal{JF}^j$. $d(\cdot, \cdot)$ calculates the Euclidean distance between vectors. σ is the heat kernel parameter.

With the similarities computed by Eq. (3), face f_i^q could not be simply named as the name with the highest $simi_{ij}$ currently, as two situations have not taken into accounts: (1) null assignments correspond to faces not belonging to any of the names, which is common for Web videos; and (2) the constraint of one-to-one assignment that prohibits the possibility of assigning multiple faces in a frame to the same name, which is not in accordance with the common sense.

To avoid the two cases, the AT pipeline proposed in [7] is employed. The pipeline first employs an *Assigning* step that constructs a bipartite graph with names and faces as nodes on two sides, and applies the Hungarian algorithm to make sure the name-face correspondences are one-to-one. Then, a *Thresholding* step, which introduces a predefined threshold, is applied to remove the low confident matched name-face pairs, i.e., force them null assigned. More details of the AT pipeline are given in [7]. After the AT pipeline, the obtained name-face pairs (including null assigned faces) constitute the results of name-face association.

3   Experiments

3.1   Dataset and Experimental Setup

To evaluate our COIM method, we construct a dataset of celebrity faces and names as follows. First, the WebV-Cele dataset [2] are employed as the repository, which consists of 75,073 hot YouTube videos crawled from Dec. 2008 to Feb. 2009, covering 2,427 celebrities and 649,001 faces. As we would like to collect videos containing multiple celebrities, ten topics occurring at this period are selected in terms of their popularity, facial appearance and the number of involved celebrities. Moreover, in order to verify the pros and cons of our method, there are topics about the same celebrity in different activities.

Descriptions of the topics, which are listed in Table 1, are used as queries to issue the index file built on top of surrounding text of the 75,073 videos. As a result, ten result lists are generated, each corresponding to a topic. We pick out the top 100 videos from each list. The videos are labeled as "relevant" or "irrelevant" one-by-one by an experienced assessor, where "relevant" means the video having at least one clip visually described the actual topic and also having face responses in WebV-Cele. The number of relevant videos, as well as the average number of faces and names found in the relevant videos of the ten topics is also listed in Table 1. The dataset finally consists of 351 videos. There are 13.3 faces and 2.2 names per video on average.

Table 1. Statistics on the selected ten topics

TID	Topic description	Time	#Video	#Face	#Name
1	Bush was attacked by shoes in Iraq	200811	56	11.5	2.2
2	Barack Obama's inauguration speech	200901	23	10.8	1.8
3	Amada Holden in Britain's Got Talent	200904	50	15.7	2.3
4	Susan Boyle's show in Britain's Got Talent	200904	73	14.7	2.7
5	Jim Carrey & Jenny McCarthy on Larry King Live	200908	14	27.7	3.0
6	Jonas Brothers on Larry King Live	200906	21	29.3	2.7
7	Lady Gaga Poker Face	200902	49	5.2	1.7
8	Lady Gaga on the Ellen DeGeneres Show	200905	22	14.8	2.6
9	Miley Cyrus's MTV – Fly on the Wall	200812	26	6.8	1.7
10	Kristen Stewart & Robert Pattinson on Movie Awards	200906	17	9.1	2.9
	Total		351	13.3	2.2

In the experiments, we run the 351 videos one-by-one, using our method and compared baseline methods. Each face appearing in these videos is assigned with a name presented in its neighborhood (e.g., $\mathcal{T}_q^{\#}$), or none of them. Three metrics measured the performance of name-face association at the face level, namely Face Accuracy (FA), Face Precision (FP) and Face Recall (FR) are adopted for evaluation, where FA calculates the fraction of correctly associated faces (including null assigned faces) over all the detected faces. FP is the same as FA, except that null assignments are not included for evaluation. FR is the fraction of correctly associated faces over all the labeled celebrity faces. As for the facial feature, we use the 1937-dimensional feature vector extracted from 13 facial regions [18].

3.2   Evaluations

In this section, sensibility analysis of the parameters is performed first to determine the optimal configuration of both COIM and IM methods. Then, the COIM method is compared with two baselines, i.e., the IM method and the GA method.

Parameter Sensibility Analysis. There are two types of parameters that affect the performance of the image matching based methods, i.e., the parameter K in Eq. (3), and the parameters α in Eq. (2).

We first fix the $\alpha = 0.5$ and analyze the influence of parameter K, which quantifies how many faces in top searched celebrity images are involved for evaluation. For both COIM and IM methods, the parameter is set to different numbers (maximal 64) and results are listed in Table 2. To make a fair comparison, we adjust thresholds such that the methods all have an FR around 0.5.

Table 2.   FPs and FAs of COIM and IM for different K at an FR around 0.5

		$K = 10$	$K = 20$	$K = 30$	$K = 64$
FA	IM	0.5911	0.609	0.6134	0.6157
	COIM	0.6603	0.6937	0.6792	0.6595
FP	IM	0.6475	0.6786	0.6946	0.7004
	COIM	0.7155	0.7754	0.7587	0.7380

As can be seen, the performance steadily improves with the increase of K for IM, showing that IM benefits from more Web image faces. In contrast, the performance experiences a first growth and then a decline for COIM. It implies that the tailored designed queries indeed collect facial images that are highly relevant to the celebrities' appearance in the video, especially for the top searched ones. On the other hand, the decline process can be explained as that there are only a reasonable number of relevant facial images. Expanding the query words is likely to confuse the query intention to some extent and results in noisy images, which also explains the reasonable of using two rather than more tags to construct the queries.

We then investigate parameter α that balances the contribution of tag relevance and tag co-occurrence. For simplicity, we range α from 0 to 1.0 with an increasing step of 0.1. Table 3 gives the results. It is seen that the optimal performance is achieved when setting $\alpha = 0.6$, showing that the tag relevance plays a more important role in the query construction. Moreover, it is also show that the combination of the two properties can generate better performance when compared with the results of considering the two properties individually (i.e., $\alpha = 0$ or $\alpha = 1.0$), indicating the merit of multiple tag property fusion. Drawing from the observations, we set $K = 64$ for IM, and fix $K = 20$ and $\alpha = 0.6$ for our COIM method in the following evaluations.

Table 3. Performance of the COIM method w.r.t parameter α at an FR around 0.5

α	0	0.1	0.2	0.3	0.4	0.5	0.6	0.7	0.8	0.9	1.0
FA	0.605	0.641	0.665	0.679	0.686	0.694	**0.701**	0.695	0.682	0.663	0.648
FP	0.688	0.703	0.734	0.749	0.765	0.775	**0.785**	0.780	0.760	0.742	0.732

Name-Face Association. To evaluate the performance in name-face association, our COIM method and two baselines, i.e., the IM method [7] and the GA method [5], are tested against the 351 videos. The performance is listed in Table 4, where the results with FRs around 0.2, 0.5 and 0.8 are given, representing typical applications of high, middle and low FAs, respectively. The main observations are:

Table 4. The overall performance of different methods on the 351 videos

	FA			FP		
	FR = 0.2	FR = 0.5	FR = 0.8	FR = 0.2	FR = 0.5	FR = 0.8
GA	0.5814	0.6204	0.5660	0.8325	0.6895	0.4986
IM	0.5828	0.6224	0.5749	0.8578	0.7087	0.5195
COIM	**0.6106**	**0.7006**	**0.6324**	**0.9283**	**0.7850**	**0.5542**

- IM performs slightly better than GA, which again demonstrates that leveraging external resources is a promising direction for improving the performance of name-face association. Moreover, the IM based methods have the merit that it does not rely on large number of faces and names to model the visual-textual consistency.
- COIM performs better than IM across different FRs, where 4.8%~12.6% improvement gains in terms of FA, and 6.7%~10.8% improvement gains in terms of FP are obtained compared with IM, showing that COIM is indeed beneficial from the facial images crawled by tailored designed queries with contextual information.
- As FR increases, FA experiences a growth and followed by a decline process. This is attributed to the influence of null assignments. When FR is low, a majority of celebrity faces are wrongly null assigned because of the rigorous set threshold. The error is gradually rectified with the growth of FR. However, when FR is high, it raises another problem that many unknown faces are also assigned with names.

We further present the FAs and FPs of our COIM method at an FR around 0.5 on the ten topics in Table 5. As can be seen, the performance varies greatly among different topics. For example, topic 5 and 8 are mainly about interviews. The detected faces are usually large and clear. Matching between images is thus easy to implement. In contrast, COIM performs poorly for topic 7 and 9, whose faces are captured from MTV with motion blur, occlusions, heavily makeup, etc, making the extracted facial feature relatively noisy. Interestingly, topic 6 is also about an interview but their performance is not as good as topic 5 and 8. This is because on one hand, Jonas Brothers is a group of three persons looked similar. On the other hand, the searched facial images of one of them often mix with the others, making the association unreliable.

Table 5. Performance of the COIM method on the ten topics at an FR around 0.5

TID	FA	FP	TID	FA	FP	TID	FA	FP
1	0.7214	0.8255	5	0.7599	0.8604	9	0.6637	0.7096
2	0.6865	0.8102	6	0.6178	0.6570	10	0.6773	0.7324
3	0.7360	0.8434	7	0.6243	0.7074			
4	0.7262	0.8368	8	0.7926	0.8673	mean	0.7006	0.7850

4   Conclusion

In this paper we have proposed the COIM method for automatically associating faces detected from Web videos with their names. Our novelty lies in the use of highly similar Web facial images to implement the association, where queries concisely describing celebrities in a specific video are derived and used to crawl the face images. Consequently, the task of name-face association is better implemented within the image matching framework. The experiments conducted on ten people-related topics basically validate our proposal, from which remarkable performance improvement are observed when compared with the GA and IM methods. While the overall performance of the COIM is promising, we observe that advanced facial feature representations such as DeepFace [18] are proposed recently. Thus, we are also interested in investigating the effectiveness of applying such representations to the COIM method in the near future.

Acknowledgements. This research is supported by National Nature Science Foundation of China (Grant No. 61303175, 61303171).

References

1. Bu, J., Xu, B., Wu, C.: Unsupervised face-name association via commute distance. ACM Multimedia **2012**, 219–228 (2012)
2. Chen, Z.N., Ngo, C.W., Zhang, W., Cao, J., Jiang, Y.G.: Name-face association in web videos: a large-scale dataset, baselines, and open issues. J. Comput. Sci. Technol. **29**(5), 785–798 (2014)
3. Zhao, M., Yagnik, J.: Large-scale learning and recognition of faces in web videos. IEEE FGR **2008**, 1–7 (2008)
4. Zhang, Y.F., Xu, C.S., Lu, H.Q.: Character identification in feature-length films using global face-name matching. IEEE Trans. Multimedia **11**(7), 1276–1288 (2009)
5. Guillaumin, M., Mensink, T., Verbeek, J.: Face recognition from caption-based supervision. Int. J. Comput. Vis. **96**(1), 64–82 (2012)
6. Chen, Z.N., Ngo, C.W., Cao, J., Zhang, W.: Community as a connector: associating faces with celebrity names in web videos. ACM Multimedia **2012**, 809–812 (2012)
7. Chen, Z.N., Feng, B.L., Ngo, C.W., Jia, C.Y., Huang, X.S.: Improving automatic name-face association using celebrity images on the web. ICMR **2015**, 623–626 (2015)
8. Pang, L., Ngo, C.W.: Unsupervised celebrity face naming in web videos. IEEE Trans. Multimedia **17**(6), 854–866 (2015)
9. Zhao, W.L., Wu, X., Ngo, C.W.: On the annotation of web videos by efficient near-duplicate search. IEEE Trans. Multimedia **12**(5), 448–461 (2010)

10. Siersdorfer, S., Pedro, J.S., Sanderson, M.: Content redundancy in YouTube and its application to video tagging. ACM Trans. Inf. Syst. **29**(3), 301–331 (2011)
11. Liu, D., Yan, S.C., Hua, X.S., Zhang, H.J.: Image retagging using collaborative tag propagation. IEEE Trans. Multimedia **13**(4), 702–712 (2011)
12. Chen, Z.N., Cao, J., Xia, T., Song, Y.C., Zhang, Y.D., Li, J.T.: Web video retagging. Multimedia Tools Appl. **55**(1), 53–82 (2011)
13. Li, X., Snoek, C.G.M., Worring, M.: Learning social tag relevance by neighbor voting. IEEE Trans. Multimedia **11**(7), 1310–1322 (2009)
14. Chen, Z.N., Cao, J., Song, Y.C., Guo, J.B., Zhang, Y.D., Li, J.T.: Context-oriented web video tag recommendation. WWW **2010**, 1079–1080 (2010)
15. Chen, Z.N., Cao, J., Song, Y.C., Zhang, Y.D., Li, J.T.: Web video categorization based on Wikipedia categories and content-duplicate open resources. In: ACM Multimedia 2010, pp. 1107–1110 (2010)
16. Chen, Z., Feng, B., Xie, H., Zheng, R., Xu, B.: Video to article hyperlinking by multiple tag property exploration. In: Gurrin, C., Hopfgartner, F., Hurst, W., Johansen, H., Lee, H., O'Connor, N. (eds.) MMM 2014, Part I. LNCS, vol. 8325, pp. 62–73. Springer, Heidelberg (2014)
17. Cao, J., Zhang, Y.D., Song, Y.C., Chen, Z.N., Zhang, X., Li, J.T.: MCG-WEBV: a benchmark dataset for web video analysis, Technical report, pp. 1–10 (2009)
18. Taigman, Y., Yang, M., Ranzato, M., Wolf, L.: DeepFace: closing the gap to human-level performance in face verification. CVPR **2014**, 1701–1708 (2014)

Social Media Profiler: Inferring Your Social Media Personality from Visual Attributes in Portrait

Jie Nie[1(✉)], Lei Huang[2], Peng Cui[1], Zhen Li[2], Yan Yan[2],
Zhiqiang Wei[2], and Wenwu Zhu[1]

[1] Department of Computer Science and Technology,
Tsinghua University, Beijing, China
niejie@tsinghua.edu.cn
[2] Department of Computer Science and Technology,
Ocean University of China, Qingdao, China

Abstract. In this paper, we introduce an interesting but challenging problem: how to infer social media personality from portrait. To address this problem, we jointly consider social media content and behavior information. Specifically, first, we represent social media personality as a reflection in accordance with user behaviors in social media. Second, by means of clustering, people are divided into eight groups and labeled with different personality types. Upon regression analysis, discriminative visual attributes for personality classification are determined. Third, low-level features of selected visual attributes are trained to predict personality from given portrait. To evaluate the proposed method, we collect images of people from the internet and the behaviors of these people from their micro-blog. Comprehensive experiments demonstrate that the proposed method can achieve significant performance gain over the existing method.

Keywords: Social media · Personality · Visual attribute · Portrait

1 Introduction

With rapid increasing of social media, we expose ourselves more and more by means of multimedia. By examining these data, psychologists could infer personality and deduce appearance, age, education, occupation, and even living habits of people. This judgment is based on the fact that our behaviors are decided by personality, which also impacts on our life, career and appearance. For example, people who smile more have deep nasolabial folds, and serious people prefer sagging their mouth. Therefore, connections exist between social media activities and appearance. To evident, in social media, people who always post selfies are usually dressed up and fancy wearing. As a contrast, people with frequent posts of technical news, almost fixed their appearance by a simple figure, e.g., Jobs. What's more, in case of data mining, it is difficult to determine initial values in the absence of empirical or historical information. By connecting behavior information with appearance, people could estimate it properly if

E. Chen et al. (Eds.): PCM 2016, Part II, LNCS 9917, pp. 640–649, 2016.
DOI: 10.1007/978-3-319-48896-7_63

given a photo. Thus, learning how to predict human personalities from portraits is important.

More recently, some works investigated connections between multimedia and personality from psychological perspective [1–4]. Machajdik et al. [1] studied inferring affections from multimedia and exploited theoretical and empirical concepts from psychology and art theory to extract and combine low-level features that represent the emotional content of an image. [2–4] extended potential information embedded in multimedia to excavate out human personality. As a result, Cristani et al. [2] inferred one's personality traits from photo corpus amount of 300 posts as his/her favorite on Flickr, and Nie's work [3] studied the perception of profile pictures and visual elements that can appear in a profile, However, the existing works only considered content information without behavior information, which contains useful clews correlative to human personality. While our work considers behavior information in addition to content information and achieves significant better performance. Moreover, the above existing methods set the ground truth of personality by introducing psychology questionnaires participated by human, which leads to a subjective estimation. While in this work, we define our personality as "social media personality" which is reflected accordance with human's social media behaviors. By being given quantitative representation of personality, our method become more reasonable and convincible.

Through the above analysis, we propose an interesting problem of how to infer social media personality from portrait image. To address this problem, we jointly consider behavior information together with content information. More specifically, we first incorporate social media content and social media behavior from microblog for grouping people by social media personality types. Then, visual attributes selection scheme is performed by using the social media personality types as ground truth. Finally, prediction model of social media personality for portrait is built by exploring low-level representation for visual attributes. Experiments are carried out on a challenging dataset containing microblog information of 1000 public people from 2009 to 2014 and 5000 corresponding portraits from "Google images". This paper reveals the existence of connection between visual attributes in human portrait and social media behaviors. What's more, it demonstrates it is possible to predict social media behaviors from portraits.

2   The Method

Our proposed method consists of three key technical components: social media personality representation by incorporating content and behavior from microblog, visual attributes selection scheme towards social media personality, and feature extraction for visual attributes. Next we will present them in details.

2.1   Social Media Personality Representation

In this paper, we define social media personality as the personality reflected accordance with human's social media content and behavior. For social media content, we applied concepts [5] and emotions detectors [6] on images posted by one user during a relatively long period in social media, and then represented by concepts and emotions histograms. For social media behavior, we utilized statistical data related to user's active period, level of attention (interests), and frequency of posts and forwards. Table 1 lists detailed description of factors we introduced to represent human's social media personality. With these representation, one user is described as a vector with 54 dimensions. Then we use the clustering algorithm to process these data. The clustering algorithm can divide the people into different groups. Each group of people have similar behaviors in social media. We use these groups as personality types.

Table 1. Factors of social media personality representation. Concepts include: animal, baby, building, commercial advertisement, crowd, dress, entertainment, face, flowers, food, greeting, handshaking, head and shoulder, maps, mountain, nighttime, oceans, office, old people, outdoor, person, rainy, river, road, shopping mall, sky, sports, sunny, traffic, and weather. Emotions include: joy, anticipation, anger, disgust, sadness, surprise, fear, and trust.

Category	No.	Name	Length	Short description
Social media content	1	Concepts	30	Normalized histogram of concepts. Posted images are applied through concept detectors, and 30 concept detectors are adopted in our paper
	2	Emotions	8	Normalized histogram of emotions. Posted images are applied through emotion detectors. Eight emotion detectors are adopted in our paper
Social media behavior	3	Active period	12	Posts (including forwards) are summed on the fact that they were released during the same time period, where the whole day is divided evenly into 12 periods. Values are normalized
	4	Level of attention	2	The mean and standard deviation of attention numbers on each post. Values are normalized by fans number
	5	Frequency of posts	2	The mean posts number and forwards number per day

2.2 Visual Attribute Selection

During the process of finding connections between social media personality and portrait visual attributes, it is important to select proper visual attributes, which are correlative towards social media personality. Therefore, we explore visual attributes within human's portrait as much as possible first, and then by regression analysis, we choose discriminative attributes on the fact that how it affects the result of distinguishing users by social media personality.

Figure 1 shows visual attributes concerned in our work. All visual attributes are labeled manually on 200 portraits, which are downloaded from "Google image" by using people's names as search queries. Here we choose public people since it is easy to obtain his/her representative portrait, what is convincible to express personality.

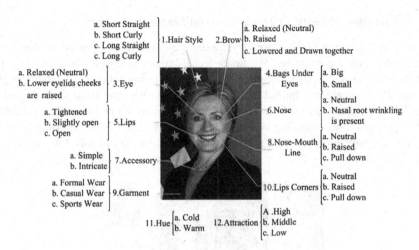

Fig. 1. Visual attribute descriptions of portrait.

Multinomial logistic regression model is introduced for unveiling the correlation between visual attributes and personality types. Here we simply represent the model as $M\_L(V, P)$, where V is the set containing all visual attributes, and P indicates personality types as discussed in Sect. 2.1. For each visual attribute v_i, we calculate its contribution value as follows.

$$Con.(v_i) = 1 - Probability(Likelihood\_Ratio\_Test(v_i))$$
$$= 1 - Probability(-2\ln(\frac{Likelihood(M\_L(V - \{v_i\}, P))}{Likelihood(M\_L(V, P))}))$$

where $Likelihood\_Ratio\_Test(v_i) \sim \chi^2$. The larger contribution value is, the more important role v_i plays. If value larger than 0.995, the corresponding visual attribute is very relevant to the social media personality. Table 2 shows the results for contribution value test of each visual attribute. From Table 2, we can find that nine visual attributes are very relevant to the social media personality, i.e., Hair style, Brow, Eye, Lips, Nose, Nose mouth lines, Garment, Lips corners and Hue.

Table 2. Contribution value test

Visual attribute	Contribution value	Visual attribute	Contribution value
v_1: Hair style	1	v_7: Accessary	0.938
v_2: Brow	0.996	v_8: Nose mouth lines	1
v_3: Eye	1	v_9: Garment	1
v_4: Bags under eyes	0.813	v_{10}: Lips corners	0.999
v_5: Lips	0.997	v_{11}: Hue	0.999
v_6: Nose	0.998	v_{12}: Attraction	0.966

2.3 Descriptor of Features Towards Social Media Personality

Leading by regression analysis, we design a descriptor considering visual attributes that affect social media personality. We firstly locate human face using face detection [7] and then extract the facial part by applying bonding boxes following methods in [8]. All facial regions are normalized into 100 * 80 pixels. We extend the facial region to both left and right sides by 16 pixels, and upper side by 40 pixels to locate the hair parts, results in three bounding box regions. Then, we locate the region of apparel 10 pixels below face with size of 200 * 180 pixels. Results are illustrated in Fig. 2(a).

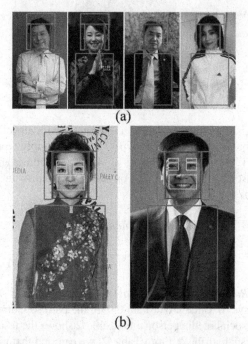

Fig. 2. Human regions location. (a) Face, hair and torso region location. (b) Eye brows, eyes, nose-mouth region location.

We detect functional regions of face, such as eyebrows, eyes, nose and mouth manually, only once, and applying to all face images by an automatic labeling system. However, not all features are helpful to distinguish different personalities. Eye brows, eyes, nose-mouth regions are selected on the fact that these factors affect personality classification referring to Sect. 2.2. as shown in Fig. 2(b). And we unified these regions to 15 * 30 pixels, 20 * 30 pixels and 40 * 80 pixels. Table 3 enumerates features we extract from each region. Features are aggregated by concatenating together.

Table 3. Description of features extracted from human regions.

Category		No.	Length	Short description
Facial regions	Eye brows	1	19	Mean of image intensity; normalized histogram of edge orientation; normalized histogram of edge magnitude
	Eyes	2	19	Mean of image intensity; normalized histogram of edge orientation; normalized histogram of edge magnitude
	Nose-mouth	3	28	Histogram of Gradients (HOG) and Local Binary Pattern Descriptors (LBP)
Hair regions		4	13	Mean of image intensity; normalized histogram of edge orientation
Apparel regions		5	22	LBP and Vision based garment descriptor [9]
Background		6	32	HSV Color space

3 Experiments

3.1 Experiment Setup

Experiments are performed in two phases: firstly, people are represented by social media data and clustered into groups. In this phase, we download social media images and data referring to user's behavior of 1000 public people from microblog in the year from 2009 to 2014. Then, with "social media personality" presentation, people are clustered by K-means algorithm. Here, K is 8 referring to the selection method in reference [10]. People and their personality types composed our ground truth listing in Table 4 with detailed numbers. Secondly, we download portrait images of these people using "Google image" by searching their names. Usually, we selected images ranked top five since these are more representative for public people. Thus, there are 5000 portraits labeled with personality types.

Table 4. Personality types

Type no.	A	B	C	D	E	F	G	H
People number	257	189	147	113	98	82	70	44
Portrait number	1285	945	735	565	490	410	350	220

For each personality type, we trained a classifier by using portrait images. Our classifiers are Support Vector Machines with RBF kernels, which been trained using LibSVM [11]. For each classifier, the sample number we use are between 50 to 250 for positive samples and 1000 for negative samples.

3.2   Results and Analysis

3.2.1   Performance Comparison

We trained a total of eight classifiers to predict social media personality from human portraits. To compare our features, we adopted the same feature types applied in the whole image other than in specific regions as the baseline. We use precision/recall and F1-measure as the evaluation metric. Since the number of negative samples are over 10 times of positive samples, we also give the performance under accuracy metric. Results are shown in Table 5. From Table 5, we can see that the accuracy of our feature, which achieves an average accuracy 80.38% on inferring personality type from portraits images, gain an improvement by 9.36% to the base line method. As shown from the recall values, our method achieves an average value 81.67%, gain an improvement by 23.26% to the base line method. This demonstrates that our features are definitely discriminative since our features are extracted from portrait regions correlated to social media personality while base line features are extracted from the whole image that may con tains a plenty of noises.

Table 5. Comparison of our method with other method.

Classifier	Precision		Recall	
	Our method	Baseline	Our method	Baseline
Type A	**71.57%**	60.24%	**84.44%**	75.10%
Type B	**68.06%**	42.08%	**94.50%**	56.51%
Type C	**53.62%**	21.32%	**82.59%**	78.64%
Type D	**35.00%**	16.45%	**69.38%**	53.63%
Type E	**14.59%**	10.72%	**57.76%**	21.02%
Type F	**25.23%**	25.66%	**98.29%**	85.37%
Type G	**45.94%**	11.28%	**79.14%**	28.86%
Type H	**20.19%**	7.16%	**87.27%**	68.18%
Average value	**41.78%**	24.36%	**81.67%**	58.41%
Classifier	F1-measure		Accuracy	
	Our method	Baseline	Our method	Baseline
Type A	**77.39%**	66.85%	**87.38%**	80.85%
Type B	**79.13%**	48.24%	**90.58%**	77.08%
Type C	**65.02%**	33.55%	**76.14%**	54.20%
Type D	**46.53%**	25.18%	**81.98%**	63.98%
Type E	**23.30%**	13.25%	**62.72%**	75.10%
Type F	**40.15%**	39.46%	**67.92%**	78.52%
Type G	**58.13%**	16.22%	**92.02%**	79.14%
Type H	**32.79%**	12.96%	**84.26%**	59.27%
Average value	**52.81%**	31.96%	**80.38%**	71.02%

3.2.2 Personality Collages

Beyond the quantitative comparisons, we highlight the qualitative performance of our method in Fig. 3. Figure 3 lists a random selection of portrait images labeled with personality types a to h corresponding to personality types A to H in Table 4. From Fig. 3, we can find that people with same personality type usually have similar property in portraits, e.g., for personality type A, people are always with short hair (83.27%) and fancy wear (75.09%). While on the other hand, for social media personalities, their active periods occurred at nighttime (89.49%) and most of them are interested in sports (67.32%). For personality type B, people are always in formal wear (55.55%) and with tightened lips (67.20%).

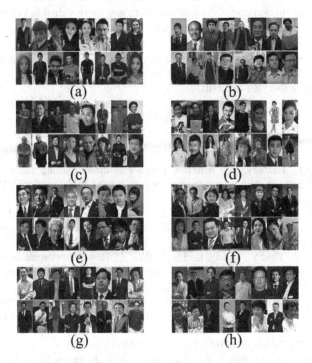

Fig. 3. Performance demonstration of personality types.

Further, we also have made comprehensive comparison between the behavior data in microblog and visual attributes in portrait. We find that long term behavior data in microblog is superior to visual attribute in portrait for social media personality inferring. For example, people in personality D are always detected as A, since both of them are fancy dressed (87.61%). However, personality D posts more selfies than personality A. People in personality E and H are falsely classified as B since their visual attributes are similar but they have big difference in social behaviors.

4 Conclusions and Future Works

In this paper, we address the problem of how to infer social media personality from portrait image by jointly considering content and behavior information. We firstly represent social media personality as a reflection in accordance with user behaviors in social media. Then, people are divided into groups and labeled with different personality types by clustering. Discriminative visual attributes for personality classification are determined. Finally, low-level features of selected visual attributes are trained to predict personality from given portrait. Comprehensive experiments strongly demonstrate the effectiveness of our method. Future work will concentrate on features refine and design [12, 13]. It is also necessary to enlarge dataset by bringing in information of common people. As a result, more and more valuable information could be reflected through the lens of multimedia.

Acknowledgements. This work is supported by the National Nature Science Foundation of China (No. 61402428, No. 61202208); the Self Innovation and Achievements Transformation of Shandong Province (No. 2014CGZH0708).

References

1. Machajdik, J., Hanbury, A.: Affective image classification using features inspired by psychology and art theory. In: Proceedings of the ACM International Conference on Multimedia (2010)
2. Cristani, M., Vinciarelli, A., Segalin, C., Perina, A.: Unveiling the multimedia unconscious: implicit cognitive processes and multimedia content analysis. In: Proceedings of the ACM International Conference on Multimedia (2013)
3. Nie, J., Cui, P., Yan, Y., Huang, L., Li, Z., Wei, Z.: How your portrait impresses people? Inferring personality impressions from portrait contents. In: Proceedings of the ACM International Conference on Multimedia (2014)
4. Yan, Y., Nie, J., Huang, L., Li, Z., Cao, Q., Wei, Z.: Is your first impression reliable? Trustworthy analysis using facial traits in portraits. In: He, X., Luo, S., Tao, D., Xu, C., Yang, J., Hasan, M.A. (eds.) MMM 2015. LNCS, vol. 8936, pp. 148–158. Springer, Heidelberg (2015). doi:10.1007/978-3-319-14442-9_13
5. Jiang, Y.-G., Yang, J., Ngo, C.-W., Hauptmann, A.G.: Representations of keypoint-based semantic concept detection: a comprehensive study. IEEE Trans. Multimedia **12**(1), 42–53 (2010)
6. Borth, D., Ji, R., Chen, T., Breuel, T., Chang, S.F.: Large-scale visual sentiment ontology and detectors using adjective noun pairs. In: Proceedings of the ACM International Conference on Multimedia (2013)
7. Viola, P., Jones, M.: Rapid object detection using a boosted cascade of simple features. In: Proceedings of the IEEE Conference on Computer Vision and Pattern Recognition (2001)
8. Cootes, T.F., Taylor, C.J., Cooper, D.H., Graham, J.: Active shape models-their training and application. Comput. Vis. Image Underst. **61**(1), 38–59 (1995)
9. Huang, L., Xia, T., Zhang, Y., Lin, S.: Finding suits in images of people. In: Schoeffmann, K., Merialdo, B., Hauptmann, Alexander, G., Ngo, C.-W., Andreopoulos, Y., Breiteneder, C. (eds.) MMM 2012. LNCS, vol. 7131, pp. 485–494. Springer, Heidelberg (2012). doi:10.1007/978-3-642-27355-1_45

10. Leskovec, J., Rajaraman, A., Ullman, J.: Mining of Massive Datasets. Cambridge University Press, Cambridge (2010)
11. Chang, C., Lin, C.: LIBSVM: a library for support vector machines. ACM Trans. Intell. Syst. Technol. 2(27), 1–27 (2011)
12. Liu, W., Mei, T., Zhang, Y., Che, C., Luo, J.: Multi-task deep visual semantic embedding for video thumbnail selection. In: IEEE Conference on Computer Vision and Pattern Recognition, pp. 3707–371 (2015)
13. Liu, W., Zhang, Y., Tang, S., Tang, J., Hong, R., Li, J.: Accurate estimation of human body orientation from RGB-D sensors. IEEE Trans. Cybern. 43(5), 1442–1452 (2013)

SSFS: A Space-Saliency Fingerprint Selection Framework for Crowdsourcing Based Mobile Location Recognition

Hao Wang[✉], Dong Zhao, Huadong Ma, and Huaiyu Xu

Beijing Key Laboratory of Intelligent Telecommunications Software and Multimedia,
School of Computer Science, Beijing University of Posts and Telecommunications,
Beijing, China
{wanghaoxc,dzhao,mhd,xuhuaiyu}@bupt.edu.cn

Abstract. With the development of the crowdsourcing technology, it is introduced to collect fingerprints including images and other sensory data for constructing location recognition database. However, when abundant crowdsourced fingerprints with diversified quality evolve, it is necessary to select high quality fingerprints to decrease the burden of storage for performing offline location recognition directly on mobile devices. To address this problem, we propose a fingerprint selection framework, i.e., **Space- Saliency Fingerprint Selection (SSFS)**, considering both the space distribution and image quality of the fingerprints. First, for all the fingerprints corresponding to the same object, we propose the **Self-adaptive Space Clustering (SSC)** algorithm to group them into several clusters for maintaining high diversity of the fingerprint database. Second, for every cluster, we propose the **Salient Part Feature Detection (SPFD)** algorithm to detect salient parts of images with various disturbances for evaluating the quality of images. Extensive experiments demonstrate that SSFS is effective and efficient for fingerprint selection requirement.

Keywords: Mobile location recognition · Crowdsourcing · Fingerprint selection · Salient part feature

1 Introduction

The proliferation of smartphones equipped with cameras and various sensors provides a great potential for implementing location-based services. Although the GPS can perform the physical localization with good accuracy in many scenarios, it is still powerless when the users tend to launch a logical location query. In contrast, the Mobile Visual Location Recognition (MVLR) [1] system utilizes the image and various sensory data captured from smartphones as a location query, and matches it to a location fingerprint database which is built in advance for providing logical location information to users.

How to construct the location fingerprint database is still an important issue for MVLR systems. One of the most popular ways is to collect images from

© Springer International Publishing AG 2016
E. Chen et al. (Eds.): PCM 2016, Part II, LNCS 9917, pp. 650–659, 2016.
DOI: 10.1007/978-3-319-48896-7_64

social networking websites, e.g., Flickr and Panoramio [2]. However, the images obtained in this way may miss important details such as shooting angle and GPS information, and tend to be poorly organized. Another widely-used way is to drive surveying vehicles with digital camera system and other mounted sensing equipments, e.g., Inertial Measurement Unit(IMU) [3], to collect rich location fingerprints. However, this way is time-consuming and labor-intensive, and may not be effective wherever the surveying vehicles cannot reach, e.g., restricted zones of campuses or streets. In order to address this issue, Wang et al. [1] introduce the crowdsourcing technology [5,6] to a location fingerprint collection framework, and construct a crowdsourced fingerprint database composed of thousands of images and various sensory data, including shooting angle, GPS, tilt, etc. Nevertheless, with the long-term running of the system, the amount of fingerprints increases rapidly, which will decrease the fingerprint searching efficiency. Moreover, in order to save users' mobile traffic, it is a popular way to realize an offline mobile location recognition system [4] directly on mobile devices by downloading the fingerprint database in advance. This way always prefers a smaller fingerprint database to decrease the burden of storage for smartphones. Thus, it is important to design a fingerprint selection framework to eliminate redundancy but without obvious loss of location recognition accuracy.

To address the fingerprint selection problem, we propose Space-Saliency Fingerprint Selection (SSFS), considering both the spatial distribution and image quality. For one thing, the framework should be capable of filtering out the redundant spatial fingerprints and maintaining the high diversity in the spatial distribution. For this purpose, we propose the Self-adaptive Space Clustering (SSC) algorithm to partition the fingerprints corresponding to the same object into several clusters. For another, we pay attention to image quality which is also an important issue. When constructing the fingerprint database, it is incvitable to take various disturbances caused by moving pedestrians or vehicles in the background. Whereas, salient parts of images may not be missed. Yang et al. [7] propose Identical Salient Point (ISP) to extract salient visual words from multiple images captured by smartphones, using which some disturbances are excluded for improving searching precision. Inspired by ISP, we propose Salient Part Features (SPF) to evaluate the image quality of crowdsourced database within the spacial clusters. Then, we propose Salient Part Feature Detection (SPFD) algorithm to distinguish the features corresponding to salient part from others. In the previous work, Chen et al. [8] propose a generic task-driven data collection framework (CrowdPic) for mobile crowd photographing. However, in addition to utilize sensory data for fingerprint selection, we focus on evaluating the image quality using Visual Hashing Bit (VHB) [9] with respect to disturbance caused by moving pedestrians or vehicles.

To testify the effectiveness of the SSFS, we compare the searching precision of the SSPF with other schemes (randomly selection, only considering the spatial distribution, and only considering the image quality), by performing experiments on 8,062 fingerprints crowdsourced from BUPT campus. By selecting 90% of fingerprints from the database, SSPF achieves around 5% precision superior to other schemes and maintains nearly the same precision as 100% of fingerprints.

The rest of the paper is organized as follows. Section 2 provides an overview of the SSFS framework. Sections 3 and 4 present the SSC algorithm and SPFD algorithm in detail, respectively. In Sect. 5, extensive experiments are conducted to demonstrate the effectiveness of the framework. At last, this paper is concluded in Sect. 6.

2   SSFS Framework

As mentioned above, SSFS framework aims at satisfying two requirements: spatial diversity distribution and high-quality image selection. Figure 1 presents the modules of the framework. The framework is mainly composed of four components: Initiation, Self-adaptive space clustering, Salient part detection, and Fingerprint filtering out.

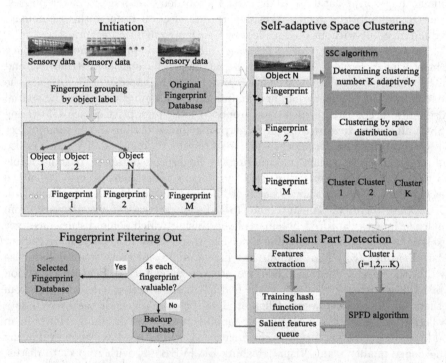

Fig. 1. Framework of Space Salient Fingerprint Selection (SSFS)

Initiation. We launch the initiation of the fingerprint grouping and prepare for fingerprint selection. Although abundant fingerprints are obtained by crowdsourcing technology, the disordered original fingerprints should be sorted out.

The original fingerprints are grouped into dozens of objects, each of which is composed of different numbers of fingerprints.

Self-adaptive Space Clustering. For all the fingerprints corresponding to the same object, it is necessary to divide them into several clusters. However, since each fingerprint is captured from distinct angles and locations, the clustering number should be adaptive for the characteristics of the fingerprints. The goal of SSC algorithm is to assign every fingerprint a cluster ID for selecting high-quality images.

Salient Part Detection. After obtaining the cluster ID of every fingerprint from the previous module, how to select high-quality subset from fingerprints with the same cluster ID is still not-trivial. Considering various disturbances of the images, we propose SPFD detection algorithm to evaluate them with respect to the salient features they contain. Then, this part can provide a sequence of queues, each of which is filled with fingerprints with the same object. Moreover, the descending queues are sorted with respect to the amount of salient part features.

Fingerprint Filtering Out. The last module of the framework is Fingerprint Filtering Out. After obtaining the queues from previous part, the system sets the proportion of the fingerprints to be selected and reserves the deleted fingerprints into backup database.

3   Self-adaptive Space Clustering

As illustrated in Fig. 2, the fingerprints which are shooting toward the object show the characteristics of spatial distribution in the scenario. When capturing the objects, sensors (accelerometer & magnetometer) which are embedded in the smartphones record the contextual distribution, e.g., shooting angles.

Then, we propose spatial grouping to separate these fingerprints into several clusters. The main goal of spatial grouping is to maintain the diversity of the selected fingerprints which should have multiple shooting angle groups. If fingerprints with similar shooting angles predominate in the selected fingerprint database, it is hard to cover the various aspects of the object, which may be inevitable to decrease the searching precision.

However, how many clusters should be designed is still a significant problem. Considering that different objects have different fingerprint distribution characteristics, we argue that the clustering number should adapt to the spatial distribution. Specifically, if the fingerprints' shooting angles vary in a large scope, the clustering number should be designed larger; whereas, if the shooting angles vary in a small scope, the clustering number should be designed smaller. Inspired by setting the azimuth value to be 20° as angular threshold parameter in Crowd-pan-360 [10], we also set each cluster's shooting angle scope to be 20°. Moreover, from the experimental results in CrowdLR [1], it is also inferred that 20° is also an appropriate threshold parameter. With the fingerprints corresponding to the same object, we denote the maximum shooting angle as Ang_{max}, and denote the

654   H. Wang et al.

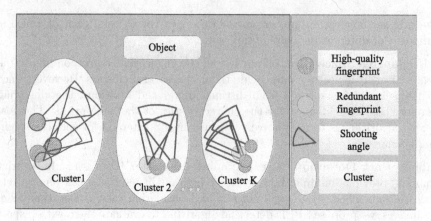

Fig. 2. Spatial grouping of the fingerprints. Fingerprints corresponding to the same object are grouped into K clusters. Then, high-quality fingerprints will be selected in each cluster.

minimum shooting angle as Ang_{min}. Then, the self-adaptive cluster number K should satisfy the Eq. (1).

$$K = \left\lceil \frac{|Ang_{max} - Ang_{min}|}{20} \right\rceil \tag{1}$$

After determining the clustering number of the fingerprints, we utilize the K-means algorithm to group the fingerprints into K clusters. At last, every fingerprint is assigned a cluster ID. Then, we summarize the SSC algorithm as Algorithm 1.

Algorithm 1. Self-adaptive Space Clustering (SSC) Algorithm

Input: fingerprints set $F : F_1, F_2, ..., F_M$
Output: assigned clusterID for each fingerprint
$\quad\quad\quad CluID : CluID_1, CluID_2, ..., CluID_M$
1 **foreach** $i \leftarrow 1$ *to* N **do**
2 $\quad$ calculate Ang_{max} and Ang_{min};
3 $\quad$ determine K by Eq. (1);
4 $\quad$ clustering fingerprints with K clusters;
5 $\quad$ **foreach** $j \leftarrow 1$ *to* $|O_i|$ **do**
6 $\quad\quad$ calculate the cluster ID $CluID : CluID_1, CluID_2, ..., CluID_M$;
7 $\quad\quad$ assign each fingerprint the cluster ID;
8 $\quad$ **end**
9 **end**

---

4   Salient Part Detection

For the crowdsourced fingerprints composed of sensory data and images, we focus on selecting high-quality images in this section. It is observed that when capturing the objects, various disturbances appear on these images. These disturbances may be moving pedestrians, vehicles and their shadows; or may be trivial objects and advertisements; or may be changing backgrounds caused by changing azimuths. How to select high-quality images with less disturbance is our goal. As shown in Fig. 3, the features corresponding to the landmark in the two images are shared commonly; whereas, the features corresponding to the background, sky and moving students in one image are not shared in the other image. Salient parts are shared by the two images; whereas, the non-salient parts are not commonly shared. Moreover, from the crowdsourced databases, we find that the non-salient parts are more likely to be missed. For example, in Fig. 3, the landmark is not missed while the moving students and trees are missed in other images. Along this line, we propose SPF to evaluate the image quality.

Fig. 3. Examples of disturbances in the crowdsourced images. Disturbance parts are presented by blue triangles while the salient features are presented by red points and linked by red lines. From the images, we can find that salient part features are more robust, compared with other features. (Color figure online)

We perform salient part features detection as follows. First, we extract all the SURF [11] features of all the images, because of the good balance between the efficiency and searching accuracy in the mobile visual search. Second, the features, each of which is saved as 64 dimensional float data, are utilized to train the hash function. The hash function is used for converting the SURF features to binary hash codes. Third, the SPFD algorithm distinguishes the SPF from other features and evaluates the images by the amount of SPF they contain.

4.1 Training the Hash Function

Inspired by VHB in mobile visual searching, we utilize hash method to translate the SURF features into a sequence of binary hash codes. The approach can decrease the searching cost on mobile location system [9]. The training stage is composed of the following steps: First, we train the spectral hash unsupervisely and obtain the hash function (i.e., h^v) shown in Eq. (2).

$$h^v = sign(\cos(W\phi)) \tag{2}$$

Second, using the learned transition parameter matrix W obtained by Eq. (2), we transform the 64-dimension float features into 80 bits binary hash codes.

4.2 SPFD Algorithm

Recently, ISP is proposed to explore contextual saliency by performing optimal matching pair determination between the images. ISP aims at improving searching precision by extracting identical visual words. However, we propose SPF to capture the salient parts and evaluate the quality of crowdsourced images. Moreover, we propose the SPFD algorithm which is based on the idea that salient parts appear more frequently than non-salient parts.

In the previous section, we group the fingerprints into several clusters and obtain their cluster ID. For fingerprints within the same cluster, we construct an image set $I = \{I_1, I_2, ..., I_l, ...\}$. Every element I_l in I is composed of features set F which is donated as $[F_1, F_2, ...]$. Every feature is presented with 80 bits $[b_1, b_2, ..., b_{80}]$. Inspired by ISP, we design best matching pair to recognise the identical features between two images. Specifically, suppose I_A has features set $F : [f_1, f_2, ...]$, and I_B has features set $F' : [f'_1, f'_2, ...]$. We determine the best matching pair as follows: for each feature f in the F, we compare the hamming distance between f and every feature in F'. Suppose the distance between f' in F' and f is the minimum hamming distance. Whereas, for f', we compare the distances between f' and every feature in F. If the distance between f in F and f' is also the minimum hamming distance, we regard (f, f') as the best matching pair. The distance between f and f' is calculated by Eq. (3).

$$Dis(f, f') = \sum_{1}^{k=80} b_f^k \bigoplus b_{f'}^k \tag{3}$$

At last, how may best matching pairs every fingerprint has will be determined. Then, we can obtain the queue which is filled of sorted fingerprints with respect to the amount of best matching pairs. We summarise the SPFD algorithm as Algorithm 2.

5 Experiments

In this section, we describe the crowdsourced fingerprint database and evaluate the performances of our method. We compare SSFS fingerprint selection approach with several baselines.

Algorithm 2. Salient Part Feature Detection (SPFD) Algorithm

Input: an image set $I = \{I_1, I_2, ..., I_l, ...\}$
Output: Number of best matching pairs the images have:$[N_1, N_2, ..., N_l, ...]$

```
 1  foreach i ← 1  to  |I| − 1 do
 2      foreach j ← i + 1  to  |I| do
 3          foreach f ∈ F_i do
 4              foreach f' ∈ F'_j do
 5                  | calculate the minimum distance by Eq. (3) ;
 6              end
 7          end
 8          foreach f' ∈ F'_j do
 9              foreach f ∈ F_i do
10                  | calculate the minimum distance by Eq. (3) ;
11              end
12          end
13          if (f, f') is a best matching pair then
14              N_i++;   N_j++;
15      end
16  end
```

5.1 Database and Implementation

Our fingerprint database is consisted of 8,062 fingerprints crowdsourced from 162 objects. The objects contain typical areas, e.g., campus landmarks, library, teaching buildings and dormitories on the BUPT campus. In total, 1,620 fingerprints are randomly selected as testing set, the rest 6,442 fingerprints are saved as training set. We implement VHB searching scheme, adopting OpenCV library to extract 661,522 SURF features from the training set. These features are used to train spectral hash function by Matlab 2011 and obtain the parameter matrix.

5.2 Experimental Results

We adopt Precision@N and MAP@N to evaluate the performances of SSFS. The two metrics are widely utilized in the state-of-the-art location recognition systems [2,7]. Based on the aforementioned SSFS, we provide three optional fingerprint selection strategies. **No Spatial diversity considering (NSD):** When performing fingerprint selection, we only consider the image quality without considering the spatial diversity. **No Salinecy Part detecting (NSPF):** When performing fingerprint selection, we only consider the spatial diversity without considering the image quality. **Randomly Selection:** We randomly select the fingerprints. For fair comparison, we select 90% fingerprints for all the strategies[1]. Precision@N considers the top 1 image candidate with the top N most

---

[1] Adopting 90% fingerprints from the database, SSFS approach maintains approximately high precisions with 100% fingerprints.

matching features as Eq. (4).

$$Precision@N = \frac{1}{N_q} \sum_{i=1}^{N_q} P_i(N) \tag{4}$$

N_q is the number of query fingerprints; $P_i(N)$ presents whether the ith fingerprint query is the correct matching with top N best matching features. From Fig. 4, we can find that SSFS outperforms other three fingerprint selection approaches. It is concluded that SSFS effectively improve the searching precision compared with other strategies. It also confirmed the effectiveness of considering both spatial distribution and image quality when selecting fingerprints from crowdsourced fingerprint database.

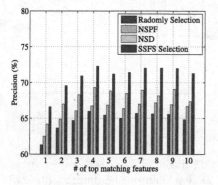

Fig. 4. Precision @N returns the best matching image with the top N features which vary from 1 to 10.

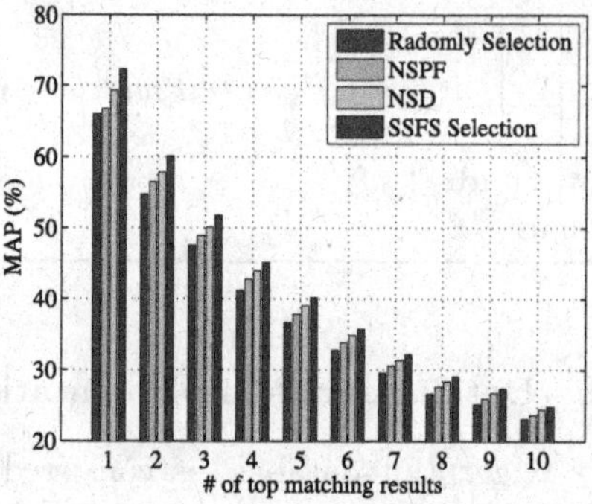

Fig. 5. MAP@N return the top N images which vary from 1 to 10.

Mean average precision at N ($MAP@N$) [2] is used to evaluate correct matching proportion in the returning results (i.e., top N candidates), revealing the position-sensitive ranking precision of the queries as Eq. (5).

$$MAP@N = \frac{1}{N_q} \sum_{i=1}^{N_q} \left(\frac{\sum_{r=1}^{N} P(r) rel(r)}{N} \right) \tag{5}$$

In this experiment, N also varies from 1 to 10; P(r) is the precision at the cut-off rank of r; rel(r) represents whether r is a correct match.

The results in Fig. 5 show SSFS also outperforms other approaches in the metric considering position-sensitive rank. It is worth mentioning that in this experiment, the number of top matching features is assigned as 4. However, when we adjust it, similar results can also be obtained. It is also confirmed that it is an useful scheme to maintain high diversity in spatial distribution and high-quality images when selecting fingerprints in the crowdsourced database.

6   Conclusion and Future Work

In this paper, we propose the SSFS framework to perform the fingerprint selection in the crowdsourced fingerprint database. Moreover, we propose the SSC algorithm to group the fingerprints into several clusters and select high-quality images using SPFD algorithm. In the future work, we will consider more sensory data to select excellent fingerprints.

Acknowledgement. This work is supported by the National Natural Science Foundation of China under Grant No. 61332005, No. 61502051 and No. 61190114, the Cosponsored Project of Beijing Committee of Education, and the Beijing Training Project for the Leading Talents in S&T (ljrc201502).

References

1. Wang, H., Zhao, D., Ma, H.D., Xu, H.Y.: Crowdsourcing based mobile location recognition with richer fingerprints from smartphone sensors. In: IEEE Conference on Parallel and Distributed Systems, pp. 156–163 (2015)
2. Ji, R.R., Duan, L.Y., Chen, J., Yao, H.X., Yuan, Y.R., Gao, W.: Location discriminative vocabulary coding for mobile landmark search. Int. J. Comput. Vis. **96**(3), 290–314 (2012)
3. Chen, D.M., Baatz, G., Koser, K., Tsai, S.S., Vedantham, R., Pylvanainen, T., Roimela, K., Chen, X., Bach, J., Pollefeys, M., Girod, B., Grzeszczuk, R.: City-scale landmark identification on mobile devices. In: IEEE Conference on Computer Vision and Pattern Recognition, pp. 737–744 (2011)
4. Guan, T., He, Y.F., Gao, J., Yang, J.Z., Yu, Q.: On-device mobile visual location recognition by integrating vision and inertial sensors. IEEE Trans. Multimedia **15**(7), 1688–1699 (2013)
5. Ma, H.D., Zhao, D., Yuan, P.Y.: Opportunities in mobile crowd sensing. IEEE Commun. Mag. **52**(8), 29–35 (2014)
6. Zhao, D., Li, X.Y., Ma, D.: Budget-feasible online incentive mechanisms for crowdsourcing tasks truthfully. IEEE/ACM Trans. Netw. **24**(2), 647–661 (2016)
7. Yang, X.Y., Qian, X.M., Xue, Y.: Scalable mobile image retrieval by exploring contextual saliency. IEEE Trans. Image Process. **24**(6), 1709–1721 (2015)
8. Chen, H.H., Guo, B., Yu, Z.W., Chen, M.: CrowdPic: a multi-coverage picture collection framework for mobile crowd photographing. In: IEEE Conference on Ubiquitous Intelligence and Computing, pp. 68–76 (2015)
9. Liu, W., Mei, T., Xhang, Y.: Instant mobile video search with layered audio-video indexing and progressive transmission. IEEE Trans. Multimedia **16**(8), 2242–2255 (2014)
10. Raychoudhury, V., Shrivastav, S., Sandha, S.S., Cao, J.N.: CROWD-PAN-360: crowdsourcing based context-aware panoramic map generation for smartphone users. IEEE Trans. Parallel Distrib. Syst. **26**(8), 2208–2219 (2015)
11. Bay, H., Tuytelaars, T., Gool, L.: SURF: speeded up robust features. In: Leonardis, A., Bischof, H., Pinz, A. (eds.) ECCV 2006. LNCS, vol. 3951, pp. 404–417. Springer, Heidelberg (2006). doi:10.1007/11744023_32

Multi-view Multi-object Tracking Based on Global Graph Matching Structure

Chao Li, Shantao Ping$^{(\boxtimes)}$, Hao Sheng, Jiahui Chen, and Zhang Xiong

State Key Laboratory of Software Development Environment,
School of Computer Science and Engineering, Beihang University,
Beijing 100191, People's Republic of China
{licc,pingst,shenghao,chenjh}@buaa.edu.cn

Abstract. We present a novel global graph matching framework based on virtual nodes for multi-object tracking in multiple views. Contrary to recent approaches, we incorporate a global graph matching structure (GGMS), allowing the tracker to better cope with long-term occlusions and tracking failure caused by interaction of targets. In our approach, the matching problem is solved as follows: Virtual detections are introduced by mapping the nodes among views, to ensure that the amount of detections in each view is the same, and then realize the whole graph matching. In addition, appropriate optimization is performed to convert this mapping problem to the Assignment Problem, which could be efficiently addressed by the Hungarian Algorithm. Finally, we demonstrate the validity of our approach on the publicly available datasets, and achieve very competitive results by quantitative evaluation.

Keywords: Multi-object tracking · Multi-view · Graph matching

1 Introduction

With the fast development of smart devices, numerous cameras lead to ubiquitous video sources. Crowd-sourced video retrieval systems [1] based on video content comparison has emerged. Multi-object tracking is a key problem for many computer vision tasks, such as surveillance [2], animation or activity recognition. The tracking in video consists of detecting all subjects in every frame, and following their complete trajectory over time. Successful research on a new generation of reliable pedestrian detectors [3, 4] has prompted the use of the tracking-by-detection paradigm [5], even for crowded or semi-crowded scenarios. Under this paradigm, the problem is often divided in two steps: detection and data association [6, 7]. The tracker first acquires a set of detections using a pedestrian detector. The individual detections are then assigned to tracks, where each track is composed of all the detections from a single individual. If all persons were to be correctly observed at every timestamp this task would be trivial, however, due to false positive detections, occlusions and missed detections, this association problem becomes very challenging.

Usually, the problem of tracking is divided into two directions: monocular tracking and multi-view tracking. In recent research, the minimum-cost network flow tracking approach [8, 9] is more popular in monocular tracking. This method can effectively

© Springer International Publishing AG 2016
E. Chen et al. (Eds.): PCM 2016, Part II, LNCS 9917, pp. 660–669, 2016.
DOI: 10.1007/978-3-319-48896-7_65

cope well with short-term occlusion, however, it tends to become unreliable when the long-term occlusion occurs.

Unlike monocular tracking, in multiple views, the information from other perspective can complement better the detection errors in the main view, which may be caused by occlusions or detection failures. While considering multi-view tracking, the additional problem of data association between views arises. Reconstruction and tracking are two main problems. Wu et al. [10] handled these works as separate stages. Leal et al. [11] attempted to jointly solve these two problems for multi-view multi-object tracking. Although excellent results have been achieved in this method, there still exists potentiality in dealing with the occlusion and missing detections.

To achieve this promotion, we continue the work of [11] which has discussed above. In our approach, we propose a method to solve the problem iteratively. Firstly, the output of [11], such as the world coordination of detections, is our input. Virtual nodes which are obtained by mapping each of the detections in each view to another are introduced to ensure that the amount of detections in each of the two views is same. Then a weight defined as the distance between different nodes and some constraints for the graph are introduced, in order to further realize the matching of the two graphs.

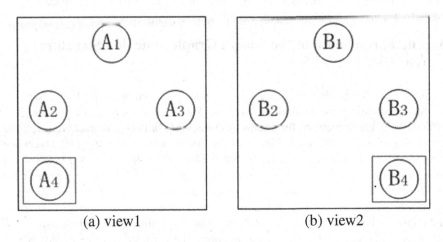

| (a) view1 | (b) view2 |

Fig. 1. These two graphs represent the 3D detections in view 1 and view 2 corresponding to the F frame. We assume that A_1, A_2, A_3 and B_1, B_2, B_3 are matched well with each other respectively, and A_4 can't match with B_4.

The rest of the paper is organized as follows. Section 2 presents related work. The formulation of our proposed method is described in Sect. 3. Section 4 describes an optimization approach to solve the problem. Next, experiments are presented in Sect. 5 and, finally, the paper is concluded in Sect. 6.

2 Related Work

Object tracking has been studied extensively. For example, Kang et al. [12] proposed to take the multi-camera tracking as a problem of maximum joint probability model based on color. By estimating the object model through Kalman filtering, it used the joint probabilistic data filtering and multi-camera homography to multi-target tracking. Lien et al. [13] presented a tracking method for multi-view object based on the cooperation of hidden Markov process and particle filtering. Nummiaro et al. [14] put forword a tracking algorithm for multi-view object based on particle filtering, but unlike the idea of information fusion, this algorithm selected the best point of view for object tracking among the different perspectives.

Many global approaches that use more information have been explored to over-come occlusion and detector failure. Leal et al. [11] attempted to jointly solve these two problems for multi-view multi-object tracking. In this work, a separate tracking graph is constructed for each view. In addition, for each pair of views, an additional tracking graph is constructed, providing the coupling constraints for the involved views. In [15], it presents a solution which only requires a single tracking graph. Multi view coupling constraints are incorporated into the reconstruction nodes within the tracking graph. Tracking therefore only needs to be done once in the world coordinate space.

3 The Formulation of the Global Graph Matching Structure (GGMS)

In this section, the problem in [11] and the methods proposed in this paper is described.

As stated earlier, we continue the work of [11] which has proven to be a mathe-matically reliable framework for multi-object tracking. In [11], one tracking graph(2D layer) is constructed for each view and the multi-camera couplings(3D layer) are incorporated by an additional tracking graph for each possible camera pair in the world coordinate space. Ideally, an object which is seen by all available cameras generates a 2D detection in each view and the corresponding projections to the common world coordinates should all come to the same location. However, due to projection errors and imprecise detections, the resulting 3D positions are unlikely to match up exactly. In 3D layer, three types of edges, reconstruction edges, camera coherency edges and temporal 3D edges are introduced. Instead, these edges act as prizes for the graph, when the reconstruction, camera coherence and temporal 3D edges are sufficiently negative, it assigns the same identity to the objects seen by all available cameras. The problem lies in that when occlusion occurs, the 3D reconstruction will be based on only one visual angle. At this time, the occlusion could not be effectively resolved.

In this paper, we introduce a graph structure, and then solve the occlusion problem demonstrated above by the matching of the graph. As shown in Fig. 1, each graph has four 3D detections corresponding to the F frame. Each 3D detection is defined by a tuple Ai = (id_i, x_i, y_i, z_i), where id_i and (x_i, y_i, z_i) are the object identity and the location in world coordinates. It is assumed that detections A_1, A_2, A_3 shown in Fig. 1(a) are matched with detections B_1, B_2, B_3 shown in Fig. 1(b) respectively. The detection A_4

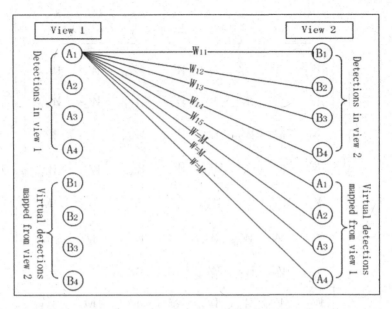

Fig. 2. This illustration shows how the detections and the virtual detections between two views matched with each other. The matching cost is expressed as W_{ij}, where $W_{ij} = M$ means these two detections can't be matched. And M is an infinite constant defined.

from view 1 cannot find corresponding matching point in view 2, and so is the detection B_4 from view 2. Our purpose is to find an algorithm to achieve the matching of the two graphs. Due to the existence of special circumstances: the amount of the detections in two views may be not same, so virtual nodes are introduced to ensure that the number of the detections is the same in each view as shown in Fig. 2. W represents the weight of detections respectively, which can be expressed as

$$W_{ij} = e^{dist-\partial} - 1 \tag{1}$$

$$dist = \sqrt{(x_i - x_j)^2 + (y_i - y_j)^2 + (z_i - z_j)^2} \tag{2}$$

where dist is the Euclidean distance between detections in world coordinates and δ reflects the reasonable threshold which represents the maximum distance between two detections when they are correctly matched. We introduce an exponential function of the (dist − δ) which guarantees the W_{ij} is negative when matching and positive when not matching. The matching of two graphs indicates that the graph has the smallest weight (Fig. 3).

To get the smallest weight, we can convert it into a Linear Program (LP), its objective function is linearized with a set flags $X_{ij} = \{0, 1\}$ which indicate if an edge $i \rightarrow j$ is in the solution or not. We define a number of variables in advance, as follows: (i) Detections in view 1 are represented by i, among which, No. 1 to No. m are inherent, while the rest are virtual detections transformed from view 2. (ii) Detections in view 2

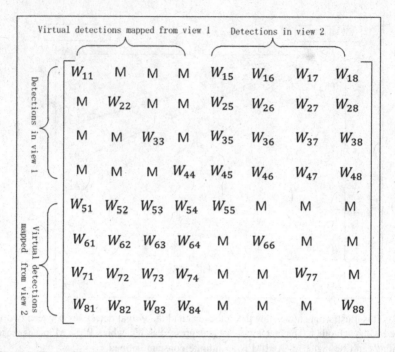

Fig. 3. This illustration shows that how the detections and the virtual detections between two views are matched with each other. The matching cost is expressed as W_{ij}, where W_{ij} = M means these two detections can't be matched. And M is an infinite constant defined.

are represented by j, among which, No. 1 to No. m are virtual nodes mapped from view 1, while the rest are inherent. The proposed graph-matching structure can be expressed as a LP with the following objective function:

$$F = \min \sum_{i=1}^{count} \sum_{j=1}^{count} X_{ij} W_{ij} \tag{3}$$

where count = m + n is the total amount of detections in view 1 and view 2. M is defined to represent the quantity of detection in view 1 and so as n in view 2. The problem is subject to the following constraints:

$$\sum_{j=m+1}^{count} X_{ij} = 1, \quad i = 1, 2, \ldots, m \tag{4}$$

The constraint ensures that each detection in view 1 has one (also the only one) corresponding detection in view 2 whether it is a detection or a virtual node mapped from view 1.

$$\sum_{i=1}^{m} X_{ij} = 1, \quad j = m+1, m+2, \ldots, count \tag{5}$$

The constraint ensures that each detection in view 2 has one (also the only one) corresponding detection in view 1 whether it is a detection or a virtual node mapped from view 2.

$$\sum_{i=1}^{m} X_{ij} \leq 1, \quad j = 1, 2, \ldots, m \tag{6}$$

This guarantees that each virtual detection (mapped from view 2) in view 1 has at most one matching detection in view 2.

$$\sum_{j=m+1}^{count} X_{ij} \leq 1, \quad i = m+1, m+2, \ldots, count \tag{7}$$

This assures that each virtual detection (mapped from view 1) in view 2 has at most one matching detection in view 1.

$$\sum_{i=1}^{m} X_{ij} = 1, \quad j = 1, 2, \ldots, m \tag{8}$$

$$\sum_{j=m+1}^{count} X_{ij} = 1, \quad i = m+1, m+2, \ldots, count \tag{9}$$

In order to solve the Linear Programming problem more conveniently, we convert the constraint conditions of the inequalities (6) and (7) depicted above to the equalities (8) and (9) expressed below.

4   Optimization Approach

In this section, we mainly talk about how to make further optimization of the above problem, as well as how to solve this problem. Firstly, it is converted into the Assignment Problem. Then we solve it efficiently with the Hungarian Algorithm.

4.1   How to Convert the Problem

From the notations in Sect. 3, the constraints of (4), (5), (8) and (9) can be optimized as the following equalities which can be expressed as:

$$\sum_{j=1}^{count} W_{ij} = 1, \quad i = 1, 2, \ldots, count \tag{10}$$

$$\sum_{i=1}^{count} X_{ij} = 1, \quad j = 1, 2, \ldots, count \tag{11}$$

where (10) denotes each detection (including the virtual detections mapped from view 2) in view 1 has one corresponding detection in view 2. And (11) represents each detection (contain the virtual detections mapped from view 1) in view 2 can only be arranged to one detection from view 1. The X_{ij} is re-expressed as below:

$$X_{ij} = 0 \, or \, 1, \quad i, j = 1, 2, \ldots, count, \tag{12}$$

The equalities (10), (11) and (12) constitute the new and optimal constraint of the problem. Then the objective function (3) with the optimal constraints has become as an Assignment Problem. The solution will be demonstrated in the next subsection.

4.2   The Solution Strategy

In order to solve this problem, we introduce a weight matrix, as shown in Fig. 4. The row vector of the matrix represents the detection in view 1, where the former m line represents the point view 1, and the remainder denotes the virtual point mapped from view 2. And meanwhile, the column vector of the matrix represents the detection in view 2, where the former m column represents the virtual point mapped from view 1, and the remainder denotes the point in view 2.

$$
\begin{bmatrix}
0 & 0 & 0 & 0 & \boxed{1} & 0 & 0 & 0 \\
0 & 0 & 0 & 0 & 0 & \boxed{1} & 0 & 0 \\
0 & 0 & 0 & 0 & 0 & 0 & \boxed{1} & 0 \\
0 & 0 & 0 & \boxed{1} & 0 & 0 & 0 & 0 \\
\boxed{1} & 0 & 0 & 0 & 0 & 0 & 0 & 0 \\
0 & \boxed{1} & 0 & 0 & 0 & 0 & 0 & 0 \\
0 & 0 & \boxed{1} & 0 & 0 & 0 & 0 & 0 \\
0 & 0 & 0 & 0 & 0 & 0 & 0 & \boxed{1}
\end{bmatrix}
$$

Fig. 4. This picture is a solution matrix, which is corresponded to the front of the weight matrix. In this matrix, element 1 means $X_{ij} = 1$. In other words, the two detections i and j are matched with each other. And all the elements of $X_{ij} = 1$ are in the final solution.

Because the detection in the same view could not be matched with each other, we define $X_{ij} = M$ (i, j = 1, 2, .., m and i, j = m + 1, m + 2, .., count and i ≠ j), which represents an infinite constant and is not likely to be contained in the solution. The weight matrix could be solved with the Hungarian Algorithm, and then a solution matrix (as in Fig. 5) consists of 0 and 1 is obtained. In the solution matrix, 0 represents unselected edge of X_{ij} and 1 represents the matching edge.

Since we evaluate on view 1, and the second view we use does not show all the pedestrians. Therefore, we consider the detections of view 1 as the main detections and

| (a) view1 | (b) view2 | (c) mapped result |

Fig. 5. Tracking results on PETS 2009 for two cameras. (a) result of single view 1— a pedestrian is occluded, (b) result of single view 2 (corresponding to view 6 in PETS 2009 S2L1), (c) our result by mapping detections between view 1 and view 2 to solve the occlusion existed in view 1.

only use the second view to further improve the 3D position. In other words, if detections in view 2 are matching with the virtual points mapped from view 2, then we add the detections (corresponding to $X_{ii} = 1, i = m + 1, m + 2, ..,$ count in the solution matrix) to the final results of view 1.

5 Experiment

In this section, we show the tracking results of the proposed method on the key problem in computer vision, namely occlusion usually exists in multi-object tracking. Evaluating results of multi-object tracking is non-trivial because errors might be present in various forms including ID switches, broken tracks, imprecisely localized tracks and false tracks. Measures such as MOTA [16, 17] combine different errors into a single score and enable the global ranking of tracking methods.

We show the tracking results (shown in Fig. 5) of our approaches on the publicly available PETS2009 dataset [18], a scene with several interacting targets, based on MOTA metrics depicted above. We compare our results to some other multi-camera tracking methods [19, 20]. As shown in Table 1, our method generally has comparable MOTA, MOTP and recall scores with [11]. The result indicates that the occlusion could be addressed in this method more effectively and our objective function is easy to construct and solve.

Table 1. Table summarizing results over PETS 2009 S2.L1 sequence. Abbreviations are as follows GT - ground truth tracks. MT - Mostly tracked. PT - partially tracked. ML - mostly lost. Comparison of several methods tracking on a variable number of cameras.

Method	Camera numbers	GT	MT	PT	ML	MOTA	MOTP	Prcn	Rcll
Berclaz [19]	5	–	–	–	–	75	62	–	–
Berclaz [20]	5	–	–	–	–	82	56	–	–
Leal [10]	3	–	–	–	–	71.4	53.4	–	–
Leal [10]	2	–	–	–	–	76.0	60.0	–	–
Ours	2	**19**	**19**	0	0	**93.2**	79.9	93.4	96.8

6 Conclusion

In this paper, we present a novel method for multi-object tracking in overlapping views. This new approach achieves the matching of two graphs, by introducing virtual nodes mapped from other corresponding view. An optimal solution is provided based on the Hungarian Algorithm. The result shows that this method can be used to complete large tracking gaps caused by occlusion or detector failure. The proposed method has shown good performance on the publicly available PETS 2009 S2.L1 sequence, solving the problem of occlusion and matching state of the art performance.

Acknowledgement. This study was partially supported by the National Natural Science Foundation of China (No. 61370122) and the National High Technology Research and Development Program of China (No. 2013AA01A603). Supported by the Programme of Introducing Talents of Discipline to Universities and the Open Fund of the State Key Laboratory of Software Development Environment under grant #SKLSDE-2015ZX-21. Thank you for the support from HAWKEYE Group.

References

1. Liu, C., Zhang, L., Liu, K., Liu, Y.: Scan without a glance: towards content-free crowdsourced mobile video retrieval system. In: International Conference on Parallel Processing, pp. 250–259 (2015)
2. Yilmaz, A., Javed, O., Shah, M.: Object tracking: a survey. ACM Comput. Surv. **38**(4), pp. 81–93 (2006)
3. Bourdev, L., Malik, J.: Poselets: body part detectors trained using 3D human pose annotations. In: Proceedings/IEEE International Conference on Computer Vision, pp. 1365–1372 (2009)
4. Felzenszwalb, P.F., Girshick, R.B., David, M.A., Deva, R.: Object detection with discriminatively trained part-based models. IEEE Trans. Pattern Anal. Mach. Intell. **32**(9), 1627–1645 (2010)
5. Breitenstein, M.D., Reichlin, F., Leibe, B., KollerMeier, E.: Robust tracking-by-detection using a detector confidence particle filter. In: IEEE International Conference on Computer Vision, pp. 1515–1522 (2009)
6. Zhang, L., Li, Y., Nevatia, R.: Global data association for multi-object tracking using network flows. In: IEEE Conference on Computer Vision and Pattern Recognition, CVPR 2008, pp. 1–8 (2008)
7. Segal, A.V., Reid, I.: Latent data association: Bayesian model selection for multi-target tracking. In: 2013 IEEE International Conference on Computer Vision (ICCV), pp. 2904–2911 (2013)
8. Butt, A.A., Collins, R.T.: Multi-target tracking by lagrangian relaxation to min-cost network flow. In: IEEE Conference on Computer Vision Pattern Recognition, pp. 1846–1853 (2013)
9. Anton, M., Stefan, R., Konrad, S.: Continuous energy minimization for multitarget tracking. IEEE Trans. Pattern Anal. Mach. Intell. **36**(1), 58–72 (2014)
10. Wu, Z., Hristov, N.I., Kunz, T.H., Betke, M.: Tracking-reconstruction or reconstruction-tracking? Comparison of two multiple hypothesis tracking approaches to interpret 3D object motion from several camera views. In: Workshop on Motion and Video Computing, WMVC 2009, pp. 1–8 (2009)

11. Leal-Taixe, L., Pons-Moll, G., Rosenhahn, B.: Branch-and-price global optimization for multiview multi-target tracking. In: 2012 IEEE Conference on Computer Vision and Pattern Recognition (CVPR), pp. 1987–1994. IEEE (2012)
12. Kang, J., Cohen, I., Medioni, G.: Persistent objects tracking across multiple non overlapping cameras. In: Proceedings of IEEE Workshop on Motion and Video Computing, pp. 112–119 (2005)
13. Lien, K.C., Huang, C.L.: Multiview-based cooperative tracking of multiple human objects. J. Image Video Process. 8(2), 1–13 (2008)
14. Nummiaro, K., et al.: Color-based object tracking in multi-camera enviroment. In: Proceedings of Pattern Recognition Symposium, pp. 591–599 (2003)
15. Hofmann, M., Wolf, D., Rigoll, G.: Hypergraphs for joint multi-view reconstruction and multi-object tracking. In: IEEE Conference on Computer Vision Pattern Recognition, pp. 3650–3657 (2013)
16. Milan, A., Schindler, K., Roth, S.: Detection- and trajectory-level exclusion in multiple object tracking. In: IEEE Conference on Computer Vision Pattern Recognition, pp. 3682–3689 (2013)
17. Hofmann, M., Haag, M., Rigoll, G.: Unified hierarchical multi-object tracking using global data association. In: 2013 IEEE International Workshop on Performance Evaluation of Tracking and Surveillance (PETS), pp. 22–28. IEEE (2013)
18. Ferryman, J., Shahrokni, A.: Pets2009: dataset and challenge. In: 2009 Twelfth IEEE International Workshop on Performance Evaluation of Tracking and Surveillance (PETS-Winter), pp. 1–6 (2009)
19. Berclaz, J., Fleuret, F., Fua, P.: Multiple object tracking using flow linear programming. In: 2009 Twelfth IEEE International Workshop on Performance Evaluation of Tracking and Surveillance (PETSWinter), pp. 1–8 (2009)
20. Berclaz, J., Fleuret, F., Turetken, E., Fua, P.: Multiple object tracking using k-shortest paths optimization. IEEE Trans. Softw. Eng. 33(9), 1806–1819 (2011)

Accelerating Large-Scale Human Action Recognition with GPU-Based Spark

Hanli Wang[1,2(✉)], Xiaobin Zheng[1,2], and Bo Xiao[1,2]

[1] Department of Computer Science and Technology,
Tongji University, Shanghai, China
hanliwang@tongji.edu.cn
[2] Key Laboratory of Embedded System and Service Computing,
Ministry of Education, Tongji University, Shanghai, China
{13xiaobin,1314xiaobo}@tongji.edu.cn

Abstract. In this paper, a large-scale human action recognition system is proposed which is built upon the combination of the rising big data processing technology Spark and the powerful Graphics Processing Unit (GPU) in order to fully utilize the efficient in-memory computing ability of Spark and the fine-grained parallel computing capacity of GPU for visual data processing. A number of key algorithms for human action recognition including trajectory based feature extraction, Gaussian Mixture Model (GMM) generation and Fisher Vector (FV) encoding are performed with the proposed GPU-based Spark framework. The experimental results on the benchmark human action dataset Hollywood-2 demonstrate that the proposed GPU-based Spark framework is able to dramatically accelerate the process of human action recognition.

Keywords: Human action recognition · Spark · GPU · MapReduce · Heterogeneous computing

1 Introduction

The past decade has witnessed a great success of social networks and multimedia technologies, leading to an explosive growth of videos. It is highly desired to effectively query, analyze, and utilize these immense video data for a number of multimedia applications, among which human action recognition has actively attracted researchers' attentions such as [1–3] to name a few. However, with multimedia big data explosion, in order to deal with large-scale video data required by human action recognition, it is necessary to exploit powerful computing techniques and systems to address the tremendous computational demands.

This work was supported in part by the National Natural Science Foundation of China under Grant 61472281, the "Shu Guang" project of Shanghai Municipal Education Commission and Shanghai Education Development Foundation under Grant 12SG23, and the Program for Professor of Special Appointment (Eastern Scholar) at the Shanghai Institutions of Higher Learning under Grant GZ2015005.

© Springer International Publishing AG 2016
E. Chen et al. (Eds.): PCM 2016, Part II, LNCS 9917, pp. 670–679, 2016.
DOI: 10.1007/978-3-319-48896-7_66

To meet this end, several parallel computing frameworks are designed in recent years which permit the horizontal scaling of large-scale workloads using High-Performance Computing (HPC) systems such as the representative MapReduce [4] and Spark [5]. Proposed by Google, MapReduce [4] is a popular parallel programming paradigm deployed on computer clusters, which applies the intuition that large-scale workloads can be processed with map and reduce operations. As one of the most successful implementations of MapReduce, Hadoop [6] offers locality-aware scheduling, fault-tolerance as well as load balancing. However, Hadoop is not suitable for iterative tasks which are common for multimedia data processing due to its acyclic data flow. As a solution, Spark [5] is designed which is a fast and general engine for large-scale data processing that supports cyclic data flow as well as in-memory distributed computing.

On the other hand, there is a new trend about HPC toward heterogeneity and hierarchy. Such heterogeneous systems are usually equipped with Graphic Processing Unit (GPU) and are more powerful than traditional HPC systems. Since the popularity of CUDA architecture [7], GPU has been widely studied and applied which is suitable for data-intensive tasks at fine-grained parallel level because it is equipped with thousands of stream processors and is able to run massive amount of threads simultaneously. Along this research line, a number of frameworks or paradigms have been recently designed. In [8], StarPU is introduced for numerical kernel design to perform parallel tasks on a shared-memory machine with heterogeneous hardwares. A high-level model for parallel programming, called merge, is proposed in [9], which runs on shared-memory machines with heterogeneous hardwares and employs the MapReduce programming paradigm to simplify the interface for users. In [10], an elastic computing framework is proposed, which uses an adapter to hide the difference of various kinds of processors, such as GPU and Field-Programmable Gate Array (FPGA). He *et al.* [11] propose a GPU-based MapReduce framework on a number of applications such as string matching and matrix multiplication. In [12], a cloud-based heterogeneous computing framework is designed for large-scale image retrieval.

Regarding large-scale human action recognition, we have performed a preliminary study [13] to employ Spark to speed up several key processes such as trajectory based feature extraction, Gaussian Mixture Model (GMM) generation and Fisher Vector (FV) encoding [14]. In this work, we further extend our previous work [13] to design a GPU-based Spark framework implemented on an 8-node heterogeneous computer cluster, which provides a promising solution to large-scale human action recognition and exploits jointly the computing power of CPUs and GPUs to accelerate the related high-throughput computing tasks. Experimental results on the benchmark Hollywood-2 dataset [15] demonstrate that the proposed GPU-based Spark framework is able to achieve a wonderful speedup in processing large amount of video data required by human action recognition, and more powerful than the CPU-only Spark framework (*i.e.*, GPU disabled). The rest of this paper is structured as follows. Section 2 details the proposed GPU-based Spark framework for human action recognition. The experimental results are given in Sect. 3 to demonstrate the performance of the proposed framework. At last, this work is concluded in Sect. 4.

2   Proposed GPU-Based Spark Framework for Human Action Recognition

The details of the proposed GPU-based Spark Framework to accelerate several typical key algorithms involved by FV-oriented human action recognition are introduced in this section, mainly including trajectory based feature extraction (Sect. 2.2), GMM generation (Sect. 2.3) and FV encoding (Sect. 2.4).

2.1   System Overview

An overview of the proposed GPU-based Spark framework is illustrated in Fig. 1. First, according to the pre-designed InputFormat, the proposed GPU-based Spark cluster reads data splits from the Hadoop Distributed File System (HDFS) and caches these input data for subsequent distributed processing. Within each Spark worker, high-efficiency native programs are implemented with C++ programming and the GPU parallel processing is fulfilled with CUDA C programming. The Java Native Interface (JNI) is employed to connect Spark workers and native functions. Moreover, the technique of Protocol Buffers (PB) [16] is utilized to guarantee the efficiency of data transmission between Spark workers and native functions since PB provides an excellent serialization/deserialization mechanism.

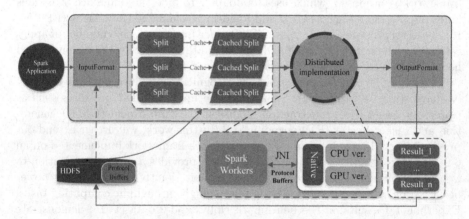

Fig. 1. Overview of the proposed GPU-based Spark framework.

2.2   Distributed Trajectory Based Feature Extraction

In the current work, the approach of FV-oriented human action recognition such as [17] is chosen as the testbed to deploy the proposed GPU-based Spark framework, since the FV model [14] is an improved version of the traditional Bag-of-Words model [18] and widely applied for human action recognition. Moreover, in order to extract features for FV encoding, the improved dense trajectory based approach [2] is employed for feature extraction and representation, because trajectory based approaches are shown to be very efficient in representing video features and thus boost the performance of human action recognition.

In our framework, we distribute the workloads of video feature extraction across the underlying computer cluster by utilizing the scalability and the fault tolerance ability of Spark, which is similar to the implementation as discussed in [13]. Specifically speaking, each Spark worker extracts the input video path to native programs which are responsible to read actual video data and write extracted features to HDFS. This kind of design is able to eliminate redundant data transmission between workers and native programs. As Spark has no knowledge about which extraction task runs faster because the running time counts on the content and length of the input video, it is easily to result in load unbalance. In order to solve this problem, the technique of priority order [13] is employed so that we reschedule the execution order by which long task is put ahead to be carried out to achieve a better workload balance.

2.3   Distributed Gaussian Mixture Model Generation

The distributed implementation of GMM generation is designed based on the EM algorithm [19] with an illustration shown in Fig. 2. Initially, the input feature data splits are cached and serialized in PB format for usage by EM algorithm which can be expressed as iterative training by Expectation Step (E-Step) and Maximization Step (M-Step). In our design, the E-Step is parallelized by partitioning the dataset and performing the relevant intermediate value calculation across the cluster.

Assume the dataset is denoted as $X = \{x_1, \ldots, x_n\}$ and the partition set is $P = \{p_1, \ldots, p_Z\}$, for a specific data partition $p_t = \{x_1^t, \ldots, x_m^t\}$, the log-likelihood $ll^t(\theta; X)$ is calculated as

$$ll^t(\theta; X) = \sum_{i=1}^{m} \log \sum_{k=1}^{K} \pi_k N_k(x_i^t | \mu_k, \Sigma_k), \qquad (1)$$

where θ is the parameter set as $\theta = \{\pi_k, \mu_k, \Sigma_k; k = 1, \cdots, K\}$ for a K-component GMM model in which μ_k and Σ_k are the mean and covariance of the kth component, and π_k is the weight of the kth component which can be regarded as the prior probability and should satisfy the conditions that $0 \le \pi_k \le 1$ and $\sum_{k=1}^{K} \pi_k = 1$; $N_k(x|\mu_k, \Sigma_k)$ is the kth Gaussian distribution.

In order to compute Eq. (1), a posterior probability $q_k(x)$ is employed as

$$q_k(x_i^t) = \frac{\pi_k N_k(x_i^t | \mu_k, \Sigma_k)}{\sum_{l=1}^{K} \pi_l N_l(x_i^t | \mu_l, \Sigma_l)}. \qquad (2)$$

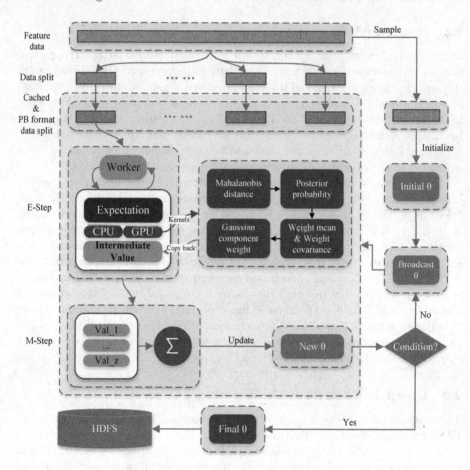

Fig. 2. Distributed GMM generation with GPU-based Spark.

And three intermediate parameters including the sum of posterior probability q_k^t, weighted mean $q\_x_k^t$ and weighted covariance $q\_d_k^t$ are computed in the E-Step to support the next M-Step as

$$q_k^t = \sum_{i=1}^{m} q_k(x_i^t),$$ (3)

$$q\_x_k^t = \sum_{i=1}^{m} q_k(x_i^t)x_i^t,$$ (4)

$$q\_d_k^t = \sum_{i=1}^{m} q_k(x_i^t)(x_i^t - \mu_k)(x_i^t - \mu_k)^T.$$ (5)

The above parameters can be calculated by GPUs at the E-Step with the GPU kernels invoked and the relevant results copied back to the host for subsequent computing. Regarding the M-Step, it fuses the aforementioned intermediate values with the Spark reduce operation and then updates the GMM parameter set

θ with the following operations.

$$\pi_k^{new} = \frac{\sum_{t=1}^{Z} q_k^t}{\sum_{l=1}^{K} \sum_{t=1}^{Z} q_l^t}, \tag{6}$$

$$\mu_k^{new} = \frac{\sum_{t=1}^{Z} q\_x_k^t}{\sum_{t=1}^{Z} q_k^t}, \tag{7}$$

$$\Sigma_k^{new} = \frac{\sum_{t=1}^{Z} q\_d_k^t}{\sum_{t=1}^{Z} q_k^t} - (\mu_k^{new} - \mu_k)^2. \tag{8}$$

2.4   Distributed Fisher Vector Encoding

FV encoding works with GMM and employs both the first and second order statistics to represent visual information. For a given GMM model with the parameter set $\theta = \{\pi_k, \mu_k, \Sigma_k; k = 1, \cdots, K\}$ and the dataset $X = \{x_1, \ldots, x_n\}$, FV is calculated by

$$u_k = \frac{1}{n\sqrt{\pi_k}} \sum_{i=1}^{n} q_k(x_i) \frac{x_i - \mu_k}{\sigma_k}, \tag{9}$$

$$v_k = \frac{1}{n\sqrt{2\pi_k}} \sum_{i=1}^{n} q_k(x_i) \left[\left(\frac{x_i - \mu_k}{\sigma_k}\right)^2 - 1 \right], \tag{10}$$

where $q_k(x)$ is the posterior probability in Eq. (2), u_k and v_k stand for the mean derivation vector and covariance derivation vector related to the kth Gaussian component, and σ_k is the diagonal vector of Σ_k with the division being element-wise. By concatenating u_k and v_k, the final FV can be generated as

$$\psi(X) = [\cdots, u_k, \cdots, v_k, \cdots]^T. \tag{11}$$

Then, the power normalization operation is usually applied on each dimension of FV as $f(z) = \mathbf{sign}(z)|z|^\alpha$ to further improve the performance of FV encoding where α is a regulation parameter.

The flowchart of the proposed distributed FV encoding is shown in Fig. 3. Similar to feature extraction, the proposed distributed FV encoding takes each video feature file as a sub-task which is assigned to a certain Spark worker. Then, GPU kernels work to calculate Eqs. (9)–(10) since they account for the primary calculations. As discussed in [13], the technique of 'Direct-pipe' (as marked by the green solid line in Fig. 3) is used to transfer the feature data directly from the extraction process to FV encoding, which is more efficient than the traditional 'Save-then-pipe' method (as illustrated by the black dashed line in Fig. 3).

3   Experimental Results

An 8-node computer cluster is used to verify the performance of the proposed GPU-base Spark framework with the hardware configuration shown in Table 1. As observed in Table 1, a middle-level configured computer node (marked as 'single*') is chosen to perform a single CPU thread version of all the following evaluations to demonstrate the speedup achieved by the proposed GPU-based Spark framework. Each node is installed with GNU/Linux Ubuntu 12.04, Java 1.7, gcc/g++ 4.6.4, CUDA 5.5, Spark 1.4.1 and Hadoop 1.2.1. The human action dataset Hollywood-2 [15] is used in our experiments, which provides 12 action categories collected from 69 Hollywood movies and includes 1,707 videos (823 for training and 884 for testing).

Currently, both the CPU and GPU versions of implementation are performed for GMM generation and FV encoding, while only the CPU version of implementation is provided for trajectory based feature extraction. Therefore, the reader can refer to our previous work [13] for the Speedup Ratio (SR) achieved by the proposed Spark framework against the single CPU thread implementation for trajectory based feature extraction. In the following, the SR performances obtained by the proposed GPU-based Spark framework are presented on GMM generation and FV encoding.

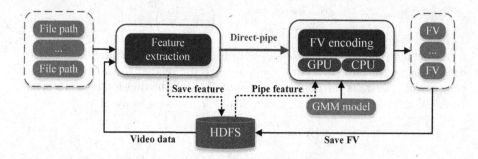

Fig. 3. Flowchart of distributed FV encoding. (Color figure online)

Table 1. Hardware configuration of the proposed GPU-based Spark framework.

Hardware	Amount		
	1	5 + 1 (single*)	2
CPU	Intel Core i5-3450	Intel Core i5-3470	Intel Core i5-4430
CPU Cores	4	4	4
Memory	32 GB DDR3	32 GB DDR3	32 GB DDR3
GPU	GeForce GTX 760 × 2	GeForce GTX 660 × 2	GeForce GTX 760 × 2
CUDA Cores	1152 × 2	960 × 2	1152 × 2
Network	1 Gbps LAN		

Table 2. Comparison of running time and SR on GMM generation.

K	128						256					
Size	2 GB			10 GB			2 GB			10 GB		
Dim	30	96	108	30	96	108	30	96	108	30	96	108
T_S	186	184	179	913	907	910	291	285	289	1495	1475	1380
T_C	56	53	54	245	276	237	103	101	98	493	492	457
T_G	2.3	2.0	2.1	8.9	9.0	8.7	3.0	3.3	3.1	11.0	10.3	10.1
$SR_{C/S}$	3.3	3.5	3.3	3.7	3.3	3.8	2.8	2.8	2.9	3.0	3.0	3.0
$SR_{G/S}$	81.0	92.0	85.2	102.6	100.8	104.6	97.0	86.4	93.2	135.9	143.2	136.6
$SR_{G/C}$	24.3	26.5	25.7	27.5	30.7	27.2	34.3	30.6	31.6	44.8	47.8	45.2

Firstly, the summary of the SR performances on GMM generation is shown in Table 2 by varying the number of GMMs (K), the video data size (Size) and the dimension of features (Dim). The performances of running time in units of seconds are presented as T_S, T_C and T_G for the single CPU thread implementation, the Spark framework without enabling GPU (*i.e.*, the framework in [13]) and the proposed GPU-based Spark framework, respectively. From the running time performance, the speedup performances can be concluded as denoted as $SR_{C/S}$, $SR_{G/S}$ and $SR_{G/C}$ which indicate the SR performance of the work in [13] over the single CPU thread implementation, the SR performance of the proposed GPU-based Spark framework over the single CPU thread implementation and the SR performance of the proposed GPU-based Spark framework between enabling and disabling GPUs.

From the results, it can be easily seen that the proposed GPU-based Spark framework is able to dramatically accelerate the GMM generation process as compared to the single CPU thread implementation with the speedup from 81× to 143×. As compared with the CPU-only Spark framework [13], an acceleration of 24× − 48× can be achieved when GPUs are enabled for fine-grained computing. Moreover, along with the increment of data to be processed (such as the number of GMMs and data size), the speedup is further improved for different features, *e.g.*, when Dim = 96 and K = 128, the $SR_{G/S}$ performance has been boosted from 92.0 to 100.8 when the data size is increased from 2 GB to 10 GB. This reveals that the proposed framework becomes more efficient when processing larger amount of data because more computational resources will be spent on the real calculations instead of the overheads for data partitioning and transferring during the task execution required by Spark.

Similar to GMM generation, the running time and SR performances achieved on FV encoding are shown in Table 3, where we use 'Input' (which is equal to the product of a single mapper data file size and the number of data files) to show the processing ability of the proposed framework in handling different sets of input data scales. As observed from the results in Table 3, although the

Table 3. Comparison of running time and SR on FV encoding.

K	128						256					
Input	64 MB $\times$ 32			128 MB $\times$ 16			64 MB $\times$ 32			128 MB $\times$ 16		
Dim	30	96	108	30	96	108	30	96	108	30	96	108
T_S	607	611	603	574	566	570	814	821	810	788	791	783
T_C	41	41	42	39	37	38	66	65	63	60	56	59
T_G	15	13	14	14	14	13	15	16	16	12	13	14
$SR_{C/S}$	14.8	14.9	14.4	14.7	15.3	15.0	12.3	12.6	12.9	13.1	14.1	13.3
$SR_{G/S}$	40.5	47.0	43.1	41.0	40.4	43.8	54.3	51.3	50.6	65.7	60.8	55.9
$SR_{G/C}$	2.7	3.2	3.0	2.8	2.6	2.9	4.4	4.1	3.9	5.0	4.3	4.2

proposed GPU-based Spark framework is able to greatly speed up FV encoding as compared with both the single CPU thread version and CPU-only Spark framework, the $SR_{G/C}$ performance is not very significant as compared to that on GMM generation. This is mainly because the amount of computations to be carried out on GPUs is less for FV encoding than that for GMM generation.

4   Conclusion

In this work, a GPU-based Spark framework is proposed for large-scale human action recognition. The proposed framework fully utilizes the computing resources of CPUs and GPUs of the underlying heterogeneous system. The FV-oriented human action recognition approach is employed as a representative to evaluate the proposed framework. The comparative experimental results demonstrate that the proposed GPU-based Spark framework is able to dramatically improve the real-time performance for human action recognition. In the future, we will further enrich the utilities of the proposed framework to other kinds of human action recognition approaches.

References

1. Wang, H., Kläser, A., Schmid, C., Liu, C.L.: Action recognition by dense trajectories. In: Proceedings of CVPR 2011, pp. 3169–3176, June 2011
2. Wang, H., Schmid, C.: Action recognition with improved trajectories. In: Proceedings of ICCV 2013, pp. 3551–3558, December 2013
3. Wang, H., Yi, Y., Wu, J.: Human action recognition with trajectory based covariance descriptor. In: Proceedings of ACM MM 2015, pp. 1175–1178, October 2015
4. Dean, J., Ghemawat, S.: MapReduce: simplified data processing on large clusters. Commun. ACM 51(1), 107–113 (2008)
5. Zaharia, M., Chowdhury, M., Franklin, M.J., Shenker, S., Stoica, I.: Spark: cluster computing with working sets. In: Proceedings of HotCloud 2010, p. 10, June 2010
6. Hadoop. http://hadoop.apache.org/

7. CUDA guide. http://docs.nvidia.com/cuda/cuda-c-programming-guide/
8. Augonnet, C., Thibault, S., Namyst, R., Wacrenier, P.-A.: STARPU: a unified platform for task scheduling on heterogeneous multicore architectures. In: Sips, H., Epema, D., Lin, H.-X. (eds.) Euro-Par 2009. LNCS, vol. 5704, pp. 863–874. Springer, Heidelberg (2009). doi:10.1007/978-3-642-03869-3_80
9. Linderman, M., Collins, J., Wang, H., Meng, T.: Merge: a programming model for heterogeneous multi-core systems. In: Proceedings of ASPLOS 2008, pp. 287–296, March 2008
10. Wernsing, J.R., Stitt, G.: Elastic computing: a portable optimization framework for hybrid computers. Parallel Comput. **38**(8), 438–464 (2012)
11. He, B., Fang, W., Luo, Q., Govindaraju, N., Wang, T.: Mars: a MapReduce framework on graphics processors. In: Proceedings of PACT 2008, pp. 260–269, October 2008
12. Wang, H., Xiao, B., Wang, L., Zhu, F., Jiang, Y.G., Wu, J.: CHCF: a cloud-based heterogeneous computing framework for large-scale image retrieval. IEEE Trans. Circ. Syst. Video Technol. **25**(12), 1900–1913 (2015)
13. Wang, H., Zheng, X., Xiao, B.: Large-scale human action recognition with Spark. In: Proceedings of MMSP 2015, pp. 1–6, October 2015
14. Perronnin, F., Dance, C.: Fisher kernels on visual vocabularies for image categorization. In: Proceedings of CVPR 2007, pp. 1–8, June 2007
15. Marszalek, M., Laptev, I., Schmid, C.: Actions in context. In: Proceedings of CVPR 2009, pp. 2929–2936, June 2009
16. Google protobuf. https://code.google.com/p/protobuf/
17. Oneata, D., Verbeek, J., Schmid, C.: Action and event recognition with Fisher vectors on a compact feature set. In: Proceedings of ICCV 2013, pp. 1817–1824, December 2013
18. Sivic, J., Zisserman, A.: Video google: a text retrieval approach to object matching in videos. In: ICCV 2003, pp. 1470–1477, October 2003
19. Dempster, A.P., Laird, N.M., Rubin, D.B.: Maximum likelihood from incomplete data via the EM algorithm. J. Royal Stat. Soc. **39**(1), 1–38 (1977)

Adaptive Multi-class Correlation Filters

Linlin Yang[1], Chen Chen[2], Hainan Wang[1], Baochang Zhang[1(✉)],
and Jungong Han[3]

[1] School of Automation Science and Electrical Engineering,
Beihang University, Beijing, China
bczhang@buaa.edu.cn
[2] Center for Research in Computer Vision, University of Central Florida,
Orlando, USA
[3] Department of Computer Science and Digital Technologies,
Northumbria University, Newcastle upon Tyne, UK

Abstract. Correlation filters have attracted growing attention due to their high efficiency, which have been well studied for binary classification. However, by setting the desired output to be a fixed Gaussian function, the conventional multi-class classification based on correlation filters becomes problematic due to the under-fitting in many real-world applications. In this paper, we propose an adaptive multi-class correlation filters (AMCF) method based on an alternating direction method of multipliers (ADMM) framework. Within this framework, we introduce an adaptive output to alleviate the under-fitting problem in the ADMM iterations. By doing so, a closed-form sub-solution is obtained and further used to constrain the optimization objective, simplifying the entire inference mechanism. The proposed approach is successfully combined with the Histograms of Oriented Gradients (HOG) features, multi-channel features and convolution features, and achieves superior performances over state-of-the-arts in two multi-class classification tasks including handwritten digits recognition and RGBD-based action recognition.

Keywords: Multi-class correlation filters · ADMM · Adaptive output

1 Introduction

In the application of object detection and localization, correlation filters have shown to be competitive with far more complicated approaches, but using only a fraction of the computational power. Correlation filters take advantage of the fact that the convolution of two image patches is equivalent to an element-wise

This work was supported in part by the Natural Science Foundation of China under Contract 61272052 and Contract 61473086, in part by PAPD, in part by CICAEET, and in part by the National Basic Research Program of China under Grant 2015CB352501. The work of B. Zhang was supported by the Program for New Century Excellent Talents University within the Ministry of Education, China, and Beijing Municipal Science & Technology Commission Z161100001616005.

E. Chen et al. (Eds.): PCM 2016, Part II, LNCS 9917, pp. 680–688, 2016.
DOI: 10.1007/978-3-319-48896-7_67

product in the fast Fourier transform (FFT) domain. Thus, by formulating the objective in the FFT domain, they can specify the desired output of a linear classifier for several translations or image shifts [7]. Bolme [1] proposed to learn a minimum output sum of squared error (MOSSE) filter for visual tracking on gray-scale images. Heriques *et al.* utilized correlation filters in a kernel space based on circulant structure (CSK) [7], which achieved very fast speed in tracking. By using HOG features, kernelized correlation filter (KCF) [7] was developed to improve the performance of CSK. Multi-channel correlation filters (MCCF) were developed to localize eye positions [5]. In [12], hierarchical convolutional features were combined with KCF to achieve robust tracking. Furthermore, maximum margin correlation filters (MMCF) [16], constraining the output at the target location, show better robustness to outliers. We can also find some works on correlation filters for multi-class tasks, such as the Distance Classifier Correlation Filter (DCCF) [13]. Although much success has been demonstrated, the existing works do not principally exploit adaptive output in the procedure of solving the optimized variable.

Problem and motivation: The multi-class output is a useful constraint and has been widely investigated in the state-of-the-art classifiers, i.e., support vector machine (SVM) [18] and Adaboost [17]. Many new applications have been developed [6]. However, to the best of our knowledge, the structured output constraint is neglected in correlation filters calculation. Since each class has its own correlation filter, each correlation filter finds the largest correlation response on its own sample set to discriminate among different classes. In traditional correlation filter methods, a fixed desired output setting could cause an under-fitting problem since the learning process cannot converge when all samples are equally treated. As another intuition, the correlation filter of each class is iteratively computed, which can actually be considered as a prior to constrain the solution [26]. Different from existing works, this paper provides new insights into correlation filters from the following aspects:

- Based on an adaptive output, we propose an iterative procedure to calculate correlation filters and obtain a closed-form solution in each iteration.
- We use sub-filters derived from the previous steps to constrain the solution in the ADMM framework for an efficient correlation filter calculation.

For easy of explanation, expressions are given for 1-dimensional (1-D) signals and can be extended to 2-D. ϕ is a kernel function and X^H is the Hermitian transpose of X. We define correlation operation as $*$, dot product as $\cdot$ and element-wise product as $\odot$. $\wedge$ denotes the Fourier transform and $\mathcal{F}^{-1}$ its inverse. Moreover, we define $\mathbf{x} \otimes \mathbf{y} = max(\mathbf{x} * \mathbf{y})$ and $Gauss(x)$ denotes Gaussian distribution response with peak value x.

The rest of the paper is organized as follows. Section 2 describes the details of the proposed method, while the algorithm and discussion are stated in Sect. 3. Experiments and results are presented in Sect. 4. Finally, Sect. 5 concludes the paper.

2 Proposed AMCF Algorithm

We first revisit the one-vs-all (OVA) framework, based on which a new adaptive correlation filters scheme is proposed by considering a multi-class constraint in the optimization process. A closed-form sub-solution is obtained in each iteration using the ADMM technique. The sub-solutions derived from ADMM iterations are used to constrain the problem in our framework.

Let $(\mathbf{x}_1, y_1), ..., (\mathbf{x}_m, y_m)$ be a set of training examples and assume that each example $\mathbf{x}_i$ is from a domain $X \subseteq R_n$ and each label y_i is an integer from the set $Y = 1, ..., k$. A multi-class classifier can be seen as a mapping $H : \mathcal{X} \to \mathcal{Y}$. Based on the OVA framework for multi-class classification, we can compute the result according to

$$H(\mathbf{x}_i) = \operatorname*{argmax}_{r=1}^{k}(W_r \otimes \phi(\mathbf{x}_i)), \tag{1}$$

where W is a matrix of size $k \times n$ over R and W_r is the tth row of W indicating the correlation filter of the rth class.

The objective is defined as the minimum squared-error between $Gauss(Y_{i,j})$ (the ith training sample's gaussian desired output in j^{th} class) and the correlation response $W_j * \phi(\mathbf{x}_i)$. Y is a matrix consists of the maximum value of response. Moreover, the iterative process results in a subset of solutions, which can be used in a ADMM framework [26]. In the ADMM optimization, the variable could be considered from a subspace, which is also used here to constrain our problem. The optimization problem is then defined as follows:

$$\min_{W,\varepsilon} \quad \frac{1}{2}\sum_{i=1}^{m}\sum_{j=1}^{k}\|Gauss(Y_{i,j}) - W_j * \phi(\mathbf{x}_i)\|^2 + \frac{\beta}{2}\sum_{i=1}^{m}\varepsilon_i^2 + \frac{\lambda}{2}\|W\|^2$$

$$subject\ to\ \forall\ i \quad W_{y_i} \otimes \phi(\mathbf{x}_i) + \delta_{y_i,q_i} - W_{q_i} \otimes \phi(\mathbf{x}_i) = 1 - \varepsilon_i$$

$$W \sim \mathcal{G} \tag{2}$$

where $q_i = \operatorname*{argmax}_{j}(W_j \otimes \phi(\mathbf{x}_i))$ and $\delta_{i,j} = \begin{cases} 0 & i \neq j \\ 1 & i = j \end{cases}$, $\lambda > 0$ is a regularization constant and $\varepsilon_i \geq 0$ are soft constraints. $\mathcal{G}$ denotes a subspace, which is generated based on sub-solutions calculated in an iterative process. β is empirically given. To incorporate subspace prior $\mathcal{G}$ into our model, we propose to perform variable cloning $W \to N \sim \mathcal{G}$. This constraint is included in the ADMM framework to solve the optimization problem with high practicability [26]. The subspace constraint can be added to our approach to simplify the inference mechanism of our algorithm. Now the constrains $W \sim \mathcal{G}$ can be written as $W - N = 0$ and $N \in \mathcal{G}$.

Based on the Lagrangian method, we have:

$$L = \frac{1}{2} \sum_{i=1}^{m} \sum_{j=1}^{k} \|Gauss(Y_{i,j}) - W_j * \phi(\mathbf{x}_i)\|^2 + \frac{\beta}{2} \sum_{i=1}^{m} \varepsilon_i^2 + \frac{\lambda}{2} \|W\|^2$$

$$+ \sum_{i=1}^{m} \alpha_i (W_{y_i} \otimes \phi(\mathbf{x}_i) + \delta_{y_i,q_i} - W_{q_i} \otimes \phi(\mathbf{x}_i) - 1 + \varepsilon_i) \qquad (3)$$

$$+ M \cdot (W - N) + \frac{\eta}{2} \|W - N\|^2$$

where M is the Lagrangian multiplier. After transferring the constraint, we simplify the algorithm by means of ADMM [2]. Specifically, at each iterative step, we compute the pth hyperplane of the tth iteration using the result of the previous iteration (i.e., the $(t-1)^{th}$ iteration). We assume that there are s positive samples and $m - s$ negative samples in the pth class. Similar to [5,7], we pose this problem equivalently in the frequency domain based on Parseval's Theorem [14] to derive a closed-form and efficient solution:

$$\hat{W}_p^t = [(\lambda + \eta)I + 2\Phi(\tilde{X})^H \Phi(\tilde{X})]^{-1} [\Phi(\tilde{X})^H \tilde{Y}_p^t + \eta \hat{N}_p^{t-1} + \hat{M}_p^{t-1}]$$

$$\hat{N}_p^t = mean(W_p^{[1:t]}) \qquad (4)$$

$$\hat{M}_p^t = \hat{M}_p^{t-1} + \eta(\hat{W}_p^t - \hat{N}_p^t)$$

and

$$\tilde{X}_p^t = \begin{pmatrix} diag(\hat{\mathbf{x}}_1) \\ \cdots \\ diag(\hat{\mathbf{x}}_m) \end{pmatrix} ; \tilde{Y}_p^t = \begin{pmatrix} \hat{Gauss}(Y_{p,1}^t) \\ \cdots \\ \hat{Gauss}(Y_{p,m}^t) \end{pmatrix} ; Y_p^t = Y_p^{t-1} + \beta \begin{pmatrix} \mathbf{a}_1 \\ \mathbf{a}_2 \end{pmatrix} ;$$

$$\mathbf{a}_1 = \begin{pmatrix} 1 + max(\mathcal{F}^{-1}(\hat{W}_{q_1}^{t-1} \odot \phi(\hat{\mathbf{x}}_1))) - \delta_{p,q_1} \\ \cdots \\ 1 + max(\mathcal{F}^{-1}(\hat{W}_{q_s}^{t-1} \odot \phi(\hat{\mathbf{x}}_s))) - \delta_{p,q_s} \end{pmatrix}$$

$$\mathbf{a}_2 = \begin{pmatrix} max(\mathcal{F}^{-1}(\hat{W}_{y_{s+1}}^{t-1} \odot \phi(\hat{\mathbf{x}}_{s+1}))) - 1 + \vartheta_{p,q_{s+1}} \\ \cdots \\ max(\mathcal{F}^{-1}(\hat{W}_{y_m}^{t-1} \odot \phi(\hat{\mathbf{x}}_m))) - 1 + \vartheta_{p,q_m} \end{pmatrix}$$

$$q_i = \underset{j}{argmax} \, (max(\mathcal{F}^{-1}(\hat{W}_j \odot \phi(\hat{\mathbf{x}}_i))))$$

$$\vartheta_{p,q_i} = \begin{cases} 0 & q_i = p \\ 1 - max(\mathcal{F}^{-1}(\hat{W}_{y_i}^{t-1} \odot \phi(\hat{\mathbf{x}}_i))) \\ \quad + max(\mathcal{F}^{-1}(\hat{W}_p^{t-1} \odot \phi(\hat{\mathbf{x}}_i))) & q_i \neq p \end{cases}$$

Here $mean(\cdot)$ denotes the mean of sub-filters and $diag(\cdot)$ is an operator that transforms a D dimensional vector into a $D \times D$ dimensional diagonal matrix.

Algorithm 1. Adaptive multi-class correlation filters with subspace constraints

1: Set Y_p^t based on label, $\eta_p^0 = 0.25$, $\varepsilon_{p,best} = +\infty$, $\beta = 1$, iteration number $t = 1$
2: Initialize $\hat{\mathbf{W}}^{[0]}, \hat{\mathbf{N}}^{[0]}$ and $\hat{\mathbf{M}}^{[0]}$ based on correlation filters
3: **repeat**
4:    **for** $i = 1 : label$ **do**
5:        $\mathbf{Y}_p^t = \mathbf{Y}_p^{t-1} + \beta \begin{pmatrix} \mathbf{a}_1 \\ \mathbf{a}_2 \end{pmatrix}$
6:        $\tilde{\mathbf{Y}}_p^t = \begin{pmatrix} \hat{\mathbf{Gauss}}(\mathbf{Y}_{p,1}^t) \\ \cdots \\ \hat{\mathbf{Gauss}}(\mathbf{Y}_{p,m}^t) \end{pmatrix}$
7:        $\hat{\mathbf{W}}_p^t = [(\lambda + \eta_p^{t-1})\mathbf{I} + 2\Phi(\tilde{\mathbf{X}})^H \Phi(\tilde{\mathbf{X}})]^{-1}[\Phi(\tilde{\mathbf{X}})^H \tilde{\mathbf{Y}}_p^t + \eta_p^{t-1}\hat{\mathbf{N}}_p^{t-1} + \hat{\mathbf{M}}_p^{t-1}]$
8:        $\varepsilon_p = \|\hat{\mathbf{W}}^{[k+1]} - \hat{\mathbf{W}}^{[k]}\|_2$
9:        **if** $\varepsilon_p < \varepsilon_{p,best}$ **then**
10:            $\eta_p^t = \eta_p^{t-1}$
11:            $\varepsilon_{p,best} = \varepsilon_p$
12:        **else**
13:            $\eta_p^t = t\eta_p^{t-1}$
14:        **end if**
15:        $\hat{\mathbf{N}}_p^t = [(\lambda + \eta_p^t)\mathbf{I} + 2\Phi(\tilde{\mathbf{X}})^H \Phi(\tilde{\mathbf{X}})]^{-1}[\Phi(\tilde{\mathbf{X}})^H \tilde{\mathbf{Y}}_p^t + \eta_p^t \hat{\mathbf{W}}_p^t + \hat{\mathbf{M}}_p^{t-1}]$
16:        $\hat{\mathbf{M}}_p^t = \hat{\mathbf{M}}_p^{t-1} + \eta_p^t(\hat{\mathbf{M}}_p^t - \hat{\mathbf{N}}_p^t)$
17:        $t = t + 1$
18:    **end for**
19: **until** some stopping criterion

3   Summary of the AMCF Algorithm and Discussion

The details of the proposed AMCF algorithm is shown in Algorithm 1. To demonstrate the advantages of AMCF, we focus on y (the maximum of response), which is the key component in the final classification. The value of y can be regarded as the weight of the training samples. When a sample is misclassified, $\|y\|$ increases, which means the weight decreases. It is known that under-fitting occurs in the setting of a fixed output since all the samples are treated equally. As evident from Fig. 1, both training and test errors are large without using adaptive y.

As far as computational complexity is considered, AMCF is very fast in the testing process given that there are only one element-wise product operation and one inverse transform operation in the FFT domain. When training K classes of D-dimensional feature vectors with T iterations, AMCF has a memory cost of $\mathcal{O}(KD)$ and a time cost of $\mathcal{O}(TKDlogD)$.

4   Experiments

To verify the effectiveness of the proposed AMCF algorithm in classification applications, we carry out experiments on a large-scale dataset, MNIST [10] dataset, for handwritten digits recognition and a challenging depth-based action datasets, MSRAction3D [11], for human action recognition.

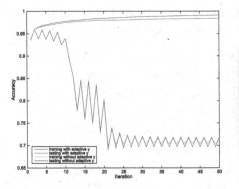

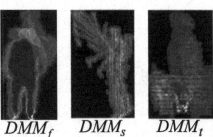

DMM_f DMM_s DMM_t

Fig. 1. Convergence comparison between the correlation filters without adaptive y and the proposed AMCF method on the MNIST dataset using hierarchical features.

Fig. 2. Three DMMs of a depth action sequence "high throw".

For the MNIST dataset, we use features based on convolutional neural networks (CNNs) which exploit rich hierarchical features [12] in images. Hierarchical convolutional features are able to preserve the neighborhood relations and spatial locality of images in their latent higher-level feature representations.

For action recognition on the MSRAction3D, we use multi-channel HOG features computed from the Depth Motion Maps (DMMs) [24] due to their computational efficiency. According to [24], each depth action sequence generates three DMMs corresponding to three projection views, i.e., front view (f), side view (s) and top view (t), denoted by DMM_f, DMM_s and DMM_t, respectively (see Fig. 2). We concatenate the HOG features extracted from the three DMMs to form the multi-channel HOG features as the final feature representation.

4.1 MNIST Dataset

We perform handwritten digits recognition on the widely used MNIST [10] dataset. It has a training set of 60,000 examples, and a test set of 10,000 examples. We use the convolutional features extracted by LeNet [9] to encode the original MNIST digits. The same experimental setup in [8] is followed. The proposed method achieves the best performance as shown in Table 1.

4.2 MSRAction3D Dataset

The MSRAction3D dataset consists of depth sequences captured by a Kinect device. It includes 20 actions performed by 10 subjects. Each subject performed each action 2 or 3 times. The size of each depth image is 240×320 pixels. The same experimental setup in [4,20,25] is adopted. The same parameters reported in [3] were used here for the sizes of DMMs and block. A total of 20 actions are employed and one half of the subjects (1, 3, 5, 7 and 9) are used for training and

Table 1. Recognition results comparison on the MNIST dataset.

Method	Accuracy (%)
LeNet [9]	98.9
MCCF [5]	93.5
SVM poly 4 [9]	98.9
K-NN Euclidean [9]	97.6
PCA+quadratic [9]	96.7
Ours	**98.9**

Table 2. Recognition results comparison on the MSRAction3D dataset.

Method	Accuracy (%)
DMM-HOG [24]	85.5
Random Occupancy [21]	86.5
HON4D [15]	88.9
Actionlet Ensemble [22]	88.2
Depth Cuboid [23]	89.3
Vemulapalli et al. [19]	89.5
Ours	**92.3**

the remaining subjects are used for testing. The recognition rates of our method and existing approaches are listed in Table 2. It is clear that our method achieves better performance than other competing methods.

5 Conclusions

In this paper, we propose an efficient framework for the multi-class correlation filters classification with subspace constraints in the ADMM framework. The new insight focuses on an adaptive output and also subspace constraints on the solution. The experimental results on handwritten digits recognition and MSR action recognition show that the proposed algorithm performs favorably against the state-of-the-art methods. Future work will focus on improving the kernel method and accelerating the convergence speed.

References

1. Bolme, D.S., Beveridge, J.R., Draper, B.A., Lui, Y.M.: Visual object tracking using adaptive correlation filters. In: Proceedings of the IEEE Conference on Computer Vision and Pattern Recognition, pp. 2544–2550. IEEE (2010)
2. Boyd, S., Parikh, N., Chu, E., Peleato, B., Eckstein, J.: Distributed optimization and statistical learning via the alternating direction method of multipliers. Found. Trends Mach. Learn. **3**(1), 1–122 (2011)
3. Chen, C., Jafari, R., Kehtarnavaz, N.: Action recognition from depth sequences using depth motion maps-based local binary patterns. In: Proceedings of the IEEE Winter Conference on Applications of Computer Vision, pp. 1092–1099. IEEE (2015)
4. Chen, C., Liu, M., Zhang, B., Han, J., Jiang, J., Liu, H.: 3d action recognition using multi-temporal depth motion maps and Fisher vector. In: Proceedings of International Joint Conference on Artificial Intelligence, pp. 3331–3337 (2016)
5. Galoogahi, H., Sim, T., Lucey, S.: Multi-channel correlation filters. In: Proceedings of the IEEE International Conference on Computer Vision, pp. 3072–3079 (2013)

6. Han, J., Zhou, P., Zhang, D., Cheng, G., Guo, L., Liu, Z., Bu, S., Wu, J.: Efficient, simultaneous detection of multi-class geospatial targets based on visual saliency modeling and discriminative learning of sparse coding. ISPRS J. Photogrammetry Remote Sens. **89**, 37–48 (2014)

7. Henriques, J.F., Caseiro, R., Martins, P., Batista, J.: High-speed tracking with kernelized correlation filters. IEEE Trans. Pattern Anal. Mach. Intell. **37**(3), 583–596 (2015)

8. Jia, Y., Shelhamer, E., Donahue, J., Karayev, S., Long, J., Girshick, R., Guadarrama, S., Darrell, T.: Caffe: convolutional architecture for fast feature embedding. In: Proceedings of the ACM International Conference on Multimedia, pp. 675–678. ACM (2014)

9. LeCun, Y., Bottou, L., Bengio, Y., Haffner, P.: Gradient-based learning applied to document recognition. Proc. IEEE **86**(11), 2278–2324 (1998)

10. LeCun, Y., Cortes, C., Burges, C.J.: The MNIST database of handwritten digits (1998)

11. Li, W., Zhang, Z., Liu, Z.: Action recognition based on a bag of 3d points. In: Proceedings of IEEE Computer Society Conference on Computer Vision and Pattern Recognition Workshops, pp. 9–14 (2010)

12. Ma, C., Huang, J.B., Yang, X., Yang, M.H.: Hierarchical convolutional features for visual tracking. In: Proceedings of the IEEE International Conference on Computer Vision, pp. 3074–3082 (2015)

13. Mahalanobis, A., Kumar, B.V., Sims, S.: Distance-classifier correlation filters for multiclass target recognition. Appl. Opt. **35**(17), 3127–3133 (1996)

14. Oppenheim, A.V., Willsky, A.S., Nawab, S.H.: Signals and Systems. Pearson, Hoboken (2014)

15. Oreifej, O., Liu, Z.: HON4D: histogram of oriented 4d normals for activity recognition from depth sequences. In: Proceedings of the IEEE Conference on Computer Vision and Pattern Recognition, pp. 716–723 (2013)

16. Rodriguez, A., Boddeti, V.N., Kumar, B.V., Mahalanobis, A.: Maximum margin correlation filter: a new approach for localization and classification. IEEE Trans. Image Process. **22**(2), 631–643 (2013)

17. Shen, C., Lin, G., van den Hengel, A.: Structboost: boosting methods for predicting structured output variables. IEEE Trans. Pattern Anal. Mach. Intell. **36**(10), 2089–2103 (2014)

18. Tsochantaridis, I., Joachims, T., Hofmann, T., Altun, Y.: Large margin methods for structured and interdependent output variables. J. Mach. Learn. Res. **6**, 1453–1484 (2005)

19. Vemulapalli, R., Arrate, F., Chellappa, R.: Human action recognition by representing 3d skeletons as points in a lie group. In: Proceedings of the IEEE Conference on Computer Vision and Pattern Recognition, pp. 588–595 (2014)

20. Vieira, A.W., Nascimento, E.R., Oliveira, G.L., Liu, Z., Campos, M.F.: On the improvement of human action recognition from depth map sequences using space-time occupancy patterns. Pattern Recogn. Lett. **36**, 221–227 (2014)

21. Wang, J., Liu, Z., Chorowski, J., Chen, Z., Wu, Y.: Robust 3D action recognition with random occupancy patterns. In: Fitzgibbon, A., Lazebnik, S., Perona, P., Sato, Y., Schmid, C. (eds.) ECCV 2012. LNCS, vol. 7573, pp. 872–885. Springer, Heidelberg (2012). doi:10.1007/978-3-642-33709-3_62

22. Wang, J., Liu, Z., Wu, Y., Yuan, J.: Mining actionlet ensemble for action recognition with depth cameras. In: Proceedings of the IEEE Conference on Computer Vision and Pattern Recognition, pp. 1290–1297. IEEE (2012)

23. Xia, L., Aggarwal, J.: Spatio-temporal depth cuboid similarity feature for activity recognition using depth camera. In: Proceedings of the IEEE Conference on Computer Vision and Pattern Recognition, pp. 2834–2841 (2013)
24. Yang, X., Zhang, C., Tian, Y.: Recognizing actions using depth motion maps-based histograms of oriented gradients. In: Proceedings of the ACM International Conference on Multimedia, pp. 1057–1060. ACM (2012)
25. Yang, Y., Zhang, B., Yang, L., Chen, C., Yang, W.: Action recognition using completed local binary patterns and multiple-class boosting classifier. In: Proceedings of Asian Conference on Pattern Recognition, pp. 336–340 (2015)
26. Zhang, B., Perina, A., Murino, V., Del Bue, A.: Sparse representation classification with manifold constraints transfer. In: Proceedings of the IEEE Conference on Computer Vision and Pattern Recognition, pp. 4557–4565 (2015)

Deep Neural Networks for Free-Hand Sketch Recognition

Yuqi Zhang[1,2], Yuting Zhang[2], and Xueming Qian[1,2(✉)]

[1] The School of Software Engineering,
Xi'an Jiaotong University, Xi'an 710049, China
zhangyuqi@stu.xjtu.edu.cn, qianxm@mail.xjtu.edu.cn
[2] The Ministry of Education Key Laboratory for Intelligent Networks
and Network Security, Xi'an Jiaotong University, Xi'an 710049, China
zhangyuting@stu.xjtu.edu.cn

Abstract. The paper presents a deep Convolutional Neural Network (CNN) framework for free-hand sketch recognition. One of the main challenges in free-hand sketch recognition is to increase the recognition accuracy on sketches drawn by different people. To overcome this problem, we use deep Convolutional Neural Networks (CNNs) that have dominated top results in the field of image recognition. And we use the contours of natural images for training, because sketches drawn by different people may be very different and databases of the sketch images for training are very limited. We propose a CNN training on contours that performs well on sketch recognition over different databases of the sketch images. And we make some adjustments to the contours for training and reach higher recognition accuracy. Experimental results show the effectiveness of the proposed approach.

Keywords: Deep convolutional neural networks · Contour · Sketch recognition

1 Introduction

Through the process of human civilization, sketch has been used as a basic and powerful communication tool. Sketches can effectively describe the aim of a recognition or search, when it is hard to get natural images sometimes. With the popularity of touchscreens, we can sketch on computers, phones and tablets and sketches have become much easier to obtain. Research on sketches has attracted more interest in the computer vision community in recent years, with the advance in technology and people needs, such as sketch classification [7, 8], sketch recognition [9–13], sketch-based image retrieval [14–16, 21] and sketch-based 3D model retrieval [18–20].

Prior work on sketch recognition generally extracts hand crafted features from sketch images followed by feeding them to a classifier. Deep Neural Networks (DNNs) have recently achieved impressive performance in the field of image recognition. But in the field of free-hand sketch recognition, there are three important questions need to solve with DNNs. The first one is that DNNs trained on natural images are not applicable to the sketches, because sketches do not contain texture and color

© Springer International Publishing AG 2016
E. Chen et al. (Eds.): PCM 2016, Part II, LNCS 9917, pp. 689–696, 2016.
DOI: 10.1007/978-3-319-48896-7_68

information. The second one is the fact that databases of the sketch images for training are very limited. And the third one is that the sketches of each person may be very different.

In this work, we propose a deep Convolutional Neural Network (CNN) training on the contours of natural images for free-hand sketch recognition. Our contributions are summarized as follows: (1) For the first time, we train on the contours of natural images for free-hand sketch recognition to increase scalability and robustness. (2) We propose a CNN architecture to make it more suitable for sketch recognition and it performs well for training the network on contours or sketches. (3) The proposed method can not only improve the recognition accuracy but also has robustness over the variations of drawing sketch. With training on large contours, the proposed method can make sketch recognition on sketches drawn by users without requiring any priori knowledge.

2   Related Work

In this section, firstly, we introduce the early studies on sketch recognition. Secondly, we present some recent researches where deep Convolutional Neural Networks (CNNs) were used for sketch recognition.

Hammond et al. [11] proposed a language to describe how sketches are drawn and edited in an area and creating a sketch recognition system. [7, 10] extract hand crafted features from sketch images and feed them to SVM (support vector machine). Li et al. [9] used a star graph and ensemble matching to exploited local features and global structures of sketches to overcome the feature sparsity problem. Their unified sketch recognition framework addressed both local and global variations.

In recent years, Deep neural networks have improved performance in the field of image recognition. In the area of natural image recognition, CNNs have achieved very satisfied results [3–5]. DNNs, especially CNNs, can automatically learn features instead of manually extracting features and its multi layers learning can get more effective expression. Yu et al. [1] proposed a novel Convolutional Neural Networks (CNN), Sketch-a-Net, for free-hand sketch recognition rather than natural photo statistics. They also suggested the effectiveness of sequential ordering information in sketches to improve sketch recognition performance. Seddati et al. [2] proposed a CNN that is both more accurate and faster for sketch recognition. [1, 2] both carried out experiments on the largest free-hand sketch benchmark dataset, the TU-Berlin sketch dataset [6].

3   Approach

The framework of the proposed method is shown in Fig. 1. At first, we extract contours from natural images by Berkeley detector [14, 15, 17, 21]. They learn to detect natural image boundaries using local brightness, color and texture cues. The extracted contours look like sketches but have more complicated lines and details. Some of them are shown in Fig. 2. Next, we train on these contours with our network. We remove the global mean for training contours and train on GPU. Finally, we use the model which was trained successfully to make recognition on testing sketches. All these sketches pass through the network that will estimate for each sketch the probabilities of belonging to each class. The output of nodes in the last layer from the network is a vector with 31 probabilities on each category and the category that has the highest probability is the winner.

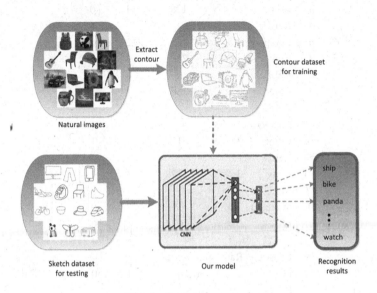

Fig. 1. System framework

Fig. 2. Examples of the extracted contours

Most deep Convolutional Neural Networks (CNNs) [3–5] for image recognition follows a typical structure of multiple convolutional layers followed by fully connected layers. Following previous work, our network architecture is described below: The size of input image is 229 × 229 × 3. Every multiple convolutional layer is followed by a rectifier layer (ReLU). We place six multiple convolutional layers when the first, second, fourth and sixth are followed by a maximum pooling layer (Maxpool). Then three fully-connected layers follow these layers. The output of the last fully-connected

Table 1. Details of our network architecture

Ind	Type	Filter size	Filter num	Stride	Pad
1	Conv	9 × 9	64	2	0
2	ReLU	–	–	–	–
3	Maxpool	3 × 3	–	2	0
4	Conv	5 × 5	128	1	0
5	ReLU	–	–	–	–
6	Maxpool	3 × 3	–	2	0
7	Conv	3 × 3	256	1	1
8	ReLU	–	–	–	–
9	Conv	3 × 3	256	1	1
10	ReLU	–	–	–	–
11	Maxpool	3 × 3	–	2	1
12	Conv	3 × 3	512	1	1
13	ReLU	–	–	–	–
14	Conv	3 × 3	512	1	1
15	ReLU	–	–	–	–
16	Maxpool	3 × 3	–	2	0
17	FC	6 × 6	1024	1	0
18	ReLU	–	–	–	–
19	Dropout	Rate : 0.5	–	–	–
20	FC	1 × 1	1024	1	0
21	ReLU	–	–	–	–
22	Dropout	Rate : 0.5	–	–	–
23	FC	1 × 1	31	1	0

layer is fed to a 31-way softmax. The details of our network architecture are shown in Table 1.

There are a few differences between our network and previous CNNs such as AlexNet [3]. At first, we use fewer and small kernels and small stride in the first convolutional layer. Our consideration is as follows: contours contain less information than the natural images and the categories we used are relatively small, so we used fewer kernels. Small kernels and small stride may be able to reduce the loss of information. Next, we place more multiple convolutional layers and more pooling layers. We find that deeper networks might get more effective expression. Next, we remove Local Response Normalization (LRN). [1, 2] both reported that LRN has no effect on training on sketches, and our experiments also show that LRN has no effect on training on contours. Then the number of kernels we use increases with the in-depth of our network and reach the maximum before the last layer. At last, we used fewer kernels in the last layer and the number of kernels is the same as the number of categories.

4   Experiments

4.1   Dataset

TU-Berlin Sketch Dataset. This dataset was used in [6] and it contains 250 categories with 80 sketches per category. We use 31 sketch categories and the selected categories are the same with our natural images categories. Then we randomly select 70 sketches per category for training and 10 sketches per category for testing. For training sketches, we do mirroring, rotation and shift.

Our Dataset. We collect a total of 43200 natural images gathered from Google using keywords to search for relevant images and it contains 31 categories with about 1400 images per category. Examples of categories are hat, ship, bike, computer, airplane, car, bed, panda and watch. We extract contours from all images for training. Then we perform mirroring, shift and expanding for all contours.

We draw 310 sketches with 10 sketches per category as our sketch dataset for testing. Some of them are shown in Fig. 3. 10 students in our lab participate in this work.

Fig. 3. Examples of our sketches

4.2   Results and Discussion

AlexNet [3] and our network were trained separately on sketches and contours. AlexNet-sketch: we re-trained AlexNet with 31 categories sketches from TU-Berlin sketch dataset. AlexNet-contour: we re-trained AlexNet with 31 categories contours extracted from natural images. Our-sketch: we trained our network with 31 categories sketches from TU-Berlin sketch dataset. Our-contour: we trained our network with 31 categories contours extracted from natural images. The classification results on TU-Berlin sketch dataset and our sketch dataset are shown in Table 2. The following observations can be made: (1) Training on contours improves the sketch recognition accuracy by an average of 3.4% over all testing sketches. It is probably because the sketches drawn by each person are different but are the same as contours of natural images. The other reason may be that the sketch images for training are very limited and natural images are easy to gain. (2) Training on sketches shows a great difference of accuracy on the two datasets from 37.9% to 75.2% averagely, and training on contours shows a roughly consistent performance on the two datasets from 54.5% to 65.45% averagely. This is, perhaps, because we used TU-Berlin sketch dataset for training and it is overfitting. Training on contours does not suffer from this question. (3) Our network improves the sketch recognition accuracy from 54.6% to 58.6% training on sketches and from 58.5% to 61.5% training on contours. The design of our network such as more multiple convolutional layers can achieve more effective expression for sketch recognition.

Table 2. Results comparison over different testing datasets

Model	TU-Berlin sketch dataset	Our sketch dataset	Both datasets
AlexNet-sketch [3]	73.9%	35.2%	54.6%
AlexNet-contour [3]	53.5%	63.5%	58.5%
Our-sketch	76.5%	40.6%	58.6%
Our-contour	55.5%	67.4%	61.5%

Table 3 compares results with our network training on contours and adjusted contours. Contour: we used the original contours for training. Contour + expanding: we used the original contours and the expanded contours for training. Contour + other: we did mirroring and shift for the original contours and train on them. Contour + all: we used the original contours and all adjusted contours for training. In this experiment, we show that adding the expanded contours improves the recognition accuracy from 56.3% to 61.9% and adding the other adjusted contours improves the recognition accuracy from 56.3% to 61.5% over all testing sketches. It is probably because the expanded contours are able to express better line and shape information and the other adjusted contours can reduce overfitting. When we used the original contours and all adjusted contours for training, we get a relatively best result that is 64.7%. And the rising trend of the recognition results is consistent with the two datasets.

Table 3. Results comparison using different training datasets

Model	TU-Berlin sketch dataset	Our sketch dataset	Both datasets
Contour	49.7%	62.9%	56.3%
Contour + expanding	56.1%	67.7%	61.9%
Contour + other	55.5%	67.4%	61.5%
Contour + all	59.0%	70.3%	64.7%

In Fig. 4, the recognition results of each class on two datasets are shown. The horizontal axis is the category number and the vertical axis is the accuracy. The proposed method further shows a roughly consistent performance on different datasets with training on contours. Some results of several categories such as bed and flower are not good. The average recognition accuracy of bed and flower are 10% and 20% respectively. This is, perhaps, because contours of beds and flowers have a lot of complex lines and details, then they can't fully reflect the shape information.

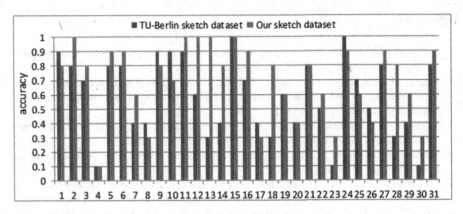

Fig. 4. Recognition results of each class

Table 4 provides four examples of recognition results. The black words are correct recognition results and the red words are wrong recognition results. Overall, the proposed method performs well in the most experimental category and is more robust for a variety of sketches drawn by different people. As we can see, the proposed method also performs well for sketches that have more complicated lines and details such as the first three sketches in Table 4.

Table 4. Examples of recognition results

Model				
AlexNet-sketch	chair	bed	butterfly	chair
AlexNet-contour	penguin	chair	computer	chair
Our-sketch	chair	guitar	butterfly	chair
Our-contour	bag	guitar	computer	chair

5 Conclusion

We first trained on the contours of natural images for sketch recognition to increase scalability and robustness. And we proposed a deep Convolutional Neural Network (CNN) training on contours that performs well over different databases of the sketch images. Finally, we discussed the adjustment of contours for training to increase recognition accuracy.

References

1. Yu, Q., Yang, Y., Song, Y.-Z., Xiang, T., Hospedales, T.: Sketch-a-net that beats humans. In: British Machine Vision Conference (BMVC) (2015)
2. Seddati, O., Dupont, S., Mahmoudi, S.: DeepSketch: deep convolutional neural networks for sketch recognition and similarity search. In: International Workshop on Content-Based Multimedia Indexing, pp. 1–6 (2015)
3. Krizhevsky, A., Sutskever, I., Hinton, G.E.: Imagenet classification with deep convolutional neural networks. Adv. Neural Inf. Process. Syst. **25**(2), 2012 (2012)
4. Simonyan, K., Zisserman, A.: Very deep convolutional networks for large-scale image recognition. Eprint Arxiv (2014)
5. Szegedy, C., Liu, W., Jia, Y., Sermanet, P., Reed, S., Anguelov, D., et al.: Going deeper with convolutions. In: Computer Vision and Pattern Recognition, pp. 1–9 (2015)
6. Eitz, M., Hays, J., Alexa, M.: How do humans sketch objects? ACM Trans. Graph. **31**(4), 44 (2012)
7. Schneider, R.G., Tuytelaars, T.: Sketch classification and classification-driven analysis using fisher vectors. ACM Trans. Graph. **33**(6), 174:1–174:9 (2014)
8. Cao, X., Zhang, H., Liu, S., Guo, X., Lin, L.: SYM-FISH: A Symmetry-Aware Flip Invariant Sketch Histogram Shape Descriptor. In: IEEE International Conference on Computer Vision, pp. 313–320. IEEE (2013)
9. Li, Y., Song, Y., Gong, S.: Sketch recognition by ensemble matching of structured features. In: British Machine Vision Conference (BMVC), pp. 1–11 (2013)
10. Li, Y., Hospedales, T.M., Song, Y.-Z., Gong, S.: Free-hand sketch recognition by multi-kernel feature learning. Comput. Vis. Image Underst. **31**, 1–11 (2015)
11. Hammond, T., Davis, R.: Ladder, a sketching language for user interface developers. Comput. Graph. **29**(4), 518–532 (2005)
12. Laviola, J.J., Zeleznik, R.C.: Mathpad 2: a system for the creation and exploration of mathematical sketches. ACM Trans. Graph. **23**(3), 432–440 (2004)
13. Sarvadevabhatla, R.K., Babu, R.V.: Freehand sketch recognition using deep features. Computer Science (2015)
14. Zhang, Y., Qian, X., Tan, X.: Sketch-based image retrieval using contour segments. In: IEEE International Workshop on Multimedia Signal Processing (2015)
15. Qian, X., Tan, X., Zhang, Y., Hong, R., Wang, M.: Enhancing sketch-based image retrieval by re-ranking and relevance feedback. IEEE Trans. Image Process. **25**(1), 195–208 (2015)
16. Eitz, M., Hildebrand, K., Boubekeur, T., Alexa, M.: Sketch-based image retrieval: benchmark and bag-of-features descriptors. IEEE Trans. Vis. Comput. Graph. **17**(11), 1624–1636 (2010)
17. Martin, D.R., Fowlkes, C.C., Malik, J.: Learning to detect natural image boundaries using local brightness, color, and texture cues. IEEE Trans. Pattern Anal. Mach. Intell. **26**(5), 530–549 (2004)
18. Wang, F., Kang, L., Li, Y.: Sketch-based 3D shape retrieval using convolutional neural networks. Eprint Arxiv (2015)
19. Eitz, M., Hildebrand, K., Boubekeur, T., Alexa, M.: Sketch-based 3D shape retrieval. ACM SIGGRAPH **31**, 13–15 (2010). ACM
20. Pu, J., Lou, K., Ramani, K.: A 2D sketch-based user interface for 3D cad model retrieval. Comput. Aided Des. Appl. **2**(6), 717–725 (2007)
21. Qian, X., Zhang, Y., Tan, X., Han, J.: Sketch-based image retrieval by salient contour reinforcement. IEEE Trans. Multimedia **18**(8), 1 (2016)

Fusion of Thermal and Visible Imagery for Effective Detection and Tracking of Salient Objects in Videos

Yijun Yan[1], Jinchang Ren[1(✉)], Huimin Zhao[4], Jiangbin Zheng[2], Ezrinda Mohd Zaihidee[1,3], and John Soraghan[1]

[1] Department of Electronic and Electrical Engineering, University of Strathclyde, Glasgow, UK
{yijun.yan,jinchang.ren}@strath.ac.uk
[2] School of Software and Microelectronics, Northwestern Polytechnical University, Xi'an, China
[3] Faculty of Electrical and Electronics Engineering, Universiti Malaysia Pahang, Pekan, Pahang, Malaysia
[4] School of Electronic and Information, Guangdong Polytechnic Normal University, Guangzhou, China

Abstract. In this paper, we present an efficient approach to detect and track salient objects from videos. In general, colored visible image in red-green-blue (RGB) has better distinguishability in human visual perception, yet it suffers from the effect of illumination noise and shadows. On the contrary, thermal image is less sensitive to these noise effects though its distinguishability varies according to environmental settings. To this end, fusion of these two modalities provides an effective solution to tackle this problem. First, a background model is extracted followed by background-subtraction for foreground detection in visible images. Meanwhile, adaptively thresholding is applied for foreground detection in thermal domain as human objects tend to be of higher temperature thus brighter than the background. To deal with cases of occlusion, prediction based forward tracking and backward tracking are employed to identify separate objects even the foreground detection fails. The proposed method is evaluated on OTCBVS, a publicly available color-thermal benchmark dataset. Promising results have shown that the proposed fusion based approach can successfully detect and track multiple human objects.

Keywords: Video salient objects · Pedestrian detection/tracking · Image fusion · Visible image · Thermal image

1 Introduction

In the past decades, detection and tracking of video objects has always been a major task in the computer vision field [1, 2]. As one subset of video object tracking, pedestrian detection and tracking has drawn massive research attention and been applied on many applications such as visual surveillance [3, 4], driver-assistance systems [5, 6], human activity recognition [7, 8], etc. For pedestrian detection and tracking, visible camera and thermal imagery are two popularly used sources of image modalities, though not necessarily in a combined solution [9–11]. However, either visible image or thermal image

© Springer International Publishing AG 2016
E. Chen et al. (Eds.): PCM 2016, Part II, LNCS 9917, pp. 697–704, 2016.
DOI: 10.1007/978-3-319-48896-7_69

has their advantages and disadvantages. Visible image can show detailed color information, however it really suffer from lighting variations, cluttered backgrounds, artificial appearances i.e. shadows and etc. Since the object is detected by its temperature and radiated heat, thermal image can eliminate the influence of color and illumination changes on the objects' appearance [12] in any weather conditions and at both day and night time. However, in some cases e.g. occlusions, thermal camera may fail to detect the object properly. In Fig. 1, there are three pedestrian templates, for the one with yellow rectangle; both visible and thermal image can detect it very well since it has high contrast to the background in visible and human temperature in thermal domain. For the template in red rectangle, it has a compact shape in the thermal image; however in visible image, we can just identify it coarsely due to similar appearance in color of the background and the person's cloth. The one in green rectangle can be seen in visible image but hardly observed in the corresponding thermal image. This is because thermography is only able to directly detect surface temperatures, and it can't work well when the object is (partially) occluded. Moreover, it will detect any objects (e.g. windows and car in Fig. 1) with surface temperature.

Fig. 1. Visible image of a scene (left) and thermal image of the same scene (right). (Color figure online)

In this paper, we present a pedestrian detection and tracking algorithm that fuse the information from both visible and thermal images. To detect the region of pedestrian in visible domain, we firstly apply a statistical method to model the background before applying background subtraction to extract the foreground regions. In thermal domain, we apply a histogram-based adaptive threshold method to detect all the objects with temperature. Then, the salient pedestrian regions can be obtained by the fusion of both visible and thermal binary maps. In addition, we also proposed a backward tracking method to automatically identify the individual pedestrian template from pedestrian group (detailed in Sect. 3).

The rest of the paper is organized as follows: Sect. 2 describes the foreground detection approach. Section 3 elaborates the backward tracking method. Experimental results are presented and discussed in Sect. 4. Finally, some concluding remarks and future work are summarized in Sect. 5.

2   Foreground Detection

To capture the region of pedestrians in visible image, we first estimate the background image by computing a median map (Fig. 2(a)) of N frames randomly selected from the video sequence. And background subtraction (Fig. 2(b)) for each visible frame is defined as:

$$BS_{vis}(x, y) = \left| I(x, y) - I_{med}(x, y) \right|$$

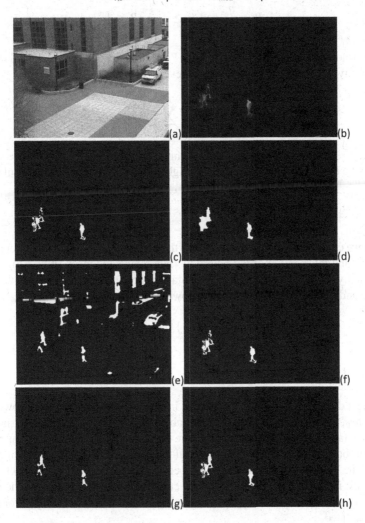

Fig. 2. (a) Median map from N frames, (b) grayscale background subtraction result, (c) binary visible image from Fig. 1, (d) filtered mask, (e) binary thermal image from Fig. 1, (f) intersection of (c) and (d), (g) intersection of (d) and (e), (h) fusion of binary visible and thermal image.

After that, we binarize the BS_{vis} with an empirical threshold (Fig. 2(c)) to get a binary image I_{vis} with coarse human body region. Then a binary mask I_{mask} with compact ROI is generated by applying morphology and filtering the insignificant region (Fig. 2(d)) on.

For thermal image, we introduce a histogram based threshold selection method inspired by [13] to segment the objects with salient temperature and get a binary image I_{thm} (Fig. 2(e)). Given a thermal map with L grey levels, the probability of each grey level is denoted by:

$$P_i = \frac{n_i}{N}, \text{ and } P_i \geq 0, \sum_{i=1}^{L} P_i = 1$$

Furthermore, the probability distribution P_i is normalized within [0, 1] and regarded as probability occurrence $\lambda(k)$ at each gray level.

$$\lambda(k) = 1 - \sum_{i=1}^{L} P_i(k)$$

Let μ, γ, σ be the mean, median and variance of the probability occurrence value in λ, and let the threshold T be defined as a weighted combination of these parameters.

$$T = \omega_\mu \mu + \omega_\gamma \gamma + \sigma$$

where $\omega_\mu, \omega_\gamma > 0$ and $\omega_\mu + \omega_\gamma = 1$.

Then we can calculate the intersection of the binary visible image and filtered mask (Fig. 2(f)), and intersection of the binary thermal image and mask (Fig. 2(g)), respectively. Finally, the salient pedestrian segmentation (Fig. 2(h)) can be done by the fusion of visible and thermal binary results as follows:

$$I_{final} = \left(I_{mask} \cap I_{vis} \right) \cup \left(I_{mask} \cap I_{thm} \right)$$

3   Object Tracking

After object detection, we can identify most individual objects very well. However, in some frames, the occlusion problem is inevitable. Figure 3 (right and middle) shows the detection detail of two adjacent frames where there should be three pedestrian patterns detected in both frames, but for the frame in the middle, the object detection method considers the left two patterns as one object because they are close to each other. Therefore, we use mean-shift method [14] to detect the individual objects from the objects group. As can be seen from the right image in Fig. 3, the identification result for second frame is updated.

Fig. 3. Initial detection result of frame 1 (left) and frame 2 (middle), and updated detection result of frame 2 after mean-shift tracking progress.

4   Experimental Results

To evaluate the performance of our method, we present our method on sequence 4, 03 OSU Color-Thermal Database from the popular benchmark database OTCBVS. Thermal sequences are captured by Raytheon PalmIR 250D thermal sensor and color sequence are captured by Sony TRV87 Handycam color sensor. All the frames in both sequences have a spatial resolution of 320 * 240 pixels.

To validate the performance of the proposed approach, three different sequences are used in our experiments. In Figs. 4, 5 and 6, detection and tracking results from these sequences are given to illustrate the extracted/tracked objects using their bounding boxes. As can be seen, the proposed method can give reliable pedestrian detection and tracking results under various conditions, including occlusion and changes in terms of illumination and scale. When the pedestrians are independent, we can detect them very well with proper scale bounding box. We can also identify the people even they are overlapped e.g. the images in first row in Fig 4. In addition, when there is some occlusion appears like tree or wall, or the object is getting out of the screen (e.g. the image in Figs. 5 and 6), we can still locate the objects and track their motion.

Fig. 4. Detection and tracking results for sequence 4.

Fig. 5. Detection and tracking results for sequence 5.

Fig. 6. Detection and tracking results for sequence 6.

5   Conclusion

In this paper, we proposed an efficient approach to fuse visible and thermal images for salient object detection and tracking in videos. By estimating the background model followed by background subtraction, foreground objects can be successfully detected with adaptive thresholding applied to the salient temperature maps of the thermal image. Prediction based forward and backward tracking is found particularly useful to separate overlapped or occluded objects. In future work, we will further improve the method and test the performance on other more challenging datasets, including those with human shadow and large scale illumination changes. Future work will be feature fusion [15, 16] for improved detection and tracking [17–19].

Acknowledgements. This work was supported by the National Natural Science Foundation of China (61272381, 61571141), Guangdong Provincial Application-oriented Technical Research and Development Special fund project (2015B010131017), Science and Technology Major Project of Education Department of Guangdong Province (2014KZDXM060), and the Natural Science Foundation of Guangdong Province (2016A030311013, 2015A030313672) and International Scientific and Technological Cooperation Projects of Education Department of Guangdong Province (2015KGJHZ021).

References

1. Li, M., Wei, C., Yuan, Y., Cai, Z.: A survey of video object tracking. Int. J. Control Autom. **8**, 303–312 (2015)
2. Yilmaz, A., Javed, O., Shah, M.: Object tracking: a survey. ACM Comput. Surv. (CSUR) **38**, 13 (2006)
3. Benfold, B., Reid, I.: Stable multi-target tracking in real-time surveillance video. In: IEEE Conference on Computer Vision and Pattern Recognition (CVPR), pp. 3457–3464 (2011)
4. Sidla, O., Lypetskyy, Y., Brandle, N., Seer, S.: Pedestrian detection and tracking for counting applications in crowded situations. In: IEEE International Conference on Video and Signal Based Surveillance, AVSS 2006, p. 70 (2006)
5. Ge, J., Luo, Y., Tei, G.: Real-time pedestrian detection and tracking at nighttime for driver-assistance systems. IEEE Trans Intell. Transp. Syst. **10**, 283–298 (2009)
6. Geronimo, D., Lopez, A.M., Sappa, A.D., Graf, T.: Survey of pedestrian detection for advanced driver assistance systems. IEEE Trans. Pattern Anal. Mach. Intell. **32**(7), 1239–1258 (2009)
7. Bodor, R., Jackson, B., Papanikolopoulos, N.: Vision-based human tracking and activity recognition. In: Proceedings of the 11th Mediterranean Conference on Control and Automation (2003)
8. Poppe, R.: A survey on vision-based human action recognition. Image Vis. Comput. **28**, 976–990 (2010)
9. Davis, J.W., Keck, M.A.: A two-stage template approach to person detection in thermal imagery. In: null, pp. 364–369 (2005)
10. Davis, J.W., Sharma, V.: Robust background-subtraction for person detection in thermal imagery. In: IEEE International Workshop on Object Tracking and Classification Beyond the Visible Spectrum (2004)
11. Davis, J.W., Sharma, V.: Robust detection of people in thermal imagery. In: Proceedings of the 17th International Conference on Pattern Recognition, ICPR 2004, pp. 713–716 (2004)
12. Kim, D.-E., Kwon, D.-S.: Pedestrian detection and tracking in thermal images using shape features. In: Ubiquitous Robots and Ambient Intelligence (URAI), pp. 22–25 (2015)
13. Ren, J., Vlachos, T.: Segmentation-assisted detection of dirt impairments in archived film sequences. IEEE Trans. Syst. Man Cybern. Part B Cybern. **37**, 463–470 (2007)
14. Comaniciu, D., Ramesh, V., Meer, P.: Real-time tracking of non-rigid objects using mean shift. In: IEEE Conference on Computer Vision and Pattern Recognition, pp. 142–149 (2000)
15. Ren, J., et al.: Fusion of intensity and inter-component chromatic difference for effective and robust colour edge detection. IET Image Proc. **4**(4), 294–301 (2010)
16. Yan, Y., et al.: Adaptive fusion of color and spatial features for noise-robust retrieval of colored logo and trademark images. Multidimension. Syst. Signal Process. **27**(4), 945–968 (2016)

17. Ren, J., et al.: Tracking the soccer ball using multiple fixed cameras. Comput. Vis. Image Underst. **113**(5), 633–642 (2009)
18. Han, J., et al.: Object detection in optical remote sensing images based on weakly supervised learning and high-level feature learning. IEEE Trans. TGRS **53**(6), 3325–3337 (2015)
19. Han, J., et al.: Background prior-based salient object detection via deep reconstruction residual. IEEE Trans. TCSVT **25**(8), 1309–1321 (2015)

RGB-D Camera based Human Limb Movement Recognition and Tracking in Supine Positions

Jun Wu[1], Cailiang Kuang[1], Kai Zeng[1], Wenjing Qiao[1], Fan Zhang[2(✉)],
Xiaobo Zhang[3], and Zhisheng Xu[4]

[1] School of Electronics and Information, Northwestern Polytechnical University,
Xi'an 710072, People's Republic of China
junwu@nwpu.edu.cn, kuangcailiang07@gmail.com, 798304055@qq.com,
qiaowenjing3190885@163.com
[2] College of Information Science and Electrical Engineering, Zhejiang University,
Hangzhou 310027, People's Republic of China
fanzhang@zju.edu.cn
[3] School of Public Health, Zhejiang University,
Hangzhou 310012, People's Republic of China
coolsurfer@zju.edu.cn
[4] Sir Run Run Shaw Hospital, Zhejiang University,
Hangzhou 310016, People's Republic of China
xu.zhisheng@outlook.com

Abstract. Human action recognition is an important topic and it has been widely applied in human-computer interaction. This work aims at human pose recognition based on RGB-D camera data streams for patients in a supine position (for example, with limb movement disorders), where bed backgrounds are misinterpreted as part of the human body. The target human limb poses include both upper and lower limbs' movements. A novel framework for human limb movement recognition in a supine position is investigated and developed. The main steps include human region locating, limb detection and segmentation, limb labeling and limb movement tracking. Based on the tracking information on human bones by the RGB-D camera, human body region detection is executed according to the depth information. Further, this system is able to solve the problem of the human limb label confusions for left and right limbs due to their occlusion cases. Our proposed tracking algorithm achieves accurate positioning of the human body, and it provides reliable mid-level data for tracking human limbs. Experiment results show that four human limbs in supine positions are able to be located successfully. It is valuable and promising in the field of medical rehabilitation.

Keywords: Human pose recognition · Supine position · Human limbs labeling · Depth tracking · RGB-D camera

This work is supported by the National Natural Science Foundation of China (No. 61103062, 61472357, 61571063), the NPU Foundation for Fundamental Research (No. JC201249), Scientific Research Foundation for Returned Scholars, Ministry of Education of China (2013), and the Fundamental Research Funds for the Central Universities under the grant 2015QNA5005.

© Springer International Publishing AG 2016
E. Chen et al. (Eds.): PCM 2016, Part II, LNCS 9917, pp. 705–714, 2016.
DOI: 10.1007/978-3-319-48896-7_70

1   Introduction

Automatic recognition and tracking of the 3D human body poses and gestures has become an interesting and emerging topics in the field of computer vision. In medical applications, human motion detection and tracking allow doctors and family members to monitor and predict the behaviors of the elderly people, such as falling down accidently, or to monitor the continuous states of the patients for further analysis of disease diagnosis.

In a traditional system of patient motion capturing, a number of special cameras in a studio needs to be setup beforehand, and one or more tags need to wear on the human body. In recent years, the human pose estimation based on no-tagging image sequence has been widely concerned because of its convenience. Especially after the RGB-D cameras come into being, it has been widely used in extensive applications, such as human posture recognition, medical rehabilitation, entertainment domain, and so on. In the field of medical rehabilitation, current somatosensory technology by the Kinect is mainly used for patients with active exercise training and rehabilitation treatment, especially suitable for community and family rehabilitation. The rehabilitation training system developed based on the Kinect is able to replace lots of traditional complicated equipments.

Yao et al. [1] propose a hand gesture recognition method, which is integrated into a vision-based hand gesture recognition framework for developing desktop applications. A hand contour model is proposed to simplify the gesture matching process, which can reduce the computational complexity of gesture matching. Shi et al. [2] present a real-time vision-based bimanual 3D gesture interaction technique that is capable of tracking both bare-hands, that is without markers nor gloves. By only recovering features calculated from images, the depth channel is not utilized. Kyriazis et al. [3] present an algorithm to recover and track the 3D position, orientation and full articulation of a human hand from markerless visual observations obtained by a Kinect sensor. Wu et al. [5] propose a 3D finger detection and tracking algorithm based on a sliding window for RGB-D sequences. It tracks the up and down movements of the fingertips in order to apply in some real-world applications.

In order to guide exercise rehabilitation of the youth movement disorder treatment, Chang et al. [6] develops a Kinect-based Kinerehab system, which automatically detect motion information of patients with movement disorder. This system matches joint point positions of a patient captured from the Kinect sensors with the existing database for movement pattern, then calculates the accuracy of the motions to its suitable expected positions. Combined with virtual reality and video game technologies, Belinda [7] applies 3D scene models based on the Unity3D engine into development platform, and develops a training game which is suitable for balance rehabilitation of patients in spinal cord injury and traumatic brain injury. Alana et al. [8] designs a Kinect-based rehabilitation training system for shoulders and elbows.

In the medical rehabilitation, to carry out rehabilitation training with the help of the Kinect, for the case that patients stand in the center of a room the Kinect has good capacity to track most of the bone structure information.

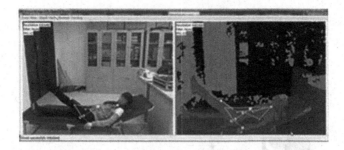

Fig. 1. An real-world example of the tracking results of human bone information by the Kinect in a supine position.

However, due to physical reasons, some patients are only able to lie on the bed to carry out certain rehabilitation training, which is very common to those seniors suffered from stroke and hemiplegia. In this case, patients are lying on a flat bed to keep a supine position. In clinical medicine, the supine positions are the most common state.

When patients lie on a soft bed, the Kinect is basically able to catch the main body parts, but there are interferences for depth information due to the depth of the bed is similar to that of the human body. Especially when parts of human body is possible to be embedded into a soft bed, their depth values are almost the same values, and the bed is might recognized as parts of human body. This results in failure cases to track the bone information of human limbs.

As shown in Fig. 1, it can be seen that, the skeleton points tracked are gathered in the middle of the human body, and the skeleton points for human limbs are not successful. It is a typical issue of human pose recognition and tracking for patients in a supine position in the field of medical rehabilitation. This paper mainly deal with this issue and investigate a human limb pose tracking algorithm in a supine position based on a RGB-D camera, such as the Kinect.

2   Human Limb Movement Recognition Algorithm in a Supine Position

The main steps of our proposed Human Limb Movement Recognition Algorithm in the supine positions includes: human region detection, human limb detection and locating, human limb labeling, and human limb movement tracking based on integration of RGB and depth information. The flowchart of the proposed system is illustrated in Fig. 2.

2.1   Human Body Detection

After the alignment of the RGB and depth data, the human body as a foreground can be segmented from the background based on the temporal differences with

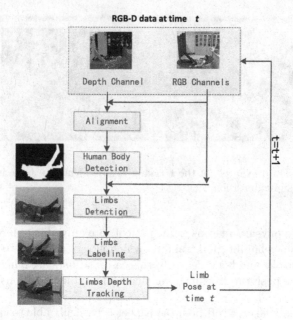

Fig. 2. The flowchart of the proposed system.

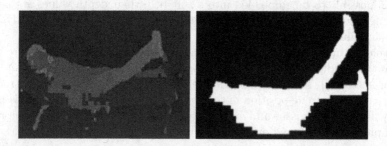

Fig. 3. Left: an example of human boy region segmentation with certain interferes and defects. Right: an example of refined results of human boy region.

the combination of RGB and depth information, as shown in Fig. 3 (left). Unfortunately, there are many interferes (scatted tiny regions) and defects (small holes within the contour) in the results of the human body segmentation. And these results will affect the following steps as human limb detection and tracking.

To get the relatively refined human body region, we apply multi-level mathematical morphological operations to eliminate defects, and utilize the connectivity property to remove interferes. The theory of mathematical morphology is based on set theory. There are four basic operations: corrosion, expansion, open operation and close operation. Open and close operations can be deduced by corrosion and expansion operations. The essence of the corrosion operation is to make the image shrink. The expansion operation is the dual form of the corrosion operation, and its essence is make image pixels be expanded. Furthermore, the open operation is defined as corrosion operation followed by expansion operation on an image. The open operation is able to eliminate the interference of isolated points, and can smooth the contour's boundary. The close operation is defined as expansion operation followed by corrosion operation on an image. The close operation is able to heal the fracture of the target region, fill small holes inside, and leads to a smooth boundary. After both the open and close operations are applied to the target image plan, the connected component of human body is formed, as in Fig. 3 (right).

2.2 Human Limb Detection

For medical rehabilitation in supine positions, when a patient is lying on the soft bed, due to similar depth information of a bed and human body from a RGB-D camera, the bed is likely to be identified as part of human body. This results in false judgment of human skeletal location information due to unavoidable interferences. Figure 1 give an example of human skeleton structure in a supine position by the Kinect. We can see that the key points of the human skeleton are gathered in the middle of human body, where the human limb detection fails. In this case, when a patient is lying on the bed, the detection and tracking of skeletal information will lead to missed information, tracking errors, or even totally failure sometimes. Based on our evaluation, the standard Kinect SDK is not able to determine the correct key points of human skeleton. To simplify this problem, considering the real requirements of rehabilitation training in the supine position, in our system we mainly detect and track the movements of human limbs, including left and right hand, left and right foot.

(1) The Left and Right Hand Detection: The human left and right hand detection is employed mainly using elliptical color models for skin detection. After the candidate hand regions are obtained, there are possibly pseudo hand areas. The hand region refinement is executed to remove these pseudo regions. Further, the center of inscribed circle of the refined hand region, to obtain the central location of a human hand. At this time, two hands are located in two separate regions, and at the same time, human head is also detected.

(2) The Left and Right Leg Detection: The human left and right leg detection is executed using the Hilditch algorithm [9] by thinning the corresponding human body region. According to the structure of human body, the human body's feet are located at the far end of the human body. Therefore, the skeleton of the human body is obtained by thinning algorithm. And then the two farthest ends of the human skeleton (to the human head) is detected, which is judged as human left and right legs. In general, image thinning algorithm is mainly used for binary images. And the image thinning process is actually the process of seeking the skeleton of an image. The key region of skeleton can be

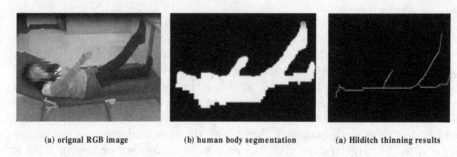

(a) orignal RGB image   (b) human body segmentation   (a) Hilditch thinning results

Fig. 4. Results of an example using Hilditch thinning algorithm.

Fig. 5. Left: an example of human limb detection. Right: an example of the actual labels of the human body skeleton.

understood as the middle axis of the image. The Hilditch algorithm is a classical skeleton extraction algorithm. The binary image using the Hilditch algorithm has two values (0/1), the Hilditch algorithm only thinning 1-value pixels, 0-value pixels are considered as the background area. The results of the Hilditch algorithm is shown in Fig. 4.

Finally, we can locate the human limbs, as in Fig. 5, which gives a result of human limb detection (left/right hand, left/right leg).

2.3   Human Limb Labeling

According to the structure characteristics of the human body skeleton, we are able to label the human limbs and the head. In the previous section, the human body limbs and the head has been detected, respectively. Compared with the human body's center, if its deviation angle to the body center is the smallest, and it is the closest point, the part of human body will be identified as the head. For the detection of human hands, in the left side of the body center, it is defined as the left hand; in the right hand side of the body center, it is defined as the right hand. For the detection of the human foot, in the left side of the body center, it is defined as the left foot; in the right side of the body center, it is defined as the right foot. Figure 5 illustrates the actual labels of the human body skeleton, where, the annotation labels of human limbs include four cases:

head (HEAD), left hand (HAND LEFT), right hand (HAND RIGHT), left foot (FOOT LEFT), right foot (FOOT RIGHT).

2.4   Human Limb Movement Tracking

In this paper, human hand detection and foot detection are processed individually. Hand detection mainly utilizes the elliptical models of skin region [4] based on the color information of RGB-D cameras. Then the hand depth tracking is executed after mapping hands in color image space to the depth image space. As mentioned above, foot detection is obtained by refining the human body contour using thinning algorithm. And foot movement tracking is processed using the depth information of the foot ends. To achieve stable results of the hand and foot tracking, when calculating the depth of the human limb ends in a image frame, we use neighborhood pixels to compute the depth information of the hand end and the foot end, as well as the head. While, to remove noises of depth in the time domain, a sliding window strategy is applied to smooth the depth values of the human limb end and the head.

$$D(i,t) = \begin{cases} D(i,t), |D(i,t) - \tilde{D}(i,t)| < \varepsilon \\ \tilde{D}(i,t), \text{otherwise}. \end{cases} \tag{1}$$

where, $D(i,t)$ is the depth values within a convex hull in a center point of hand or foot ends, and i belong to a label set for left/right hand/foot, ε is a predefined threshold.

$$\tilde{D}(i,t) = \alpha_1 D(i,t-1) + \alpha_2 D(i,t-2), s.t.\alpha_1 + \alpha_2 = 1. \tag{2}$$

When the left foot and the right foot have a case with occlusion, especially they are in one straight line in certain direction, it is very likely to assign wrong LEFT/RIGHT labels for both foots due to the occlusion issue. We name this case as wrongly-exchanging labels. To solve this problem, we utilize and combine the depth information and the continuous movement to avoid these wrongly-exchanging labels. As the patients do certain exercises on the bed, the speed is relatively slow enough, the RGB-D camera is able to capture the trajectory of the limbs movements.

2.5   Human Pose Recognition in a Supine Position

Based on the labels of the human limbs, the movement patterns of the limbs ends, and the corresponding smoothed depth information, the types of human poses can be recognized. The patterns of human limb movements include: the left hand up (LHandUP), the left hand down (LHandDown), the right hand up (RHandUp), the right hand down (RHandDown), the left foot up (LFootUp), the left foot down (LFootDown), the right foot up (RFootUp), the right foot down (RFootDown). The depth information of recent five continuous frames are collected to judge the body pose types. In order to reduce the influences of fluctuation of depth information in time domain, if the pattern of four frames as a time sequence meet the case of up movement or down movement, we are able to give a judgement using the majority rule.

3   Experiment Results

In this section, we first introduce the basic setup of our experiments, and give the results for human limb labeling, human limb depth tracking, human limb movements recognition, respectively. Finally, we give out a short summary.

3.1   Experiment Setup

The Kinect for Xbox 360 is used as the RGB-D camera to obtain the image sequences. The initial angle of the Kinect camera is set to $-12°$. The vertical height from the camera to the bed surface is about 112 cm, and the horizontal distance from the camera to the bed is about 143 cm. The bed height is approximately 40 cm. In order to verify our proposed algorithm, 15 volunteers with different heights and ages in supine positions on the bed are captured using Kinect camera respectively. To evaluate the influences with different positions for the camera, we set several different modes including from the left side or the right side of the human body, close to the head, or close to the foot, or close to the middle part of the body. From Case 1 to case 6, the positions of the RGB-D camera are set up as: (1) in the right side of the human body, right over the middle of body (Case 1), close to the head (Case 2), close to the foot (Case 3); (2) in the left side of the human body, right over the middle of body (Case 4), close to the head (Case 5), close to the foot (Case 6).

3.2   Results of Human Limb Depth Tracking

Here, we mainly evaluate the accuracy of the depth values for the human limb ends. The upward and downward movements of human limbs are both considered. At the same time, the RGB-D camera is placed on the six different locations. The accuracy of the human limb ends' depth value tracking is listed in Table 1, where each pair of accuracies in the table cell represents the cases of the upward and downward movements of the human body's limbs, respectively. Based on our observations on the target data set, the parameters in Eqs. (1) and (2) are set as: $\varepsilon = 0.54$, $\alpha_1 = 0.5$, $\alpha_2 = 0.5$.

From the Table 1, we can see that the accuracy of the left limb depth tracking and the accuracy of the right limb depth tracking is symmetrical. Similarly, it can be concluded that, in a certain range, farer from the RGB-D camera, the higher the accuracy of the human limbs depth tracking. In addition, the accuracy of the depth tracking is more sensitive to the locations of the RGB-D camera.

Table 1. Accuracy of human limbs depth tracking for upward/downward movements.

Camera mode	Left hand	Right hand	Left foot	Right foot
Case 1	92.2/92.6	91.4/91.3	87.8/87.5	86.9/87.0
Case 2	91.2/91.5	91.2/91.3	90.7/90.5	89.1/89.2
Case 3	93.3/93.5	93.1/93.2	85.4/85.7	84.3/84.6
Case 4	92.5/92.3	92.6/92.4	86.5/87.2	87.7/87.4
Case 5	91.4/91.7	91.2/91.6	89.3/89.1	90.4/90.3
Case 6	93.1/93.5	93.1/93.3	84.8/84.2	85.4/85.6

3.3   Results of Human Limb Movements Type Recognition

Here, we evaluate the accuracy of the movements type recognition for the human limbs. The upward and downward movements of human limbs are both considered. At the same time, the RGB-D camera is placed on the six different locations. The accuracy of the human limb movement type recognition is listed in Table 2, where each pair of accuracies in the table cell represents the cases of the upward and downward movements of the human body's limbs, respectively.

When the RGB-D camera is placed in the right side of the human body (Case 1), the distances from the bed surface are set to different values as: 143 cm, 160 cm, 180 cm, 200 cm, respectively. We track the individual up and down movement of the human body. The accuracy of human posture recognition is illustrated in Table 3. Each pair of values in the table cell represents the accuracy of the upper and downward movement of the human limbs, respectively. We can conclude from Table 3 that the accuracy of the human limb movements type recognition is better for shorter distance, and worse for longer distance.

Table 2. Accuracy of the human limbs movements type recognition for upward and downward movements, for six cases.

Camera mode	Left hand	Right hand	Left foot	Right foot
Case 1	87.2/87.6	87.4/87.3	82.2/82.3	82.1/81.9
Case 2	86.9/87.2	86.5/87.1	83.6/83.4	83.4/83.0
Case 3	88.9/88.1	88.1/88.4	80.6/80.3	80.5/80.7
Case 4	87.3/87.2	87.1/87.5	82.4/82.8	82.1/82.4
Case 5	86.4/86.7	86.2/87.6	83.6/83.1	84.0/83.3
Case 6	88.1/88.4	88.3/88.3	80.8/80.5	80.4/80.6

Table 3. Accuracy of the human limbs movements type recognition for different distance from the bed surface to the camera, for case 1 only.

Distance	Left hand	Right hand	Left foot	Right foot
143 cm	87.2/87.6	87.4/87.3	82.2/82.3	82.1/81.9
160 cm	86.1/86.3	86.2/86.7	81.4/80.6	81.4/80.3
180 cm	85.2/85.4	85.4/85.9	79.8/79.3	79.1/79.0
200 cm	83.2/83.6	83.4/83.3	76.2/76.8	75.1/75.9

4   Conclusions

This work proposes a method to execute human pose recognition for patients in supine positions based on the RGB-D camera. First, human body region are located, and human limbs are detected and segmented according to the depth information. Then human limbs are labeled as left hand, right hand, left foot, and right foot. Next, the human limb movement including up and down movements for four limbs are tracked and recognized. Our proposed tracking algorithm achieves accurate the human body region and provides reliable mid-level data for tracking the movement patterns of four human limbs. Experiment results show that the correct location of human limbs in supine positions is able to be achieved successfully. The accuracy of the human limb tracking system is more than 85%, and the accuracy of the human body supine posture recognition is more than 82%. Future works will go on improving the accuracy of the human limb tracking, and establish a more elaborate model of human limb structure with elbow and knee joint points to obtain more accurate tracking results.

References

1. Yao, Y., et al.: Real-time hand gesture recognition using RGB-D sensor. In: CVPR (2014)
2. Shi, J., et al.: A real-time bimanual 3D interaction method based on bare-hand tracking. In: ACM Multimedia (2011)
3. Kyriazis, N., et al.: Efficient model-based 3D tracking of hand articulations using kinect. In: BMVC (2011)
4. Tang, H., et al.: Hand's skin detection based on ellipse clustering. In: ISCSCT (2008)
5. Jun, W., et al.: A 3D fingertips detecting and tracking algorithm based on the sliding window. In: ACM Multimedia (2014)
6. Chang, Y.J., et al.: A Kinect-based system for physical rehabilitation: a pilot study for young adults with motor disabilities. Res. Dev. Disabil. **32**(6), 2566–2570 (2011)
7. Lange, B., et al.: Development and evaluation of low cost game-based balance rehabilitation tool using the Microsoft kinect sensor. In: EMBC (2011)
8. Da Gama, A., et al.: Improving motor rehabilitation process through a natural interaction based system using kinect sensor. In: 3DUIC (2012)
9. Naccache, N.J., et al.: An investigation into the skeletonization approach of Hilditch. Pattern Recognit. **17**(3), 279–284 (1984)

Scene Parsing with Deep Features and Spatial Structure Learning

Hui Yu[1], Yuecheng Song[2], Wenyu Ju[1], and Zhenbao Liu[2(✉)]

[1] Shanghai Aircraft Design and Research Institute, Shanghai 200232, China
yuhui@comac.cc
[2] Northwestern Polytechnical University, Xi'an 710072, China
liuzhenbao@nwpu.edu.cn

Abstract. Conditional Random Field (CRF) is a powerful tool for label-ing tasks, and has always played a key role in object recognition and semantic segmentation. However, the quality of CRF labeling depends on selected features, which becomes the bottleneck of the accuracy improve-ment. In this paper, our semantic segmentation problem is calculated in the same way within the framework of Conditional Random Field. Dif-ferent from other CRF-based strategies, which use appearance features of image, revealing only little information, we combined our framework together with deep learning strategy, such as Convolutional Neural Net-works (CNNs), for feature extraction, which have shown strong ability and remarkable performance. This combination strategy is called deep-feature CRF (dCRF). Through dCRF, the deep informantion of image is illustrated and gets ultilized, and the segmentation accuracy is also increased. The proposed deep CRF strategy is adopted on SIFT-Flow and VOC2007 datasets. The segmentation results reveals that if we use features learned from deep networks into our CRF framework, the per-formance of our semantic segmentation strategy would increase signifi-cantly.

Keywords: Convolutional Neural Networks (CNNs) · Conditional Ran-dom Fields (CRFs) · Scene parsing · Deep learning · deep feature CRF

1 Introduction

For most aircraft safety problems, scene parsing has always been a critical prob-lem and become challenging in recent years. Given an image as input, what we need is to segment and recognize every object out. Obviously, as we all know, the goal of semantic segmentation [1–3] is identifying every pixel from the image with a high accuracy, which is also the core technology.

In recent studies, a variety of strategies based on the framework of Markov Random Fields or Conditional Random Fields [4,5] have been investigated and well learned. The difference between these methods is features, classifiers, and the graphic models it constructed. Besides, a majority of segmentation meth-ods are introduced by superpixels generated from over-segmentation algorithms

© Springer International Publishing AG 2016
E. Chen et al. (Eds.): PCM 2016, Part II, LNCS 9917, pp. 715–722, 2016.
DOI: 10.1007/978-3-319-48896-7_71

[6–8] on specific images. However, the disadvantage of these methods is feature selection. The features these method selected are often hand-crafted, like HOG [9], SURF [10], and so on, which would be useful in some datasets. However, these features are often low-level, and reveals only a little information, which would make results inconsistent.

To overcome the shortages, deep learning strategies have been introduced for feature extraction. Over past few years, these methods have gained great popularity in machine learning and related fields. This type of methods typically take the original image as input, learning the deep representation, and have found notable success in various tasks such as image classification, object recognition, etc. The success of deep learning methods basicly due to the ability to learn rich-level features within class variance.

In this paper, to increase the accuracy of semantic segmentation, we take the both advantages of deep learning strategies and CRFs, proposing a strategy based on the framework of Conditional Random Fields with extracted deep learning features, called deep-feature CRF (dCRF). Unlike [7] and [8], we learn our features from Convolutional Neural Network (CNN) and constructed a graph model based on Conditional Random Fields. We perform our scene parsing on a SIFT-Flow dataset, containing 2,688 outdoor photographs.

The paper is organized as follows: Sect. 2 briefly describes the details of the Conditional Random Fields algorithm and the features we select. Section 3 presents and discusses the experiments results of proposed dCRF segmentation scheme. Finally, we present our concluding remarks in Sect. 4.

2   Scene Parsing Method

In this section, we formulate our scene parsing based on Conditional Random Fields with deep learning features. The process of proposed dCRF starts with feature extraction of Convolutional Neural Networks and superpixel segmentation. For each superpixel, all deep features are computed in average. In CRF training stage, the data terms are calculated from the distribution classified with deep learning features, whereas the pairwise are determined with the difference of nearby superpixels. We construct our graph model in the framework of Conditional Random Fields.

Unlike [11], which uses an Structured SVM for image classification and constructs a spatial structure for graph model, the process of Conditional Random Fields is applied on a individual architecture through Convex Optimization [12].

The flowchart of purposed dCRF is shown in Fig. 1, whereas the details are illustrated as follows.

2.1   Conditional Random Fields

Given an image, we cut it into superpixels with the method of Simple Linear Iterative Clustering (SLIC) [13] algorithm, and create a graph model $G = (V, E)$, in which vertices are defined as $v \in V$ and edges $e \in E \in \mathbb{R}^{V \times V}$. In this

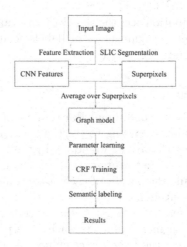

Fig. 1. The flowchart of purposed method.

definition, each superpixel is considered as a vertex node, whereas the edge the connections between each neighbouring node pairs. The expression e_{ij} refers to the edge consisting vertex v_i and v_j, whereas the observation of nodes are denoted as data $\mathbf{x}$, and states $\mathbf{y} = \langle \mathbf{y}_1, \mathbf{y}_2, ... \mathbf{y}_n \rangle$. The conditional distribution of each graph model can be factorized into potentials on nodes $\phi_N(\mathbf{x}_i, \mathbf{y}_i)$ (unary) and edges $\psi_E(\mathbf{x}_{ije}, \mathbf{y}_i, \mathbf{y}_j)$ (pairwise). Consider the potentials with a weight $\mathbf{w}$ for training in a graph model, which is transformed into problem of pairwise CRF, apparently. With the definition of potentials and parameters, the conditional distribution of each graph model can be rewritten as:

$$p(\mathbf{y}|\mathbf{x}, \mathbf{w}) = \frac{1}{Z(\mathbf{x}, \mathbf{w})} \prod_{i \in V} \phi_N(\mathbf{x}_i, \mathbf{y}_i) \prod_{e_{ij} \in E} \psi_E(\mathbf{x}_{ije}, \mathbf{y}_i, \mathbf{y}_j), \tag{1}$$

in which $Z(\mathbf{x}, \mathbf{w})$ is defined as a partition function with unary or pairwise potentials on the constructed graph model.

Through the definition, the potentials can be described as the log-linear combination of feature functions, $\mathbf{f}_N$ and $\mathbf{f}_E$. With a set of example training images $D = \{(\mathbf{x}^n, \mathbf{y}^n)\}, n = 1, 2 ... M$ as a sample of graphical model, Regulized Maximum Conditional Likelihood defined in [12] is applied and the training process can be transformed into an optimization of conditional log-likelihood written as:

$$\mathbf{w}^* = \arg\min_{\mathbf{w}} \lambda \|\mathbf{w}\|^2 - \sum_{n=1}^{M} (\sum_{i \in V} \mathbf{w}_N^T \mathbf{f}_N(\mathbf{x}_i^n, \mathbf{y}_i^n) + \sum_{e_{ij} \in E} \mathbf{w}_E^T \mathbf{f}_E(\mathbf{x}_{ije}^n, \mathbf{y}_i^n, \mathbf{y}_j^n)) + \sum_{n=1}^{M} \log Z(\mathbf{x}^n, \mathbf{w})$$
$$\tag{2}$$

In Eq. 2, $\mathbf{w} = [\mathbf{w}_N, \mathbf{w}_E]$ is the weight representing the importance of unary and pairwise terms, whereas λ is a non-negative L2-regulizer in parameter learning.

The conditional distribution over the class variable can be obtained by solving Eq. 2, and the most likely assignment of all labels $\mathbf{y}$ at the same time when $p(\mathbf{y}|\mathbf{x}, \mathbf{w}^*)$ reaches maximum.

2.2 Feature Selection

For each problem based on Conditional Random Fields, the most important process is feature selection. According to [1], the more information the feature takes, the higher accuracy the results would be. In this paper, we select Convolutional Neural Network as the feature extractor. The deep network is trained with multiple stages, while the output of each stage is always the input of next stage. These inputs and outputs, on the basis of [1], are called feature maps.

By the same time of feature extraction, the image is also cut into superpixels by the way of SLIC segmentation. For each superpixel, the average of all hierarchical features among the region is calculated as the deep feature of the superpixel, which is different from the method introduced in [1]. The feature selection of proposed dCRF are illustrated as follows.

Unary terms. With the graph model of CRF constructed, the feature function $\mathbf{f}_N$ and $\mathbf{f}_E$ in Eq. 2 need to be computed. The form of unary features is defined as:

$$\mathbf{f}_N(\mathbf{x}, \mathbf{y}_k) = \log \mathbf{P}_k(\mathbf{y}_{k,a}) \tag{3}$$

where $\mathbf{P}_k(\mathbf{y}_{k,a})$ is the distribution of superpixel $\mathbf{x}$. The distribution $\mathbf{P}_k(\mathbf{y}_{k,a})$ is computed from a softmax classifier proposed by [1].

Pairwise terms. Similar to definition in [7], the pairwise feature $\mathbf{f}_E(\mathbf{x}_{ije}, \mathbf{y}_i, \mathbf{y}_j)$ of our graphical model calculated for every edge is defined as:

$$\mathbf{f}_E(\mathbf{x}_{ije}, \mathbf{y}_i, \mathbf{y}_j) = \begin{cases} 1 - \exp(-\gamma_K ||\mathbf{c}_i - \mathbf{c}_j||_2^2) & : & l_i = l_j \\ \exp(-\gamma_K ||\mathbf{c}_i - \mathbf{c}_j||_2^2) & : & l_i \neq l_j, \end{cases} \tag{4}$$

where $\mathbf{c}_i$ and $\mathbf{c}_j$ are the mean color of superpixel i and j in LAB color space and l is the class label.

There is difference between our method and the method in [11], in which the inference of graph model is computed in a spatial structure, and a Structured SVM classifier is applied in model training. However, in this paper, a Pseudo-Likelihood CRF training is used for parameter learning instead. With all features computed and the graph structure constructed, a max-product loopy belief-propagation inference [12] is computed to optimize the Eq. 2 with the strategy of Limited-Memory BFGS.

3 Experiments and Results

In this paper, in order to test the performance of proposed dCRF, we take our method on SIFT-Flow and VOC2007 datasets. From the experiments, it can be clearly found that compared to other methods, the proposed dCRF can have a better performance.

3.1 SIFT-Flow

First, we use the SIFT-Flow dataset [18], which contains 2,688 labeled frames. The author of the dataset also provides a training and testing splits and a mapping from 59 categories and 34 classes: 33 labeled objects and one void. We take 2,488 training frames for CRF parameter learning and 200 for testing, and make a comparison to other state-of-art semantic segmentation strategies.

Some experimental results are revealed in Fig. 2, whereas the per-pixel and per-class accuracy of proposed dCRF are illustrated in Table 1, with comparison of other semantic segmentation strategies. From Table 1, it can be obviously found that the higher result accuracy can be reached if our graphical model is trained in the method of Conditional Random Fields with deep learning features from networks.

Table 1. Comparison of parsing performance about per-pixel and per-class accuracy with different strategy on SIFT-Flow dataset

Method	Per-pixel accuracy	Per-class accuracy
Our methods (dCRF)	83.5%	36.8%
Pinheiro et al. (2013) [14]	77.7%	29.8%
Farabet et al. (2013) [1]	78.5%	29.6%
Singh et al. (2013) [15]	79.2%	33.8%
Eigen et al. (2012) [16]	77.1%	32.5%
Tighe et al. (2010) [17]	76.9%	29.4%

Some results are illustrated in Fig. 2. From Fig. 2, these issues should be paid special attention: First, the proposed dCRF, like many other superpixel based on Conditional Random Fields, the rough area of objects with clear boundaries could be found, except for those with smaller-than-superpixel-size ones. Actually, the dataset contains 34 categories, making semantic labeling into a problem full of challenge. However, smaller objects like poles is too hard to search out. The results due to: Conditional Random Fields is a powerful tool in object recognition, the more information the feature brings, the higher the segmentation accuracy would be. While Convolutional Neural Networks has great ability of feature selection, of which the advantages the CRF takes. However, because of small objects is often cut into superpixels through semantic segmentation, the information of small objects is lost, which would cause recognition errors.

3.2 VOC2007

Our experiment is also taken on the VOC2007 dataset [19]. This dataset contains 9,963 images, in which there are 5,011 images for training and 4,952 images for testing. The dataset contains 20 labeled objects and one background.

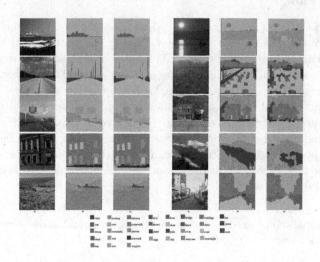

Fig. 2. Segmentation results on SIFT-Flow dataset, from left to right are image, ground truth, and our results.

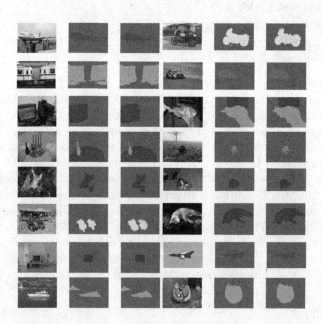

Fig. 3. The segmentation results on VOC2007 dataset, from left to right are image, ground truth, and our results.

Table 2. Comparison of parsing performance of average per-class accuracy with different strategy on VOC2007 dataset

Method	Average per-class accuracy
Our methods (dCRF)	60.8%
Girshick et al. (2014) [20]	54.1%
Zhu et al. (2014) [21]	55.3%

The experiments of the dataset is similar to SIFT-Flow. The results of VOC2007 dataset is illustrated in Fig. 3, and the per-class accuracy is shown in Table 2, which is also compared to other similar strategies. From the experiments of the VOC datasets, it can be clearly found that with the deep features considered into our framework, the accuracy may have a significantly increase duo to the ability of expression the features of deep learning networks, and the stability of Conditional Random Fields.

4 Conclusion

In this work, we have shown the basic corresponding performance on effective Conditional Random Fields with deep features generated from neural networks, which is able to achieve better accuracy of semantic labeling compared to other state-of-art strategies within the same framework.

References

1. Farabet, C., Couprie, C., Najman, L., LeCun, Y.: Learning hierarchical features for scene labeling. IEEE Trans. Pattern Anal. Mach. Intell. **35**(8), 1915–1929 (2013)
2. Philipp, K., Vladlen, K.: Efficient inference in fully connected CRFs with Gaussian edge potentials. In: Advances in Neural Information Processing Systems, pp. 109–117 (2011)
3. Jamie, S., John, W., Carsten, R., Antonio, C.: Textonboost for image understanding: multi-class object recognition and segmentation by jointly modeling texture, layout, and context. Comput. Vision **81**(1), 1–23 (2009)
4. Li, S.Z., Singh, S.: Markov Random Field Modeling in Image Analysis, vol. 26. Springer, London (2009)
5. Lafferty, J., McCallum, A., Pereira, F.C.: Conditional random fields: probabilistic models for segmenting and labeling sequence data. In: Eighteenth International Conference on Machine Learning (ICML), pp. 282–289 (2001)
6. Kae, A., Sohn, K., Lee, H., Learned-Miller, E.: Augmenting CRFs with boltzmann machine shape priors for image labeling. In: 2013 IEEE Conference on Computer Vision and Pattern Recognition (CVPR), pp. 2019–2026. IEEE (2013)
7. Cesar, C., Jana, K.: Semantic parsing for priming object detection in RGB-D scenes. In: Semantic Perception, Mapping and Exploration (SPME) (2013)
8. Cesar, C., Jana, K.: Semantic segmentation with heterogeneous sensor coverages. In: IEEE Robotics and Automation Society (IRAS) (2014)

 9. Dalal, N., Triggs, B.: Histograms of oriented gradients for human detection. In: IEEE Computer Society Conference on Computer Vision and Pattern Recognition, CVPR 2005, vol. 1. IEEE, pp. 886–893 (2005)
10. Bay, H., Ess, A., Tuytelaars, T., Van Gool, L.: Speeded-up robust features (surf). Comput. Vis. Image Underst. **110**(3), 346–359 (2008)
11. Liu, F., Lin, G., Shen, C.: CRF learning with CNN features for image segmentation. Pattern Recognit. **48**, 2983–2992 (2015)
12. Sebastian, N., Christoph, H.L.: Structured learning and prediction in computer vision, the essence of knowledge (2011)
13. Radhakrishna, A., Appu, S., Kevin, S., Aurelien, L., Pascal, F., Sabine, S.: Slic superpixels compared to state-of-the-art superpixel methods. IEEE Trans. Pattern Anal. Mach. Intell. **34**(11), 2274–2282 (2012)
14. Pinheiro, P.H.O., Collobert, R.: Recurrent convolutional neural networks for scene labeling. In: International Conference on Machine Learning (ICML) (2014)
15. Singh, G., Kosecka, J.: Nonparametric scene parsing with adaptive feature relevance and semantic context. In: 2013 IEEE Conference on Computer Vision and Pattern Recognition (CVPR), pp. 3151–3157. IEEE (2013)
16. Eigen, D., Fergus, R.: Nonparametric image parsing using adaptive neighbor sets. In: 2012 IEEE Conference on Computer Vision and Pattern Recognition (CVPR), pp. 2799–2806. IEEE (2012)
17. Tighe, J., Lazebnik, S.: SuperParsing: scalable nonparametric image parsing with superpixels. In: Daniilidis, K., Maragos, P., Paragios, N. (eds.) ECCV 2010. LNCS, vol. 6315, pp. 352–365. Springer, Heidelberg (2010). doi:10.1007/978-3-642-15555-0_26
18. Liu, C., Yuen, J., Torralba, A.: Nonparametric scene parsing via label transfer. IEEE Trans. Pattern Anal. Mach. Intell. **33**(12), 2368–2382 (2011)
19. Everingham, M., VanGool, L., Williams, C., Winn, J., Zisserman, A.: The PASCAL Visual Object Classes Challenge 2007 (VOC2007) Results. http://www.pascal-network.org/challenges/VOC/voc2007/workshop/index.html
20. Girshick, R., Donahue, J., Darrell, T., Malik, J.: Rich feature hierarchies for accurate object detection and semantic segmentation. In: IEEE Conference on Computer Vision and Pattern Recognition (CVPR 2014), pp. 580–587. IEEE (2014)
21. Zhu, J., Mao, J., Yuille, A.: Learning from weakly supervised data by the expectation loss SVM (e-SVM) algorithm. In: Advances in Neural Information Processing Systems (NIPS), pp. 1125–1133 (2014)

Semi-supervised Learning for Human Pose Recognition with RGB-D Light-Model

Xinbo Wang[1,2], Guoshan Zhang[1], Dahai Yu[2(✉)], and Dan Liu[2,3]

[1] Tianjin University, Tianjin 300072, China
[2] Tianjin Optical Electrical Gaosi Communication
Engineering Technology Co., Ltd., Tianjin 300384, China
yudahai@toec-gdgs.com
[3] Xi'an University of Architecture and Technology, Xi'an 710043, China

Abstract. This work targets human pose recognition based on RGB-D videos. In recently, RGB-D based methods can be typically represented as either maps-based approaches or skeleton-based approaches. This paper proposes a semi-supervised learning method for evaluating human posture via RGB-D and light-model. The light-model is generated to represent depth sequence, by using the dynamic-fusion strategy. In this regard, light-model has richer information than depth image, and a CNN classifier is further constructed to recognize human pose with trained labeled light model data. Soft correlation and hard correlation are used to adjust the CNN output of non-labeled data. This paper constructs a set of posture data which consist of RGB images and light model. The experiments results show that our method is more accuracy than the state of the art, and the efficient is also competitive. This study implies that feature extracted from 3D models is reliable for human pose recognition, especially for sitting posture.

Keywords: Semi-supervised learning · RGB-D · Light model · Convolutional neural networks · Pose recognition

1 Introduction

Human pose recognition is important to video surveillance and kinematic analysis. It is a fundamental step for scene understanding. With depth image and skeleton data [8], human pose recognition has significant progress in recent years. However, initialization heavily influence the effect of skeleton extraction, and this method usually becomes invalid in sitting posture. Another problem is the poor depth image quality. Textureless and noisy images influence the recognition. Fortunately, with dense mapping strategy, we can obtain high quality 3D points, but very seldom paper concentrate on dense mapping method for non-rigid recognition. Our purpose in this paper is using CNNs to recognize human posture with rich feature of human 3D model.

As the development of sensor technology, RGB-D camera such as Kinect becomes cheaper and more prevalent in recent years. RGB-D cameras can generate 3D points from an infrared pattern, and it offers a different way to represent human poses. Evaluating human posture via the random forest and Kinect-based skeleton tracking

© Springer International Publishing AG 2016
E. Chen et al. (Eds.): PCM 2016, Part II, LNCS 9917, pp. 723–737, 2016.
DOI: 10.1007/978-3-319-48896-7_72

has many effective works. With the RGB-D data, a lot of works also develop the CNN-based method for human pose recognition. However, the skeleton tracking always failed when human is sitting. With more scale invariant information compared with the color cameras, algorithm can be more reliable. But most of the method on color image can not be used on depth image directly, because the depth images do not have as much texture as color images do, and they are usually too noisy. In literatures, there are two main method to recognize human poses through depth images, the first is maps-based Approaches [24–26, 29, 30], the second is skeleton-based approaches [8, 27, 28]. Human pose recognition from single depth images [8, 27] is based on uses the randomized decision forests to label body parts. In another hand, skeleton tracking, with Kinect-based algorithms are accurate and robust for pose estimation. However, Kinect-based methods need an initialization to confirm the body parts.

For the last decade, many works [1, 2] focus on the statistical representations of local features, and these representations of motion patterns are powerful for dynamic scene. Recently, deep learning [3] and Convolutional Neural Networks [4] has attracted great interest in computer vision. It has great ability for feature extraction, and with large number of data, CNNs have shown many amazing results. Some works use CNNs for human pose recognition, for instance, P-CNN [5] propose a pose-based CNN descriptor which tracks human body parts. C3D [6, 7] is a modified CNN to support 3-Dimensional Convolutional Networks, and it proved its recognition ability for sports action.

With the depth sensor, we can construct 3D model from depth images to describe human posture. Kinfu [9] firstly propose an real-time 3D fusion strategy from a single depth sensor, but it is only suitable for static scene. Dynamic fusion [10] can reconstructs non-rigid objects, for example, human. With dual-quaternion blending to warp the canonical model to live model, dynamic fusion reconstructs the non-rigid objects real-time. We propose a fusion strategy based on time nodes, which fuse depth images between two time nodes. Indeed, this method constructs an averaging weighted signed distance function. The obtained 3D model is smoother and less noisy than single depth image, and it contains all the information of depth images between two time nodes.

This paper uses the light model to represent 3D model, and with light from different positions, we can get various light models from a single 3D model. This expanded data set shows richer characteristics of human sitting posture. Our motivation is to get a more natural and diverse sitting posture description. Our experiment shows that light model is valid for human posture recognition.

The rest of the paper is organized as follows. In Sect. 2, how we get the sitting posture data set is presented, and we propose a semi-supervised method which uses soft correlation and hard correlation to adjust unlabeled data. In Sect. 3, we conduct experiments on the data sets and discuss the performance of our model. Review of related work is presented in Sect. 4. In Sect. 5, we conclude the paper.

2   Related Work

Many works on human action recognition focused on local features. In particular [19] calculates ratios between the height and the width of the bounding box around a detected human, used to detect standing, crawling/bending, lying down, and sitting of transit surveillance. In [20, 21], the approach attempts to track specific joints and body parts. In [22], Due to self-occlusion and background clutter, some approaches also use the motion generated from each body part as a feature for pose change. Since movements from each joint are shown to be interdependent. In [23], the observed motion is compared with registered motion exemplars, whereas action models are used to estimate possible future poses. IDT-FV (improved version of DT with FV encoding) [2] was considered as an outstanding work to many challenging benchmarks.

With depth sensor, we can get more scale invariant information. Two main methods on depth sensor before are maps-based Approaches and skeleton-based Approaches. Much works have been done with RGB and depth, we do our research with RGB and light model which obtains from depth. DSTIP (depth spatio-temporal interest points) and DCSF (depth cuboid similarity feature) [11] were proposed to model human activities from depth video. HON4D [12] (oriented 4D surface normals) was extracted to get spatio-temporal changes of action by using a histogram. Randomized decision forests with skeleton tracking [8] has led a great success in commercial application. Experiment with skeleton dataset captured by depth camera in [35], the results demonstrate the effectiveness of their algorithm. [40] shows that a significant performance is achieved when they extract interest points solely from RGB channels and combine the RGB based descriptors and depth map based descriptors. Based on human 3D skeleton model which generates from RGB-D sensor, we could extract periodical joints motion and distances to describe multi-classes of actions [41]. The similar method with us in [42] fuse the depth and RGB information for activity recognition. This method based on a video dataset collected by a kinect camera, and show that adding depth information in the descriptor can distinctly improve the accuracy of human activity recognition.

Recently, Convolution Neural Networks (CNNs) have made image classification in significant progress. There are also some work on CNNs to pose recognition [5, 13, 14]. [13, 14] use the CNN to classify whole frame in rgb video. [5] proposed a pose-based CNN descriptor, and it aggregates motion and appearance information along tracks of human body parts. C3D [6, 7] use a modified network from caffe, and it can support 3-Dimensional Convolution. With CNNs and RGBD data, [15] propose reconfigurable convolution neural networks, and it extends the convolution neural networks by incorporating structure alternatives.

Usually, large amount of labeled data must be required when we want to achieve a good recognition performance. Due to the ability of handling both the labeled and unlabeled data, this paper proposes a semi-supervised learning framework. Although there are many successful semi-supervised methods [38, 39] in the action recognition, a lot of work are mainly about how to reduce the time of manually labeling data. In [35], the paper proposes a novel algorithm named semi-supervised discriminant analysis with global constraint (SDG) which can better estimate the data distribution with both insufficient labeled data and sufficient unlabeled data. This method cuts down the time-consuming of manually labeling data. [36] proposes a boosted multi-class semi-supervised learning algorithm in which the co-EM algorithm is adopted to leverage the information from unlabeled data. All of the [34–36] focus on refining learning techniques to utilize the small amount of labeled data. In [37], the paper proposes a novel semi-supervised learning algorithm named En-Co-training which use ensemble method to extend the co-training paradigm.

Our work also rely on 3D reconstruction. With light model from 3D points, we can train a CNN to recognize human posture. Recent years, dense mapping based on depth sensor like kinect has many amazing works [9, 10, 16–18]. Kinfu [9] firstly propose a real-time method to reconstruct 3D model using GPU and kinect. Elasticfusion [18] use rgb and depth image to calculate camera position, and apply local loop closure and global loop closure to adjust 3D model. To reconstruct non-rigid object, dynamicfusion [10] apply node graph to 3D model, and all the 3D points can translate through warp-field based node graph (Fig. 1).

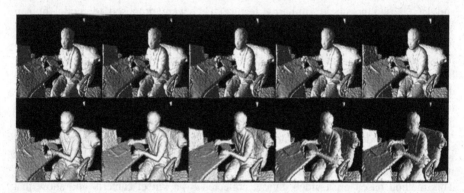

Fig. 1. Light models from the same surface points with different diffuse light

3 Acquire Light Model

In image recognition, the main difficulty is that the change of illumination and scale zooming. 3D point clouds are doing well in these two aspects. In the recognition of human body posture. At present, some papers utilize the depth map to get the human skeleton point information for the identification of human body posture. But this method has strict restrictions on the initial posture, and the effect of sitting posture recognition is particularly bad. The goal of this paper is to identify the human body posture directly through 3D point clouds. It also has two challenges, one is the Identification of 3D point clouds, and the other is non-rigid 3D reconstruction. For the Identification of 3D point clouds, some papers use spin image [2, 3], but this method is of high computing complexity and often can not be achieved in real time. Some methods use voting strategies to identify 3D point clouds [4], however, it requires exactly the same or high similarity of 3D point clouds and the recognition effect of non-rigid body is usually not good. In this paper, we map 3D point clouds to light model and different light directions determine different light models. Compared with the depth map, the pixel value of the light model does not change with the distance between human and camera. In this way, we try to restore the shape of the object in the view of the camera as far as possible. As 2D images, Light models can be classified using CNN (convolutional neural networks) to get the recognition result. For the non-rigid 3D reconstruction, elastic fusion is realized on local deformation correction, dynamic fusion realizes the real-time non-rigid 3D reconstruction by depth camera. The method of dynamic fusion is amazing but also has some disadvantages. For example, the effect is poor for fast moving objects, objects with topological changes and large scenes. Analysis the reasons, we can find the most important is that ICP algorithm is sensitive to initial value, reconstruction often fails due to the dramatic changes of one frame. Therefore, this paper adopts the method of time node fusion. By non-rigid fusion, we get a de-noising 3D point cloud fused by depth maps for a short period in the view of the camera rather than getting a complete point cloud.

In the following sections, we describes how to integrate time nodes and get the light model. Our goal is training a Convolutional Neural Network for human posture recognition by semi-supervised learning. We found that the pixel values of light model would not change due to distance compared to the depth image, so our training dataset contains not only RGB images but also light model which could obtained by non-rigid 3D reconstruction.

3.1 Non-rigid 3D Reconstruction

We note that the reconstruction model obtained by fusion can get more sitting information than depth image. We fuse the given depth between two time nodes into a 3D model and get light model by lighting. Similar to the dynamic fusion and kinfu, we allocate a space in GPU memory, including 256^3 voxels. We achieve the fusion of three-dimensional model by updating the SDF function which defined on voxel, 3D point cloud can be expressed by zerocrossing of SDF function. We can also obtain 3D point cloud of person surface through raycast method.

We achieve the 3D surface by estimating the transformation matrix of each 3D node. Due to non-rigid of person, the relative position between each surface patch will change. Like dynamic fusion, we use a series of nodes to form the skeleton of 3D surface and restrict node by regularization to make the transformation more smooth. The difference between dynamic fusion and us is to fix camera position instead of estimating camera pose. While obtained a new frame of depth image, we calculate the transformation matrix of each 3D node by using ICP algorithm. We can obtain warp volume by transform volume space with node transformation matrix, and get non-rigid 3D point cloud and normal by raycast the warp volume.

3.2 Time Node Fusion

In the 3D modeling process, a possible approach is to track the position of the human body constantly and fuse depth images into the 3D model. However, non-rigid 3D reconstruction is usually not stable and perform weak for the fast-moving and topology changes of human, such as hands cross and separate. Therefore, the non-rigid reconstruction is defined between two time nodes in our experiments.

We need to merge the depth images between two time nodes into a 3D model. Assuming t1 and t2 represent two neighboring time nodes and we set the time interval sets between two nodes is 1 s. We reinitialize the volume and warp volume at time t1 and fuse the depth images between t1 and t2 into the new 3D model. For a single depth image, although camera noise and the hole area is usually serious, but the resulting 3D model can get more complete information of human after weighted update the SDF function constantly in the reconstruction. By fusing depth images between two time nodes, the 3D model can represent the information of the depth images sequence in this period of time. In this way, we can get a non-rigid 3D point cloud. In the next section, we will use it to generate the required training samples - light model.

3.3 Light Model

Light model is often used to texture 3D objects in graphics, it often simulate 3D object in the light by defining a virtual light source. The most common light sources are ambient light, diffuse light and specular light. We use light model to show the results of non-rigid reconstruction, and get a series of light model by changing the diffuse light angle. These light models can represent the 3D model under different light sources, and also can enrich our data set.

$$L = norm(P_{light} - P) * n_P + L_{ambient} \tag{1}$$

$$L_{model} = \begin{cases} 0, L \leq 0 \\ 255 * L, 0 < L < 1 \\ 255, L \geq 1 \end{cases} \tag{2}$$

Where L_{model} represents pixel value of light model, P_{light} represents diffuse light position, P represents 3D point clouds, n_P represents the normal of vertex point, $norm()$ is normalized function, $L_{ambient}$ is ambient brightness. In our experiment, we choose (0.1, 0.1, 0.1) as the ambient light. The initial position of diffuse light is (−5.0, 1.0, −1.0) and light position changing formula is:

$$P_{light} = P_{light} + (1.0, 0.0, 0.0)$$

Thus, we can get the series of light model under the lights.

4 Semi-supervised Learning

We introduced the non-rigid 3D reconstruction and obtained light model in the previous section. Now, we recognize the sitting basis events by semi-supervised learning of the existing time series RGB and light model pictures. Here we first classify the labeled data, then we show how to do semi-supervised learning with the classified model and a large number of unlabeled data.

In order to train with the large number of unlabeled data stably, we establish two forms of correlation: hard correlation and soft correlation. Hard correlation means that RGB image and light model should represent the same basic event at the same time, and soft correlation means that basic event should happen sequentially, for example, forward event changes to the backward event usually after normal sitting; after raising hand event, the most likely event is to continue raising hand, second possible event is normal sitting. In order to train CNN for semi-supervised with soft and hard correlation, we construct a quadruple network. The inputs are both the RGB images and light models of current time node and previous time node. Training results area mended through hard correlation and soft correlation, and corrected results adjust the network weights.

In this paper, we divide sitting basic events into seven categories named forward, backward, raising hand, stoop, left-leaning, right-leaning and normal sitting respectively. We believe that the basis of seven categories can constitute the behavior of sitting.

4.1 Data Acquisition

With RGB video and depth video, we need to extract patches of interest, like human or chairs which are movable. ROIs of movable objects such as person and chair can be obtained by depth background modeling. We adopt a method in which the background is not updated. Background modeling and foreground detection are important steps in video processing used to detect robustly moving objects in challenging environments. In our method, it requires no movable objects in the scene when we start the camera in the data acquisition process, we can get the depth of the background model by the weighted average of 10 frame depth, and the process time is about 0.3 s. For a new depth image, subtract it with the depth background model, and a difference depth map can be obtained. The depth difference threshold is set to 200 mm and contour length threshold is set to 50 pixels, then we do binarization of difference depth map with different threshold, and detect contours of binary image. It can be regarded as movable object if contour length is greater than the threshold, and the bounding box of movable object can be taken as ROI. In our experiment, the 3D point cloud can be obtained directly from the depth map, so we can get the ROI of the foreground object stably. The ROI can also be applied to color images after registration to get the foreground object in color images. Light model and the ROI of color images will be used as a sample of the data set. We set interval of time node 1 s, each quadruple data includes ROI of RGB image in current time, ROI of RGB image in previous time, ROI of light mode incurrent time and ROI of light model in previous time (Fig. 2).

4.2 Network Structure

Alexnet architecture was selected as our single network, and we take the image with size 227 * 227 as input. In our experiment, the output is 7 dimensional feature space. The entire network consists of four single network, which take the RGB image and light model of current time and previous time respectively as input. The four single networks are Net for previous color images (N_{pc}), Net for current color images (N_{cc}), Net for previous light model images (N_{plm}) and Net for current light model images

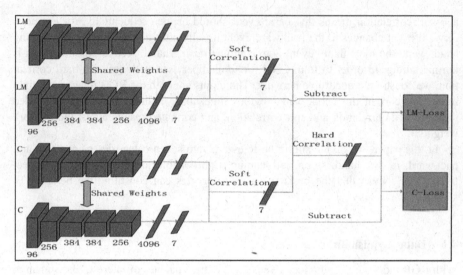

Fig. 2. Framework of quadruple network

(N_{clm}). Where N_{cc} and N_{pc} share weights, and N_{plm} shares weights with N_{clm}. For a few labeled patch pairs sampled from the light models and color images, we don't distinguish previous time node and current time node. All the light model patchs will be used to train N_{clm}. N_{clm} network will also be trained at the same time due to the shared weights. Similarly, all the color image patchs will be used to train N_{cc} and N_{pc}. Through the above process, we will complete the initialization of the quadruple network.

We need a large number of unlabeled data to complete semi-supervised learning. With pre-labeled data, we could obtain a CNN model to classify unlabeled data. There must be two result for existing pre-trained model to classify unlabeled: correct recognition and error recognition. In order to suppress the wrong results, We introduce hard correlation and soft correlation, and restrict the relationship between previous output and current output. Specifically, for a given set of input data, the output of N_{pc} is O_{pc}, the output of N_{cc} is O_{cc}, the output of N_{plm} is O_{plm} and the output of N_{clm} is O_{clm}. O_{pc} and O_{cc} satisfy the sequence of events. We define the order relation as soft correlation. The soft correlation generates the soft correlation space. In the soft correlation space, given a priori events, we can get the posterior probability. Similarly, O_{plm} and O_{clm} also satisfy the soft association limit. O_{clm} and O_{cc} are the output of the current time node, they should represent the same event and we will use a hard correlation to limit. We adjust O_{cc} and O_{clm} by hard correlation and soft correlation. After the adjustment, we take output as the label of unlabeled sample, and back-propagation algorithm is used to adjust the N_{cc} and N_{clm} network weights, we use the Adam algorithm [32] as the optimization method. Through the above process, we have defined the complete semi-supervised learning process.

4.3 Hard Correlation and Soft Correlation

Soft correlation represents the continuity of basic events. We believe that the occurrence of the basis event is interconnected. In order to establish contact latecomer event with the former event, we construct a soft correlation which weighted sum the latecomer event and the former event. The soft correlation will achieve quantitative description between priori events and posterior events. For a priori event, it is mapped to the soft correlation space and we can know the probability of several basic events that may occur in the following. In semi-supervised learning, the input is an unlabeled quadruple data. Firstly, considering the color images, the priori event is O_{pc}, which is mapped to the soft correlation space, we can get the probability distribution of the posterior event. Actually, due to the uncertainty of the unlabeled samples, this probability distribution can only be used as a reference. The output O_{cc} of N_{cc} provides another more important reference for the posterior event. Here, we use the correlation coefficient to sum the results. (The same results can be obtained for light model) its adjustment formulas can be expressed as:

$$\begin{cases} O_{csoft} = \phi * \Phi(\Psi(O_{pc})) + (1 - \phi) * O_{cc} \\ O_{lmsoft} = \phi * \Phi(\Psi(O_{plm})) + (1 - \phi) * O_{clm} \end{cases} \tag{3}$$

Where the $\Psi()$ extract label from the 7 dimensional output vector. $\Phi()$ maps the label to the soft correlation space which represents the possibility of basic events after current event. ϕ is the correlation coefficient, in our experiment, we choose it as 0.4. We note that ϕ is a critical parameter, which determines the impact degree between the former event to latecomer event.

Hard correlation restrict O_{cc} to be consistent with O_{clm} at the same time. Through the above steps, we obtain the soft correlation output O_{csoft} of N_{cc} and the soft correlation output O_{lmsoft} of N_{clm}. We will compare the soft correlation results of two networks: O_{csoft} and O_{lmsoft}, then decide what basic event happen in this time. After adjusting soft correlation, we do hard correlation adjustment, the formula is:

$$\begin{cases} O_{chard} = onehot((O_{csoft} + O_{lmsoft})/2) \\ O_{lmhard} = O_{chard} \end{cases} \tag{4}$$

Wherein $onehot()$ function changes maximum value of vector into 1, and the rest goes to zero.

4.4 Soft Correlation Space

Soft correlation space represents the interrelated of the basic events. Given a priori event, the label is mapped to a soft correlation space and we can get the probability distribution of posterior events. For example, backward event most likely to occur after the backward event, second possible is after normal event, but impossible occur after forward event. To describe this interrelated, we introduce soft correlation space. Since we have defined seven basic events, so soft correlation space will be 7D space.

With $\Phi()$ function, it can map basic event label i into 7D vector of soft correlation space, which represents the probability of each basic event occur after basic event i. The establishment of soft correlation space consists of two steps. Firstly, initialization, all the labeled samples will be used to statistics the order of events. For each of the basic events, the probability of the occurrence of posterior events can be obtained by marking samples, and the soft correlation space is initialized; Secondly, Update, for an unlabeled sample, if it satisfies the confidence condition, it will be used as a confidence sample, and the soft correlation space is updated. All labeled samples are confidence samples, we note that for the labeled samples, color image's basic event of previous time node and light model's basic event of previous time node is the same. Meanwhile, color image's basic event of current time node and light model's basic event of current time node is the same. We will use the condition to determine whether the quadruple data is a confidence sample.

We first initialize the soft correlation space with pre-labeled data. Count all the pre-labeled quadruple data, assume N is the total number. For previous time node of quadruple data, the number of basic event i is N_i, $N = \Sigma N\_i$, then

$$\Phi(i)[j] = \frac{M_{ij}}{N_i}, i,j = 1,2,\ldots,7 \tag{5}$$

Where M_ij represents the number of basic event j happen after the basic event i. We need to update the soft correlation space in the semi-supervised learning process, if an unlabeled quadruple data meet the following criteria:

$$\begin{cases} \Psi(O_{pc}) == \Psi(O_{cc}) == p \\ \Psi(O_{plm}) == \Psi(O_{clm}) == q \end{cases} \tag{6}$$

Then we assume the quadruple data is definite sample, and update the soft correlation space.

$$N = N+1, N_i = N_i + 1, M_{ij} = M_{ij} + 1$$

Then we recalculate $\Phi()$ function.

5   Experiment

This section describes our experimental results. First, we evaluate time node fusion and compare the light model to depth image. We then train the CNNs with light model and depth image, respectively, our goal is to demonstrate the advantages of light model. Next, semi-supervised learning with hard correlation and soft correlation is compared with supervised learning. Finally, our method is compared with the state of the art.

5.1 Performance of Light Model

We tested our algorithm on an Intel Core E5-1620 3.5 GHz CPU with an Quadro K620 GPGPU processor. Our input data are captured using a single Kinect camera with a resolution of 640 × 480 and sampling frequency of 30 FPS. Method in Sect. 3.3 was used to construct light model. Figure 3 compares the performance of light model and depth image. We notice that, compared to the depth image, noise of light model is suppressed, and the number of holes decreased. With normal information, light model can describe body posture more intuitive.

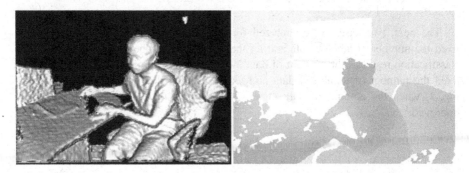

Fig. 3. Light model and depth image

To verify this, we selected two sets of data. The first data set is different postures of light model, and the second data set is depth images corresponding to light model. Since the light model has timing information and each light model is fused by depth images in 1 s, we select the intermediate depth image corresponding to the light model. Body posture will be divided into seven categories, namely anteversion, hypsokinesis, raising hand, hands up, turn left, turn right and sit straight. In our experiment, 2500 light models and its corresponding depth images are selected as testing data, while 7500 light models and its corresponding depth images are selected as training data. We train the two groups of data with AlexNet, and compare the results of their classification. As shown in Table 1, light model has a better result.

Table 1. Comparision of depth image and light model

	Precision (%)
Depth image	87.2
Light model	92.3

5.2 Semi-supervised Learning

In order to evaluate our proposed algorithm, we perform experiments to compare supervised learning and semi-supervised learning. Similar to above section, we use the same data in comparative experiments. The images for supervised learning are all labeled, and 25% images for semi-supervised learning are labeled. In the experiment for semi-supervised learning, we adopt hard correlation and soft correlation method which are described in Sect. 4.3. The result is shown in Table 2, and we can see that semi-supervised learning got a competitive results.

Table 2. Comparision of supervised and semi-supervised learning

	Precision (%)
Supervised learning	92.7
Semi-supervised learning	91.3

The next, two cases were analyzed for semi-supervised learning. First case, we fixed the number of labeled data and let the number of unlabeled data increases. The classification result as the amount of data increases was examined. The other case, we fixed the number of unlabeled data and let the labeled data increases. As shown in Fig. 4, when the amount of data increases, the effect of classification results were improved.

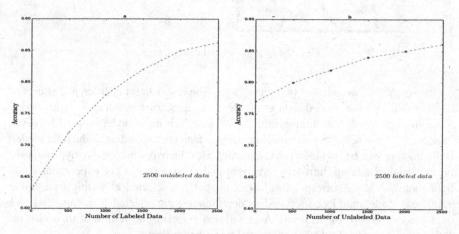

Fig. 4. Semi-supervised learning

6   Conclusion

This paper introduces light model which is constructed with time node fusion method. We demonstrate the effectiveness of light model for human pose recognition. With the light model and RGB data, we construct a semi-supervised CNN classifier which use the hard correlation and soft correlation.

References

1. Schuldt, C., Laptev, I., Caputo, B.: Recognizing human actions: a local SVM approach. In: 17th International Conference on Proceedings of the Pattern Recognition (ICPR 2004), vol. 3, pp. 32–36. IEEE Computer Society (2004)
2. Heng, W., Schmid, C.: Action recognition with improved trajectories. In: 2013 IEEE International Conference on Computer Vision (ICCV). IEEE (2013)
3. Krizhevsky, A., Sutskever, I., Hinton, G.E.: ImageNet classification with deep convolutional neural networks. In: Advances in Neural Information Processing Systems (2012)
4. Jia, Y., et al.: Caffe: convolutional architecture for fast feature embedding. In: ACM Multimedia, vol. 2 (2014)
5. Chéron, G., Laptev, I., Schmid, C.: P-CNN: pose-based CNN features for action recognition. In: Proceedings of the IEEE International Conference on Computer Vision (2015)
6. Tran, D., et al.: Learning spatiotemporal features with 3D convolutional networks. In: Proceedings of the IEEE International Conference on Computer Vision (2015)
7. Karpathy, A., et al.: Large-scale video classification with convolutional neural networks. In: 2014 IEEE Conference on Computer Vision and Pattern Recognition (CVPR). IEEE (2014)
8. Shotton, J., et al.: Real-time human pose recognition in parts from single depth images. Commun. ACM **56**(1), 116–124 (2013)
9. Newcombe, R.A., et al.: KinectFusion: real-time dense surface mapping and tracking. In: 2013 IEEE International Conference on Computer Vision (ICCV). IEEE (2013)
10. Newcombe, R.A., Fox, D., Seitz, S.M.: DynamicFusion: reconstruction and tracking of non-rigid scenes in real-time. In: Proceedings of the IEEE Conference on Computer Vision and Pattern Recognition (2015)
11. Lu, X., Aggarwal, J.K.: Spatio-temporal depth cuboid similarity feature for activity recognition using depth camera. In: 2013 IEEE Conference on Computer Vision and Pattern Recognition (CVPR). IEEE (2013)
12. Oreifej, O., Liu, Z.: HON4D: histogram of oriented 4d normals for activity recognition from depth sequences. In: 2013 IEEE Conference on Computer Vision and Pattern Recognition (CVPR). IEEE (2013)
13. Simonyan, K., Zisserman, A.: Two-stream convolutional networks for action recognition in videos. In: Advances in Neural Information Processing Systems (2014)
14. Ng, J.Y.-H., et al.: Beyond short snippets: deep networks for video classification. arXiv preprint arXiv:1503.08909a (2015)
15. Wang, K., Wang, X., Lin, L., et al.: 3D human activity recognition with reconfigurable convolutional neural networks. In: Proceedings of the ACM International Conference on Multimedia. ACM (2014)
16. Whelan, T., et al.: Kintinuous: spatially extended kinectfusion. MIT-CSAIL-TR-2012-020 (2012)
17. Nießner, M., et al.: Real-time 3d reconstruction at scale using voxel hashing. ACM Trans. Graph. (TOG) **32**(6) (2013). Article No. 169
18. Whelan, T., et al.: ElasticFusion: dense SLAM without a pose graph. In: RSS (2015)
19. Blan, A.O., et al.: Shining a light on human pose: on shadows, shading and the estimation of pose and shape. In: IEEE 11th International Conference on Computer Vision, ICCV 2007. IEEE (2007)
20. Lee, M.W., Nevatia, R.: Body part detection for human pose estimation and tracking. In: IEEE Workshop on Motion and Video Computing, WMVC 2007. IEEE (2007)

21. Lee, M.W., Nevatia, R.: Dynamic human pose estimation using Markov chain Monte Carlo approach. In: Seventh IEEE Workshops on Application of Computer Vision, WACV/MOTIONS 2005, vol. 1–2. IEEE (2005)

22. Fathi, A., Mori, G.: Human pose estimation using motion exemplars. In: IEEE 11th International Conference on Computer Vision, ICCV 2007. IEEE (2007)

23. Baumberg, A.M., Hogg, D.C.: An efficient method for contour tracking using active shape models. In: Proceedings of the 1994 IEEE Workshop on Motion of Non-rigid and Articulated Objects. IEEE (1994)

24. Li, W., Zhang, Z., Liu, Z.: Action recognition based on a bag of 3d points. In: 2010 IEEE Computer Society Conference on Computer Vision and Pattern Recognition Workshops (CVPRW). IEEE (2010)

25. Vieira, A.W., Nascimento, E.R., Oliveira, G.L., Liu, Z., Campos, M.F.M.: STOP: Space-Time Occupancy Patterns for 3D action recognition from depth map sequences. In: Alvarez, L., Mejail, M., Gomez, L., Jacobo, J. (eds.) CIARP 2012. LNCS, vol. 7441, pp. 252–259. Springer, Heidelberg (2012). doi:10.1007/978-3-642-33275-3_31

26. Wang, J., Liu, Z., Chorowski, J., Chen, Z., Wu, Y.: Robust 3d action recognition with random occupancy patterns. In: Fitzgibbon, A., Lazebnik, S., Perona, P., Sato, Y., Schmid, C. (eds.) ECCV 2012. LNCS, vol. 7441, pp. 872–885. Springer, Heidelberg (2012). doi:10.1007/978-3-642-33709-3_62

27. Mao, Y., et al.: Accurate 3d pose estimation from a single depth image. In: 2011 IEEE International Conference on Computer Vision (ICCV). IEEE (2011)

28. Criminisi, A., Shotton, J., Robertson, D., Konukoglu, E.: Regression forests for efficient anatomy detection and localization in CT studies. In: Menze, B., Langs, G., Tu, Z., Criminisi, A. (eds.) MCV 2010. LNCS, vol. 6533, pp. 106–117. Springer, Heidelberg (2011). doi:10.1007/978-3-642-18421-5_11

29. Jalal, A., et al.: Recognition of human home activities via depth silhouettes and transformation for smart homes. Indoor Built Environ. **21**(1), 184–190 (2011)

30. Yang, X., Zhang, C., Tian, Y.: Recognizing actions using depth motion maps-based histograms of oriented gradients. In: Proceedings of the 20th ACM International Conference on Multimedia. ACM (2012)

31. Wu, S.-L., Cui, R.-Y.: Human behavior recognition based on sitting postures. In: 2010 International Symposium on Computer Communication Control and Automation (3CA), vol. 1. IEEE (2010)

32. Kingma, D., Ba, J.: Adam: a method for stochastic optimization. arXiv preprint arXiv:1412.6980 (2014)

33. Wang, X., Gupta, A.: Unsupervised learning of visual representations using videos. arXiv preprint arXiv:1505.00687 (2015)

34. Stikic, M., Van Laerhoven, K., Schiele, B.: Exploring semi-supervised and active learning for activity recognition. In: 12th IEEE International Symposium on Wearable Computers, ISWC 2008. IEEE (2008)

35. Zhao, X., et al.: Human action recognition based on semi-supervised discriminant analysis with global constraint. Neurocomputing **105**, 45–50 (2013)

36. Zhang, T., et al.: Boosted multi-class semi-supervised learning for human action recognition. Pattern Recogn. **44**(10), 2334–2342 (2011)

37. Guan, D., et al.: Activity recognition based on semi-supervised learning. In: 13th IEEE International Conference on Embedded and Real-Time Computing Systems and Applications, RTCSA 2007. IEEE (2007)

38. Dempster, A.P., Laird, N.M., Rubin, D.B.: Maximum likelihood from incomplete data via the EM algorithm. J. Roy. Stat. Soc.: Ser. B (Methodol.) **39**, 1–38 (1977)

39. Miller, D.J., Uyar, H.S.: A mixture of experts classifier with learning based on both labelled and unlabelled data. In: Advances in Neural Information Processing Systems (1997)
40. Zhao, Y., et al.: Combing RGB and depth map features for human activity recognition. In: 2012 Asia-Pacific on Signal and Information Processing Association Annual Summit and Conference (APSIPA ASC). IEEE (2012)
41. Faria, D.R., Premebida, C., Nunes, U.: A probabilistic approach for human everyday activities recognition using body motion from RGB-D images. In: 2014 RO-MAN: The 23rd IEEE International Symposium on Robot and Human Interactive Communication. IEEE (2014)
42. Ming, Y., Ruan, Q., Hauptmann, A.G.: Activity recognition from RGB-D camera with 3d local spatio-temporal features. In: 2012 IEEE International Conference on Multimedia and Expo (ICME). IEEE (2012)

Author Index